Psychological Testing

PRINCIPLES, APPLICATIONS, & ISSUES

Ninth Edition

ROBERT M. KAPLAN
Stanford University

DENNIS P. SACCUZZO
San Diego State University

CENGAGE
Learning

Australia • Brazil • Mexico • Singapore • United Kingdom • United States

Psychological Testing: Principles, Applications, and Issues, **Ninth Edition**
Robert M. Kaplan and Dennis P. Saccuzzo

Product Director: Star M. Burruto

Product Manager: Carly McJunkin

Content Developer: Tangelique Williams-Grayer

Product Assistant: Katie Chen

Marketing Manager: James Findlay

Art and Cover Direction, Production Management, and Composition: Lumina Datamatics, Inc.

Manufacturing Planner: Karen Hunt

Cover Image: Christian Offenberg/iStock/ Thinkstock

Unless otherwise noted all items © Cengage Learning®

For product information and technology assistance, contact us at **Cengage Learning Customer & Sales Support, 1-800-354-9706.**

For permission to use material from this text or product, submit all requests online at **www.cengage.com/permissions.** Further permissions questions can be e-mailed to **permissionrequest@cengage.com.**

Library of Congress Control Number: 2016948139

Student Edition:
ISBN: 978-1-337-09813-7

Cengage Learning
20 Channel Center Street
Boston, MA 02210
USA

Cengage Learning is a leading provider of customized learning solutions with employees residing in nearly 40 different countries and sales in more than 125 countries around the world. Find your local representative at **www.cengage.com.**

Cengage Learning products are represented in Canada by Nelson Education, Ltd.

To learn more about Cengage Learning Solutions, visit **www.cengage.com.**

Purchase any of our products at your local college store or at our preferred online store **www.cengagebrain.com.**

Printed in the United States of America
Print Number: 01   Print Year: 2017

Brief Contents

PART I   **PRINCIPLES**

1   Introduction   1
2   Norms and Basic Statistics for Testing   23
3   Correlation and Regression   63
4   Reliability   99
5   Validity   133
6   Writing and Evaluating Test Items   159
7   Test Administration   187

PART II   **APPLICATIONS**

8   Interviewing Techniques   203
9   Theories of Intelligence and the Binet Scales   225
10   The Wechsler Intelligence Scales: WAIS-IV, WISC-V, and WPPSI-IV   247
11   Tests for Infants, Disabilities, and Special Populations   267
12   Standardized Tests in Education, Civil Service, and the Military   299
13   Applications in Clinical and Counseling Settings   329
14   Projective Personality Tests   371
15   Computers and Basic Psychological Science in Testing   401
16   Testing in Counseling Psychology   425
17   Testing in Health Psychology and Health Care   443
18   Testing in Industrial and Business Settings   483

PART III   **ISSUES**

19   Test Bias   513
20   Testing and the Law   547
21   The Future of Psychological Testing   587

Contents

PART I   PRINCIPLES

1   Introduction   1

Basic Concepts   6
   What a Test Is   6
   Types of Tests   7

Overview of the Book   9
   Principles of Psychological Testing   10
   Applications of Psychological Testing   10
   Issues of Psychological Testing   11

Historical Perspective   11
   Early Antecedents   11
   Charles Darwin and Individual Differences   12
   Experimental Psychology and Psychophysical Measurement   13
   The Evolution of Intelligence and Standardized Achievement Tests   14
   Personality Tests: 1920–1940   16
   The Emergence of New Approaches to Personality Testing   18
   The Period of Rapid Changes in the Status of Testing   20
   The Current Environment   21

Summary   21

2   Norms and Basic Statistics for Testing   23

Why We Need Statistics   24

Scales of Measurement   25
   Properties of Scales   25
   Types of Scales   27
   Permissible Operations   28

Frequency Distributions   29

Percentile Ranks   32

Percentiles   36

Describing Distributions   37
   Mean   37
   Standard Deviation   38

Z Score   40
Standard Normal Distribution   41
McCall's *T*   48
Quartiles and Deciles   50

Norms   51
Age-Related Norms   54
Tracking   54
Criterion-Referenced Tests   58

Summary   61

3 Correlation and Regression   63

The Scatter Diagram   64

Correlation   66

Regression   67
The Regression Line   67
The Best-Fitting Line   68
Testing the Statistical Significance of a Correlation Coefficient   74
How to Interpret a Regression Plot   76

Other Correlation Coefficients   80

Terms and Issues in the Use of Correlation   82
Residual   82
Standard Error of Estimate   83
Coefficient of Determination   83
Coefficient of Alienation   83
Shrinkage   84
Cross Validation   84
The Correlation-Causation Problem   84
Third Variable Explanation   85
Restricted Range   86

Multivariate Analysis (Optional)   87
General Approach   87
An Example Using Multiple Regression   87
Discriminant Analysis   88
Factor Analysis   89

Summary   92

APPENDIX 3.1: Calculation of a Regression Equation and a Correlation Coefficient   93

Calculation of a Regression Equation (Data from Table 3.5)   94

4 Reliability   99

History and Theory of Reliability   100
Conceptualization of Error   100

Spearman's Early Studies   101
Basics of Test Score Theory   101

The Domain Sampling Model   103

Item Response Theory   104

Models of Reliability   106
Sources of Error   106
Time Sampling: The Test–Retest Method   107
Item Sampling: Parallel Forms Method   108
Split-Half Method   109
KR_{20} Formula   111
Coefficient Alpha   112
Reliability of a Difference Score   113

Reliability in Behavioral Observation Studies   115

Connecting Sources of Error with Reliability Assessment Method   119

Using Reliability Information   122
Standard Errors of Measurement and the Rubber Yardstick   122
How Reliable Is Reliable?   123
What to Do about Low Reliability   124

Summary   129

APPENDIX 4.1: Using Coefficient Alpha to Estimate Split-Half Reliability When the Variances for the Two Halves of the Test Are Unequal   130

APPENDIX 4.2: The Calculation of Reliability Using KR_{20} 130

5   **Validity   133**

Defining Validity   135

Aspects of Validity   136
Face Validity   136
Content-Related Evidence for Validity   136
Criterion-Related Evidence for Validity   138
Construct-Related Evidence for Validity   149
Relationship between Reliability and Validity   155

Summary   157

6   **Writing and Evaluating Test Items   159**

Item Writing   160
Item Formats   161
Guessing   163
Other Possibilities   170

Item Analysis   173
Item Difficulty   173

Discriminability   175
Pictures of Item Characteristics   177
Linking Uncommon Measures   182
Items for Criterion-Referenced Tests   184
Limitations of Item Analysis   185

Summary   186

7   Test Administration   187

Why We Changed Our Minds   188

The Examiner and the Subject   188
The Relationship Between Examiner and Test Taker   188
The Race of the Tester   189

Stereotype Threat   190
How Stereotype Threat Does Damage   191
Remedies for Stereotype Threat   192
Language of Test Taker   193
Training of Test Administrators   193
Expectancy Effects   193
Effects of Reinforcing Responses   196
Computer-Assisted Test Administration   197
Mode of Administration   199
Subject Variables   201

Summary   201

PART II   APPLICATIONS

8   Interviewing Techniques   203

The Interview as a Test   207

Reciprocal Nature of Interviewing   208

Principles of Effective Interviewing   208
The Proper Attitudes   209
Responses to Avoid   209
Effective Responses   211
Responses to Keep the Interaction Flowing   212
Measuring Understanding   215
Mental Status Examination   217
Developing Interviewing Skills   218

Sources of Error in the Interview   219
Interview Validity   219
Interview Reliability   222

Summary   223

9   Theories of Intelligence and the Binet Scales   225

The Problem of Defining Intelligence   226

Binet's Principles of Test Construction   228
Principle 1: Age Differentiation   228
Principle 2: General Mental Ability   229

Spearman's Model of General Mental Ability   229
Implications of General Mental Intelligence (*g*)   230
The *gf-gc* Theory of Intelligence   230

The Early Binet Scales   231
The 1905 Binet-Simon Scale   231
The 1908 Scale   232

Terman's Stanford-Binet Intelligence Scale   234
The 1916 Stanford-Binet Intelligence Scale   234
The Intelligence Quotient (IQ)   234
The 1937 Scale   235
The 1960 Stanford-Binet Revision and Deviation IQ (SB-LM)   237

The Modern Binet Scale   238
Model for the Fourth and Fifth Editions of the Binet Scale   238
Characteristics of the 1986 Revision   240
Characteristics of the 2003 Fifth Edition   242
Psychometric Properties of the 2003 Fifth Edition   243
Median Validity   244

Summary   244

10   The Wechsler Intelligence Scales: WAIS-IV, WISC-V, and WPPSI-IV   247

The Wechsler Intelligence Scales   249
Point and Performance Scale Concepts   249

From the Wechsler–Bellevue Intelligence Scale to the WAIS-IV   251

Scales, Subtests, and Indexes   251
A Closer Look at Subtests   252
From Raw Scores to Scaled and Index Scale Scores   257
Index Scores   258
FSIQs   258

Interpretive Features of the Wechsler Tests   259
Index Comparisons   259
Pattern Analysis   260
Hypothetical Case Studies   260

Psychometric Properties of the Wechsler Adult Scale   262
Standardization   262
Reliability   263
Validity   263

Evaluation of the Wechsler Adult Scales   263

Downward Extensions of the WAIS-IV: The WISC-V and the WPPSI-IV   264
    The WISC-V   264
    The WPPSI-IV   265

Summary   266

11   Tests for Infants, Disabilities, and Special Populations   267

Alternative Individual Ability Tests Compared With the Binet and Wechsler Scales   268

Alternatives Compared With One Another   270
    Early Tests   272
    Infant Scales   272
    Major Tests for Young Children   279
    General Individual Ability Tests for Handicapped and Special Populations   284

Testing Learning Disabilities   287
    Visiographic Tests   292
    Creativity: Torrance Tests of Creative Thinking (TTCT)   294
    Individual Achievement Tests: Wide Range Achievement Test-4 (WRAT-4)   296

Summary   297

12   Standardized Tests in Education, Civil Service, and the Military   299

Comparison of Group and Individual Ability Tests   301
    Advantages of Individual Tests   302
    Advantages of Group Tests   302

Overview of Group Tests   303
    Characteristics of Group Tests   303
    Selecting Group Tests   303
    Using Group Tests   304

Group Tests in the Schools: Kindergarten Through 12th Grade   305
    Achievement Tests Versus Aptitude Tests   305
    Group Achievement Tests   305
    Group Tests of Mental Abilities (Intelligence)   308

College Entrance Tests   312
    The New (2016) SAT   312
    The American College Test   313

Graduate and Professional School Entrance Tests   314
    Graduate Record Examination Aptitude Test   314

Miller Analogies Test   318
The Law School Admission Test   319

Nonverbal Group Ability Tests   321
Raven Progressive Matrices   322
Goodenough-Harris Drawing Test (G-HDT)   324
The Culture Fair Intelligence Test   325
Standardized Tests Used in the U.S. Civil Service System   326
Standardized Tests in the U.S. Military: The Armed Services
Vocational Aptitude Battery   326

Summary   327

**13   Applications in Clinical and Counseling
Settings   329**

Strategies of Structured Personality Test Construction   331
Deductive Strategies   332
Empirical Strategies   332
Criteria Used in Selecting Tests for Discussion   334

The Logical-Content Strategy   334
Woodworth Personal Data Sheet   334
Early Multidimensional Logical-Content Scales   335
Mooney Problem Checklist   335
Criticisms of the Logical-Content Approach   336

The Criterion-Group Strategy   336
Minnesota Multiphasic Personality Inventory   336
California Psychological Inventory (CPI)–Third Edition   347

The Factor Analytic Strategy   349
Guilford's Pioneer Efforts   349
Cattell's Contribution   350
Problems With the Factor Analytic Strategy   352

The Theoretical Strategy   353
Edwards Personal Preference Schedule (EPPS)   353
Personality Research Form, Third Edition (PRF-III) and
Jackson Personality Inventory Revised (JPI-R)   355
Self-Concept   357

Combination Strategies   358
Positive Personality Measurement and the NEO Personality
Inventory–Three (NEO-PI-3)   358
The NEO Personality Inventory–Three (NEO PI-R™)   359

Frequently Used Measures of Positive Personality Traits   362
Rosenberg Self-Esteem Scale   362
General Self-Efficacy Scale (GSE)   363
Ego Resiliency Scale Revised   363
Dispositional Resilience Scale (DRS)   363
Hope Scale   364

Life Orientation Test-Revised (LOT-R)   364
Satisfaction with Life Scale (SWLS)   365
Positive and Negative Affect Schedule (PANAS)   365
Coping Intervention for Stressful Situations (CISS)   366
Core Self-Evaluations   366

Future of Positive Personality Research   367
Summary   368

14   Projective Personality Tests   371

The Projective Hypothesis   373
The Rorschach Inkblot Test   374
Historical Antecedents   374
Stimuli, Administration, and Interpretation   375
Psychometric Properties   380
An Alternative Inkblot Test: The Holtzman   389
The Thematic Apperception Test   390
Stimuli, Administration, and Interpretation   391
Psychometric Properties   394
Alternative Apperception Procedures   395
Nonpictorial Projective Procedures   395
Word Association Test   396
Sentence Completion Tasks   396
Figure Drawing Tests   398
Summary   398

15   Computers and Basic Psychological Science in Testing   401

Cognitive-Behavioral Assessment Procedures Versus the Medical Model of Assessment   403
The Rationale for Cognitive-Behavioral Assessment   403
Early Procedures Based on Operant Conditioning   405
Self-Report Techniques   407
The Dysfunctional Attitude Scale   411
Irrational Beliefs Test   411
Irrational Beliefs Inventory (IBI)   412
Cognitive Functional Analysis   412
Psychophysiological Procedures   414
Physiological Variables With Treatment Implications   414
Evaluation of Psychophysiological Techniques   415
Computers and Psychological Testing   416
Computer-Assisted Interview   416
Computer-Administered Tests   417
Computer Diagnosis, Scoring, and Reporting of Results   418

Internet Usage for Psychological Testing   419
The Computerization of Cognitive-Behavioral Assessment   420
Tests Possible Only by Computer   420
Computer-Adaptive Testing   421

Summary   423

16   Testing in Counseling Psychology   425

Measuring Interests   426
The Strong Vocational Interest Blank   427
The Evolution of the Strong Measures   428
The Campbell Interest and Skill Survey   429
The Reemergence of the Strong Interest Inventory   430
The Kuder Occupational Interest Survey   432
The Career Assessment Inventory   436
The Self-Directed Search   436
Eliminating Gender Bias in Interest Measurement   437
Aptitudes and Interests   439

Measuring Personal Characteristics for Job Placement   439
Are There Stable Personality Traits?   440
Other Uses of Interest Matching Methods: The Case
of Internet Dating   440

Summary   441

17   Testing in Health Psychology and Health Care   443

Neuropsychological Assessment   444
Clinical Neuropsychology   444
Developmental Neuropsychology   449
Adult Neuropsychology   453
California Verbal Learning Test (CVLT)   459
Automated Neuropsychological Testing   462
Anxiety and Stress Assessment   463
Stress and Anxiety   464
The State-Trait Anxiety Inventory   464
Measures of Coping   466
Ecological Momentary Assessment   466
Depression   467
NIH Toolbox   470

Quality-of-Life Assessment   472
What Is Health-Related Quality of Life?   472
Common Methods for Measuring Quality of Life   473
mHealth and New Mobile Technologies   476
The 2015 Medical College Admissions Test (MCAT)   477

Summary   482

18   Testing in Industrial and Business Settings   483

Personnel Psychology—The Selection of Employees   484
   Employment Interview   484

Base Rates and Hit Rates   486
   Taylor-Russell Tables   489
   Utility Theory and Decision Analysis   493
   Value-Added Employee Assessments   495
   Incremental Validity   499

Personnel Psychology From the Employee's Perspective: Fitting People to Jobs   501
   The Myers-Briggs Type Indicator   501
   Tests for Use in Industry: Wonderlic Personnel Test (WPT)   502

Measuring Characteristics of the Work Setting   503
   Classifying Environments   503

Job Analysis   505

Measuring the Person–Situation Interaction   508

Summary   511

PART III   ISSUES

19   Test Bias   513

Why Is Test Bias Controversial?   514

The Traditional Defense of Testing   520
   Content-Related Evidence for Validity   521
   Criterion-Related Sources of Bias   524

Other Approaches to Testing Minority Group Members   529
   Ignorance Versus Stupidity   529

Suggestions for Solutions   531
   Ethical Concerns and the Definition of Test Bias   531
   Thinking Differently: Finding New Interpretations of Data   535
   Developing Different Criteria   535
   When Tests Harm   536
   Does It Matter? More Testing and Less Testing   537
   Changing the Social Environment   540

Summary   544

20   Testing and the Law   547

Laws Governing the Use of Tests   549
   Federal Authorities   549
   Specific Laws   553

Federal Initiatives in Education   555
The Common Core   556

Major Lawsuits That Have Affected Psychological Testing   558

Early Desegregation Cases   558
Stell v. Savannah-Chatham County Board of Education   559
Hobson v. Hansen   560
Diana v. State Board of Education   561
Larry P. v. Wilson Riles   561
Parents in Action on Special Education v. Hannon   563
Crawford et al. v. Honig et al.   564
Marchall v. Georgia   568
Debra P. v. Turlington   568
Regents of the University of California v. Bakke   571
Golden Rule Insurance Company et al. v. Washburn et al.   571
Adarand Constructors, Inc. v. Peña, Secretary of Transportation, et al.   572
Affirmative Action in Higher Education   572
Grutter v. Bollinger and *Gratz v. Bollinger*   573
Parents v. Seattle   575
Meredith v. Jefferson County Board of Education   576
Fisher v. University of Texas   576
Personnel Cases   577
Cases Relevant to the Americans With Disabilities Act (ADA)   583
A Critical Look at Lawsuits   584

Summary   585

21 The Future of Psychological Testing   587

Issues Shaping the Field of Testing   588

Professional Issues   588
Moral Issues   591
Social Issues   594

Current Trends   596

The Proliferation of New Tests   596
Higher Standards, Improved Technology, and Increasing Objectivity   597
Greater Public Awareness and Influence   598
The Computerization of Tests   599
Testing on the Internet   599

Future Trends   599

Future Prospects for Testing Are as Promising as Ever Before   600
Controversy, Disagreement, and Change Will Continue   600
The Integration of Cognitive Science and Computer Science Will Lead to Several Innovations in Testing   601

Summary   601

APPENDIX 1   Areas of a Standard Normal Distribution   603

APPENDIX 2   Critical Values of r for $\alpha = .05$ and $\alpha = .01$
(Two-Tailed Test)   606

APPENDIX 3   Critical Values of t 607

APPENDIX 4   Code of Fair Testing Practices in Education   609

GLOSSARY   614
REFERENCES   618
NAME INDEX   683
SUBJECT INDEX   700

List of Sample Test Profiles

FIGURE **9.7** Cover page of Stanford-Binet Intelligence Scale 239

FIGURE **12.1** Example of a score report for the Stanford Achievement Test 307

FIGURE **12.2** A sample student profile from the ACT 313

FIGURE **12.3** GRE verbal ability sample items 315

FIGURE **12.4** GRE quantitative ability sample items 317

FIGURE **12.5** MAT sample items 319

FIGURE **13.2** An MMPI profile sheet 337

FIGURE **13.3** An MMPI-2 profile sheet 344

FIGURE **13.4** Jackson Personality Inventory profile sheet 356

FIGURE **13.5** NEO Personality Inventory profile sheet 360

TABLE **14.1** Summary of Rorschach scoring 381

FOCUSED EXAMPLE **14.2** The danger of basing Rorschach interpretations on insufficient evidence 386–387

Sentence completion tasks 396

FIGURE **17.5** Profile of a patient tested with the Luria-Nebraska battery 459

FIGURE **18.2** Sample questions from the Wonderlic 503

FIGURE **19.8** Sample SOMPA profile 525

TABLE **20.1** Examples of items from a minimum competence test 569

Preface

Psychology is a broad, exciting field. Psychologists work in settings ranging from schools and clinics to basic research laboratories, pharmaceutical firms, and private international companies. Despite this diversity, all psychologists have at least two things in common: They all study behavior, and they all depend to some extent on its measurement. This book concerns a particular type of measurement, psychological tests, which measure characteristics pertaining to all aspects of behavior in human beings.

Psychological Testing is the result of a long-standing partnership between the authors. As active participants in the development and use of psychological tests, we became disheartened because far too many undergraduate college students view psychological testing courses as boring and unrelated to their goals or career interests. In contrast, we see psychological testing as an exciting field. It has a solid place in the history of psychology, yet it is constantly in flux because of challenges, new developments, and controversies. A book on testing should encourage, not dampen, a student's interest. Thus, we provide an overview of the many facets of psychological tests and measurement principles in a style that will appeal to the contemporary college student.

To understand the applications and issues in psychological testing, the student must learn some basic principles, which requires some knowledge of introductory statistics. Therefore, some reviewing and a careful reading of Part I will pave the way for an understanding of the applications of tests discussed in Part II. Part III examines the issues now shaping the future of testing. Such issues include test anxiety, test bias, and the interface between testing and the law. The future of applied psychology may depend on the ability of psychologists to face these challenging issues.

Throughout the book, we present a series of focused discussions and focused examples. These sections illustrate the material in the book through examples or provide a more detailed discussion of a particular issue. We also use box features called "Psychological Testing in Everyday Life" to demonstrate material such as statistical calculations.

Increased Emphasis on Application

Students today often favor informal discussions and personally relevant examples. Consequently, we decided to use models from various fields and to write in an informal style. However, because testing is a serious and complicated field in which major disagreements exist even among scholars and experts, we have treated the controversial aspects of testing with more formal discussion and detailed referencing.

The first edition of *Psychological Testing: Principles, Applications, and Issues* was published in 1982. The world has changed in many ways in the 35 years since the text was first introduced. For example, personal computers were new in 1982. Most students and professors had never heard of the Internet, nobody communicated by e-mail, and the inventor of Facebook had not yet been born. Nobody had even imagined smart portable phones. The first edition of *Psychological Testing* was produced on typewriters, before word processors were commonly used. At the time, few professors or students had access to private computers. The early editions of the book offered instruction for preparing the submission of statistical analyses to mainframe computers. There were far fewer applications of psychological testing than there are today. On the other hand, principles of psychological testing have remained relatively constant. Thus, newer editions have included improvements and refinements in the Principles chapters. The later chapters on Applications and Issues have evolved considerably.

Not only has the field of psychological testing changed, but so have the lives of the authors. One of us (RMK) spent most of his career as a professor in a school of medicine, eventually moved to a school of public health, then to the federal government, and back again to a school of medicine. The other (DPS) completed law school and works extensively with attorneys and the U.S. legal system on many of the applied issues discussed in this book. While maintaining our central identities as psychologists, we have also had the opportunity to explore cutting-edge practice in medicine, public health, government regulation, education, and law. The ninth edition goes further than any previous edition in spelling out the applications of psychological testing in a wide variety of applied fields.

In developing this edition, we have organized topics around the application areas. Chapter 11 considers psychological testing in education and special education. Chapter 12 looks at the use of standardized tests in education, civil service, and the military. Chapters 13 and 14 consider the use of psychological tests in clinical and counseling settings.

The age of computers has completely revolutionized psychological testing. We deal with some of these issues in the Principles chapters by discussing computer-adaptive testing and item response theory. In Chapter 15, we discuss applications of psychological science in the computer age. Chapter 16 discusses the use of psychological testing in the field of counseling psychology and focuses primarily on interest inventories. Chapter 17 explores the rapidly developing fields of psychological assessment in health psychology, medicine, and health care. Chapter 18 reviews psychological testing in industry and business settings. Several of these chapters discuss the role of new electronic technologies, such as cell phones and sensors, in the acquisition of information about human behavior.

Over the last 35 years psycholological testing has faced important challenges related to fairness and to social justice. Chapter 19 takes a careful look at these controversies and attempts to spell out some of the differering perspectives in these detates. Chapter 20 focuses on legal challenges to testing practices. Ethical issues relevant to psychological tests are considered in Chapter 21.

Following a trend in our recent editions, the final chapters on issues in psychological testing have been extensively updated to reflect new developments in social justice, law, and ethics.

Organization of the Ninth Edition: A Note to Professors for Planning

Producing nine editions of *Psychological Testing* over the course of more than 35 years has been challenging and rewarding. We are honored that hundreds of professors have adopted our text, and that it is now used in hundreds of colleges and universities all over the world. However, some professors have suggested that we reorganize the book to facilitate their approach to the class. To accommodate the large variety of approaches, we have tried to keep the chapters independent enough for professors to teach them in whatever order they choose. For example, one approach to the course is to go systematically through the chapter sequence.

Professors who wish to emphasize psychometric issues, however, might assign Chapters 1 through 7, followed by Chapters 19 and 20. Then, they might return to certain chapters from the Applications section. On campuses that require a strong statistics course as a prerequisite, Chapters 2 and 3 might be dropped. Professors who emphasize applications might assign Chapters 1 through 5 and then proceed directly to Part II, with some professors assigning only some of its chapters. Although Chapters 9 through 13 are most likely to be used in a basic course, we have found sufficient interest in Chapters 14 through 18 to retain them. Chapters 17 and 18 represent newer areas into which psychological testing is expanding. Finally, Chapters 19 and 20 were written so that they could be assigned either at the end of the course or near the beginning. For example, some professors prefer to assign Chapters 19 and 20 after Chapter 5.

MindTap for Kaplan and Saccuzzo's *Psychological Testing*

MindTap is a personalized teaching experience with relevant assignments that guide students to analyze, apply, and improve thinking, allowing instructors to measure skills and outcomes with ease.

▶ Guide Students: A unique learning path of relevant readings, media, and activities that moves students up the learning taxonomy from basic knowledge and comprehension to analysis and application.

▶ Personalized Teaching: Becomes yours with a Learning Path that is built with key student objectives. Control what students see and when they see it. Use it as-is or match to your syllabus exactly—hide, rearrange, add and create your own content.

▶ Promote Better Outcomes: Empower instructors and motivate students with analytics and reports that provide a snapshot of class progress, time in course, engagement and completion rates.

Supplements Beyond Compare

Cognero

Cengage Learning Testing Powered by Cognero is a flexible, online system that allows you to:

- ▶ author, edit, and manage test bank content from multiple Cengage Learning solutions
- ▶ create multiple test versions in an instant
- ▶ deliver tests from your LMS, your classroom or wherever you want.

Instructor's Resource Manual and Test Bank

The Instructor's Resource Manual (IRM) was written by Katherine Nicolai of Rockhurst University the Test Bank by TBD. The IRM includes suggestions for:

- ▶ designing your course,
- ▶ using psychological tests in your course,
- ▶ using student data to teach measurement,
- ▶ using class time,
- ▶ demonstrations, activities, and activity-based lectures.

The IRM also provides a description of integrative assignments found on the instructor's companion Web site and *unique* mock projectives and much more.

The test bank contains more than 800 multiple-choice questions in addition to many "thought" essay questions.

Acknowledgments

We are highly indebted to the many reviewers and professors who provided feedback that helped shape this textbook. Special thanks go to reviewers of all editions of the text: Glen M. Adams, *Harding University*, John Dale Alden III, *Lipscomb University*, Steven Anolik, *St. Francis College*; Michael DeDonno, *Barry University*, John C. Hotz, *St. Cloud State University*, Jacqueline Massa, *Kean University*, Katherine Noll, *University of Illinois at Chicago*; Janet Panter, *Rhodes College*; and Joneis Frandele Thomas, *Howard University*; Virginia Allen, *Idaho State University*, David Bush, *Utah State University*; Ira Bernstein, *University of Texas, Arlington*; Jeff Conte, *San Diego State University*, Imogen Hall, *University of Windsor*, Maureen Hannah, *Siena College*; Ronald McLaughlin, *Juniata College*; Michael Mills, *Loyola Marymount University*, Philip Moberg, *University of Akron*; M. J. Monnot, *Central Michigan University*, Jennifer Neemann, *University of Baltimore*; Karen Obremski Brandon, *University of South Florida*; Frederick Oswald, *Michigan State University*, S. Mark Pancer, *Wilfrid Laurier University*, Christopher Ralston, *Iowa State University*, Sharon Rostosky, *University of Kentucky*, Stefan Schulenberg, *University of Mississippi*; Theresa Sparks, *Clayton State University*; Chockalingam Viswesvaran, *Florida International University*, Mark Wagner, *Wagner College*; and Nancy Zook *SUNY Purchase*.

The nine editions of this book have been developed under seven different Cengage editors. The earlier editions benefited from the patient and inspired supervision of Todd Lueders, C. Deborah Laughton, Phil Curson, Marianne Taflinger, and Jim Brace-Thompson, and Tim Matray. We are most appreciative of the support we have received from current content developer, Tangelique Williams-Grayer. She has been patient, helpful, and very well organized in directing the development of the current edition. Each of our editors has come to the task with a different personality and a different set of insights. We learned immensely from each of them and the ninth edition represents a collection of what we have gained from advice and consultations over many years. We want to give particular thanks to Kate Nicolai for preparing the student workbook for past editions, and the ninth edition online Instructor's Manual. And, we also thank the editorial and production teams, including Jennifer Ziegler, content production manager; Katie Chen, product assistant; and Sharib Asrar of Lumina Datamatics.

The ninth edition was completed while one of us (RMK) was a fellow at the Center for Advanced Studies in the Behavioral Sciences at Stanford University. The Center gratiously provided office space, library services, and collegial support that greatly facilitated the timely revision of the manuscript.

Robert M. Kaplan
Dennis P. Saccuzzo
September 2016

Robert M. Kaplan

ROBERT M. KAPLAN has served as Chief Science Officer at the US Agency for Health Care Research and Quality (AHRQ) and Associate Director of the National Institutes of Health, where he led the behavioral and social sciences programs. He is also a Distinguished Emeritus Professor of Health Services and Medicine at UCLA, where he led the UCLA/RAND AHRQ health services training program and the UCLA/RAND CDC Prevention Research Center. He was Chair of the Department of Health Services from 2004 to 2009. From 1997 to 2004 he was Professor and Chair of the Department of Family and Preventive Medicine, at the University of California, San Diego. He is a past President of several organizations, including the American Psychological Association Division of Health Psychology, Section J of the American Association for the Advancement of Science (Pacific), the International Society for Quality of Life Research, the Society for Behavioral Medicine, and the Academy of Behavioral Medicine Research. Kaplan is a former Editor-in-Chief of *Health Psychology* and of the *Annals of Behavioral Medicine*. His 20 books and over 500 articles or chapters have been cited nearly 30,000 times and the ISI includes him in the listing of the most cited authors in his field (defined as above the 99.5th percentile). Kaplan is an elected member of the National Academy of Medicine (formerly the Institute of Medicine). Dr. Kaplan is currently Regenstrief Distinguished Fellow at Purdue University and Adjunct Professor of Medicine at Stanford University, where he works with Stanford's Clinical Excellence Research Center (CERC).

Robert M. Kaplan

DENNIS P. SACCUZZO is a professor emeritus at San Diego State University, president and co-founder of Applications of Psychology to Law, Inc., an educational corporation devoted to applying cutting-edge psychological concepts to the law, and a founding partner of Saccuzzo Johnson & Poplin, LLP, a law firm from which he uses his knowledge of testing and his legal background to fight for the rights of special education students and other vulnerable groups of individuals He has been a scholar and practitioner of psychological testing for over 40 years. He has authored numerous peer-reviewed publications and professional presentations in the field. Dr. Saccuzzo's research has been supported by the National Science Foundation, the National Institutes of Mental Health, the National Institutes of Health, the U.S. Department of Education, the Scottish Rite Foundation, and the U.S. armed services. He is also a California-licensed psychologist and a California-licensed attorney. He is board certified in clinical psychology by the American Board of Professional Psychology (ABPP). In addition, he is a diplomate of the American Board of Assessment Psychology (ABAP). He is a fellow of the American Psychological Association and American Psychological Society for outstanding and unusual contributions to the field of psychology. Dr. Saccuzzo is the author or co-author of over 300 peer-reviewed papers and publications, including 12 textbooks and over 20 law manuals.

Introduction

LEARNING OBJECTIVES

When you have completed this chapter, you should be able to:

▶ Define the basic terms pertaining to psychological and educational tests

▶ Distinguish between an individual test and a group test

▶ Define the terms *achievement, aptitude,* and *intelligence* and identify a concept that can encompass all three terms

▶ Distinguish between ability tests and personality tests

▶ Define the term *structured personality test*

▶ Explain how structured personality tests differ from projective personality tests

▶ Explain what a normative or standardization sample is and why such a sample is important

▶ Identify the major developments in the history of psychological testing

▶ Explain the relevance of psychological tests in contemporary society

You are sitting at a table. You have just been fingerprinted and have shown a picture ID. You look around and see over 200 nervous people. A test proctor with a stopwatch passes out booklets. You are warned not to open the booklet until told to do so; you face possible disciplinary action if you disobey. This is not a nightmare or some futuristic fantasy—this is real.

Finally, after what seems like an eternity, you are told to open your booklet to page 3 and begin working. Your mouth is dry; your palms are soaking wet. You open to page 3. You have 10 minutes to solve a five-part problem based on the following information.[1]

A car drives into the center ring of a circus and exactly eight clowns—Q, R, S, T, V, W, Y, and Z—get out of the car, one clown at a time. The order in which the clowns get out of the car is consistent with the following conditions:

V gets out at some time before both Y and Q.
Q gets out at some time after Z.
T gets out at some time before V but at some time after R.
S gets out at some time after V.
R gets out at some time before W.

Question 1. If Q is the fifth clown to get out of the car, then each of the following could be true *except*:

Z is the first clown to get out of the car.
T is the second clown to get out of the car.
V is the third clown to get out of the car.
W is the fourth clown to get out of the car.
Y is the sixth clown to get out of the car.
Not quite sure how to proceed, you look at the next question.

Question 2. If R is the second clown to get out of the car, which of the following must be true?

S gets out of the car at some time before T does.
T gets out of the car at some time before W does.
W gets out of the car at some time before V does.
Y gets out of the car at some time before Q does.
Z gets out of the car at some time before W does.

Your heart beats a little faster and your mind starts to freeze up. You glance at your watch and notice that 2 minutes have elapsed and you still don't have your bearings. The person sitting next to you looks a bit faint. Welcome to the world of competitive, "high stakes," standardized psychological tests. The questions you just faced were actual problems from a past version of the LSAT—the Law School Admission Test. Whether or not a student is admitted into law school in the United States is almost entirely determined by that person's score on the LSAT and undergraduate college grade point average. Thus, one's future can depend to a tremendous extent on a single score from a single test given in a tension-packed morning or afternoon. Despite

[1] Used by permission from the Law School Admission Test, October 2002. Answer to Question 1 is D; answer to Question 2 is E.

efforts to improve tests like the LSAT to increase diversity (Kirkland & Hansen, 2011; Pashley, Thornton, & Duffy, 2005), standardized tests tend to disadvantage women, test takers whose parents have lower incomes and levels of education, and ethnic minorities (Atkinson & Geiser, 2009).

Partly because of diversity concerns, growing numbers of 4-year colleges are not relying on the SAT test (Berger 2012; Espenshade & Chung, 2010). In 2011, the website of the National Center for Fair and Open Testing named hundreds of 4-year colleges that do not use the SAT test to admit substantial numbers of freshmen (Fair Test, 2011), and updates the list to keep its website current, http://www.fairtest .org/university/optional. As a result, there continues to be changes to the SAT to make it more responsive to modern realities (Wainer, 2014). Similar problems have appeared on the GRE—the Graduate Record Exam, a test that plays a major role in determining who gets to study at the graduate level in the United States. (Later in this book, we discuss how to prepare for such tests and what their significance, or predictive validity, is.) ETS, creator of the GRE General Test, recently revised the test in several significant ways. The revised GRE General Test was introduced on August 1, 2011 (http://www.ets.org/gre/ institutions/about/general), and is now even being used to evaluate European students (Schwager, Hülsheger, Lang, & Bridgeman, 2015)

Today, some careers do ride on a single test. Perhaps you have already taken the GRE or LSAT. Or perhaps you have not graduated yet but are thinking about applying for an advanced degree or professional program and will soon be facing the GRE, LSAT, or MCAT (Medical College Admission Test). Clearly, it will help you have a basic understanding of the multitude of psychological tests people are asked to take throughout their lives.

From birth, tests have a major influence on our lives. When the pediatrician strokes the palms of our hands and the soles of our feet, he or she is performing a test. When we enter school, tests decide whether we pass or fail classes. Testing may determine if we need special education. In the United States, Europe, and many other industrialized countries, competence tests determine if students will graduate from high school (Lamb, 2011; Reardon, Nicole, Allison, & Michal, 2010). More tests determine which college we may attend. And, of course, we still face more tests once we are in college.

After graduation, those who choose to avoid tests such as the GRE may need to take tests to determine where they will work. In the modern world, a large part of everyone's life and success depends on test results. Indeed, tests even have worldwide significance.

For example, 15-year-old children in 32 nations were given problems such as the following from the Organization for Economic Co-operation and Development (OECD) and the Programme for International Student Assessment (PISA) (Schleicher & Tamassia, 2000):

A result of global warming is that ice of some glaciers is melting.
  Twelve years after the ice disappears, tiny plants, called lichen, start to grow on the rocks. Each lichen grows approximately in the shape of a circle.

  The relationship between the diameter of the circles and the age of the lichen can be approximated with the formula: $d = 7.0 \times$ the square root of $(t - 12)$ for any/less

FIGURE 1.1

Approximate average scores of 15-year-old students on the OECD mathematical literacy test.

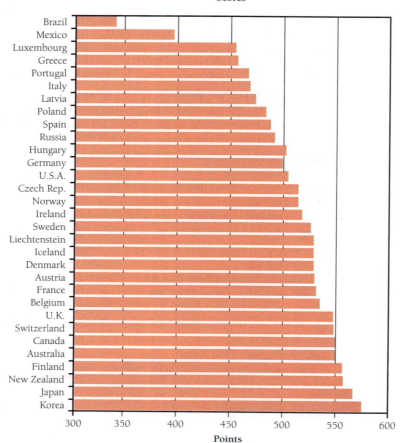

International Mathematical Literacy Scores

Statistics used by permission of the OECD and PISA. Figure courtesy of W. J. Koen

than or equal to 12, where d represents the diameter of the lichen in millimeters, and t represents the number of years after the ice has disappeared.

Calculate the diameter of the lichen 16 years after the ice disappeared. The complete and correct answer is:

$$d = 7.0 \times \text{the square root of } (16 - 12 \text{ mm})$$

$$d = 7.0 \times \text{the square root of } 4 \text{ mm}$$

$$d = 14 \text{ mm}$$

Eighteen countries ranked above the United States in the percentage of 15-year-olds who had mastered such concepts (see Figure 1.1).

The results were similar for an OECD science literacy test (see Figure 1.2), which had questions such as the following:

A bus is moving along a straight stretch of road. The bus driver, named Ray, has a cup of water resting in a holder on the dashboard. Suddenly Ray has to slam on the brakes.

FIGURE 1.2

Approximate average scores of 15-year-old students on the OECD scientific literacy test.

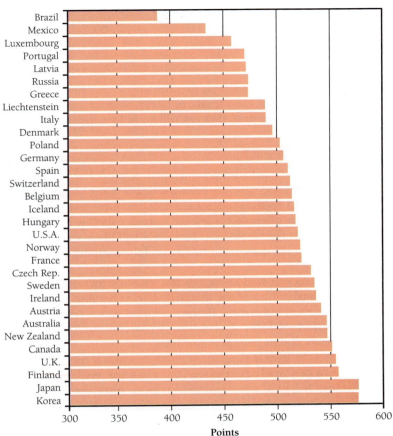

International Scientific Literacy Scores

Statistics used by permission of the OECD and PISA. Figure courtesy of W. J. Koen

What is most likely to happen to the water in the cup immediately after Ray slams on the brakes?

A. The water will stay horizontal.

B. The water will spill over side 1.

C. The water will spill over side 2.

D. The water will spill but you cannot tell if it will spill over side 1 or side 2.

The correct answer is C.

How useful are tests such as these? Do they measure anything meaningful? How accurate are they? Such questions concern not only every U.S. citizen but also all members of the highly competitive international community. To answer them, you must understand the principles of psychological testing that you are about to learn.

To answer questions about tests, you must understand the concepts presented in this book, such as reliability, validity, item analysis, and test construction. A full understanding of these concepts will require careful study and knowledge of basic statistics, but your efforts will be richly rewarded. When you finish this book, you will be a better consumer of tests.

Basic Concepts

You are probably already familiar with some of the elementary concepts of psychological testing. For the sake of clarity, however, we shall begin with definitions of the most basic terms so that you will know how they are used in this textbook.

What a Test Is

Everyone has had experience with tests. A **test** is a measurement device or technique used to quantify behavior or aid in the understanding and prediction of behavior. A spelling test, for example, measures how well someone spells or the extent to which someone has learned to spell a specific list of words. At some time during the next few weeks, your instructor will likely want to measure how well you have learned the material in this book. To accomplish this, your instructor may give you a test.

As you well know, the test your instructor gives may not measure your full understanding of the material. This is because a test measures only a sample of behavior, and error is always associated with a sampling process. Test scores are not perfect measures of a behavior or characteristic, but they do add significantly to the prediction process, as you will see.

An **item** is a specific stimulus to which a person responds overtly; this response can be scored or evaluated (e.g., classified, graded on a scale, or counted). Because psychological and educational tests are made up of items, the data they produce are explicit and hence subject to scientific inquiry.

In simple terms, items are the specific questions or problems that make up a test. The problems presented at the beginning of this chapter are examples of test items. The overt response would be to fill in or blacken one of the spaces:

A **psychological test** or educational test is a set of items that are designed to measure characteristics of human beings that pertain to behavior. There are many types of behavior. *Overt* behavior is an individual's observable activity. Some psychological tests attempt to measure the extent to which someone might engage in or "emit" a particular overt behavior. Other tests measure how much a person has previously engaged in some overt behavior. Behavior can also be *covert*—that is, it takes place within an individual and cannot be directly observed. For example, your feelings and thoughts are types of covert behavior. Some tests attempt to measure such behavior. Psychological and educational tests thus measure past or current behavior. Some also attempt to predict future behavior, such as success in college or in an advanced degree program.

Scores on tests may be related to traits, which are enduring characteristics or tendencies to respond in a certain manner. "Determination," sometimes seen as "stubbornness," is an example of a trait; "shyness" is another. Test scores may also be related to the state, or the specific condition or status, of an individual. A determined individual after many setbacks may, for instance, be in a weakened state and therefore be less inclined than usual to manifest determination. Tests measure many types of behavior.

What does it mean when someone gets 75 items correct on a 100-item test? One thing it means, of course, is that 75% of the items were answered correctly. In many situations, however, knowing the percentage of correct items a person obtained can be misleading. Consider two extreme examples. In one case, out of 100 students who took the exam, 99 had 90% correct or higher, and 1 had 75% correct. In another case, 99 of the 100 students had scores of 25% or lower, while 1 had 75% correct. The meaning of the scores can change dramatically, depending on how a well-defined sample of individuals scores on a test. In the first case, a score of 75% is poor because it is in the bottom of the distribution; in the second case, 75% is actually a top score. To deal with such problems of interpretation, psychologists make use of **scales,** which relate raw scores on test items to some defined theoretical or empirical distribution. Later in the book you will learn about such distributions.

Types of Tests

Just as there are many types of behavior, so there are many types of tests. Those that can be given to only one person at a time are known as **individual tests** (see Figure 1.3). The examiner or **test administrator** (the person giving the test) gives

FIGURE 1.3
An individual test administration.

Steve Debenport/Getty Images

the test to only one person at a time, the same way that psychotherapists see only one person at a time. A **group test,** by contrast, can be administered to more than one person at a time by a single examiner, such as when an instructor gives everyone in the class a test at the same time.

One can also categorize tests according to the type of behavior they measure. Ability tests contain items that can be scored in terms of speed, accuracy, or both. On an ability test, the faster or the more accurate your responses, the better your scores on a particular characteristic. The more algebra problems you can correctly solve in a given amount of time, the higher you score in ability to solve such problems.

Historically, experts have distinguished among achievement, aptitude, and intelligence as different types of ability. **Achievement** refers to previous learning. A test that measures or evaluates how many words you can spell correctly is called a *spelling achievement test*. **Aptitude,** by contrast, refers to the potential for learning or acquiring a specific skill. A spelling aptitude test measures how many words you might be able to spell given a certain amount of training, education, and experience. Your musical aptitude refers in part to how well you might be able to learn to play a musical instrument given a certain number of lessons. Traditionally distinguished from achievement and aptitude, **intelligence** refers to a person's general potential to solve problems, adapt to changing circumstances, think abstractly, and profit from experience. When we say a person is "smart," we are usually referring to intelligence. When a father scolds his daughter because she has not done as well in school as she can, he most likely believes that she has not used her intelligence (general potential) to achieve (acquire new knowledge).

The distinctions among achievement, aptitude, and intelligence are not always so cut-and-dried because all three are highly interrelated. Attempts to separate prior learning from potential for learning, for example, have not succeeded. In view of the considerable overlap of achievement, aptitude, and intelligence tests, all three concepts are encompassed by the term **human ability.**

There is a clear-cut distinction between ability tests and personality tests. Whereas ability tests are related to capacity or potential, **personality tests** are related to the overt and covert dispositions of the individual—for example, the tendency of a person to show a particular behavior or response in a given situation. Remaining isolated from others, for instance, does not require any special skill or ability, but some people typically prefer or tend to remain thus isolated. Personality tests measure typical behavior.

There are several types of personality tests. In Chapter 13, you will learn about structured, or objective, personality tests. **Structured personality tests** provide a statement, usually of the "self-report" variety, and require the subject to choose between two or more alternative responses such as 'True" or "False" (see Figure 1.4).

In contrast to structured personality tests, projective personality tests are unstructured. In a **projective personality test,** either the stimulus (test materials) or the required response—or both—are ambiguous. For example, in the highly controversial Rorschach test, the stimulus is an inkblot. Furthermore, rather than being asked to choose among alternative responses, as in structured personality tests, the individual is asked to provide a spontaneous response. The inkblot is presented

FIGURE 1.4
Self-report test items.

	True	False
1. I like heavy metal music.	☐	☐
2. I believe that honesty is the best policy.	☐	☐
3. I am in good health.	☐	☐
4. I am easily fatigued.	☐	☐
5. I sleep well at night.	☐	☐

TABLE 1.1   Types of Tests

I. **Ability tests:** Measure skills in terms of speed, accuracy, or both.

   A. **Achievement:** Measures previous learning.

   B. **Aptitude:** Measures potential for acquiring a specific skill.

   C. **Intelligence:** Measures potential to solve problems, adapt to changing circumstances, and profit from experience.

II. **Personality tests:** Measure typical behavior—traits, temperaments, and dispositions.

   A. **Structured (objective):** Provides a self-report statement to which the person responds "True" or "False," "Yes" or "No."

   B. **Projective:** Provides an ambiguous test stimulus; response requirements are unclear.

to the subject, who is asked, "What might this be?" Projective tests assume that a person's interpretation of an ambiguous stimulus will reflect his or her unique characteristics (see Chapter 14).

See Table 1.1 for a brief overview of ability and personality tests.

Psychological testing refers to all the possible uses, applications, and underlying concepts of psychological and educational tests. The main use of these tests, though, is to evaluate individual differences or variations among individuals. Such tests measure individual differences in ability and personality and assume that the differences shown on the test reflect actual differences among individuals. For instance, individuals who score high on an IQ test are assumed to have a higher degree of intelligence than those who obtain low scores. Thus, the most important purpose of testing is to differentiate among those taking the tests. We shall discuss the idea of individual differences later in this chapter.

Overview of the Book

This book is divided into three parts: *Principles, Applications,* and *Issues.* Together, these parts cover psychological testing from the most basic ideas to the most complex. Basic ideas and events are introduced early and stressed throughout to reinforce what you have just learned. In covering principles, applications, and issues, we intend to provide not only the *who's* of psychological testing but also the *how's* and *why's* of major developments in the field. We also address an important concern of many students—relevance—by examining the diverse uses of tests and the resulting data.

Principles of Psychological Testing

By *principles of psychological testing,* we mean the basic concepts and fundamental ideas that underlie all psychological and educational tests. Chapters 2 and 3 present statistical concepts that provide the foundation for understanding tests. Chapters 4 and 5 cover two of the most fundamental concepts in testing: reliability and validity. **Reliability** refers to the accuracy, dependability, consistency, or repeatability of test results. In more technical terms, reliability refers to the degree to which test scores are free of measurement errors. As you will learn, there are many ways a test can be reliable. For example, test results may be reliable over time, which means that when the same test is given twice within any given time interval, the results tend to be the same or highly similar. **Validity** refers to the meaning and usefulness of test results. More specifically, validity refers to the degree to which a certain inference or interpretation based on a test is appropriate. When one asks the question, "What does this psychological test measure?" one is essentially asking "For what inference is this test valid?"

Another principle of psychological testing concerns how a test is created or constructed. In Chapter 6, we present the principles of test construction. The act of giving a test is known as **test administration,** which is the main topic of Chapter 7. Though some tests are easy to administer, others must be administered in a highly specific way. The final chapter of Part I covers the fundamentals of administering a psychological test.

Applications of Psychological Testing

Part II, on applications, provides a detailed analysis of many of the most popular tests and how they are used or applied. It begins with an overview of the essential terms and concepts that relate to the application of tests. Chapter 8 discusses interviewing techniques. An **interview** is a method of gathering information through verbal interaction, such as direct questions. Not only has the interview traditionally served as a major technique of gathering psychological information in general, but also data from interviews provide an important complement to test results.

Chapters 9 and 10 cover individual tests of human ability. In these chapters, you will learn not only about tests but also about the theories of intelligence that underlie them. In Chapter 11, we cover testing in education with an emphasis on special education. In Chapter 12, we present group tests of human ability. Chapter 13 covers structured personality tests, and Chapter 14 covers projective personality tests. In Chapter 15, we discuss the important role of computers in the testing field. We also consider the influence of cognitive psychology, which today is the most prominent of the various schools of thought within psychology (Gentner, 2010; Klauer, Voss, & Stahl, 2011; Rips, 2011).

These chapters not only provide descriptive information but also delve into the ideas underlying the various tests. Chapter 16 examines interest tests, which measure behavior relevant to such factors as occupational preferences. Chapter 17 reviews the relatively new area of medical testing for brain damage and health status. It also covers important recent advancements in developmental neuropsychology. Finally, Chapter 18 covers tests for industrial and organizational psychology and business.

Issues of Psychological Testing

Many social and theoretical issues, such as the controversial topic of racial differences in ability, accompany testing. Part III covers many of these issues. As a compromise between breadth and depth of coverage, we focus on a comprehensive discussion of those issues that have particular importance in the current professional, social, and political environment.

Chapter 19 examines test bias, one of the most volatile issues in the field (Cormier, McGrew, & Evans, 2011; Moreno & Mickie, 2011). Because psychological tests have been accused of being discriminatory or biased against certain groups, this chapter takes a careful look at both sides of the argument. Because of charges of bias and other problems, psychological testing is increasingly coming under the scrutiny of the law (Caffrey, 2009; Saccuzzo, 1999). Chapter 20 examines test bias as related to legal issues and discusses testing and the law. Chapter 21 presents a general overview of other major issues currently shaping the future of psychological testing in the United States with an emphasis on ethics. From our review of the issues, we also speculate on what the future holds for psychological testing.

Historical Perspective

We now briefly provide the historical context of psychological testing. This discussion touches on some of the material presented earlier in this chapter.

Early Antecedents

Most of the major developments in testing have occurred over the last century, many of them in the United States. The origins of testing, however, are neither recent nor American. Evidence suggests that the Chinese had a relatively sophisticated civil service testing program more than 4000 years ago (DuBois, 1970, 1972). Every third year in China, oral examinations were given to help determine work evaluations and promotion decisions.

By the Han Dynasty (206–220 B.C.E.), the use of **test batteries** (two or more tests used in conjunction) was quite common. These early tests related to such diverse topics as civil law, military affairs, agriculture, revenue, and geography. Tests had become quite well developed by the Ming Dynasty (1368–1644 C.E.). During this period, a national multistage testing program involved local and regional testing centers equipped with special testing booths. Those who did well on the tests at the local level went on to provincial capitals for more extensive essay examinations. After this second testing, those with the highest test scores went on to the nation's capital for a final round. Only those who passed this third set of tests were eligible for public office.

The Western world most likely learned about testing programs through the Chinese. Reports by British missionaries and diplomats encouraged the English East India Company in 1832 to copy the Chinese system as a method of selecting employees for overseas duty. Because testing programs worked well for the company, the British government adopted a similar system of testing for its civil service in 1855. After the British endorsement of a civil service testing system, the French and German governments followed suit. In 1883, the U.S. government established the American Civil Service Commission, which developed and administered competitive examinations for certain government jobs. The impetus of the testing movement in the Western world grew rapidly at that time (Wiggins, 1973).

Charles Darwin and Individual Differences

Perhaps the most basic concept underlying psychological and educational testing pertains to individual differences. No two snowflakes are identical, no two fingerprints the same. Similarly, no two people are exactly alike in ability and typical behavior. As we have noted, tests are specifically designed to measure these individual differences in ability and personality among people.

Although human beings realized long ago that individuals differ, developing tools for measuring such differences was no easy matter. To develop a measuring device, we must understand what we want to measure. An important step toward understanding individual differences came with the publication of Charles Darwin's highly influential book *The Origin of Species* in 1859. According to Darwin's theory, higher forms of life evolved partially because of differences among individual forms of life within a species. Given that individual members of a species differ, some possess characteristics that are more adaptive or successful in a given environment than are those of other members. Darwin also believed that those with the best or most adaptive characteristics survive at the expense of those who are less fit and that the survivors pass their characteristics on to the next generation. Through this process, he argued, life has evolved to its currently complex and intelligent levels.

Sir Francis Galton, a relative of Darwin, soon began applying Darwin's theories to the study of human beings (see Figure 1.5). Given the concepts of survival of the fittest and individual differences, Galton set out to show that some people possessed characteristics that made them more fit than others, a theory he articulated in his book *Hereditary Genius,* published in 1869. Galton (1883) subsequently began a series of experimental studies to document the validity of his position. He concentrated on demonstrating that individual differences exist in human sensory and motor functioning, such as reaction time, visual acuity, and physical strength. In doing so, Galton initiated a search for knowledge concerning human individual differences, which is now one of the most important domains of scientific psychology.

FIGURE 1.5
Sir Francis Galton.

(From the National Library of Medicine)

Galton's work was extended by the U.S. psychologist James McKeen Cattell, who coined the term *mental test* (Cattell, 1890). Cattell's doctoral dissertation was based on Galton's work on individual differences in reaction time. As such, Cattell perpetuated and stimulated the forces that ultimately led to the development of modern tests.

Experimental Psychology and Psychophysical Measurement

A second major foundation of testing can be found in experimental psychology and early attempts to unlock the mysteries of human consciousness through the scientific method. Before psychology was practiced as a science, mathematical models of the mind were developed, in particular those of J. E. Herbart. Herbart eventually used these models as the basis for educational theories that strongly influenced 19th-century educational practices. Following Herbart, E. H. Weber attempted to demonstrate the existence of a psychological threshold, the minimum stimulus necessary to activate a sensory system. Then, following Weber, G. T. Fechner devised the law that the strength of a sensation grows as the logarithm of the stimulus intensity.

Wilhelm Wundt, who set up a laboratory at the University of Leipzig in 1879, is credited with founding the science of psychology, following in the tradition of Weber and Fechner (Hearst, 1979). Wundt was succeeded by E. B. Titchner, whose student, G. Whipple, recruited L. L. Thurstone. Whipple provided the basis for immense changes in the field of testing by conducting a seminar at the Carnegie Institute in 1919 attended by Thurstone, E. Strong, and other early prominent U.S. psychologists. From this seminar came the Carnegie Interest Inventory and later the Strong Vocational Interest Blank. Later in this book, we discuss in greater detail the work of these pioneers and the tests they helped develop.

Thus, psychological testing developed from at least two lines of inquiry: one based on the work of Darwin, Galton, and Cattell on the measurement of individual differences, and the other (more theoretically relevant and probably stronger) based on the work of the German psychophysicists Herbart, Weber, Fechner, and Wundt. Experimental psychology developed from the latter. From this work also came the idea that testing, like an experiment, requires rigorous experimental control. Such control, as you will see, comes from administering tests under highly standardized conditions.

The efforts of these researchers, however necessary, did not by themselves lead to the creation of modern psychological tests. Such tests also arose in response to important needs such as classifying and identifying the mentally and emotionally handicapped. One of the earliest tests resembling current procedures, the Seguin Form Board Test (Seguin, 1866/1907), was developed in an effort to educate and evaluate the mentally disabled. Similarly, Kraepelin (1912) devised a series of examinations for evaluating emotionally impaired people.

An important breakthrough in the creation of modern tests came at the turn of the 20th century. The French minister of public instruction appointed a commission to study ways of identifying intellectually subnormal individuals in order to provide them with appropriate educational experiences. One member of that commission was Alfred Binet. Working in conjunction with the French physician T. Simon, Binet developed the first major general intelligence test. Binet's early effort launched the first systematic attempt to evaluate individual differences in human intelligence (see Chapter 9).

The Evolution of Intelligence and Standardized Achievement Tests

The history and evolution of Binet's intelligence test are instructive. The first version of the test, known as the Binet-Simon Scale, was published in 1905. This instrument contained 30 items of increasing difficulty and was designed to identify intellectually subnormal individuals. Like all well-constructed tests, the Binet-Simon Scale of 1905 was augmented by a comparison or standardization sample. Binet's standardization sample consisted of 50 children who had been given the test under *standard conditions*—that is, with precisely the same instructions and format. In obtaining this standardization sample, the authors of the Binet test had norms with which they could compare the results from any new subject. Without such norms, the meaning of scores would have been difficult, if not impossible, to evaluate. However, by knowing such things as the average number of correct responses found in the standardization sample, one could at least state whether a new subject was below or above it.

It is easy to understand the importance of a standardization sample. However, the importance of obtaining a standardization sample that represents the population for which a test will be used has sometimes been ignored or overlooked by test users. For example, if a standardization sample consists of 50 white men from wealthy families, then one cannot easily or fairly evaluate the score of an African American girl from a poverty-stricken family. Nevertheless, comparisons of this kind are sometimes made. Clearly, it is not appropriate to compare an individual with a group that does not have the same characteristics as the individual.

Binet was aware of the importance of a standardization sample. Further development of the Binet test involved attempts to increase the size and representativeness of the standardization sample. A **representative sample** is one that comprises individuals similar to those for whom the test is to be used. When the test is used for the general population, a representative sample must reflect all segments of the population in proportion to their actual numbers.

By 1908, the Binet-Simon Scale had been substantially improved. It was revised to include nearly twice as many items as the 1905 scale. Even more significantly, the size of the standardization sample was increased to more than 200. The 1908 Binet-Simon Scale also determined a child's **mental** age, thereby introducing a historically significant concept. In simplified terms, you might think of mental age as a measurement of a child's performance on the test relative to other children of that particular age group. If a child's test performance equals that of the average 8-year-old, for example, then his or her mental age is 8. In other words, in terms of the abilities measured by the test, this child can be viewed as having a similar level of ability as the average 8-year-old. The chronological age of the child may be 4 or 12, but in terms of test performance, the child functions at the same level as the average 8-year-old. The mental age concept was one of the most important contributions of the revised 1908 Binet-Simon Scale.

In 1911, the Binet-Simon Scale received a minor revision. By this time, the idea of intelligence testing had swept across the world. By 1916, L. M. Terman of Stanford University had revised the Binet test for use in the United States. Terman's revision, known as the Stanford-Binet Intelligence Scale (Terman, 1916), was the only American version of the Binet test that flourished. It also characterizes one of the most important trends in testing—the drive toward better tests.

Terman's 1916 revision of the Binet-Simon Scale contained many improvements. The standardization sample was increased to include 1,000 people, original items were revised, and many new items were added. Terman's 1916 Stanford-Binet Intelligence Scale added respectability and momentum to the newly developing testing movement.

World War I

The testing movement grew enormously in the United States because of the demand for a quick efficient way of evaluating the emotional and intellectual functioning of thousands of military recruits in World War I. The war created a demand for large-scale group testing because relatively few trained personnel could evaluate the huge influx of military recruits. However, the Binet test was an individual test.

Shortly after the United States became actively involved in World War I, the army requested the assistance of Robert Yerkes, who was then the president of the American Psychological Association (see Yerkes, 1921). Yerkes headed a committee of distinguished psychologists who soon developed two structured group tests of human abilities: the Army Alpha and the Army Beta. The Army Alpha required reading ability, whereas the Army Beta measured the intelligence of illiterate adults.

World War I fueled the widespread development of group tests. About this time, the scope of testing also broadened to include tests of achievement, aptitude, interest, and personality. Because achievement, aptitude, and intelligence tests overlapped considerably, the distinctions proved to be more illusory than real. Even so, the 1916 Stanford-Binet Intelligence Scale had appeared at a time of strong demand and high optimism for the potential of measuring human behavior through tests. World War I and the creation of group tests had then added momentum to the testing movement. Shortly after the appearance of the 1916 Stanford-Binet Intelligence Scale and the Army Alpha test, schools, colleges, and industry began using tests. It appeared to many that this new phenomenon, the psychological test, held the key to solving the problems emerging from the rapid growth of population and technology.

Achievement Tests

Among the most important developments following World War I was the development of standardized achievement tests. In contrast to essay tests, standardized achievement tests provide multiple-choice questions that are standardized on a large sample to produce norms against which the results of new examinees can be compared.

Standardized achievement tests caught on quickly because of the relative ease of administration and scoring and the lack of subjectivity or favoritism that can occur in essay or other written tests. In school settings, standardized achievement tests allowed one to maintain identical testing conditions and scoring standards for a large number of children. Such tests also allowed a broader coverage of content and were less expensive and more efficient than essays. In 1923, the development of standardized achievement tests culminated in the publication of the Stanford Achievement Test by T. L. Kelley, G. M. Ruch, and L. M. Terman.

By the 1930s, it was widely held that the objectivity and reliability of these new standardized tests made them superior to essay tests. Their use proliferated widely. It is interesting, as we shall discuss later in the book that teachers of today appear to have come full circle. Currently, many people favor written tests and work samples (portfolios) over standardized achievement tests as the best way to evaluate children, and reduce or prevent marginalization of minority children (Watson, 2015).

Rising to the Challenge

For every movement there is a countermovement, and the testing movement in the United States in the 1930s was no exception. Critics soon became vocal enough to dampen enthusiasm and to make even the most optimistic advocates of tests defensive. Researchers, who demanded nothing short of the highest standards, noted the limitations and weaknesses of existing tests. Not even the Stanford-Binet, a landmark in the testing field, was safe from criticism. Although tests were used between the two world wars and many new tests were developed, their accuracy and utility remained under heavy fire.

Near the end of the 1930s, developers began to reestablish the respectability of tests. New, improved tests reflected the knowledge and experience of the previous two decades. By 1937, the Stanford-Binet had been revised again. Among the many improvements was the inclusion of a standardization sample of more than 3000 individuals. A mere 2 years after the 1937 revision of the Stanford-Binet test, David Wechsler published the first version of the Wechsler intelligence scales (see Chapter 10), the Wechsler-Bellevue Intelligence Scale (W-B) (Wechsler, 1939). The Wechsler-Bellevue scale contained several interesting innovations in intelligence testing. Unlike the Stanford-Binet test, which produced only a single score (the so-called IQ, or intelligence quotient), Wechsler's test yielded several scores, permitting an analysis of an individual's pattern or combination of abilities.

Among the various scores produced by the Wechsler test was the performance IQ. Performance tests do not require a verbal response; one can use them to evaluate intelligence in people who have few verbal or language skills. The Stanford-Binet test had long been criticized because of its emphasis on language and verbal skills, making it inappropriate for many individuals, such as those who cannot speak or who cannot read. In addition, few people believed that language or verbal skills play an exclusive role in human intelligence. Wechsler's inclusion of a nonverbal scale thus helped overcome some of the practical and theoretical weaknesses of the Binet test. In 1986, the Binet test was drastically revised to include performance subtests. More recently, it was overhauled again in 2003, as we shall see in Chapter 9. (Other important concepts in intelligence testing will be formally defined in Chapter 10, which covers the various forms of the Wechsler intelligence scales.)

Personality Tests: 1920–1940

Just before and after World War II, personality tests began to blossom. Whereas intelligence tests measured ability or potential, personality tests measured presumably stable characteristics or traits that theoretically underlie behavior. **Traits** are relatively enduring dispositions (tendencies to act, think, or feel in a certain manner in any given circumstance) that distinguish one individual from another. For example, we say that some people are optimistic and some pessimistic. Optimistic people tend to remain so regardless of whether or not things are going well. A pessimist, by contrast, tends to look at the negative side of things. Optimism and pessimism can thus be viewed as traits. One of the basic goals of traditional personality tests is to measure traits. As you will learn, however, the notion of traits has important limitations.

The earliest personality tests were structured paper-and-pencil group tests. These tests provided multiple-choice and true-false questions that could be administered to a large group. Because it provides a high degree of structure—that is, a definite stimulus and specific alternative responses that can be unequivocally scored—this sort of test is a type of structured personality test. The first structured personality test, the Woodworth Personal Data Sheet, was developed during World War I and was published in final form just after the war (see Figure 1.6).

As indicated earlier, the motivation underlying the development of the first personality test was the need to screen military recruits. History indicates that tests such as the Binet and the Woodworth were created by necessity to meet unique challenges. Like the early ability tests, however, the first structured personality test was simple by today's standards. Interpretation of the Woodworth test depended on the now-discredited assumption that the content of an item could be accepted at face value. If the person marked "False" for the statement "I wet the bed," then it was assumed that he or she did not "wet the bed." As logical as this assumption seems, experience has shown that it is often false. In addition to being dishonest, the person responding to the question may not interpret the meaning of "wet the bed" the same way as the test administrator does. (Other problems with tests such as the Woodworth are discussed in Chapter 13.)

The introduction of the Woodworth test was enthusiastically followed by the creation of a variety of structured personality tests, all of which assumed that a subject's response could be taken at face value. However, researchers scrutinized, analyzed, and criticized the early structured personality tests, just as they had done with the ability tests. Indeed, the criticism of tests that relied on face value alone became so intense that structured personality tests were nearly driven out of existence. The development of new tests based on more modern concepts followed, revitalizing the use of structured personality tests. Thus, after an initial surge of interest and optimism during most of the 1920s, structured personality tests declined

FIGURE 1.6
The Woodworth Personal Data Sheet represented an attempt to standardize the psychiatric interview. It contains questions such as those shown here.

	Yes	No
1. I wet the bed.	☐	☐
2. I drink a quart of whiskey each day.	☐	☐
3. I am afraid of closed spaces.	☐	☐
4. I believe I am being followed.	☐	☐
5. People are out to get me.	☐	☐
6. Sometimes I see or hear things that other people do not hear or see.	☐	☐

FIGURE 1.7
Card 1 of the Rorschach inkblot test, a projective personality test. Such tests provide an ambiguous stimulus to which a subject is asked to make some response.

by the late 1930s and early 1940s. Following World War II, however, personality tests based on fewer or different assumptions were introduced, thereby rescuing the structured personality test.

During the brief but dramatic rise and fall of the first structured personality tests, interest in projective tests began to grow. In contrast to structured personality tests, which in general provide a relatively unambiguous test stimulus and specific alternative responses, projective personality tests provide an ambiguous stimulus and unclear response requirements. Furthermore, the scoring of projective tests is often subjective.

Unlike the early structured personality tests, interest in the projective Rorschach inkblot test grew slowly (see Figure 1.7). The Rorschach test was first published by Herman Rorschach of Switzerland in 1921. However, several years passed before the Rorschach came to the United States, where David Levy introduced it. The first Rorschach doctoral dissertation written in a U.S. university was not completed until 1932, when Sam Beck, Levy's student, decided to investigate the properties of the Rorschach test scientifically. Although initial interest in the Rorschach test was lukewarm at best, its popularity grew rapidly after Beck's work despite suspicion, doubt, and criticism from the scientific community. Today, however, the Rorschach is under a dark cloud (see Chapter 14).

Adding to the momentum for the acceptance and use of projective tests was the development of the Thematic Apperception Test (TAT) by Henry Murray and Christina Morgan in 1935. Whereas the Rorschach test contained completely ambiguous inkblot stimuli, the TAT was more structured. Its stimuli consisted of ambiguous pictures depicting a variety of scenes and situations, such as a boy sitting in front of a table with a violin on it. Unlike the Rorschach test, which asked the subject to explain what the inkblot might be, the TAT required the subject to make up a story about the ambiguous scene. The TAT purported to measure human needs and thus to ascertain individual differences in motivation.

The Emergence of New Approaches to Personality Testing

The popularity of the two most important projective personality tests, the Rorschach and TAT, grew rapidly by the late 1930s and early 1940s, perhaps because of disillusionment with structured personality tests (Dahlstrom, 1969a). However, as we shall see in Chapter 14, projective tests, particularly the Rorschach, have not withstood a vigorous examination of their psychometric properties (Wood, Lilienfeld, Nezworski, Garb, Allen, & Wildermuth, 2010).

In 1943, the Minnesota Multiphasic Personality Inventory (MMPI) began a new era for structured personality tests. The idea behind the MMPI—to use empirical methods to determine the meaning of a test response—helped revolutionize structured personality tests. The problem with early structured personality tests such as the Woodworth was that they made far too many assumptions that subsequent scientific investigations failed to substantiate. The authors of the MMPI, by contrast, argued that the meaning of a test response could be determined only by empirical research. The MMPI, along with its updated companion the MMPI-2 (Butcher, 1989, 1990), is currently the most widely used and referenced personality test. Its emphasis on the need for empirical data has stimulated the development of tens of thousands of studies.

Just about the time the MMPI appeared, personality tests based on the statistical procedure called *factor analysis* began to emerge. **Factor analysis** is a method of finding the minimum number of dimensions (characteristics, attributes), called *factors,* to account for a large number of variables. We may say a person is outgoing, is gregarious, seeks company, is talkative, and enjoys relating to others. However, these descriptions contain a certain amount of redundancy. A factor analysis can identify how much they overlap and whether they can all be accounted for or subsumed under a single dimension (or factor) such as extroversion.

In the early 1940s, J. R. Guilford made the first serious attempt to use factor analytic techniques in the development of a structured personality test. By the end of that decade, R. B. Cattell had introduced the Sixteen Personality Factor Questionnaire (16PF); despite its declining popularity, it remains one of the most well-constructed structured personality tests and an important example of a test developed with the aid of factor analysis. Today, factor analysis is a tool used in the design or validation of just about all major tests. (Factor analytic personality tests will be discussed in Chapter 13.) See Table 1.2 for a brief overview of personality tests.

TABLE 1.2 Summary of Personality Tests

Woodworth Personal Data Sheet: An early structured personality test that assumed that a test response can be taken at face value.

The Rorschach Inkblot Test: A highly controversial projective test that provided an ambiguous stimulus (an inkblot) and asked the subject what it might be.

The Thematic Apperception Test (TAT): A projective test that provided ambiguous pictures and asked subjects to make up a story.

The Minnesota Multiphasic Personality Inventory (MMPI): A structured personality test that made no assumptions about the meaning of a test response. Such meaning was to be determined by empirical research.

The California Psychological Inventory (CPI): A structured personality test developed according to the same principles as the MMPI.

The Sixteen Personality Factor Questionnaire (16PF): A structured personality test based on the statistical procedure of factor analysis.

The Period of Rapid Changes in the Status of Testing

The 1940s saw not only the emergence of a whole new technology in psychological testing but also the growth of applied aspects of psychology. The role and significance of tests used in World War I were reaffirmed in World War II. By this time, the U.S. government had begun to encourage the continued development of applied psychological technology. As a result, considerable federal funding provided paid, supervised training for clinically oriented psychologists. By 1949, formal university training standards had been developed and accepted, and clinical psychology was born. Other applied branches of psychology—such as industrial, counseling, educational, and school psychology—soon began to blossom.

One of the major functions of the applied psychologist was providing psychological testing. The Shakow, Hilgard, Kelly, Sanford, and Shaffer (1947) report, which was the foundation of the formal training standards in clinical psychology, specified that psychological testing was a unique function of the clinical psychologist and recommended that testing methods be taught only to doctoral psychology students. A position paper of the American Psychological Association published 7 years later (APA, 1954) affirmed that the domain of the clinical psychologist included testing. It formally declared, however, that the psychologist would conduct psychotherapy only in "true" collaboration with physicians. Thus, psychologists could conduct testing independently, but not psychotherapy. Indeed, as long as psychologists assumed the role of testers, they played a complementary but often secondary role vis-à-vis medical practitioners. Though the medical profession could have hindered the emergence of clinical psychology, it did not, because as tester the psychologist aided the physician. Therefore, in the late 1940s and early 1950s, testing was the major function of the clinical psychologist (Shaffer, 1953).

For better or worse, depending on one's perspective, the government's efforts to stimulate the development of applied aspects of psychology, especially clinical psychology, were extremely successful. Hundreds of highly talented and creative young people were attracted to clinical and other applied areas of psychology. These individuals, who would use tests and other psychological techniques to solve practical human problems, were uniquely trained as practitioners of the principles, empirical foundations, and applications of the science of psychology.

Armed with powerful knowledge from scientific psychology, many of these early clinical practitioners must have felt frustrated by their relationship to physicians (see Saccuzzo & Kaplan, 1984). Unable to engage independently in the practice of psychotherapy, some psychologists felt like technicians serving the medical profession. The highly talented group of post-World War II psychologists quickly began to reject this secondary role. Further, because many psychologists associated tests with this secondary relationship, they rejected testing (Lewandowski & Saccuzzo, 1976). At the same time, the potentially intrusive nature of tests and fears of misuse began to create public suspicion, distrust, and contempt for tests. Attacks on testing came from within and without the profession. These attacks intensified and multiplied so fast that many psychologists jettisoned all ties to the traditional tests developed during the first half of the 20th century. Testing therefore underwent another sharp decline in status in the late 1950s that persisted into the 1970s (see Holt, 1967).

The Current Environment

Beginning in the 1980s and through the present, several major branches of applied psychology emerged and flourished: neuropsychology, health psychology, forensic psychology, and child psychology. Because each of these important areas of psychology makes extensive use of psychological tests, psychological testing again grew in status and use. Neuropsychologists use tests in hospitals and other clinical settings to assess brain injury. Health psychologists use tests and surveys in a variety of medical settings. Forensic psychologists use tests in the legal system to assess mental state as it relates to an insanity defense, competency to stand trial or to be executed, and emotional damages. Child psychologists use tests to assess childhood disorders. Tests are presently in use in developed countries throughout the world (Black & William, 2007; Schwager et al., 2015). As in the past, psychological testing remains one of the most important yet controversial topics in psychology.

As a student, no matter what your occupational or professional goals, you will find the material in this text invaluable. If you are among those who are interested in using psychological techniques in an applied setting, then this information will be particularly significant. From the roots of psychology to the present, psychological tests have remained among the most important instruments of the psychologist in general and of those who apply psychology in particular.

Testing is indeed one of the essential elements of psychology. Though not all psychologists use tests and some psychologists are opposed to them, all areas of psychology depend on knowledge gained in research studies that rely on measurements. The meaning and dependability of these measurements are essential to psychological research. To study any area of human behavior effectively, one must understand the basic principles of measurement.

In today's complex society, the relevance of the principles, applications, and issues of psychological testing extends far beyond the field of psychology. Even if you do not plan to become a psychologist, you will likely encounter psychological tests. Attorneys, physicians, social workers, business managers, educators, and many other professionals must frequently deal with reports based on such tests. Even as a parent, you are likely to encounter tests (taken by your children). To interpret such information adequately, you need the information presented in this book.

The more you know about psychological tests, the more confident you can be in your encounters with them. Given the attacks on tests and threats to prohibit or greatly limit their use, you have a responsibility to yourself and to society to know as much as you can about psychological tests. The future of testing may well depend on you and people like you. A thorough knowledge of testing will allow you to base your decisions on facts and to ensure that tests are used for the most beneficial and constructive purposes.

Summary

The history of psychological testing in the United States has been brief but intense. Although these sorts of tests have long been available, psychological testing is very much a product of modern society with its unprecedented technology and population growth and unique problems. Conversely, by helping solve the challenges posed by modern developments, tests have played an important role in recent U.S. and world history. You should realize, however, that despite advances in the theory and technique of psychological testing, many unsolved technical problems and hotly debated social, political, and economic issues remain. Nevertheless, the prevalence of tests despite strong opposition indicates that, although they are far from perfect, psychological tests must fulfill some important need in the decision-making processes permeating all facets of society. Because decisions must be made, such tests will probably flourish until a better or more objective way of making decisions emerges.

Modern history shows that psychological tests have evolved in a complicated environment in which hostile and friendly forces have produced a balance characterized by innovation and a continuous quest for better methods. One interesting thing about tests is that people never seem to remain neutral about them. If you are not in favor of tests, then we ask that you maintain an open mind while studying them. Our goal is to give you enough information to assess psychological tests intelligently throughout your life.

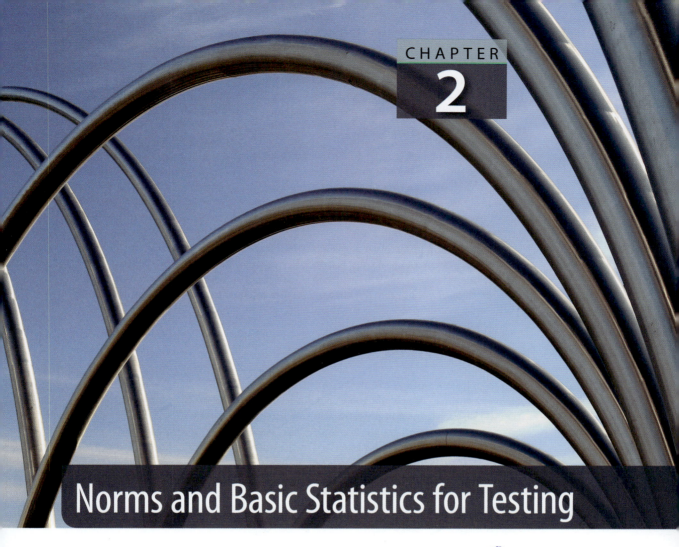

Norms and Basic Statistics for Testing

LEARNING OBJECTIVES

When you have completed this chapter, you should be able to:

▶ Discuss three properties of scales of measurement

▶ Determine why properties of scales are important in the field of measurement

▶ Identify methods for displaying distributions of scores

▶ Calculate the mean and the standard deviation for a set of scores

▶ Define a *Z* score and explain how it is used

▶ Relate the concepts of mean, standard deviation, and *Z* score to the concept of a standard normal distribution

▶ Define quartiles, deciles, and stanines and explain how they are used

▶ Tell how norms are created

▶ Relate the notion of tracking to the establishment of norms

We all use numbers as a basic way of communicating: Our money system requires us to understand and manipulate numbers, we estimate how long it will take to do things, we count, we express evaluations on scales, and so on. Think about how many times you use numbers in an average day. There is no way to avoid them.

One advantage of number systems is that they allow us to manipulate information. Through sets of well-defined rules, we can use numbers to learn more about the world. *Tests* are devices used to translate observations into numbers. Because the outcome of a test is almost always represented as a score, much of this book is about what scores mean. This chapter reviews some of the basic rules used to evaluate number systems. These rules and number systems are important tools for learning about human behavior.

If you have had a course in basic statistics, then this chapter will reinforce the basic concepts you have already learned. If you need additional review, reread your introductory statistics book. Most basic statistics books cover the information in this chapter. If you have not had a course in statistics, then this chapter will provide some of the information needed for understanding other chapters in this book.

Why We Need Statistics

Through its commitment to the scientific method, modern psychology has advanced beyond centuries of speculation about human nature. Scientific study requires systematic observations and an estimation of the extent to which observations could have been influenced by chance alone (Gravetter & Wallnau, 2016). Statistical methods serve two important purposes in the quest for scientific understanding.

First, statistics are used for purposes of description. Numbers provide convenient summaries and allow us to evaluate some observations relative to others (Maul, Irribarra, & Wilson, 2016). For example, if you get a score of 54 on a psychology examination, you probably want to know what the 54 means. Is it lower than the average score, or is it about the same? Knowing the answer can make the feedback you get from your examination more meaningful. If you discover that the 54 puts you in the top 5% of the class, then you might assume you have a good chance for an A. If it puts you in the bottom 5%, then you will feel differently.

Second, we can use statistics to make **inferences**, which are logical deductions about events that cannot be observed directly. For example, you do not know how many people watched a particular television movie unless you ask everyone. However, by using scientific sample surveys, you can infer the percentage of people who saw the film. Data gathering and analysis might be considered analogous to criminal investigation and prosecution (Schweder & Hjort, 2016; Tukey, 1977). First comes the detective work of gathering and displaying clues, or what the statistician John Tukey calls *exploratory data analysis*. Then comes a period of *confirmatory data analysis*, when the clues are evaluated against rigid statistical rules. This latter phase is like the work done by judges and juries.

Some students have an aversion to numbers and anything mathematical. If you find yourself among them, you are not alone. Professional psychologists can also feel uneasy about statistics. However, statistics and the basic principles of measurement lie at the center of the modern science of psychology. Scientific statements are usually based on careful study, and such systematic study requires some numerical analysis.

This chapter reviews both descriptive and inferential statistics. **Descriptive statistics** are methods used to provide a concise description of a collection of quantitative information. **Inferential statistics** are methods used to make inferences from observations of a small group of people known as a *sample* to a larger group of individuals known as a *population*. Typically, the psychologist wants to make statements about the larger group but cannot possibly make all the necessary observations. Instead, he or she observes a relatively small group of subjects (sample) and uses inferential statistics to estimate the characteristics of the larger group (Schweder & Hjort, 2016).

Scales of Measurement

One may define *measurement* as the application of rules for assigning numbers to objects. The rules are the specific procedures used to transform qualities of attributes into numbers (Lane, Raymond, & Haladyna, 2015). For example, to rate the quality of wines, wine tasters must use a specific set of rules. They might rate the wine on a 10-point scale, where 1 means extremely bad and 10 means extremely good. For a taster to assign the numbers, the system of rules must be clearly defined. The basic feature of these types of systems is the scale of measurement. For example, to measure the height of your classmates, you might use the scale of inches; to measure their weight, you might use the scale of pounds.

There are numerous systems by which we assign numbers in psychology. Indeed, the study of measurement systems is what this book is about. Before we consider any specific scale of measurement, however, we should consider the general properties of measurement scales.

Properties of Scales

Three important properties make scales of measurement different from one another: magnitude, equal intervals, and an absolute 0.

Magnitude

Magnitude is the property of "moreness." A scale has the property of magnitude if we can say that a particular instance of the attribute represents more, less, or equal amounts of the given quantity than does another instance (Gravetter & Wallnau, 2016; Howell, 2008; McCall, 2001). On a scale of height, for example, if we can say that John is taller than Fred, then the scale has the property of magnitude. A scale that does not have this property arises, for example, when a gym coach assigns identification numbers to teams in a league (team 1, team 2, etc.). Because the numbers only label the teams, they do not have the property of magnitude. If the coach were to rank the teams by the number of games they have won, then the new numbering system (games won) would have the property of magnitude.

Equal Intervals

The concept of equal intervals is a little more complex than that of magnitude. A scale has the property of equal intervals if the difference between two points at any place on the scale has the same meaning as the difference between two other points that differ by the same number of scale units. For example, the difference between inch 2 and inch 4 on a ruler represents the same quantity as the difference between inch 10 and inch 12: exactly 2 inches.

As simple as this concept seems, a psychological test rarely has the property of equal intervals. For example, the difference between intelligence quotients (IQs) of 45 and 50 does not mean the same thing as the difference between IQs of 105 and 110. Although each of these differences is 5 points ($50 - 45 = 5$ and $110 - 105 = 5$), the 5 points at the first level do not mean the same thing as 5 points at the second. We know that IQ predicts classroom performance. However, the difference in classroom performance associated with differences between IQ scores of 45 and 50 is not the same as the differences in classroom performance associated with IQ score differences of 105 and 110. In later chapters, we will discuss this problem in more detail.

When a scale has the property of *equal intervals*, the relationship between the measured units and some outcome can be described by a straight line or a linear equation in the form $Y = a + bX$. This equation shows that an increase in equal units on a given scale reflects equal increases in the meaningful correlates of units. For example, Figure 2.1 shows the hypothetical relationship between scores on a test of manual dexterity and ratings of artwork. Notice that the relationship is not a straight line. By examining the points on the figure, you can see that at first the relationship is nearly linear: Increases in manual dexterity are associated with increases in ratings of artwork. Then the relationship becomes nonlinear. The figure shows that after a manual dexterity score of approximately 5, increases in dexterity produce relatively small increases in quality of artwork.

Absolute 0

An absolute 0 is obtained when nothing of the property being measured exists. For example, if you are measuring heart rate and observe that your patient has a rate of 0 and has died, then you would conclude that there is no heart rate at all.

FIGURE 2.1

Hypothetical relationship between ratings of artwork and manual dexterity. In some ranges of the scale, the relationship is more direct than it is in others.

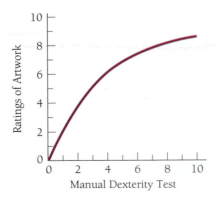

For many psychological qualities, it is extremely difficult, if not impossible, to define an absolute 0 point. For example, if one measures shyness on a scale from 0 through 10, then it is hard to define what it means for a person to have absolutely no shyness (McCall, 2001).

Types of Scales

Table 2.1 defines four scales of measurement based on the properties we have just discussed. You can see that a nominal scale does not have the property of magnitude, equal intervals, or an absolute 0. **Nominal scales** are really not scales at all; their only purpose is to name objects. For example, the numbers on the backs of football players' uniforms are nominal. Nominal scales are used when the information is qualitative rather than quantitative. Social science researchers commonly label groups in sample surveys with numbers (such as 1 = African American, 2 = white, and 3 = Mexican American). When these numbers have been attached to categories, most statistical procedures are not meaningful. On the scale for ethnic groups, for instance, what would a mean of 1.87 signify?

A scale with the property of magnitude but not equal intervals or an absolute 0 is an **ordinal scale**. This scale allows you to rank individuals or objects but not to say anything about the meaning of the differences between the ranks. If you were to rank the members of your class by height, then you would have an ordinal scale. For example, if Fred was the tallest, Susan the second tallest, and George the third tallest, you would assign them the ranks 1, 2, and 3, respectively. You would not give any consideration to the fact that Fred is 8 inches taller than Susan, but Susan is only 2 inches taller than George.

For most problems in psychology, the precision to measure the exact differences between intervals does not exist. So, most often one must use ordinal scales of measurement. For example, IQ tests do not have the property of equal intervals or an absolute 0, but they do have the property of magnitude. If they had the property of equal intervals, then the difference between an IQ of 70 and one of 90 should have the same meaning as the difference between an IQ of 125 and one of 145. Because it does not, the scale can only be considered ordinal. Furthermore, there is no point on the scale that represents no intelligence at all—that is, the scale does not have an absolute 0.

TABLE 2.1   Scales of Measurement and Their Properties

Type of scale	Magnitude	Equal intervals	Absolute 0
Nominal	No	No	No
Ordinal	Yes	No	No
Interval	Yes	Yes	No
Ratio	Yes	Yes	Yes

When a scale has the properties of magnitude and equal intervals but not absolute 0, we refer to it as an **interval scale**. The most common example of an interval scale is the measurement of temperature in degrees Fahrenheit. This temperature scale clearly has the property of magnitude, because 35°F is warmer than 32°F, 65°F is warmer than 64°F, and so on. Also, the difference between 90°F and 80°F is equal to a similar difference of 10° at any point on the scale. However, on the Fahrenheit scale, temperature does not have the property of absolute 0. If it did, then the 0 point would be more meaningful. As it is, 0 on the Fahrenheit scale does not have a particular meaning. Water freezes at 32°F and boils at 212°F. Because the scale does not have an absolute 0, we cannot make statements in terms of ratios. A temperature of 22°F is not twice as hot as 11°F, and 70°F is not twice as hot as 35°F.

The Celsius scale of temperature is also an interval rather than a ratio scale. Although 0 represents freezing on the Celsius scale, it is not an absolute 0. Remember that an absolute 0 is a point at which nothing of the property being measured exists. Even on the Celsius scale of temperature, there is still plenty of room on the thermometer below 0. When the temperature goes below freezing, some aspect of heat is still being measured.

A scale that has all three properties (magnitude, equal intervals, and an absolute 0) is called a **ratio scale**. To continue our example, a ratio scale of temperature would have the properties of the Fahrenheit and Celsius scales but also include a meaningful 0 point. There is a point at which all molecular activity ceases, a point of absolute 0 on a temperature scale. Because the Kelvin scale is based on the absolute 0 point, it is a ratio scale: 22°K is twice as cold as 44°K. Examples of ratio scales also appear in the numbers we see on a regular basis. For example, consider the number of yards gained by running backs on football teams. Zero yards actually means that the player has gained no yards at all. If one player has gained 1000 yards and another has gained only 500, then we can say that the first athlete has gained twice as many yards as the second.

Another example is the speed of travel. For instance, 0 miles per hour (mph) is the point at which there is no speed at all. If you are driving onto a highway at 30 mph and increase your speed to 60 when you merge, then you have doubled your speed.

Permissible Operations

Level of measurement is important because it defines which mathematical operations we can apply to numerical data (Streiner, Norman, & Cairney, 2014). For nominal data, each observation can be placed in only one mutually exclusive category. For example, you are a member of only one gender. One can use nominal data to create frequency distributions (see the next section), but no mathematical manipulations of the data are permissible. Ordinal measurements can be manipulated using arithmetic; however, the result is often difficult to interpret because it reflects neither the magnitudes of the manipulated observations nor the true amounts of the property that have been measured. For example, if the heights of 15 children are rank ordered, knowing a given child's rank does not reveal how tall he or she stands. Averages of these ranks are equally uninformative about height.

With interval data, one can apply any arithmetic operation to the differences between scores. The results can be interpreted in relation to the magnitudes of the underlying property. However, interval data cannot be used to make statements about ratios. For example, if IQ is measured on an interval scale, one cannot say that an IQ of 160 is twice as high as an IQ of 80. This mathematical operation is reserved for ratio scales, for which any mathematical operation is permissible (Gravetter & Wallnau, 2016).

Frequency Distributions

A single test score means more if one relates it to other test scores. A *distribution* of scores summarizes the scores for a group of individuals. In testing, there are many ways to record a distribution of scores.

The **frequency distribution** displays scores on a variable or a measure to reflect how frequently each value was obtained. With a frequency distribution, one defines all the possible scores and determines how many people obtained each of those scores. Usually, scores are arranged on the horizontal axis from the lowest to the highest value. The vertical axis reflects how many times each of the values on the horizontal axis was observed. For most distributions of test scores, the frequency distribution is bell shaped, with the greatest frequency of scores toward the center of the distribution and decreasing scores as the values become greater or less than the value in the center of the distribution.

Figure 2.2 shows a frequency distribution of 1000 observations that takes on values between 61 and 90. Notice that the most frequent observations fall toward the center of the distribution, around 75 and 76. As you look toward the extremes of the distribution, you will find a systematic decline in the frequency with which the scores occur. For example, the score of 71 is observed less frequently than 72, which is observed less frequently than 73, and so on. Similarly, 78 is observed more frequently than 79, which is noted more often than 80, and so forth.

FIGURE 2.2

Frequency distribution approximating a normal distribution of 1000 observations.

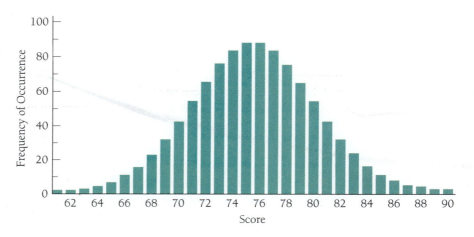

Though this neat symmetric relationship does not characterize all sets of scores, it occurs frequently enough in practice for us to devote special attention to it. We explain this concept in greater detail in the section on the normal distribution.

Table 2.2 lists the rainfall amounts in San Diego, California, between 1965 and 2015. Figure 2.3 is a histogram based on the observations. The distribution is slightly skewed, or asymmetrical. We say that Figure 2.3 has a *positive* skew because the tail goes off toward the higher or positive side of the *X* axis. There is a

TABLE 2.2 Inches of Rainfall in San Diego, 1964–2011

Year (Oct–Sept)	Rainfall (Inches)	Year (Oct–Sept)	Rainfall (Inches)
1965	8.81	1991	12.31
1966	14.76	1992	12.48
1967	10.86	1993	18.26
1968	7.86	1994	9.93
1969	11.48	1995	17.13
1970	6.33	1996	5.18
1971	8.03	1997	7.73
1972	6.12	1998	17.16
1973	10.99	1999	6.5
1974	6.59	2000	5.75
1975	10.64	2001	8.57
1976	10.14	2002	3.3
1977	9.18	2003	10.31
1978	17.3	2004	5.18
1979	14.93	2005	22.6
1980	15.62	2006	5.36
1981	8.13	2007	3.85
1982	11.85	2008	7.2
1983	18.49	2009	9.15
1984	5.37	2010	10.6
1985	9.6	2011	12.7
1986	14.95	2012	7.9
1987	9.3	2013	6.55
1988	12.44	2014	5.09
1989	5.88	2015	11.91
1990	7.62	Mean	10.11

FIGURE 2.3

Histogram for San Diego rainfall, 1965–2015.

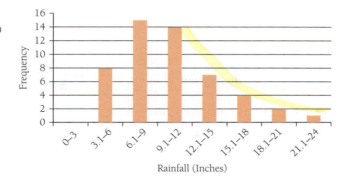

FIGURE 2.4

Frequency polygon for San Diego rainfall, 1965–2015.

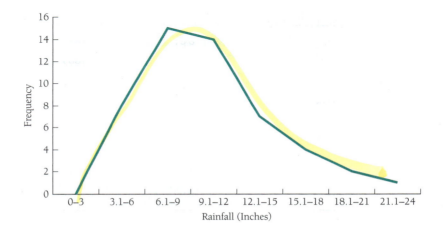

slight skew in Figures 2.3 and 2.4, but the asymmetry in these figures is relatively hard to detect. Figure 2.5 gives an example of a distribution that is clearly skewed. The figure summarizes annual household income in the United States at the time of the last census in 2010. Very few people make high incomes, while the great bulk of the population is bunched toward the low end of the income distribution. Of particular interest is that this figure only includes household incomes less than $100,000. For household incomes greater than $100,000, the government only reports incomes using class intervals of $50,000. In 2011, about 16% of the U.S. households had incomes greater than $100,000. Because some households have extremely high incomes, you can imagine that the tail of this distribution would go very far to the right. Thus, income is an example of a variable that has positive skew.

One can also present this same set of data as a frequency polygon (see Figure 2.4). Here the amount of rainfall is placed on the graph as a point that represents the frequencies with which each interval occurs. Lines are then drawn to connect these points.

Whenever you draw a frequency distribution or a frequency polygon, you must decide on the width of the class interval. The **class interval** for inches of rainfall is the

FIGURE 2.5

Household income up to $100,000 in the United States for 2010. This is an example of positive skew.

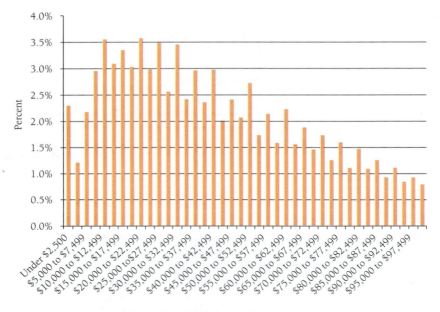

Personal Income (US$)

(Data from the United States Department of Labor Statistics and the Bureau the Census, http://ferret.bls.census.gov/macro/032003/hhinc/new06_000.htm)

unit on the horizontal axis. For example, in Figures 2.3 and 2.4, the class interval is 3 inches—that is, the demarcations along the X axis increase in 3-inch intervals. This interval is used here for convenience; the choice of 3 inches is otherwise arbitrary.

Percentile Ranks

Percentile ranks replace simple ranks when we want to adjust for the number of scores in a group. A **percentile rank** answers the question, "What percent of the scores fall below a particular score (X_i)?" To calculate a percentile rank, you need only follow these simple steps: (1) determine how many cases fall below the score of interest, (2) determine how many cases are in the group, (3) divide the number of cases below the score of interest (Step 1) by the total number of cases in the group (Step 2), and (4) multiply the result of Step 3 by 100.

The formula is

$$P_r = \frac{B}{N} \times 100 = \text{percentile rank of } X_i$$

where

P_r = percentile rank
X_i = the score of interest
B = the number of scores below X_i
N = the total number of scores

This means that you form a ratio of the number of cases below the score of interest and the total number of scores. Because there will always be either the same or fewer cases in the numerator (top half) of the equation than there are in the denominator (bottom half), this ratio will always be less than or equal to 1. To get rid of the decimal points, you multiply by 100.

As an example, consider the runner who finishes 62nd out of 63 racers in a gym class. To obtain the percentile rank, divide 1 (the number of people who finish behind the person of interest) by 63 (the number of scores in the group). This gives you 1/63, or .016. Then multiply this result by 100 to obtain the percentile rank, which is 1.6. This rank tells you the runner is below the 2nd percentile.

Now consider the Bay to Breakers race, which attracts 50,000 runners to San Francisco. If you had finished 62nd out of 50,000, then the number of people who were behind you would be 49,938. Dividing this by the number of entrants gives you .9988. When you multiply by 100, you get a percentile rank of 99.88. This tells you that finishing 62nd in the Bay to Breakers race is exceptionally good because it places you in the 99.88th percentile.

Psychological Testing in Everyday Life 2.1 presents the calculation of percentile ranks of the infant mortality rates of selected countries as reported by the Central Intelligence Agency (CIA). Infant mortality is defined as the number of babies out of 1000 who are born alive but die before their first birthday. Before proceeding, we should point out that the meaning of this calculation depends on which countries are used in the comparison.

In this example, the calculation of the percentile rank is broken into five steps and uses the raw data in the table. In Step 1, we arrange the data points in ascending order. Singapore has the lowest infant mortality rate (2.31), Japan is next (2.79), and Afghanistan has the highest rate (151.95).

In Step 2, we determine the number of cases with worse rates than that of the case of interest. In this example, the case of interest is the United States. Therefore, we count the number of cases with a worse rate than that of the United States. Ten countries—Saudi Arabia, Colombia, China, Turkey, Morocco, Bolivia, Laos, Ethiopia, Mozambique, and Afghanistan—have infant mortality rates greater than 6.26.

In Step 3, we determine the total number of cases (18).

In Step 4, we divide the number of scores worse than the score of interest by the total number of scores:

$$\frac{10}{18} = .55$$

Technically, the percentile rank is a percentage. Step 4 gives a proportion. Therefore, in Step 5, you transform this into a whole number by multiplying by 100:

$$.55 \times 100 = 55$$

Thus, the United States is in the 55th percentile.

The percentile rank depends absolutely on the cases used for comparison. In this example, you calculated that the United States is in the 55th percentile for

2.1 PSYCHOLOGICAL TESTING IN EVERYDAY LIFE

Infant Mortality in Selected Countries, 2011

Country	1000 Live Births
Afghanistan	151.95
Australia	4.75
Bolivia	44.96
China	20.25
Colombia	18.90
Ethiopia	80.80
France	3.33
Israel	4.22
Italy	5.51
Japan	2.79
Laos	77.82
Morocco	36.88
Mozambique	105.80
Saudi Arabia	11.57
Singapore	2.31
Spain	4.21
Turkey	25.78
United States	6.26
Mean	33.78
Standard Deviation	42.99

To calculate the percentile rank of infant mortality in the United States in comparison to that in selected countries, use the following formula:

$$P_r = \frac{B}{N} \times 100$$

where

P_r = the percentile rank
B = the number of cases with worse rates than the case of interest
N = the total number of cases

Country	1000 Live Births
Singapore	2.31
Japan	2.79
France	3.33
Spain	4.21
Israel	4.22
Australia	4.75
Italy	5.51
United States	6.26
Saudi Arabia	11.57
Colombia	18.90
China	20.25
Turkey	25.78
Morocco	36.88
Bolivia	44.96
Laos	77.82
Ethiopia	80.80
Mozambique	105.80
Afghanistan	151.95

Data from US Central Intelligence Agency, 2011

Steps

1. Arrange data in ascending order—that is, the lowest score first, the second lowest score second, and so on.

$$N = 18, \text{mean} = 33.78, \text{standard deviation} = 42.99$$

2. Determine the number of cases with worse rates than the score of interest. There are 10 countries in this sample with infant mortality rates greater than that in the United States.

3. Determine the number of cases in the sample (18).

4. Divide the number of scores worse than the score of interest (Step 2) by the total number of scores (Step 3):

$$\frac{10}{18} = .55$$

5. Multiply by 100:

$$.55 \times 100 = 55\text{th percentile rank}$$

infant mortality within this group of countries. If all countries in the world had been included, then the ranking of the United States have been different.[1]

Using this procedure, try to calculate the percentile rank for Bolivia. The calculation is the same, except that there are four countries with worse rates than Bolivia (as opposed to 11 worse than the United States). Thus, the percentile rank for Bolivia is

$$\frac{4}{18} = .22 \times 100 = 22$$

or the 22nd percentile. Now try France. You should get a percentile rank of 83.

Percentiles

Percentiles are the specific scores or points within a distribution. Percentiles divide the total frequency for a set of observations into hundredths. Instead of indicating what percentage of scores fall below a particular score, as percentile ranks do, percentiles indicate the particular score, below which a defined percentage of scores falls.

Try to calculate the percentile and percentile rank for some of the data in Psychological Testing in Everyday Life 2.1. As an example, look at Italy. The infant mortality rate in Italy is 5.51/1000. When calculating the percentile rank, you exclude the score of interest and count those below (in other words, Italy is not

---

[1] We put these numbers together for an example, but it is not representative of all countries in the world. The complete CIA data set includes 224 counties; among them, the United States ranks 46th in infant mortality. There are 178 countries with higher (worse) So, the United States is in about the 79th percentile among all nations (178/224 = 0.79). This means that about one fifth of the countries have lower infant mortality rates, but that the US does better than about 4 fifths of the counties. Further, the distribution of infant mortality is highly skewed, with many counties having low rates and a few having high rates. The following graph presents a complete and more accurate picture.

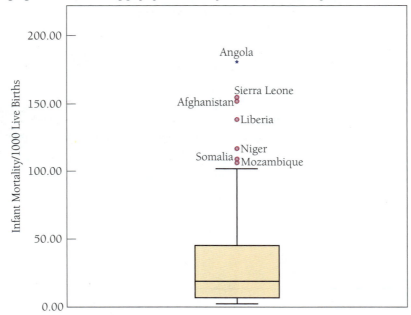

included in the count). There are 11 countries in this sample with infant mortality rates worse than Italy's. To calculate the percentile rank, divide this number of countries by the total number of cases and multiply by 100:

$$P_r = \frac{B}{N} \times 100 = \frac{11}{18} \times 100 = .61 \times 100 = 61$$

Thus, Italy is in the 61st percentile rank, or the 61st percentile in this example is 5.51/1000 or 5.51 deaths per 1000 live births.

Now take the example of Israel. The calculation of percentile rank requires looking at the number of cases below the case of interest. In this example, 13 countries in this group have infant mortality rates worse than Israel's. Thus, the percentile rank for Israel is 13/18 = 100 = 72. The 72nd percentile corresponds with the point or score of 6.75 (6.75/1000 live births).

In summary, the percentile and the percentile rank are similar. The percentile gives the point in a distribution below which a specified percentage of cases fall (4.22/1000 for Israel). The percentile is in raw score units. The percentile rank gives the percentage of cases below the percentile; in this example, the percentile rank is 56.

When reporting percentiles and percentile ranks, you must carefully specify the population you are working with. Remember that a percentile rank is a measure of relative performance. When interpreting a percentile rank, you should always ask the question, "Relative to what?" Suppose, for instance, that you finished in the 17th percentile in a swimming race (or fifth in a heat of six competitors). Does this mean that you are a slow swimmer? Not necessarily. It may be that this was a heat in the Olympic games, and the participants were the fastest swimmers in the world. An Olympic swimmer competing against a random sample of all people in the world would probably finish in the 99.99th percentile. The example for infant mortality rates depends on which countries in the world were selected for comparison. The United States actually does quite poorly when compared with European countries and the advanced economies in Asia (Singapore and Japan). However, the U.S. infant mortality rate looks much better compared with countries in the developing world.

Describing Distributions

Mean

Statistics are used to summarize data. If you consider a set of scores, the mass of information may be too much to interpret all at once. That is why we need numerical conveniences to help summarize the information. An example of a set of scores that can be summarized is shown in Table 2.2 (see page 30): amounts of rainfall in San Diego. We signify the variable as X. A *variable* is a score that can have different values. The amount of rain is a variable because different amounts of rain fell in different years.

The arithmetic average score in a distribution is called the **mean**. To calculate the mean, we total the scores and divide the sum by the number of cases, or N. The capital Greek letter sigma (Σ) means summation. Thus, the formula for the mean, which we signify as $\overline{X}$ is

$$\overline{X} = \frac{\Sigma X}{N}$$

In words, this formula says to total the scores and divide the sum by the number of cases. Using the information in Table 2.2, we find the mean by following these steps:

1. Obtain ΣX, or the sum of the scores: $8.81 + 14.76 + 10.86 + 7.86 + \cdots + 11.91 = 515.97$
2. Find N, or the number of scores: Data are from the 51 years between 1965 and 2015. So, $N = 51$
3. Divide ΣX by N: $515.97/51 = 10.11$

Psychological Testing in Everyday Life 2.2 summarizes common symbols used in basic statistics.

Standard Deviation

The standard deviation is an approximation of the average deviation around the mean. The standard deviation for the amount of rainfall in San Diego is 4.31. To understand rainfall in San Diego, you need to consider at least two dimensions: first, the amount of rain that falls in a particular year; second, the degree of variation from year to year in the amount of rain that falls. The calculation suggests that, on the average, the variation around the mean is approximately 4.31 inches.

However informative, knowing the mean of a group of scores does not give you that much information. As an illustration, look at the following sets of numbers.

Set 1	Set 2	Set 3
4	5	8
4	5	8
4	4	6
4	4	2
4	3	0
4	3	0

Calculate the mean of the first set. You should get 4. What is the mean of the second set? If you calculate correctly, you should get 4 again. Next find the mean for Set 3. It is also 4. The three distributions of scores appear quite different but have the same mean, so it is important to consider other characteristics of the distribution of scores besides the mean. The difference between the three sets lies in *variability*. There is no variability in Set 1, a small amount in Set 2, and a lot in Set 3.

2.2 PSYCHOLOGICAL TESTING IN EVERYDAY LIFE

Common Symbols

You need to understand and recognize the symbols used throughout this book. $\overline{X}$ is the mean; it is pronounced "X bar." Σ is the summation sign. It means sum, or add, scores together and is the capital Greek letter sigma. X is a variable that takes on different values. Each value of X_i represents a raw score, also called an *obtained score*.

Measuring this variation is similar to finding the average deviation around the mean. One way to measure variability is to subtract the mean from each score $(X - \overline{X})$ and then total the deviations. Statisticians often signify this with a lowercase x, as in $x = (X - \overline{X})$. Try this for the data in Table 2.2. Did you get 0? You should have, and this is not an unusual example. In fact, the sum of the deviations around the mean will always equal 0. However, you do have an alternative: You can square all the deviations around the mean in order to get rid of any negative signs. Then you can obtain the average squared deviation around the mean, known as the **variance**. The formula for the variance is

$$\sigma^2 = \frac{\Sigma(X - \overline{X})^2}{N}$$

where $(X - \overline{X})$ is the deviation of a score from the mean. The symbol σ is the lowercase Greek sigma; σ^2 is used as a standard description of the variance.

Though the variance is a useful statistic commonly used in data analysis, it shows the variable in squared deviations around the mean rather than in deviations around the mean. In other words, the variance is the average squared deviation around the mean. To get it back into the units that will make sense to us, we need to take the square root of the variance. The square root of the variance is the standard deviation (σ), and it is represented by the following formula:

$$\sigma = \sqrt{\frac{\Sigma(X - \overline{X})^2}{N}}$$

The **standard deviation** is thus the square root of the average squared deviation around the mean. Although the standard deviation is not an average deviation, it gives a useful approximation of how much a typical score is above or below the average score.

Because of their mathematical properties, the variance and the standard deviation have many advantages. For example, knowing the standard deviation of a normally distributed batch of data allows us to make precise statements about the distribution. The formulas just presented are for computing the variance and the standard deviation of a population. That is why we use the lowercase Greek sigma $(\sigma$ and $\sigma^2)$. Psychological Testing in Everyday Life 2.3 summarizes when you should use Greek and Roman letters. Most often, we use the standard deviation for a sample to estimate the standard deviation for a population. When we talk about a sample, we replace the Greek σ with a Roman letter S. Also, we divide by $N - 1$ rather than N to recognize that S of a sample is only an estimate of the variance of the population.

$$S = \sqrt{\frac{\Sigma(X - \overline{X})^2}{N - 1}}$$

In calculating the standard deviation, it is often easier to use the raw score equivalent formula, which is

$$S = \sqrt{\frac{\Sigma X^2 - \dfrac{(EX)^2}{N}}{N - 1}}$$

This calculation can also be done automatically by some minicalculators, iPhones, or Excel.

2.3   **PSYCHOLOGICAL TESTING IN EVERYDAY LIFE**

Terms and Symbols Used to Describe Populations and Samples

	Population	Sample
Definition	All elements with the same definition	A subset of the population, usually drawn to represent it in an unbiased fashion
Descriptive characteristics	Parameters	Statistics
Symbols used to describe	Greek	Roman
Symbol for mean	μ	$\overline{X}$
Symbol for standard deviation	σ	S

In reading the formula, you may be confused by a few points. In particular, be careful not to confuse ΣX^2 and $(\Sigma X)^2$. To get ΣX^2, each individual score is squared and the values are summed. For the scores 3, 5, 7, and 8, ΣX^2 would be $3^2 + 5^2 + 7^2 + 8^2 = 9 + 25 + 49 + 64 = 147$. To obtain $(\Sigma X)^2$, the scores are first summed and the total is squared. Using the example, $(\Sigma X)^2 = (3 + 5 + 7 + 8)^2 = 23^2 = 529$.

Z Score

One problem with means and standard deviations is that they do not convey enough information for us to make meaningful assessments or accurate interpretations of data. Other metrics are designed for more exact interpretations. The Z score transforms data into standardized units that are easier to interpret. A Z score is the difference between a score and the mean, divided by the standard deviation:

$$Z = \frac{X_i - \overline{X}}{S}$$

In other words, a Z score is the deviation of a score X_i from the mean in standard deviation units. If a score is equal to the mean, then its Z score is 0. For example, suppose the score and the mean are both 6, then $6 - 6 = 0$. Zero divided by anything is still 0. If the score is greater than the mean, then the Z score is positive; if the score is less than the mean, then the Z score is negative.

Let's try an example. Suppose that $X_i = 6$, the mean $\overline{X} = 3$, and the standard deviation $S = 3$. Plugging these values into the formula, we get

$$Z = \frac{6 - 3}{3} = \frac{3}{3} = 1$$

Let's try another example. Suppose $X_i = 4$, $\overline{X} = 5.75$, and $S = 2.11$. What is the Z score? It is $-.83$:

$$Z = \frac{4 - 5.75}{2.11} = \frac{-1.74}{2.11} = -.83$$

This means that the score we observed (4) is .83 standard deviation below the average score, or that the score is below the mean but its difference from the mean is slightly less than the average deviation.

Example of Depression in Medical Students: Center for Epidemiologic Studies Depression Scale (CES-D)

The CES-D is a general measure of depression that has been used extensively in epidemiological studies. The scale includes 20 items and taps dimensions of depressed mood, hopelessness, appetite loss, sleep disturbance, and energy level. Each year, students at the University of California, San Diego, School of Medicine are asked to report how often they experienced a particular symptom during the first week of school on a 4-point scale ranging from rarely or none of the time [0 to 1 days (0)] to most or all of the time [5 to 7 days (3)]. Items 4, 8, 12, and 16 on the CES-D are reverse scored. For these items, 0 is scored as 3, 1 is scored as 2, 2 as 1, and 3 as 0. The CES-D score is obtained by summing the circled numbers. Scores on the CES-D range from 0 to 60, with scores greater than 16 indicating clinically significant levels of depressive symptomatology in adults.

Feel free to take the CES-D measure yourself. Calculate your score by summing the numbers you have circled. However, you must first reverse the scores on items 4, 8, 12, and 16. As you will see in Chapter 5, the CES-D does not have high validity for determining clinical depression. If your score is less than 16, the evidence suggests that you are not clinically depressed. If your score is high, it raises suspicions about depression—though this does not mean you have a problem. (Of course, you may want to talk with your college counselor if you are feeling depressed.)

Table 2.3 shows CES-D scores for a selected sample of medical students. You can use these data to practice calculating means, standard deviations, and Z scores.

In creating the frequency distribution for the CES-D scores of medical students, we used an arbitrary class interval of 5.

Standard Normal Distribution

Now we consider the standard normal distribution because it is central to statistics and psychological testing. However, you should first participate in a short exercise. Take any coin and flip it 10 times. Repeat this exercise of 10 coin flips 25 times. Record the number of heads you observe in each group of 10 flips. When you are done, make a frequency distribution showing how many times you observed 1 head in your 10 flips, 2 heads, 3 heads, and so on.

Your frequency distribution might look like the example shown in Figure 2.6. The most frequently observed events are approximately equal numbers of heads and tails. Toward the extremes of 10 heads and 0 tails or 10 tails and 0 heads, events are observed with decreasing frequency. For example, there were no occasions in which fewer than 2 heads were observed and only one occasion in which more than 8 heads were observed. This is what we would expect from the laws of probability. On average, we would expect half of the flips to show heads and half to show tails if heads and tails are equally probable events. Although observing a long string of heads or tails is possible, it is improbable. In other words, we sometimes see the coin come up heads in 9 out of 10 flips. The likelihood that this will happen, however, is quite small.

Center for Epidemiologic Studies Depression Scale (CES-D)

Instructions: *Circle the number for each statement that best describes how often you felt or behaved this way DURING THE PAST WEEK.*

	Rarely or none of the time (less than 1 day)	Some or a little of the time (1–2 days)	Occasionally or a moderate amount of the time (3–4 days)	Most or all of the time (5–7 days)
1. I was bothered by things that usually don't bother me.	0	1	2	3
2. I did not feel like eating.	0	1	2	3
3. I felt that I could not shake off the blues even with help from my family or friends	0	1	2	3
R 4. I felt that I was just as good as other people.	0	1	2	3
5. I had trouble keeping my mind on what I was doing	0	1	2	3
6. I felt depressed.	0	1	2	3
7. I felt that everything I did was an effort.	0	1	2	3
R 8. I felt hopeful about the future.	0	1	2	3
9. I thought my life had been a failure.	0	1	2	3
10. I felt fearful.	0	1	2	3
11. My sleep was restless.	0	1	2	3
R 12. I was happy.	0	1	2	3
13. I talked less than usual.	0	1	2	3
14. I felt lonely.	0	1	2	3
15. People were unfriendly.	0	1	2	3
R 16. I enjoyed life	0	1	2	3
17. I had crying spells.	0	1	2	3
18. I felt sad.	0	1	2	3
19. I felt that people disliked me	0	1	2	3
20. I could not get "going."	0	1	2	3

TABLE 2.3 The Calculation of Mean, Standard Deviation, and Z Scores for CES-D Scores

Name	Test score (X)	X^2	Z score
John	14	196	.42
Carla	10	100	−.15
Fred	8	64	−.44
Monica	8	64	−.44
Eng	26	676	−.13
Fritz	0	0	−1.58
Mary	14	196	.42
Susan	3	9	−1.15
Debbie	9	81	−.29
Elizabeth	10	100	−.15
Sarah	7	49	−.58
Marcel	12	144	.14
Robin	10	100	−.15
Mike	25	625	1.99
Carl	9	81	.29
Phyllis	12	144	.14
Jennie	23	529	1.70
Richard	7	49	−.58
Tyler	13	169	.28
Frank	1	1	−1.43
	$\Sigma X = 221$	$\Sigma X^2 = 3377$	

$$\bar{X} = \frac{\Sigma X}{N} = \frac{221}{20} = 11.05$$

$$S = \sqrt{\frac{\Sigma X^2 - \frac{(\Sigma X)^2}{N}}{N - 1}} = \sqrt{\frac{3377 - \frac{(22)^2}{20}}{20 - 1}} = 7.01$$

$$\text{Monica's } Z \text{ score} = \frac{X - \bar{X}}{S} = \frac{8 - 11.05}{7.01} = -.44$$

$$\text{Marcel's } Z \text{ score} = \frac{X - \bar{X}}{S} = \frac{12 - 11.05}{7.01} = .14$$

$$\text{Jennie's } Z \text{ score} = \frac{X - \bar{X}}{S} = \frac{23 - 11.05}{7.01} = 1.70$$

FIGURE 2.6

Frequency distribution of the number of heads in 25 sets of 10 flips.

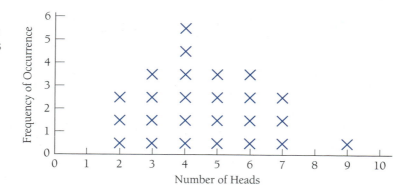

FIGURE 2.7

The theoretical distribution of the number of heads in an infinite number of coin flips.

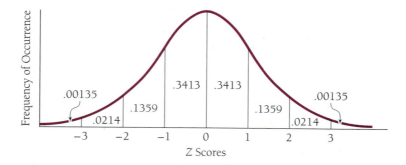

Figure 2.7 shows the theoretical distribution of heads in an infinite number of flips of the coin. This figure might look a little like the distribution from your coin-flipping exercise or the distribution shown in Figure 2.6. This is a normal distribution, or what is technically known as a *symmetrical binomial probability distribution.*

On most occasions, we refer to units on the X (or horizontal) axis of the normal distribution in Z score units. Any variable transformed into Z score units takes on special properties. First, Z scores have a mean of 0 and a standard deviation of 1.0. If you think about this for a minute, you should be able to figure out why this is true. Recall that the sum of the deviations around the mean is always equal to 0. The numerator of the Z score equation is the deviation around the mean, while the denominator is a constant. Thus, the mean of Z scores can be expressed as

$$\frac{\Sigma(X_i - \bar{X})/S}{N} \quad \text{or} \quad \frac{\Sigma Z}{N}$$

Because $\Sigma(X_i - \bar{X})$ will always equal 0, the mean of Z scores will always be 0. In Figure 2.7, the standardized, or Z score, units are marked on the X axis. The numbers under the curve are the proportions of cases (in decimal form) that we would expect to observe in each area. Multiplying these proportions by 100 yields percentages. For example, we see that 34.13% or .3413 of the cases fall between the mean and one standard deviation above the mean. Do not forget that 50% of the cases fall below the mean. Putting these two bits of information together, we can conclude that if a score is one standard deviation above the mean, then it is at about the 84th percentile rank (50 + 34.13 = 84.13 to be exact). A score that is one standard deviation below the mean would be about the 16th percentile rank (50 − 34.13 = 15.87). Thus, you can use what you have learned about means, standard deviations, Z scores, and the normal curve to transform raw scores, which have little meaning, into percentile scores, which are easier to interpret. These methods can be used only when the distribution of scores is normal or approximately normal. Methods for nonnormal distributions are discussed in most statistics books under "nonparametric statistics."

Percentiles and Z Scores

These percentile ranks are the percentage of scores that fall below the observed Z score. For example, the Z score −1.6 is associated with the percentile rank of 5.48. The Z score 1.0 (third column) is associated with the percentile rank of 84.13.

Part I of Appendix 1 is a simplified version of Part II, which you need for more advanced use of Z scores. Part II gives the areas between the mean and various Z scores. Standard scored values are listed in the "Z" column. To find the proportion of the distribution between the mean of the distribution and a given Z score, you must locate the entry indicated by a specific Z score. Z scores are carried to a second decimal place in the columns that go across the table. First, consider the second column of the table because it is similar to Part I of Appendix 1. Take the Z score of 1.0. The second column is labeled .00, which means that the second decimal place is also 0. The number listed in the table is .3413. Because this is a positive number, it is above the mean. Because the area below the mean is .5, the total area below a Z score of 1.0 is .5 +.3413 = .8413. To make this into a percentile (as shown in Part I of the appendix), multiply by 100 to get 84.13. Now try the example of a Z score of 1.64. To locate this value, find 1.6 in the first column. Then, move your hand across the row until you get to the number below the heading .04. The number is .4495. Again, this is a positive Z score, so you must add the observed proportion to .5 that falls below the mean. The proportion below 1.64 is .9495. Stated another way, 94.95% of the cases fall below a Z score of 1.64. Now try to find the percentile rank of cases that fall below a Z score of 1.10. If you are using the table correctly, you should obtain 86.43.

Now try −.75. Because this is a negative Z score, the percentage of cases falling below the mean should be less than 50. But there are no negative values in Part II of Appendix 1. For a negative Z score, there are several ways to obtain the appropriate area under the curve. The tables in Appendix 1 give the area from the mean to the Z score. For a Z score of −.75, the area between the mean and the Z score is .2734. You can find this by entering the table in the row labeled .7 and then moving across the row until you get to the figure in that row below the heading .05. There you should find the number .2734. We know that .5 of the cases fall below the mean. Thus, for a negative Z score, we can obtain the proportion of cases falling below the score by subtracting .2734, the tabled value listed in the appendix, from .5. In this case, the result is

$$.5 - .2734 = .2266$$

Because finding the percentile ranks associated with negative Z scores can be tricky, you might want to use Part I of Appendix 1 to see if you are in the right ballpark. This table gives both negative and positive Z scores but does not give the detail associated with the second decimal place. Look up $-.7$ in Part I. The percentile rank is 24.20. Now consider a Z score of $-.8$. That percentile rank is 21.19. Thus, you know that a Z score of $-.75$ should be associated with a percentile rank between 21.19 and 24.20. In fact, we have calculated that the actual percentile rank is 22.66.

Practice with Appendix 1 until you are confident that you understand how it works. Do not hesitate to ask your professor or teaching assistant if you are confused. This is an important concept that you will need throughout the rest of the book. After you have mastered using the Tables in Appendix 1, you might try a nifty website (https://www.easycalculation.com/statistics/p-value-for-z-score.php) that can find the probabilities for you.

Look at one more example from Table 2.2 (rainfall in San Diego, page 30). California had a dry year in 1999 and in 2007 and then experienced a serious 3-year drought between 2012 and 2014. In each of these years, the newscasters frequently commented that this was highly unusual. They described it as the "La Nina" effect; some even claimed that it signaled global warming. The question is whether the amount of rainfall received in 1999, 2007, 2012, 2013, and 2014 was unusual given what we know about rainfall in general. To help gain a better understanding of variability from year to year, we created a graph that shows how rainfall in San Diego changes from year to year (see Figure 2.8). It does not rain that much in San Diego, but the amount of rain varies considerably from year to year and it is necessary to put this variability into context. To evaluate this, calculate the Z score for rainfall. According to Table 2.2, there were 6.50 inches of rainfall in 1999 and 3.85 inches in 2007. The mean for rainfall is 10.11 inches and the standard deviation is 4.31. Thus, the Z score for 1999 is

$$Z = (6.50 - 10.11) / 4.31 = -0.84$$

Next determine where a Z score of $-.84$ falls within the Z distribution. According to Appendix 1, a Z score of $-.84$ is equal to the 20th percentile ($.5 - .2995 = .2005$).

FIGURE 2.8
Year-to-year variability of rainfall in San Diego: 1965–2015.

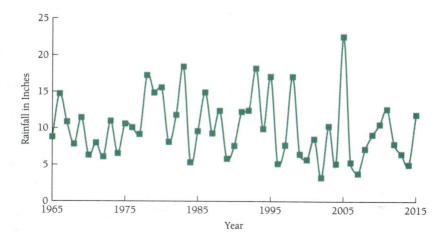

Thus, the low rainfall year in 1999 was unusual—given all years, it was in about the 20th percentile. However, it was not *that* unusual. You can estimate that there would be less rainfall in approximately 20% of all years. 2007 was a different case. The Z score for 2007 was -1.45. This is obtained by subtracting the mean rainfall (10.11) from the 2007 value (3.85) and dividing by the standard deviation of rainfall (4.31).

$$(3.85 - 10.11)/4.31 = -1.45$$

Rainfall in 2007 was in the 7.35th percentile. (Using Appendix 1, you can look up the Z score of -1.45 and find an area below the mean of 0.4265. Then you can estimate the percentile as $50 - 42.65 = 7.35$.) In fact, 2007 was more unusual than 2014, which was the worst of the three draught years with a cumulative rainfall of 5.09 inches. That was associated with a Z score of -1.16, placing the year in the 12.30 percentile among this sequence of 51 consecutive years.

You can also turn the process around. Instead of using Z scores to find the percentile ranks, you can use the percentile ranks to find the corresponding Z scores. To do this, look in Part II of Appendix 1 under percentiles and find the corresponding Z score. For example, suppose you wish to find the Z score associated with the 90th percentile. When you enter Part II of Appendix 1, look for the value closest to the 90th percentile. This can be a little tricky because of the way the table is structured. Because the 90th percentile is associated with a positive Z score, you are actually looking for the area above the 50th percentile. So you should look for the entry closest to .4000 ($.5000 + .4000 = .9000$). The closest value to .4000 is .3997, which is found in the row labeled 1.2 and the column labeled .08. This tells you that a person who obtains a Z score of 1.28 is at approximately the 90th percentile in the distribution.

Now return to the example of CES-D scores for medical students (Table 2.3). Monica had a Z score on the CES-D of $-.44$. Using Appendix 1, you can see that she was in the 33rd percentile (obtained as $.50 - .1700 = .33 \times 100 = 33$). Marcel, with his Z score of .14, was in the 56th percentile; and Jennie, with a Z score of 1.70, was in the 96th percentile. You might have few worries about Monica and Marcel. However, it appears that Jennie is more depressed than 96% of her classmates and may need to talk to someone.

An Example Close to Home

One of the difficulties in grading students is that performance is usually rated in terms of raw scores, such as the number of items a person correctly answers on an examination. You are probably familiar with the experience of having a test returned to you with some number that makes little sense to you. For instance, the professor comes into class and hands you your test with a 72 on it. You must then wait patiently while he or she draws the distribution on the board and tries to put your 72 into some category that you understand, such as B+.

 An alternative way of doing things would be to give you a Z score as feedback on your performance. To do this, your professor would subtract the average score (mean) from your score and divide by the standard deviation. If your Z score was positive, you would immediately know that your score was above average; if it was negative, you would know your performance was below average.

TABLE 2.4 *Z* Score Cutoffs for a Grading System

Grade	Percentiles	Z score cutoff
A	85–100	1.04
B	60–84	.25
C	20–59	−.84
D	6–19	−1.56
F	0–5	<−1.56

Suppose your professor tells you in advance that you will be graded on a curve according to the following rigid criteria. If you are in the top 15% of the class, you will get an A (85th percentile or above); between the 60th and the 84th percentiles, a B; between the 20th and the 59th percentiles, a C; between the 6th and the 19th percentiles, a D; and in the 5th percentile or below, an F. Using Appendix 1, you should be able to find the *Z* scores associated with each of these cutoff points for normal distributions of scores. Try it on your own and then consult Table 2.4 to see if you are correct. Looking at Table 2.4, you should be able to determine what your grade would be in this class on the basis of your *Z* score. If your *Z* score is 1.04 or greater, you would receive an A; if it were greater than .25 but less than 1.04, you would get a B; and so on. This system assumes that the scores are distributed normally.

Now try an example that puts a few of these concepts together. Suppose you get a 60 on a social psychology examination. You learned in class that the mean for the test was 55.70 and that the standard deviation was 6.08. If your professor uses the grading system that was just described, what would your grade be?

To solve this problem, first find your *Z* score. Recall the formula for a *Z* score:

$$Z = \frac{X_i - \overline{X}}{S}$$

So your *Z* score would be

$$Z = \frac{60 - 55.70}{6.08} = \frac{4.30}{6.08} = .707$$

Looking at Table 2.4, you see that .707 is greater than .25 (the cutoff for a B) but less than 1.04 (the cutoff for an A). Now find your exact standing in the class. To do this, look again at Appendix 1. Because the table gives *Z* scores only to the second decimal, round .707 to .71. You will find that 76.11% of the scores fall below a *Z* score of .71. This means that you would be in approximately the 76th percentile, or you would have performed better on this examination than approximately 76 out of every 100 students.

McCall's *T*

There are many other systems by which one can transform raw scores to give them more intuitive meaning. One system was established in 1939 by W. A. McCall, who originally intended to develop a system to derive equal units on mental quantities.

He suggested that a random sample of 12-year-olds be tested and that the distribution of their scores be obtained. Then percentile equivalents were to be assigned to each raw score, showing the percentile rank in the group for the people who had obtained that raw score. After this had been accomplished, the mean of the distribution would be set at 50 to correspond with the 50th percentile. In McCall's system, called **McCall's T,** the standard deviation was set at 10.

In effect, McCall generated a system that is exactly the same as standard scores (Z scores), except that the mean in McCall's system is 50 rather than 0 and the standard deviation is 10 rather than 1. Indeed, a Z score can be transformed to a **T score** by applying the linear transformation

$$T = 10Z + 50$$

You can thus get from a Z score to McCall's T by multiplying the Z score by 10 and adding 50. It should be noted that McCall did not originally intend to create an alternative to the Z score. He wanted to obtain one set of scores that could then be applied to other situations without standardizing the entire set of numbers.

There is nothing magical about the mean of 50 and the standard deviation of 10. It is a simple matter to create systems such as standard scores with any mean and standard deviation you like. If you want to say that you got a score 1000 points higher than a person who was one standard deviation below you, then you could devise a system with a mean of 100,000 and a standard deviation of 1000. If you had calculated Z scores for this distribution, then you would obtain this with the transformation

$$NS(\text{for new score}) = 1000Z + 100,000$$

In fact, you can create any system you desire. To do so, just multiply the Z score by "whatever you would like the standard deviation of your distribution to be and then add the number you would like the mean of your new distribution to be."

An example of a test developed using standardized scores is the Scholastic Aptitude Test SAT Reasoning Test. When this test was created in 1941, the developers decided to make the mean score 500 and the standard deviation 100. Thus, they multiplied the Z scores for those who took the test by 100 and added 500. For a long time, the basic scoring system was used and the 1941 norms were applied. In other words, if the average score of test takers was below the 1941 reference point, the mean for any year could be less than or more than 500. However, in 1995, the test was changed so that the mean each year would be 500 and the standard deviation would be 100. In other words, the test is recalibrated each year. However, drifts continue. For example, in 2016, the average scores on the SAT math test taken by high school juniors and seniors 510 was for a representative sample of all students and 541 for college bound students. For both groups, the standard deviation was 103 (data from www.collegeboard.com).

It is important to make the distinction between standardization and normalization. McCall's T and the other methods described in this section standardize scores by applying a linear transformation. These transformations do not change the characteristics of the distributions. If a distribution of scores is skewed before the transformation is applied, it will also be skewed after the transformation has been used. In other words, transformations standardize but do not normalize.

Quartiles and Deciles

The terms *quartiles* and *deciles* are frequently used when tests and test results are discussed. The two terms refer to divisions of the percentile scale into groups. The quartile system divides the percentage scale into four groups, whereas the decile system divides the scale into 10 groups.

Quartiles are points that divide the frequency distribution into equal fourths. The first quartile is the 25th percentile; the second quartile is the **median**, or 50th, percentile; and the third quartile is the 75th percentile. These are abbreviated Q1, Q2, and Q3, respectively. One-fourth of the cases will fall below Q1, one-half will fall below Q2, and three-fourths will fall below Q3. The interquartile range is the interval of scores bounded by the 25th and 75th percentiles. In other words, the **interquartile range** is bounded by the range of scores that represents the middle 50% of the distribution.

Deciles are similar to quartiles except that they use points that mark 10% rather than 25% intervals. Thus, the top decile, or D9, is the point below which 90% of the cases fall. The next decile (D8) marks the 80th percentile, and so forth.

Another system developed in the U.S. Air Force during World War II is known as the **stanine system**. This system converts any set of scores into a transformed scale, which ranges from 1 to 9. Actually the term *stanine* comes from "standard nine." The scale is standardized to have a mean of 5 and a standard deviation of approximately 2. It has been suggested that stanines had computational advantages because they required only one column on a computer card (Anastasi & Urbina, 1997). But, it has been many decades since anyone has used computer cards. Even in the modern computer era, the concept of stanines is still used.

Table 2.5 shows how percentile scores are converted into stanines. As you can see, for every 100 scores, the lowest 4 (or bottom 4% of the cases) fall into the 1st stanine. The next 7 (or 7% of the cases) fall into the 2nd stanine, and so on.

Finally, the top 4 cases fall into the top stanine. Using what you have learned about Z scores and the standard normal distribution, you should be able to figure

TABLE 2.5 Transformation of Percentile Scores into Stanines

Percentage of cases	Percentiles	Stanines
4	1–4	1 Bottom 4 percent
7	5–11	2
12	12–23	3
17	24–40	4
20	41–60	5
17	61–77	6
12	78–89	7
7	90–96	8
4	97–100	9 Top 4 percent

out the stanine for a score if you know the mean and the standard deviation of the distribution that the score comes from. For example, suppose that Igor received a 48 on his normally distributed chemistry midterm. The mean in Igor's class was 42.6, and the standard deviation was 3.6. First, you must find Igor's Z score. Do this by using the formula

$$ Z = \frac{X_i - \overline{X}}{S} \text{ so } Z = \frac{48 - 42.6}{3.6} = 1.5 $$

Now you need to transform Igor's Z score into his percentile rank. To do this, use Appendix 1. Part I shows that a Z score of 1.5 is in approximately the 93rd percentile. Thus, it falls into the 8th stanine.

Actually, you would rarely go through all these steps to find a stanine. There are easier ways of doing this, including computer programs that do it automatically. However, working out stanines the long way will help you become familiar with a variety of concepts covered in this chapter, including standard scores, means, standard deviations, and percentiles. First, review the five steps to go from raw scores to stanines:

1. Find the mean of the raw scores.
2. Find the standard deviation of the raw scores.
3. Change the raw scores to Z scores.
4. Change the Z scores to percentiles (using Appendix 1).
5. Use Table 2.5 to convert percentiles into stanines.

An alternative method is to calculate the percentile rank for each score and use Table 2.5 to obtain the stanines. Remember: In practice, you would probably use a computer program to obtain the stanines. Although stanines are not used much in the modern computer era, you can still find them in popular educational tests such as the Stanford Achievement Test.

Norms

Norms refer to the performances by defined groups on particular tests. There are many ways to express norms, and we have discussed some of these under the headings of Z scores, percentiles, and means. The norms for a test are based on the distribution of scores obtained by some defined sample of individuals. The mean is a norm, and the 50th percentile is a norm. Norms are used to give information about performance relative to what has been observed in a standardization sample.

Much has been written about norms and their inadequacies. In later chapters, we shall discuss this material in relation to particular tests. We cover only the highlights here. Whenever you see a norm for a test, you should ask how it was established. Norms are obtained by administering the test to a sample of people and obtaining the distribution of scores for that group.

For example, say you develop a measure of anxiety associated with taking tests in college. After establishing some psychometric properties for the test, you administer the test to normative groups of college students. The scores of these groups of students might then serve as the norms. Say that, for the normative groups of students, the average score is 19. When your friend Alice comes to take the test and obtains a score of 24, the psychologist using the test might conclude that Alice is above average in test anxiety.

The SAT, as indicated earlier, has norms for all of its subject tests. The current SAT includes 20 subject tests. These subject tests represent five general subject areas: English, history, languages, mathematics, and science. For each subject area, the test taker gets a score ranging from 200 to 800. The test was administered to millions of high-school seniors from all over the United States. With distributions of scores for this normative group, one could obtain a distribution to provide meaning for particular categories of scores. The scoring system has changed only slightly over the last 75 years. For example, in the 1941 national sample, a person who scored 650 on the verbal portion of the SAT was at the 93rd percentile of high-school seniors. However, if you took the test before 1995 and scored 650, it did not mean that you were in the 93rd percentile of the people who took the test when you did. Rather, it meant that you would have been at the 93rd percentile if you had been in the group the test had been standardized on. However, if the normative group was a representative sample of the group to which you belonged (and there is every reason to believe it was), then you could reasonably assume that you were in approximately the 93rd percentile of your own group.[2] After 1995, a SAT score of 650 would place you in the 93rd percentile of the people who took the test during the year you completed it. In the current versions of the SAT, test takers do not respond to exactly the same questions. It is hard to assure that all versions of the test are equally difficult. To adjust for differences in how hard different test editions are, the SAT uses a process known as equating. The process uses average level of test performance in each group of test takers to make this adjustment. Some controversies surrounding norms are discussed in Psychological Testing in Everyday Life 2.4.

In Chapters 9 and 10, we will review intelligence tests. Most intelligence tests are transformed to have a mean of 100 and a standard deviation of 15. Thus, an IQ score of 115 is one standard deviation above the mean and an IQ score of 130 is two standard deviations above the mean. Using the information we have reviewed, you can determine that an IQ score of 115 is approximately in the 84th percentile, while an IQ score of 85 is approximately in the 16th percentile. Only some 0.13% of the population obtains an IQ score of 145, which is three standard deviations above the mean. Figure 2.9 shows the standard normal distribution with the Z scores, T scores, IQ scores, and stanines. Examining the figure, locate the point that is one standard deviation above the mean. That point is associated with a Z score of 1.0, a T score of 60, an IQ score of 115, and the 7th stanine. Using the figure, try to find the score on each scale for an observation that falls two standard deviations below the mean. You should get a Z score of −2.0, a T score of 30, an IQ score of 70, and a stanine of 1.

---

[2] Based on the *American Testing Program Guide for 1989–1991*, College Board of the Educational Testing Service, Princeton, New Jersey.

FIGURE 2.9

Standard normal distribution with cumulative percentages, percentiles, *Z* scores, *T* scores, IQ scores, and stanines.

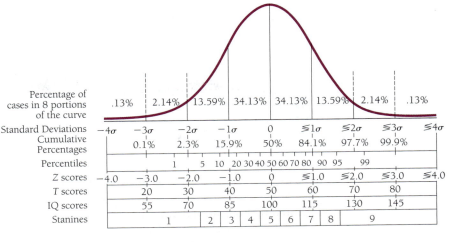

Percentage of cases in 8 portions of the curve	.13%	2.14%	13.59%	34.13%	34.13%	13.59%	2.14%	.13%
Standard Deviations	−4σ	−3σ	−2σ	−1σ	0	≤1σ	≤2σ	≤3σ ≤4σ
Cumulative Percentages		0.1%	2.3%	15.9%	50%	84.1%	97.7%	99.9%
Percentiles			1	5 10 20 30 40 50 60 70 80	90 95	99		
Z scores	−4.0	−3.0	−2.0	−1.0	0	≤1.0	≤2.0	≤3.0 ≤4.0
T scores		20	30	40	50	60	70	80
IQ scores		55	70	85	100	115	130	145
Stanines		1	2	3	4 5 6	7	8	9

2.4 PSYCHOLOGICAL TESTING IN EVERYDAY LIFE

Within-Group Norming Controversy

One of the most troubling issues in psychological testing is that different racial and ethnic groups do not have the same average level of performance on many tests (see Chapter 19). When tests are used to select employees, a higher percentage of majority applicants are typically selected than their representation in the general population would indicate. For example, employers who use general aptitude tests consistently overselect white applicants and underselect African Americans and Latinos or Latinas. *Overselection* is defined as selecting a higher percentage from a particular group than would be expected on the basis of the representation of that group in the applicant pool. If 60% of the applicants are white and 75% of those hired are white, then overselection has occurred.

The U.S. Department of Labor uses the General Aptitude Test Battery (GATB) to refer job applicants to employers. At one point, however, studies demonstrated that the GATB adversely affected the hiring of African Americans and Latinos and Latinas. To remedy this problem, a few years ago the department created separate norms for different groups. In other words, to obtain a standardized score, each applicant was compared only with members of his or her own racial or ethnic group. As a result, overselection based on test scores was eliminated. However, this provoked other problems. For example, consider two applicants, one white and one African American, who are in the 70th percentile on the GATB. Although they have the same score, they are compared with different normative groups. The raw score for the white applicant would be 327, while that for the African American would be 283 (Brown, 1994).

(continues)

This was seen as a problem because an African American applicant might be selected for a job even though he or she had a lower raw score, or got fewer items correct, than did a white applicant.

The problem of within-group norming is highlighted by opposing opinions from different prestigious groups. The National Academy of Sciences, the most elite group of scholars in the United States, reviewed the issue and concluded that separate norms were appropriate. Specifically, they argued that minority workers at a given level of expected job performance are less likely to be hired than are majority group members. The use of separate norms was therefore required in order to avoid adverse impact in hiring decisions (Gottfredson, 1994; Hartigan & Wigdor, 1989).

In contrast to this conclusion, legislation has led to different policies. Section 106 of the Civil Rights Act of 1991 made it illegal to use separate norms. The act states that it is unlawful for employers

> in connection with the selection or referral of applicants or candidates for employment or promotion to adjust the scores of, use different cut-offs for, or otherwise alter the results of employment-related tests on the basis of race, color, religion, sex, or national origin.

Employers may have a variety of different objectives when making employment decisions. One goal may be to enhance the ethnic and racial diversity of their workforce. Another goal may be to hire those with the best individual profiles. Often these goals compete. The law may now prohibit employers from attempting to balance these competing objectives (Sackett & Wilk, 1994).

Age-Related Norms

Certain tests have different normative groups for particular age groups. Most IQ tests are of this sort. When the Stanford-Binet IQ test was originally created, distributions of the performance of random samples of children were obtained for various age groups. When applying an IQ test, the tester's task is to determine the mental age of the person being tested. This is accomplished through various exercises that help locate the age-level norm at which a child is performing.

Tracking

One of the most common uses of age-related norms is for growth charts used by pediatricians. Consider the question "Is my son tall or short?" The answer will usually depend on a comparison of your son to other boys of the same age. Your son would be quite tall if he were 5 feet at age 8 but quite short if he were only 5 feet at age 18. Thus, the comparison is usually with people of the same age.

Beyond this rather obvious type of age-related comparison, child experts have discovered that children at the same age level tend to go through different growth patterns. Children who are small as infants often remain small and continue to grow at a slower pace than do others. Pediatricians must therefore know more than a child's age; they must also know the child's percentile within a given age group. For a variety of physical characteristics, children tend to stay at about their same percentile level, relative to other children in their age group, as they grow older. This tendency to stay at about the same level relative to one's peers is known as **tracking.** Height and weight are good examples of physical characteristics that track. Figures 2.10 and 2.11 show the expected rates of growth in terms of length (height) for boys and girls.

FIGURE 2.10

Tracking chart for boys' physical growth from birth to 36 months.

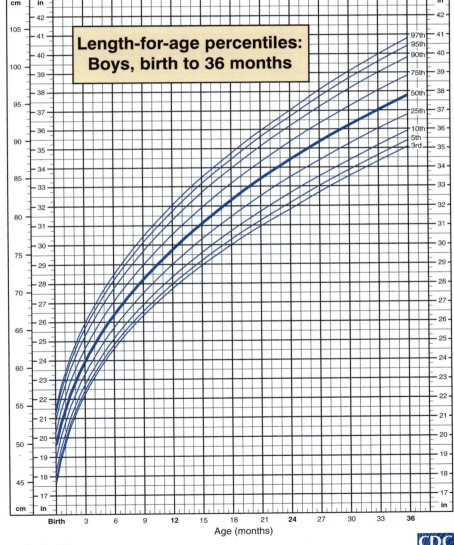

CDC Growth Charts: United States

Length-for-age percentiles: Boys, birth to 36 months

Published May 30, 2000.
SOURCE: Developed by the National Center for Health Statistics in collaboration with the National Center for Chronic Disease Prevention and Health Promotion (2000).

FIGURE 2.11

Tracking chart for girls' physical growth from birth to 36 months.

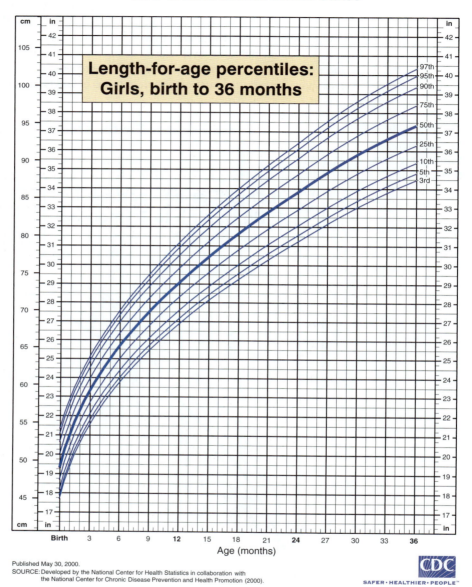

CDC Growth Charts: United States

Length-for-age percentiles: Girls, birth to 36 months

Published May 30, 2000.
SOURCE: Developed by the National Center for Health Statistics in collaboration with the National Center for Chronic Disease Prevention and Health Promotion (2000).

The charts are based on national norms from the U.S. Centers for Disease Control and Prevention (CDC). Notice that the children who were the largest as babies are expected to remain the largest as they get older.

Pediatricians use the charts to determine the expected course of growth for a child. For example, if a 3-month-old boy was 24 inches in length (about 61 cm), the doctor would locate the child on the center line on the bottom half of Figure 2.10. By age 36 months, the child would be expected to be about 37.5 inches (or about 95 cm). The tracking charts are quite useful to doctors because they help determine whether the child is going through an unusual growth pattern. A boy who had a length of 24 inches at age 3 months might come under scrutiny if at age 36 months he had a length of 35 inches. He would have gone from the 50th percentile to about the 3rd percentile in relation to other boys. This might be normal for 3-year-olds if the boy had always been in the 3rd percentile, but unusual for a boy who had been in the middle of the length distribution. The doctor might want to determine why the child did not stay in his track.

Figure 2.12 shows an example of a child going off track. There is some concern that children who are fed a fat-restricted diet experience stunted growth (Kaplan & Toshima, 1992). The consequences of a slightly restricted vegetarian diet are mild if they exist at all. However, highly restricted diets may affect growth. For instance, Pugliese, Lifshitz, Grad, Fort, and Marks-Katz (1983) studied 24 adolescents who had voluntarily undergone severe caloric restrictions because they wanted to lose weight. Though they did not have anorexia nervosa, they consumed only a small percentage of the calories recommended for their age. Figure 2.12 shows the growth

FIGURE 2.12
Growth in the case of severe dietary restriction. The scales represent percentile standards for height and weight, and the plotted values are for the clinical case.

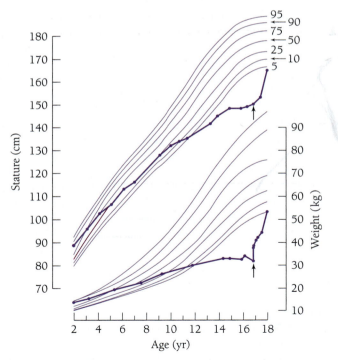

(From Pugliese et al., 1983, p. 514; reprinted by permission of *The New England Journal of Medicine, 309*, 513–518, 1983.)

pattern for one of these children. As the figure suggests, the child grew normally until age 9. At that point, highly restricted dieting began. Within a few years, growth was interrupted. The arrow in the figure shows the point at which psychotherapy began. After this point, normal feeding resumed, and growth started once again. However, at age 18, the child was still below the 5th percentile in height and weight. Given normal tracking, this child should have been between the 25th and 50th percentiles.

Although the tracking system has worked well for medicine, it has stirred considerable controversy in education. Some people believe there is an analogy between the rates of physical growth and the rates of intellectual growth: Just as there are some slow growers who eventually will be shorter than average adults, there are slow learners who will eventually know less as adults. Furthermore, some suggest that children learn at different rates. Children are therefore separated early in their educational careers and placed in classrooms that correspond with these different tracks. Many educators have attacked the tracking system because it discriminates against some children. Because people use psychological tests to place children in these tracks, some tests have come under severe scrutiny and attack. We shall return to this controversy in Chapters 19 and 20.

Criterion-Referenced Tests

The purpose of establishing norms for a test is to determine how a test taker compares with others. A **norm-referenced test** compares each person with a norm. Many critics have objected that this use of tests forces competition among people. Young children exposed to many norm-referenced tests in elementary school can get caught up in a never-ending battle to perform better than average. In addition to ranking people according to performance, however, tests can play an important role in identifying problems and suggesting new directions for individualized programs of instruction. During the last two decades, interest has grown in tests that are applied to determine whether students know specific information. These tests do not compare students with one another; they compare each student's performance with a criterion or an expected level of performance (Hartman & Looney, 2003; Wiberg, 2003).

A **criterion-referenced test** describes the specific types of skills, tasks, or knowledge that the test taker can demonstrate such as mathematical skills. The results of such a test might demonstrate that a particular child can add, subtract, and multiply but has difficulty with both long and short division. The results of the test would not be used to make comparisons between the child and other members of his or her class. Instead, they would be employed to design an individualized program of instruction that focuses on division. Thus, the criterion-referenced testing movement emphasizes the diagnostic use of tests—that is, using them to identify problems that can be remedied. Criterion-referenced tests became an important trend in clinical psychology in the 1980s and 1990s. In educational testing, the same ideas formed the basis of the standards-based testing movement. Instead of comparing how well children were performing

2.5 PSYCHOLOGICAL TESTING IN EVERYDAY LIFE

Within High-School Norms for University Admission

Beginning in 2002, the University of California changed its admissions policy. The university had discovered that its admissions did not reflect the demographic characteristics of the state. In particular, students from underrepresented groups and those from low-income neighborhoods were not gaining admission to the university. When the university was required to give up its affirmative action program, there were serious concerns that the student classes would not reflect the diversity of the state of California.

To address this problem, the university created the Eligibility in Local Context (ELC) program. This program guarantees eligibility for university admission to the top 4% of graduates of California high schools. The plan focuses only on high-school grades and does not require the SAT test.

The purpose of this policy is to provide norming within particular high schools. In other words, students are not competing with all other students in the state but are being compared only with those who have had similar educational exposures. The policy was designed to increase the number of students from underrepresented ethnic and minority groups who were admitted to the university. Unfortunately, the program was not successful. Latino acceptance rates dropped from 68% in 1995 to 45% in 2003. African American acceptance rates were 58% in 1995 and dropped to 35% by 2003. As a result, the program was abandoned. The California case was linked to a variety of rules relevant selection of the top portion of high-school classes. We will return to this discussion when we review the case of Abigail N. Fisher versus the University of Texas in Chapter 20.

Details can be obtained from www.ucop.edu/sas/elc.

in relation to other children, schools were evaluated on the basis of how many students exceeded a criterion score. Under the No Child Left Behind legislation, schools could lose funding if the number of students failing to meet the criterion was too high. By 2011, it became apparent that too many districts could meet the criterion, and the Obama administration offered relief from the criterion standard for districts willing to engage in other reform. Thus, the criterion-referenced testing movement, originally thought to be a humanistic trend, became associated with a more conservative approach to public education. Advocates for standards-based testing emphasize that schools must enforce high standards. Critics of the standards movement argue that the cut points for passing high stakes tests are often arbitrary (see Psychological Testing in Everyday Life 2.6).

2.6 PSYCHOLOGICAL TESTING IN EVERYDAY LIFE

Are 4th Graders Smarter than 3rd Graders?

One of the most important instruments for measuring school performance is the standardized achievement test. California uses a standardized testing and reporting (STAR) system. STAR is very important because it evaluates performance for high stakes programs such as No Child Left Behind. In an average year, nearly 5 million children are tested in the STAR program. The evaluation of information from the STAR program reveals some interesting trends. The test reveals several indicators of school performance, and these measures are taken quite seriously. Figure 2.13 summarizes the percentage of students who perform at an advanced level in different grades. The data are from three separate years: 2005, 2006, and 2007. The graph shows that each year, relatively few 3rd graders perform at the advanced level while many 4th graders perform at the advanced level. Does this mean that 4th-grade students are smarter than 3rd-grade students? Norm-referenced test results would never lead to this conclusion because students at each level are compared relative to other students in their same grade level. Standards-based testing does not attend to how students are performing in relation to other students. Instead, the tests consider performance relative to a defined standard. One explanation for the data shown in the graph is that there was an exceptional crop of good students in a particular 4th grade. However, this explanation seems unlikely because the effect occurs each year. A more plausible explanation is that the definition of performing at an advanced level is somewhat arbitrary. The test may be too hard for 3rd graders but perhaps too easy for 4th graders.

FIGURE 2.13
STAR test performance by grade in 3 years.

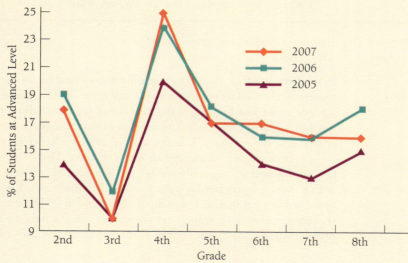

<table>
<tr><td>**2.7**</td><td>**PSYCHOLOGICAL TESTING IN EVERYDAY LIFE**</td></tr>
</table>

Big Data

Since the last time we revised *Psychological Testing*, there has been a revolution in social science research associated with "Big Data." Instead of performing studies on small samples of people, we are now encouraged to use of ever-larger data sets with massive numbers of measured variables. "Big data" generally refers to *data sets with sizes beyond the ability of commonly used software tools to capture, curate, manage, and process the data within a tolerable elapsed time.* Big data are clearly an important new direction for most areas of science. There are new opportunities to capture the opportunities and challenges facing all biomedical researchers to use massive amounts of information available on the Internet to study human and animal behavior. The new data sets exceed the abilities of currently used approaches to manage and analyze behavior. In the next few chapters, we speculate on how the new approaches to data will affect the future of our science and practice.

Summary

In this chapter, we discussed some basic rules for translating observations of behaviors into numbers. The use of number systems is important for precision in all scientific exercises. Measures of psychological processes are represented by one of four types of scales. A *nominal scale* simply assigns numbers to categories. This type of scale has none of the properties of a numbered scale. An *ordinal scale* has the property of magnitude and allows us to rank objects, but it does not have the property of equal intervals or an absolute 0. An *interval scale* can describe the distances between objects because it has the property of equal intervals in addition to the property of magnitude. A *ratio scale* has an absolute 0 in addition to equal intervals and magnitude. Any mathematical operation on a ratio scale is permissible.

To make sense out of test scores, we have to examine the score of an individual relative to the scores of others. To do this requires creating a distribution of test scores. There are several ways to display the distribution of scores, including frequency distributions and frequency polygons. We also need statistics to describe the distribution. The *mean* is the average score, the *variance* is the averaged squared deviation around the mean, and the *standard deviation* is the square root of the variance. Using these statistics, we can tell a lot about a particular score by relating it to characteristics of a well-known probability distribution known as the standard normal distribution.

Norms are used to relate a score to a particular distribution for a subgroup of a population. For example, norms are used to describe where a child is on some measure relative to other children of the same age. In contrast, *criterion-referenced tests* are used to document specific skills rather than to compare people. Criterion-referenced tests are the basis for standards-based assessment in public education. Standards-based assessment requires that students pass tests demonstrating that they have critical knowledge and skills in defined areas. Some critics believe the cut points for passing the tests are arbitrary.

In summary, this chapter reviewed basic statistical methods for describing scores on one variable. In Chapter 3, we shall discuss statistical methods for showing the relationship between two or more variables.

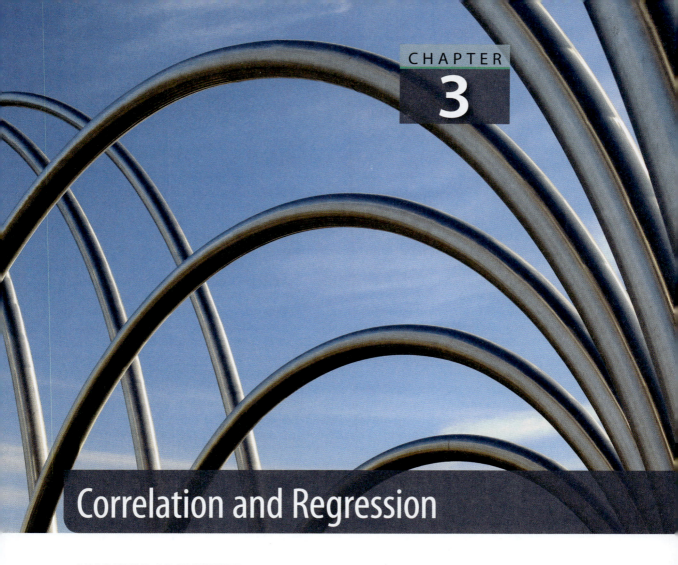

Correlation and Regression

LEARNING OBJECTIVES

When you have completed this chapter,[1] you should be able to:

▶ Express the extent to which two measures are associated

▶ Explain what a scatter diagram is and how it is used

▶ Define a positive correlation and a negative correlation

▶ Discuss some of the differences between correlation and regression

▶ Tell how a regression line describes the relationship between two variables

▶ Discuss under which circumstances you would use the point biserial correlation, the phi coefficient, and the tetrachoric correlation

▶ Outline the procedure you would use to predict one score from the linear combination of several scores

▶ Explain factor analysis and how it is used

[1]Portions of this chapter are taken from *Basic Statistics for the Behavioral Sciences* by Robert M. Kaplan (Newton, MA: Allyn & Bacon, 1987).

A banner headline in an issue of a tabloid news report read, "Food Causes Most Marriage Problems." The article talked about the "startling results of studies by doctors and marriage counselors." Before we are willing to accept the magazine's conclusion, we must ask many questions. Did the tabloid report enough data for us to evaluate the hypothesis? Do we feel comfortable concluding that an association between diet and divorce has been established?

There were many problems with the tabloid news report. The observation was based on the clinical experiences of some health practitioners who found that many couples who came in for counseling had poor diets. One major oversight was that there was no control group of people who were not having marriage problems. We do not know from the study whether couples with problems have poor diets more often than do people in general. Another problem is that neither diet nor marital happiness was measured in a systematic way. Thus, we are left with subjective opinions about the levels of these variables. Finally, we do not know the direction of the causation: Does poor diet cause unhappiness, or does unhappiness cause poor diet? Another possibility is that some other problem (such as stress) may cause both poor diet and unhappiness. So it turns out that the article was not based on any systematic study. It merely cited the opinions of some physicians and marriage counselors who felt that high levels of blood sugar are related to low energy levels, which in turn cause marital unhappiness.

This chapter focuses on one of the many issues raised in the report—the level of association between variables. The tabloid report tells us that diet and unhappiness are associated, but not to what extent. Is the association greater than we would expect by chance? Is it a strong or is it a weak association?

Lots of things seem to be related. For example, long-term stress is associated with heart disease, training is associated with good performance in athletics, and overeating is associated with indigestion. People often observe associations between events. For some events, the association is obvious. For example, the angle of the sun in the sky and the time of day are associated in a predictable way. This is because time was originally defined by the angle of the sun in the sky. Other associations are less obvious, such as the association between performing well on the Scholastic Aptitude Test SAT Mathematics Subject Test and obtaining good grades in college.

Sometimes, we do not know whether events are meaningfully associated with one another. If we do conclude that events are fundamentally associated, then we need to determine a precise index of the degree. This chapter discusses statistical procedures that allow us to make precise estimates of the degree to which variables are associated. These methods are quite important; we shall refer to them frequently in the remainder of this book. The indexes of association used most frequently in testing are *correlation, regression,* and *multiple regression.*

The Scatter Diagram

Before discussing the measures of association, we shall look at visual displays of the relationships between variables. In Chapter 2, we concentrated on univariate distributions of scores, which involve only one variable for each individual under study. This chapter considers statistical methods for studying *bivariate distributions,* which

FIGURE 3.1

A scatter diagram. The circled point shows a person who had a score of 21 on *X* and 14 on *Y*.

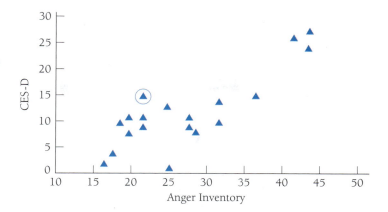

have two scores for each individual. For example, when we study the relationship between test scores and classroom performance, we are dealing with a bivariate distribution. Each person has a score on the test and a score for classroom performance. We must examine the scores of all the individuals to know whether these two variables are associated.

The American Psychological Association's Task Force on Statistical Inference has suggested that visual inspection of data is an important step in data analysis (Wilkinson, 1999) and there is increasing interest in data visualization (Cook, Lee, & Majumder, 2016). A **scatter diagram** is a picture of the relationship between two variables. An example of a scatter diagram is shown in Figure 3.1, which relates scores on a measure of anger for medical students to scores on the Center for Epidemiologic Studies Depression Scale CES-D. The axes in the figure represent the scales for two variables. Values of *X* for the anger inventory are shown on the horizontal axis, and values of *Y* for the CES-D are on the vertical axis. Each point on the scatter diagram shows where a particular individual scored on both *X* and *Y*. For example, one person had a score of 14 on the CES-D and a score of 21 on the anger inventory. This point is circled in the figure. You can locate it by finding 21 on the *X* axis and then going straight up to the level of 14 on the *Y* axis. Each point indicates the scores for *X* and *Y* for one individual. As you can see, the figure presents a lot of information. Each point represents the performance of one person who has been assessed on two measures.

The next sections present methods for summarizing the information in a scatter diagram by finding the straight line that comes closest to more points than any other line. One important reason for examining the scatter diagram is that the relationships between *X* and *Y* are not always best described by a straight line. For example, Figure 3.2 shows the hypothetical relationship between levels of antidepressant medication in the blood of depressed patients and the number of symptoms they report. However, the relationship is systematic. Patients who have too little or too much medication experience more symptoms than do those who get an intermediate amount. The methods of linear correlation or linear regression to be presented in this chapter are not appropriate for describing nonlinear relationships such as this.

FIGURE 3.2
A scatter diagram
showing a nonlinear
relationship.

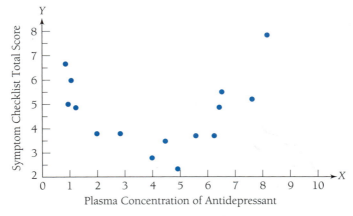

(From R. M. Kaplan & Grant, 2000).

Correlation

In correlational analysis, we ask whether two variables covary. In other words, does Y get larger as X gets larger? For example, does the patient feel dizzier when the doctor increases the dose of a drug? Do people get more diseases when they are under more stress? Correlational analysis is designed primarily to examine linear relationships between variables. Although one can use correlational techniques to study nonlinear relationships, doing so lies beyond the scope of this book.[2]

A **correlation coefficient** is a mathematical index that describes the direction and magnitude of a relationship. Figure 3.3 shows three different types of relationships between variables. Part (a) of the figure demonstrates a *positive correlation*. This means that high scores on Y are associated with high scores on X, and low scores on Y correspond to low scores on X. Part (b) shows *negative correlation*. When there is a negative correlation, higher scores on Y are associated with lower scores on X, and lower scores on Y are associated with higher scores on X. This might describe the relationship between barbiturate use and amount of activity: The higher the drug dose, the less active the patients are. Part (c) of Figure 3.3 shows no correlation, or a situation in which the variables are not related. Here, scores on X do not give us information about scores on Y. An example of this sort of relationship is the lack of correlation between shoe size and IQ.

There are many ways to calculate a correlation coefficient. All involve pairs of observations: For each observation on one variable, there is an observation on one other variable for the same person.[3] Appendix 3.1 (at the end of this chapter) offers an example of the calculation of a correlation. All methods of calculating a correlation coefficient are mathematically equivalent. Before we present methods for calculating the correlation coefficient, however, we shall discuss regression, the method on which correlation is based.

---

[2]Readers who are interested in studying nonlinear relationships should review German and Hill (2007).
[3]The pairs of scores do not always need to be for a person. They might also be for a group, an institution, a team, and so on.

FIGURE 3.3
Three hypothetical relationships:
(a) positive correlation,
(b) negative correlation,
(c) no correlation.

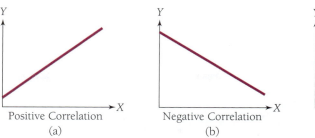
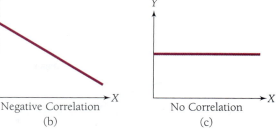

Positive Correlation
(a)

Negative Correlation
(b)

No Correlation
(c)

Regression

The Regression Line

We use correlation to assess the magnitude and direction of a relationship. A related technique, known as *regression,* is used to make predictions about scores on one variable from knowledge of scores on another variable. These predictions are obtained from the **regression line,** which is defined as the best-fitting straight line through a set of points in a scatter diagram. It is found by using the *principle of least squares,* which minimizes the squared deviation around the regression line. Let us explain.

The mean is the point of least squares for any single variable. This means that the sum of the squared deviations around the mean will be less than it is around any value other than the mean. For example, consider the scores 5, 4, 3, 2, and 1. The mean is $\Sigma X_i / N = 15/5 = 3$. The squared deviation of each score around the mean can be found. For the score 5, the squared deviation is $(5-3)^2 = 4$. For the score 4, it is $(4-3)^2 = 1$. The score 3 is equal to the mean, so the squared deviation around the mean will be $(3-3)^2 = 0$. By definition, the mean will always be the point of least squares.

The regression line is the running mean or the line of least squares in two dimensions or in the space created by two variables. Consider the situation shown in the scatter diagram in Figure 3.1. For each level of X (or point on the X scale), there is a distribution of scores on Y. In other words, we could find a mean of Y when X is 3, another mean of Y when X is 4, and so on. The least squares method in regression finds the straight line that comes as close to as many of these Y means as possible. In other words, it is the line for which the squared deviations around the line are at a minimum.

Before we get to the regression equation, we must define some of the terms it includes. The term on the left of the equation is Y'. This is the predicted value of Y. When we create the equation, we use observed values of Y and X. The equation is the result of the least squares procedure and shows the best linear relationship between X and Y. When the equation is available, we can take a score on X and plug it into the formula. What results is a predicted value of Y, or Y'.

The most important term in the equation is the *regression coefficient,* or *b,* which is the slope of the regression line. The regression coefficient can be expressed as the ratio of the sum of squares for the covariance to the sum of squares for X. *Sum of squares* is defined as the sum of the squared deviations around the mean. For X, this is the sum of the squared deviations around the X variable. *Covariance* is used to express how much two measures covary, or vary together. To understand covariance, let's look at the extreme case of the relationship between two identical sets of scores. In this case, there will be a perfect association. We know that we can create a new score that exactly repeats the scores on any one variable. If we created this new twin variable, then it would covary perfectly with the original variable. Regression analysis attempts to determine how similar the variance between two variables is by dividing the covariance by the average variance of each variable. The covariance is calculated from the cross products, or products of variations around each mean. Symbolically, this is

$$\Sigma XY = \Sigma(X-\overline{X})(Y-\overline{Y})$$

The regression coefficient or slope is:

$$b = \frac{N(\Sigma XY) - (\Sigma X)(\Sigma Y)}{N\Sigma X^2 - (\Sigma X)^2}$$

The *slope* describes how much change is expected in Y each time X increases by one unit. For example, Figure 3.4 shows a regression line with a slope of .67. In this figure, the difference between 1 and 2 in units of X is associated with an expected difference of .67 in units of Y (for $X = 1$, $Y = 2.67$ and for $X = 2$, $Y = 3.34$; $3.34 - 2.67 = .67$). The regression coefficient is sometimes expressed in different notation. For example, the Greek β is often used for a population estimate of the regression coefficient.

The **intercept,** *a*, is the value of Y when X is 0. In other words, it is the point at which the regression line crosses the Y axis. This is shown in Figure 3.4. It is easy to find the intercept when we know the regression coefficient. The intercept is found by using the following formula:

$$a = \overline{Y} - b\overline{X}$$

The Best-Fitting Line

Correlational methods require finding the best-fitting line through a series of data points. In Figure 3.4, a regression line is shown that is based on a series of observations for particular individuals. Each individual had actually obtained a score on X and on Y. Take the example of someone who obtained a score of 4 on

FIGURE 3.4

The regression equation. The slope *a* is the change in Y per unit change in X. The intercept *b* is value of Y when X is 0.

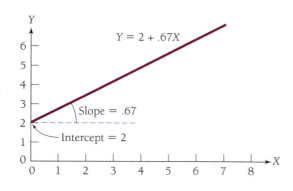

$Y = 2 + .67X$

Slope = .67

Intercept = 2

X and 6 on Y. The regression equation gives a predicted value for Y, denoted as Y'. Using the regression equation, we can calculate Y' for this person. It is

$$Y' = 2 + .67X$$

so

$$Y' = 2 + .67(4)$$
$$= 4.68$$

The actual and predicted scores on Y are rarely exactly the same. Suppose that the person actually received a score of 4 on Y and that the regression equation predicted that he or she would have a score of 4.68 on Y. The difference between the observed and predicted score $(Y - Y')$ is called the **residual.** The best-fitting line keeps residuals to a minimum. In other words, it minimizes the deviation between observed and predicted Y scores. Because residuals can be positive or negative and will cancel to 0 if averaged, the best-fitting line is most appropriately found by squaring each residual. Thus, the best-fitting line is obtained by keeping these squared residuals as small as possible. This is known as *the principle of least squares.* Formally, it is stated as

$$\Sigma(Y - Y')^2 \text{ is at a minimum}$$

An example showing how to calculate a regression equation is given in Appendix 3.1. Whether or not you become proficient at calculating regression equations, you should learn to interpret them in order to be a good consumer of research information.

Table 3.1 and Figure 3.5 present an example of a regression problem. The data come from international studies on the relationship between price per pack of cigarettes and the number of cigarettes consumed per capita. There is considerable variability in the price per pack of cigarettes among European countries. The differences between countries are primarily defined by the level of taxation. Some countries, such as Norway, have high taxes on tobacco; therefore, the price per pack for cigarettes is much higher. Figure 3.5 shows the scatter diagram as it relates price to number of cigarettes consumed.

Although the relationship is not strong, there is a negative trend, which is defined by the regression equation. The intercept in this equation is 2764.6. This means the line intersects the Y axis at 2764.6. The intercept provides an estimate of the number of cigarettes that would be consumed if cigarettes were free. The regression coefficient for this model is $b = -243.99$ and tells how much cigarette consumption should decline for each dollar that is added to the price of a pack of cigarettes. In other words, this equation suggests that, on average, people will smoke 244 fewer cigarettes per year for each dollar added to the price of cigarettes. Thus, according to this simple model, adding a $2 tax to cigarettes would decrease consumption on average by approximately 488 cigarettes per year (Kaplan et al., 1995).

Correlation is a special case of regression in which the scores for both variables are in standardized, or Z, units. Having the scores in Z units is a nice convenience because it eliminates the need to find the intercept. In correlation, the intercept is always 0. Furthermore, the slope in correlation is easier to interpret because it is in a standardized unit. An example of how to calculate a correlation coefficient is given in Appendix 3.1. In calculating the correlation coefficient, we can bypass the step

TABLE 3.1   Relationship of Cigarette Price and Consumption

	Country	Average cigarettes/year	Price per pack ($)
1.	Belgium	1990	1.54
2.	Czechoslovakia	2520	1.90
3.	Denmark	2110	3.60
4.	Finland	1720	2.50
5.	France	2400	0.80
6.	GFR	2380	2.90
7.	GDR	2340	1.78
8.	Greece	3640	0.48
9.	Hungary	3260	0.36
10.	Iceland	3100	3.51
11.	Ireland	2560	2.77
12.	Italy	2460	**1.21**
13.	Netherlands	1690	1.65
14.	Norway	710	4.17
15.	Portugal	1730	0.72
16.	Romania	2110	0.37
17.	Spain	2740	0.55
18.	Sweden	1660	2.30
19.	Switzerland	2960	1.84
20.	Turkey	3000	0.54
21.	USSR	2170	0.80
22.	UK	2120	2.45

of changing all the scores into Z units. This gets done as part of the calculation process. You may notice that Steps 1–13 are identical for calculating regression and correlation (Appendix 3.1). Psychological Testing in Everyday Life 3.1 gives a theoretical discussion of correlation and regression.

The **Pearson product moment correlation** coefficient is a ratio used to determine the degree of variation in one variable that can be estimated from knowledge about variation in the other variable. The correlation coefficient can take on any value from -1.0 to 1.0.

Table 3.2 gives the raw data for CES-D scores (X) and anger inventory scores (Y) for medical students. Try to find the regression of anger on CES-D and the correlation between these two measures. The correct answer is $r = .82$.

As you will see from Appendix 3.1, calculations of the correlation coefficient and the regression can be long and difficult. You may be able to avoid the many computational steps by using a calculator or one of the many calculation tools on the Internet. Many inexpensive pocket calculators automatically perform correlation and regression.

FIGURE 3.5

Scatter diagram relating price to number of cigarettes consumed.

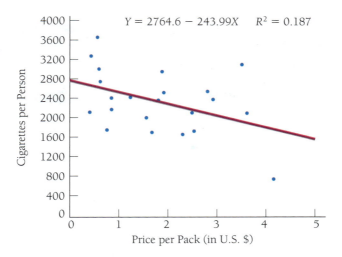

$Y = 2764.6 - 243.99X \quad R^2 = 0.187$

Cigarettes per Person

Price per Pack (in U.S. $)

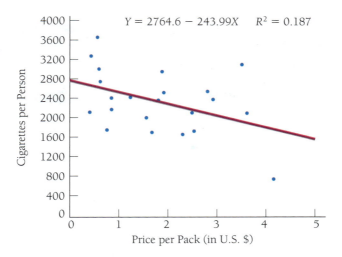

3.1 PSYCHOLOGICAL TESTING IN EVERYDAY LIFE

A More Theoretical Discussion of Correlation and Regression

The difference between correlation and regression is analogous to the difference between standardized scores and raw scores. In correlation, we look at the relationship between variables when each one is transformed into standardized scores. In Chapter 2, standardized scores (Z scores) were defined as $(X - \overline{X})/S$. In correlation, both variables are in Z scores, so they both have a mean of 0. In other words, the mean for the two variables will always be the same. As a result of this convenience, the intercept will always be 0 (when X is 0, Y is also 0) and will drop out of the equation. The resulting equation for translating X into Y then becomes $Y = rX$. The correlation coefficient (r) is equal to the regression coefficient when both X and Y are measured in standardized units. In other words, the predicted value of Y equals X times the correlation between X and Y. If the correlation between X and Y is .80 and the standardized (Z) score for the X variable is 1.0, then the predicted value of Y will be .80. Unless there is a perfect correlation (1.0 or −1.0), scores on Y will be predicted to be closer to the Y mean than scores on X will be to the X mean. A correlation of .80 means that the prediction for Y is 80% as far from the mean as is the observation for X. A correlation of .50 means that the predicted distance between the mean of Y and the predicted Y is half of the distance between the associated X and the mean of X. For example, if the Z score for X is 1.0, then X is one unit above the mean of X. If the correlation is .50, then we predict that Y will have a Z score of .50.

(continues)

One benefit of using the correlation coefficient is that it has a reciprocal nature. The correlation between X and Y will always be the same as the correlation between Y and X. For example, if the correlation between drug dose and activity is .68, the correlation between activity and drug dose is .68.

On the other hand, regression does not have this property. Regression is used to transform scores on one variable into estimated scores on the other. We often use regression to predict raw scores on Y on the basis of raw scores on X. For instance, we might seek an equation to predict a student's grade point average (GPA) on the basis of his or her SAT score. Because regression uses the raw units of the variables, the reciprocal property does not hold. The coefficient that describes the regression of X on Y is usually not the same as the coefficient that describes the regression of Y on X.

The term *regression* was first used in 1885 by an extraordinary British intellectual named Sir Francis Galton. Fond of describing social and political changes that occur over successive generations, Galton noted that extraordinarily tall men tended to have sons who were a little shorter than them and that unusually small men tended to have sons closer to the average height (but still shorter than average). Over time, individuals with all sorts of unusual characteristics tended to produce offspring who were closer to the average. Galton thought of this as a regression toward mediocrity, an idea that became the basis for a statistical procedure that described how scores tend to regress toward the mean. If a person is extreme on X, then regression predicts that he or she will be less extreme on Y. Karl Pearson developed the first statistical models of correlation and regression in the late 19th century.

Statistical Definition of Regression

Regression analysis shows how change in one variable is related to change in another variable. In psychological testing, we often use regression to determine whether changes in test scores are related to changes in performance. Do people who score higher on tests of manual dexterity perform better in dental school? Can IQ scores measured during high school predict monetary income 20 years later? Regression analysis and related correlational methods reveal the degree to which these variables are linearly related. In addition, they offer an equation that estimates scores on a criterion (such as dental-school grades) on the basis of scores on a predictor (such as manual dexterity).

In Chapter 2, we introduced the concept of variance. You might remember that *variance* was defined as the average squared deviation around the mean. We used the term *sum of squares* for the sum of squared deviations around the mean. Symbolically, this is

$$\Sigma(X - \overline{X})^2$$

The variance is the sum of squares divided by $N - 1$. The formula for this is

$$S_X^2 = \frac{\Sigma(X - \overline{X})^2}{N - 1}$$

We also gave some formulas for the variance of raw scores. The variance of X can be calculated from raw scores using the formula

$$S_X^2 = \frac{\Sigma X^2 - \dfrac{(\Sigma X)^2}{N}}{N - 1}$$

If there is another variable, Y, then we can calculate the variance using a similar formula:

$$S_Y^2 = \frac{\Sigma Y^2 - \dfrac{(\Sigma Y)^2}{N}}{N - 1}$$

To calculate regression, we need a term for the covariance. To calculate the covariance, we need to find the sum of cross products, which is defined as

$$\Sigma XY = \Sigma(X - \overline{X})(Y - \overline{Y})$$

and the raw score formula, which is often used for calculation, is

$$\Sigma XY - \frac{(\Sigma X)(\Sigma Y)}{N}$$

The covariance is the sum of cross products divided by $N - 1$.

Now look at the similarity of the formula for the covariance and the formula for the variance:

$$S_{XY}^2 = \frac{\Sigma XY - \dfrac{(\Sigma X)(\Sigma Y)}{N}}{N - 1}$$

$$S_X^2 = \frac{\Sigma X^2 - \dfrac{(\Sigma X)^2}{N}}{N - 1}$$

Try substituting X for Y in the formula for the covariance. You should get

$$\frac{\Sigma XX - \dfrac{(\Sigma X)(\Sigma X)}{N}}{N - 1}$$

(continues)

▼ **3.1** **PSYCHOLOGICAL TESTING IN EVERYDAY LIFE** *(continued)*

If you replace ΣXX with ΣX^2 and $(\Sigma X)(\Sigma X)$ with $(\Sigma X)^2$, you will see the relationship between variance and covariance:

$$\frac{\Sigma X^2 - \dfrac{(\Sigma X)^2}{N}}{N-1}$$

In regression analysis, we examine the ratio of the covariance to the average of the variances for the two separate measures. This gives us an estimate of how much variance in one variable we can determine by knowing about the variation in the other variable.

Testing the Statistical Significance of a Correlation Coefficient

One of the most important questions in evaluating a correlation is whether it is larger than we would expect by chance. The correlation between two randomly created variables will not always be 0.0. By chance alone, it is possible to observe a correlation higher or lower than 0.0. However, the expected value the correlation averaged over many randomly created data sets is 0.0, and we can estimate the probability that correlations of various magnitudes occurred by chance alone. We begin with the null hypothesis that there is no relationship between variables. The null hypothesis is rejected if there is evidence that the association between two variables is significantly different from 0. Correlation coefficients can be tested for statistical significance using the t distribution. The t distribution is not a single distribution (such as the Z distribution) but a family of distributions, each with its own degrees of freedom. The *degrees of freedom* (df) are defined as the sample size minus two, or $N - 2$. The formula for calculating the t value is

$$t = r\sqrt{\frac{N-2}{1-r^2}}$$

The significance of the t value—where, $df = N - 2$ and N is the number of pairs—can then be obtained by using Appendix 3.1.

Let's take one example of a correlation of .37 based on 50 pairs of observations. Using the formula, we obtain

$$t = .37\sqrt{\frac{48}{.86}}$$
$$= .37(7.47)$$
$$= 2.76$$

Suppose we had stated the null hypothesis that the population association between these two variables is 0. Test statistics are used to estimate whether the

TABLE 3.2 CES-D Correlation Example

X, anger inventory	Y, CES-D	X^2	Y^2	XY	Predicted	Residual
21	14	441	196	294	7.31	6.69
21	10	441	100	210	7.31	2.69
21	8	441	64	168	7.31	.69
27	8	729	64	216	11.35	−3.35
43	26	1849	676	1118	22.14	3.86
24	0	576	0	0	9.33	−9.33
36	14	1296	196	504	17.42	−3.42
17	3	289	9	51	4.61	1.61
31	9	961	81	279	14.05	−5.05
19	10	361	100	190	5.96	4.04
19	7	361	49	133	5.96	1.04
24	12	576	144	288	9.33	2.67
27	10	729	100	270	11.35	−1.35
41	25	1681	625	1025	20.79	4.21
18	9	324	81	162	5.29	3.71
24	12	576	144	288	9.33	2.67
43	23	1849	529	989	22.14	.86
28	7	784	49	196	12.03	−5.03
31	13	961	169	403	14.05	−1.05
16	1	256	1	16	3.94	−2.94

See Appendix 3.1 for definitions of steps.

Step 1: $N = 20$

Step 2: $\Sigma X = 531$

Step 3: $\Sigma Y = 221$

Step 4: $\Sigma X^2 = 15,481$

Step 5: $\Sigma Y^2 = 3377$

Step 6: $\Sigma XY = 6800$

Step 7: 281,961

Step 8: 48,841

Steps 9, 10, 11: $20(6800) - (531)(221) = 18,649$

Steps 12, 13: $20(15,481) - (531)(531) = 27,659$

Step 14: $b = .67$

Step 15: $\bar{X} = 26.55$

Step 16: $\bar{Y} = 11.05$

Steps 17, 18: $a = 6.85$

Step 19: CES-D $= -6.85 + .67(\text{anger})$

For correlation:

Step 16: 22, 741.93

Step 17 correlation: .82

observed correlation based on samples is significantly different from 0. This would be tested against the alternative hypothesis that the association between the two measures is significantly different from 0 in a **two-tailed test.** A significance level of .05 is used. Formally, then, the hypothesis and alternative hypothesis are

$$H_0: \quad r = 0$$
$$H_1: \quad r \neq 0$$

Using the formula, we obtain a *t* value of 2.76 with 48 degrees of freedom. According to Appendix 3.1, this *t* value is sufficient to reject the null hypothesis. Thus, we conclude that the association between these two variables was not the result of chance.

There are also statistical tables that give the critical values for *r*. One of these tables is included as Appendix 2. The table lists critical values of *r* for both the .05 and the .01 alpha levels according to degrees of freedom. For the correlation coefficient, $df = N - 2$. Suppose, for example, that you want to determine whether a correlation coefficient of .45 is statistically significant for a sample of 20 subjects. The degrees of freedom would be 18 ($20 - 2 = 18$). According to Appendix 2, the critical value for the .05 level is .444 with 18 *df*. Because .45 exceeds .444, you would conclude that the chances of finding a correlation as large as the one observed by chance alone would be less than 5 in 100. However, the observed correlation is less than the criterion value for the .01 level (that would require .561 with 18 *df*).

How to Interpret a Regression Plot

Regression plots are pictures that show the relationship between variables. A common use of correlation is to determine the **criterion validity evidence** for a test, or the relationship between a test score and some well-defined criterion. The association between a test of job aptitude and the criterion of actual performance on the job is an example of criterion validity evidence. The problems dealt with in studies of criterion validity evidence require one to predict some criterion score on the basis of a predictor or test score. Suppose that you want to build a test to predict how enjoyable someone will turn out to be as a date. If you selected your dates randomly and with no information about them in advance, then you might be best off just using normative information.

You might expect the distribution of enjoyableness of dates to be normal. In other words, some people are absolutely no fun for you to go out with, others are exceptionally enjoyable, and the great majority are somewhere between these two extremes. Figure 3.6 shows what a frequency distribution of enjoyableness of dates might look like. As you can see, the highest point, which shows where dates are most frequently classified, is the location of the average date.

If you had no other way of predicting how much you would like your dates, the safest prediction would be to pick this middle level of enjoyableness because it is the one observed most frequently. This is called *normative* because it uses information gained from representative groups. Knowing nothing else about an individual, you can make an educated guess that a person will be average in enjoyableness because past experience has demonstrated that the mean, or average, score is also the one

FIGURE 3.6

Hypothetical distribution of the enjoyableness of dates. Few dates are extremely enjoyable or extremely unenjoyable. The greatest number fall near the middle.

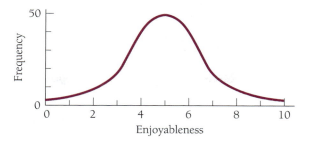

FIGURE 3.7

Hypothetical relationship between dating desirability and the enjoyableness of dates. Each point summarizes the dating desirability score and the enjoyableness rating for a single subject. The line was derived from a mathematical procedure to come as close to as many points as possible.

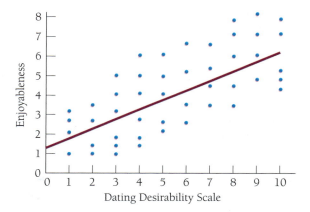

observed most frequently. In other words, knowing about the average date gives you some information about what to expect from a particular date. But it is doubtful that you would really want to choose dates this way. You probably would rather use other information such as educational background, attitudes, and hobbies to predict a good date.

Most of us, in fact, use some system to help us make important personal choices. The systems we come up with, however, are never perfect, but they are better than using normative information alone. In regression studies, researchers develop equations that help them describe more precisely where tests fall between being perfect predictors and being no better than just using the normative information. This is done by graphing the relationship between test scores and the criterion. Then a mathematical procedure is used to find the straight line that comes as close to as many of the points as possible. (You may want to review this chapter's earlier section on the regression line.)

Figure 3.7 shows the points on hypothetical scales of dating desirability and the enjoyableness of dates. The line through the points is the one that minimizes the squared distance between the line and the data points. In other words, the line is the one straight line that summarizes more about the relationship between dating desirability and enjoyableness than does any other straight line.

Figure 3.8 shows the hypothetical relationship between a test score and a criterion. Using this figure, you should be able to find the predicted value on the criterion variable by knowing the score on the test or the predictor. Here is how

FIGURE 3.8

Predicted relationship between a test score and a criterion. The dotted line shows how you should have obtained a predicted criterion score of 7.4 from the test score of 8.

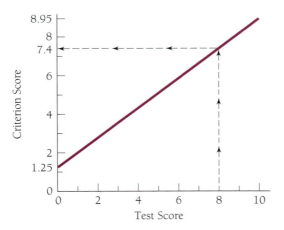

you read the graph. First, pick a particular score on the test—say, 8. Find 8 on the axis of the graph labeled "Test Score." Now draw a line straight up until you hit the slanted line on the graph. This is the regression line. Now make a 90-degree left turn and draw another line until it hits the other axis, which is labeled "Criterion Score." The dashed line in Figure 3.8 shows the course you should take. Now read the number on the criterion axis where your line has stopped. On the basis of information you gained by using the test, you would thus expect to obtain 7.4 as the criterion variable.

Notice that the line in Figure 3.8 is not at a 45° angle and that the two variables are measured in the same units. If it were at a 45° angle, then the test would be a perfect (or close to perfect) forecaster of the criterion. However, this is almost never the case in practice. Now, do the same exercise you did for the test score of 8 with test scores from the extremes of the distributions. Try the scores 0 and 10. You will find that the score of 10 for the test gives a criterion score of 8.95, and the test score of 0 gives a criterion score of 1.25. Notice how far apart 0 and 10 are on the test. Now look at how far apart 1.25 and 8.95 are on the criterion. You can see that using the test as a predictor is not as good as perfect prediction, but it is still better than using the normative information. If you had used only the normative information, you would have predicted that all scores would be the average score on the criterion. If there were perfect prediction, then the distance between 1.25 and 8.95 on the criterion would be the same as the distance between 0 and 10 on the test.

Figure 3.9 shows a variety of different regression slopes. Notice that the higher the standardized regression coefficient (*b*), the steeper the line. Now look at the regression line with a slope of 0. It is parallel to the "Test Score" axis and perpendicular to the "Criterion Score" axis. A regression line such as this shows that the test score tells us nothing about the criterion beyond the normative information. Whatever test score you choose, the criterion score will be the same—the average score on the criterion. The slope of 0 tells you that the test and the criterion are unrelated and that your best bet under these circumstances is to predict the average score on the criterion.

FIGURE 3.9

Regression lines with different standardized slopes.

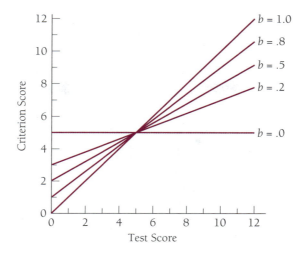

TABLE 3.3 Expected Criterion Scores for Two Test Scores When Predicted from Regression Lines with Different Slopes

Test score	Slope	Predicted criterion score
11	1.0	11.00
3	1.0	3.00
11	.8	9.90
3	.8	3.50
11	.5	8.25
3	.5	4.25
11	.2	6.60
3	.2	5.00
11	.0	5.50
3	.0	5.50

Now try to find the predicted score on the criterion for test scores of 11 and 3 for several of the different slopes shown in Figure 3.9. Notice that the steeper the slope of the regression line, the farther apart the predicted scores on the criterion. Table 3.3 shows the predicted scores for all of the different slopes. You can use it to check your answers.

When the regression lines have slopes of 0 or nearly 0, it is best not to take any chances in forecasting the criterion. Instead, you should depend on the normative information and guess the mean of Y. As the slope becomes steeper, it makes more sense to take some chances and estimate that there will be differences in criterion scores.

Figure 3.9 is also instructive regarding psychological tests. For example, if SAT scores have a slope of 0.5 for predicting grades in college, this means that the relationship between the SAT and performance is defined by the "$b = 0.5$" line. Using this sort of information, college administrators can infer that SAT scores may predict differences in college performance. However, because the slope is not steep, those predictions are not far from what they would get if they used the normative information.

Other Correlation Coefficients

The Pearson product moment correlation is only one of many types of correlation coefficients. It is the most commonly used because most often we want to find the correlation between two continuous variables. Continuous variables such as height, weight, and intelligence can take on any values over a range of values. But sometimes we want to find the correlations between variables scaled in other ways.

Spearman's rho is a method of correlation for finding the association between two sets of ranks. The rho coefficient (r) is easy to calculate and is often used when the individuals in a sample can be ranked on two variables but their actual scores are not known or have a normal distribution.

One whole family of correlation coefficients involves dichotomous variables. Dichotomous variables have only two levels. Examples are yes-no, correct-incorrect, and male-female. Some dichotomous variables are called *true dichotomous* because they naturally form two categories. For example, gender is a true dichotomous variable. Other dichotomous variables are called *artificially dichotomous* because they reflect an underlying continuous scale forced into a dichotomy. Passing or failing a bar examination is an example of such an artificial dichotomy; although many scores can be obtained, the examiners consider only pass and fail. The types of correlation coefficients used to find the relationship between dichotomous and continuous variables are shown in Table 3.4.

The **biserial correlation** expresses the relationship between a continuous variable and an artificial dichotomous variable. For example, the biserial correlation

TABLE 3.4 Appropriate Correlation Coefficients for Relationships between Dichotomous and Continuous Variables*

	Variable *X*		
Variable *Y*	Continuous	Artificial dichotomous	True dichotomous
Continuous	Pearson *r*	Biserial *r*	Point biserial *r*
Artificial dichotomous	Biserial *r*	Tetrachoric *r*	Phi
True dichotomous	Point biserial *r*	Phi	Phi

*The entries in the table suggest which type of correlation coefficient is appropriate given the characteristics of the two variables. For example, if variable *Y* is continuous and variable *X* is true dichotomous, you would use the point biserial correlation.

might be used to assess the relationship between passing or failing the bar examination (artificial dichotomous variable) and GPA in law school (continuous variable). If the dichotomous variable had been "true" (such as gender), then we would use the *point biserial correlation*. For instance, the point biserial correlation would be used to find the relationship between gender and GPA. When both variables are dichotomous and at least one of the dichotomies is "true," then the association between them can be estimated using the *phi coefficient*. For example, the relationship between passing or failing the bar examination and gender could be estimated using the phi coefficient. If both dichotomous variables are artificial, we might use a special correlation coefficient known as the *tetrachoric correlation*. Among these special correlation coefficients, the point biserial, phi, and Spearman's rho coefficients are probably used most often. The formulas for calculating these correlations are given in Psychological Testing in Everyday Life 3.2.

3.2 PSYCHOLOGICAL TESTING IN EVERYDAY LIFE

Formulas for Spearman's Rho, the Point Biserial Correlation, and the Phi Coefficient

$$\textbf{Spearman's rho formula: } \rho = 1 - \frac{6\Sigma d_i^2}{N^3 - 3}$$

where

ρ = Spearman's rho coefficient

d_i = a subject's rank order on variable 2 minus his or her rank order on variable 1

N = the number of paired ranks

When used: To find the association between pairs of observations, each expressed in ranks.

$$\textbf{Point biserial correlation formula: } r_{\text{pbis}} = \left[\frac{\bar{Y}_1 - \bar{Y}}{S_y} \right] \sqrt{\frac{P_x}{1 - P_x}}$$

where

r_{pbis} = the point biserial correlation coefficient

X = a true dichotomous (two-choice) variable

Y = a continuous (multilevel) variable

Y_1 = the mean of Y for subjects have a "plus" score on X

P = the mean of Y for all subjects

S_y = the standard deviation for scores

P_x = the proportion of subjects giving a "plus" score on X

(continues)

Terms and Issues in the Use of Correlation

When you use correlation or read studies that report correlational analysis, you will need to know the terminology. Some of the terms and issues you should be familiar with are *residual, standard error of estimate, coefficient of determination, coefficient of alienation, shrinkage, cross validation, correlation—causation problem,* and *third variable.* Brief discussions of these terms and concepts follow.

Residual

A regression equation gives a predicted value of Y' for each value of X. In addition to these predicted values, there are observed values of Y. The difference between the predicted and the observed values is called the **residual.** Symbolically, the residual is defined as $Y - Y'$.

Consider the example of the CES-D. Earlier we calculated the regression equation that predicted CES-D scores from scores on the anger inventory. The equation suggested that predicted CES-D = $-6.85 + .67 \times$ anger score. Let's take the example of a person who had an anger score of 19 and an observed CES-D score of 7. The predicted CES-D score is

$$-6.85 + (.67 \times 19) = 5.88$$

In other words, the person had an observed score of 7 and a predicted score of 5.88. The residual is[4]

$$7 - 5.88 = 1.12$$

In regression analysis, the residuals have certain properties. One important property is that the sum of the residuals always equals 0 $[\Sigma(Y - Y') = 0]$. In addition, the sum of the squared residuals is the smallest value according to the principle of least squares $[\Sigma(Y - Y')^2 = \text{smallest value}]$.

Standard Error of Estimate

Once we have obtained the residuals, we can find their standard deviation. However, in creating the regression equation, we have found two constants (a and b). Thus, we must use two degrees of freedom rather than one, as is usually the case in finding the standard deviation. The standard deviation of the residuals is known as the **standard error of estimate**, which is defined as

$$S_{yx} = \sqrt{\frac{\Sigma(Y - Y')^2}{N - 2}}$$

The standard error of estimate is a measure of the accuracy of prediction. Prediction is most accurate when the standard error of estimate is relatively small. As it becomes larger, the prediction becomes less accurate.

Coefficient of Determination

The correlation coefficient squared is known as the **coefficient of determination.** This value tells us the proportion of the total variation in scores on Y that we know as a function of information about X. For example, if the correlation between the SAT score and performance in the first year of college is .40, then the coefficient of determination is .16. The calculation is simply $.40^2 = .16$. This means that we can explain 16% of the variation in first-year college performance by knowing SAT scores. In the CES-D and anger example, the correlation is .82. Therefore, the coefficient of determination is .67 (calculated as $.82^2 = .67$), suggesting that 67% of the variance in CES-D can be accounted for by the anger score.

Coefficient of Alienation

The **coefficient of alienation** is a measure of nonassociation between two variables. This is calculated as $\sqrt{1 - r^2}$, where r is the coefficient of determination. For the SAT example, the coefficient of alienation is $\sqrt{1 - .16} = \sqrt{.84} = .92$. This means that there is a high degree of nonassociation between SAT scores and college performance. In the CES-D and anger example, the coefficient of alienation is $\sqrt{1 - .67} = .57$. Figure 3.10 shows the coefficient of determination and the coefficient of alienation represented in a pie chart.

---

[4]There is a small discrepancy between 1.12 and 1.04 for the example in Table 3.2, page 77. The difference is the result of rounding error.

FIGURE 3.10

Proportion of variance in first-year college performance explained by SAT score. Despite a significant relationship between SAT and college performance ($r = .40$), the coefficient of determination shows that only 16% of college performance is explained by SAT scores. The coefficient of alienation is .92, suggesting that most of the variance in college performance is not explained by SAT scores.

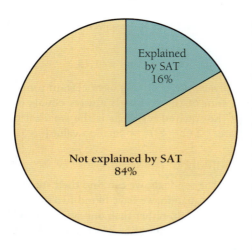

Shrinkage

Many times a regression equation is created on one group of subjects and then used to predict the performance of another group. One problem with regression analysis is that it takes advantage of chance relationships within a particular sample of subjects. Thus, there is a tendency to overestimate the relationship, particularly if the sample of subjects is small. **Shrinkage** is the amount of decrease observed when a regression equation is created for one population and then applied to another. Formulas are available to estimate the amount of shrinkage to expect given the characteristics of variance, covariance, and sample size (Gravetter & Wallnau, 2016; Wang & Thompson, 2007).

Here is an example of shrinkage. Say a regression equation is developed to predict first-year college GPAs on the basis of SAT scores. Although the proportion of variance in GPA might be fairly high for the original group, we can expect to account for a smaller proportion of the variance when the equation is used to predict GPA in the next year's class. This decrease in the proportion of variance accounted for is the shrinkage.

Cross Validation

The best way to ensure that proper references are being made is to use the regression equation to predict performance in a group of subjects other than the ones to which the equation was applied. Then a standard error of estimate can be obtained for the relationship between the values predicted by the equation and the values actually observed. This process is known as **cross validation.**

The Correlation-Causation Problem

Just because two variables are correlated does not necessarily imply that one has caused the other (see Focused Example 3.1). For example, a correlation between aggressive behavior and the number of hours spent viewing television does not mean that excessive viewing of television causes aggression. This relationship could mean that an aggressive child might prefer to watch a lot of television. There are many examples of misinterpretation of correlations. We know, for example, that physically active elderly people live longer than do those who are sedentary. However, we do not know if physical activity causes long life or if healthier people are more likely to be physically active. Usually, experiments are required to determine whether manipulation of one variable causes changes in another variable. A correlation alone does not prove causality, although it might lead to other research that is designed to establish the causal relationships between variables.

3.1 FOCUSED EXAMPLE

The Danger of Inferring Causation from Correlation

A newspaper article once rated 130 job categories for stressfulness by examining Tennessee hospital and death records for evidence of stress-related diseases such as heart attacks, ulcers, arthritis, and mental disorders. The 12 highest and the 12 lowest jobs are listed in the table to the right.

The article advises readers to avoid the "most stressful" job categories. The evidence, however, may not warrant the advice offered in the article. Although certain diseases may be associated with particular occupations, holding these jobs does not necessarily cause the illnesses. Other explanations abound. For example, people with a propensity for heart attacks and ulcers might tend to select jobs as unskilled laborers or secretaries. Thus, the direction of causation might be that a health condition causes job selection rather than the reverse. Another possibility involves a third variable, some other factor that causes the apparent relationship between job and health. For example, a certain income level might cause both stress and illness. Finally, wealthy people tend to have better health than poor people. Impoverished conditions may cause a person to accept certain jobs and also to have more diseases.

These three possible explanations are diagrammed in the right-hand column. An arrow indicates a causal connection. In this example, we are not ruling out the possibility that jobs cause illness. In fact, it is quite plausible. However, because the nature of the evidence is correlational, we cannot say with certainty that a job causes illness.

Most Stressful	Least Stressful
1. Unskilled laborer	1. Clothing sewer
2. Secretary	2. Garment checker
3. Assembly-line inspector	3. Stock clerk
4. Clinical lab technician	4. Skilled craftsperson
5. Office manager	5. Housekeeper
6. Foreperson	6. Farm laborer
7. Manager/administrator	7. Heavy equipment operator
8. Waiter	8. Freight handler
9. Factory machine operator	9. Child-care worker
10. Farm owner	10. Factory package wrapper
11. Miner	11. College professor
12. House painter	12. Personnel worker

Job → Illness	Illnes → Job	Economic Status
		Job Illness
Job causes illness	Tendency toward illness causes people to choose certain jobs	Economic status (third variable) causes job selection and illness

Third Variable Explanation

There are other possible explanations for the observed relationship between television viewing and aggressive behavior. One is that some third variable, such as poor social adjustment, causes both. Thus, the apparent relationship between viewing and aggression actually might be the result of some variable not included in the analysis. In the example of the relationship between physical activity and life expectancy, chronic disease may cause both sedentary lifestyle and shortened life expectancy. We usually refer to this external influence as a **third variable.**

Restricted Range

Correlation and regression use variability on one variable to explain variability on a second variable. In this chapter, we use many different examples such as the relationship between smoking and the price of a pack of cigarettes, the relationship between anger and depression, and the relationship between dating desirability and satisfaction. In each of these cases, there was meaningful variability on each of the two variables under study. However, there are circumstances in which the ranges of variability are restricted. Imagine, for example, that you were attempting to study the relationship between scores on the Graduate Record Examination GRE quantitative test and performance during the first year of graduate school in the math department of an elite Ivy League university. No students had been admitted to the program with GRE verbal scores less than 700. Further, most grades given in the graduate school were A's. Under these circumstances, it might be extremely difficult to demonstrate a relationship even though a true underlying relationship may exist.

This is illustrated in Figure 3.11. The squares in the hypothetical example represent the relationship between SAT quantitative and graduate school GPA across all potential students. For all students, the correlation is 0.53. The open circles in the figure show the same relationship for the elite group of students under consideration. Because the elite students (closed circles in Figure 3.11) do not vary much on GRE quantitative, it is difficult to observe significant correlation between GRE quantitative (GRE-Q) and any other variable. In this example, the correlation is 0.08. This is called the **restricted range problem.** Correlation requires variability. If the variability is restricted, then significant correlations are difficult to find.

FIGURE 3.11

Hypothetical relationship between GRE-Q and GPA for all students and for students in elite program.

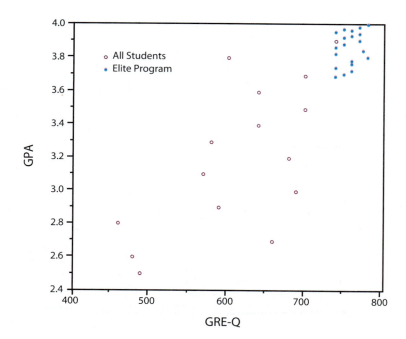

Multivariate Analysis (Optional)

Multivariate analysis considers the relationship among combinations of three or more variables. For example, the prediction of success in the first year of college from the linear combination of SAT verbal and quantitative scores is a problem for multivariate analysis. However, because the field of multivariate analysis requires an understanding of linear and matrix algebra, a detailed discussion of it lies beyond the scope of this book.

On the other hand, you should have at least a general idea of what the different common testing methods entail. This section will familiarize you with some of the multivariate analysis terminology. It will also help you identify the situations in which some of the different multivariate methods are used. Several references are available in case you would like to learn more about the technical details (Brown, 2015; Gravetter & Wallnau, 2016; Vogt & Johnson, 2015).

General Approach

The correlational techniques presented to this point describe the relationship between only two variables such as stress and illness. To understand more fully the causes of illness, we need to consider many potential factors besides stress. Multivariate analysis allows us to study the relationship between many predictors and one outcome, as well as the relationship among the predictors.

Multivariate methods differ in the number and kind of predictor variables they use. All of these methods transform groups of variables into linear combinations. A *linear combination* of variables is a weighted composite of the original variables. The weighting system combines the variables in order to achieve some goal. Multivariate techniques differ according to the goal they are trying to achieve.

A linear combination of variables looks like this:

$$Y' = a + b_1 X_1 + b_2 X_2 + b_3 X_3 + \cdots + b_k X_k$$

where Y' is the predicted value of Y, a is a constant, X_1 to X_k are variables and there are k such variables, and the b's are regression coefficients. If you feel anxious about such a complex-looking equation, there is no need to panic. Actually, this equation describes something similar to what was presented in the section on regression. The difference is that instead of relating Y to X, we are now dealing with a linear combination of X's. The whole right side of the equation creates a new composite variable by transforming a set of predictor variables.

An Example Using Multiple Regression

Suppose we want to predict success in law school from three variables: undergraduate GPA, rating by former professors, and age. This type of multivariate analysis is called **multiple regression,** and the goal of the analysis is to find the linear combination of the three variables that provides the best prediction of law school success. We find the correlation between the criterion (law school GPA) and some composite of the predictors (undergraduate GPA plus professor rating plus age). The combination of the three predictors, however, is not just the sum of the three scores. Instead, we program the computer to find a specific way of adding the predictors that will make the correlation between the composite and the criterion as high as possible. A weighted composite might look something like this:

$$\text{law school GPA} = .80 \, (Z \text{ scores of undergraduate GPA})$$
$$+ .54 \, (Z \text{ scores of professor ratings})$$
$$+ .03 \, (Z \text{ scores of age})$$

This example suggests that undergraduate GPA is given more weight in the prediction of law school GPA than are the other variables. The undergraduate GPA is multiplied by .80, whereas the other variables are multiplied by much smaller coefficients. Age is multiplied by only .03, which is almost no contribution. This is because .03 times any Z score for age will give a number that is nearly 0; in effect, we would be adding 0 to the composite.

The reason for using Z scores for the three predictors is that the coefficients in the linear composite are greatly affected by the range of values taken on by the variables. GPA is measured on a scale from 0 to 4.0, whereas the range in age might be 21 to 70. To compare the coefficients to one another, we need to transform all the variables into similar units. This is accomplished by using Z scores (see Chapter 2). When the variables are expressed in Z units, the coefficients, or weights for the variables, are known as *standardized regression coefficients* (sometimes called B's or betas). There are also some cases in which we would want to use the variables' original units. For example, we sometimes want to find an equation we can use to estimate someone's predicted level of success on the basis of personal characteristics, and we do not want to bother changing these characteristics into Z units. When we do this, the weights in the model are called *raw regression coefficients* (sometimes called b's).

Before moving on, we should caution you about interpreting regression coefficients. Besides reflecting the relationship between a particular variable and the criterion, the coefficients are affected by the relationship among the predictor variables. Be careful when the predictor variables are highly correlated with one another. Two predictor variables that are highly correlated with the criterion will not both have large regression coefficients if they are highly correlated with each other as well. For example, suppose that undergraduate GPA and the professors' rating are both highly correlated with law school GPA. However, these two predictors also are highly correlated with each other. In effect, the two measures seem to be of the same thing (which would not be surprising, because the professors assigned the grades). As such, professors' rating may get a lower regression coefficient because some of its predictive power is already taken into consideration through its association with undergraduate GPA. We can only interpret regression coefficients confidently when the predictor variables do not overlap and are uncorrected. They may do so when the predictors are uncorrected.

Discriminant Analysis

Multiple regression is appropriate when the criterion variable is continuous (not nominal). However, there are many cases in testing where the criterion is a set of categories. For example, we often want to know the linear combination of variables that differentiates passing from failing. When the task is to find the linear combination of variables that provides a maximum discrimination between categories, the appropriate multivariate method is **discriminant analysis.** An example of discriminant analysis involves attempts to determine whether a set of measures predicts success or failure on a particular performance evaluation.

Sometimes we want to determine the categorization in more than two categories. To accomplish this, we use multiple discriminant analysis.

Discriminant analysis has many advantages in the field of test construction. One approach to test construction is to identify two groups of people who represent two distinct categories of some trait. For example, say that two groups of children are classified as "language disabled" and "normal." After a variety of items are presented, discriminant analysis is used to find the linear combination of items that best accounts for differences between the two groups. With this information, researchers could develop new tests to help diagnose language impairment. This information might also provide insight into the nature of the problem and eventually lead to better treatments.

Factor Analysis

Discriminant analysis and multiple regression analysis find linear combinations of variables that maximize the prediction of some criterion. Factor analysis is used to study the interrelationships among a set of variables without reference to a criterion. You might think of factor analysis as a data-reduction technique. When we have responses to a large number of items or a large number of tests, we often want to reduce all this information to more manageable chunks. In Figure 3.1, we presented a two-dimensional scatter diagram. The task in correlation is to find the best-fitting line through the space created by these two dimensions. As we add more variables in multivariate analysis, we increase the number of dimensions. For example, a three-dimensional plot is shown in Figure 3.12. You can use your imagination to visualize what a larger set of dimensions would look like. Some people claim they can visualize more than three dimensions, while others feel they cannot. In any case, consider that points are plotted in the domain created by a given dimension.

In factor analysis, we first create a matrix that shows the correlation between every variable and every other variable. Then we find the linear combinations, or *principal components,* of the variables that describe as many of the interrelationships among the variables as possible. We can find as many principal components as there are variables. However, each principal component is extracted according to mathematical rules that make it independent of or uncorrected with the other principal components. The first component will be the most successful in describing the variation among the variables, with each succeeding component somewhat less successful. Thus, we often decide to examine only a few components that account for larger proportions of the variation. Technically, principal components analysis and true factor analysis differ in how the correlation matrix is created. Even so, principal components are often called *factors.*

Once the linear combinations or principal components have been found, we can find the correlation between the original items and the factors. These correlations are called *factor loadings.* The expression "item 7 loaded highly on factor I" means

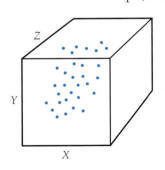

FIGURE 3.12

A three-dimensional scatter plot might be represented by this box. In addition to plotting points on the *X* and *Y* axes, we must locate them in relation to a third *Z* axis.

3.2 FOCUSED EXAMPLE

The Factors of Trust

Rotter (1967) described a scale for the measurement of interpersonal trust. *Trust* was defined as "an expectancy held by an individual or a group that the word, promise, verbal or written statement of another individual or group can be relied upon" (p. 651). However, after the publication of the original trust article, several authors reported that trust seems to be composed of several independent factors (Chun & Campbell, 1974; Kaplan, 1973; Wright & Tedeschi, 1975). In each case, the items were given to a large group of people, and the results were subjected to factor analysis. This procedure reduces the many items down to a smaller number of *factors,* or linear combinations of the original items. Then *item loadings,* or the correlations of the original items with the factors, are studied in order to name the factors. The table that follows shows the loadings of the items on three of the factors (Kaplan, 1973).

Once they have obtained the factor loadings, researchers must attempt to name the factors by examining which items load highly on them. In this case, an item was used to help interpret a factor if its item loading on the factor was greater than .35 or less than −.35. Three factors of trust were found.

Factor I: Institutional trust. This represented trust toward major social agents in society. It included items regarding the competence of politicians, such as "This country has a dark future unless we can attract better people into politics" (−.67). Many of the items conveyed the idea of misrepresentation of public events by either the government or the mass media. For example, some items with high loadings were "Most people would be horrified if they knew how much news the public hears and sees is distorted" (−.69) and "Even though we have reports in newspapers, radio, and TV, it is hard to get objective accounts of public events" (−.67).

Factor II: Sincerity. Items loading highly on sincerity tended to focus on the perceived sincerity of others. These items included "Most idealists are sincere and usually practice what they preach" (.62) and "Most people answer public opinion polls honestly" (.58). Nearly all the items with high loadings on the second factor began with the word "most." Because of this loose wording, it would be possible for people to agree with the items because they believe in the sincerity of most people in a given group but still feel little trust for the group because of a few "rotten eggs." Thus, a woman could believe most car repairers are sincere but still service her car herself because she fears being overcharged.

Factor III: Caution. This contained items that expressed fear that some people will take advantage of others, such as "In dealing with strangers, one is better off being cautious until they have provided evidence that they are trustworthy" (.74) and "In these competitive times you have to be alert or someone is likely to take advantage of you" (.53). Note that caution appears to be independent of perceived sincerity.

The data imply that generalized trust may be composed of several dimensions. It also implies that focusing on specific components of trust rather than the generalized case will likely help researchers the most in using this trust scale.

Focused Example adapted from Rotter (1967); table taken from Kaplan (1973).

there is a high correlation between item 7 and the first principal component. By examining which variables load highly on each factor, we can start interpreting the meanings of the factors. Focused Example 3.2 shows how the meanings of various factors in a scale on interpersonal trust are evaluated.

Factor analysis is a complex and technical method with many options the user must learn about. For example, users frequently use methods that help them get a clearer picture of the meaning of the components by transforming the variables in

Item number	Item	Loading factor I	II	III
A. Items with high loadings on institutional factor				
4.	This country has a dark future unless we can attract better people into politics.	−.67	−.12	−.06
5.	Fear of social disgrace or punishment rather than conscience prevents most people from breaking the law.	−.54	.02	−.06
13.	The United Nations will never be an effective force in keeping world peace.	−.41	.09	−.21
16.	The judiciary is a place where we can all get unbiased treatment.	.37	.23	.00
19.	Most people would be horrified if they knew how much news the public hears and sees is distorted.	−.69	.18	.28
21.	Most elected public officials are really sincere in their campaign promises.	.44	.17	−.02
24.	Even though we have reports in newspapers, radio, and TV, it is hard to get objective accounts of public events.	−.67	−.08	.00
28.	If we really knew what was going on in international politics, the public would have more reason to be more frightened than it now seems to be.	−.49	.01	.24
33.	Many major national sports contests are fixed in one way or another.	−.55	−.04	.28
B. Items with high loadings on sincerity factor				
1.	Hypocrisy is on the increase in our society.	.09	−.52	.08
12.	Most students in school would not cheat even if they were sure of getting away with it.	.29	.45	.07
27.	Most experts can be relied upon to tell the truth about the limits of their knowledge.	.20	.66	.20
34.	Most idealists are sincere and usually practice what they preach.	.12	.62	−.20
38.	Most repair persons will not overcharge even if they think you are ignorant of their specialty.	.11	.48	−.35
44.	Most people answer public opinion polls honestly.	.04	.58	.16
C. Items with high loadings on caution factor				
2.	In dealing with strangers, one is better off being cautious until they have provided evidence that they are trustworthy.	−.22	−.03	.74
7.	Using the honor system of not having a teacher present during examinations would probably result in increased cheating.	.13	.08	.45
32.	In these competitive times, you have to be alert or someone is likely to take advantage of you.	−.12	−.01	.53
42.	A large share of the accident claims filed against insurance companies are phony.	−.07	−.14	.57

a way that pushes the factor loadings toward the high or the low extreme. Because these transformational methods involve rotating the axes in the space created by the factors, they are called *methods of rotation*. Researchers have many options for transforming variables. They can choose among several methods of rotation, and they can explore the many characteristics of the matrix originally used in their analyses. If you are interested, several books discuss factor analysis methods in great detail (Brown, 2015; Kline, 2015).

Summary

This chapter began with a discussion of a claim made in a grocery store tabloid that poor diet causes marital problems. Actually, there was no specific evidence that diet causes the problems—only that diet and marital difficulties are associated. However, the *Enquirer* failed to specify the exact strength of the association. The rest of the chapter was designed to help you be more specific than the *Enquirer* by learning to specify associations with precise mathematical indexes known as *correlation coefficients*.

First, we presented pictures of the association between two variables; these pictures are called *scatter diagrams*. Second, we presented a method for finding a linear equation to describe the relationship between two variables. This regression method uses the data in raw units. The results of regression analysis are two constants: A *slope* describes the degree of relatedness between the variables, and an *intercept* gives the value of the *Y* variable when the *X* variable is 0. When both of the variables are in standardized or *Z* units, the intercept is always 0 and drops out of the equation. In this unique situation, we solve for only one constant, which is *r*, or the *correlation coefficient*.

When using correlational methods, we must take many things into consideration. For example, correlation does not mean the same thing as causation. In the case of the *National Enquirer* article, the observed correlation between diet and problems in marriage may mean that diet causes the personal difficulties. However, it may also mean that marriage problems cause poor eating habits or that some *third variable* causes both diet habits and marital problems. In addition to the difficulties associated with causation, we must always consider the strength of the correlational relationship. The *coefficient of determination* describes the percentage of variation in one variable that is known on the basis of its association with another variable. The *coefficient of alienation* is an index of what is not known from information about the other variable.

A *regression line* is the best-fitting straight line through a set of points in a scatter diagram. The regression line is described by a mathematical index known as the regression equation. The *regression coefficient* is the ratio of covariance to variance and is also known as the slope of the regression line. The regression coefficient describes how much change is expected in the *Y* variable each time the *X* variable increases by one unit. Other concepts discussed were the *intercept*, the *residual* (the difference between the predicted value given by a regression equation and the observed value), and the *standard error of estimate* (the standard deviation of the residuals obtained from the regression equation).

The field of *multivariate analysis* involves a complicated but important set of methods for studying the relationships among many variables. *Multiple regression* is a multivariate method for studying the relationship between one criterion variable and two or more predictor variables. A similar method known as *discriminant analysis* is used to study the relationship between a categorical criterion and two or more predictors. *Factor analysis* is another multivariate method for reducing a large set of variables down to a smaller set of composite variables.

Correlational methods are the most commonly used statistical techniques in the testing field. The concepts presented in this overview will be referred to throughout the rest of this book.

APPENDIX 3.1:
Calculation of a Regression Equation and a Correlation Coefficient

In this appendix, we consider the relationship between team performance and payroll for teams in baseball's National League. The Data are from the 2016 season and available on the Internet at www.espn.com. The 2016 season was of particular interest to baseball fans because the World Series pitted the Chicago Cubs with a payroll of more than $154 million against the Cleveland Indians with a payroll of a mere $74 million. The Cubs won the Series, raising the question of whether there is a relationship between expenditure and performance of professional baseball teams.

In this example, payroll for National League teams is measured as mean player salary (expressed in millions of dollars) whereas performance is measured by the number of games won[1]. The data are shown in Table 3.5 and summarized in Figure 3.13. Each dot in the figure represents one team. In 2016, there was a positive relationship between payroll and performance. In other words, teams with higher median salaries had better performance. As Figure 3.13 indicates, each increase in expenditure

TABLE 3.5 Games Won and Median Salaries for Teams in Baseball's National

Team	Average Salary (X)	Games Won (Y)	X^2	Y^2	XY
Dodgers	$8.85	91	$78.35	8,281	805.49
Giants	$6.89	87	$47.47	7,569	599.44
Cubs	$6.18	103	$38.23	10,609	636.85
Cardinals	$5.72	86	$32.74	7,396	492.10
Nationals	$5.67	95	$32.10	9,025	538.28
Mets	$5.36	87	$28.68	7,569	465.93
Rockies	$4.51	75	$20.30	5,625	337.94
Pirates	$4.15	78	$17.23	6,084	323.79
Padres	$4.06	68	$16.46	4,624	275.88
Reds	$3.60	68	$12.95	4,624	244.68
Diamondbacks	$3.57	69	$12.75	4,761	246.37
Phillies	$3.36	71	$11.28	5,041	238.50
Marlins	$3.09	79	$9.56	6,241	244.31
Brewers	$2.77	73	$7.68	5,329	202.31
Braves	$2.76	68	$7.62	4,624	187.70
SUM (Σ)	$70.53	1,198	373.42	97,402	5,839.57

---

[1]In this example we use total payroll divided by 25, which is the number of players allowed on the roster. Some of the clubs pay more than 25 players. This may explain why estimates of average salary differ in different data sets.

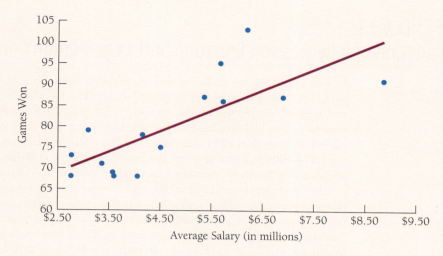

FIGURE 3.13
Average Salary in millions of dollars versus games won by National League baseball teams in 2016.

is associated with an increase in performance. The regression coefficient (4.93) suggests that for each million dollar increase in mean salary, the team's performance increases by an average of 4.93 games per season. We also did the same exercise for total payroll. In 2016 the Los Angeles Dodgers had the highest payroll in the National League, at $221 million. In contrast, the Atlanta Brave had a total payroll of $69 million. The correlation between total payroll and games won was 0.77 and the regression equation was:

$$Y = 4.93X + 56.70$$

This tells us that an owner must spend about $5,070,994 (or about $202,840 for each of 25 players) to win one game. Overall, the relationship is significant, and the best explanation is that there is an association between payroll and performance.

Calculation of a Regression Equation (Data from Table 3.5)
Formulas:

$$b = \frac{N(\Sigma XY) - (\Sigma Y)(\Sigma Y)}{N \Sigma X^2 - (\Sigma X)^2}$$

$$a = \overline{Y} - b\overline{X}$$

STEPS

1. Find N by counting the number of pairs of observations. $N = 15$.
2. Find ΣX by summing the X scores.

$$\$8.85 + \$6.89 + \$6.18 + \ldots + \$2.76 = \$70.53$$

3. Find ΣY by summing the Y scores.

$$91 + 87 + 103 + \ldots + 1198$$

4. Find ΣX^2. Square each X score and then sum them.

$$(8.85)^2 + (6.89)^2 + (6.18)^2 + \ldots (2.76)^2 = 373.42$$

5. Find ΣY^2. Square each Y score and then sum them.

$$(8281)^2 + (7569)^2 + (10609)^2 + \dots (4624)^2 = 97,402$$

6. Find ΣXY. For each pair of observations multiply X by Y. Then sum the products.

$$805.49 + 599.44 + 636.85 + \dots + 187.70 + 5,839.57$$

7. Find $(\Sigma X)^2$ by squaring the results of Step 2.

$$70.53^2 = 4,974.48$$

8. Find $(\Sigma Y)^2$ by squaring the results of Step 3.

$$1,198^2 = 1,435,204$$

9. Find $N\Sigma XY$ by multiplying the results of Step 1 by Step 6.

$$15 \times 5,839.57 = 87,593.55$$

10. Find $(\Sigma X)(\Sigma Y)$ by multiplying the results of Steps 2 and 3.

$$70.53 \times 1,198 = 84,500.36$$

11. Find $(N\Sigma XY) - (\Sigma X)(\Sigma Y)$ by subtracting the results of Step 10 from the result of Step 9.

$$87,593.55 - 84,500.36 = 3,093.12$$

12. Find $N\Sigma X^2$ by multiplying the results of Steps 1 and 4.

$$15 \times 373.42 = 5601.30$$

13. Find $N\Sigma X^2 - (\Sigma X)^2$ by subtracting the result of Step 7 from that of Step 12.

$$5601.30 - 4,974.48 = 626.82$$

14. Find b by dividing the result of Step 11 by that of Step 13.

$$3,093.12/626.82 = 4.93$$

15. Find the mean of X by dividing the result of Step 2 by that of Step 1.

$$\$70.53/15 = \$4.70$$

16. Find the mean of Y by dividing the result of Step 3 by that of Step 1.

$$1,198/15 = 79.87$$

17. Find $b\overline{X}$ by multiplying the results of Steps 14 and 15.

$$4.93 \times 4.70 = 23.17$$

18. Find a by subtracting the results of Step 17 from Step 16.

$$79.87 - 23.17 = 56.70$$

19. The resultant regression equation is

$$Y = a + bX$$
$$Y = 56.70 + 4.93X$$

Games won $= 56.70 + (4.93X$ average salary in millions of dollars$)$

Calculation of a Correlation Coefficient (Data from Table 3.5)

Formula:

$$r = \frac{N\Sigma XY - (\Sigma X)(\Sigma Y)}{\sqrt{[N\Sigma X^2 - (\Sigma X)^2][N\Sigma Y^2 - (\Sigma Y)^2]}}$$

1. Find N by counting the number of pairs of observations. $N = 15$.
2. Find ΣX by summing the X scores.

$$\$8.85 + \$6.89 + \$6.18 + \ldots + \$2.76 = \$70.53$$

3. Find ΣY by summing the Y scores.

$$91 + 87 + 103 + \ldots + 1198$$

4. Find ΣX^2. Square each X score and then sum them.

$$(8.85)^2 + (6.89)^2 + (6.18)^2 + \ldots (2.76)^2 = 373$$

5. Find ΣY^2. Square each Y score and then sum them.

$$(8281)^2 + (7569)^2 + (10609)^2 + \ldots (4624)^2 = 97{,}402$$

6. Find ΣXY. For each pair of observations multiply X by Y. Then sum the products.

$$805.49 + 599.44 + 636.85 + \ldots + 187.70 + 5{,}839.57$$

7. Find $(\Sigma X)^2$ by squaring the results of Step 2.

$$70.53^2 = 4{,}974.48$$

8. Find $(\Sigma Y)^2$ by squaring the results of Step 3.

$$1{,}198^2 = 1{,}435{,}204$$

9. Find $N\Sigma XY$ by multiplying the results of Step 1 by Step 6.

$$15 \times 5{,}839.57 = 87{,}593.55$$

10. Find $(\Sigma X)(\Sigma Y)$ by multiplying the results of Steps 2 and 3.

$$70.53 \times 1{,}198 = 84{,}500.36$$

11. Find $(N\Sigma XY) - (\Sigma X)(\Sigma Y)$ by subtracting the results of Step 10 from the result of Step 9.

$$87{,}593.55 - 84{,}500.36 = 3{,}093.12$$

12. Find $N\Sigma X^2$ by multiplying the results of Steps 1 and 4.

$$15 \times 373.42 = 5601.30$$

13. Find $N\Sigma X^2 - (\Sigma X)^2$ by subtracting the result of Step 7 from that of Step 12.

$$5601.30 - 4{,}974.48 = 626.82$$

14. Find $N\Sigma Y^2$ by multiplying the results of Steps 1 and 5.

$$15 \times 97{,}402 = 1{,}461{,}030$$

15. Find $N\Sigma Y^2 - (\Sigma Y)^2$ by subtracting the result of Step 8 from that of Step 14.

$$1,461,030 - 1,435,204 = 25,826$$

16. Find $\sqrt{[N\Sigma X^2 - (\Sigma X)^2][N\Sigma Y^2 - (\Sigma Y)^2]}$ by multiplying the results of Steps 13 and 15 and taking the square root of the product.

$$\sqrt{626.82 \times 25,826} = 4023.46$$

17. Find $r = \dfrac{N\Sigma XY - (\Sigma X)(\Sigma Y)}{\sqrt{[N\Sigma X^2 - (\Sigma X)^2][N\Sigma Y^2 - (\Sigma Y)^2]}}$, by dividing the result of Step 11 by that of Step 16.

$$3,093.12/4023.46 = 0.77$$

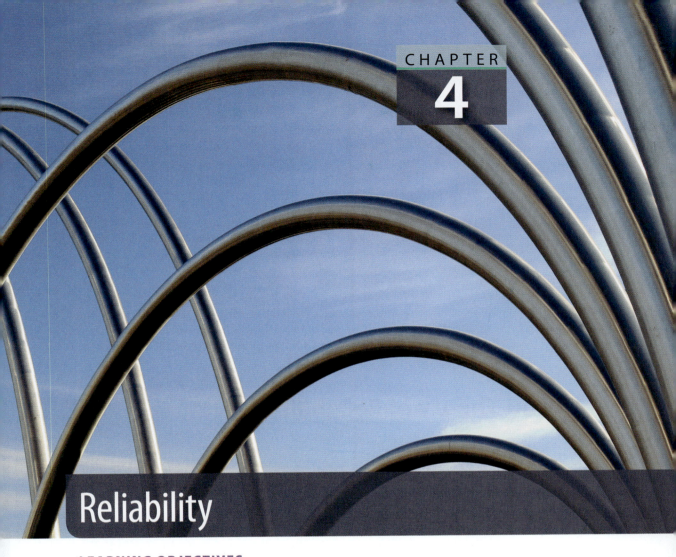

Reliability

LEARNING OBJECTIVES

When you have completed this chapter, you should be able to:

► Describe the role of measurement error in scientific studies of behavior

► Know that reliability is the ratio of true variability to observed variability and explain what this tells us about a test with a reliability of .30, .60, or .90

► Describe how test–retest reliability is assessed

► Explain the difference between test–retest reliability estimates and split-half reliability estimates

► Discuss how the split-half method underestimates the reliability of a short test and what can be done to correct this problem

► Know the easiest way to find average reliability

► Define *coefficient alpha* and tell how it differs from other methods of estimating reliability

► Discuss how high a reliability coefficient must be before you would be willing to say the test is "reliable enough"

► Explain what can be done to increase the reliability of a test

► Tell how the reliability of behavioral observations is assessed

n the gymnastics competition at an international meet, a young Romanian woman received an 8.9 for the first portion of her routine. As she reappeared for the second portion, the television commentator said, "The 8.9 rating for her first routine does not accurately represent her ability. This young woman is clearly a 9.5 performer." With this remark, the commentator indicated a discrepancy between the gymnast's score for the first routine and her true ability, a common occurrence in the measurement of human abilities. For example, after an examination, students sometimes feel that the questions on the test did not allow them to display their real knowledge. And actors sometimes complain that a 5-minute audition is not an adequate measure of their talents.

Discrepancies between true ability and measurement of ability constitute errors of measurement. In psychological testing, the word *error* does not imply that a mistake has been made. Rather than having a negative connotation, *error* implies that there will always be some inaccuracy in our measurements. Our task is to find the magnitude of such errors and to develop ways to minimize them. This chapter discusses the conceptualization and assessment of measurement error. Tests that are relatively free of measurement error are deemed to be *reliable*, hence the name of this chapter. Tests that have "too much" measurement error are considered unreliable. We shall see the ways we can determine "how much is too much" in these cases.

History and Theory of Reliability

Conceptualization of Error

Students who major in physical science have chosen to study phenomena that are relatively easy to measure with precision. If you want to measure the width of this book, for example, you need to only apply a ruler and record the number of inches or centimeters.

In psychology, the measurement task is more difficult. First, researchers are rarely interested in measuring simple qualities such as width. Instead, they usually pursue complex traits such as intelligence or aggressiveness, which one can neither see nor touch. Further, with no rigid yardsticks available to measure such characteristics, testers must use "rubber yardsticks"; these may stretch to overestimate some measurements and shrink to underestimate others (Kline, 2015b; Thomas, 2012). Psychologists must assess their measuring instruments to determine how much "rubber" is in them. A psychologist who is attempting to understand human behavior on the basis of unreliable tests is like a carpenter trying to build a house with a rubber measuring tape that never records the same length for the same piece of board.

As you will learn from this chapter, the theory of measurement error is well developed within psychology. This is not to say that measurement error is unique to psychology. In fact, serious measurement error occurs in most physical, social, and biological sciences. For example, measures of the gross national product (economics) and blood pressure (medicine) are known to be less reliable than well-constructed psychological tests. However, the concern with reliability has been a particular obsession for psychologists and provides evidence of the advanced scientific status of the field (Kline, 2015a).

Spearman's Early Studies

Psychology owes the advanced development of reliability assessment to the early work of the British psychologist Charles Spearman. In 1733, Abraham De Moivre introduced the basic notion of sampling error (Stanley, 1971); and in 1896, Karl Pearson developed the product moment correlation (see Chapter 3 and Pearson, 1901). Reliability theory puts these two concepts together in the context of measurement. A contemporary of Pearson, Spearman actually worked out most of the basics of contemporary reliability theory and published his work in a 1904 article entitled "The Proof and Measurement of Association between Two Things." Because the *British Journal of Psychology* did not begin until 1907, Spearman published his work in the *American Journal of Psychology*. Spearman's work quickly became known in the United States. The article came to the attention of measurement pioneer Edward L. Thorndike, who was then writing the first edition of *An Introduction to the Theory of Mental and Social Measurements* (1904).

Thorndike's book is remarkably sophisticated, even by contemporary standards. Since 1904, many developments on both sides of the Atlantic Ocean have led to further refinements in the assessment of reliability. Most important among these is a 1937 article by Kuder and Richardson, in which several new reliability coefficients were introduced. Later, Cronbach and his colleagues (Cronbach, 1989, 1995) made a major advance by developing methods for evaluating many sources of error in behavioral research. Reliability theory continues to evolve. In recent years, sophisticated mathematical models have been developed to quantify "latent" variables based on multiple measures (Bentler, 2015).

Basics of Test Score Theory

Classical test score theory assumes that each person has a true score that would be obtained if there were no errors in measurement. However, because measuring instruments are imperfect, the score observed for each person almost always differs from the person's true ability or characteristic. The difference between the true score and the observed score results from measurement error. In symbolic representation, the observed score (X) has two components; a true score (T) and an error component (E):

$$X = T + E$$

| Observed score | True score | Error |

Or we can say that the difference between the score we obtain and the score we are really interested is the error of measurement:

$$X - T = E$$

A major assumption in classical test theory is that errors of measurement are random. Although systematic errors are acknowledged in most measurement

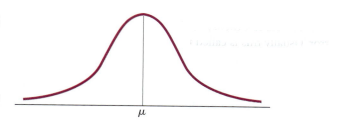

μ

problems, they are less likely than other errors to force an investigator to make the wrong conclusions. A carpenter who always misreads a tape measure by 2 inches (or makes a systematic error of 2 inches) would still be able to cut boards the same length. Using the rubber-yardstick analogy, we would say that this carpenter works with a ruler that is always 2 inches too long. Classical test theory, however, deals with rubber-yardstick problems in which the ruler stretches and contracts at random.

Using a rubber yardstick, we would not get the same score on each measurement. Instead, we would get a distribution of scores like that shown in Figure 4.1. Basic sampling theory tells us that the distribution of random errors is bell shaped. Thus, the center of the distribution should represent the true score, and the dispersion around the mean of the distribution should display the distribution of sampling errors. Though any one application of the rubber yardstick may or may not tell us the true score, we can estimate the true score by finding the mean of the observations from repeated applications.

Figure 4.2 shows three different distributions. In the far left distribution, there is a great dispersion around the true score. In this case, you might not want to depend on a single observation because it might fall far from the true score. The far-right distribution displays a tiny dispersion around the true score. In this case, most of the observations are extremely close to the true score so that drawing conclusions on the basis of fewer observations will likely produce fewer errors than it will for the far-left curve.

The dispersions around the true score in Figures 4.1 and 4.2 tell us how much error there is in the measure. Classical test theory assumes that the true score for an individual will not change with repeated applications of the same test. Because of random error, however, repeated applications of the same test can produce different scores. Random error is responsible for the distribution of scores shown in Figures 4.1 and 4.2. Theoretically, the standard deviation of the distribution of

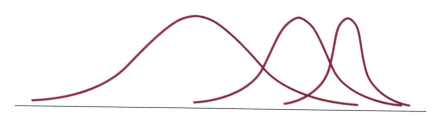

errors for each person tells us about the magnitude of measurement error. Because we usually assume that the distribution of random errors will be the same for all people, classical test theory uses the standard deviation of errors as the basic measure of error. Usually this is called the **standard error of measurement**:

$$\sigma_{meas}$$

The rubber-yardstick analogy may help you understand this concept. Suppose you have a table that is 30 inches high. You measure the height of the table several times using a steel yardstick and keep coming up with the same height: 30 inches. Next, you try to measure the table with the rubber yardstick. The first time you try, the stick has stretched, and you record 28 inches. The next time, you discover the stick has shrunk and it gives you 32 inches. Now you are in trouble, because repeated applications of the yardstick do not always give you the same information about the height of the table.

There is one way out of this situation. Assuming that the yardstick stretches and shrinks randomly, you can say that the distribution of scores given by the yardstick will be normal. Most scores will be close to the actual or true score. Scores that greatly differ from the true score will occur less frequently—that is, you will rarely observe a score as low as 5 inches or as high as 53 inches. The mean of the distribution of scores from repeated applications of the rubber yardstick will be an estimate of the table's true height. The standard deviation will be the standard error of measurement. Remember from Chapter 3 that the standard deviation tells us something about the average deviation around the mean. The standard error of measurement tells us, on the average, how much a score varies from the true score. In practice, the standard deviation of the observed score and the reliability of the test are used to estimate the standard error of measurement.

The Domain Sampling Model

The domain sampling model is another central concept in classical test theory. This model considers the problems created by using a limited number of items to represent a larger and more complicated construct. For example, suppose we want to evaluate your spelling ability. The best technique would be to go systematically through a dictionary, have you spell each word, and then determine the percentage you spelled correctly. However, it is unlikely that we would have time for this. Instead, we need to find a way to evaluate your spelling without having you spell every word. To accomplish this evaluation, we decide to use a *sample* of words. Remember that what we are really attempting to evaluate is how well you can spell, which would be determined by your percentage correct if you had been given all the words in the English language. This percentage would be your "true score." Our task in reliability analysis is to estimate how much error we would make by using the score from the shorter test as an estimate of your true ability.

This model conceptualizes reliability as the ratio of the variance of the observed score on the shorter test and the variance of the long-run true score. The measurement considered in the domain sampling model is the error introduced by using a sample of items (or words in this case) rather than the entire domain.[1] As the sample gets larger, it represents the domain more and more accurately. As a result, the greater the number of items, the higher the reliability. A later section of this chapter shows how a larger number of items increases test reliability.

When tests are constructed, each item is a sample of the ability or behavior to be measured. Long tests have many such samples, and short tests have few. However, each item should equally represent the studied ability. When testing your spelling ability, for example, we could use 5 words, 100 words, or 5000 words.

Reliability can be estimated from the correlation of the observed test score with the true score.[2] This would be easy to find if we knew the true score. However, finding the true scores is not practical and is rarely possible. In the spelling example, finding the true score would involve testing people on all of the words in the English language.

Because true scores are not available, our only alternative is to estimate what they would be. Given that items are randomly drawn from a given domain, each test or group of items should yield an unbiased estimate of the true score. Because of sampling error, however, different random samples of items might give different estimates of the true score. The distribution of these estimates should be random and normally distributed. If we create many tests by sampling from the same domain, then we should get a normal distribution of unbiased estimates of the true score. To estimate reliability, we can create many randomly parallel tests by drawing repeated random samples of items from the same domain. In the spelling example, we would draw several different lists of words randomly from the dictionary and consider each of these samples to be an unbiased test of spelling ability. Then, we would find the correlation between each of these tests and each of the other tests. The correlations then would be averaged.[3] Psychological Testing in Everyday Life 4.1 considers one of the technical issues in estimating true reliability.

Item Response Theory

Perhaps the most important new development relevant to psychometrics is item response theory. Most of the methods for assessing reliability depend on classical test theory (DeVellis, 2006; Kline, 2015a; Thomas, 2012). Classical test theory has been around for over 100 years and it has served the field well. However, a growing movement is turning away from the classical test theory for a variety of different reasons. First, classical test theory requires that exactly the same test items be administered to each person. For a trait such as intelligence, a relatively small number of items concentrate on an individual's particular level of ability. For example, many of the items are too easy and some of them may be too hard. Because so few of the items

---

[1]The term *domain* is used to describe an extremely large collection of items. Some authors prefer the term *universe* or *population* to describe the same concept (Nunnally & Bernstein, 1994).
[2]As M. J. Allen and Yen (1979) point out, there are at least six alternative interpretations of the reliability coefficient. The interpretation we offer here is the one most commonly used.
[3]Technically, it is inappropriate to average correlation coefficients. The appropriate method is to use Fisher's *r* to *Z* transformation to convert the correlations into approximate *Z* scores. Then the *Z* scores are averaged, and the mean *Z* is transformed back into a correlation (Silver & Dunlap, 1987).

4.1 PSYCHOLOGICAL TESTING IN EVERYDAY LIFE

The Unbiased Estimate of Reliability

Theorists have demonstrated mathematically that an unbiased estimate of a test's reliability is given by the square root of the average correlation between all other randomly parallel tests from the domain. Symbolically,

$$r_{1t} = \sqrt{\bar{r}_{1j}}$$

where

1 = scores on test 1

t = the true score for the ability of interest

$\bar{r}_{1j}$ = the average correlation between test 1 and all other randomly parallel tests

As you learned in Chapter 3, product moment correlation coefficients always take on values between –1 and 1. When we estimate reliability, the correlation will always be positive. When a number is less than 1.0, its square root will always be larger than itself. Thus, the correlation between two randomly parallel tests will be smaller than the estimated correlation between one of the tests and the true score according to the formula. For example, if the correlation between two randomly parallel tests is .64, the estimated reliability of the test will be $\sqrt{.64} = .80$. This is built into the estimation of reliability because it would be impossible for a test to correlate more highly with any other test than it would correlate with its own true score. Thus, the correlation between two randomly parallel tests would be expected to be less than the correlation of either test with the true score.

concentrate on a person's exact ability level, the reliability of the intelligence score may not inspire confidence.

A newer approach, known as item response theory (IRT), has been the subject of intense development over the few decades (DeMars, 2010; Templin, 2016). Using IRT, the computer is used to focus on the range of item difficulty that helps assess an individual's ability level. For example, if the person gets several easy items correct, the computer might quickly move to more difficult items. If the person gets several difficult items wrong, the computer moves back to the area of item difficulty where the person gets some items right and some wrong. Then, this level of ability is intensely sampled. The overall result is that a more reliable estimate of ability is obtained using a shorter test with fewer items. Of course, there are many difficulties with applications of IRT. For instance, the method requires a bank of items that have been systematically evaluated for level of difficulty (Templin, 2016). Considerable effort must go into test development, and complex computer software is required. Because of the importance of IRT in current testing, we will return to discuss this issue in more detail in Chapter 6.

Models of Reliability

Federal government guidelines require that a test be reliable before one can use it to make employment or educational placement decisions (Wilcox & Youngsmith, 2015). In this section, we hope to justify the need for high standards of reliability. Most reliability coefficients are correlations; however, it is sometimes more useful to define reliability as its mathematically equivalent ratio. The reliability coefficient is the ratio of the variance of the true scores on a test to the variance of the observed scores:

$$r = \frac{\sigma_T^2}{\sigma_X^2}$$

where

r = the theoretical reliability of the test

σ_T^2 = the variance of the true scores

σ_X^2 = the variance of the observed scores

We have used the Greek σ^2 instead of S^2 to symbolize the variance because the equation describes theoretical values in a population rather than those actually obtained from a sample. The ratio of true score variance to observed score variance can be thought of as a percentage. In this case, it is the percentage of the observed variation (σ_X^2) that is attributable to variation in the true score. If we subtract this ratio from 1.0, then we will have the percentage of variation attributable to random error. $\sigma_T^2 + \sigma_E^2$ could also be used as the denominator because

$$(\sigma_X^2) = \sigma_T^2 + \sigma_E^2$$

Suppose you are given a test that will be used to select people for a particular job, and the reliability of the test is .40. When the employer gets the test back and begins comparing applicants, 40% of the variation or difference among the people will be explained by real differences among people, and 60% must be ascribed to random or chance factors. Now you can see why the government needs to insist on high standards of reliability.

Sources of Error

An observed score may differ from a true score for many reasons. There may be situational factors such as loud noises in the room while the test is being administered. The room may be too hot or too cold. Some of the test takers may have a cold or be feeling depressed. Also, the items on the test might not be representative of the domain. For example, suppose you could spell 96% of the words in the English language correctly but the 20-item spelling test you took included five items (20%) that you could not spell.

Test reliability is usually estimated in one of three ways. In the *test–retest method,* we consider the consistency of the test results when the test is administered on different occasions. Using the method of *parallel forms,* we evaluate the test across different forms of the test. With the method of *internal consistency,* we examine how people perform on similar subsets of items selected from the same form of the measure. Each approach is based on a different source of variability. We shall consider each method separately.

Time Sampling: The Test–Retest Method

Test–retest reliability estimates are used to evaluate the error associated with administering a test at two different times. This type of analysis is of value only when we measure "traits" or characteristics that do not change over time. For instance, we usually assume that an intelligence test measures a consistent general ability. As such, if an IQ test administered at two points in time produces different scores, then we might conclude that the lack of correspondence is the result of random measurement error. Usually we do not assume that a person got more or less intelligent in the time between tests.

Tests that measure some constantly changing characteristic are not appropriate for test–retest evaluation. For example, the value of the Rorschach inkblot test seems to be to tell the clinician how the client is functioning at a particular time. Thus, differences between Rorschach scores at two times could reflect one of two things: (1) a change in the true score being measured or (2) measurement error. Clearly the test–retest method applies only to measures of stable traits.

Test–retest reliability is relatively easy to evaluate: Just administer the same test on two well-specified occasions and then find the correlation between scores from the two administrations using the methods presented in Chapter 3.

However, you need to consider many other details besides the methods for calculating the test–retest reliability coefficient. Understanding and using the information gained from these mechanical exercises requires careful thought. One thing you should always consider is the possibility of a *carryover effect*. This effect occurs when the first testing session influences scores from the second session. For example, test takers sometimes remember their answers from the first time they took the test. Suppose we ask someone the trivia question "Who was the half sister of Dr. Grey on the television program *Grey's Anatomy?*" Then we ask the same question 2 days later. Some of the test takers might have watched the show in the meantime and found out they were wrong the first time. When there are carryover effects, the test–retest correlation usually overestimates the true reliability.

Carryover problems are of concern only when the changes over time are random. In cases where the changes are systematic, carryover effects do not harm the reliability. An example of a systematic carryover is when everyone's score improves exactly 5 points. In this case, no new variability occurs. Random carryover effects occur when the changes are not predictable from earlier scores or when something affects some but not all test takers. If something affects all the test takers equally, then the results are uniformly affected and no net error occurs.

Practice effects are one important type of carryover effect. Some skills improve with practice. When a test is given a second time, test takers score better because they have sharpened their skills by having taken the test the first time. Asking people trivia questions about old movies might stimulate them to think more about the movies or may actually give them some of the information. Practice can also affect tests of manual dexterity: Experience taking the test can improve dexterity skills. As a result, scores on the second administration are usually higher than they were on the first. Practice may affect test takers in different ways, so the changes are not constant across a group.

Because of these problems, the time interval between testing sessions must be selected and evaluated carefully. If the two administrations of the test are close in time, there is a relatively great risk of carryover and practice effects. However, as the time between testing sessions increases, many other factors can intervene to affect scores. For example, if a test is given to children at ages 4 and 5, and the scores from the two administrations of the test correlate at .43, then we must deal with many possible explanations. The low correlation might mean that (1) the test has poor reliability, (2) children change on this characteristic between ages 4 and 5, or (3) some combination of low reliability and change in the children is responsible for the .43 correlation. Further, most test–retest evaluations do not indicate a most likely choice among alternative explanations.

When you find a test–retest correlation in a test manual, you should pay careful attention to the interval between the two testing sessions. A well-evaluated test will have many retest correlations associated with different time intervals between testing sessions. Most often, you want to be assured that the test is reliable over the time interval of your own study. You also should consider what events occurred between the original testing and the retest. For example, activities such as reading a book, participating in a course of study, or watching a TV documentary can alter the test–retest reliability estimate.

Of course, sometimes poor test–retest correlations do not mean that a test is unreliable. Instead, they suggest that the characteristic under study has changed. One of the problems with classical test theory is that it assumes that behavioral dispositions are constant over time. For example, if you are an aggressive person, it is assumed that you will be aggressive all the time. However, some authors have suggested that important behavioral characteristics, such as motivation, fluctuate over time. In fact, important variables such as health status are expected to vary (Hanmer et al., 2016; Kaplan & Ries, 2007; Morera & Stokes, 2016). In classical test theory, these variations are assumed to be errors. Because advanced theories of motivation actually predict these variations, test theorists have been challenged to develop models to account for systematic variations.

Item Sampling: Parallel Forms Method

Building a reliable test also involves making sure that the test scores do not represent any one particular set of items or a subset of items from the entire domain. For example, if you are developing a test of spelling ability, then you would include a particular subset of words from the dictionary in the test. But, as we saw earlier, a test taker may get a score different from the ideal precisely because of the items you have chosen. One form of reliability analysis is to determine the error variance that is attributable to the selection of one particular set of items.

Parallel forms reliability compares two equivalent forms of a test that measure the same attribute. The two forms use different items; however, the rules used to select items of a particular difficulty level are the same.

When two forms of the test are available, one can compare performance on one form versus the other. Some textbooks refer to this process as *equivalent forms reliability,* whereas others call it simply *parallel forms.* Sometimes the two forms are administered to the same group of people on the same day. The Pearson product moment correlation coefficient (see Chapter 3) is used as an estimate of the reliability. When both forms of the test are given on the same day, the only sources of variation are random error and the difference between the forms of the test. (The order of administration is usually counterbalanced to avoid practice effects.) Sometimes the two forms of the test are given at different times. In these cases, error associated with time sampling is also included in the estimate of reliability.

The method of parallel forms provides one of the most rigorous assessments of reliability commonly in use. Unfortunately, the use of parallel forms occurs in practice less often than is desirable. Often test developers find it burdensome to develop two forms of the same test, and practical constraints make it difficult to retest the same group of individuals. Instead, many test developers prefer to base their estimate of reliability on a single form of a test.

In practice, psychologists do not always have two forms of a test. More often, they have only one test form and must estimate the reliability for this single group of items. You can assess the different sources of variation within a single test in many ways. One method is to evaluate the internal consistency of the test by dividing it into subcomponents.

Split-Half Method

In split-half reliability, a test is given and divided into halves that are scored separately. The results of one half of the test are then compared with the results of the other. The two halves of the test can be created in a variety of ways. If the test is long, the best method is to divide the items randomly into two halves. For ease in computing scores for the different halves, however, some people prefer to calculate a score for the first half of the items and another score for the second half. Although convenient, this method can cause problems when items on the second half of the test are more difficult than items on the first half. If the items get progressively more difficult, then you might be better advised to use the *odd-even system,* whereby one subscore is obtained for the odd-numbered items in the test and another for the even-numbered items.

To estimate the reliability of the test, you could find the correlation between the two halves. However, this would be an underestimate because each subtest is only half as long as the full test. As we discussed earlier, test scores gain reliability as the number of items increases. An estimate of reliability based on two half-tests would be deflated because each half would be less reliable than the whole test.

The correlation between the two halves of the test would be a reasonable estimate of the reliability of half the test. To correct for half-length, you can apply the *Spearman-Brown formula,* which allows you to estimate what the correlation between the two halves would have been if each half had been the length of the whole test:

$$\text{corrected } r = \frac{2r}{1 + r}$$

where r is the estimated correlation between the two halves of the test if each had had the total number of items, and r is the correlation between the two halves of

TABLE 4.1   Estimates of Split-Half Reliability Before and After Correction for Half-Length Using the Spearman-Brown Formula

Before correction	After correction	Amount of change
.05	.09	.04
.15	.26	.11
.25	.40	.15
.35	.52	.17
.45	.62	.17
.55	.71	.16
.65	.79	.14
.75	.86	.11
.85	.92	.07
.95	.97	.02

the test. (There are different forms of the estimation formula, as you will see later in the chapter.) For example, when the CES-D (which was described in Chapter 3) is divided into two equal parts, the correlation between the two halves of the test (for medical students) is .78. According to the formula, the estimated reliability would be

$$\text{corrected } r = \frac{2(.78)}{1 + .78} = \frac{1.56}{1.78} = .876$$

Using the Spearman-Brown formula increases the estimate of reliability. The left-hand column in Table 4.1 shows several estimates of reliability that are not corrected using the Spearman-Brown procedure. The middle column shows the same values after they have been corrected. The right-hand column shows the amount of change the correction introduces. As you can see, the Spearman-Brown procedure has a substantial effect, particularly in the middle ranges.

Using the Spearman-Brown correction is not always advisable. For instance, when the two halves of a test have unequal variances, Cronbach's (1951) coefficient alpha (*a*) can be used. This general reliability coefficient provides the lowest estimate of reliability that one can expect. If alpha is high, then you might assume that the reliability of the test is acceptable because the lowest boundary of reliability is still high; the reliability will not drop below alpha. A low alpha level, on the other hand, gives you less information. Because the alpha coefficient marks only the lower bound for the reliability, the actual reliability may still be high. Thus, if the variances for the two halves of the test are unequal, coefficient alpha can confirm that a test has substantial reliability; however, it cannot tell you that a test is unreliable. (Appendix 4.1 provides an example.) The formula for coefficient alpha is

$$\alpha = \frac{2[\sigma_x^2 - (\sigma_{y1}^2 \sigma_{y2}^2)]}{\sigma_x^2}$$

where

$$\alpha = \text{the coefficient alpha for estimating split-half reliability}$$
$$\sigma_x^2 = \text{the variance for scores on the whole test}$$
$$\sigma_{y1}^2 \sigma_{y2}^2 = \text{the variance for the two separate halves of the test}$$

When the variances for the two halves of the test are equal, the Spearman-Brown coefficient and coefficient alpha give the same results. Although there have been conceptual advances in reliability assessment, Cronbach's alpha remains the most commonly used reliability index.

KR_{20} Formula

In addition to the split-half technique, there are many other methods for estimating the internal consistency of a test. Many years ago, Kuder and Richardson (1937) greatly advanced reliability assessment by developing methods for evaluating reliability within a single test administration.

Their approach does not depend on some arbitrary splitting of the test into halves. Decisions about how to split tests into halves cause many potential problems for split-half reliability. The two halves may have different variances. The split-half method also requires that each half be scored separately, possibly creating additional work. The Kuder-Richardson technique avoids these problems because it simultaneously considers all possible ways of splitting the items.

The formula for calculating the reliability of a test in which the items are dichoto-mous, scored 0 or 1 (usually for right or wrong), is known as the **Kuder-Richardson 20,** or KR_{20} or $KR20$. The formula came to be labeled this way because it was the 20th formula presented in the famous article by Kuder and Richardson.

The formula is

$$KR_{20} = r = \frac{N}{N-1}\left(\frac{S^2 - \Sigma pq}{S^2}\right)$$

where

$$KR_{20} = \text{the reliability estimate } (r)$$
$$N = \text{the number of items on the test}$$
$$S^2 = \text{the variance of the total test score}$$
$$p = \text{the proportion of the people getting each item correct (this is found}$$
$$\text{separately for each item)}$$
$$q = \text{the proportion of people getting each item incorrect. For each item,}$$
$$q \text{ equals } 1 - p.$$
$$\Sigma pq = \text{sum of the products of } p \text{ times } q \text{ for each item on the test}$$

Studying the components of the formula may give you a better understanding of how it works. First, you will recognize the term S^2 from Chapter 2. This is the variance of the test scores. The variance appears twice in the formula: once on the top of the right portion in the equation and once on the bottom of the right portion. The other term in the right portion is Σpq. This is the sum of the product of the proportion of people passing each item times the proportion of people failing each item. The product pq is the variance for an individual item. Thus, Σpq is the sum of the individual item variances.

Think about conditions that would make the term on the right side of the equation either large or small. First, consider the situation in which the variance (S^2) is equal to the sum of the variances of the individual items. Symbolically, this would be $S^2 = \Sigma pq$. In this case, the right-hand term in the formula would be 0 and, as a result, the estimate of reliability would be 0. This tells us that to have nonzero reliability, the variance for the total test score must be greater than the sum of the variances for the individual items. This will happen only when the items are measuring the same trait. The total test score variance is the sum of the item variances and the covariances between items (Crocker & Algina, 1986).

The only situation that will make the sum of the item variance less than the total test score variance is when there is covariance between the items. Covariance occurs when the items are correlated with each other. The greater the covariance, the smaller the Σpq term will be. When the items covary, they can be assumed to measure the same general trait, and the reliability for the test will be high. As Σpq approaches 0, the right side of the equation approaches 1.0. The other factor in the formula is an adjustment for the number of items in the test. This will allow an adjustment for the greater error associated with shorter tests. (Appendix 4.2 provides an example.)

In addition to the KR_{20}, Kuder and Richardson presented Formula 21, or KR_{21}, a special case of the reliability formula that does not require the calculation of the p's and q's for every item. Instead, the KR_{21} uses an approximation of the sum of the pq products—the mean test score. The KR_{21} procedure rests on several important assumptions. The most important is that all the items are of equal difficulty, or that the average difficulty level is 50%. *Difficulty* is defined as the percentage of test takers who pass the item. In practice, these assumptions are rarely met, and it is usually found that the KR_{21} formula underestimates the split-half reliability:

$$KR_{21} = \frac{N}{N-1}\left[1 - \frac{\overline{X}(1 - \overline{X}/N)}{S^2}\right]$$

where all terms are as previously defined.

Mathematical proofs have demonstrated that the KR_{20} formula gives the same estimate of reliability that you would get if you took the mean of the split-half reliability estimates obtained by dividing the test in all possible ways (Cronbach, 1951). You can see that because the Kuder-Richardson procedure is general, it is usually more valuable than a split-half estimate of internal consistency (Kline, 2015a).

Coefficient Alpha

The KR_{20} formula is not appropriate for evaluating internal consistency in some cases. The KR_{20} formula requires that you find the proportion of people who got each item "correct." There are many types of tests, though, for which there are no right or wrong answers, such as many personality and attitude scales. For example, on an attitude questionnaire, you might be presented with a statement such as, "I believe extramarital sexual intercourse is immoral." You must indicate whether you *strongly disagree, disagree, are neutral, agree,* or *strongly agree*. None of these choices is incorrect, and none is correct. Rather, your response indicates where you stand on the continuum between agreement and disagreement. To use the Kuder-Richardson method with this sort of item, Cronbach developed a formula that estimates the internal consistency of tests in which the items are not scored as 0 or 1 (right or wrong). In doing so, Cronbach developed a more general reliability estimate, which he called **coefficient alpha,** or α. The formula for coefficient alpha is[4]

$$r = \alpha = \left(\frac{N}{N-1}\right)\left(\frac{S^2 - \Sigma S_i^2}{S^2}\right)$$

As you may notice, this looks quite similar to the KR_{20} formula. The only difference is that Σpq has been replaced by ΣS_i^2. This new term, S_i^2, is for the variance of the individual items (i). The summation sign informs us that we are to sum the individual item variances. S^2 is for the variance of the total test score. The only real difference is the way the variance of the items is expressed. Actually, coefficient alpha is a more general reliability coefficient than KR_{20} because S_i^2 can describe the variance of items whether or not they are in a right-wrong format. Thus, coefficient alpha is the most general method of finding estimates of reliability through internal consistency.

All of the measures of internal consistency evaluate the extent to which the different items on a test measure the same ability or trait. They will all give low estimates of reliability if the test is designed to measure several traits. Using the domain sampling model, we define a domain that represents a single trait or characteristic, and each item is an individual sample of this general characteristic. When the items do not measure the same characteristic, the test will not be internally consistent.

Factor analysis is one popular method for dealing with the situation in which a test apparently measures several different characteristics (see Chapter 3). This can be used to divide the items into subgroups, each internally consistent; however, the subgroups of items will not be related to one another (Brown, 2015; Raykov & Zinbarg, 2011). Factor analysis can help a test constructor build a test that has submeasures for several different traits. When factor analysis is used correctly, these subtests will be internally consistent (highly reliable) and independent of one another. For example, you might use factor analysis to divide a group of items on interpersonal communication into two subgroups, perhaps assertiveness items and self-esteem items. The reliability of the self-esteem and the assertiveness subscales might be quite high; however, the correlation between assertiveness and self-esteem scores could be quite low. The nature of the factor analysis method ensures these characteristics. Thus, factor analysis is of great value in the process of test construction.

Reliability of a Difference Score

Some applications of psychological testing require a *difference score,* which is created by subtracting one test score from another. This might be the difference between performances at two points in time—for example, when you test a group of children before and after they have experienced a special training program. Or it may be the difference between measures of two different abilities, such as whether a child is doing better in reading than in math. Whenever comparisons between two different attributes are being made, one must make the comparison in Z, or standardized, units (see Chapter 2).

---

[4]Although this formula appears different from the formula for coefficient alpha from the section "Split-Half Method," the equations are mathematically equivalent.

Difference scores create a host of problems that make them more difficult to work with than single scores. To understand the problems, you must refer back to the definition of an observed score as composed of both true score (7) and error (E). In a difference score, E is expected to be larger than either the observed score or T because E absorbs error from both of the scores used to create the difference score. Furthermore, T might be expected to be smaller than E because whatever is common to both measures is canceled out when the difference score is created. As a result of these two factors, the reliability of a difference score is expected to be lower than the reliability of either score on which it is based. If two tests measure exactly the same trait, then the score representing the difference between them is expected to have a reliability of 0.

As we have previously mentioned, it is most convenient to find difference scores by first creating Z scores for each measure and then finding the difference between them (score 2 − score 1). The reliability of scores that represent the difference between two standard scores (or Z scores) is given by the formula

$$r = \frac{\frac{1}{2}(r_{11} + r_{22}) - r_{12}}{1 - r_{12}}$$

where

r_{11} = the reliability of the first measure

r_{22} = the reliability of the second measure

r_{12} = the correlation between the first and the second measures

Using this formula, you can calculate the reliability of a difference score for any two tests for which the reliabilities and the correlation between them are known. For example, suppose that the correlation between two measures is .70 and the reliabilities of the two measures are .90 and .70, respectively. The reliability of the difference between these two measures is

$$r = \frac{\frac{1}{2}(.90 + .70) - .70}{1 - .70}$$

$$= \frac{.10}{.30}$$

$$= .33$$

As this example demonstrates, the reliability of the difference score between tests with reliabilities as high as .90 and .70 is only .33. The situation in which the reliability of the difference score is lower than the average reliabilities of the two initial measures is not unusual. In fact, it occurs in all cases except when the correlation between the two tests is 0.

The low reliability of a difference score should concern the practicing psychologist and education researcher. Because of their poor reliabilities, difference scores cannot be depended on for interpreting patterns.

For example, it may be difficult to draw the conclusion that a patient is more depressed than the schizophrenic on the basis of an Minnesota Multiphasic Personality Inventory MMPI profile that shows a lower depression than the schizophrenia score. Any differences between these two scales must be interpreted cautiously because the reliability of the score that represents the difference between the two scales can be expected to be low. The difficulties associated with using difference scores have been well studied. In a widely cited article, Cronbach and Furby (1970) demonstrated that there are many pitfalls associated with using difference scores to measure change. For example, it appears impossible to make a meaningful interpretation of the difference between scores on the same children that are taken at the beginning and at the end of a school year. Measuring the "change" that occurred during that school year requires the use of sophisticated experimental designs in which children are randomly assigned to experimental and control conditions.

Although reliability estimates are often interpreted for individuals, estimates of reliability are usually based on observations of populations, not observations of the same individual. One distinction is between reliability and information. Low reliability implies that comparing gain scores in a population may be problematic. For example, average improvements by schools on a statewide achievement test may be untrustworthy if the test has low reliability. Low information suggests that we cannot trust *gain-score* information about a particular person. This might occur if the test taker was sick on one of the days a test was administered, but not the other. However, low reliability of a change score for a population does not necessarily mean that gains for individual people are not meaningful (Mellenbergh, 1999). An improvement for an individual student might offer important information even though the test may have low reliability for the population.

Although reliability is often difficult to calculate, computer programs that do much of the work are now available.

Reliability in Behavioral Observation Studies

Psychologists with behavioral orientations usually prefer not to use psychological tests. Instead, they favor the direct observation of behavior. To measure aggression, for example, they would record the number of times a child hits or kicks another child. Observers would tabulate the number of observable responses in each category. Thus, there would be one score for "hits," another for "kicks," and so on.

Some people feel that behavioral observation systems are so simple that they have no psychometric problems, but they have many sources of error. Because psychologists cannot always monitor behavior continuously, they often take samples of behavior at certain time intervals.

Sources of error introduced by time sampling are similar to those with sampling items from a large domain. When each time sample is thought of as an "item," these problems can be handled using sampling theory and methods such as alpha reliability.

In practice, behavioral observation systems are frequently unreliable because of discrepancies between true scores and the scores recorded by the observer. For example, an observer might miss one or two times a child hits or kicks; another observer might catch them all. The problem of error associated with different observers presents unique difficulties. To assess these problems, one needs to estimate the reliability of the observers (Ladd, Tomlinson, Myers, & Anderson, 2016). These reliability estimates have various names, including *interrater, interscorer, interobserver,* or *interjudge reliability.* All of the terms consider the consistency among different judges who are evaluating the same behavior. There are at least three different ways to do this. The most common method is to record the percentage of times that two or more observers agree. Unfortunately, this method is not the best one, for at least two reasons. First, this percentage does not consider the level of agreement that would be expected by chance alone. For instance, if two observers are recording whether a particular behavior either occurred or did not occur, then they would have a 50% likelihood of agreeing by chance alone. A method for assessing such reliability should include an adjustment for chance agreement. Second, percentages should not be mathematically manipulated. For example, it is not technically appropriate to average percentages. Indexes such as Z scores are manipulable and thus better suited to the task of reliability assessment.

The *kappa statistic* is the best method for assessing the level of agreement among several observers. The kappa statistic was introduced by J. Cohen (1960) as a measure of agreement between two judges who each rate a set of objects using nominal scales. Fleiss (1971) extended the method to consider the agreement between any number of observers. *Kappa* indicates the actual agreement as a proportion of the potential agreement following correction for chance agreement. Values of kappa may vary between 1 (perfect agreement) and −1 (less agreement than can be expected on the basis of chance alone). A value greater than .75 generally indicates "excellent" agreement, a value between .40 and .75 indicates "fair to good" ("satisfactory") agreement, and a value less than .40 indicates "poor" agreement (Fleiss, 1981). The calculation of kappa is beyond the scope of this presentation, but interested readers can find more details in some good summary references (Warrens, 2015). An example of a study using behavioral assessment is discussed in Psychological Testing in Everyday Life 4.2. Behavioral observation is difficult and expensive. In the future, we expect that more of the observation will be done with new technologies and smart software. This is discussed in Psychological Testing in Everyday Life 4.3.

4.2   PSYCHOLOGICAL TESTING IN EVERYDAY LIFE

Behavioral Observation and Physical Activity in Children

Determining levels of physical activity has become one of the most crucial goals of research in child development. Physical activity is an important determinant of weight management and the risk for obesity. To address these measurement needs, researchers developed the System for Observing Children's Activity and Relationships during Play (SOCARP). This system is used to keep track of a variety of behaviors, including physical activity levels, type of activity, the size of social groups, and the amount of social behavior that occurs during play. The reliability of the system was evaluated over 24 days in eight elementary schools using a total sample of 48 boys and 66 girls. Among the children, 42% were overweight. On half of the days, the activity was videotaped. To get an objective measure of activity, a uniaxial accelerometer was attached to 99 during the period recess observation. The study showed that activity could be reliably assessed by trained observers. Interobserver reliabilities (i.e., percentage agreement) were 89% for activity level, 88% for group size, 90% for activity type, and 88% for interactions. Further, the level of energy expenditure estimated by the SOCARP system correlated $r = 0.67$ with objective measurement using the accelerometer (Ridgers, Stratton, & McKenzie, 2011).

4.3 PSYCHOLOGICAL TESTING IN EVERYDAY LIFE

Behavioral Observation in the Era of Big Data

Psychologists have advocated for behavioral observation for decades. However, the actual use of behavioral observation in research and practice still remains rare. The difficulty is that behavioral observation is hard to do, expensive, and labor intensive. In addition, it requires hundreds and hundreds of observational data points. However, with the advent of new technologies and big data analysis programs, behavioral observation may soon be revolutionized. For example, much of the observation can be done with sensors and cameras. Smart software can be developed to identify and record particular behaviors. Cameras placed on playgrounds might capture levels of physical activity, episodes of pushing, or other evidence of bullying. New software using machine learning technologies can become expert in differentiating these from other behaviors. There are growing opportunities to observe people in a wide variety of naturalistic settings (Kaplan & Stone, 2013).

One practical example of the use of these new technologies involved placing motion detectors in the homes of elderly people living alone. Most older people are very hesitant to relinquish their independence. Home monitoring provides the opportunity for independent living while continuing to protect safety. In addition, continuous monitoring can identify when problems develop. These new technologies for continuous behavioral observation study of individuals living with chronic illnesses have now been applied in a variety of settings. The Oregon Center for Aging and Technology (ORCATECH) was able to monitor individuals living in private homes over the course of a year. Figure 4.3 shows the amount of time that a single elderly person spent in the bedroom, the bathroom, living room, near the front door, and in the kitchen over the course of the year. Starting from the center of the circle shown in the figure, each small circle represents a single day. The concentric circles drawn going out from the center represent a month of observation. The overall circle represents the 24-hour clock. It shows that between about 10 PM and midnight, the person spent most of the time in the bedroom awake and moving around. The time between midnight and about 6 AM was when the person usually slept. You can see that during the first part of the year (shown in the area closer to the center of the circle) it was relatively rare for her to be moving around the bedroom between midnight and 6:00 AM. Later in the year, movement became much more common. This suggests that a sleep problem was developing. The figure shows that the person was spending time in the kitchen at mealtimes, although less so around the dinner hour. Overall, the study demonstrates new technologies can automate behavioral observation. Although it will be necessary to systematically study the reliability of these methods, the

(continues)

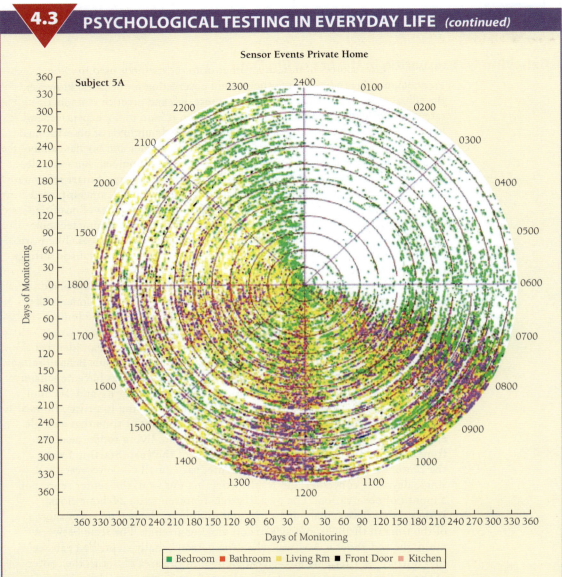

Sensor Events Private Home

Pavel M, Jimison HB, Wactlar HD, Hayes TL, Barkis W, Skapik J, Kaye J. The role of technology and engineering models in transforming healthcare. IEEE Rev Biomed Eng. 2013; 6:156-77. Reproduced by permission.

FIGURE 4.3 Spiral plot of activity observed over the period of a year. Each day is represented by a circle starting at day 0 in the origin and moving out to the last day in the periphery. Some of the subject's periodic behaviors are visualized as spokes on this wheel, e.g., sleeping and meal-preparation activities.

potential for widespread application of behavioral observation is now technically possible. This particular example shows clever data visualization techniques can be used to summarize massive amounts of data.

Connecting Sources of Error with Reliability Assessment Method

Table 4.2 relates sources of measurement error to the methods used to assess reliability. Remember that *reliability* is a generic term. Psychologists use different methods of reliability assessment to describe different sources of measurement error, and each has a different meaning. As Table 4.2 suggests, one source of measurement error is *time sampling*. The same test given at different points in time may produce different scores, even if given to the same test takers. This source of error is typically assessed using the test–retest method. Another source of error is *item sampling*. The same construct or attribute may be assessed using a wide pool of items. For example, no one item is used to assess human intelligence, yet different items used to measure this general construct may not always give the same reflection of the true ability. This sort of error is assessed using alternate forms, or parallel forms reliability. Typically, the correlation between two forms of a test is created by randomly sampling a large pool of items believed to assess a particular construct. This correlation is used as an estimate of this type of reliability.

The *internal consistency* of a test refers to the intercorrelations among items within the same test. If the test is designed to measure a single construct and all items are equally good candidates to measure that attribute, then there should be a high correspondence among the items. This internal consistency is evaluated using split-half reliability, the KR_{20} method, or coefficient alpha. Another source of measurement error occurs when different observers record the same behavior. Even though they have the same instructions, different judges observing the same event may record different numbers. To determine the extent of this type of error, researchers can use an adjusted index of agreement such as the kappa statistic.

As you can see, the term *reliability* refers to several methods that are used to assess different sources of error. Sometimes different sources of error occur in the

TABLE 4.2   Sources of Measurement Error and Methods of Reliability Assessment

Source of error	Example	Method	How assessed
Time sampling	Same test given at two points in time	Test–retest	Correlation between scores obtained on the two occasions
Item sampling	Different items used to assess the same attribute	Alternate forms or parallel forms	Correlation between equivalent forms of the test that have different items
Internal consistency	Consistency of items within the same test	1. Split-half	1. Corrected correlation between two halves of the test
		2. KR_{20}	2. See Appendix 4.2
		3. Alpha	3. See Appendix 4.1
Observer differences	Different observers recording	Kappa statistic	See Fleiss (1981)

same situation—for example, an error associated with item sampling and additional error linked to time sampling. When evaluating reliability information, you should take into consideration all potential sources of error. Interrater agreement can be a problem in basic medical as well as behavioral studies (see Focused Example 4.1). A summary of the standards for reporting information about reliability is presented in Focused Example 4.2.

4.1 FOCUSED EXAMPLE

Interrater Agreement in Pathology

Psychologists have always been self-critical about the less-than-perfect reliability rates in behavioral studies. They assume that agreement must be higher in other fields, particularly when there is an opportunity for more careful study. For example, we would expect high interrater agreement among pathologists who study tissue under a microscope. However, many studies suggest that agreement among pathologists who study the same specimens is often no better than among behavioral scientists who observe the activities of the same individuals. For example, one study evaluated the reliability of pathologist-assessed ductal carcinoma in situ (DCIS). Six pathologist subjects were given written guidelines and examples of each of the problems they were looking for. Following this training, these experienced pathologists were given 24 high-quality slides of breast tissue. There was considerable variability in the propensity to see DCIS: One pathologist saw cancer in 12% of the slides, while another saw DCIS in 33% of the same slides.

Figure 4.4 summarizes the results for 10 slides where at least one pathologist saw DCIS. The columns represent women, and the rows represent pathologists. Hatched squares indicate that the pathologist saw DCIS; open squares indicate that DCIS was not seen. No two pathologists had the same pattern of identification. One pathologist saw cancer in eight of the ten cases, while another saw DCIS in only three. One case was diagnosed by only one pathologist, and only two cases were seen by all six. These variations in diagnostic patterns imply that patients with the same problem, going to different doctors, may get different diagnoses (Welch, 2004).

FIGURE 4.4
Interobserver agreement among six pathologists on DCIS for 10 cases.

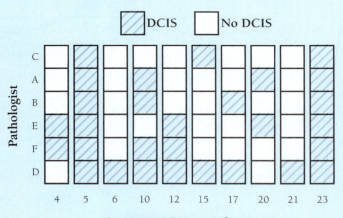

From Welch H. G., and Black W. C. (2007, December 1). Using autopsy series to estimate the disease "reservoir" for ductal carcinoma in situ of the breast: "How much more breast cancer can we final" *Ann Intern Med.,* 127(11): 1023–1028. Copyright © 1997 American College of Physicians. Reprinted by permission.

4.2 FOCUSED EXAMPLE

Summary of Guidelines for Reliability

The American Psychological Association, American Educational Research Association, and National Council on Measurement in Education (2014) suggest 20 standards for reliability.* Here is a summary of these standards:

1. Estimates of reliabilities and standard errors of measurement should be provided for each total score, subscore, or combination of scores.

2. The standard error of measurement should be reported in both raw score units and derived score units.

3. Sometimes test interpretation involves comparison between two observed scores for an individual or average scores for two groups. In these situations, reliability data, including standard errors, should be reported for differences.

4. When reporting reliability, information on the method of subject selection, sample size, and characteristics of the groups under study should be reported.

5. Reliability coefficients and standard errors, typically derived using a particular technique, should not be used interchangeably with estimates obtained using other methods.

6. If reliability coefficients are adjusted for a restricted range, these adjustments must be reported.

7. If a test has multiple factors or measures multiple traits simultaneously, this multifactorial structure must be recognized in the reports of reliability.

8. Those who take the test must be told if the rate of work may affect their performance.

9. For tests that are timed, reliability estimates should be obtained using alternate form or test–retest methods that adjust for the amount of time subjects have to complete the test.

10. Judges can make subjective errors in rating behavior. When subjective errors are possible, an interrater consistency evaluation should consider within-examinee comparisons as well as between rater reliability.

11. Whenever feasible, test publishers should provide reliability evidence for major subpopulations. For example, they should provide separate reliability estimates for white, African American, Asian American, and Hispanic groups.

12. If a test is applied to different grade levels or different age groups and separate norms are provided for each group, reliability data should be provided for each age or population group separately.

13. Sometimes national tests are applied in local areas. Whenever possible, reliability data should be evaluated and reported at the local level.

14. Conditional standard errors of measurement should be reported. This means that if the test divides examinees into specific subgroups, the standard error of measurement for each of these subgroups should be considered.

15. If a test is used to divide examinees into categories, estimates should be reported for the percentage of people who would be placed in the same category if the test were administered on two separate occasions.

16. Sometimes different examinees complete tests with different items. The items might be randomly selected from some larger pool of items (as is often the case using item response theory). Under these circumstances, reliability should be estimated on the basis of successive administrations of the test under conditions similar to those under which the test is typically administered.

17. Some tests are available in both long and short versions. Under these circumstances, reliability should be reported for each version of the test.

18. If variations are allowed in the procedures for test administration, separate reliability estimates should be provided under each of the major variations.

19. When average scores for groups are used to evaluate programs, the groups tested should be considered samples from a larger population. The standard error of the group mean should be reported.

20. Sometimes, program evaluation administrators give small subsets of items to many subsamples of examinees. Then the data are aggregated to estimate performance for the group. When these procedures are used, the reliability analysis must take the sampling scheme into consideration.

*Standards not applicable to basic psychometrics are not listed here. Adapted from American Educational Research Association et al. (1999, pp. 31–36).

Using Reliability Information

Now that you have learned about reliability theory and methods, you will benefit from reviewing some practical aspects of reliability assessment. Different situations call for different levels of reliability.

Standard Errors of Measurement and the Rubber Yardstick

Earlier in this chapter, we used the rubber yardstick to introduce the concept of the standard error of measurement. Remember that psychologists working with unreliable tests are like carpenters working with rubber yardsticks that stretch or contract and misrepresent the true length of a board. However, as all rubber yardsticks are not equally inaccurate, all psychological tests are not equally inaccurate. The standard error of measurement allows us to estimate the degree to which a test provides inaccurate readings; that is, it tells us how much "rubber" there is in a measurement. The larger the standard error of measurement, the less certain we can be about the accuracy with which an attribute is measured. Conversely, a small standard error of measurement tells us that an individual score is probably close to the measured value. Some textbooks refer to the standard error of measurement as the standard error of a score. To calculate the standard error of measurement, we need to use the standard deviation and the reliability coefficient. The formula for this calculation is

$$S_m = S\sqrt{1 - r}$$

where

S_m = the standard error for the measurement

S = the standard deviation of the scores

r = the reliability coefficient

For example, suppose that an IQ test has a mean of 100 for a particular sample, with a standard deviation of 14. You are particularly interested in a person with a score of 106. The reliability of the test is .89. Plugging these values into the formula, you find

$$S_m = 14\sqrt{1 - .89} = 4.64$$

Researchers use standard errors of measurement to create confidence intervals around specific observed scores. You may want to review the concept of a confidence interval in your introductory statistics textbook. Briefly, we never know whether an observed score is the "true" score. However, we can form intervals around an observed score and use statistical procedures to estimate the probability that the true score falls within a certain interval. Common intervals used in testing are the 68% interval, the 95% interval, and the 99% interval. These intervals are created using Z scores (see Chapter 2).

Let's suppose we wish to create the 95% confidence interval for this specific IQ test. The 95% confidence interval is associated with the Z score of 1.96. The upper bound of the confidence interval is equal to the mean plus $1.96(S_m)$, or, in this example,

$$106 + 1.96(4.64) = 115.09$$

The lower bound of the interval is equal to the mean minus

$$1.96 \times S_m$$

So, in this example, the lower bound would be

$$106 - 1.96(4.64) = 96.91$$

Although we do not know the true score for a person who received the score of 106, we can be 95% confident that the true score falls between 96.9 and 115.1. As you can see, however, the scores of 96 and 115 on an IQ test (see Chapters 11 and 12) are quite different. Tests with more measurement error include more "rubber." In other words, the larger the standard error of measurement, the larger the confidence interval. When confidence intervals are especially wide, our ability to make precise statements is greatly diminished. Psychological Testing in Everyday Life 4.4 applies these principles to the interpretation of changes in the average Scholastic Aptitude Test SAT score.

How Reliable Is Reliable?

People often ask how high a reliability coefficient must be before it is "high enough." The answer depends on the use of the test. It has been suggested that reliability estimates in the range of .70 and .80 are good enough for most purposes in basic research. In many studies, researchers attempt to gain only approximate estimates of how two variables are related. For research, it may be appropriate to estimate what the correlation between two variables would have been if the measures had been more reliable. Promising results can justify spending extra time and money to make the research instruments more reliable. Some people have argued that it would be a waste of time and effort to refine research instruments beyond a reliability of .90. In fact, it has even been suggested that reliabilities greater than .95 are not very useful because they suggest that all of the items are testing essentially the same thing and that the measure could easily be shortened. Although the higher reliability is usually desirable, it may not be worth the added burden and costs (Nunnally & Bernstein, 1994). A report from the National Academy of Sciences notes that extremely high reliability might be expected for tests that are highly focused. For example, a test of skill at using the multiplication tables for one-digit numbers would be expected to have an especially high reliability.

In clinical settings, high reliability is extremely important. When tests are used to make important decisions about someone's future, evaluators must be certain to minimize any error in classification. Thus, a test with a reliability of .90 might not be good enough. For a test used to make a decision that affects some person's future, evaluators should attempt to find a test with a reliability greater than .95.

Perhaps the most useful index of reliability for the interpretation of individual scores is the standard error of measurement. This index is used to create an interval around an observed score. The wider the interval, the lower the reliability of the score.

Are Scores Really Getting Worse?

In September 2011, newspapers across the nation reported that declining SAT scores mean that the U.S. educational system is losing ground. According to the College Board, SAT reading scores have dropped 3 points, while math scores have dropped 1 point and writing scores 2 points.

What do we make of these declines? Education journalists are quick to cite declining investments in public education. Further, they attribute some of the decline to more poorly prepared teachers, to student apathy, and to a general decline in the academic preparation of American students.

There are other explanations for the decline and, before we even go there, it is worth considering whether there has been, indeed, a measureable decline. First, we must consider the reliability of the SAT components. The Educational Testing Service ETS reports that the reliability of the SAT is quite high. For critical reading, mathematics, and writing, it suggests that reliabilities tend to be about 0.90. However, there may be some problems with the reliability of the scoring of essays. For example, different readers who evaluate the same essay do not always agree. For a group of 2006 college-bound seniors, the interrater reliability of the evaluation of essays ranged from 0.77 to 0.81. When students were asked to write more than one essay, the reliability of the estimates was only 0.67 (Ridgers et al., 2011).

Using the formula for the standard error of measurement, we can calculate the 95% confidence interval around the mean of 489 for the writing component of the SAT. For simplicity, we will use the SD of 100, which is the standard for the SAT.

The standard error of measurement is:

$$S_m = 100\sqrt{1 - .67} = 57.45$$

Using the standard error of measurement, we can say that we are 95% confident that a person's true score falls between two values.

What to Do about Low Reliability

Often, test constructors want their tests to be used in applied settings, but analysis reveals inadequate test reliability. Fortunately, psychometric theory offers some options. Two common approaches are to increase the length of the test and to throw out items that run down the reliability. Another procedure is to estimate what the true correlation would have been if the test did not have measurement error.

Increase the Number of Items

According to the domain sampling model, each item in a test is an independent sample of the trait or ability being measured. The larger the sample, the more likely that the test will represent the true characteristic. In the domain sampling model, the reliability of a test increases as the number of items increases.

Many thousands of college-bound students take the SAT, so there is a lot of precision for estimating mean scores. However, we can use the formula to estimate the usual range to be expected around different scores. For example, we can estimate the 68% confidence interval, which would be equivalent to one standard deviation above or below the mean score of 489 for the writing component of the SAT. This would result in a range from 432 to about 546. The observed difference of 2 points is well within the range defined by one adjusted standard deviation from the mean.

Sampling is another explanation for the changes in scores between 2010 and 2011. We would expect the average performance on the test to be the same if the population of test takers was also the same. Increasing the number of less-prepared test takers is another alternative explanation for the decline in the average score. In 2011, more people than ever before took the SAT. Historically, the SAT had been taken by students most directed toward obtaining an education at a 4-year college. When the population of test takers expands, it is most likely that the population becomes more inclusive of students who have not had exposure to college preparation, including coaching for standardized tests. In 2011, not all test takers had completed the college preparative curriculum, which includes 4 years of English, 3 years of math, 3 years of natural science, and 3 years of social science and history. Those who did not complete the college prep core scored an average of 143 points lower than those who had finished the traditional preparation. This might be regarded as a positive sign because it represents increasing access to college and greater interest in more people obtaining a college education.

A medical example will clarify why longer tests are more reliable. Suppose that you go to the doctor with indigestion. You want the doctor to make a reliable judgment about what is causing it. How comfortable would you feel if the doctor asked only one question before making a diagnosis? You would probably feel more comfortable if the doctor asked many questions. In general, people feel that the more information a doctor obtains by asking questions and performing tests, the more reliable the diagnosis will be. This same principle applies to psychological tests.

A decision to increase the number of items in a test might engender a long and costly process. With new items added, the test must be reevaluated; it may turn out to fall below an acceptable level of reliability. In addition, adding new items can be costly and can make a test so long that few people would be able to sit through it. Fortunately, by applying the Spearman-Brown prophecy formula, one can estimate how many items will have to be added in order to bring a test to an acceptable level of reliability.

The prophecy formula for estimating how long a test must be to achieve a desired level of reliability is another case of the general Spearman-Brown method for estimating reliability. Algebraic manipulations of the general formula allow one to solve it for the length needed for any desired level of reliability:

$$N = \frac{r_d(1 - r_o)}{r_o(1 - r_d)}$$

where

N = the number of tests of the current version's length that would be needed

r_d = the desired level of reliability

r_o = the observed level of reliability based on the current version of the test

Consider the example of the 20-item CES-D test that had a reliability for medical students of .87. We would like to raise the reliability to .95. Putting these numbers into the prophecy formula, we get

$$N = \frac{.95(1 - .87)}{.87(1 - .95)} = \frac{.124}{.044} = 2.82$$

These calculations tell us that we would need 2.82 tests of the same length as the current 20-item test to bring the reliability up to the desired level. To find the number of items required, we must multiply the number of items on the current test by N from the preceding formula. In the example, this would give 20 × 2.82 = 56.4. So the test would have to be expanded from 20 to approximately 56 items to achieve the desired reliability, assuming that the added items come from the same pool as the original items and that they have the same psychometric properties.

The decision to expand a test from 20 to 56 items must depend on economic and practical considerations. The test developer must first ask whether the increase in reliability is worth the extra time, effort, and expense required to achieve this goal. If the test is to be used for personnel decisions, then it may be dangerous to ignore any enhancement of the test's reliability. On the other hand, if the test is to be used only to see if two variables are associated, the expense of extending it may not be worth the effort and cost.

When the prophecy formula is used, certain assumptions are made that may or may not be valid. One of these assumptions is that the probability of error in items added to the test is the same as the probability of error for the original items in the test. However, adding many items may bring about new sources of error, such as the fatigue associated with taking an extremely long test.

As an example of a situation in which increasing the reliability of a test may not be worthwhile, consider a 40-item test with a reliability of .50. We would like to bring the reliability up to .90. Using the prophecy formula, we get

$$N = \frac{.90(1 - .50)}{.50(1 - .90)} = \frac{.90(.50)}{.50(.10)} = \frac{.45}{.05} = 9$$

These figures tell us that the test would have to be nine times its present length to have a projected reliability of .90. This is calculated as 9 × 40 = 360 items long. Creating a test that long would be prohibitively expensive, and validating it would require a considerable investment of time for both test constructors and test takers. Also, new sources of error might arise that were not present in the shorter measure.

For example, many errors may occur on the longer test simply because people get tired and bored during the long process of answering 360 questions. There is no way to take these factors into account by using the prophecy formula.

Factor and Item Analysis

The reliability of a test depends on the extent to which all of the items measure one common characteristic. Although psychologists set out to design test items that are consistent, often some items do not measure the given construct. Leaving these items in the test reduces its reliability. To ensure that the items measure the same thing, two approaches are suggested. One is to perform factor analysis (see Chapter 3 and Brown, 2015). Tests are most reliable if they are *unidimensional*. This means that one factor should account for considerably more of the variance than any other factor. Items that do not load on this factor might be best omitted.

Another approach is to examine the correlation between each item and the total score for the test. This form of item analysis (see Chapter 6) is often called **discriminability analysis.** When the correlation between the performance on a single item and the total test score is low, the item is probably measuring something different from the other items on the test. It also might mean that the item is so easy or so hard that people do not differ in their response to it. In either case, the low correlation indicates that the item drags down the estimate of reliability and should be excluded.

Correction for Attenuation

Low reliability is a real problem in psychological research and practice because it reduces the chances of finding significant correlations between measures. If a test is unreliable, information obtained with it is of little or no value. Thus, we say that potential correlations are attenuated, or diminished, by measurement error.

4.3 FOCUSED EXAMPLE

Measurement Error in the Era on Big Data

For any measured variable, the difference between the true score and the observed score results from measurement error. This error is common in all biological, social, and behavioral sciences, but it can be controlled through systematic measure development. Small controlled studies often devote great attention to measurement precision. In contrast, users of big data sets may be unaware of how study variables were measured and low reliability of some measures can be expected. This can be a serious problem because it reduces the chances of finding significant relationships among measures. Thus, estimates of correlations and effect sizes are attenuated by measurement error. Large sample size may help reduce this bias, but if the measures are of very low reliability, the analysis will be focused on random variation. For example, suppose two variables in a big data set have reliability coefficients of .050 and 0.30. Even if these two variables were perfectly correlated in the real world ($r = 1.0$), the maximum expected observed correlation would be only 0.38. A modest correlation would be unlikely to be detected, even in a very large data set. Having more observations does not necessarily resolve the issue of measurement error.

Fortunately, measurement theory does allow one to estimate what the correlation between two measures would have been if they had not been measured with error. These methods "correct" for the attenuation in the correlations caused by the measurement error. To use the methods, one needs to know only the reliabilities of two tests and the correlation between them. The **correction for attenuation** is

$$\hat{r}_{12} = \frac{r_{12}}{\sqrt{r_{11}r_{22}}}$$

where

$\hat{r}_{12}$ = the estimated true correlation between tests 1 and 2

r_{12} = the observed correlation between tests 1 and 2

r_{11} = the reliability of test 1

r_{22} = the reliability of test 2

Suppose, for example, that the correlation between the CES-D and ratings of clinical skill was .34; the reliabilities of the tests were .87 and .70 for the CES-D and the clinical skill tests, respectively. The estimated true correlation between depression and clinical skill would be

$$\frac{.34}{\sqrt{(.87)(.70)}} = \frac{.34}{\sqrt{.609}} = \frac{.34}{.78} = .44$$

As the example shows, the estimated correlation increases from .34 to .44 when the correction is used.

Sometimes one measure meets an acceptable standard of reliability but the other one does not. In this case, we would want to correct for the attenuation caused only by the one unreliable test. To do this, we use the formula

$$\hat{r}_{12} = \frac{r_{12}}{\sqrt{r_{11}}}$$

where

$\hat{r}_{12}$ = the estimated true correlation

r_{12} = the observed correlation

r_{11} = the reliability of the variable that does not meet our standard of reliability

For example, suppose we want to estimate the correlation between the CES-D score and GPA in medical school. The reliability of the CES-D test is .75, which is not quite as good as we would like, but medical school GPA is assumed to be measured without error. Using the fallible CES-D depression test, we observe the correlation to be .53. Plugging these numbers into the formula, we get

$$\frac{.53}{\sqrt{.75}} = \frac{.53}{.87} = .61$$

This informs us that correcting for the attenuation caused by the CES-D test would increase our observed correlation from .53 to .61.

Summary

Measurement error is common in all fields of science. Psychological and educational specialists, however, have devoted a great deal of time and study to measurement error and its effects. Tests that are relatively free of measurement error are considered to be reliable, and tests that contain relatively large measurement error are considered unreliable. In the early part of the 20th century, Charles Spearman worked out the basics of contemporary theories and methods of reliability. Test score and reliability theories have gone through continual refinements.

When we evaluate *reliability,* we must first specify the source of measurement error we are trying to evaluate. If we are concerned about errors that result from tests being given at different times, then we might consider the *test–retest method* in which test scores obtained at two different points in time are correlated. On other occasions, we may be concerned about errors that arise because we have selected a small sample of items to represent a larger conceptual domain. To evaluate this type of measurement error, we could use a method that assesses the internal consistency of the test such as the *split–half method.* The KR_{20} method and *alpha coefficient* are other methods for estimating the internal consistency of a test.

The standard of reliability for a test depends on the situation in which the test will be used. In some research settings, bringing a test up to an exceptionally high level of reliability may not be worth the extra time and money. On the other hand, strict standards for reliability are required for a test used to make decisions that will affect people's lives. When a test has unacceptably low reliability, the test constructor might wish to boost the reliability by increasing the test length or by using factor analysis to divide the test into homogeneous subgroups of items. In research settings, we can sometimes deal with the problem of low reliability by estimating what the correlation between tests would have been if there had been no measurement error. This procedure is called *correction for attenuation.*

Evaluating the reliability of behavioral observations is also an important challenge. The percentage of items on which observers agree is not the best index of reliability for these studies because it does not take into consideration how much agreement is to be expected by chance alone. Correlation-like indexes such as kappa or phi are better suited to estimate reliability in these behavioral studies.

Reliability is one of the basic foundations of behavioral research. If a test is not reliable, then one cannot demonstrate that it has any meaning. In the next chapter, we focus on how the meaning of tests is defined.

APPENDIX 4.1:
Using Coefficient Alpha to Estimate Split-Half Reliability
When the Variances for the Two Halves of the Test Are Unequal

Formula:

$$\alpha = \frac{2[S_x^2 - (S_{y1}^2 + S_{y2}^2)]}{S_x^2}$$

Data:

$$S_x^2 = 11.5$$
$$S_{y1}^2 = 4.5$$
$$S_{y2}^2 = 3.2$$

STEPS

1. Find the variance for the whole test.

$$S_x^2 = 11.5$$

2. Add the variances for the two halves of the test.

$$S_{y1}^2 = 4.5 \qquad S_{y2}^2 = 3.2 \qquad 4.5 + 3.2 = 7.7$$

3. Find $S_x^2 - (S_{y1}^2 + S_{y2}^2)$ by subtracting the result of Step 2 from that of Step 1.

$$11.5 - 7.7 = 3.8$$

4. Find $2[S_x^2 - (S_{y1}^2 + S_{y2}^2)]$ by multiplying the result of Step 3 times 2.

$$2(3.8) = 7.6$$

5. Find alpha by dividing the result of Step 4 by that of Step 1.

$$\frac{7.6}{11.5} = .66$$

APPENDIX 4.2:
The Calculation of Reliability Using KR_{20}

Formula:

$$KR_{20} = \frac{N}{N - 1}\left(\frac{S^2 - \Sigma pq}{S^2}\right)$$

Data:

$$NS = \text{number of test takers} = 50$$
$$N = \text{number of items} = 6$$
$$S^2 = \text{variance (Step 6)} = 2.8$$

Item	Number of test takers responding correctly	p (from Step 2)	q (from Step 3)	pq (from Step 4)
1	12	.24	.76	.18
2	41	.82	.18	.15
3	18	.36	.64	.23
4	29	.58	.42	.24
5	30	.60	.40	.24
6	47	.94	.06	$\Sigma pq = 1.10$ (from Step 5)

STEPS

1. Determine the number of test takers *NS*.

$$NS = 50$$

2. Find *p* by dividing the number of people responding correctly to each item by the number of people taking the test (Step 1). This is the level of difficulty.

$$\frac{12}{50} = .24 \qquad \frac{41}{50} = .48 \ldots$$

3. Find *q* for each item by subtracting *p* (the result of Step 2) from 1.0. This gives the proportion responding incorrectly to each item.

$$1.0 - 2.4 = .76 \qquad 1.0 - .82 = .18 \ldots$$

4. Find *pq* for each item by multiplying the results of Steps 2 and 3.

$$(.24)(.76) = .18 \qquad (.82)(.18) = .15 \ldots$$

5. Find Σpg by summing the results of Step 4 over the *N* items.

$$.18 + .15 + .23 + .24 + .24 + .06 = 1.1$$

6. Find S^2, which is the variance for the test sources. To do this, you need the scores for each individual in the group. The formula for the variance is

$$S^2 = \frac{\Sigma X^2 - \left[\dfrac{(\Sigma X)^2}{NS}\right]}{NS - 1}$$

In this example, $S^2 = 2.8$.

7. Find $S^2 - \Sigma pq$ by subtracting the result of Step 5 from that of Step 6.

$$2.8 - 1.1 = 1.7$$

8. Find $(S^2 - \Sigma pq)/S^2$ by dividing the result of Step 7 by that of Step 6.

$$\frac{1.7}{2.8} = .607$$

9. Find N or the number of items.

$$N = 6$$

10. Find $N/(N - 1)$ by dividing the result of Step 9 by Step 9 minus 1.

$$\frac{6}{5} = 1.2$$

11. Find KR_{20} by multiplying the results of Steps 8 and 10.

$$(1.2)(.607) = .73$$

Validity

LEARNING OBJECTIVES

When you have completed this chapter, you should be able to:

▶ Determine the relationship between establishing test validity and using the scientific method

▶ Explain why it is inappropriate to refer to so-called face validity as real evidence of validity

▶ List the categories of validity evidence recognized in the booklet *Standards for Educational and Psychological Testing*

▶ Tell how the strategy for establishing evidence for content validity differs from the strategy used to obtain evidence for other types of validity

▶ Discuss the difference between predictive and concurrent criterion validity evidence

▶ Relate the concept of the coefficient of determination (from Chapter 3) to the interpretation of the validity coefficient in criterion validity evidence

► Tell how to interpret the results of a test that, for example, had a validity coefficient of .35 for predicting success on a particular job

► List some of the issues to consider when you interpret a validity coefficient

► Know how to evaluate evidence for construct validity

► Select a hypothetical construct and describe how you would go about developing a measure for it

The case of Willie Griggs was argued before the U.S. Supreme Court in October 1970. Griggs and 12 other African American laborers were employees of the Dan River Steam Station of the Duke Power Company in Draper, North Carolina. The company classified Griggs and the other complainants as laborers whose primary work assignment was sweeping and cleaning. The men would have preferred promotion to the next higher classification level of coal handler. However, the company required a passing score on a general intelligence test for that promotion. Of the 95 employees at the power station, 14 were African American. Among the 14 African American workers, 13 were assigned to sweeping and cleaning duties. The main obstacle for the men who wanted to move up in the company was their performance on the test.

Because the test appeared to render ineligible a much higher proportion of African American employees than white ones, the power company was sued for engaging in discriminatory employment practice. The lawsuit centered on the meaning of the test scores. The power company managers argued that using the test "would improve the overall quality of the work force." They suggested that they did not intend to discriminate on the basis of race and that the test only helped them find the most capable employees (*Griggs v. Duke Power*, 1971).

In court, the power company was required to show why the test had meaning for the particular jobs within its establishment. In other words, the company had to prove that the test had a specific meaning for particular jobs such as laborer or coal handler. On hearing the arguments, the Supreme Court ruled that the tests served as "built-in head winds" for minority groups and had no meaning for the purpose of hiring or promoting workers to the classification of coal handler. In other words, the test did not measure specific job capabilities. The decision has been reaffirmed and eventually became the basis of the Civil Rights Bill of 1991.

As a result of the *Griggs v. Duke Power* decision, employers must provide evidence that a test used for the selection or promotion of employees has a specific meaning (Bills & Kaufman, 2016). In the field of testing, we refer to this meaning as *validity*. The meaning of a test is defined by specific evidence acquired by specific methods. Not only must there be evidence that a test has meaning in general, but also there must be evidence that it has validity for the particular situation in which it is applied. This evidence—not the word of a psychologist—is what establishes the meaning of a test. As in a legal court proceeding, a psychologist must obey specific rules of evidence in establishing that a test has a particular meaning for a specific purpose. This chapter reviews the rules of evidence that people use the most. Cases similar to the one involving Willie Griggs continue to be heard by the courts and some of these will be discussed in Chapter 20.

Obtaining data in validity studies is like gathering evidence for a court trial. For instance, psychologists always begin by assuming that there is no reason to believe a measure is valid. Evidence for validity comes from showing the association between the test and other variables. The rules strictly forbid saying there is a relationship without showing some proof, which is similar to the legal notion of innocent until proven guilty. Proof of guilt must be persuasive. In a similar manner, one must have convincing proof that there is a relationship between two variables before one justifiably touts the connection.

Psychologists and other professionals continually attempt to convince the public that their discipline is meaningful. Regarding psychological tests, certain segments of the public may have become too trusting. After you read this chapter, we hope that you can determine when test results are meaningful and when they are questionable.

Defining Validity

Validity can be defined as the agreement between a test score or measure and the quality it is believed to measure. Validity is sometimes defined as the answer to the question, "Does the test measure what it is supposed to measure?" To address this question, we use systematic studies to determine whether the conclusions from test results are justified by evidence. Throughout the 20th century, psychologists created many subcategories of validity. Definitions of validity blossomed, making it hard to determine whether psychologists who referred to different types of validity were really talking about different things. Though validity defined the meaning of tests and measures, the term itself was beginning to lose its meaning. In 1985, a joint committee of the American Educational Research Association (AERA), the American Psychological Association (APA), and the National Council on Measurement in Education (NCME) published a booklet entitled *Standards for Educational and Psychological Testing*. These standards were revised in 1999 and again in 2014 (Worrell & Roberson, 2016). The latest version of *Standards* is organized into three sections: foundations, operations, and applications. In many ways, this organization follows the way we have organized the eight editions of this book into principles, applications, and issues. In *Standards*, foundations is similar to our principles and focuses on basic psychometric concepts such as validity and reliability. Operations in the *Standards* considers how tests are designed and built and how they are administered, scored, and reported. It also reviews standards for test manuals and other documentation. The applications section of *Standards* takes on a wide range of issues, ranging from training required to administer and interpret tests. We shall refer to the standards frequently because they provide a sensible set of psychological test guidelines that have won approval by major professional groups (Reeves & Marbach-Ad, 2016).

In their original work, the joint committee set aside numerous possible definitions of validity by suggesting the following: Validity is the evidence for inferences made about a test score. There are three types of evidence: (1) construct related, (2) criterion related, and (3) content related. People have many other names for different aspects of validity, but most aspects can be seen in terms of these categories.

The most recent standards emphasize that validity is a unitary concept that represents all of the evidence that supports the intended interpretation of a measure.

The consensus document cautions against separating validity into subcategories such as content validity, predictive validity, and criterion validity. Though categories for grouping different types of validity are convenient, the use of categories does not imply that there are distinct forms of validity. Sometimes psychologists have been overly rigorous about making distinctions among categories when, indeed, the categories overlap (Reeves & Marbach-Ad, 2016).

Aspects of Validity

In this section, we discuss the three aspects of validity suggested by the joint committee. First, however, we address what some call *face validity*. The joint committee refused to recognize face validity as a legitimate category because it is not technically a form of validity. The term needs to be mentioned because it is commonly used in the testing literature.

Face Validity

Face validity is the mere appearance that a measure has validity. We often say a test has face validity if the items seem to be reasonably related to the perceived purpose of the test. For example, a scale to measure anxiety might include items such as "My stomach gets upset when I think about taking tests" and "My heart starts pounding fast whenever I think about all of the things I need to get done." On the basis of positive responses to these items, can we conclude that the person is anxious? Remember that validity requires evidence in order to justify conclusions. In this case, we can only conclude that the person answers these two items in a particular way. If we want to conclude that the person has a problem with anxiety, then we need systematic evidence that shows how responses to these items relate to the psychological condition of anxiety. Face validity is really not validity at all because it does not offer evidence to support conclusions drawn from test scores.

We are not suggesting that face validity is unimportant. In many settings, it is crucial to have a test that "looks like" it is valid. These appearances can help motivate test takers because they can see that the test is relevant. For example, suppose you developed a test to screen applicants for a training program in accounting. Items that ask about balance sheets and ledgers might make applicants more motivated than items about fuel consumption. However, both types of items might be testing the same arithmetic reasoning skill.

Content-Related Evidence for Validity

How many times have you studied for an examination and known almost everything only to find that the professor has come up with some strange items that do not represent the content of the course? If this has happened, you may have encountered a test with poor content-related evidence for validity. Content-related evidence for validity of a test or measure considers the adequacy of representation of the conceptual domain the test is designed to cover. For example, if you are being tested on the first six chapters of this book, then content-related evidence of validity is provided by the correspondence between the items on the test and the information in the chapters.

5.1 FOCUSED EXAMPLE

Challenging the Professor

Most professors have had the content validity evidence of their tests challenged at some time or other. A student may complain, "Your test did not give me an opportunity to demonstrate what I know" or "You assigned Chapters 1 through 5, but nearly all of the items came from Chapters 1 and 2—how can you evaluate whether we know anything about the other material we were supposed to read?" In the process of creating good and fair tests, professors should continually face this sort of questioning and attempt to create tests that will not evoke legitimate criticism. Good judgment is always required in test development: We can never get around the need for careful planning (Cureton, Cronbach, Meehl, Ebel, & Ward, 1996).

Traditionally, **content validity evidence** has been of greatest concern in educational testing (Gafni, 2016) and more recently in tests developed for medical settings (Edwards et al., 2016). The score on your history test should represent your comprehension of the history you are expected to know. Many factors can limit performance on history tests, however, making the professor's inferences about your knowledge less valid. These factors could include characteristics of the items (such as vocabulary words that some students do not understand) and the sampling of items (such as items on World War I in a test on ancient Chinese culture).

Because the boundaries between content and other types of evidence for validity are not clearly defined, we no longer think of content validity evidence as something separate from other types of validity evidence (Miller & Lovler, 2015). However, content validity evidence offers some unique features. For example, it is the only type of evidence besides face validity that is logical rather than statistical.

In looking for content validity evidence, we attempt to determine whether a test has been constructed adequately. (See Focused Example 5.1.) For example, we ask whether the items are a fair sample of the total potential content. Establishing content validity evidence for a test requires good logic, intuitive skills, and perseverance. The content of the items must be carefully evaluated. For example, test developers must consider the wording of the items and the appropriateness of the reading level (Kline, 2015; Messick, 1998a, 1998b). Determination of content validity evidence is often made by expert judgment. There are several methods for aggregating judgments into an index of content representation. Typically, multiple judges rate each item in terms of its match or relevance to the content (Edwards et al., 2016). Statistical methods such as factor analysis have also been used to determine whether items fit into conceptual domains (Brown, 2015).

Two new concepts that are relevant to content validity evidence were emphasized in the latest version of the standards for educational and psychological tests (Worrell & Roberson, 2016): construct underrepresentation and construct-irrelevant variance. *Construct underrepresentation* describes the failure to capture important components of a construct. For example, if a test of mathematical knowledge included algebra but not geometry, the validity of the test would be threatened by construct underrepresentation. *Construct-irrelevant variance* occurs when scores are influenced by factors irrelevant to the construct. For example, a test of intelligence might be influenced by reading comprehension, test anxiety, or illness.

Often, test scores reflect many factors besides what the test supposedly measures. For example, many students do poorly on tests because of anxiety or reading problems. A slow reader may get a low score on an examination because he or she did not have adequate time to read through all of the questions. Only by taking such factors into account can we make accurate generalizations about what the test score really means. Chapter 7 will present a more detailed discussion of this problem.

Criterion-Related Evidence for Validity

Folklore includes stories about fortune tellers who can look into crystal balls and see the future. Most people in our society do not believe that anyone can actually do this. When we want to know how well someone will do on a job, which students we should select for our graduate program, or who is most likely to get a serious disease, we often depend on psychological testing to forecast behavior and inclinations.

Criterion validity evidence tells us just how well a test corresponds with a particular criterion. Such evidence is provided by high correlations between a test and a well-defined criterion measure. A criterion is the standard against which the test is compared. For example, a test might be used to predict which engaged couples will have successful marriages and which ones will get divorced. Marital success is the criterion, but it cannot be known at the time the couples take the premarital test. The reason for gathering criterion validity evidence is that the test or measure is to serve as a "stand-in" for the measure we are really interested in. In the marital example, the premarital test serves as a stand-in for estimating future marital happiness.

Predictive and Concurrent Evidence

The forecasting function of tests is actually a type or form of criterion validity evidence known as **predictive validity evidence.** For example, the SAT Critical Reading Test serves as predictive validity evidence as a college admissions test if it accurately forecasts how well high-school students will do in their college studies. The SAT, including its quantitative and verbal subtests, is the *predictor variable*, and the college grade point average (GPA) is the *criterion*. The purpose of the test is to predict the likelihood of succeeding on the criterion—that is, achieving a high GPA in college. A valid test for this purpose would greatly help college admissions committees because they would have some idea about which students would most likely succeed. Unfortunately, many tests do not have exceptional prediction records, and we must search continually for better ways to predict outcomes.

Data from an analysis of scores from students at 110 colleges and universities that participated in the College Board's National SAT Validity Study (Korbin, 2008) suggest that high-school GPA remains the best predictor of first-year college GPA. The study had data on SAT scores obtained in 2006 and first-year GPAs obtained during the spring term of 2007. There were 195,099 participants in the study. Among these, 150,377 had data available on all of the elements needed to complete the analysis. However, the correlation is quite modest *(r = 0.36)*. Among the SAT components, the SAT Writing score correlates with first-year GPA at 0.33. SAT-Critical reading is slightly less correlated ($r = 0.29$), followed by SAT-Math ($r = 0.26$). A similar study that aggregated data for 169,818 students who completed the American College Test (ACT) and then entered a variety of different colleges also showed that high-school GPA was the best predictor of first-year college GPA ($r = 0.47$) followed by ACT overall score ($r = 0.38$). The results were very similar in highly selective and in less selective institutions (Westrick, Le, Robbins, Radunzel, & Schmidt, 2015).

Correcting for restricted range boosts the correlations significantly. Restricted range occurs when colleges do not have the full range of GPA scores or SAT scores because they select only the best students. This problem may reduce the level of observed correlation. When corrections for restricted range are made, correlations between the SAT components and first-year college GPA typically approach about $r = 0.50$ (Korbin, Sinharay, et al., 2011; Westrick et al., 2015). However, there is some debate about whether correction for a restricted range is appropriate.

Another type of evidence for criterion validity is concurrent. Concurrent-related evidence for validity comes from assessments of the simultaneous relationship between the test and the criterion—such as between a learning disability test and school performance. Here the measures and criterion measures are taken at the same time because the test is designed to explain why the person is now having difficulty in school. The test may give diagnostic information that can help guide the development of individualized learning programs. Concurrent evidence for validity applies when the test and the criterion can be measured at the same time.

Job samples provide a good example of the use of **concurrent validity evidence** (Highhouse, Doverspike, & Guion, 2015). Industrial psychologists often have to select employees on the basis of limited information. One method is to test potential employees on a sample of behaviors that represent the tasks to be required of them. Because these samples were shown to correlate well with performance on the job, the samples alone could be used for the selection and screening of applicants. Impressive results support the use of work samples for selecting employees in a variety of areas, including motor skills (Asher & Sciarrino, 1974) and work in the petroleum industry (Dunnette, 1972). However, samples seem to be more meaningful for blue-collar trades or jobs that require the manipulation of objects. They may not be equally meaningful for all jobs (Callinan & Robertson, 2000).

According to current standards for equal employment opportunity, employers must demonstrate that tasks used to test potential new employees relate to actual job performance (Larson, 2011). Thompson and Thompson (1982) reviewed 26 federal court decisions in which the validity of tests used to screen employees was challenged. The judgments in the various cases show that the job-related test must focus on tasks, should be in a written form, and must include several data sources with large samples. In other words, the courts require good scientific evidence that a test used to screen employees is valid in terms of how job candidates will perform if employed (Zedeck & Cascio, 1984). Similar validation processes are used in measures of mental health. Focused example 5.2 describes the process of validating a measure of depression.

Another use of concurrent validity evidence occurs when a person does not know how he or she will respond to the criterion measure. For example, suppose you do not know what occupation you want to enter. In each occupation, some people are happy and others are less satisfied. The Strong Interest Inventory (SII) uses as

5.2 FOCUSED EXAMPLE

Validation of a Self-Report Measure of Depression

In Chapters 2, 3, and 4, we offered some data on depression based on the Center for Epidemiologic Studies Depression Scale (CES-D). The CES-D is a general measure of depressive symptoms that has been used extensively in epidemiologic studies (Weissman, Sholomskas, Pottenger, Prusoff, & Locke, 1977). Recall that the scale includes 20 items and taps dimensions of depressed mood, feelings of guilt and worthlessness, appetite loss, sleep disturbance, and energy level. These items are assumed to represent all the major components of depressive symptomatology. Sixteen of the items are worded negatively, whereas the other four are worded positively to avoid the possibility of patterned responses. The respondents are asked to report how often they experienced a particular "symptom" during the past week on a 4-point scale: 0 (rarely or none of the time—less than 1 day), 1 (some or a little of the time—1 to 2 days), 2 (occasionally or a moderate amount of the time—3 or 4 days), and 3 (most or all of the time—5 to 7 days). The responses to the four positive items are reverse scored. Scores on the CES-D scale can range from 0 to 60, with scores greater than 18 suggesting clinically significant levels of depression.

Validity studies have demonstrated that the CES-D is highly correlated with other measures of depression. For example, one validity study demonstrated significant correlations with the more complete Beck Depression Inventory. The CES-D, however, was designed for studies of nonpsychiatric populations (Gottlib & Cine, 1989). A series of studies have demonstrated that the CES-D is associated with clinical diagnoses of depression; however, the CES-D is a better screening instrument than diagnostic tool. Lewinsohn and Teri (1982) demonstrated that scores of less than 16 on the CES-D were highly associated with clinical judgments of nondepression. Conversely, scores of 17 or greater had only a moderate association with psychiatric diagnoses of depression.

Because the CES-D has only moderate evidence of validity for the evaluation of clinical depression, one needs more complex methods for such evaluations. It has been suggested that as much as 3% of the population experiences major depressive problems at any given time. The diagnosis of major depressive disorder involves three components:

1. A clinician identifies a series of specific symptoms.
2. The symptoms persist for at least 2 weeks.
3. The diagnosis is not ruled out for another reason.

A diagnosis of depression thus requires the active involvement of a trained psychiatrist or psychologist. Most measures of depression do not provide enough information for anyone to make such a complex judgment.

M. Zimmerman and Coryell (1987) have offered a 22-item self-report scale that can be used to diagnose major depressive disorder. They suggest that the scale may give an accurate estimate of the prevalence of these problems in the general population. Thus, researchers can estimate the proportion of the

criteria patterns of interest among people who are satisfied with their careers. (See Chapter 16.) Then the patterns of interest for people taking the tests before they have chosen an occupation are matched to patterns of interest among people who are happy in various occupations. Vocational interests are better predictors of perceived job fit than are personality characteristics (Ehrhart & Makransky, 2007).

Validity Coefficient

The relationship between a test and a criterion is usually expressed as a correlation called a *validity coefficient*. This coefficient tells the extent to which the test is valid for making statements about the criterion.

general population that suffers from depression but not incur the expense of having a psychiatrist or psychologist interview large samples. Zimmerman and Coryell call their measure the Inventory to Diagnose Depression (IDD). The IDD includes 22 items. For each item, the person records a score of 0 (which represents no disturbance) through 4 (which indicates that the symptom is present). The numbers 1, 2, and 3 suggest different gradations of the symptom. For example, the IDD item about insomnia includes the following choices:

0 = I am not sleeping less than usual.

1 = I occasionally have slight difficulty sleeping.

2 = I clearly don't sleep as well as usual.

3 = I sleep about half my normal amount of time.

4 = I sleep less than 2 hours per night.

The IDD also considers whether the symptoms have been present for less than or more than 2 weeks. Some of the depressive symptoms considered by the IDD are decreased energy, decreased interest in sex, guilt, weight gain, anxiety, irritability, and weight loss.

Although the IDD seems to measure the concept of depression (face validity), systematic evidence obtained in validity studies is required. In other words, we need to ask, "What is the evidence that self-reports on this scale actually measure depression?"

The first step in establishing the validity of the IDD is to demonstrate that it is related to other measures designed to assess depression. For example, studies have shown it to be significantly correlated with the Hamilton Rating Scale for Depression in 234 adults ($r = .80$), the Beck Depression Inventory in 234 adults ($r = .87$), and the Carroll Depression Scale in 105 adults ($r = .81$). In addition, reports of the experience of specific symptoms on the IDD were systematically related to clinicians' judgments of individual symptoms for the same patients.

In another study, first-degree relatives of patients with psychiatric disorders were interviewed using a highly structured system known as the *diagnostic interview schedule*. The system uses a computer program to generate diagnoses for specific disorders. In 97.2% of the 394 cases, the IDD gave the same diagnostic classification of depression as did the more complex interview. Though the detailed interview identified some cases not detected by the IDD, the estimates of the rates of major depression assessed with the IDD came quite close to those found in major studies of the general population. In other studies, the IDD has helped gain an understanding of some of the determinants of depression. For example, 4332 women who had recently given birth completed the IDD. The study demonstrated that postpartum depression was significantly more common among low-income women in comparison to those with more financial resources. Postpartum depression was also associated with lower occupational prestige and having more children at home (Segre, O'Hara, Arndt, & Stuart, 2007).

There are many other measures of depression besides the IDD. However, most of these are not designed to make the specific diagnosis of major depressive disorder. Discriminant evidence for validity demonstrates the advantage of the IDD over other approaches. In particular, other measures do not feed directly into the DSM-IV classification system.

There are no hard-and-fast rules about how large a validity coefficient must be to be meaningful. In practice, one rarely sees a validity coefficient larger than .60, and validity coefficients in the range of .30 to .40 are commonly considered adequate. A coefficient is statistically significant if the chances of obtaining its value by chance alone are quite small: usually less than 5 in 100. For example, suppose that the SAT had a validity coefficient of .40 for predicting GPA at a particular university. Because this coefficient is likely to be statistically significant, we can say that the SAT score tells us more about how well people will do in college than we would know by chance.

College students differ in their academic performance for many reasons. You probably could easily list a dozen. Because there are so many factors that contribute

5.3 FOCUSED EXAMPLE

The Testing Industry and the Public: A Brief History of Controversy

Aptitude testing has become a major industry. Most college-bound high-school students must take the SAT or the American College Test (ACT). Often these tests are taken several times. In addition, students often take subject area tests (SAT-II) and enroll in preparation courses, such as the Princeton Review or the Stanley Kaplan preparation class.

Concern about the power of the testing industry is not new. Ralph Nader, an aggressive attorney and consumer advocate, earned a solid reputation over the years for his attacks on giant corporations, including automobile manufacturers and food producers. Nader "exposed" the misdeeds of corporations to the public. Early in 1980, Nader released the results of his 6-year investigation of the Educational Testing Service (ETS)—the largest test producer in the United States. At a press conference, he exclaimed, "What this report makes clear is that ETS's claims to measure aptitude and predict success are false and unsubstantiated and can be described as a specialized kind of fraud" (Kaplan, 1982).

What Nader disputed was the use of ETS tests such as the SAT and Graduate Record Examination (GRE) as evidence for predictive validity. The data used by Nader and his team of researchers were no different from those used by ETS officials; however, the way Nader chose to interpret the data was markedly different. ETS has consistently reported that the SAT, for example, accounts for a small but significant percentage of the variance in first-year college grade point averages. Nader did not interpret the results in the typical terms of percentage of variance. Instead, he reported the percentage of cases the test successfully predicted according to his own criteria. On the basis of this approach, he concluded that the test predicted successfully in only 12% of the cases; however, Nader's calculations were not based on an appropriate statistical model (Kaplan, 1982, 1985). On the basis of his interpretation, Nader suggested that there should be more regulation of the testing industry. Referring to ETS, he explained, "They have assumed a rare kind of corporate power, the power to change the way people think about their own potential, and through the passive acceptance of their test scores by admissions officers, to decide who will be granted and who will be denied access to education and career opportunities" [from *APA Monitor*, 1980, *11*(2), 1-7].

Though Nader uncovered an important problem, it is not certain that the ETS deserves all of the blame. ETS puts out its own guidelines for the use of the SAT and other tests. Designed to be read by college admissions officers, these booklets clearly acknowledge the limitations of the tests. For example, college administrators are told that the test accounts for a small but significant percentage of the variation in college performance, and they are advised to look at other criteria in addition to test scores. Thus, much of the problem lies with admissions committees and with college

to college performance, it would be too much to expect the SAT to explain all of the variation. The question we must ask is "How *much* of the variation in college performance will we be able to predict on the basis of SAT scores?"

The validity coefficient squared is the percentage of variation in the criterion that we can expect to know in advance because of our knowledge of the test scores. Thus, we will know .40 squared, or 16%, of the variation in college performance because of the information we have from the SAT test. This is the coefficient of determination that was discussed in Chapter 3. The remainder of the variation in college performance is actually the greater proportion: 84% of the total variation is still unexplained. In other words, when students arrive at college, most of the reasons they perform differently will be a mystery to college administrators and professors. (See Focused Examples 5.3 and 5.4.) In many circumstances, using a test

administrators who passively accept SAT scores as the ultimate predictor of college performance. However, the Nader report started the process of questioning the value of testing. Personnel testing is now more closely regulated (Tenopyr, 1998), and some people have seriously questioned aptitude testing.

In 1997, President Bill Clinton proposed to create voluntary national tests in reading and mathematics. The Clinton proposal aroused considerable debate about the value of tests. As a result, the administration and Congress asked the National Research Council of the prestigious National Academy of Sciences to study test use. In 1999, the committee released a report entitled *High Stakes: Testing for Tracking, Promotion, and Graduation*. Although generally supportive of testing, the report raised some of the same issues originally surfaced by Nader. In particular, the National Academy expressed concern that test results are commonly misinterpreted and that misunderstanding of test results can damage individuals (Heubert & Hauser, 1999).

In response to these criticisms, a new SAT was released in 2005 for the entering college classes of 2006. The SAT verbal section was replaced by a new test called *Critical Reading*. The SAT no longer uses analogies and instead focuses on reading short passages. A new writing section was also added to the test. It includes both multiple-choice questions on grammar and a written essay. Further, the SAT math section was completely revised. Previously, the SAT math section covered only geometry and algebra I. Because so many more high-school students take advanced math,

the new math section covers 3 years of high-school math and includes material covered in Algebra II.

By 2016, the rebellion against standardized tests had gained significant momentum. Colleges and universities began challenging the value of testing for making admissions decisions. According to the website, "FairTest," more than 850 institutions are now test optional. This means that taking the SAT or ACT is no longer required of all applicants. In 2015 alone, 47 major institutions announced new test optional policies. Institutions deciding they would stop requiring tests included some of the most elite and selective universities in the country.

The decision to go test optional was supported by systematic research. William Hiss, a former Dean of admissions at Bates College published an evaluation involving 33 private and public universities that had adopted a test optional policy. It had been assumed that those who got into college without test score evidence would be less likely to perform well or to graduate. The data did not confirm this belief. Hiss found there was no difference in graduation rates between those submitting test scores and those who did not. Further, cumulative GPA for those who submitted test scores (2.88) were not statistically distinguishable from GPAs of students who did not submit test scores (2.83). On the other hand, those who did not submit test scores were more likely to be first-generation college attenders and to be from underrepresented ethnic and minority groups (Hiss & Franks, 2014). Going test optional may result in a more diversified student body without reducing academic preparedness.

is not worth the effort because it contributes only a few percentage points to the understanding of variation in a criterion. However, low validity coefficients (.30 to .40) can sometimes be especially useful even though they may explain only 10% of the variation in the criterion. For example, Dunnette (1967) demonstrated how a simple questionnaire used for military screening could save taxpayers millions of dollars every month even though the validity was not remarkably high. Landy, Farr, and Jacobs (1982) found that a performance evaluation and feedback system for computer programmers with a validity of .30 could translate into increased earnings of $5.3 million in 1 year. If we adjust for inflation between 1983 and 2016, $5.3 million in 1983 is equal to about $12.7 million in 2016. In some circumstances, though, a validity coefficient of .30 or .40 means almost nothing. In Chapter 18, we show how validity coefficients are translated into specific decision models and how industrial psychologists use information about test validity to save money (Landy, 2003; Landy & Shankster, 1994). Focused Example 5.5 discusses the validity of tests used in the medical field.

Evaluating Validity Coefficients

To be an informed consumer of testing information, you should learn to review carefully any information offered by a test developer. Because not all validity coefficients of .40 have the same meaning, you should watch for several things in evaluating such information. We will cover some of these issues here and go into more depth in Chapter 7.

In its booklet *Standards for Educational and Psychological Testing*, the joint committee of the AERA, the APA, and the NCME (2014) lists several issues of concern when interpreting validity coefficients. Here are some of its recommendations.

Look for Changes in the Cause of Relationships   Be aware that the conditions of a validity study are never exactly reproduced. For example, if you take the GRE to gain admission to graduate school, the conditions under which you take the test may not be exactly the same as those in the studies that established the validity of the GRE. Many things may differ, including the way grades are assigned in graduate school and the population taking the test.

The logic of criterion validation presumes that the causes of the relationship between the test and the criterion will still exist when the test is in use. Though this presumption is true for the most part, there may be circumstances under which the relationship changes. For example, a test might be used and shown to be valid

---

5.4 FOCUSED EXAMPLE

Why the University of California Rejected the SAT-I

In 2001, Richard Atkinson, a psychologist and president of the University of California (UC) system, proposed that the statewide university no longer require the SAT Reasoning Test (SAT-I) for freshman admission. This made the University of California the first major university system to reject the use of the SAT-I. The decision was based on a major study of 78,000 first-time UC freshmen. The study compared the SAT-I with the SAT-II. The SAT-I is the traditional test that evaluates reasoning ability, while the SAT-II is an achievement test that evaluates student knowledge in particular areas.

The study found that the SAT-II achievement tests were consistently better predictors of grades during the freshman year than was the SAT-I. In fact, controlling for SAT-II and high-school grades, the SAT-I contributes little or nothing to the prediction of first-year grades in the university. Furthermore, the study found that SAT-I scores were more sensitive to the socioeconomic background of students than were SAT-II scores. When compared against students with similar socioeconomic backgrounds, the SAT-I was unable to predict college performance. However, even after statistically controlling for socioeconomic background, the SAT-II remained a good predictor.

To learn more about this issue, see http://www.ucop.edu/pathways/ucnotes/march05/news1.html.

for selecting supervisors in the industry; however, the validity study may have been done at a time when all the employees were men, making the test valid for selecting supervisors for male employees. If the company hires female employees, then the test may no longer be valid for selecting supervisors because it may not consider the abilities necessary to supervise a sexually mixed group of employees.

What Does the Criterion Mean?   Criterion-related validity studies mean nothing at all unless the criterion is valid and reliable. Some test constructors attempt to correlate their tests with other tests that have unknown validity. A meaningless group of items that correlates well with another meaningless group remains meaningless.

For applied research, the criterion should relate specifically to the use of the test. Because the SAT attempts to predict performance in college, the appropriate criterion is GPA, a measure of college performance. Any other inferences made on the basis of the SAT require additional evidence. For example, if you want to say that the SAT tells you something about adaptability, then you must obtain evidence on the relationship between the SAT and a separate measure of adaptability.

Review the Subject Population in the Validity Study   Another reason to be cautious of validity coefficients is that the validity study might have been done on a population that does not represent the group to which inferences will be made. For example, some researchers have debated whether validity coefficients for intelligence

5.5 FOCUSED EXAMPLE

The Cholesterol Test: Predictive Validity Evidence

The concept of predictive validity evidence applies to medical tests as well as to psychological measures. A major issue in contemporary public health is the relationship between cholesterol levels and death from heart disease. Systematic studies have demonstrated that high levels of cholesterol in the blood can help predict early death from heart disease and stroke. To learn more about these problems, physicians take blood samples to examine cholesterol levels. To evaluate this information, they must consider the relationship between the test (blood cholesterol level) and the criterion (premature death). Although this relationship has been established in many studies, the level of association is actually quite low. Some studies show the relationship to fall near 0.10, or to account for about 1% of the variance in mortality.

Furthermore, those with high levels of blood cholesterol are advised to eat foods low in saturated fats and cholesterol. However, some systematic studies have failed to find strong, statistically significant relationships between these dietary habits and mortality rates (Stallones, 1983). These low-validity coefficients suggest that these measures tell us little about what can be predicted for a particular individual. However, heart disease is a profoundly serious problem for the general population. Each year, more than 600,000 Americans die of these problems. Thus, even weak associations help explain a significant number of cases. As a society, if we reduce blood cholesterol levels, there will be a significant reduction in the number of deaths associated with cholesterol. The low correlation between cholesterol tests and heart disease suggests that we cannot say precisely which specific individuals will benefit. However, the small but significant statistical relationship tells us that there is some important predictive value in cholesterol tests (Clarke et al., 2007; Golomb, Stattin, & Mednick, 2000; Kaplan & Golomb, 2001).

and personnel tests that are based primarily on white samples are accurate when used to test African American students (Daley & Onwuegbuzie, 2011; Murphy, 2003b; Sackett, 2003). We review this problem in detail in Chapter 19.

In industrial settings, attrition can seriously jeopardize validity studies. Those who do poorly on the job either drop out or get fired and thus cannot be studied when it comes time to do the job assessment. If there was a group that did well on the test but failed on the job, then it might not be represented and could be systematically eliminated from the study because the workers were already off the job by the time the assessment came around.

Be Sure the Sample Size Was Adequate

Another problem to look for is a validity coefficient that is based on a small number of cases. Sometimes a proper validity study cannot be done because there are too few people to study. A common practice is to do a small validity study with the people available. Unfortunately, such a study can be quite misleading. You cannot depend on a correlation obtained from a small sample, particularly for multiple correlation and multiple regression. The smaller the sample, the more likely chance variation in the data will affect the correlation. Thus, a validity coefficient based on a small sample tends to be artificially inflated.

A good validity study will present some evidence for cross validation. A cross validation study assesses how well the test actually forecasts performance for an independent group of subjects.[1] In other words, the initial validity study assesses the relationship between the test and the criterion, whereas the cross validation study checks how well this relationship holds for an independent group of subjects. The larger the sample size in the initial study, the better the likelihood that the relationship will cross validate.

Never Confuse the Criterion with the Predictor

In at least one university, students are required to meet a certain cutoff score on the GRE before they can be admitted to a graduate program. Occasionally, the department admits a student who did not get the cutoff score and these students go on to complete all of the requirements for graduation. But it still requires the student to meet the minimum GRE score before it confers a degree. The logic behind this policy represents a clear misunderstanding of the test and its purpose.

In this case, the GRE is the predictor, and success in graduate school is the criterion. The only reason for using the test in the first place is to help select students who have the highest probability of success in the program. By completing the program, the students have already succeeded on the criterion (success in the program). Before the university would acknowledge that the students indeed had succeeded, the students had to go back and demonstrate that they would have been predicted to do well on the criterion. This reflects a clear confusion between predictor and criterion. Further, most of the students provisionally admitted because of low GRE scores succeeded by completing the program.

---

[1]Correct cross validation methodology requires that the raw score weights from the original sample be applied to the validation sample (Hand, 2011; Raykov & Marcoulides, 2010).

Check for Restricted Range on Both Predictor and Criterion A variable has a "restricted range" if all scores for that variable fall very close together. For example, the GPAs of graduate students in Ph.D. programs tend to fall within a limited range of the scale—usually above 3.5 on a 4-point scale. The problem this creates is that correlation depends on variability. If all the people in your class have a GPA of 4.0, then you cannot predict variability in graduate-school GPA. Correlation requires that there be variability in both the predictor and the criterion.

One major problem with the GRE is that it does not correlate well with graduate-school GPAs. Sternberg and Williams (1997) did a detailed study of predictors of success among Yale psychology graduate students. They found that GRE verbal scores were weakly correlated with GPA at Yale ($r = 0.17$) but that GRE quantitative scores were not significant predictors of graduate-school performance. Further GRE scores were not significantly related to faculty ratings of analytical skills, creativity, practicality, research skills, teaching skills, or the quality of doctoral dissertations. Some studies make a strong argument in favor of the GRE, but the results are actually quite similar. For example, Kuncel and colleagues aggregated results from 100 studies involving more than 10,000 students. When predicting first-year graduate GPA in doctoral programs, the predictive validity of the GRE Verbal and GRE Quantitative was statistically significant, but quite modest (GRE-Verbal $r = .22$, GRE-Quantitative $r = .24$). Of course, GPA is not the best criterion for graduate school success. Yet ratings of student performance by faculty were in the same range (GRE-Verbal $r = .23$, GRE-Quantitative $r = .20$) (Kuncel, Wee, Serafin, & Hezlett, 2010). Other measures, such as career success, are rarely available.

There are at least three explanations for the modest performance of the GRE for predicting graduate-school performance. First, the GRE may not be a valid test for selecting graduate students. Second, those students who are admitted to graduate school represent such a restricted range of ability that it is not possible to find significant correlations. Students with low GRE scores are usually not admitted to graduate school and, therefore, are not considered in validity studies. Third, grades in graduate school often represent a restricted range. Once admitted, students in graduate programs usually receive As and Bs. A grade of C is usually considered a failing grade. Although the restricted-range problem cannot be ruled out, many studies do show substantial variability in GRE scores and in graduate-school grades. Even in the study of the prestigious Yale program, GRE verbal scores ranged from 250 to 800 (mean = 653), and GRE quantitative scores ranged from 320 to 840 (mean = 672). Ratings by professors had substantial variability (Sternberg & Williams, 1997).

In addition to graduate schools, most schools of veterinary medicine use the GRE. Because veterinary schools are larger than most graduate programs, estimating veterinary school success from the GRE provides a good opportunity for study. There are 27 schools of veterinary medicine in the United States. One study obtained data from approximately 1400 students who had applied to 16 schools. The study suggested that undergraduate GPA is the best predictor of grades in veterinary school ($r = .53$). The correlation for the GRE-V verbal was 0.41; the correlation for the quantitative portion of the GRE (GRE-Q) was 0.47; and the correlation for the analytic section (GRE-A) was 0.45. The authors of the study corrected for the restricted range and measurement error in the GRE. As would be expected, these validity coefficients increase with these corrections (Powers, 2001). However, not all reviewers believe that correction is appropriate. In summary, even the best evidence suggests that GRE accounts for only one fifth of the variation in veterinary school success ($0.47^2 = 0.22$).

Review Evidence for Validity Generalization   Criterion-related validity evidence obtained in one situation may not be generalized to other similar situations. *Generalizability* refers to the evidence that the findings obtained in one situation can be generalized—that is, applied to other situations. This is an issue of empirical study rather than judgment. In other words, we must prove that the results obtained in a validity study are not specific to the original situation. There are many reasons why results may not be generalized. For example, there may be differences in the way the predictor construct is measured or in the type of job or curriculum involved—in the actual criterion measure—between the groups of people who take the test; there may also be differences in the time period—year or month—when the test is administered. Because of these problems, we cannot always be certain that the validity coefficient reported by a test developer will be the same for our particular situation. An employer, for example, might use a work sample test based on information reported in the manual, yet the situation in which he or she uses the test may differ from the situations of the original validation studies. When using the test, the employer might be using different demographic groups or different criterion measures or else predicting performance on a similar but different task. Generalizations from the original validity studies to these other situations should be made only on the basis of new evidence.

Consider Differential Prediction   Predictive relationships may not be the same for all demographic groups. The validity for men could differ in some circumstances from the validity for women. Or the validity of the test may be questionable because it is used for a group whose native language is not English, even though the test was validated for those who spoke only English. Under these circumstances, separate validity studies for different groups may be necessary. This issue will be discussed in more detail in Chapter 19.

Although criterion-related validity evidence is common in psychological and educational research, it simply does not apply in some instances. By definition, the criterion must be the most accurate measure of the phenomenon if it is to serve as the "gold standard." If a criterion exists, then only greater practicality or less expense justifies the use of concurrent measures as proxies or substitutes for the criterion. If the criterion is not a superior measure, then failure of correspondence by any new measure may reveal a defect in the criterion itself. For example, studies on the validity of measures of general health have been hindered because a clear criterion of health has never been defined (Kaplan, 2002). The development of a health index helped define the meaning of the term *health*. Often work on a psychological test involves the simultaneous development of a concept and the instrumentation to measure the concept. This cannot be accomplished by criterion-related validity studies. Instead, we need a more involved approach that involves construct-related evidence for validity.

Construct-Related Evidence for Validity

Before 1950, most social scientists considered only criterion and content evidence for validity. By the mid-1950s, investigators concluded that no clear criteria existed for most of the social and psychological characteristics they wanted to measure. Developing a measure of intelligence, for example, was difficult because no one could say for certain what intelligence was. Studies of criterion validity evidence would require that a specific criterion of intelligence be established against which tests could be compared. However, there was no criterion for intelligence because it is a hypothetical construct. A *construct* is defined as something built by mental synthesis. As a construct, intelligence does not exist as a separate thing we can touch or feel, so it cannot be used as an objective criterion.

Contemporary psychologists often want to measure intelligence, love, curiosity, or mental health. None of these constructs are clearly defined, and there is no established criterion against which psychologists can compare the accuracy of their tests. These are the truly challenging problems in measurement.

Construct validity evidence is established through a series of activities in which a researcher simultaneously defines some construct and develops the instrumentation to measure it. This process is required when "no criterion or universe of content is accepted as entirely adequate to define the quality to be measured" (Cronbach & Meehl, 1955, p. 282; Sackett, 2003). Construct validation involves assembling evidence about what a test means. This is done by showing the relationship between a test and other tests and measures. Each time a relationship is demonstrated, one additional bit of meaning can be attached to the test. Over a series of studies, the meaning of the test gradually begins to take shape. The gathering of construct validity evidence is an ongoing process that is similar to amassing support for a complex scientific theory. Although no single set of observations provides crucial or critical evidence, many observations over time gradually clarify what the test means. An example of construct validity evidence is given in Focused Example 5.6.

Years ago, D. T. Campbell and Fiske (1959) introduced an important set of logical considerations for establishing evidence of construct validity. They distinguished between two types of evidence essential for a meaningful test: convergent and discriminant. To argue that a test has meaning, a test constructor must be armed with as much of these two types of evidence as possible.

Convergent Evidence

When a measure correlates well with other tests believed to measure the same construct, **convergent evidence** for validity is obtained. This sort of evidence shows that measures of the same construct *converge*, or narrow in, on the same thing. In many ways, convergent evidence that is also construct validity evidence is like criterion validity evidence. In each case, scores on the test are related to scores on some other measure. In the case of convergent evidence for construct-related validity, however, there is no criterion to define what we are attempting to measure. Criterion-related evidence for validity is fine for situations in which we are attempting to predict performance on a particular variable, such as success in graduate school. Here the task is well defined, and all we need to do is find the items that are good predictors of this graduate-school criterion. Because there is no well-defined criterion in construct-related validity, the meaning of the test comes to be defined by the variables it can be shown to be associated with.

The Meaning of Love

An interesting example of construct validity evidence comes from the work of Zick Rubin (1970, 1973), who noted that love has been one of the most discussed issues of all time. Throughout history, men and women have written and sung about love more than any other topic. The index to Bartlett's *Familiar Quotations* shows that references to love are second only to citations to "man" (with "love" cited 769 times and "man" cited 843 times). All this preoccupation with love, however, has not led to a better understanding of its true meaning. Perhaps it is something we can feel but not necessarily understand well enough to describe in a definite way.

In the mid-1970s, there was a famous trial in Los Angeles in which singer Michelle Triola Marvin sued actor Lee Marvin for half the earnings he gained while the couple lived together. A major issue in the trial was the couple's unmarried status during the period in which the earnings occurred. During the trial, Lee's attorney questioned the actor about the extent to which he loved Michelle while they lived together. If he had been asked his height, he could have used the scale of inches. But love? How could he put that into a number? The actor instead resorted to a gas-tank analogy. He said his love for the singer was like when you are driving your car and you look over at your gas gauge and find it "about half full." That is about how much he loved Michelle—about half a tank. If there had been a measure of love, he would not have needed to use such a vague analogy (Rubin, 1979).

In developing his love scale, Rubin first had to create a list of items that represented all the different things people might call love. This was not an easy task because we all have different ideals. To create a measure of love, Rubin had to condense conventional wisdom about loving and liking into sets of statements to which people could respond on a scale. He eventually developed statements that subjects could agree or disagree with on a 5-point scale (where 1 is for strong disagreement and 5 is for strong agreement).

Collecting a set of items for construct validation is not easy because we never know which items eventually will be relevant to the construct we are attempting to measure. Building the love scale was particularly difficult in this regard. To prepare his measure, Rubin read extensively about love. Elizabeth Barrett Browning wrote, "How do I love thee? Let me count the ways." Indeed, after reading the many diverse views of love, Rubin hardly knew where to begin counting. However, because this was a study in construct validity evidence, it was important that Rubin consider counting. Construct validity evidence requires that there be content validity evidence. Content validity evidence in turn requires that the items fully represent the domain of inference (in this case, love). All the ways that love is defined by different people must be included in this collection.

Rubin began his study with his sets of statements that people could respond to on a scale ranging from disagreement to agreement. Some of the items were intended to measure love, whereas others were supposed to tap liking. Next, he gave the pool of items to 198 students from the University of Michigan. Each item had a blank in which a name could be filled in.

An example of the need to obtain construct validation evidence comes from studies that attempt to define and measure the construct "health," a complex concept. Because of this complexity, no single measure can serve as the criterion against which a measure of health can be assessed. This situation requires establishment of evidence for construct validity. Some of the construct validation studies were used to demonstrate the convergent validity evidence for the measure of health that the authors called a *health index.*

Convergent evidence is obtained in one of two ways. In the first, we show that a test measures the same things as other tests used for the same purpose. In the second, we demonstrate specific relationships that we can expect if the test is

The students responded to the questions twice, one time filling in the name of their lover and another time filling in the name of a friend. Then the items were subjected to factor analysis. Recall from Chapter 3 that this is a method for reducing a large number of items or variables into smaller and more manageable composites of items called *factors*.

In the love scale, three factors were obtained: attachment, caring, and intimacy. The items on the attachment scale emphasized desire to be with the loved person or to seek him or her out if lonely. The caring scale included items about empathy and concern for the loved person's welfare. The intimacy scale considered exclusive aspects of the relationship— for example, the willingness to confide in him or her about intimate personal problems. The items on the liking scale focused on favorable aspects of the other person along such dimensions as adjustment, maturity, good judgment, and intelligence.

The data from these scales were subjected to several statistical procedures that helped discriminate between the responses of lovers and friends and eventually led to the establishment of two measures: a love scale and a liking scale. With these measures of liking and loving in hand, Rubin next had to determine whether they were really measuring what they were supposed to measure. One study using the test with dating couples suggested that loving and liking were not necessarily related. There was a modest relationship between scores on the two scales, which was weaker for women than for men. This suggested, especially for women, that we can love someone we do not particularly like.

Several things indicated that the love scale really was measuring "love." For example, men and women scored higher on the love scale when they filled in the names of their lovers than when they filled in the name of a same-sex friend (all were assumed to be heterosexual). There also was a substantial correlation between love scale scores and estimates of the likelihood of marriage. The greater the love score, the more probable marriage was considered to be.

Finally, some of the dating couples were separated into groups of "strong love" (high love scores) and "weak love" (low love scores). From behind a one-way mirror, the researchers noted how much eye contact the lovers had with each other. Strong lovers spent more time simply gazing into each other's eyes than did weak lovers. When paired with a strong opposite-sex lover from another couple, strong lovers made no more mutual eye contact than did weak lovers.

In summary, Rubin began his study of love with neither a clear definition of love nor a method of measuring it. Through a series of structured exercises, he gradually came to have a better grasp of the construct. For example, he discovered that lovers mark some items differently than do couples who are just friends. He also discovered that "love" may have at least three independent components. Once the basic scale was developed, each new application defined a new meaning. For instance, one study showed that the scale predicts how much time lovers will spend gazing into each other's eyes. Thus, in future applications of the love scale, we would expect couples who score as strong lovers (for one another) to spend much time in mutual gazing.

really doing its job. The studies on the health index included both types of evidence. In demonstrating the meaning of the health index, the authors continually asked themselves, "If we were really measuring health, which relationships would we expect to observe between the health index and other measures?" The simplest relationship, between health index scores and the way people rate their own health status, was strong and clearly showed that the index captured some of the same information that individuals used to evaluate their own health. However, a good measure must go beyond this simple bit of validity evidence because self-ratings are unreliable. If they were not, then we would use self-perceived health status itself as the index of health and not bother to develop another health index.

In construct validity evidence, no single variable can serve as the criterion. In the case of the health index, other studies were used to show a variety of other relationships. For example, people who scored as less healthy on the health index also tended to report more symptoms and chronic medical conditions. The authors also hypothesized that health status would be related to age, and they observed that these two variables were indeed systematically related: Older people in the sample tended to have a lower health status than did younger people.

The researchers also evaluated specific hypotheses based on certain theoretical notions about the construct. In the health index studies, the authors reasoned that "if the index really measures health, then we would expect that people who score low on the measure will visit doctors more often." A study confirming that those scoring lower on health status visited doctors more often provided evidence for one more inference. Also, certain groups (such as disabled people) should have lower average scores on the index than do other groups (such as nondisabled people). Again, a study confirmed this hypothesis (Kaplan, Ganiats, Sieber, & Anderson, 1998; Fryback et al., 2007).

In another series of studies, investigators argued that a health index should correlate with specific physiological measures representing disease states. In one study, for example, patients with chronic lung diseases took measures of lung function. These measures were more strongly correlated with the general health index than they were with a variety of other physiological and social variables (Kaplan & Ries, 2007). Other studies demonstrated that the measures were related to clinical indicators of arthritis, Alzheimer's disease, depression, schizophrenia, and other conditions. If a health index really measures health, then treatments designed to improve health should be reflected by changes in the measure. In one study, patients with arthritis underwent a new treatment believed to remedy their condition. The general health index demonstrated the significant improvements caused by the treatment (Bombardier, Ware, Russell, et al., 1986). Other studies showed the measure was related to improvements in conditions such as Alzheimer's disease (Kerner, Patterson, Grant, & Kaplan, 1998), schizophrenia (Patterson et al., 1996), arthritis (Groessl, Kaplan, & Cronan, 2003), diseases of the veins (Kaplan, Criqui, Denenberg, Bergan, & Fronek, 2003), depression (Pyne et al., 2003), aging (Groessl et al., 2007), and several other conditions (Kaplan & Ries, 2007).

A series of studies thus expanded the number of meanings that could be given to the health index. Yet, convergent validity evidence does not constitute all of the evidence necessary to argue for the meaning of a psychological test or measure. In this case, we also must have discriminant evidence (see Focused Example 5.7).

Discriminant Evidence

Scientists often confront other scientists with difficult questions such as, "Why should we believe your theory if we already have a theory that seems to say the same thing?" An eager scientist may answer this question by arguing that his or her theory is distinctive and better. In testing, psychologists face a similar challenge. Why should they create a new test if there is already one available to do the job? Thus, one type of evidence a person needs in test validation is proof that the test measures something unique. For example, if a health index measures the same thing that self-ratings of health, symptoms, and chronic medical conditions measure, then why

5.7 FOCUSED EXAMPLE

Construct Validity of the Women's Health Initiative Insomnia Rating Scale

A brief measure known as the Women's Health Initiative Insomnia Rating Scale (WHIIRS) was administered to 67,999 postmenopausal women. The study also measured a wide variety of other variables.

Validity of the WHIIRS is defined by its associations with other measures. Some of the validity coefficients are shown in Figure 5.1. In the figure, three of these validity coefficients are negative. For example, higher scores on insomnia that represents poor sleep are associated with low levels of emotional well-being, energy, and general health. The researchers did not expect emotional expression to be associated with sleep. Indeed, they observed little correlation between emotional expression and the WHIIRS. The WHIIRS was positively correlated with hot flashes and sleep duration. This suggests that women with high scores on insomnia experienced more hot flashes at night and slept fewer hours. Overall, these findings support the validity of the WHIIRS (Levine et al., 2003).

FIGURE 5.1
Validity correlations for WHIIRS.

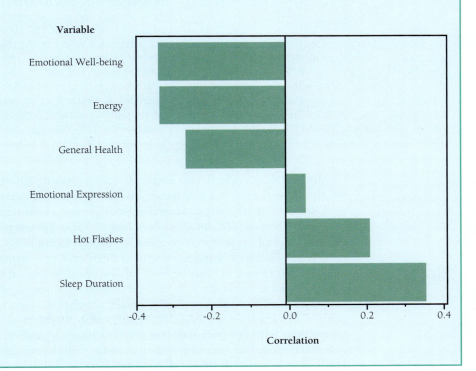

do we need it in addition to all these other measures? The answer is that the index taps something other than the tests used in the convergent evidence studies. This demonstration of uniqueness is called **discriminant evidence,** or what some call *divergent validation.* To demonstrate discriminant evidence for validity, a test should have low correlations with measures of unrelated constructs, or evidence for what the test does not measure.

5.8 FOCUSED EXAMPLE

Discriminant validity interviews versus online testing for employment decisions

Human Resources (HR) managers are experts in making hiring decisions. These decisions are usually based on reviews of resumes and on job interviews. But how good are the employment decisions based on resumes and interviews? The decision process often depends on the values and the personal biases of the particular manager. Further, these decisions might not be aligned with the goals and values of the firm. An alternative is to use validated tests as a tool for employee selection. Even though employment testing has a very long history, the use of tests to select employees remains controversial.

One analysis completed by the National Bureau of Economic Research compared testing versus manager discretion in hiring people for low-skill jobs. The job test consisted of an online questionnaire comprising questions on technical skills, personality, and cognitive functioning. The questions had been validated against subsequent work performance.

For many of these lower skilled jobs, employee retention is crucial. It may take several weeks to train new employees, while the median duration of employment is less than 100 days. The study demonstrated that those selected on the basis of the test had a longer tenure than those selected by managers. On average, those selected on the basis of the test stayed with the company 15% longer. The study also considered people who were passed over by the manager even though they had higher test scores. Some of these individuals were then hired by the company 1 month later. This allowed a comparison between people who had high test scores but were rejected by the managers versus those who had lower test scores but had been hired by the managers. The evaluation showed that those who had high test scores, even though they had been rejected at first, outperformed other employees and stayed on the job longer (Hoffman, Kahn, & Li, 2015).

By providing evidence that a test measures something different from other tests, we also provide evidence that we are measuring a unique construct. Discriminant evidence indicates that the measure does not represent a construct other than the one for which it was devised. An example of how an online job test provides discriminate evidence beyond job interviews is given in Focused Example 5.8.

As this discussion implies, construct-related validity evidence actually subsumes all the activities used in other types of validity evidence studies. In construct-related validation, for example, content-related validation is an essential step. Furthermore, convergent and discriminant studies actually correlate the tests with many different criteria. For example, a measure of health status might be validated by showing correlations with symptoms, doctor visits, or physiological variables. Assembling construct-related evidence for validity requires validation against many criteria. Until quite recently, textbooks divided validity into different types. However, this was often confusing because there is a similarity between what was called *construct*- and *criterion-related validity*. Many psychologists now believe that construct-related evidence for validity actually is the only major type of validity that need concern us. Validity is defined by evidence and other categories (such as criterion-related and convergent) that might be thought of as subcategories of validity evidence (Anastasi & Urbina, 1997; Borsboom, 2015; Heubert & Häuser, 1999; Landy, 2003;

Messick, 1998a, 1998b, 1999; Murphy, 2003a, 2003b; Raykov & Marcoulides, 2010; Ridgers, Stratton, et al., 2011; Rothstein, 2003; Sackett, 2003; Schmidt & Hunter, 2003; Thomas, 2012). According to the testing pioneer Lee Cronbach, it may not be appropriate to continue to divide validity into three parts: "All validation is one, and in a sense all is construct validation" (1980, p. 99). Recall that the 2014 edition of *Standards for Educational and Psychological Testing* no longer recognizes different categories of validity. Instead, it recognizes different categories of evidence for validity.

Criterion-Referenced Tests

The procedures for establishing the validity of a criterion-referenced test resemble those for studying the validity of any other test. As you may recall from Chapter 2, criterion-referenced tests have items that are designed to match certain specific instructional objectives. For example, if the objective of some educational program is for children to be able to list 75% of the countries in Europe, then the criterion-referenced test could ask that the countries be listed. Children who listed 75% of the countries would pass the test. They would be evaluated against this specific criterion rather than on the basis of how they perform relative to other students. Validity studies for the criterion-referenced tests would compare scores on the test to scores on other measures that are believed to be related to the test. Specific procedures for evaluating the validity of a criterion-referenced test have been discussed in more technical articles (Alger, 2016). The idea of comparing an individual with himself or herself rather than to the norms of a group remains appealing (Royal & Guskey, 2015).

Relationship between Reliability and Validity

Attempting to define the validity of a test will be futile if the test is not reliable. Theoretically, a test should not correlate more highly with any other variable than it correlates with itself. The maximum validity coefficient (r_{12max}) between two variables is equal to the square root of the product of their reliabilities, or $r_{12max} = \sqrt{r_{11}r_{22}}$, where r_{11} and r_{22} are the reliabilities for the two variables.

Because validity coefficients are not usually expected to be exceptionally high, a modest correlation between the true scores on two traits may be missed if the test for each of the traits is not highly reliable. Table 5.1 shows the maximum validity you can expect to find given various levels of reliability for two tests. Sometimes we cannot demonstrate that a reliable test has meaning. In other words, we can have reliability without validity. However, it is logically impossible to demonstrate that an unreliable test is valid.

Reliability and validity are related concepts. Figure 5.2 divides the total variation of a test score into different parts. The example used is a test with a validity coefficient of .40. If we consider the total variability on some measure, such as college performance, approximately 16% of the variation might be explained by performance on a predictor test. There is also variation in the score, part of which is explained by measurement error. As noted in Chapter 4, this error might be

TABLE 5.1   How Reliability Affects Validity*

Reliability of test	Reliability of criterion	Maximum validity (correlation)
1.0	1.0	1.00
.8	1.0	.89
.6	1.0	.77
.4	1.0	.63
.2	1.0	.45
.0	1.0	.00
1.0	.5	.71
.8	.5	.63
.6	.5	.55
.4	.5	.45
.2	.5	.32
.0	.5	.00
1.0	.0	.00
.8	.0	.00
.6	.0	.00
.4	.0	.00
.2	.0	.00
.0	.0	.00

*The first column shows the reliability of the test. The second column displays the reliability of the validity criterion. The numbers in the third column are the maximum theoretical correlations between tests, given the reliability of the measures.

related to time sampling, internal consistency, item sampling, and so forth. The figure hypothetically shows these relationships. Finally, some of the variability is "un-explained" or explained by factors of which we are unaware.

FIGURE 5.2
Division of total variation on a performance measure as a function of validity and reliability. Many sources of variation are reflected in a test score. Most of the variance in scores remains unexplained (60%). Internal error (14%) and time sampling error (10%) are two types of reliability that reduce the validity of the test. Validity accounts for approximately 16% of the total variance in this example.

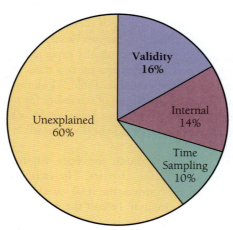

Summary

Validity is a basic idea in measurement and in the science of psychology. Although we have emphasized the validity of psychological tests, the ideas we discussed apply equally to all measures. To make any inference, a good scientist must have substantiating data.

Once a test is "validated," many psychologists mistakenly think it can be used to support many different inferences. Actually, there should be as many validity studies as there are inferences about the scores. Validity really refers to evidence supporting what can be said on the basis of the test scores and not to the tests themselves. Any time we claim that a test score means something different from before, we need a new validity study. Acquiring evidence about the meaning of tests should be an ongoing process. The more a test or a measure is used, the more we learn about what it means.

To establish the validity of a test, we need to gather several types of evidence. It is usually valuable to have *face validity,* or the appearance that a measure has meaning, even though this is not a formally recognized type of validity. *Content validity evidence* is based on the correspondence between the item content and the domain the items represent. Sometimes tests are evaluated against a well-defined criterion. *Predictive validity evidence* comes from studies that use a test to forecast performance on a criterion that is measured at some point in the future. *Concurrent validity evidence* is obtained from correlations between the test and a criterion when both are measured at the same point in time. *Construct validity evidence* is used when a specific criterion is not well defined. *Convergent evidence* comes from correlations between the test and other variables that are hypothetically related to the construct. *Discriminant evidence* shows that the measure does not include superfluous items and that the test measures something distinct from other tests. Reliability and validity are related because it is difficult to obtain evidence for validity unless a measure has reasonable validity. On the other hand, a measure can have high reliability without supporting evidence for its validity. Validity is central to the understanding of psychological tests and measures. We shall refer to validity in all of the remaining chapters.

Writing and Evaluating Test Items

LEARNING OBJECTIVES

When you have completed this chapter, you should be able to:

▶ Describe two types of item formats commonly used in objective classroom examinations

▶ Know whether or not you should guess on a multiple-choice examination when you are not sure of the correct answer

▶ Explain the types of measurement problems the Likert format is used for

▶ Discuss what sorts of problems you might encounter if you used a 10-point category scale to rate the abilities of a group of similar individuals

▶ Set the level of item difficulty needed for a test that discriminates well among individuals

▶ Describe the process of assessing item discriminability

▶ Define an item characteristic curve and tell how it is used

▶ Draw an item characteristic curve for an item that discriminates well at high but not low levels of performance

▶ Explain how item response theory can lead to more accurate tests and also require fewer responses

▶ Discuss some of the limitations of item analysis for tests that are designed to find specific learning problems

At this point in your studies, you are almost certainly an experienced test taker. Most of these have been classroom exercises; however, you have also been exposed to standardized tests such as the SAT Reasoning Test or the Iowa Test of Basic Skills. As a seasoned test taker, you also may have become an experienced test critic. After taking a test, most students are willing to judge whether it was a fair or good test. When you feel that you have taken a bad test, you might ask yourself how it could have been better. As an exercise, you might consider creating a fair test of the material covered in the first five chapters of this book. In this chapter, we offer the basics of creating test items. In the next chapter, we discuss how to administer the tests.

Item Writing

When a professor announces that there will be a test, one of the first questions is "What kind of test?" Will it be a true-false, multiple-choice, essay, or fill-in-the-blank test? As you will learn later in this book, personality and intelligence tests require different sorts of responses. The test constructor must determine the best format for getting these responses(Rodriguez, 2016). In part, this choice stems from the objectives and purpose of the test. For example, if the test requires right or wrong answers, then it will usually be a true-false, multiple-choice, matching, or essay task.

Writing test items can be difficult. (DeVellis, (2016) provided several simple guidelines for item writing. Here are six of them:

1. *Define clearly what you want to measure.* To do this, use substantive theory as a guide and try to make items as specific as possible.
2. *Generate an item pool.* Theoretically, all items are randomly chosen from a universe of item content. In practice, however, care in selecting and developing items is valuable. Avoid redundant items. In the initial phases, you may want to write three or four items for each one that will eventually be used on the test or scale.
3. *Avoid exceptionally long items.* Long items are often confusing or misleading.
4. *Keep the level of reading difficulty appropriate for those who will complete the scale.*
5. *Avoid "double-barreled" items that convey two or more ideas at the same time.* For example, consider an item that asks the respondent to agree or disagree with the statement, "I vote Democratic because I support social programs." There are two different statements with which the person could agree: "I vote Democratic" and "I support social programs."
6. *Consider mixing positively and negatively worded items.* Sometimes, respondents develop the "acquiescence response set." This means that the respondents will tend to agree with most items. To avoid this bias, you can include items that are worded in the opposite direction. For example, in asking about depression, the CES-D (see Chapter 2) uses mostly negatively worded items (such as "I felt

depressed"). However, the CES-D also includes items worded in the opposite direction ("I felt hopeful about the future").

Times change, and tests can get outdated (Kline, 2015). When "writing items, you need to be sensitive to ethnic and cultural differences. For example, items on the CES-D concerning appetite, hopefulness, and social interactions may have a different meaning for African American respondents than for white respondents (DeVellis, 2012; Foley, Reed, Mutran, & DeVellis, 2002). Sometimes, the factor structure, or the way items aggregate, may be different from African American respondents in comparison to white respondents (Allen, DeVellis, Renner, Kraus, & Jordan, 2007) or it may be different at different points in time (Zimbardo & Boyd, 2015). It is also important to recognize that tests may become obsolete. In one study, the reliability of items in the Armed Services Vocational Aptitude Battery was studied over a 16-year period. Approximately 12% of the items became less reliable over this time. Items that retained their reliability were more likely to focus on skills, while those that lost reliability focused on more abstract concepts.

Item Formats

The type of test you have probably experienced most in the classroom is one in which you receive credit for a specific response, or selection of the single "correct" alternative for each test item. True-false and multiple-choice examinations use this system. Similar formats are used for many other purposes such as evaluating attitudes, determining knowledge about traffic laws, or deciding whether someone has characteristics that are associated with a particular health condition. The simplest test of this type uses a dichotomous format.

The Dichotomous Format

The **dichotomous format** offers two alternatives for each item. Usually a point is given for the selection of one of the alternatives. The most common example of this format is the true-false examination. This test presents students with a series of statements. The student's task is to determine which statements are true and which are false. There are many virtues of the true-false test, including ease of construction and ease of scoring, but the method has also become popular because a teacher can easily construct a test by copying lines out of a textbook. The lines that are copied verbatim are designated as "true." Other statements are altered so that they are no longer true.

The advantages of true-false items include their obvious simplicity, ease of administration, and quick scoring. Another attractive feature is that the true-false items require absolute judgment. The test taker must declare one of the two alternatives. However, there are also disadvantages. For example, true-false items encourage students to memorize material, making it possible for students to perform well on a test that covers materials they do not really understand. Furthermore, "truth" often comes in shades of gray, and true-false tests do not allow test takers the opportunity to show they understand this complexity. Also, the mere chance of getting any item correct is 50%. Thus, to be reliable, a true-false test must include many items. Overall, dichotomous items tend to be less reliable, and therefore less precise than some of the other item formats.

The dichotomous format does not appear only as true-false on educational tests. Many personality tests require responses in a true-false or some other two-choice format, such as yes-no. Personality test constructors often prefer this type of format because it requires absolute judgment. For example, in response to an item such as "I often worry about my sexual performance," people cannot be ambivalent—they must respond "True" or "False." Dichotomous items have many advantages for personality tests with many subscales. One is that they make the scoring of the subscales easy. All that a tester needs to do is count the number of items a person endorses from each subscale.

Although the true-false format is popular in educational tests, it is not used as frequently as the multiple-choice test, which represents the polytomous format.

The Polytomous Format

The **polytomous format** (sometimes called *polychotomous)* resembles the dichotomous format except that each item has more than two alternatives. Typically, a point is given for the selection of one of the alternatives, and no point is given for selecting any other choice. Because it is a popular method of measuring academic performance in large classes, the multiple-choice examination is the polytomous format you have likely encountered most often. Multiple-choice tests are easy to score, and the probability of obtaining a correct response by chance is lower than it is for true-false items. A major advantage of this format is that it takes little time for test takers to respond to a particular item because they do not have to write. Thus, the test can cover a large amount of information in a relatively short time.

When taking a multiple-choice examination, you must determine which of several alternatives is "correct." Incorrect choices are called **distractors.** As we shall demonstrate in the section on item analysis, the choice of distractors is critically important.

Because most students are familiar with multiple-choice tests and related formats such as matching, there is no need to elaborate on their description. However, it is worthwhile to consider some of the issues in the construction and scoring of multiple-choice tests.

First, how many distractors should a test have? Psychometric theory suggests that adding more distractors should increase the reliability of the items. However, in practice, adding distractors may not actually increase the reliability because it is difficult to find good ones. The reliability of an item is not enhanced by distractors that no one would ever select. Studies have shown that it is rare to find items for which more than three or four distractors operate efficiently. Ineffective distractors actually may hurt the reliability of the test because they are time-consuming to read and can limit the number of good items that can be included in a test. A review of the problems associated with selecting distractors suggests that it is usually best to develop three or four good distractors for each item (Anastasi & Urbina, 1997). Well-chosen distractors are an essential ingredient of good items.

Sometimes psychometric analysis can pave the way for simpler tests. For example, most multiple-choice tests have followed the suggestion of four or five alternatives. However, this traditional practice may not be the best use of resources. In one evaluation of tests for entry-level police officers, applicants completed a test battery with either five alternative multiple-choice items or three alternative items. Psychometric analysis showed that the validity and reliability were about equal for the two types of tests. This result suggests that three alternative multiple-choice

TABLE 6.1 Common Problems in Multiple-Choice Item Writing.

Problem	Description
Unfocused Stem	The stem should include the information necessary to answer the question. Test takers should not need to read the options to figure out what question is being asked.
Negative Stem	Whenever possible, the stem should exclude negative terms such as *not* and *except*
Window Dressing	Information in the stem that is irrelevant to the question or concept being assessed is considered "window dressing" and should be avoided.
Unequal Option Length	The correct answer and the distractors should be about the same length.
Negative Options	Whenever possible, response options should exclude negatives such as "not"
Clues to the Correct Answer	Test writers sometimes inadvertently provide clues by using vague terms such as *might*, *may*, and *can*. Particularly in the social sciences where certainty is rare, vague terms may signal that the option is correct.
Heterogeneous Options	The correct option and all of the distractors should be in the same general category.

Adapted From (DiSantis et al., 2015).

items may be better than five alternative items because they retain the psychometric value but take less time to develop and administer (Sidick, Barrett, & Doverspike, 1994). A review of more than 80 years of psychometric research confirms that three-option multiple-choice items are as good as, if not better than, items that have more than three alternatives (Rodriguez, 2005).

Poorly written distractors can adversely affect the quality of the test. Sometimes a test maker will throw in "cute" distractors that are extremely unlikely to be chosen. If distractors are too easy, then a poorly prepared test taker has a high chance of guessing the correct answer. As a result, the test will have lower reliability and validity.

Table 6.1 summarizes some of the rules in item writing developed by Rodriguez (2005). These principles have now been adapted for different fields such as continuing medical education (DiSantis, Ayoob, & Williams, 2015).

Even though multiple-choice tests have been used for hundreds of years, problems in item writing are common. One analysis of items used in professional medical continuing education courses showed that 43% of test times included at least one of the problems described in Table 6.1 (DiSantis et al., 2015).

Guessing

Another issue concerns the scoring of multiple-choice examinations. Suppose you bring your roommate to your sociology test, and he or she fills out an answer sheet without reading the items. Will your roommate get any items correct? The answer is yes—by chance alone. If each test item has four choices, the test taker would be expected to get 25% of the total number of items correct. If the test items had three choices, then a 33.33% rate of success would be expected. Because test takers get some "correct" answers simply by guessing, a correction for guessing is sometimes used. The formula to correct for guessing on a test is

$$\text{corrected score} = R - \frac{W}{n - 1}$$

where

R = the number of right responses

W = the number of wrong responses

n = the number of choices for each item

Omitted responses are not included; they provide neither credit nor penalty. The expression $W/(n - 1)$ is an estimate of how many items the test taker is expected to get right by chance. For example, suppose that your roommate randomly filled out the answer sheet to your sociology test. The test had 100 items, each with four choices. By chance, her expected score would be 25 correct. Let's assume that she got exactly that, though in practice this may not occur, because 25 is the *average* random score. The expected score corrected for guessing would be

$$R - \frac{W}{n - 1}$$

$$= 25 - \frac{75}{4 - 1}$$

$$= 25 - \frac{75}{3}$$

$$= 25 - 25 = 0$$

In other words, when the correction for guessing is applied, the expected score is 0.

A question that students frequently ask is "Should I guess on multiple-choice items when I don't know the answer?" The answer depends on how the test will be scored. If a correction for guessing is not used, then the best advice is "guess away." By guessing, you have a chance of getting the item correct. You do not have this chance if you do not guess. However, if a correction for guessing is used, then random guessing will do you no good. Some speeded tests are scored so that the correction for the guessing formula includes only the items that were attempted—that is, those that were not attempted are not counted either right or wrong. In this case, random guessing and leaving the items blank have the same expected effect.

How about cases where you do not know the right answer but can eliminate one or two of the alternatives? How many times have you narrowed your answer down to two alternatives but could not figure out which of the two was correct? In this case, we advise you to guess. The correction formula assumes that you are equally likely to respond to each of the four categories. For a four-choice item, it would estimate your chance of getting the item correct by chance alone to be 1 in 4. However, if you can eliminate two alternatives, then the chances are actually 1 in 2. This gives you a slight advantage over the correction formula.

Research has shown that students are more likely to guess when they anticipate a low grade on a test than when they are more confident (Bereby-Meyer, Meyer, &

Flascher, 2002). Other schemes discourage guessing by giving students partial credit for items left blank (Campbell, 2015). Mathematical methods have been introduced to summarize information in multiple-choice tests and dichotomous-item tests (Huibregtse, Admiraal, & Meara, 2002; Ling & Cavers, 2015). These methods summarize the mean, the reliability as calculated from the binomial distribution, and a guessing threshold. The *guessing threshold* describes the chances that a low-ability test taker will obtain each score. These newer methods are highly technical and are beyond the scope of this book. In summary, the techniques are derived from the first three moments of the test score distribution. Mathematically inclined readers who are interested in the methods should consult Carlin and Rubin (1991).

As you have seen, true-false and multiple-choice formats are common to educational and achievement tests. Similar formats are found on personality tests. For example, frequently used personality inventories such as the Minnesota Multiphasic Personality Inventory (MMPI) or the California Psychological Inventory (CPI) present subjects with a long list of statements to which one responds either "True" or "False" (see Chapter 15).

Other personality and attitude measures do not judge any response as "right" or "wrong." Rather, they attempt to quantify characteristics of the response. These formats include the Likert format, the category scale, and the Q-sort. Some of these formats will be discussed in more detail in Chapter 15.

Another format, the essay, is commonly used in classroom evaluation, and the Educational Testing Service now uses a writing sample as a component of its testing programs. Essay exams can be evaluated using the same principles used for structured tests. For example, the validity of the test can be established through correlations with other tests. The reliability of the scoring procedure should be assessed by determining the association between two scores provided by independent scorers. In practice, however, the psychometric properties of essay exams are rarely evaluated.

The Likert Format

One popular format for attitude and personality scales requires that a respondent indicate the degree of agreement with a particular attitudinal question. This technique is called the **Likert format** because it was used as part of Likert's (1932) method of attitude scale construction. A scale using the Likert format consists of items such as "I am afraid of heights." Instead of asking for a yes-no reply, five alternatives are offered: *strongly disagree, disagree, neutral, agree,* and *strongly agree.* Examples of Likert scale items are given in Table 6.2. In some applications, six options are used to avoid allowing the respondent to be neutral. The six responses might be *strongly disagree, moderately disagree, mildly disagree, mildly agree, moderately agree,* and *strongly agree.* Scoring requires that any negatively worded items be reverse scored and the responses are then summed. This format is especially popular in measurements of attitude. For example, it allows researchers to determine how much people endorse statements such as "The government should not regulate private business."

Because responses in a Likert format can be subjected to factor analysis, test developers can find groups of items that go together. The Likert format is often used to create Likert scales (Clark & Watson, 1998). The scales require assessment of item discriminability, a concept that we address later in the chapter.

TABLE 6.2 Examples of Likert Scale Items

Following is a list of statements. Please indicate how strongly you agree or disagree by circling your answer to the right of the statement.

Five-choice format with neutral point

Some politicians can be trusted	Strongly disagree	Somewhat disagree	Neither agree nor disagree	Somewhat agree	Strongly agree
I am confident that I will achieve my life goals	Strongly disagree	Somewhat disagree	Neither agree nor disagree	Somewhat agree	Strongly agree
I am comfortable talking to my parents about personal problems	Strongly disagree	Somewhat disagree	Neither agree nor disagree	Somewhat agree	Strongly agree

Alternative set of choices: strongly disagree, disagree, undecided, agree, strongly agree

Six-choice format without neutral point

Some politicians can be trusted	Strongly disagree	Moderately disagree	Mildly disagree	Mildly agree	Moderately agree	Strongly agree
I am confident that I will achieve my life goals	Strongly disagree	Moderately disagree	Mildly disagree	Mildly agree	Moderately agree	Strongly agree
I am comfortable talking to my parents about personal problems	Strongly disagree	Moderately disagree	Mildly disagree	Mildly agree	Moderately agree	Strongly agree

Alternative set of choices: strongly disagree, disagree, lean toward disagree, lean toward agree, agree, strongly agree

A variety of technical approaches to Likert scale development are available (AsÃºn, Rdz-Navarro, & Alvarado, 2016). Some studies have demonstrated that the Likert format is superior to methods such as the visual analogue scale for measuring complex coping responses (Flynn, Schaik, & van Wersch, 2004). Others have challenged the appropriateness of using traditional parametric statistics to analyze Likert responses because the data are at the ordinal rather than at an interval level (Bishop & Herron, 2015). Nevertheless, the Likert format is familiar and easy to use. It is likely to remain popular in personality and attitude tests.

The Category Format

A technique that is similar to the Likert format but that uses an even greater number of choices is the **category format.** Most people are familiar with 10-point rating systems because we are regularly asked questions such as, "On a scale from 1 to 10, with 1 as the lowest and 10 as the highest, how would you rate your new boyfriend in terms of attractiveness?" Doctors often ask their patients to rate their pain on a scale from 1 to 10, where 1 is little or no pain and 10 is intolerable pain. A category scale need not have exactly 10 points; it can have either more or fewer categories.

Although the 10-point scale is common in psychological research and everyday conversation, controversy exists regarding when and how it should be used. We recently encountered a college basketball coach who rates the quality of high-school prospects on a 10-point rating scale. It is assumed that this rating provides a reliable estimate of the players' abilities. However, experiments have shown that responses to items on 10-point scales are affected by the groupings of the people or things being rated. For example, if coaches are asked to rate the abilities of a group of 20 talented players, they may tend to make fine distinctions among them so as to use most or all of the categories on the 10-point scale. A particular player rated as a 6 when he was on a team with many outstanding players might be rated as a 9 if he were judged with a group of poorly coordinated players (Leibovitch, 2015; Parducci, 1968, 1995). We know from a variety of studies that people will change ratings depending on context (Norman, 2003). When given a group of objects to rate, subjects have a tendency to spread their responses evenly across the 10 categories (Stevens, 1966). See Focused Example 6.1 for more on the effect of context on value ratings. Other advice on creating category items involves making the response options clearer for the respondent. For example, reliability and validity may be higher if all response options are clearly labeled, as opposed to just labeling the categories at the extremes (Green & Yang, 2009).

Experiments have shown that this problem can be avoided if the endpoints of the scale are clearly defined and the subjects are frequently reminded of the definitions of the endpoints. For example, instead of asking coaches to rate the ability of basketball players on a 10-point scale, testers might show them films that depict the performance of a player rated as 10 and other films showing what the rating of 1 means. Under these circumstances, the subjects are less likely to offer a response that is affected by other stimuli in the group (Kaplan & Ernst, 1983).

People often ask, "Why use a 10-point scale instead of a 13-point or a 43-point scale?" This question has generated considerable study. More than 90 years ago, researchers argued that the optimal number of points is 7 (Symonds, 1924), whereas others have suggested that the optimal number of categories should be three times this number (Champney & Marshall, 1939). As is often the case, the number of categories required depends on the fineness of the discrimination that subjects are willing to make. If the subjects are unconcerned about a given topic, then they will not make fine discriminations about it, and a scale with a few categories will do about as well as a scale with many. However, when people are highly involved with some issue, they will tend to respond best to a greater number of categories. For most rating tasks, however, a 10-point scale seems to provide enough discrimination. N. H. Anderson (1991) has found that a 10-point scale provides substantial discrimination among objects for a wide variety of stimuli. Some evidence suggests that increasing the number of response categories may not increase reliability and validity. In fact, increasing the number of choices beyond nine or so can reduce reliability because responses may be more likely to include an element of randomness when there are so many alternatives that respondents cannot clearly discriminate between the fine-grained choices (Clark & Watson, 1998). One analysis showed that the optimum number of categories is between four and seven. Reliability suffers when fewer than four categories are used, but the increase in reliability does not increase much when form than seven categories are available (Lozano, García-Cueto, et al., 2008). An approach related to category scales is the *visual analogue* scale. Using this method, the respondent is given a 100-millimeter line and asked to place a mark between two well-defined endpoints. The scales are scored according to the measured distance from the first endpoint to

The Effect of Context on Value Ratings

The numbers we assign when using rating scales are sometimes influenced by the context or the background against which objects are rated. In one experiment, college students were asked to rate how immoral they believed certain acts to be. The students were divided into two groups. One group rated the items that typically represented "mild" actions (List 1) with items ranging from keeping a dime found in a phone booth to avoiding criticism by contributing money to a cause you don't believe in. The other group rated items that typically represented more severe actions (List 2). These ranged from failure to repay money borrowed from friends to murdering your mother. The numbers on the right represent average ratings by a large number of college students. The six items included on both lists are marked with asterisks. These items are judged more leniently when included in List 2 than when in List 1. This experiment shows that the numbers we assign when using rating scales are affected by context (Parducci, 1968).

List 1

Registering in a hotel under a false name.	1.68
Bawling out servants publicly.*	2.64
Contributing money to a cause in which you do not believe in order to escape criticism.	3.03
Keeping a dime you find in a telephone booth.	1.08
Publishing under your own name an investigation originated and carried out without remuneration by a graduate student working under you.*	3.95
Failing to pay your bus fare when the conductor overlooks you.	2.36
Playing poker on Sunday.	1.17
Failing to put back in the water lobsters shorter than the legal limit.*	2.22
Cheating at solitaire.	1.53
Fishing without a license.	2.27
Habitually borrowing small sums of money from friends and failing to return them.*	2.93
Stealing towels from a hotel.	2.58
Stealing a loaf of bread from a store when you are starving.	1.79

the mark (see Figure 6.1). Visual analogue scales are popular for measuring self-rated health. However, they are not used often for multi-item scales, because scoring is time-consuming (Clark & Watson, 1998). Methods are available for creating confidence intervals around item means for rating scales (Penfield, 2003b).

Checklists and Q-Sorts

One format common in personality measurement is the adjective checklist (Gough, 1960). With this method, a subject receives a long list of adjectives and indicates whether each one is characteristic of himself or herself. Adjective checklists can be

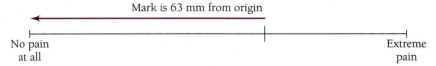

FIGURE 6.1

The 100-mm visual analogue scale. The subject has rated her pain 63 mm from the base of no pain at all. On a scale ranging from 0 to 100, this level of pain is scored as 63.

Poisoning a neighbor's dog whose barking bothers you.*	4.19	Having a sane person committed to a mental hospital in order to get rid of him.	4.46
Lying about your whereabouts to protect a friend's reputation.	1.60	Failing to put back in the water lobsters that are shorter than the legal limit.*	1.82
Wearing shorts on the street where it is illegal.	1.59	Having sexual relations with a sibling (brother or sister).	3.72
Pocketing the tip the previous customer left for the waitress.*	3.32	Putting your deformed child in the circus.	3.81
Getting your own way by playing on people's sympathies.	2.90	Habitually borrowing small sums of money from friends and failing to return them.*	2.37
		Having incestuous relations with your parent.	3.88
List 2		Murdering your mother without justification or provocation.	4.79
Using guns on striking workers.	3.82	Poisoning a neighbor's dog whose barking bothers you.*	3.65
Bawling out servants publicly.*	2.39	Testifying falsely against someone for pay.	4.07
Stealing $10 from an impecunious acquaintance.	3.79	Teaching adolescents to become dope addicts.	4.51
Selling to a hospital milk from diseased cattle.	4.51	Pocketing the tip the previous customer left for the waitress.*	2.46
Publishing under your own name an investigation originated and carried out without remuneration by a graduate student working under you.*	3.47	Sending another person to take a civil service exam for you.	3.39
Spreading rumors that an acquaintance is a sexual pervert.	3.91	*Items followed by an asterisk appear on both lists. From Parducci (1968).	

used for describing either oneself or someone else. For example, in one study at the University of California at Berkeley, raters checked the traits they thought characterized a group of 40 graduate students. Half of these students had been designated by their instructors as exceptional in originality, and the other half low in originality. The results demonstrated that the adjectives chosen to describe members of these two groups differed. The highly original students were described most often by the traits *adventurous, alert, curious, quiet, imaginative,* and *fair minded.* In contrast, the low-originality students were seen as *confused, conventional, defensive, polished, prejudiced,* and *suggestible.*

The adjective checklist requires subjects either to endorse such adjectives or not, thus allowing only two choices for each item. A similar technique known as the *Q-sort* increases the number of categories. The Q-sort can be used to describe oneself or to provide ratings of others (Stephenson, 1953). With this technique, a subject is given statements and asked to sort them into nine piles. For example, Block (1961) gave observers 100 statements about personal characteristics. The statements were sorted into piles that indicated the degree to which they appeared to describe a given person accurately. If you were using this method, you might be asked to rate your

FIGURE 6.2 The California Q-sort. The numbers of items distributed in the nine piles of the California Q-sort approach a normal distribution.

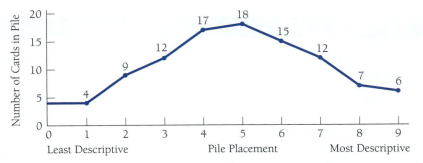

roommate. You would receive a set of 100 cards, each with a statement on it such as the following:

Has a wide range of interests.

Is productive; gets things done.

Is self-dramatizing; is histrionic.

Is overreactive to minor frustrations; is irritable.

Seeks reassurance from others.

Appears to have a high degree of intellectual capacity.

Is basically anxious.

If a statement really hit home, you would place it in pile 9. Those that were not at all descriptive would be placed in pile 1. Most of the cards are usually placed in piles 4, 5, and 6. The frequency of items placed in each of the categories usually looks like a bell-shaped curve (see Figure 6.2). The items that end up in the extreme categories usually say something interesting about the person. Even though the Q-sort method was developed decades ago, it is still actively used in contemporary research (Holden, Kellett, Davies, & Scott, 2016).

Other Possibilities

We have discussed only a few of many item formats. The forced-choice (such as multiple-choice and Q-sort) and Likert formats are clearly the most popular in contemporary tests and measures. Other formats have become less popular in recent years. For example, checklists have fallen out of favor because they are more prone to error than are formats that require responses to every item. If you are interested in learning more about item writing and item formats, then you might check some general references (Kline, 2015; Lane, Raymond, & Haladyna, 2015; Worrell & Roberson, 2016).

Unfortunately, there is no simple recipe for item writing. One group analyzed 20 different textbooks that offered rules on item writing. The textbooks reviewed offered 40 different bits of advice. These are summarized in Table 6.3. The table also summarizes whether there is research support for each suggestion in relation

TABLE 6.3   Summary of Advice About Item Writing From 20 Textbooks

	Frequency	%	Research support	Multiple-choice	Matching	True-false	Completion
1. "All of the Above" should not be an answer option	16	80.0	X	X			
2. "None of the Above" should not be an answer option	15	75.0		X			
3. All answer options should be plausible	14	70.0		X	X		
4. Order of answer options should be logical or vary	13	65.0	X	X			
5. Items should cover important concepts and objectives	12	60.0		X	X	X	X
6. Negative wording should not be used	11	55.0		X			
7. Answer options should include only one correct answer	11	55.0		X	X		
8. Answer options should all be grammatically consistent with stem	10	50.0		X	X		
9. Specific determiners (e.g., *always, never*) should not be used	10	50.0		X			
10. Answer options should be homogenous	10	50.0		X	X		
11. Stems must be unambiguous and clearly state the problem	10	50.0		X			
12. Correct answer options should not be the longest answer option	9	45.0		X			
13. Answer options should not be longer than the stem	8	40.0	X				
14. Items should use appropriate vocabulary	8	40.0	X	X	X	X	
15. In fill-in-the-blank items, a single blank should be used, at the end	8	40.0				X	
16. Items should be independent of each other	8	40.0	X				
17. In matching, there should be more answer options than stem	8	40.0		X			
18. All parts of an item or exercise should appear on the same page	8	40.0	X	X	X	X	
19. True-false items should have simple structure	6	30.0				X	

(continues)

TABLE 6.3   Summary of Advice About Item Writing From 20 Textbooks (*continued*)

	Frequency	%	Research support	Multiple-choice	Matching	True-false	Completion
20. True-false items should be entirely true or entirely false	6	30.0				X	
21. There should be 3–5 answer options	6	30.0	X	X	X		
22. Answer options should not have repetitive wording	6	30.0	X	X			
23. Point value of items should be presented	6	30.0	X	X	X	X	
24. Stems and examples should not come directly from textbook	5	25.0	X	X	X		X
25. Matching item directions should include basis for match	5	25.0			X		
26. Answer options should be logically independent of one another	5	25.0	X	X			
27. Directions should be included	5	25.0	X	X	X	X	
28. Questions using the same format should be together	5	25.0	X	X	X	X	
29. Vague frequency terms (e.g., often, usually) should not be used	4	20.0	X		X		
30. Multiple-choice stems should be complete sentences	4	20.0	X				
31. There should be an equal number of true and false statements	4	20.0				X	
32. True-false statements should be of equal length	4	20.0				X	
33. Individual items should be short	4	20.0	X	X	X		
34. Answer options should be available more than once	4	20.0		X			
35. Number of answer options should be <7 for elementary age tests	4	20.0		X			
36. Number of answer options should be <17 for secondary age tests	4	20.0		X			
37. Complex item formats ("a and b, but not c") should not be used	3	15.0	X	X			
38. All items should be numbered	3	15.0	X	X	X	X	
39. Test copies should be clear, readable, and not handwritten	2	10.0	X	X	X	X	
40. Stems should be on the left, and answer options on the right	2	10.0		X			

to multiple-choice, matching, true-false, or completion items. The most frequent advice (given in 80% of the textbooks) was not to use "all of the above" as a response option. As a student, you may have noticed that this frequent advice is commonly ignored (Frey, Petersen, Edwards, Pedrotti, & Peyton, 2005). However, writing good items remains an art rather than a science. There is no substitute for using precise language, knowing the subject matter, being familiar with the level of examinees, and using your imagination. Once the items are written and have been administered, you can use item-analysis techniques to evaluate them.

Item Analysis

A good test has good items. But what are good items? How many times have you been in a class in which students launched a full-scale battle over particular items in a multiple-choice test? Tests with good items are hard to create. Good test making requires careful attention to the principles of test construction. **Item analysis,** a general term for a set of methods used to evaluate test items, is one of the most important aspects of test construction. The basic methods involve assessment of item difficulty and item discriminability.

Item Difficulty

For a test that measures achievement or ability, **item difficulty** is defined by the number of people who get a particular item correct. For example, if 84% of the people taking a particular test get item 24 correct, then the difficulty level for that item is .84. Some people have suggested that these proportions do not really indicate item "difficulty" but item "easiness." The higher the proportion of people who get the item correct, the easier the item.

How hard should items be in a good test? This depends on the uses of the test and the types of items. The first thing a test constructor needs to determine is the probability that an item could be answered correctly by chance alone. A true-false item could be answered correctly half the time if people just guessed randomly. Thus, a true-false item with a difficulty level of .50 would not be a good item. A multiple-choice item with four alternatives could be answered correctly 25% of the time. Therefore, we would require difficulty greater than 25% for an item to be reasonable in this context. Other obvious limits are the extremes of the scale. An item that is answered correctly by 100% of the respondents offers little value because it does not discriminate among individuals.

The optimal difficulty level for items is usually about halfway between 100% of the respondents getting the item correct and the level of success expected by chance alone. Thus, the optimum difficulty level for a four-choice item is approximately .625. To arrive at this value, we take the 100% success level (1.00) and subtract from it the chance performance level (.25). Then, we divide the result by 2 to find the halfway point and add this value to the expected chance level. The steps are outlined here.

Step 1. Find half of the difference between 100% (or 1.00) success and chance performance.

$$\frac{1.0 - .25}{2} = \frac{.75}{2} = .375$$

Step 2. Add this value to the probability of performing correctly by chance.

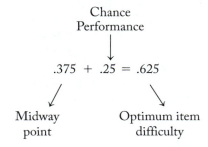

A simpler method for obtaining the same result is to add 1.00 to chance performance and divide by 2.0. For this example, the result would be

$$\frac{.25 + 1.0}{2.00} = .625$$

In most tests, the items should have a variety of difficulty levels because a good test discriminates at many levels. For example, a professor who wants to determine how much his or her students have studied might like to discriminate between students who have not studied at all and those who have studied just a little, or between those who have studied just a little and those who have studied a fair amount, or perhaps between those students who have studied more than average and those who have worked and studied exceptionally hard. In other words, the professor needs to make many discriminations. To accomplish this, he or she requires items at many different levels of difficulty.

For most tests, items in the difficulty range of .30 to .70 tend to maximize information about the differences among individuals. However, some tests require a concentration of more-difficult items. For example, if a test is to be used to select medical students and only a small number of qualified applicants can be accepted, then a test with especially difficult items will make fine discriminations in a way that a test with a broader range of difficulty would not. Conversely, a test used to select students for educable mentally challenged classes should have a greater concentration of easier items to make fine discriminations among individuals who ordinarily do not perform well on tests (Allen & Yen, 1979). In constructing a good test, one must also consider human factors. For example, though items answered correctly by all students will have poor psychometric qualities, they may help the morale of the students who take the test. A few easier items may help keep test anxiety in check, which in turn adds to the reliability of the test. Although we have discussed item analysis in relation to achievement tests, the same methods can be used to evaluate other measures. For example, instead of considering an item as right or wrong, one could set it up to indicate whether it is or is not associated with a particular diagnosis, group membership, and so forth.

Item difficulty is only one way to evaluate test items. Another way is to examine the relationship between performance on particular items and performance on the whole test. This is known as discriminability.

Discriminability

In the previous section, we discussed the analysis of item difficulty, which determines the proportion of people who succeed on a particular item. Another way to examine the value of items is to ask "Who gets this item correct?" Assessment of **item discriminability** determines whether the people who have done well on particular items have also done well on the whole test. One can evaluate the discriminability of test items in many ways.

The Extreme Group Method

This method compares people who have done well with those who have done poorly on a test. For example, you might find the students with test scores in the top third and those in the bottom third of the class. Then, you would find the proportions of people in each group who got each item correct. The difference between these proportions is called the *discrimination index*. Psychological Testing in Everyday Life 6.1 demonstrates this method.

The Point Biserial Method

Another way to examine the discriminability of items is to find the correlation between performance on the item and performance on the total test. You might remember from Chapter 3 that the correlation between a dichotomous (two-category) variable and a continuous variable is called a *point biserial correlation*. The point biserial correlation between an item and a total test score is

$$r_{pbis} = \left[\frac{\bar{Y}_1 - \bar{Y}}{S_y} \right] \sqrt{\frac{P_x}{1 - P_x}}$$

where

r_{pbis} = the point biserial correlation or index of discriminability
$\bar{Y}_1$ = the mean score on the test for those who got item 1 correct
$\bar{Y}$ = the mean score on the test for all persons
S_y = the standard deviation of the exam scores for all persons
P_x = the proportion of persons getting the item correct (Allen & Yen, 1979)

For example, suppose that 58% of the students in a psychology class gave the correct response to item 15 on their midterm exam. The mean score on the whole test for these students who got item 15 correct was 57.6, and the mean score for the entire class was 54.3. The standard deviation on the test was 9.7. To calculate the discriminability of item 15 by the point biserial method, you would enter this information into the formula:

$$\left[\frac{57.6 - 54.3}{9.7} \right] \sqrt{\frac{.58}{.42}} = .34 \times \sqrt{1.38} = (.34)(1.17) = .40$$

In other words, the correlation between succeeding on item 15 and total test performance is .40.

On tests with only a few items, using the point biserial correlation is problematic because performance on the item contributes to the total test score. For example, if a

6.1 PSYCHOLOGICAL TESTING IN EVERYDAY LIFE

Finding the Item Discrimination Index by Using the Extreme Group Method

Step 1.   Identify a group of students who have done well on the test—or example, those in the 67th percentile and above. Also identify a group that has done poorly—for example, those in the 33rd percentile and below.

Step 2.   Find the proportion of students in the high group and the proportion of students in the low group who got each item correct.

Step 3.   For each item, subtract the proportion of correct responses for the low group from the proportion of correct responses for the high group. This gives the item discrimination index (d_i).

Example

Item Number	Proportion Correct for Students in the Top Third of Class (P_t)	Proportion Correct for Students in the Bottom Third of Class (P_b)	Discriminability Index ($d_i = P_t - P_b$)
1	.89	.34	.55
2	.76	.36	.40
3	.97	.45	.52
4	.98	.95	.03
5	.56	.74	−.18

In this example, items 1, 2, and 3 appear to discriminate reasonably well. Item 4 does not discriminate well because the level of success is high for both groups; it must be too easy. Item 5 appears to be a bad item because it is a "negative discriminator." This sometimes happens on multiple-choice examinations when overprepared students find some reason to disqualify the response keyed as correct.

test has six items, there is bound to be a positive correlation between getting a particular item correct and the total test score because one-sixth of the total score is performance on that item. To compensate for this problem, it is sometimes advisable to exclude the item from the total test score. For the six-item test, we might look at the point biserial correlation between passing item 1 and the test score derived from items 2 through 6.

The point biserial correlation (r_{pbis}) between an item and the total test score is evaluated in much the same way as the extreme group discriminability index. If this value is negative or low, then the item should be eliminated from the test. The closer the value of the index is to 1.0, the better the item. Note that the easiest items, such as those answered correctly by 90% or more, usually do not appear to be good items on the discriminability index. If 90% of test takers get an item correct, then there is too little variability in performance for there to be a substantial correlation with the total test score. Similarly, if items are so hard that they are answered correctly by 10% or fewer of the test takers, then there is too little room to show a correlation between the items and the total test score.

Pictures of Item Characteristics

A valuable way to learn about items is to graph their characteristics, which you can do with the **item characteristic curve.** For particular items, one can prepare a graph for each individual test item. On these individual item graphs, the total test score is plotted on the horizontal (X) axis and the proportion of examinees who get the item correct is plotted on the vertical (Y) axis. The total test score is used as an estimate of the amount of a "trait" possessed by individuals. Because we can never measure traits directly, the total test score is the best approximation we have. Thus, the relationship between performance on the item and performance on the test gives some information about how well the item is tapping the information we want.

Drawing the Item Characteristic Curve

To draw the item characteristic curve, we need to define discrete categories of test performance. If the test has been given to many people, we might choose to make each test score a single category (65, 66, 67, and so on). However, if the test has been given to a smaller group, then we might use a smaller number of class intervals (such as 66–68, 69–71). When only a small number of people took the test, some scores would not be observed and would appear as gaps on the graph. Using fewer class intervals allows the curve to take on a smoother appearance. Once you have arrived at these categories, you need to determine what proportion of the people within each category got each item correct. For example, you must determine what proportion of the people with a total test score of 65 got item 34 correct, what proportion of the people with a total test score of 66 got item 34 correct, and so on. Once you have this series of breakdowns, you can create a plot of the proportions of correct responses to an item by total test scores. Examples of these graphs are shown in Figures 6.3 through 6.7.

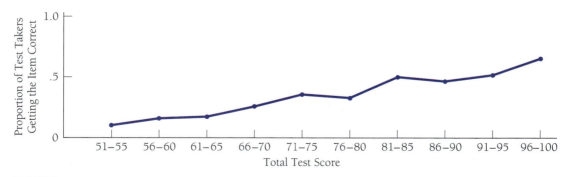

FIGURE 6.3
Item characteristic curve for a "good" test item. The proportion of test takers who get the item correct increases as a function of the total test score.

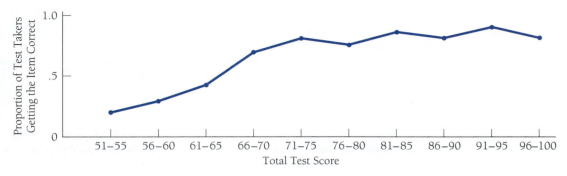

FIGURE 6.4
Item characteristic curve for a test item that discriminates well at low levels of performance but not at higher levels.

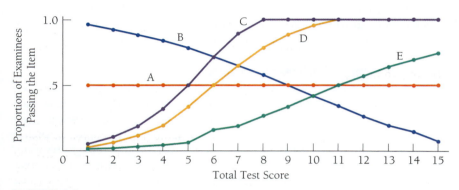

FIGURE 6.5
Item characteristic curves for several items.

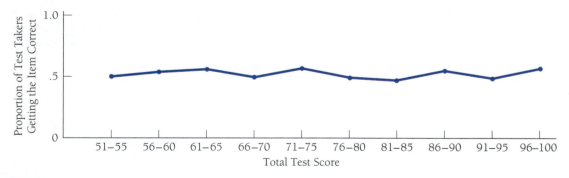

FIGURE 6.6
Item characteristic curve for a poor item. People with different test scores were equally likely to get the item correct.

Figure 6.3 shows the item characteristic curve for a "good" test item. The gradual positive slope of the line demonstrates that the proportion of people who pass the item gradually increases as test scores increase. This means that the item successfully discriminates at all levels of test performance. The curve shown in Figure 6.4

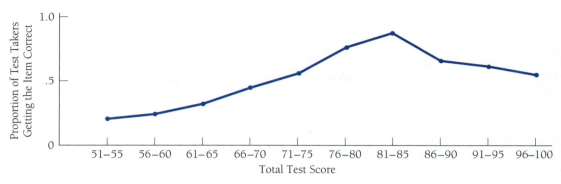

FIGURE 6.7

Another example of a problem item. Sometimes test takers who "know too much" will rule out the alternative designated as correct.

illustrates an item that discriminates especially well among people at the lower level of performance. However, because all of the people who scored above average on the test got this item correct, it did not provide much discrimination in the higher ranges of performance.

Figure 6.5 shows a variety of item characteristic curves. Ranges in which the curve changes suggest that the item is sensitive, while flat ranges suggest areas of low sensitivity. The items are each sensitive in a particular range. Figures 6.6 and 6.7 show item characteristic curves for poor items. The flat curve in Figure 6.6 indicates that test takers at all levels of ability were equally likely to get the item correct. Figure 6.7 demonstrates a particularly troublesome problem. The item characteristic curve gradually rises, showing that the item is sensitive to most levels of performance. Then, it turns down for people at the highest levels of performance, suggesting that those with the best overall performance on the test did not have the best chances of getting the item correct. This can happen on multiple-choice examinations when one of the alternatives is "none of the above." Students who are exceptionally knowledgeable in the subject area can sometimes rule out all the choices even though one of the alternatives has actually been designated as correct.

Another convenient picture of item characteristics is shown in Figure 6.8. This graph plots the item numbers within the space created by difficulty on one axis and discriminability (in this case, point biserial correlation between item passage and test score) on the other axis. Item 12 has been circled on the graph so that you can identify it. Of all respondents, 46% got this item correct, and its discriminability level is .60. Thus, item 12 on the graph is aligned with 46 on the difficulty axis and .60 on the discriminability axis. Earlier in the discussion we noted that "good" items usually fall within a difficulty range of 30% and 70%. In Figure 6.8, the shaded region bound by the dotted lines represents the region in which acceptable levels of difficulty and discriminability are achieved. Thus, items for the final version of the test should be selected from this area.

In summary, item analysis breaks the general rule that increasing the number of items makes a test more reliable. When bad items are eliminated, the effects of chance responding can be eliminated and the test can become more efficient,

FIGURE 6.8

Items from a 30-item test are plotted on a graph with discriminability on one axis and difficulty on the other. Each number on the graph represents a test item: 1 is for item 1 and so on. The shaded area represents items above a discriminability level of .30 and between 30% and 70% in difficulty level. These items would be the best candidates to include in the final version of the test. Item 12 (circled) was passed by 46% of the respondents and was correlated .60 with total test score, so it should be retained.

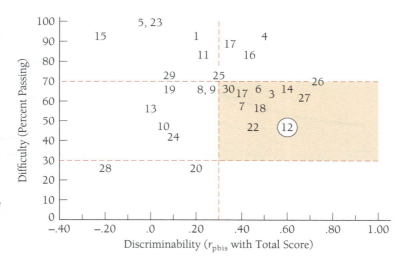

reliable, and valid. In the next section, we will consider item response theory, which is a modern method to improve test efficiency even further.

Item Response Theory

New approaches to item analysis have generated a new model of psychological testing (Templin, 2016). According to classical test theory, a score is derived from the sum of an individual's responses to various items, which are sampled from a larger domain that represents a specific trait or ability. Newer approaches to testing based on item analysis consider the chances of getting particular items right or wrong. These approaches, now known as *item response theory* (IRT), make extensive use of item analysis (DeMars, 2010; De Ayala & Santiago, 2016; DeVellis, 2012; Templin, 2016). According to these approaches, each item on a test has its own item characteristic curve that describes the probability of getting each particular item right or wrong given the ability level of each test taker. With the computer, items can be sampled, and the specific range of items where the test taker begins to have difficulty can be identified (Bolt, 2003; Schmidt & Embretson, 2003). In this way, testers can make an ability judgment without subjecting the test taker to all of the test items. Computer programs are now available to teach the complex theory underlying IRT (De Ayala & Santiago, 2016; DeMars, 2010; DeVellis, 2012).

This theory has many technical advantages. It builds on traditional models of item analysis and can provide information on item functioning, the value of specific items, and the reliability of a scale (Templin, 2016; van der Linden, 2016). Perhaps the most important message for the test taker is that his or her score is no longer defined by the total number of items correct, but instead by the level of difficulty of items that he or she can answer correctly. The implications of IRT are profound. In fact, some people believe that IRT was the most important development in psychological testing in the second half of the 20th century. However, many psychology training programs have not yet added these methods to their curriculum (Aiken, 2008).

There are various approaches to the construction of tests using IRT. Some of the approaches use the two dimensions shown in Figure 6.8: difficulty and discriminability. Other approaches add a third dimension for the probability that test takers with the lowest levels of ability will get a correct response. Still other approaches use only the difficulty parameter. All of the approaches grade items in relation to the probability that those who do well or poorly on the exam will have different levels of performance. One can average item characteristic curves to create a test characteristic curve that gives the proportion of responses expected to be correct for each level of ability.

Perhaps the most attractive advantage of tests based on IRT is that one can easily adapt them for computer administration. The computer can rapidly identify the specific items that are required to assess a particular ability level. With this approach, test takers do not have to suffer the embarrassment of attempting multiple items beyond their ability. Conversely, they do not need to waste their time and effort on items far below their capability. In addition, each test taker may get different items to answer, greatly reducing the chances of cheating. It has been suggested that computer-adaptive testing will increase efficiency by 50% or more by reducing the amount of time each test taker spends responding to items (Schmidt & Embretson, 2003).

Figure 6.9 shows the measurement precision associated with conventional and computer-adaptive tests. Most conventional tests have the majority of their items at or near an average level of difficulty; this is represented by the "peaked conventional" portion of the figure. Though the precision of the test is best for those at average ability levels, those with the lowest or highest ability levels are not well assessed by this type of test. An alternative approach, labeled "rectangular conventional" in Figure 6.9, requires that test items be selected to create a wide range in level of difficulty. These items are pretested and selected to cover evenly the span from easiest to most difficult. The problem with this approach is that only a few items of the test are appropriate for individuals at each ability level; that is, many test takers spend much of their time responding to items either considerably below their ability level or too difficult to solve. As a result, measurement precision is constant across the range of test-taker abilities but relatively low for all people, as shown in Figure 6.9.

FIGURE 6.9

Measurement precision as a function of trail level for adaptive, peaked, and rectangular conventional tests. Adaptive tests based on item response theory (IRT) have higher precision across the range of ability levels.

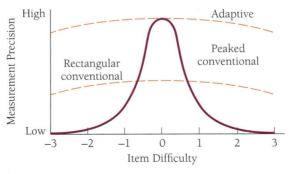

(From Weiss, 1985)

The supporters of IRT believe that the solution to this problem lies in computer-adaptive testing. The computer samples items and determines the range of ability that best represents each test taker. Then testing time is spent focusing on the specific range that challenges the respondent—specifically, items that have a 50% probability of a correct response (assuming no guessing) for each individual. This results in a measurement instrument of equally high precision for all test takers.

IRT is now widely used in many areas of applied research, and there are specialized applications for specific problems such as the measurement of self-efficacy (Smith, Wakely, De Kruif, & Swartz, 2003), psychopathology (Nugent, 2003; Reise & Waller, 2003), industrial psychology (Schneider, Goff, Anderson, & Borman, 2003), and health (Carle, Riley, Hays, & Cella, 2015). Along with the many technical developments in IRT, new technical problems have sprung up. For example, difficulties arise when tests measure multiple dimensions. However, IRT addresses traditional problems in test construction well. For example, IRT can handle items that are written in different formats (Hayes, 2000; Hays, Liu, Spritzer, & Cella, 2007) . In addition, IRT can identify respondents with unusual response patterns and offer insights into cognitive processes of the test taker (Primi, Morsanyi, Chiesi, Donati, & Hamilton, 2015; Sijtsma & Verweij, 1999). Use of IRT may also reduce the biases against people who are slow in completing test problems. In other words, by presenting questions at the test taker's ability level, IRT and computer-adaptive testing allow the defined time spent on taking the test to be used most efficiently by test takers (van der Linden, Scrams, & Schnipke, 1999). Psychological Testing in Everyday Life 6.2 describes how IRT is now being used in medical care.

External Criteria

Item analysis has been persistently plagued by researchers' continued dependence on *internal criteria,* or total test score, for evaluating items. The examples we have just given demonstrate how to compare performance on an item with performance on the total test. You can use similar procedures to compare performance on an item with performance on an external criterion. For example, if you were building a test to select airplane pilots, you might want to evaluate how well the individual items predict success in pilot training or flying performance. The advantages of using external rather than internal criteria against which to validate items were outlined by Guttman (1950) more than 60 years ago. Nevertheless, external criteria are rarely used in practice (Linn, 1994a, 1994b).

Linking Uncommon Measures

One challenge in test applications is how to determine linkages between two different measures. There are many cases in which linkages are needed. For example, the SAT uses different items each time it is administered. Interpretation of the test results for students who took the test at different times requires that scores on each administration have the same meaning, even though the tests include different items—that is, we assume that a score of 600 means the same thing for two students even though the two students completed different tests. Attempts to link scores on a test such as the SAT with those of an equivalent test, such as the American College Test (ACT), pose a more difficult problem. Often these linkages are

6.2 PSYCHOLOGICAL TESTING IN EVERYDAY LIFE

IRT Meets Medicine

PROMIS Initiative

One of the major users of IRT and computer-adaptive testing is being evaluated by the National Institutes of Health (NIH). Many people feel that diagnoses in medicine can be done exclusively from biological tests, and for many years, doctors simply ignored most of the information that was told to them by their patients. However, it has become increasingly clear that patient-reported outcomes provide the key to understanding many important chronic illnesses. People come to doctors because they experience symptoms and problems, and it is important to have these issues addressed. Further, many problems are embarrassing to talk about. For example, many people are uncomfortable talking about bowel habits or sexual functioning. Yet they may feel more comfortable responding to questions about these common problems using a standardized questionnaire.

In response to these concerns, the National Institutes of Health funded the Patient Reported Outcomes Measurement Information System or PROMIS. The purpose of this exercise was to develop highly reliable and precise measures that described how patients report their health status, including physical, mental, and social well-being. The PROMIS initiative is designed to provide practicing clinicians with highly valid and reliable measures that can be used in clinical practice and in research. PROMIS operates through a series of centers throughout the United States, including Boston University, Children's Hospital of Philadelphia, Cincinnati's Children's Hospital, Duke University, Georgetown University, Stanford University, Stony Brook University, University of North Carolina at Chapel Hill, University of Maryland, University of Pittsburgh, UCLA, University of Washington, and several related sites.

The PROMIS study is evaluating measures in a variety of different areas, including HIV infection, drug safety, sexual function, GI distress, mental health, and self-efficacy. Some specialized centers focus on problems associated with children. In all of these areas, a large item bank is created. Using IRT and computer-adaptive testing, patients are able to communicate information about their health problems through questioning that gets the most information using the fewest number of questions (Schalet et al., 2016; Thissen et al., 2016).

---

achieved through statistical formulas. This is analogous to converting a temperature from Celsius to Fahrenheit. Between tests, however, such conversions are not so straightforward. For instance, public schools often give reading and mathematics tests. Although researchers can create a formula that will link mathematics scores to reading scores, it makes little sense to try to interpret mathematical ability in terms of reading skill.

Problems in test linkages became important in the late 1990s when the National Assessment of Educational Progress (NAEP) program was proposed. As part of the program, different students took different tests and were compared on these "uncommon measures." The National Research Council of the National Academy of Sciences was asked if it was feasible to develop equivalency measures that would allow commercial and state test developers to link their measures together. After a detailed study, the committee concluded that it was not feasible to compare the wide array of commercial and state achievement tests to one another. Further, they concluded that developing transformation methods for individual scores should not be done (Feuer et al., 1999).

Items for Criterion-Referenced Tests

In Chapter 2, we briefly mentioned criterion-referenced testing. The traditional use of tests requires that we determine how well someone has done on a test by comparing the person's performance to that of others. For example, the meaning of Jeff's 67 on a geography test is interpreted by his percentile rank in the geography class. Another way of evaluating Jeff's performance is to ask how much he learned in comparison to how much he "should have" learned. Jeff is no longer in competition with everyone else. Instead, we have defined what Jeff must do to be considered knowledgeable about a certain unit. How much Jeff knows rather than whether or not he knows more than someone else determines his grade.

A *criterion-referenced test* compares performance with some clearly defined criterion for learning. This approach is popular in individualized instruction programs. For each student, a set of objectives is defined that state exactly what the student should be able to do after an educational experience. For example, an objective for a middle-school algebra student might be to solve linear equations with two unknowns. The criterion-referenced test would be used to determine whether this objective had been achieved. After demonstrating this knowledge, the student could move ahead to another objective. Many educators regard criterion-referenced tests as diagnostic instruments. When a student does poorly on some items, the teacher knows that the individualized education program needs more focus in a particular area.

The first step in developing criterion-referenced tests involves clearly specifying the objectives by writing clear and precise statements about what the learning program is attempting to achieve. These statements are usually stated in terms of something the student will be able to do. For example, a unit in high-school civics might aim at getting students to understand the operation of municipal government. Test items that assess the attainment of this objective might ask about the taxation powers of local governments, the relation of municipal to state government, and so on.

To evaluate the items in the criterion-referenced test, one should give the test to two groups of students—one that has been exposed to the learning unit and one that has not. Figure 6.10 shows what the distribution of scores would look like. The frequency polygon looks like a V. The scores on the left side of the V are probably those from students who have not experienced the unit. Scores on the right represent those who have been exposed to the unit. The bottom of the V is the *antimode,* or the least frequent score. This point divides those who have been exposed to the unit from those who have not been exposed and is usually taken as the *cutting score* or *point,* or what marks the point of decision. When people get scores higher than the

FIGURE 6.10

Frequency polygon used to evaluate a criterion-referenced test.

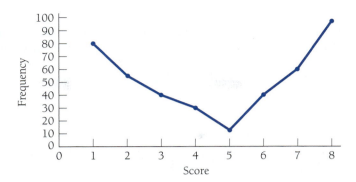

antimode, we assume that they have met the objective of the test. When they get lower scores, we assume they have not. In Figure 6.10, the cutting score is 5.

Criterion-referenced tests offer many advantages to newer educational approaches. For example, in computer-assisted instruction, each student works at his or her own pace on an individualized program of instruction, after which a criterion-referenced test is used to evaluate progress. Students who pass the test can move on to the next unit. Students who do not pass can repeat some of the instruction until they pass.

Similarly, the Internet has provided abundant opportunities for "distance learning" (Anderson, 2016). Using the Internet, students can gain educational experiences interactively. As more college courses come online, there will be a variety of challenges for evaluation and student assessment.

Limitations of Item Analysis

The growing interest in criterion-referenced tests has posed new questions about the adequacy of item-analysis procedures. The main problem is this: Though statistical methods for item analysis tell the test constructor which items do a good job of separating students, they do not help the students learn. Young children do not care as much about how many items they missed as they do about what they are doing wrong. Many times children make specific errors and will continue to make them until they discover why they are making them.

For example, an achievement test might ask a fourth-grade student to add .40 and .30. One of the multiple-choice alternatives would be .07 because item analysis had demonstrated that this was a good distractor. The child who selected .07 would not receive a point on the item and also might continue to make similar errors. Although the data are available to give the child feedback on the "bug" in his or her thinking, nothing in the testing procedure initiates this guidance (Linn, 1994a). One study that involved 1300 fourth, fifth, and sixth graders found that 40% of the children made the same type of error when given problems of a particular kind (Brown & Burton, 1978). Some researchers in educational measurement now appear to be moving toward testing programs that diagnose as well as assess (Miller, Linn, & Gronlund, 2012). Tests can have different purposes. In the past, many have placed too much emphasis on ranking students and not enough on discovering specific weaknesses or gaps in knowledge. There are other disadvantages of criterion-referenced tests. One that has caused considerable concern is that teachers "teach to the test"(Ashwin, 2016). For example, they may concentrate on skills that are easy to test while ignoring more important skills such as critical thinking, judgment, reading comprehension, and self-expression.

Summary

There is an art and a science to test construction. Writing good items is a complex and demanding task. In the first step, developers decide what sort of information they are trying to obtain. If they want to know whether or not test takers know "the right information," developers may use true-false items—that is, a *dichotomous format*. They may also use for the same purpose multiple-choice items, a *polytomous format,* in which a correct choice must be selected among several alternatives. With these types of formats, the test constructor must always consider the probability that someone will get an answer correct by chance.

Many formats are available for tests that do not have right or wrong answers. The *Likert format* is popular for attitude scales. In this format, respondents check on a 5-point scale the degree to which they agree or disagree with the given statements. Similarly, in the category-scaling method, ratings are obtained on a scale with defined endpoints. The familiar 10-point scale is an example of a category scale. Unfortunately, category scales are subject to some bias when the endpoints are not clearly defined. Checklists and Q-sorts are among the many item formats used in personality research. These methods require people to make judgments about whether or not certain items describe themselves or others.

Once developers have created test items, they can administer them to groups of individuals and systematically assess the values of the items. One method of item analysis requires evaluation of item difficulty, which is usually assessed by examining the number of people who get each item correct. In addition to difficulty analysis, test constructors usually examine the correlation between getting any item correct and the total test score. This correlation is used as an index of *discriminability*.

Another way to learn about the value of items is to draw a picture of the *item characteristic curve*. For example, the proportion of people who get an item correct can be plotted as a function of the total test score. The best items are those for which the probability of getting the item correct is highest among those with the highest test scores.

The most important contemporary development in psychological testing is *item response theory* (IRT). In this method, a computer identifies the specific items that characterize the skill level of a particular test taker. The test is tailored to that individual. This method allows more precision and less burden on the test taker. Although all test takers may be scored on the same dimensions, the actual items they complete are likely to differ.

Criterion-referenced tests require a different approach to test construction. With such tests, a person's knowledge is evaluated against what he or she is expected to know rather than against what others know. To evaluate items in criterion-referenced tests, one compares the performance of those who would be expected to know the material with the performance of others who would not be expected to have learned the information.

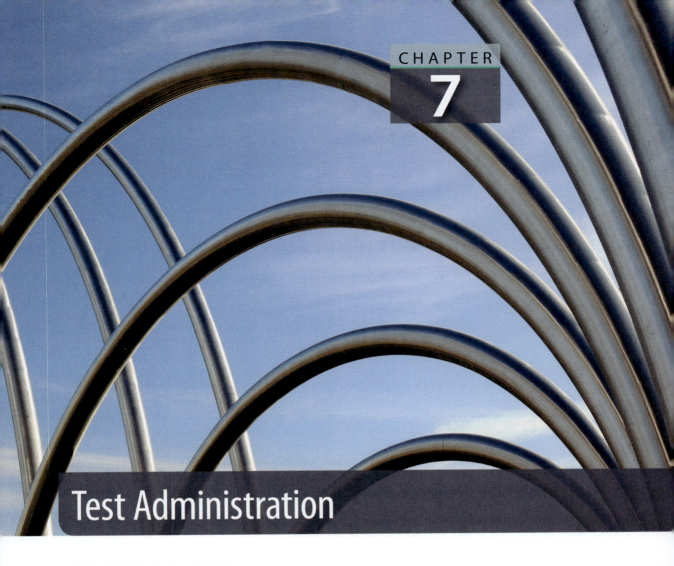

Test Administration

LEARNING OBJECTIVES

When you have completed this chapter, you should be able to:

► Discuss how the relationship between the examiner and the test taker can affect test scores

► Explain how an expectancy effect might affect a test score

► Describe stereotype threat and how it can affect test scores

► Examine the relationship between test performance and reinforcing particular responses

► Outline some of the advantages of computer-assisted test administration

► List what characteristics of the state of the subject should be considered when a test score is evaluated

n the last six chapters, we discussed many topics related to test construction. Before we move on to applications of the tests, one final methodological issue needs to be covered: the administration of tests.

Many factors influence test scores. We have a tendency to think that an observed score really represents the true ability or trait we are trying to measure. In Chapter 4, we reviewed the concept of reliability and introduced measurement error, or the difference between the true score and the observed score. Reliability theory is primarily concerned with random sources of error. In the actual application of tests, we must consider many other potential sources of error, including the testing situation, tester characteristics, and test-taker characteristics.

Why We Changed Our Minds

Sometimes new evidence forces us to rethink our beliefs. Studies on biases associated with test administration are a case in point. When this book was first published in 1982, leaders in the field were persuaded that the test scores were relatively unaffected by the environment in which the test was administered. In particular, it was widely believed that the interaction between the test administrator and test taker had little effect on scores. Or, the little bias caused by these circumstances could be mitigated by following standardized testing procedures.

In the 35 years following the initial publication of this book, new evidence has emerged suggesting that testing circumstances do make a difference. In particular, discomfort resulting from stereotyping can adversely affect test takers. As a result of this new evidence, it may be time to rethink the traditional beliefs about test-taking biases. This chapter will summarize the evidence that led to the earlier conclusion that test results are not affected by the testing situation. Then, we consider the emerging evidence that context matters and we will examine new approaches to mitigate these concerns.

The Examiner and the Subject

The Relationship Between Examiner and Test Taker

Both the behavior of the examiner and his or her relationship to the test taker can affect test scores. In one study reported more than 50 years ago, 1st- through 7th-grade children were given the Wechsler Intelligence Scale for Children (WISC; see Chapter 10) under one of two conditions. Half of the children were given the test under an enhanced rapport condition in which the examiner used friendly conversation and verbal reinforcement during the test administration. The other children took the test under a neutral rapport condition in which the examiner neither initiated conversation nor used reinforcement (Feldman & Sullivan, 1960). The examiner's rapport had little effect on the scores of the younger children (through 3rd grade). However, average IQ scores for the 5th-grade through 9th-grade students were higher for those who had received the test under the enhanced rapport condition (mean IQ = 122) than for those with a neutral administrator (mean IQ = 109). This difference (122 − 109) is almost a full standard deviation.

Another study compared scores obtained by examiners who made approving comments (such as "good" or "fine") with scores obtained by examiners who used disapproving comments ("I thought you could do better than that") or neutral comments. Children who took the test under a disapproving examiner received lower scores than did children exposed to a neutral or an approving examiner (Witmer, Bernstein, & Dunham, 1971). For younger children, a familiar examiner may make a difference. In one study, 137 children took a reading test, half with a familiar proctor, half with an unfamiliar proctor. Reading scores were significantly lower when the proctor was unfamiliar (DeRosa & Patalano, 1991). Because of these early observations, systematic procedures were developed to reduce this biasing effect.

Observations of children with academic performance problems show that it is common for these test takers to show evidence of opposition, restlessness, and overactivity (Venkatesan, 2015). In a quantitative review of the literature, Fuchs and Fuchs (1986) considered 22 different studies that involved 1489 children. Averaged across the studies, they found that the test performance was approximately 0.28 standard deviation (roughly 4 IQ points) higher when the examiner was familiar with the test taker than when not. In those studies that involved children from lower socioeconomic classes, familiarity accounted for approximately 7.6 IQ points. The review raises important concerns because it demonstrates that familiarity with the test taker, and perhaps preexisting notions about the test taker's ability, can either positively or negatively bias test results.

In most testing situations, examiners should be aware that the interaction with test takers can influence the results. They should also keep in mind that subtle cues given by the test administered can affect the level of performance expected by the examiner.

The Race of the Tester

Because of concern about bias, the effects of the tester's race have generated considerable attention. Some groups feel that their children should not be tested by anyone except a member of their own race. For example, some people claim that African American children receive lower test scores when tested by white examiners than by examiners of their own race. Although the effects of racial bias in test administration are discussed frequently, relatively few experimental studies have examined the exact impact of these effects. Sattler reviewed such effects on several occasions (Sattler, 2002, 2004, 2014). After careful consideration of the problem and occasional reanalysis of the data, Sattler concluded that there is little evidence that the race of the examiner significantly affects intelligence test scores. Sattler and Gwynne (1982) have referred to the belief that white examiners impede the test performance of African American children as a myth widely held but unsupported by scientific studies.

Until about 2000, it was widely believed that the examiner's race did not affect the results of IQ tests because the procedures for properly administering an IQ test are so specific. Anyone who gives the test should do so according to a strict procedure. In other words, well-trained African American and white test administrators should act almost identically. Deviation from this procedure might produce differences in performance associated with the race of the examiner. For example, in the next sections, we show how subtle nonverbal cues can affect test scores. Even though most standardized tests require a strict administration procedure, the examiner can still communicate a hostile or a friendly atmosphere, a hurried or a relaxed manner, or an inquisitorial or a therapeutic role. Rather than race, these effects may reflect individual or cultural differences.

However, if the literature was examined carefully, there were hints decades ago that some biases were creeping in. Way back in the 1970s, Sattler (1973b, 1973c) had shown that the race of the examiner affects test scores in some situations. Examiner effects tend to increase when examiners are given more discretion about the use of the tests. In one study in which a small effect of the examiner's race was found, the examiners were paraprofessionals rather than psychologists. The white examiners obtained higher scores from white than from African American children, whereas scores for both groups of children were comparable when tested by African American examiners (Abramson, 1969).

There may be some biases in the way items are presented. One study compared African American and white preschool children on the Preschool Language Assessment Instrument. All children completed the test in two formats during two sessions that were separated by 2 weeks. In one session, the administration was standard; in the other, the administrators were allowed a greater use of context and themes in explaining the test. The African American children obtained higher test scores when the items were administered in the thematic mode. In particular, the researchers noted a significant increase in performance on the more complex and difficult items (Fagundes, Haynes, Haak, & Moran, 1998).

Stereotype Threat

Being evaluated by others can be very threatening. Most people worry about how well they will perform on tests. The situation may be made worse for groups victimized by negative stereotyping. Test takers may face a double threat. First, there is personal concern about how one will be evaluated and whether they will do well on the test (Spencer, Steele, & Quinn, 1999). For people who come from groups haunted by negative stereotypes, there may be a second level of threat. As a member of a stereotyped group, there may be extra pressure to disconfirm inappropriate negative stereotypes. For example, some people hold the inaccurate belief that women have less mathematical aptitude than men. Studies have shown that women underperform on difficult mathematic status, but not on easy tests. When men and women are told they are taking a test that captures gender differences in test performance, men score higher than equally qualified women. However, these differences can be eliminated by lowering stereotype threat. This is accomplished by describing the test as one that does not identify gender differences (Finnigan & Corker, 2016).

Stereotype threat might have very important effects on test scores. One review of the literature indicated that these threats may explain 50% to 80% of the difference between males and females on the SAT Math section. Other analyses suggest that 25% to 41% of the differences in SAT performance between white non-Hispanic students and those of Hispanic heritage can be explained by stereotype threat while 17% to 29% of the SAT performance differences between white non-Hispanic and African American students can be explained by threat (Walton, Spencer, & Erman, 2013).

Several studies have shown that African American college students tend to get lower grades in college in comparison to white students who are equally prepared. Stereotype threat is a common explanation for this finding. Simply being aware of the negative stereotype may inhibit performance on tests and academic performance. Part of the problem is the belief that intelligence is a fixed trait that is genetically determined. As we will see in Chapter 19, the belief that intelligence is a fixed trait has lost credibility in recent years. Some interventions designed to change mindset have been particularly helpful in addressing this problem. In one study, students were told that intelligence is malleable and adaptable to environmental circumstances. African American students in this condition became more engaged with their university experience, obtained higher grade point averages, and reported greater enjoyment with the college experience in comparison to students who had not been assigned to the mindset condition (Aronson, Fried, & Good, 2002). Studies have shown that these results generalize to other groups that may be victims of negative stereotypes. For example, one very similar study suggested an advantage of a stereotype threat intervention for Turkish-origin migrants who live in Germany. In German culture, people whose families originated in Turkey are often the victims of negative attitudes. Interventions that tell test takers that intelligence can be modified by the environment help reduce the impact of stereotype threat (Froehlich, Martiny, Deaux, Goetz, & Mok, 2016). There have been several meta-analyses that summarize large numbers of studies on stereotype threat. These analyses show that the effect is robust and can be replicated in a wide range of circumstances (Lamont, Swift, & Abrams, 2015; Spencer, Logel, & Davies, 2016)

How Stereotype Threat Does Damage

Much of the literature has focused on the test administrator. It asks what the test giver can do to minimize bias. The problem with this literature is that it failed to consider the test taker and the context of testing. People come to testing situations with fears and anxieties that can be provoked by the context. Cues about the testing environment can exacerbate these concerns. For example, if a person from a stereotyped group is reminded that members of his or her group may not perform well on the test, lower performance might be expected.

There are a variety of hypotheses about why stereotype threat affects performance. One theory holds that stereotype threat depletes working memory (Mazerolle, Régner, Rigalleau, & Huguet, 2015). People who are threatened may engage in cognitive processes that focus their attention on themselves rather than on the test task. They overattend to the treat and have less attentional capacity to concentrate on the test. Efforts to suppress these interfering thoughts may deplete working memory.

Another explanation for the effects of stereotype threat is "self-handicapping." Test takers, when faced with the expectation that they may not perform well, might reduce their level of effort. Not trying hard offers a good explanation for poor performance. In order to protect self-worth, they might give themselves an alternative explanation for disappointing performance. They can legitimately say that they did not try very hard (Beilock, Rydell, & McConnell, 2007).

Others have argued that stereotype threat cause physiological arousal. Arousal might facilitate performance on easy tests but can interfere with performance on more challenging assessments (Walton, Murphy, & Ryan, 2015).

Remedies for Stereotype Threat

One of the criticisms of the stereotype threat literature is that most of the studies were conducted in the laboratory, not in real-life situations. Performance on high-stakes tests, such as the SAT, provides real-life examples of the impact of stereotype threat (Stricker, Rock, & Bridgeman, 2015). One series of studies demonstrated how stereotype threat might work in real-world testing situations. Laboratory studies have demonstrated that simple triggers can activate thoughts about stereotypes and that these cognitive processes are enough to hinder test performance. For example, it is common for the first section of a testing form to include information about age, race, and sex. For someone concerned about test performance, responding to these questions might activate concerns about how their group is perceived. Asking a woman to indicate her sex just prior to beginning the Advanced Placement (AP) calculus test may stimulate her to think about negative stereotypes that incorrectly imply that women have low math aptitude. This threat could be avoided by simply moving the questions about age, race, and sex from the beginning of the test to the end. By doing so, the questions that serve as stereotype triggers would be completed after the substantive math questions on the test were done. One study estimated that simply moving information about sex from the beginning to the end of the AP calculus test might result in about 4700 more women each year achieving a high enough score on the AP calculus test to get college credit for their AP calculus course (Danaher & Crandall, 2008).

A variety of interventions to mitigate the effects of stereotype threat have been tested (Spencer et al., 2016). Many of these interventions are effective, not because they change the situation, but rather because they reduce the level of threat. For example, telling test takers that they are completing a nondiagnostic test can sometimes reduce the amount of threat. In one study, telling women that the math test they were about to take is not expected to show sex differences in performance resulted in women outperforming men in a math class (Good, Aronson, & Harder, 2008).

Perhaps one of the most damaging effects of stereotypes is the subtle communication that some groups possess a fixed trait that cannot be changed. For example, the suggestion that IQ is inherited and is not subject to environmental influence may lead some groups to develop a fixed mindset that they will not do well on tests. Ultimately, this mindset might result in reduced effort. Providing African American students with well-documented evidence that intelligence is not a trait and that it can be changed with experience may result in better academic performance and higher grade point averages (Aronson et al., 2002). Other interventions help test takers cope with stress while others help students move from a fixed mindset that underscores that tests are evaluating immovable traits to a growth mindset that emphasizes capacity for improvement. Some early experiments show that interventions that promote a growth mindset result in higher GPAs and fewer students receiving D and F grades in the 9th grade (Yeager et al., 2016).

In summary, the stereotype threat phenomenon has received significant attention in recent years. Although there is substantial evidence that it threatens test performance in some groups, we are also beginning to see evidence that relatively simple interventions can be used to mitigate some of the negative consequences of stereotyping (Spencer et al., 2016).

Language of Test Taker

The amount of linguistic demand can put non-English speakers at a disadvantage. Even for tests that do not require verbal responses, it is important to consider the extent to which test instructions assume that the test taker understands English (Cormier, McGrew, & Evans, 2011). Some of the new standards concern testing individuals with different linguistic backgrounds. The standards emphasize that some tests are inappropriate for people whose knowledge of the language is questionable. For example, the validity and reliability of tests for those who do not speak English is suspect. Translating tests is difficult, and it cannot be assumed that the validity and reliability of the translation are comparable to the English version. Concern about the internal validity of research studies often compromises external validity (Rabin et al., 2016). External validity concerns the use of research findings in groups other than those who participated in the original validation studies. The standard is that, for test takers who are proficient in two or more languages, the test should be given in the language that the test takers feel is their best. Evidence for test comparability across languages should be available. Furthermore, interpreters should be used only with great caution because test interpreters can introduce bias into the testing situation [American Educational Research Association (AERA), American Psychological Association (APA), & National Council on Measurement in Education (NCME), 2014].

Training of Test Administrators

Different assessment procedures require different levels of training (Oakland & Wechsler, 2016). Many behavioral assessment procedures require training and evaluation but not a formal degree or diploma. Psychiatric diagnosis is sometimes obtained using the Structured Clinical Interview for DSM-V (SCID) (Tolin et al., 2016). Typical SCID users are licensed psychiatrists or psychologists with additional training on the test. There are no standardized protocols for training people to administer complicated tests such as the Wechsler Adult Intelligence Scale-Revised (WAIS-R; see Chapter 10), although these tests are usually administered by licensed psychologists. Many training programs have students complete only four practice administrations of the WAIS-R. In a study of 22 graduate students, there were numerous errors in scoring the test, with no improvement over five practice administrations. The error rate went down only after approximately 10 administrations, suggesting that students need at least 10 practice sessions to begin gaining competence with the WAIS-R (Patterson, Slate, Jones, & Steger, 1995).

Expectancy Effects

The literature on stereotype threat concentrates on how cues in the testing environment can affect the test taker. Beliefs held by people administering and scoring tests might also get translated into inaccurate test scores. A well-known line of research in psychology has shown that data sometimes can be affected by what an experimenter expects to find. Robert Rosenthal and his colleagues at Harvard University conducted many experiments on such **expectancy effects**, often called **Rosenthal effects** (Rosenthal & Rubie-Davies, 2015). In a typical experiment, Rosenthal employed a large number of student experimenters to help collect data on a task such as rating human faces for success or failure. Half of the student experimenters were led to believe that the average response would fall toward the success side of the scale, and the other half were told that the average response would fall on the failure side. The results of these experiments have consistently demonstrated that the subjects actually provide data that confirm the experimenter's expectancies. However, the magnitude of the effects is small—approximately a 1-point difference on a 20-point scale (Rosenthal, 1966).

The experimenter's influence is not limited to human subjects. Other experiments have demonstrated that rats that are expected to be "maze bright" will learn to run through a maze more quickly than will rats that are expected to be "maze dull." In reality, all of the rats were from the same litter and they were randomly assigned to be labeled as maze bright or maze dull (Rosenthal & Fode, 1963).

Several authors have challenged the Rosenthal experiments, claiming that they are based on unsound statistical procedures or faulty design (Barber & Silver, 1968; Elashoff & Snow, 1971; Thorndike, 1968). Rosenthal has acknowledged some problems in his early work and has greatly improved his own skills as a methodologist (Rosenthal, 2015; Rosenthal & Rubie-Davies, 2015).

Expectancies shape our judgments in many important ways (Rosenthal & Rubie-Davies, 2015). One of the most important responsibilities for faculty in research-oriented universities is to apply for grant funding. Grant reviewers are supposed to judge the quality of proposals independently of the reputation of the applicant. However, studies suggest that reviewers' expectancies about the investigators do influence their judgment (Ginther et al., 2011). Psychological Testing in Everyday Life Box 7.1 summarizes the problem of racial bias in the review of grants submitted to the National Institutes of Health. On the basis of these analyses, the Institutes initiated a program on racial sensitivity and stereotype threat.

Two aspects of the expectancy effect relate to the use of standardized tests. First, the expectancy effects observed in Rosenthal's experiments were obtained when all of the experimenters followed a standardized script. Although gross forms of bias are possible, Rosenthal argued that the expectancy effect results from subtle nonverbal communication between the experimenter and the subject. The experimenter may not even be aware of his or her role in the process. In one recent study, teachers were trained to raise expectations for math performance for all students. A control group did not get this training. Over the course of a school year, students whose teachers had high expectations training achieved significantly great gains in math performance in comparison to those whose teachers did not get this training (Rubie-Davies, Peterson, Sibley, & Rosenthal, 2015). The expectancy effect can impact intelligence testing in many ways, such as scoring. In a series of experiments, graduate students with some training in intelligence testing were asked to score ambiguous responses from intelligence tests. Sometimes they were told that the responses had been given by "bright" people, and other times they were told the responses were from "dull" people. The students tended to give more credit to

7.1   PSYCHOLOGICAL TESTING IN EVERYDAY LIFE

Racial Bias in the Review of NIH Grants

The U.S. National Institutes of Health (NIH) has a long-standing commitment to support the highest quality research. The 27 NIH institutes and centers take pride in their commitment to fairness in the grant review process. However, one study raised concerns about equity in the review process. The study analyzed the probability of having a research grant funded by the NIH as a function of the race or ethnicity of the applicant. The study systematically controlled for a wide variety of factors that might explain the result. For example, the grant success rate is statistically adjusted to control for the influence of the applicant's institution, for years of experience, and for level of training. The analysis, which included a review of 106,368 applications, found that African American and Asian applicants were significantly less likely to receive funding for their applications. However, among Asians, the difference was largely explained by whether the applicant was a U.S. citizen. Overall, African American applicants were 10% less likely than white applicants to receive funding for their grant (see figure). There was some evidence that African American applicants were discouraged by the system. For example, African American and Hispanic applicants were less likely to resubmit their grant applications after they had received feedback. As a result of this important study, the NIH created a variety of programs to investigate the problem further and to develop recommendations for increased equity in grant review (Ginther et al., 2011; Tabak & Collins, 2011).

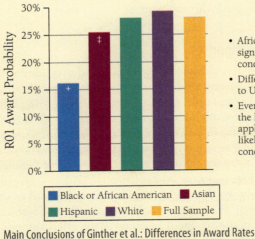

- African American and Asian R01 applicants are significantly less likely to receive a grant to conduct original research.
- Differences in Asian applicant award rates related to U.S. citizenship.
- Even after controlling for factors that influence the likelihood of success, African American applicants are still <u>10 percentage points</u> less likely than white applicants to receive a grant to conduct original research.

Main Conclusions of Ginther et al.: Differences in Award Rates

responses purportedly from bright test takers (Sattler, Hillix, & Neher, 1970; Sattler & Winget, 1970). Other studies have demonstrated that the expectancy effect can occur even if the responses are not ambiguous (Sattler, 1998).

A variety of interpersonal and cognitive process variables have been shown to affect our judgment of others (Pawling, Kirkham, Tipper, & Over, 2016). Even something as subtle as a physician's voice can affect the way patients rate their doctors (Haskard, Williams, DiMatteo, Heritage, & Rosenthal, 2008). These biases may also affect test scoring. For example, Donahue and Sattler (1971) demonstrated that students who scored the WAIS would most likely give credit for selected items to examinees they liked or perceived to be warm. Thus, examiners must remain aware that their relationships with examinees can affect their objectivity when they score certain types of tests.

Many studies have attempted to find subtle variables that affect test responses. For example, Rappaport and McAnulty (1985) presented tape-recorded responses to people scoring IQ tests. Though the children on the recording gave the same response with or without an accent, no difference between these two conditions surfaced.

In reviewing these studies, Sattler (2014) noted that studies demonstrating an expectancy effect tended to have an administrator test only two children (one under a high and one under a low expectancy condition). The studies that did not find an expectancy effect tended to have more subjects tested by each test administrator. The studies that used more samples of each tester's behavior should produce more reliable estimates of the expectancy effect; therefore, the studies that failed to show an expectancy effect may be more credible than those that showed it.

In spite of these inconsistent results, you should pay careful attention to the potentially biasing effect of expectancy. Even Rosenthal's harshest critics do not deny the possibility of this effect. And, the expectancy effect has withstood the test of time. Some of the findings have been continuously replicated over the course of more than 50 years (Babad, 2016). Thus, it is always important to do as much as you can to eliminate bias associated with expectation.

Effects of Reinforcing Responses

Because reinforcement affects behavior, testers should always administer tests under controlled conditions. Several studies have shown that reward can significantly affect test performance. For example, incentives can help improve performance on IQ tests for specific subgroups of children. In one study, 6- to 13-year-olds received tokens they could exchange for money each time they gave a correct response on the WISC verbal scale. This incentive improved the performance of white children from lower-income families but not for children from middle-income families or African American children from lower-income homes (Sweet, 1970).

Many studies have shown that children will work quite hard to obtain praise such as, "You are doing well" (Eisenberger & Cameron, 1998). Several studies have shown that the effects of praise are about as strong as the effects of money or candy (Merrell, 1999). The results of these studies, however, are sometimes complicated. For instance, one study found that girls increased their accuracy on the WISC block design subtest when given any type of reinforcement for a correct response. Boys increased their accuracy only when given chips that could be exchanged for money

(Bergan, McManis, & Melchert, 1971). It also appears that the type of praise is important. For example, praising the process ("you worked hard") results in better performance than praising the person ("you are clever") (Skipper & Douglas, 2011).

Some of the most potent effects of reinforcement arise in attitudinal studies. In survey research, the answer given by a respondent is not necessarily right or wrong but rather an expression of how someone feels about something. Repeated studies have demonstrated that the way an interviewer responds affects the content of responses in interview studies (Cannell & Henson, 1974). In one of the most interesting of these, respondents in a household survey were asked if they suffered from certain physical symptoms. For half of the subjects, the interviewer gave an approving nod each time a symptom was reported. For the other half, the interviewer remained expressionless. The number of symptoms reported increased significantly with such approval. In a similar study, two symptoms that no one should report were added to the list: "Are your intestines too long?" and "Do the ends of your hair itch?" More people reported these symptoms if they had been reinforced for reporting other symptoms than if they had not.

The potency of reinforcement requires that test administrators exert strict control over the use of feedback. Because different test takers give different responses, one cannot ensure that the advantages resulting from reinforcement will be the same for all people. As a result, most test manuals and interviewer guides insist that no feedback be given.

Testing also requires standardized conditions because situational variables can affect test scores. The book *Standards for Educational and Psychological Testing*, published by the APA and other professional groups (AERA, APA, & NCME, 2014), emphasizes that a test manual should clearly spell out the directions for administration. These directions should be sufficiently detailed to be duplicated in all situations in which the test is given. A good test manual gives the test examiner instructions that include the exact words to be read to the test takers. It also includes questions that testers will likely ask and instructions on how administrators should answer them.

Inexperienced test administrators often do not fully appreciate the importance of standardization in administration. Whether they give a test or supervise others who do, they must consider that the test may not remain reliable or valid if they deviate from the specified instructions.

A few occasions do require deviation from standardized testing procedures. Sattler (1988) acknowledges that the blind need special considerations, and Edelstein and Kalish (1999) discuss the testing needs of the aged. However, many widely used tests have now developed special standardized methods for testing particular populations. To ensure that tests are given under standardized conditions, some examiners prefer to give instructions through a tape recorder. Others have opted for computer-assisted test administration.

Computer-Assisted Test Administration

Computer technology affects many fields, including testing and test administration. Today, virtually all educational institutions and most households enjoy access to the Internet. This easy access has caused test administration on computers to blossom.

Interactive testing involves the presentation of test items on a computer terminal or personal computer and the automatic recording of test responses. The computer can also be programmed to instruct the test taker and to provide instruction when parts of the testing procedure are not clear. As early as 1970, Cronbach recognized the value of computers as test administrators. Here are some of the advantages that computers offer:

▶ excellence of standardization,
▶ individually tailored sequential administration,
▶ precision of timing responses,
▶ release of human testers for other duties,
▶ patience (test taker not rushed), and
▶ control of bias.

Since the publication of the first edition of this book in 1982, computer technology has bloomed in testing. Today, many of the major psychological tests are available for use on a personal computer. The influential aptitude tests, such as the SAT and GRE, are now administered by computer. Furthermore, the computer is playing an increasingly important role in test administration. Some older people, though, feel uneasy interacting with computers, or suffer from "keyboard phobia."

The computer offers many advantages in test administration, scoring, and interpretation, including ease of application of complicated psychometric issues and the integration of testing and cognitive psychology. Most importantly, computer administration reduces a variety of biases in test administration (Green, 2011). In most cases, scores obtained via electronic administration are equivalent to those captured through other methods, such as paper and pencil (Rutherford et al., 2015).

Computer-assisted test administration does not necessarily depend on a structured order of test items. Indeed, one advantage of this approach is that the items can be given in any order or in a unique random order for every test taker. Computers are objective and cost-effective. Furthermore, they allow more experimental control than do other methods of administration. For example, if you want a precise limit on the amount of time any one item can be studied, the computer can easily be programmed to flash the items on the screen for specific durations. The computer-assisted method also prevents test takers from looking ahead at other sections of the test or going back to sections already completed (Green, 2011; Lane, Raymond, & Haladyna, 2015). Comparisons of test scores have not tended to show large differences between computer-assisted and paper-and-pencil tests (Ward, Hooper, & Hannafin, 1989), yet the computer method ensures standardization and control and also reduces scoring errors. It was once thought that people would rebel against interactions with machines. However, evidence suggests that test takers find interactions with computers more enjoyable than paper-and-pencil tests (Rosenfeld, Doherty, Vicino, Kantor, & Greaves, 1989).

One of the most interesting findings concerns the use of computers to obtain sensitive information. In one study, 162 college students were assessed on the Minnesota Multiphasic Personality Inventory (MMPI) and questionnaires that concerned drinking and other personal information. The information was obtained in one of three ways: computer, questionnaire, or interview. The results suggested that students were less likely to disclose socially undesirable information during a personal interview than on a computer. In fact, students may be more honest when tested by a computer than by a person. Furthermore, most people are comfortable providing information to questionnaires via computers, even if the questions address sensitive issues such as substance abuse (Spear, Shedlin, Gilberti, Fiellin, & McNeely, 2016). Some studies show that young people are willing to disclose more personal health information online than in face-to-face conversation. This seems to be an even stronger effect in Hong Kong than in South Korea or the United States (Lin, Zhang, Song, & Omori, 2016).

There has been a substantial increase in the number of studies devoted to computer-administered testing. Most studies show that computer administration is at least as reliable as traditional assessment (Kröhne & Martens, 2011). Computer assessment has been applied in a variety of areas, including the administration of the MMPI (Blazek & Forbey, 2011), personnel selection (Hanson, Borman, Mogilka, Manning, & Hedge, 1999), and cognitive process (Senior, Phillips, Barns, & David, 1999). As more and more types of tests are prepared for computer administration, independent reliability and validity studies will be needed. There are many advantages of computer-administered tests. For example, in medical studies, repeated assessments of cognitive function are often needed. Studies have demonstrated that cognitive tests given at home using an iPad produce results similar to those obtained in the clinic (Rentz et al., 2016). Not all observers endorse the rapid development of computerized test administration. For example, J. D. Matarazzo (1986) suggested that computer-generated test reports in the hands of an inexperienced psychologist cannot replace clinical judgment. In such cases, computerized reports may actually cause harm if misinterpreted. Other problems include computerized scoring routines that have errors or are poorly validated; such problems are often difficult to detect within the software. Hartman (1986b) accurately predicted an increase over the last 15 years in consumer liability cases involving software products. Groth-Marnat and Schumaker (1989) outlined several problems caused by faulty computerized testing systems. For example, some programs have untested claims of validity, and computerized reports might be based on an obsolete database. A clinical psychologist who lets the computer do too much of the thinking may misinterpret test responses. With the growth in computerized testing, the industry has needed to create new guidelines.

In response to these concerns, there are now guidelines for computer-based Internet testing (van de Vijver, Schweizer, & DiStefano, 2016). The guidelines emphasized the need for the highest quality computer displays, protection against technical problems such as poor Internet connections, assurance of high psychometric properties of the tests, and the need to consider differential experience with computers by test takers. Test takers might be at a disadvantage if they are taking the test with an older computer or with a poor Internet connection. In addition, people with poorer technical computer or keyboard skills might get lower scores independent of their knowledge or aptitude.

Mode of Administration

A variety of studies have considered the difference between self-administered measures and those that are administered by a tester or a trained interviewer. Studies on health, for example, have shown that measures administered by an interviewer are more likely to show people in good health than are measures that are self-completed. Another study showed that measures administered via telephone yielded higher

7.1 FOCUSED EXAMPLE

Test Administration Types and Self-Reporting

Behaviors are a very important part of cancer screening. Asking about cancer-related behaviors often requires very personal information. Cancer researchers need to ask about sexual behavior or about very personal health practices, and they need to obtain the information in the most sensitive way. The National Cancer Institute has developed questionnaires to ask about the use of cancer screening tests. Some screening tests require that a person test his or her own stool for the presence of blood. Other tests require that a medical scope be inserted into the anal cavity. Asking about these topics can be embarrassing for both the patient and the interviewer.

In one study, investigators had the opportunity to compare the mode of administration. Men and women between the ages of 51 and 74 were asked about their use of colon and rectal cancer screening tests, but not all people were asked in the same way. The participants were randomly assigned to provide the information by mail, by telephone, or in a face-to-face survey. The self-reports about cancer screening were then compared to their actual medical records. This allowed a comparison to determine which way of asking best corresponded to actual test use. The study found that the mode of administration did not make much difference. Mail, telephone, and face-to-face methods were about equally accurate when compared to medical records. However, there was a tendency to overreport the use of some of the tests. In particular, people overreported the use of the test that required people to gather their own stool for testing. Although there are some biases in self-reports, it does not appear that they are systematically related to mode of administration (Vernon et al., 2008).

health scores than those that required people to fill out the questionnaires on their own (Hanmer, Hays, & Flyback, 2007). Most studies show that computer administration leads to more accurate results. Men, in particular, may be more likely to offer random responses using the older paper-and-pencil versions of tests (Blazek & Forbey, 2011). Studies of dietary recall suggest that information obtained through Web-based automated data collection systems is about equivalent to that collected through more expensive interviewer-administered systems (Thompson et al., 2015). Even though mode of administration has only small effects in most situations, it should be constant within any evaluation of patients (Bowling, 2005).

For studies of psychiatric disability, the mode of asking the questions makes a difference. Particularly for younger people, more distress and disability is reported in self-completed questionnaires compared with questionnaires completed using an interviewer (Moun, 1998). In other instances, the mode of administration is less important. Focused Example 7.1 suggests that the type of test administration has little effect on personal reports about the use of cancer screening tests.

In educational testing, it is less clear that the mode of test administration has a strong impact. One study synthesized all published investigations on the mode of administration for reading tests administered to K-12 students. Analysis compared performance of computer-administered tests with those administered using traditional paper-and-pencil measures. The analysis did not find significant differences between scores from computer-administered versus paper-and-pencil modes (Wang, Jiao, Young, Brooks, & Olson, 2008).

Subject Variables

A final variable that may be a serious source of error is the state of the subject. Motivation and anxiety can greatly affect test scores. For example, many college students suffer from a serious debilitating condition known as **test anxiety** (Spielberger, Anton, & Bedell, 2015). Such students often have difficulty focusing attention on the test items and are distracted by other thoughts such as, "I am not doing well" or "I am running out of time" (Zuckerman & Spielberger, 2015). Test anxiety appears to have three components: worry, emotionality, and lack of self-confidence (Oostdam & Meijer, 2003).

It may seem obvious that illness affects test scores. When you have a cold or the flu, you might not perform as well as when you are feeling well. Many variations in health status affect performance in behavior and in thinking (Kaplan, 2004). In fact, medical drugs are now evaluated according to their effects on the cognitive process (Gordon et al., 2016). Some populations need special consideration. For example, the elderly may do better with individual testing sessions, even for tests that can be administered to groups (Martin, Johnson, Poon, Clayton, & Olsen, 1994). The measurement of the effects of health status on functioning will also be discussed in more detail in Chapter 17.

Summary

Standardized test administration procedures are necessary for valid results. Extensive research in social psychology has clearly demonstrated that situational factors can affect scores on mental and behavioral tasks. These effects, however, can be subtle and may not be observed in all studies. For example, stereotype threat can have significantly detrimental effects on test takers. Similarly, the examiner's rapport and expectancies may influence scores on some but not all occasions. Direct reinforcement of specific responses does have an acknowledged impact and therefore should not be given in most testing situations. In response to these problems, several remedies have been suggested. These include standardization of the test instructions. The threat of the testing situation might be reduced by maneuvers as simple as asking demographic information at the end rather than at the beginning of the test.

Interest has increased in computer-assisted test administration because it may reduce examiner bias. Computers can administer and score most tests with great precision and with minimum bias. This mode of test administration has become the norm for many types of tests.

The state of the subject also affects test scores. For example, some students suffer from debilitating *test anxiety*, which seriously interferes with performance.

Interviewing Techniques

LEARNING OBJECTIVES

When you have completed this chapter, you should be able to:

▶ Explain the difference between a structured and an unstructured interview

▶ Discuss the importance of setting the proper tone for an interview

▶ Describe the role of the interviewer's attitude in the interviewing process

▶ Identify some of the characteristics of effective interviewing

▶ List which types of statements tend to keep the interaction flowing or to elicit self-exploration in the interviewee

▶ Explain the effects of empathy statements on interviewee responses

▶ Identify the various sources of error in the interview

▶ Appreciate the role of cultural, ethnic, and socioeconomic factors in the interview process

▶ Explain how interview skills are acquired and developed

203

simple Google search of the term *interview techniques* will reveal a plethora of sites offering advice on how to answer job interview questions. Some of these sites are useful, others not. How can you decide? Consider Maria predicament. Maria was being considered for a high-level public relations position with the computer firm for which she worked. The job duties would require her to interact with a wide variety of people, ranging from heads of state and corporation presidents to rank-and-file employees and union officials. In addition, the position would involve making formal policy statements for news media. Any poorly phrased statement or inappropriate reaction on her part could result in adverse publicity, which could cost the firm millions of dollars. The application process therefore involved an elaborate testing procedure, including two lengthy interviews. The first was with the firm's personnel selection officer, and the second was with the firm's clinical psychologist (see Figure 8.1).

Knowing the importance of first and last impressions (Reece, 2009; Roeckelein, 2002), Maria took care to appear neat and well groomed. In her first interview, the personnel officer read from a form as she conducted the interview, which went something like this:

OFFICER: I've read your application form and have gone over your qualifications. Would you now please outline your educational experiences, beginning with high school?

MARIA: I graduated from high school in June 2001 with an emphasis in history and social studies. I began attending college in September 2001. I graduated in June 2006 with a major in psychology and minor in business management. I then entered the university's graduate program in business. I earned my master's degree in business administration in 2008.

OFFICER: What is your work history? Begin with your first full-time employment.

FIGURE 8.1
An interview.

pan_kung/Shutterstock.com

Maria described her work history from 2008 through the present. The personnel officer then continued a series of questions, which Maria systematically answered. The questions went something like this:

How do your education and experience relate to the job for which you are applying?

What educational experiences have you had that might help you function in the job for which you are applying?

What employment experiences have you had that might help you function in the job for which you are applying?

Identify any deficiencies in your educational and work experiences.

What educational and work experiences have you had that might impair your ability to function in the job for which you are applying?

The interview continued in a similar manner. With each question, the personnel officer attempted to relate Maria's educational and work experiences to the particular job duties she hoped to assume. For her final question, the personnel officer asked, "Why do you believe you are a good candidate for this position?"

Maria felt good about her interview with the personnel officer. She thought the questions were clear and straightforward, and she was pleased by her answers. The next day she appeared for her interview with the clinical psychologist. Unlike the personnel officer, the psychologist conducted the interview without using written interview questions. This second interview, quite different from the first, went something like this:

PSYCHOLOGIST: Maria, why don't you tell me a little bit about yourself?

MARIA: Where do you want me to begin?

PSYCHOLOGIST: Oh, it doesn't matter. Just tell me about yourself.

MARIA: I graduated from high school in June of 2001. I majored in history and social studies.

PSYCHOLOGIST: Yes, I see.

MARIA: I then attended college and finally finished graduate school in 2008. My master's degree should help me assume the duties of the new position.

PSYCHOLOGIST: You feel that your master's degree is a useful asset in your application.

MARIA: Yes, my graduate experiences taught me how to work with others.

PSYCHOLOGIST: With these graduate experiences, you learned the art of working with other people.

MARIA: Well, I guess I didn't learn it all in graduate school. I've always managed to get along well with others.

PSYCHOLOGIST: As far as you can tell, you work pretty well with people.

MARIA: That's right. As the oldest of four children, I've always had the responsibility for supervising others. You know what I mean?

PSYCHOLOGIST: Being the oldest, you were given extra responsibilities as a child.

MARIA: Not that I resented it. Well, maybe sometimes. It's just that I never had much time for myself.

PSYCHOLOGIST: And having time for yourself is important to you.

MARIA: Yes, of course it is. I guess everybody needs some time alone.

PSYCHOLOGIST: As a person who deals with others all day long, you must treasure those few moments you have to yourself.

MARIA: I really do. Whenever I get a chance I like to drive up to the lake all by myself and just think.

PSYCHOLOGIST: Those moments are precious to you.

The interview continued like this for about an hour. After it was over, Maria wasn't sure how she had done. Think about the two interviews. In what ways were they alike? How did they differ? As you contemplate your answers, you will soon realize that there is more than one type of interview, and that interviews can differ considerably.

The first interview with the personnel officer was highly structured (Levashina, Hartwell, Morgeson, & Campion, 2014). The interviewer read from a printed set of questions, using a standardized interview. Thus, all applicants for the position were asked the same questions in the same sequence. By contrast, the second was an unstructured interview and therefore unstandardized. The clinical psychologist didn't appear to have any specific or particular questions in mind, and the sequence of questions followed from Maria's statements. Each applicant, no doubt, would be asked different questions, depending on his or her responses.

Can you identify other differences between the two interviews? The first was narrow and restricted. It focused on two specific areas: Maria's education and her work experiences. The second was broad and unrestricted. Although the interview clearly focused on Maria herself, it touched on a variety of areas. The first interview was *directive*. The personnel officer directed, guided, and controlled the course of the interview. The second interview was *nondirective*. The clinical psychologist let Maria determine the direction of the interview. When Maria talked about her master's degree, the psychologist discussed it. When Maria talked about being the oldest of four children, this became the focus of the psychologist's response. Furthermore, unlike the personnel officer, the psychologist rarely asked questions. Instead, the psychologist tended to comment or reflect on Maria's previous statement. Last, but perhaps most important, Maria's interview with the personnel officer can best be described as an employment interview, also called a *selection interview*; it was designed to elicit information pertaining to Maria's qualifications and capabilities for particular employment duties (employment interviews are discussed in greater detail in Chapter 18). The second interview, on the other hand, was a diagnostic interview, centered on Maria's emotional functioning rather than her qualifications—that is, the clinical psychologist was interested in uncovering those feelings, thoughts, and attitudes that might impede or facilitate Maria's competence. Interviews are pervasive and increasingly are becoming important in all matters of life (Jong & Jung, 2015).

The Interview as a Test

In many respects, an interview resembles a test (see Table 8.1). Like any psychological or educational test, an interview is a method for gathering data or information about an individual. This information is then used to describe the individual, make future predictions, or both. Like tests, interviews can be evaluated in terms of standard psychometric qualities such as reliability and validity. Furthermore, there are several types of interview procedures; each is chosen according to the type of information sought and the interviewer's goals.

Like any test, the interview involves the interaction of two or more people. Some interviews proceed like individually administered tests, with the interviewer interacting with a single individual at a time. In others, such as the family interview, a single interviewer works with two or more individuals at the same time, as in a group test. Like all tests, an interview has a defined purpose. Furthermore, just as the person who gives a test must take responsibility for the test administration process, so the interviewer must assume responsibility for the conduct of the interview.

Many tests, such as the Thematic Apperception Test (TAT), cannot be properly used without adequate interview data. The interview, on the other hand, is often the only or most important source of data. The interview remains one of the most prevalent selection devices for employment (Huffcutt, 2011; Levashina et al., 2014; Schneider, Powell, & Roulin, 2015). Good interviewing skills may be one of the most important tools for functioning in today's society. Furthermore, interviewing is the chief method of collecting data in clinical psychiatry (Machado, Beutler, Harwood, Mohr, & Lenore, 2011). It is also used in all health-related professions, including general medicine and nursing (Eggly, 2002; Gao, Tilse, Wilson, Tuckett, & Newcombe, 2015). Interviewing is an essential testing tool in subspecialties such as clinical, industrial, counseling, school, and correctional psychology.

A wide variety of other professions depend on interviewing. Indeed, interview skills are important in most professions that involve people: social workers, vocational and guidance counselors, and marriage and family counselors; parole boards; researchers; businesspeople (to evaluate employees as well as potential clients); courtroom attorneys; contractors or architects (to determine exactly what their customers want them to do)—the list goes on and on. Interviewing also plays a role in our nonprofessional lives, such as when a parent questions a group of children to find out whose soccer ball broke the window. To begin new relationships on a

TABLE 8.1 Similarities Between an Interview and a Test

Method for gathering data

Used to make predictions

Evaluated in terms of reliability

Evaluated in terms of validity

Group or individual

Structured or unstructured

positive note, one must possess a degree of interviewing skill. Given such a broad application, no introductory text on psychological tests could be complete without reference to the interview.

Reciprocal Nature of Interviewing

Although there are many types and purposes of interviews, all share certain factors. First, all interviews involve mutual interaction whereby the participants are interdependent—that is, they influence each other (Breggin, 2002; Elmir, Schmied, Jackson, & Wilkes, 2011; Ridge, Campbell, & Martin, 2002). A study by Akehurst and Vrij (1999) illustrates the transactional or reciprocal nature of the interview process. Criminal suspects were observed while being interrogated. The researchers found that if one of the participants in the interview increased his or her activity level, then the activity of the other participant also increased. Similarly, a reduction in activity by one triggered a reduction in the other. The researchers concluded that the participants in an interview profoundly affect each other. Unfortunately for the suspects, a second experiment demonstrated that increased activity on the part of the suspect was related to increased suspiciousness on the part of the interrogator. Results revealed that highly active interrogators increased activity in the suspects, which, in turn, increased the interrogators' suspiciousness (Akehurst & Vrij, 1999).

Interview participants also affect each other's mood. In a classic study, Heller (1971) found that when professional actors responded with anger to highly trained, experienced interviewers, the interviewers became angry themselves and showed anger toward the actors. In this phenomenon, called *social facilitation*, we tend to act like the models around us (see Augustine, Mehl, & Larsen, 2011). If the interviewer is tense, anxious, defensive, and aloof, then the interviewee tends to respond in kind. Thus, if the interviewer wishes to create conditions of openness, warmth, acceptance, comfort, calmness, and support, then he or she must exhibit these qualities.

Because the participants in an interview influence each other, the good interviewer knows how to provide a relaxed and safe atmosphere through social facilitation. However, although both parties influence each other, the good interviewer remains in control and sets the tone. If he or she reacts to the interviewee's tension and anxiety with more tension and anxiety, then these feelings will mount. By remaining relaxed, confident, and self-assured, the interviewer has a calming effect on the interviewee. Even potentially violent prison inmates or disturbed psychotic people can become manageable when the interviewer sets the proper tone. Clearly, social facilitation is one of the most important concepts underlying the interview process.

Principles of Effective Interviewing

Naturally, specific interviewing techniques and approaches vary, depending on such factors as the type of interview (e.g., employment versus diagnostic) and the goals of the interviewer (e.g., description versus prediction). Thus, there are no set rules that apply to all interviewing situations. However, some principles facilitate the conduct of almost any interview. Knowing these principles will not only increase your understanding of the factors and processes that underlie the interview but also help you acquire interview skills of your own.

The Proper Attitudes

Good interviewing is actually more a matter of attitude than skill (Duan & Kivlighan, 2002; Jackle, Lynn, Sinibaldi, & Tipping, 2013). Experiments in social psychology have shown that *interpersonal influence* (the degree to which one person can influence another) is related to *interpersonal attraction* (the degree to which people share a feeling of understanding, mutual respect, similarity, and the like) (Dillard & Marshall, 2003; Krause, Back, Egloff, & Schmukle, 2014). Attitudes related to good interviewing skills include warmth, genuineness, acceptance, understanding, openness, honesty, and fairness. For example, in a study of the initial psychotherapeutic interviews of first-year clinical psychology graduate students, patients and therapists both responded to a questionnaire. Their task was to rate the quality of the interview and indicate the topics, concerns, problems, and feelings of the patient as well as the feelings of the therapist.

The most important factor in the patients' evaluation was their perception of the interviewer's feelings. The session received a good evaluation by both participants when the patient saw the interviewer as warm, open, concerned, involved, committed, and interested, regardless of subject matter or the type or severity of the problem. On the other hand, independent of all other factors, when the interviewer was seen as cold, defensive, uninterested, uninvolved, aloof, and bored, the session was rated poorly (Saccuzzo, 1975). To appear effective and establish rapport, the interviewer must display the proper attitudes.

Responses to Avoid

In a "stress interview," the interviewer may deliberately induce discomfort or anxiety in the interviewee. As a rule, however, making interviewees feel uncomfortable tends to place them on guard, and guarded or anxious interviewees tend to reveal little information about themselves. However, because one purpose of the stress interview is to determine how well an individual functions in adversity, the types of responses that interviewers should avoid might be used in a stress interview. If the goal is to elicit as much information as possible or to receive a good rating from the interviewee, then interviewers should avoid certain responses, including judgmental or evaluative statements, probing statements, hostility, and false reassurance.

Judgmental or evaluative statements are particularly likely to inhibit the interviewee. Being *judgmental* means evaluating the thoughts, feelings, or actions of another. When we use such terms as *good, bad, excellent, terrible, disgusting, disgraceful,* and *stupid*, we make evaluative statements. By judging others, we put them on guard because we communicate the message, "I don't approve of this aspect of you." Such judgments also inhibit others' ease in revealing important information. Thus, unless the goal of the interview is to determine how a person responds to being evaluated, evaluative or judgmental statements should usually be avoided.

Most interviewers should also avoid probing statements. These demand more information than the interviewee wishes to provide voluntarily. The most common way to phrase a probing statement is to ask a question that begins with "Why?" Asking "Why?" tends to place others on the defensive. When we ask "Why?," as in "Why did you stay out so late?," we are demanding that the person explain his or her behavior. Such a demand has an obvious judgmental quality. Furthermore, in probing we may induce the interviewee to reveal something that he or she is not yet ready to reveal. If this happens, the interviewee will probably feel anxious and thus not well disposed to revealing additional information.

In some circumstances, probes are appropriate and necessary. With children or individuals with mental retardation, for instance, one often needs to ask questions to elicit meaningful information (Devoe & Faller, 2002). Highly anxious or withdrawn individuals may also need a probe to get beyond a superficial interchange. In such circumstances, one must use the probe wisely, avoiding "Why?" statements and replacing them with "Tell me" or "How?" statements, as illustrated in Table 8.2.

The hostile statement directs anger toward the interviewee. Clearly, one should avoid such responses unless one has a specific purpose, such as determining how an interviewee responds to anger.

The reassuring statement attempts to comfort or support the interviewee: "Don't worry. Everything will be all right." Though reassurance is sometimes appropriate, you should almost always avoid false reassurance. For example, imagine a friend of yours flunks out of college, loses her job, and gets kicked out of her home by her parents. You are lying to this person when you say, "Don't worry; no problem; it's okay." This false reassurance does nothing to help your friend except perhaps make her realize that you are not going to help her. What has happened to your friend is terrible and will require specific action on her part to prevent even more disastrous developments. Naturally, you should not overwhelm your friend with all the facts at once, but she needs to come to grips with the situation in manageable doses before taking the necessary steps to constructively solve the problem. The person who gives false reassurance usually knows he or she is doing it, as does the person who receives it (see Figure 8.2).

TABLE 8.2 Effective Probing Statements

Poor	Better
Why did you yell at him?	1. Tell me more about what happened.
	2. How did you happen to yell at him?
	3. What led up to the situation?
Why did you say that?	1. Can you tell me what you mean?
	2. I'm not sure I understand.
	3. How did you happen to say that?
Why can't you sleep?	1. Tell me more about your sleeping problem.
	2. Can you identify what prevents you from sleeping?
	3. How is it that you are unable to sleep?

FIGURE 8.2

Responses to avoid in an unstructured interview.

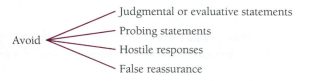

Avoid — Judgmental or evaluative statements
— Probing statements
— Hostile responses
— False reassurance

Effective Responses

Knowing what types of responses to avoid, how does one go about conducting an effective interview? One major principle of effective interviewing is keeping the interaction flowing. The interview is a two-way process; one person speaks first, then the other, and so on. Furthermore, the interviewer usually exerts a minimum amount of effort to keep the interaction flowing. As long as the interviewee's verbalizations relate to the purpose of the interview, the interviewer listens with interest by maintaining face-to-face contact.

Except in structured interviews or for a particular purpose, one can effectively initiate the interview process by using an open-ended question. This is a question that usually cannot be answered specifically, as opposed to a closed-ended question, which can be. Examples of open-ended questions include, "Tell me a little bit about yourself," "Tell me about what interests you," and "What is it that brings you here to see me?" Examples of closed-ended questions include, "Do you like sports?," "Are you married?," and "How old are you?"

A closed-ended question brings the interview to a dead halt, thus violating the principle of keeping the interaction flowing. In the example at the beginning of this chapter, even the personnel officer's opening question—"Would you now please outline your educational experiences, beginning with high school?"—was sufficiently open-ended to permit a variety of responses, depending on the interviewee. Where one individual might provide every minute detail of his or her education, a second might simply include major events. The clinical psychologist's opening statement—"Maria, why don't you tell me a little bit about yourself?"—was even more open-ended. Maria could have replied with just about anything.

Open-ended questions give the interviewee wide latitude in choosing the topics that he or she feels are important. Except for highly specific structured interviews, we usually can learn a lot more about people when they tell us what they think is important than when we try to guess by asking a series of closed-ended questions. The open-ended question requires the interviewee to produce something spontaneously and the closed-ended question to recall something. Table 8.3 presents some closed-ended questions along with corresponding open-ended ones.

Conducting an interview requires flexibility. If not structured, most interviews cannot be conducted in precisely the same way. In therapeutic or diagnostic

TABLE 8.3 Closed- and Open-Ended Questions

Closed-ended	Open-ended
Do you like sports cars?	What kinds of cars do you like?
Do you like baseball?	What kinds of recreational activities do you prefer?
Are you having a problem?	Can you tell me about your problems?
Is your father strict?	What is your father like?
Would you like to vacation in Hawaii?	What are your favorite vacation spots?

interviews, interviewers usually follow only general guidelines in conducting the interview. Their goal is to get to know the interviewees as well as possible to understand them and predict their behavior.

Responses to Keep the Interaction Flowing

After asking the open-ended question, the interviewer as a rule lets the interviewee respond without interruption; that is, the interviewer remains quiet and listens. Unless the interview is structured, once the interviewee's response dies down, the interviewer usually responds in a way that will keep the interaction flowing. (See Table 8.4 for a summary of responses that do this.) He or she should use minimum effort to maintain the flow, such as using a transitional phrase such as 'Yes," "And," or "I see." These phrases imply that the interviewee should continue on the same topic. In Maria's interview with the clinical psychologist, for example, Maria stated, "I graduated from high school in June 1995. I majored in history and social studies." The clinical psychologist simply responded with the transition, "Yes, I see." Maria then elaborated.

Sometimes the transitional phrase fails to have the desired effect. When this occurs, the interviewer should make a response relevant to what has just been communicated. In other words, the interview is thematic; it does not jump from one unrelated topic to another as it might if the interviewer asked a series of set questions. The theme in Maria's interview with the clinical psychologist was Maria. Although the topics changed from Maria's education to her feelings about being the oldest of four, Maria herself remained the central focus. The psychologist accomplished this by making statements relevant to what Maria was saying.

To make such a response, the interviewer may use any of the following types of statements: verbatim playback, paraphrasing, restatement, summarizing, clarifying, and understanding. You can view these statements on a continuum ranging from being totally interchangeable with the interviewee's response to adding to or going beyond it.

In a *verbatim playback*, the interviewer simply repeats the interviewee's last response. For example, in her interview with the clinical psychologist, Maria stated, "I majored in history and social studies." The psychologist replied with the transitional

TABLE 8.4 Responses to Keep the Interaction Flowing

Response	Definition or example
Transitional phrase	"Yes," "I see," "Go on"
Verbatim playback	Repeats interviewee's exact words
Paraphrasing and restatement	Repeats interviewee's response using different Words
Summarizing	Pulls together the meaning of several responses
Clarification response	Clarifies the interviewee's response
Empathy and understanding	Communicates understanding

phrase "Yes, I see." A verbatim playback, "You majored in history and social studies," would have been equally effective. In either case, Maria most likely would continue to elaborate on her previous response. Thus, like the transitional phrase, the verbatim playback generally leads to an elaboration of the interviewee's previous response.

Paraphrasing and *restatement* responses are also interchangeable with the interviewee's response. A paraphrase tends to be more similar to the interviewee's response than a restatement, but both capture the meaning of the interviewee's response. When Maria said, "My master's degree should help me assume the duties of the new position," the psychologist replied, "You feel that your master's degree is a useful asset in your application"—a restatement. A paraphrase might have taken the form, "You feel that your master's degree will be an important aid in taking on the responsibilities of the new position." In his restatement, the psychologist introduced "useful asset" to restate Maria's attitude toward her master's degree. The paraphrase, on the other hand, simply substituted "important aid" for "help" and "taking on the responsibilities" for "assuming the duties." Neither statement added anything to Maria's. Both, however, communicated to Maria that the interviewer was listening and made it easy for Maria to elaborate.

Summarizing and *clarification* statements go just beyond the interviewee's response. In summarizing, the interviewer pulls together the meaning of several interviewee responses. To Maria's last statement in the example, the psychologist could have replied with the summarizing statement, "As a youth, you never had much time to yourself because you were responsible for taking care of your three younger siblings. Today you enjoy those few moments you have to be alone. Whenever you get a chance to be alone, you drive to the lake all by yourself and just think." Notice that this summarizing statement involves verbatim playback, paraphrasing, and restating. With these three types of statements, the psychologist summarizes an entire sequence of responses.

The clarification statement, as its name implies, serves to clarify the interviewee's response. When Maria stated, "Not that I resented it. Well, maybe sometimes. It's just that I never had much time for myself," the psychologist attempted to clarify what Maria was trying to say. It was not that Maria resented the extra responsibilities; rather, she simply wanted some time to be alone. Thus, the psychologist clarified Maria's statement by saying, "And having time for yourself is important to you."

Like summarizing, paraphrasing, restatement, and verbatim playback, the clarification statement remains close to the meaning of the interviewee's response. Each of these interviewer responses communicates a degree of understanding. At the lowest level, the verbatim playback communicates that the interviewer at least heard the communication. The restatement, paraphrase, and summarizing responses go a bit further by communicating that the interviewer has a good idea of what the interviewee is trying to communicate. And clarification shows yet further comprehension.

Even more powerful is the empathy or understanding response. This response communicates that the interviewer understands how the interviewee *feels*. When the psychologist stated, "These moments are precious to you," he did not simply paraphrase or restate. Instead, he communicated that he understood how Maria felt about having time to herself.

Many students find it difficult to see the value of statements that stay close to the interviewee's response. Some consider such statements artificial and weak because of their noncommittal quality. However, the rationale for such responses is based on the well-known and well-documented finding that when we show people we understand, they will talk about or explore themselves at ever deeper levels (Maj, Gaebel, Lopez-Ibor, & Sartorius, 2002; Rogers, 1980; Walker, 2001). Accurate empathy elicits self-exploration. Consider the following example:

PSYCHOLOGIST: What's been happening today, Kerry? (*open-ended question*)

KERRY: My physics teacher yelled at me in front of the whole class.

PSYCHOLOGIST: That's embarrassing. (*understanding*)

KERRY: Not only that, she seems to pick on me all the time.

PSYCHOLOGIST: That bothers you. (*understanding*)

KERRY: Yeah, I guess so. It seems like she's always finding fault with my work. No matter what I do, she just doesn't like it.

PSYCHOLOGIST: That is really frustrating, Kerry. You just can't seem to please her. (*understanding*)

KERRY: The other day we had an exam, and I got an F. I checked my answers with Hector, and mine were the same as his. Yet I got an F and Hector got a B.

PSYCHOLOGIST: Hey, that doesn't seem fair. (*clarification and understanding*)

KERRY: You bet it isn't fair. But when I tried to talk to her about it, she refused to listen.

PSYCHOLOGIST: That's scary. (*understanding*)

KERRY: It sure is. If I get one more F, I'll be kicked out of school.

PSYCHOLOGIST: This is really serious. (*clarification*)

KERRY: Yeah. If I got kicked out of school, I couldn't face my parents or friends.

PSYCHOLOGIST: This whole thing has got you really upset. (*understanding*)

Certainly, the psychologist's responses are not the only ones that would work. However, note how the psychologist, in providing a series of understanding responses, "uncovered" the real source of Kerry's anguish. The feelings Kerry expressed moved from embarrassment to anger to fear of being kicked out of school and finally to fear of how his friends and family would view his failure.

Let's consider four other responses that the psychologist could have made to Kerry's initial statement, "My physics teacher yelled at me in front of the whole class."

1.   "Why did she do that?" With this probing statement, Kerry has to defend himself or explain why it happened. He has to go over the circumstances that preceded the incident, actually leading away from Kerry's real feelings and concerns.

2.   "Why did you let her do that to you? That wasn't very smart of you." This evaluative statement places Kerry on the defensive, criticizes him, and possibly hurts his feelings. Given this type of reaction from the psychologist, Kerry will not feel safe exploring his real feelings.

3.   "That woman is always yelling at somebody. You should report her to the dean." With this off-the-cuff advice, the psychologist again removes himself

from Kerry's real concerns. The two might spend the rest of their time together weighing the pros and cons of reporting Kerry's physics teacher. Still worse, Kerry might impulsively follow the advice and get into real trouble if he cannot substantiate his claims.

4. "Don't worry. That physics teacher yells at everyone. It doesn't mean a thing." With this false reassurance, Kerry is no longer free to express his real concern. The psychologist has already dismissed the whole matter as insignificant.

In short, understanding responses that stay close to the content and underlying feeling provided by interviewees permit them to explore their situations more and more fully. Effective unstructured interviewing serves to uncover information from the interviewee. One good way to accomplish this involves what we call *understanding statements*. To establish a positive atmosphere, interviewers begin with an open-ended question followed by understanding statements that capture the meaning and feeling of the interviewee's communication. See Figure 8.3 for an exercise in keeping the interaction flowing.

Measuring Understanding

We can further appreciate understanding statements by analyzing measures of understanding. Attempts to measure understanding or empathy originated with Carl Rogers's seminal research into the effects of client-centered therapy (Rogers, 1959a, 1959b; Walker, Rablen, & Rogers, 1960). It culminated in a 5-point scoring system (Truax & Carkhuff, 1967, pp. 46–58). Each level in this system represents a degree of empathy. The levels range from a response that bears little or no relationship to the previous statement to a response that captures the precise meaning and feeling of the statement. The highest degrees of empathy, levels four and five, are relevant primarily for therapeutic interviews. Level three represents various degrees of true empathy or understanding and may be used in all types of unstructured or semistructured (i.e., partially structured) interviews. The lowest levels, one and two, have no place in a professional interview and should be avoided. Low-level responses, however, occur frequently in everyday conversations. We discuss these levels to illustrate one way to measure understanding.

Level-One Responses

Level-one responses bear little or no relationship to the interviewee's response. A level-one conversation might proceed as follows:

Sarah: Victor, look at my new dress.

Victor: I sure hope it doesn't rain today.

Sarah: See, it's red with blue stripes.

Victor: If it rains, my baseball game might get canceled.

Sarah: I really love this dress, it's my favorite.

Victor: It's sure going to tick me off if that game gets canceled.

The two people are really talking only to themselves.

FIGURE 8.3
Exercise in keeping the interaction flowing.

Directions: Below is a list of statements, each followed by two possible replies. Select the one that would tend to keep the interaction flowing.

1. I hate school.
   ☐ a. It sounds like you're fed up with school.
   ☐ b. What's wrong with school?

2. My dad is a jerk.
   ☐ a. Why don't you just tell him to "chill out"?
   ☐ b. You're angry with your dad.

3. Most people are liars.
   ☐ a. Don't be so negative.
   ☐ b. You feel that most people can't be trusted.

4. We were ahead until the last minute of the game.
   ☐ a. That's disappointing.
   ☐ b. Why didn't you win?

5. She stood me up again.
   ☐ a. If I were you, I wouldn't ask her out again.
   ☐ b. It hurts to be treated like that.

6. I hope I passed the test.
   ☐ a. You're worried about how you did on the test.
   ☐ b. Don't worry. I'm sure you passed.

Answers: 1. a; 2. b; 3. b; 4. a; 5. b; 6. a

Notes:
1b is a probing statement.
2a is advice.
3a is advice.
4b is a probing statement.
5a is advice.
6b is false reassurance.

Level-Two Responses

The level-two response communicates a superficial awareness of the meaning of a statement. The individual who makes a level-two response never quite goes beyond his or her own limited perspective. Level-two responses impede the flow of communication. For example:

SARAH: Boy, I feel good. I just got a beautiful new dress.

VICTOR: I feel bad. It's probably going to rain.

SARAH: I'll wear this dress to your baseball game.

VICTOR: If it rains, there won't be a game.

Here the conversation is related, but only superficially. Neither person really responds to what is going on with the other.

Level-Three Responses

A level-three response is interchangeable with the interviewee's statement. According to Carkhuff and Berenson (1967), level three is the minimum level of responding that can help the interviewee. Paraphrasing, verbatim playback, clarification statements, and restatements are all examples of level-three responses.

Level-Four and Level-Five Responses

Level-four and level-five responses not only provide accurate empathy but also go beyond the statement given. In a level-four response, the interviewer adds "noticeably" to the interviewee's response.

In a level-five response, the interviewer adds "significantly" to it (Carkhuff & Berenson, 1967). We recommend that beginning interviewers learn to respond at level three before going on to the more advanced levels. In the example with Sarah and Victor, a level-four interchange might proceed as follows:

SARAH: I just got a new dress.

VICTOR: You feel happy because you like new clothes.

SARAH: This one is beautiful; it has red and blue stripes.

VICTOR: You really love that new dress. It is a nice addition to your wardrobe.

Active Listening

An impressive array of research has accumulated to document the power of the understanding response (Fitzgerald & Leudar, 2010; Rock, 2007; Rogers, 1980; Truax & Mitchell, 1971). This type of responding, sometimes called *active listening*, is the foundation of good interviewing skills for many different types of interviews.

Mental Status Examination

An important tool in psychiatric and neurological examinations, the mental status examination is used primarily to diagnose psychosis, brain damage, and other major mental health problems. Its purpose is to evaluate a person suspected of having neurological or emotional problems in terms of variables known to be related to these problems.

The areas covered in the mental status examination include the person's appearance, attitudes, and general behavior. The interviewer is also alert to the interviewee's emotions. For example, is there one dominant emotion that fluctuates little? Is there an absence of emotion (i.e., a flat affect)? Are the emotions appropriate? Do the emotions fluctuate widely? The person's thought processes are also evaluated. Intelligence can be evaluated by such factors as speed and accuracy of thinking, richness of thought content, memory, judgment, and ability to interpret proverbs. Especially important in the assessment of schizophrenia, a major form of psychosis that involves loss of contact with reality, is the quality of the person's thought processes. This can be assessed through an analysis of thought content. For example, is there anything unusual or peculiar about the person's thoughts? Is the person preoccupied with any particular idea? Are the person's ideas realistic?

Other important areas evaluated in the mental status examination include the person's ability to direct and deploy attention. Is the person distracted? Can he or she stick to a task as long as needed to complete it? Sensory factors also are considered. Is the person seeing things that are not there? What is the accuracy of the person's perceptions? Several guides for conducting mental status exams are available (see, e.g., Groth-Marnat, 2009; Levitas, Hurley, & Pary, 2002). A fairly recent development is a mental status exam for autism spectrum disorders (Grodberg et al., 2014).

Keep in mind that to make proper use of the mental status examination, you must have a broad understanding of the major mental disorders and the various forms of brain damage. There is no room for amateurs or self-appointed practitioners when a mental status examination is needed. However, knowledge of those areas covered in the mental status examination can be useful to interviewers who are interested in knowing the important variables in observing and evaluating another human being.

Developing Interviewing Skills

A continuing controversy in the field of interviewing concerns whether interviewing skills can be learned. In fact, a Goggle search on interviewing skills will reveal numerous sites offering to teach such skills. Although you should always exercise caution on the Internet, the general consensus among psychologists is that people can acquire them (Boegels, van der Vleuten, Blok, & Kreutzkamp, 1996; Levinson, Lesser, & Epstein, 2010; Posthuma, Morgeson, & Campion, 2002; Prinstein, 2004). Otherwise, why would we bother to have clinical, counseling, and other types of training programs where interviews are used?

The first step in doing so is to become familiar with research and theory on the interview in order to understand the principles and underlying variables in the interview. A second step in learning such skills is supervised practice. Experience truly is the best teacher. No amount of book learning can compare with having one's taped interview analyzed by an expert. Maurer, Solamon, and Troxtel (2001) found that applicants who received coaching performed better in an interview than applicants who did not.

As a third step, one must make a conscious effort to apply the principles involved in good interviewing, such as guidelines for keeping the interaction flowing. This application includes constant self-evaluation—for example, continually asking oneself questions such as, "What does this person mean? Am I communicating that I understand? Is the person exploring at deeper levels? What is being communicated nonverbally?"

The initial phase of learning any new skill seems to involve attending to a hundred things at once—an impossible task. However, with persistent effort, people eventually respond appropriately by habit. Thus, experienced interviewers automatically attend to the person's appearance, nonverbal communications, emotional tone, and so on. They do so not because they are endowed with special abilities but because they have trained themselves to do so. To facilitate this process, cognitive interviews, a relatively recent innovation, are used to assess a respondent's understanding of information (Lee, 2014; Madrid, Kalpakjian, Hanks, & Rapport, 2015; Priede, Jokinen, Ruuskanen, & Farrall, 2014).

Sources of Error in the Interview

To make appropriate use of the interview, people must develop an awareness of the various sources of error or potential bias in data from interviews. Then they can try to compensate for these negative effects. Furthermore, this knowledge allows one to develop a better awareness of the limitations inherent in judging human beings on the basis of the interview.

Interview Validity

Many sources of interview error come from the extreme difficulty we have in making accurate, logical observations and judgments (Rapp, Hinze, Kohlhepp, & Ryskin, 2014). Suppose, for example, in the first day of teaching a 5th-grade class, a teacher observes that one child follows all of the rules and directions, but a second child just cannot seem to stay out of trouble. If that teacher is not careful, then he or she might develop a bias. The teacher might see the first child as good even if she breaks the rules for several weeks in a row. On the other hand, the teacher might see the second child as bad even if she follows the rules for the rest of the school term. Similarly, a child may turn in a paper replete with grammatical and spelling errors. This child may have just had a bad day. However, even if his or her next paper is relatively free of errors, the teacher will have a tendency to look for them and to view the child as weak in grammar. Furthermore, the teacher may see the child as weak in other areas just on the basis of his or her early impression of the child's grammatical skills.

It has been demonstrated that interviewers form an impression of the interviewee within the first minute or so and spend the rest of the interview trying to confirm that impression (Metzger, 2005). Long ago, E. L. Thorndike (1920) labeled this tendency to judge specific traits on the basis of a general impression the *halo effect*. Thorndike became aware of this effect when he noticed that ratings of behavioral tendencies (traits) based on interview data tended to correlate more highly than reasonably expected.

People apparently tend to generalize judgments from a single limited experience (Li, Wang, & Zhang, 2002). In the interview, halo effects occur when the interviewer forms a favorable or unfavorable early impression. The early impression then biases the remainder of the judgment process. Thus, with an early favorable impression or positive halo, the interviewer will have difficulty seeing the negatives. Similarly, with an early negative halo, the interviewer will have difficulty seeing the positives. In short, halo effects impair objectivity and must be consciously avoided.

Similarly, people tend to judge on the basis of one outstanding characteristic (Sim, Saperia, Brown, Bernieri, & Hackett, 2015). Hollingworth (1922) first called this error *general standoutishness*. One prominent characteristic can bias the interviewer's judgments and prevent an objective evaluation. In an early classic paper, Burtt (1926) noted the tendency of interviewers to make unwarranted inferences from personal appearance. A well-groomed, attractive individual might be rated higher in intelligence than would a poorly groomed, unattractive individual, even if the latter was actually more intelligent than the former. Thus, physical appearance can play a major role in how a job applicant is perceived and rated (Kanazawa, 2011;

Reed, 2000). It is important to note, however, that appearance factors that contribute most to the decision-making process are factors that are controllable by the applicant, such as grooming. When it appears that applicants have attempted to manage the controllable factors, they are viewed more favorably, even if they are viewed as unattractive (Posthuma, Morge-son, & Campion, 2002). Another potential source of error in the interview can be found in cross-ethnic, cross-cultural, and cross-class interviewing (Fish, 2001; Miyamoto, 2005; Vatrapu & Pérez-Quifiones, 2006). In the international business community, ignorance of cultural differences is becoming increasingly apparent. Japanese and Arabs consider direct eye contact a sign of aggression. The Japanese person avoids eye contact as a sign of deference and respect. The Japanese also tend to pay more attention to the entire social surrounding, as indicated by eye-tracking data (Takahiko et al., 2008). In the middle-class United States, by contrast, direct eye contact is expected as a sign of honesty and sincerity. Unless we understand and take cultural differences into account, we can easily send the wrong message or misinterpret others' intentions.

The misunderstanding of cultural differences within the United States also leads to interviewer bias (McCarthy, Lee, Itakura, & Muir, 2008; Schouten & Meeuwesen, 2006). Researchers are making some progress, however, in attempts to reduce interviewer bias. For example, organizations that adopt carefully administered interviews that conform to the key components of structure can minimize concerns of applicant discrimination on the basis of gender and race (McCarthy, Van Iddekinge, & Campion, 2010).

Although reviews of the literature (Nevo & Jager, 1993; Ralston, 1988) have failed to provide a framework from which to understand bias in the interview process, careful structuring and administering of the selection interview improves its psychometric properties (Sander, Johann, Wilhelm, & Wittmann, 2000). That does not mean error such as cultural distortions do not still reduce the validity of interview data. Even in a highly structured interview, initial impressions formed during rapport building appear to influence the evaluation, whether they are clearly relevant or not (Barrick et al., 2011).

Given the choice between alternative selection processes, such as relying on intelligence test alone, the highly structured interview continues to be the most effective means of eliminating, or at least reducing, bias (Ployhart & Holtz, 2008). Research suggests that highly structured interviews draw "individuating information" from the interviewee and this, in turn, overrides initial perceptions, providing resistance against bias (McCarthy et al., 2010, p. 336). Thus, to override initial perceptions, interviews must be structured to accomplish three goals. First, the interviewers must be motivated to form an accurate impression of the interviewee. Second, the interviewer must focus more attention on the interviewee in order to notice, remember, and use individuating information that is *not* consistent with initial perceptions. Finally, interviewers must focus on information that is predictive of job performance. Table 8.5 details the process of accomplishing these three goals.

Mean score differences between racioethnic minority (African American, Hispanic, Asian) or female subgroups and racioethnic majority (white) or male subgroups contribute to adverse impact (Pyburn, Ployhart, & Kravitz, 2008). Sources of error such as cultural distortions can reduce the validity of interview data. Recall that validity tells us about the meaning of test scores. Errors that reduce the

TABLE 8.5 Suggestions for Structuring Cross-Ethnic, Cross-Cultural, and Cross-Class Interviews

Increase interviewers' motivation to form an accurate impression
- When interviewers expect that their judgments will be made known or compared to the judgments of other interviewers, they are more motivated to present an accurate impression. Thus, in structured interviews, the use of panels increases the interviewer motivation to attend to individuating information.

Provide structure that innately moves interviewers past initial judgments
- Interviewers move past their initial judgment when the interview is structured so that the interviewers ask a series of predetermined, job-relevant questions and then rate each of the interviewees' responses.

Focus attention on the interviewee
- Interviewers who are forced to focus on the interviewee by being required to retrieve and record specific information about the interviewee are less able to remember the interviewee's stereotyped traits. Thus, simply taking notes reduces the impact of preexisting bias.
- Highly structured interviews tend to take longer than less structured interviews, allowing more opportunity for interviewers to obtain individuating information.

Focus attention on information predictive of job performance
- The questions in high-structure interviews are designed to measure the interviewees' knowledge, skills, abilities, and characteristics as well as compatibility with behaviors required for a specific job.
- The interviewer rates each interviewee as low, moderate, or high for each category. This focuses attention on the information vital for making a valid judgment about each interviewee.
- Highly structured interviews minimize the extent to which applicants can express irrelevant information by limiting opportunity for the interviewee to ask questions.

(Information used in Table 8.5 is from: McCarthy, J. M, Van Iddekinge, C. H., & Campion, M. A. (2010). Are highly structured job interviews resistant to demographic similarity effects? *Personnel Psychology, 63*(2), 325–359, 336–338.)

objectivity of the interviewer produce inaccurate judgments, thus biasing the validity of the evaluation. These tendencies perhaps explain why the predictive validity of interview data varies so widely. R. Wagner (1949), for example, earlier reported studies that attempted to correlate judgments from interview data with such factors as grades, intelligence, and performance on standardized tests. The correlations ranged from .09 to .94, with a median of .19. Studies reviewed in a classic work by Ulrich and Trumbo (1965) revealed a similar range of predictive validity coefficients, with correlations as low as −.05 and as high as .72 when ratings based on interview data were correlated with a variety of indexes such as job performance. Subsequent research reported similar findings (Arvey & Campion, 1982; Carlson, Thayer, Mayfield, & Peterson, 1971). Other reviews have suggested higher and more consistent coefficients especially when specific characteristics such as cognitive ability are being assessed. In a meta-analytic review of 49 studies, for example, Huffcutt, Roth, and McDaniel (1996) found that .4 provided a good estimate of the relationship between test scores and interview ratings of cognitive abilities.

When examining the relationship between structured interviews and subsequent supervisor ratings, researchers found correlations from 0.30 to 0.60; however, unstructured interviews typically correlate less than 0.20 with the same outcome measures (Ebmeier, Dillon, & Ng, 2007).

Although one can question the validity of interview data, the interview does provide a wealth of unique data. The safest approach is to consider interview data as tentative: a hypothesis or a set of hypotheses to be confirmed by other sources of data. Interview data may have dubious value without the support of more standardized procedures. Results from standardized tests, on the other hand, are often meaningless if not placed in the context of case history or other interview data. The two go together, each complementing the other, each essential in the process of evaluating human beings.

Interview Reliability

Recall that reliability refers to the stability, dependability, or consistency of test results. For interview data, the critical questions about reliability have centered on inter-interviewer agreement (agreement between two or more interviewers). As with the validity studies, reliability coefficients for inter-interviewer agreement vary widely. For example, in R. Wagner's (1949) classic study, reliability coefficients ranged from .23 to .97 (median .57) for ratings of traits. The range of coefficients for ratings of overall ability was even wider ($-.20$ to .85; median .53). Ulrich and Trumbo's (1965) widely cited review reported similar findings.

Research consistently indicates unstructured interviews have low levels of reliability (U.S. Office of Personnel Management, 2008). Research also shows that in terms of adverse impact, interviews give fairer outcomes than many other widely used selection tools, including psychometric tests of ability and intelligence (Moscoso, 2000).

McCarthy et al. (2010) argued that one reason for fluctuations in interview reliability is, in part, because interview procedures vary considerably in their degree of standardization in terms of interview development, administration, and/or scoring. Simply, different interviewers look for different things. Thus, whereas one interviewer might focus on strengths, another might focus on weaknesses. The two interviewers would disagree because their judgments are based on different aspects of the individual.

As we have noted, agreement among interviewers varies for different types of interviews. The research suggests that a highly structured interview in which specific questions are asked in a specific order can produce highly stable results (Huff-cutt, Conway, Roth, & Stone, 2001). For example, if we ask a person his or her name, date of birth, and parents' names as well as the addresses of all residences within a particular time span, and then ask the same questions a year later, results should be nearly identical. Reliability would be limited only by the memory and honesty of the interviewee and the clerical capabilities of the interviewer. Although extreme, this example should make it clear that highly structured interviews should produce fairly dependable results. In fact, the internal consistency reliability for scores on highly structured interviews was .79 where the interviewer was gathering information about the interviewee's experience, .90 where interviewees responded to hypothetical dilemmas they may experience on the job, and .86 where the interviewer was gathering information about the interviewees' past behavior (McCarthy et al., 2010). The problem is that such structure can limit the content of the interview, thus defeating the purpose of providing a broad range of data.

Unstructured or semistructured interviews frequently provide data that other sources cannot provide. However, the dependability of such results is clearly limited. The same question may not be asked twice, or it may be asked in different ways. Thus, interviewers readily acknowledge the limited reliability of interview data.

Summary

In a *structured interview,* the interviewer asks a specific set of questions. In the structured *standardized* interview, these questions are printed. The interviewer reads the questions in a specific order or sequence. In the *unstructured interview*, there are no specific questions or guidelines for the interviewer to follow. Thus, each unstructured interview is unique. Such interviews provide considerable flexibility at the expense of data stability.

An interview is an *interactive* process. The participants (interviewer and interviewee) influence each other. The tendency for people to behave like the models around them is called *social facilitation*. Good interviewers thus can set a good tone in an interview by maintaining a warm, open, and confident atmosphere.

Good interviewing involves developing the proper *attitudes* and displaying them during the interview. Interviewees give positive evaluations to interviewers when the interviewer is seen as warm, genuine, accepting, understanding, open, committed, and involved. Poor evaluations result when interviewers exhibit the opposite attitudes and feelings.

The process of interviewing involves facilitating the flow of communication. An interviewer should avoid statements that are *judgmental* or *evaluative, probing, hostile,* or *reassuring*. An unstructured interview should begin with an *open-ended question*—that is, one that cannot be answered briefly. The process of interviewing then involves facilitating the flow of communication. *Closed-ended questions*, which can be answered with a "yes" or "no" or a specific response, usually bring the interview to a halt and typically should be reserved for instances where less directive procedures fail to produce the desired information. Furthermore, transitional phrases such as "I see" help keep the interview flowing. Statements that communicate understanding or are interchangeable with the interviewee's responses tend to elicit self-exploration at increasingly deeper levels. These interviewer responses include *verbatim playback, paraphrasing, restatement, summarizing, clarification,* and *understanding. Confrontation* is another response that experienced interviewers use for specific purposes, but it is not recommended as a general strategy.

Efforts to assess the quality of understanding or empathetic statements have led to a 5-point scale system developed by Rogers, Truax, Carkhuff, and coworkers. Understanding statements are extremely powerful in helping the interviewee uncover and explore underlying feelings. Types of interviews include the *evaluation or assessment interview*, the *structured clinical interview*, the *case history interview*, the *mental status examination*, and the *employment interview*.

There are two primary sources of error in the interview: those pertaining to the *validity* or meaning of data and those pertaining to its dependability or *reliability*. Tendencies to draw general conclusions about an individual that are based on just the data of a first impression limit the meaning and accuracy of interview data. Such tendencies have been labeled *the halo effect* and *standoutishness*. Cultural misunderstandings can also bias interview data and lead to inaccurate conclusions. Furthermore, predictive validity coefficients for interview data vary widely. The reliability of interview data has been measured primarily in terms of agreement among interviewers on variables, such as intelligence and traits. The more structured the interview, the more the interviewers agree. Thus, like predictive validity coefficients, reliability coefficients for interview data vary widely. Training tends to enhance reliability.

One develops interviewing skills through knowledge about good interviewing behavior and principles, supervised practice, and a conscious effort to form the right habits. However, the interview is fallible. Interview data can best be seen as the complement of other data sources.

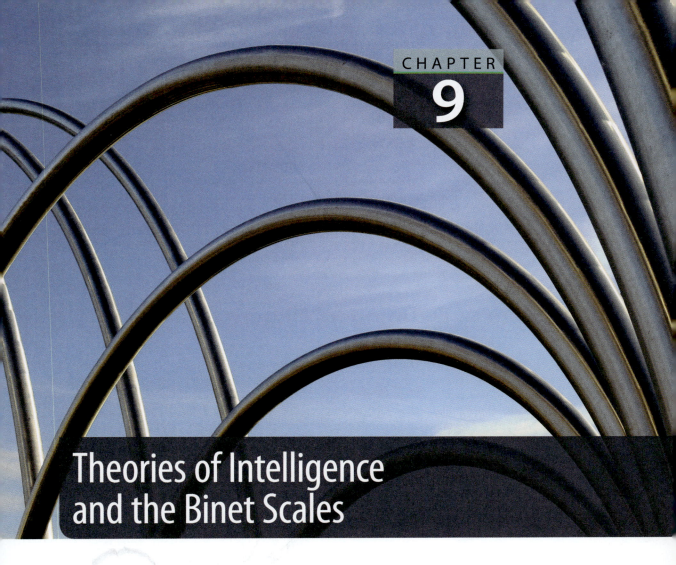

Theories of Intelligence and the Binet Scales

LEARNING OBJECTIVES

When you have completed this chapter, you should be able to:

▶ Explain how Binet and other psychologists have defined intelligence

▶ Compare Spearman's *g* with contemporary *gf-gc* theory

▶ Identify Binet's two guiding principles of test construction

▶ Describe the concept of age differentiation

▶ Describe the concept of mental age (MA)

▶ Describe the intelligence quotient (IQ) concept

▶ Define deviation IQ

▶ Discuss the various editions of the Stanford-Binet Intelligence Scale

225

Three 8-year-old children, Fred, Maria, and Roberto, were being evaluated for a special program for the gifted in a magnet school. Those who qualified would be placed in a special accelerated program in which the student–teacher ratio was 15 to 1 rather than the usual 25 to 1. The gifted program also had special funds for enrichment programs such as field trips and hands-on exposure to computers. To qualify, a child had to score three standard deviations above the mean on the Stanford-Binet Intelligence Scale (fifth edition; Roid, 2003a, 2003b, 2003c).

Because the Stanford-Binet is standardized, all three children were exposed to the same conditions. The test began with a set of vocabulary items.

Only Maria scored high enough on the test to be placed in the gifted program. Given that all children were exposed to the same test conditions, can we rest assured that the procedure was fair and that Maria was indeed the most intelligent of the three? As critical thinkers, we of course cannot give an unqualified "Yes" to the question. We need much more information.

The Problem of Defining Intelligence

To say that one person is more intelligent than a second, we must be prepared to define *intelligence*. Unfortunately, of all the major concepts in the field of testing, intelligence is among the most elusive (see Anderson, 2013; Fletcher & Hattie, 2011). Alfred Binet, one of the original authors of the test that bears his name, defined intelligence as "the tendency to take and maintain a definite direction; the capacity to make adaptations for the purpose of attaining a desired end, and the power of autocriticism" (cited in Terman, 1916, p. 45). Spearman (1923), by contrast, defined intelligence as the ability to educe either relations or correlates. According to Freeman (1955), intelligence is "adjustment or adaptation of the individual to his total environment," "the ability to learn," and "the ability to carry on abstract thinking" (pp. 60–61). And Das (1973) defined intelligence as "the ability to plan and structure one's behavior with an end in view" (p. 27). H. Gardner (1983) defined intelligence in terms of the ability "to resolve genuine problems or difficulties as they are encountered" (p. 60), while Sternberg (1986, 1988) defined intelligence in terms of "mental activities involved in purposive adaptation to, shaping of, and selection of real-world environments relevant to one's life" (1986, p. 33). For Anderson (2001, 2013), intelligence is two-dimensional and based on individual differences in information-processing speed and executive functioning influenced largely by inhibitory processes. Other views depict intelligence as a blend of abilities, including personality and various aspects of memory (Deary, Penke, & Johnson, 2010).

T. R. Taylor (1994) identified three independent research traditions that have been employed to study the nature of human intelligence: the psychometric, the information-processing, and the cognitive approaches. The *psychometric approach* examines the elemental structure of a test (DiStefano & Dombrowski, 2006; Taylor, 1994). Following the psychometric approach, we examine the properties of a test through an evaluation of its correlates and underlying dimensions (Helmbold & Rammsayer, 2006). In the *information-processing* approach, we examine the processes that underlie how we learn and solve problems (Gary, 2010). Finally, the cognitive tradition focuses on how humans adapt to real-world demands (Sternberg, Mio, & Mio, 2009). Of the three approaches, the psychometric is the oldest and is the focus of this chapter. (The information-processing and cognitive approaches will be discussed more thoroughly in Chapter 15.) As you will see, Binet's approach is based heavily on the psychometric tradition.

Returning to our example, how can we begin to judge whether the Binet test allowed testers to judge the three children fairly? A test such as the Binet that examines one's ability to define words and identify numerical sequences certainly does not meet the standards of all or even most definitions of intelligence. Even if we assume that the Stanford-Binet scale is a valid measure of intelligence, can we safely say that the evaluation procedure for Fred, Maria, and Roberto was fair?

Again, we cannot answer unequivocally. Roberto, a Mexican American, had Spanish-speaking parents, neither of whom finished high school. His father spent most of his life working as a farmer. Fred, an African American, came from a family of five children. As with Roberto, neither of Fred's parents completed high school. Although Fred's father worked long hard hours as a machine operator on an assembly line, the family was poor. Maria's parents, by contrast, had a combined income of $300,000 per year and were well educated. Her mother was a clinical psychologist, her father an attorney.

There is a correlation between socioeconomic background and scores on all standardized intelligence tests (Bornstein, Hahn, Suwalsky, & Haynes, 2003; Hart, Petrill, Deckard, & Thompson, 2007), including Stanford-Binet (Sangwan, 2001). Thus, many people have charged that intelligence tests are biased, especially against ethnic minorities, the poor (Hays, 2001), and non-native speakers (te Nijenhuis, Willigers, Dragt, & van der Flier, 2016). Ironically, intelligence tests were initially developed to eliminate subjectivity in the evaluation of children's ability. And it should be noted that among standardized tests, the Stanford-Binet fifth edition is among the best in providing appropriate cautions for test users.

For many people, the topic of intelligence testing arouses strong feelings and sometimes strong personal biases, even among experts (Naglieri & Goldstein, 2009; Reynolds & Ramsay, 2003). Proponents hold that properly used intelligence tests provide an objective standard of competence and potential (Greisinger, 2003). Critics charge that intelligence tests are biased (McDermott, Watkins, & Rhoad, 2014), not only against certain racial and economic groups (Jones, 2003) but also used by those in power to maintain the status quo (Gould, 1981). In fact, intelligence tests have been under attack almost from their inception.

Formal intelligence testing began with a decision of a French minister of public instruction around the turn of the 20th century. Some people today might criticize the minister's decision to create a procedure for identifying intellectually limited individuals, so they could be removed from the regular classroom and receive special educational experiences. This decision provided the force behind the development of modern intelligence tests and the heated controversy now associated with them.

In 1904, the French minister officially appointed a commission, to which he gave a definite assignment: to recommend a procedure for identifying so-called subnormal (intellectually limited) children. One member of this commission, Alfred Binet, had demonstrated his qualifications for the job by his earlier research on human abilities (Binet, 1890a, 1890b). The task of the commission was indeed formidable. No one doubted that human beings were capable of incredible accomplishments, which obviously reflected intelligence. Nor was there much doubt that differences existed among individuals in their level of intelligence. But how was one to define intelligence?

Binet and his colleagues had few guideposts. A study by Wissler (1901) indicated that simple functions such as reaction time and sensory acuity failed to discriminate well among individuals of high and low scholastic ability. Therefore, Binet looked for complex processes in his struggle to understand human intelligence. However, unlike today, there were few available definitions of intelligence. Binet's first problem was to decide what he wanted to measure—that is, to define intelligence. Beginning with this definition, Binet and his colleagues developed the world's first intelligence test.

Binet's Principles of Test Construction

As you have seen, Binet defined intelligence as the capacity (1) to find and maintain a definite direction or purpose, (2) to make necessary adaptations—that is, strategy adjustments—to achieve that purpose, and (3) to engage in self-criticism so that necessary adjustments in strategy can be made. In choosing a definition, Binet took the necessary first step in developing a measure of intelligence.

However, he still faced the problem of deciding exactly what he wanted to measure. Because Binet believed that intelligence expressed itself through the judgmental, attentional, and reasoning facilities of the individual (Binet & Simon, 1905), he decided to concentrate on finding tasks related to these three facilities. In developing tasks to measure judgment, attention, and reasoning, Binet used trial and error as well as experimentation and hypothesis-testing procedures. He was guided by two major concepts that to this day underlie not only the Binet scale but also major modern theories of intelligence: age differentiation and general mental ability. These principles, which perhaps represent Binet's most profound contribution to the study of human intelligence, provided the foundation for subsequent generations of human ability tests.

Principle 1: Age Differentiation

Age differentiation refers to the simple fact that one can differentiate older children from younger children by the former's greater capabilities. For example, whereas most 9-year-olds can tell that a quarter is worth more than a dime, a dime is worth more than a nickel, and so on, most 4-year-olds cannot. In employing the principle of age differentiation, Binet searched for tasks that could be completed by between 66.67% and 75% of the children of a particular age group and also by a smaller proportion of younger children but a larger proportion of older ones. Thus, Binet eventually assembled a set of tasks that an increasing proportion of children could complete as a function of increases in age.

Using these tasks, he could estimate the mental ability of a child in terms of his or her completion of the tasks designed for the average child of a particular age, regardless of the child's actual or chronological age. A particular 5-year-old child might be able to complete tasks that the average 8-year-old could complete. On the other hand, another 5-year-old might not be capable of completing even those tasks that the average 3-year-old could complete. With the principle of age differentiation, one could determine the equivalent age capabilities of a child independent of his or her chronological age. This equivalent age capability was eventually called *mental age*. If a 6-year-old completed tasks that were appropriate for the average 9-year-old, then the 6-year-old had demonstrated that he or she had capabilities equivalent to those of the average 9-year-old, or a mental age of 9. Today, psychologists use the more sophisticated technique of item response theory (see Chapter 6) and other techniques to accomplish the goal of evaluating age equivalent capabilities (Horn, 2005; Huang & Wang, 2014; Roid, 2003a).

Principle 2: General Mental Ability

Binet was also guided in his selection of tasks by his decision to measure only the total product of the various separate and distinct elements of intelligence, that is, *general mental ability*. With this concept, Binet freed himself from the burden of identifying each element or independent aspect of intelligence. He also was freed from finding the relation of each element to the whole. Binet's decision to measure general mental ability was based, in part, on practical considerations. He could restrict the search for tasks to anything related to the total or the final product of intelligence. He could judge the value of any particular task in terms of its correlation with the combined result (total score) of all other tasks. Tasks with low correlations could be eliminated, and tasks with high correlations retained. The notion of general mental ability is critical to understanding modern conceptions of human intelligence as well as the various editions of the Binet from the first through the present modern fifth edition.

Spearman's Model of General Mental Ability

Binet was not alone in his conception of general mental ability. Before Binet, this notion was propounded by F. Galton (1869) in his classic work, *Hereditary Genius: An Inquiry into Its Laws and Consequences* (see Chapter 1). Independently of Binet, in Great Britain, Charles Spearman (1904, 1927) advanced the notion of a general mental ability factor underlying all intelligent behavior (see Thorndike, 1990a, 1990b). According to Spearman's theory, intelligence consists of one general factor (g) plus a large number of specific factors (see Figure 9.1). Spearman's

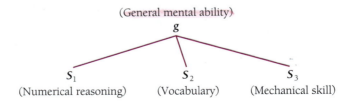

FIGURE 9.1

Spearman's model of intelligence. According to the model, intelligence can be viewed in terms of one general underlying factor (g) and a large number of specific factors ($S_1, S_2, \ldots, S_n$). Thus, intelligence can be viewed in terms of g (general mental ability) and S (specific factors). Spearman's theory was consistent with Binet's approach to constructing the first intelligence test.

notion of general mental ability, which he referred to as *psychometric g* (or simply *g*), was based on the well-documented phenomenon that when a set of diverse ability tests are administered to large unbiased samples of the population, almost all of the correlations are positive. This phenomenon is called *positive manifold*, which, according to Spearman, resulted from the fact that all tests, no matter how diverse, are influenced by *g*. For Spearman, *g* could best be conceptualized in terms of mental energy.

To understand how a single general factor can underlie all intelligent behavior, consider the analogy of a central power station for a large metropolitan city. The same station provides the power for lights of all sizes and types. Although some lights may be brighter or better than others, all depend on power from the central power source. Reducing the output from the central source affects all of the lights.

To support the notion of *g*, Spearman developed a statistical technique called *factor analysis* (Willis, Dumont, & Kaufman, 2011), which today has become quite sophisticated (Rostami, Abdollahi, & Maeder, 2016). Traditionally, factor analysis is a method for reducing a set of variables or scores to a smaller number of hypothetical variables called *factors*. Through factor analysis, one can determine how much variance a set of tests or scores has in common (Abbott, Amtmann, & Munson, 2003; Lorenzo-Seva, 2003; Timmerman & Kiers, 2003). This common variance represents the *g* factor. The *g* in a factor analysis of any set of mental ability tasks can be represented in the first unrotated factor in a principal components analysis (Saccuzzo, Johnson, & Guertin, 1994). Spearman found that, as a general rule, approximately half of the variance in a set of diverse mental ability tests is represented in the *g* factor. Today, Spearman's *g* "is the most established and ubiquitous predictor of occupational and educational performance" (Willis, Dumont, & Kaufman, 2011).

Implications of General Mental Intelligence (*g*)

The concept of general intelligence implies that a person's intelligence can best be represented by a single score, *g*, that presumably reflects the shared variance underlying performance on a diverse set of tests. True performance on any given individual task can be attributed to *g* as well as to some specific or unique variance (just as the luminance of a light depends on the central power source as well as the individual qualities of the light). However, if the set of tasks is large and broad enough, the role of any given task can be reduced to a minimum. Differences in unique ability stemming from the specific task tend to cancel each other, and overall performance comes to depend most heavily on the general factor. Such reasoning guided the development of the Binet scale as well as all its subsequent revisions through the most current fifth edition (Roid, 2003a).

The *gf-gc* Theory of Intelligence

Recent theories of intelligence have suggested that human intelligence can best be conceptualized in terms of multiple intelligences rather than a single score (Furnham & Petrides, 2003; Mulhollen, 2007; Riggio, Murphy, & Pirozzolo, 2002). One such theory is called the *gf-gc* theory (Horn & Blankson, 2005; Horn & Noll, 1997).

According to *gf-gc* theory, there are two basic types of intelligence: fluid (*f*) and crystallized (*c*). Fluid intelligence can best be thought of as those abilities that allow us to reason, think, and acquire new knowledge (Kane & Engle, 2002; Primi, 2002; Stankov, 2003). Crystallized intelligence, by contrast, represents the knowledge and understanding that we have acquired (Bates & Shieles, 2003; Horn & Masunaga, 2006; Thorsen, Gustafsson, & Cliffordson, 2014). You might think of this distinction in terms of the abilities that allow us to learn and acquire information (fluid) and the actual learning that has occurred (crystallized).

The Binet began with the notion of a single intelligence, *g*. As the test progressed to its modern form, it has implicitly adopted a model of intelligence that acknowledges these two forms of intelligence. Thus, the evolution of the Binet has in many ways reflected and paralleled the evolution of modern psychometric theory and approaches to intelligence.

The Early Binet Scales

Using the principles of age differentiation and general mental ability, Binet and another appointee of the French minister of public instruction, T. Simon, collaborated to develop the first version of what would eventually be called the Stanford-Binet Intelligence Scale. The first version, the 1905 Binet-Simon scale, was quite limited compared with current applications of intelligence tests. Its purpose was restricted to identifying mentally disabled children in the Paris school system.

The 1905 Binet-Simon Scale

The 1905 Binet-Simon scale was an individual intelligence test consisting of 30 items presented in an increasing order of difficulty. Item 4, for example, tested the subject's ability to recognize food (e.g., to discriminate between chocolate and wood). Item 14 required subjects to define familiar objects such as a fork. The most difficult item, 30, required subjects to define and distinguish between paired abstract terms (e.g., *sad* and *bored*).

In Binet's time, three levels of intellectual deficiency were designated by terms no longer in use today because of the derogatory connotations they have acquired. *Idiot* described the most severe form of intellectual impairment, *imbecile* moderate levels of impairment, and *moron* the mildest level of impairment. Binet believed that the ability to follow simple directions and imitate simple gestures (item 6 on the 1905 scale) was the upper limit of adult idiots. The ability to identify parts of the body or simple objects (item 8) would rule out the most severe intellectual impairment in an adult. The upper limit for adult imbeciles was item 16, which required the subject to state the differences between two common objects such as wood and glass.

The collection of 30 tasks of increasing difficulty in the Binet-Simon scale provided the first major measure of human intelligence. Binet had solved two major problems of test construction: He determined exactly what he wanted to measure, and he developed items for this purpose. He fell short, however, in several other areas. The 1905 Binet-Simon scale lacked an adequate measuring unit to express

FIGURE 9.2
Schematic summary of the evolution of the 1905 Binet scale.

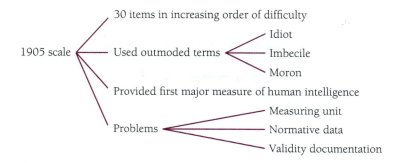

results; it also lacked adequate normative data and evidence to support its validity. The classifications Binet used (idiot, imbecile, and moron) can hardly be considered sufficient for expressing results and, as Binet himself knew, little had been done to document the scale's validity. Furthermore, norms for the 1905 scale were based on only 50 children who had been considered normal based on average school performance (see Figure 9.2).

The 1908 Scale

In the 1908 scale, Binet and Simon retained the principle of age differentiation. Indeed, the 1908 scale was an **age scale**, which means items were grouped according to age level rather than simply one set of items of increasing difficulty, as in the 1905 scale (see Table 9.1). The age scale provided a model for innumerable tests still used in educational and clinical settings. However, the age scale format also presented several challenges and, as we will see, is used in only a modified or "hybrid" fashion in the most recent, fifth edition. When items are grouped according to age level, comparing a child's performance on different kinds of tasks is difficult, if not impossible, unless items are exquisitely balanced as in the fifth edition. For example, does the child perform exceptionally well on one type of item? The current edition has a procedure that allows test users to combine all verbal items into a single scale and all nonverbal items into a single scale to overcome such problems with the age scale format.

Despite its limitations, the 1908 Binet scale clearly reflected improvement over the 1905 scale. However, Binet had done little to meet one persistent criticism: The scale produced only one score, almost exclusively related to verbal, language, and reading ability. Binet claimed that a single score was consistent with the notion of general mental ability and therefore appropriate. Unfortunately, Binet made little effort to diversify the range of abilities tapped. As a result, the scale remained heavily weighted on language, reading, and verbal skills at the expense of other factors such as the integration of visual and motor functioning (e.g., eye–hand coordination). Not until the 1986 revision were these problems seriously addressed, and in the fifth revision major efforts were made to provide a wide diversity of scores as well as a balance of verbal and nonverbal items.

Perhaps the main improvement in the 1908 scale was the introduction of the concept of mental age. Here Binet attempted to solve the problem of expressing the

TABLE 9.1 Sample Items From the 1908 Binet-Simon Scale

Age level 3 (five items)	**Age level 4 (four items)**
1. Point to various parts of face.	1. Name familiar objects.
2. Repeat two digits forward.	2. Repeat three digits forward.
Age level 5 (five items)	**Age level 6 (seven items)**
1. Copy a square.	1. State age.
2. Repeat a sentence containing 10 syllables.	2. Repeat a sentence containing 16 syllables.
Age level 7 (eight items)	**Age level 8 (six items)**
1. Copy a diamond.	1. Recall two items from a passage.
2. Repeat five digits forward.	2. State the differences between two objects.
Age level 9 (six items)	**Age level 10 (five items)**
1. Recall six items from a passage.	1. Given three common words, construct a sentence.
2. Recite the days of the week.	2. Recite the months of the year in order.
Age level 11 (five items)	**Age level 12 (five items)**
1. Define abstract words (for example, *justice*).	1. Repeat seven digits forward.
2. Determine what is wrong with absurd statements.	2. Provide the meaning of pictures.
Age level 13 (three items)	
1. State the differences between pairs of abstract terms.	

results in adequate units. A subject's mental age was based on his or her performance compared with the average performance of individuals in a specific chronological age group. In simple terms, if a 6-year-old can perform the tasks that can be done by two-thirds to three-fourths of the representative group of 8-year-old children, then this child has a mental age of 8. A 10-year-old who can do no more than pass items that two-thirds to three-fourths of the representative group of 5-year-olds can pass is said to have a mental age of 5.

To summarize, the 1908 Binet-Simon scale introduced two major concepts: the age scale format and the concept of mental age. However, even though the mental age concept was eventually abandoned and the age scale format modified, these two concepts found widespread use and application in a host of new tests that are still in use today (see Figure 9.3).

FIGURE 9.3

Schematic summary of the evolution of the 1908 Binet scale.

1908 scale
— Retained principle of age differentiation
— Used age scale format
— Introduced concept of mental age

Terman's Stanford-Binet Intelligence Scale

Though Binet and Simon again revised their intelligence scale in 1911, this third version contained only minor improvements. Indeed, it was the 1916 Stanford-Binet version, developed under the direction of L. M. Terman, that flourished and served for quite some time as the dominant intelligence scale for the world.

In this section, we continue our look at the evolution of the Binet scale and its relation to theories of intelligence. First, we examine Terman's 1916 version of the scale and see how he related the concepts of mental age and intelligence quotient (IQ). Then, we look at the 1937 and 1960 revisions before we move on to the modern versions of the Binet. Each version illustrates important test concepts as well as the evolution of intelligence tests throughout the world.

The 1916 Stanford-Binet Intelligence Scale

In developing the 1916 Stanford-Binet version, Terman relied heavily on Binet's earlier work. The principles of age differentiation, general mental ability, and the age scale were retained. The mental age concept also was retained (see Figure 9.4). Terman's 1916 revision increased the size of the standardization sample. Unfortunately, the entire standardization sample of the 1916 revision consisted exclusively of white, native-Californian children. Thus, although the standardization sample was markedly increased, it was far from representative. In fact, given that even geographic location may affect test performance, this sample cannot even be considered to represent white, native-born Americans. Nevertheless, the increased sample size clearly marked an improvement over the meager 50 and 203 individuals of the 1905 and 1908 Binet-Simon versions.

The Intelligence Quotient (IQ)

The 1916 scale provided the first significant application of the now outdated **intelligence quotient (IQ)** concept. This particular IQ concept, recommended by Stern (1912), used a subject's mental age in conjunction with his or her chronological age to obtain a ratio score. This ratio score presumably reflected the subject's rate of mental development. Table 9.2 illustrates how IQ is determined.

In calculating IQ, the first step is to determine the subject's actual or chronological age. To obtain this, we need only know his or her birthday. In the

FIGURE 9.4
Schematic summary of the evolution of the 1916 Binet scale.

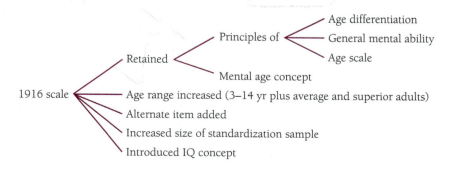

TABLE 9.2 The Intelligence Quotient Concept

Child 1:

Chronological age (CA): 6 years

Mental age (MA): 6 years

$$IQ = \frac{MA}{CA} \times 100 = \frac{6}{6} \times 100 = 100$$

Child 2:

Chronological age (CA): 6 years

Mental age (MA): 3 years

$$IQ = \frac{MA}{CA} \times 100 = \frac{3}{6} \times 100 = 50$$

Child 3:

CA = 6; MA = 12; IQ = 200

Adult 1:

CA = 50; MA = 16

$$IQ = \frac{16^*}{16} \times 100 = 100$$

*(the maximum CA)

second step, the subject's mental age is determined by his or her score on the scale. Finally, to obtain the IQ, the chronological age (CA) is divided into the mental age (MA) and the result multiplied by 100 to eliminate fractions: IQ = MA/CA × 100.

As you can see in Table 9.2, when MA is less than CA, the IQ is below 100. In this case, the subject was said to have slower-than-average mental development. When MA exceeded CA, the subject was said to have faster-than-average mental development.

The IQ score altered the nature of the measuring unit used to express the results. However, the method may have actually been a step backward; the MA/CA method of calculating IQ scores was ultimately abandoned in all major tests. The 1916 scale had a maximum possible mental age of 19.5 years; that is, if every group of items was passed, this score would result. Given this limitation, anyone older than 19.5 would have an IQ of less than 100 even if all items were passed. Therefore, a maximum limit on the chronological age had to be set. Because back in 1916 people believed that mental age ceased to improve after 16 years of age, 16 was used as the maximum chronological age.

The 1937 Scale

The 1937 scale extended the age range down to the 2-year-old level. Also, by adding new tasks, developers increased the maximum possible mental age to 22 years, 10 months. Scoring standards and instructions were improved to reduce ambiguities, enhance the standardization of administration, and increase interscorer

FIGURE 9.5
Schematic summary
of the evolution of the
1937 Binet scale.

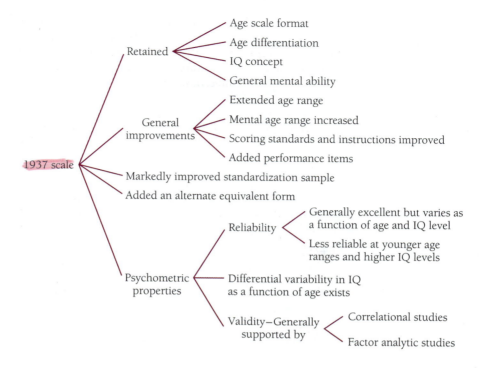

reliability. Furthermore, several performance items, which required the subject to do things such as copy designs, were added to decrease the scale's emphasis on verbal skills.

The standardization sample was markedly improved. Whereas the 1916 norms were restricted to Californians, the new subjects for the 1937 Stanford-Binet standardization sample came from 11 U.S. states representing a variety of regions. Subjects were selected according to their fathers' occupations. In addition, the standardization sample was substantially increased. Unfortunately, the sample included only whites and more urban subjects than rural ones. Nevertheless, this improved sample represented a desirable trend.

Perhaps the most important improvement in the 1937 version was the inclusion of an alternate equivalent form. Forms L and M were designed to be equivalent in terms of both difficulty and content. With two such forms, the psychometric properties of the scale could be readily examined (see Figure 9.5).

Problems With the 1937 Scale

A major problem with the 1937 scale was that its reliability coefficients were higher for older subjects than for younger ones. Thus, results for the latter were not as stable as those for the former. Reliability figures also varied as a function of IQ level, with higher reliabilities in the lower IQ ranges (i.e., less than 70) and poorer ones in the higher ranges. The lowest reliabilities occurred in the youngest age groups in the highest IQ ranges. These findings apply generally to all modern intelligence tests: Scores are most unstable for young children in high IQ ranges.

Along with the differing reliabilities, each age group in the standardization sample produced a unique standard deviation of IQ scores. This differential variability in IQ scores as a function of age created the single most important problem in the 1937 scale. More specifically, despite the great care taken in selecting the standardization sample, different age groups showed significant differences in the standard deviation of IQ scores. For example, the standard deviation in the IQ scores at age 6 was approximately 12.5. The standard deviations at ages 2.5 and 12, on the other hand, were 20.6 and 20.0, respectively. Because of these discrepancies, IQs at one age level were not equivalent to IQs at another (see Focused Example 9.1).

The 1960 Stanford-Binet Revision and Deviation IQ (SB-LM)

The developers of the 1960 revision (SB-LM) tried to create a single instrument by selecting the best from the two forms of the 1937 scale. Tasks that showed an increase in the percentage passing with an increase in age—a main criterion and guiding principle for the construction of the Binet scale—received the highest priority, as did tasks that correlated highly with scores as a whole—a second guiding principle of the Binet scale. In addition, instructions for scoring and test administration were improved, and IQ tables were extended from age 16 to 18. Perhaps most important, the problem of differential variation in IQs was solved by the deviation IQ concept.

As used in the Stanford-Binet scale, the *deviation IQ* was simply a standard score with a mean of 100 and a standard deviation of 16 (today the standard deviation is set at 15). With the mean set at 100 and assigned to scores at the 50th percentile, the deviation IQ was ascertained by evaluating the standard deviation of mental age for a representative sample at each age level. New IQ tables were then constructed that corrected for differences in variability at the various age levels. By correcting for these differences in variability, one could compare the IQs of one age level with those of another. Thus, scores could be interpreted in terms of standard deviations and percentiles with the assurance that IQ scores for every age group corresponded to the same percentile. Today, the deviation IQ method

Combo ot
okey

▼ **9.1** **FOCUSED EXAMPLE**

Differential Variability in IQ Scores

Recall our discussion of standard deviations and percentiles in Chapter 2. A score that is two standard deviations above the mean is approximately at the 98th percentile. Therefore, if the mean IQ is 100, a 6-year-old, where the standard deviation is 12.5, would need an IQ of 125 to be two standard deviations above the mean, or the 98th percentile. However, at 12 years of age, where the standard deviation is 20, the same child would need an IQ of 140 to be two standard deviations above the mean and in the 98th percentile. Say a child at age 6 with an IQ of 125 also obtained an IQ of 125 at age 12. He or she would then be only 1.25 standard deviations above the mean (because the standard deviation at age 12 is 20) and thus at only about the 89th percentile. You can see that in the 1937 scale, an IQ at one age range was not comparable to an IQ at another age range in terms of percentiles.

FIGURE 9.6
Schematic summary of the evolution of the 1960 Binet scale.

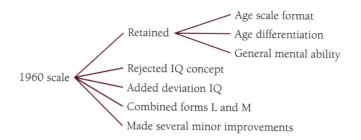

is considered the most precise way of expressing the results of an intelligence test (see Figure 9.6).

The 1960s revision did not include a new normative sample or restandardization. However, by 1972, a new standardization group consisting of a representative sample of 2100 children (approximately 100 at each Stanford-Binet age level) had been obtained for use with the 1960 revision (Thorndike, 1973). Unlike all previous norms, the 1972 norms included nonwhites. For many, however, the general improvements in the 1960 revision, even with the new 1972 norms, did not suffice. In 1986, a new and drastically revised version of the Binet scale was published (Thorndike, Hagen, & Sattler, 1986). Then, in 2003, there was another major revision in which many of the concepts added to the 1986 edition were abandoned in favor of concepts used in the 1960 (SB-LM) version. The changes in 1986 and the possible reasons for the return to the older 1960 model are instructive.

The Modern Binet Scale

Our discussion of the evolution of the Binet scale has illustrated many of the concepts that have dominated intelligence testing from its inception to the present. The fourth and fifth editions of the Stanford-Binet scale continue this tradition of innovation and incorporation of central psychometric and theoretical concepts. In this section, we examine the fourth and fifth editions of the scale, which its authors developed in response to cultural and social changes and new research in cognitive psychology. First, we consider the basic model that guided this development and briefly discuss the features common to both editions. Next, we compare these latest editions to their predecessors. We begin with a brief look at how the fourth edition was changed. Then, we consider the 2003 edition in greater detail—the various subtests, summary scores, and procedures. We also examine the scale's psychometric properties. Finally, we examine the 2003 edition of the Binet in light of a relatively new theory of intelligence.

Model for the Fourth and Fifth Editions of the Binet Scale

The model for the latest editions of the Binet (Figure 9.7) is far more elaborate than the Spearman model that best characterized the original versions of the scale. These versions incorporate the *gf-gc* theory of intelligence. They are based on a hierarchical model. At the top of the hierarchy is *g* (general intelligence), which

9-74534

RECORD BOOKLET

Stanford-Binet Intelligence Scale: Fourth Edition

Name _____

Sex _____

Ethnicity NA H B W/NH O/AA PI Other _____

	YEAR	MONTH	DAY
Date of Testing			
Birth Date			
Age			

School _____

Grade _____

Examiner _____

Father's Occupation: _____

Mother's Occupation: _____

FACTORS AFFECTING TEST PERFORMANCE
Overall Rating of Conditions

Optimal	Good	Average	Detrimental	Seriously detrimental

	RAW SCORE	STANDARD AGE SCORE
Verbal Reasoning		
1 Vocabulary	_____	_____
6 Comprehension	_____	_____
7 Absurdities	_____	_____
14 Verbal Relations	_____	_____
Sum of Subtest SAS's		
Verbal Reasoning SAS		░░░
Abstract/Visual Reasoning		
5 Pattern Analysis	_____	_____
9 Copying	_____	_____
11 Matrices	_____	_____
13 Paper Folding & Cutting	_____	_____
Sum of Subtest SAS's		
Abstract/Visual Reasoning SAS		░░░
Quantitative Reasoning		
3 Quantitative	_____	_____
12 Number Series	_____	_____
15 Equation Building	_____	_____
Sum of Subtest SAS's		
Quantitative Reasoning SAS		░░░
Short-Term Memory		
2 Bead Memory	_____	_____
4 Memory For Sentences	_____	_____
8 Memory For Digits	_____	_____
10 Memory For Objects	_____	_____
Sum of Subtest SAS's		
Short-Term Memory SAS		░░░
Sum of Area SAS's		

		COMPOSITE SCORE
Test Composite		_____
Partial Composite		_____
Partial Composite based on _____		

	1	2	3	4	5	
Attention						
a) Absorbed by task						Easily distracted
Reactions During Test Performance						
a) Normal activity level						Abnormal activity level
b) Initiates activity						Waits to be told
c) Quick to respond						Urging needed
Emotional Independence						
a) Socially confident						Insecure
b) Realistically self-confident						Distrusts own ability
c) Comfortable in adult company						Ill-at-ease
d) Assured						Anxious
Problem-Solving Behavior						
a) Persistent						Gives up easily
b) Reacts to failure realistically						Reacts to failure unrealistically
c) Eager to continue						Seeks to terminate
d) Challenged by hard tasks						Prefers only easy tasks
Independence of Examiner Support						
a) Needs minimum of commendation						Needs constant praise and encouragement
Expressive Language						
a) Excellent articulation						Very poor articulation
Receptive Language						
a) Excellent sound discrimination						Very poor sound discrimination

Was it difficult to establish rapport with this person?
Easy └──┴──┴──┴──┴──┘ Difficult

The Riverside Publishing Company

Robert L. Thorndike
Elizabeth P. Hagen
Jerome M. Sattler

FIGURE 9.7
Cover page of Stanford-Binet Intelligence Scale.
(Stanford-Binet Intelligence Scales, Fifth Edition (SB-5). © 2003 by PRO-ED. Reproduced with permission.)

reflects the common variability of all tasks. At the next level are three group factors. *Crystallized abilities* reflect learning—the realization of original potential through experience. *Fluid-analytic abilities* represent original potential, or the basic capabilities that a person uses to acquire crystallized abilities (Horn, 1994; Horn & Cattell, 1966; Horn & Noll, 1997). *Short-term memory* refers to one's memory during short intervals—the amount of information one can retain briefly after a single, short presentation (Colom, Flores-Mendoza, Quiroga, & Privado, 2005). In addition, crystallized ability has two subcategories: verbal reasoning and nonverbal reasoning (Pomplun & Custer, 2005).

The Role of Thurstone's Multidimensional Model

Today's Binet test attempts to evaluate *g* in the context of a multidimensional model of intelligence. The impetus for a multidimensional model stemmed from the work of Thurstone (1938). He argued that, contrary to Spearman's notion of intelligence as a single process, intelligence could best be conceptualized as comprising independent factors, or "primary mental abilities." In this approach, instead of viewing all specific abilities as being powered by a *g* factor, some groups of abilities were seen as independent. For example, the ability to code and all associated abilities might be completely independent of the ability to select the best investments. Group abilities were seen as broad capabilities that were independent of each other rather than each being the result of a single underlying factor. Years of painstaking work ultimately revealed evidence for group abilities factors that were relatively, but not totally, independent. The group factors were correlated, and from them a *g* factor could be extracted, as in the hierarchical model of the fourth and fifth editions of the Binet. The bottom line is that so far all roads point to a single factor correlated with abilities of all types. However, as will be seen, certain skills group together more strongly with so-called group abilities, such as verbal group ability and nonverbal group ability.

Characteristics of the 1986 Revision

The 1986 revision attempted to retain all of the strengths of the earlier revisions while eliminating the weaknesses. This was no easy task, nor was it a complete success as indicated by the backtracking that occurred in the fifth edition. To continue to provide a measure of general mental ability, the authors of the 1986 revision decided to retain the wide variety of content and task characteristics of earlier versions. However, to avoid having this wide content unevenly distributed across age groups, the age scale format was entirely eliminated, which as you recall grouped items according to age level so that the test starts and stops at an age-appropriate level. In place of the age scale, items with the same content were placed together into any one of 15 separate tests to create point scales. For example, all vocabulary items were placed together in one test; all matrix items were placed together in a second. In this way, we could see how many points one obtained in the vocabulary arena and how many points one obtained in solving matrix problems. Then, one could compare a subject's vocabulary ability with that same subject's ability at solving matrix problems.

The more modern 2003 fifth edition provided a standardized hierarchical model with five factors, as illustrated in Figure 9.8. At the top of the hierarchy is

FIGURE 9.8
Three-level hierarchical model of the 2003 fifth edition.

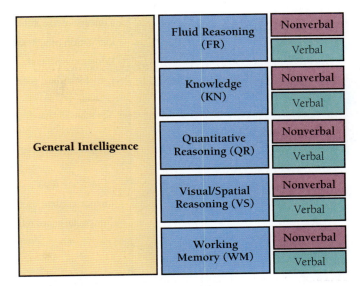

(Adapted from Figure 2.1, p. 24 in G. H. Roid, 2003b.)

FIGURE 9.9
Verbal and nonverbal tasks on 2003 fifth edition.

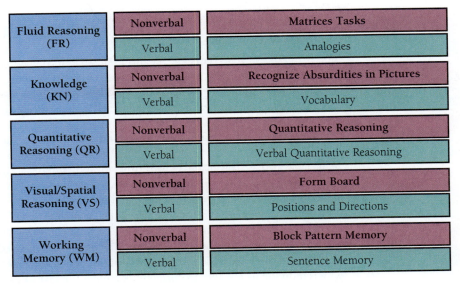

(Adapted from Figure 2.1, p. 24 in G. H. Roid, 2003b.)

general intelligence, just as in the 1986 edition. However, there are now five rather than four main factors. Each factor, in turn, has an equally weighted nonverbal and verbal measure. Figure 9.9 indicates the types of activities used to measure the various factors.

Placing together items of similar content in a point scale permits the calculation of specific scores for each of the 15 tests. Thus, in addition to an overall score that presumably reflects *g*, one can obtain scores related to each specific content area.

FIGURE 9.10
Characteristics of the modern (1986) Binet.

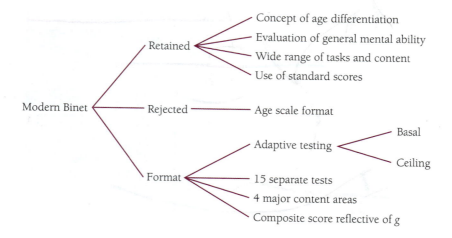

The drawback is less variety to the items. In addition, each of the specific 15 tests were grouped into one of four content areas or factors. Figure 9.10 summarizes the characteristics of the 1986 fourth edition.

Characteristics of the 2003 Fifth Edition

The fifth edition represents an elegant integration of the age-scale and point-scale formats. First, the nonverbal and verbal scales are equally weighted. The test examination process begins with one of two "routing measures" (subtests): one nonverbal, one verbal. The routing tests are organized in a point scale, which means that each contains items of similar content and of increasing difficulty. For example, the verbal routing test consists of a set of vocabulary items of increasing difficulty.

The purpose of the routing tests is to estimate the examinee's level of ability in order to guide the examination process by estimating the level of ability at which to begin testing for any given subject. The nonverbal routing test is used to estimate nonverbal ability; the verbal routing test is used to estimate verbal ability. The remaining eight subtests are arranged in an age-scale format. This means that tasks of differing content are grouped together on the basis of difficulty. For example, an age scale-based subtest might have a mixture of different types of verbal and nonverbal tasks, with the tasks grouped according to the typical age at which individuals are able to correctly complete the task. This mixing of tasks was the procedure used in all prior versions of the Binet except the fourth edition. The difference with the 2003 fifth edition is that because of the equal weighting of verbal and nonverbal items, it is possible to summarize an examinee's score on all items of similar content. As a result, the fifth edition retains the advantage of the point scale by allowing examiners to summarize scores within any given content area while also using a mixture of tasks to maintain an examinee's interest.

Using the routing tests to estimate ability, the examiner then goes to an age scale-based subtest at the appropriate level for the examinee. In that way, items that are too easy are skipped to save time and provide for a more efficient examination.

FIGURE 9.11
Characteristics of the 2003 fifth edition.

2003 Fifth Edition	Uses a "hybrid" of point and age scales
	Has an equal balance of nonverbal and verbal items
	Has 5 factors plus — Nonverbal IQ / Verbal IQ / Full-Scale IQ
	Uses a standard deviation of 15 for IQ and factor scores

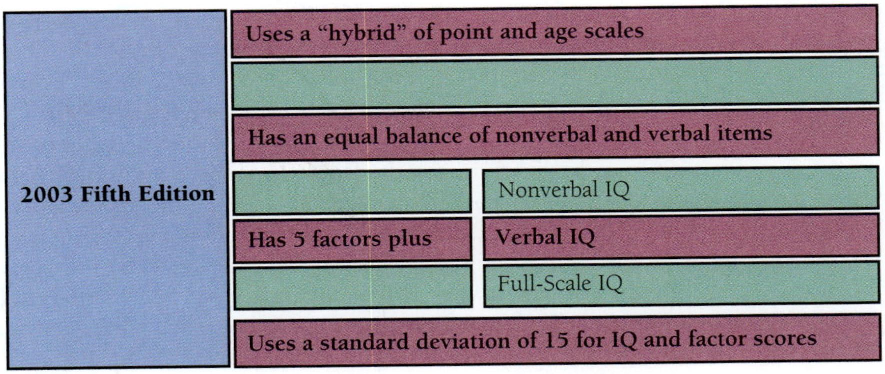

The estimated level of ability is called the *start point*. However, if a certain number of early items are missed, then the examiner moves to a lower (and therefore easier) level. The level at which a minimum criterion number of correct responses is obtained is known as the **basal**. Testing continues until examinees reach the **ceiling**, which is a certain number of incorrect responses that indicate the items are too difficult.

Examiners can complete scaled scores for each of the five nonverbal subtests and each of the five corresponding verbal subtests. These scaled scores have a mean of 10 and a standard deviation of 3. In addition, a standard score with a mean of 100 and a standard deviation of 15 is computed for nonverbal IQ, verbal IQ, full-scale IQ, and each of the five factors: fluid reasoning, knowledge, quantitative reasoning, visual-spatial processing, and working memory. Nonverbal and verbal IQ scores are based on summing the five nonverbal and five verbal subtests. The full-scale IQ is based on all 10. The standard scores for each of the five factors are based on summing the nonverbal and corresponding verbal subtest for each respective factor. Figure 9.11 summarizes the characteristics of the 2003 fifth edition.

Psychometric Properties of the 2003 Fifth Edition

The 2003 fifth edition was constructed with exceptional diligence. It continues the tradition of its predecessors in providing a state-of-the-art model for intelligence tests in terms of its psychometric standards and construction.

The awkward standard deviation of 16 for major indexes was finally abandoned in favor of the more common standard deviation of 15. Several new subtests were added, while those that were retained were updated with new artwork, toys, and better items. A major goal of the fifth edition is to tap the extremes in intelligence— the major historical strength of the Binet that had been essentially lost in the fourth edition. The age range touted by the fifth edition spans from 2 to 85+ years of age.

Norms were based on a representative sample of 4800 individuals from age 2 through 85+, stratified by gender, ethnicity, region, and education according to the 2001 census. To augment the standardization sample, 3000 additional individuals were included, encompassing various subpopulations such as gifted, mentally retarded, attention-deficit/hyperactivity disorder (ADHD), and those with speech, language, and hearing problems. The range of possible scores runs from a low of 40 to a high of 160, reestablishing the Binet as one of the most appropriate tests for evaluating extremes in intelligence (see Canivez, 2008; Silverman et al., 2010).

Overall, the reliability of the fifth edition is quite good. Coefficients for the full-scale IQ are either .97 or .98 for each of the 23 age ranges reported in the manual. Average reliabilities for the three IQ scores are .98 (full-scale IQ), .95 (nonverbal IQ), and .96 (verbal IQ). Coefficients for the five-factor index scores range from .90 to .92. Coefficients for verbal and nonverbal subtests are comparable and consistently in the high .8's. Test–retest coefficients are likewise excellent, with a range from the high .7's to the low .9's, depending on age and testing interval. Interscorer agreement was made high by eliminating items where such agreement was low, with an overall median of .9 reported in the technical manual (Roid, 2003c).

However, Canivez reports that results from more recent independent studies have seriously challenged the claim that the fifth edition measures five factors (Canivez, 2008, citing DiStefano & Dombrowski, 2006). DiStefano and Dombrowski concluded that the fifth edition was probably best explained as a unidimensional test of intelligence. Canivez opines that failure to find support for Roid's (2003c) five factors and limited support for even two factors may be the result of Roid extracting too many factors due to not considering exploratory factor analyses and multiple factor extraction criteria (Canivez, citing Frazier & Youngstrom, 2007). As a result, clinical interpretation of the fifth edition should primarily reside at the global, general intelligence level until research adequately supports interpretation of lower-order (Stratum II) dimensions. As of late 2016, such research was lacking.

Median Validity

The technical manual reports four types of evidence that support the validity of the test: (1) content validity, (2) construct validity, (3) empirical item analysis, and (4) considerable criterion-related evidence of validity. Full-scale IQs for the fifth edition correlate in the low to mid .8's, with established measures including the Wechsler scales, which are discussed in the next chapter.

Summary

Binet defined *intelligence* as the capacity (1) to find and maintain a definite direction or purpose; (2) to make necessary adaptations—that is, strategy adjustments—to achieve that purpose; and (3) to engage in self-criticism so that necessary adjustments in strategy can be made.

Binet's two principles of test construction were age differentiation and general mental ability. *Age differentiation* refers to the fact that with increasing age, children develop their abilities. Thus, older children have greater abilities than do younger ones. Spearman developed his own theory of general mental ability, or *g*, based on the idea that a single general factor underlies all intelligence. Modern theorists have taken this concept further in *gf-gc* theory, in which there are two basic types of intelligence: fluid (*gf*) and crystallized (*gc*).

Mental age is a unit of measurement for expressing the results of intelligence tests. The concept was introduced in the second revision of the Binet scale in 1908. A subject's mental age is based on his or her performance compared with the average performance of individuals in a specific chronological age group. For example, if a 6-year-old child can perform tasks that the average 8-year-old can do, then the 6-year-old child is said to have a mental age of 8.

Like mental age, the *intelligence quotient* (IQ) is a unit of measure for expressing the results of intelligence tests. Introduced in the Terman 1916 Stanford-Binet revision of the Binet scale, the IQ is a ratio score. Specifically, the IQ is the ratio of a subject's mental age (as determined by his or her performance on the intelligence scale) and chronological age. This ratio is then multiplied by 100 to eliminate fractions.

The *deviation IQ*, as it is now used in the Stanford-Binet Scale (fifth edition), is a standard score with a mean of 100 and a standard deviation of 15. Older versions had a standard deviation of 16.

The most recent revision of the Binet scale, the fifth edition, was released in 2003. This edition combines the age and point scale methods of test construction.

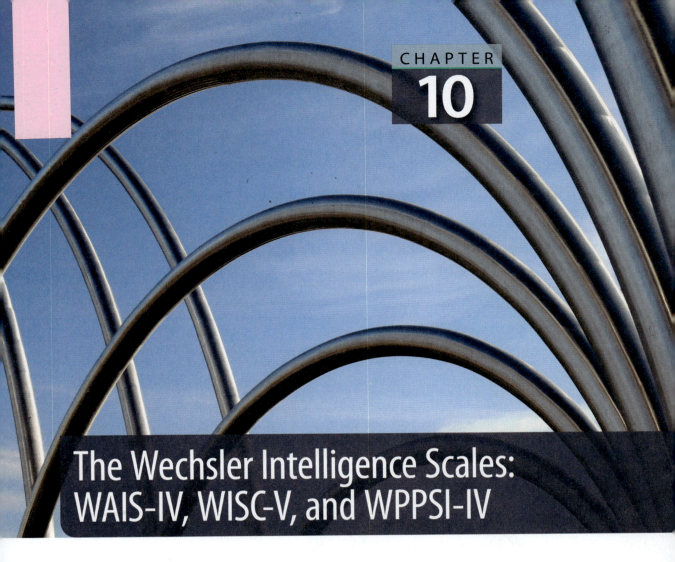

The Wechsler Intelligence Scales: WAIS-IV, WISC-V, and WPPSI-IV

LEARNING OBJECTIVES

When you have completed this chapter, you should be able to:

▶ Identify the major motivation for the development of the Wechsler scales

▶ Briefly describe the point and performance scale concepts

▶ Distinguish between verbal and performance tasks

▶ Explain how IQ scores are determined on the Wechsler scales

▶ Describe the reliability of the Wechsler scales

▶ Describe the validity of the Wechsler scales

▶ Identify some of the major advantages and disadvantages of the Wechsler scales

▶ Describe the advances in testing reflected in the WISC-V and WPPSI-IV

247

S usan's family has just moved from a small rural town to a large city on the East Coast of the United States. At age 9, she remains shy around strangers and lacks confidence. Her attempt to adjust to a new school has been disastrous. Because she started in the middle of the school term, all of the other children seem way ahead of her; she feels hopelessly behind. To make matters worse, she has an unusually strong fear of failure. Rather than make an error, she remains silent even if she knows an answer. With all of her negative experiences in the new school, she begins to develop a poor attitude toward school tasks and therefore avoids them. Eventually, her teacher refers her to the school psychologist for testing. To Susan, this referral is the school's way of punishing her for not doing her homework. Fearful, upset, and angry, she makes up her mind not to cooperate with the psychologist.

When the time finally comes for her appointment, Susan begins to cry. The principal is called in to accompany her to the psychologist's office. Although she appears to calm down, Susan remains fearful and anxious. Finally, the psychologist decides to begin the testing. He starts with a relatively simple task that requires Susan to repeat digits. The psychologist states, "I want you to repeat some numbers that I'm going to say to you. Please say them as I do." He begins the first set of digits and states in a soft, clear voice, "Six, one, three." Susan does not even respond. She has been staring blankly at the walls and has not heard what the psychologist has said. The psychologist attracts her attention and says, "Now say what I say: four, two, seven." This time Susan hears him but again remains silent.

Now think for a moment. How many different factors are involved in the psychologist's ostensibly simple request to repeat three digits forward? To comply with this request, Susan has to direct her attention to the words of the psychologist, possess adequate hearing, and understand the instructions. She also has to cooperate, make an effort, and be capable of repeating what she has heard. Certainly her familiarity with numerals—that is, her previous learning and experience—can influence her performance. If the children in her new school have had more exposure to numerals than she has, then they might have an advantage over her in this regard. Furthermore, her lack of confidence, negative attitude toward school, fear of failure, and shyness have all played a role in her performance. A more confident, less fearful child with positive attitudes toward school would have a clear advantage over Susan. Thus, in addition to memory and other indicators of intelligence, many nonintellective factors (e.g., attitude, experience, and emotional functioning) play an extremely important role in a person's ability to perform a task even as "simple" as repeating three digits forward.

Though both Binet and Terman considered the influence of nonintellective factors on results from intelligence tests, David Wechsler, author of the Wechsler scales, has been perhaps one of the most influential advocates of the role of nonintellective factors in these tests. Throughout his career, Wechsler emphasized that factors other than intellectual ability are involved in intelligent behavior. Today, there are three Wechsler intelligence tests, the Wechsler Adult Intelligence Scale, Fourth Edition (WAIS-IV), the Wechsler Intelligence Scale for Children, Fifth Edition (WISC-V), and the Wechsler Preschool and Primary Scale of Intelligence, Fourth Edition (WPPSI-IV).

The Wechsler Intelligence Scales

The role of nonintellective factors is apparent in the Wechsler intelligence scales. Just 2 years after the Binet scale's monumental 1937 revision, the Wechsler–Bellevue Intelligence Scale challenged its supremacy as a measure of human intelligence. With so many different and varied abilities associated with intelligence, Wechsler objected to the single score offered by the 1937 Binet scale. In addition, although Wechsler's test did not directly measure nonintellective factors, it took these factors into careful account in its underlying theory. In constructing his own intelligence test, Wechsler deviated considerably from many of the Binet scale's central concepts.

Wechsler (1939) capitalized on the inappropriateness of the 1937 Binet scale as a measure of the intelligence of adults. Because the Binet scale items were selected for use with children, Wechsler concluded that these items lacked validity when answered by adults. Further, examiner–subject rapport was often impaired when adults were tested with the Binet scale. Wechsler (1939) also correctly noted that the Binet scale's emphasis on speed, with timed tasks scattered throughout the scale, tended to unduly handicap older adults. Furthermore, mental age norms clearly did not apply to adults. Finally, Wechsler criticized the then existing Binet scale because it did not consider that intellectual performance could deteriorate as a person grew older. (As noted in Chapter 9, the modern Binet scale has addressed these and many other criticisms of its earlier predecessors.)

Point and Performance Scale Concepts

Many of the differences between the Wechsler and the original Binet scales were profound. Two of the most critical differences were (1) Wechsler's use of the point scale concept rather than an age scale used in the early Binet Tests and (2) Wechsler's inclusion of a nonverbal performance scale.

The Point Scale Concept

Recall that from 1908 to 1972, the Binet scale grouped items by age level. Each age level included a group of tasks that could be passed by two-thirds to three-fourths of the individuals at that age level. In an age-scale format, the arrangement of items has nothing to do with their content. At a particular year level, there might be one task related to memory, a second to reasoning, and a third to skill in using numerical data. Another level might also include a task related to memory but then include other tasks related to concentration or language skills. Thus, various types of content are scattered throughout the scale. Furthermore, on the earlier Binet scale, subjects did not receive a specific amount of points or credit for each task completed. For example, if a Binet scale subject is required to pass three out of four tasks in order to receive credit for a particular test, then passing only two tasks would produce no credit at all for that test.

In a point scale, credits or points are assigned to each item. An individual receives a specific amount of credit for each item passed. The point scale offers an inherent advantage. This scale makes it easy to group items of a particular content together, which is exactly what Wechsler did. The effect of such groupings appeared so powerful that a similar concept was used in the 1986 Binet scale. By arranging items according to content and assigning a specific number of points to each item, Wechsler constructed an intelligence test that yielded not only a total overall score but also scores for each content area. Thus, the point scale concept allowed Wechsler to devise a test that permitted an analysis of the individual's ability in a variety of content areas (e.g., judgment, vocabulary, and range of general knowledge). Today, Wechsler's concept is the standard.

The Performance Scale Concept

The early Binet scale had been persistently and consistently criticized for its emphasis on language and verbal skills. To deal with this problem, Wechsler included an entire scale that provided a measure of nonverbal intelligence: a performance scale. Thus, in addition to measuring intelligence in adults and yielding separate scores, Wechsler's approach offered a third major advantage over the early Binet scales. The performance scale consisted of tasks that require a subject to do something (e.g., copy symbols or point to a missing detail) rather than merely answer questions (see Figure 10.1).

Although the early Binet scales contained some performance tasks, these tended to be concentrated at the younger age levels. Furthermore, the results of a subject's response to a performance task on the Binet scale were extremely difficult to separate from the results for verbal tasks, as can be done today. As a result, one could not determine the precise extent to which a subject's response to a nonverbal performance task increased or decreased the total score. The original Wechsler scale, however, included two separate scales. The verbal scale provided a measure of verbal intelligence, and the performance scale a measure of nonverbal intelligence. As we will see, the most recent editions of the Wechsler scales, the WAIS-IV, the WISC-V, and the WPPSI-IV, now have as many as five major scales instead of the original two.

The concept of a performance scale was far from new. Before the Wechsler scale, several performance tests served as supplements or alternatives to the then verbally weighted Binet scale (such as the Leiter International Performance Scale, discussed in Chapter 11). However, Wechsler's new scale was the first to offer the possibility of directly comparing an individual's verbal and nonverbal intelligence—that is, both

FIGURE 10.1
Advantages of
Wechsler's scale.

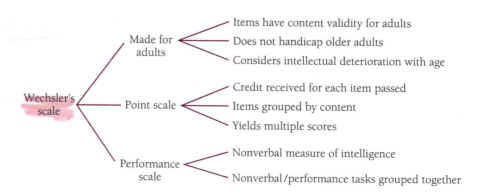

the verbal and performance scales were standardized on the same sample, and the results of both scales were expressed in comparable units. Again, this procedure of standardizing multiple scales on the same sample represents the current standard in modern psychological testing.

A performance scale attempts to overcome biases caused by language, culture, and education. Furthermore, if verbal tasks provide a useful context in which to observe problem solving, then tasks that require the subject to do something physical, such as pointing, can offer an even richer and more varied context. Indeed, performance tasks tend to require a longer interval of sustained effort, concentration, and attention than most verbal tasks. Therefore, they not only measure intelligence but also provide the clinician with a rich opportunity to observe behavior in a standard setting.

From the Wechsler–Bellevue Intelligence Scale to the WAIS-IV

Despite his conceptual improvements, Wechsler's first effort to measure adult intelligence, the Wechsler–Bellevue scale (Wechsler, 1939), was poorly standardized. Its normative sample consisted of a nonrepresentative sample of 1081 whites from the eastern United States (primarily New York residents). By 1955, however, Wechsler had revised the Wechsler–Bellevue scale into its modern form, the Wechsler Adult Intelligence Scale (WAIS), which was revised in 1981 (the WAIS-R), again in 1997 (the WAIS-III), and yet again in 2008 (WAIS-IV) with the WAIS-V no doubt soon to come. To better understand the modern Wechsler scales, it is important to reflect on the concepts underlying the original distinction between the verbal and performance IQs.

Scales, Subtests, and Indexes

Like Binet, Wechsler defined intelligence as the capacity to act purposefully and to adapt to the environment. In his words, intelligence is "the aggregate or global capacity of the individual to act purposefully, to think rationally and to deal effectively with his environment" (1958, p. 7). Wechsler believed that intelligence comprised specific elements that one could individually define and measure; however, these elements were interrelated—that is, not entirely independent. This is why he used the terms *global* and *aggregate*. Wechsler's definition implies that intelligence comprises several specific interrelated functions or elements and that general intelligence results from the interplay of these elements. Modern research overwhelmingly supports this view (Canivez, 2015; Corballis, 2011; Goldstein & Beers, 2003; Sternberg, 2000; Weiss, Saklofske, Coalson, & Engi Raiford, 2010). Theoretically, by measuring each of the elements, one can measure general intelligence by summing the individual's capacities on each element. Thus, Wechsler tried to measure separate abilities, which Binet had avoided in adopting the concept of general mental ability.

TABLE 10.1   Core Wechsler Subtests

Subtest	Major function measured by various subtests
Vocabulary	Vocabulary level
Similarities	Abstract thinking
Arithmetic	Concentration
Digit span	Immediate memory, anxiety
Information	Range of knowledge
Coding	Visual–motor functioning
Block design	Nonverbal reasoning
Matrix reasoning	Inductive reasoning
Visual puzzles	Perceptual reasoning
Symbol search	Information-processing speed

In the WAIS-IV, as well as in the WISC-V and WPPSI-IV, Wechsler's basic approach is maintained. First, there are individual subtests, each of which is related to a basic underlying skill or ability (see Table 10.1). For example, the information subtest measures one's range of knowledge. Each of the various subtests is also part of a broader "index." On the WAIS-IV, the subtests are sorted into four indexes: verbal comprehension, perceptual reasoning, working memory, and processing speed. The full-scale IQ (FSIQ) is then based on the summed scores of these four indexes.

An *index* is created where two or more subtests are related to a basic underlying skill. Figure 10.2 shows the WAIS-IV's four indexes and their corresponding subtests.

A Closer Look at Subtests

To get a better understanding of subtests, let's look at some of these in greater detail. In describing these and all other tests in this book, our examples are not those actually used in the test itself unless express permission has been obtained. Our goal is merely to illustrate the type of content to give readers a better understanding of how the actual subtest works.

The Vocabulary Subtest

The ability to define words is not only one of the best single measures of intelligence but also the most stable. Vocabulary tests appear on nearly every individual test that involves verbal intelligence. The relative stability of the vocabulary subtest and verbal comprehension index of which it is a part is one of its most important features. If an individual has shown *deterioration* (i.e., lowered performance compared with a previously higher level) because of emotional factors or brain damage, for example, vocabulary is one of the last functions to be affected. It is more stable and less

FIGURE 10.2

Schematic overview of WAIS-IV index scores.

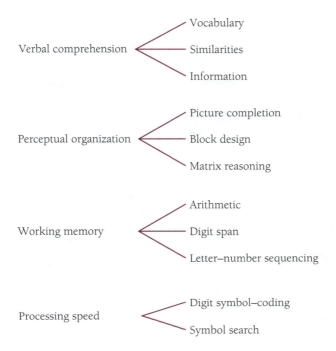

Verbal comprehension
- Vocabulary
- Similarities
- Information

Perceptual organization
- Picture completion
- Block design
- Matrix reasoning

Working memory
- Arithmetic
- Digit span
- Letter–number sequencing

Processing speed
- Digit symbol–coding
- Symbol search

vulnerable than other aspects of intelligence. For example, the poor concentration of schizophrenic people lowers their performance on arithmetic or digit span tasks (respecting numbers spoken out loud) long before vocabulary is affected (Behrwind et al., 2011; Michel, Goldberg, Heinrichs, Miles, & Ammari, 2013; Schwarz, Gfeller, & Oliveri, 2006). Also, whereas mild concentration difficulties lower optimal performance on arithmetic and digit span tasks, such difficulties generally do not affect vocabulary until they become quite severe (Almkvist, Adveen, Henning, & Tallberg, 2007; Weiss et al., 2010). Because the vocabulary subtest provides a relatively stable estimate of general verbal intelligence, one can use it to evaluate baseline or premorbid intelligence (i.e., what a person's intellectual capacity probably was prior to an emotional illness, brain injury, or trauma) (Carlozzia et al., 2011; Seidman, Buka, Goldstein, & Tsuang, 2006).

The Similarities Subtest

The similarities subtest consists of paired items of increasing difficulty. The subject must identify the similarity between the items in each pair. The examiner asks, for example, "In what way are bread and water alike?" Many of the early, easier items are so well known that responses simply reflect previously learned associations (Kaufman, 1990). However, the more difficult items might be something like, "In what way are an ant and a rose alike?" Some items definitely require the subject to think abstractly. This subtest measures the subject's ability to see the similarity between apparently dissimilar objects or things.

The character of a person's thought processes can be seen in many cases. For example, individuals with schizophrenia may give *idiosyncratic* concepts, or concepts that have meaning only to them. Such a response to the bread and water item might be "Both are used for torture." Such a response has meaning only to the schizophrenic person.

The Arithmetic Subtest

The arithmetic subtest contains approximately 15 relatively simple problems in increasing order of difficulty. The ninth most difficult item is as easy as this: "A person with $28.00 spends $.50. How much does he have left?" Obviously, you need not be a mathematician to figure this one out; however, you must be able to retain the figures in memory while manipulating them. In a few cases, such as in mentally handicapped or educationally deprived subjects, arithmetic skills can play a significant role. Generally, however, concentration, motivation, and memory are the main factors underlying performance. Figure 10.3 illustrates some of the intellective and nonintellective components of the arithmetic subtest as revealed by factor analytic and logical analyses.

The Digit Span Subtest

The digit span subtest requires the subject to repeat digits, given at the rate of one per second, forward and backward. In terms of intellective factors, the digit span subtest measures short-term auditory memory and is one of the core subtests in the working memory index. As with other Wechsler subtests, however, nonintellective factors (e.g., attention) often influence the results (Davidson & Kemp, 2011; Hale,

FIGURE 10.3
Arithmetic subtest: intellective and nonintellective components.

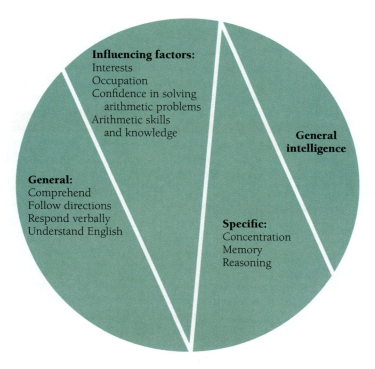

Influencing factors:
Interests
Occupation
Confidence in solving
   arithmetic problems
Arithmetic skills
   and knowledge

General intelligence

General:
Comprehend
Follow directions
Respond verbally
Understand English

Specific:
Concentration
Memory
Reasoning

Hoeppner, & Fiorello, 2002; Hopko, Hunt, & Armento, 2005). For example, anxiety in the test situation may impair performance on the digit span subtest (Gass & Curiel, 2011; Hopko et al., 2005; Marchand, Lefebvre, & Connolly, 2006).

The Information Subtest

College students typically find the information subtest relatively easy and fun. As in all Wechsler subtests, items appear in order of increasing difficulty. Item 6 asks something like, "Name two people who have been generals in the U.S. Army" or "How many members are there in the U.S. Congress?" Like all Wechsler subtests, the information subtest involves both intellective and nonintellective components, including the abilities to comprehend instructions, follow directions, and provide a response. Although purportedly a measure of the subject's range of knowledge, nonintellective factors such as curiosity and interest in the acquisition of knowledge tend to influence test scores. The subtest is also linked to alertness to the environment and alertness to cultural opportunities. Figure 10.4 illustrates how one can parcel a score on the information subtest.

The Comprehension Subtest

The comprehension subtest has three types of questions. The first asks the subject what should be done in a given situation, as in, "What should you do if you find an injured person lying in the street?" The second type of question asks the subject to

FIGURE 10.4
Information subtest: intellective and nonintellective components.

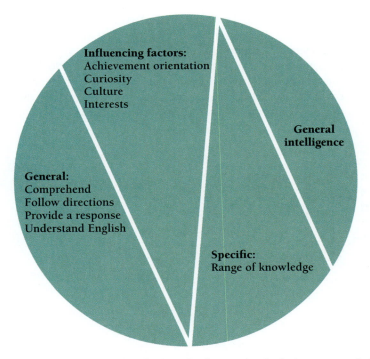

Influencing factors:
Achievement orientation
Curiosity
Culture
Interests

General
intelligence

General:
Comprehend
Follow directions
Provide a response
Understand English

Specific:
Range of knowledge

(Based on factor analytic and logical analyses of intellective and nonintellective components in the information subtest.)

provide a logical explanation for some rule or phenomenon, as in, "Why do we bury the dead?" The third type asks the subject to define proverbs such as, "A journey of 1000 miles begins with the first step." Generally, the comprehension subtest measures judgment in everyday practical situations, or common sense. Emotional difficulties frequently reveal themselves on this subtest and lower the person's score (Goldstein, Minshew, Allen, & Seaton, 2002). For example, to the question concerning what to do if you find an injured person, a psychopathic individual might respond, "Tell them I didn't do it." A phobic neurotic might respond, "Make sure I don't get any blood on myself." A schizophrenic might say, "Run!" In each case, the person's emotional disturbance interferes with his or her judgment and results in an inappropriate response.

The Letter–Number Sequencing Subtest

The letter–number sequencing task is supplementary on the working memory index; it is not required to obtain an index score, but it may be used as a supplement for additional information about the person's intellectual functioning (Phares & Trull, 2000; Wechsler, Coalson, & Engi Raiford, 2008). It is made up of items in which the individual is asked to reorder lists of numbers and letters. For example, Z, 3, B, 1, 2, A, would be reordered as 1, 2, 3, A, B, Z. This subtest is related to working memory and attention (Phares & Trull, 2000; Wechsler, 2008).

The Digit Symbol–Coding Subtest

The coding subtest (formerly called digit symbol) requires the subject to copy symbols. In the standard WAIS-IV response form, the numbers 1 through 9 are each paired with a symbol (see Figure 10.5). After completing a short practice sample, the subject has 120 seconds to copy as many symbols as possible. The subtest measures such factors as ability to learn an unfamiliar task, visual-motor dexterity, degree of persistence, and speed of performance (Kaufman, 1990; Weschler, 2008). Naturally, the subject must have adequate visual acuity and appropriate motor capabilities to complete this subtest successfully, and factors that affect these capabilities, such as age, may affect test results (Kreiner & Ryan, 2001).

FIGURE 10.5

Digit symbol–coding: an illustrative example. The top row contains divided boxes with a number in the upper half and a mark underneath. The bottom row contains divided boxes with numbers on top but no marks. The subject must supply the appropriate mark in the lower half of the bottom row.

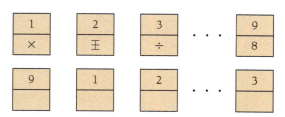

The Block Design Subtest

Block design tasks have long been included in nonverbal measures of intelligence (Arthur, 1930; Kohs, 1923). Materials for the block design subtest include nine variously colored blocks. The materials also include a booklet with pictures of the blocks arranged according to a specific geometric design or configuration. The subject must arrange the blocks to reproduce increasingly difficult designs. This subtest requires the subject to reason, analyze spatial relationships, and integrate visual and motor functions. The input information (i.e., pictures of designs) is visual, but the response (output) is motor. The subtest provides an excellent measure of nonverbal concept formation, abstract thinking, and neurocognitive impairment (Lysaker, Clements, Wright, Evans, & Marks, 2001; Paul et al., 2001). It is one of the core measures of the perceptual reasoning index scale in the WAIS-IV.

The Matrix Reasoning Subtest

As indicated in the previous chapter, modern theories of intelligence emphasize its multidimensional quality (Flanagan, McGrew, & Ortiz, 2000; Vogt, Dolan, & Hoelzle, 2015). The matrix reasoning subtest was included in the WAIS-IV as a core subtest in the perceptual reasoning index scale in an effort to enhance the assessment of fluid intelligence, which involves our ability to reason. In the matrix reasoning subtest, the subject is presented with nonverbal, figural stimuli. The task is to identify a pattern or relationship between the stimuli. In addition to its role in measuring fluid intelligence, this subtest is a good measure of information-processing and abstract-reasoning skills (Phares & Trull, 2000; Wechsler, 2008).

The Symbol Search Subtest

Symbol search is a relatively new subtest. It was optional in WAIS-III, but now is a core measure in the processing speed index scale. It was added in recognition of the role of speed of information processing in intelligence (Joy, Kaplan, & Fein, 2004; Kaufman, DeYoung, Reis, & Gray, 2011; Saccuzzo, Johnson, & Guertin, 1994). In this subtest, the subject is shown two target geometric figures. The task is then to search from among a set of five additional search figures and determine whether the target appears in the search group. Presumably, the faster a subject performs this task, the faster his or her information-processing speed will be. Chapter 15 discusses other measures of information-processing speed.

From Raw Scores to Scaled and Index Scale Scores

Each subtest produces a raw score—that is, a total number of points—and has a different maximum total.

To allow testers to compare scores on individual subtests, raw scores can be converted to standard or scaled scores with a mean of 10 and a standard deviation of 3. In deriving a subtest scaled score for the WAIS-IV, the test developers used a statistical method called inferential norming (Wilkins, Rolfhus, Weiss, & Zhu, 2005). A variety of statistical indexes or "moments," such as means and standard deviations, were calculated for each of the 13 age groups of the stratified normative sample (Weschler, 2008, p. 39). These were plotted across age groups to derive estimates of age group midpoint population moments. In the end, the test developers were able to derive reference group norms, which allow the test user to compare subjects at the subtest level. As will be seen later, such reference group norms can be extremely valuable in interpreting scores.

The four composite index scales are then derived by summing the core subtest scores (see Figure 10.2). For example, the verbal comprehension index is determined from scaled scores on the vocabulary, similarities, and information subtests. Each of the four index scores was normalized to have a mean of 100 and a standard deviation of 15. Let's look more closely at these index scores.

Index Scores

As indicated in Figure 10.2, there are four such scores: verbal comprehension, perceptual organization, working memory, and processing speed.

As a measure of acquired knowledge and verbal reasoning, the verbal comprehension index might best be thought of as a measure of crystallized intelligence. According to the test developers, this index is a "more refined," "purer" measure of verbal comprehension than is the verbal IQ (VIQ) because it excludes the arithmetic and digit span subtests, which have attentional or working memory components (Tulsky, Zhu, & Ledbetter, 1997, p. 186; Weschler, 2008).

The perceptual reasoning index, consisting of visual puzzles, block design, and matrix reasoning (see Figure 10.2), is believed to be a measure of fluid intelligence. Other factors that influence one's performance on this group of tests are attentiveness to details and visual-motor integration (Tulsky et al., 1997; Weschler, 2008).

The notion of working memory is perhaps one of the most important innovations on the modern WAIS. *Working memory* refers to the information that we actively hold in our minds, in contrast to our stored knowledge, or long-term memory (James & Rix, 2013; Pascanu & Jaeger, 2011). Consider the following question: "If you have $10.00, and you have given $4.50 to your brother and spent 75¢ on candy, how much do you have left?" To answer this question, you must mentally hold $10.00 in your head, subtract $4.50, and then hold that result while you subtract 75¢. It is your working memory that allows you to do this.

Finally, the processing speed index attempts to measure how quickly your mind works. For example, while one person may require 20 seconds to solve the given problem, another may require only 5 seconds.

FSIQs

The FSIQ follows the same principles of index scores. It is obtained by summing the age-corrected scaled scores of all four index composites. Again, a deviation IQ with a mean of 100 and a standard deviation of 15 is obtained. The FSIQ represents a measure of general intelligence.

The WAIS-IV follows a hierarchical model with general intelligence (FSIQ) at the top. The index scores form the next level, with the subtests providing the base (see Figure 10.6). When it comes to theories of intelligence, Figure 10.6 represents the consensus model of today and likely for some time to come—a general factor at the top followed by group factors and finally individual abilities.

FIGURE 10.6
Hierarchical structure of the WAIS-IV.

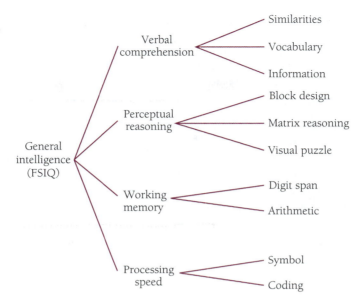

Interpretive Features of the Wechsler Tests

The WAIS-IV provides a rich source of data that often furnishes significant cues for diagnosing various conditions. The comparison of index scores and analysis of the pattern of subtest scores may be helpful, for example, in evaluating brain damage and disordered states. (The original Wechsler scale, through the WAIS-III, was based on just two indexes, called verbal and performance IQs.) As with modern index scores, these had a mean of 100 and standard deviations of 15. As the vast bulk of assessment is based on comparing the old verbal and performance IQs, these will be used to illustrate the process of index comparisons.

Index Comparisons

In providing measures of nonverbal intelligence in conjunction with a nonverbal IQ measure, the Wechsler offers an extremely useful opportunity not offered by the early Binet scales. First, the nonverbal measures aid in the interpretation of the verbal measures (now called the verbal comprehension subtest). Assume, for example, that a subject obtains a VIQ in the low ranges (such as VIQ = 60). If the performance IQ (PIQ) is also approximately 60, then the VIQ has been confirmed, and we have a good indication that the individual is, in fact, intellectually retarded. Remember, however, that a diagnosis of mental retardation should not be made on the basis of IQ alone. The individual must show significant deficits in adaptive functioning as well as an FSIQ below 70. What if the PIQ exceeds 100, but the VIQ is 55? In this case, the individual is at least average in his or her nonverbal skills but three standard deviations below the mean in the verbal area. Even though the FSIQ might still fall well below normal, it is quite unlikely that such a person is mentally retarded. Instead, language, cultural, or educational factors might account for the differences in the two measures of intellectual performance. However, there are limits to index comparisons as well.

In one study of verbal versus performance IQs, Saccuzzo, Johnson, and Russell (1992) examined approximately 5000 gifted children from four ethnic backgrounds: African American, Caucasian, Filipino, and Hispanic. Results showed that even though all children had IQs of 125 or greater, the nature of the verbal–performance discrepancy, if any, depended on ethnic background. The African American and Caucasian groups had higher verbal than performance IQs. The reverse was found for the Filipinos, who had significantly higher PIQs. No differences were found between the verbal and performance IQs for the Hispanics. Results such as these indicate that it is not appropriate to make sweeping generalizations about the meaning of index discrepancies and should provide a warning as new research begins to look at comparisons among index scores.

Pattern Analysis

The separate subtest scores of the WAIS-IV and other Wechsler tests offer an opportunity for *pattern analysis*. In such analysis, one evaluates relatively large differences between subtest scaled scores. Wechsler (1958) reasoned that different types of emotional problems might have differential effects on the subtests and cause unique score patterns. For example, people with conversion disorders often use denial and repression—that is, they put things out of awareness as a defense mechanism. Therefore, they should show lapses in their long-term store of knowledge, which might produce a relatively low score on the information subtest. Schizophrenia involves poor concentration and impaired judgment, which might turn up as relatively low scores on arithmetic and comprehension. Wechsler (1958) provided a host of patterns tentatively proposed as diagnostically significant.

Following Wechsler's (1958) proposed patterns, many investigators empirically studied the potential validity of pattern analysis. As is the case in many fields of psychology, results were inconclusive and contradictory.

Years of investigation have revealed that analysis of patterns must be done cautiously. At best, such analysis should be used to generate hypotheses. Such hypotheses must then be either corroborated or refuted by other sources of data, such as historical information, medical records, family interviews, and direct observation (Tulsky et al., 1997; Weschler, 2008). The next section presents two hypothetical case studies to illustrate how hypotheses might be generated from an administration of the WAIS, using only two indexes—a verbal (VIQ) and a performance (PIQ) IQ score.

Hypothetical Case Studies

A Drop in Grades

Consider the following example of a 16-year-old high-school junior who has a D average, although he previously had a stable B average. Standard achievement tests found his reading and arithmetic grades appropriate. Table 10.2 shows his age-corrected scaled scores (remember, the mean is 10 and the standard deviation is 3).

The previously stable B average indicates that this individual is probably of at least average intelligence. The rapid decline in his grades, however, suggests some

TABLE 10.2 Hypothetical Scaled Scores for a High-School Junior

Verbal scales	Performance scales
Vocabulary: 11	Picture completion: 10
Similarities: 11	Digit symbol–coding: 4
Arithmetic: 7	Block design: 5
Digit span: 5	Matrix reasoning: 6
Information: 11	Picture arrangement: 1
Comprehension: 9	
Scaled score sum: 54	Scaled score sum: 36
Verbal IQ: 104	Performance IQ: 83
Full-scale IQ: 93	

dramatic change or shift in functioning. His scaled score of 11 on vocabulary is above the mean. Because vocabulary is a relatively stable measure of IQ, the scaled score of 11 also indicates this individual's IQ of 93 is most likely an underestimate of his intelligence. Assuming that this individual's typical scaled score performance would be approximately 11, as reflected in his scaled score on vocabulary and confirmed by his scaled scores on information and similarities, we find evidence for deterioration in his judgment (comprehension), concentration (arithmetic), and immediate memory (digit span) in the verbal areas. We also find deterioration in his visual-motor speed and integration (digit symbol–coding), nonverbal reasoning (block design), and fluid intelligence (matrix reasoning) in the performance areas.

With no evidence to the contrary, the clinician would strongly suspect that the subject's shift in grades may be the result of a brain injury or tumor, because these impair performance on the subtests in which the subject has shown evidence of deterioration. However, the clinician would consider other possibilities as well. Environmental or situational factors could lead to impairment on the various subtests. For example, because the subject may have become involved with drugs, this possibility must be examined. Furthermore, schizophrenia may cause similar decrements in performance. Therefore, signs of peculiar behavior or other symptoms of schizophrenia should be ruled out by an interview and other tests. Ruling out situational, environmental, and schizophrenic factors, the examiner might interview to determine whether the subject has suffered a recent blow to the head. If these possibilities prove to be negative, then the subject should be immediately referred for a neurological examination. As you no doubt have observed, this analysis resulted in several speculations, and the clinician exercised the usual caution in using the results.

A Slow Learner

Table 10.3 shows the hypothetical age-corrected scaled scores of a 16-year-old girl with chronic school problems. Identified as a slow learner in the earlier grades, she reads far below her grade level.

TABLE 10.3   Hypothetical Scaled Scores for a Slow Learner

Verbal scales	Performance scales
Vocabulary: 8	Picture completion: 11
Similarities: 11	Digit symbol–coding: 12
Arithmetic: 4	Block design: 13
Digit span: 10	Matrix reasoning: 12
Information: 3	Picture arrangement: 10
Comprehension: 7	
Scaled score sum: 43	Scaled score sum: 58
Verbal IQ: 89	Performance IQ: 112
Full-scale IQ: 99	

The subject is nearly one standard deviation above the mean in her PIQ; all her subtests in the performance area are at or greater than the mean. Clearly, she does not lack intellectual potential. Thus, her VIQ of 89 most likely underestimates her intellectual capacity. Furthermore, she obtains an above-average score on similarities, a noneducationally related measure of abstract thinking skills. Her major weaknesses arise in the subtests related to academic achievement, information, and arithmetic. In addition, she shows some impairment in her judgment. Her VIQ thus appears to be lowered because of her lack of motivation for academic achievement and her poor judgment. Her pattern of subtest scores is one typically found in poor readers and delinquents.

In considering these illustrations, remember that the validity of pattern analysis is still questionable. Evidence supporting the validity of most patterns, for reasons we shall discuss more fully, is questionable. So far our analysis has only considered the original verbal versus performance discrepancy, which has generated volumes of research. Now the WAIS-IV has four-index scores. If comparing two was hazardous, comparing four- is even more prone to errors (Grégoire, Coalson, & Zhu, 2011). Our illustrations are designed to give you a flavor of the approach taken by many practicing psychologists. Most real-life examples are nowhere nearly as clear-cut as our hypothetical ones.

Psychometric Properties of the Wechsler Adult Scale

Standardization

The WAIS-VI standardization sample consisted of a stratified sample of 2200 adults divided into 13 age groups from 16:00 through 90:11 as well as 13 specialty groups (Tulsky et al., 1997, p. 19; Weschler, 2008). The sample was stratified according to gender, race, education, and geographic region based on 2005 census data.

Reliability

The impressive reliability coefficients for the WAIS-IV attest to the internal and temporal reliability of the four index scores and full-scale IQ. When the split-half method is used for all subtests except speeded tests (digit symbol–coding and symbol search), the typical average coefficients across age levels are .98 for the FSIQ, .96 for the verbal comprehension index VIQ, .95 for the perceptual reasoning index, .94 for the working memory index, and .90 for the processing speed index (Weschler, 2008, p. 42). Test–retest coefficients reported in the manual are only slightly lower.

The technical manual reports an overall standard error of measurement of 2.16 for the FSIQ and 2.85 for the verbal comprehension index. The error is a bit higher for the other indexes (Weschler, 2008, p. 45). As you may recall from our discussion of correlation and reliability (see Chapter 4), all tests possess a certain degree of measurement error. The standard error of measurement (SEM) is the standard deviation of the distribution of error scores. According to classical test theory, an error score is the difference between the score actually obtained by giving the test and the score that would be obtained if the measuring instrument were perfect. In practice, the SEM is based on the reliability coefficient, given by the formula

$$SEM = SD\sqrt{1 - r_{xx}}$$

where SD is the standard deviation of the test scores and r_{xx} is the reliability coefficient. In practice, the SEM can be used to form a confidence interval within which an individual's true score is likely to fall. More specifically, we can determine the probability that an individual's true score will fall within a certain range a given percentage of the time. To be roughly at the 68% level, an obtained score must fall within the range of one SEM. The 95% confidence interval is approximately two SEMs.

Using this information, we can see that the smaller SEM for the verbal comprehension index and full-scale IQs means that we can have considerably more confidence that an obtained score represents an individual's true score than we can have for the other indexes. Thus, given an FSIQ of 110, we can assume that 95% of the time the subject's true score would fall at $(+/-)$ 4.32 (two SEMs) of the true score. In other words, 95% of subjects with a score of 110 have a true score between 105.68 and 114.32, and only 5% do not.

Validity

The validity of the WAIS-IV rests heavily on its correlation with earlier versions of the test. However, the Wechsler tests are considered among the most valid in the world today for measuring IQ.

Evaluation of the Wechsler Adult Scales

The Wechsler adult scale is extensively used as a measure of adult intelligence. This scale is well constructed and its primary measures—the four index components and full-scale IQ (FSIQ)—are highly reliable. As with all modern tests, including the modern Binet, the reliability of the individual subtests is lower and therefore makes analysis of subtest patterns dubious for the purpose of making decisions about individuals. Yet making such conclusions is commonplace. As we have noted, though such analysis may be useful for generating hypotheses, it calls for extreme caution.

Downward Extensions of the WAIS-IV: The WISC-V and the WPPSI-IV

Many of the basic ideas of the WAIS-IV apply to its downward extension, the WISC-V, first published in 1949, revised in 1974, 1991, and 2003, and most recently revised in 2014. The WISC-V measures intelligence from ages 6 through 16 years, 11 months. Many basic ideas of the WAIS-IV also apply to the Wechsler Preschool and Primary Scale of Intelligence, Fourth Edition (WPPSI-IV). The WPPSI-IV, first published in 1967, revised in 1989 and 2003, and most recently in 2012, measures intelligence in children from 2.5 to 7 years, 7 months. Because you already know the basic ideas that apply to all Wechsler scales, we present here only some of the interesting features of the WISC-V and the WPPSI-IV.

The WISC-V

If ever there truly was a 21st-century test, it must be the WISC-V (Wechsler, 2014). The WISC-V can be administered and scored by two coordinated iPads, one for the examiner and one for the subject being tested. According to the test authors, administration is faster and more efficient. The scores can then be forwarded for interpretation and even report generation to a Web-based platform called "Q-global scoring and reporting."

The WISC-V has all the bells and whistles that early test users could only dream of and is an excellent demonstration of the best in psychological testing. Standardization, reliability, and validity support provided in the interpretative manual are as good as or better than those of its predecessor, the WISC-IV, and most other individual tests. The test is heavily based on speed of a response based on the findings that faster responding is associated with higher ability for most tasks. Descriptive classifications, such as very *superior* and *borderline*, have been replaced with more neutral sounding terms such as *extremely high* and *very low*. All of this is a far cry from the original descriptive terms, such as *imbecile*, used in the original Binet.

The WISC-V follows the model we have already seen for the WAIS-IV. Based on results of factor analyses, the data continue to reveal a hierarchical structure. At the top of the hierarchy is FSIQ. Next are the five indexes or primary scores. The five indexes are called verbal comprehension, visual spatial, fluid reasoning, working memory, and processing speed. Each index is associated with at least two subtest scores. To enhance assessment, there are five ancillary scales, each based on two or more subtests. These are called quantitative reasoning, auditory working memory, nonverbal, general ability, and cognitive processing. Finally, there are three "complementary" scales, called naming speed, symbol translation, and storage and retrieval.

As we discussed earlier, the use of pattern analysis and comparison of index scores are controversial. As of this writing, perhaps the largest controversy centers are on the number of factors and their stability. Recall that the WAIS-IV had four factors. Factor analysis of the WISC-V indicated five: verbal comprehension, visual–spatial reasoning, fluid reasoning (ability to abstract), working memory, and processing speed. The basic controversy centers around is it really five different factors, or perhaps only four, three, two, or even one (Canivez, 2015; Vogt, Dolan, & Hoelzle, 2015).

If the factors are unstable, then comparing the index scores to make diagnostic conclusions would be dubious. Even so, clinicians have been making such interpretations since the original version of the Wechsler test appeared long ago, and today's WISC-V is as good as it gets. And with its use of iPads for testing and scoring, the WISC-V is likely to represent the standard for the future. (For more on the future of testing, see Chapter 21.)

An important feature of the WISV-V is a number of special group studies, which support its validity (Wechsler, 2014). In an effort to provide insights into the impact of various cognitive deficits on academic performance, various groups were targeted and carefully studied. These included various specific learning disabilities, attention-deficit/hyperactivity disorder (ADHD), traumatic brain injury, and autism spectrum disorders. Numerous tables and findings are presented in the interpretative manual to aid clinicians (Wechsler, 2014). There are also a number of YouTube videos that explain the WISC-V and how it works. A Google search will easily yield numerous hits to keep users and parents up to date.

In sum, with the WISC-V, the future is now. Some of its features could not have even been imagined when individual ability tests were first introduced. It is much like the difference between the first airplanes flew by the Wright brothers at the turn of the 20th-century and a 21st-century navy jet.

The WPPSI-IV

In 1967, Wechsler published a scale for children 4 to 6 years of age, the WPPSI. In its revised (1989) version, the WPPSI-R paralleled the WAIS-IV and WISC-III in format, method of determining reliabilities, and subtests.

The WPPSI-III was then published in 2002 (Wechsler, 2002). It contained most of the new features of the WISC-IV, including five composites. Ten years later, the WPPSI was published (Wechsler, 2012). The WPPSI-IV covers the age ranges from 2:6 through 7:7. The WPPSI-IV is more flexible than its predecessors and gives the test user the option of using more or less subtests depending on how complete an evaluation is needed and how young the child is. Younger children required less testing.

Like the WISC-V, the WPPSI is based on the familiar hierarchical model. General mental ability, or g, is at the top and reflected in the full-scale IQ. Then, there are three group factors, represented by index or primary scores: verbal comprehension, visual spatial, and working memory. Finally, each of the indexes is composed of two or more subtest scores.

To support legislation that recommends multiple assessments for the identification of children in need of special educational services, WPPSI-IV, like the earlier WPPSI-III, is compatible with measures of adaptive functioning and achievement. As we have seen, the WISC-V shares this feature as well. Like other Wechsler tests, the WPPSI-IV is well constructed, has excellent reliabilities, and is well grounded in modern theory.

Numerous research studies have supported the validity and use of the WPPSI-IV (Syeda & Climie, 2014), and like the WPPSI-III (Gordon, 2004), the WPPSI-IV is an excellent modern test (Syeda, & Climie, 2014). There has been considerable interest in the new working memory index (Coalson, Wahlstrom, Raiford, & Holdnack, 2011). However, the larger issue relates to the stability and validity of all three indexes (Watkins & Beaujean, 2014). According to Watkins and Beaujean (2014), factor analysis of the standardization sample best fits a bifactor structure. These authors concluded that the general g factor as represented by full-scale IQ accounted for more variance in every subtest than did its corresponding domain-specific factor, that is, index. Moreover, the g factor accounted for more total and common variance than all domain-specific factors combined. These findings bring us back full circle in the general versus specific factor debate discussed earlier in this chapter. Do we have just one general factor that accounts for the majority of variance and is there room for group factors? The debate continues to rage on.

Summary

Motivation for the development of the Wechsler scales began with the search for a more appropriate measure of adult intelligence than that provided by the 1937 Binet scale. The first product of this effort was the Wechsler–Bellevue scale.

In a *point scale*, a specific number of credits or points is assigned to each item. A *performance scale* measures nonverbal intelligence, as opposed to a *verbal scale*, which measures verbal intelligence. On a performance scale, the subject is required to do something other than merely answer questions. Today, performance scales on the Wechsler tests have been replaced by various index scores, such as a visual-spatial scale and a working memory scale.

The WAIS-IV contains four index composites in addition to a measure of general intelligence. The indexes are obtained by (1) converting the raw score of each subtest to a *scaled score*, or an age-corrected standard score of 10 with a standard deviation of 3; (2) adding the corresponding core scores to obtain a separate summary or composite score for each index; and (3) converting these to standardized scores with a mean of 100 and a standard deviation of 15. The FSIQ is then based on the index scores and also has a mean of 100 and a standard deviation of 15.

The reliability coefficients of the WAIS-IV are excellent for the four index scores and FSIQ. Reliabilities for the individual subtests, however, vary. Evidence for the validity of the WAIS-IV comes from its high correlation with its earlier predecessors. The WISC-V is a downward extension of the WAIS-IV for measuring children's intelligence. First published in 1949, the WISC was revised in 1974, 1991, 2003, and most recently in 2014. It contains many significant changes from earlier versions as well as several important innovations, including empirical testing of item bias.

The WPPSI-IV is a downward extension of the WISC-V for measuring intelligence in the youngest children. It was first published in 1967 and revised in 1989, 2002, and again in 2012.

Tests for Infants, Disabilities, and Special Populations

LEARNING OBJECTIVES

When you have completed this chapter, you should be able to:

▶ Identify the advantages and disadvantages of various individual ability tests compared with the Binet and Wechsler scales

▶ List six differences among the various individual ability tests

▶ Discuss the strengths and weaknesses of the Bayley Scales of Infant Development compared with other measures of infant intelligence

▶ Identify some of the purposes of the Columbia Mental Maturity Scale

▶ Explain the main theory behind tests of learning disability

▶ Explain the main idea behind testing for brain damage

▶ List three possible reasons for errors on the Bender Visual Motor Gestalt Test

▶ Describe the general reaction among reviewers to the Torrance Tests of Creative Thinking

▶ Briefly discuss the Wide Range Achievement Test

267

I n Long Beach, California, a student was being evaluated for a learning disability. At issue was whether the student qualified for special education. The evaluation used a variety of tests but did not use the Binet or Wechsler test. The student was found not eligible. The parents challenged the evaluation, claiming the district was required to use a standardized IQ test like the Binet or Wechsler in its evaluation. Siding with the school district, the 9th U.S. Circuit Court of Appeals held that the district was not required to use a traditional standardized test such as the Binet or Wechsler in its evaluation of the student (*Ford and Ford v. Long Beach Unified School District*, 37 IDELR I, 9th Circuit 2002). As noted in the *Special Educator 2003 Desk Book* (Norlin, 2003), an important reference book in special education that summarizes recent court decisions in the field, tests must be considered valid for a particular student or they cannot be used. In this case, the Binet and Wechsler apparently were not the only tests to meet this standard. Indeed, there are numerous alternatives to the Binet and Wechsler in the assessment of learning disabilities, brain damage, and numerous other problems.

For assessing general intelligence in relatively normal individuals or to obtain baseline information, the Binet and Wechsler scales are exceptionally good instruments. However, both have their limitations and are not valid for all individuals.

How, then, can one fairly evaluate the performance on the Binet scale of someone who has been blind for life? What about individuals who cannot speak?

Clearly, numerous circumstances arise where a score on the major scales would be either impossible to obtain or seriously biased against the individual. Thus, several individual tests have been created to meet special problems, measure specific abilities, or address the limitations of the Binet and Wechsler scales. Such tests are widely used in education and, in particular, in the important field of special education.

There is quite an array of individual ability tests. Because many were designed to supplement or provide an alternative to the Binet and Wechsler scales, we begin this chapter by comparing the general features of these tests with those of the Binet and Wechsler scales. We move on to compare the alternative tests to each other, and then we discuss them one at a time.

Alternative Individual Ability Tests Compared With the Binet and Wechsler Scales

The tests discussed in this section are generally less well established than the Binet and Wechsler scales; however, this does not sufficiently explain why no other individual test is used as much as these two major scales. Despite the limitations of the Binet and Wechsler scales, none of the alternatives is clearly superior from a psychometric standpoint. Although a few of the most recently revised tests are quite good, some of the alternative tests are weaker in terms of the representativeness or quality of the standardization sample. Some are less stable, and most are more limited in their documented validity. Some have weaknesses in the test manual, such as unclear or poorly standardized administration instructions, and others provide insufficient information about psychometric adequacy, appropriate uses, and limitations. Except for some specific advantages, perhaps none of the alternatives can be considered better than the two major scales when one considers all relevant factors, except for individuals with special needs.

Though usually weaker in psychometric properties, many of the alternatives to the major scales do not rely on a verbal response as much as the Binet and Wechsler verbal scales do. Many require the individual only to point or to make any response indicating "Yes" or "No," and thus do not depend as much on the complex integration of visual and motor functioning. Like the Wechsler scales, most of the alternatives contain a performance-type scale or subscale. Indeed, the dearth of performance tasks in the early Binet scales helped to stimulate the development of many alternative individual tests of ability.

In providing a performance component (many alternatives are exclusively performance scales), alternatives to the Binet and Wechsler have particular relevance for special populations. Some were designed for special populations, such as individuals with sensory limitations (e.g., deaf people) or physical limitations (e.g., people who are paralyzed or partially paralyzed). Others were designed to evaluate those with language limitations, such as culturally deprived people, certain brain-damaged individuals, and foreign-born or non-English-speaking individuals. Still others were designed to assess learning disabilities.

Because the tests were designed for special populations or purposes, the existence of alternatives is justifiable. However, their specificity often limits the range of functions or abilities that they can measure. Thus, one may consider the greater specificity of some alternatives as a weakness as well as a strength. Although the alternatives may be much more suitable for special populations than the major scales would be, an IQ score based on one of the alternatives, with rare exception, cannot be compared directly with a score from one of the major scales. However, the alternatives are often useful as a supplement for results obtained with one of the major scales, such as for screening purposes, for follow-up or reevaluations, or when insufficient time is available to administer one of the major scales. In addition, when several such tests are used in conjunction, limitations in one can be reduced or overcome by a particular strength in another. For example, in the case cited at the beginning of this chapter, the evaluation used six alternative measures, and this was considered acceptable (Norlin, 2003).

Because they are designed for special populations, some alternatives can be administered totally without verbal instructions (e.g., through pantomime or chalkboard instructions) (Naglieri & Ford, 2003; Parissea & Maillartb, 2009). Furthermore, most are less related than the Binet and Wechsler scales to reading ability, and a few are almost totally independent of reading ability. As a consequence, the scores from many alternatives contain less variability because of scholastic achievement than either the Binet or the Wechsler scale, both of which correlate strongly with scholastic achievement.

See Table 11.1 for a summary of alternative tests versus the major scales.

TABLE 11.1   Comparison of General Features of Alternatives With the Wechsler and Binet Scales

Disadvantages of alternatives

    Weaker standardization sample

    Less stable

    Less documentation on validity

    Limitations in test manual

    Not as psychometrically sound

    IQ scores not interchangeable with Binet or Wechsler

Advantages of alternatives

Can be used for specific populations and special purposes:

    Sensory limitations

    Physical limitations

    Language limitations

    Culturally deprived people

    Foreign-born individuals

    Non-English-speaking people

Not as reliant on verbal responses

Not as dependent on complex visual–motor integration

Useful for screening, supplementing, and reevaluations

Can be administered nonverbally

Less variability because of scholastic achievement

Alternatives Compared With One Another

To construct and publish a useful test, we must develop a better method than is currently available. We may develop a test to measure some factor not tapped by any existing measure or provide a test for a particular group for whom existing procedures have not worked. If a new test offers no specific advantages, most examiners will probably stay with a more established test. Therefore, most alternatives tend to differ from one another in some important way. Alternatives to the major scales that do no more than attempt to measure abilities in the same way, only better, have met with little success.

    In comparing tests other than the Binet and Wechsler scales, we find that some apply to only the youngest children, others to older children and adolescents, and still others to both children and adults. Thus, some of the alternatives to the major scales differ in their targeted age ranges. A second important difference concerns what is measured. Some of the alternatives attempt to measure language or vocabulary skills through nonverbal techniques, some to measure nonverbal or nonlanguage intelligence, and others to measure perceptual or motor skills. Alternatives also differ in the type of score they produce. Some give only a single score, as in the early Binet scales, whereas others produce several scores, as in the modern Binet and the Wechsler scales. The alternatives differ also in the type of response required of subjects. Some present the items in a multiple-choice format, requiring that the subject choose or point to a correct alternative; others simply require the subject to indicate "Yes" or "No" by whatever means possible.

Other important differences mark the alternative individual tests of human ability. Some require simple motor skills, whereas others demand relatively complex motor behavior. A few sample a wide range of abilities, but most focus on a narrow range. Still another difference concerns the target population, which may include deaf, blind, physically handicapped, learning disabled, language-impaired, or foreign-born people. Furthermore, some provide timed tasks; others do not. Some claim to have significance for personality and clinical diagnoses; others are exclusively related to ability.

Another difference is the amount of examiner skill and experience necessary for administration. Whereas some tests require as much skill and experience as the Binet or Wechsler scales do, others require only minimal examiner skill and could probably be administered by a trained paraprofessional under supervision. To avoid confusing the various tests in this chapter, you should compare the various alternatives with the Binet and Wechsler scales; you should also compare them with each other in terms of their main distinguishing features, as summarized in Table 11.2.

TABLE 11.2 Summary of Differences Among Individual Ability Tests Other Than the Binet and Wechsler Scales

Difference	Definition or example
Age range	Different tests are designed for specific age groups
What is measured	Verbal intelligence, nonverbal intelligence, and so on
Type of score	Single score versus multiple scores
Type of skill required	Simple motor, complex motor, and so on
Range of abilities sampled	Single specific ability versus a wide range of abilities
Target population	Deaf, blind, learning disabled, and so on
Timing	Some are timed; others are not
Personality versus ability	Some are relevant for personality and clinical diagnoses, others for ability
Examiner skill and experience	Some require far less examiner skill and experience to administer and interpret than others

Early Tests

The earliest individual ability tests were typically designed for specific purposes or populations. One of the first, the Seguin Form Board Test (Seguin, 1907) first published in the 1800s, actually preceded the Binet. This test, of the performance variety, produced only a single score. It consisted of a simple form board with objects of various shapes placed in appropriately shaped holes (such as squares or circles). The Seguin Form Board Test was used primarily to evaluate mentally retarded adults and emphasized speed of performance. A version of this test is still available (Bhave, Bhargava, & Kumar, 2011). Quite a while after the development of the Seguin test, the Healy–Fernald Test was developed as an exclusively nonverbal test for adolescent delinquents. Although it produced only a single score, the Healy–Fernald Test provided several types of tasks, rather than just one, as in the Seguin Form Board Test, and there was less emphasis on speed. Then, Knox (1914) developed a battery of performance tests for non-English-speaking adult immigrants to the United States. The test was one of the first that could be administered without language. Speed was not emphasized.

In sum, early individual ability tests other than the Binet scale were designed for specific populations, produced a single score, and had nonverbal performance scales. The emphasis on speed gradually decreased from the earliest to the more recent tests. These early procedures demonstrated the feasibility of constructing individual nonverbal performance tests that could provide an alternative to the then verbally dependent Binet scale. They could be administered without visual instructions and used with children as well as adults.

Infant Scales

An important category of individual tests of ability attempts to measure intelligence in infants and young children. Generally, there is not much point to estimating the IQ of an infant or preschool toddler. However, where mental retardation or developmental delays are suspected, these tests can supplement observation, genetic testing, and other medical procedures. Thus, our discussion of educational tests begins with tests that can be used well before the child enters the school system.

Brazelton Neonatal Assessment Scale (BNAS)

The BNAS is an individual test for infants between 3 days and 4 weeks of age (Brazelton, 1973, 1984; Nugent, 2013). It purportedly provides an index of a newborn's competence (Nugent, 2013). Developed by a Harvard pediatrician, the Brazelton scale produces 47 scores: 27 behavioral items and 20 elicited responses. These scores are obtained in a variety of areas, including the neurological, social, and behavioral aspects of a newborn's functioning. Factors such as reflexes, responses to stress, startle reactions, cuddliness, motor maturity, ability to habituate to sensory stimuli, and hand–mouth coordination are all assessed. Reviews of the Brazelton scale have been favorable (Aylward, 2011; Guzzetta, 2009). As Sostek (1978) stated, the Brazelton has "the greatest breadth of the available neonatal examinations" (p. 208). The Brazelton also has a considerable research base (e.g., Costa Figueiredo, Tendais, Conde, Pacheco, & Teixeira, 2010; Hays, 2004; Johnson, 2003; Nugent, 2013). Indeed, we found about 2000 research articles that used the test in some way, and much information is available using a Google search.

The Brazelton scale has found wide use as a research tool and as a diagnostic tool for special purposes (Lundqvist-Persson, Lau, Nordin, Bona, & Sabel, 2011; Majnemer & Mazer, 1998). For example, the scale has been used to evaluate the effects of low birth weight on premature infants (Lundqvist-Persson et al., 2011; Medoff-Cooper, McGrath, & Bilker, 2000). Researchers have used it to study the effects of cocaine use in pregnancy (Morrow et al., 2001), prenatal alcohol exposure (Oberlander et al., 2010), prenatal iron deficiency (Hernández-Martínez et al., 2011), prenatal maternal mood (Field, Diego, & Hernandez-Reif, 2010; Field, Diego, Hernandez-Reif, Schanberg, & Kuhn, 2002), prenatal maternal dopamine levels (Marcus et al., 2011), and environmental agents (Tronick, 1987). Others have used the scale to study parent–infant attachment (Beal, 1991), gender differences in newborns (Lundqvist & Sabel, 2000), and high-risk neonates (Emory, Tynan, & Dave, 1989). Reviews of the relevant literature have been highly enthusiastic (El-Dib, Massaro, Glass, & Aly, 2011; Majnemer & Mazer, 1998).

The BNAS remains one of the most commonly used scales for the assessment of neonates (Berger, Hopkins, Bae, Hella, & Strickland, 2010). Despite the enthusiasm for the scale, it has several significant drawbacks. No norms are available. Thus, although examiners and researchers can state that one infant scored higher than another in a particular area, there is no standard sample against which to compare test results. In addition, more research is needed concerning the meaning and implication of scores. The scale purportedly helps one assess the infant's role in the mother–infant social relationship (Guzzetta, 2009; Stern, 2010), and high scores presumably imply high levels of intelligence (Brazelton, 1993; Canals, Hernández-Martínez, Esparó, & Fernández-Ballart, 2011). Like most infant intelligence measures, however, the Brazelton scale has poorly documented predictive and construct validity. The scale has not been shown to be of value in predicting later intelligence (McGregor, 2001; Tronick & Brazelton, 1975). Furthermore, despite relatively good interrater reliability for trained examiners, with coefficients ranging from .85 to .90 (McGregor, 2001), the test–retest reliability (i.e., reliability over time) leaves much to be desired. As for all measures of intelligence when development is rapid and uneven, test–retest reliability coefficients for the Brazelton scale are typically poor and unstable for subjects younger than 8 years (see Figure 11.1).

In conclusion, although the Brazelton scale may offer much as a research tool and a supplement to medical testing procedures, as an individual test of infant intelligence it is unsatisfactory. Its lack of norms is a serious shortcoming, and its failure to predict future intelligence leaves us wondering what the scale is really measuring. In fairness to the Brazelton, the scale is extremely well constructed.

FIGURE 11.1

Schematic summary of the Brazelton Neonatal Assessment Scale.

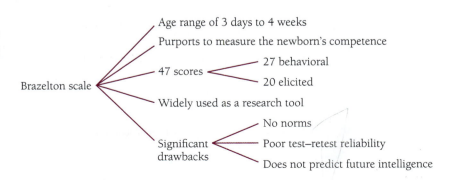

Moreover, as you will see, *all* infant ability tests based on sensorimotor functioning have proven ineffective in predicting later intelligence except in the lowest ranges.

Gesell Developmental Schedules (GDS)

The GDS (also known as the Gesell Maturity Scale, the Gesell Developmental Observation, and the Yale Tests of Child Development) is one of the oldest and most established infant intelligence measures. First published in 1925 (Gesell, 1925), the Gesell scale has been subjected to extensive research and refinement and was updated in 1940, 1965, 1979, and most recently in 2011 (The Gesell Institute, 2011). To gather supportive data for the GDS, the Gesell Institute completed a nationwide study in March 2010, which included 1300 assessments of children aged 2.3 through 6.3 years (The Gesell Institute, 2010).

One of the leading infant intelligence measures from the 1930s through the 1960s, the Gesell scale continues to be used as a research tool by those interested in assessing infant intellectual development after exposure to mercury (Marques et al., 2009), diagnoses of abnormal brain formation (Dror et al., 2009), in utero diagnoses of hyperthyroidism (Sun et al., 2011), assessing infants with autism (Abel & Russell, 2005; Yurong, Dun, & Xiurong, 2001), and validating newer psychological measures (Mammen, Russell, Nair, Russell, & Kishore, 2013). However, because the Gesell scale suffers from several psychometric weaknesses, interest in and use of the scale has fallen despite revisions and improvements.

The Gesell Developmental Schedules claim to provide an appraisal of the developmental status of children from 2.3 months to 6.3 years of age. The original scale is based on normative data from a carefully conducted longitudinal study of early human development (Gesell et al., 1940). The idea behind procedures based on developmental data is that human development unfolds in stages or in sequences over time. Gesell and colleagues obtained normative data concerning these various stages in maturation. With data on when specific developmental milestones manifest themselves (e.g., when the infant first rolls from back to stomach unassisted, when the child first utters words, or when the child learns to walk), one can compare the rate of development of any infant or young child with established norms. If the child shows behavior or responses that are associated with a more mature level of development than is typically found for his or her chronological age, then one can assume that the child is ahead in development compared with others of the same age. Accelerated development can be related to high intelligence.

In the Gesell scale, an individual's **developmental quotient (DQ)** is determined according to a test score, which is evaluated by assessing the presence or absence of behavior associated with maturation. The DQ concept parallels the mental age (MA) concept. Thus, the Gesell produces an intelligence quotient (IQ) score similar to that of the Binet scale. The formula for IQ in the Gesell scale is as follows:

$$IQ = \frac{\text{Development Quotient}}{\text{Chronological Age}} \times 100$$

or more simply,

$$IQ = \frac{DQ}{CA} \times 100$$

FIGURE 11.2

Schematic summary of the Gesell Developmental Schedules.

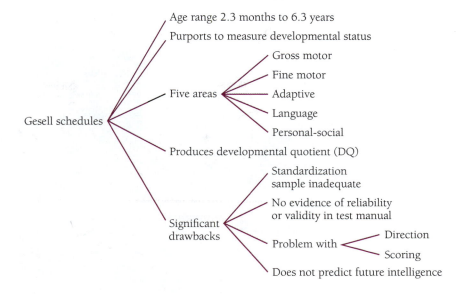

Despite years of extensive use and updating, the Gesell scale has fallen short of acceptable psychometric standards (Walker, 1992). The standardization sample has not been representative of the population. The data gathered in the 2010 national study may serve to improve the standardization sample but so far the research continues only to be supportive of the test in predicting intelligence at the lower ends of the scale (Accardo, 2013) In addition, as with most infant tests, evidence of reliability or validity is poorly documented. Like all sensorimotor infant tests, the Gesell does not predict later intelligence except at the low end of scores (see Figure 11.2). Thus, its main value is in obtaining an early estimate of possible mental retardation.

In conclusion, Gesell's concept of empirically determining developmental sequence norms in evaluating infants and young children is logical and promising. When first constructed, the Gesell scale was nothing short of a breakthrough in infant ability testing. The use of a nonrepresentative sample in its initial development, furthermore, was not at all unusual. The Gesell scale has recently undergone revisions that should help it meet today's more rigorous standards for standardization samples. By providing a standard format for observing behavior, the Gesell scale may be of value to the highly trained and experienced examiner. Even so, the available empirical data indicate that it is not highly accurate for predictive purposes except at the low ranges (Accardo, 2013). The scale does appear, however, to help uncover subtle deficits in infants (Williamson, Wilson, Lifschitz, & Thurbers, 1990).

Bayley Scales of Infant and Toddler Development–Third Edition (BSID-III)

Like the Gesell scale, the Bayley Scales of Infant Development base assessments on normative maturational developmental data. Originally published only 4 years before the Brazelton scale, the Bayley scales were the product of 40 years of study (Bayley, 1969; Kimble & Wertheimer, 2003). Revised in 1994, and then again

FIGURE 11.3
Bayley Scales of Infant
Development.

Bayley Scales of Infant Development. ©1969 by NCS Pearson, Inc. Reproduced with permission. All rights reserved.
"Pearson" and "Bayley Scales of Infant Development" are trademarks, in the United States and/or other countries, of
Pearson Education, Inc. or its affiliates (s).

in 2005, the BSID-III, or Bayley-III, was designed for infants between 1 and
42 months of age (Geisinger, Spies, Carlson, & Plake, 2007) and assesses development across five domains: cognitive, language, motor, socioemotional, and adaptive
(Aylward, 2011). A more focused measure of test observations has also been incorporated into the Bayley-III with the express goal of better informing intervention
planning (Geisinger et al., 2007). To assess mental functions, the Bayley-III uses
measures such as the infant's response to a bell, the ability to follow an object with
the eyes, and, in older infants, the ability to follow oral instructions. The heart of the
Bayley-III is the motor scale because it assumes that later mental functions depend
on motor development (Flanagan & Alfonso, 1995) (see Figure 11.3).

Unlike the Gesell and Brazelton scales, the Bayley-III scales have an excellent
standardization. With a large normative sample of infants between 1 and 42 months
of age divided into subgroups by gender, race, socioeconomic status, rural versus
urban area, and geographic region, the Bayley-III is currently the best standardized
test of its kind available (Geisinger et al., 2007). Nevertheless, more recent studies
have indicated that the Bayley-III standardization sample is lower in ability than the
general population and thereby underestimates developmental impairment (Chinta,
Walker, Halliday, Loughran-Fowlds, & Badawi, 2014; Milne, McDonald, &
Comino, 2012).

Bayley-III scores include scaled scores, composite scores, and percentile ranks
for all five scales. Confidence intervals are available for the scores from the five scales.
Growth scores and developmental age scores are available for the cognitive, language,

and motor scales. The growth scores are used to create a chart of progress over time for each subtest. The growth scores range from 200 to 800 with a mean of 500 and a standard deviation of 100. Given the care and effort put into its development, the generally positive reviews of the Bayley-III come as no surprise (Geisinger et al., 2007). The overall reliability coefficients (coefficient alpha for individual scales), as calculated with Fisher's z transformation, ranged from .86 (fine motor) to .91 (cognitive, expressive communication, and gross motor) (Geisinger et al., 2007). The reliabilities of the social-emotional and adaptive behavior scales were similarly strong (.83 to .94; .79 to .98, respectively). Taken together, these results suggest strong internal consistency for the measurement of functioning within these five domains (Geisinger et al., 2007).

Research interest in the Bayley scales continues to grow (Torras-Mana, Guillamon-Valenzuela, Ramirez-Mallafre, Brun-Gasca, & Fornieles-Deu, 2014; Weiss, Oakland, & Aylward, 2010). Evidence to support the construct validity of the instrument included a factor analysis of the subtests. This study used the overall sample of 1700 children. The results supported a three-factor model and confirmed that the instrument measures motor, language, and cognitive development (Geisinger et al., 2007). More recent studies have supported the validity of the Bayley including its usefulness in making an early diagnosis of language disorder (Torras-Mana et al., 2014; Yu et al., 2013).

In terms of construct validity, scores on the performance scale increase with increasing chronological age. However, the bulk of available research casts considerable doubt on the assumption of a relationship between motor behavior and later mental functions (Janssen et al., 2011). In its favor, even the earlier editions of the Bayley predict mental retardation (Chung et al., 2010; Patrianakos-Hoobler et al., 2010). Infants who score two standard deviations below the mean have a high probability of testing in the retarded ranges later in life (DeWitt, Schreck, & Mulick, 1998; Goldstein, Fogle, Wieber, & O'Shea, 1995). However, for infants who score within the normal ranges, there is no more than low correlation between Bayley scores and those obtained from standard intelligence tests such as the WISC-III and Binet scale (Flanagan & Alfonso, 1995).

Like the Brazelton, the Bayley-III is widely used in research. It has been used to assess children with Down syndrome, with pervasive developmental disorders, with cerebral palsy, with language impairment, who are at risk for developmental delay, who suffered asphyxiation at birth, with prenatal alcohol exposure, who are small for gestational age, and with premature or low birth weight (Geisinger et al., 2007). A major research use is to assess infants of drug-using mothers (e.g., Miller-Loncar et al., 2005; Moe, 2002), infants whose mothers suffer from postpartum depression (Righetti-Veltema, Bousquet, & Manzano, 2003), human immunodeficiency virus (HIV)-positive infants (Llorente et al., 2003), and other at-risk infants (Lai, Guo, Guo, & Hsu, 2001; Leslie, Gordon, Ganger, & Gist, 2002; Misri, Corral, Wardrop, & Kendrick, 2006) (see Figure 11.4).

In conclusion, the Bayley-III is among the most psychometrically sound test of its kind (Geisinger et al., 2007). The question remains as to whether tests of this type can predict future intelligence. Available research indicates that although the Bayley-III may be a good predictor for disabled populations, it does not predict well within the normal ranges. Moreover, users must keep in mind the possibility that the test underestimates developmental impairment (Chinta et al., 2014).

FIGURE 11.4

Schematic summary of the Bayley Scales of Infant Development.

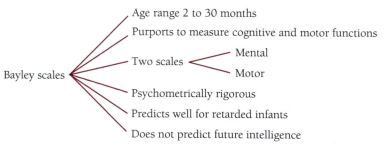

Bayley scales
- Age range 2 to 30 months
- Purports to measure cognitive and motor functions
- Two scales
  - Mental
  - Motor
- Psychometrically rigorous
- Predicts well for retarded infants
- Does not predict future intelligence

Description of ITPA-3 Subtests from the Illinois Test of Psycholinguistic Abilities–Third Edition ITPA-3 Manual 9476 by Hammill, Mather, and Roberts. Copyright © 2001 PRO-ED, Inc.

Cattell Infant Intelligence Scale (CIIS)

Another noteworthy infant ability test is the CIIS, which is also based on normative developmental data. Designed as a downward extension of the Stanford-Binet scale for infants and preschoolers between 2 and 30 months of age, the Cattell scale purports to measure intelligence in infants and young children. Patterned after the 1937 Binet in an age scale format, the Cattell scale contains five test items for each month between 2 and 12 months of age and five items for each 2-month interval between 12 and 36 months of age. The items are similar to those on other infant tests, such as the Gesell scale. Tasks for infants include attending to a voice and following objects with his or her eyes. Tasks for young children involve using a form board and manipulating common objects. The ability to follow oral instructions becomes more and more important as age increases.

Today, the Cattell is rarely used. It was copyrighted nearly three decades before the original Bayley scale and has not been revised. Normative data for the Cattell scale compare unfavorably with those for the original Bayley scales, and even worse with the Bayley-II in several respects, not to mention the Bayley-III. In addition to being outdated and more than four times smaller, the Cattell standardization sample is based primarily on children of parents from the lower and middle classes and therefore does not represent the general population.

In one of the few available published studies comparing the Cattell scale with the Bayley, scores derived from the Bayley predicted Stanford-Binet IQs better than the Cattell scores did (Atkinson, 1990) (see Figure 11.5).

FIGURE 11.5

Schematic summary of the Cattell Infant Intelligence Scale.

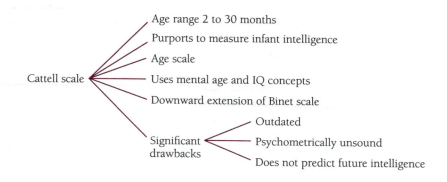

Cattell scale
- Age range 2 to 30 months
- Purports to measure infant intelligence
- Age scale
- Uses mental age and IQ concepts
- Downward extension of Binet scale
- Significant drawbacks
  - Outdated
  - Psychometrically unsound
  - Does not predict future intelligence

TABLE 11.3 Summary of Infant Scales

Scale	Age range	Standardization sample	Psychometric properties
Brazelton	3 days–4 weeks	None	Good interrater reliability, poor test–retest reliability
Gesell	2.3 months–6.3 years	1300 infants	Little evidence, some support for construct validity
Bayley	2–30 months	1262 infants	Very good split-half reliability
Cattell	2–30 months	285 infants	Little evidence, some support for construct validity

General: For children younger than 18 months, these measures do not correlate significantly with IQ later in life. After 18 months, there are significant but small and clinically unhelpful correlations. Correlations tend to increase with the age of the infant at the time of testing.

Major alternative: Tests of memory, particularly visual memory and abstraction. Such tests do correlate with IQs in later life, even for infants tested in the first few days after birth.

In sum, the Cattell scale has remained relatively unchanged for more than 60 years. It is psychometrically unsatisfactory. Reliability coefficients vary widely, with many being less than acceptable (see Hooper, Conner, & Umansky, 1986). Moreover, what the scale measures is unclear; it does not predict future intelligence for infants in the normal ranges. Its use in clinical settings is highly suspect, and it is presented here only for historical value.

See Table 11.3 for a summary of the properties of infant scales.

Major Tests for Young Children

In this section, we discuss two major individual tests specifically developed to evaluate intelligence in young children: the McCarthy Scales of Children's Abilities (MSCA) and the Kaufman Assessment Battery for Children (KABC).

McCarthy Scales of Children's Abilities (MSCA)

A product of the early 1970s, the MSCA measure ability in children between 2 and 8 years old. Overall, the McCarthy scales present a carefully constructed individual test of human ability. However, because of its relatively meager validity data and the absence of recent norms, the McCarthy no longer competes with the Wechsler scale. McCarthy died before the test was published, and although the test is still for sale, no one has taken up the task of strengthening and modernizing the McCarthy (see Figure 11.6).

FIGURE 11.6
McCarthy Scales of
Children's Abilities.

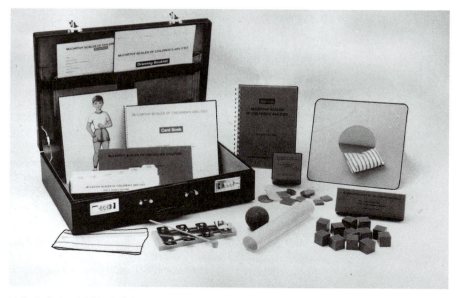

McCarthy Scales of Children's Abilities. ©1970, 1992 by NCS Pearson, Inc. Reproduced with permission. All rights reserved. Pearson is a trademark, in the United States and/or other countries, of Pearson Education, Inc. or its affiliates (s).

On the positive side, the McCarthy produces a pattern of scores as well as a variety of composite scores. Its battery of 18 tests samples a wide variety of functions long held to be related to human intelligence. Of the 18 scales, 15 are combined into a composite score known as the **general cognitive index (GCI)**, a standard score with a mean of 100 and a standard deviation of 16. Presumably, the index reflects how well the child has integrated prior learning experiences and adapted them to the demands of the scales. The concept of combining various subtests to form composite scores is an important idea in testing, and it is one of the main features of the most recent edition of the Stanford-Binet scale (see Figure 11.7).

The psychometric properties of the McCarthy scales are relatively good. Picone, Regine, and Ribaudo (2001) have shown evidence of factorial validity, and a 2002 longitudinal study (Stannard, Wolfgang, Jones, & Phelps, 2001) shows evidence of predictive validity.

The McCarthy scales have been used in a variety of research studies (Hansen, Dinesen, Hoff, & Greisen, 2002; Smith, 2005). The McCarthy was used to evaluate the effects of nutritional supplements given to nursing mothers on the development of the nursing infants (Jensen et al., 2010), the effects of air pollution on children's cognitive development (Freire et al., 2010), and the effects of early intervention on the cognitive development of preterm infants (Nordhov et al., 2010). Hoekstra et al. used the McCarthy to evaluate the relationship between autism and intelligence in a longitudinal study of over 8000 twin pairs (Hoekstra, Happé, Baron-Cohen, & Ronald, 2010). Genetic model fitting showed that autistic traits and IQ were influenced by a common set of genes and a common set of environmental influences that continuously affect these traits throughout childhood. Another longitudinal

FIGURE 11.7

Schematic overview of the general cognitive index of the McCarthy scales.

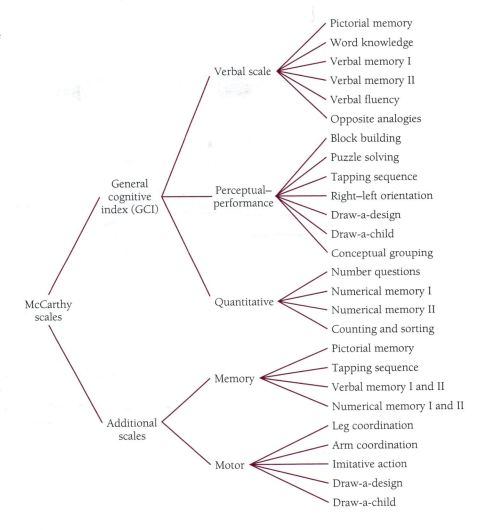

study evaluated the effects of early intervention on the development of children worldwide (Nores & Barnett, 2010). The study found that children from different contexts and countries receive substantial cognitive, behavioral, health, and schooling benefits from early childhood interventions. The benefits are sustained over time. Interventions that have an educational or stimulation component evidenced the largest cognitive effects. The McCarthy scales were used to show positive effects of parental cognitive stimulation and emotional support on children's cognitive abilities (Hubbs-Tait, Culp, Culp, & Miller, 2002). A study by McGill-Evans and Harrison (2001) used the McCarthy scales to show that preterm birth, parental age, and infant gender accounted for more than 30% of the variance in cognitive-motor skills. Finally, a 2011 study used the McCarthy scales to assess the effect of the mode of delivery (vaginal or caesarean section) on the long-term psychomotor development of extremely low-birth weight infants (Minguez-Milio, Alcázar, Aubá,

Ruiz-Zambrana, & Minguez, 2011). Results suggested that a caesarean section provides lower morbidity and better prognosis for neurodevelopment long-term outcome in extremely low-birth weight infants.

Kaufman Assessment Battery for Children–Second Edition (KABC-II)

Originally a product of the early 1980s, the current (2004) version of the KABC-II is an individual ability test for children between 3 and 18 years of age. The KABC-II consists of 18 subtests combined into five global scales called sequential processing, simultaneous processing, learning, planning, and knowledge.

According to the stated purposes and intentions in its test manuals, the KABC-II is quite ambitious (Kaufman & Kaufman, 1983a, 1983b, 2004a). It is intended for psychological, clinical, minority group, preschool, and neuropsychological assessment as well as research. The test also purports to enable the psychoeducational evaluation of learning disabled and other exceptional children and educational planning and placement. Before we examine the extent to which the KABC succeeds in meeting such lofty goals, let's look at some of its underlying concepts.

Theoretically, the KABC is based on several approaches (see Kaufman, 1984; Kaufman & Kaufman, 2004a), including the neuropsychological model of brain functioning of renowned Russian neuroscientist Aleksander Luria (1966); the theory of split brain functioning of U.S. Nobelist Roger Sperry (1968); and the theories of information processing, most notably that of cognitive scientist Ulric Neisser (1967). In the work of these and other scientists, the Kaufmans noted a major distinction between two types of higher brain processes, which they referred to as the *sequential–simultaneous distinction* (Kaufman, 1984). *Sequential processing* refers to a child's ability "to solve problems by mentally arranging input in sequential or serial order." Examples of sequential processing are number and word order recall. Presented one at a time, items must be dealt with sequentially rather than all at once. In contrast, simultaneous processing takes place in parallel. It refers to a child's ability to "synthesize information (from mental wholes) in order to solve a problem" (Kaufman & Kaufman, 1985, p. 250).

The sequential–simultaneous distinction of the KABC is one of the test's most distinguishing characteristics (Bain & Gray, 2008; Reynolds & Kamphaus, 1997). The KABC-II does not claim to provide a pure measure of either sequential or simultaneous processing. Instead, the test developers selected tasks that, from a rational analysis, appeared to distinguish one type of processing from the other. A major intent of providing separate measures of simultaneous and sequential processing is to identify the child's unique strengths and problem-solving strategies. Presumably, such information can help others develop educational and remedial intervention strategies for a child.

The KABC-II was conformed with the Kaufman Test of Educational Achievement, Second Edition (KTEA-II), which provides an achievement score. Offering independent and comparable scores for both intelligence and achievement in the same test is a major advantage. In addition, the KABC-II has a nonverbal measure of ability that is specifically designed to be as fair as possible to children who are linguistically different or handicapped.

The KABC-II and its counterpart, the KTEA-II, are well constructed and psychometrically sound. Raw scores for each of the 18 subtests can be converted to standard scores with a mean of 10 (SD = 3). The global scales can be converted to standard scores (mean = 100, SD = 15), percentiles, and age-equivalent norms.

Validity data reported in the original KABC test manual have received considerable attention. Factor analytic studies support their sequential–simultaneous and mental processing achievement distinctions (Potvin, Keith, Caemmerer, & Trundt, 2015). The KABC intelligence estimates also tend to show smaller (approximately 8 points) differences between African Americans and whites than either the Wechsler or Binet scales, in which whites typically score some 15 points higher than African Americans (see Jensen, 1985; Rushton & Jensen, 2005). Thus, the KABC tends to be less biased against African Americans (Dale, McIntosh, Rothlisberg, Ward, & Bradley, 2011; Lamp & Krohn, 2001). However, the KABC also tends to underestimate the scores of gifted children (compared with the Binet Form L-M and the WISC-R), so its validity for evaluating giftedness is questionable (McCallum, Karnes, & Oehler-Stinnett, 1985). Moreover, at least one group of researchers has found KABC items biased against Mexican Americans (Valencia, Rankin, & Livingston, 1995). Since its original publication in April 1983, the KABC has generated considerable interest. Reactions have varied widely. On the positive side, Kaufman and Kaufman (1985, p. 268) point to its strong theoretical orientation, separate intelligence and achievement scales, separate nonverbal scale, limited oral instructions, limited verbal responding, colorful and interesting items, inclusion of sociocultural norms, and empirical documentation of smaller differences between groups (Kaufman, 2009). For instance, their studies have established smaller differences between African Americans and whites (Dale et al., 2011), Latinos or Latinas and whites (Tomes, 2011), and Indians and whites on the KABC compared with other tests (Malda, van de Vijver, Srinivasan, Transler, & Sukumaar, 2010). These strengths are acknowledged by independent reviewers (Aiken, 1987; Anastasi, 1984), and the KABC-II has smoothed many of the edges of the original KABC (Kaufman, Lichtenberger, Fletcher-Janzen, & Kaufman, 2005).

Despite these strengths, criticism has been harsh (Williams, Voelker, & Ricciardi, 1995). According to Jensen (1984), one can attribute the smaller differences between whites and minorities on the KABC to its poorer predictive validity for school achievement and its less effective measurement of general intelligence compared with the Binet and Wechsler scales. Other critics point to the KABC's imperfect match with its theoretical foundation and disproportionate contribution of the simultaneous and mental processing composites (Bracken, 1985). Moreover, the neuropsychological model that underlies the sequential–simultaneous distinction is at best poorly supported and at worst inaccurate and outmoded (Herbert, 1982). None of these criticisms appear to have been clearly addressed by the newer KABC-II.

Perhaps the most severe criticism of the KABC has come from Sternberg (1984), who charged that the KABC manual misrepresents the support for the theory underlying the KABC. He also maintained that the test suffers from a noncorrespondence between its definition and its measurement of intelligence. This criticism continues to be voiced and empirically supported by Cahan and Noyman (2001). Furthermore, Sternberg found that empirical support for the theory underlying the KABC is questionable. And, like Jensen (1984), he noted an overemphasis on rote learning at the expense of ability to learn. Indeed, test scores do show a decrease in g saturation as ability levels increase (Reynolds & Keith, 2007).

Although the criticisms of the KABC are largely valid and generally apply to the KABC-II, it is important to see them in context. First, many of these criticisms, such as lack of correspondence between definition and measurement of intelligence, also apply to the test's major competitors. Even the best available instruments have shortcomings and limitations. Although the underlying theory of the test has yet to be fully established, the test at least *has* a theoretical structure. Perhaps the biggest problem for the KABC is that it has fallen behind, especially with the WISC-V, which was discussed in Chapter 10.

General Individual Ability Tests for Handicapped and Special Populations

Many alternative tests are specifically designed to provide a more valid measure of intellectual functioning for cases in which the Binet and Wechsler may be biased or inappropriate. Each of these general individual ability tests for handicapped and special populations contains unique strengths and limitations.

Columbia Mental Maturity Scale–Third Edition (CMMS)

A variety of sensory and physical limitations often make a valid administration of the Binet, Wechsler, or even many of the major alternative scales (such as the McCarthy) quite impossible. Therefore, for children who experience physical limitations (such as cerebral palsy), speech impairments, language limitations, or hearing loss, instruments are needed that do not create negative bias. One attempt at such an instrument is the CMMS, which purports to evaluate ability in normal and variously handicapped children from 3 through 12 years of age. When used for individuals with special needs, the test often provides a more suitable measure of intelligence than do the more established scales (Kroese, 2003).

The Columbia scale requires neither a verbal response nor fine motor skills. Presented as a measure of general reasoning ability, the scale requires the subject to discriminate similarities and differences by indicating which drawing does not belong on a 6-by-9-inch card containing three to five drawings, depending on the level of difficulty. The task, then, is multiple-choice.

The Columbia scale contains 92 different cards grouped into eight overlapping levels, or scales, according to chronological age. Testing begins at a scale appropriate for the child's age. Advantages of the Columbia scale include its relative independence of reading skills, the ease of its administration and scoring, and the clarity of its test manual. Because subjects are not timed, pressure is minimal.

Though somewhat outdated, the standardization sample is impressive. It consists of 2600 children divided into 13 levels from 3 years, 6 months to 9 years, 11 months. Each level contains 200 children. The sample is stratified according to the U.S. population in terms of variables that include gender, race, geographic region, and parental occupation.

The scale's manual contains data on both split-half and test–retest reliability for some age groups in the standardization sample. The scale is consistent internally as well as over short intervals of time. Coefficients range between .85 and .90 for both split-half and test–retest reliabilities.

The Columbia scale is highly vulnerable to random error. A young child can obtain a score of 82 simply on chance alone, and a score in the average ranges can be obtained with just a few lucky guesses (Kaufman, 1978). In conclusion, the Columbia scale is a reliable instrument that is useful in assessing ability in many people with sensory, physical, or language handicaps. Because of its multiple-choice nature, however, and consequent vulnerability to chance variance, one should use results with caution. When used with individuals for whom the major scales would be appropriate, the Columbia scale might best be seen as a screening device. Although its standardization sample is somewhat outdated, the Columbia scale can be used to test a variety of special populations for whom the Wechsler, Binet, and other scales are inappropriate. Even for these populations, however, the Columbia scale might be best used in conjunction with whatever Wechsler subtests can be given.

Peabody Picture Vocabulary Test–Fourth Edition (PPVT-IV)

Similar to the Columbia scale in several respects, the PPVT-IV was originally developed by L. M. Dunn and I. M. Dunn (1981). The most recent revision was published in 2007. Although the age range of 2 through 90 years is considerably wider than the range of the Columbia scale, both are multiple-choice tests that require a subject to indicate only "Yes" or "No" in some manner. Primarily for the physically or language handicapped, the PPVT-IV is not usually used with people who are deaf, because the instructions are administered aloud. Nonetheless, the test has been used in research with deaf persons to evaluate their ability to define words (Beal-Alvarez, Lederberg, & Easterbrooks, 2011).

The test purports to measure hearing or receptive (hearing) vocabulary, presumably providing a nonverbal estimate of verbal intelligence (Dunn & Dunn, 1997). One can use it as a screening instrument or as a supplement to other measures in evaluating learning problems (Camaioni, Ercolani, Penge, Riccio, & Bernabei, 2001), linguistic problems (Bayles, 1990), brain tumor survivors (Castellino, Tooze, Flowers, & Parsons, 2011), and many other special problems (Fielding-Barnsley & Purdie, 2003; Marchman, Saccuman, & Wulfeck, 2004; Ment et al., 2003). Though untimed, the PPVT-IV can be administered in 15 minutes or less, and it requires no reading ability. Two forms (IIIA and IIIB) are available. Each form has 204 plates, with each plate presenting four numbered pictures. The subject must indicate which of the four pictures best relates to a word read aloud by the examiner. Items are arranged in increasing order of difficulty, and the administrator must determine a basal and ceiling performance, as in the modern Binet scale. The number of incorrect responses is subtracted from the ceiling to produce a total score. This score can then be converted to a standard score (mean = 100, SD = 15), percentile rank, stanine, or age-equivalent score.

The PPVT-IV purports a split-half internal consistency of .86 to .97, alternate form reliability from .88 to .94, and retest reliability of .91 to .94. Its validity has been reported as good, with respectable correlations with the WISC-III VIQ at .91.

The Peabody may underestimate Wechsler or Binet IQs for retarded children (Prout & Sheldon, 1984), gifted children (Hayes & Martin, 1986), and adults (Bell, Lassiter, Matthews, & Hutchinson, 2001; Campbell, Bell, & Keith, 2001; Washington & Craig, 1999). Research has supported its use for certain adults, such as those with neurocognitive deficits (Edelstein et al., 2011) or language impairment (Fidler, Plante, & Vance, 2001). Because it evaluates only receptive vocabulary and not problem solving, abstract thinking, and other functions tapped by the major IQ tests, the Peabody test should never be used as a substitute for a Wechsler or Binet IQ. Indeed, researchers have repeatedly noted that the Peabody test cannot be used as a substitute for a major intelligence test (Castellino et al., 2011). Nevertheless, much care went into the latest revision, and the test meets rigorous psychometric standards. According to the test developers, the PPVT-IV test was standardized on a national sample of individuals aged 2 years 6 months to over 90 years. More than 5500 individuals were tested; data from approximately 3500 subjects were used for the normative scores. The sample matches the U.S. Census for gender, race, ethnicity, region, socioeconomic status (SES), and clinical diagnosis or special education placement (Dunn & Dunn, 2007).

The authors were careful to indicate the limitations of the test as well as its appropriate uses. These include "establishing and restoring rapport," "testing preschool children," "screening for verbal ability," "screening for giftedness and mental retardation," and "measuring English language proficiency" (see Dunn & Dunn, 1997) and testing language performance of low-income African American preschool children (Oi, Kaiser, Milan, & Hancock, 2006).

In conclusion, the modern Peabody test can be an important component in a test battery or used as a screening device. It is easy to administer and is useful for a variety of groups. However, its tendency to underestimate IQ scores, in conjunction with the problems inherent in the multiple-choice format, indicates that the Peabody test cannot be used in place of the Binet and Wechsler scales. One should use it for general screening purposes and to evaluate receptive vocabulary, and heed the careful instructions specified in the test manual.

Leiter International Performance Scale–Third Edition

Whereas the Columbia and Peabody tests measure verbal aspects of intelligence, the LIPS-3 (Leiter scale) is strictly a performance scale (Roid, Miller, Pomplun, & Koch, 2013). It aims at providing a nonverbal measure of intelligence in individuals 3 to 75 years and older (see Figure 11.8). First developed in the 1930s, and revised most recently in 2013, the Leiter scale is still used by researchers (see Vicario et al., 2010), although one finds it more frequently used in clinical settings, where it is still widely utilized to assess the intellectual function of children with pervasive developmental disorders, especially those who cannot be tested with standard intelligence tests (Portoghese et al., 2010). The Leiter scale purports to provide a nonverbal measure of general intelligence by sampling a wide variety of functions from memory to nonverbal reasoning. One can administer it without using language, and it requires no verbal response from subjects. For this reason, it is often used when assessing children with autism (see Makkonen et al., 2011).

Presumably, one can apply it to a large range of disabled individuals, particularly the deaf and language-disabled. Like the Peabody test and the Columbia scale, the Leiter-3 scale is untimed. The Leiter-3 has considerable utility for subjects who cannot or will not provide a verbal response (Bay, 1998; Bos, 1996; Makkonen et al., 2011). The Leiter scale merits consideration as an aid to clinical diagnosis in disabled children (Bradley-Johnson, 2001; Tsatsanis et al., 2003). However, the test user must exercise caution in interpreting Leiter test results because the meaning of test scores requires more research (Hooper & Mee Bell, 2006).

FIGURE 11.8
Leiter International
Performance Scale.

Courtesy of Stoelting Company

Porteus Maze Test (PMT)

The PMT is a popular but poorly standardized nonverbal performance measure of intelligence. Since it was first published at about the time of World War I, it has served as an important individual ability test (Krikorian & Bartok, 1998). As its name implies, the PMT consists of maze problems. Specifically, it includes 12 mazes that increase in complexity across age levels. The participant is required to trace the maze from the starting point to the goal while following certain rules (Kar, Rao, Chandramouli, Thennarasu, & Satishchandra, 2011). Like the Leiter scale, the Porteus test can be administered without verbal instruction and thus can be used for a variety of special populations (Kugler, 2007; Leshem & Glicksohn, 2007; May, Tuvblad, Baker, & Raine, 2015).

The Porteus test's standardization sample is quite old (Doctor, 1972). Despite its problems, the Porteus test meets an important need in providing a measure of ability for many groups to whom the Binet and Wechsler scales do not apply. Like many similar tests, a restandardization would greatly improve the quality of the Porteus.

In sum, the widespread use and interest in tests such as the Peabody, Leiter, and Porteus clearly indicate the need for strictly nonverbal or performance measures of intelligence, especially for the disabled.

Testing Learning Disabilities

One of the most important areas in education involves the study of specific learning disabilities. A major concept in this field is that a child average in intelligence may fail in school because of a specific deficit or disability that prevents learning.

A learning disability is just one of the many types of disabilities that may entitle a child to receive special education services under the Individuals with Disabilities Education Act (IDEA) (20 U.S.C. 1400 et seq.) and its state law counterparts. Federal law entitles every eligible child with a disability to a free appropriate public education that emphasizes special education and related services designed to meet his or her unique needs and prepare him or her for further education, employment, and independent living. To qualify for special education services under IDEA and its state law counterparts, a child must not only have a disability but also have his or her educational performance adversely affected by the disability. Thus, the beginning point for evaluating a learning disability is a problem in how a child is performing in school.

Prior to the 2004 amendment of IDEA, schools were required to wait until a child fell considerably behind grade level before the child became eligible for special education services. That is, it was only when there was a severe discrepancy between a child's potential to achieve and actual school achievement that a child became eligible for special education services on the basis of a "specific learning disability" under federal and most state law counterparts.

Today, school districts are no longer required to follow this discrepancy model. Educators can now find other ways to determine when a child needs extra help (Coleman, Buysse, & Neitzel, 2006). This new way of intervention is being implemented throughout the country through a process called response to intervention, or RTI (Robins & Antrim, 2013). The major premise of RTI is that early intervening services can prevent academic failure for many students with learning difficulties. It can also determine which students actually have learning disabilities, and whose underachievement cannot be attributed to other factors such as inadequate instruction (Robins & Antrim, 2013).

School problems may be the result of any one or a combination of many factors including very low potential (intelligence) and emotional upset resulting from such factors as divorce, parental separation, bereavement, drug intoxication, and a host of others. However, a child will not be found to have a learning disability if problems in school are the result of a lack of basic instruction in math or reading, or based on limited English proficiency.

Identifying a learning disability is a complex process, and parents are advised to seek professional help. A good resource for parents and teachers is Barbara Z. Novick and Maureen M. Arnold's book *Why Is My Child Having Trouble at School?* (Tarcher, 1995). These authors identify several "signs of a learning problem," including:

disorganization—for example, sloppy homework or papers crumpled or out of place;

careless effort—for example, misreads instructions or mishears directions;

forgetfulness—for example, the child's best excuse is "I forgot";

refusal to do school work or homework—for example, turns in work half-finished or needs somebody closely supervising in order to complete assignments;

slow performance—for example, takes far more than the expected time to complete an assignment;

poor attention—for example, mind seems to wander or frequently does not know what she or he is supposed to be doing; and

moodiness—for example, child shows anger, sadness, or irritability when asked to complete a school or home assignment.

Illinois Test of Psycholinguistic Abilities (ITPA-3)

Of the major tests designed specifically to assess learning disabilities, none better illustrates the theory of learning disabilities and has generated more interest than the controversial ITPA-3. Based on modern concepts of human information processing, the ITPA assumes that failure to respond correctly to a stimulus can result not only from a defective output (response) system but also from a defective input or information-processing system. This test assumes that a human response to an outside stimulus can be viewed in terms of discrete stages or processes. In stage 1, the senses receive input or incoming environmental information. Thus, the information must first be received by the senses before it can be analyzed. During stage 2, this information is analyzed or processed. Finally, having processed the information, the individual must make a response—stage 3 (see Figure 11.9).

Assuming that a learning disability can occur at any level of processing, the Illinois test theorizes that the child may be impaired in one or more specific sensory modalities. Input may be visual, auditory, or tactile. The Illinois test provides 12 subtests that measure the individual's ability to receive visual, auditory, or tactile input independently of processing and output factors. The 12 subtests also have been designed and selected to represent three "global" composites: general language, spoken language, and written language.

The general language composite is formed by combining the results of all 12 subtests; this serves as the test's best single estimate of linguistic ability because it reflects the broadest array of spoken and written language abilities. Other composites are assessed by combinations of two or more subtests. For instance, the spoken language composite is formed by combining the results of the six subtests that measure aspects of oral language. The subtests assess oral language's semantical, grammatical, and phonological aspects. The remainder of the composites that may be formed include the written language composite, semantics composite, grammar composite, phonology composite, comprehension composite, spelling composite, sight–symbol processing composite, and sound–symbol processing composite.

By providing relatively independent measures for each of these areas, the Illinois test purports to help isolate the specific site of a learning disability. For example, a child may receive age-appropriate scores for the written language composite while receiving unusually low scores on the spoken language composite. This result would indicate that although the child can receive and process information as well as others do when tasks are based on written language, he or she has trouble with tasks based on spoken language. The treatment intervention can therefore focus on enhancing the child's specific area of weakness. Similarly, if the problem involves auditory processing, then this area becomes the focus.

Designed for use with children ages 5 through 12, the Illinois test has found widespread use and interest among educators, psychologists, learning disability specialists, and researchers (Garayzábal Heinze et al., 2011; Klausen, Moller, Holmefjord, Reiseaeter, & Asbjornsen, 2000; Kohnen & Nickels, 2010; Ottem,

FIGURE 11.9
Three-stage information-processing model.

2002a, 2002b; Sun & Buys, 2013; Tong & Zhu, 2006). Original claims of the test's ability to isolate information-processing deficiencies proved to be overly optimistic and led to severe criticism (Bell, 1990). The most recent version of the test makes much more modest claims. According to the test manual, the test is useful in determining "specific strengths and weaknesses among linguistic abilities" and "can be used to assess linguistic delays."

The first two versions of the test were criticized because it was difficult to administer and presented no reliability or validity data. Efforts were made to improve the properties of the ITPA-3. According to the test developers, internal consistency, stability, and interscorer reliability for all subtests and composites are high enough to allow ITPA-3 scores to be used as the basis for making clinical judgments (i.e., rs greater than .90) (see ProEd, 2011; Towne, 2003). Validity evidence shows that all ITPA-3 subtests are useful for measuring both spoken and written language.

Studies showing the absence of gender, ethnic, and racial bias have been included in the manual and normative data are now provided (Towne, 2003). The ITPA-3 was normed using a sample of 1522 children aged 5 to 12 years from 27 states. This new normative information was collected during the years 1999 and 2000. The normative sample reflects the population characteristics of the United States relative to ethnicity, race, gender, disability status, geographic region, parental education, rural/urban residence, and family income.

The substantial changes made to the ITPA-3 represent a major improvement over previous versions (Towne, 2003). However, although the ITPA-3 can be considered a comprehensive assessment tool, it should be remembered that specific constructs are evaluated with only two subtests (i.e., the spelling and comprehension composites). Clinicians should conduct further assessment with children who demonstrate potential problems in these two areas (Towne, 2003). Overall, the ITPA-3 now appears to be a psychometrically sound measure of children's psycholinguistic abilities.

Woodcock-Johnson IV

One of the better tests for evaluating learning disabilities is the Woodcock-Johnson IV (Woodcock, McGrew, & Mather, 2001). The Woodcock-Johnson III was designed as a broad-range individually administered test to be used in educational settings. It assesses general intellectual ability (g), specific cognitive abilities, scholastic aptitude, oral language, and achievement (Schrank, Mather, & McGrew, 2014). The 2014 version of the Woodcock-Johnson was created to go beyond the Cattell-Horn-Carroll (CHC) three-stratum theory of intelligence, which formed the basis of the earlier 2001 third edition (Schank, Mcgrew, &Woodcock, 2001). Nevertheless, despite the addition of seven new tests, most of the basic ideas remain the same as the earlier version.

The WJ-IV actually provides three independent but coordinated test batteries that the publishers state can be used separately or independently: tests of cognitive abilities, tests of achievement, and tests of oral language.

By comparing a child's score on cognitive ability with his or her score on achievement, one can evaluate possible learning problems (Mather & Schrank, 2001; Ofiesh, Mather, & Russell, 2005; Schrank, Flanagan, Woodcock, & Mascolo, 2002). Because both the cognitive abilities battery and the achievement battery

TABLE 11.4 Description of Illinois Test of Psycholinguistic Abilities (ITPA-3) Subtests

Subtest	Description
Spoken Analogies:	The examiner says a four-part analogy, of which the last part is missing. The child then tells the examiner the missing part. For example, in response to "Birds fly, fish _____," the child might say, "swim."
Spoken Vocabulary:	The examiner says a word that is actually an attribute of some noun. For example, the examiner may say, "I am thinking of something with a roof," to which the child might respond, "house."
Morphological Closure:	The examiner says an oral prompt with the last part missing. For example, the examiner says, "big, bigger, _____," and the child completes the phrase by saying the missing part, "biggest."
Syntactic Sentences:	The examiner says a sentence that is syntactically correct but semantically nonsensical (e.g., "Red flowers are smart"). The child repeats the sentence.
Sound Deletion:	The examiner asks the child to delete words, syllables, and their phonemes from spoken words. For example, the examiner might ask the student to say "weekend" without the "end."
Rhyming Sequences:	The examiner says strings of rhyming words that increase in length, and the child repeats them (e.g., "noon," "soon," "moon").
Sentence Sequencing:	The child reads a series of sentences silently and then orders them into a sequence to form a plausible paragraph. For example, if the following three sentences were rearranged in B, C, A order they would make sense: A. I go to school. B. I get up. C. I get dressed.
Written Vocabulary:	After reading an adjective (e.g., "A broken _____"), the child responds by writing a noun that is closely associated with the stimulus word (e.g., "vase" or "mirror").
Sight Decoding:	The child pronounces a list of printed words that contain irregular parts (e.g., "would," "laugh," "height," "recipe").
Sound Decoding:	The child reads aloud phonically regular names of make-believe animal creatures (e.g., Flant, Yang).
Sight Spelling:	The examiner reads aloud irregular words one by one in a list. The child is given a printed list of these words, in which the irregular part of the words and one or more phonemes are missing. He or she writes in the omitted part of the words. For example, the examiner says, "said," the child sees s_____d, and he or she writes in the missing letters, "ai."
Sound Spelling:	The examiner reads aloud phonically regular nonsense words, and the child writes the word or the missing part.

ITPA-3: Illinois Test of Psycholinguistic Abilities–Third Edition, online pamphlet, retrieved from http://www.proedinc.com/customer/productView.aspx?ID=788.

were normed together, they provide for evaluating the presence of discrepancies without the errors associated with comparing results based on separately normed tests (Villarreal, 2015). Conormed batteries have also enabled the creators of the Woodcock-Johnson to incorporate specific regression coefficients between all predictor and criterion variables for each age and population group. This allows evaluators to calculate the presence and significance of both intra-ability discrepancies (such as a discrepancy between an individual test taker's scores on processing speed and fluid reasoning) and ability–achievement discrepancies (such as a high score on the cognitive abilities battery and a low score on the achievement battery). Such discrepancies are defined in terms of a major discrepancy (usually 1.5 to 2 standard deviations) between cognitive ability (intelligence) and achievement. If a child is at the mean for cognitive ability (i.e., 50th percentile) and is two standard deviations below the mean in achievement (i.e., 2.2 percentile rank), evaluators would suspect a learning disability and call for further evaluation. The Woodcock-Johnson also allows an evaluator to pinpoint specific deficits in cognitive ability. For instance, in evaluating a child who is struggling to keep up with the class in reading and has scored one standard deviation above the mean on the cognitive ability battery, it would be beneficial to discover that the child's results on the processing speed subtest were slightly below average. In this way, diagnosis of learning disabilities using the Woodcock-Johnson can help to isolate specific areas of concern, provide accurate diagnoses, and even suggest avenues of intervention.

The Woodcock-Johnson has relatively good psychometric properties. The standardization included a large sample representative of the U.S. population in terms of gender, race, occupational status, geographic region, and urban versus rural status. Median test reliabilities have split-half reliabilities in the .80's and .90's.

The field of learning disability assessment is relatively new and so are tests in this area. As a result, with the possible exception of the KABC, new tests of learning disability are in the same stage as early intelligence instruments. When judged by modern standards for individual ability tests, especially those that purportedly measure intelligence, these tests compare unfavorably in many respects.

For learning disability tests, three conclusions seem warranted. First, test constructors appear to be responding to the same criticisms that led to changes in the Binet and Wechsler scales and ultimately to the development of the KABC. Second, much more empirical and theoretical research is needed (Miller, McCardle, & Hernandez, 2010). Finally, users of learning disabilities tests should take great pains to understand the weaknesses of these procedures and not overinterpret results.

Visiographic Tests

Visiographic tests require a subject to copy various designs. Such tests are used in education and have achieved a central position in neuropsychological testing because of their sensitivity to many different kinds of brain damage (Jacobson, Delis, & Bondi, 2002). In this section, we briefly describe three such tests and then, in Chapter 18, discuss neuropsychological testing in greater detail.

Benton Visual Retention Test–Fifth Edition (BVRT-V)

Tests for brain damage are based on the concept of *psychological deficit*, in which a poor performance on a specific task is related to or caused by some underlying deficit. By knowing the underlying function or ability measured by a specific psychological test, the test examiner can relate a poor performance on that test to this underlying function (Dige & Wik, 2005). Such is the idea behind the BVRT-V, which assumes

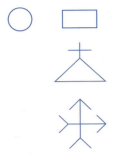

FIGURE 11.10

Designs similar to those on the Benton Visual Retention Test.

that brain damage easily impairs visual memory ability. Thus, a deficit on a visual memory task is consistent with possible brain damage or brain diseases such as Alzheimer's (Yan, Yang, & Wang, 2001).

Designed for individuals ages 8 and older, the Benton test consists of geometric designs briefly presented and then removed (see Figure 11.10). The subject must then reproduce the designs from memory. The responses are scored according to criteria in the manual. The subject loses points for mistakes and omissions and gains points for correct or partially correct responses. Norms are then available to evaluate scores. As the number of errors increases, the subject approaches the organic (brain-damaged) range (Lockwood, Mansoor, Homer-Smith, & Moses, 2011). Errors are also associated with normal aging (Resnick, Trotman, Kawas, & Zonderman, 1995), learning disabilities (Snow, 1998), and schizophrenia (Karageorgiou et al., 2011; Rollnick et al., 2002). More recently, a computerized version has been developed (Thompson & Chinnery, 2011; Thompson, Ennis, Coffin, & Farman, 2007).

Bender Visual Motor Gestalt Test (BVMGT)

Also used in the assessment of brain damage, the BVMGT has a variety of uses and is one of the most popular individual tests. It consists of nine geometric figures (such as a circle and a diamond) that the subject is simply asked to copy (see Figure 11.11). With specific errors identified for each design, the Bender test is scored according to

FIGURE 11.11

The figures of the Bender Visual Motor Gestalt Test.

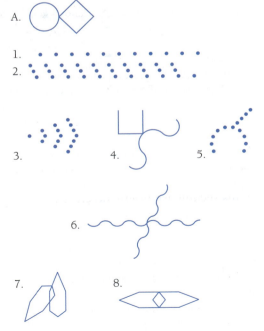

(From the Bender Visual Motor Gestalt Test by L. Bender, 1962.)

the number of errors the subject makes (Bolen, Hewett, Hall, & Mitchell, 1992; Xu, Fu, & Zhang, 1996). Developmental norms are available that describe the number of errors associated with children ages 5 through 8 (see Koppitz, 1964). By age 9, any child of normal intelligence can copy the figures with only one or two errors. Therefore, anyone older than 9 who cannot copy the figures may suffer from some type of deficit.

Research on the Bender test has shown that errors can occur for people whose mental age is less than 9 (e.g., because of low intelligence), those with brain damage (Bobic, Pavicevic, & Gomzi, 2000), those with nonverbal learning disabilities (Jing, Deqing, & Longhui, 2001), and those with emotional problems (Biswas, Malhotra, Malhotra, & Gupta, 2006; Uber, 2005). Errors associated with brain damage have been identified, and a variety of scoring systems for brain damage are available. However, the reliability of such systems has been questioned (Fuller & Vance, 1995; Lubin & Sands, 1992; Wagner & Flamos, 1988). Nevertheless, the Bender ranks among the top 10 most widely used assessment instruments (Pio-trowski, 1995; also see Blasi, Elia, Buono, Ramakers, & di Nuovo, 2007).

Memory-for-Designs (MFD) Test

Another simple drawing test that involves perceptual–motor coordination is the MFD test. Requiring only a 10-minute administration, the MFD test can be used for individuals 8 to 60 years of age. Empirical data have tended to support its use as an indicator of brain injury and brain disease (Strauss & Brandt, 1990; Teng et al., 1989). As in the Benton test, the subject attempts to draw a briefly presented design from memory. Drawings are scored from 0 to 3, depending on how they compare with representative drawings from normal controls and people with varying degrees of brain injury. A raw score total based on all 15 drawings can then be corrected for age and intelligence by reference to a table. This corrected score can then be evaluated against a relatively large normative sample.

Reported split-half reliability indexes are quite good (.92), and test–retest indexes range from .81 to .90 (Graham & Kendall, 1960). Like so many psychological tests, the MFD needs additional validity documentation. Available studies have been quite supportive (Goldstein, Canavan, & Polkey, 1988; Mandes & Gessner, 1988).

To summarize, like all visiographic psychological tests used in isolation, the Benton, Bender, and MFD have been criticized because of their limitations in reliability and validity documentation. However, all three can be used as screening devices. An excessive number of errors on any of these procedures provide a signal for the examiner that in-depth testing or a medical evaluation may be necessary, and further results may help explain why a student is not performing well in school.

Creativity: Torrance Tests of Creative Thinking (TTCT)

The measurement of creativity is one of the most underdeveloped areas in the field of psychological testing. One can define *creativity* as the ability to be original, to combine known facts in new ways, or to find new relationships between known facts.

Evaluating creativity may provide a possible alternative to IQ testing. Creativity tests may also be useful in a battery to help explain the nature of a student's difficulty in the classroom. However, like learning disability tests, most creativity tests are still in the early stages of development. One of the best, most established, and most popular of these creativity tests is the TTCT.

The Torrance test was originally developed in 1966 and reformed five times in 1974, 1984, 1990, 1998, and 2008. The total sample size combined has reached a staggering 272,599. The TTCT separately measures aspects of creative thinking such as fluency, originality, and flexibility (Palaniappan & Torrance, 2001). In measuring fluency, administrators ask an individual to think of as many different solutions to a problem as possible. The more distinct solutions a person can find, the greater his or her fluency. To evaluate originality, a test maker attempts to evaluate how new or unusual a person's solutions to problems are. Finally, flexibility is measured in terms of an individual's ability to shift directions or try a new approach to problem solving. For example, if the way you study for exams has not met your goals, then you would show flexibility if you tried a new approach. Instead of spending all your time passively rereading, you might try the recall method in which you spend half your study time trying to recall and synthesize what you have learned.

Like individual ability tests for the handicapped and tests of learning disability, the TTCT does not meet the Binet and Wechsler scales in terms of standardization, reliability, and validity. Reliability studies have varied widely (e.g., correlations of .35 to .73 for a 3-year period), and validity studies have tended to be varied as well as inconclusive (Kim, Cramond, & Bandalos, 2006). Unlike some creativity tests, the TTCT was conservatively presented as a research tool, but little has been done to prevent it from being applied in educational settings. Caution is indicated. On the positive side, several research studies have supported the utility of the Torrance tests as an unbiased indicator of giftedness (Kim, 2006; Santosa, 2007).

Factor analytic studies have suggested that the various types of creative thinking (fluency, flexibility, originality) tend to load on a single, general factor (Clapham, 1998). A 2006 study indicated that the two-factor model had a much better fit than the one general factor model (Kim, 2006, p. 257). The TTCT consists of two factors, innovative and adaptive, rather than a single factor, contrary to the majority of earlier research. The findings of this study are consistent with several researchers' (e.g., Isaksen & Puccio, 1988; Puccio et al., 1995; Torrance & Horng, 1980) interpretation of Kirton's (1976, 1978, 1987, 1989) model. Clearly, far more work is needed; today, human creativity surprisingly remains a largely unexplained field.

An interesting phenomenon is that we as a society may be becoming less creative. Kim (2011) compared scores from the various standardizations and found that even though IQ scores have been rising, creativity scores have been going down. Objectively, with modern electronics and apps, it would seem like creativity is going up, but the researchers found just the opposite. More research in this area seems highly warranted.

In sum, the Torrance tests are typical of creativity tests. Applied practitioners demand such a tool for their work. Though inconsistent, available data reflect the tests' merit and fine potential. As with so many other tests, however, more work is needed. One should view results from creativity tests as tentative and to be used only in conjunction with other tests.

Individual Achievement Tests: Wide Range Achievement Test-4 (WRAT-4)

We have discussed the widely made distinction between intelligence and achievement. As you know, intelligence tests measure potential ability, whereas achievement tests measure what the person has actually acquired or done with that potential. Although scores from intelligence tests and achievement tests often overlap, discrepancies sometimes arise between the two, for instance, when a person of average potential has not made full use of that potential. Such a person would tend to score higher on a general ability test than on a specific achievement test, especially if the general ability test minimizes the effects of learning and the achievement test is highly specific. Similarly, a person may score average on a general intelligence test but, because of a high level of interest, motivation, or special training, score above average on achievement. Thus, despite the overlap of intelligence and ability tests, comparing their data can sometimes be extremely revealing. Indeed, as we indicated, discrepancies between IQ and achievement have traditionally been the main defining feature of a learning disability.

Most achievement tests are group tests, which will be discussed in the next chapter. Among the most widely used individual achievement tests is the WRAT-4, which purportedly permits an estimate of grade-level functioning in word reading, spelling, math computation, and sentence comprehension (Snelbaker, Wilkinson, Robertson, & Glutting, 2001; Wilkinson & Robertson, 2006). It can be used for children ages 5 and older and has two levels for each of the three achievement areas.

The WRAT-4 is easy to administer and is highly popular. Despite its research and clinical uses (Casaletto et al., 2014; Jantz et al., 2015), however, it has some problems (Johnstone, Holland, & Larimore, 2000).

The earlier WRAT-R had been severely criticized for its inaccuracy in evaluating grade-level reading ability. The test merely required participants to pronounce words from a list. The 1993 version retained this format, which led one reviewer to conclude that "on no grounds can this be considered a test of reading" (Mabry, 1995, p. 1108). Because the basic concept of the test has not changed for nearly 60 years, it is "already outdated" (Mabry, 1995, p. 1109). The test authors believe that the WRAT-4 provides a quick, simple, and psychometric sound measure of fundamental academic skills. Quick and simple, yes, but the jury is still out on psychometrically sound. From a purely technical standpoint, the reliability and validity evidence provided in the manual surpasses that of many small tests (Hoff, 2010). Internal consistency and alternate-form reliability estimates are high, and the inclusion of validity evidence is an improvement over previous editions. Unfortunately, many of the validity studies have sample sizes too small to demonstrate convergent and discriminant validity sufficiently (Hoff, 2010).

Summary

The number of individual ability tests is almost overwhelming. Most of these tests serve highly specific purposes, and their strength lies in their specificity. Table 11.2 summarizes the major differences among the various individual tests of ability. Of the infant and preschool scales, the Bayley Scales of Infant Development are the most psychometrically sound. The McCarthy Scales of Children's Abilities appear to be promising tests for measuring intelligence in young children, but more work is needed. The KABC-II appears to have considerable value, but it has been strongly criticized. Overall, general ability tests for handicapped and special populations should be used cautiously. Among ability tests for the handicapped, the Columbia Mental Maturity Scale–Third Edition is one of the most promising.

Learning disability tests are based on information-processing theory. Because these tests are relatively new, one should view their results with caution. As with creativity tests, these tests still have a long way to go to reach the standards of the Binet and Wechsler scales. Drawing tests such as the Bender, the Benton, and the Memory-for-Designs are all excellent and economical screening devices for brain damage. These tests attempt to measure an ability related to brain functioning. In addition to being a screening device for brain damage, the Bender Visual Motor Gestalt Test can be used to measure intellectual and emotional functioning.

Although achievement and intelligence tests often overlap, a comparison of the two can be useful. A major individual achievement test, the Wide Range Achievement Test-4 is a quick and relatively simple way to evaluate certain achievement scores, but its psychometric adequacy remains an issue.

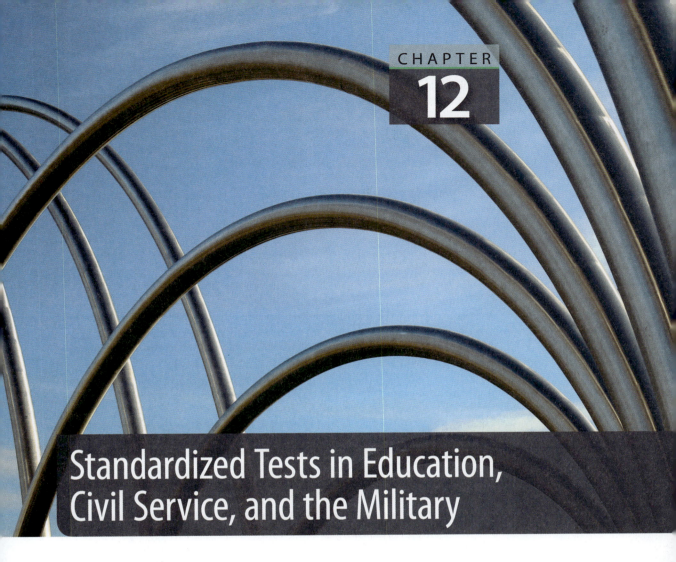

Standardized Tests in Education, Civil Service, and the Military

LEARNING OBJECTIVES

When you have completed this chapter, you should be able to:

▶ Compare group and individual ability tests

▶ Identify the major characteristics of group tests

▶ List four general rules for using results from group ability tests

▶ Evaluate the adequacy of the group ability tests used in kindergarten through 12th grade

▶ Identify and evaluate two major group ability tests for college entrance

▶ Identify and evaluate two major group ability tests for graduate-school entrance

▶ Identify some of the advantages of the Goodenough-Harris Drawing Test

▶ Identify some group ability tests widely used in business and industry

299

You no doubt have experienced taking a standardized group test. Such tests are given in kindergarten through 12th grade. Most colleges require standardized group entrance exams.

One test that has been the bane of many psychology and education majors is the GRE Revised General Test (GRE). Each year hundreds of thousands of GREs are administered in more than 160 countries at more than 700 test centers worldwide (Educational Testing Service (ETS), 2011). The GRE is one of the most widely used tests for admission into postgraduate programs. If you plan to go on to graduate school, you will probably face the GRE. The extent to which graduate programs rely on the GRE can best be summed up by Sternberg and Williams (1997). Applications for admission into the Ph.D. program of one major research university are sorted on arrival into one of four boxes: below 1200, 1200–1300, 1301–1400, and above 1400, where the mean is 1000 and the standard deviation is 200. The first applications to be read are from the box above 1400 or two standard deviations above the mean. Applicants who score below 1301 are "rarely admitted" (Sternberg & Williams, 1997). The question is, how do we tell if this approach to admissions is justified?

When justifying the use of group standardized tests, test users often have problems defining what exactly they are trying to predict, or what the test *criterion* is (Thayer, 1992; Thayer & Kalat, 1998). With the GRE, the best criterion appears to be first-year grades in graduate school (Leavitt, Lombard, & Morris, 2011, p. 448). However, historically, the GRE has typically correlated only in the high teens to low twenties with first-year grades (Fairtest, 2007; Schneider & Briel, 1990). According to the National Center for Fair and Open Testing (Fairtest, 2007), the ability of the GRE to predict first-year graduate grades is incredibly weak. Fairtest reports that in one ETS study of 12,000 test takers, the exam accounted for a mere 9% of the variation among students' first-year grades. Undergraduate grades proved to be a stronger predictor of academic success, explaining 14% of the variation in graduate-school grades. Considering that a correlation of .2 accounts for only 4% of the variance, it is clear that a lot of weight is placed on a test that contributes relatively little to the criterion. Moreover, tests such as the GRE predict neither clinical skill nor even the ability to solve real-world problems (see Neisser et al., 1996).

To investigate the criterion problem, Saccuzzo and Johnson (2000) examined scores on the Law School Admission Test (LSAT) as they related to first-time bar pass rates. The LSAT was found to correlate from .063 to .146 with bar pass rates, depending on the sample. Strikingly, a student's cumulative law school grade point average (GPA) correlated between .587 and .591 with bar pass rates. Using multiple regression analysis, the researchers found that cumulative law school GPA accounted for 35.2% of the variation in bar pass rate, but the LSAT accounted for only an additional 2.3% of the variance. The implication was clear: Although the test did contribute to prediction, its weight was miniscule compared to actual performance as measured by a student's law school GPA.

In this chapter, we continue our discussion of testing in education, evaluating many of the group tests used on a daily basis in schools, colleges, and graduate and professional schools. We also examine standardized tests used in the U.S. civil service and military. Tests used in business and industry are discussed in Chapter 18. As you encounter these tests, keep in mind that even though they do add accuracy in the selection process, the amount of variability they account for is relatively small.

If the test correlates with a criterion at the .4 level, then it accounts for 16% of the variability in that criterion, with the other 84% resulting from unknown factors and errors. Before discussing specific tests, we compare group and individual tests and also reexamine the distinctions among achievement, aptitude, and intelligence.

Comparison of Group and Individual Ability Tests

Individual tests (as discussed in Chapters 9, 10, and 11) require a single examiner for a single subject. The examiner provides the instructions according to a standardized procedure stated in the test manual. The subject responds, and the examiner records the response verbatim. The examiner then evaluates and scores the subject's responses. This scoring process usually involves considerable skill. In contrast, a single examiner can administer group tests to more than one person at the same time. The examiner may read the instructions and impose time limits. Subjects record their own responses, which are usually choices between two or more alternatives. Scoring is usually objective and requires no skill on the part of the examiner, who simply adds the number of correct responses and in some cases subtracts a certain percentage for incorrect responses.

Further, in most individual tests, the examiner takes responsibility for eliciting a maximum performance. If a problem exists that might inhibit a maximum performance—for example, if a subject is frightened, nervous, uncooperative, or unmotivated—the examiner takes action to address this problem. For example, the examiner may encourage guessing by saying in a warm, friendly, and supportive tone, "Sure you know that; just guess." On the other hand, those who use the results of group tests must *assume* that the subject was cooperative and motivated. Subjects are not praised for responding, as they may be on individual tests, and there are no safeguards to prevent a person from receiving a low score for reasons other than low ability—such as lack of motivation, lack of cooperation, or emotional upset. As a result, low scores on group tests are often difficult to interpret. With high scores, and especially high scores, one can logically assume that the subject was motivated and has mental abilities commensurate with the obtained score. Low scores, however, may have resulted from low ability, lack of interest, inadequate motivation, clerical errors in recording responses, or a host of other factors. Table 12.1 compares individual and group tests.

TABLE 12.1　Individual Versus Group Tests

Individual tests	Group tests
One subject is tested at a time.	Many subjects are tested at a time.
Examiner records responses.	Subjects record own responses.
Scoring requires considerable skill.	Scoring is straightforward and objective.
Examiner flexibility can elicit maximum performance if permitted by standardization.	There are no safeguards.

Advantages of Individual Tests

Individual tests can provide a wealth of information about a subject beyond the test score. In these tests, the instructions and methods of administration are as identical as possible, so subjects take an individual test in typically the same circumstances. Therefore, differences observed in behavior and attitudes most likely reflect differences in the individuals taking the test. One person may respond quickly and enthusiastically when correct but may become hesitant or withdrawn following failure. Another person may react to failure by trying harder and may actually do better in the face of frustration and failure.

After examiners have gained experience with an individual test and know how to use it properly, they can observe different reactions from individuals placed in the same situation. Experienced examiners eventually develop internal norms. They have an idea of how most subjects react to a certain task or situation and can easily identify unusual reactions. The opportunity to observe behavior in a standard situation can be invaluable to an examiner who is trying to understand the unique attributes of a person and interpret the meaning of a test score.

By providing the opportunity to observe behavior under standardized conditions, individual tests add a whole new dimension to the information that one can obtain from an interview. Some subjects will not talk; some cannot talk. How can the examiner gain an understanding of such individuals? Information provided by friends or relatives cannot be relied on because they are rarely objective and not usually trained in observing human behavior. Simply observing the person in a natural setting may provide some useful information, but then the examiner has nothing with which to compare these observations. Thus, by allowing observations of behavior under standard conditions, individual tests provide an invaluable opportunity for the examiner to get information beyond what he or she can obtain in an interview.

Advantages of Group Tests

Group tests also offer unique advantages. Group tests are cost-efficient because they minimize the time needed for administration and scoring; they also involve less expensive materials and usually require less examiner skill and training than do individual tests. Scoring for group tests is more objective and hence typically more reliable than the subjective scoring of many individual tests. Group tests can be used with large numbers of individuals. When combined with data from other sources, group test results can yield information that is as useful and meaningful as that obtained from individual tests.

Whereas individual tests find their greatest application in the assessment and diagnosis of psychological or medical problems, the application of group tests is far broader. Group tests are used in schools at every level. The military, industry, and researchers also use them extensively. Group test results can be used for screening and selection purposes; to assess mental, vocational, or special abilities; to assess learning in a particular discipline or subject area; and to assess interests and aptitudes for specific occupations or job duties.

If the examiner's purpose does not require the benefits of individual tests, or if many individuals must be tested in a limited time with limited personnel, then

TABLE 12.2 Unique Advantages of Individual and Group Tests

Individual tests	Group tests
Provide information beyond the test score	Are cost-efficient
Allow the examiner to observe behavior in a standard setting	Minimize professional time for administration and scoring
Allow individualized interpretation of test scores	Require less examiner skill and training
	Have more objective and more reliable scoring procedures
	Have especially broad application

carefully administered and interpreted group tests can be extremely valuable tools. Table 12.2 summarizes the advantages of individual and group tests.

Overview of Group Tests

Characteristics of Group Tests

In general, group tests can be characterized as paper-and-pencil or booklet-and-pencil tests because the only materials required are a printed booklet of test items, a test manual, a scoring key, an answer sheet, and a pencil. However, computerized group testing is becoming more popular (Wang, Lin, Chang, & Douglas, 2016), and the clear trend is toward more computerized testing and less paper and pencil (see Mattson, 2011). Most group tests are multiple choice, but some require a free response such as completing a sentence or design, or writing an essay, as in the modern GRE.

Group tests by far outnumber individual tests. Like the latter, group tests vary among themselves in many respects. One major difference is whether the test is primarily verbal (thus requiring reading or language skills), primarily nonverbal, or a combination.

Some group tests group items by type (e.g., all verbal analogy problems are in the same section, with items arranged in order of increasing difficulty). A test of this kind is ideally suited for producing a variety of scores such as those obtained from the Wechsler scales. Other group tests present different tasks arranged in no particular or systematic order. A test of this kind typically produces a single score related to general ability.

Group test scores can be converted to a variety of units. Most produce percentiles or some type of standard score, but a few produce ratio or deviation IQs.

Selecting Group Tests

Because there are a sufficient number of psychometrically adequate group tests for most purposes, the test user need never settle for anything but well-documented and psychometrically sound tests. This is especially true for ability tests used in the schools.

In view of the large number of psychometrically sound instruments, this chapter will not discuss poorly standardized or marginally reliable tests. However, tests excluded from this discussion are not necessarily psychometrically unsound. We gave highest priority to established, highly used tests that continue to generate interest among researchers and practitioners. We also include tests that illustrate concepts or meet specific needs. Finally, we include a few recent tests as well as tests of historical value.

Using Group Tests

Overall, the tests included in our discussion are about as reliable and well standardized as the best individual tests. However, as for some individual tests, validity data for some group tests are weak, meager, or contradictory—or all three. Therefore, all users of group tests must carefully interpret and make use of test scores. These tests should not be seen as a simple way of making decisions but as a tool to be used in conjunction with other data.

Test use is an especially important issue for group tests because the results from these procedures are used by more people than are the results from individual tests. All routine users of these tests—thousands of teachers, educators, school administrators, personnel staff, counselors, and so forth—as well as the many consumers of group test information can benefit from the following suggestions.

Use Results With Caution

Never consider scores in isolation or as absolutes. Try to include the test score as only one bit of data, tentatively accepted unless not confirmed by other data. Be especially careful in using these tests for prediction, except for predicting relatively limited factors over a brief time. Avoid overinterpreting test scores or attributing more to test scores than their limitations warrant.

Be Especially Suspicious of Low Scores

Users of group tests must assume that subjects understand the purpose of testing, want to do well, and are equally rested and free of emotional problems. Many group tests also require reading ability as well as an interest in solving test problems. Failing to fulfill any of these assumptions and requirements can produce an artificially low score.

Consider Wide Discrepancies a Warning Signal

When an individual exhibits wide discrepancies either among test scores or between a test score and other data, all may not be well with the individual (assuming no clerical errors). The discrepancy may reflect emotional problems or severe stress. For example, a child with high test scores may obtain poor grades because of emotional upset. Or a child with good grades may obtain a poor test score because of a crisis, such as a death in the family.

When in Doubt, Refer

With low scores, wide discrepancies, or sufficient reason to doubt the validity or fairness of a test result, the safest course is to refer the subject for individual testing. Given the reasons for the referral, a professional who is trained in individual test use can generally ascertain the cause of the problem and provide the unique interpretation called for in such cases. It is often dangerous as well as reckless to take on a responsibility meant only for a trained specialist.

Group Tests in the Schools: Kindergarten Through 12th Grade

The purpose of these tests is to measure educational achievement in schoolchildren. Before proceeding to a discussion of the specific tests, this section reviews the nature of achievement tests and how they differ from aptitude tests.

Achievement Tests Versus Aptitude Tests

Achievement tests attempt to assess what a person has learned following a specific course of instruction. The first achievement tests used in the schools were essay tests. These were rapidly replaced in the 1930s by standardized achievement tests such as the Stanford Achievement Test, which is still in use today. These tests were more cost-effective than their essay counterparts, and scoring was far more objective and reliable. However, like their predecessors, standardized achievement tests had as their goal the endpoint evaluation of a student's knowledge after a standard course of training. In such tests, validity is determined primarily by content-related evidence. In other words, these tests are considered valid if they adequately sample the domain of the construct (e.g., math, science, or history) being assessed.

On the other hand, aptitude tests attempt to evaluate a student's potential for learning rather than how much a student has already learned. Unlike achievement tests, aptitude tests evaluate a wide range of experiences obtained in a variety of ways. They evaluate the effects of unknown and uncontrolled experiences. The validity of an aptitude test is judged primarily on its ability to predict future performance. Thus, such tests rely heavily on criterion-oriented evidence for validity. Table 12.3 summarizes the differences between achievement and aptitude tests.

As you know, the intelligence test measures general ability. Like aptitude tests, intelligence tests attempt to predict future performance. However, such tests predict generally and broadly, as opposed to aptitude tests, which typically predict potential in a specific area such as math, science, or music.

Clearly, achievement, aptitude, and intelligence are highly interrelated. For example, an algebra achievement test might be used to predict success (aptitude) in a geometry course. The following discussion examines all three types, beginning with achievement tests. Then we consider group intelligence tests used in the school system. Finally, we examine tests used to measure scholastic aptitude.

Group Achievement Tests

The Stanford Achievement Test is one of the oldest of the standardized achievement tests widely used in the school system (Gardner, Rudman, Karlsen, & Merwin, 1982). Now in its 10th edition, this test is well normed and criterion-referenced,

TABLE 12.3   Achievement Tests Versus Aptitude Tests

Achievement tests	Aptitude tests
1. Evaluate the effects of a known or controlled set of experiences	1. Evaluate the effects of an unknown, uncontrolled set of experiences
2. Evaluate the product of a course of training	2. Evaluate the potential to profit from a course of training
3. Rely heavily on content validation procedures	3. Rely heavily on predictive criterion validation procedures

with exemplary psychometric documentation. It evaluates achievement in kindergarten through 12th grades in the following areas: spelling, reading comprehension, word study and skills, language arts, social studies, science, mathematics, and listening comprehension. Figure 12.1 shows an example of the scoring output for the Stanford Achievement Test.

Another well-standardized and psychometrically sound group measure of achievement is the Metropolitan Achievement Test (MAT), which measures achievement in reading by evaluating vocabulary, word recognition, and reading comprehension. Now in its eighth edition, the MAT-8 was renormed in 2000, and alternate versions of the test including Braille, large print, and audio formats were made available for use with children having visual limitations (Harcourt Educational Measurement, 2000). An example of a reading item follows:

> Jennifer _____ to play house.
>
> Pick the word that best completes the sentence.
>
> **A.** wood   **B.** book   **C.** likes   **D.** hopes

The MAT-8 also measures mathematics by evaluating number concepts (e.g., measurement, decimals, factors, time, money), problem solving (e.g., word problems), and computation (addition, subtraction, multiplication, division). For example, a child might be presented with this item:

> Jason had four candy bars. He gave one to Mary and one to Bill. Which number sentence below shows how many candy bars he had left?
>
> **A.** $4 - 2 =$ **B.** $4 - 1 =$ **C.** $2 - 2 =$ **D.** $2 - 1 =$

Spelling is evaluated on the MAT-8 in a normal spelling test format in which the student is asked to spell an orally dictated word presented in a sentence. Language skills are evaluated with a grammar test as well as a measure of alphabetizing skills. Science knowledge is evaluated in items such as the following:

> A thermometer is used to measure. _____
>
> (Mark the best answer.)
>
> **A.** light   **B.** dark   **C.** temperature   **D.** planets

FIGURE 12.1
Example of a score report for the Stanford Achievement Test.

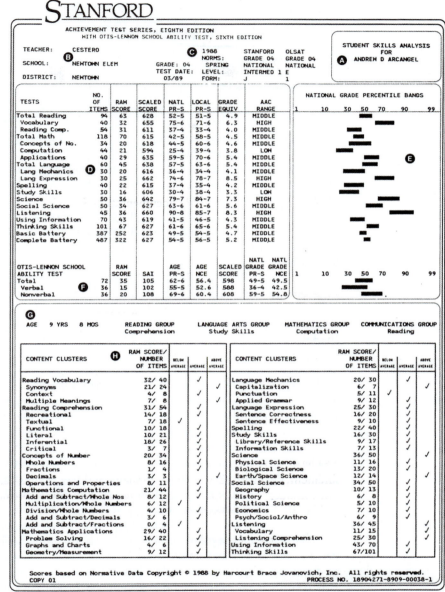

(Reproduced by permission from the Score Report for the Stanford Achievement Test, 8th Edition. Copyright © 1991 by Harcourt Brace Jovanovich, Inc. All Rights Reserved.)

Finally, the MAT-8 has several social studies items. Students are tested on their knowledge of geography, economics, history, political science, anthropology, sociology, and psychology, as in the following:

Paris is in _____

(Mark the best answer.)

    A. England   **B.** Spain   **C.** Canada   **D.** France

The MAT-8 standardization sample reflects a diverse nationwide student population. The sample was stratified by school size, public versus nonpublic school affiliation, geographic region, socioeconomic status, and ethnic background. Reliabilities of the total scores run in the high .90's, while those for the five major content areas range from .90 to .96.

The SAT and the MAT are state-of-the-art achievement tests. Their psychometric documentation is outstanding. The tests are reliable and normed on exceptionally large samples. They sample a variety of school subjects and cover all grade levels.

Group Tests of Mental Abilities (Intelligence)

This section discusses four group tests of mental abilities: the Kuhlmann-Anderson, the Henmon-Nelson, the Cognitive Abilities Test, and the Developing Cognitive Abilities Test.

Kuhlmann-Anderson Test (KAT)–Eighth Edition

The KAT is a group intelligence test with eight separate levels covering kindergarten through 12th grade. Each level of the KAT contains several tests with a variety of items on each. As in most multilevel batteries that cover many age or grade ranges, KAT items are primarily nonverbal at lower levels, requiring minimal reading and language ability. However, whereas most multilevel batteries become increasingly verbal with increasing age or grade level, the KAT remains primarily nonverbal throughout. Thus, the KAT is suited not only to young children but also to those who might be handicapped in following verbal procedures. It might even be suitable for adaptation for non-English-speaking populations, assuming proper norming.

The results of the most recent (eighth) edition of the KAT can be expressed in verbal, quantitative, and total scores. At some levels, total scores can be expressed as deviation IQs. Scores at other levels can be expressed as percentile bands. A **percentile band** is like a confidence interval. It provides the range of percentiles that most likely represent a subject's true score. One creates it by forming an interval one standard error of measurement above and below the obtained score and then converting the resulting values to percentiles.

An overwhelming majority of reviews have praised the KAT for its construction, standardization, and other excellent psychometric qualities. Normative data have been continually improved and are based on more than 10,000 subjects. Reliability coefficients are quite good, with split-half coefficients running in the low .90's and test–retest coefficients ranging from the low .80's to the low .90's. Validity is also

12.1 PSYCHOLOGICAL TESTING IN EVERYDAY LIFE

Changes in School Policies on Testing

By 2015, the tide against excessive testing in the schools began to change. In the last year of his presidency, Barack Obama surprised many in the policy community when he argued that there was too much testing in the schools (see https://www.youtube.com/watch?v=zYZ4qtN6KVM). The president proclaimed, "learning is about so much more than just filling in the right bubble." He went on to say, "So we're going to work with states, school districts, teachers, and parents to make sure that were not obsessing about testing." The announcement was a surprise because the Obama administration had promoted the use of standardized tests. Secretary of Education Arnold Duncan, following the No Child Left Behind momentum from the George W. Bush Presidency, had initiated several programs that accelerated the use of these tests. Some of these programs were highly controversial. For example, accountability programs were created in which teachers were evaluated, and sometimes even fired, on the basis of improvements in standardized test scores. Yet these policies had become politically sensitive. For example, one Gallup poll showed that 63% of parents with children in school were against using test scores of students as part of the evaluation of their teachers.

The presidents shift in policy was stimulated by an evaluation study conducted by the Council of the Great City Schools. The evaluation was conducted in 66 large school districts. Among the many problems identified in the report was a lack of standardization. Within the 66 districts that participated in the study, 401 different tests were administered during the 2014–2015 school year. The average student took about eight standardized tests per year, and the amount of time spent on testing was completely uncorrelated with performance in math or reading. There was no correlation between how much time was spent in testing and how well students performed in reading and math. Perhaps the biggest concern was the time that it took to take the tests. In 2015, students in the 66 largest school districts were spending 20 to 25 hours each school year taking standardized tests. In addition to the time actually taken for the test, it was estimated that a considerably larger number of hours were spent preparing the students to take the exams. This left less time for other forms of classroom instruction.

The standardized tests that were the focus of the study were independent of the tests used by teachers to evaluate their students. In 71% of the districts participating in the study, students were required to take final exam or end-of-course tests in addition to the state-required tests. In nearly half the districts, students also took career and technical education tests.

Feedback from test performance was also a problem. In 39% of the districts, for example, there was no feedback on test performance for 2 to 4 months. This

(continues)

made it difficult to use the feedback constructively to improve performance for the students.

The word *test* itself raise some concerns. For example, as part of the evaluation, parents were asked if they agreed or strongly agreed with the statement "accountability for how well my child is educated is important, and it begins with accurate measurement of what he/she is learning in school." This high level of support drops very significantly if the word *accurate measurement* is substituted with *test*. Parents also reacted negatively to the words *harder* tests or *more rigorous* tests.

When President Obama made his announcement in October 2015, it was noted that 2% of all classroom time was spent completing standardized tests.

well documented. The KAT correlates highly with a variety of ability and IQ tests. In sum, the KAT is an extremely sound, sophisticated group test. Its nonverbal items make it particularly useful for special purposes. Its impressive validity and reliability also make it one of the most popular group ability tests for all grade levels. Its potential for use and adaptation for non-English-speaking individuals or even non-English-speaking countries needs to be explored.

Henmon-Nelson Test (H-NT)

A second well-standardized, highly used, and carefully constructed test for all grade levels is the H-NT of mental abilities. Although it produces only a single score that is believed to reflect general intelligence, two sets of norms are available. One set is based on raw score distributions by age, and the other on raw score distributions by grade. Raw scores can be converted into deviation IQs as well as percentiles. The availability of only a single score has continued to spur controversy. However, a single score is consistent with the purpose of the test, which is to obtain a relatively quick measure of general intelligence (it takes approximately 30 minutes to complete the 90 items).

As in the other tests for school-aged individuals, most of the reported reliability coefficients, both split-half and test–retest, run in the .90's. Furthermore, the H-NT correlates well with a variety of intelligence tests (median .76, range .50–.84) and achievement test scores (median .79, range .64–.85). Correlations with grades, though not as high, are impressive, with a median coefficient of .60, which would account for 36% of the variability.

In sum, the H-NT is an extremely sound instrument. It can help predict future academic success quickly. However, the H-NT has some important limitations when used as the sole screening instrument for selecting giftedness or identifying learning disabilities in minority, culturally diverse, and economically disadvantaged children.

By providing only a single score related to Spearman's *g* factor, the H-NT does not consider multiple intelligences. When the test was being developed, no special effort was made to check for content bias, either by judges or by statistical analysis. The manual presents no data pertaining to the norms for special racial, ethnic, or socioeconomic groups, nor was the test designed to be used for culturally diverse children. Indeed, the manual pointedly calls for caution when using the H-NT for individuals from an educationally disadvantaged subculture. It also advises caution when extreme scores (below 80 or above 130) are obtained. Consistent with these cautions, research suggests that the H-NT tends to underestimate Wechsler full-scale IQ scores by 10 to 15 points for certain populations (Watson & Klett, 1975). A major problem with the H-NT is its relatively low ceiling. For example, to achieve an IQ of 130, a ninth-grade child would have to answer approximately 85 of the items correctly. This leaves only five items to discriminate all those above 130.

Cognitive Abilities Test (COGAT) Form 7

The **COGAT Form 7** (Lohman, 2012) stands out as a measure of fluid intelligence (Warne, 2015). In terms of its reliability and validity, the COGAT is comparable to the H-NT. Unlike the H-NT, however, the COGAT provides three separate scores: verbal, quantitative, and nonverbal. Reliabilities (KR_{20}) for the verbal score are in the high .90's; for the quantitative, the low .90's; and for the nonverbal, the high .90's.

The COGAT's item selection is superior to that of the H-NT in terms of selecting minority, culturally diverse, and economically disadvantaged children. Unlike the H-NT, the COGAT was specifically designed for poor readers, poorly educated people, and people for whom English is a second language. As with the KAT, it can potentially be adopted for use outside of the United States.

The test authors of the COGAT took special steps to eliminate irrelevant sources of test difficulty, especially those pertaining to cultural bias. All items were scrutinized for content that might be biased for or against any particular group. Statistical tests were then performed to eliminate items that might predict differentially for white and minority students. To eliminate the effect of test-taking skills, the test administration includes extensive practice exercises.

The COGAT offers advantages over the H-NT in evaluating minority, culturally diverse, and economically disadvantaged children. It provides reliable assessment of the academic abilities of both English language learners and those whose primary language is English (Lakin & Lai, 2011; Walrath, 2014). Moreover, research has revealed that the COGAT is a sensitive discriminator for giftedness (Chong, 2000) and a good predictor of future performance (Henry & Bardo, 1990; Luo, Thompson, & Detterman, 2003). It also is a good measure of verbal underachievement (Langdon, Rosenblatt, & Mellanby, 1998). Research on the new Form 7 is promising (Walrath, 2014; Warne, 2015) and suggests that the COGAT will have an important role in today's diverse environment.

Summary of K–12 Group Tests

The Stanford Achievement Test, MAT, KAT, H-NT, and COGAT are all sound, viable instruments. The Stanford Achievement Test and MAT provide outstanding measures of achievement. A particular strength of the KAT in evaluating intelligence is its set of nonverbal items. The H-NT provides a quick estimate of *g* (general intelligence) for most children but is not as valid as the COGAT for assessing minority or culturally diverse children. Each test should be used only by those who know its particular properties, strengths, and limitations.

College Entrance Tests

Two of the most widely used and well-known entrance tests are the 2016 SAT and the American College Test (ACT).

The New (2016) SAT

The motto for the SAT should be: If at first you don't succeed, try again. In March of 2016, the world saw yet another version of one of the most widely used tests in the world, the so-called SAT Suite of Assessments. Gone was earlier SAT Reasoning Test of 1995. The problem is that of the 1.7 million students who took the 1995 version in 2015, less than half, specifically, only 42% were college ready and the older test was not doing a thing to solve this problem.

In continuous use since 1926, the SAT is well known in college communities. From 1941 through April 1995, norms for the SAT were based on a sample of 10,000 students who took the test in 1941. When compared with these original norms, users in the late 1980s and early 1990s tended to score approximately 20 to 80 points lower for each of the two main sections of the test, the SAT-V (Verbal) and the SAT-M (Math). With the original mean at 500 for each of the two sections, national averages in the 1980s and early 1990s tended to run 420 for the SAT-V and 480 for the SAT-M. Numerous explanations were advanced to explain the decline, which became somewhat of a national embarrassment (Hanford, 1986).

In June 1994, the test developers announced that they would restore the national average to the 500-point level of 1941. They accomplished this by renorming the test on 1.8 million students and converting raw scores to standard scores with a mean of 500 and a standard deviation of 100. The new norms pushed up national SAT averages approximately 75 points for the verbal section and 20 points for the math. In 2002, the average scores on the SAT were 504 for the verbal section and 516 for the math section. This facelift did not, unfortunately, do much to alter the usual advantages of white and upper socioeconomic individuals. Minorities continued to be disadvantaged (Artze, 2003).

The modern 2016 SAT appears to be much more of an achievement test than an aptitude test. It corresponds to the high-school curriculum and covers the common core benchmarks adopted by most states. It is also easier than the earlier versions, testing words that students have actually encountered in college, rather than esoteric words that one is likely to encounter only on a former version of the test. According to the college board, extensive testing was conducted to ensure that no differential advantage is given to any racial or income group.

Scores on the 2016 SAT are based on a scale ranging from 400 to 1600 points, along with an optional essay for which scores range between 2 and 8. This compares to the 1995 version, for which the scale ranged from 600 to 2400 points and the essay was a mandatory part of the total score. Other important changes included reducing the answer choices from 5 to 4, reducing the number of sections, having no penalty for guessing, and, perhaps most importantly, less emphasis on speed.

While there still appears to be a consensus that familiarity with the test influences test scores, effective steps have been taken to ensure that all students get an equal opportunity to prepare for the test. The college board has partnered with Khan Academy, a nonprofit educational organization. Using items supplied by the college board, Khan Academy provides efficient and effective study programs free of charge for everyone.

To date, it has been unclear whether the new SAT will realize its promise. The holy grail of testing has been to find a valid and reliable test that is unbiased and that does not advantage rich versus poor, white versus African American, man versus woman, and so on. Hopefully, as we reach the end of the second decade of the 21st century, this goal will be achieved.

The American College Test

The ACT is another popular and widely used college entrance test. It was updated in 2005 and is particularly useful for non-native speakers of English. The ACT produces specific content scores and a composite. The content scores are in English, mathematical usage, social studies reading, and natural science reading. In expressing results, the ACT makes use of the Iowa Test of Educational Development (ITED) scale. Scores on this scale can vary between 1 and 36, with a standard deviation of 5 and a mean of 16 for high-school students and a mean of 19 for college aspirants. Figure 12.2 shows a sample profile report from the ACT.

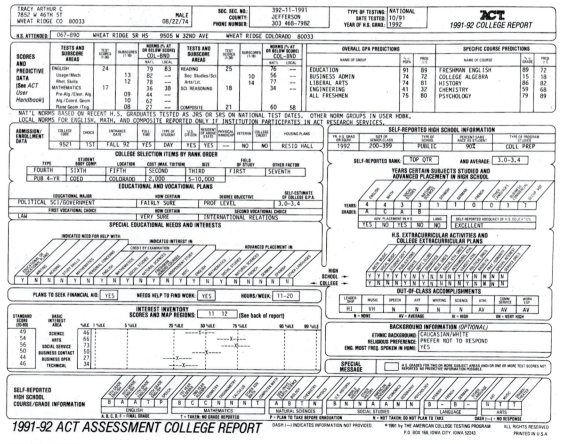

1991-92 ACT ASSESSMENT COLLEGE REPORT

FIGURE 12.2

A sample student profile from the ACT.

The ACT compares with the pre-2016 SAT in terms of predicting college GPA alone or in conjunction with high-school GPA (Stumpf & Stanley, 2002). In fact, the correlation between the two tests is quite high—in the high .80's (Pugh, 1968). However, internal consistency coefficients are not as strong in the ACT, with coefficients in the mid .90's for the composite and in the high .70's to high .80's for the four content scores.

Graduate and Professional School Entrance Tests

If you plan to go to graduate school, then you will probably have to take a graduate-school entrance test. The two most widely used tests are the GRE and the Miller Analogies Test. Tens of thousands of potential applicants also take entrance tests for professional-degree programs such as medical and law school. The LSAT serves to illustrate such tests.

Graduate Record Examination Aptitude Test

The GRE is one of the most commonly used tests for graduate-school entrance. Offered throughout the year at designated examination centers located mostly at universities and colleges in the United States and numerous other countries worldwide, the GRE purports to measure general scholastic ability. It is most frequently used in conjunction with GPA, letters of recommendation, and other academic factors in the highly competitive graduate-school selection process. The GRE contains a general section that produces verbal (GRE-V) and quantitative (GRE-Q) scores. In 2002, the third section of the GRE, which evaluates analytical reasoning (GRE-A), was changed from a multiple-choice format to an essay format. It consists of two essays that require the test taker to analyze an argument based on the evidence presented and to articulate and support an argument (Educational Testing Service, 2002). In addition to this general test for all college majors, the GRE contains an advanced section that measures achievement in at least 20 majors, such as psychology, history, and chemistry (see Figures 12.3 and 12.4).

For a number of years, plans had been underway to launch a major revision of the GRE. On April 2, 2007, the Educational Testing Service (ETS) canceled the plans; instead, two new question types were added gradually from 2007 through 2009. In December 2009, ETS announced plans to move forward with major revisions to the GRE in 2011 (Lewin, 2009). Changes include a new 130–170 scoring scale, the elimination of certain question types such as antonyms and analogies, the addition of an online calculator, and the elimination of the CAT format of question-by-question adjustment, in favor of a section-by-section adjustment (Lewin, 2009). In August 2011, the GRE revised General Test replaced the GRE® General Test (ETS, 2011). According to ETS, the GRE features a new test taker-friendly design and new questions and more closely reflects the kind of thinking required in graduate school.

With a standard mean score of 500 and a standard deviation of 100, the verbal section covers reasoning, identification of opposites, use of analogies, and paragraph comprehension. The quantitative section covers arithmetic reasoning, algebra, and geometry. However, the normative sample for the GRE is relatively small. The

FIGURE 12.3
GRE verbal ability sample items.

Directions*

In each of the following questions, a related pair of words or phrases is followed by five lettered pairs of words or phrases. Select the lettered pair that best expresses a relationship similar to that expressed in the original pair.

Sample Question

COLOR : SPECTRUM :
(A) tone : scale
(B) sound : waves
(C) verse : poem
(D) dimension : space
(E) cell : organism

Strategies for Answering

- Establish a relationship between the given pair before reading the answer choices.
- Consider relationships of kind, size, spatial contiguity, or degree.
- Read all of the options. If more than one seems correct, try to state the relationship more precisely.
- Check to see that you haven't overlooked a possible second meaning for one of the words.
- *Never* decide on the best answer without reading all of the answer choices.

Answer

The relationship between *color* and *spectrum* is not merely that of part to whole, in which case (E) or even (C) might be defended as correct. A *spectrum* is made up of a progressive, graduated series of *colors*, as a *scale* is of a progressive, graduated sequence of *tones*. Thus, (A) is the correct answer choice. In this instance, the best answer must be selected from a group of fairly close choices.

Sentence Completions

Sentence completions measure your ability to recognize words or phrases that both logically and stylistically complete the meaning of a sentence.

Directions*

Each sentence below has one or two blanks, each blank indicating that something has been omitted. Beneath the sentence are five lettered words or sets of words. Choose the word or set of words for each blank that *best* fits the meaning of the sentence as a whole.

---
* The directions are presented as they appear on the actual test.

Sample Question

Early _____ of hearing loss is _____ by the fact that the other senses are able to compensate for moderate amounts of loss, so that people frequently do not know that their hearing is imperfect.
(A) discovery . . indicated
(B) development . . prevented
(C) detection . . complicated
(D) treatment . . facilitated
(E) incidence . . corrected

Strategies for Answering

- Read the incomplete sentence carefully.
- Look for key words or phrases.
- Complete the blank(s) with your own words; see if any options are like yours.
- Pay attention to grammatical cues.
- If there are two blanks, be sure that both parts of your answer choice fit logically and stylistically into the sentence.
- After choosing an answer, read the sentence through again to see if it makes sense.

Answer

The statement that the other senses compensate for partial loss of hearing indicates that the hearing loss is not *prevented* or *corrected*; therefore, choices (B) and (E) can be eliminated. Furthermore, the ability to compensate for hearing loss certainly does not facilitate the early *treatment* (D) or the early *discovery* (A) of hearing loss. It is reasonable, however, that early *detection* of hearing loss is *complicated* by the ability to compensate for it. The best answer is (C).

Reading Comprehension Questions

Reading comprehension questions measure your ability to
- read with understanding, insight, and discrimination
- analyze a written passage from several perspectives

Passages are taken from the humanities, social sciences, and natural sciences.

Directions*

The passage is followed by questions based on its content. After reading the passage, choose the best answer to each question. Answer all questions following the passage on the basis of what is *stated* or *implied* in the passage.

GRE materials selected from GRE Practice General Test 2003–2004, 2003. Reprinted by permission of Education Testing Service, the copyright owner. Permission to reprint GRE materials does not constitute review or endorsement by Education Testing Service of this publication as a whole or of any other testing information it may contain.

psychometric adequacy of the GRE is also less spectacular than that of the SAT, both in the reported coefficients of validity and reliability and in the extensiveness of documentation. Nevertheless, the GRE is a relatively sound instrument. *but less sound than SAT*

The stability of the GRE based on Kuder-Richardson and odd–even reliability is adequate, with coefficients only slightly lower than those of the SAT. However, the predictive validity of the GRE is far from convincing.

Independent studies of the GRE vary from those that find moderate correlations between the GRE and GPA to those that find no or even a negative relationship between the two. House and Johnson (1998), for example, reported correlations ranging from .22 to .33 between GRE scores and various graduate-school courses, which would account for 4.84% to 10.89% of the variance. In 1999, House found that higher GRE scores were significantly correlated with higher grades in specific courses. Using regression analysis, Ji (1998) reported that GRE scores account for 16% to 6% of the variance in graduate GPA, indicating a correlation from .4 to approximately .25. In another study, House (1997) found that even though GRE scores were significantly correlated with students' degree completion, they were not significant predictors of grades for a group of Native American students. Another independent study found an even weaker correlation with the GRE and grad school GPA—just 6% of the variation in grades could be predicted by GRE scores (Fairtest, 2007). Moreover, false-negative rates are high, which means that students whose GRE scores would not predict success in graduate school succeed at high rates (Holmes & Beishline, 1996). Perhaps one reason for this is that students who are more willing to change tier answers tend to get higher scores (Liu, Bridgeman, Gu, Xu, & Kong, 2015).

The GRE overpredicts the achievement of younger students while underpredicting the performance of older students (House, 1998). It is noteworthy that in one program that offers a GRE waiver to students who are typically older and more experienced, a study found that students who requested and received GRE test waivers tended to perform at a higher level in an MBA program, as measured by grade point average (Leavitt, Lombard, & Morris, 2011, pp. 447–448). There are still African American–white differences, and studies that proposed a so-called "Obama Effect," which held that such differences were reduced or eliminated during certain critical points in the Obama administration, have not been supported (Stricker & Rock, 2015).

At this point, those who aspire to enter graduate school might be asking, "With its limitations, why is it that the GRE has such a critical effect on my chances for going to graduate school and on my future career?" One answer is that many schools have developed their own norms and psychometric documentation and can use the GRE, either independently or with other sources of data, to predict success in their programs. Furthermore, many graduate selection committees use the GRE broadly, as in requiring a minimum cutoff score to apply. Because more qualified students apply for graduate school than the available resources can train and job markets can absorb, the difficult job of selection must begin somewhere.

Finally, by looking at a GRE score in conjunction with GPA, graduate success can be predicted with greater accuracy than without the GRE (Morrison & Morrison, 1995). A 2001 meta-analysis of the GRE's predictive validity indicated that the GRE and undergraduate GPA can be valid predictors of graduate GPA, comprehensive examination scores, number of publications authored, and ratings by faculty (Kuncel, Hezlett, & Ones, 2001). That same year, a regression analysis conducted by Fenster, Markus, Wiedemann, Brackett, and Fernandez (2001) indicated that a linear combination of the verbal and quantitative sections of the GRE and undergraduate GPA correlated .63 with the GPA achieved in graduate school. As Melchert (1998) has noted, high achievement in any profession relies

FIGURE 12.4

GRE quantitative ability sample items.

the answer choices given.

Sample Question

When walking, a certain person takes 16 complete steps in 10 seconds. At this rate, how many complete steps does the person take in 72 seconds?
(A) 45
(B) 78
(C) 86
(D) 90
(E) 115

Strategies for Answering

- Determine what is given and what is being asked.
- Scan all answer choices before answering a question.
- When approximation is required, scan answer choices to determine the degree of approximation.
- Avoid long computations. Use reasoning instead, when possible.

Answer

72 seconds represents 7 ten-second intervals plus 2/10 of such an interval. Therefore, the person who takes 16 steps in 10 seconds will take (7.2)(16) steps in 72 seconds.

$$(7.2)(16) = (7)(16) + (0.2)(16)$$
$$= 112 + 3.2$$
$$= 115.2$$

Since the question asks for the number of complete steps, the best answer choice is (E).

Problem Solving–Data Interpretation Questions

Data interpretation questions measure your ability
- to synthesize information and select appropriate data for answering a question
- to determine that sufficient information for answering a question is not provided

The data interpretation questions usually appear in sets and are based on data presented in tables, graphs, or other diagrams.

Directions*

Each of the following questions has five answer

choices. For each of these questions, select the best of the answer choices given.

Sample Question

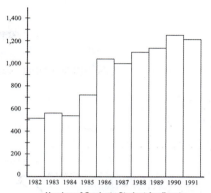

Number of Graduate Student Applicants at University X, 1982–1991

In which of the following years did the number of graduate student applicants increase the most from that of the previous year?
(A) 1985
(B) 1986
(C) 1988
(D) 1990
(E) 1991

Strategies for Answering

- Scan the set of data to see what it is about.
- Try to make visual comparisons and estimate products and quotients rather than perform computations.
- Answer questions only on the basis of data given.

Answer

This question can be answered directly by visually comparing the heights of the bars in the graph. The greatest increase in height between two adjacent bars occurs for the years 1985 and 1986. The best answer

---

* The directions are presented as they appear on the actual test.

on a "confluence" of factors. Therefore, any single predictor such as the GRE will necessarily correlate only modestly with success in a profession.

Graduate schools also frequently complain that grades no longer predict scholastic ability well because of *grade inflation*—the phenomenon of rising average college grades despite declines in average SAT scores (Kuh & Hu, 1999). Thus, many people claim that a B today is equivalent to a C 15 or 20 years ago, and that

[margin note: stop here:)]

[margin note: GRE is useful because of grade inflation + student's ability to read recommendation letters.]

an A today is equivalent to a B then. This grade inflation has led to a corresponding restriction in the range of grades. Thus, the median GPA for applicants to clinical psychology Ph.D. programs can exceed 3.5. Another reason for reliance on GRE scores is that the Freedom of Information Act grants students the right to examine their files, including letters of recommendation. Schools argue that professors and others cannot be candid while knowing the student may someday read the letter. Thus, as the validity of grades and letters of recommendation become more questionable, reliance on test scores increases, fair or not. However, students with relatively poor GRE scores can take heart in the knowledge that their score does not necessarily predict performance in graduate school.

In any case, there is a definite overall decline in verbal scores while quantitative and analytical scores are gradually rising. The mean of verbal scores in 1965 was 530. In the decades to follow, the mean continued to decline until reaching a low of 468 in 1999 and 456 in 2009—a drop of 64 points. Conversely, quantitative mean scores rose from 533 in 1965 to 565 in 1999 and 590 in 2009, an increase of 57 points (National Center for Education Statistics, 2011). This increase is mirrored in the mean analytical scores. This decrease in verbal scores has partially been explained by an increase in non-U.S. test takers that started in 1976 (National Center for Education Statistics, 1995). Because non-U.S. students tend to score higher on the quantitative portion of the GREs and lower on the verbal section, the increase from 7.5% non-U.S. examinees in 1976 to 20.5% non-U.S. examinees in 1988 is a plausible explanation for the overall pattern. However, the fact that American high-school students taking the older SATs experienced a similar pattern leads one to question if the number of non-U.S. examinees taking the GREs is the only explanation for the pattern of GRE scores. As any student knows, correlation does not imply causation.

Miller Analogies Test

A second major graduate-school entrance test is the Miller Analogies Test. Like the GRE, the Miller Analogies Test is designed to measure scholastic aptitudes for graduate studies. However, unlike the GRE, the Miller Analogies Test is strictly verbal. In 60 minutes, the student must discern logical relationships for 120 varied analogy problems, including the most difficult items found on any test (see Figure 12.5). Knowledge of specific content and a wide vocabulary are extremely useful in this endeavor. However, the most important factors appear to be the ability to see relationships and a knowledge of the various ways analogies can be formed (by sound, number, similarities, differences etc.). Used in a variety of specializations, the Miller Analogies Test offers special norms for various fields.

Odd–even reliability data for the Miller Analogies Test are adequate, with coefficients in the high .80's reported in the manual. Unfortunately, as with the GRE, the Miller Analogies Test lacks predictive validity support. Despite a substantial correlation with the GRE (coefficients run in the low .80's), validity coefficients reported in the manual for grades vary considerably from sample to sample and are only modest (median in the high .30's).

Like the GRE, the Miller Analogies Test has an age bias. Miller Analogies Test scores overpredicted the GPAs of a 25- to 34-year-old group and underpredicted the GPAs of a 35- to 44-year-old group. However, it also overpredicted achievement

FIGURE 12.5
MAT sample items.

Look at the first sample analogy below. **Pain** is the right answer because **pain** is related to PLEASURE as DARK is related to LIGHT. On the **Answer Sheet** mark **c** for the first sample to show that choice **c. pain** is the right answer. The diagram at the right shows you how to mark on your **Answer Sheet**.

SAMPLES

1. LIGHT : DARK :: PLEASURE : (*a.* picnic, *b.* day, *c.* pain, *d.* night)
2. LEAVE : DEPART :: (*a.* stay, *b.* go, *c.* home, *d.* come) : REMAIN
3. STAPLE : (*a.* clamp, *b.* paper, *c.* glue, *d.* food) :: NAIL : WOOD
4. (*a.* 4, *b.* 5, *c.* 7, *d.* 6) : 12 :: 12 : 24

How to Mark on Answer Sheet

1 ⓐ ⓑ ⬤c ⓓ

2 ⬤a ⓑ ⓒ ⓓ

Choose the proper word in the **parentheses** in Sample 2 and mark the corresponding letter in the proper place on **your Answer Sheet**. Do the same thing in the third and fourth samples.

of a 45-year-old group (House & Keeley, 1996). According to House and Keeley (1996), motivation for academic achievement may be highest in the middle adult years, causing these students to obtain grades that were higher than predicted by their test scores. These same investigators have found that the Miller Analogies Test underpredicts the GPAs of women and overpredicts those of men (House & Keeley, 1995).

Generally, the psychometric adequacy of the Miller Analogies Test is reasonable when compared with ability tests in general, but GRE scores and GPA continue to be its primary correlates. Furthermore, the Miller Analogies Test does not predict research ability, creativity, and other factors important to graduate-school and professional performance. However, as an aid in discriminating among graduate-school applications and adults at the highest level of verbal ability, the Miller Analogies Test is an excellent device as long as one keeps in mind its possible biases.

The Law School Admission Test

The LSAT provides a good example of tests for professional degree programs. LSAT problems require almost no specific knowledge. Students of any major can take it without facing bias. As with the Miller Analogies Test, some of the problems on the LSAT are among the most difficult that one can encounter on a standardization test. The LSAT is taken under extreme time pressure.

The LSAT contains three types of problems: reading comprehension, logical reasoning, and analytical reasoning. Reading comprehension problems are similar to those found on the GRE. The student is given four 450-word passages followed by approximately seven questions per passage. The content of the passages may be drawn from just about any subject—history, the humanities, the women's movement, African American literature, science, and so forth. Each passage is purposefully chosen to be complicated and densely packed with information. The questions that follow may be long and complicated. Students may be asked what was not covered as well as to draw inferences about what was covered. All of this must be done in 35 minutes.

Approximately half of the problems on the LSAT are logical reasoning problems. These provide a test stimulus as short as four lines or as long as half a page and ask for some type of logical deduction. Here is an example of a logical reasoning question, as provided by law services:

"Electrons orbit around the nucleus of an atom the way the earth orbits around the sun. It is well known that gravity is a major force that determines the orbit of the earth. We may therefore, expect that gravity is the main force that determines the orbit of an electron."

The argument attempts to prove its case by:

(A) applying well-known general laws to a specific case

(B) appealing to well-known specific cases to prove a general law about them

(C) testing the conclusion by a definite experiment

(D) appealing to an apparently similar case

(E) stating its conclusions without giving any kind of reason to think that it might be true

---

Source: *LSAT/LSDAS Registration and Information Handbook,* 1994–1995, p. 42. Copyright 1994 Law School Admission Council. Reprinted by permission.

According to Law Services, this question is a "middle difficulty" item. Approximately 60% of test takers answered correctly (D). Approximately 25% chose A. A student has some 35 minutes to complete 25 problems such as this.

Applying for law school is a little less mystical than applying to graduate school. Unlike graduate schools, the weight given to the LSAT score is openly published for each school approved by the American Bar Association. Although many law schools consider special factors such as overcoming hardship, entrance into most approved schools is based heavily on a weighted sum of GPA and LSAT scores.

The publishers of the LSAT have made available every single previously administered test since the format changed in 1991. With little variation from year to year, one can know what to expect by examining old tests. For each administration, scores are adjusted according to test difficulty; one can then compare scores from one test to the next. Law Services also provides booklets that analyze questions from past tests and explain various test-taking strategies.

The LSAT is psychometrically sound, with reliability coefficients in the .90's. It predicts first-year GPA in law school. Its content validity is exceptional in that the skills tested on the LSAT resemble the ones needed for success in the first year of law school. Although women tend to obtain lower scores than men, this does not prevent women from applying to prestigious schools. Moreover, a large-scale study found no evidence of bias in the law-school admission process (Wrightsman, 1998). The Law School Admissions Council maintains that the LSAT items go through a rigorous screening and pretesting process to eliminate bias, and that the primary reason that minorities perform less well on the LSAT is lack of preparation (Law School Admissions Council, 2011). Still, it must be said that African Americans do perform more poorly on the LSAT (Johnson, 2013). The Council advises that minority group members, particularly African Americans, are more vulnerable to test anxiety than other test takers and that the best way to avoid test anxiety is to prepare thoroughly for the LSAT.

Controversy over the bias issue continues, however (Johnson, 2013; Shultz & Zedeck, 2011). Jay Rosner, executive director of the Princeton Review Foundation, concludes that every question chosen to appear on every LSAT and SAT in the past 10 years has favored whites over African Americans (Rosner, 2003). In his view, if a test item is more likely to be answered correctly by nonminorities than by minorities, then it is a biased item. He found this to be true for every question on the LSAT. In addition, it is clear that women and minorities tend to score slightly lower on the LSAT; by some standards, this differential result also defines test bias (Black Issues in Higher Education, 2001) and has led the Law School Admissions Council to create a $10 million initiative to increase diversity in American law schools. Thus far, the Council has established a diversity committee, which has spent in excess of $5 million on projects designed to increase the number of minority men and women who attend law schools. The money has been spent, in part, on grants provided to projects that increase the enrollment of minorities in law schools (Law School Admissions Council, 2011).

However, there is evidence that may tend to nullify the arguments based on differential test results. If bias is defined not on the basis of differential item or test results but by how well these test results predict actual success in law school for each group, then the conclusions are much different. Using this second definition, if there is bias, it is in favor of minorities and women (Klein, 2002). Specifically, Klein found that even though females and minorities tend to score lower on the LSAT, the LSAT and undergraduate GPA index scores tend to overpredict their success in the first year of law school. Conversely, nonminority males tend to earn a slightly higher first-year GPA than would be predicted by their index scores. The same is generally true of the GRE and other standardized tests. It is a puzzling paradox in testing that has yet to be solved.

Nonverbal Group Ability Tests

As we have noted, nonverbal tests are needed for evaluating certain individuals. Like their individual test counterparts, nonverbal group tests may be performance tests that require the subject to do something (draw, solve maze problems), or they may be paper-and-pencil tests that provide printed nonverbal items and instruct the subject to select the best of two or more multiple-choice responses. Some nonverbal group tests can be administered without the use of language.

Raven Progressive Matrices

The Raven Progressive Matrices (RPM) test is one of the best known and most popular nonverbal group tests. Although used primarily in educational settings, the Raven is a suitable test anytime one needs an estimate of an individual's general intelligence. Only the SAT, Wechsler, and Binet tests are referenced more in the *Mental Measurements Yearbook.* One may administer the RPM to groups or individuals, from 5-year-olds to elderly adults. Instructions are simple and, if necessary, the RPM can be administered without the use of language. In fact, the test is used throughout the modern world. The RPM consists exclusively of one of the most common types of stimuli in nonverbal tests of any kind—matrices (see Figures 12.6 and 12.7). The 60 matrices of the Raven Plus are graded in difficulty (Raven, Raven, & Court, 1998). Each contains a logical pattern or design with a missing part. The subject must select the appropriate design from as many as eight choices. The test can be used with or without a time limit.

The original RPM also has 60 items, which were believed to be of increasing difficulty. However, item response and other analyses demonstrated that there were three items in the middle that were of roughly comparable difficulty. This resulted in an overestimation of the IQs of those individuals who were at the level of these items, because if they got one, they tended to get the other two. The newer 1998 Raven Plus corrects this problem (Raven et al., 1998).

Research supports the RPM as a measure of general intelligence, or Spearman's *g* (see Raven et al., 1998 for an extensive review; see also Colom, Flores-Mendoza, & Rebello, 2003). In fact, the Raven may be the best single measure of g available, as shown by a multidimensional scaling by Marshalek, Lohman, and Snow (1983) (see Figure 12.8). Because of the Raven's ability to measure general fluid intelligence, it was used in a brain-imaging study that evaluated how the differences in ability to reason and solve problems translate into differences in the firing of neurons in the brain (Gray, 2003). By conducting magnetic resonance imaging (MRI) while participants completed the matrices, brain activity involved with the task was

FIGURE 12.6
Sample Progressive
Matrices items.

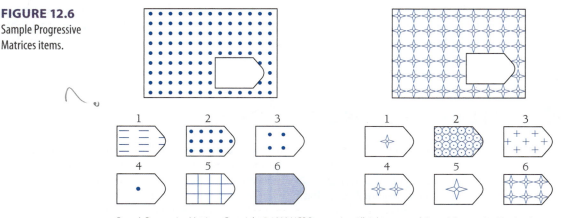

FIGURE 12.7

An advanced problem from the alternate Raven by N. E. Johnson et al., 1993.

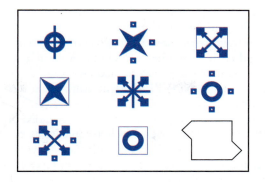

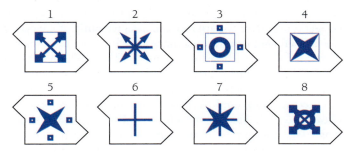

FIGURE 12.8

Marshalek, Lohman, and Snow's radix analysis of the Raven.

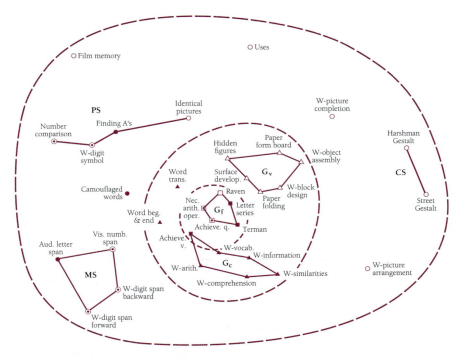

(Courtesy of Richard Snow.)

observed. The study revealed that variations in test performances were reflected in brain activity in the lateral prefrontal cortex. In addition, participants who scored highly on the Raven showed an increased amount of brain activity in the anterior cingulated cortex and the cerebellum. As well as providing insight concerning the function of different areas of the brain, the study confirmed that standard intelligence tests such as RPM are measuring the workings of essential and specific brain activities.

Figure 12.6 is the only illustration of an RPM problem that the test publisher allows to be reproduced. Recently, Johnson et al. (1993) developed a parallel research form for the RPM. Initial studies with the parallel form have revealed an alternate form reliability coefficient of .90 with comparable internal reliability coefficients between the two versions of the test (.94). Figure 12.7 illustrates one of the more difficult items from the parallel form. A product of England, the RPM was originally designed to assess military recruits independently of educational factors. For years, the lack of adequate norms for the RPM and weaknesses in the manual received criticism. In spite of these limitations, the RPM and other tests like it flourished. One can see the versatility of matrices in their wide application for such groups as young children, the culturally deprived, the language handicapped (Saccuzzo, Johnson, & Guertin, 1994), and those suffering traumatic brain injury (Hiscock, Inch, & Gleason, 2002). Analysis of available reliability studies shows a rather respectable range of coefficients, from the high .70's to low .90's (see Raven et al., 1998).

The manual for the Raven has been updated, and an impressive set of norms have been published (Raven, 1986, 1990; Raven et al., 1998). With these new norms, one can compare the performance of children from major cities around the world. Thus, a major criticism of the Raven has finally been addressed in an extremely useful and far-reaching way.

The Raven appears to minimize the effects of language and culture (Raven, 2000). For example, whereas Latinos, Latinas, and African Americans typically score some 15 points lower on the Wechsler and Binet scales than do Caucasians, there is less difference—only 7 or 8 points—with the Raven. Thus, the Raven tends to cut in half the selection bias that occurs with the Binet or Wechsler. Consequently, it has great utility in selecting disadvantaged African American and Latino and Latina children for giftedness (Saccuzzo & Johnson, 1995). Moreover, unlike the Kaufman (see Chapter 11), which also has a lower discrepancy between white and other racial groups, the Raven is actually a better measure of general intelligence than the Wechsler scales (Colom et al., 2003). With its worldwide norms and updated test manual, as well as its successful computer administered version, the Raven holds promise as one of the major players in the testing field.

Goodenough-Harris Drawing Test (G-HDT)

A remarkable nonverbal intelligence test that can be either group or individually administered is the G-HDT. Although not a standardized test in the strictest sense, the G-HDT is one of the quickest, easiest, and least expensive to administer of all ability tests. Therefore, it is widely used in educational and other settings, including clinical. A pencil and white unlined paper are the only materials needed. The subject is instructed to draw a picture of a whole man and to do the best job possible. The

G-HDT was standardized by determining those characteristics of human figure drawings that differentiated subjects in various age groups. Subjects get credit for each item included in their drawings. As a rule, each detail is given one point, with 70 points possible. For example, if only a head is included with no facial features, then the subject receives only one point. Points are added for additional details such as facial features and clothing.

The G-HDT was originally standardized in 1926 and restandardized in 1963 (Harris, 1963). Scoring of the G-HDT follows the principle of age differentiation—older children tend to get more points because of the greater accuracy and detail of their drawings. Thus, one can determine mental ages by comparing scores with those of the normative sample. Raw scores can be converted to standard scores with a mean of 100 and a standard deviation of 15. Split-half, test–retest, and interscorer reliability coefficients are good, with ranges in the high .60's to the low .90's for both old and revised forms (Dunn, 1972). Scores begin leveling off at age 14 or 15, so the use of the G-HDT is restricted primarily to children and works best with younger children (Scott, 1981). Despite the relatively outdated norms, scores on the G-HDT remain significantly related to Wechsler IQ scores (Abell, Horkheimer, & Nguyen, 1998; Alexopoulos, Haritos-Fatouros, Sakkas, Skaltsas, & Vlachos, 2000).

Because of their ease of administration and short administration time, the G-HDT and other human figure drawing tests are used extensively in test batteries. The test allows an examiner to obtain a quick but rough estimate of a child's intelligence. The G-HDT is most appropriately used in conjunction with other sources of information in a battery of tests; results based on G-HDT data alone can be quite misleading (Abell et al., 1998).

The Culture Fair Intelligence Test

All cultures tend to reinforce certain skills and activities at the expense of others. One purpose of nonverbal and performance tests is to remove factors related to cultural influences so that one can measure pure intelligence independently of learning, culture, and the like. Experience and empirical research have shown that such a test has yet to be developed. Indeed, many doubt whether such an accomplishment is even possible, although the Raven probably comes close to this goal.

The IPAT Culture Fair Intelligence Test was designed to provide an estimate of intelligence relatively free of cultural and language influences. Although this test succeeds no more in this regard than any other such attempt, the popularity of the Culture Fair Intelligence Test reflects the strong desire among users for a test that reduces cultural factors as much as possible (Tan & Tan, 1998).

Constructed under the direction of R. B. Cattell, the Culture Fair Intelligence Test is a paper-and-pencil procedure that covers three levels (ages 4–8 and mentally disabled adults, ages 8–12 and randomly selected adults, and high-school age and above-average adults). Two parallel forms are available.

Standardization varies according to age level. Kuder-Richardson reliabilities are only in the .70's, with substantially lower test–retest coefficients. The test has been correlated with a wide variety of other tests with mixed results. Correlations with the Wechsler and Binet tests are quite good, with a range of .56 to .85. Also, normative data from Western European countries, the United States, and

Australia are comparable. Thus, if one wishes to estimate intelligence in a Western European or Australian individual, the Culture Fair Intelligence Test is probably the instrument of choice. The Culture Fair Test is viewed as an acceptable measure of fluid intelligence (Colom & Garcia-Lopez, 2002; Rammsayer & Brandler, 2002), although the norms are becoming outdated, and more work is needed if the Culture Fair Test is to compete with the Raven.

Standardized Tests Used in the U.S. Civil Service System

The number and variety of group ability tests for measuring aptitude for various occupations are staggering. The General Aptitude Test Battery (GATB), for example, is a reading ability test that purportedly measures aptitude for a variety of occupations.

The U.S. Employment Service developed the GATB for use in making employment decisions in government agencies. It attempts to measure a wide range of aptitudes from general intelligence (g) to manual dexterity. The GATB also produces scores for motor coordination, form perception (awareness of relevant details and ability to compare and discriminate various shapes), and clerical perception (e.g., the ability to proofread). Scores are also available for verbal, numerical, and spatial aptitudes.

The GATB was originally standardized in 1952 on a sample of 4000 people believed to represent the working population of the United States in 1940. Stratified according to gender, education, occupation, and geographic location, the sample ranged in age from 18 to 54. The mean educational level of the sample, 11.0 years, reveals that the GATB is most appropriate for those who have not graduated from college. Moreover, with rapidly changing times and the advent of high technology, the GATB may be out of date (see, e.g., Avolio & Waidman, 1990; Vandevijer & Harsveld, 1994).

The GATB has engendered considerable controversy because it used within-group norming prior to the passage of the Civil Rights Act of 1991. In within-group norming, individuals are compared with others within a specific subgroup. For example, women may be compared only with other women; African Americans only with other African Americans. Such norming practices were justified on the basis of fairness. If men consistently outperform women on a particular test, then, given an equal number of men and women applying for a job, more men will be selected. However, the Civil Rights Act of 1991 outlawed within-group norming, arguing that such norming was reverse discrimination (see Brown, 1994). Today, any kind of score adjustments through within-group norming in employment practices is strictly forbidden by law (see Kittaeff, 2011, p. 83). (For more on these issues, see Chapter 21.)

Standardized Tests in the U.S. Military: The Armed Services Vocational Aptitude Battery

Designed for the Department of Defense, the Armed Services Vocational Aptitude Battery (ASVAB) is administered to more than 1.3 million individuals each year. A multiple aptitude battery, the ASVAB was designed for students in grades 11 and 12 and in postsecondary schools. The test yields scores used in both educational and military settings. In the latter, ASVAB results can help identify students who potentially qualify for entry into the military and can recommend assignment to various military occupational training programs.

The ASVAB consists of 10 subtests: general science, arithmetic reasoning, word knowledge, paragraph comprehension, numeral operations, coding speed, auto and shop information, mathematics knowledge, mechanical comprehension, and electronics information. These subtests are grouped into various composites, including three academic composites—academic ability, verbal, and math; four occupational composites—mechanical and crafts, business and clerical, electronics and electrical, and health and social; and an overall composite that reflects general ability.

The psychometric characteristics of the ASVAB are excellent. The most recent form was produced in 2002 when the earlier version underwent a major revision.

Since the late 1990s, the military has presented the ASVAB via computer rather than in the traditional paper-and-pencil format (see Hambrick et al., 2011; Moreno, Segall, & Hetter, 1997). Through this computerized format, subjects can be tested *adaptively*, meaning that the questions given to each person can be based on his or her unique ability. Briefly, adaptive testing of ability involves presenting an item of a known level of difficulty and then presenting either a more difficult or a less difficult item, depending on whether the subject is correct. The procedure cuts testing time almost in half and is far less fatiguing than the complete test. (We discuss computer-adaptive testing in depth in Chapter 15.) After many political battles, the adaptive version of the ASVAB was finally put into use in the late 1990s (Sands, Waters, & McBride, 1997).

Summary

Standardized ability tests are available for just about any purpose. There appears to be no end to the construction of this type of test. Relative ease in scoring and administration gives group ability tests a major advantage over individual tests. In many cases, the results from group tests are as stable and valid as those from individual tests. However, low scores, wide discrepancies between two group test results, or wide discrepancies between a group test result and some other indicator such as grades are reasons for exercising caution in interpreting results. When in doubt, users of group ability tests should refer the problem to a competent professional who can administer an individual ability test. The public school system makes the most extensive use of group ability tests. Indeed, many sound tests exist for all levels from kindergarten through 12th grade. Achievement tests for this age include the Stanford Achievement Test and the Metropolitan Achievement Test (MAT).

College and graduate-school entrance tests also account for a large proportion of the group ability tests used in the United States. The most popular college entrance tests include the SAT and the American College Test (ACT). Students looking toward postgraduate work may have to take the GRE, the Miller Analogies Test, or a more specialized test such as the Law School Admission Test (LSAT).

Several nonverbal group ability tests have proven helpful for determining intelligence in certain populations. The Raven Progressive Matrices (RPM) and the Goodenough-Harris Drawing Test (G-HDT) can provide helpful data on intelligence; the latest edition of the former has norms that allow worldwide comparisons. The IPAT Culture Fair Intelligence Test also provides good data on intelligence; however, it may soon be obsolete without further revisions.

Other group ability tests can help vocational counselors assess ability for certain occupations; the General Aptitude Test Battery (GATB) is one. Still other group ability tests measure aptitude for advanced or professional training. Developed for the military, the Armed Services Vocational Aptitude Battery (ASVAB) provides helpful data for both military and civilian applications.

In viewing group ability tests, one gets the impression that there is almost no limit to the scope and applicability of psychological tests.

Applications in Clinical and Counseling Settings

LEARNING OBJECTIVES

When you have completed this chapter, you should be able to:

▶ Identify the major characteristics of a structured personality test

▶ Identify the underlying assumption of the first structured personality test (the Woodworth Personal Data Sheet)

▶ Identify the assumptions of early structured personality tests based on the logical-content strategy

▶ Briefly discuss the strategy used in construction of the MMPI and MMPI-2

▶ Describe the K and F scales on the MMPI and MMPI-2

▶ Identify strengths and weaknesses of the MMPI and MMPI-2

▶ Explain how one uses factor analysis to build structured personality tests

▶ Explain the approach to test construction used in the NEO Personality Inventory

▶ Briefly describe the EPPS and explain the meaning of an ipsative score

dichotomous

Personality test

n his junior year in college, Mike went to the university counseling center for help in finding a direction in life. To aid him in his quest, a psychologist suggested that he respond to a long list of items known as the California Psychological Inventory (CPI). The CPI is a structured personality test used in counseling settings that provides a list of statements and asks the subject to respond "True" or "False" to each. It is widely used as a tool in career assessment (Gasser, Larson, & Borgen, 2004, p. 349; Gough, 1995). The statements included such choices as these: "I like to read mystery stories." "I am usually alert to my environment." "I would rather follow others than be the leader." "I like to solve difficult problems." "My father is a good man." It took Mike approximately an hour to respond to the 462 items.

A week later, Mike returned for an interpretation of his test scores. The psychologist told him that the test indicated he was highly effective in dealing with other people; his response pattern resembled the pattern of individuals who make effective leaders. The CPI also indicated that Mike could control his desires and impulses and express them effectively and appropriately.

How did the counseling psychologist decide that Mike's responses reflected specific traits and characteristics such as leadership ability and impulse control? Did the interpretations really reflect Mike's characteristics? How stable were the results? Will the CPI indicate after 10 years that Mike still has leadership qualities? This chapter explores these and related questions.

Recall that people have developed tests in part to help solve the problems that face modern societies. Tests of mental ability were created to distinguish those with subnormal mental abilities from those with normal abilities in order to enhance the education of both groups. However, there is far more to being human than having normal or subnormal mental capabilities. It is not enough to know that a person is high or low in such factors as speed of calculation, memory, range of knowledge, and abstract thinking. To make full use of information about a person's mental abilities, one must also know how that person uses those abilities. All the mental abilities in the world remain inert in someone who sits in the corner of a room all day. But even modest mental abilities can go far in a high-energy individual who relates well to others and is organized, persistent, determined, and motivated. These nonintellective aspects of human behavior, typically distinguished from mental abilities, are called *personality characteristics*. Such characteristics are of vital concern in clinical and counseling settings.

One can define *personality* as the relatively stable and distinctive patterns of behavior that characterize an individual and his or her reactions to the environment. Structured personality tests attempt to evaluate personality traits, personality types, personality states, and other aspects of personality, such as self-concept. *Personality traits* refer to relatively enduring dispositions—tendencies to act, think, or feel in a certain manner in any given circumstance and that distinguish one person from another. *Personality types* refer to general descriptions of people; for example, avoiding types have low social interest and low activity and cope by avoiding social situations. *Personality states* refer to emotional reactions that vary from one situation to another. Finally, *self-concept* refers to a person's self-definition or, according to C. R. Rogers (1959a), an organized and relatively consistent set of assumptions that a person has about himself or herself. This chapter focuses on the measurement of personality traits, with some discussion of personality types and self-concept.

Before the first Binet scale was developed, Alfred Binet hypothesized that a person's pattern of intellectual functioning might reveal information about personality factors (Binet & Henri, 1895, 1896). Subsequent investigators agreed with Binet's hypothesis (Hart & Spearman, 1912; Terman, 1916; Thorndike, 1921), and this hypothesis continues to find support (Groth-Marnat, 1999; Kossowska, 2002; von Stumm, Chamorro-Premuzic, & Ackerman, 2011). However, specific tests of human personality were not developed until World War I, which created a need to distinguish people on the basis of emotional well-being.

Like pioneers in the measurement of mental ability, the early developers of personality tests traveled in uncharted territory. Imagine yourself faced with the task of measuring some aspect of human behavior. How would you begin? You could observe and record a person's behavior. However, this approach did not work for early investigators because their task was to identify emotionally unstable military recruits; the volume of applicants for military service in the United States during World War I was so great that it became impossible to use the one available method of the time—the psychiatric interview. Psychologists needed a measure of emotional functioning so they could evaluate large numbers of people and screen out those who were unfit for military service. To meet this need, psychologists used **self-report questionnaires** that provided a list of statements and required subjects to respond in some way to each, such as marking "True" or "False" to indicate whether the statement applied to them.

The general procedure in which the subject is asked to respond to a written statement is known as the *structured,* or objective, method of personality assessment, as distinguished from the *projective* method (see Chapter 14). As their name implies, structured measures of personality, also known as "objective" measures, are characterized by structure and lack of ambiguity. A clear and definite stimulus is provided, and the requirements of the subject are evident and specific. An example of a structured personality test item is "Respond 'yes' or 'no' to the statement 'I am happy.'" In contrast, a projective test item may provide a picture of an inkblot and ask "What might this be?" In a projective personality test, the stimulus is ambiguous and the subject has few guidelines about what type of response is required.

Strategies of Structured Personality Test Construction

Like measures of mental ability, personality measures evolved through several phases. New features appeared as problems with older approaches became evident. In the realm of structured personality testing, many approaches or strategies have been tried. Psychologists disagree on how these strategies should be classified, what they should be called, and even how many distinctly different strategies exist. At the broadest level, the strategies are deductive and empirical. One can in turn divide each of these strategies as follows. Deductive strategies comprise the logical-content and the theoretical approach. Empirical strategies comprise the criterion-group and the factor analysis method. (See Figure 13.1.) Some procedures combine two or more of these strategies.

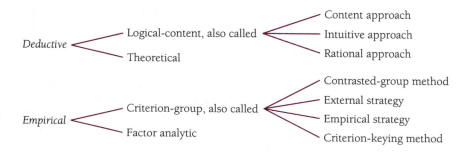

Deductive Strategies

Deductive strategies use reason and deductive logic to determine the meaning of a test response. The logical-content method has test designers select items on the basis of simple face validity; in the theoretical approach, test construction is guided by a particular psychological theory.

Logical-Content Strategy

The logical-content strategy, as its name implies, uses reason and deductive logic in the development of personality measures. In the most general use of this strategy, the test designer tries to logically deduce the type of content that should measure the characteristic to be assessed. For example, if one wants to measure eating behavior, it makes sense to include statements such as "I frequently eat between meals." Statements that have no direct logical relevance to eating behavior, such as "I enjoy solving complex puzzles," would not be included in tests that use the logical-content strategy. The principal distinguishing characteristic of this strategy is that it assumes that the test item accurately describes the subject's personality and behavior. If a person marks "True" for the statement "I am outgoing," then testers assume that he or she *is* outgoing. Initial efforts to measure personality used the logical-content approach as the primary strategy.

Theoretical Strategy

As its name implies, the theoretical strategy begins with a theory about the nature of the particular characteristic to be measured. As in the logical-content approach, an attempt is then made to deduce items. In the theoretical approach, however, items must be consistent with the theory. If the theory hypothesizes that personality can be broken down into six major areas, then developers strive to create items that tap each of these six areas. In addition, theoretical strategies demand that every item in a scale be related to the characteristic being measured. Thus, the theoretical approach attempts to create a homogeneous scale and, toward this end, may use statistical procedures such as item analysis.

Empirical Strategies

Empirical strategies rely on data collection and statistical analyses to determine the meaning of a test response or the nature of personality and psychopathology. These strategies retain the self-report features of the deductive strategies in that subjects are asked to respond to items that describe their own views, opinions, and feelings. However, empirical strategies attempt to use experimental research to determine empirically the meaning of a test response, the major dimensions of personality, or both. In the criterion-group approach, test designers choose items to distinguish a group of individuals with certain characteristics, the *criterion group,* from a control group; the factor analytic approach uses the statistical technique of factor analysis to determine the meaning of test items.

Criterion-Group Strategy

The criterion-group strategy begins with a criterion group, or a collection of individuals who share a characteristic such as leadership or schizophrenia. Test constructors select and administer a group of items to all the people in this criterion group as well as to a control group that represents the general population. Constructors then attempt to locate items that distinguish the criterion and control groups, or how the two groups *contrast.*

Suppose that a group of aggressive individuals mark "True" to items such as "I am not aggressive," "I like to attend concerts," and "I would rather read than write" significantly more often than did individuals in a control group. These items could then be included on an aggression scale. When new subjects endorse a large proportion of items on the aggression scale, one may hypothesize that they are aggressive because they endorsed the same items that distinguished aggressive individuals from control individuals. The content of the items is of little consequence. What matters is that aggressive individuals marked "True" to these items, thereby discriminating the aggressive individuals from the control group. As J. S. Wiggins (1973, p. 394) noted some time ago, depressed individuals respond "False" significantly more than controls do to the statement "I sometimes tease animals." There is no logical or rational reason for this response. The actual content or face validity of an item in the criterion-group strategy is of little importance. Instead, the approach attempts to determine which items discriminate the criterion and control groups.

Once distinguishing items have been determined for one sample of subjects to represent the criterion group, the next step is to *cross-validate* the scale by checking how well it distinguishes an independent criterion sample—individuals also known to possess the same characteristics to be measured—from a control group. If the scale significantly distinguishes the two groups, then it is said to have been cross-validated. Once a scale has been developed, data from the normal controls can be used to obtain standard scores. One can then determine how far above or below the mean of the normal group each new subject scores in standardized units. Thus, a subject's score on each scale can be converted to percentiles (see Chapter 2).

After a scale has been constructed and cross-validated, the third step in the criterion approach is to conduct additional research to ascertain empirically what it means when subjects endorse a large number of items on a particular scale. An independent group of people who score two standard deviations above the mean on an aggression scale, for example, may be studied intensely to determine how they describe themselves, how others describe them, the characteristics of their family backgrounds, and so on.

Factor Analytic Strategy

The factor analytic strategy uses factor analysis to derive empirically the basic dimensions of personality. Recall from Chapter 3 that factor analysis boils down or reduces data to a small number of descriptive units or dimensions. A test, for example, may have two scales that correlate highly, such as hostility and aggression. This correlation means that the two overlap in what they measure; that is, they share common variance. Both, for example, may be related to paranoid personality, a problem characterized in part by aggression and hostility. The same test may also have two other scales, suspicion and defensiveness, variables also associated with the paranoid personality. These two scales may correlate not only with each other but also with the hostility and aggression scales. Thus, all four scales may share common variance. If one can show that a substantial proportion of the variability in all four scales is related to some common factor, then a factor analyst could argue that the test actually has only one scale that is related to the paranoid personality.

common

Factor analysts begin with an empirical database consisting of the intercorrelation of a large number of items or tests. They then factor analyze these intercorrelations, typically to find the minimum number of factors that account for as much of the variability in the data as possible. They then attempt to label these factors by ascertaining what the items related to a particular factor have in common.

Criteria Used in Selecting Tests for Discussion

There are far too many structured personality tests to discuss them all adequately in a book devoted exclusively to the subject, let alone in a single chapter. (We prefer the term *tests* for general purposes, although for specific procedures other terms such as *inventories, techniques, scales,* and *assessment procedures* are often preferred.) However, all available structured personality tests can be classified according to whether they use one or some combination of the four strategies just discussed: logical-content, theoretical, criterion-group, and factor analytic. The tests in the discussion that follows have been chosen because (1) they illustrate each of the major strategies; (2) they are widely used, as indicated by surveys of psychological test usage in the United States (Archer, Buffington-Vollum, Stredny, & Handel, 2006; Lubin, Larson, & Matarazzo, 1984; Watkins, Campbell, Nieberding, & Hallmark, 1995); (3) they interest the research community, as determined by publication in major journals; and (4) they show historical value, as determined by the introduction of new concepts in structured personality testing.

The Logical-Content Strategy

We begin our discussion with the first personality test ever developed—the Woodworth Personal Data Sheet. We then present other examples of tests based on the logical-content approach.

Woodworth Personal Data Sheet

The first personality inventory ever, the Woodworth Personal Data Sheet, was developed during World War I and published in its final form after the war (Woodworth, 1920). Its purpose was to identify military recruits who would be likely to break down in combat. The final form of the Woodworth contained 116 questions to which the individual responded "Yes" or "No." The items were selected from lists of known symptoms of emotional disorders and from the questions asked by psychiatrists in their screening interviews. In effect, the scale was a paper-and-pencil psychiatric interview (Gibby & Zickar, 2008). The Woodworth consisted of questions similar to these: "Do you drink a fifth of whiskey a day?" "Do you wet the bed at night?" "Do you frequently daydream?" "Do you usually feel in good health?" "Do you usually sleep soundly at night?" The Woodworth yielded a single score, providing a global measure of functioning. Only those recruits who reported many symptoms received an interview. In this way, the military could concentrate its efforts on the most likely candidates for rejection. *interesting*

Although its items were selected through the logical-content approach, the Woodworth had two additional features. First, items endorsed by 25% or more of a normal sample in the scored direction were excluded from the test. This technique tended to reduce the number of *false positives*—that is, subjects identified by the test as risks but who would most likely be cleared in an actual interview. Second, only those symptoms that occurred twice as often in a previously diagnosed neurotic group as in normals were included in the first version of the test.

The success of the Woodworth in solving the problem of mass screening stimulated the development of a host of structured tests aimed at measuring personality characteristics. These tests borrowed items from each other, particularly the Woodworth, and used a variety of methods for clustering and scoring items. However, all of them assumed that test responses had items that could be taken at face value; that is, they assumed the face validity of a test response. If someone marked "No" to "I wet the bed," for example, it was assumed that he or she had not wet the bed. *issue w face v.*

Early Multidimensional Logical-Content Scales

Two of the best-known early tests developed with the logical-content strategy were the Bell Adjustment Inventory and the Bernreuter Personality Inventory. The Bell attempted to evaluate the subject's adjustment in a variety of areas such as home life, social life, and emotional functioning. The Bernreuter could be used for subjects as young as age 13 and included items related to six personality traits such as introversion, confidence, and sociability. Each was first published in the 1930s and, in contrast to the Woodworth, produced more than one score. These multidimensional procedures laid a foundation for the many modern tests that yield multiple scores rather than a single overall index.

Mooney Problem Checklist

Clinical

Few modern tests rely extensively on the logical-content method of test construction. One of the few such tests still in use is the Mooney Problem Checklist (see Steverink, Veenstra, Oldehinkel, Gans, & Rosmalen, 2011; Woolfson, Taylor, & Mooney, 2011), published in 1950. The Mooney contains a list of problems that recurred in clinical case history data and in the written statements of problems submitted by approximately 4000 high-school students. It resembles the Woodworth in that subjects who check an excessive number of items are considered to have difficulties. The main interpretive procedure, as with any checklist test, is to assume the face validity of a test response (Wood & McMurran, 2013). Thus, if a subject checks an item related to finances, then testers assume that the person is having financial difficulties.

Criticisms of the Logical-Content Approach

Psychologists involved in the development of the Woodworth and the plethora of subsequent tests satisfied an important need. These tests proved extremely useful as screening devices and methods of obtaining information about a person without an extensive interview. Before long, however, the weaknesses of the logical-content strategy became evident.

In assuming that one can interpret test items at face value, the logical-content strategy also assumes that the subject takes a normal approach to the test, complies with the instructions, reads each item, and answers as honestly as possible. Even if this were all so, subjects might not be able to evaluate their own behavior objectively in the area covered by the test item (e.g., "I never drink too much alcohol"). And even if subjects can provide accurate self-evaluation, they still may not interpret the test item in the same way as the test constructor or test user, which is also an implicit assumption of the logical content strategy. For example, what does "wet the bed" really mean?

None of these assumptions is necessarily true, and assuming that they are true is certain to produce errors. Indeed, structured personality tests based on the logic of face validity were so sharply criticized that the entire structured approach to personality was all but discarded (Ellis, 1946; Landis, 1936; Landis, Zubin, & Katz, 1935; McNemar & Landis, 1935). It was finally rescued by the introduction of a new conceptualization in personality testing, the empirical criterion-group strategy.

The Criterion-Group Strategy

Just when the development of an adequate structured personality test seemed nothing more than a pipe dream, the Minnesota Multiphasic Personality Inventory (MMPI) introduced several innovations in the construction of structured personality tests. Though not entirely new, the main idea—assume nothing about the meaning of a subject's response to a test item—was the only way of meeting objections to face validity. Because making assumptions had been the downfall of the logical-content approach, developers of the MMPI argued that the meaning of a test response could be determined only through empirical research. This section discusses the MMPI as well as its most recent offspring, the MMPI-2.

Minnesota Multiphasic Personality Inventory

The Minnesota Multiphasic Personality Inventory (MMPI and MMPI-2) is a true–false self-report questionnaire. Statements are typically of the self-reference type such as "I like good food" and "I never have trouble falling asleep." Subjects mark "True" or "False" for each statement as it applies to themselves. The heart of the test consists of its validity, clinical, and content scales. The validity scales provide information about the person's approach to testing, such as whether an attempt was made either to "fake bad" by endorsing more items of pathological content than any person's actual problems could justify or to "fake good" by avoiding pathological items. The clinical scales were designed to identify psychological disorders such as depression and schizophrenia. Today, clinicians use formulas, the pattern of scores, codebooks that provide extensive research summaries on the meaning of test scores, and clinical judgment to assess the meaning of the clinical scales. The content scales consist of groups of items that are empirically related to a specific content area. For example, the anger scale contains references to irritability, hotheadedness, and other symptoms of anger or control problems. Subjects obtain a raw score on each scale based on the number of items they have marked in the scored direction. Raw scores are then converted to T scores, with a mean of 50 and a standard deviation of 10 (see Figure 13.2).

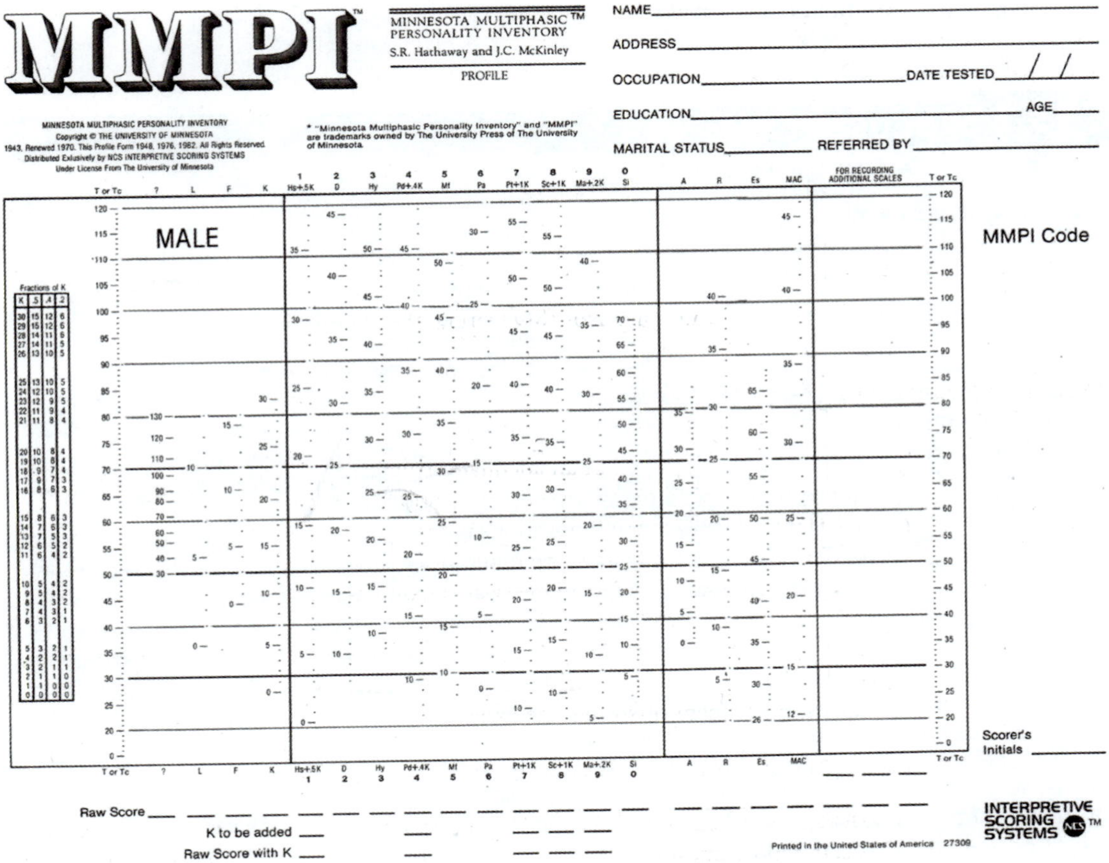

FIGURE 13.2

An MMPI profile sheet.

(Reproduced by permission of University of Minnesota Press.)

Purpose

Like the Woodworth, the purpose of the MMPI and MMPI-2 is to assist in distinguishing normal from abnormal groups. Specifically, the test was designed to aid in the diagnosis or assessment of the major psychiatric or psychological disorders. For the most part, it is still used for this purpose. The MMPI requires at least a sixth-grade reading ability; the MMPI-2 requires an eighth-grade reading ability. Administrators must take great care to make sure the individual can read at the appropriate level and has an IQ within normal limits (see Focused Example 13.1).

Original Development of the Scales

Beginning with a pool of 1000 items selected from a wide variety of sources, including case histories, psychological reports, textbooks, and existing tests, the original authors of the MMPI, S. R. Hathaway, a psychologist, and J. C. McKinley, a physician, selected 504 items judged to be relatively independent of one another. The scales were then determined empirically by presenting the items to criterion and control groups.

13.1   FOCUSED EXAMPLE

Reading the MMPI

In one interesting case, a 16-year-old girl was detained by the juvenile court. Her mother had reported her to the police, stating she could not be controlled. A few hours before the girl's preliminary hearing, the judge requested psychological testing to aid in the assessment process. A psychology intern was the only professional staff member available. Though relatively inexperienced with the MMPI, he tried to carry out the judge's orders by administering the test. The intern warned the girl of the validity scales, stating that he could tell if she tried to fake. When presented with the test booklet, the girl groaned and stated, "This test is too hard." The intern assured her not to worry, that there were no right or wrong answers. "Oh, I hope I pass," the girl said. "I'm not good at tests."

Rather than the usual 1 to 2 hours, she took more than 3 hours to complete the MMPI, finishing moments before her court hearing began. The intern immediately scored it and found that she had marked nearly half of the 64 items in the scored direction on the F scale, one of the validity scales containing highly pathological content. Because the average for the general population on this scale is four items in the scored direction, with an average of eight items in the scored direction for adolescents, the girl's endorsement of 30 items indicated she had not taken a normal approach to testing and suggested to the intern that she had "faked bad" by deliberately endorsing pathological items.

In court, the judge asked the intern what the results showed. "I can't tell," said the intern, "because she tried to fake." "Did you fake?" asked the judge. "No sir," said the girl, "I swear I didn't." The judge told her to go back and take the test again.

Irate, the intern again warned the girl not to fake. "Oh, I hope I pass," she moaned. "Just answer truthfully and you'll pass," said the intern. She completed the test, and the intern immediately scored it. The results were almost identical to those for the previous testing. The intern rushed into the testing room and scolded the girl for faking again. "I knew I'd flunk that test," she said. "It was too hard for me." Finally, it dawned on the intern to ask whether she could read the test. A reading test revealed that she could read at only the fourth-grade level. Most of the items were therefore incomprehensible to her. The embarrassed intern was forced to go back into court and explain what had happened. No doubt he never again administered the MMPI without checking the subject's reading level.

The criterion groups used to develop the original MMPI consisted of psychiatric inpatients at the University of Minnesota Hospital. These psychiatric patients were divided into eight groups according to their psychiatric diagnoses. Though the original pool of patients had 800 people, this number was substantially reduced in order to find homogeneous groupings with sufficient agreement on diagnoses. The final eight criterion groups each consisted of approximately 50 patients:

▶ *hypochondriacs*—individuals preoccupied with the body and fears of illness;
▶ *depressed patients*;
▶ *hysterics*—primarily individuals who showed a physical problem with no physical cause, such as physical pain without cause;
▶ *psychopathic deviates*—delinquent, criminal, or antisocial individuals;
▶ *paranoids*—individuals who showed symptoms such as poor reality testing (e.g., delusions in which they falsely believed that people were plotting against them);
▶ *psychasthenics*—individuals with a disorder characterized by excessive doubts and unreasonable fears;
▶ *schizophrenics*—individuals with a psychotic disorder involving dramatic symptoms (such as hallucinations) and thinking problems (such as illogical reasoning); and
▶ *hypomanics*—individuals with a disorder characterized by hyperactivity and irritability (see Table 13.1).

Those in the criterion groups were then compared with some 700 controls consisting primarily of relatives and visitors of the patients, excluding mental patients, in the University of Minnesota Hospital. The use of this control group was perhaps the original MMPI's greatest source of criticism. There is little basis for saying that

TABLE 13.1 Original Criterion Groups for the MMPI

Hypochondriacs	Patients who suffer from overconcern of bodily symptoms and express conflicts through bodily (somatic) symptoms
Depressives	Patients with depressed mood, loss of appetite, loss of interest, suicidal thoughts, and other depressive symptoms
Hysterics	Immature individuals who overdramatize their plight and may exhibit physical symptoms for which no physical cause exists
Psychopathic deviates	Individuals who are antisocial and rebellious and exploit others without remorse or anxiety
Paranoids	Individuals who show extreme suspicions, hypersensitivity, and delusions
Psychasthenics	Individuals plagued by excessive self-doubts, obsessive thoughts, anxiety, and low energy
Schizophrenics	Disorganized, highly disturbed individuals out of contact with reality and having difficulties with communication, interpersonal relations, sensory abnormalities (e.g., hallucinations), or motor abnormalities (e.g., catatonia)
Hypomanics	Individuals in a high-energy, agitated state with poor impulse control, inability to sleep, and poor judgment

the relatives of patients in a large city university hospital are representative of the general population, although the control group was augmented by other subjects such as a group of recent high-school graduates. The MMPI-2, by contrast, has a large and relatively good representative control sample.

Despite its weakness, the original control group did provide a reference sample. After an item analysis was conducted, items that separated the criterion from the control group were included on one or more of the eight scales.

To cross-validate the scales, independent samples of the criterion and control groups were administered the items. To qualify as cross-validated, a scale had to distinguish the criterion group from the control group at the .05 level of significance (i.e., the probability of obtaining differences by chance is less than 5 out of 100).

In addition to the eight scales just described, two content scales were added: the masculinity-femininity (MF) scale, which contained items differentially endorsed by men and women, and the social-introversion (Si) scale, which measures introversion and extroversion. These two scales plus the eight scales already described constitute the original 10 clinical scales of the MMPI.

Because the logical-content approach had been criticized for its many assumptions, Hathaway and McKinley developed special scales called *validity scales* to measure test-taking attitude and to assess whether the subject took a normal, honest approach to the test (see Table 13.2). The L, or lie, scale was designed to detect individuals who attempted to present themselves in an overly favorable way.

The K scale served the same purpose but was empirically constructed. In deriving the K scale, Hathaway and McKinley compared the MMPI scores of nondisturbed individuals showing normal patterns with the MMPI scores of disturbed individuals who produced normal MMPI patterns—that is, they showed no scales that deviated significantly from the mean. The K scale thus attempts to locate those items that distinguished normal from abnormal groups when both groups produced a normal test pattern. It was assumed that pathological groups would produce normal patterns because of defensiveness, a tendency to hide or deny psychological problems, and

TABLE 13.2   Original Validity Scales of the MMPI

Lie scale (L)		Fifteen rationally derived items included in both the MMPI and MMPI-2 designed to evaluate a naive attempt to present oneself in a favorable light. The items reflect personal weaknesses, such as "I never lose control of myself when I drive." Most people are willing to admit to these weaknesses. People who score high on this scale are unwilling to acknowledge minor flaws.
Infrequency scale (F)		Of the original 64 items from the MMPI developed to detect deviant response patterns, 60 were retained for the MMPI-2. These are items that are scored infrequently (less than 10%) by the normal population. The F scale contains items such as "I am aware of a special presence that others cannot perceive." High scores on the F scale invalidate the profile.
K scale		Thirty items included on both the MMPI and MMPI-2 that detect attempts to deny problems and present oneself in a favorable light. People who score high on this scale are attempting to project an image of self-control and personal effectiveness. Extremely high scores on this scale invalidate the profile.

that this defensiveness could be determined by comparing these individuals to nondisturbed normals.

The F or infrequency scale, which is designed to detect individuals who attempt to fake bad, consists of those items endorsed by less than 10% of the control group. Of the 64 items on the F scale, most of which contain pathological content such as "Odd odors come to me at times," the average number of items endorsed in the scored direction is four. Anyone who marks a lot of these items is taking an unusual approach to the test. Thus, high F scores bring the validity of the whole profile into question.

Finally, although it is referred to as a validity scale, the "cannot say" scale consists simply of the items to which the subject failed to respond either "True" or "False." If as few as 10% of the items are omitted, then the entire profile is invalid.

Initial Interpretations

For all of the scales, the control group provided the reference for which standard scores were determined. McCall's *T*, with a mean of 50 and a standard deviation of 10, was used to compute standard scores. Subjects with *T* scores of 50 were thus at the mean of the control sample for any given scale. *T* scores of 70, two standard deviations above the mean, were considered significantly elevated for the MMPI. With the new norms for the MMPI-2, *T* scores of 65 are now considered significant.

The original approach taken to interpret the MMPI was simple and straightforward. Because the scales significantly discriminated the criterion groups from control groups and withstood the test of cross-validation, most users assumed that individuals with characteristics similar to those of a criterion group would have significant elevation on the appropriate scale. Schizophrenics, for example, would show significant elevation on the schizophrenia scale, hysterics would show elevation on the hysteria scale, and so on. Unfortunately, this assumption turned out to be false. Experience with the MMPI rapidly revealed that only a relatively small number of disturbed subjects showed elevation on only a single scale. More often, elevation was found in two, three, four, or even all of the scales. Thus, a problem had arisen: What did the test mean when someone showed elevation on the hysteria, psychopathic deviate, schizophrenia, and hypomania scales? Thank goodness there is no such thing as a hysterical psychopathic hypomanic schizophrenic!

To deal with multiple-scale elevations, clinicians made use of pattern (configural) analysis, which the test authors had originally suggested (Hathaway & McKinley, 1943). This change led to an avalanche of studies and proposals for identifying clinical groups on the basis of patterns of MMPI scores (e.g., Meehl & Dahlstrom, 1960). However, early investigations soon revealed the futility of this approach (Garfield & Sineps, 1959; Loy, 1959; Meikle & Gerritse, 1970). Either the rules were so complex that only an extremely small portion of the profiles met the criteria, such as the Gilberstadt and Duker (1965) rules, or the rules led to diagnoses that were no more accurate than those made by untrained nonprofessionals (Meehl, 1954, 1956, 1957; Meehl & Rosen, 1955). Led by Meehl, clinicians began to look at the two highest scales.

Meehl's Extension of the Empirical Approach

Pointing to the possible advantages of analyzing the two highest scales, or *two-point code*, Meehl (1951) emphasized the importance of conducting research on individuals who showed specific two-point codes and other configural patterns. This way, developers could empirically determine the meaning of MMPI elevations. Thus, the validity of the MMPI was extended by finding homogeneous profile patterns and determining the characteristics of individuals who show these patterns. In other words, new criterion groups were established of individuals grouped on the basis of similarities in their MMPI profiles. In this approach, the characteristics of a criterion group, consisting of subjects who showed elevation on two scales (e.g., the psychopathic deviate and hypomania scales), could be empirically determined. The difference in approach meant that MMPI configural patterns, rather than psychiatric diagnosis, became the criterion for the selection of homogeneous criterion groups.

Because the original idea of the contrasted-group method was extended by the use of criterion groups, we use the term *criterion-group strategy* rather than *contrasted-group strategy* to describe the MMPI and related tests. The most recent approach does not attempt to distinguish the criterion group from a control group. Instead, the characteristics of the criterion groups are evaluated through empirical means such as peer ratings, physician ratings, and demographic characteristics. The upshot has been numerous studies that describe the characteristics of individuals who show specific MMPI patterns (Archer, Hagan, Mason, Handel, & Archer, 2011; Deskovitz, Weed, Chakranarayan, Williams, & Walla, 2016). Along with an empirical approach, Meehl and others began to advocate a change in the names of the clinical scales. Because elevation on the schizophrenia scale did not necessarily mean the person was schizophrenic, the use of such a name was awkward as well as confusing. Meehl and others therefore suggested that the scales be identified by number rather than by name. Table 13.3 lists the scales by their number. The validity scales retained their original names.

At this point, MMPI patterns could have a numerical code. For each of the two most commonly used coding systems, the clinical scales are listed in rank order from highest T score to lowest. A symbol indicates the level of elevation. In Welsh's (1948) well-established system, for example, T scores of 90 (four standard deviations above the mean) and greater are designated by *; T scores between 80 and 89 are designated by "; T scores between 70 and 79, by '; T scores between 60 and 69, by –; and so on for each 10-point interval down to # placed to the right of T scores below 29. For example, the code 13* 2" 7' 456890– means that Scales 1 and 3 have T scores above 90, Scale 2 above 80, Scale 7 above 70, and the remaining scales between 60 and 69. This pattern is referred to as a one-three two-point pattern or, more simply, a *13 code*, based on the two highest scales.

The Restandardization: MMPI-2

Beginning in 1982, a major effort was made to update and restandardize the MMPI. The result was the MMPI-2 (Butcher, Graham, Dahlstrom, Tellegen, & Kaernmer, 1989). The purpose of the revision was to update and expand the norms; revise items that were out of date, awkward, sexist, or problematic; and broaden the item pool to extend the range of constructs that one could evaluate. At the same time, developers strove to retain all the features of the original MMPI, including the original validity and clinical scales (Rogers, Sewell, Harrison, & Jordan, 2006). Finally, they wanted

TABLE 13.3   Original MMPI Scales

Symbol currently in use	Old name	Number of items in scale*	Common interpretation of elevation
Validity Scales			
L	Lie scale	13	Naive attempt to fake good
K	K scale	30	Defensiveness
F	F scale	64	Attempt to fake bad
Clinical Scales			
1	Hypochondriasis	33	Physical complaints
2	Depression	60	Depression
3	Hysteria	60	Immaturity
4	Psychopathic deviate	50	Authority conflict
5	Masculinity–femininity	60	Masculine or feminine interests
6	Paranoia	40	Suspicion, hostility
7	Psychasthenia	48	Anxiety
8	Schizophrenia	78	Alienation, withdrawal
9	Hypomania	46	Elated mood, high energy
0	Social introversion	70	Introversion, shyness

*Because of item overlap, the total number of items here is 654.

Note: The validity scales (L, K, and F) determine the individual's approach to testing (normal or honest, fake bad, or fake good). Of the 10 clinical scales, two were developed rationally (5 and 0). The remaining eight scales were developed through the criterion-group method. Numerous interpretive hypotheses can be associated with each MMPI scale; however, the meaning of any MMPI scale depends on the characteristics of the subject (age, race, sex, socioeconomic status, education, IQ, etc.).

to develop a separate form for adolescents. Each of these goals was well accomplished (see Figure 13.3).

The original MMPI contained 550 items, with 16 items repeated on the back of the scoring sheets for convenience of scoring, for a total of 566 items. The MMPI-2 has 567 items. Changes included dropping the 16 repeated items, dropping 13 items from the clinical scales, and dropping 77 items from the range 399 and 550, leaving 460 items from the original test. Then 81 items were added for the new content scales, two items were added to pick up severe pathology (critical items), and 24 unscored items were added for experimental purposes, for a total of 567. An additional 68 items were rewritten with no change in meaning (Ben-Porath & Butcher, 1989). Reasons for rewriting items included outdated language (24), sexist language (11), awkward language (6), and minor changes or simplifications (33).

Interpretation of the clinical scales remained the same because not more than four items were dropped from any scale, and the scales were renormed and scores transformed to uniform *T* scores. On the original MMPI, more people were scoring above a *T* score of 70 than a normal distribution would predict, and the scales were

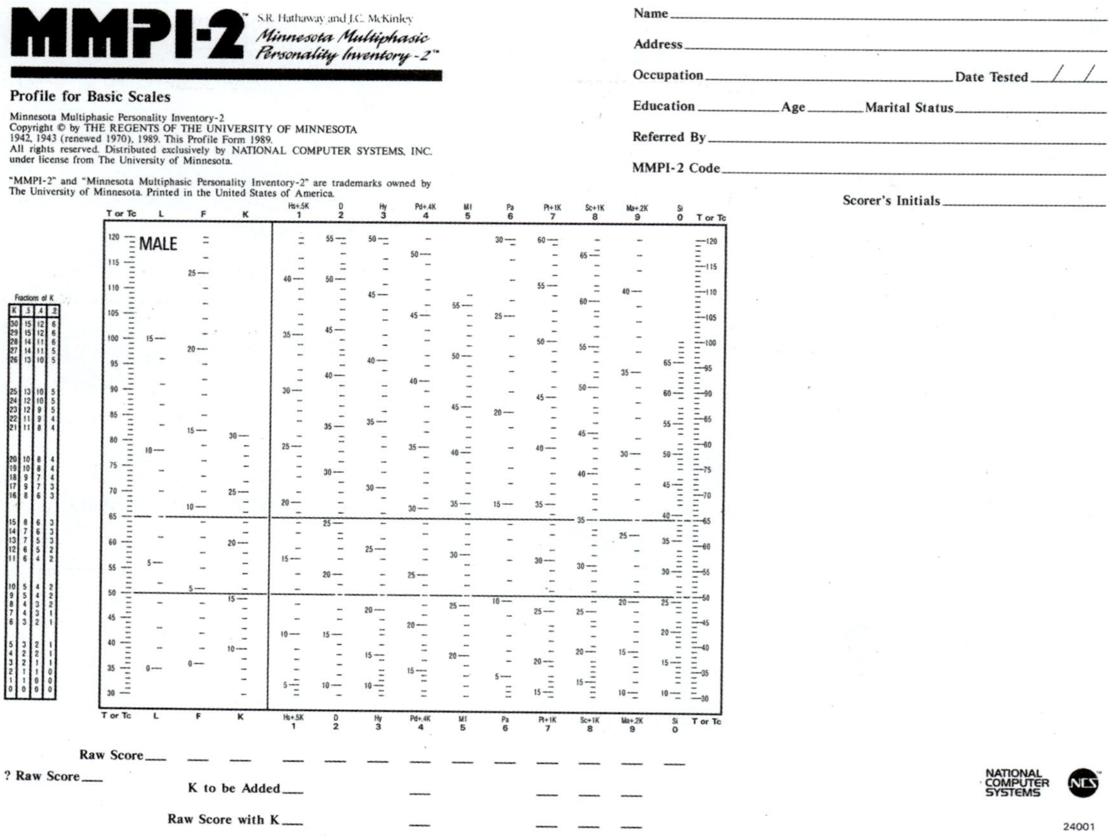

FIGURE 13.3
An MMPI-2 profile sheet.
(Reproduced by permission of University of Minnesota Press.)

not uniform. To maintain consistency with previous research and interpretation, the cut score was lowered to 65. With uniform T scores, the distribution is the same on all scores, with 8% scoring above 65, and 4% above 70.

In developing new norms, the MMPI project committee (James Butcher of the University of Minnesota, Grant Dahlstrom of the University of North Carolina, Jack Graham of Kent State University, and Auke Tellegen of the University of Minnesota) selected 2900 subjects from seven geographic areas of the United States: California, Minnesota, North Carolina, Ohio, Pennsylvania, Virginia, and Washington. Of these, 300 were eliminated because of incomplete or invalid profiles, resulting in a final sample of 2600 men and women. Potential subjects for the restandardization were initially identified by telephone and then contacted by letter. Testing centers were set up in major cities to make personal contact and arrange for the testing. The goal was to obtain a sample that reflected the demographics of the 1980 census. However, because participation was completely voluntary, the final sample was more educated and had greater economic means than the general population.

A major feature of the MMPI-2 is the inclusion of additional validity scales. On the original MMPI, all of the F items are in the first 370 items and appear on the front of the answer sheet. The MMPI-2 expanded the F scale to the back of the scoring sheet as well. The FB (Back F) score provides a check on validity and cooperation throughout the test and permits a confirmation of F scores obtained in the first half of the test. Two additional validity scales, the Variable Response Inconsistency Scale (VRIN) and the True Response Inconsistency Scale (TRIN), are included to evaluate response styles (see Baer & Sekirnjak 1997; Martino et al., 2016). The VRIN attempts to evaluate random responding. The scale consists of matched pairs of items that have similar content. Each time the pairs are marked in opposite directions, a point is scored on the scale. The TRIN attempts to measure **acquiescence**—the tendency to agree or mark "True" regardless of content (Handel, Arnau, Archer, & Dandy, 2006). This scale consists of matched pairs of items with opposite content. For example, to receive a point on the TRIN Scale, the person might mark "True" to both "I feel good" and "I feel bad."

There are 154 items on the MMPI-2 that permit the evaluation of various content areas (Arita & Baer, 1998; Strassberg, 1997). The MMPI-2 contains 15 content scales, including HEA (health concerns) and TPA, which evaluate for the hard-driving, irritable, impatient Type A personality. Other MMPI-2 content scales include FAM (family problems), which evaluates family disorders and possible child abuse, and WRK (work interference), which examines behaviors or attitudes likely to interfere with work performance.

Psychometric Properties

The psychometric properties of the MMPI and MMPI-2 are comparable (Gaston et al., 1994); the newer version maintains strong continuity with the original. For example, the factor structures of the new and original versions are quite similar.

Median split-half reliability coefficients for both the original MMPI and the MMPI-2 run in the .70's, with some coefficients as high as .96 but others much lower. Median test–retest coefficients range from the low .50's to the low .90's (median .80's). Although these coefficients are not as solid as those for the major ability tests such as the Binet and Wechsler, they are as high as or better than those reported in comparable tests. Moreover, when one looks at the basic higher-order factor structure, the MMPI and MMPI-2 are extremely reliable, with coefficients running in the high .90's.

Although the reliability of the MMPI is generally adequate, developers have not yet dealt with some notable problems. For example, because of the way scales were originally constructed, many items are on more than one scale, with some items on as many as six. Scale 8, which has more items than any other scale, contains only 16 unique items. This problem of item overlap was not confronted in the MMPI-2 revision because the goal was to retain all the original scales.

Perhaps as a result of item overlap, intercorrelations among the clinical scales are extremely high. For example, Scales 7 and 8 correlate between .64 and .87, depending on the sample studied (Butcher et al., 1989; Dahlstrom & Welsh, 1960). This high intercorrelation among the scales has led to several factor analytic studies (Johnson, Null, Butcher, & Johnson, 1984), which consistently show that two factors account for most of the variance in the original MMPI scales. These factors have been variously labeled throughout the literature (for instance, as negative or positive affectivity). Because of the high intercorrelations among the scales and the results of factor analytic studies, the validity of pattern analysis has often been questioned (Nichols & Greene, 1997).

Another problem with the MMPI and MMPI-2 is the imbalance in the way items are keyed. Many individuals approach structured tests with a **response style,** or bias, which is a tendency to mark an item in a certain way regardless of content. One of these tendencies, as you have seen, is acquiescence. Given the possibility of response tendencies, one would expect an equal number of items keyed true and keyed false. Not so: All of the items on the L scale and 29 of the 30 items on the K scale are keyed false. Scales 7, 8, and 9 are keyed on a 3:1 true–false ratio. The VRIN and TRIN scales of the MMPI-2 allow the examiner to evaluate response tendencies and represent a clear positive step toward overcoming this imbalance.

Major works devoted to the MMPI and MMPI-2 strongly emphasize the importance of taking into account the subject's demographic characteristics when interpreting profiles (Butcher, 1990; Butcher, Graham, Williams, & Ben-Porath, 1990; Nelson, Novy, Averill, & Berry, 1996). This advice is indeed warranted in that most of the studies have shown that age (Butcher, Aidwin, Levenson, & Ben-Porath, 1991; Osberg & Poland, 2002), gender (Butcher et al., 1989), race (Butcher, 1990), place of residence (Erdberg, 1969), and other demographic factors such as intelligence, education, and socioeconomic status (Butcher, 1990) are all related to the MMPI and MMPI-2 scales (Slatkoff, 2007). This overwhelming evidence supporting the covariation between demographic factors and the meaning of MMPI and MMPI-2 scores clearly shows that two exact profile patterns can have quite different meanings, depending on the demographic characteristics of each subject. Despite these differences in interpretation, some evidence suggests that the MMPI-2 predicts equally well for at least whites and African Americans (Arbisi, Ben-Porath, & McNulty, 2002; Stewart, 2007; Timbrook & Graham, 1994), but there is also evidence of bias (Arbisi et al., 2002).

The major source of validity for the MMPI and MMPI-2 comes from the many research studies that describe the characteristics of particular profile patterns. Tens of thousands of studies have been conducted, with the number of new studies increasing every year (Groth-Marnat, 1999). In fact, our survey of the relevant literature through 2016 revealed more citations for the MMPI and MMPI-2 than for any other personality test. This body of research provides ample evidence for the construct validity of the MMPI and MMPI-2. Many studies, for example, have related MMPI response patterns to alcoholism and substance abuse (Egger et al., 2007; Galli et al., 2011). For instance, evidence indicates that the MMPI and MMPI-2 might help detect individuals who might later become alcoholics (Kammeier, Hoffman, & Loper, 1973; Malinchoc, Oxford, Colligan, & Morse, 1994). The items of the original MMPI were administered to a group of men while they were still in college. The response patterns of those individuals who later became alcoholics were compared with those of a control group who did not become alcoholics. Results showed that the subjects who eventually became alcoholics had significantly higher scores on one validity scale (F) and two clinical scales (4 and 9). Thus, these scales may be related to characteristics that contribute to alcoholism in men. Interestingly, the response pattern of those in the alcoholic group was the same as their retest pattern after they had become alcoholics.

Indeed, the range of problems that the MMPI and MMPI-2 can help with spans everything from eating disorders (Berg, Peterson, Frazier, & Crow, 2011; Exterkate, Bakker-Brehm, & de-Jong, 2007), soldiers' reaction in battle (Leach, 2002), posttraumatic stress syndrome (Pupo et al., 2011), the detection of sexual abuse in children (Holifield, Nelson, & Hart, 2002), the characteristics of child sexual abusers (Sullivan, Beech, Leam, & Gannon, 2011), risk factors of female criminals (Lui et al., 2002), the effects of acculturation (Kwon, 2002), differentiating criminal types (Glaser, Calhoun, & Petrocelli, 2002), and prediction of delinquent behavior (Cumella & O'Connor, 2009) to prediction of probability of dropout from cognitive behavioral therapy for PTSD (Garcia, Kelley, Rentz, & Lee, 2011) and prediction of psychosis (Miettunen et al., 2011). Of course, not all MMPI studies report positive results (Levenson, Olkin, Herzoff, & DeLancy, 1986), but the vast majority attest to its utility and versatility (Harkness, McNulty, & Ben-Porath, 1995; Iverson, Franzen, & Hammond, 1995). This large database and sound construction explain in part why the MMPI is accepted as evidence in the judicial system (Saccuzzo, 1999).

The effectiveness of the MMPI as a tool in treatment has also been established. Using the MMPI, psychologists can now conduct integrated assessments that take the complexities of an individual's personality into account, serve as the basis for developing an effective treatment plan, and facilitate meaningful reporting and client feedback (Harwood, Beutler, & Groth-Marnat, 2011). Another study provided further insight into the value of the MMPI-2 in assessing clients with chronic personality disorders in long-term psychotherapy and using the results for providing feedback to patients (Finn, 2011). Results in therapy were improved with the repeated use of the MMPI-2 in incorporating feedback in treatment.

Current Status

The restandardization of the MMPI has eliminated the most serious drawback of the original version: the inadequate control group. With its already widespread use and acceptance, the future of the MMPI appears extremely bright. A new set of clinical scales (MMPI-2 Restructured Clinical Scales) was introduced in 2003 and includes contemporary norms, additional content domains, and a revision of items that eliminates sexist content and dated references (Tellegen, 2003). The addition of new items is sure to generate many new applications. Furthermore, the newer items can be added to the original scales when appropriate to increase their reliability as well as their predictive validity. Indeed, the MMPI and MMPI-2 are without question the leading personality test of the 21st century.

California Psychological Inventory (CPI)–Third Edition

The CPI (Gough, 1987) is a second example of a structured personality test constructed primarily by the criterion-group strategy. For three of the 36 CPI scales in the most recent revision, criterion groups (e.g., men versus women; homosexual men versus heterosexual men) were contrasted to produce measures of personality categorized as (1) introversion–extroversion, (2) conventional versus unconventional in following norms, and (3) self-realization and sense of integration.

In contrast to the MMPI and MMPI-2, the CPI attempts to evaluate personality in normally adjusted individuals and thus finds more use in counseling settings. The test contains 20 scales, each of which is grouped into one of four classes. Class I scales measure poise, self-assurance, and interpersonal effectiveness. Individuals who score high on these scales tend to be active, resourceful, competitive, outgoing, spontaneous, and self-confident. They are also at ease in interpersonal situations. Individuals who score high on Class II scales, which evaluate socialization, maturity, and responsibility, tend to be conscientious, honest, dependable, calm, practical, cooperative, and alert to ethical and moral issues. Class III scales measure achievement potential and intellectual efficiency. High scores in this class tend to indicate organized, efficient, sincere, mature, forceful, capable, and well-informed people. Class IV scales examine interest modes. High scorers tend to respond well to the inner needs of others and adapt well socially.

In addition, the CPI also includes 13 scales that are designed for special purposes such as managerial potential, tough-mindedness, and creativity as well as several experimental scales evaluating dimensions of operating style (Gough, 1996).

More than a third of the 434 items are almost identical to items in the original MMPI, and many others resemble them. However, the test does more than share items with the MMPI. Like the MMPI, the CPI shows considerable intercorrelation among its scales. Factor analytic studies have shown that only two factors in the CPI, associated with internal controls (Class II scales) and interpersonal effectiveness (Class I scales), account for a large part of the variance (Megargee, 1972). In a more recent meta-analysis, Rushton and Irwing (2009) found evidence of one overarching general factor, not only in the CPI but also in other major tests including the Big five and the Guildford-Zimmerman tests to be discussed later in the chapter. Rushton and Irwing (2009) propose that this overarching general factor is related to "social efficacy," much like Spearman's *g* factor is related to overall cognitive efficiency.

Like the MMPI, true–false scale keying for the CPI is often extremely unbalanced. Reliability coefficients are similar to those reported for the MMPI. Short-term test–retest coefficients range from .49 to .90, depending on the sample; long-term coefficients range from .38 to .77. However, the method used to establish some of the criterion groups for the CPI has been questioned. For example, for some of the scales, subjects were placed in criterion groups on the basis of ratings by friends. Nevertheless, one must consider the psychometric properties of the CPI adequate by today's standards because they are comparable to those of most widely used personality tests.

The CPI is commonly used in research settings to examine everything from typologies of sexual offenders (Burtona, Dutyb, & Leibowitzc, 2011; Worling, 2001) to personnel choices (Dantzker, 2011; Doherty & Nugent, 2011). The advantage of the CPI is that it can be used with normal subjects. The MMPI and MMPI-2 generally do not apply to normal subjects, and the meaning of nonelevated profiles is not well established. Therefore, if one intends to assess normal individuals for interpersonal effectiveness and internal controls, then the CPI is a good candidate for the measure. Furthermore, as with the MMPI and MMPI-2, a considerable body of literature has focused on the CPI. Each new piece of literature extends the utility of the test and adds to its construct validity. Therefore, the future of the CPI as a measure of normal personalities has good potential despite its limitations.

The Factor Analytic Strategy

Structured personality tests, as they exist today, share one common set of assumptions. These assumptions, simply stated, are that humans possess characteristics or traits that are stable, vary from individual to individual, and can be measured. Nowhere are these assumptions better illustrated than in the factor analytic strategy of test construction.

Recall that factor analysis is a statistical procedure for reducing the redundancy in a set of intercorrelated scores. For example, one major technique of factor analysis, the principal-components method (Bentler & de Leeuw, 2011), finds the minimum number of common factors that can account for an interrelated set of scores. As noted in the previous section, no more than two factors, perhaps only one, can account for most of the variance in both the CPI and the MMPI, which suggests that these tests are actually measuring no more than two unique components and that all scales are related to these one or two components.

The advantages of factor analysis are quite evident. However, before computers, even simple factor analyses required several weeks or even months of tedious arithmetic operations on a hand calculator. Therefore, the development of the factor analytic strategy awaited computer technology. R. B. Cattell has particularly distinguished himself in using the factor analytic strategy of structured personality assessment; this section focuses largely on his work.

Guilford's Pioneer Efforts

One usual strategy in validating a new test is to correlate the scores on the new test with the scores on other tests that purport to measure the same entity. J. R. Guilford's approach was related to this procedure. However, instead of comparing one test at a time to a series of other tests, Guilford and his associates determined the interrelationship (intercorrelation) of a wide variety of tests and then factor analyzed the results in an effort to find the main dimensions underlying all personality tests. If the results from existing personality tests could be reduced to a few factors, then items that correlated highly with these factors could be used in a new test, which would therefore capture the major dimensions of personality.

The result of the initial attempt to apply this strategy was a series of inventories that Guilford and his associates published in the 1940s and which were ultimately collapsed into a single scale—the Guilford-Zimmerman Temperament Survey (Guilford & Zimmerman, 1956).

This survey reduces personality to 10 dimensions, each of which is measured by 30 different items. The 10 dimensions are general activity, restraint, ascendance (leadership), sociability, emotional stability, objectivity, friendliness, thoughtfulness, personal relations, and masculinity. The test presents a list of statements, most of which are self-statements as in the MMPI and MMPI-2.

The subject must indicate "Yes" or "No" for each statement. Three verification keys are included to detect falsification and to evaluate the validity of the profile. However, this first major factor analytic structured personality test failed to catch on, perhaps because it was overshadowed by the MMPI and because of its arbitrary, subjective way of naming factors. Today, the Guilford-Zimmerman Temperament Survey primarily serves as a research tool, with strong indications based on the latest and most powerful research tools that the 10 factors have an overarching, higher-order single factor, social efficacy, as discussed earlier in this chapter (Rushton & Irwing, 2009).

Cattell's Contribution

Rather than attempting to uncover the major dimensions of personality by intercorrelating personality tests, R. B. Cattell began with all the adjectives applicable to human beings so that he could empirically determine and measure the essence of personality. Beginning with a monumental catalog of all the adjectives (trait names) in an unabridged dictionary that apply to humans, Allport and Odbert (1936) reduced their list to 4504 "real" traits. Adding to the list traits found in the psychological and psychiatric literature, Cattell then reduced the list to 171 items that he believed accounted for the meaning of all items on the original list. College students then rated their friends on these 171 terms, and the results were intercorrelated and factor analyzed. The 171 terms were reduced to 36 dimensions, called *surface traits*. Subsequent investigation by factor analysis finally produced 16 distinct factors that accounted for all the variables. Thus, Cattell had reduced personality to 16 basic dimensions, which he called *source traits* (see Table 13.4).

Source traits

The product of Cattell's marathon task was the Sixteen Personality Factor Questionnaire, better known as the 16PF (Cattell & Cattell, 1995; Schuerger, 1995), which was subsequently revised following continued factor analysis. Consistent with the factor analytic strategy, items that correlated highly with each of the 16 major factors, or source traits, were included, and those with relatively low correlations were excluded.

Developers took great care in standardizing the 16PF. Separate norms were provided for men alone, women alone, and men and women combined for each of three U.S. groups: adults, college students, and high-school seniors. Thus, nine sets of norms are available. To deal further with the covariation of structured personality test data and demographic variables that plagues the MMPI, the 16PF provides age corrections for those scales that change significantly with age. Six forms of the test are available: two parallel forms for each of the three levels of vocabulary proficiency, ranging from newspaper-literate adults through the educationally disadvantaged. For the latter, a tape-recorded (oral) form is also available. Norms for the various forms are based on more than 15,000 subjects representative of geographic area, population density, age, family income, and race according to figures provided by the U.S. census. Unlike the MMPI and CPI, the 16PF contains no item overlap, and keying is balanced among the various alternative responses.

Short-term test–retest correlation coefficients for the 16 source traits are impressive, with a range of .65 to .93 and a median coefficient of .83. Long-term test–retest coefficients, however, are not so impressive (.21 to .64), and

TABLE 13.4 The Primary Source Traits Covered by the 16PF Test

Factor	Low Sten score description (1–3)	High Sten score description (8–10)
A	*Cool,* **reserved, impersonal, detached, formal, aloof** Sizothymia*	*Warm,* **outgoing, kindly, easygoing, participating, likes people** Affectothymia
B	*Concrete-thinking,* **less intelligent** Lower scholastic mental capacity	*Abstract-thinking,* **more intelligent, bright** Higher scholastic mental capacity
C	*Affected by feelings,* **emotionally less stable, easily annoyed** Lower ego strength	*Emotionally stable,* **mature, faces reality, calm** Higher ego strength
E	*Submissive,* **humble, mild, easily led, accommodating** Submissiveness	*Dominant,* **assertive, aggressive, stubborn, competitive, bossy** Dominance
F	*Sober,* **restrained, prudent, taciturn, serious** Desurgency	*Enthusiastic,* **spontaneous, heedless, expressive, cheerful** Surgency
G	*Expedient,* **disregards rules, self-indulgent** Weaker superego strength	*Conscientious,* **conforming, moralistic, staid, rule bound** Stronger superego strength
H	*Shy,* **threat-sensitive, timid, hesitant, intimidated** Threctia	*Bold,* **venturesome, uninhibited, can take stress** Parmia
I	*Tough-minded,* **self-reliant, no-nonsense, rough, realistic** Harria	*Tender-minded,* **sensitive, overprotected, intuitive, refined** Premsia
L	*Trusting,* **accepting conditions, easy to get on with** Alaxia	*Suspicious,* **hard to fool, distrustful, skeptical** Protension
M	*Practical,* **concerned with "down-to-earth" issues, steady** Praxernia	*Imaginative,* **absent-minded, absorbed in thought, impractical** Autia
N	*Forthright,* **unpretentious, open, genuine, artless** Artlessness	*Shrewd,* **polished, socially aware, diplomatic, calculating** Shrewdness
O	*Self-assured,* **secure, feels free of guilt, untroubled, self-satisfied** Untroubled adequacy	*Apprehensive,* **self-blaming, guilt prone, insecure, worrying** Guilt proneness
Q1	*Conservative,* **respecting traditional ideas** Conservatism of temperament	*Experimenting,* **liberal, critical, open to change** Radicalism
Q2	*Group-oriented,* **a "joiner" and sound follower, listens to others** Group adherence	*Self-sufficient,* **resourceful, prefers own decisions** Self-sufficiency
Q3	*Undisciplined self-conflict,* **lax, careless of social rules** Low integration	*Following self-image,* **socially precise, compulsive** High self-concept control
Q4	*Relaxed,* **tranquil, composed, has low drive, unfrustrated** Low ergic tension	*Tense,* **frustrated, overwrought, has high drive** High ergic tension

*Titles in roman type are the technical names for the factors and are explained more fully in the *Handbook*.

(From the *Administrator's Manual for the Sixteen Personality Factor Questionnaire*. Copyright © 1972, 1979, 1986 by the Institute for Personality and Ability Testing, Inc. Reproduced by permission.)

most such coefficients reported in the literature are lower than those reported for the MMPI and MMPI-2 (Schuerger, Tait, & Tavernelli, 1982). Also a bit disappointing are the correlations between the various forms, which range from a low of .16 to a high of .79, with median coefficients in the .50's and .60's, depending on which forms are correlated. Moreover, despite the method used for deriving the factors, the 16 source traits of the 16PF do intercorrelate, with some correlations as high as .75. To deal with this overlap, the 16 factors themselves were factor analyzed, resulting in four second-order factors, for which one can obtain scores.

Other important features of the test are its provision of a parallel inventory for ages 12 to 18, the Junior Senior High School Personality Questionnaire, and still another parallel extension for use with ages 8 to 12, the Children's Personality Questionnaire. Cross-cultural studies have been conducted in Western Europe, Eastern Europe, the Middle East, Australia, Canada (Schuerger, 1995), and Korea (Sohn, 2002). To extend the test to the assessment of clinical populations, items related to psychological disorders have been factor analyzed, resulting in 12 new factors in addition to the 16 needed to measure normal personalities. These new factors were then used to construct a clinical instrument, the Clinical Analysis Questionnaire (CAQ) (Delhees & Cattell, 1971).

Despite the care that has gone into the 16PF, its research base and use pale when compared with those of the MMPI and MMPI-2. The fact is, neither clinicians nor researchers have found the 16PF to be as useful as the MMPI. Moreover, the claims of the 16PF to have identified the basic source traits of the personality are simply not true. However, various research investigations have supported the validity of Cattell's personality test (see Meyer, 1993).

Factor analysis is one of many ways of constructing tests. It will identify only those traits about which questions are asked, however, and it has no more claim to uniqueness than any other method. Even so, the 16PF remains an exemplary illustration of the factor analytic approach to structured personality testing.

Problems With the Factor Analytic Strategy

One major criticism of factor analytic approaches centers on the subjective nature of naming factors. To understand this problem, one must understand that each score on any given set of tests or variables can be broken down into three components: common variance, unique variance, and error variance. *Common variance* is the amount of variance a particular variable holds in common with other variables. It results from the overlap of what two or more variables are measuring. *Unique variance* refers to factors uniquely measured by the variable. In other words, it refers to some construct measured *only* by the variable in question. *Error variance* is variance attributable to error.

Factor analytic procedures generally identify sources of common variance at the expense of unique variance. Thus, important factors may be overlooked when the data are categorized solely on the basis of blind groupings by computers. Furthermore, all the computer can do is identify the groupings. The factor analyst must determine which factors these groupings measure, but no definite criteria or rules exist for naming factors. If five items such as *daring, outgoing, determined, excitable*, and *fearless* load high on a factor, then what should one call this factor? In factor analysis, one name for this factor has about as much validity as any other.

The Theoretical Strategy

To avoid the potential disagreement and biases that stem from factor analytic approaches, developers have proposed using theory as a way to guide the construction of structured personality tests. In this approach, items are selected to measure the variables or constructs specified by a major theory of personality. After the items have been selected and grouped into scales, construct-related evidence for validity is sought. In other words, predictions are made about the nature of the scale; if the predictions hold up, then the scale is supported.

Edwards Personal Preference Schedule (EPPS)

One of the best-known and earliest examples of a theoretically derived structured personality test is the EPPS (Edwards, 1954, 1959). According to Edwards, the EPPS is not actually a test in the strictest sense of the word because there are no right or wrong answers. At one time, the EPPS was used widely in counseling centers (Lubin, Wallis, & Paine, 1971). It has also been widely researched (Nittono, 1997; Thorson & Powell, 1996). Today, the test is not used extensively. However, in addition to illustrating the theoretical strategy, the EPPS elucidates some interesting concepts in personality test construction, such as the concept of ipsative scores, which we shall discuss later.

The theoretical basis for the EPPS is the need system proposed by Murray (1938), probably the most influential theory in personality test construction to date. The human needs proposed by Murray include the need to accomplish (achievement), the need to conform (deference), and the need for attention (exhibition). In developing the EPPS, Edwards selected 15 needs from Murray's list and constructed items with content validity for each.

Having selected items based on theory, Edwards could avoid the blind, subjective, and atheoretical approaches of other strategies. However, he still faced the perpetual problems of response styles and biases, which the MMPI had dealt with by including special scales to detect faking or unusual test-taking approaches. Edwards was especially concerned about faking and social desirability, the tendency to say good things about yourself or to mark items that you believe will be approved by the examiner, regardless of accuracy.

To deal with these sources of bias, Edwards attempted to rate each of his items on social desirability. He then formed pairs of items roughly comparable in social desirability and required subjects to select the item in the pair that was more characteristic of their likes or feelings. Subjects cannot simply provide the socially desirable or expected response because both items in the pair are presumably equal on social desirability. There is also not much point in faking—that is, selecting the less characteristic item. In addition, no problem of balancing scored items arises, as it does from the true–false imbalance of the MMPI.

As a further check on the validity of EPPS results, Edwards included a consistency scale with 15 pairs of statements repeated in identical form. In other words, of the 210 pairs of statements, only 195 are unique. The 15 that occur twice are presented more or less randomly throughout the test. With this format, the number of times a subject makes the identical choice can be converted to a percentile based on normative data. The approach provided the precursor to the VRIN and TRIN scales of the MMPI-2. The EPPS also permits an analysis of within-subject consistency, which consists of the correlation of odd and even scores in the 15 scales.

Norms for the EPPS were based on more than 1500 college men and women and approximately 9000 adults from the general population selected from urban and rural areas in 48 states. Separate normative data are available for each of these two groups and high-school students as well. For a given raw score on each of the 15 scales, a percentile can be obtained immediately from the profile sheet.

In constructing the EPPS, Edwards listed items for each of the scales and then paired them with items from the other 14 scales. When subjects make a choice, they select between one of two needs. In other words, in each choice, a subject selects one need at the expense of another. With this procedure, one can express the selection of items on one scale relative to the selection of items on another, thereby producing an **ipsative score**. Ipsative scores present results in relative terms rather than as absolute totals. Thus, two individuals with identical relative, or ipsative, scores may differ markedly in the absolute strength of a particular need. Ipsative scores compare the individual against himself or herself and produce data that reflect the relative strength of each need for that person; each person thus provides his or her own frame of reference.

Although the manual presents only short-term (1-week) test–retest reliability figures, the coefficients, which range from .74 to .88, are quite respectable for personality test data. Though not as impressive, split-half reliabilities, which range from .60 to .87 as reported in the manual, are generally satisfactory. Furthermore, intercorrelations among the scales are lower than those for either the MMPI or 16PF, ranging between −.34 and +.46. The lower intercorrelation is good because it supports the possibility of pattern analysis.

The EPPS has several interesting features. Its forced-choice method, which requires subjects to select one of two items rather than to respond "True" or "False" ("yes" or "no") to a single item, is an interesting solution to the problem of faking and other sources of bias. Because each subject provides his or her own frame of reference, testers can determine the relative strength of needs as well as the internal consistency of each individual subject. Item content follows established theoretical lines. The 15 identical pairs help researchers evaluate the profile's validity. Norms are based on large samples and are available for adults from the general population as well as for high-school and college students. Ipsative scores based on these norms can be converted to percentiles. Reliability data generally are adequate for the short term, and the 15 scales of the EPPS have lower intercorrelations than do the scales of the major tests developed by using factor analytic and criterion-group strategies. Last, but not least, the test is among the most researched of the personality inventories and is used widely in applied settings (Ali & Aslam, 2011).

Despite its impressive features and the widespread interest and use it has engendered, the EPPS has not been well received by reviewers (e.g., Heilbrun, 1972). Studies have shown that, like other structured personality tests, the EPPS can be faked in spite of its forced-choice procedure (Burnsa & Christiansen, 2011). Other data raise questions about the test's ability to control social desirability effects (Kim, 2011). The appropriateness of converting ipsative scores, which are relative, to normative percentiles is also questionable.

Since the first attempts at test construction, tests have followed a trend of gradual improvement following criticism and the identification of problems. The EPPS seems to have originated in this spirit, but efforts are not being made to improve it. Many more validity studies are needed, and new norms are long overdue.

Personality Research Form, Third Edition (PRF-III) and Jackson Personality Inventory Revised (JPI-R)

Other attempts to use the theoretical strategy in constructing a structured personality test are the PRF-III (Jackson, 1967) and the JPI-R (Jackson, 1976a, 1976b, 1997). Like the EPPS, the original PRF and JPI were based on Murray's (1938) theory of needs. However, unlike Edwards, the constructors of these tests developed specific definitions of each need. In this way, items for each scale could be as independent as possible, an important consideration in creating homogeneous scales. To further increase the homogeneity of scales, more than 100 items were tentatively written for each scale and administered to more than 1000 college students. Biserial correlational analysis then located the items that correlated highest with the proposed scale while showing relatively low correlations with other scales, particularly social desirability. In other words, strict definitional standards and statistical procedures were used in conjunction with the theoretical approach. This use of a combination of procedures is the latest trend in personality test construction.

To help assess validity, a scale analogous to the F scale of the MMPI was constructed. Like the F scale, the PRF and JPI infrequency scales consist of items with low endorsement rates in a standard sample. Thus, high rates of endorsement on this scale throw doubt on the validity of the results. A social desirability scale similar to the K scale of the MMPI is also included in the PRF. Two sets of parallel forms (four forms in all) as well as a form based on the best items from other forms were developed for the PRF. The latest revision of the JPI (JPI-R) has one form consisting of 300 true-false items and 15 scales for use with high-school students through college students and adults. These 15 scales have been organized in terms of five higher-order dimensions termed analytical, extroverted, emotional, opportunistic, and dependable. College norms have been updated and new norms for blue- and white-collar workers are now included. The PRF, as its name implies, is intended primarily for research purposes (Paunonen & Ashton, 1998; Randolph, Smart, & Nelson, 1997). The JPI is intended for use on normal individuals to

Jackson Personality Inventory

PROFILE SHEET: MALE

Name _____ Age _____ Form Administered _____

Date Tested _____ Other Information _____

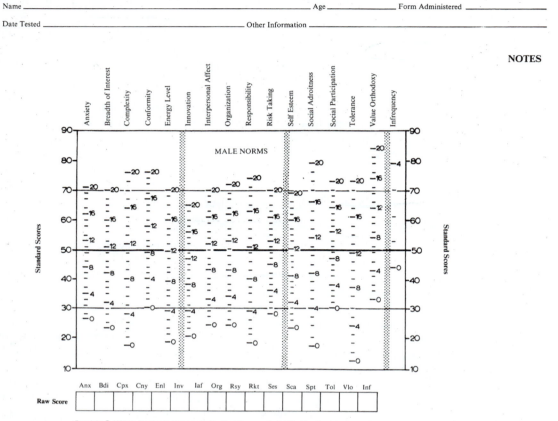

Copyright © 1984 by Douglas N. Jackson, Ph.D. All rights reserved. Published by Sigma Assessment Systems, Inc., Research Psychologists Press Division, P.O. Box 610984, Port Huron, MI 48061-0984. Published simultaneously in Canada.

FIGURE 13.4

Jackson Personality Inventory profile sheet.

(Reprinted with permission of Sigma Assessment Systems, Inc., P.O. Box 610984, Port Huron, MI 48061-0984, copyright 1976.)

assess various aspects of personality including interpersonal, cognitive, and value orientations (Ashton, 1998; Moneta & Wong, 2001). Figure 13.4 shows a profile sheet from the JPI.

Items for the PRF and JPI are balanced in true-false keying. Unlike the scales of the MMPI, the PRF and JPI scales have no item overlap. Furthermore, the scales are relatively independent (see Table 13.5).

By combining theory with rigorous statistical procedures, these tests appear to have established a new trend in the construction of structured personality tests. As with other structured personality tests, however, the PRF has yet to challenge the MMPI and MMPI-2 in terms of use (both clinical and research) and status.

TABLE 13.5 Trait Descriptions for the Jackson Personality Inventory

Scale trait	
Anxiety	Tendency to worry over minor matters
Breadth of interest	Curiosity; inquisitiveness
Complexity	Preference for abstract versus concrete thought
Conformity	Compliance; cooperativeness
Energy level	Energy; enthusiasm
Innovation	Originality; imagination
Interpersonal affect	Ability to identify with others
Organization	Planfulness; systematic versus disorganized
Responsibility	Responsibility; dependability
Risk taking	Reckless and bold versus cautious and hesitant
Self-esteem	Self-assured versus self-conscious
Social adroitness	Skill in persuading others
Social participation	Sociable and gregarious versus withdrawn and a loner
Tolerance	Broad-minded and open versus intolerant and uncompromising
Value orthodoxy	Moralistic and conventional versus modern and liberal
Infrequency	Validity of profile

Self-Concept

Many personality tests have evolved from a theoretical strategy to evaluate *self-concept*—the set of assumptions a person has about himself or herself. Presumably, what you believe to be true about yourself will strongly affect your behavior (Swann, Chang-Schneider, & McClarty, 2007). If you believe you are honest, then you will tend to act in conformity with this belief (Mazar, Amir, & Ariely, 2008). If you believe you are effective with others, then you will more likely assume a leadership role than you would if you believed you were ineffective. The extent to which you use your leadership skills or other abilities is influenced by your self-concept.

Several adjective checklists have been developed to evaluate self-concept. In these, a list of adjectives is presented and subjects are asked to indicate which apply to them. Gough's Adjective Checklist, for instance, contains 300 adjectives in alphabetical order (Gough & Heilbrun, 1980). The Piers-Harris Children's Self-Concept Scale–Second Edition contains 80 self-statements (e.g., "I like my looks") and requires a "Yes" or "No" response (Piers, Harris, & Herzberg, 1999). Beyond checklists, the Tennessee Self-Concept Scale–Second Edition is a formal paper-and-pencil test that is designed to measure self-concept data (Fitts & Warren, 1996).

A novel approach to the assessment of self-concept is based on Carl Rogers's theory of the self. According to Rogers, the self is organized to remain consistent.

New experiences that are consistent with a person's self-concept are easily integrated; experiences that are inconsistent with the self-concept tend to be denied or distorted. For example, if you view yourself as honest and moral and find yourself looking at another student's exam during the pressure of a difficult test, then you might try to distort the experience by thinking your classmate purposefully flashed her paper in front of your eyes.

To evaluate self-concept, Rogers uses a *Q-sort technique,* in which a person receives a set of cards with appropriate self-statements such as "I am a good person." The individual then sorts the cards in piles from least to most personally descriptive. The person is asked to make two sorts of the cards. The first describes who the person really is (real self). The second describes what the person believes he or she should be (ideal self). Rogers's theory predicts that large discrepancies between the real and ideal selves reflect poor adjustment and low self-esteem (Rogers, 1961).

Combination Strategies

Clearly, the modern trend is to use a mix of strategies for developing structured personality tests. Indeed, almost all of the tests we have examined use factor analytic methods regardless of their main strategy. In this section, we briefly discuss a test of positive personality characteristics that relies on a combination of strategies in scale development: the NEO Personality Inventories.

Positive Personality Measurement and the NEO Personality Inventory—Three (NEO-PI-3)

The early history of personality measurement focused on negative characteristics such as anxiety, depression, and other manifestations of psychopathology. Although the reasons to assess negative affect and psychopathology are numerous and compelling, research suggests that it may be advantageous to evaluate individuals' positive characteristics in an attempt to understand the resources that an individual is endowed with and how this endowment affects behavior and well-being. Early research (Kobasa, 1979) suggested that stressful situations can be better endured by people high on the trait of "hardiness," defined as a way of characterizing stressful situations as meaningful, changeable, and challenging. Similarly, Bandura (1986) has espoused the view that individuals with a strong sense of "self-efficacy" or strong belief in their ability to organize resources and manage situations, are better able to persevere in the face of hardships. Assuming these authors are correct, the ability to live a satisfying life even in the midst of stress and hardship depends on positive personal characteristics rather than only on the *absence* of psychopathology or negative affect.

Although relatively little is known about the structure of positive human characteristics, their measurement, or their effects in mitigating adversity, there has been a recent worldwide surge of interest in positive personality (Bermant, Talwar, & Rozin, 2011; Jayawickreme & Blackie, 2014; Laborde, Guillen, Dosseville, & Allen, 2015; Mazaheri, Nikneshan, Daghaghzadeh, & Afshar, 2015). Currently, several such measures of positive characteristics exist that evaluate traits such as conscientiousness, hope, optimism, self-efficacy, and other positive traits.

The NEO Personality Inventory—Three (NEO PI-R™)

Forefront in the evaluation of positive personality characteristics has been the NEO-PI-III (Costa & McCrae, 1985, 1995; Costa, McCrae, & Jonsson, 2002; Costa, McCrae, & Kay, 1995; McCrae & Costa, 2003; Sutin & Costa, 2011). The developers of this test used both factor analysis and theory in item development and scale construction. Quite ambitious, the NEO-PI-3 attempts to provide a multipurpose inventory for predicting interests, health and illness behavior, psychological well-being, and characteristic coping styles. Of the personality tests, the NEO-PI-3 has been among the most heavily researched during the last decade (e.g., Bech, Carrozzino, Austin, Møller, & Vassend, 2016; Furnham, Guenole, Levine, & Chamorro-Premuzic, 2013; Sutin & Costa, 2011; Vassend & Skrondal, 2011).

Based on their review of extensive factor analytic studies and personality theory, the authors of the NEO-PI-3 identified three broad domains: neuroticism (N), extroversion (E), and openness (O)—thus the name NEO. Each domain has six specific facets. Neuroticism (N) is defined primarily by anxiety and depression. The six facets of this domain are anxiety, hostility, depression, self-consciousness, impulsiveness, and vulnerability (describing people who do not feel safe). Extraversion (E) refers to the degree of sociability or withdrawal a person tends to exhibit. Its six facets are warmth, gregariousness, assertiveness, activity, excitement seeking, and positive emotions. Finally, openness (O) refers to the breadth of experience to which a person is amenable. Its six facets are fantasy, aesthetics, feelings (openness to feelings of self and others), actions (willingness to try new activities), ideas (intellectual curiosity), and values. Figure 13.5 is a profile from the original NEO Personality Inventory.

Guided by personality theory and factor analytic findings, the authors of the NEO-PI-R took a rational approach in constructing items. For each of the 18 facets, 14 items were written. Seven were positively worded and seven negatively worded to create a balance. Subjects respond on a 5-point Likert format ranging from "strongly disagree" to "strongly agree." Initial items were then refined using a variety of statistical procedures.

Data in the manual and from a variety of research reports support the NEO-PI-R and its earlier version, the NEO. Factor analytic studies support the grouping of three major areas and associated facets. Reliabilities for the three domains are in the high .80's to the low .90's for both internal consistency and test–retest reliability. As is true of all major personality tests, reliabilities of the individual facets are lower. Predictive and concurrent validity studies are encouraging, with coefficients ranging into the .80's.

The NEO-PI-R has supported what is perhaps becoming one of the most accepted notions in personality and personality assessment—the *five-factor model* of personality (Costa et al., 2002; Poropat, 2009; Sutin & Costa, 2011). Recall that through factor analysis, researchers have repeatedly attempted to find the minimum number of independent personality dimensions to describe the human personality.

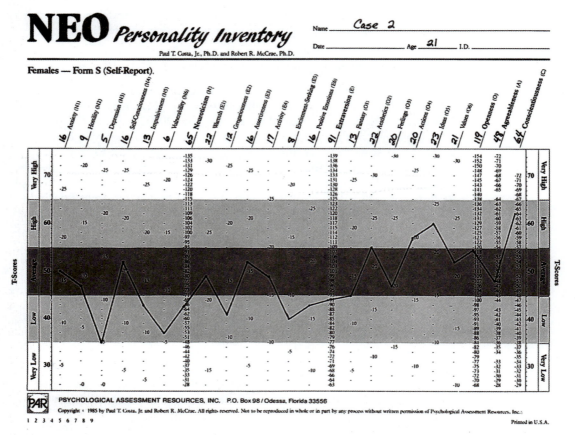

FIGURE 13.5

NEO Personality Inventory profile sheet.

(Reprinted by permission of Psychological Assessment Resources, Inc.)

Research with the NEO has supported the notion of the following five dimensions (Poropat, 2009; Wiggins, 1994):

1. *Extroversion* is the degree to which a person is sociable, leader-like, and assertive as opposed to withdrawn, quiet, and reserved.

2. *Neuroticism* is the degree to which a person is anxious and insecure as opposed to calm and self-confident.

3. *Conscientiousness* is the degree to which a person is persevering, responsible, and organized as opposed to lazy, irresponsible, and impulsive.

4. *Agreeableness* is the degree to which a person is warm and cooperative as opposed to unpleasant and disagreeable.

5. *Openness to experience* is the degree to which a person is imaginative and curious as opposed to concrete-minded and narrow in thinking.

Among positive characteristics, conscientiousness as identified on the NEO has been of particular interest. Conscientiousness is constructed of two major facets: achievement and dependability. Conscientiousness, which emerges in childhood (Eisenberg, Duckworth, Spinrad, & Valiente, 2014), has been found to be valid as a positive predictor of performance in all occupations studied (Bakker, Demerouti, & ten Brummelhuis, 2011; Barrick et al., 2001; Di Fabio & Busoni, 2007) and to be positively correlated with effective styles of coping with stressful situations (Bartley & Roesch, 2011; Haren & Mitchell, 2003; Hu et al., 2002) and with the Satisfaction with Life Scale (Baudin, Aluja, Rolland, & Blanch, 2011; Hayes & Joseph, 2003), which is discussed later. Barrick, Mount, and Judge (2001) also suggested that results from meta-analysis underscore the importance of the dimension of conscientiousness as a "fundamental individual difference variable that has numerous applications" (p. 21), setting it apart as central in theories seeking to explain positive personality traits.

Other NEO factors have been evaluated by Barrick et al. (2001), who found that an absence of the factor neuroticism could be predictive of performance, though to a lesser degree than was conscientiousness, and with a less consistent relationship to specific performance criteria. Neuroticism was also negatively correlated with effective styles of coping with stressful situations (Hu et al., 2002). In addition, high neuroticism predicted lower scores on the Satisfaction with Life Scale (Hayes & Joseph, 2003).

The trait openness correlated significantly with crystallized intelligence (Bates & Sheiles, 2003), and the traits of openness, agreeableness, and extraversion were found to be beneficial in predicting success in specific job settings. In addition, Judge and Bono (2000) found that extraversion and agreeableness were effective in predicting transformational leadership.

Two converging areas of research with the NEO and NEO-PI-3 discuss whether the five-factor model is actually the best way to categorize the minimum dimensions of human personality, and, if so, whether these dimensions hold up across cultures. Some researchers, including the authors of the JPI, have found support for an alternative model with a six-factor solution (Jackson, Paunonen, Fraboni, & Goffin, 1996; Maltby, Wood, Day, & Pinto, 2011; Rolland, Parker, & Stumpf, 1998). When six factors are found, five tend to parallel the "big five" of NEO-PI-R (Detwiler & Ramanaiah, 1996). However, evidence for the six-factor model is weak and inconclusive (Heuchert, Parker, Stumpf, & Heinrich, 2000; Piedmont, 1998; Thalmayer, Saucier, & Eigenhuis, 2011).

As indicated earlier in this chapter, researchers have turned to the question of whether there is one general factor of personality (GFP) that occupies the apex of the hierarchies of both personality and personality disorders (Rushton & Irwing, 2009, 2011). First, Rushton and Irwing cross-validated data that indicated a two-factor solution. The alpha was labeled stability and the beta was labeled plasticity. Then, using meta-analysis, these researchers found evidence of a single model, which was then tested and confirmed in a representative sample (Rushton & Irwing, 2009, 2011). A subsequent meta-analysis of 212 published sets of big-five scores further corroborated this single-factor model (van der Linden, te Nijenhuis, & Bakker, 2010). Although the existence of a GFP does not mean that other personality factors lower on the hierarchy are meaningless, knowledge of the GFP is useful where a compound measure of personality is needed (van der Linden et al., 2010). An understanding of the GFP has contributed to both theoretical and practical usage of personality tests. In a related line of research, investigators have attempted to determine whether the five factors can be applied across cultures. Testing of this hypothesis is possible because the NEO-PI-R has been translated into numerous languages. The taxonomic structure of the NEO has become widely accepted because its five factors of personality have remained robust across cultures and measures (Egger, DeMay, Derksen, & van der Staak, 2003; Ispas, Iliescu, Ilie, & Johnson, 2014).

Finding that data from Filipino (Katigbak, Church, Guanzon-Lapena, Carlota, & del Pilar, 2002) and French translations tend to parallel U.S. data in support of the five-factor solution, some researchers have made the bold claim that the five-factor model is a "biologically based human universal" (McCrae, Costa, Del Pilar, Rolland, & Parker, 1998). This work is further supported by research on a Korean version of the NEO-PI-R (Spirrison & Choi, 1998; Yoon, Schmidt, & Ilies, 2002). However, Huang, Church, and Katigbak (1997) reported that even though the factor structure may be similar for Filipino populations, the mean scores tended to differ across populations. Klimstra, Crocetti, Hale, Fermani, and Meeus (2011) also advised caution when interpreting test results from Dutch and Italian adolescence. The translated testing materials had slightly different meanings to the Dutch and Italian adolescent respondents, resulting in subtle cross-national differences in personality. And in a study of approximately 3500 university students and employees in Kuwait, El-Ansarey (1997) reported that the NEO is not a valid or reliable inventory to assess personality in Kuwait society. Finally, a study of father–offspring and mother–offspring correlations indicated significant but "weak" family resemblances for the five personality dimensions (Bratko & Marusic, 1997).

Given its general amenability to cross-cultural and international studies, along with the potential significance of biologically based universal human traits, the NEO-PI-R is likely to engender considerable research for some time. Moreover, the NEO-PI-R reflects modern trends in personality test construction by its reliance on theory, logic, and the liberal use of factor analysis and statistical approaches in test construction. It appears to be exceptionally promising for measuring a wide range of characteristics in the world community.

Frequently Used Measures of Positive Personality Traits

Rosenberg Self-Esteem Scale

The Rosenberg Self-Esteem Scale (Rosenberg, 1965) is widely used today for diverse samples in the United States (Heatherton & Wyland, 2003; Supple, Su, Plunkett, Peterson, & Bush, 2013) and in various countries worldwide such as Hungary (Bödecs, Horváth, & Szilágyi, 2011), Germany (Gudjonsson & Sigurdsson, 2003), the United Kingdom (Huang & Dong, 2011; Schaefer, Koeter, Wouters, Emmelkamp, & Schene, 2003), and Turkey (Kugu, Akyuez, Dogan, Ersan, & Izgic, 2002). This scale measures global feelings of self-worth using 10 simple and straight-forward statements that examinees rate on a 4-point Likert scale. The Rosenberg scale was created for use with adult populations. The scale has strong psychometric properties, with considerable evidence of concurrent, known-groups, predictive, and construct validity. Internal reliability is .92, and test–retest reliability shows correlations of .85 and .88 over a 2-week period. One of the measure's greatest strengths is the amount of research conducted using a wide range of populations such as adolescents (Whiteside-Mansell & Corwyn, 2003; Yarcheski, Mahon, & Yarcheski, 2003) and individuals with eating disorders (Beato, Cano, & Belmonte, 2003; Chen et al., 2003) and hearing loss (Crowe, 2003).

General Self-Efficacy Scale (GSE)

The GSE (Jerusalem & Schwarzer, 1992) was developed to measure an individual's belief in his or her ability to organize resources and manage situations, to persist in the face of barriers, and to recover from setbacks. The scale consists of 10 items and takes only 4 minutes to complete. Internal reliabilities for the GSE range from .76 to .90. Research from 25 countries indicates that the GSE is configurally equivalent across cultures and that the underlying construct of self-efficacy is global (Scholz, Dona, Sud, & Schwarzer, 2002; also see Löve, Moore, & Hensing, 2011). The GSE has been found to be positively correlated with favorable emotions, dispositional optimism, self-esteem, and work satisfaction. Negative correlations have been found with depression, anxiety, stress, burnout, and health complaints.

Ego Resiliency Scale Revised   *Universal*

This measure of ego resiliency or emotional intelligence was developed by Block and Kremen in 1996 (see Alessandri, Vecchione, Caprara1, & Letzring, 2011). The Ego Resiliency Scale (ER89-R) consists of 14 items, each answered using a 4-point Likert scale to rate statements such as "I am regarded as a very energetic person," "I get over my anger at someone reasonably quickly," and "Most of the people I meet are likeable." ER89-R scores correlated highly with ratings for being sympathetic, considerate, dependable, responsible, cheerful, warm, assertive, socially adaptive, and not hostile. Fredrickson (2001) provided evidence of the scale's validity. The scales have been translated into several languages, including French (Callahan et al., 2001), Italian (Alessandri et al., 2011), and Korean (Min, Kim, Hwang, & Jahng, 1998), and are widely used in psychological research.

Dispositional Resilience Scale (DRS)

The DRS was developed by Bartone, Wright, Ingraham, and Ursano (1989) to measure "hardiness," which is defined as the ability to view stressful situations as meaningful, changeable, and challenging. The coefficient alpha for the short version of the DRS, referred to as the Short Hardiness Scale, is .70, and the 3-week test–retest reliability coefficient is .78 (Bartone, 2007). In an earlier study by Bartone (1995) using the Short Hardiness Scale, hardiness emerged as a significant predictor of grades among West Point cadets. Furthermore, research has indicated that those who measure high in hardiness have lower levels of worry (Hanton, Evans, & Neil, 2003); others have suggested that hardiness, as measured by the DRS, can function as an index of mental health (Taylor, Pietrobon, Taverniers, Leon, & Fern, 2011).

Hope Scale

Snyder et al. (1991) proposed a cognitive model that characterizes hope as goal-driven energy (agency) in combination with the capacity to construct systems to meet goals (pathways) (Tennen, Affleck, & Tennen, 2002). The Hope Scale, also referred to as the Dispositional Hope Scale, was developed by Snyder et al. (1991) and measures the components of this cognitive model. The scale consists of 12 items that are rated on an 8-point Likert scale ranging from "definitely false" to "definitely true." Of the 12 items, four measure pathways, four measure agency, and four are distracters that are not scored. Snyder et al. (1991) have reported adequate internal reliability (alphas ranging from .74 to .84) and test–retest reliability (ranging from .76 to .82 over 10 weeks), and it appears that the Hope Scale is particularly invulnerable to faking (Terrill, Friedman, Gottschalk, & Haaga, 2002). High scores on the scale have been shown to be predictive of college graduation (Snyder et al., 2002), healthy psychological adjustment, high achievement, good problem-solving skills, and positive health-related outcomes (Snyder, Sympson, Michael, & Cheavens, 2001). It has also been found to be a good measure of hope in traumatized population (Creamer et al., 2009). The Hope Scale takes 2 to 5 minutes to complete and is useful for examinees who read at the seventh-grade level or higher. Snyder et al. (1991) report that scores on the Hope Scale are positively correlated with measures of dispositional optimism and positive affect and negatively correlated with hopelessness and depression. Magalette and Oliver (1999) indicate that the Hope Scale predicts variance independent of measures of self-efficacy and optimism, suggesting it measures a related, but not identical, construct.

Life Orientation Test-Revised (LOT-R)

The LOT-R is the most widely used self-report measure of dispositional optimism, which is defined as an individual's tendency to view the world and the future in positive ways. The LOT-R consists of 10 items developed to assess individual differences in generalized optimism versus pessimism. Items are answered on a 5-point response scale ranging from "strongly disagree" to "strongly agree." Cronbach's alpha is estimated at .82. Test–retest reliability for the LOT-R appears adequate ($r = .79$ over 4 weeks, as reported by Smith, Pope, Rhodewalt, & Poulton, 1989). The LOT-R and its predecessor, the LOT, have been used extensively in studies of stress and coping (Chico-Libran, 2002; Vassend, Quale, Røise, & Schanke, 2011). Dispositional optimism scores correlate highly with self-esteem (.54), neuroticism ($-.50$), and trait anxiety ($-.59$) (Scheier, Carver, & Bridges, 1994). Scheier and Carver (1985) found that the LOT correlates negatively with depression ($-.49$), perceived stress ($-.55$), and hopelessness ($-.47$). A 2002 study by Creed, Patton, and Bartrum replicates these findings. In addition, the LOT-R is strongly positively correlated with active coping strategies (Chico-Libran, 2002; Horney et al., 2011) and with emotional regulation strategies (Scheier, Weintraub, & Carver, 1986). Although the LOT-R is widely used and has been shown to be a psychometrically sound instrument, it is notable that studies have suggested the LOT-R is more susceptible to faking good than are other tests of optimism (Terrill et al., 2002).

Satisfaction with Life Scale (SWLS) *universal*

The five-item SWLS (Diener, Emmons, Larsen, & Griffin, 1985) was developed as a multi-item scale for the overall assessment of life satisfaction as a cognitive-judgmental process, rather than for the measurement of specific satisfaction domains. This simple and flexible instrument is one of the most widely used measures of life satisfaction or global well-being (Lucas, Deiner, & Larson, 2003). As an extremely popular research tool, the SWLS has been used to assess life satisfaction in many groups such as minorities (Constantine & Watt, 2002), cancer patients (Ferrario, Zotti, Massara, & Nuvolone, 2003), the elderly (Richeson & Thorson, 2002), immigrants (Neto, 2002), university students (Matheny et al., 2002; Paolini, Yanez, & Kelly, 2006), those suffering from traumatic injury (Corrigan, Bogner, Mysiw, Clinchot, & Fugate, 2001), and psychiatric patients (Arrindell, van Nieuwenhuizen, & Lutejin, 2001). It has also been translated and validated for use in several countries, including China (Bai, Wu, Zheng, & Ren, 2011) and Germany (Glaesmer, Grande, Braehler, & Roth, 2011). Pons, Atienza, Balaguer, and Garcia-Merita (2002) report adequate internal reliability, and Diener et al. (1985) report satisfactory test–retest stability for a 2-month period ($r = .82$). Others have shown that life satisfaction as measured by the SWLS can be relatively stable between years (Corrigan et al., 2001). Deiner et al. (1985) note that the inventory is designed to assess both fluctuations in life satisfaction and global ratings of this construct. A 6th- to 10th-grade reading level is necessary in order to complete the inventory accurately, and it takes only a minute or two to complete. The SWLS has been found to be positively correlated with healthy psychological and social functioning and negatively associated with measures of psychological distress (Arrindell et al., 2001). The SWLS has been adapted for use with children and is an appropriate measure for life satisfaction in children (Gadermann, Guhn, & Zumbo, 2011).

Positive and Negative Affect Schedule (PANAS) *universal*

The PANAS was developed by Watson, Clark, and Tellegen (1988) to measure two orthogonal dimensions of affect. One of the most widely used measures of affect (Schmukle, Egloff, & Burns, 2002), the instrument has two scales—one for positive affect (PA) and one for negative affect (NA). Each scale consists of 10 adjectives such as *distressed, interested, guilty, afraid,* and *nervous.* The respondents are asked to rate the extent to which their moods have mirrored the feelings described by each adjective during a specified period of time. Watson et al. (1988) have presented extensive evidence demonstrating that the PANAS scales are internally consistent with coefficient alphas ranging from .84 to .90, and that they are largely uncorrelated with each other and stable over a 2-month period. Watson et al. (1988) have also presented evidence showing that the PANAS scales are valid measures of the underlying NA and PA constructs, with moderately high correlations between the NA scale of the PANAS and other measures of psychological distress. In addition, there is some evidence that the PANAS can be successfully translated into other languages and used across cultures and ethnic groups (Karim, Weisz, & Ur Rehman, 2011; Terraciano, McCrae, & Costa, 2003).

Coping Intervention for Stressful Situations (CISS)

Active behavioral and cognitive coping strategies have been shown to be associated with measures of positive affect, and the strategy of coping by avoidance has been shown to be associated with high levels of negative affect (Pernas et al., 2001). Understanding individuals' styles of coping is key to understanding components of their personality. Endler and Parker (1990) created the CISS as a 48-item questionnaire that measures coping styles by asking subjects how they would respond to a variety of stressful situations. Using a 5-point Likert scale with choices ranging from "not at all" to "very much," this inventory assesses individuals according to three basic coping styles: task-oriented coping, emotion-oriented coping, and avoidance-oriented coping.

Core Self-Evaluations

The widespread use of the NEO and other popular tests of positive characteristics has led to a deeper understanding of the fundamentals of personality. It has been suggested that measures of personality, to some extent, are all tapping into a single core construct (Judge, Erez, Bono, & Thoresen, 2002). Core self-evaluations is a framework for understanding and evaluating this core (Judge & Larsen, 2001). This broad-based personality construct is composed of four specific traits: self-esteem, generalized self-efficacy, neuroticism, and locus of control. The construct is not simply a descriptive system but explanatory of the dispositional source of life satisfaction and performance. In other words, the system not only describes the positive traits of individuals but also suggests ways in which these positive traits affect emotions and behaviors. Judge, Locke, Durham, and Kluger (1998) showed consistent effects of core evaluations on job satisfaction, with self-esteem and self-efficacy contributing most to the core self-evaluation conception. Heller, Judge, and Watson (2002) suggest that life satisfaction is largely the result of dispositional factors explained through core self-evaluations. Moreover, factor analytic evaluations of the core self-evaluation construct, though limited, have resulted in evidence of its validity for motivation, life satisfaction, and performance (Erez & Judge, 2001).

In 2011, Chang et al. conducted a review spanning 15 years of CSE theory and research. The study focused in particular on the outcomes, mediators, and moderators of CSE via both and quantitative literature reviews (Chang, Ferris, Johnson, Rosen, & Tan, 2011). Meta-analytic results support the relation of CSE with various outcomes, including job and life satisfaction, in-role and extra-role job performance, and perceptions of the work environment such as job characteristics and fairness.

In light of all evidence to date, the core self-evaluation construct remains a better predictor of job performance than do individual traits and should give direction to further evaluation (Erez & Judge, 2001). When focusing on life or job satisfaction, a combination of the personality characteristics neuroticism and extroversion as well as measures of positive and negative affect appear to be best suited for prediction. Nevertheless, the interrelatedness among the various measures of positive characteristics remains largely unexplored and has provoked many questions.

Future of Positive Personality Research

Among the questions raised in the area of positive personality research is whether the various measures are capturing a series of unique and independent traits or are more generally related to a single underlying construct. There also is debate about whether positive characteristics are independent constructs or merely represent the absence of negative traits. The question also has been raised whether the presence of positive characteristics mitigates detrimental effects of negative characteristics, and, if so, to what extent.

In an attempt to answer these questions, Saccuzzo et al. (2003) analyzed the results of 15 separate tests of positive personality completed by 313 college-aged students. The findings were clear in demonstrating that the various measures of positive affect, from hope through resiliency, are best conceptualized as a single construct or dimension. These measures shared considerable common variance, with no evidence at all for independence. Thus, regardless of what they are called, measures of positive affect measure just that and at varying levels of success. It appears to be feasible to create a robust single measure by locating those items with the highest correlation with the general factor. Furthermore, given the consistency among the measures, it would appear as though positive affect can be reliably and validly measured with relative economy in terms of number of items.

The data likewise indicated that measures of negative affect constitute a single dimension. Although there may be some utility from a clinical perspective in distinguishing among constructs such as anxiety and depression, negative affect can best be thought of as tapping into a broader, more general construct. This negative affect construct, however, has a strong and negative relationship with its positive affect counterpart.

There was strong empirical support to indicate that measures of positive and negative affect fall along a continuum ranging from the highest measures of positive affect through the highest measures of negative affect. In general, individuals who are high on positive are low on negative. Conversely, individuals who are high on negative are not high on positive. Thus, when measures of both positive and negative affect were evaluated in a single factor analysis, positive measures consistently loaded positively, while negative measures loaded negatively.

In effect, scoring high on measures of positive affect has the same meaning as scoring low on measures of negative affect. Conversely, scoring high on negative affect has the same meaning as scoring low on measures of positive affect.

These findings confirm other research that suggests the understanding of personal characteristics is improved by considering both the positive and negative affect dimensions. At the simplest level, individuals who score high on positive and low on negative represent those best able to function. Conversely, those high on negative affect and low on positive will tend to have a diminished capacity to deal with stressful situations. However, within the negative affect group, there may be a significant number of individuals whose scores in the positive dimension have a counterbalancing effect. Obviously, individuals in the mixed category should be further studied in order to confirm the findings of this study. Clearly, positive personality characteristics and their measurement are only beginning to be understood, and the decades ahead should prove interesting to those following the progress of this research.

Summary

Structured personality tests are self-report procedures that provide statements to which the subject must either respond "True" or "False" ("Yes" or "No") or choose the most characteristic of two or more alternatives. These tests are highly structured and provide a definite, unambiguous stimulus for the subject. Scoring is straightforward and usually involves summing the number of items marked in a scored direction.

The original pressure to develop personality tests came from the demands created by the military in World War I for a screening instrument to identify emotionally unstable recruits who might break down under the pressures of combat. The first structured personality instrument, the Woodworth Personal Data Sheet, was based on a logical-content strategy in which items were interpreted in terms of face validity.

Not long after, tests based on the logical-content strategy fell into disrepute. The problem with these tests was the numerous assumptions underlying them, including the following: The subject complies with the instructions and provides an honest response; the subject understands the items and is an accurate observer capable of evaluating his or her own behavior and responding in a nondefensive manner; and the subject, test constructor, and test interpreter all define the questions in the same way. A wide body of research seriously questioned all of these assumptions.

The first major advance in structured personality assessment came with the MMPI, which used a strategy involving criterion groups. In this criterion-group strategy, groups with known characteristics were contrasted with a control population. Items that distinguished the criterion group were included in a scale that was then cross-validated on an independent sample of criterion and control subjects. The MMPI revitalized structured personality tests. Rather than making assumptions about the meaning of a subject's response to a test item, it attempted to discern empirically the response's meaning. In the criterion-group strategy, the content of the item is irrelevant. If a subject marks "True" to the statement "I hear loud voices when I'm alone," testers do not assume that he or she really does hear loud voices when alone.

In addition to its advantages over logical-content tests in avoiding assumptions, the MMPI featured validity scales. The two most important MMPI validity scales are the K scale, which measures social desirability, and the F scale, which consists of 64 infrequently endorsed items to pick out subjects who take an unusual or unconventional approach to testing. Theoretically, excessively high scores on the validity scales can identify biased results, thus avoiding the problems of faking and social desirability inherent in the logical-content approach.

Despite its extensive use, researchers' widespread interest in it, and its recent restandardization (the MMPI-2), the MMPI has its problems, including item overlap among the scales, an imbalance in true-false keying, high intercorrelation among the scales, and a lack of generalizability across demographic variables.

The factor analytic strategy of test construction attempts to overcome some of the problems inherent in the criterion strategy. Factor analytic strategies try to find areas of common variance in order to locate the minimum number of variables or factors that account for a set of intercorrelated data. R. B. Cattell has been the most important representative of this approach.

Using the factor analytic approach to find the common variance of all trait-descriptive terms in the dictionary, Cattell reduced an original pool of more than 4000 items to 16 and created the 16PF. Great care was taken to provide adequate norms. Nine separate normative samples based on demographic variables, plus an age-correction scale, are available. Also available are three sets of parallel forms that accommodate different levels of subjects' vocabulary proficiency.

The EPPS has found its primary use in counseling centers. It employs a forced-choice strategy that requires subjects to choose the more applicable of two statements. Ipsative scores, which use the subject as his or her own frame of reference, express results in terms of the relative strength of a need.

Several tests have been developed with the theoretical strategy. Among these is the Q-sort technique, which measures self-concept.

The modern trend is to use a combination of strategies in scale construction. This approach is used in the NEO Personality Inventory-Revised (NEO-PI-R), which is the most commonly used measure of positive personality characteristics. Of the structured personality tests, the NEO, along with the MMPI-2, promise to be the dominant tests of the 21st century.

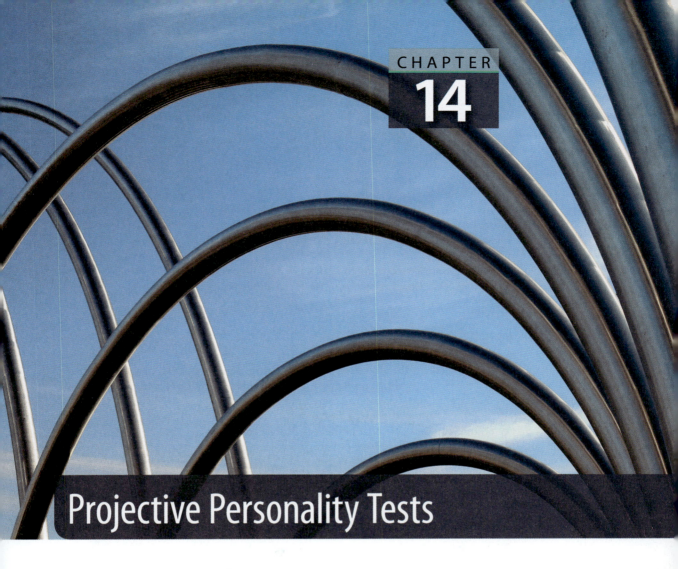

Projective Personality Tests

LEARNING OBJECTIVES

When you have completed this chapter, you should be able to:

▶ Define the projective hypothesis

▶ Identify five individuals who played a dominant role in the development of the Rorschach

▶ Describe the Rorschach stimuli

▶ Briefly describe Rorschach administration and scoring

▶ List the pros and cons of the Rorschach

▶ Describe the Holtzman Inkblot Test

▶ Describe the TAT stimuli

▶ Briefly describe TAT administration

▶ Identify the factors that should be considered in evaluating the TAT

▶ List some of the major similarities and differences between the Rorschach and the TAT

few years ago, the wife of an army sergeant sued him for divorce after 14 years of marriage. She claimed that her husband was "mentally unstable and deranged." She accused him of beating her for no apparent reason. The sergeant went to a forensic psychologist to "prove" his sanity. In addition to an interview, an ability test [the Wechsler Adult Intelligence Scale, Third Edition (WAIS-IV)], and an objective personality test [the Minnesota Multiphasic Personality Inventory-2 (MMPI-2)], the psychologist administered the Rorschach Inkblot Test. The Rorschach is one of the best known as well as the most controversial of the projective personality tests (Musewicz, Marczyk, Knauss, & York, 2009). According to the psychologist's evaluation, the Rorschach indicated that the sergeant was free of unusual or bizarre thought processes. The psychologist concluded that, based on the Rorschach and other test results, the sergeant was mentally stable, contrary to his wife's claims.

When the matter went to court, the psychologist was called to the witness stand. The cross-examination by the wife's attorney proceeded as follows:

ATTORNEY: Based on the Rorschach and other tests, you concluded that this man is mentally stable.

PSYCHOLOGIST: I did.

ATTORNEY: What is the Rorschach?

PSYCHOLOGIST: The Rorschach is a projective psychological test that contains 10 cards with inkblots on them. Five of the inkblots are black and gray; two are black, gray, and red; and the remaining three are composed of a variety of pastel colors of various shades.

ATTORNEY: How do you administer a Rorschach?

PSYCHOLOGIST: The subject—that is, the person taking the test—is shown each of the cards, one at a time. The subject is required to state what the inkblot might be.

ATTORNEY: You mean to say that you can tell whether a person is sane or insane by the way he or she interprets 10 black, gray, and variously colored inkblots?

In fact, a competent psychologist would never assert that a single test, or even several tests used in combination, can be used to prove or disprove one's sanity. In practice, psychologists conduct *assessments,* in which tests are used in conjunction with historical data, face-to-face contact, interview procedures, and experience to test hypotheses about individuals. Nevertheless, the ability of psychologists to draw accurate inferences has always been questioned, and nowhere is this more true than where the Rorschach is concerned (see Blasczyk-Schiepa, Kazénb, Kuhlb, & Grygielskic, 2011, for a discussion on criticism of the Rorschach; also see Gacono & Evans, 2007; Garb, Wood, Lilienfeld, & Nezworski, 2005; Mattlar, 2004; Meyer, Mihura, & Smith, 2005).

Projective personality tests such as the Rorschach are perhaps the most controversial and most misunderstood psychological tests (Aronow, Reznikoff, & Moreland, 1995; Blatt, 1990; Lilienfeld, Wood, & Garb, 2000). The Rorschach has been vigorously attacked on a variety of scientific and statistical grounds (Krishnamurthy, Archer, & Groth-Marnat, 2011, p. 283; Wood, Lilienfeld, Nezworski, & Garb, 2003; Wood, Nezworski, & Stejskal, 1996), yet surveys of psychological test usage in the United States consistently find that the Rorschach continues to be one of the most widely used tests in clinical settings (see Musewicz et al., 2009; Schwartz, 2014; Wood et al., 2003). In addition, it was found that five projective techniques (two of which were the Rorschach and the TAT) were among the 10 testing instruments most frequently used in clinical settings (Musewicz et al., 2009; Watkins, Campbell, Nieberding, & Hallmark, 1995). The Rorschach is used extensively by psychologists and widely taught in doctoral training programs for clinical psychologists (Hunsley & DiGiulio, 2001; Meloy & Singer, 1991; Piotrowski, 1984; Piotrowski, Sherry, & Keller, 1985; Ritzler & Alter, 1986; Weiner, 2003). Moreover, our survey of the testing literature revealed that between 2012 and 2016, the Rorschach remained the most referenced projective personality test. Feelings against the Rorschach run so high that reviewers of this book have threatened that they would not use it if it includes a discussion of the Rorschach! Proponents of the Rorschach frequently e-mail or send copies of favorable articles to keep us up-to-date with their side of the argument. Why is there such a widespread acceptance of projective tests such as the Rorschach in spite of severe attacks from prominent researchers and psychometricians? And what among clinicians is the true story? To answer these questions, we need to begin with a look at the rationale for and the nature of projective tests.

The Projective Hypothesis

Numerous definitions have been advanced for the primary rationale underlying projective tests, known as the **projective hypothesis**, with credit for the most complete analysis usually given to L. K. Frank (1939). Simply stated, this hypothesis proposes that when people attempt to understand an ambiguous or vague stimulus, their interpretation of that stimulus reflects their needs, feelings, experiences, prior conditioning, thought processes, and so forth. When a frightened little boy looks into a dark room and sees a huge shadow that he interprets as a monster, he is projecting his fear onto the shadow. The shadow itself is neutral—neither good nor bad, neither fearsome nor pretty. What the child really sees is a reflection of the inner workings of his mind.

The concept of projection is not new. Exner (1993) notes, for example, that Leonardo da Vinci used ambiguous figures to evaluate young art students. The artist presented potential students with an ambiguous figure and presumably evaluated their imaginations according to the quality of the artistic forms the students created from it. The concept of projection is also reflected in Shakespeare's "Nothing is either good or bad, but thinking makes it so."

Although what the subject finally sees in a stimulus is assumed to be a reflection of personal qualities or characteristics, some responses may be more revealing than others. If, for example, you say that a round figure is a ball, you provide a relatively straightforward interpretation of the stimulus. The stimulus itself has little ambiguity; it is round and shaped like a ball. In viewing this stimulus, a high percentage of people probably see, though not necessarily report, a ball. Theoretically, however, even this simple response can reveal a lot about you. For example, your response may indicate that you accurately perceive simple objects in the external environment and are willing to provide a conventional response. Suppose you said that this same stimulus looked like a square peg in a round hole. Assuming the stimulus is actually round and contains no lines or shapes resembling a square peg, your perception of the stimulus does not conform to its actual property (roundness). Thus, your perceptions in general may not be accurate. Your response may also indicate that you are unwilling to provide the obvious, conventional response. Or it may indicate that you feel out of place, like a square peg in a round hole.

Of course, examiners can never draw absolute, definite conclusions from any single response to an ambiguous stimulus. They can only hypothesize what a test response means. Even the same response to the same stimulus may have several possible meanings, depending on the characteristics of the people who make the response. A problem with all projective tests is that many factors can influence one's response to them. For example, a response may reflect a recent experience or an early experience one has forgotten. It may reflect something one has witnessed (a bloody murder) or something one imagines (flunking out of college) rather than something one has actually experienced directly. It may reflect day-to-day problems, such as an argument with a boyfriend or girlfriend. With all of these possible factors influencing a response, it is no wonder that the validity of projective tests has been questioned. Arguably, the interpretation of projective tests requires highly trained, experienced practitioners, but as in any field, even an expert can draw the wrong conclusions. Further, even the most experienced experts often disagree among themselves (Exner, 1995; Nezworski & Wood, 1995). As in the example at the beginning of the chapter, Rorschach users believe that they can use projective tests to draw valid conclusions. Many researchers, however, remain firmly unconvinced (Erickson, Lilienfeld, & Vitacco, 2007; Sechrest, Stickle, & Stewart, 1998; Wood et al., 1996, 2003).

The Rorschach Inkblot Test

As an example of a psychological test based on the projective hypothesis, the Rorschach has few peers. Indeed, no general discussion of psychological tests is complete without reference to the Rorschach, despite heated scientific controversies. The Rorschach has been called everything from a psychological X-ray (Piotrowski, 1980) and "perhaps the most powerful psychometric instrument ever envisioned" (Board of Professional Affairs, 1998, p. 392) to an instrument that "bears a charming resemblance to a party game" (Wood et al., 2003, p. 1) and should be "banned in clinical and forensic settings" (Garb, 1999, p. 316). Strangely, the Rorschach is both revered and reviled (compare, e.g., Erickson et al., 2007 and Mattlar, 2004).

Historical Antecedents

Like most concepts, the notion of using inkblots to study human functioning did not simply appear out of thin air. More than 25 years before the birth of Herman Rorschach, the originator of the test that bears his name, J. Kerner (1857) noted that individuals frequently report idiosyncratic or unique personal meanings when viewing inkblot stimuli. The wide variety of possible responses to inkblots does provide a rationale for using them to study individuals. Indeed, Binet proposed the idea of using inkblots to assess personality functioning (Binet & Henri, 1896) when Rorschach was only 10 years old. Several historic investigators then supported Binet's position concerning the potential value of inkblots for investigating human personality (Dearborn, 1897; Kirkpatrick, 1900). Their support led to the publication of the first set of standardized inkblots by Whipple (1910). Rorschach, however, receives credit for finding an original and important use for inkblots: identifying psychological disorders. His investigation of inkblots began in 1911 and culminated in 1921 with the publication of his famous book *Psychodiagnostik*. A year later, he suddenly and unexpectedly died of a serious illness at age 37.

Rorschach's work was viewed with suspicion and even disdain right from the outset. Not even the sole psychiatric journal of Switzerland, Rorschach's homeland, reviewed *Psychodiagnostik* (Allison, Blatt, & Zimet, 1968). In fact, only a few foreign reviews of the book appeared, and these tended to be critical. When David Levy first brought Rorschach's test to the United States from Europe, he found a cold, unenthusiastic response. U.S. psychologists judged the test to be scientifically unsound, and psychiatrists found little use for it. Nevertheless, the use of the test gradually increased, and eventually it became quite popular.

Five individuals have played dominant roles in the use and investigation of the Rorschach. One of these, Samuel J. Beck, was a student of Levy's. Beck was especially interested in studying certain patterns or, as he called them, "configurational tendencies" in Rorschach responses (Beck, 1933). Beck, who died in 1980, eventually wrote several books on the Rorschach and influenced generations of Rorschach practitioners (Beck, 1944, 1945, 1952). Like Beck, Marguerite Hertz stimulated considerable research on the Rorschach during the years when the test first established its foothold in the United States (Hertz, 1937, 1938). Bruno Klopfer, who immigrated to the United States from Germany, published several key Rorschach books and articles and played an important role in the early development of the test (Klopfer & Davidson, 1944; Klopfer & Kelley, 1942). Zygmunt Piotrowski (1947, 1964) and David Rapaport (Rapaport, Gill, & Schafer, 1945–1946) came somewhat later than Beck Hertz, and Klopfer, but like them continues to exert an influence on clinical practitioners who use the Rorschach. The development of the Rorschach can be attributed primarily to the efforts of these five individuals. Like most experts, however, the five often disagreed. Their disagreements are the source of many of the current problems with the Rorschach. Each expert developed a unique system of administration, scoring, and interpretation; they all found disciples who were willing to accept their biases and use their systems.

Stimuli, Administration, and Interpretation

Rorschach constructed each stimulus card by dropping ink onto a piece of paper and folding it. The result was a unique, bilaterally symmetrical form on a white background. After experimenting with thousands of such blots, Rorschach selected 20. However, the test publisher would only pay for 10. Of the 10 finally selected, five were black and gray; two contained black, gray, and red; and three contained pastel colors of various shades. An example of a Rorschach card is shown in Figure 14.1.

The Rorschach is an individual test. In the administration procedure, each of the 10 cards is presented to the subject with minimum structure. After preliminary remarks concerning the purpose of testing, the examiner hands the first card to the

FIGURE 14.1
A Rorschach-type image is created by dropping ink onto a piece of paper and folding it. This is a reproduction of an actual card from the Rorschach.

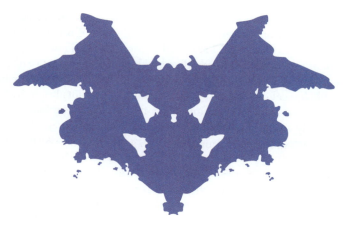

subject and asks something like, "What might this be?" No restriction is placed on the type of response permitted, and no clues are given concerning what is expected. If the subject asks for guidance or clarification, the examiner gives little information. If, for example, the subject asks, "Do I use the whole thing or just part of it?" the examiner replies, "As you like" or "Whatever you choose." Anxious subjects or individuals who are made uncomfortable by unstructured situations frequently ask questions, attempting to find out as much as possible before committing themselves. The examiner, however, must not give any cues that might reveal the nature of the expected response. Furthermore, in view of the finding that the examiner may inadvertently reveal information or reinforce certain types of responses through facial expressions and other forms of nonverbal communication (Lord, 1950; Wood, Lilienfeld, Garb, & Nezworski, 2000a), Exner (1993) advocated an administration procedure in which the examiner sits next to the subject rather than face-to-face as in Rapaport's system (Blais, Norman, Quintar, & Herzog, 1995).

Notice that the examiner is nonspecific and largely vague. This lack of clear structure or direction with regard to demands and expectations is a primary feature of all projective tests. The idea is to provide as much ambiguity as possible so that the subject's response reflects only the subject. If the examiner inadvertently provides too many guidelines, the response may simply reflect the subject's tendency to perform as expected or to provide a socially desirable response, as discussed in Chapter 13. Therefore, an administration that provides too much structure is antithetical to the main idea behind projective tests.

Each card is administered twice. During *the free-association* phase of the test, the examiner presents the cards one at a time. If the subject gives only one response to the first card, then the examiner may say, "Some people see more than one thing here." The examiner usually makes this remark only once. If the subject rejects the card—that is, states that he or she sees nothing—then the examiner may reply, "Most people do see something here, just take your time." The examiner records every word and even every sound made by the subject verbatim. In addition, the examiner records how long it takes a subject to respond to a card (reaction time) and the position of the card when the response is made (upside down, sideways).

In the second phase, the *inquiry*, the examiner shows the cards again and scores the subject's responses. Responses are scored according to at least five dimensions, including location (where the perception was seen), determinant (what determined the response), form quality (to what extent the response matched the stimulus properties of the inkblot), content (what the perception was), and frequency of occurrence (to what extent the response was popular or original; popular responses occur once in every three protocols on average). A complete discussion of these special scoring categories is beyond the scope of this text. For more information on scoring and interpretation, see Exner's (1993; Exner & Erdberg, 2005) Rorschach textbooks.

In scoring for location, the examiner must determine where the subject's perception is located on the inkblot. To facilitate determining this location, a small picture of each card, known as the *location chart*, is provided. If necessary, on rare occasions, an examiner may give a subject a pencil and ask the subject to outline the perception on the location chart. In scoring for location, the examiner notes whether the subject used the whole blot (W), a common detail (D), or an unusual detail (Dd). Location may be scored for other factors as well, such as the *confabulatory response* (DW). In this response, the subject overgeneralizes from a part to the whole.

According to such Rorschach proponents as Exner, a summary of a subject's location choices can be extremely valuable. The examiner may, for example, determine the number and percentage of W, D, and Dd responses. This type of information, in which scoring categories are summarized as a frequency or percentage, is known as the quantitative, structural, or statistical aspect of the Rorschach as opposed to the qualitative aspects, which pertain to the content and sequence of responses. Normal subjects typically produce a balance of W, D, and Dd responses. When a subject's pattern deviates from the typical balance, the examiner begins to suspect problems (Tarafder, Mukhopadhyay, & Basu, 2004). However, no one has been able to demonstrate that a particular deviation is linked to a specific problem (e.g., see Acklin, 1995; Bartell & Solanto, 1995; Frank, 1995). A substantial deviation from what is typical or average may suggest several possibilities. The protocol may be invalid. The subject may be original or unconventional and thus fail to respond according to the typical pattern. Or the subject may have a perceptual problem associated with certain types of brain damage or severe emotional problems. The relative proportion of W, D, and Dd location choices varies with maturational development. Ames, Metraux, and Walker (1971), for example, noted that W responses occur most frequently in the 3- to 4-year-old group. As the child grows older, the frequency of W responses gradually decreases until young adulthood. Theoretically, adult protocols with a preponderance of W responses suggest immaturity or low mental age.

Like other quantitative aspects of the Rorschach, location patterns and frequencies have been studied in experimental investigations. Presumably, these investigations provide information about the meaning of various response patterns and thus contribute to the construct validity of the Rorschach. Unfortunately, many of the results of the studies conflict with the opinions of experts. Furthermore, many studies that support the validity of the Rorschach have been denounced as unreplicated, methodologically unsound, and inconsistent (Gacono & Evans, 2007; Wood et al., 2003). There appears to be no room for compromise in this area of psychological testing.

Having ascertained the location of a response, the examiner must then determine what it was about the inkblot that led the subject to see that particular percept. This factor is known as the *determinant*. One or more of at least four properties of an inkblot may determine or lead to a response: its form or shape, its perceived movement, its color, and its shading. If the subject uses only the form of the blot to determine a response, then the response is scored F and is called a *pure form response*. Responses are scored for form when the subject justifies or elaborates a response by statements such as "It looks like one," "It is shaped like one," or "Here are the head, legs, feet, ears, and wings." In all of these examples, the response is determined exclusively on the basis of shape. In addition to form, a perception may be based on movement, color, shading, or some combination of these factors. These other determinants can be further subdivided. Movement may be human (M), such as two people hugging; animal (FM), such as two elephants playing; or inanimate (m), such as sparks flying. As you can see, the scoring can become quite complex.

As with location, several attempts have been made to link the presence (or absence) of each determinant as well as the relative proportion of the various determinants to various hypotheses and empirical findings (Daini & Bernardini, 2007; Exner, 1999; Perry, Sprock, Schaible, & McDougall, 1995). Consider the movement response. Most Rorschach practitioners agree that whether and how a subject uses movement can be revealing. Like most Rorschach indicators, however, the meaning of movement is unclear because of disagreements among experts and contradictory or unclear experimental findings. Many experts believe that the movement response is related to motor activity and impulses. Numerous movement responses, for example, may suggest high motor activity or strong impulses. The ratio of M (human movement) to FM (animal movement) responses has been linked by some experts to a person's control and expression of internal impulses.

A special type of movement response is called *cooperative movement*. Such responses involve positive interaction between two or more humans or animals (Exner, 1999). Exner and colleagues believe that such responses provide information about a subject's attitude concerning how people interact. One study, for example, reported that individuals who give more than two such responses tended to be rated by others as fun to be with, easy to be around, and trustworthy (Exner & Farber, 1983). The conclusion seemed to be that such responses were positive. Subsequent research, however, could not confirm the initial findings (Shaffer & Erdberg, 1996). In a study of 20 individuals who had committed sexual homicide, 14 gave cooperative movement responses. Clearly, there is no simple or clear-cut approach to Rorschach interpretation (Gacono & Evans, 2007; Gacano & Meloy, 1994).

As you think about the inferences that can be drawn from the Rorschach, keep in mind that they are at best hypotheses. Competent psychologists never blindly accept one interpretation of a particular quantitative aspect of the Rorschach. Certainly, one who blindly accepts a particular interpretation of a Rorschach pattern is ignoring the available literature. Focused Example 14.1 explains some of the ways that highly trained experts use the Rorschach to make clinically useful inferences.

Identifying the determinant is the most difficult aspect of Rorschach administration. Because of the difficulties of conducting an adequate inquiry and the current lack of standardized administration procedures, examiners vary widely in the conduct of their inquiries (Blais et al., 1995). It has been known for years

14.1 FOCUSED EXAMPLE

Expert Interpretation of the Rorschach

Rorschach experts resolutely maintain that, if properly used, the Rorschach can be an invaluable tool. Modern scientists are completely unconvinced. At best, Rorschach interpretations should be viewed only as tentative hypotheses. Hypotheses that are confirmed by other sources of data usually have more validity than do those that cannot be confirmed. When the Rorschach is rigidly or blindly interpreted, scientific skepticism is justified. When the Rorschach is interpreted cautiously and in conjunction with other sources of data, however, a highly trained expert may surprise even the most critical scientist.

When Dennis Saccuzzo had a predoctoral internship at a Veterans Administration hospital, Marguerite Hertz, one of the five original Rorschach experts, was a consultant there. Every second Thursday of the month, Hertz would interpret an actual Rorschach protocol presented by interns or staff members. Her interpretations were so detailed and exact that Saccuzzo, who was inexperienced with the Rorschach, doubted their validity. When other interns or staff agreed with everything Hertz said, he became even more skeptical. He thought they were merely awed by Hertz's reputation and were afraid to challenge this spirited woman.

When Saccuzzo's turn came to present a Rorschach, he used the protocol of a patient he had

been seeing in psychotherapy for several months. He knew this patient well and fully expected Hertz to make errors in her interpretation. He was surprised, however, when Hertz was able to describe this patient after reading only the first four or five responses and examining the quantitative summary of the various scoring categories and ratios. Within 25 minutes, Hertz told him not only what he already knew but also things he had not seen but were obviously true once pointed out. This experience was most unsettling. Having started with a strong bias against the Rorschach, and still doubting its scientific underpinnings, he could not dismiss what Hertz had done.

Later, he came to believe that Hertz's secret was her experience. She had given or studied so many Rorschachs that she had great insight into the meaning of each pattern. After having seen the Rorschach patterns of dozens, if not hundreds, of disturbed individuals, she could identify a problem. Indeed, her knowledge and experience were so broad that she could even distinguish specific types of disturbances based on the Rorschach.

However, until the experts can specify the exact processes underlying correct interpretations from the Rorschach, the criticism from scientists will continue, as Hertz herself (1986), who has repeatedly called for innovation and rigorous research, has acknowledged.

that examiner differences influence the subject's response (Gibby, Miller, & Walker, 1953; Hartman, 2001; Lis, Parolin, Calvo, Zennaro, & Meyer, 2007). As a result of this problem, much of the Rorschach literature is confounded by differences in administration and scoring alone, let alone interpretation. This is one reason why reliable experimental investigations of the Rorschach are rare (Lewandowski & Saccuzzo, 1976).

On the other hand, scoring content is relatively simple. Most authorities list content categories such as human (H), animal (A), and nature (N). An inquiry is generally not necessary to determine content.

Similarly, most experts generally agree on the so-called populars, those responses frequently given for each card. Exner's (1993, 2003) Comprehensive System, which includes as populars only those responses that occur once in three protocols on the average, provides a standardized method for scoring populars.

Form quality is the extent to which the percept (what the subject says the inkblot is) matches the stimulus properties of the inkblot. Scoring form quality is difficult. Some experts argue that if the examiner can also see the percept, then the response has adequate form quality, but if the examiner cannot see it, then the response has poor form quality and is scored F–. Obviously, such a subjective system is grossly inadequate because scoring depends on the intelligence, imagination, skill, and psychological state of the examiner. Exner's (1993) Comprehensive System, which uses the usual frequency of the occurrence of various responses in evaluating form quality, is more objective and thus more scientifically acceptable than the subjective method.

Table 14.1 summarizes our discussion of Rorschach scoring. Though the discussion has been incomplete, we hope it has shown how a projective test can be scored to yield quantitative data. These quantitative data, in turn, permit the accumulation of norms for particular groups. If subjects deviate from the typical or expected performance, then the examiner must determine the reason underlying the deviation. Proponents argue that this process can lead to valuable information about individuals (Acklin, 1995; Groth-Marnat, 1999; Hilsenroth, Fowler, & Padawer, 1998).

Rorschach scoring is obviously difficult and complex. Use of the Rorschach requires advanced graduate training. You should not attempt to score or use a Rorschach without formal and didactic graduate instruction and supervised experience. Without this detailed training, you might make serious errors because the procedure is so complex.

Rorschach protocols may be evaluated not only for its quantitative data but also for qualitative features, including specific content (Moreland, Reznikoff, & Aronow, 1995) and sequence of responses (Exner, 1999). One important aspect of a qualitative interpretation is an evaluation of content reported frequently by emotionally disturbed, mentally retarded, or brain-damaged individuals but infrequently by the normal population. Such responses have been used to discriminate normal from disordered conditions (Moreland et al., 1995).

Confabulatory responses also illustrate the idea behind qualitative interpretations. In this type of response, the subject overgeneralizes from a part to a whole: "It looked like my mother because of the eyes. My mother has large piercing eyes just like these." Here the subject sees a detail—"large piercing eyes"—and overgeneralizes so that the entire inkblot looks like his or her mother. Although one such response has no clear or specific meaning, experts believe that the more confabulatory responses a subject makes, the more likely that she or he is in a disordered state.

Psychometric Properties

Clinical Validation

The mystique and popularity of the Rorschach became widespread in the 1940s and 1950s. This popularity was widely based on clinical evidence gathered from a select group of Rorschach virtuosos who had the ability to dazzle with blind analysis, a process by which a clinician conducts a Rorschach analysis of a patient with no former knowledge of the patient's history or diagnosis and then validates the results of the Rorschach evaluation by checking other sources (Klopfer & Davidson,

TABLE 14.1   Summary of Rorschach Scoring

I. Location

Definition:	Where on the blot was the percept seen (located)?
Types:*	1. Whole (W). The whole inkblot was used.
	2. Common detail (D). A common or well-defined part of the inkblot was used.
	3. Unusual detail (Dd). An unusual or poorly defined part of the inkblot was used.

II. Determinant

Definition:	What feature of the inkblot determined the response?
Types:*	1. Form (F). The shape or outline of the blot determined the response ("because the inkblot looked like one").
	2. Movement (M, FM, m). Movement was seen ("two animals walking up a hill").
	3. Color (C). Color played a role in determining the response ("a brown bear," "pink clouds").
	4. Shading (T). Texture or shading features played a role in determining the response ("a furry bear because of the shading").

III. Form quality

Definition:	To what extent did the percept match the stimulus properties of the inkblot?
Types:*	1. F+ or +. Percept matched stimulus properties of the inkblot in an exceptionally good way.
	2. F. Percept matched stimulus properties of the inkblot.
	3. F− or −. Percept matched the stimulus properties of the inkblot poorly.

IV. Content

Definition:	What was the percept?
Types:*	1. Human (H).
	2. Animal (A).
	3. Nature (N).

V. Popular-original

Definition:	How frequently is the percept seen in normative samples? (Popular responses are seen in about one of every three protocols.)

*This list is incomplete and does not cover the entire range of possibilities. The information given is designed to illustrate quantitative scoring of a projective test.

1962). For those who were interested in forming an opinion about the validity of the Rorschach, the impact of one stunning display of insightful blind analysis was far greater than the impact of vast collections of empirical evidence that disputed the Rorschach's scientific validity, and these displays were responsible for much of the wide and unquestioning acceptance of the Rorschach as a sound diagnostic tool (Zubin, 1954).

However, in the early 1960s, research began a long trend that has lasted to the present and has revealed that the Rorschach was less than miraculous. With the application of scientific methods of evaluation, there continue to be clear indications that even the Rorschach elite did not possess the ability to divine true diagnoses (Holtzman & Sells, 1954; Little & Schneidman, 1959). The astounding successes in clinical validation became an enigma that has been explained in several ways. First, it has been suggested that the great successes in blind analysis were the product of a few simple tricks (Wood et al., 2003). One of these tricks, labeled the Barnum effect by Bertram Forer, is illustrated by a demonstration he used with his introductory psychology class (Forer, 1949). Forer prepared a personality profile for each of his new students based on a questionnaire he had administered. He then requested that each of his students rate their personal profile for accuracy, 0 being inaccurate and 5 being perfect. Forer's students gave an average rating of 4.2 (highly accurate), and more than 40% of the students said their profiles were a perfect description of their personality. The catch is that Forer had given each of the students the exact same profile, which he had compiled from a book of horoscopes. Forer had selected statements that seemed precise but that actually fit most people. He demonstrated the degree to which people overestimate the uniqueness and precision of general statements concerning their personality. Wood et al. (2003) suggest that much of the overwhelming acceptance of diagnosis based on blind analysis resulted from the Barnum effect and not from stunning accuracy.

It has also been suggested that the extraordinary early success of blind analysis could be attributed to the evaluator giving several different, or even contradictory, analyses for an individual client. When the information from other psychological tests and interviews was then revealed, the accuracy of many results of the blind reading could be supported by some of the statements, and the reading only appeared to be a success (Wittenborn & Sarason, 1949).

Others have explained the early successes not by trickery, but by the level of genius of the Rorschach virtuosos and by their ability to succeed in blind analysis because of their vast experience with the Rorschach (Klopfer & Kelly, 1946). But these explanations fall short when considering that the same virtuosos who stunned others with their success in clinical settings were able to perform no better than chance when tested in controlled studies (Holtzman & Sells, 1954). In addition, it has also been suggested that experience with the Rorschach does not lend itself to a greater degree of accuracy in diagnosis (Turner, 1966).

Regardless of the means by which early success of blind analysis and clinical proof of the validity of the Rorschach were obtained, scientists contend that clinical evaluation is unreliable, subject to self-deception (Meehl, 1997), and unscientific (Zubin, 1954). Confirmation bias, the tendency to seek out and focus on information that confirms ardent beliefs and to disregard information that tends to contradict those beliefs, can mislead even the most honest and well-meaning clinicians. Consider a clinician who hopes to prove the validity of the Rorschach. The clinician makes an evaluation based on the patient's responses to the inkblots and is then presented with a myriad of details about the patient gleaned from different psychological tests, interviews, and the client's background. From that myriad of information, the data that support the diagnosis based on the Rorschach would tend to be automatically focused on and retained; information not supporting the Rorschach's findings could be easily passed over.

In response to several studies in the late 1950s and early 1960s that served to debunk the greatness of Rorschach, Exner, as indicated, began to develop a system to remedy many of the problems with which the Rorschach was plagued. Exner attempted to address these problems with his creation of the Comprehensive System for scoring. Because the Comprehensive System for scoring the Rorschach is widely taught and the most largely accepted method in use today (Gacono & Evans, 2007; Guarnaccia, Dill, Sabatino, & Southwick, 2001; Mattlar, 2004), research concerning the reliability of this system is valuable when discussing the Rorschach (Lis et al., 2007; Mattlar, 2004; Palm, 2005). Lis et al. (2007) investigated the impact of administration and inquiry skills on Rorschach Comprehensive System. The results indicate that administration skills can have a dramatic impact and may contribute to variations in samples collected by different investigators (Lis et al., 2007).

Many scientifically minded evaluators of the Rorschach are in agreement that the Comprehensive System has failed to remedy the inadequacies of the Rorschach. In their 2003 book entitled *What's Wrong with the Rorschach?* Wood and colleagues outlined several facets of the Rorschach that raise doubt about its use in situations, such as forensic and clinical settings, which require a high degree of diagnostic accuracy. The following summarizes their contentions.

Norms

As we have emphasized throughout the book, unless the scores of a client can be compared to the scores of a reference group, they are of no use. Although it has been estimated that the Rorschach is administered yearly to more than 6 million people worldwide (Sutherland, 1992), it has never been adequately normed (Wood et al., 2003). Attempts to create representative national norms have failed on several levels. Today, most clinicians who use the Rorschach depend on the norming carried out by Exner. By 1986, Exner had established norms for average adult Americans; by 1990, Exner's books were filled with normative tables that included norms for practically every Rorschach variable. Although Exner was given credit for establishing the Rorschach's first reliable, nationally representative norms, Wood et al. (2003) contend that his attempt was significantly flawed because of a computational error created by using the same 221 cases twice in his sample. In other words, his sample of what was reported to be 700 individuals consisted of 479 individuals, 221 of whom were entered twice. Many clinicians now use Exner's revised norms. Exner (2007) conducted a normative project and released new nonpatient norms. The norms were based on a population of 450 adults recruited from 22 states and assessed by 22 examiners (Krishnamurthy et al., 2011). Although this revision is a positive step, it cannot undo the decade of inaccurate diagnoses that may have resulted because of faulty norms. Also, the revised norms have been criticized as being seriously flawed and differing significantly from those of other researchers. Furthermore, a review of the results from 32 separate studies concluded that the norms used in the Comprehensive System are inaccurate and tend to overidentify psychological disorders in nonpatient populations (Wood et al., 2010; Wood, Nezworski, Garb, & Lilienfeld, 2001b), a problem discussed in depth in the next section (Sakuragi, 2006).

Overpathologizing

Research has suggested that diagnoses from the Rorschach, whether using the older system for scoring or Exner's Comprehensive System, wrongly identify more than half of normal individuals as emotionally disturbed. The problem of overpathologizing has been seen not only in the diagnosis of healthy adults (Drogin, Dattilio, Sadoff, & Gutheil, 2011; Shaffer, Erdberg, & Haroian, 1999) but also in children (Erard, 2005; Hamel, 2000). Hamel found that slightly above-average children were labeled as suffering from significant social and cognitive impairments when evaluated with the Rorschach. The possible harm from mislabeling individuals as sick when they are not is immeasurable. Consider the consequences of wrongly diagnosing an individual in the family court setting, where a faulty finding could lead to a parent losing custody of a child. Equally devastating repercussions could result from mislabeling in clinical and forensic settings. Although the Rorschach is not advised in the child custody evaluation (Drogin et al., 2011), according to clinician surveys, it is used in more than 50% of parent assessments in the child custody determination process (Ackerman & Pritzl, 2011, Table 3). Also, consider the life-altering consequences of mislabeling a child as psychologically unwell, such as the stigma and differential treatment associated with mental or emotional illness and the implementation of costly and time-consuming treatment plans.

Unreliable Scoring

The traditional belief, especially among opponents of the Rorschach, is that the Rorschach is unreliable. Indeed, when one views individual studies in isolation, especially those published before 1985, the results appear confusing.

For every study that has reported internal consistency coefficients in the .80's and .90's, one can find another with coefficients of .10 or even .01. Psychologists who hope to shed light on this picture through meta-analysis, however, have found themselves in the midst of controversy.

Meta-analysis is a statistical procedure in which the results of numerous studies are averaged in a single, overall investigation. In an early meta-analysis of Rorschach reliability and validity, K. Parker (1983) reported an overall internal reliability coefficient of .83 based on 530 statistics from 39 papers published between 1971 and 1980 in *the Journal of Personality Assessment,* the main outlet for research on projective techniques.

Meta-analyses conducted by Parker and others were subsequently criticized as flawed on the grounds that results on validity were not analyzed separately from results on reliability (Garb, Florio, & Grove, 1998, p. 402). Exner (1999) has countered, finding it "reasonable" to argue for test–retest coefficients in the .70's. Moreover, the lack of separate results on reliability and validity should affect only the assessment of the validity of the Rorschach, not its reliability.

Furthermore, when one uses the Kuder-Richardson formula (which examines all possible ways of splitting the test in two) to calculate internal consistency coefficients rather than the more traditionally used odd–even procedure, Rorschach reliability coefficients are markedly increased. In one study, E. E. Wagner and coworkers (1986) compared the split-half coefficients using the odd–even and the Kuder-Richardson techniques for 12 scoring categories.

With the odd–even technique, coefficients ranged between $-.075$ and $+.785$. However, with the Kuder-Richardson, the coefficients ranged from .55 to .88, with a mean of .77. Thus, results from both meta-analysis and application of Kuder-Richardson techniques reveal a higher level of Rorschach reliability than has generally been attributed to the test.

Lack of Relationship to Psychological Diagnosis

Although a few Rorschach scores accurately evaluate some conditions characterized by thought disorder and anxiety, there is a notable absence of proven relationships between the Rorschach and psychological disorders and symptoms. Several classic studies examined the Rorschach's ability as a psychodiagnostic test and were disappointing to those who hoped to prove its accuracy (Holtzman & Sells, 1954; Little & Schneidman, 1959; Newton, 1954). More recently, Nezworski and Garb (2001) contend that Comprehensive System scores do not demonstrate a relationship to psychopathy, conduct disorder, or antisocial personality disorder, and the original and revised versions of the Depression Index have little relationship to depression diagnosis. Wood, Lilienfeld, Garb, and Nezworski (2000) reviewed hundreds of studies examining the diagnostic abilities of the Rorschach and found these studies did not support it as a diagnostic tool for such disorders as major depressive disorder, posttraumatic stress disorder, dissociative identity disorder, conduct disorder, psychopathy, anxiety disorders, or dependent, narcissistic, or antisocial personality disorders. Although even proponents of the Rorschach often agree that it is not a valid diagnostic tool, the Rorschach continues to be used in both clinical and forensic settings for the purpose of diagnosis hundreds of thousands of times each year in the United States alone (Wood et al., 2003).

The Problem of "R"

Those who are being evaluated with the Rorschach are free to give as many responses ("R") to each inkblot as they wish. As early as 1950, it was determined that this aspect unduly influenced scores (Fiske & Baughman, 1953). As the number of responses goes up, so do other scores on the test. This causes several problems. If a person is generally more cooperative or intellectual, then they are more likely to give more responses. Those who are more likely to give more responses are also more likely to give what are labeled *space responses* (responding to the white space within or around the inkblot instead of responding to the inkblot). More space responses are interpreted by clinicians as indicating oppositional and stubborn characteristics in the test taker. Thus, those who are most cooperative with the test are more likely to be falsely labeled as oppositional. This is just one example of how "R" can negatively affect Rorschach scores (see also Focused Example 14.2). Although the problem with "R" was determined in the early history of the Rorschach, clinicians who use the Rorschach generally ignore the problem.

In sum, evaluating the Rorschach on classical psychometric properties (standardization, norms, reliability, validity) has proven exceptionally difficult. Indeed, this attempt to document or refute the adequacy of the Rorschach has produced one of the greatest divisions of opinion within psychology. Time and again, psychologists heatedly disagreed about the scientific validity of the Rorschach. Despite numerous negative evaluations, the Rorschach has flourished in clinical settings.

14.2 FOCUSED EXAMPLE

The Danger of Basing Rorschach Interpretations on Insufficient Evidence

We had the opportunity to become involved in a forensic case in which an individual claimed that the negligence of a large company in sealing pipes together caused a gas leak that resulted in brain damage. This individual consulted an attorney, who sent him to a psychologist. The psychologist administered a Rorschach test. Based on her findings, the psychologist concluded that the person was brain damaged and thus had a legitimate case. The company called us and asked whether the Rorschach could be used to diagnose or identify brain damage. We replied that there is absolutely no support for the idea that one can prove a person is brain damaged simply on the basis of Rorschach results.

Lawyers for the company brought in the psychologist's report and a copy of the Rorschach protocol. The person suspected of brain damage provided only six responses, far fewer than the 22 to 32 responses typically found for the 10 Rorschach cards. The protocol was as follows:

	Free Association	Inquiry	Scoring
Card 1	A bat.	Here are the wings; there is the head.	W F A P

Discussion

The W indicates the whole inkblot was used in the percept. The F indicates that only the form or shape (not color, movement, or shading) determined the response. The A stands for animal content. The P indicates this response is a popular (that is, one that is commonly given).

Card 2	I don't know.	No, I still don't.	Rejection

Discussion

When the subject fails to provide a response, this is known as a *rejection*. Some examiners present the card again in the inquiry and ask, "Now do you see anything?" A rejection could have several meanings. The typical or classical interpretation of a rejection is guardedness or defensiveness.

Card 3	I don't know. (Q) No, I don't see anything.	I said I don't know.	Rejection

Discussion

The (Q) indicates the examiner questioned the subject further, thus attempting to elicit a response. Notice the defensive quality in the subject's response during the inquiry.

Card 4	A gorilla.	All of it; big feet, head, body.	W F A
Card 5	A moth.	Whole thing; wings, feelers, head.	W F A P
Card 6	I don't know.	No, nothing.	Rejection
Card 7	A bird without a head.	Wings, but no head. (Q) All of it.	W F–A

In evaluating the Rorschach, keep in mind that there is no universally accepted method of administration. Some examiners provide lengthy introductions and explanations; others provide almost none. Most of the experts state that the length, content, and flavor of administrative instructions should depend on the subject. Empirical evidence, however, indicates that the method of providing instructions and the content of the instructions influence a subject's response to the Rorschach

Discussion

The F− indicates a poor correspondence between the response, bird, and the stimulus properties of the inkblot. *Bird* is an unusual response to this inkblot.

	Free Association	*Inquiry*	*Scoring*
Card 8	Animals, maybe rats, trying to steal something	Just two animals on the sides.	D F A P

Discussion

The two animals were formed from two common details (D). It was scored P because this response is popular (that is, frequently occurring).

Card 9	I don't know.	No, it doesn't look like anything to me.	Rejection
Card 10	Nothing, wait, looks like a bug here.	Just a bug, legs, pinchers, head.	D F Insect

In our judgment, the psychologist who conducted this Rorschach administration more than stretched the interpretation when she claimed this person was brain damaged. In fact, her conduct may be viewed as unethical. The argument presented was that a small number of responses, a preponderance of W responses, a lack of determinants other than form, and misperception (the poor form quality response to Card 7) were all consistent with brain damage. Because the protocol contained qualities commonly found in the protocols of brain-damaged individuals, the psychologist argued that she had found evidence for brain damage.

We looked at this Rorschach protocol and concluded that its information alone could in no way be considered sufficient evidence for brain damage. First, a small number of responses in itself cannot be attributed to any single factor (Exner, 1999). A small number of responses can be found in retarded, depressed, and extremely defensive individuals as well as in those who are brain damaged. Second, the small number of responses led to an imbalance in the proportion of W to D responses. Data on the typical ratio of W to D responses are based on protocols with 20 to 30 responses. With only six responses, all bets are off. No one can say anything about the balance with so few responses. In any case, there is no clear evidence that brain-damaged people give a preponderance of W responses. Third, the one F− response proves nothing. Furthermore, the subject gave three popular responses, indicating he was capable of accurate perceptions. Fourth, the lack of determinants other than form can have several possible interpretations. The significance of the exclusive use of form in this protocol is dubious, however, in view of the small number of responses. A protocol with 30 responses, all determined exclusively by form, would have quite a different meaning. Notice how the total number of responses can influence or alter the meaning of Rorschach data. As indicated, the Rorschach places no limit on the number of possible responses.

We suggested that other tests be used to evaluate brain damage in this individual. Taking a conservative approach, we did not deny that this person was brain damaged. We simply stated that the Rorschach in no way documented the presence of brain damage. The person in question, however, dropped his suit after our analysis was communicated to his attorney and psychologist.

(Blais et al., 1995; Hartman, 2001). Given the lack of standardized instructions, which has no scientifically legitimate excuse, comparisons of the protocols of two different examiners are tenuous at best (see Wood et al., 1996).

Suppose, for example, one hypothesizes that the total number of responses to a Rorschach is related to the level of defensiveness. Even with an adequate criterion measure of defensiveness, if examiner instructions influence the number of responses, then one examiner might obtain an average of 32 responses whereas a second might obtain 22, independent of defensiveness. If protocols from both examiners are averaged in a group, then any direct relationship between number of responses and defensiveness can easily be masked or distorted.

Like administration, Rorschach scoring procedures are not adequately standardized. One system scores for human movement whenever a human is seen, whereas another has elaborate and stringent rules for scoring human movement. The former system obviously finds much more human movement than does the latter, even when the same test protocols are evaluated. Without standardized scoring, determining the frequency, consistency, and meaning of a particular Rorschach response is extremely difficult.

One result of unstandardized Rorschach administration and scoring procedures is that reliability investigations have produced varied and inconsistent results. Even when reliability is shown, validity is questionable. Moreover, scoring as well as interpretation procedures do not show criterion-related evidence for validity and are not linked to any theory, which limits construct-related evidence for validity. Researchers must also share in the responsibility for the contradictory and inconclusive findings that permeate the Rorschach literature. Many research investigations of tests such as the Rorschach have failed to control important variables, including race, sex, age, socioeconomic status, and intelligence. If race, for example, influences test results as research indicates (see Garb, Wood, Nezworski, Grove, & Stejskal, 2001; Saccuzzo, Johnson, & Guertin, 1995; Velox, 2005; Wood, 1999), then studies that fail to control for race may lead to false conclusions. Other problems that are attributable to the research rather than to psychometric properties include lack of relevant training experience in those who score the protocols, poor statistical models, and poor validating criteria (Frank, 1995; Meloy & Singer, 1991).

Whether the problem is lack of standardization, poorly controlled experiments, or both, there continues to be disagreement regarding the scientific status of the Rorschach (Exner, 1995; Garb, Wood, Lilienfeld, & Nezworski, 2004; Garfield, 2000; Hunsley, 2001; Nezworski & Wood, 1995; Viglione & Hilsenroth, 2001; Wood et al., 1996, 2003). As Buros (1970) noted some time ago, "This vast amount of writing and research has produced astonishingly little, if any, agreement among psychologists regarding the specific validities of the Rorschach" (p. xxvi). In brief, the meaning of the thousands of published Rorschach studies is still debatable. For every supportive study, there appears to be a negative or damaging one (see Table 14.2). These words are as true today as they were in 1970.

Clearly, the final word on the Rorschach has yet to be spoken. Far more research is needed, but unless practitioners can agree on a standard method of administration and scoring, the researchers' hands will be tied.

In the first edition of this book, published in 1982, we predicted that the 21st century would see the Rorschach elevated to a position of scientific respectability because of the advent of Exner's Comprehensive System. Over the years, we backed away from this position. Now, no less than 35 years later, we must acknowledge that we do not know the answer. However, it would appear as though the ethical burden rests with the test's users. Any user must be conversant with the literature and ready against attack.

TABLE 14.2 Summary of Arguments Against and in Favor of the Rorschach

Against	In favor
1. Lacks a universally accepted standard of administration, scoring, and interpretation.	1. Lack of standardized procedures is a historical accident that can be corrected.
2. Evaluations of data are subjective.	2. Test interpretation is an art, not a science; all test interpretation involves a subjective component.
3. Results are unstable over time.	3. A new look at the data reveals that the Rorschach is much more stable than is widely believed.
4. Is unscientific.	4. Has a large empirical base.
5. Is inadequate by all traditional standards.	5. Available evidence is biased and poorly controlled and has therefore failed to provide a fair evaluation.

An Alternative Inkblot Test: The Holtzman

Among the prime problems of the Rorschach, from a psychometric viewpoint, are its variable number of responses from one subject to another, lack of standard procedures, and lack of an alternative form. The Holtzman Inkblot Test was created to meet these difficulties while maintaining the advantages of the inkblot methodology (Holtzman, Thorpe, Swartz, & Herron, 1961; also see Wong & Jamadi, 2010). In this test, the subject is permitted to give only one response per card. Administration and scoring procedures are standardized and carefully described. An alternate form is available that correlates well with the original test stimuli. Interscorer as well as split-half reliabilities are comparable to those found for objective personality tests.

Both forms, A and B, of the Holtzman contain 45 cards. Each response may be scored on 22 dimensions. Many of these dimensions resemble those found in the Rorschach and include location, determinant, and content. Responses may also be scored for such factors as anxiety and hostility. For each scoring category or variable, well-established norms are presented for several samples ranging from 5-year-olds through adults. Given the psychometric advantages of the Holtzman, it is interesting that the test hasn't even begun to challenge the Rorschach's popularity. Current references to the Holtzman are few and far in between.

There are several factors that contributed to the relative unpopularity of the Holtzman, the most significant of which may have been Holtzman's refusal to exaggerate claims of the test's greatness and his strict adherence to scientifically founded evidence of its utility (Wood et al., 2003). The main difficulty with the Holtzman as a psychometric instrument is its validity (Gamble, 1972; Zubin, 1972). Modern studies are rare and unimpressive. Those studies that show a positive relationship between the Holtzman and various criterion measures are based on qualitative rather than quantitative features. Thus, the available supportive evidence is highly subjective, depending on examiner skill rather than formal interpretive standards. In short, one cannot currently consider the Holtzman any more useful than the Rorschach, despite the former's superior psychometric features. Perhaps the best that can be said is that there simply is not enough information to judge its clinical utility compared with the Rorschach (Darolia & Joshi, 2004; Leichsenring, 1990, 1991).

The Thematic Apperception Test

The Thematic Apperception Test (TAT) was introduced in 1935 by Christina Morgan and Henry Murray of Harvard University. It is comparable to the Rorschach in many ways, including its importance and psychometric problems. As with the Rorschach, use of the TAT grew rapidly after its introduction; with the exception of the Rorschach, the TAT is used more than any other projective test (Wood et al., 2003). Though its psychometric adequacy was (and still is) vigorously debated (Alvarado, 1994; Keiser & Prather, 1990; Lilienfeld et al., 2000; Weiner & Craighead, 2010), unlike the Rorschach, the TAT has been relatively well received by the scientific community (Miller, 2015). Also, the TAT is based on Murray's (1938) theory of needs (see Chapter 13), whereas the Rorschach is basically atheoretical. The TAT and the Rorschach differ in other respects as well. The TAT authors were conservative in their evaluation of the TAT and scientific in their outlook. The TAT was not oversold as was the Rorschach, and no extravagant claims were made. Unlike the Rorschach, the TAT was not billed as a diagnostic instrument—that is, a test of disordered emotional states. Instead, the TAT was presented as an instrument for evaluating human personality characteristics (see Table 14.3). This test also differs from the Rorschach because the TAT's nonclinical uses are just as important as its clinical ones (Dhar & Mishra, 2014). Indeed, the TAT is one of the most important techniques used in personality research (Harrati, Mazoyer, & Vavassori, 2014; McClelland, 1999; Serfass & Sherman, 2013).

As stated, the TAT is based on Murray's (1938) theory, which distinguishes 28 human needs, including the needs for sex, affiliation, and dominance. Many of these needs have been extensively researched through use of the TAT (McClelland, 1999; Sun, Pan, & Tong, 2004). The theoretical need for achievement—"the desire or tendency to do things as rapidly and/or as well as possible" (Murray, 1938, p. 164)—alone has generated a very large number of studies involving the TAT (Hofer & Chasiotis, 2011; McClelland, 1999; Miller, 2015). The TAT measure of the achievement need has been related to factors such as parental perceptions, parental expectations, and parental attitudes toward offspring. Need achievement is

TABLE 14.3 A Comparison of the Rorschach and the TAT

Rorschach	TAT
Rejected by scientific community	Well received by scientific community
Atheoretical	Based on Murray's (1938) theory of needs
Oversold by extravagant claims	Conservative claims
Purported diagnostic instrument	Not purported as diagnostic
Primarily clinical use	Clinical and nonclinical uses

also related to the standards that you as a student set for yourself (e.g., academic standards). The higher your need for achievement, the more likely you are to study and ultimately achieve a high economic and social position in society (Hofer & Holger, 2011). Studies such as those on the achievement motive have provided construct-related evidence for validity and have increased the scientific respectability of the TAT (Annalakshmi, 2006).

Stimuli, Administration, and Interpretation

The TAT is more structured and less ambiguous than the Rorschach. TAT stimuli consist of pictures that depict a variety of scenes. There are 30 pictures and one blank card. Specific cards are designed for male subjects, others for female. Some of the cards are appropriate for older people, others for young ones. A few of the cards are appropriate for all subjects, such as Card 1. This card shows a boy, neatly dressed and groomed, sitting at a table on which lies a violin. In his description of Card 1, Murray stated that the boy is "contemplating" the violin. According to experts such as Bellak (1986), Card 1 of the TAT tends to reveal a person's relationship toward parental figures.

Other TAT cards tend to elicit other kinds of information. Card 4 is a picture of a woman "clutching the shoulders of a man whose face and body are averted as if he were trying to pull away from her" (Bellak, 1975, p. 51). This card elicits information concerning male–female relationships. Bellak (1986, 1996) and others provide a description of the TAT cards along with the information that each card tends to elicit. This knowledge is essential in TAT interpretation. Figure 14.2 shows Card 12F, which sometimes elicits conflicting emotions about the self. Other feelings may also be elicited.

FIGURE 14.2

Card 12F from the Thematic Apperception Test. This card often gives the subject a chance to express attitudes toward a mother or daughter figure. Sometimes attitudes toward marriage and aging also emerge.

Lewis J Merrim/Getty Images

Standardization of the administration, especially the scoring procedures of the TAT, is about as poor as, if not worse than, those of the Rorschach. Most examiners typically state something like, "I am going to show you some pictures. I want you to tell me a story about each picture. Tell me what led up to the story, what is happening, what the characters are thinking and feeling, and what the outcome will be." In the original design of the test, 20 cards were to be administered to each subject, 10 cards in each of two separate 1-hour sessions. In actual practice, however, only 10 or 12 cards are typically used (Bellak, 1996) and administration of the entire test typically takes place during one session (Lilienfeld et al., 2000). As with the Rorschach and almost all other individually administered tests, the examiner records the subject's responses verbatim. The examiner also records the *reaction time*—the time interval between the initial presentation of a card and the subject's first response. By recording reaction time, the examiner can determine whether the subject has difficulty with a particular card. Because each card is designed to elicit its own themes, needs, and conflicts, an abnormally long reaction time may indicate a specific problem. If, for example, the reaction time substantially increases for all cards involving heterosexual relationships, then the examiner may hypothesize that the subject is experiencing difficulty in this area.

There are by far more interpretive and scoring systems for the TAT than for the Rorschach. In his comprehensive review of the TAT literature, Murstein (1963, p. 23) states, "There would seem to be as many thematic scoring systems as there were hairs in the beard of Rasputin." Murstein summarizes most of the major methods of interpretation for the TAT, grouping them into quantitative and nonquantitative methods. Unlike the quantitative aspects of the Rorschach, which most examiners consider extremely important, the quantitative methods of TAT interpretation are unpopular (Alvarado, 1994; Groth-Marnat, 1999). Most TAT examiners find the available scoring systems to be overly elaborate, complex, and time-consuming. They therefore tend to use only nonquantitative methods of interpretation. In a survey of more than 100 psychologists who practiced in juvenile and family courts in North America, most clinicians (97%) reported that they did not use any scoring system at all but relied on their clinical judgment and intuition to interpret and score the TAT (Lilienfeld et al., 2000; Seewaldt, 2006).

Almost all methods of TAT interpretation take into account the *hero, needs, press, themes,* and *outcomes.* The *hero* is the character in each picture with whom the subject seems to identify (Bellak, 1996). In most cases, the story revolves around one easily recognizable character. If more than one character seems to be important, then the character most like the storyteller is selected as the hero. Of particular importance are the motives and *needs* of the hero. Most systems, including Murray's original, consider the intensity, duration, and frequency of each need to indicate the importance and relevance of that need. In TAT interpretation, *press* refers to the environmental forces that interfere with or facilitate satisfaction of the various needs. Again, factors such as frequency, intensity, and duration are used to judge the relative importance of these factors. The frequency of various *themes* (e.g., depression) and *outcomes* (e.g., failures) also indicates their importance.

To understand the potential value of the TAT in evaluating personality characteristics, you should realize that different individuals offer quite different responses to the same card. For example, given Card 1, in which a boy is contemplating a violin, one subject may say, "This boy's mother has just reminded him to practice the violin. The boy hates the violin and is wondering what he can do to make his practice session less boring. As he daydreams, his mother scolds him, so he picks up the violin and plays, resenting every minute." Another subject may respond, "The boy has just come home from school and is getting ready to practice the violin. He hopes to become a great violin player someday but realizes he's just an average, ordinary person. He picks up the violin and plays, dreaming about success." A third story may go as follows: "It's violin practice again and the boy is fed up. Do this, do that; his parents are always trying to live his life. This time he fixes them. He picks up the violin, smashes it, and goes out to play baseball."

Think about these three stories. Because the stimulus was the same in each case, differences in the stories must in some way reflect differences in the storytellers. The primary issue is exactly what is revealed in these stories. Many years ago, Lindzey (1952) analyzed several assumptions underlying the TAT. Table 14.4 lists these major assumptions. Although there were problems with many of the studies cited by Lindzey, positive evidence was found to support these assumptions, the validity of which has never been refuted (Bellak, 1996; Johnson, 1994). By understanding these assumptions, you can get an idea of the complexity of TAT interpretation.

TABLE 14.4 Lindzey's Assumptions for TAT Interpretation

Primary assumption

In completing an incomplete or unstructured situation, the individual may reveal his or her own characteristics (strivings, dispositions, conflicts).

Other assumptions

1. The storyteller ordinarily identifies with one person in the drama. The characteristics (wishes, strivings, conflicts) of this imaginary person may reflect those of the storyteller.

2. The storyteller's characteristics may be represented indirectly or symbolically.

3. All stories are not of equal importance.

4. Themes directly related to stimulus material are less likely to be significant than those unrelated to stimulus material.

5. Recurrent themes (those that show up in three or four different stories) are particularly likely to mirror the characteristics of the storyteller.

6. The stories may reflect momentary characteristics of the storyteller (those aroused by temporary environmental factors) as well as enduring characteristics.

7. Stories may reflect events from the past that the storyteller has only observed or witnessed. However, the selection of these stories suggests that the events may still reflect the storyteller's own characteristics.

8. The stories may also reflect group membership or sociocultural factors.

9. Dispositions and conflicts inferred from the storyteller's creations may be unconscious and thus may not always be reflected directly in overt behavior or consciousness.

Adapted from Lindzey (1952).

Although Lindzey's analysis was conducted some time ago, many TAT practitioners are guided by the assumptions listed in Table 14.4. The primary assumption—in completing an incomplete or unstructured situation, the individual may reveal his or her own strivings, dispositions, and conflicts—provides a rationale and support for projective tests in general. Most of the other assumptions, however, pertain specifically to the TAT. As these assumptions indicate, although a story reflects the storyteller, many other factors may influence the story. Therefore, all TAT experts agree that a complete interview and a case history must accompany any attempt to interpret the TAT. No matter how careful and thorough such an interview is, however, final conclusions and interpretations are still based on many factors, including the skill and experience of the examiner.

Psychometric Properties

Many experts consider the TAT to be psychometrically unsound (see Karp, 1999; Lilienfeld et al., 2000). Given the TAT's unstandardized procedures for administration, scoring, and interpretation, one can easily understand why psychometric evaluations have produced inconsistent, unclear, and conflicting findings. As with the Rorschach, divisions of opinion run deep. Subjectivity affects not only the interpretation of the TAT, but also analysis of the TAT literature. In other words, as with the Rorschach, two experts can look at the same research data and draw different or even opposite conclusions. It should be no surprise, then, that for almost every positive empirical finding there is a negative counterpart.

Even so, an analysis of existing results reveals that the study of specific variables, such as the achievement need, produces respectably high reliability figures. Test–retest reliabilities appear to fluctuate, however, and to diminish as the interval between the two testing sessions increases. The median test–retest correlation across studies is only approximately .30 (Kraiger, Hakel, & Cornelius, 1984; Winter & Stewart, 1977). However, J. W. Atkinson (1981) has argued that the validity of the TAT does not depend on test–retest reliability. Split-half reliabilities have been consistently poor. Many TAT proponents, though, do not consider the split-half method appropriate because each card is designed to produce its own theme and content (Cramer, 1999). What is needed is a study using Kuder-Richardson reliabilities, as has been done with the Rorschach. Gruber and Kreuzpointner (2013) maintain that the problem has stemmed from the incorrect use of internal consistency coefficients, especially Cronbach's α. When these investigators analyzed the original data set of the Thematic Apperception Test and two additional data sets, they found generally higher values when using the category scores as items instead of picture scores. To date, no one has followed up on this promising line of research.

Validity studies of the TAT have produced murky findings. Most experts agree that there is content-related validity evidence for using the TAT to evaluate human personality; however, criterion-related evidence for validity has been difficult to document. In an early but often cited study, Harrison (1940a, 1940b) found that his own inferences based on TAT stories correlated at .78 with hospital records for specific variables. He reported that he was 75% correct in diagnosing patients into major categories, such as psychotic versus neurotic, using TAT data. Little and Shneidman (1959) found, however, that when 12 specialists for each of four tests (TAT, Make-a-Picture Story, Rorschach, MMPI) were asked to match the judgments of a group of criterion judges who had conducted extensive interviews with each of the subjects, not only was there little agreement between the test judges and the criterion judges, but also the TAT had the lowest reliability and the poorest predictive validity of the four tests. Newer studies also report discouraging reliability coefficients (Singh, 1986). A more recent meta-analysis by Spangler (1992) found average correlations between the TAT and various criteria to run between .19 and .22, which is hardly impressive.

In short, like the Rorschach, the TAT has several significant problems. In spite of these problems, however, the TAT continues to find widespread application in clinical as well as research settings (see Ackerman & Pritzl, 2011, Tables 2 & 3; Pirelli, Gottdiener, & Zapf, 2011). As with the Rorschach, the most pressing need appears to be establishing standardized administration and scoring procedures. Until such standardization is achieved, the TAT will continue to fare poorly according to traditional psychometric standards.

Alternative Apperception Procedures

The versatility and usefulness of the TAT approach are illustrated not only by attempts such as those of Ritzler, Sharkey, and Chudy (1980) to update the test but also by the availability of special forms of the TAT for children and others for the elderly. The Children's Apperception Test (CAT) was created to meet the special needs of children ages 3 through 10 (Bellak, 1975; also see Meersand, 2011). The CAT stimuli contain animal rather than human figures as in the TAT.

A special children's apperception test has been developed specifically for Latino and Latina children (Malgady, Constantino, & Rogler, 1984). The Tell Me a Story Test (TEMAS) is a TAT technique that consists of 23 chromatic pictures depicting minority and nonminority characters in urban and familial settings (Constantino, Malgady, Colon-Malgady, & Bailey, 1992; Goodyear-Brown, 2011). Initial research has shown the promise of the TEMAS as a multicultural projective test for use with minority children (Constantino & Malgady, 1999; Costantino, Dana, & Malgady, 2007).

The Gerontological Apperception Test uses stimuli in which one or more elderly individuals are involved in a scene with a theme relevant to the concerns of the elderly, such as loneliness and family conflicts (Verdon, 2011; Wolk & Wolk, 1971). The Senior Apperception Technique is an alternative to the Gerontological Apperception Test and is parallel in content (Bellak, 1975; Bellak & Bellak, 1973).

All of these alternative perception tests hold promise as clinical tools (Mark, 1993; Verdon, 2011).

Nonpictorial Projective Procedures

Projective tests need not involve the use of a pictorial stimulus. Words or phrases sometimes provide the stimulus, as in the Word Association Test and incomplete sentence tasks. Or a subject can be asked to create or draw something, as in the Draw-a-Man Test. This final section briefly describes each of these procedures.

Word Association Test

Imagine yourself comfortably seated in a psychologist's examining office. Your task is simple, or at least it seems so. The psychologist says a word and you say the first word that comes to mind. The test begins. The first word is *hat*. You reply *coat*, the most common response of college students according to Rapaport, Gill, and Schafer (1968). The test goes on as follows:

Lamp

Love

Father

Paper

Masturbation

Chair

Breast

Car

Penis

Suicide

Do some of these words arouse any feelings in you? Words such as *love, father, breast,* and *masturbation* do in many people. The purpose of word association tests is to infer possible disturbances and areas of conflict from an individual's response to specific words.

The use of word association tests dates back to Galton (1879) and was first used on a clinical basis by Jung (1910) and G. H. Kent and Rosanoff (1910). In the first to attempt to standardize word association procedures, Kent and Rosanoff developed a list of 100 standard words and presented them to a sample of 1000 normal adults who were partially stratified by geographic location, education, occupation, age, and intelligence. An objective scoring system was developed, and the Kent-Rosanoff word association test enjoyed moderate popularity in the 1920s and 1930s.

Rapaport et al. (1968) subsequently developed a 60-item word association test. The range of words covered familial, household, oral, anal, aggressive, and phobic content. Responses were quantified by collecting norms on college students and schizophrenics, although interpretations were clearly psychoanalytic in nature.

Interest in word association techniques dropped considerably after Rapaport et al. (1968) concluded that the procedures did not live up to their clinical promise. Although the techniques are still in use (Mao, 2011; Oral, Güleç, Aydin, Ozan, & Kırpınar, 2011; Petchkovsky et al., 2013), they play only a limited role in clinical and counseling settings.

Sentence Completion Tasks

Another family of projective techniques involving words is incomplete sentence tasks. These tasks provide a stem that the subject is asked to complete.

Computers and Basic Psychological Science in Testing

LEARNING OBJECTIVES

When you have completed this chapter, you should be able to:

▶ Identify the differences between cognitive-behavioral assessment and traditional assessment procedures

▶ Identify the difference between the *beliefs* underlying traditional tests and the beliefs underlying behavioral tests

▶ Briefly describe cognitive-behavioral assessment based on operant conditioning

▶ Identify the main difference between cognitive-behavioral self-report techniques and traditional self-report techniques

▶ List three types of behavioral self-report techniques

▶ Briefly describe psychophysical assessment

▶ Discuss the role of computers in modern psychological testing

A high-school teacher once contacted us regarding her 7-year-old son. At the age of 4, the boy had suffered from an illness in which he could not eat solid food for 25 days because it made him gag. If he managed to swallow, he became extremely nauseous. Ever since he had recovered from the illness, he was reluctant to eat all but a few select foods. His usual menu was cold cereal for breakfast, a peanut butter sandwich for lunch, and plain spaghetti for dinner. He refused to eat meat or vegetables of any kind. His parents tried everything, but nothing worked. The mother was concerned that the boy was not developing properly. She had taken him to a pediatrician who told her that unless something could be done to get the boy to eat, he would have to be hospitalized. The physician suggested psychiatric intervention and gave the boy 1 month to improve.

After explaining this problem, the mother asked us whether we could administer a test that might explain why the child wasn't eating. A school psychologist had suggested to her that psychological tests might help facilitate the treatment process. If we could understand why the boy wasn't eating, perhaps this information would help us treat him. During our interview, we discovered that the boy had been in psychiatric treatment when he was 5. The treatment had lasted approximately 1 year, with little improvement. Partly because of this previous failure and partly because of her desperation, the mother insisted we do some testing. As we thought about the various tests we might use, we could see little value in using any of the traditional tests for this problem.

We did administer the Wechsler Intelligence Scale for Children, Fifth Edition (WISC-V) and found that the boy had above-average intelligence (full-scale IQ = 115). In achievement, the boy was functioning about half a grade level above his current grade placement in both reading and arithmetic. Thus, intellectual and achievement factors could not account for the problem. Unfortunately, personality tests were not much more useful than the ability tests had been. After administering the Children's Apperception Test and conducting extensive interviewing and observation (see Chapter 14), our interpretation confirmed our suspicion that the boy's eating problem originated with the trauma he had suffered when he could not eat solid foods. In simple terms, the boy had a fear of eating.

Knowing why the boy wasn't eating certainly wasn't much help. One of the weaknesses of the original model of testing as reflected in traditional tests is that they provide little information concerning possible treatment approaches. When we explained the situation to the mother, she pleaded, "Isn't there any other type of test you can give him? Isn't there a test that might also indicate what type of treatment would be most effective?" Thanks to advances within scientific psychology, we could answer, "Yes."

We told the mother that numerous alternatives to traditional tests had been developed by psychologists in the specialty based on cognitive-behavioral principles known as *cognitive behavior assessment or, sometimes, simply behavioral assessment* (Reh, Schmidt, Lam, Schimmelmann, & Hebebrand, 2015). In the hands of highly trained experts, traditional psychological tests may be extremely valuable, but they still fall short on several grounds. The traditional tests discussed thus far in this book offer little information concerning treatment approaches. As a rule, these traditional procedures also provide little information about how a person might behave in a

TABLE 15.1 Varieties of Alternatives to Traditional Testing Procedures

Operant conditioning techniques

Self-report techniques

Cognitive techniques

Psychophysiological techniques

Psychophysiological procedures

particular situation. Even if these traditional procedures do explain the reason behind a particular symptom, this information usually offers little to the overall treatment process. The result of such shortcomings in traditional tests has been an explosion of alternative approaches based on principles of scientific psychology, and more recently the advent of personal computers.

The techniques we discuss in this chapter can be divided into several categories. These include procedures based on conditioning, self-report techniques (Arentoft, Van Dyk, Thames, Sayegh, & Thaler, 2016), Kanfer and Saslow's behavior-analytic approach, a variety of cognitive techniques, psychophysiological techniques, and signal-detection procedures. Each of these is discussed in turn (see Table 15.1).

Cognitive-Behavioral Assessment Procedures Versus the Medical Model of Assessment

The Rationale for Cognitive-Behavioral Assessment

Traditional testing procedures are based on a medical model. According to this model, the overt manifestations of a disordered psychological condition (e.g., overeating or undereating) are only symptoms—surface expressions of an underlying cause. Disordered behavior is believed to be caused by some underlying characteristic such as an early traumatic experience. In the example at the beginning of this chapter, the boy's avoidance of food was, in a sense, caused by the trauma of an illness in which solid food made him nauseous. Treatment in the medical model is based on the idea that unless the cause of a symptom is removed, a new symptom may develop. Thus, one major function of traditional psychological tests is to ascertain the possible underlying causes of disordered behaviors.

In cognitive-behavioral assessment, by contrast, the behaviors, thought processes, or physiological responses that define a disordered condition are considered the real problem. If the person eats too much, then the problem is simply overeating and not some underlying cause. The overeating may, in fact, have been caused by some early experience, just as in the 7-year-old boy. However, in cognitive-behavioral assessment, the eating behavior becomes the direct target of treatment. Therefore, the testing procedure in this case would evaluate eating behavior.

This is not to say that cognitive-behavioral assessment denies, ignores, or negates the causes of psychological disorders. On the contrary, certain techniques of cognitive-behavioral assessment include an evaluation of the factors that precede, coexist with, and follow (maintain) disordered behavior (DiCaccavo, 2010; Kounti, Tsolaki, & Kiosseoglou, 2006). These may be environmental factors (such as working conditions, home situation), thought processes (such as internal dialogue), or both. Thus, cognitive-behavioral assessment often includes an evaluation of the internal and external factors that lead to and maintain disordered behavior as well as an evaluation of the behavior itself (Mack & Rybarczyk, 2011, p. 89; Sheldon, 2011, pp. 3–4).

Cognitive-behavioral assessment is more direct than traditional psychological tests. It is characterized by fewer inferential assumptions and remains closer to observable phenomena (Sheldon, 2011). Through cognitive-behavioral assessment, one might find that, just before eating, the 7-year-old boy in our example says to himself, "I don't want to eat; it will make me sick." Subsequently, the boy refuses to eat. As he leaves the dinner table, his mother says, "That's okay, honey, you don't have to eat." The boy's statement, "I don't want to eat," precedes the disordered behavior. His avoidance of food is the core of the disorder. His mother's comment, plus the boy's relief that he doesn't have to eat, reinforces or maintains the disorder. In cognitive-behavioral assessment, psychologists analyze preceding and subsequent factors and focus on a direct change in overt behavior, thoughts, or physiological processes. The treatment process thus involves an attempt to alter the disordered behavior (e.g., increasing the frequency of eating). Treatment may also involve modifying the internal dialogue before and after the boy eats and modifying the mother's behavior so that she no longer reinforces avoidance of food but instead reinforces eating.

In traditional procedures, the boy's failure to eat would be viewed as only a symptom. Testing would be aimed at determining the cause of this symptom (the early trauma of the illness he had when he was 4), and treatment would be directed at the cause rather than at the behavior itself. Presumably, by giving the boy insight into the causes of his behavior, a psychologist could get the boy to understand why he wasn't eating. When he achieved this understanding, he would no longer need to avoid eating. Table 15.2 compares traditional and cognitive-behavioral assessment.

It is beyond the scope of this text to debate the pros and cons of the cognitive-behavioral and medical models. Our goal is to help you understand the differences between the two. Suffice it to say that cognitive-behavioral testing procedures, based on psychology's scientific base, have added a whole new dimension to the field of psychological testing.

TABLE 15.2 Traditional Versus Cognitive-Behavioral Assessment

	Traditional assessment	**Cognitive-behavioral assessment**
Target	Underlying cause	Disordered behavior
Symptoms	Superficial	Focus of treatment
Assessment	Indirect; not related to treatment	Direct; related to treatment
Theory	Medical model	Behavioral model
Goal	Determine cause of symptoms	Analyze disordered behavior

Early Procedures Based on Operant Conditioning

In operant conditioning, psychologists observe the behaviors of an individual. After the individual has made a response, they can do something to the individual to alter the probability of the recurrence of the response. They may present something positive or remove something negative following the response, which should increase the rate of recurrence, or else they may present something aversive or remove something positive following the response, which should reduce the rate of recurrence.

In cognitive-behavioral assessment based on operant conditioning, one must first identify the critical response or responses involved in the disorder. One can then evaluate these critical responses for frequency, intensity, or duration. This evaluation establishes the baseline (usual rate of occurrence) for the particular behavior. According to an early system developed by Kanfer and Saslow (1969), if the behaviors occur too frequently, then they are called *behavioral excesses*. If they occur too infrequently, they are called *behavioral deficits*. Obviously, with a behavioral excess, treatment centers on reducing the frequency, intensity, or duration of the behavior in question. With a behavioral deficit, treatment focuses on increasing the behavior. Table 15.3 outlines the steps in cognitive-behavioral assessment based on operant conditioning.

After attempting to increase or decrease the behavior (treatment intervention), psychologists observe the effect of the intervention on the behavior in question relative to the baseline. If the goal was to decrease the behavior, then there should be a decrease relative to the baseline. If the critical behavior remains at or above baseline levels, then the intervention has failed.

In the example at the beginning of this chapter, we decided to use cognitive-behavioral assessment based on operant conditioning. The critical behavior was obvious: frequency of eating. Furthermore, the critical behavior was a deficit; that is, the boy wasn't eating enough. To evaluate the critical behavior (Step 3), we asked the boy's mother to record the amount and kind of food that the boy ate each day. Using standard calorie references, we converted the amount of food the boy ate into calories. The baseline looked something like the graph in Figure 15.1. The boy was eating an average of approximately 800 calories a day, with a range of 600 to 1000 calories on any given day. This number of calories is too few to prevent a small, gradual weight loss.

Because the behavior was a deficit, we tried to increase the boy's frequency of eating. For our intervention, we used a reward system based on points. The boy received points for everything he ate. The more he ate, the more points he got.

TABLE 15.3 Steps in a Cognitive-Behavioral Assessment

Step 1:	Identify critical behaviors.
Step 2:	Determine whether critical behaviors are excesses or deficits.
Step 3:	Evaluate critical behaviors for frequency, duration, or intensity (i.e., obtain a baseline).
Step 4:	If excesses, attempt to decrease frequency, duration, or intensity of behaviors; if deficits, attempt to increase behaviors.

FIGURE 15.1

Baseline in eating difficulty example.

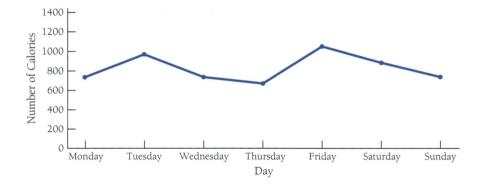

Following each meal, his mother recorded the number of points that he received as well as the cumulative total. She posted this record on a bulletin board in the boy's room so that he could observe his own progress. She also posted a chart that we had worked out with the two of them. The chart listed toys and other rewards that he could trade for points. For example, he could exchange 10 points for a package of baseball cards any time he wanted. He could also save his points for bigger prizes. For 350 points, he could get an iPad game he had been wanting, and so on. In the treatment procedure, his mother recorded exactly what he ate each day just as she had during the pretreatment assessment in which the baseline was obtained. This record was then converted into calories, and each week we made a graph of his day-to-day calorie intake.

The intervention proved highly effective. Within 1 week, the boy had earned some 200 points and was well on the way to securing his iPad game. The graph for this first week of treatment is shown in Figure 15.2. As the graph indicates, the boy doubled his average intake of calories to some 1600 (range 1400 to 1800). Thus, his intake of calories was far above baseline following the intervention. Assessment continued throughout the treatment and also provided feedback about the effects of the treatment. In the second week, the boy's consumption of calories fell below the dramatic increases of the first week, but it never fell below baseline levels. In 6 weeks, the boy gained approximately 8 pounds. He had earned just about every toy

FIGURE 15.2

Eating behavior during the first week of intervention.

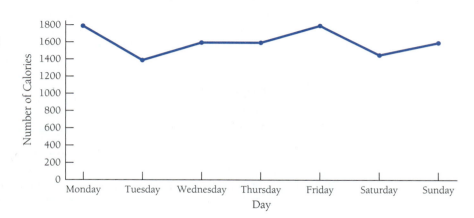

or game he had ever wanted. At this point, his mother became concerned that he might gain too much weight or that she might go broke paying for rewards. After consultation with us, she terminated the point system. Following termination, there was a substantial drop in his eating behavior for 3 or 4 days, but then it increased to about a normal level for his age.

Over the course of treatment, the boy's parents had developed a different attitude about his eating behavior. So had the boy. Everybody concerned now knew that the boy could eat without negative consequences. The parents refused to permit the boy to get away without eating, and the boy no longer had an excuse not to eat. Although the therapy never attempted to get at an original or hypothetical underlying cause of the behavior, the boy was in every sense cured. He wasn't hospitalized, and his eating behavior was adequate 6 months following treatment. His mother complained that he was still a finicky eater, but his weight was within normal limits.

Practitioners can use the operant approach to solve a variety of problems, including smoking (Hogarth, Dickinson, & Duka, 2005; Hogarth, Dickinson, Wright, Kouvaraki, & Duka, 2007; Winkler et al., 2011), poor study habits (Gallo & Rinaldo, 2010), coping with chronic pain (Hölzl, Kleinböhl, & Huse, 2005; Vlaeyen, de Jong, Onghena, Kerckhoffs-Hanssen, & Kole-Snijders, 2002), addiction (Treisman & Clark, 2011), and poor diet (Douglas, 2002; Tazaki & Landlaw, 2006). In each case, one first calculates a baseline. Then, one implements an intervention. Finally, one observes the effects of this intervention on the baseline. If you feel you don't study enough, for instance, you can try the approach yourself. To assess your study behavior, record the number of minutes you study each day for 1 week. This is your baseline. Then decide on a reward for yourself. Every day record how long you study. Give yourself the reward whenever you study longer than 25% above the average time for your baseline. See whether this procedure doesn't increase the time you spend studying.

Self-Report Techniques

In our example, the frequency of the 7-year-old boy's disordered eating behavior was recorded by his mother because the assessment process required that someone observe the boy. Not all problems, however, can be so easily and readily observed. Further, when a parent or other relative of the subject does the observing and recording, the practitioner must depend on the skill, accuracy, and honesty of the well-meaning but untrained relative. Thus, in the ideal situation, the practitioner or a trained assistant observes the individual to be assessed. The practitioner directly observes and records specific problem behaviors in a variety of situations and notes the factors that precede and maintain these behaviors. Like any observer, the practitioner must make him- or herself as inconspicuous and as unobtrusive as possible to avoid interfering with or influencing the subject. Unfortunately, following a subject around to record behaviors is difficult, time-consuming, and often unrealistic. In most cases, the observer can hardly avoid influencing the subject. Indeed, psychologists have long known that the mere presence of an observer may alter the behavior of an individual (Polansky et al., 1949).

One attempt to deal with the problems inherent in observation is the *self-report technique* (Muris & Field, 2011, p. 77). The typical self-report is a list of statements

TABLE 15.4 Examples of a Behavioral Self-Report

Circle	1 if the item elicits no fear
	2 if the item elicits some fear
	3 if the item elicits a little fear
	4 if the item elicits a lot of fear
	5 if the item elicits extreme fear

Worms	1	2	3	4	5
Bats	1	2	3	4	5
Psychological tests	1	2	3	4	5
Dogs	1	2	3	4	5
Snakes	1	2	3	4	5
Highways	1	2	3	4	5
Men	1	2	3	4	5

Circle true or false as the item applies to you.

I like to talk when in a group.	True	False
I relate easily to persons of the opposite sex.	True	False
I like to walk in dark places.	True	False
I like to give speeches to large groups.	True	False
I feel most comfortable with strangers.	True	False
I feel most comfortable with family.	True	False
I feel most comfortable with friends.	True	False
I like to be the leader in a group.	True	False
I would rather follow than lead in a group.	True	False

about particular situations. The subject's task may be either to respond "True" or "False" to each statement or to circle a number (1 to 5, for example) to indicate the importance or relevance of the statement. Table 15.4 gives examples of the types of statements used. Self-report techniques assume that the person's responses reflect individual differences and measure some other observable behavior. If, for example, one person circles 5 for fear of snakes and another person circles 1, then psychologists assume that direct observation of these two individuals in the presence of snakes would reveal different, measurable responses. The person who circled 5 might scream and run. The person who circled 1 might simply ignore the snakes. In place of direct observation, the practitioner accepts the face validity of the subject's responses.

 That cognitive-behavioral assessment has concentrated on phenomena such as fear illustrates the major distinction between cognitive-behavioral and traditional self-report procedures. Cognitive-behavioral procedures focus on situations that lead to particular response patterns; that is, situations are the primary determinant of behavior. Traditional self-report procedures focus on relatively enduring internal characteristics of the individual (personality traits) that lead to particular response patterns. In the cognitive-behavioral approach, one sees situations as the primary determinant of behavior. In the traditional approach, one sees characteristics that the person brings to a situation (e.g., traits) as the primary determinant of behavior. Thus, in the cognitive-behavioral approach, a person is not simply fearful and therefore fearful no matter what the situation; a person is fearful only in certain circumstances or situations because these circumstances elicit fear in that person (Ramirez & Andreu, 2006).

The Fear Survey Schedule (FSS)

The FSS is the oldest and most researched of the cognitive-behavioral self-report procedures. In clinical and experimental use since the 1950s, it continues to be used for a variety of purposes (Kushnir, Gothelf, & Sadeh, 2015; O'Hare, & Dien, 2008; Westenberg, Gullone, Bokhorst, Heyne, & King, 2007). Since the FSS was introduced into the literature by Akutagawa (1956) as a 50-item test, it has undergone a variety of changes, and various versions have from 50 to 122 items, with ratings of fear on either 5-point or 7-point scales (Burnham, 2005). It has been adapted for use with children (Burnham & Giesen, 2005; Murisa, Huijdinga, Mayera, & de Vriesa, 2011), and there even is a version for parents of preschool children (Kushnir et al., 2015). There are also versions for adolescents (Muris & Field, 2011) as well as adults with intellectual disabilities (Hermans, van der Pas, & Evenhuis, 2011). One adaptation of the FSS was created for measuring specific phobias (Antony, 2001; Ten Berge & Veerkamp, 2005). From its worldwide use (Bajrić, Kobašlija, & Hrvoje, 2011; Diercke, Ollinger, Bermejo et al., 2012; Du, Lee, & Christinam, 2011), numerous cross-cultural studies are available (e.g., Hawkins-Gilligan, Dygdon, & Conger, 2011; Lahikainen, Kraav, Kirmanen, & Taimalu, 2006).

Items are typically related to situations that involve fear and avoidance behaviors, such as fear of open places, fear of snakes, fear of dead animals. Subjects rate each item according to the degree to which they experience that particular fear. Developers have derived items on the FSS from clinical observation of actual cases (Wolpe & Lang, 1964) and from experimental investigations in laboratory settings (Geer, 1965). The FSS attempts to identify those situations that elicit fear and thus avoidance. Once psychologists have identified these situations, they can aim treatment at helping people deal with these situations, thus reducing fear.

Assertiveness

Some individuals have difficulty speaking up for themselves. When they finally do speak up, they are often aggressive. Suppose someone cuts in front of you in a long line to see a popular movie. Assertiveness experts might suggest that you calmly and firmly inform this person of the location of the end of the line. If you encounter resistance, you calmly explain that everyone has been waiting in line and that the only polite and appropriate thing for the intruder to do is to go to the end of the line. Many people have difficulty acting appropriately in this type of situation. They may stew inside or go to the other extreme and display aggression, such as striking the intruder or throwing a temper tantrum.

TABLE 15.5 Sample Questions From a Behavioral Assertiveness Questionnaire

I. Suppose you were in the following situations. How would you respond? Indicate by circling number 1, 2, or 3.

   A. You have ordered filet mignon for you and your date at an expensive restaurant. You wanted yours cooked rare. The waiter brings it well done. What would you do?

      1. Tell the waiter to bring you another, cooked the way you wanted it.

      2. Complain to the waiter, but eat what he had brought for you anyway.

      3. Say nothing.

   B. You are at a bank. You've been waiting in line for nearly 10 minutes. Finally, you reach the head of the line. A man with a large briefcase comes from the outside and steps right in front of you. What would you do?

      1. Tell him to go to the end of the line.

      2. Tell him there is a long line, but let him go in front of you anyway.

      3. Say nothing.

II. In those situations in which you say nothing, what are you afraid of? (Check the best answer.)

   A. Being yelled at ( )

   B. Being beat up ( )

   C. Being embarrassed ( )

   D. Being rejected ( )

   E. Violating a personal or religious belief ( )

   F. Expending excessive energy ( )

Adapted from Cautela and Upper (1976, pp. 97–98).

Clinical practitioners have constructed various measures of assertiveness. Table 15.5 illustrates the type of item found in a self-report questionnaire for assertiveness, such as the Assertive Behavior Survey Schedule (ABSS). If you were taking the ABSS, you would indicate the responses you would make in specific situations that call for assertiveness. You would also be asked to speculate on the consequences of assertiveness for you. Thus, the ABSS can help determine whether you can be assertive if necessary, situations in which you might have difficulty being assertive, and your personal attitude toward assertiveness.

Evaluation of Self-Report Procedures

Obviously, any practitioner with a problem to assess can simply devise and publish a self-report device. Indeed, there appears to be no shortage of such practitioners. Unfortunately, psychometric data have rarely been presented to help evaluate these devices, although this trend seems to be shifting (see Dubowitz et al., 2011; Vorstenboscha, Antonya, Koernera, & Boivinb, 2012; Wuyek, Antony, & McCabe, 2011).

In their use of self-report techniques, some psychologists "reinvent the wheel." For example, Cautela and Upper (1976) did not hesitate to admit that the prototypes of current self-report techniques are tests such as the Woodworth Personal Data Sheet. Early paper-and-pencil structured personality tests, finally abandoned in the 1930s, are indeed difficult to distinguish from many modern self-report procedures. Both implicitly assume that test responses have face validity. Thus, all of the problems associated with face validity—subject capacity and willingness to be truthful, response bias, poor reliability, poor validity, and lack of norms—usually plague cognitive-behavioral self-report techniques. Unfortunately, only one of these self-report techniques, the FSS, has been subjected to anything close to an adequate psychometric analysis, with over 1000 published research articles through 2016.

Practitioners have a long way to go before they can offer cognitive-behavioral self-report procedures as established clinical tools. However, when used in conjunction with other sources of data, such as psychophysiological recordings and direct observation, self-report data can provide useful information in clinical as well as research settings. Indeed, this is the modern trend.

The Dysfunctional Attitude Scale

A major pillar of cognitive-behavioral assessment that focuses primarily on thinking patterns rather than overt behavior is A. T. Beck's (1967, 1976, 2002) Cognitive Model of Psychopathology. The model is based on *schemas*, which are cognitive frameworks or organizing principles of thought. For example, in your first impression of an individual, you create a schema of that person. In your subsequent interactions with that person, you add to or subtract from that original schema. Moreover, the original schema influences your subsequent perceptions. For instance, if you originally pegged the person as a "techie," then you will likely label subsequent behavior accordingly. According to Beck, schemas serve to organize prior experience, guide the interpretations of new experiences, and shape expectancies and predictions. Beck's theory holds that dysfunctional schemas predispose an individual to develop pathological behaviors (Lomax & Lam, 2011; Newman, Leahy, Beck, Reilly-Harrington, & Gyulia, 2003).

To evaluate negative schemas, Beck and colleagues have developed the Dysfunctional Attitude Scale (DAS) (Weissman, 1979; Weissman & Beck, 1978). The DAS has two parallel forms (Power, Katz, McGuffin, & Duggan, 1994). It identifies beliefs that might interact with a stressor to produce psychopathology (Whisman, Johnson, & Smolen, 2011). For instance, a person may believe that he cannot find happiness without being loved by another or that turning to someone else for advice or help is an admission of weakness. The subject is provided with a list of statements such as "Others can care for me even if they know all my weaknesses" and is asked to respond on a 7-point Likert scale ranging from "totally agree" to "totally disagree." The validity of the scale is supported by a variety of factor analytic data (Beck et al., 1991; Ruiz, Suárez-Falcón, Barón-Rincón, Barrera-Acevedo, & Martínez-Sánchez, 2016; Whisman et al., 2011). A Spanish version is also available (Ruiz, Suarez-Falcon, Odriozola-Gonzalez, Barbero-Rubio, & Lopez-Lopez, 2015).

Irrational Beliefs Test

According to the cognitive viewpoint, human behavior is often determined by beliefs and expectations rather than reality. If, for example, your instructor announces that there will be an exam in the third week of classes, you will do most of your studying for it the day or two before it if you are like most students. Suppose, however, you miss the class just before the announced exam. And suppose that a "friend" of yours plays a trick on you and tells you the exam has been canceled. If you believe your friend and therefore expect that there will be no exam, will you study as hard as you would have (if at all) had you known there would be a test? It's unlikely. The exam will still be given (reality), but your behavior will have changed because of your belief that the exam has been canceled. In view of the influence of beliefs and expectations, several cognitive-behavioral tests have been developed to measure them. In an early study, R. A. Jones (1968), for example, developed a 100-item Irrational Beliefs Test (IBT) to measure irrational beliefs (e.g., the belief that you must always succeed to be worthwhile).

The IBT requires subjects to indicate their level of agreement or disagreement with each of the 100 items on a 5-point scale (e.g., "I frequently worry about things over which I have no control"). Half of the items indicate the presence of a particular irrational belief; the other half, its absence.

The IBT found widespread use in clinical as well as research settings and has received considerable attention (Bridges & Sanderman, 2002; Taghavi, Goodarzi, Kazemi, & Ghorbani, 2006; Warren, 2011). Although the IBT was initially one of the most popular measures of irrational beliefs, its use has gradually diminished due to criticisms that these beliefs were not measured independently of the emotional consequences they were hypothesized to cause (Bridges & Harnish, 2010, p. 871). The reliability of the IBT appears to be similar to that of structured personality tests, with test–retest coefficients for short intervals (2 weeks or less) ranging from .48 to .90 for individual scales and .88 for the full scale. The validity documentation of the IBT is weak (Smith & Zurawski, 1983), although the IBT does appear to be related to both anxiety and depression (Cook & Peterson, 1986; Deffenbacher et al., 1986).

Irrational Beliefs Inventory (IBI)

The IBI was developed to improve upon some of the weaknesses of the IBT. This 50-item scale, developed in the Netherlands by Koopmans, Sanderman, Timmerman, and Emmelkamp, is based in part on the item pool of the IBT. Because it measures cognitions rather than negative affect, the IBI avoids the criticisms leveled at the IBT—that beliefs were not measured separately from the negative consequences of those beliefs. The IBI uses a 5-point scale and consists of five subscales (worrying, rigidity, need for approval, problem avoidance, and emotional irresponsibility) plus a total score.

The IBI has consistent psychometric properties across several cultures (Bridges & Sanderman, 2002), including Arabic (Al-Heeti, Hamid, & Alghorani, 2012) as well as Spanish-speaking populations (Amutio & Smith, 2007). Its internal consistency is acceptable, and the five subscales were found to be independent of each other. It has been useful in clinical and research settings when exploring the role of irrational beliefs in obsessive-compulsive disorder, social phobias, and therapy for depression (Bridges & Sanderman, 2002).

Cognitive Functional Analysis

What people say to themselves also influences behavior. If you tell yourself that you can't learn statistics, then you will likely avoid statistics. Furthermore, when confronted with a difficult statistics problem, you will tend to give up quickly. If you tell

Mindset

yourself you like statistics, you will probably confront difficult statistics problems by taking your time and systematically figuring out the answers. Self-statements have been shown to influence behaviors as diverse as coping behavior in patients with fear of public speaking (Gallego, Emmelkamp, van der Kooij, & Mees, 2011), pain during pregnancy (Chang, Yang, Jensen, Lee, & Lai, 2011), treatment of schizophrenia (Bennouna-Greene, Berna, Conway, Rathbone et al., 2011), and athletic performance (Perkos, Theodorakis, & Chroni, 2002). Interestingly, positive and negative self-statements do not function in the same way. Apparently, negative self-statements do far more harm than positive self-statements do good. Thus, treatment generally involves identifying and then eliminating negative self-statements rather than increasing positive self-statements. Try to become aware of your own self-statements for a moment. What do you say to yourself as you go about your daily activities? Odds are, if you make a lot of negative self-statements, you are hindering your personal efficiency and ability to cope.

interesting

One of the most important examples of cognitive-behavioral assessment is called *cognitive-functional analysis* (Meichenbaum, 1976, 2003). The premise underlying a cognitive-functional analysis is that what a person says to him- or herself plays a critical role in behavior. The cognitive-functional analyst is thus interested in internal dialogue such as self-appraisals and expectations. Again, what do you say to yourself about yourself as you go about your daily activities? Do you constantly criticize or belittle yourself? Or do you always reassure yourself of your capabilities? Research clearly indicates these self-statements influence your behavior and even your feelings (Longe, Maratos, & Gilbert, 2010; Martin & Swinson, 2000; Masuda, Twohig, Stormo et al., 2010).

Cognitive-functional analysis is concerned with ascertaining the environmental factors that precede behavior (environmental antecedents) as well as those that maintain behavior (environmental consequences). In addition, however, a cognitive-functional analysis attempts to ascertain the internal or cognitive antecedents and consequences for the behavioral sequence (the internal dialogue). What does the person say to him- or herself before, during, and following the behavior? What is said before the behavior may influence what is done. What is said during the behavior may influence the way the behavior manifests itself. What is said following the behavior may influence its probability of recurrence.

If thoughts influence overt behavior, then modifying one's thoughts can lead to modifications in one's actions. In other words, to the extent that thoughts play a role in eliciting or maintaining one's actions, modification of the thoughts underlying the actions should lead to behavioral changes. For example, if the thought "I must have a cigarette" is consistently associated with the behavioral sequence involved in smoking, then changing that thought to "My lungs are clean, I feel healthy, and I have no desire to smoke" could help to modify the person's pattern of smoking behavior.

Parallel to Meichenbaum's technique of cognitive-functional analysis are procedures and devices that allow a person to test him- or herself, or *self-monitoring devices*. Because cognitive-behavioral practitioners value the role and responsibility of the individual in the therapeutic process, they have developed a wide variety of these devices. In the simplest case, an individual must record the frequency of a particular behavior—that is, to monitor it so that he or she becomes aware of the behavior. To monitor your smoking behavior, simply count the number of cigarettes you smoke each day. To monitor your weight, weigh yourself each morning and record the number of pounds.

Some self-monitoring procedures are quite sophisticated. For example, a mechanical counter, marketed to the general public, can be attached to the jaw to count the number of bites a person takes when eating. The idea is to take fewer bites each day, even if only one less than the day before. Presumably, this procedure will ultimately result in a lower intake of food and eventually weight loss. Similarly, timing devices and procedures allow people to assess how long they engage in an activity. In one method, the subject plugs in a clock every time she studies, thus recording total study time. The goal is to increase this length of time, either by increasing the length of individual study sessions or by increasing the total study time within a specific period. These self-monitoring assessment tools are limited only by the imagination of the practitioner. One of us (DPS) recently bought a smartphone that was equipped with a health meter that counted the number of stets, number of flight of stairs, and distance traveled per day. Later in this chapter in our section about computerized psychological tests and measurement, we discuss the latest computer equipment used to analyze thoughts and behaviors regarding everything from social regulation of emotion (Perrez, Wilhelm, Schoebi, & Horner, 2001) to fear responses (South, Larson, White, Dana, & Crowley, 2011).

Psychophysiological Procedures

Seen as a variant of cognitive-behavioral assessment by some and as an independent category by others, psychophysiological methods of assessment use such indicators as heart rate, blood pressure, galvanic skin response (GSR), and skin temperature to assess psychological problems (Hsieh et al., 2011). In essence, psychophysiological assessment procedures attempt to quantify physiological responses (Humphreys et al., 2011).

Physiological Variables With Treatment Implications

The feasibility of psychophysiological assessment received support in an early study conducted by Ax (1953). Ax demonstrated that the fear response was related to specific physiological changes such as increases in blood pressure and skin conductance levels. He found that he could distinguish fear and anger based on physiological data. Ax's early work, subsequently supported (see Ekman, Levenson, & Friesen, 1983; Turpin, 1991), had interesting implications. For instance, it suggested the possibility of assessing abnormally chronic and intense anger or fear through strictly physiological methods.

This type of assessment represents a quantum leap from traditional procedures, which depend on voluntary responses from subjects. In addition, as with other methods of behavioral assessment, psychophysiological assessment has direct implications for treatment (Wichers, Lothmann, Simons, Nicolson, & Peeters, 2011).

The polygraph and related devices that measure blood pressure, heart rate, and GSR have been the primary tools of the psychophysiological assessment specialist.

However, imaginative researchers continue to develop tools for special purposes. For example, psychophysiologists have been particularly interested in measuring adult sexual responses. Measures of sexual arousal make use of the fact that it is directly related to the flow of blood into the penis in men and into the vagina in women (Janssen, 2002; Masters & Johnson, 1966). Using this knowledge, researchers have developed measures of human sexual arousal. For example, penile erection can be measured by the penile transducer, a device that encircles the penis (Baxter, Barbaree, & Marshall, 1986; Zuckerman, 1971). As erection occurs, an electrical signal is generated, and this signal can then be recorded. The procedure can be used to determine the type of stimuli (pictures, fantasies, men, women, and so forth) that lead to arousal in men as well as the strength of the male sexual response. The penile transducer and related devices are much more objective than traditional tools.

Evaluation of Psychophysiological Techniques

Support for psychophysiological assessment has come from investigations that have revealed a systematic covariation between measurable physiological processes and cognitive processes (Jacobson, Bondi, & Salmon, 2002; Kossowsky, Wilhelm, Roth, & Schneider, 2011). For example, in a classic study, Ahern and Beatty (1979) found that more intelligent subjects show smaller task-evoked pupillary dilations than do less intelligent subjects (as evaluated by their scores on the SAT Reasoning Test). These results reveal physiological differences in individuals with differing mental abilities. Later research supports these findings (Langer et al., 2011). In other studies, Beatty and colleagues (e.g., Geiselman, Woodward, & Beatty, 1982) used measures of heart rate variability and skin conductance to evaluate *processing intensity*, the amount of effort or energy devoted to a cognitive task. Presumably, brighter individuals expend less of their total available processing resources in solving a difficult problem, either because they have greater resources or because they make more efficient use of them.

   Psychophysiological hardware seems to hold considerable promise for raising the scientific respectability of psychological testing. Problems still remain, however. One of the most serious of these concerns artifacts. For instance, movement by a subject may result in the recording of a physiological response that did not occur. In many cases, furthermore, direct measurement is difficult if not impossible. To measure brain wave patterns, for example, one places electrodes on the head, whereas the electrical current measured actually comes from the brain. Thus, the skull distorts the electrical impulse measured by the recording device. There are other problems as well, including the long-known effect of initial values (Wilder, 1950), by which the strength of a response is influenced by the absolute prestimulus strength. Which is the stronger response: an increase in heart rate from 60 to 85 beats per minute or an increase from 110 to 125 beats per minute? Obviously, one must take initial values into account in evaluating the strength, intensity, and significance of a physiological response. Another problem, which you have seen throughout this book, is that demographic factors such as age, gender, and ethnicity influence psychophysiological responses (Anderson & McNeilly, 1991). Thus, one must always consider cultural, ethnic, economic, gender, and other variables in making any kind of assessment. In spite of these problems, psychophysiological procedures appear to hold great promise for the future of psychological testing.

Computers and Psychological Testing

The application and use of computers in testing have been a major development in the field (Florell, 2011; Stochl, Böhnke, Pickett, & Croudace, 2015). For testing, one can use computers in two basic ways: (1) to administer, score, and even interpret traditional tests as in the new dual iPad approach to the WISC-V (see Chapter 10) and (2) to create new tasks and perhaps measure abilities that traditional procedures cannot tap. We will briefly look at the history and development of computers and psychological testing and recent applications of computers to the testing field, particularly to cognitive-behavioral assessment.

In 1966, a Rogerian therapist named Eliza marked the beginning of a new phase in psychological testing and assessment (Epstein & Klinkenberg, 2001). With a great amount of empathy, Eliza encouraged her clients to talk about their experiences and how these experiences made them feel. Clients responded warmly and enjoyed the sense of empathy resulting from their interaction. The warmth and connection between Eliza and her clients came as a big surprise to researcher Dr. Joseph Weizenbaum. Eliza was his creation, a computer program developed to emulate the behavior of a psychotherapist. Weizenbaum had produced the program in an attempt to show that human–computer interaction was superficial and ineffective for therapy. Dr. Weizenbaum discovered that sessions with Eliza engendered positive emotions in the clients who had actually enjoyed the interaction and attributed human characteristics to the program. The research by Weizenbaum gave credence to the theory that human–computer interaction may be beneficial and opened the door for further study.

Computer-Assisted Interview

As it became apparent that the computer could be an effective means of gathering information from individuals, psychological computer testing began to encompass the presentation of interviews and assessments traditionally completed in paper-and-pencil form. The computer-assisted interview has been used for everything from comprehensive behavioral psychological assessment and diagnostics (Coid et al., 2006) to special topic evaluations such as screenings for suicide (Kohli et al., 2010), human immunodeficiency virus (HIV) risk (Fenton et al., 2005; Millett et al., 2011; Morin et al., 2005), depression (Leventhal et al., 2011), sexual behaviors (Dolezal et al., 2011), drug abuse (Chan, Gelernter, Oslin, Farrer, & Kranzler, 2011), and phobias (Crome et al., 2010).

Although there has been some controversy as to the equivalence of computer-based interviewing and paper-and-pencil forms, much of the research has indicated that the validity of computer-administered interviews is equal to or better than that of paper-and-pencil forms (Dolezal et al., 2011; Porter, Forbes, Manzi, & Kalish, 2010). In part, this equivalence can be attributed to the fact that in creating computer-administered versions, it has been the goal to make these tests as similar to the original versions as possible (Epstein & Klinkenberg, 2001).

The explanation for computer versions that produce more accurate assessment is slightly more complicated and often debated. Computer interview success may exceed the interview accomplishments of some clinicians because the computer programs ask more standardized questions, covering areas that a clinician may neglect. More important, computer-administered interviews appear to reduce the likelihood of clients skewing their responses in an attempt to appear socially acceptable to the clinician. When gathering information about more sensitive topics, such as sexual behaviors, the popularity of computer-assisted interviews is steadily increasing (Dolezal et al., 2011). It has been shown that participants are more likely to share sensitive information about other personal subjects when computer-assisted interviewing is used. This has been the case for the evaluation of potentially embarrassing conditions such as incontinence (Parnell et al., 2011). Research consistently shows that the computer-based versions of psychological interviews make individuals more at ease and willing to disclose information concerning issues that might otherwise not be discussed (see Cooley et al., 2001; Hewitt, 2002; Lessler, Caspar, Penne, & Barker, 2000). Although some studies show the effects of social desirability may be reducing over time (Dwight & Feigelson, 2000), studies of distortion caused by social desirability support the idea that social desirability has less of an impact with computer-assisted interviewing than with traditional administration (Dolezal et al., 2011; Lowndes et al., 2011).

It is interesting to note that as computers become more sophisticated and begin to more closely emulate human characteristics, prompting clients to respond as if they are responding to a human, the likelihood of responding to sensitive personal questions in socially desirable ways does not increase (Tourangeau, Couper, & Steiger, 2003). In fact, people are sometimes more frank and candid in response to a computer than to a skilled therapist.

Computer-Administered Tests

Traditional assessments other than computer-assisted interviews have also been made available as computer-based tests and the use of computerized testing in assessment has steadily increased in recent years (Blazek & Forbey, 2011). As with computer-assisted interviews, there has been much discussion about the equivalence of the paper-and-pencil forms and the computer-administered versions. A preponderance of the research suggests that, in general, tests such as the Minnesota Multiphasic Personality Inventory (MMPI-2) (Blazek & Forbey, 2011), Big Five Personality tests (Vecchione, Alessandri, & Barbaranelli, 2011), and the Ansell-Casey Life Skills Assessment (Bressani & Downs, 2001) result in similar evaluations when administered by computer or by paper and pencil.

A small number of psychological tests that measure negative affect tend to produce different results than their paper-and-pencil forms (Clay, Lankford, & Wilson, 1992). Some have found that negative affect scores are particularly elevated when testing computer-anxious individuals and using the Beck Depression Inventory. However, more recent analyses have validated the computer administration of the BDI-II against paper-and-pencil administration (Satre, Chi, Eisendrath, & Weisner, 2011). Computer anxiety also has an effect on educational testing and appears to be most pronounced when evaluating math skills (Kröhne & Martens, 2011; Stone & Davey, 2011, p. 20).

Although questions remain about the impact of computer anxiety on test takers (Shermis, Mzumara, & Bublitz, 2001), research suggests the benefits of computer administration outweigh the benefits of paper-and-pencil administration in several ways (Norris, Pauli, & Bray, 2007). Computer administration is generally less time-consuming for both the individual being tested and the test administrator, more cost-effective, better accepted by test takers who are adults or children, and often more accurate (Konradt, Syperek, & Hertel, 2011; Kröhne & Martens, 2011).

Computer-administered psychological testing is not without drawbacks. The finer subtleties of human communication cannot be read by a computer program. Body language that may suggest hesitation or distortion of the truth to a human would not be captured by computer. The use of subtle techniques by the clinician also cannot be emulated by a computer. To gather sensitive information, a clinician's line of questioning must be flexible and selective based on the client's responses. Although some programs are becoming sophisticated to the extent that they can sense emotion and adjust responses accordingly (Lopatovska & Arapakis, 2011; Picard & Klein, 2002), they have yet to match the clinician's ability to detect subtle emotional cues.

Computer Diagnosis, Scoring, and Reporting of Results

From educational testing to tests that evaluate personality and psychopathology, computers are taking a prominent role in the scoring of tests, reporting of results, and diagnosis of clients (Greenea, 2011).

The effectiveness of computer scoring, computer-generated diagnosis, and narrative reports has been the issue of controversy since their inception (Tallent, 1987). From neuropsychological assessments such as the Halstead-Reitan Battery (Russell, 2000) to personnel screening tests, the scoring and report generation of certain tests seem to be straightforward, efficient, and accurate (Vale, Keller, & Bentz, 1986). Since early in the history of computers in psychological testing, there has been evidence suggesting computer diagnosis provides reliability comparable to that of psychiatrists (Sletten, Ulett, Altman, & Sundland, 1970).

Projective tests have also been successfully scored by computer for decades. When examining the computer-scoring version of the Holtzman Inkblot Test, validity was confirmed by acceptable correlations between the computer-scoring methods and traditional methods of scoring (Gorham, Moseley, & Holtzman, 1968). Evaluation of the online version of the Rorschach determined that the computer can provide a report similar to that of a clinician (Harris, Robinson, & Menzies, 1981). Similarly, the Rotter Incomplete Sentence Blank showed only small differences between administration types that were not significant once attitudes toward computers were adjusted for (Rasulis, Schuldberg, & Murtagh, 1996).

For every study that confirms the reliability of computer-generated scores, diagnoses, and reports, there is one that suggests caution is in order. Even the most popular tests such as the MMPI have been criticized for including scoring errors (Pope, Butcher, & Seelen, 2000) and generating reports that are markedly less accurate than those of clinicians (Epstein & Rotunda, 2000). Allard and Faust (2000) also detected scoring errors when evaluating the MMPI, the Beck Depression Inventory, and the Spielberger State-Trait Anxiety inventory. The overall message gathered from decades of research concludes that computers are a tool, and interpretations of the scores, reports, and diagnoses they produce are appendages to clinical judgment (Butcher, Perry, & Atlis, 2000) that require the assessment and expertise of clinicians (Russell, 2000).

Internet Usage for Psychological Testing

The advent of computers and the Internet has revolutionized testing and played a major role in the proliferation of modern techniques. In the early 1990s, the Internet began to thrive, and its growth, development, and diversity of use have exploded since 1995 (Crespin & Austin, 2002). Today the Internet is inundated with a wide variety of psychological tests: from personality tests that are neither reliable nor valid and meant only for entertainment to tests used in the selection of qualified employees and massive scientifically complex research projects that use the Internet as a source of large numbers of participants and data collection. The Internet has already shown itself to be useful to the science of psychological testing and measurement.

Any interested person can easily find free psychological tests on the World Wide Web. Humanmetrics.com offers an online test based on Jung and Briggs Myers' personality approaches, the results of which provide personality type and guidance on career choices. Teamtechnology.co.uk offers an online test that analyzes styles of leadership, while free-iqtest.net will tell you how intelligent you are. These tests are touted as statistically sound instruments based on decades of research. Because individuals are often interested in evaluations about themselves, by offering free psychological tests, sites can gather massive amounts of useful data for research purposes.

Although some researchers doubt the quality of data gathered online, the use of the Web to gather data has generally been shown to be adequate (McGraw, Tew, & Williams, 2000; Sethuraman, Kerin, & Cron, 2005). Problems concerning the inability to standardize testing conditions when participants are testing at different locations, using different types of computers, and with different amounts of distraction in their environments may be compensated for by the massive sample sizes available to Web-based laboratories. Davis (1999) has shown that results gathered from Web-based participants in different environments did not covary. A study that compared Web-based assessment, traditional paper-and-pencil assessment, and Web-based assessment in a disruptive environment found no significant differences between assessment techniques and resulted in significantly high test–retest reliability coefficients for all three types of administration (Miller et al., 2002). Traditional tests conducted via the Internet are found to have similar results to their paper-and-pencil versions (Cronk & West, 2002) and to include less error in data collection (Miller et al., 2002; Pettit, 2002). It is also becoming evident that Web-based samples can more closely match the intended sample (McCabe, Boyd, Couper, Crawford, & D'Arcy, 2002), especially when methods that are used to publicize the project target specific interests (Epstein & Klinkenberg, 2002). And, once again, some evidence suggests that, as with the use of the computer alone, Web-based testing facilitates more thorough self-disclosure from participants (Davis, 1999).

The ease at which participants can be recruited to participate in online testing, the ease of data collection, and the reduction of error make Web-based data collection appealing to researchers (Pettit, 2002) and ensure its use in the future.

The Computerization of Cognitive-Behavioral Assessment

As with other computer-based psychological assessments, computer-based cognitive-behavioral evaluations appear to have equivalent results as their paper-and-pencil counterparts (Franceschina, Dorz, & Bari, 2001). In addition to success in computer-based evaluation, computer-based cognitive-behavioral treatments have been found effective for the motivation, engagement, and treatment of drug-dependent individuals (Bickel, Christensen, & Marsch, 2011) and for treating anxiety disorders (Khanna, Aschenbrand, & Kendall, 2007), including generalized anxiety disorder (Lorian, Titov, & Grisham, 2011), panic disorder (Carper, McHugh, & Barlow, 2011), and social phobia (Heimberg, 2001). They have also been found useful for evaluating body image disturbance in individuals with eating disorders (Shibata, 2002), levels of conflict and cooperation in individuals' social interactions (Aidman & Shmelyov, 2002), and different aspects of individuals' natural social, linguistic, and psychological lives (Mehl, Pennebaker, Crow, Dabbs, & Price, 2001).

Newman, Szkodny, Llera, and Przeworski (2011) conducted a review of research on the efficacy of computer-assisted self-help in conjunction with minimal contact therapies for drug and alcohol abuse and smoking addiction. They found that, in the treatment of substance use and abuse, self-administered and predominantly self-help computer-based cognitive and behavioral interventions are efficacious, but some therapist contact is important for greater and more sustained reductions in addictive behavior. The use of computers in cognitive-behavioral therapy substantially improves the quality and effectiveness of traditional techniques. The ability for a client to instantly record a target behavior and to access a tool to help deal with the behavior as it occurs is efficient and reduces the length of time needed to alter a pattern of behavior.

Computer programs can also generate schedules of reinforcement including fixed ratio, variable ratio, fixed interval, and variable interval schedules (Wolach & McHale, 2002). A cumulative recording of subjects' responses can then be documented, simplifying the evaluation concerning the effectiveness of the type of schedule used.

Tests Possible Only by Computer

In addition to tests that are merely computer-friendly versions of their traditional paper-and-pencil forms and tests conducted over the Internet, there are developments in psychological testing made possible only with the use of computers.

The use of computer-generated virtual reality programs for psychological testing and treatment of phobias has grown rapidly in the past decade (Bohil, Alicea, & Biocca, 2011). Virtual reality technology is ideal for safely and efficiently exposing clients to the objects of their phobias while evaluating physiological responses (Wiederhold, Jang, Kim, & Wiederhold, 2002), systematically recording those responses, and evaluating patient improvement (Bohil et al., 2011). Equipment that measures heart rate, skin resistance, and skin temperature informs clinicians of the level of distress caused by a phobia and levels of improvement as treatment continues.

Virtual reality environments that mimic an airplane ride, an encounter with a spider, social situations, and being in front of an audience have all been found to engender the same reactions as the actual environment, only to a lesser degree and with the added confidence of the client being in control of the program. Studies that have measured physiological responses have found that controlled exposure to virtual environments can desensitize individuals to the object of their fear (Wiederhold et al., 2002). When using virtual reality to treat and measure fear responses associated with spider phobia, Garcia-Palacios, Hoffman, Karlin, Furness, and Botella (2002) found that 83% of those being treated showed clinical signs of improvement. There have also been studies boasting success rates of 65 to 80% when treating fear of flying (Maltby, Kirsch, Mayers, & Allen, 2002; Mühlberger, Weik, Pauli, & Wiedemann, 2006; Rothbaum et al., 2006; Wiederhold, Gervirtz, & Spira, 2001), and great improvements have been seen when treating clients with claustrophobia (Safir & Wallach, 2011), fear of public speaking (Lee et al., 2002), fear of driving (Mühlberger, Bülthoff, & Wiedemann, 2007; Wald & Taylor, 2000), and fear of heights (Cottraux, 2005; Pull, 2005).

Because of the relative safety of facing one's fear in a virtual environment, because virtual reality reduces the possibility of embarrassment to clients (Bohil, Alicea, & Biocca, 2011), and because virtual reality requires less time and money to conduct than does in vivo desensitization, it is seen as ideal for the treatment and measurement of phobic responses. These positive attributes of virtual reality also make individuals with phobias more likely to seek and complete treatment (Garcia-Palacios, Hoffman, See, Tsai, & Botella, 2001). The success of virtual reality in the treatment of phobias has spawned interest in those who are looking for improved ways to evaluate and treat those with schizophrenia, attention-deficit hyperactivity disorder, autism (Costa, De Carvalho, Drummond, Wauke, & De Sa Guimaraes, 2002), posttraumatic stress disorder (Wood et al., 2007), obsessive-compulsive disorder, body image disorders (North, North, & Coble, 2002), and sexual dysfunction (Vincelli & Riva, 2000). Interesting concepts, including the use of interactive computer games with embedded recording and assessment facilities that measure responses to virtual situations, are beginning to be used in the assessment of personality and psychopathology (Aidman & Shmelyov, 2002). Interactive virtual reality programs are also being appraised as a tool for educational assessment (Byers, 2001). As computer technology advances, computer-generated virtual reality will play a major role in several areas of psychological testing and measurement in the coming decades.

Computer-Adaptive Testing

Although to a smaller extent traditional tests allow for some adaptation according to the test taker's responses, advancements in computer technology have allowed for the construction of tests that adapt and metamorphize according to each response given. After each response, the computer updates the estimation of the test taker's ability. That estimation is then used to select the next item on the test. The selection of only items necessary for the evaluation of the test taker limits the number of items needed for an exact evaluation. Computer-adaptive tests have been found to be more precise and efficient than fixed-item tests (Kantrowitz, Dawson, & Fetzer, 2011). Over the past two decades, computer-adaptive tests have been used for classroom testing (Wang, Chang, & Huebner, 2011), for evaluating general intelligence (Murphy, 2010), in the selection process for remedial instruction (Saine, Lerkkanen, Ahonen, Tolvanen, & Lyytinen, 2011), to assess military personnel (PACE, 2011) and employees (Kantrowitz, Dawson, & Fetzer, 2011), for college and graduate student placement, and in nursing licensure (Economides & Roupas, 2007; Schmidt, 2000).

There are several practical benefits of computer-adaptive testing. One benefit that is enjoyed by test takers is the decrease in time needed for test taking. In addition, efficiency is increased as scores are immediately recorded and made available. Expenses are reduced because no highly trained test administrators are needed since the computer acts as administrator. Finally, computer-adaptive tests are self-paced and provide accurate scores for test takers whose abilities range from gifted to impaired.

However, there are limitations to computer-adaptive tests. There may be some difficulty in presenting long reading passages, intricate graphs, or artwork. Computer-adaptive tests may not be suitable for all test subjects or skills. They may not calibrate with paper-and-pencil versions. Administrator facility with a large number of computers is required for group testing. The computer literacy levels of test takers may significantly affect performance. Finally, examinees often question the equity of computer-adaptive tests as each test taker answers a different set of questions.

One of the most frequently debated drawbacks of computer-adaptive testing is the inability of test takers to go back and change previously answered questions (Wise, Finney, Enders, Freeman, & Severance, 1999). If allowed to do so, a test taker could purposefully answer the initial items incorrectly. The computer would then generate a simpler test for which the examinee is overqualified. After answering the simpler questions correctly, the examinee could then go back to the initial questions and change them to the right answer. Although some feel that this strategy would not be attractive to test takers (Wise et al., 1999), caution is still in order when considering item review.

In addition, there is concern that a test taker who is reviewing a completed test may be able to distinguish easier items from difficult items. The examinee would then be aware of which items were answered incorrectly and change the incorrect answers according to that feedback. Although this argument against item review in computer-adaptive testing appears to be sound, Wise, Finney, Enders, Freeman, and Severance (1999) and others (Green, 1983) have found that test takers do not discriminate well between easy and difficult questions and therefore would not be informed of which items were answered incorrectly.

Regardless of the drawbacks, computer-adaptive testing is highly effective and frequently used. Of the Educational Testing Service's 11 million test administrations worldwide each year, some of its most frequently used tests [Graduate Record Examination (GRE), GMAT, and Test of English as a Foreign Language (TOEFL)] are computer-adaptive.

Summary

Cognitive-behavioral procedures differ from traditional tests in that they are more direct, have fewer inferential assumptions, and remain closer to observable phenomena. Traditional tests are based on the medical model, which views the overt manifestations of psychological disorders merely as symptoms of some underlying cause. This underlying cause is the target of the traditional procedures. Cognitive-behavioral tests are based on the belief that the overt manifestations of psychological disorders are more than mere symptoms. Although possibly caused by some other factor, the behaviors themselves—including actions, thoughts, and physiological processes—are the targets of behavioral tests.

In cognitive-behavioral assessment based on *operant conditioning*, one must first identify the critical response or responses involved in a disorder. These critical responses are then evaluated for frequency, intensity, or duration. The resulting data provide the baseline for the particular behaviors. Once a baseline is obtained, an intervention is introduced. The effect of this intervention on the baseline is then observed.

Self-report techniques focus on situations that lead to particular response patterns, whereas traditional procedures focus on determining the internal characteristics of the individual that lead to particular response patterns. Furthermore, the cognitive-behavioral procedures purport to be more related to observable phenomena than are traditional procedures.

One of the most important examples of the cognitive-behavioral assessment approach is Meichenbaum's technique, *cognitive-functional analysis*. The premise underlying cognitive-functional analysis is that what a person says to him- or herself plays a critical role in determining behavior. A cognitive-functional analysis ascertains the environmental factors that precede behavior as well as those that maintain it. In addition, this kind of analysis attempts to ascertain the internal or cognitive antecedents and consequences of a behavioral sequence.

An important development is the application of computers to testing. Computers are used more and more frequently for testing in all its phases, from administration to analysis; however, care must be taken in using computers wisely.

Testing in Counseling Psychology

LEARNING OBJECTIVES

When you have completed this chapter, you should be able to:

▶ Describe the use of the criterion-keying method in the development of the SVIB

▶ List some of the criticisms of the SVIB and how they were addressed in later versions of the measure

▶ Describe how the KOIS differs from the SII

▶ Outline some of the controversial issues in interest measurement

▶ Evaluate the proposition that personality traits are stable over time

▶ Discuss the newer uses of matching interest profiles, including Internet dating

425

At age 35, Harry found himself faced with a dilemma. He had studied hard for many years to become a dentist, but what he had suspected for many years was becoming obvious: He did not like dentistry. Although Harry had chosen this occupation, he had not considered dentistry in detail before making a commitment to the field.

Harry could trace his interest in becoming a dentist to an experience he had during his childhood. As a young boy, he liked to play golf. While on the course one day, Harry met a dentist who explained that the practice of dentistry was lucrative but still allowed practitioners enough time to play golf and engage in other activities. Harry was a good student, and the encounter with the golfer-dentist made him think that dentistry would afford him the ideal lifestyle. Harry liked his science classes when he entered college, and he continued to be an outstanding student. After 4 years at a state university, he was accepted by a good dental school.

In dental school, Harry began to question his career choice. Two things were apparent by the end of his third year. First, he did not really enjoy doing dental work. He found himself uneasy when his patients fussed in the chair, and he disliked subjecting people to the discomfort associated with some dental procedures. Second, Harry discovered that he did not share many interests with other people in the field of dentistry.

After completing dental school, Harry did a brief tour of duty as a dentist in the U.S. Air Force. When he left the service, he decided he wanted to get away from dentistry for a while and enrolled in art school. However, despite his dislike for dentistry, he returned to the practice because of the large personal and financial investment he had already made in the profession. Dentistry paid well, and retraining in a field of more interest to him would be difficult and costly. In the 35 years that had passed since he had graduated from dental school, Harry quit and reentered his dental practice on five separate occasions. Throughout the entire experience, he remained unhappy with his choice of profession.

This true story recounts the lives of many people who feel they have made the wrong career choice. Some of the misery that talented people like Harry experience could be avoided with proper career counseling and guidance (Savickas, 2015). In this chapter, we examine the contribution of psychological tests to the selection of and preparation for a career.

The term *career* connotes "adventure" to many people. As a noun, it means "swift course"; as a verb, it means "to go swiftly or wildly." The Latin root is *carrus*, "chariot." Thus, the term for today's rat race has its roots in the exciting Roman races (Super & Hall, 1978). Careers can indeed be exciting and the essence of life if they are properly selected. They can also lead to misery if not carefully chosen. Psychological tests can help people select the right career. The first step in the identification of an appropriate career path is the evaluation of interests.

Measuring Interests

If you want to enter an appropriate career, you must identify your interests. Some people need little help finding work that interests them; others can benefit from the guidance given by a psychological test. In the nearly 90 years since the introduction of interest inventories, millions of people have received feedback about their own interests to help them make wise career choices.

The first interest inventory, introduced in 1921, was called the Carnegie Interest Inventory. When the *Mental Measurements Yearbook* was first published in 1939, it discussed 15 different interest measures (Datta, 1975). The two most widely used interest tests were introduced relatively early: the Strong Vocational Interest Blank in 1927 and the Kuder Preference Survey in 1939.

Today, there are more than 80 interest inventories in use; however, the Strong remains one of the most widely used tests in research and practice. Because the Strong is so important, we will take some time to review the various iterations of the test that have evolved over the years.

The Strong Vocational Interest Blank

Shortly after World War I, E. K. Strong, Jr. and some of his colleagues began to examine the activities that members of different professions liked and disliked. They came to realize that people in different professional groups had different patterns of interests. To some extent, one might expect this, because people tend to choose lines of work that interest them. One might expect carpenters to like woodworking, and painting might interest an artist more than a salesperson. However, Strong and his colleagues also found that people in the same line of work had similar hobbies, liked the same types of entertainment, and read the same sorts of books and magazines.

With this research as a base, Strong set out to develop a test that would match the interests of a subject to the interests and values of a criterion group of people who were happy in the careers they had chosen. This procedure is called criterion keying, or the *criterion-group approach* (see Chapter 15). The test they created with this method was the Strong Vocational Interest Blank (SVIB).

In preliminary studies of the test, groups of individuals from many professions and occupations responded to approximately 400 items dealing with likes and dislikes related to these occupations and to leisure activities. The criterion keying then determined how the interests of new subjects resembled those of the criterion groups.

In the revised 1966 version of the SVIB, the 399 items were related to 54 occupations for men. A separate form presented 32 different occupations for women. Items in the SVIB were weighted according to how frequently an interest occurred in a particular occupational group as opposed to how frequently it occurred in the general population. Raw scores were converted to standard scores, with a mean of 50 and a standard deviation of 10. Each criterion group used in the construction of the SVIB contained approximately 300 people, a good normative sample. Numerous reliability studies produced impressive results, with odd–even and short-term test–retest figures generally running between the low .80's and the low .90's. Long-term (20-year) test–retest coefficients ran in the respectable .60's. Validity data indicated that the SVIB predicted job satisfaction well (e.g., Strong & Campbell, 1966). In addition, studies have shown that achieving one's career aspirations contributes to job satisfaction (Iliescu, Ispas, Sulea, & Ilie, 2015).

One of the most interesting findings to emerge from the hundreds of published studies using the SVIB is that patterns of interest remain relatively stable over time.

Strong made a practice of asking a group of Stanford University students who took the test in the 1930s to take the test again as they grew older. These studies showed that interests remain relatively stable for as long as 22 years. Of course, most people did modify their interests slightly over this period, and a few people made complete turnabouts; nevertheless, the great majority remained consistent. Newer studies confirm the stability of most vocational interests (Xu & Tracey, 2016).

Studies also showed that interest patterns are fairly well established by age 17. For example, Stanford premed students who eventually became physicians scored high on the physician scale of the SVIB. When recontacted throughout life, they tended to remain high on that scale (Tyler & Walsh, 1979). Other studies showed some instability of interests during adolescence, with the patterns becoming stable by the senior year of high school (Hansen & Campbell, 1985).

Despite the widespread acceptance and use of the SVIB, disenchantment with the test began to mount in the late 1960s and early 1970s. Critics cited a gender bias in the scales because different tests were used for men and women. Others complained about the lack of theory associated with the test.

The Evolution of the Strong Measures

Although the original Strong Vocational Interest Inventory is no longer used, the measure evolved over the last 80 years. In 1974, D. P. Campbell published a new version of the SVIB, which he called the Strong-Campbell Interest Inventory (SCII). The SCII was Campbell's (1974) response to the shortcomings of the SVIB. Items from both the men's and women's forms of the SVIB were merged into a single form that included scales devoid of gender bias. For example, the scales for waiter and waitress were merged, and items that referred to gender (e.g., salesman) were appropriately modified.

Campbell also introduced more theory into the measurement strategy. He became interested in J. L. Holland's (1975) theory of vocational choice. After many years of study, Holland had postulated that interests express personality and that people can be classified into one or more of six categories according to their interests (see Table 16.1).

TABLE 16.1   Holland's Six Personality Factors

Factor	Interest pattern
Realistic	Enjoys technical material and outdoor activities
Investigative	Is interested in science and the process of investigation
Artistic	Enjoys self-expression and being dramatic
Social	Is interested in helping others and in activities involving other people
Enterprising	Is interested in power and political strength
Conventional	Likes to be well organized and has clerical interests

Adapted from J. L. Holland (1985).

Over the years, research has generally supported Holland's ideas (Brown & Lent, 2016). For example, one detailed study that used all 437 occupational titles from the Bureau of the Census demonstrated that Holland's system can better describe work activities, general training requirements, and occupational rewards than can a variety of competing vocational classification systems (Gottfredson, 1980). Over the course of last 60 years, research has consistently supported the claim that occupational interests reflect personality (Rossier, 2015).

The Campbell Interest and Skill Survey

The Strong scales have had an interesting and turbulent recent history. David Campbell began working on the Strong Vocational Interest Blank in 1960 when he was a graduate student at the University of Minnesota (Campbell, 2002). When Strong died in 1963, Campbell, then an assistant professor at the University of Minnesota, became the primary representative of the SVIB. Later versions were published under the authorship of Strong and Campbell. The first version of the Strong-Campbell Interest Inventory was published in 1974. Because Strong had been a professor at Stanford University, Stanford and the University of Minnesota became engaged in a legal dispute over ownership. In an out-of-court settlement in 1988, Stanford received the rights to publish the Strong Interest Inventory while Campbell received the rights to most of the cumulative work. In 1992, Campbell published the Campbell Interest and Skill Survey (CISS) (Campbell, 2002; Campbell, Hyne, & Nilsen, 1992).

The CISS asks respondents to assess their degree of interest in 200 academic and occupational topics. Furthermore, it assesses the degree of skill in 120 specific occupations. The system produces an 11-page profile and a 2-page report summary (Campbell, 1995). The CISS ultimately yields a variety of different types of scales. These are summarized in Table 16.2. For each of these scales, an interest level and a skill score are offered.

In addition to these specific scales, the CISS offers an academic focus scale that helps test takers understand how comfortable or successful they may be in an

TABLE 16.2 Summary of the Components of the Campbell Interest and Skill Survey

Orientation scales

Seven scales describe the test taker's occupational orientation: influencing, organizing, helping, creating, analyzing, producing, and adventuring.

Basic scales

The basic scales provide an overview for categories of occupations. Examples of basic scales include law/politics, counseling, and mathematics.

Occupational scales

Sixty occupational scales describe matches with particular occupations, including attorney, engineer, guidance counselor, and math teacher.

From the Campbell Interest and Skills Survey. Paper presented at the annual meeting of the American Psychological Association, New York, August 1995. Reprinted by permission of David P. Campbell.

academic setting, and an extroversion scale that helps guide them to occupations with the appropriate amount and intensity of interpersonal relations. Recently, Campbell teamed up with *US News & World Report* to offer the CISS online (see https://www .profiler.com). For $19.25 plus tax, you can gain access to the 320-question survey. The fee includes a personalized report that compares your results to the responses of people who are successfully employed in 60 occupations, along with a comprehensive career planner and a guide to help you interpret the results.

To a large extent, the CISS is a continuation of the research on the SVIB and the SCII. The CISS is now shorter and more efficient than the older SCII. The scales are standardized with means of 50 and standard deviations of 10. As with the earlier versions, the CISS uses the theoretical structure of John Holland. The manual provides extensive evidence for validity and reliability (Campbell, 1995). New evidence continues to support the validity of the CISS and its subscales (Hansen & Leuty, 2007).

The Reemergence of the Strong Interest Inventory

As noted in the previous paragraph, supporters of the Strong and the Campbell inventories engaged in a legal dispute resulting in a "divorce" between Stanford University and the University of Minnesota. In 2007, Stanford released the new Strong, known as the Strong Interest Inventory (SII). The Strong SII represents a substantial revision of the previous measure and features a different item format. Previous editions had used a three-choice format, while the revised version offers a five-choice, Likert-type format with icons for "Strongly Like," "Like," "Indifferent," "Dislike," and "Strongly Dislike." A core component of the SII is the Basic Interest Scales (BIS). Since the original development of the SVIB, there had been substantial changes in work life and workplaces, and the new SII includes 41 content scales to represent these areas. The new Strong includes 244 occupational scales. In comparison to earlier versions, there is more focus on careers in business and technology for both men and women. For example, 122 of the scales include different pairs for men and women. Examples of the new normative groups include greater diversity in terms of ethnic groups, race, and diversity in the workforce.

Over more than 35 years that we have worked on this book, we have had the opportunity to test the same person using Strong tests at different life phases. A summary of this exercise is given in Focused Example 16.1. Psychological Testing in Everyday Life 16.1 shows components of the computerized interpretation of the SII.

The first published evaluation of the SII considered 31 college majors in a national college sample of 1403 women and 469 men to evaluate the relationships between content scales and choice of college major. The study showed substantial concurrent validity for a wide variety of college major choices (Gasser, Larson, & Borgen, 2007). The basic interest scales were the best predictors of selection of major.

In summary, the Strong has reemerged as a major competitor among interest inventories. We expect continuing research to evaluate its validity. If you are interested in taking the SII, you can complete the measure for a fee of between $39 and $59 at http://www.personalityreports.com.

16.1 FOCUSED EXAMPLE

Stability of Vocational Interests—a 28-Year Case Study

One of the challenges in interest testing is in determining if career preferences are stable. We all change over time, and we would not want to advise someone to follow a particular career path only to discover that his or her interests had changed just a few years later. Most studies do suggest that career-related interests are stable over time (Ehrhart & Makransky, 2007). As an example, we offer a case study. When we wrote the first edition of this book in 1980, we tested Jean A, a 28-year-old psychology graduate student who had not yet started her professional career. Jean was married but did not have children and was uncertain what career path she would follow. Using the SCII, we retested Jean 11 years later. During this 11-year interval, Jean completed her Ph.D., held three different jobs, and had given birth to two children. She was now a 39-year-old university professor engaged in research and teaching. In 2008, we retested Jean a third time using the new version of the Strong Interest Inventory. A tremendous amount had changed for both Jean and the test. Jean's career had flourished, and she had risen through the ranks as a senior university administrator in the sciences. Although she remained at the university, the demands on her had changed considerably. Instead of teaching students, she had become responsible for solving problems across many different university departments and programs. Further, her personal life had changed. She had separated from her husband and her children had left home, graduated from college, and started their own lives. Her circle of friends had evolved and she had lost her father, who had instilled in her a strong work ethic. In many ways, Jean had reinvented herself, but had her basic interests changed?

In addition to the changes Jean had experienced, the tests had also changed. The initial test and 11-year follow-up were completed using the SCII.

The 28-year follow-up was done using the new SII. The SII is much improved over the earlier tests and has much more advanced scoring templates, particularly for professional women. From the few occupations scales available to women in the 1970s, the SII now has 122 validated occupational scales for women.

Table 16.3 compares Jean A's SCII profiles at ages 28, 39, and 56. As the table shows, her interests remained remarkably stable. Despite the passage of 28 years, not to mention the use of a different testing instrument, the picture we get of Jean is very similar. Her highest theme remained investigative, suggesting interests in science, math, and research. The investigative cluster usually comes with skills in analysis, research, and writing. Jean had always scored high on the investigative theme, and this became stronger as she aged. Although the rank orders changed some, Jean tended to score low on the enterprising theme, a cluster associated with interests in business, politics, and entrepreneurship.

TABLE 16.3 Scores on Occupational Themes for Jean A at Ages 28, 39, and 56

Theme	1980, Age 28	1991, Age 39	2008, Age 56
Investigative	58	58	69
Artistic	51	51	56
Social	45	46	60
Enterprising	42	37	43
Conventional	37	44	54
Realistic	36	36	50

(continues)

16.1   **FOCUSED EXAMPLE** *(continued)*

People scoring high on entrepreneurship enjoy selling, persuading, and marketing. Clearly, this was not Jean as a younger woman nor as a more mature adult.

In 1980, the SCII steered Jean toward four professions: physician, optometrist, psychologist, and university professor. At ages 28 and 39, physician was identified as the best career match for Jean, but university professor had emerged as her second-best match by age 39. By age 56, psychologist was noted as the best match, but university professor was very close. In fact, most of the professions identified at the top of the list in 1980 remained in the top 10 among 122 different occupations when Jean was evaluated in 2008. Given the changes that both Jean and the test experienced, the stability of the picture is quite remarkable (see Table 16.4). In 1980, the SCII suggested that Jean avoid certain professions such as librarian, beautician, flight attendant, and army officer. The 2008 test suggested that her worst matches were art teacher, interior designer, florist, and cosmetologist. At both times, Jean's interests did not match those of women who had chosen more traditionally female roles.

In 2012, as Jean A approached her 60th birthday, she remained happy in her career. It is likely that guidance given by interest inventories early in her adulthood would have directed her toward career fields that would remain good matches throughout her working life.

TABLE 16.4   Scores on Occupational Scales for Jean A at Ages 28, 39, and 56

Profession	1980, Age 28	1991, Age 39	2008, Age 56
Physician	58	53	48
Optometrist	52	47	51
Psychologist	50	47	57
University professor	49	50	56

The Kuder Occupational Interest Survey

Although the SCII is probably the most widely used interest inventory today, it competes with many other interest inventories. The Kuder Occupational Interest Survey (KOIS) ranks second in popularity. It is one of several interest scales that grew out of the original Kuder Preference Survey published in 1939. Throughout the years, the Kuder has offered a unique alternative to the SVIB, SCII, and CISS.

The KOIS presents the test taker with 100 triads (sets of three) of alternative activities. For each triad, the test taker selects the most preferred and the least preferred alternatives. Scoring of the KOIS scales gives the same information yielded by the earlier Kuder Preference Surveys—data on 10 general occupational interests (e.g., outdoor interests versus social service interests). However, in its current form, the KOIS examines the similarity between a test taker's interests and those of people employed in various occupations in a manner much like that of the SCII and CISS. Furthermore, the KOIS has developed separate norms for men and women. The KOIS also has a separate set of scales for college majors. Thus, in addition to suggesting which occupational group might work best with a test taker's interests, the KOIS may also help students choose a major (Diamond & Zytowski, 2000).

16.1 PSYCHOLOGICAL TESTING IN EVERYDAY LIFE

Interpreting the SII

In the example of Jean A, the thematic interests ranked by the SII report are as follows:

THEME	CODE	STANDARD SCORE & INTEREST LEVEL	STD SCORE
Investigative	I	VERY HIGH	69
Social	S	HIGH	60
Artistic	A	MODERATE	55
Conventional	C	MODERATE	54
Realistic	R	MODERATE	50
Enterprising	E	MODERATE	43

The charts above display your GOT results in descending order, from your highest to least level of interest. Referring to the Theme Descriptions provided, determine how well your results fit for you. Do your highest Themes ring true? Look at your next highest level of interest and ask yourself the same question. You may wish to highlight the Theme descriptions on this page that seem to fit you best.

(From National Career Assessment Sciences, Inc.™, Report of Scores, Kuder Occupational Survey, Form DD, copyright © 1965, 1968, 1970, 1979. National Career Assessment Services, Inc. Reprinted by permission.)

The report then goes on to suggest specific professions that may be a good or a poor match:

YOUR TOP TEN STRONG OCCUPATIONS

1. Psychologist (IA)
2. Geographer (IA)
3. Biologist (IRA)
4. Software Developer (IR)
5. University Professor (IAR)
6. Rehabilitation Counselor (SAI)
7. Computer Systems Analyst (C)
8. Sociologist (IAR)
9. Science Teacher (IRS)
10. Optometrist (IR)

Occupations of Dissimilar Interest

Art Teacher (ASE)

Interior Designer (EA)

Medical Illustrator (AIR)

Florist (EAC)

Cosmetologist (EC)

SII reports are very detailed and offer lots of specific guidance. For example, they identify next steps, what training should be undertaken, and what skills need to be developed. The end of the report provides a "snapshot summary." Here is the summary for Jean A:

(continues)

16.1 PSYCHOLOGICAL TESTING IN EVERYDAY LIFE *(continued)*

SNAPSHOT OF RESULTS

YOUR HIGHEST THEMES

· Investigative
· Social
· Artistic

PERSONAL AND WORK ENVIRONMENT DESCRIPTORS

· Analytical, independent, research oriented
· Helpful, collaborative, cooperative
· Creative, flexible, self-expressive

SPECIFIC INTERESTS FOR WORK, LEISURE, AND LEARNING

· Conducting experiments
· Operating scientific equipment
· Studying scientific theory
· Performing statistical analyses
· Using math to solve problems

· Teaching math
· Analyzing research results
· Conducting scientific experiments
· Writing reports

CAREERS THAT MIGHT BE MOST APPEALING TO YOU

· Psychologist
· Geographer
· Biologist
· Software Developer
· University Professor

· Rehabilitation Counselor
· Computer Systems Analyst
· Sociologist
· Science Teacher
· Optometrist

HOW YOU LIKE TO WORK AND LEARN

· Balance between working with colleagues and working alone
· Learning new ideas to apply to abstract problems
· Taking charge of some projects but not others

· Playing it safe and making decisions carefully
· With others, sharing responsibility and achievement

To emphasize nontraditional occupations for men and women, a series of new scales has been added to the KOIS. Examples of these new scales are architect (female norms), journalist (female norms), and film and television producer or director (male norms) (Zytowski, 1985).

Although each test taker is evaluated with regard to the norms for many occupational and college major groups, the KOIS provides a summary of an individual's highest scores by marking them with an asterisk.

The report is divided into four sections. The first summarizes the dependability of the results. An analysis of answer patterns considers consistency. The report shown in the table suggests that the results appear to be dependable for this particular test taker. The second section rank orders interest patterns in comparison to the normative sample of men and women. In this example, the person taking the test has exceptionally high interests in literary and outdoor areas in comparison to both men and women. The female test taker had low interests in comparison to other women in the mechanical, social service, and persuasive areas.

The core of the KOIS report is shown in the third section. This section ranks the test taker in relation to men and women who are employed in different occupations and are satisfied with their career choices. The report shows that the woman who completed the measure has a pattern of interests that best matches those of journalists who are satisfied with their work. The pattern also shows good correspondence with interests of lawyers, personnel managers, and physicians. The pattern matches most poorly with bank clerk, beautician, and department store sales. The fourth section of the report matches patterns of interests to those of students who have selected different college majors. The woman whose results are shown in this example matches interest patterns most closely with women who are majoring in history, English, or political science. Her interests match most poorly with women majoring in physical education, nursing, and art.

Studies show that the psychometric properties of the KOIS are very good. Short-term reliabilities tend to be high (between .80 and .95), and increasing evidence indicates that scores remain stable for as long as 30 years (Zytowski, 1996). One study on the predictive validity of the KOIS showed that half of one group of adults who had taken an early version of the KOIS while they were high-school students were working in fields that the high-school KOIS suggested they enter. Predictive validity for the college major scales was even better. There was closer correspondence between interests and the occupation a person was working in for those who had completed college than for those who had not. A college degree thus provides more freedom than a high-school diploma does in finding personally desirable work (Zytowski, 1976).

In other studies, high-school students reported greater confidence in their knowledge of themselves when they received KOIS results than when they did not. But knowing the results of the KOIS did not make the high-school students more confident or more satisfied with their career plans, except when the students expressed a special interest in learning about the test results (Zytowski, 1977). Other studies have considered self-efficacy for the specific occupational tasks in the KOIS. *Self-efficacy* represents a person's expectation that he or she could perform the tasks in the occupational groups. The research suggests that, in comparison to women, men have higher expectations that they will succeed in mechanical and physical work, and women have greater expectations that they will succeed when working with people than do men (Lucas, Wanberg, & Zytowski, 1997). Even though the KOIS has been less thoroughly studied than the SVIB-SCII, a growing amount of evidence indicates that it may be quite useful for guidance decisions for high-school and college students. The KOIS, although still in common use, has not undergone a major revision since 1991 (Zytowski, 1992). However, research using the KOIS continues. Studies using the KOIS have shown that career preferences are quite stable over the course of time. For example, one study tested 107 high-school juniors and seniors in 1975 and then retested them 30 years later in 2005. In general, occupational interests remained very stable, but some of the particular interest scales were associated with instability in occupational interests (Rottinghaus, Coon, Gaffey, & Zytowski, 2007).

The Jackson Vocational Interest Survey (JVIS), revised in 1995 and copyrighted in 1999, is used for the career education and counseling of high-school and college students. It can also be used to plan careers for adults, including those who want to make midlife career changes. Douglas Jackson, the developer of the measure, was strongly influenced by the psychometric pioneers from the Educational Testing Service (Jackson, 2002). The JVIS consists of 289 statements describing job-related activities. It takes 45 minutes to complete, and the scoring yields 34 basic interest scales. The test construction carefully avoided gender bias. The scale employs forced-choice formats in which the respondent must indicate a preference between two equally popular interests.

Studies suggest that the reliability for 10 general occupational themes is approximately .89 and that the test–retest stability of the 44 basic interest scales ranges from .84 to .88. Validity studies suggest that the JVIS predicts university and academic majors more accurately than do most other interest inventories. Available in both hand-scored and machine-scored forms, the JVIS offers computer software to administer and score the measure (Jackson & Livesley, 1995; Walsh & Osipow, 2013).

The Career Assessment Inventory

Developed by Charles B. Johansson, the Career Assessment Inventory (CAI) is designed for people not oriented toward careers requiring college or professional training. The CAI is written at the sixth-grade reading level and is designed for the 80% of U.S. citizens who have fewer than 4 years of postsecondary education. The CAI provides information similar to that yielded by the SII and CISS. Each test taker is evaluated on Holland's six occupational theme scales: realistic, investigative, artistic, social, enterprising, and conventional. The second portion of the CAI report describes basic interests. Each test taker is evaluated in 22 specific areas, including carpentry, business, and food service. The third section of the report is a series of occupational scales. Scores for the 89 occupational scales on the CAI were obtained by using a criterion-keying method. The interests of the test takers are matched to the interests of truck drivers, secretaries, waitpersons, and so forth.

Validity and reliability studies reported in the test manual suggest that the CAI has desirable psychometric properties. Scores tend to be quite stable, and people who find employment in occupations for which they have expressed strong interest tend to remain at their jobs and find more satisfaction with work than do those with low scores for those occupations. The test developer also took special pains to make the CAI culturally fair and eliminate gender bias. In many ways, the CAI has become the working person's CISS (Johannson, 1976; Johannson & Johannson, 1978).

The Self-Directed Search

Most interest inventories require professional or computer-automated scoring. In addition, they typically require interpretation by a trained counselor. J. L. Holland developed the Self-Directed Search (SDS) to be a self-administered, self-scored, and self-interpreted vocational interest inventory (Holland, 2013). The SDS attempts to simulate the counseling process by allowing respondents to list occupational aspirations, indicate occupational preferences in six areas, and rate abilities and skills in these areas (Srsic, Stimac, & Walsh, 2001). Then the test takers can score their

own inventory and calculate six summary scores, which they can use to obtain codes that reflect the highest areas of interest. Using the SDS, test takers can develop a meaningful personal career theory. The personal theory goes beyond interests and includes readiness for career decision making and readiness to obtain guidance (Reardon & Lenz, 2015). The SDS is linked to an occupational finder. In the 1994 edition of the system, the individual can locate more than 1300 occupations and match his or her own interest codes to corresponding occupational choices.

The SDS includes 228 items. Six scales with 11 items each describe activities. Another 66 items assess competencies, with six scales of 11 items each. Occupations are evaluated in six scales of 14 items each. Self-estimates are obtained in two sets of six ratings. Studies have demonstrated that respondents accurately score their own tests. Validity studies reflect a moderate, but not high, association between SDS categories and stated vocational aspirations (Holland, 2013). Computer-assisted approaches to the self-directed search are now available (see http://www.self-directed-search.com/How-does-it-work/Sample-reports).

Despite the common and enthusiastic use of interest inventories, several problems have repeatedly surfaced, including faking, sex bias, and mismatches between abilities and interests.

Eliminating Gender Bias in Interest Measurement

Not all members of the society have found the use and development of interest inventories acceptable. In particular, advocates of women's rights justifiably pointed out that the early interest inventories discriminated against women (Birk, 1974; Campbell, 1995; Diamond, 1979; Peoples, 1975; Tittle, 1983). The Association for Evaluation in Guidance appointed the Commission on Sex Bias in Measurement, which concluded that interest inventories contributed to the policy of guiding young men and women into gender-typed careers. The interest inventories tended to direct women into their traditional work roles, such as nursing, clerical service, and elementary-school teaching. The SVIB, the main interest inventory at the time of the commission report, had separate forms for men and women. Careers on the women's form, it was noted, tended to be lower in status and to command lower salaries (Joshi, Neely, Emrich, Griffiths, & George, 2015).

In response to these criticisms, the test developers began using the same forms for both men and women. However, in the 1977 SCII manual, Campbell noted that if Strong were alive, he may have felt that using the same norming tables for both men and women would have harmed the validity of the test. A unisex interest inventory, according to Strong, ignores the social and statistical reality that men and women have different interests. In other words, knowing the sex of the test taker tells us a lot about his or her interests. Nevertheless, the measure developers began to make major efforts to reduce gender bias, and newer measures, such as the CISS (Campbell, 1995), have gone even further. In the most recent versions, normative samples have been expanded to ensure larger and more representative samples. The 2007 SII has separate normative scales for men and women.

Most measures have reduced but not eliminated gender bias. Contemporary studies show that many items in the Strong Interest Inventory function differently for men and for women. Furthermore, these differences have been observed in cultures as different as the United States and Iceland (Einarsdottir, 2002). Interest inventory developers have worked hard to address these concerns. Although the basic interest and general theme portions of the SII and CISS compare a respondent's responses with those from a combined male and female reference group, the occupational scales are normed separately for men and women. Furthermore, the interpretive comments that are provided by most scoring services are geared toward the test taker's gender (Minton & Schneider, 1980). We expect that using the same or different norms for men and women will continue to engender controversy and debate. The current versions of the CISS, KOIS, and SII reflect the growing concern about gender bias (Campbell, 1995; Hansen & Campbell, 1987). Because career choices for many women are complex, interest inventories alone may be inadequate and more comprehensive approaches are needed (McLennan & Arthur, 1999).

Interest inventories have been around for several generations, making it possible to compare interests of groups born at different points in time. In the 1940s and 1950s, when career interest inventories got their start, the world was a very different place. Only a small percentage of women completed college and there was little ethnic and racial variability on most campuses (see Figure 16.1). By 1971, about 42% of college graduates were female and 58% were male. By 2016, that trend had reversed, with women earning nearly 60% of bachelor's degrees.

iStockphoto.com/Christopher Futcher

FIGURE 16.1

A crowd of Notre Dame University students

Ralph Crane/Getty Images

Budany and Hansen (2011) studied changes in vocational interests across birth cohorts of college students by integrating samples collected between 1976 and 2004. They identified doctoral dissertations and journal articles that had used the Strong Interest Inventory and the Strong-Campbell Interest Inventory and had information on the Holland's RIASEC typology. Across all studies included in the analysis, there were 12,039 females and 9550 subjects. They combined results across studies using meta-analysis and broke down the results by the year the data were collected. Between 1976 and 2004, college women showed an increase in enterprising interests, while college men demonstrated a decrease in the realistic and investigative interests. Back in the 1970s, there were significant differences between college men and women in investigative, enterprising, and conventional interests. As time went on, these differences diminished, suggesting that a greater emphasis on egalitarianism was helping change the basic career interests of young men and women.

Aptitudes and Interests

Extensive research on interest inventories reinforces an important but often overlooked point: Interest inventories measure interests, not the odds that people will succeed in the jobs that they find interesting.

The norm groups for the Strong inventories consist of people successful enough in various fields to remain working in them for defined periods. However, *degree* of success is not defined. If you obtain a high score for a particular occupation, then it means that you have interests similar to those of the people in that field. Self-rated satisfaction with chosen careers does appear to be higher for people whose interests match those of others working in the field, but repeated studies have emphasized that the chances of succeeding in that job depend on aptitudes and abilities.

Measuring Personal Characteristics for Job Placement

Interests are just one of the many factors to be considered in career planning and placement. Career choices also depend on matches between skills and jobs. Employers want to find the right person for the job, and job hunters continually seek that one position that perfectly suits their personal skills and interests. Thus, psychologists and vocational guidance specialists look at job placement from many different perspectives. Some focus on the person and his or her characteristics, others attend the work environment, while still others concentrate on unique combinations of people and situations. To begin, let's look at some of the theories and measurement methods that focus on the person. This approach involves the administration of an extensive battery of tests, including many we have already covered, such as the SCII and the KOIS. The results of this large battery of tests were factor analyzed (see Chapter 3) to find common factors or traits that characterize different occupational groups. People who require guidance take the battery of tests to learn about their traits. Then the counselor matches their traits to those that characterize the different occupations.

Are There Stable Personality Traits?

Imagine that you are responsible for hiring employees for a large business, and you want to do everything you can to convince your supervisors that you are doing a good job. You need to make decisions about the personalities of the people you interview, and you need to communicate this information to the people who will supervise them. For example, you might ask whether interviewees have the traits of kindness, honesty, trustworthiness, reliability, and dedication. People often believe that knowledge of such personality traits provides them with a convenient way of organizing information about others—for describing how they have behaved in the past and for predicting how they will act in the future (Anusic & Schimmack, 2016; Carver & Schier, 2012).

Indeed, all of the approaches to occupational interest assessment that we have presented in this chapter assume that interests are relatively stable personality characteristics. Much of the study of personality has been devoted to creating categories of traits, developing methods for measuring them, and finding out how groups of traits cluster. Indeed, the very concept of personality assumes that the characteristics of a person are stable over time. If Richard is "hardworking," then we expect him to work hard in many different situations. Although we commonly use trait names in this way to describe other people, the evidence that personality characteristics are stable is a little shaky. For example, Mischel (1984) showed that personality traits are simply not good predictors of how people will behave in particular situations (Linehan, 2016). In a classic, well-argued attack on trait theorists, Mischel (1968) demonstrated that knowing how someone scores on measures of psychological traits sometimes gives little better than chance insight into how the person will act in a given situation. Career assessments may be a good exception to Mischel's criticism. The career inventories do not assess personality traits. Instead, they evaluate how people will respond to some well-defined situations. In fact, most studies do suggest that career interests are quite stable over long periods of time (Xu & Tracey, 2016). Furthermore, Mischel and his colleagues eventually softened on their belief about consistency of behaviors over time. For example, they had tested children's ability to delay gratification over 40 years ago. When some of the same people performed similar tasks 40 years later, they found that impulsiveness tended to be relatively stable (Shermer, 2015). Children who were unable to delay gratification were more likely to be impulsive as adults (Casey et al., 2011).

Other Uses of Interest Matching Methods: The Case of Internet Dating

Developing computer algorithms for matching interest profiles was once technologically difficult. However, in the modern era, matching profiles can be done quickly and inexpensively. As result, methods for matching interests are now used in a variety of different fields relevant to counseling psychology. Perhaps the most rapid growth has taken place in Internet dating.

Estimates provided by the Pew Charitable Trust indicate that about 11% out of the 38% of American adults who are currently single and considering a new relationship have used Internet dating services. Among those who have used the services, about two-thirds have gone on a date with someone they met online and about a quarter met a spouse or someone they engaged in a long-term relationship with through Internet matching services. Most people using the services agree that online dating is a good way to meet a partner (Madden & Lenhart, 2013).

There are a lot of different Internet dating websites. Most relevant to our discussion are services that are based on scientific algorithms. These came online around 2000 with the development of eHarmony.com. eHarmony was developed by a clinical psychologist with training in personality psychology (Warren, 1994). The methodology uses self-report questionnaires to identify preferences, interests, and values. Within a few years, a variety of very similar services were developed, including PerfectMatch and Chemistry.

One of the biggest problems in evaluating Internet dating sites is that the actual methods are hidden from the public. We do not know exactly how the computer makes the matches. The eHarmony survey includes 13 sections with approximately 300 items. These 300 items provide scores on 29 dimensions that they believe are related to successful long-term relationships. The items ask for endorsement of personality adjectives such as *warm* and *competitive*, and also ask about interests including volunteering and being physically fit. In addition, they ask about descriptions of emotions, such as being happy or angry. Respondants are also asked to provide self-reports about characteristics such as the ability to make other people laugh. We were able to retrieve the patent application for eHarmony.com, which suggests that the matches are based on personality, socioeconomic status, religion, appearance, ethnic background, energy level, education, and interests (Buckwalter, Carter, Forgatch, Parsons, & Warren, 2013). Other dating services use different questionnaires and items, but most of them focus on personality traits of both the clients and their idealized partners.

The idea behind some of the more sophisticated Internet dating services builds upon decades of research on human interests. Matching partners in relationships may not be that dissimilar to finding the match between interests and job placement. However, there is surprisingly little research that is available for public scrutiny. Despite claims of the success of scientific couple matching, most of the methods used to create these matches remain secret and unavailable for public scrutiny (Finkel, Eastwick, Karney, Reis, & Sprecher, 2012).

Summary

The beginning of this chapter presented the real-life case of Harry, a dentist who felt he had made the wrong career choice. Harry's problem might have been avoided through proper interest testing and career counseling. Several methods for assessing vocational interests are available. The best known of these is the Strong (now called the SII), an empirically keyed test that matches the interests of male and female test takers with those of people satisfied with their career choices. Although one of the most widely used tests in the history of psychology, the early version of the Strong (SVIB) was criticized for its sexist and atheoretical orientation. Newer versions, such as the SII and the CISS, respond to these criticisms by including male and female keys in the same form and by embracing Holland's theory of occupational themes.

The KOIS is the next most frequently used interest test. In contrast to earlier versions, the present KOIS provides occupational scores similar to those given by the SII. A unique feature of the KOIS is that it provides scores for college majors. Other occupational interest measures are also available, including the CAI, designed for use with non-college-oriented individuals.

In 1968, Mischel demonstrated that personality measures do not always accurately predict behavior in particular situations. At about the same time, many attribution theorists began demonstrating that people explain the behavior of others by using personality traits; however, when asked about their own behavior, they tend to attribute cause to the situation. These ideas gave rise to the development of measures to assess the characteristics of social environments and work settings and we will discuss these in Chapter 17. Studies of the stability of occupational interests suggest that some aspects of personal preference are fairly stable over long periods of time.

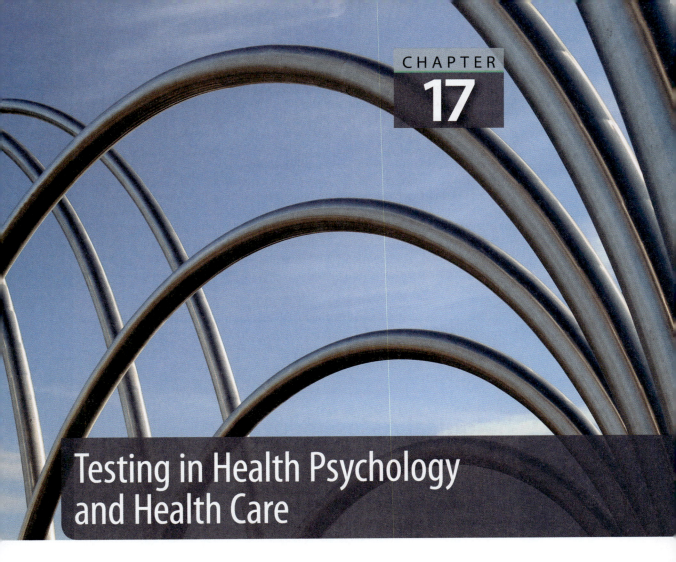

Testing in Health Psychology and Health Care

LEARNING OBJECTIVES

When you have completed this chapter, you should be able to:

- ▶ Describe at least three important health-care situations in which psychological tests are used
- ▶ Define *clinical neuropsychology*
- ▶ Discuss the use of neuropsychological instruments in both childhood and adulthood
- ▶ Describe the Halstead-Reitan test battery
- ▶ Describe the Luria-Nebraska test battery
- ▶ Discuss the advantages of the California Verbal Learning Test

- ▶ Discuss some of the theoretical orientations that underlie anxiety measures
- ▶ Describe the strengths and weaknesses of two different approaches for the assessment of life stress
- ▶ Discuss the relationship among measures of coping, measures of life stress, and measures of social support
- ▶ Differentiate psychometric and decision theory approaches to quality-of-life measurement
- ▶ Describe the SF-36
- ▶ Discuss the concept of a quality-adjusted life-year

443

t has been estimated that about 15% all psychologists are directly employed by hospitals, medical centers, and clinics, and this figure is increasing. One of the main functions of psychologists in these settings is to use and interpret measurement instruments (Norcross, VandenBos, Freedheim, & Domenech Rodríguez, 2016). When the first edition of psychological testing was written, there was a clear separation of physical and mental health in the practice of medicine. Physicians evaluated physical health problems and often put aside psychological complaints. In severe cases, those with apparent mental health problems were referred to mental health providers. Over the last several decades, the situation has changed. Today, management of depression and anxiety is considered to be core components of primary health care. In fact, depression is one of the most commonly treated problems in primary care clinics. In previous generations, assessment of depression, anxiety, or cognitive function was considered outside the domain of primary care physicians. Today, practicing internists, pediatricians, neurologists, and family physicians must understand the basics of psychological testing.

Although this chapter cannot discuss all of the measures used in medical settings, it focuses on three areas that have experienced rapid development in the last few years: neuropsychological assessment, anxiety and stress assessment, and quality-of-life assessment. Unlike other chapters, this chapter covers three separate topics—that is, the topics are not directly related to one another, except that each describes a common approach to assessment in contemporary health care.

Neuropsychological Assessment

Clinical Neuropsychology

Linda was an intelligent, extremely cooperative 7-year-old when she was hit by a car. Unconscious for only a short time, she appeared to show a rapid physical recovery from the accident. However, by the time 1 year had passed, her parents had become concerned about the behavioral changes they had observed since the accident. Linda was now introverted, did not interact well with others, and seemed anxious, prone to temper tantrums, frustrated, and unable to take criticism. The doctor who had originally examined Linda referred her to a neurologist, who could not find anything abnormal in her computed tomography (CT) scans and electroencephalogram (EEG) tests. Unable to determine the source of her difficulties, the neurologist referred Linda to a specialized psychologist trained in neuropsychological assessment. The psychologist discovered that Linda's visual functioning and her ability to talk were superior; however, she had difficulties in hearing and in writing down phonemes she had heard. Furthermore, tests showed that she did quite well on things she had learned before the accident but that she had lost the ability to discriminate among the sounds of letters closely related to one another. This in turn generated a great deal of strain and caused her to believe that she was stupid and unable to keep up with other children. The test that helped identify Linda's specific problem is called the Luria-Nebraska Neuropsychological Battery. After discovering that Linda's problem was highly specific, her teachers designed a special education program that used a visual approach and avoided auditory presentations. Her parents could also adapt to their child's problem once they realized its nature. Given this support and the reduced pressure, Linda's introversion, sensitivity to criticism, and frustration decreased. As her injuries healed, she returned to normal (Golden, 1981).

Linda's case shows the importance of a rapidly expanding new field known as *clinical neuropsychology*. This field is a scientific discipline that focuses on psychological impairments of the central nervous system and their remediation (Morgan & Ricker, 2016). *Clinical neuropsychology* is defined as the scientific discipline that studies the relationship between behavior and brain functioning in the realms of cognitive, motor, sensory, and emotional functioning (Spencer & Adams, 2016). The activities of neuropsychologists include the identification, description, multivariate quantification, and treatment of diseases of the brain and spinal cord.

A multidisciplinary endeavor, clinical neuropsychology overlaps neurology, psychiatry, and psychometric testing in the following ways: Neuropsychology and neurology both focus on sensations and perceptions and on motor movements. Neuropsychology and psychiatry both study mood and adaptations to psychosocial situations (Zane et al., 2016). Finally, neuropsychology and psychometrics both use psychological tests. Neuropsychology differs from these other clinical disciplines because it is finely specialized, focusing on attention, memory, learning, language and communication, spatial integration, and cognitive flexibility. In summary, neuropsychology is a field of study that actively attempts to relate brain dysfunction and damage to observable and measurable behavioral functioning (Cubelli & Sala, 2007).

The practice of clinical neuropsychology has benefited from remarkable advances in neuroimaging. New methods have made it possible to see diseases in the brain among living people. A few short years ago, the only way to learn about these problems was to study the brains of people who had already died. The rapid advances in neuroimaging (see Figure 17.1) produced some surprises for the evolving field of clinical neuropsychology. For example, many people assumed that improvements in brain scanning would eliminate the need for clinical neuropsychology. If tumors can be easily detected with CT or magnetic resonance imaging (MRI), why would we need functional tasks to determine if there was a lesion in the brain? As the field of neuroimaging advanced, it became increasingly clear that behavior and functional assessments were important. One of the problems was that there is remarkable variability among people in the structure of their brains. The early neuroanatomists of the 19th century mapped the brain on the basis of one or two people. Now that thousands of people have had their brains imaged, it has become apparent that there is remarkable variability from person to person in how their brains are structured and organized (Shattuck et al., 2008). In clinical situations, identification of a lesion or tumor does not necessarily relate to functioning. Similarly, people may have important functioning problems that are not clearly traced to specific regions of the brain. Neurologists now believe that performance on neuropsychological tests gives them clues about which part of the brain to examine (Richards, Sanchez, Phillips-Meek, & Xie, 2016). In addition to identifying tumors, neuropsychological tests have proven valuable in characterizing the effects of serious medical conditions, such as human immunodeficiency virus (HIV), that might influence the brain and behavior (Woods et al., 2016).

Despite these major advances in imaging of the brain, neuropsychology is able to detect problems that are often missed even with the latest neuroimaging devices.

FIGURE 17.1

Advances in functional magnetic resonance imaging (fMRI) can detect responses to stimulation and brain activity associated with blood flow. This activity lights up affected brain areas on MRI images.

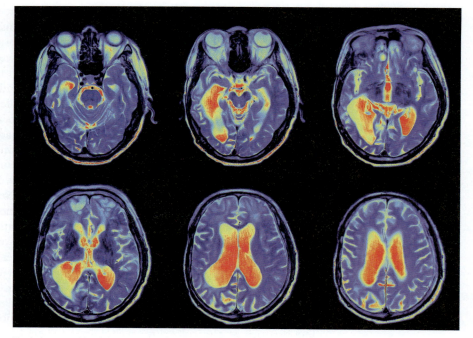

iStockphoto.com/akesak

Furthermore, neuropsychological testing can detect Alzheimer's disease and other clinical problems in their earliest stages and tests are now used to detect a wide range of clinical problems (Burnham et al., 2016). It remains the primary method to diagnose the effects of minor traumatic injury (Barnes et al., 2004; Hanten et al., 2004; Marceau, Lunn, Berry, Kelly, & Solowij, 2016). It is unclear how much we will ever be able to understand about human memory and thought on the basis of physiology alone. Beyond physiologic findings, motivation or desire to perform well can profoundly affect performance (Green, 2003).

The roots of clinical neuropsychology can be traced to studies by Pierre Broca and Carl Wernicke in the 19th century. These early investigators recognized that functions such as the recognition of speech were localized in the left hemisphere of the brain. By the first decade of the 20th century, Brodmann had developed the first functional map of the cerebral cortex. A variety of investigators, including Benton, Tuber, and Geschwind developed methods for associating function with different areas of the brain. Early neuropsychologists, including Luria and Reitan, used psychological tests to estimate areas of brain damage. However, major advances in brain imaging reduced the need for these types of services. MRI and CT scanning now allow clinicians to examine the brains of living people.

Clinical neuropsychology has developed rapidly over the last few decades (Benton & Sivan, 2007; Morgan & Ricker, 2016). In 1970, neuropsychology was viewed as a new field characterized by rapid growth (Parsons, 1970). During the 1970s and early 1980s, research in neuropsychology exploded, and a practice specialty rapidly developed. Currently, neuropsychology has formally joined the ranks of other neurosciences. Using powerful measurement techniques, neuropsychologists have developed many procedures for identifying the relationship between brain problems and behavioral problems (Butters, Delis, & Lucas, 1995). The activities of neuropsychologists are extremely varied and require complex technology. An exploration of this important new discipline in any depth would require a review of neuroanatomy and other topics in neuroscience that we cannot discuss here. Instead, we describe some current activities of active neuropsychological research and practice. Neuropsychologists are quite specialized. Some focus on brain dysfunction in children (Abramovitch et al., 2015) whereas others work with adults or older adults (Morgan & Ricker, 2016). Neuropsychologists focus mainly on brain dysfunction, but some are actively developing interventions for those who suffer brain injuries or related problems (Albrecht, Masters, Ames, & Foster, 2016). Neuropsychologists also study how cognitive processes are affected by mental illness (Reilly et al., 2016) as well as alcohol abuse (Valsan, Veetil, & Beevi, 2016) or serious diseases such as AIDS (Kabuba, Menon, Franklin Jr, Heaton, & Hestad, 2016). Some specialize in the evaluation of older adults (Taylor, Livingston, Kreutzer, & West, 2016). Some neuropsychologists prefer to use batteries of psychological tests, whereas others prefer specific tasks derived from experimental psychology (Savage, 2016).

Neuropsychological assessment has been used to evaluate specific problems in memory. Clearly, memory is a heterogeneous phenomenon; scientists make distinctions among memory systems such as short- and long-term memory. Short-term memory occurs when one recollects or produces material immediately after it has been presented. The capacity for short-term memory is probably limited; without repetition, one can hold information only a few minutes. Conversely, long-term memory may be stored for a long time (more than a few days), and the capacity for long-term memory is quite large.

Examiners use a variety of clinical techniques to measure memory dysfunction, including the Wechsler Memory Scale–Revised (WMS-R), the Memory Assessment Scales (MAS), the Randt Memory Test (RMT), and the Luria-Nebraska battery. Short-term memory is best assessed using verbal tests. These include the immediate recall span, the digit span, and several word tests (Butters et al., 1995). The techniques used to assess short-term memory include tests that evaluate memory for specific stories or memory for lists of unrelated words.

Significant progress has been made in linking performance on neuropsychological tests to specific clinical problems (Morgan & Ricker, 2016). For example, alcoholic dementia, which is caused by long-term chronic alcoholism, is characterized by dysfunction in visuospatial skills. Patients with Huntington's disease perform much better on recognition than do patients with Alzheimer's disease; however, the former may have retrograde amnesia with equally deficient recall of events from all decades, while the latter have more severe difficulties with recall for recent events and less for long-term memories (Butters et al., 1995).

Another example of a study that used neuropsychological evaluations compared recently detoxified alcoholics with nonalcoholic controls who were the same age and with recovering alcoholics who had been abstinent for at least 18 months. The groups were comparable in education, age, and IQ. However, comparisons on learning and retention of new information differed. Figure 17.2 shows some of these differences. Recently detoxified alcoholics scored lower on measures of immediate

FIGURE 17.2

Learning and memory performance by recently detoxified alcoholics (abstinent 2 weeks), long-term abstinent alcoholics (abstinent 18 months), and nonalcoholic controls.

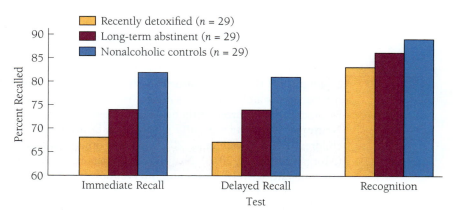

(Adapted from data in Dawson & Grant, 2000.)

recall, 20-minute delayed recall, and recognition than did comparable subjects who had been off alcohol for 18 months. Both groups of former alcoholics performed more poorly that did the nonalcoholic controls. These findings suggest that there may be some recovery of learning and memory when alcoholics are abstinent for 18 months or more. However, chronic alcohol use may permanently affect some neuropsychological functioning (Boelema et al., 2016).

New research also challenges the idea that functional problems are related to specific locations within the brain. New evidence suggests that complex cognitive, perceptual, and motor functioning are determined by neural systems rather than specific single structures. There are complicated circuits and dense interconnections between different locations in the brain. Neuropsychological evaluation estimates localized problems as well as problems with the brain's complex interconnections.

One of the most studied areas of neuropsychology is the identification of deficits in the left or right hemisphere of the brain. Evidence for left hemisphere control of language in right-handed individuals comes from studies on brain damage, studies of brain stimulation during surgery for patients with epilepsy, and from evaluation of people who have suffered a stroke on one side of the brain. However, approximately two-thirds of left-handed people have language organized on the left side of the brain, approximately 20% have language organized in the right hemisphere, and the remainder appear to have language represented on both sides. Table 17.1 summarizes some of the problems associated with left or right hemisphere damage (Swanda, Haaland, & LaRue, 2000).

Trained neuropsychologists can identify specific problems. For example, Wernicke's aphasia is characterized by impaired verbal comprehension and ability to repeat information. People with this pattern of impairment have damage to Wernicke's area of the brain (the superior temporal gyrus), problems monitoring their language output, and often have difficulty with the syntax of their spoken sentences. Sometimes people affected by Wernicke's aphasia utter unintelligible strings of words that can be confused with schizophrenic symptoms.

Neuropsychological tests can also be used to diagnose motor problems. For example, right-handed people who have damage to their right hemisphere often develop spatial disorders such as the inability to copy or draw objects or difficulties

TABLE 17.1 Selected Neuropsychological Deficits Associated With Left or Right Hemisphere Damage

Left hemisphere	Right hemisphere
Word memory problems	Visual–spatial deficits
Right–left disorientation	Impaired visual perception
Finger agnosia	Neglect
Problems recognizing written words	Difficulty writing
Problems performing calculations	Problems with spatial calculations
Problems with detailed voluntary motor activities, not explained by paralysis	Problems with gross coordinated voluntary motor not explained by paralysis activities
Problems dressing	Inability to recognize a physical deficit (e.g., denial of a paralyzed limb)

Adapted from Swanda, Haaland, and LaRue (2000).

assembling certain objects. Some individuals may develop specific problems associated with right hemisphere damage, such as dressing apraxia. People with this condition have difficulty identifying the top or the bottom of a garment, and sometimes the left or the right side as well. Although these individuals may function well in other aspects of their lives, they have a great deal of difficulty dressing.

Neuropsychologists are also skilled at identifying which aspects of the information-processing systems may be damaged. For example, information retrieval and storage are related but different functions. Some people have problems in recall or retrieval of information. Tests can be used to determine whether the problem is in recognition or actual retrieval of information. Recognition might be evaluated using multiple-choice format items. Patients who have difficulty recognizing information may have deficiencies in storage, which is associated with the medial temporal lobes or the diencephalic system. Impaired retrieval of information may be associated with problems in the frontal lobes, for example. (See Focused Example 17.1.)

Developmental Neuropsychology

Testing is typically done as part of a complex evaluation. When children are not performing well in school, a medical, educational, and psychological evaluation might be ordered. Sometimes, neuropsychological testing is done to provide a baseline. For example, a child who is undergoing intense medical therapy or a child with a serious medical illness such as epilepsy may face neurological changes over time. Repeated neuropsychological evaluations can help identify such changes (Baron & Fennell, 2000).

Neuropsychological assessment of children presents unique challenges. For example, a young child with a brain injury may adapt well to most situations, but she may later have problems with, say, her geometry class, which would require more complex visual–perceptual functioning than she had encountered before. Earlier brain injury may be missed until children reach the age where they are challenged with new types of problems.

17.1   FOCUSED EXAMPLE

Case Study: Neuropsychological Consequences of Long-Term Alcohol Abuse

Neuropsychological evaluation uses a variety of approaches to identify problems with brain functioning. One task that is often informative is to have the patient draw a clock. Damage to the right hemisphere of the brain is sometimes reflected in inaccurate global features of the drawing. Left hemisphere damage is associated with the reproduction of small features and details.

A case study helps illustrate the value of the clock drawing task. The patient in this study had been admitted to the hospital after he had called 911 and stated he was suicidal. He was intoxicated at the time of admission and had a significant history of alcohol abuse. The same patient had received neurological evaluations on several previous occasions. The patient was well educated and had completed college. He had good verbal skills, with a Wechsler Adult Intelligence Scale (WAIS) verbal IQ of 103. However,

some of his WAIS subscores were lower. For example, the digit span subtest was in the 25th percentile, and his performance on the memory domain was in the 1st percentile.

Figure 17.3 shows the subject's performance on the Draw-a-Clock task from the Boston Diagnostic Aphasia Examination. The task asks the patient, "Draw a clock, put in all of the numbers, and set the hands for ten after 11." The left-hand portion of the figure shows the clock drawn in 1996. The center section shows the clock drawn in 1998, while the third panel shows the clock drawn during the hospital admission in 1999.

The pattern of performance suggests a deterioration in parietal lobe functioning indicated by poor visuospatial functioning. It is likely that long-term alcohol abuse contributed to these problems.

FIGURE 17.3
Results from the
Draw-a-Clock task.

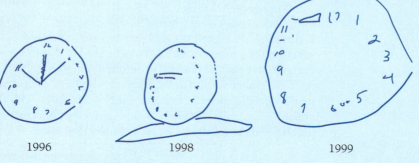

1996   1998   1999

(Dean Delis, Ph.D., provided this example.)

Another challenge in evaluating children is brain plasticity. The human brain is remarkable in its potential to reorganize in response to injury. Although recovery is often impressive, it usually is not complete, and these problems are often hard to evaluate using neuropsychological tests.

Neuropsychological tests for children differ widely. One category of measures tests general development and adaptive functioning. Examples include the Child Development Inventory, Child Behavior Checklist, Reynolds Depression Scale, and Children's State-Trait Anxiety Scale.

A second group of measures estimates attention and executive function. These tests typically evaluate functioning related to several different aspects of information processing. The Trail Making Tests, for example, scatter sequential numbers (e.g., 1, 2, 3, 4) around different locations on a sheet of paper. The child is asked to draw lines to connect the numbers in sequence. Part B of the test adds scattered sequential letters, and the child must, for example, start at 1, go to *A*, then go to 2, then *B*, and so on. The test evaluates several cognitive skills, including attention, sequencing, and thought processing.

Attention and executive function are believed to be separate. Executive function includes volition, such as forming and executing a goal, planning, and taking action to complete a task. It also includes the self-control and self-monitoring to complete the task. Mirsky and colleagues (Mirsky, 1989, 1996; Mirsky, Kugelmass, Ingraham, & Frenkel, 1995) have identified four different factors of mental processing and related them to specific anatomical regions in the brain. One factor is *focus execute.* This refers to the child's ability to scan information and respond in a meaningful way. A second factor is *sustain,* which describes the child's capacity to pay close attention for a defined interval of time. The third factor is *encode* and is related to information storage, recall, and mental manipulation. The final factor, called *shift,* refers to the ability to be flexible. Different neuropsychological tests are used to assess each of these four factors (Baron & Fennell, 2000).

The study of childhood brain dysfunction is extremely important. Neuropsychological problems appear in speech and reading disorders known generally as *learning disabilities,* which account for problems in significant numbers of young children. **Dyslexia** is a specific reading disorder characterized by difficulties in decoding single words. The problem may have a genetic base and may result from difficulties in processing phonemes. Unfortunately, it is difficult to estimate the exact number of children who are affected by dyslexia because different studies apply different definitions. The problem likely affects approximately 4% of school-aged children and approximately 80% of children identified as having a learning disability.

Federal law now requires that children with specific disabilities receive individualized instructional programs and special attention. Thus, the identification of a disability means that considerable attention will be devoted to the child at enormous public expense. In other words, learning disabilities represent major public health problems. As such, considerable effort has been devoted to defining subcategories of learning disabilities, developing procedures to identify them, and instituting methods for helping children overcome these problems (Cubelli, Pedrizzi, & Della Sala, 2016).

In addition to identification of brain injury, neuropsychological evaluations have been used for a variety of other purposes. For example, neuropsychological testing has been used to determine if people are faking illness. One application is the detection of malingering for adults who have traumatic brain injury. In one study, 65 patients who had previous brain injury were referred for a neuropsychological evaluation. Twenty-eight of these patients had been identified as having exaggerated their cognitive dysfunction in order to gain greater benefits or to escape reassignment to work. All subjects completed the WAIS (See Chapter 10). Using discriminate function analysis, which is a specialized method for identifying the linear combination of variables that separate groups, the researchers developed an equation that successfully separated malingerers from those who were not exaggerating their brain injury (Greve, Bianchini, Mathias, & Houston, 2003).

17.2   FOCUSED EXAMPLE

Neuropsychological Consequences of Football Head Injuries

Head injuries and concussions are very common among football players (Guskiewicz & Broglio, 2011). Concussions occur when the head accelerates rapidly and then is stopped, or when the head is spun rapidly. Concussions are not bruises to the brain caused by hitting something hard, and there is usually no physical evidence that the brain is swollen or bleeding. However, violent shaking of the brain may cause some cells to become depolarized and fire their neurotransmitters all at one time. This might result in a flood of neurotransmitters in the brain resulting in a downregulation of receptors that are related to learning and memory. The experience can also result in blurred vision, nausea, and memory loss. In some cases, rapid release of neurotransmitters might result in loss of consciousness. Sequential concussions can cause serious problems because it takes some time for the brain to recover (Ocwieja et al., 2012).

Concussions are particularly common among players in the National Football League (NFL). One study of retired athletes suggested that 61% had had at least one concussion and about a quarter had had three or more concussions (Guskiewicz et al., 2005). Among retired NFL players who reported sustaining one or more concussions while playing football, at least one in five also reported experiencing depression. That rate is about three times higher than the rate of depression among football players who had not experienced multiple concussions. Players who had experienced three or more concussions had a fivefold risk of mild cognitive impairment (Guskiewicz et al., 2007). Those who play in offensive skill positions are at particularly high risk (Nathanson et al., 2016).

One famous case involved Junior Seau, a celebrated Hall of Fame linebacker who played 20 seasons in the NFL. After a documented history of changes in behavior and other neurological symptoms, Seau committed suicide by a gunshot to the chest. He shot himself in the chest so that his brain could be preserved for autopsy. That autopsy revealed chronic traumatic encephalopathy (CTE) presumably caused by multiple concussions (Azad, Li, Pendharkar, Veeravagu, & Grant, 2016). More than a dozen lawsuits were filed in the later part of 2011, and about 120 former players were considering legal action. Several studies of the long-term neuropsychological consequences of football head injuries are underway, and evidence for neuropsychological effects of football head trauma continues to accumulate (Wright et al., 2016). In April of 2015, the NFL offered to pay over $1 billion to former players over a period of 65 years to compensate them for their injuries.

Another application of neuropsychological testing is to determine the seriousness of concussions among athletes (Erlanger et al., 2003). Head injury for athletes is common, particularly in sports such as boxing and football. An injured athlete often wants to return to play promptly. Returning the athlete to the playing field too soon might put him or her at serious risk. One application of clinical neuropsychology is the development of a concussion resolution index (CRI) to track the recovery following a sports-related concussion. CRI is made up of six subtests, including reaction time, visual recognition, and speed of information processing. Validity studies show that the CRI is associated with other neuropsychological tests. For example, it correlates with the grooved pegboard test. Studies using athletes who have been injured demonstrated that this computer-based test can identify ongoing neuropsychological difficulties in cases where symptom reports and clinical examinations are normal. Ongoing problems in psychomotor speed and speed of information processing may put athletes at risk for future injury. Use of these new methods could be exceptionally helpful for determining when it is safe for athletes to return to the playing field (Erlanger et al., 2003).

Other clinical neuropsychologists have been busy identifying the cognitive consequences of early brain lesions. For example, studies have shown that high-risk infants show poor performance on tests of verbal ability, coordination, visual–spatial ability, and the like by the time they are 3 years old (Francis-Williams, 1974). Other studies focus on recovery from accidents and trauma. For example, a few years after children have been in accidents involving head injuries, neurological tests often show no remaining problems. Nevertheless, neuropsychological tests of intellectual abilities often show that these functions remain somewhat impaired (Tolomeo et al., 2016). In summary, developmental neuropsychologists actively work toward understanding brain-behavior relationships in children. They have created extensive diagnostic procedures for identifying learning disabilities such as articulation disorders, speech disorders, and dyslexia. Furthermore, they have attempted to link specific medical problems such as birth complications and prematurity to later intellectual function. Finally, they have attempted to identify the cognitive consequences of early brain disease and injury.

Developmental neuropsychology is a difficult field because it requires several levels of assessment. Figure 17.4 shows a seven-step model that is used by neuropsychologists in the development of rehabilitation plans. The first step requires the application of formal tests to determine the nature of the problem. The second step calls for an assessment of the environment, such as the demands of the school environment and other academic expectations. The third and fourth steps require the formulation of treatment plans, which involve a prediction of the short- and long-term consequences of the brain problem and the chances that intervention will make a difference. The fifth step concerns the availability of resources. For example, is there a family member who can assist in treatment? Are there facilities and therapists in the community? The sixth step calls for the development of a realistic treatment plan that considers the information gained in Steps 1 to 5. Even if the neuropsychologist does not deliver the treatment, he or she may remain involved in the seventh step, evaluating progress made in the course of clinical care. When treatment is not achieving its objectives, modifications may be suggested (Fletcher, Taylor, Levin, & Satz, 1995).

As suggested by Figure 17.4, the neuropsychologist has many complex and important tasks that require the administration and interpretation of assessment devices.

Adult Neuropsychology

There are many different approaches to identifying the consequences of brain injury in adults. Perhaps the two best-known approaches involve administration of the Halstead-Reitan and Luria-Nebraska test batteries.

Halstead-Reitan Neuropsychological Battery

In 1935, Ward Halstead opened a laboratory to study the impact of impairments of brain function on a wide range of human abilities. Some of Halstead's observations were formal, while others involved observations in work and social settings. The

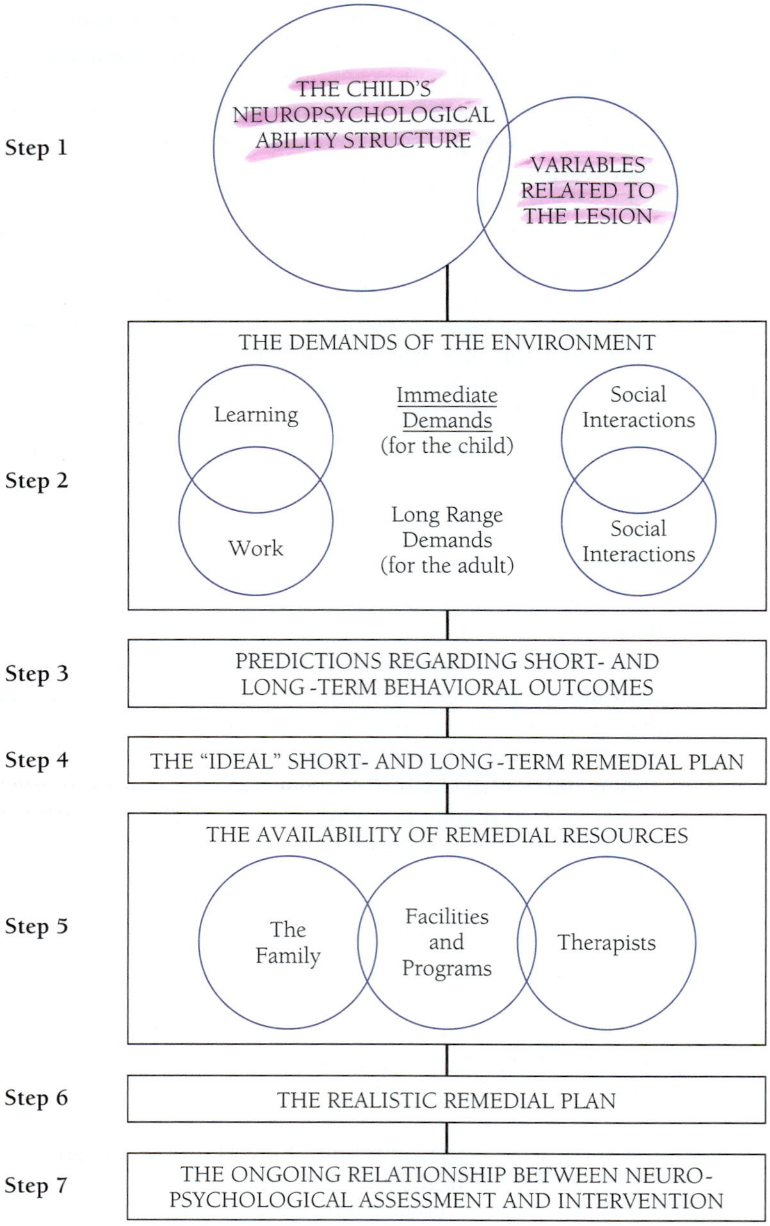

FIGURE 17.4

The process of rehabilitation requires at least seven steps: (1) assessment of the child, (2) assessment of the environment, (3) predictions about short- and long-term outcomes, (4) development of an ideal plan, (5) assessment of resources, (6) development of a realistic intervention plan, and (7) ongoing assessment.

Step 1

THE CHILD'S NEUROPSYCHOLOGICAL ABILITY STRUCTURE

VARIABLES RELATED TO THE LESION

Step 2

THE DEMANDS OF THE ENVIRONMENT

Learning

Immediate Demands (for the child)

Social Interactions

Work

Long Range Demands (for the adult)

Social Interactions

Step 3

PREDICTIONS REGARDING SHORT- AND LONG-TERM BEHAVIORAL OUTCOMES

Step 4

THE "IDEAL" SHORT- AND LONG-TERM REMEDIAL PLAN

Step 5

THE AVAILABILITY OF REMEDIAL RESOURCES

The Family

Facilities and Programs

Therapists

Step 6

THE REALISTIC REMEDIAL PLAN

Step 7

THE ONGOING RELATIONSHIP BETWEEN NEURO-PSYCHOLOGICAL ASSESSMENT AND INTERVENTION

(From J. M. Fletcher et al., 1995, p. 585. Reprinted by permission of Lippincott, Williams, & Wilkins.)

formal observations were obtained through modifications of existing psychological tests. Over time, Halstead realized that determining inadequacy in brain function required a wide range of tests that measured characteristics and abilities beyond those targeted by existing psychological tests (Reed & Reed, 2015). In 1944, Halstead was joined in his neuropsychological laboratory by his first graduate student, Ralph M.

17.3 FOCUSED EXAMPLE

Should Adolescents Be Tried as Adults? The Developing Adolescent Brain

Our criminal justice system usually has separate processes for trying children and adults. But some terrible crimes have been committed by children and adolescents. When crimes are very serious, many states allow children to be tried as adults. One compelling case was *United States vs. Omar Khadr.* Mr. Khadr was imprisoned at Guantánamo Bay for building improvised explosive devices (IEDs). Khadr was only 15 years old when he allegedly committed these crimes. The prosecution argued that building a bomb requires adultlike cognitive maturity. But is the brain of a 15-year-old the same as an adult brain?

Although adolescents may be similar in size to adults, there is increasing evidence that their brains continue to mature well into their 20s (Albert, 2012). For example, late in adolescence the gray matter in the prefrontal regions decreases in volume. This probably happens because there is a pruning of

synapses that had not been used. In addition, there is a proliferation and then a reduction of dopamine receptors in the paralimbic and prefrontal cortical regions of the brain. These components of the brain are active in reward systems, including the sensitivity to drugs. There is also an increase of white matter in the prefrontal regions and an extension of the white matter tracks to different areas of the brain. In short, the brain of an adolescent is not the same as the brain of an adult (Albert, 2012). The differences affect a wide variety of behaviors ranging from sleep to attention to the ability to operate complex machinery, such as an automobile (Steinberg, 2010). Evidence on the developing brain has only emerged in the last 10 to 15 years, and it has been slow to affect public policy (Midson, 2011). Nevertheless, the role of the developing brain is now gaining greater consideration in public policy discussions.

Reitan. Halstead and Reitan worked together until 1950, when Reitan received his Ph.D. Reitan contributed by adding several tests to the assessment procedures. The full battery includes many psychological tests and sometimes requires 8 to 12 hours to administer. In addition, patients assessed by the Halstead-Reitan battery often receive the full Minnesota Multiphasic Personality Inventory (MMPI) to evaluate their emotional state in response to a medical situation. The battery also includes a full WAIS.

The full Halstead–Reitan Neuropsychological Battery is available in different versions for children and adults. See Table 17.2 for a summary of the components in the adult battery.

A large number of studies validate the Halstead and Reitan procedures (Silk-Eglit, Stenclik, Miele, Lynch, & McCaffrey, 2015). Most of the studies show that performance on specific subtasks of the Halstead-Reitan battery is associated with dysfunction in one of the two hemispheres of the brain. For example, tactile, visual, and auditory problems on one side of the body reflect damage in the opposite hemisphere of the brain. Difficulty on the right side of the body indicates a problem in the left side of the brain (Wheeler & Reitan, 1962). Later studies by Reitan (1968) demonstrated that the battery can locate tumors or lesions in the right or left hemisphere of the brain and in the front or back portion of the brain in a significant number of cases. By studying performance in a systematic way, neuropsychologists have been able to provide important information about the location and the impact of brain problems (Reitan & Wolfson, 1997, 1999).

TABLE 17.2 Components of the Halstead-Reitan Neuropsychological Battery for Adults

Test	Description
Halstead category test	This test is a learning experiment for current learning skills, mental efficiency, and abstract concept formation.
Tactual test (time, memory, localization)	The patient must put variously shaped blocks into holes of the same shape. The test assesses several abilities, including motor speed and tactual and kinesthetic psychomotor performance, as well as memory.
Rhythm test	Thirty pairs of rhythm beats are presented, and the patient is to identify which pairs are the same and which are different. The task measures auditory perception, concentration, and attention.
Speech-sounds perception test	Sixty nonsense words are presented on a tape recorder. After hearing each word, the patient must choose the word from among four alternatives presented visually. The test measures auditory–verbal perception, auditory–visual coordination, and some aspects of language and concentration.
Finger oscillation test	The patient taps the index finger as rapidly as possible, alternating hands on consecutive trials. The test is used to analyze motor speed and right–left hand preference.
Related Procedures	The following tests are often given in conjunction with the Halstead-Reitan battery.
Trail-making test	This test requires patients to connect numbers and letters as rapidly as possible. The test measures speed, visual scanning, and ability to process information in sequence.
Strength-of-grip test	A mechanical device (the hand dynamometer) is used to measure the strength of grip in each hand.
Sensory–perceptual examination	In a variety of sensory modalities, such as touch, hearing, and vision, the patient receives information on one side of the body and then on the other side. The test is used to determine whether stimuli presented on one side of the body are perceived when presented alone and also to determine whether competition with other stimulation reduces the perception of the stimulus.

From Saccuzzo & Kaplan (1984, pp. 226–227).

Critics of the Halstead-Reitan battery point out that the major advantage of the test may not be worth the effort in applying the measures. The battery can assist in localizing injury in either the left or right hemisphere of the brain. However, this advantage may be meager in relation to the many hours it takes to complete the test. New methods of brain imaging (MRI and CT scan) may be more efficient for locating injury (Toga & Mazziotta, 2015).

Luria-Nebraska Neuropsychological Battery

A different approach to neuropsychological assessment is found in the work of Luria, who was recognized for many years as an expert on the functions of the human brain (Luria, 1966, 1973). While other researchers such as Halstead and Reitan attempted to find specific areas within the brain that correspond to particular behaviors, Luria did not acknowledge that any single area was solely responsible for any particular behavior (Golden, 2015). Instead, Luria saw the brain as a functional system, with a limited number of brain areas involved in each behavior. Each area in the functional system might be considered a necessary link in a chain. If any link is injured, the total system will break down.

Luria also introduced the concept of *pluripotentiality*—that any one center in the brain can be involved in several different functional systems (Golden, 2015). For example, one center in the brain may be involved in both visual and tactile senses. Luria also felt that multiple systems might be responsible for the same behavior. Thus, if a child's injury affects one system, another system may take over. Many clinical examples show the value of Luria's methods, particularly for severely disabled patients who may have multiple health problems and cannot complete traditional psychological tests (Guedalia, Finkelstein, Drukker, & Frishberg, 2000).

In practice, Luria applied his theory clinically to make intuitive judgments about deficits in functional systems. Because he did not use a standardized procedure, the amount of time he spent testing individuals varied greatly. In addition, it was difficult for others to repeat the exact steps Luria had used to reach conclusions about particular patients. Reitan (1976) criticized him on the grounds that Luria's opinion was the only known evidence for the validity of the tests.

Although Luria's procedures were widely regarded as important, they did not meet the psychometric standards of many U.S. psychologists. To face these criticisms, Golden (1981) developed a standardized version of Luria's procedures. Because Golden worked at the University of Nebraska, the test has become known as the Luria-Nebraska Neuropsychological Battery. The battery includes 269 items that can be administered in approximately 24 hours. The items are divided into 11 subsections; these are listed in Table 17.3. A similar test for children has also been developed (Plaisted, Gustavson, Wilkening, & Golden, 1983).

The inventory is scored by finding a standardized performance level for each of the 11 subtests. In addition, three more scores are reported. First, a pathognomonic scale consists of 32 items found in previous studies to be highly sensitive to brain dysfunction. The other two scores indicate whether dysfunction is in the right or the left hemisphere of the brain. They are taken from the sections of the battery that independently test the function of the right or left side of the body.

A variety of studies (summarized by Golden, 1981) have demonstrated that the Luria-Nebraska battery can make fine distinctions in neuropsychological functions. Many of these studies used the battery to estimate the area of the brain damaged by a tumor or lesion. In many of these studies, confirmation of localization is made by surgery, angiogram, or CT scan. In one study, the Luria-Nebraska battery localized problems in 22 of 24 right hemisphere and 29 of 36 left hemisphere cases (Golden, 1981). Some evaluations of the Luria-Nebraska battery are highly encouraging, whereas others show that these tests give little more information than

TABLE 17.3   Subsections of Luria-Nebraska Neuropsychological Battery

Test	Description
Motor functions	Examines basic and complex motor skills. Some items ask patients to perform fine tasks with the right and left hand and with the eyes open or closed. Other items involve mouth, tongue, and speech movements.
Rhythm	Evaluates rhythm and pitch skills. Patients must reproduce melodic sounds such as those from the song "Home on the Range." They are also to identify soft and loud sounds and musical patterns.
Tactile	Evaluates a variety of kinesthetic (movement) and tactile (touch) abilities. Patients are blindfolded and asked to identify where they have been touched. Then they must identify a variety of shapes and letters written on the back of the patients' hands. In addition, patients must identify common objects such as quarters, keys, paper clips, and so on.
Visual	Investigates visual and spatial skills. Patients are asked to identify objects through pictures and through progressively more difficult items. They are asked to put pieces together or identify objects in overlapping sketches.
Receptive speech	Tests ability to understand the spoken language. Items range from simple phonemes to comprehension of complex sentences.
Expressive speech	Estimates ability to express speech orally. The word sounds range from "see" to "Massachusetts" to "episcopal." Writing identifies basic writing skills, including simple spelling, copying letters and words, and writing names.
Reading	Similar to writing section. It tests whether patients can identify individual letters and read symbols, words, sentences, and stories.
Arithmetic skills	Tests a variety of simple numeric and algebraic abilities.
Memory	Assesses verbal and nonverbal memory skills. Items range from simple recall to complex memorization tasks.
Intellectual processes	Evaluates intellectual level using items similar to those on traditional intelligence tests.

From Saccuzzo & Kaplan (1984, p. 230).

do IQ tests (Carr, Sweet, & Rossini, 1986). Statistical methods for interpreting results are continually improving (Moses, Pritchard, & Faustman, 1994; Reynolds, 1982; Webster & Dostrow, 1982); nevertheless, the approach still has serious critics (Spiers, 1982).

An example of a profile from a patient tested with the Luria-Nebraska battery is shown in Figure 17.5. The two dark horizontal lines in the figure represent the normal ranges for performance on the various subtests. Scores above the top dark line indicate significant problem areas. As the figure shows, the patient demonstrates significant impairment in both expressive and receptive language, as well as problems in arithmetic and writing. Neuropsychologists have learned that memory problems are often associated with damage in the temporal lobe of the brain. Thus, the good performance on memory rules out a temporal lobe problem. Receptive and expressive language abilities seem to be localized more in the left than the right side of the brain. Comparing the profile with information acquired in other studies, the

FIGURE 17.5
Profile of a patient tested with the Luria-Nebraska battery.

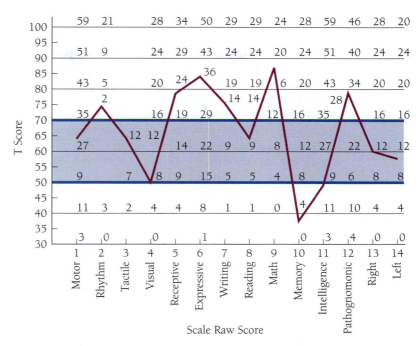

(From Golden, 1981. Copyright © 1981 by John Wiley & Sons, Inc. Reprinted by permission of John Wiley & Sons, Inc.)

neuropsychologists estimated that there was damage in the left side of the brain in the parietal-occipital area (toward the back of the left side). A neurological report confirmed that a stroke had damaged this very area.

Using information from neuropsychological test batteries, clinicians can evaluate damage and suggest programs for rehabilitation. Despite important improvements in the Luria-Nebraska battery, several methodological questions still remain. After a detailed review of the test and the standardization procedures, Lezak (1995) argued that it is important to interpret results of these tests with great caution. Some neuropsychologists prefer to use specific experimental tasks in addition to test batteries. One of the ongoing debates among neuropsychologists concerns the value of qualitative versus quantitative approaches. The Halstead-Reitan is an example of a fixed quantitative battery. Psychologists using this approach simply follow a set of standardized procedures. Qualitative approaches allow greater flexibility in the assessment process. Often the measures are designed to identify a specific information-processing problem and the psychologist can choose the components that may address specific clinical problems (Baron & Fennell, 2000). The California Verbal Learning Test is an example of this more recent approach.

California Verbal Learning Test (CVLT)

For decades, psychologists have known that people can get a wrong response for different reasons. For example, Werner (1937) objected to the use of global scores based only on the number of right or wrong items. Instead, Werner favored tests that assess how problems are solved in addition to assessing overall level of achievement.

Modern cognitive psychology has identified many levels of human information processing (Lachman, Lachman, & Butterfield, 2015). Contemporary cognitive psychology suggests that many factors determine performance on any given task (Berninger, Abbott, Cook, & Nagy, 2016; Delis & Wetter, 2007). It is not enough to know that there is an impairment in cognitive functioning. Instead, one needs to know which aspects of the human information-processing system are defective and which aspects are functioning well. This information is essential in designing rehabilitation strategies for patients who have selective problems.

The CVLT builds on research in psychological testing, cognitive psychology, and computer science (Delis, Kramer, Kaplan, & Ober, 1987). The test determines how errors are made in learning tasks. In other words, the intent is to identify different strategies, processes, and errors that are associated with specific deficits. The test attempts to link memory deficits with impaired performance on specific tasks for people who have known neurological problems. The CVLT assesses various variables, including levels of recall and recognition, semantic and serial strategies, serial position effects, learning rates across trials, consistency of item recall across trials, degree of vulnerability to proactive and retroactive interference, retention of information over short and long delays, and learning errors in recall and recognition.

In one component of the CVLT, the subject is asked to imagine that he or she is going to go shopping. Then the subject receives a list of items to buy. The examiner lists 16 items orally at a pace of approximately one word per second. The respondent is asked to repeat the list. This process is repeated through a series of five trials.

Performance on these tasks is analyzed in many ways. For example, learning across trials gives the test taker considerable information. Those who are highly anxious may perform poorly on the first trial but improve as the task is repeated (Lezak, 1995). However, adults with limited learning capacity may do relatively well on early trials but reach a plateau where repeated trials do not reflect improved performance. Adults with limited learning capacity may also have inconsistent recall across trials. This can happen when they abandon one strategy and adopt another. Studies have demonstrated that inconsistent recall across trials characterizes patients with amnesia caused by frontal lobe pathology.

The CVLT also includes other features derived from experimental cognitive psychology. For example, after five trials of exposure to the 16-word lists, a second interference list of 16 words is given. Subjects are tested immediately, and again after 20 minutes, for free recall, cued recall, and recognition of the first list.

Another unique feature of the CVLT is that one can administer it either in a paper-and-pencil form or with a microcomputer. Versions for both the PC and the Macintosh are available. The computer does not replace test administrators but instead assists them. In the computer-assisted form of the test, the examiner can enter responses directly into the computer using a single key or a light pen to touch the words on a monitor screen. This greatly facilitates and speeds up the scoring process.

Several studies have evaluated the CVLT's validity. For example, the test correlates with other measures such as the Wechsler memory scale (Mottram & Donders, 2005). In addition, factor analysis studies of the CVLT suggest independent factors for learning strategy, acquisition rate, serial position, discriminability, and learning performance. These constructs correspond to empirical findings from modern cognitive psychology. The diversity of deficits identified by the CVLT could not be identified using more-traditional psychometric tests (Delis et al., 1987).

The CVLT has been used to compare patients with Alzheimer's disease, Korsakoff's syndrome, and Huntington's disease. Alzheimer's disease is a serious neurological disorder that causes the inability to form short-term memories. Korsakoff's syndrome is an organic brain disorder often associated with long-term alcohol use that also results in the loss of short-term memory. Finally, Huntington's disease is an inherited disorder emerging in adulthood and associated with memory loss. Although all three organic brain problems are associated with memory loss, the nature of the deficit may be different. For example, patients with Alzheimer's and Huntington's may score about the same on measures of recall and memory tests but may differ in measures of forgetting (Bondi et al., 2003). Studies of brain pathology show that these two diseases affect different parts of the brain. An advantage of the CVLT is that it allows a more precise evaluation of the nature of the problems than do other tests.

When representative groups of patients from these three diagnostic groups are compared on the CVLT, those with Alzheimer's disease and Korsakoff's syndrome appear quite similar, with comparable scores for recall, learning and forgetting, semantic clustering, and several other cognitive factors. However, each of these groups performed at a lower level than did patients with Huntington's disease on measures of retention, intrusion errors, and recognition (Graves et al., 2016).

Studies of patients with Huntington's disease, Alzheimer's disease, and other neuropsychological impairments can help us understand properties of the tests. In one experiment, for example, normal patients, those with Huntington's disease, and those with Alzheimer's disease completed the CVLT. The patients were tested on immediate recall and long-delay free recall. As expected, the controls did significantly better than those with either Alzheimer's disease or Huntington's disease (see Figure 17.6). However, the correlations between the two tests were not the same for the different groups. Immediate recall and long-delayed recall were highly correlated (above $r = .80$) for normal patients and for patients with Huntington's disease. However, the two variables were correlated only .36 for patients with Alzheimer's disease. These findings are critically important because we often assume that the correlations among variables are the same for all patient groups. These findings suggest that the very nature of the association among variables is different for

FIGURE 17.6

Long-delay recall on CVLT in three patient groups.

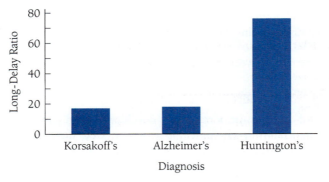

(Adapted from Delis et al., 1991.)

different patient populations. This challenges the idea that measures have the same validity for different patient groups (Delis et al., 2003). Another study demonstrated that tests of executive functioning can discriminate between conditions that have different anatomical underpinnings. MRI was used to locate sections of the brain that had reduced volumes. Adults with dementia associated with the frontal lobes made more rule violation errors in comparison to those with Alzheimer's disease or healthy adults who were about the same age (Carey et al., 2007; Graves et al., 2016).

Figure 17.6 compares CVLT scores for immediate and for long-delay savings for the two patient groups in comparison to a control group. *Long-delay savings* require that subjects learn a list of words. Then, after a long delay, they are given a free-recall test. The results are reported as the average number of correct responses. The figure shows that Huntington's patients have significantly higher recall than do those with Alzheimer's disease but fewer correct responses than controls. These results are consistent with the neuroanatomy of the illnesses. Huntington's disease is a subcortical dementia, whereas Alzheimer's disease is associated with cortical lesions. The CVLT may be helpful in identifying the location of the organic problem.

In 1994, Delis and colleagues released a children's version of the CVLT, the CVLT-C. Appropriate for children aged 5 to 16, this individually administered test can be used to evaluate mild to severe learning disabilities, attention deficit disorder (ADD), mental retardation, and other neurological disorders. In addition, the CVLT-C provides information for the diagnosis of psychiatric disorders. Like the adult version, the CVLT-C assesses both recall and recognition of words. In a typical testing session, the child may receive a list of 15 words on Monday and an interference list of 15 words on Tuesday. After the interference list, the child is tested on the Monday list. After a 20-minute delay, a nonverbal test is administered, followed by tests of long-delay free recall and long-delay cued recall, and then a test designed to assess recognition of the words that were administered the day before. These procedures produce several different scores, including total recall, learning strategy, serial position effect, learning rate, consistency of item recall, proactive and retroactive interference, and retention over long and short delays.

The test was standardized on a large national sample. Internal consistency and alpha reliabilities for the test are generally high (usually above .80 for all age levels). Validity studies consistently show that the test is moderately correlated (between .32 and .40) with the Revised Wechsler Intelligence Scale for Children (WISC-R) vocabulary subtest (Delis et al., 2004). In contrast to other tests, however, the CVLT-C provides substantially more diagnostic information (Delis et al., 1994). It is beginning to find a variety of clinical uses. For example, recent studies suggest that the CVLT can be used to detect whether patients are faking head injury in order to gain benefits (Sweet et al., 2000).

Automated Neuropsychological Testing

One of the most important new developments in clinical neuropsychology is automated neuropsychological assessment. New methods have been developed to provide quick computerized interpretation of neuropsychological tests. The Automated Neuropsychological Metrics (ANAM) test system is one such development. The ANAM was developed by the U.S. Department of Defense in order to evaluate changes in human performance when people were exposed to difficult environmental circumstances. The measure has now been used in a variety of clinical populations, including studies of patients with multiple sclerosis, lupus, Parkinson's disease, Alzheimer's disease, brain injury (Zane et al., 2016), and migraine headache (Nguyen, Williams, Silverman, & Levy, 2015). In each of these patient populations, the ANAM was responsive to cognitive changes that result from neurological disorders. A variety of studies suggested that the ANAM can efficiently screen people with cognitive changes and that it may be a valuable tool for monitoring cognitive changes as diseases progress (Kane et al., 2007).

The ANAM includes a variety of different tasks, including code substitution, code substitution recognition, matching two samples, mathematics, running memory, and logical reasoning. The reliability of performance on these tasks tends to be in the moderate range with few coefficients above .8. The ANAM has been used to evaluate military personnel who are deployed to combat. In these applications, it is important to establish a baseline for all soldiers so that it can be determined whether new injuries caused changes in mental status. It appears that the baseline scores are relatively stable with moderate reliabilities (0.72–0.86) over a short interval (Dretsch, Parish, Kelly, Coldren, & Russell, 2015). Studies have suggested that the math and running memory tasks are associated with measures that would be expected to correlate with cognitive functioning. These include performances on time-limited attention tasks and working memory tasks. On the other hand, some concerns have been raised about how people interact with computers. Familiarity with computer mouse and keyboard features varies across people, and some studies show that results from ANAM are not always the same as those obtained using paper-and-pencil tests or tests administered by a trained examiner (Parsons, 2016). In addition to applications in the military, the ANAM has been used extensively to evaluate the effects of head injury in athletes (De Marco & Broshek, 2016). Overall, there is reasonably good evidence for the validity of the ANAM (Short et al., 2007).

In summary, clinical neuropsychology is an emerging and important area in psychological testing. It is linked closely to basic research in both neuroscience and cognitive psychology. We expect this field to continue its rapid development over the next few decades.

Anxiety and Stress Assessment

It is the day of your final exam. You have studied hard and have every reason to expect an A. As you enter the classroom, the back of your neck feels stiff. Your hands sweat as you get out your pencil. Instead of concentrating on the task of test taking, you worry about not doing well, or you think about running out of time. When it is all over, you feel cheated. You knew the material well, but your grade on the exam did not reflect your knowledge.

If this story describes a situation you have experienced, then you have company. Test anxiety is a common problem among college students and a major factor in diminishing the validity of tests.

Test anxiety is also an important and active area in psychological research. Many theories about the relationship of anxiety to performance have led to the development of specific test-anxiety scales and measures (Cheng & Liao, 2016;

Tempel & Neumann, 2016). In this section, we review the general concepts of anxiety and stress, and then we review in some detail the theory and measurement of the same.

Stress and Anxiety

Stress is a response to situations that involve demands, constraints, or opportunities (Sarason & Sarason, 1999). We all experience psychological stress at some point in our lives. For some people, stress is a debilitating problem that interferes with virtually every aspect of their lives. For others, stress causes problems in particular situations. Stress helps still others to accomplish important goals. The study of psychological stress has gained an increasingly central position within the psychological and biomedical sciences (Dalton, Hammen, Brennan, & Najman, 2016). Psychological stress can interfere with performance on mental and academic tests (Duty, Christian, Loftus, & Zappi, 2016; Oostdam & Meijer, 2003), and some medical investigators now believe that stress is involved in 50% to 80% of all illnesses.

Psychological stress has three components: frustration, conflict, and pressure. *Frustration* occurs when the attainment of a goal is blocked. Though frustration takes different forms, the principle remains the same. A fourth-year premed student will likely become frustrated if she is rejected by every major medical school. Or if someone wants to get into a concert and is refused entrance, he may become frustrated. In each case, something or someone has blocked the attainment of a goal. *Conflict* is a type of stress that occurs when we must make a choice between two or more important goals, such as deciding between going to law school and going to graduate school in psychology. The final type of stress is *pressure* to speed up activities. External pressure occurs when your professor assigns a lot of extra reading right before the midterm exam; internal pressure occurs when no such reading is assigned but you take it on yourself because it fits your style and aspirations. Test anxiety does respond to treatment, particularly interventions that combine skills for test taking with cognitive and behavioral modification (Ergene, 2003).

Exposure to stressful situations can cause an observable reaction known as **anxiety,** an emotional state marked by worry, apprehension, and tension. When you are anxious, your autonomic nervous system becomes activated: Your heart beats fast, your pulse rate goes up, and your hands tend to sweat. The amount of anxiety you experience depends in part on the intensity of the stress-producing stimulus as you perceive it or your evaluation of a situation (Pelletier, Lytle, & Laska, 2016; Shavitt et al., 2016). How potentially harmful is the situation for you?

The State-Trait Anxiety Inventory

Actually, there are two types of anxiety. *State anxiety* is an emotional reaction that varies from one situation to another. *Trait anxiety* is a personality characteristic. Interest in these two types of anxiety led Charles D. Spielberger to develop the state-trait anxiety theory, which in turn led to the development of the State-Trait Anxiety Inventory (STAI). The STAI provides two separate scores: one for state anxiety (A-State) and another for trait anxiety (A-Trait). The STAI A-Trait scale consists of 20 items. On a 4-point scale, subjects indicate how they generally feel about each item. A similar set of items is used to evaluate the A-State.

Good evidence exists for the validity and the reliability of the STAI. Test–retest reliabilities range from .73 to .86 for the trait scale. The state scale, which is supposed to be inconsistent over time, indeed has low test–retest reliability (.16 to .54). Validity studies show that the STAI can be used to make several important and useful generalizations. For example, concurrent validity studies have shown that the STAI trait scale correlates well with other measures of trait anxiety. The STAI trait scale is significantly correlated with the Taylor Manifest Anxiety Scale (see Spielberger & Sydeman, 1994); it was also associated with another trait-anxiety scale known as the Institute for Personality and Ability Testing (IPAT) Anxiety Scale (Cattell & Scheier, 1961) for the same groups of college students and psychiatric patients. The correlations with the Taylor and the IPAT ranged from .75 to .85, which are quite impressive and suggest that these three scales measure much of the same psychological dimension. A variety of studies support the validity of the STAI for use in medical settings. For example, it is used to identify high levels of state and trait anxiety among patients with multiple sclerosis (Santangelo et al., 2016). It has also been shown to be useful for the evaluation of cognitive and somatic anxiety (Roberts, Hart, & Eastwood, 2016), for estimating the anxiety trajectories of patients receiving chemotherapy for breast and colorectal cancer (Schneider et al., 2016), and for evaluating the role of anxiety for people who have difficulty sleeping (Horváth et al., 2016). Overall, the STAI seems to measure the same thing as other scales that purport to assess trait anxiety.

To give a test a positive recommendation, we must also find discriminant evidence for construct validity (see Chapter 5). In one validity study for the STAI (Spielberger, Auerbach, Wadsworth, Dun, & Taulbee, 1975), patients scheduled to undergo surgery took the STAI before and after the medical procedure. Patients who had undergone major surgery showed less state anxiety after they had been told they were recovering well than they had before the operation. This finding demonstrates that state anxiety fluctuates with the situation—just as the test constructors said it would. Trait anxiety was not affected by the situation; it remained the same before and after surgery. People high in trait anxiety continued to respond in an anxious way, even in situations that evoked little or no anxiety among people low in trait anxiety (Trotter & Endler, 1999). Each component of the STAI thus appears to measure what it is supposed to measure, and the two components clearly assess different aspects of anxiety. The STAI is useful because behavior is influenced by both situations and personality traits. Studies using the STAI to evaluate tobacco use showed that smoking is influenced by situations, such as enjoyment and stimulation, and that it managed emotions among those with high levels of trait anxiety (Spielberger, Foreyt, Reheiser, & Poston, 1998).

The STAI has been translated into many different languages and is available in both adult and children's versions. There are good psychometric evaluations of many of these forms. For example, the psychometric properties of the French-Canadian STAI for children have been reported (Turgeon & Chartrand, 2003) and a Korean version has been used to evaluate medical students (Kim & Lee, 2016). There are also comparisons showing modest evidence for the validity of parent reports of their children's anxiety (Turgeon & Chartrand, 2003).

Measures of Coping

As we just saw in the case of test anxiety, different people confronted with the same stressful situation may respond quite differently. For instance, one group of investigators evaluated coping styles among adults suffering from heart failure. Patients with better coping skills were able to see more meaning in life, which in turn was related to better outcomes in both physical and mental health status (Svensson et al., 2016).

Several measures have been developed to assess the ways in which people cope with stress (Audulv, Packer, Hutchinson, Roger, & Kephart, 2016). One of these measures, the Ways of Coping Scale (Lazarus, 1995; Lazarus & Folkman, 1984), is a 68-item checklist. Individuals choose those thoughts and actions that they use to deal with stressful situations. The scale includes seven subscales for problem solving, growth, wishful thinking, advice seeking, minimizing threat, seeking support, and self-blame. Studies have suggested that the seven subscales can be divided into problem-focused and emotion-focused strategies for dealing with stressful situations. Problem-focused strategies involve cognitive and behavioral attempts to change the course of the stress; these are active methods of coping. Emotion-focused strategies do not attempt to alter the stressor but instead focus on ways of dealing with the emotional responses to stress (Cohen & Lazarus, 1994). The Ways of Coping questionnaire is one of the most widely used measures in health psychology (Stein, Hearon, Beard, Hsu, & Björgvinsson, 2016). A related measure is the Coping Inventory (Horowitz & Wilner, 1980), a 33-item measure derived from clinical interview data. Of three categories of items, the first describes activities and attitudes that people use to avoid stress. The second involves items that characterize strategies for working through stressful events. The third category considers socialization responses, or how each strategy would help the respondent cope with a specific stressful event. These measures and related tests, such as the Coping Resources Inventory (Hammer & Marting, 1985), have been useful in research on both adults and adolescents. For example, one study demonstrated that having good coping capabilities is important whether or not you are under stress (Zeidner & Hammer, 1990).

Ecological Momentary Assessment

Most psychological tests are designed to evaluate traits, which are constant over the course of time. Even measures of state anxiety are presumed to be reliable. However, levels of stress vary over the course of time. Measuring today's stress may tell us little about stress experienced next week. If we ask today about experiences last week, then the measurements may be inaccurate because memory fades over time. Recall affects virtually all autobiographical information.

New technical developments have made it possible to obtain information on an ongoing basis (Kaplan & Stone, 2013). One can obtain information repeatedly and average the results to get an overall impression of stress. Or information can be assessed with reference to a particular event. For example, suppose that you wanted to determine if levels of perceived stress coincide with particular stressors. Using computer technology, Ecological Momentary Assessment (EMA) would allow you to collect information on a continuing basis (Hoppmann & Ho, 2016). The equipment might measure blood pressure or hormonal state at specific points in time. Furthermore, a subject might be prompted to record information about mood, symptoms, or fatigue.

Most information in clinical studies is collected in clinics, offices, or laboratories—not necessarily the situations in which people ordinarily experience life events. One of the advantages of EMA is that the information is collected in the subject's natural environment. The EMA method usually involves a substantial number of repeated observations and shows variability within the subject over time (Deaton & Stone, 2016).

Studies of the co-use of alcohol and tobacco illustrate the use of EMA. Traditional studies of alcohol consumption might actually miss much of the information about drinking because the assessment is typically done during the day, whereas alcohol consumption often occurs in the evening. EMA allows the continual assessment of these behaviors in the subject's own environment. In one study, 57 subjects were given minicomputers that randomly prompted them to record their behaviors. The study showed that drinking was likely to occur between 8 PM and midnight. Smoking was more than twice as likely when subjects had been drinking as when they had not. In other words, smoking and drinking were linked (Shiffman et al., 1995). Some investigators use the latest technologies, including cell phones, to collect information in natural environments (Schneider & Stone, 2016).

Other studies have used daily assessments to evaluate life stress (Todd, 2004). In one study, 74 patients with arthritis rated stress, mood, and pain for 75 days. Those who had experienced major stresses were more likely to experience pain on the day after a stressful event than on other days. This suggests that life stress may amplify the relationship between life events and pain (Affleck et al., 1994). Further technical developments such as the EMA should significantly improve the assessment of variable behaviors, pain, and emotions (Hoppmann & Ho, 2016).

Depression

Major depressive disorders (MDDs) are the leading cause of disability among women worldwide (Kessler, 2003). Depression among women is also associated with a variety of different health-care conditions. For example, about 9% of pregnant women experience depression and about 10% of women who have recently given birth meet the criteria for a major episode of depression (Hoertel et al., 2015). Maternal depression can have important impacts on young children. It can affect the way young mothers interact with their children and it may result in increased risks of behavioral or emotional problems early in life. Further, studies suggest that children of depressed mothers have greater difficulty with school performance, peer relationships, and the development of social skills (Kersten-Alvarez et al., 2012).

Because of the importance of depression in young mothers, primary care physicians needed to consider whether it was necessary to screen for depression among pregnant women and women who have recently given birth. This decision is taken very seriously and must be based on the very best scientific evidence. In the United States, this task is often evaluated by the U.S. Preventive Services Task Force (USPSTF) (O'Connor, Rossom, Henninger, Groom, & Burda, 2016). The task force is an independent group of physicians and behavioral scientists appointed by the director of a federal agency known as the Agency for Healthcare Research and Quality. All of the recommendations of the task force depend on the latest scientific evidence. The recommendations of the task force are very important because they affect how primary care physicians are paid. If the task force gives the service a high grade (A or B), insurance companies are required to pay for the service without asking for a copayment from the patient (Murray et al., 2015).

Because of the importance of the task force recommendations, the criteria they use for the recommendations are very rigid. In the case of screening for depression, they look carefully at the validity and reliability of the screening test. In addition, they ask for evidence that something valuable will result from identifying cases. For example, just identifying cases is not enough. The task force requires evidence that a diagnosis leads to a treatment that will result in a remedy for the condition.

In the case of screening for maternal depression, the task force reviewed everything in the published literature that addressed the question of whether or not screening for depression in primary care for pregnant and postpartum women resulted in improved health outcomes. The outcomes were defined as decreased depressive symptoms, decreased deaths associated with suicide, reduced suicide attempts, reduced thoughts of suicide, improved physical functioning, improved quality of life, and improved health status. Each of the many studies the task force reviewed was graded for methodological quality.

The review began with the evaluation of measures of depression that can be applied in primary care settings. Typically, these are short questionnaires that can be completed in just a few minutes. One example is the Patient Health Questionnaire (PHQ). The PHQ is used to evaluate and monitor depressive symptoms. It considers both the frequency and severity of nine different symptoms of depression. It is particularly attractive to primary care physicians because it is self-administered and can be completed briefly in a waiting room. In addition to the PHQ, the committee identified the Edinburgh Postnatal Depression Scale (EPDS) as the most appropriate screening tool for prenatal and postnatal depression (Bina & Harrington, 2016). The scale along with scoring instructions are shown in Figure 17.7.

The task force identified 23 studies involving 5398 women that had evaluated the EPDS. Averaged across studies, the cutoff score of 13 indicated a threshold for major depressive disorder. Across the studies, the application of the EPDS resulted in a high likelihood of detecting women who were judged to be clinically depressed through other more intensive methods. The sensitivity of the method was 0.79; and the specificity was 0.87 (see Chapter 18 for more detailed discussion of sensitivity and specificity). In addition, the study showed that the EPDS functioned well for low-income and African American women and was also capable of identifying both major and minor depression in pregnant women (O'Connor et al., 2016).

Being able to diagnose depression is only part of the task. After the diagnosis of depression, the task force asked whether treatment with either psychotherapy or antidepressant medications resulted in improved health outcomes. They systematically reviewed all of the published studies in the literature. This included 10 high-quality clinical trials evaluating cognitive behavior therapy and related interventions. Although not all trials showed a significant benefit, on average, cognitive behavior therapy resulted in a significant likelihood of remission from depression and short-term benefits on a variety of outcomes. Increasing the duration of therapy also appeared to improve outcomes. Antidepressant medication also helped the women, but medicine use was associated with more harms (O'Connor et al., 2016).

FIGURE 17.7
Edinburgh Postnatal
Depression Scale.

Edinburgh Postnatal Depression Scale[1] (EPDS)

Name: _____   Address: _____

Your Date of Birth: _____   _____

Baby's Date of Birth: _____   Phone: _____

_____

As you are pregnant or have recently had a baby, we would like to know how you are feeling. Please check
the answer that comes closest to how you have felt **IN THE PAST 7 DAYS**, not just how you feel today.

Here is an example, already completed.

I have felt happy:
☐ Yes, all the time
☒ Yes, most of the time   This would mean: "I have felt happy most of the time" during the past week.
☐ No, not very often   Please complete the other questions in the same way.
☐ No, not at all

In the past 7 days:

1. I have been able to laugh and see the funny side of things
    ☐ As much as I always could
    ☐ Not quite so much now
    ☐ Definitely not so much now
    ☐ Not at all

2. I have looked forward with enjoyment to things
    ☐ As much as I ever did
    ☐ Rather less than I used to
    ☐ Definitely less than I used to
    ☐ Hardly at all

*3. I have blamed myself unnecessarily when things went wrong
    ☐ Yes, most of the time
    ☐ Yes, some of the time
    ☐ Not very often
    ☐ No, never

4. I have been anxious or worried for no good reason
    ☐ No, not at all
    ☐ Hardly ever
    ☐ Yes, sometimes
    ☐ Yes, very often

*5 I have felt scared or panicky for no very good reason
    ☐ Yes, quite a lot
    ☐ Yes, sometimes
    ☐ No, not much
    ☐ No, not at all

*6. Things have been getting on top of me
    ☐ Yes, most of the time I haven't been able to cope at all
    ☐ Yes, sometimes I haven't been coping as well as usual
    ☐ No, most of the time I have coped quite well
    ☐ No, I have been coping as well as ever

*7 I have been so unhappy that I have had difficulty sleeping
    ☐ Yes, most of the time
    ☐ Yes, sometimes
    ☐ Not very often
    ☐ No, not at all

*8 I have felt sad or miserable
    ☐ Yes, most of the time
    ☐ Yes, quite often
    ☐ Not very often
    ☐ No, not at all

*9 I have been so unhappy that I have been crying
    ☐ Yes, most of the time
    ☐ Yes, quite often
    ☐ Only occasionally
    ☐ No, never

*10 The thought of harming myself has occurred to me
    ☐ Yes, quite often
    ☐ Sometimes
    ☐ Hardly ever
    ☐ Never

Administered/Reviewed by _____   Date _____

[1]Source: Cox, J.L., Holden, J.M., and Sagovsky, R. 1987. Detection of postnatal depression: Development of the 10-item
Edinburgh Postnatal Depression Scale.   *British Journal of Psychiatry* 150:782-786 .

[2]Source: K. L. Wisner, B. L. Parry, C. M. Piontek, Postpartum Depression N Engl J Med vol. 347, No 3, July 18, 2002,
194-199

Users may reproduce the scale without further permission providing they respect copyright by quoting the names of the
authors, the title and the source of the paper in all reproduced copies.

On the basis of this review, the task force concluded that there is value in
screening all adults, including pregnant and postpartum women, for depression. They
concluded that there is high certainty of at least a moderate benefit. Screening using
the EPDS or related instruments can be accomplished in primary care practices and
has the potential to identify women in need of help. For women who are identified
as candidates for intervention, CBT and other treatments are available and these
treatments are associated with significant reductions in depressive symptoms. On the
basis of this review, the task force recommended depression screening for pregnant
and postpartum women. As a result, screening and treatment are now available to

FIGURE 17.7
(continued)

Edinburgh Postnatal Depression Scale[1] (EPDS)

Postpartum depression is the most common complication of childbearing.[2] The 10-question Edinburgh Postnatal Depression Scale (EPDS) is a valuable and efficient way of identifying patients at risk for "perinatal" depression. The EPDS is easy to administer and has proven to be an effective screening tool.

Mothers who score above 13 are likely to be suffering from a depressive illness of varying severity. The EPDS score should not override clinical judgment. A careful clinical assessment should be carried out to confirm the diagnosis. The scale indicates how the mother has felt *during the previous week*. In doubtful cases it may be useful to repeat the tool after 2 weeks. The scale will not detect mothers with anxiety neuroses, phobias or personality disorders.

Women with postpartum depression need not feel alone. They may find useful information on the web sites of the National Women's Health Information Center <www.4women.gov> and from groups such as Postpartum Support International <www.chss.iup.edu/postpartum> and Depression after Delivery <www.depressionafterdelivery.com>.

SCORING

QUESTIONS 1, 2, & 4 (without an *)
Are scored 0, 1, 2 or 3 with top box scored as 0 and the bottom box scored as 3.

QUESTIONS 3, 5-10 (marked with an *)
Are reverse scored, with the top box scored as a 3 and the bottom box scored as 0.

    Maximum score: 30
    Possible Depression: 10 or greater
    Always look at item 10 (suicidal thoughts)

Users may reproduce the scale without further permission, providing they respect copyright by quoting the names of the authors, the title, and the source of the paper in all reproduced copies.

Instructions for using the Edinburgh Postnatal Depression Scale:

1. The mother is asked to check the response that comes closest to how she has been feeling in the previous 7 days.

2. All the items must be completed.

3. Care should be taken to avoid the possibility of the mother discussing her answers with others. (Answers come from the mother or pregnant woman.)

4. The mother should complete the scale herself, unless she has limited English or has difficulty with reading.

[1]Source: Cox, J.L., Holden, J.M., and Sagovsky, R. 1987. Detection of postnatal depression: Development of the 10-item Edinburgh Postnatal Depression Scale. *British Journal of Psychiatry* 150:782-786.

[2]Source: K. L. Wisner, B. L. Parry, C. M. Piontek, Postpartum Depression N Engl J Med vol. 347, No 3, July 18, 2002, 194-199

women who have health insurance and the services are covered without the need for the woman to make a copayment.

NIH Toolbox

Many of the measures reviewed in this book are proprietary. When measures are proprietary, users must pay a fee to apply them. However, there has been a trend toward making measures publicly available. In the health area, one of the best examples is the National Institutes of Health (NIH) Toolbox. NIH is the largest supporter of biomedical and behavioral research in the world. Traditionally, NIH focused on basic biological research. More recently, it has developed a significant behavioral program and has become increasingly interested in psychological and behavioral measures. As part of this effort, it developed public domain state-of-the-art measures for assessing cognitive, emotional, motor, and sensory functioning for people ages 3 to 85. One of the rationales for developing the toolbox was the realization that people use many different measures to evaluate the same constructs in clinical studies. As a result, it was very hard to compare results across different studies. The toolbox offers well-validated measures that can serve as a common currency so that results from different investigations can be compared with one another (Gershon et al., 2013).

Ultimately, the goal of the toolbox is to provide measures that can assess neurological and behavioral function over the course of time. The measures are appropriate for different developmental stages and can be used for evaluating the effects of treatments and interventions. Table 17.4 summarizes the content of the four demands that make up the toolbox.

To administer measures in the toolbox, users can employ an app for an iPad. The app can be downloaded from https://itunes.apple.com/us/app/id1002228307. Unfortunately, there is a significant charge for the use of the software that administers the public domain measures.

TABLE 17.4 Components of the NIH Toolbox

Domain	Description	Components
Cognition	The cognition domains of the toolbox cover mental processes required for thinking, remembering, problem solving, and language.	Executive function, attention, episodic memory, language, processing speed, working memory
Emotion	Emotions are strong feelings, including joy, sorrow, or fear. Emotions reflect the state of consciousness involving affect.	Psychological well-being, social relationships, stress and self-efficacy, negative affect
Motor	The motor domain evaluates the ability to use and control muscles and movements, either voluntary or involuntary. Multiple body systems are involved in motor actions, including the nervous system, the musculoskeletal system, the brain, and the cardiovascular system.	Balance, dexterity, endurance, locomotion, strength
Sensation	The toolbox sensation domain evaluates the central nervous system processes required for incoming nerve impulses. These processes are essential to the interpretation of information that comes to the sense organs.	Audition, olfaction, pain, taste, vestibular, vision

Quality-of-Life Assessment

Have you ever thought about what you value most in life? Most people say that their health is more important than anything else. In fact, studies on the preference for different states of being sometimes exclude ratings of health because people show so little variability in their attitudes toward it. The actual definition of health status, however, has remained ambiguous.

Among the many definitions of health, we find two common themes. First, everyone agrees that premature mortality is undesirable, so one aspect of health is the avoidance of death. The health status of nations is often evaluated in terms of mortality rates or infant mortality rates (the number of children who die before 1 year of age per 1000 live births). Second, quality of life is important. In other words, disease and disability are of concern because they affect either life expectancy or life quality. For example, cancer and heart disease are the two major causes of premature death in the United States. A person with heart disease may face restrictions on daily living activities and may be unable to work or participate in social activities. Even relatively minor diseases and disabilities affect quality of life. Think about how a common cold interferes with your ability to attend school or to concentrate. Then think about how a serious problem, such as traumatic brain injury, affects quality of life (Brown et al., 2016).

Within the last few years, medical scientists have come to realize the importance of quality-of-life measurement (Brown et al., 2013; Groessl et al., 2016; Hanmer et al., 2016). Many major as well as minor diseases are evaluated in terms of the degree to which they affect life quality and life expectancy (Hanmer et al., 2016). One can also evaluate treatments by the amount of improvement they produce in quality of life. The Food and Drug Administration now considers quality-of-life data in its evaluations of new products, and nearly all major clinical trials in medicine use quality-of-life assessment measures. In the remainder of this chapter, we review several approaches to quality-of-life measurement.

What Is Health-Related Quality of Life?

Numerous quality-of-life measurement systems have evolved during the last 30 years and represent various traditions in measurement. Recent articles have presented at least two different conceptual approaches. One grows out of the tradition of health status measurement. In the late 1960s and early 1970s, the National Center for Health Services Research funded several major projects to develop general measures of health status. All of the projects were guided by the World Health Organization's (WHO) definition of health status: "Health is a complete state of physical, mental, and social well-being and not merely absence of disease" (WHO, 1948). The projects resulted in a variety of assessment tools, including the Sickness Impact Profile (Bergner, Babbitt, Carter, & Gilson, 1981), the Quality of Well-Being Scale (Kaplan & Anderson, 1990), the McMaster Health Index Questionnaire (Chambers, 1996), the SF-36 (Ware et al., 1995), and the Nottingham Health Profile (McEwen, 1992). Many of the measures examine the effect of disease or disability on performance of social role, ability to interact in the community, and physical functioning. Some of the systems have separate components for the measurement of social and mental health. The measures also differ in the extent to which they consider subjective aspects of life quality (Naughton & Shumaker, 2003).

There are two major approaches to quality-of-life assessment: psychometric and decision theory (Hanmer et al., 2016). The psychometric approach attempts to provide separate measures for the many different dimensions of quality of life. Perhaps the best-known example of the psychometric tradition is the Sickness Impact Profile (SIP). The SIP is a 136-item measure that yields 12 different scores displayed in a format similar to an MMPI profile.

The decision theory approach attempts to weight the different dimensions of health in order to provide a single expression of health status. Supporters of this approach argue that psychometric methods fail to consider that different health problems are not of equal concern. One hundred runny noses are not the same as 100 missing legs. In an experimental trial using the psychometric approach, one will often find that some aspects of quality of life improve while others get worse. For example, a medication might reduce high blood pressure but also produce headaches and impotence. Many argue that the quality-of-life notion is the subjective evaluation of observable or objective health states. The decision theory approach attempts to provide an overall measure of quality of life that integrates subjective function states, preferences for these states, morbidity, and mortality.

Common Methods for Measuring Quality of Life

This chapter presents some of the most widely used methods for measuring quality of life. Readers who are interested in more detailed reviews should consult Shumaker and Berzon (1995), Walker and Rosser (1993), or McDowell and Newell (1996).

SF-36

Perhaps the most commonly used outcome measure in the world today is the Medical Outcome Study Short Form-36 (SF-36). The SF-36 grew out of work by the RAND Corporation and the Medical Outcomes Study (MOS) (Ware & Gandek, 1998). The MOS attempted to develop a short, 20-item instrument known as the Short Form-20 or SF-20. However, the SF-20 did not have appropriate reliability for some dimensions. The SF-36 includes eight health concepts: physical functioning, role-physical, bodily pain, general health perceptions, vitality, social functioning, role-emotional, and mental health (Huber, Oldridge, & Höfer, 2016). The SF-36 can be either administered by a trained interviewer or self-administered.

It has many advantages. For example, it is brief, and there is substantial evidence for its reliability and validity. The SF-36 can be machine scored and has been evaluated in large population studies. The reliability and validity of the SF-36 are well documented (Atabakhsh & Mazaheri, 2016).

The SF-36 also presents some disadvantages. For example, it does not have age-specific questions, and one cannot clearly determine whether it is equally appropriate across age levels (Stewart & Ware, 1992). Nevertheless, the SF-36 has become the most commonly used behavioral measure in contemporary medicine (Ware, 2003).

Nottingham Health Profile (NHP)

Another major approach, the NHP, has particularly influenced the European community (Hagell, Whalley, McKenna, & Lindvall, 2003; Hinz, Klaiberg, Schumacher, & Brahler, 2003; Sivas et al., 2003; Uutela, Hakala, & Kautiainen, 2003). The NHP has two parts. The first includes 38 items divided into six categories: sleep, physical mobility, energy, pain, emotional reactions, and social isolation. Items within each section are rated in terms of relative importance. Items are rescaled in order to allow them to vary between 0 and 100 within each section.

The second part of the NHP includes seven statements related to the areas of life most affected by health: employment, household activities, social life, home life, sex life, hobbies and interests, and holidays. The respondent indicates whether or not a health condition has affected his or her life in these areas. Used in a substantial number of studies, the NHP has considerable evidence for its reliability and validity.

The NHP is consumer-based and arises from definitions of health offered by individuals in the community. Furthermore, this scale uses language that is easily interpreted by people in the community and conforms to minimum reading requirements. Substantial testing has been performed on the NHP; however, the NHP does not provide relative-importance weightings across dimensions. As a result, it is difficult to compare the dimensions directly with one another (Bureau-Chalot et al., 2002). In comparison to the SF-36, there is some evidence that the NHP is more reliable for studies of elderly adults living in the community (Faria et al., 2011).

Decision Theory Approaches

Within the last few years, interest has grown in using quality-of-life data to help evaluate the cost/utility or cost-effectiveness of health-care programs. Cost studies have gained in popularity because health-care costs have rapidly grown in recent years. All health-care interventions do not return equal benefit for the expended dollar. Cost studies might guide policymakers toward an optimal and equitable distribution of scarce resources. A cost-effectiveness analysis typically quantifies the benefits of a health-care intervention in terms of years of life or quality-adjusted life-years (QALYs). Cost/utility is a special use of cost-effectiveness that weights observable health states by preferences or utility judgments of quality (Bentley et al., 2011). In cost/utility analysis, the benefits of medical care, behavioral interventions, or preventive programs are expressed in terms of well-years (Kaplan & Ries, 2007).

If a man dies of heart disease at age 50 and we expected him to live to age 75, then we might conclude that the disease precipitated 25 lost life-years. If 100 men died at age 50 (and also had a life expectancy of 75 years), then we might conclude that 2500 life-years (100 men × 25 years) had been lost. Death is not the only relevant outcome of heart disease. Many adults suffer myocardial infarctions that leave them disabled for a long time and suffering diminished quality of life. QALYs take into consideration such consequences. For example, a disease that reduces quality of life by one half will take away .5 QALY over the course of each year.

If the disease affects two people, then it will take away 1 year (2 × .5) over each year. A medical treatment that improves quality of life by .2 for each of five individuals will result in the equivalent of 1 QALY if the benefit persists for 1 year. This system has the advantage of considering both benefits and side effects of programs in terms of the common QALY units.

The need to integrate mortality and quality-of-life information is clear in studies of heart disease. Consider hypertension. People with high blood pressure may live shorter lives if untreated, longer if treated. Thus, one benefit of treatment is to add years to life. However, for most patients, high blood pressure does not produce symptoms for many years. Conversely, the treatment for high blood pressure may cause negative side effects. If one evaluates a treatment only in terms of changes in life expectancy, then the benefits of the program will be overestimated because one has not taken side effects into consideration. On the other hand, considering only current quality of life will underestimate the treatment benefits because information on mortality is excluded. In fact, considering only current function might make the treatment look harmful because the side effects of the treatment might be worse than the symptoms of hypertension. A comprehensive measurement system takes into consideration side effects and benefits and provides an overall estimate of the benefit of treatment (Kaplan et al., 2011).

Most approaches for obtaining quality-adjusted life-years are similar. The approach that we prefer involves several steps. First, patients are classified according to objective levels of functioning. These levels are represented by the scales of mobility, physical activity, and social activity. Next, once observable behavioral levels of functioning have been classified, each individual is placed on the 0 to 1.0 scale of wellness, which describes where a person lies on the continuum between optimum function and death.

Most traditional measures used in medicine and public health consider only whether a person is dead or alive. In other words, all living people get the same score. Yet we know that there are different levels of wellness, and a need to score these levels exists. To accomplish this, the observable health states are weighted by quality ratings for the desirability of these conditions. Human value studies have been conducted to place the observable states onto a preference continuum, with an anchor of 0 for death and 1.0 for completely well (Kaplan et al., 2011). Studies have shown that the weights are highly stable over a 1-year period and consistent across diverse groups of raters (Kaplan, 1994b). Finally, one must consider the duration of stay in various health states. Having a cough or a headache for 1 day is not the same as having the problem for 1 year.

This system has been used to evaluate many different health-care programs. For example, it was used to demonstrate that a new medication for patients with arthritis produced an average of .023 QALY per year, whereas a new medication for acquired immunodeficiency syndrome (AIDS) produced nearly .46 of these units per year. However, the benefit of the arthritis medication may last as long as 20 years, ultimately producing .023 × 20 years = .46 year. The AIDS treatment produced a benefit for only 1 year, so its total effect was .46 × 1 year = .46 year. In other words, the general system allows the full potential benefits of these two completely different treatments to be compared (Kaplan et al., 1995).

mHealth and New Mobile Technologies

One of the most important new developments in health research and practice is "mHealth." mHealth is defined as diverse applications of wireless and mobile technologies designed to improve health research, health-care services, and health outcomes. This includes any wireless device carried by or on the person that can be used to transmit health data/information. The major categories include sensors (e.g., implantable miniature sensors and "nanosensors"), monitors (e.g., wireless accelerometers, blood pressure, and glucose monitors), and mobile phones (see Figure 17.8).

mHealth should not be confused with telehealth. The main difference is that mHealth is fundamentally a revolution in measurement. Devices used for mHealth are portable, real-time systems that provide a rich, potentially continuous data stream and capture information in the context of real, everyday life experiences. These new technologies give the concept of personalized health care a whole new meaning. Importantly, in these fiscally challenging times, mobile technologists are also scalable because they move away from the researcher and clinician working with a patient to a model where data are collected and often processed automatically (Istepanian, Philip, Wang, & Laxminarayan, 2011).

It is possible that mHealth technologies will revolutionize measurement, change diagnostics and treatment, and ultimately impact health at a global level (Chang et al., 2011).

One of the greatest challenges in improving human health is accounting for and addressing all of the possible exposures a human being encounters during his or her life. mHealth technologies are likely to play a major role in advancing our approach to measuring behavioral and environmental exposures in everyday life (Dobkin & Dorsch, 2011). For example, we now have smartphone applications that

Kim Kulish/Getty Images

Bloomberg/Getty Images

FIGURE 17.8

Examples of mHealth technologies.

help improve dietary choices through digital imaging. The phone captures a picture of a potential meal, identifies the food, and calculates portion size and recommended intake.

Medical diagnosis might also undergo major changes. For example, high-resolution fiber-optic microendoscopes are small portable devices that can be used to make cancer detection in the field. In some locations in the developing world, health workers can take images of skin problems and use cell phone technologies to beam images back to major medical centers around the globe. There they can get quick diagnosis and treatment directions.

Finally, mHealth can help with treatment, such as chronic disease management. Smartphone applications are being developed for disease self-management for asthma, alcohol dependence, and lung cancer.

The promise of mHealth deserves serious scrutiny (Dobkin & Dorsch, 2011). The Affordable Care Act of 2010 allowed providers to bill for remote monitoring beginning in 2014. Mobile technologies are likely to have a profound impact on health care and biomedical research, and we will soon be surrounded by more data than we can store, analyze, and interpret. New analysis methods may be necessary. In addition, there will be serious challenges in securing of data and protecting the privacy of people being monitored by the devices.

The 2015 Medical College Admissions Test (MCAT)

The Medical College Admission Test (MCAT) has become a rite of passage for entrance into medical school. The MCAT has evolved over the course of years to identify students who are most likely to succeed with a difficult medical school curriculum. The MCAT is administered by computer, and the current version tests physical and biological sciences, verbal reasoning, and writing skills. The test is quite demanding and it takes 5.5 hours to complete.

In 2015, the MCAT underwent significant change. The most important series of changes involved a new section focusing on several conceptual areas from the behavioral and social sciences. The change in the MCAT follows a comprehensive review by a series of prestigious groups, including the Institute of Medicine of the National Academy of Sciences and the American Association of Medical Colleges.

The new psychological, social, and biological foundations of behavior section of the test assesses a wide range of knowledge and draws upon concepts from psychology, sociology, biology, research methods, and statistics. These sections go into detail about the understanding of the social cultural determinants of health. Increasingly, medical scientists have come to recognize that health outcomes, to a large extent, are determined by the circumstances in which people live. In Los Angeles, for example, we can consider how long people live as a function of their racial sex in social circumstances. The discrepancies can be substantial. Asian women, for example, live on average to be about 87 years in Los Angeles. Asian African men, on the other hand, live an average of 69 years. The discrepancy of 18 years is difficult to explain without taking into consideration the social circumstances in which people live (see Figure 17.9).

FIGURE 17.9

Difference in the expected length of life from birth for African American and Asian men and women in Los Angeles, California. On average, Asian men live 11 years longer and Asian women live nearly 10 years longer than African American men and women.

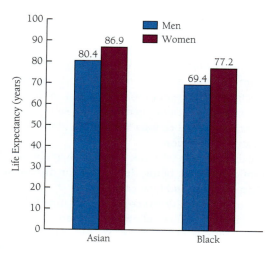

Data adapted from the Los Angeles Department of Public Health, Office of Health Assessment and Epidemiology, July 2010.

A related issue is the relationship between economic hardship and how long people live. Within the 88 cities that make up Los Angeles County, life expectancies and economic hardships vary dramatically. For example, life expectancy in wealthy Beverly Hills is 85.6 years, while in tony La Canada-Flintridge, it is 87.8 years. In tough neighborhoods like Compton, people live, on average, 75.7 years; in Willowbrook, life expectancy is only 75.6 years. Figure 17.10 is a scatter diagram showing the relationship between life expectancy and an index of hardship for cities and communities in Los Angeles County in 2010. There is a negative relationship, suggesting that the greater the economic hardship, the shorter the life expectancies of community residents.

The MCAT section on psychological, social, and behavioral foundations of behavior covers a wide range of topics. It considers perceptions and reactions to the world, behavior and behavior change, what people think about themselves and others, and the cultural and social differences that influence well-being. The section also considers how differences in social and economic status affect health, the effects of different resources and access to health care, and the broad social determinants of health.

The new subtest, "Psychological, Social, and Biological Foundations of Behavior," will measure Behavioral and Social Science (BSS) foundational knowledge. Test takers will have 95 minutes to complete the new section primarily composed of brief stimulus paragraphs illustrating behavioral and social science constructs followed by a total of approximately 55 multiple-choice questions. Components of the section include five core content areas: (1) ways that individuals perceive, think about, and react to the world; (2) factors that influence behavior and behavior change; (3) factors that influence how we think about ourselves and others; (4) ways in which culture and social differences influence well-being; and (5) ways

FIGURE 17.10

Scatter diagram showing the negative relationship between community hardship and life expectancy for cities and communities in Los Angeles County.

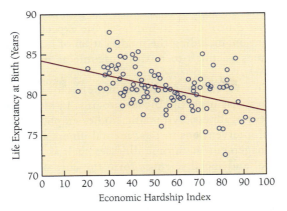

From *Life Expectancy in Los Angeles County. How Long Do We Live and Why?* Office of Health Assessment and Epidemiology: Los Angeles County Department of Public Health, 2010.

in which social stratification affects access to resources and well-being. Each of these content areas emphasizes established theory and concepts as well as experimental and observational science. For example, the section on the perception considers sensory processes (vision, hearing, chemosensory senses) and the integration of these senses through attention, cognition, memory, and language. It also considers the role of stress and emotions in the sensory processes. Clinical applications of behavioral and social science foundational knowledge are reserved for medical school instruction; however, as with the basic sciences, students will be expected to enter medical school with a sufficient scientific foundation upon which to build medical knowledge.

Medical sciences focus on biological processes. So, what value would be obtained from adding yet another MCAT component? Many lines of evidence converge to suggest that behavioral and social factors have profound effects on health—both as determinants and as key factors for preventive or treatment interventions. In November 2011, the Association of American Medical Colleges (AAMC) released a report on behavioral and social science foundations for future physicians—an important companion piece to the influential Scientific Foundations for Future Physicians report on the basic sciences in medical education. The AAMC BSS report emphasized that health is influenced by a wide variety of factors, including biological, genetic, behavioral, interpersonal relationships, cultures, and physical environments. Furthermore, several models have been developed to estimate factors that explain increases in the U.S. life expectancy since 1970. Most of the increase in life expectancy is attributable to declines in premature deaths from heart disease and stroke. These models suggest that between 23% and 46% of the decline in deaths from coronary heart disease are attributable to medical care. On the other hand, between 44% and 72% of the increased life expectancy is attributable to modification of coronary risk factors, including tobacco use, lipids, and blood pressure. In fact, reductions in tobacco use and increases in physical activity appear to be the largest contributors to improved life expectancy in the United States. Primary prevention, including the modification of health behaviors, contributes about four times as much to health outcome as medically based secondary prevention efforts.

In addition to the importance of behavioral approaches to disease prevention, there has been significant progress in biobehavioral approaches to the management of illness. Systematic studies emphasize the value of cognitive and behavioral interventions to treat mental illness and substance abuse and to aid in the management in chronic illnesses such as diabetes and heart failure. The behavioral and social sciences form the core of evaluations of cognitive impairment, many neurological diseases, and the gene–environment interaction. Moreover, disparities in health outcomes among racial and ethnic groups persist. In Los Angeles, for example, the difference in life expectancy between African American men and Asian American women is a full 19 years. Disparities in life expectancy between income, race, sex, or age subgroups are usually traceable to differences in tobacco use, obesity, physical activity, alcohol use, and risky sexual behavioral. Tomorrow's physician will need to understand changes in demographic patterns, the impact of culture on adherence to medications, and the rapidly changing economic incentives associated with emerging health-care environments.

Although nearly all medical schools include some behavioral and social science instruction, students arrive with widely varied levels of preparation, and no minimally sufficient level of training has been established. Just as for biology or chemistry, students are unlikely to comprehend complex research studies without some basic background. The behavioral and social sciences are built upon complex methodologies, theories, and a mature database. Teaching cognitive behavioral intervention to students with no background in learning theory is analogous to teaching pathophysiology to students who have not been exposed to basic biological principles. For all of these reasons, the MCAT committee and the AAMC recognized that future physicians need better, standardized training in the behavioral and social sciences both before and during medical school.

The new MCAT also includes a section on critical analysis and reasoning. This section was added to replace the writing samples sections. Analysis of data from older MCATs had suggested that the writing samples were not valid predictors of medical school success. The new critical analysis and reasoning skills section uses traditional test formats and presents passages that need to be read. Test items then assess the test takers' ability to comprehend the topics in the passages. These topics include ethics and philosophy, cross-cultural studies, and population health.

Creating the new MCAT was a significant undertaking. In response, undergraduate curricula may need to be revised to prepare students for this important hurdle on their way to medical school. Focused Example 17.4 shows a sample item from the new MCAT.

Sample Items From the 2015 MCAT

Sample Passage

Psychologists have identified two distinct forms of bias: explicit and implicit bias. An explicit bias is a conscious preference, whereas an implicit bias is an unconscious preference. Research investigating racial disparities in treatments for heart attacks has found that African Americans are significantly less likely than whites to receive thrombolytic therapy (i.e., the administration of drugs to break up or dissolve blood clots).

A recent study investigated the relationship between physicians' implicit and explicit biases and their decisions to provide thrombolytic therapy to African American and white patients. Residents were recruited to participate in an online study. Participants received a vignette describing a 50-year-old male who displayed heart attack symptoms. Half the sample's vignettes included a photo of an African American patient, while the other half were provided with a photo of a white patient.

After indicating whether or not they would refer the patient for thrombolysis therapy, participants' explicit preferences for African Americans and whites were measured using a 5-point Likert scale. Next, participants completed an implicit association task (IAT). The IAT assessed participants' implicit bias by measuring their response time to valenced words (e.g., words with good or bad connotations) presented with images of African American and white individuals. No effect was found for levels of explicit bias and the likelihood of providing thrombolysis therapy. Figure 17.11 summarizes the study's findings related to implicit bias.

(1) Which concept is the focus of this study?

    A. Fundamental attribution error
    B. Elaboration likelihood model
    C. Modern prejudice
    D. Self-serving bias

Answer: C

Foundational Concept: 8

Content Category: 8B

Skill: 1

(2) Which of the following explanations describes why the amygdala would most likely be activated by the use of the IAT in this study? The amygdala is important for:

    A. Learning
    B. Fear
    C. Anxiety
    D. Value judgments

Answer: B

Foundational Concept: 7

Content Category: 7A

Skill: 1

From: MCAT 2015: Better Best for Tomorrow's Doctors. Association of American Medical Colleges (AAMC). Available at www.aamc.org/mcat2015. (permission required)

FIGURE 17.11

Percent of participants referring patients for thrombolytic therapy as a function of participants' levels of implicit bias and patient race.

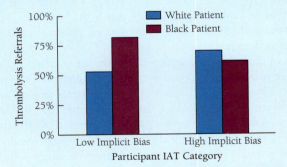

Adapted from R. A. Green et al. (2007). "Implicit Bias Among Physicians and Its Prediction of Thrombolysis Decisions for Black and White Patients." *Journal of General Internal Medicine*, 22, 1231–1238. The Preview Guide for MCAT 2015 © 2011 AAMC. May not be reproduced without permission. 123

Summary

In this chapter, we considered three broad areas relevant to testing in health-care settings. First, we reviewed clinical neuropsychology. This important new area of investigation has generated new research and clinical opportunities for psychologists. Neuropsychology involves the application of tests to evaluate the status of the central nervous system. Some of the more common approaches are the Halstead-Reitan and the Luria-Nebraska batteries. Each of these approaches is based on different principles of cognitive psychology. A newer approach, the California Verbal Learning Test, attempts to evaluate brain function by considering not only errors but also how people make errors.

Second, we reviewed some of the existing research on the theory and measurement of anxiety and stress. Research on test anxiety grew from general theories of learning. Early studies by J. Taylor identified anxiety as a motivational state that one could measure with a short scale. Using the scale, she could relate anxiety to a general theory that had previously depended primarily on evidence from animal studies. Later developments divided anxiety into state and trait components. The State-Trait Anxiety Inventory (STAI) provides two separate scores: one for state anxiety (A-State) and another for trait anxiety (A-Trait).

A variety of measures quantify adaptation to stressful situations. These include measures of coping and measures of social support. Not all individuals faced with the same stresses have the same reactions. Measures of depression are now commonly used in primary care medical settings. The U.S. Preventive Services Taskforce supported screening for depression in primary care and emphasized the value of assessing pregnant and postpartum women. Because of its recommendation, adults can be screened for depression and the services are covered by health insurance.

The third area for the application of tests in health-care settings involves health status and quality-of-life assessment. Health-care practitioners try to help people live longer and higher-quality lives than they might without health care. The quantification of life quality, however, is difficult. Two approaches to this type of assessment are psychometric methods and decision theory methods. Psychometric methods include the MOS Short Form-36 and the Nottingham Health Profile. Decision theory approaches include methods for estimating the value of the equivalent of a life-year, or a quality-adjusted life year (QALY). We expect the fields of psychological measurement and health-outcome measurement to continue to merge over the next few decades.

One of the biggest challenges in health care practice and research is the harmonization of measures. In clinical practice, there are many alternative ways to measure constructs like quality of life, executive functioning, anxiety, and functional capacity. In order to address this problem, the National Institutes of Health is developing the NIH "Toolbox." The goal of this project is to stimulate the use of a common set of measures in research and clinical care. In recognition of the importance of behavioral and social sciences in health care, the Medical College Admissions Test (MCAT) now devotes about 20% of its content to these sciences.

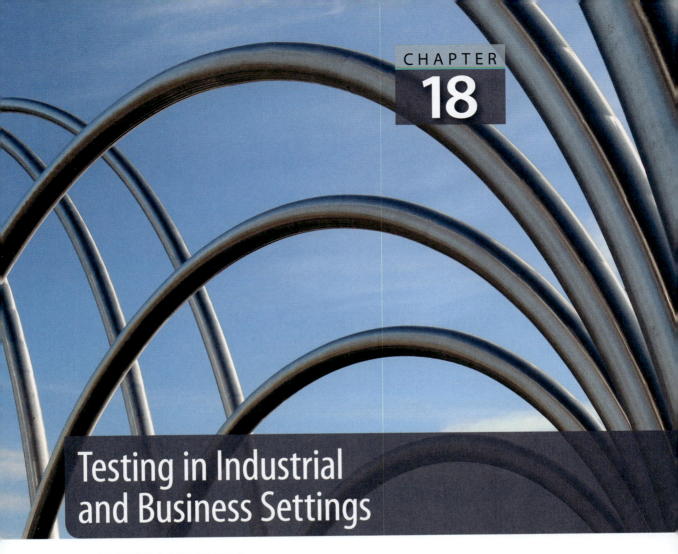

Testing in Industrial and Business Settings

LEARNING OBJECTIVES

When you have completed this chapter, you should be able to:

- ▶ Discuss the application of tests in employee selection

- ▶ Identify the first consideration in determining whether it is worthwhile to administer a test

- ▶ Explain the meaning of base rates in personnel selection

- ▶ Identify three methods for estimating the amount of information a test gives beyond what is known by chance

- ▶ Define incremental validity

- ▶ Discuss the significance of utility and decision theory

- ▶ Explain some problems with utility theory equations

- ▶ Describe the characteristics of the MBTI and the WPI

- ▶ List the components of job analysis

- ▶ Explain the person–situation interaction

- ▶ Describe the advantages and disadvantages of employment interview

483

*I*ndustrial/organizational (I/O) *psychology* involves the application of psychological principles to the workplace. This field is quite similar to the human resource management that is often taught in schools of business. However, I/O psychologists establish themselves by the methods they apply. One of the most important differences is I/O's emphasis on structured psychological testing (Cook, 2016). I/O psychologists rely extensively on research, quantitative methods, and testing procedures (Cook, 2016; Landy & Conte, 2016). Two major areas of I/O psychology are personnel psychology and organizational psychology. *Personnel psychology* is the study and practice of job analysis, job recruitment, employee selection, and the evaluation of employee performance (Schmitt, 2012). *Organizational psychology* considers leadership, job satisfaction, employee motivation, and a variety of factors surrounding the functioning of organizations (Burke, 2016). In this chapter, we focus on some of the interfaces between I/O psychology and psychological testing. We begin by reviewing the oldest approach to employee selection—the employment interview.

Personnel Psychology—The Selection of Employees

Employment Interview

The employment interview helps people make selection and promotion decisions in business and industry. These interviews are complicated because the applicant and the employer are motivated to slant their presentation in order to make an impression, not necessarily to be completely honest (Bangerter, Roulin, & König, 2011).

Studies of the validity of the employment interview have revealed extremely valuable information about interviews in general and the employment interview in particular (Huffcutt & Youngcourt, 2007; Swider, Barrick, & Harris, 2016). Most research supports a structured format for the employment interview. Several studies clearly pointed to the superiority of structured interviews for enabling interviewers to reach agreement on their employment decisions. In addition, evidence suggests that structured interviews are less subject to sex bias and are less likely to result in discrimination against women or men (Alonso, Moscoso, & Salgado, 2016). Thus, the loss of flexibility in structured interviews can be balanced by increases in reliability. Meta-analytic investigations of the literature have found that structured interviews produced mean validity coefficients twice as high as did unstructured interviews (Wiesner & Cronshaw, 1988; Williamson, Campion, Malos, Roehling, & Campion, 1997) and the validities are highest when the same assessor evaluates all candidates (Morris, Daisley, Wheeler, & Boyer, 2015). On the other hand, interviewee performance may play a very important role, even in structured interviews. For example, candidates who work hard at impression management are given higher ratings (Huffcutt, 2011).

Later we shall discuss sources of error in the interview, which studies have found to affect many employment interviews (Swider et al., 2016). For now, we briefly touch on what interviewers look for in employment interviews and methods of presenting oneself in an interview.

It has long been known that the employment interview often involves a search for negative or unfavorable rather than favorable evidence about a person (Schmitt, 2012). If negative evidence is found, the person will probably not be hired unless there is a high demand for workers and few individuals are available to fill open positions. A classic study by E. C. Webster (1964) noted that as few as one unfavorable impression was followed by final rejection in 90% of the cases. This rejection rate, however, is as low as 25% when early impressions were favorable. Webster and others caution employment interviewers against forming an early bias that might result in rejecting a competent individual. Despite widespread knowledge of Webster's cautions, interviewers continue to make basic errors when formulating personnel decisions (Huffcutt, 2011; Swider et al., 2016).

Negative factors that commonly lead to the rejection of candidates include poor communication skills, lack of confidence or poise, low enthusiasm, nervousness, and failure to make eye contact (Bolino, Long, & Turnley, 2016). Positive factors include the ability to express oneself, self-confidence and poise, enthusiasm, the ability to sell oneself, and assertiveness (Bragger et al., 2016).

Can you increase your chances of presenting yourself favorably in a job interview? As Heimberg, Keller, and Peca-Baker (1986) noted, competent performance in job interviews is widely regarded as one of the most important factors in obtaining employment. As such, several prospective employees who wish to tip the balance in their favor can choose any of several recommendations (Huffcutt, 2011).

A good first impression is one of the most important factors in a successful job interview (Swider et al., 2016). To make a good first impression, one needs to wear professional attire and show good grooming (Cash, 1985; Kennedy, 1994), project an aura of competence and expertise (Baron, 1986; Price & Garland, 1983), and give an impression of friendliness or personal warmth through nonverbal cues (Williams, 2016). But going too far with these tactics can sometimes backfire.

R. A. Baron (1986) had female confederates pose as applicants for an entry-level management position. Some wore perfume, others did not. In addition, some attempted to convey friendliness through nonverbal behaviors including a high level of eye contact with the interviewer, an informal friendly posture (such as leaning forward at predetermined points), and frequent smiling.

Interviewees in the neutral cue condition refrained from these nonverbal behaviors. The results revealed that when used alone, either perfume or positive nonverbal behaviors produced enhanced ratings for the applicants. When used together, however, these tactics produced negative reactions among interviewers, probably because they caused the applicant to be perceived as manipulative (Baron, 1986). Thus, while putting one's best foot forward in an interview is important, one must be careful not to overdo it.

Interviews remain the primary tool for selecting employees. However, personnel psychology places a strong emphasis on formal quantitative models and the use of tests for employee selection.

For many industrial applications, other factors also must be considered, such as the amount of information a selection strategy gives beyond what would be known without it (Sackett & Lievens, 2008). This can be derived from an analysis of base rates and hit rates.

Base Rates and Hit Rates

Tests must be evaluated in terms of how much they contribute beyond what would be known without them. Often, tests are used to place individuals into one of two categories. For example, on the basis of an employment test, a candidate can be deemed acceptable or unacceptable. In a medical setting, a test may determine whether or not a person has a tumor in a certain area of the brain. Because tests vary in their accuracy, test administrators must examine the possibility of erroneously assigning someone to a category.

If a test is used to make a dichotomous (two-choice) decision, then a cutoff score usually is used. Values above this score might go into the plus category, and values below it into the minus category. The plus category might indicate that the person is suitable for the job (or, in medical testing, that he or she has the tumor). The score marking the point of decision is called the *cutting score*. Those at or above the cutting score might be selected for employment, while those below the score might be turned away. Establishing a cutting score does not ensure correct decisions. For example, suppose that a person scores above the cutting score for an employment test but later fails on the job. This suggests that the test has not done its job.

Tests can be evaluated by how well they sort people into the right categories. For example, in a test that determines which people to hire for a particular job, those who score above the cutting score might be labeled "acceptable" and those below it "unacceptable." In addition to the scores on the test, the employer must have some data on how people really do on the job. To do this, he or she must define some criterion for deciding whether job performance has been acceptable or unacceptable. Using these two sets of categories, the employer can construct a chart such as the one shown in Table 18.1. There are four cells in this table. Two of the four cells are labeled "Hit" because the test has made the correct prediction. Hits occur when (1) the test predicts that the person will be unacceptable and he or she does fail, or (2) the test indicates that the person is acceptable and he or she does succeed. Misses occur when the test makes an inaccurate prediction. The **hit rate** is the percentage of cases in which a test accurately predicts success or failure.

Often, a test does not need a good hit rate because the rate of predicting success on the job is high without the test. For example, admissions officers might predict who will do well in law school on the basis of information other than scores on the Law School Admission Test (LSAT). They might use college grades. Success on the criterion in this case might be passing the bar examination on the first attempt.

TABLE 18.1 Hits and Misses for Predicting a Dichotomous Outcome Using a Cutting Score

	Decision on the basis of cutting score	
Performance on the job	Acceptable	Unacceptable
Success	Hit	Miss
Failure	Miss	Hit

The pass rate without using the LSAT would be called the **base rate**. The real value of a test comes from a comparison of the hit rate with the base rate. In other words, the hit rate must tell us how much information a test contributes to the prediction of success beyond what we would know by just examining the proportion of people who succeed.

For example, suppose the LSAT has a hit rate of 76% for predicting who will pass the bar examination in a certain state. However, 85% of the people who take the test for the first time in that state pass. The LSAT in this case tells us less than we would have known without it. In other cases, you could imagine a low hit rate and an even lower base rate. For example, suppose you need to select people for a position that will involve world-class competition. Under the circumstances, very few people could be expected to do well—say only 3% would be expected to succeed. If a test could be developed that had a 10% hit rate, it might be considered valuable.

Another problem to consider with regard to hit and miss rates is relative cost. Medical situations provide good examples of costly misses. Consider the cost of concluding on the basis of a test that a tumor is benign (not cancerous) when it is really malignant (cancerous). The cost of this sort of miss is that the life of the patient is seriously endangered. In a psychological application, concluding that someone is not suicidal because he or she is below the cutoff score when, in fact, he or she is suicidal may allow a preventable suicide. These cases are examples of **false negatives**. If the cost of a false negative is high, then a test developer might lower the cutting score. With a lower cutting score, the test will make more but safer errors.

The other type of miss is the **false positive**. For example, say someone is selected for a job on the basis of a test. Once on the job, the person does poorly and gets fired. High costs sometimes accompany this type of error. For instance, time and money might be invested to train a person who cannot really do the job. In addition, job failure can hurt the person's self-esteem and self-confidence. If the costs of a false positive are high, then you may want to raise the cutting score.

A few examples may help clarify the concepts of hits and misses for different base rates. Although this chapter is about employment testing, our students often find medical examples best illustrate these concepts. Table 18.2 presents a medical example in which a test indicates whether or not a patient has brain damage. In a validation study, an expensive radiological procedure is used to confirm whether the patient actually has brain damage. The radiological test suggests that 23 of 100 patients have brain damage, while the other 77 are normal. The table also shows the actual number of patients who have brain damage or are normal. In reality, 10 of the 100 have damage, while 90 are normal.

There are two types of hits in Table 18.2. For the 10 patients who actually have brain damage, eight are detected by the tests. In other words, the test has a detection rate of 80%. In addition, the test says that 75 individuals are normal who, it is confirmed, are actually normal. Both of these cases are hits because the test produces the correct result. There are 83 cases out of 100 when the test produces an accurate conclusion; that is, the test has 83% accuracy.

There are also two types of misses. In two cases, the test suggests that a person is normal when he or she actually has brain damage. Those are false negatives. In addition, there are 15 false positives, or cases in which the test suggests that a person has a problem when in fact he or she is normal.

TABLE 18.2 Hypothetical Example of Hits and Misses, With 83% Accuracy and 80% Detection*

		Test result		
		Brain damage	**Normal**	**Total**
	Brain damage	A	B	A + B
		8	2	10
Actual	Normal	C	D	C + D
		15	75	90
	Total	23	77	100

A = hit

A + B = base rate

B = false negative

C = false positive

D = hit

A/(A + B) = detection rate (sensitivity)

D/(C + D) = specificity base rate

(A + D)/(A + B + C + D) = accuracy rate

*We are grateful to Dr. Frank M. Rosekrans, Eastern Washington University, for suggesting this example.

The cells in Table 18.2 are labeled A, B, C, and D. Cells A and D are hit cells. The sum of these cells divided by the sum of all cells (A + B + C + D) is the accuracy rate. Cell B is a false negative, Cell C a false positive. Cell A divided by the sum of A and B is the *detection rate.*

The example in Table 18.2 suggests that the test is relatively good at detecting brain damage. One of the reasons the test works well in this situation is that the base rate for brain damage is relatively low. In actuality, only 10% of the patients have this problem, and the test detects 80% of the cases.

Now consider the example in Table 18.3. In this case, a test is used on a population with a quite high base rate for brain damage (90%). The test suggests that 50 of 100 people have brain damage when, in fact, 90 of 100 people have the problem. The test is accurate in 44% (40/90 = .44) of the cases. In this example, there are only 10 false positives. The test, however, has a high false negative rate. Finally, the table suggests that the test never concludes that someone is normal when he or she does not have a problem.

False negatives and false positives may have different meanings, depending on their context. For example, a variety of methods have been developed to predict antisocial behavior in children. Childhood aggression is a good predictor of later aggressive behavior (Dubow, Huesmann, Boxer, & Smith, 2016). However, measures of childhood aggression identify some children as potentially dangerous who turn out not to be aggressive when they are older (Fazel & Bjørkly, 2016). Similarly, measures used to predict sexual misconduct also identify many people who will not commit sexual offenses (Studer, Aylwin, Sribney, & Reddon, 2011). These are

TABLE 18.3 Hypothetical Example of Hits and Misses, With 40% Accuracy and 44% Detection*

		Test result		
		Brain damage	**Normal**	**Total**
	Brain damage	A	B	A + B
		40	50	90
Actual	Normal	C	D	C + D
		10	0	10
	Total	50	50	100

A = hit

A + B = base rate

B = false negative

C = false positive

D = hit

A/(A + B) = detection rate (sensitivity)

D/(C + D) = specificity base rate

(A + D)/(A + B + C + D) = accuracy rate

*We are grateful to Dr. Frank M. Rosekrans, Eastern Washington University, for suggesting this example.

false positives. In fact, as many as half the cases may be false positives (Lochman, 1995). A program that identifies and treats high-risk youth may subject many to unnecessary treatment. On one extreme, some people believe high-risk youth should be under police surveillance. Among adults, many people can be identified as potentially dangerous, but the number of people who commit serious violent crimes remains low (Reidy, Sorensen, & Davidson, 2015). Because of false positives, these programs would unjustly deprive some youth of their rights. Many controversies in health care are affected by the hit and miss rates of testing.

Using cutting scores to find hits and misses involves criterion validity (see Chapter 5). Many years ago, H. C. Taylor and J. T. Russell (1939) demonstrated how to relate validity coefficients to accuracy rates in selection.

Taylor-Russell Tables

The decision to use a test must depend on what the test offers. In Chapter 5, we showed that tests with significant predictive or concurrent validity coefficients did better than chance in forecasting performance on a criterion. However, knowing that a test is better than chance is not good enough for some applications. In other words, a worthwhile test must provide more information than do the base rates alone.

A very long time ago, in 1939, Taylor and Russell developed a method for evaluating the validity of a test in relation to the amount of information it contributes beyond the base rates. This method is neatly summarized in a series of tables known as the **Taylor-Russell tables**. The tables remain one of the best ways to understand the value of personnel testing. To use them, you must have the following information:

1. *Definition of success.* For each situation in which the test is to be used, success on the outcome must be defined. This could be that the patient lived, that the person succeeded on the job, or that the student did well in college. One must define success clearly by dichotomizing some outcome variable. For example, first-year grade point averages above 2.3 might be defined as success in college, and those below 2.3 might be defined as failures. Or salespeople who achieve average monthly sales of more than $20,000 might be deemed successful, and those who sell less than $20,000 might be thought of as unsuccessful.

2. *Determination of base rate.* The percentage of people who would succeed if there were no testing or screening procedure must be determined.

3. *Definition of selection ratio.* The **selection ratio** must be defined. This is the percentage of applicants who are selected or admitted.

4. *Determination of validity coefficient.* Finally, a validity coefficient for the test, usually the correlation of the test with the criterion, is required.

The Taylor-Russell tables give the likelihood that a person selected on the basis of the test score will actually succeed. There is a different table for each base rate. Table 18.4 is a Taylor-Russell table for a base rate of .60.

To use the table, find the row that represents the validity of the test that would be used for selection. Then find the column that is associated with the proportion of people who can be selected. The number in the body of the table that is associated with a particular row and a particular column gives an estimate of the percentage of people who could be expected to succeed when selected on the basis of the test.

For example, suppose that you are put in charge of deciding who will be admitted to a program to train secondary education teachers. The first thing you must do is decide on a definition of success. After meeting with a committee, you may decide that success will be defined as completing the program and obtaining a satisfactory performance evaluation in student teaching. By studying records, you determine that when no selection procedure was used, 60% of the applicants to the program succeeded on this task. Thus, the base rate would be 60%, and the Taylor-Russell table for a base rate of .60 would be used. You then consider using the Graduate Record Examination (GRE) to select people for your program because you can accept only 70% of the applicants. A study is done and determines that the correlation between GRE scores and success (completing the program and obtaining a satisfactory evaluation in student teaching) is .30. This is the validity of the test for predicting the criterion.

Now you must estimate how many people would be expected to succeed if they were selected on the basis of GRE scores. Using the Taylor-Russell table (Table 18.4) for a base rate of .60, find the row associated with the .30 validity and move across the table until you are in the column for a selection ratio of .70 (the percentage of applicants you can admit to your program). You should arrive at the number .66, which is the proportion of applicants you would expect to be successful if the selection was based on the GRE. This analysis tells you that 66% of those selected on the basis of GRE scores can be expected to be successful, compared with a success rate of 60% for those selected at random. Should the GRE be required for admittance to your program? To answer this question, you must decide whether the increment of 6% associated with the use of the test is worth the extra effort and expense of requiring it.

TABLE 18.4   Taylor-Russell Table for a Base Rate of .60

Validity (ρ_{xy})	Selection Ratio										
	.05	**.10**	**.20**	**.30**	**.40**	**.50**	**.60**	**.70**	**.80**	**.90**	**.95**
.00	.60	.60	.60	.60	.60	.60	.60	.60	.60	.60	.60
.05	.64	.63	.63	.62	.62	.62	.61	.61	.61	.60	.60
.10	.68	.67	.65	.64	.64	.63	.63	.62	.61	.61	.60
.15	.71	.70	.68	.67	.66	.65	.64	.63	.62	.61	.61
.20	.75	.73	.71	.69	.67	.66	.65	.64	.63	.62	.61
.25	.78	.76	.73	.71	.69	.68	.66	.65	.63	.62	.61
.30	.82	.79	.76	.73	.71	.69	.68	.66	.64	.62	.61
.35	.85	.82	.78	.75	.73	.71	.69	.67	.65	.63	.62
.40	.88	.85	.81	.78	.75	.73	.70	.68	.66	.63	.62
.45	.90	.87	.83	.80	.77	.74	.72	.69	.66	.64	.62
.50	.93	.90	.86	.82	.79	.76	.73	.70	.67	.64	.62
.55	.95	.92	.88	.84	.81	.78	.75	.71	.68	.64	.62
.60	.96	.94	.90	.87	.83	.80	.76	.73	.69	.65	.63
.65	.98	.96	.92	.89	.85	.82	.78	.74	.70	.65	.63
.70	.99	.97	.94	.91	.87	.84	.80	.75	.71	.66	.63
.75	.99	.99	.96	.93	.90	.86	.81	.77	.71	.66	.63
.80	1.00	.99	.98	.95	.92	.88	.83	.78	.72	.66	.63
.85	1.00	1.00	.99	.97	.95	.91	.86	.80	.73	.66	.63
.90	1.00	1.00	1.00	.99	.97	.94	.88	.82	.74	.67	.63
.95	1.00	1.00	1.00	1.00	.99	.97	.92	.84	.75	.67	.63
1.00	1.00	1.00	1.00	1.00	1.00	1.00	1.00	.86	.75	.67	.63

From Taylor, H. C., and Russell, J. T. The relationship of validity coefficients to the practical effectiveness of tests in selection: Discussion and tables. *Journal of Applied Psychology, 23,* 565–578. Copyright © 1939 American Psychological Association. Reprinted by permission.

Try to work through a real-life example using the data from the Yale Ph.D. program in psychology.[1] The correlation between the GRE quantitative score and grade point average (GPA) was approximately 0.10, rounded up (Sternberg & Williams, 1997). In fact, the 0.10 level is common among studies of the relationship between GRE and graduate school GPA (Wao, Ries, Flood, Lavy, & Ozbek, 2016). Assume that Yale is selective and admits only some 10% of its applicants and that the base rate for success is 60%. Using the Taylor-Russell table, you should find that 67% of the applicants would be successful if selected on the basis of the Graduate

---

[1]One problem with the Yale study is that it is based on students admitted to the program, not all who apply. If data on all applicants were available, it is possible that the validity of the GRE may have been higher because there would have been a greater range of scores.

Record Exam's quantitative component (GRE-Q), while 60% would be successful if selected by chance. This 67% figure comes from the third row (validity = .10) and second column (selection ratio = .10) of Table 18.4.

Looking at Table 18.4, you can see that tests will be more valuable in some situations than in others. For example, a test is most useful when the validity of the test is high and the selection ratio is low, as the lower left-hand portion of Table 18.4 shows. Conversely, when the validity is low and the selection ratio is high (the upper right-hand portion of the table), the test will be of little value. When the test has no validity (the first row of the table), using the test will be no better than selecting applicants by chance. Similarly, when nearly everyone is selected (last column), there is little reason to use a test.

Whenever a selection procedure is used, always remember that some qualified applicants will be turned away. The use of rational selection procedures should help make the system more fair by decreasing the number of qualified applicants not selected (Sackett & Lievens, 2008). One way to evaluate the selection procedure is to show the ratio of people selected by the test who then succeed and the ratio of those who would have succeeded but were not selected.

Suppose that you are the personnel manager for a company and that you can choose 30 of 100 applicants for a job. To make this decision, you have the results of a test with a validity of .70. You also know that the base rate for success on the job is .60. Using the Taylor-Russell table for a base rate of .60, you find that 91% of those selected on the basis of the test would be expected to succeed on the job. Because you can select 30 people, the table implies that approximately 27 of them will succeed and three will fail (91% of 30 = 27.3).

When you decide to hire 30 of the applicants, you also are deciding not to hire 70 people. It is important to realize that not all of the 70 people would fail if they were selected. In fact, many of them are capable people whom the testing procedure has "misdiagnosed." To justify your use of the test, it would be your responsibility to explain why your selection procedure is worthwhile even though it turns down some people who would succeed and selects some who fail.

Table 18.5 shows what would happen to all of the applicants. Of 100, 30 would be accepted and 70 rejected (the selection ratio equals .30). However, because the base rate for success is .60, 60 of the 100 applicants would have succeeded on the job and 40 would have failed. As you have seen, the Taylor-Russell table shows that

TABLE 18.5   What Would Happen to 100 Applicants if 30 People Were Selected on the Basis of a Test With a Validity of .70 for a Job With a 60% Base Success Rate?

Performance	Decision		Total
	Select	**Reject**	
Success*	27	33	60
Failure	3	37	40
Total	30	70	100

*Success ratio given selection = 27/30 = .90 (actually .91 without rounding; see Table 7.6). Success ratio given rejection = 33/70 = .47.

91% of those selected on the basis of the test will succeed, or 27 of the 30 selected ($.9 \times 30 = 27.3$), while only 3 of the 30 will likely fail.

Among the 60 people who would have succeeded, only 27 could be selected. This means that 33 people who would have been good choices were rejected. However, among the 40 people who would have failed, an estimated 37 would be in the rejected group. Using Table 18.5, we also can calculate the proportion of those rejected on the basis of the test who would be expected to succeed: $33/70 = .47$. Although the procedure leads to the rejection of many capable applicants, it can be defended as rational because the proportion of those who succeed is much higher among those who are selected by the procedure than among those who are rejected.

Let's suppose that average scores on a test for members of a minority group are lower than average scores for members of a majority group. A common argument is that increased minority hiring will result in lower average job performance because some applicants with lower test scores will be hired. However, systematic study of this issue has not always supported these arguments. For example, increased minority hiring in some industries has not resulted in a loss in job performance. There may be circumstances in which average job performance declines with an overselection of low-scoring job applicants, but the data from these studies are typically complex (Farr & Tippins, 2013).

The Taylor-Russell tables also help reveal the futility of certain types of assessment procedures. For example, some employers believe that routine background information may be useful in predicting employee success (Aamodt, 2016). In one study, McDaniel (1989) used information on school suspension, drug use, quitting school, participation in social clubs, school grades, contacts with the legal system, and socioeconomic status to predict success in the military service. The criterion for success was keeping from being discharged for being unsuitable. The study demonstrated that though most of the background variables predicted unsuitability discharges, the validity coefficients were extremely low, with the highest being approximately .15. Let us assume that the selection ratio for the armed services is .9. In other words, 9 out of every 10 applicants are admitted to the military service. Let us also assume the base rate of success of 60%. (In the McDaniel study, the base rate was approximately 85%, but assuming 60% allows us to do this exercise with Table 18.4.) When we use the Taylor-Russell table for a validity of .15 and a selection ratio of .90, we find that the proportion who succeed in military service goes to .61. Using only base-rate information, we would have predicted that 60% succeed. The information on dropping out of school improves this prediction by only 1%! The low validity for the background information is the reason for this negligible improvement. Although background information may be useful, it may provide only a minimum of information about future success.

Utility Theory and Decision Analysis

The use of Taylor-Russell tables requires that the criterion be a dichotomous variable. However, success usually is measured on a more refined numerical scale. By considering success only in terms of a dichotomous variable, one ignores much of the information available to the analyst. For example, it seems more reasonable to use a continuum of job performance as the criterion than to consider merely whether or not someone failed on a job. Since the publication of the

Taylor-Russell tables, researchers have attempted to define levels besides success and failure. These formulations are based on utility theory (Boudreau & Ramstad, 2003; Cook, 2016).

Although the use of decision and utility theory serves the industrial psychologist, the equations used to calculate the value of test data are quite complex (Boudreau & Ramstad, 2003). Furthermore, the equations require some information that is hard to estimate. For example, to use the equations, you must estimate the dollar value that is associated with different levels of performance on the job, an estimation that is difficult for most jobs (Borman, Brantley, & Hanson, 2014). Schmidt and Hunter (1983) presented mathematical arguments showing that 40% of the average salary produces a reasonable estimate of the standard deviation of the output.

Several other approaches have been suggested to solve the problems of utility analysis, although progress has been slow(Cook, 2016). For example, Raju, Burke, Normand, and Lezotte (1993) developed a new approach to utility assessment that does not require an estimate of the dollar value for performance. They proposed that the value of each individual can be estimated from the total value of his or her compensation package. A compensation package includes the value of the combination of salary and benefits. This approach simplifies the calculations and produces results similar to those of other methods; however, the Raju method may shift the subjective judgment of the standard deviation of the criterion to estimating the coefficient of variation of the criterion. In other words, the estimation problem has not been solved (Cook, 2016) . Other industrial psychologists believe that utility analysis may actually make managers less likely to use data in personnel selection. They suggest that there is a "futility of utility" (Whyte & Latham, 1997).

Clearly, the utility methods hold great promise for making rational personnel decisions, yet the difficulty in applying utility formulations has prevented their widespread use. Even so, studies do demonstrate financial advantages for companies that select employees on the basis of these formal models. Furthermore, the methodology for utility analysis continues to improve (Schmidt et al., 1993). See Focused Example 18.2 for an example of utility calculation.

Although utility theory is used only occasionally in personnel selection, it is beginning to find applications in other fields, including education (Sackett, 1998) and medicine (Drummond, Sculpher, Claxton, Stoddart, & Torrance, 2015). In education, placement decisions may have serious consequences. With tests being considered for tracking, promotion, and graduation, any decisions based on poor information may cause personal and financial harm (Eggen & Stobart, 2015). Medical researchers have long been aware that tests have false positive and false negative results. For some problems, such as the screening test for prostate cancer in younger men, there are many false positives for each true positive. Each false positive has financial and personal ramifications: In addition to costing money, a false positive may lead to other painful and unnecessary medical procedures. Analysts often consider such consequences when they interpret test data. The growing interest in utility analysis for medical decisions has led to the formation of the Society for Medical Decision Making and publication of a specialized journal entitled *Medical Decision Making*.

How Much Money Can Be Saved Through Valid Selection?

A major issue in business and industrial psychology is how to get the most productivity out of employees. Employers often use tests to select employees who have the greatest chance of being productive. Some industrial psychologists, however, may have failed to realize just how much economic value can be gained from effective selection procedures. Although Cronbach and Gleser (1965) developed methods for evaluating the cost-effectiveness of testing many years ago, their technique was not frequently used because it required estimating the standard deviation of the dollar value of employee performance. However, newer methods developed to estimate this quantity allow one to determine how much money one saves by using a valid selection procedure.

In one study, a group of personnel psychologists evaluated measures for the selection of bus drivers.

They reasoned that some bus drivers who demonstrated safer driving behaviors should be selected to work more hours. This selection procedure should make the transit companies more efficient. To select the bus drivers, researchers developed several different measures that were administered to 864 bus drivers at nine locations. After a detailed analysis of the skills required for bus drivers, it was concluded that being a good bus operator required the three "Be's": "Be there, be safe, and be courteous." Analysis also showed that supervisor's ratings could be successfully predicted, as could the absence of accidents. Furthermore, a utility analysis of the composite predictor variable demonstrated that use of the selection procedure could reduce overall operating expenses for the bus agencies by more than $500,000 per year (Jacobs, Conte, Day, Silva, & Harris, 1996).

Value-Added Employee Assessments

Personnel psychologists typically offer advice on which employees to hire. However, there are also significant challenges in determining which employees should be retained and which should be promoted. These decisions are usually made on the basis of a supervisor's appraisal. However, it might be argued that we should judge work performance on the basis of achieving long-term goals. For example, we should judge doctors on the basis of whether their patients recover from illness (Roland & Dudley, 2015) and judge teachers on the basis of their students' performance (Britton & Propper, 2016). When evaluating teachers, for example, studies have shown that it is very difficult to identify teaching quality (Adnot, Dee, Katz, & Wyckoff, 2016; Strong, Gargani, & Hacifazlioglu, 2011) and that retention decisions are often made on the basis of other factors, such as days of work missed (Jacob, 2011). Why not judge teachers on the basis of the achievement of the people they have taught?

A controversy has erupted over the appraisal of teachers on the basis of student performance. With the advent of "high-stakes testing," it is even more apparent that some schools are not performing well and that students enrolled in these schools are not getting good educational experiences. Not all teachers are the same: Some do an outstanding job of advancing the learning of their students, while others provide less value for the students they teach. What if we could evaluate teachers on the basis of the value they add?

The value-added approach to teacher assessment proposes to promote teachers when their students perform better than expected and deny reappointment for

FIGURE 18.1

Expected student growth based on standardized tests as a function of teacher for 5th grade. Teacher 1 outperformed expectations while teacher 2 underperformed. Under these circumstances, teacher 2 might face challenges in being reappointed.

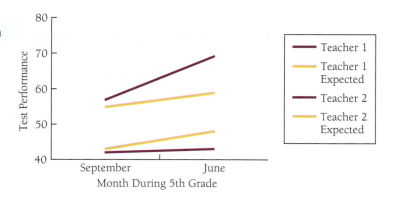

teachers whose students perform poorly. The big challenge is that, in addition to differences in teaching ability, students come to the classroom with different levels of ability. Thus, it would be unfair to punish a teacher whose students come to the classroom with lower performance capabilities. To address this problem, quantitative methods known as the value-added approach can be applied. Statistical modeling can be used to estimate the growth trajectories of students. Then, using a common technique known as multiple regression, an analyst can estimate the value added by a particular teacher. In other words, a statistical model uses a variety of variables to estimate expected student growth over the course of a school year. So it is possible to estimate whether, on average, a class of students outperformed or underperformed the expectation (Blazar, Litke, & Barmore, 2016). A teacher whose class overperforms might be rewarded, while the contract of the teacher whose class underperformed might not be renewed. (Figure 18.1 provides a summary of this model.)

The value-added approach to teacher assessment has gone beyond theory and well into application. It was supported by the Bill and Melinda Gates Foundation and some policymakers have argued that traditional credentials, such as having a degree in education or holding a master's degree, were unrelated to the value teachers provide to their students (Chingos & Peterson, 2011). On the other hand, value-added scores, at least among math teachers, are correlated with independent estimates of the quality of a teacher's instruction (Goldhaber, 2016; Hill, Kapitula, & Umland, 2011). But there are significant problems. First, measuring growth has always been challenging. Nearly 50 years ago, Cronbach and Furby (1970) published their classic article, "How Should We Measure "Change"—or Should We?" The article outlined some of the mathematical and statistical problems in estimating rates of intellectual growth. The major statistical problems discussed in this classical article remain unresolved. Simply subtracting beginning-of-the-year from end-of-the-year performance is problematic, particularly because different schools start at different levels and the level of expected growth may be related to the point at which children start. The relationships are not linear. A child who knows basic arithmetic may be ready to grow into algebra while children at a lower level of understanding of arithmetic might be expected to grow more slowly. Perhaps more challenging, creating a growth score by subtracting beginning-of-the-year from end-of-the-year performance violates statistical assumptions because the errors are correlated, while the measurement model assumes they are independent.

One way to attend this problem is to compare students who are in similar schools. However, there are nearly an infinite number of combinations of children's background and school characteristics, and some combinations are too rare to allow reliable modeling. Many factors affect the likelihood of school success, including class size, funding, preparedness of teachers, availability of high-quality teaching materials, and so on. So having enough children in each unique combination can be problematic, even for large school districts.

Many other factors bias the assessment. For example, during summer breaks, some students lose a significant amount of what they learned during the school year. This is much more likely to happen among disadvantaged children whose parents cannot afford summer camps and enrichment programs. Children from more advantaged homes may be more likely to engage in academic-related experiences during the summer months. As a result, teachers assigned to classrooms with more disadvantaged students may start the school year with the cards stacked against them. The value-added approach attempts to take a student's demographic background into consideration, but these unknown or unappreciated variables have been difficult to model. Not all of the value-added approaches disadvantage teachers assigned to low-income schools—in some cases, teachers in high-performing schools face biases. These might result from ceiling effects on standardized tests. For example, suppose that a teacher is assigned to teach math for a group of highly gifted students. At the beginning of the school year, the students, on average, get 95% of the test items correct. Because they are already near the ceiling performance for that test, the students have little room to grow, and the teacher has little opportunity to demonstrate overperformance.

There are a variety of unintended consequences for the value-added approach to teacher performance. One is known as assortative selection. In general, it takes a few years for a teacher to learn how to teach. So, most teachers perform poorly the first few years (Koedel & Betts, 2011; Ravitch, 2016). However, those teachers who perform very poorly are likely to exit the system while those who perform well tend to be promoted to a school of their choice (Feng & Sass, 2016). Rarely do highly performing teachers move to the inner city. Instead, they end up teaching in highly performing schools while novice and less well-performing teachers drift toward more poorly performing schools. If the school districts seek to dismiss teachers who underperform, they are much more likely to dismiss teachers who are working with the most challenging students. Those teachers are then replaced with novice teachers, who are known to have the greatest difficulty in managing students.

Another major criticism of the value-added approach is that it forces "teaching to the test" or "bubble children." There is more to an education than the ability to perform well on standardized tests. Yet the value-added approach evaluates teachers almost exclusively on the basis of student test performance. The consequences may be decreased classroom time devoted to psychosocial development, recreation, and the development of peer relationships. Further, cheating scandals have broken out in several school districts (see Psychological Testing in Everyday Life 18.1). When teachers and principals know that they may lose their jobs if their students perform poorly on tests, the temptation to fudge results may be almost irresistible.

18.1 **PSYCHOLOGICAL TESTING IN EVERYDAY LIFE**

Teacher Cheating Scandals

Value-added assessment puts pressure on teachers to ensure that their students perform well on standardized tests. In June 2011, a major scandal broke out in Atlanta when it was learned that teachers and administrators had made changes on student test answer sheets. The following section from the *Los Angeles Times* describes a similar set of problems among Los Angeles teachers.

Focus on standardized tests may be pushing some teachers to cheat

The number of California teachers who have been accused of cheating, lesser misconduct or mistakes on standardized achievement tests has raised alarms about the pressure to improve scores.

November 07, 2011 | By Howard Blume, *Los Angeles Times*

The stress was overwhelming.

For years, this veteran teacher had received exemplary evaluations but now was feeling pressured to raise her students' test scores. Her principal criticized her teaching and would show up to take notes on her class. She knew the material would be used against her one day.

"My principal told me right to my face that she—she was feeling sorry for me because I don't know how to teach," the instructor said.

The Los Angeles educator, who did not want to be identified, is one of about three dozen in the state accused this year of cheating, lesser misconduct or mistakes on standardized achievement tests.

The teachers came from 23 schools and 21 districts—an unprecedented number that has raised alarms about the pressure California educators are under to improve test scores. In the worst alleged cases, teachers are accused of changing incorrect responses or filling in missing ones after students returned answer booklets.

Many accused teachers have denied doing anything wrong. But documents and interviews suggest that an increasing focus on test scores has created an atmosphere of such intimidation that the idea teachers would cheat has become plausible.

"One teacher has personally confided in me that if her job was on the line, she indeed would cheat to get the higher test scores," one Los Angeles–area instructor said. "The testing procedures haven't been secure over the past 10-plus years. Some of the 'most effective' teachers could be simply the 'most cunning.'"

As attractive as it sounds to fire teachers who are underperforming, value-added assessment does not address a major concern facing public school systems. Public school teaching does not pay well, the hours are long, and the emotional and physical challenges are substantial. In the past, the most attractive feature of public school teaching was job security. Now, with the threat of easy dismissal combined with low pay and stressful circumstances, there is a significant decline in the number of people entering the teaching profession. At the same time, many teachers are preparing to exit the profession. For example, there are about 300,000 teachers in the state of California. Among those, about one-third are on the verge of retirement.

Finally, there are consequences to transparency. Not only are some school districts eager to discipline poorly performing teachers, but in some cases, reporters are willing to shame teachers publicly. The *Los Angeles Times*, for example, acquired a list of value-added scores for all the teachers in the Los Angeles unified school district and made it public, including the teachers' names. This led to the suicide of a competent but underperforming teacher. Colleagues reported that the teacher was depressed about the value-added score that the *LA Times* had posted on its website. Although the teacher scored as "average" for boosting his students' English scores, scores on the math section showed him to be "less effective." Although his overall rating suggested that he was slightly "less effective" than other teachers, he was also known as a teacher who went the extra mile for children, even though this contribution would never show on a standardized test. He sought out the kids facing the greatest personal difficulties and tutored them on weekends and after school. He visited their homes, encouraging them to stay in school and to go on to college (Zavis & Barboza, 2010). Many people think the *LA Times* went too far. This doesn't mean we should ignore evidence about underperforming teachers. But we must recognize that among all the factors that determine student performance, the value added by a teacher is a relatively small part. For example, the effects of the location of the school on persistent student outcomes are stronger than the effects of teachers (Briggs & Weeks, 2011). As an alternative to firing teachers, we can help them improve by giving feedback, offering additional training, and providing better mentoring (Stronge, Ward, & Grant, 2011). If all of this does not work, teaching might not be the best professional match for those individuals. But there may be many alternatives short of dismissal.

Incremental Validity

Validity defines the inferences that one can make on the basis of a score or measure (see Chapter 5). Evidence that a test is valid for particular inferences does not necessarily mean that the test is valuable. Though a test may be reliable and valid, the decision to use it depends on additional considerations. For example, does the test give you more information than you could find if it were not used? If so, how much more information does it give? The unique information gained through using the test is known as *incremental validity*.

In the discussions of base and hit rates and Taylor-Russell tables, we presented methods for evaluating what a test contributed beyond what was known from base rates. This kind of evaluation provides evidence for incremental validity. However, the assessment of incremental validity is not necessarily limited to comparisons with base rates. A particularly important form of evidence for incremental validity is the determination of how much information a test contributes beyond some simpler method for making the same prediction.

Most of the examples given in the preceding sections concerned tests used for selection purposes. However, the same rules and methods apply to tests used for the evaluation of personality or in the practice of clinical psychology. One concern is that assessments of personality by trained observers do not correspond well with self-assessments. One analysis aggregated data over thousands of people and found that self and observer ratings of personality have significant overlap. However, self and observer ratings offer unique and different information (Connolly, Kavanagh, & Viswesvaran, 2007). Until recently, we have tended to disregard self-ratings. Growing evidence now suggests that self-ratings offer important and valid information.

Recent research on the prediction of behavior in particular situations has yielded some simple but startling results. Although it is difficult to predict behavior on the basis of reports by trained clinical psychologists (Meehl, 1995), people are remarkably good at predicting their own behavior (Drieling et al., 2016; Martin et al., 2016). We can learn a lot simply by asking someone whether he or she will be able to perform a particular behavior.

Frequently, expensive and time-consuming psychological tests are given in order to predict future behavior. Before exerting this effort, one should ask what the tests might reveal beyond information obtained in some simpler manner. For example, for predicting functioning and life expectancy for lung patients, a simple self-rating of health serves about as well as a complex set of medical tests. Detailed interviews and tests give little information beyond the simple patient self-report. In addition, simple self-reports about smoking, completed education, and risky behaviors predict the chances of living for 10 more years about as well as measures of blood pressure, diabetes, and cholesterol (Kaplan, Howard, Manely, & Howard, 2017). Through a variety of tests and self-ratings, other studies have attempted to determine how a person will be rated by peers. The results often demonstrate that, in predicting peer ratings, simple self-ratings are as good as complex personality tests that make inferences about underlying traits. Several studies have demonstrated that self-rated emotional intelligence is a reasonably good predictor of job performance (Joseph, Jin, Newman, & O'Boyle, 2015).

Alternatively, work supervisors are known to be inaccurate raters. One variable that may affect ratings is the supervisor's own level of security. For example, studies have demonstrated that supervisors who have conflict over their own roles give relatively higher ratings of the performance of their subordinates (Fried & Tiegs, 1995). A variety of investigations have considered the validity of employment interviews. The most comprehensive summary of these studies, reported by McDaniel, Whetzel, Schmidt, and Maurer (1994), combined results from a variety of other investigations involving a combined total of 86,331 individuals. The analysis suggested that the validity of interview information depends on many variables. Situational interviews had higher validity than did job-related interviews. Psychologically based interviews had the lowest validity of all the categories studied. Structured interviews had higher validity than did unstructured ones. Initial impressions in job interviews may have strong effects on overall evaluations, even though initial impressions are often not accurate (Swider et al., 2016). Other studies have demonstrated that biographical information used for employment decisions is often unreliable (Shackleton, 2015). There is some hope for improving ratings. Studies have shown that rating accuracy can improve with specific cognitive training (Day & Sulsky, 1995).

Often, the predictive validity of selection tests is modest. For example, one investigation attempted to predict who would be the best support people for insurance agencies. A battery of tests involving cognitive ability, personality, and biographical data was administered to 357 subjects. Among these, 337 were eventually hired and rated by their immediate supervisor for job performance. The range of the validity coefficients was .17 to .28. In other words, the extensive testing battery explains only about 4% to 9% of the variance in job performance (Bosshardt, Carter, Gialluca, Dunnette, & Ashworth, 1992). Another study evaluated applicants for eight telecommunications companies. Using structural behavioral interviews to estimate job performance yielded criterion validity estimates of approximately .22 (Motowidlo et al., 1992). After decades of research on the value of personality tests for employee selection, we still have very little evidence that personality measures are meaningful predictors of job performance (Cook, 2016).

We do not offer these examples to convince you that personality tests are meaningless. As you see in Chapters 13 and 14, personality measures make many important contributions. However, test users always should ask themselves whether they can gain the same information with a simpler or less expensive method or with one that will cause the subject less strain. Tests should be used when they provide significantly more information than simpler methods would obtain. To ensure that testing is a worthwhile use of time and resources, one must carefully select the testing materials to be used.

Personnel Psychology From the Employee's Perspective: Fitting People to Jobs

One challenge in personnel psychology is to find the best matches between characteristics of people and characteristics of jobs. Temperament may be a critical component of job satisfaction. In this section, we review the Myers-Briggs Type Indicator (MBTI), which is perhaps the most widely used measure of temperament in I/O psychology.

The Myers-Briggs Type Indicator

The MBTI, developed by I. B. Myers and K. C. Briggs, is a theoretically constructed test based on Carl Jung's theory of psychology types (Quenk, 2000). Jung theorized that there are four main ways in which we experience or come to know the world:

► *sensing,* or knowing through sight, hearing, touch, and so on;
► *intuition,* inferring what underlies sensory inputs;
► *feeling,* focusing on the emotional aspect of experience; and
► *thinking,* reasoning or thinking abstractly.

Jung argued that although we must strive for balance in the four modes, each person tends to emphasize one way of experiencing the world over the others. In addition, Jung believed that one could distinguish all individuals in terms of introversion versus extroversion.

The purpose of the Myers-Briggs test is to determine where people fall on the introversion–extroversion dimension and on which of the four modes they most rely (Quenk, 2000, Tate, 2016). In line with Jung's theory, the underlying assumption of the MBTI is that we all have specific preferences in the way we construe our experiences, and these preferences underlie our interests, needs, values, and motivation.

The MBTI is widely used and has been extensively researched (Tate, 2016). It has been used to study such issues as communication styles (Evert & Lang, 2016), career choices (Yang, Richard, & Durkin, 2016), emotional intelligence (Shirzad, 2016), leadership (Day, 2016), and self-efficacy (de Haan, Grant, Burger, & Eriksson, 2016). The MBTI has even been used to study the relationship between personality and financial success (Lounsbury, Sundstrom, Gibson, Loveland, & Drost, 2016; Mabon, 1998) and sensitivity and purpose in life (Doerries & Ridley, 1998). In fact, our review of studies published between 1996 and 2016 revealed literally hundreds of studies that have used the MBTI in creative ways to study human personality and its correlates (Lounsbury et al., 2016).

Tests for Use in Industry: Wonderlic Personnel Test (WPT)

Business and industry make extensive use of tests, especially as an aid in making decisions about employment, placement, and promotion. One such test widely used is the WPT (Hinton & Stevens-Gill, 2016). Based on another popular instrument, the Otis Self-Administering Tests of Mental Ability, the WPT is a quick (12-minute) test of mental ability in adults. The Wonderlic company, which has been in business for more than 70 years, also provides assessments of motivational potential, knowledge and skills, personality and integrity, and interview prescreening. Normative data are available on more than 50,000 adults 20 to 65 years old. Five forms, whose intercorrelations range from .82 to .94, are available. Odd–even reliability coefficients are also excellent, with a range of .88 to .94 reported in the manual. The main drawback of the WPT is its validity documentation, although available studies tend to support it (Dodrill & Warner, 1988; Rosenstein & Glickman, 1994).

In short, the WPT is a quick and stable paper-and-pencil or computer-administered intelligence test with extensive norms. Widely used for employee-related decisions in industry, it has its greatest value when local validity data are available (Saltzman, Strauss, Hunter, & Spellacy, 1998). However, there have been some concerns about the validity of the Wonderlic. In particular, some studies show that the test discriminates well between those with low fluid intelligence, but does less well differentiating people with high fluid intelligence (Hicks, Harrison, & Engle, 2015). In the absence of local data, test scores must be interpreted with some caution. Figure 18.2 shows some sample questions from the Wonderlic.

In 2014, the newest version of the Wonderlic, known as the Wonderlic Personnel Test–Revised (WRT-R), was released. In addition, an abbreviated Wonderlic Personnel Test–Quicktest (WRT-Q) is also available. The newer versions update the traditional Wonderlic and use newer technologies for test administration and scoring. For most test takers, the new version can be completed in about 12 minutes.

FIGURE 18.2
Sample questions from the Wonderlic.

Sample Questions

Look at the row of numbers below. What number should come next?

8   4   2   1   1/2   1/4   ?

Assume the first 2 statements are true. Is the final one: (1) true, (2) false, (3) not certain?
The boy plays baseball. All baseball players wear hats. The boy wears a hat.

One of the numbered figures in the following drawing is most different from the others. What is the number in that figure?

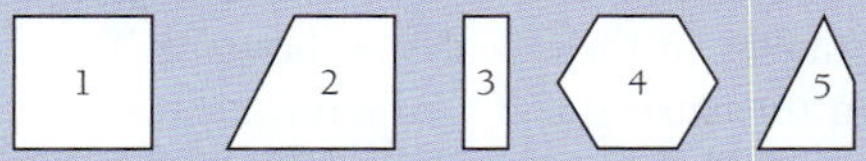

A train travels 20 feet in 1/5 second. At this same speed, how many feet will it travel in three seconds?

How many of the six pairs of items listed below are exact duplicates?

3421	1243
21212	21212
558956	558956
10120210	10120210
612986896	612986896
356471201	356571201

The hours of daylight and darkness in SEPTEMBER are nearest equal to the hours of daylight and darkness in
(1) June   (2) March   (3) May   (4) November

(Copyright © Wonderlic Personnel Test, Inc. Reprinted by permission.)

Measuring Characteristics of the Work Setting

To study the influence of situations, we need methods to describe and measure them. This section describes these methods.

Classifying Environments

How do different environments affect our behavior? Can we work better when the sun is out? Or do we get more tired and irritable on hot days? Most of social psychology is based on the premise that situations influence behavior (Moos, 2003). Some of the earliest work in the field of environmental psychology involved building elaborate systems to classify the characteristics of environments that had been shown to affect individual or group behavior (Holahan, 1986). (This was similar to the work done by many early personality psychologists who built elaborate systems to classify personality types.) We now have extensive evidence that local environments can have a big impact on physical activity and other health behaviors. The "Walkableness" of cities can be found on the Internet (see walkscore.com) and it has been shown that the level of regular exercise is related to the availability of parks, sidewalks, and public transportation (Sallis et al., 2016; Stewart et al., 2016).

Table 18.6 shows a classification system created by Moos (1973). It includes six characteristics of environments and gives examples. Many studies demonstrate that the characteristics of the people in one's environment affect one's behavior. The likelihood that a high-school girl will begin to smoke, for example, can be greatly influenced by how many girls she knows who already smoke or who approve of smoking (Gilpin & Pierce, 2003). Over the years, Moos and his colleagues have developed many different measures to evaluate the characteristics of environments (Moos, 2003). A summary of these scales is shown in Table 18.7.

Moos's work on measuring the characteristics of environments demonstrates the ways in which personal characteristics of the work environment affect job choice and worker satisfaction (Schaefer & Moos, 1996). For example, workers are more satisfied with work environments that promote quality interactions between workers and supervisors than they are with environments that keep these relationships more distant. The quality of the relationship between workers and supervisors also enhances productivity (Moos, 1987c). Some evidence indicates that workers in supportive work environments are less likely to develop disabilities caused by stress on the job than are workers in nonsupportive environments (Holahan & Moos, 1986). A pleasant work environment is also good for business. Bank customers who

TABLE 18.6 Six Characteristics of Environments

Characteristics	Examples
Ecological dimensions	Architectural design, geographic location, weather conditions
Behavioral settings	Office, home, store
Organizational structure	Percentage of women in the student body, number of people per household, average age of group
Characteristics of inhabitants	Proportion of students who date, drink, or vote
Psychosocial and organizational climate	Work pressure, encouragement of participation, orientation toward helping with personal problems
Functional or reinforcing properties	Is aggression reinforced on the football field? Is it reinforced at home?

Adapted from Moos (1973).

TABLE 18.7 Summary of Scales Used to Evaluate Different Environments

Type of environment	Scale	Reference
Treatment	Ward Atmosphere Scale	Moos (1987e)
	Community-Oriented Programs	
	Environment Scale	Moos (1987a)
Institutional	Correctional Institutions	
	Environment Scale	Moos (1987b)
Educational	University Residence Environment Scale	Moos (1987d)
	Classroom Environment Scale	Moos and Truckett (1986)
Community	Work Environment Scale	Moos (1986b)
	Group Environment Scale	Moos (1986a)
	Family Environment Scale	Moos and Moos (1986)

perceive employees as friendly and supportive tend to stay at their bank more than do customers who dislike the bank's social environment (Moos, 1986b).

In Chapter 17, we discussed the potential of electronic devices to capture information. These devices have enormous potential for assessing the environment. One of the most important problems in contemporary research is determining how much of our behavior is influenced by genetics and how much is determined by our environments. Most behaviors are the result of complex interactions between genes and environments. Recent advances in molecular biology have made measurement of genetic exposures feasible. In contrast, measurement of environment remains very challenging. Unlike our genomes, which are relatively constant throughout life, environmental exposures are dynamic and constantly changing throughout life. But, the game is changing because new electronic technologies are capable of capturing many of our exposures and behaviors. For example, environmental scientists have developed a sensor system that measures dangerous chemicals in the environment with a sensitivity at the level that we need for the most detailed studies of exposure. The goal is to be able to move beyond assigning everyone in a given geographical region an "average" exposure level to assessing individual exposures as people go about their daily routine.

In sum, behavioral settings and social environments are coming to be recognized as important factors in job and personal satisfaction. The study of work environments is a relatively new area that we expect to blossom in the coming decade.

Job Analysis

In addition to classifying work environments, the industrial psychologist must describe and measure characteristics of the job. Employers often want to detail the activities of their workplace to determine what type of personnel is needed or why

TABLE 18.8   Job Checklist for Research Assistant*

Activity	Frequency of occurrence				
	Per hour	Per day	Per week	Per month	Per year
Photocopying		1			
Typing			2		
Attending meetings				1	
Meeting with subjects			3		
Ordering supplies				1	
Writing reports					1

*The assistant would be expected to photocopy materials once per day, type twice per week, meet with subjects three times per week, and so on.

some employees are unhappy working in the setting. Zedeck and Blood (1974) summarize five basic methods for doing so: checklists, critical incidents, observations, interviews, and questionnaires.

Checklists are used by job analysts to describe the activities and working conditions usually associated with a job title. An example of a checklist for a research assistant in behavioral research is shown in Table 18.8. The first column of the checklist shows the activities associated with the job title, while the other columns list the frequency of occurrence of these activities. The job analyst must simply record how frequently each activity occurs for people in this job classification.

One of the concerns about job analysis is whether ratings are reliable. Dierdorff and Wilson (2003) reviewed 46 studies involving more than 299 estimates of reliability of job analysis. Ratings of tasks produced higher estimates of interrater reliability than did generalized ratings of jobs. The goals of a rater can also affect the ratings. One study had evaluators rate group projects. Their ratings were higher when they were told that the goal of their ratings was to produce harmony. Harmony goals also reduced the variability between projects. Emphasizing fairness also increased the mean ratings but did not affect the variability of completed projects (Wong & Kwong, 2007).

In addition to evaluating jobs, employers must evaluate job performance. This is a complex field that is beyond the scope of this text. However, there are excellent summaries of performance evaluation. Although there is some evidence for the validity of job ratings (Salgado, Moscoso, & Anderson, 2016), suffice it to say that problems in performance evaluation are challenging (Wu, Sears, Coberley, & Pope, 2016). For example, there is controversy over whether there is racial bias in the evaluation of job performance. Some researchers still argue that there are important differences in performance across racial groups. For example, Roth and colleagues summarized studies on differences in job performance (Roth, Huffcutt, & Bobko, 2003). They compared differences between African American and white employees on subjective measures such as supervisor ratings versus objective measures based on more formal evaluations. Their analysis suggested that the objective measures showed even larger differences between African American and white employees than the subjective measures for work quality, quantity, and absenteeism. Differences between Hispanic and white employees were not as large as those between African American and white employees. Studies have also shown that the racial composition of the workforce can affect the evaluation of leaders (Hernandez et al., 2016).

Critical incidents are observable behaviors that differentiate successful from unsuccessful employees. The critical incident method was developed by J. C. Flanagan (1954) and is still used in practice today (Durand, 2016). By acquiring specific descriptions of the behaviors of successful employees and their unsuccessful counterparts, one can learn something about the differences between the two groups. For example, a critical incident that might describe a successful employee is "always arrives at meetings on time." A critical incident that describes an unsuccessful employee might be "leaves work area disorganized."

Observation is another method for learning about the nature of the job (Bragger et al., 2016). As we discussed in Chapter 8, information gathered through observational methods can sometimes be biased because people change their behavior when they know they are being watched. To avoid this problem, the participant-observation method is sometimes used. A participant-observer is someone who participates in the job and functions as though he or she were one of the workers.

Interviews can also be used to find out about a job. However, some workers may give an interviewer information that differs from what they would give another employee because they are uncomfortable or fear that what they say will be held against them. Another problem is that an interviewer unfamiliar with the job may not ask the right questions.

Questionnaires are commonly used to find out about job situations, but their use calls for special precautions. Many employers favor questionnaires because they are inexpensive. However, the employer may never know whether the respondent understood the questions. Furthermore, the type of information gained is limited to the specific questions. A more serious problem concerns the selective return rate in questionnaire studies. Those employees who feel highly favorable or highly unfavorable toward the company are the most likely to complete the questionnaire and return it.

Another approach to job description is the Occupational Information Network (O*NET) (Peterson, Mumford, Levin, Green, & Waksberg, 1999). The network was developed because traditional job descriptions in the U.S. Department of Labor's *Dictionary of Occupational Titles* did not provide enough information about how tasks and skills generalized across occupations. Job content can be described by both job-oriented and work-oriented tasks. The system includes three categories: (1) worker requirements, such as skills, knowledge, and abilities; (2) experience requirements, including training and licensure; and (3) job requirements, such as work activities, work context, and characteristics of the organization (Hanson, Borman, Kubisiak, & Sager, 1999). Using O*NET, one can understand divergent occupations in relation to tasks and skills that generalize across occupational categories (Jeanneret, Borman, Kubisiak, & Hanson, 1999). O*NET continues to evolve. The entire database is available to the public at no cost (see ONETCEN-TER.ORG). The 2012 database includes thousands of occupational definitions and the system is continually updated.

Measuring the Person–Situation Interaction

In this chapter, we have presented two different perspectives. First, we reviewed research and methods from counseling psychology that emphasized the importance of people's characteristics or traits in their career satisfaction (Campbell, 2000). Then we discussed how the characteristics of work environments and job requirements affect people.

To a growing number of psychologists, whether traits or situations are more important in determining behavior is a "pseudoquestion." Established leaders, for example, change their behavior to fit different situations (Michel & LeBreton, 2011). It is meaningless to ask whether traits or situations are more important in explaining behavior, because behavior is clearly a joint function of both, *or person–situation interaction* (Sauerberger & Funder, 2016). And new methodologies are available to offer greater precision for the measurement of situations (Funder, 2016).

The interactionists support their position by reporting the proportion of variance in behavior explained by person, by situation, and by the interaction between person and situation. You might think of this as a pie divided to represent all the different influences on human behavior, including unknown causes (see Figure 18.3). Unique combinations of traits and situations cause this interaction. The beginning of Chapter 16 featured the case of Harry, a man who suffered throughout his life because he had made a bad career choice to become a dentist. For example, an interaction might describe how Harry reacts to being a dentist. This cause is different from the characteristics of Harry (in all situations) or the effects of anyone performing the role of a dentist. Careful studies that apply a statistical method known as *analysis of variance* have separated the proportion of variance attributable to each of these factors. As shown in Figure 18.3, the interaction accounts for a larger portion of the variance in behavior than does either the person or the situation (Endler, Parker, Bagby, & Cox, 1991).

FIGURE 18.3

Factors influencing behavior. A pie is divided according to the proportion of variation in behavior accounted for by person, situation, and the interaction between person and situation. The interaction is greater than either of the other two sources of influence. However, unexplained or error variance is much greater than any other factor.

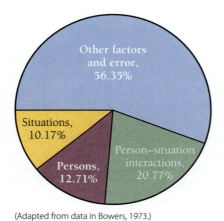

Other factors and error, 56.35%

Situations, 10.17%

Persons, 12.71%

Person–situation interactions, 20.77%

(Adapted from data in Bowers, 1973.)

As you can see, the interaction position explains only some of the people some of the time (Funder, 2015). As Figure 18.3 shows, the largest slice of the pie represents *error variance,* the proportion of the total not explained by the three sources of influence. After reviewing many studies on the influences of person and situation, I. G. Sarason, Smith, and Diener (1975) concluded that none of the three sources account for an impressive share of the variation when compared with the amount of variation left unexplained. Although the interaction is a better predictor than either trait or situation, it is only slightly better.

To help predict more of the people more of the time, Bem and Funder (1978) introduced the *template-matching technique,* a system that takes advantage of people's ability to predict their own behavior in particular situations. The system attempts to match personality to a specific template of behavior. For example, consider how to answer the question "Should Tom become an insurance salesperson?" Assuming you know nothing about Tom, perhaps the best way to guide him would be to describe how several hypothetical people might react to working in this job. You might say that shy people may have difficulty approaching new customers or that people with families may not like insurance sales because of the irregular work hours. Tom could then predict his own reaction to the job by matching his characteristics with the set of templates you have provided for him.

Along the same lines, Bem and Funder proposed that "situations be characterized as sets of template-behavior pairs, each template being a personality description of an idealized type of person expected to behave in a specified way in that setting" (1978, p. 486). The probability that a particular person will behave in a particular way in a situation is a function of the match between his or her characteristics and a template. For example, if Tom's personality characteristics matched the template for those who hated being insurance salespeople, then he might be best advised to avoid that career.

Because the template-matching idea arose from research in personality and social psychology, it is not often discussed in other areas of psychology. However, the person–situation interaction resembles what educational psychologists call the *aptitude–treatment interaction* (Yeh, 2012). The template-matching idea also resembles a popular theory of career choice that J. L. Holland (1997) proposed. Holland suggested that there are six clusters of personality and interest traits; these are the same clusters represented as the six general themes on the Strong-Campbell Interest Inventory (SCII) (realistic, investigative, artistic, social, enterprising, and conventional). Holland contended that six vocational environments correspond to these traits and that people will be happiest if they can match their traits to the characteristics of the work environment (Holland, 1975; Holland & Gottfredson, 1976). For example, an investigative individual will be most content if he or she can work in an investigative field such as science.

The fit between employers and their work environments has been of interest to industrial and organizational psychologists for many years. The relationship between characteristics of job environments and psychological status of employees has been evaluated in many studies. Reviews of this literature show that little job latitude, job strain, and bullying by other employees can lead to significant psychological depression in both male and female employees (Theorell et al., 2015).

Recently, a group developed a measure of fit between employees and the environments in which they work. The Perceived Person–Environment Fit

Scale (PPEFS) is composed of four subscales. One subscale measures the fit between a person and a job. The second component measures the fit between the person and the organization. The third subscale measures the fit among the people working in a group and a final component evaluates the fit between the person and a supervisor. The measure was evaluated in a study of 532 employees and 122 managers. Overall, there was good validity evidence demonstrating that measures of these characteristics of persons and jobs were significant predictors of job satisfaction, intention to quit, and citizenship within organizations (Chuang, Shen, & Judge, 2016).

The idea of matching traits to situations is intuitively appealing. The concept of "different strokes for different folks" seems like a good way to structure one's search for the right job, the right apartment, or the right psychotherapist. However, this approach has some problems. First, there is an enormous number of combinations of persons and situations. For example, predicting how 10 personality types will perform in 20 different work environments produces $10 \times 20 = 200$ unique combinations. Most real-life decisions require many more factors. Second, research has not yet supported specific examples of matching traits and situations. Psychotherapists, for example, often account for lack of effectiveness by arguing that weak results should be expected because therapies must be tailored to the specific personalities of clients. In other words, some people will do well in behavior therapy, whereas others will have better success with a more cognitive approach. However, research has typically failed to correlate personalities with treatments. When these interactions are found, other studies tend not to replicate them (Smith & Sechrest, 1991). As a result, researchers must go back to the theoretical drawing board for new insights into the selection of treatment.

The fit between persons and situations may depend on how we ask the questions. In one study, university students worked intensively with teams over an extended period of time. Their ratings of their fit with the team remained stable over time, but their ratings of their personal fit with their individual role on the team were less stable. Individuals who receive positive feedback for their contributions tend to feel they have a closer fit with their roles on the team (DeRue & Morgeson, 2007).

One finding that has been supported by research is that people often predict their own behavior better than do experts. However, some people tend to be overly positive in self-evaluations. This enhancement can be evaluated by comparing self-ratings with those provided by friends and professionals (Funder, 2010; Funder & West, 1993). Longitudinal studies show that self-enhancers tend to have poor social skills and poor psychological adjustment. Positive mental health may be associated with accurate self-appraisal (Funder, 2010). Cognitive ability may also play a role in how well people are able to assess their own test performance. For example, people with higher cognitive ability more accurately assess their own performance on a situational test of consumer services skills than people with lower cognitive ability do (Truxillo, Seitz, & Bauer, 2008).

In general, career satisfaction depends on an appropriate match between person and job (Rumsey, 2013). The developing technology for finding job–person matches holds great promise for the field of career counseling and guidance testing (Das & Sahoo, 2015). Counseling interventions must be tailored to individual needs (Hartung & Santilli, 2016). Trying to use the same approach with every client might be like a shoe store attempting to sell the same size of shoe to each customer.

Summary

Making a selection among the many published tests has become a technical skill. One of your first considerations should always be whether it is worthwhile to administer a given test. How much information does the test promise beyond what can be learned without the test? Interviews remain the most common method for employee selection. However, the traditional interview has significant limitations. Modern personnel psychology makes extensive use of systematic selection procedures, often based on tests, performance samples, and job analysis. In personnel selection, the *base rate* is the probability of succeeding without any selection procedure. A variety of methods have been developed to estimate the amount of information a test gives beyond what is known by chance. This estimate depends on the validity of the test, the percentage of people being selected, and the proportion of people who can be expected to succeed if no selection test is used. *Taylor–Russell tables* can be used for outcomes defined in terms of success and failure. You can use utility and decision theories for some outcomes involving more than these two levels. However, the application of the utility theory equations is fairly difficult in most circumstances. To enhance productivity in business and industry, personnel psychologists study characteristics of people, work environments, and the interactions between people and the places they may work. Learning about the interface between people and work environments may hold the key to finding the best methods for employee selection.

Test Bias

LEARNING OBJECTIVES

When you have completed this chapter, you should be able to:

▶ Discuss some of the current controversies surrounding the use of intelligence tests

▶ Give arguments for and against the belief that the content of standardized tests is biased in favor of white, middle-class children

▶ Explain how criterion-related validity studies, which review the slopes and intercepts of regression lines, are used in the study of test bias

▶ Discuss some of the problems with tests such as the Chitling Test and the BITCH

▶ List the components of the SOMPA and some of its advantages and disadvantages

▶ Describe how different social, political, and ethical viewpoints are represented by different definitions of test fairness

▶ Discuss some of the opportunities for developing improved predictors for minority group members

▶ Describe some of the problems with the criteria commonly used to evaluate standardized tests

513

▶ Describe how one can use differences in test scores to justify efforts to change the social environment

▶ Using the information from this chapter and from other sources, write an essay for or against the use of standardized tests for minority children

For the last 60 years, serious emotional debates have flourished about the meaning of tests for the placement and classification of individuals. This chapter reviews test bias, an issue so controversial that it has inspired court evaluations of the meaning of tests for racial and ethnic minority group members.

Although test bias is an unmistakably important issue (Ajayi, 2016; Cottrell, Newman, & Roisman, 2015; Reynolds & Livingston, 2012), it was not the first controversy surrounding mental testing. Mental testing has faced serious questions since test reports began in 1905, and psychologists and others have debated the issues since the 1920s (Cronbach, 1975; Haney, 1981; Mukherjee, 2016).

We feel that it is important to offer some context for this chapter. Differences in educational attainment not only predict wealth, but are also associated with health, well-being, and life expectancy. Inequality is perhaps the most challenging social problem we face (Cabieses, Pickett, & Wilkinson, 2016; Pickett & Wilkinson, 2015). Some people believe that differences in educational achievement are a reflection of basic traits, such as intelligence. Many textbooks avoid the topic because it is controversial and emotionally loaded. It is repugnant when someone suggests that some ethnic and racial groups do not have the same potential. Yet, over the course of the last 60 years, this discussion has appeared in the scholarly literature and we felt it was our responsibility to attempt to summarize what has been said. We do our best to explain the differing points of view without taking a position on whether we agree or disagree with each position. In this chapter and in Chapter 20, we also try to offer some historical context by discussing points of view that have evolved over the last 60 years. The goal is to help you understand how scholars have dealt with this topic without taking a position about which point of view is correct or incorrect.

Why Is Test Bias Controversial?

That all persons are created equal is the cornerstone of political and social thought in U.S. society, yet all individuals are not treated equally. The history of social action is replete with attempts to remedy this situation. However, psychological tests are designed to measure differences among people, often in terms of desirable personal characteristics such as intelligence and aptitude. Test scores that demonstrate differences among people may suggest to some that people are not created with the same basic abilities.

The most difficult problem is that some ethnic groups obtain lower average scores on some psychological tests. The most controversial case concerns intelligence tests. On average, African Americans score about 15 points lower than white Americans on standardized IQ tests. (See Chapter 11 for the meaning of IQ scores.) This difference equates to approximately one standard deviation. Few people disagree that the two distributions overlap greatly and that some African Americans

FIGURE 19.1

SAT Math score distributions for African American, white, and Asian American college-bound seniors, 1999.

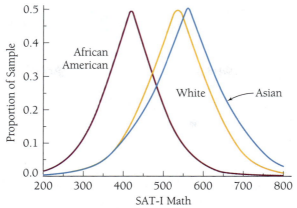

(Data provided by the College Board.)

score as high as the highest whites. Similarly, some whites score as low as the lowest African Americans. Yet only some 15% to 20% of the African American population score above the average white score, and only approximately 15% to 20% of the white population score below the average African American score. Figure 19.1 shows the overlap between African American, white, and Asian American college-bound seniors on the SAT math section. All distributions significantly overlap, but Asian American students obtain the highest average scores, followed by white and African American students.

This finding has appeared in many different studies. If you were to administer the Stanford-Binet or the Wechsler scale (see Chapter 11) to large random samples of African Americans and white Americans, it is likely you would get the same results. The dispute has not been over *whether* these differences exist but over *why* they do. Many have argued that the differences result from environmental factors (Chu, Maruyama, Elefant, & Bongar, 2016; Cottrell et al., 2015; Kamin, 1974; Mukherjee, 2016; Nisbett, 2005; Rosenthal & Jacobson, 1968; Shenk, 2011b; Tong, Baghurst, Vimpani, & McMichael, 2007; Turkheimer, 1991; Walker, Spohn, & DeLone, 2011; Wiggan, 2007; Zuckerman, 1990), while others have suggested that the differences are biological (Eysenck, 1991; Hoekstra, Bartels, Hudziak, Van Beijsterveldt, & Boomsma, 2007; Jensen, 1969, 1972; Munsinger, 1975; Rushton, 1991; van Leeuwen, van den Berg, & Boomsma, 2008) and related to the general (*g*) factor measured by IQ tests (Nyborg & Jensen, 2000). This debate lies beyond our concerns here, which center on the problems inherent in tests apart from environmental and biological factors (Fancher, 2011; Flynn, 2016). See Focused Example 19.1 for a brief look at the issue of genes and IQ. Then see Focused Example 19.2 offers for a possible environmental source of differences in test results. Finally, Focused Example 19.3 examines the very idea of race.

Beyond the other issues relevant to race and ethnicity, an increasing number of people no longer report their race when asked. Each year the College Board releases a report that summarizes SAT scores. In 2015, the report showed that overall SAT scores peaked in 2005 and have been trending down very slightly over the last decade. However, the gap between African American and Hispanic students and Asian and

Genes and Improving IQ

If intelligence were really determined genetically, then we would expect average IQ scores for different groups to be relatively constant over time. However, performance on intelligence tests has improved rather dramatically for some groups over the last 60 years. Figure 19.2 shows gains in IQ as estimated from the progressive matrix tests. These changes have been observed in a variety of Western countries, including Great Britain, the Netherlands, and Israel. Jensen has argued that environment may affect IQ, suggesting that equalizing environments would reduce the 15-point gap between African Americans and their white counterparts by approximately 10 points. Indeed, in recent years, African Americans have gained more in IQ than have whites. Since 1945, it appears that African Americans have increased average IQ by 16 points. By 1995, African Americans were performing on IQ tests at about the same level as whites in 1945 (Flynn, 1999), and this trend toward narrowing the gap has continued (Flynn, 2016).

There have also been slow improvements in achievement tests. School performance differences between African American and white children persist, despite a variety of efforts by The National Assessment

FIGURE 19.2

Gains in average IQ over time in five countries.

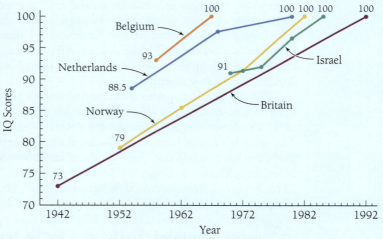

Note: Every nation is normed on its own samples. Therefore, although nations can be roughly compared in terms of different rates of IQ gain, they cannot becompared in terms of IQ scores. That is, the fact that the mean IQ of one nationappears higher than another at a given time is purely an artifact.

From J. R. Flynn. Searching for justice: The discovery of IQ gains over time. *American Psychologist*, Jan V 54 (n1), 1999, 5–20. Copyright © 1999 American Psychological Association. Reprinted by permission.

non-Hispanic white peers was not closing. One of the difficulties in evaluating the report is that about 4% of the test takers did not disclose their ethnicity and another 4% did not find a standard category. As a result, it is difficult to determine why the performance gap is not narrowing. Previous studies have shown that students who did not report ethnicity tended to get lower scores on the SAT. More recent studies indicate that the test performance of the nonresponder group is comparable to the

of Educational Programs (NAEP). The good news is that mathematics scores for both African American and white public schools students in the 4th and 8th grade have been improving since the early 1990s. Similarly, performance on reading has also been improving. For all of the years of the assessment, there has been a gap in performance between African American and white students. However, that gap is beginning to narrow. But, progress has been slow. Figure 19.3 shows the trends of improving mathematics scores for 13 year olds between 1978 and 2004. As the figure shows, all students are generally performing better, but there is a gap between African American and white students. That gap narrows over the course of time, but still persists. It is likely that the gap reflects substantial differences in access to high-quality education and inadequate financing of schools that serve the poorest students (Baker, Farrie, & Sciarra, 2016).

Because genetic change takes several generations, only an environmental hypothesis can explain these results. Many features of contemporary society have been used to explain these gains. One interesting suggestion is that heavy use of interactive video games may contribute to the IQ gains or the prevention of cognitive decline in older people (Coyle, Traynor, & Solowij, 2015). Others have suggested that the core components of intelligence represented by the *g* factor have not changed, but that other factors in the IQ tests are responsible for the trends in IQ improvement (Nijenhuis & van der Flier, 2007). One of the most challenging findings for the genetic hypothesis is related to adoption studies. When children are adopted into new homes that promote learning, the *g* component in IQ tests increases (te Nijenhuis, Jongeneel-Grimen, & Armstrong, 2015). This improvement is much more easily explained by environmental rather than a genetic hypothesis.

FIGURE 19.3

Gradual closing of African American–white achievement differences in 8th-grade mathematics.

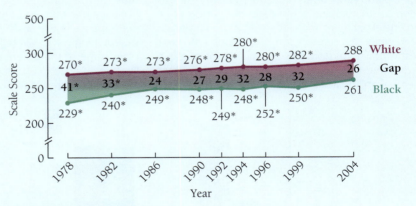

* Significantly different (p<.05) from 2004.

Note: Detail may not sum to totals due to rounding.

Source: U.S. Department of Education, Institute of Education Sciences, National Center for Education Statistics, National Assessment of Educational Progress (NAEP), various years, 1978–2004 Long-Term Trend Mathematics Assessments.

rest of the SAT takers. It is not clear why so many students failed to report their racial identity. Steele believes that African American students, because of stereotype threat, perform more poorly on tests when they reveal their race (Steele & Aronson, 2004). (See Chapter 7 for a more detailed discussion of this issue.) Whittington (2004) reports that many white students decline to report their race because they feel there is discrimination in favor of ethnic minorities and that their majority

Can Stereotyping Affect Test Performance?

Some research suggests that being a member of a group that is negatively stereotyped may adversely affect performance on standardized tests (Mayer & Hanges, 2003). As noted in this chapter, large studies consistently show that standardized tests (such as the SAT) overpredict college performance for African American, Latino, Latina, and Native American students. The overprediction occurs because many students from underrepresented groups do not get high grades in college. Steele argues that stereotyping adversely affects the victims' college grades, performance on standardized tests, and employment testing (Steele & Davies, 2003). In particular, he argues that doing well requires identification with one's school and other features of the school environment. Through a series of experiments, Steele and Aronson demonstrated how victimization by stereotyping could affect test performance. In one experiment, they subjected African American and white students to a test that included the hardest verbal items from the GRE. Half of the students were told that the test was measuring their intellectual ability, while the others were told that the

test was about problem solving unrelated to ability. They hypothesized that informing subjects that they are going to take an ability test makes people who have been victims of stereotyping worry about their performance. This threatening experience, in turn, interferes with actual test performance (Spencer et al., 2016).

When told they were taking a test of intellectual abilities, white students scored significantly higher than African American students. However, some subjects were randomly assigned to take the same test but under conditions where there was no threat. Without a threat present, white and African American students performed equivalently. The results are summarized in Figure 19.4 (Steele, 1997). A related experiment showed that simply having African American students complete a demographic questionnaire that asks about their race also suppresses performance. These clever experiments suggest that stereotyping can create self-doubts that, in turn, explain some of the difference in test performance (Spencer et al., 2016). Chapter 7 also explores this issue of stereotype threat in relation to test administration.

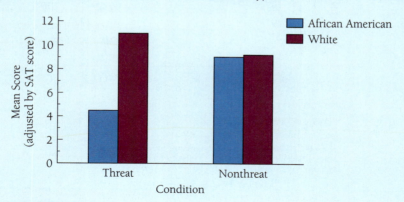

FIGURE 19.4

Effects of stereotyping upon test performance. When told they were taking a test of intellectual abilities, white students scored significantly higher than African American students. However, some students were randomly assigned to take the same test but under conditions where there was no threat. Without a threat present, white and African American students performed equivalently.

(Adapted from Steele, 1997, p. 621.)

19.3 FOCUSED EXAMPLE

Is Race a Meaningful Concept?

Race is one of the most commonly reported variables in social science. However, there has been considerable debate about the genetic basis for racial differences. One side argues that human races are highly similar to one another and that the construct of race has no biological meaning (Swallen, 2003). The evidence comes from studies in population genetics, the human genome, and physical anthropology (Freeman & Payne, 2000). Significant investigation has shown that the populations of the world are significantly intermingled—that is, humans have common genetic roots and the races of the world are not independent. The biological similarities among peoples of the world greatly outnumber the few differences.

There are many reasons to believe that classifying people as simply African American or white is extremely misleading. For example, variations in human skin tone evolved to represent different adaptations to the amount of sunlight people were exposed to. There is a wide continuum of skin tones among human populations (see Figure 19.5). Assigning people to groups based on the color of their skin or other physical features ignores the massive amount of information that defines people as individuals (Jablonski & Chaplin, 2010).

Because very strong sun exposure can damage the body, there is a biological adaptation favoring darker skin for people living closer to the equator. Those with darker skin tones were more likely to

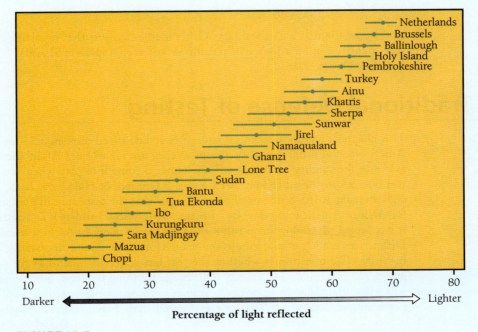

FIGURE 19.5

Range of skin colors in human populations. This wide variation suggests that classifying humans as "African American" or "white" ignores most of the information on skin tone.

(continues)

survive to the age of reproduction. Variations in skin color had little to do with race but instead were an adaptation to different levels of sunlight exposure (Singer, Erickson, Leatherman, & Goodman, 2011).

The other side of the argument suggests that there are, indeed, important genetic differences between the populations in the world. Advocates for this position acknowledge that at least 85% of a person's genetic makeup is shared by all human groups. But, they suggest that the genetic information that differentiates human populations is hidden in the interactions between genes. Newer methods are able to identify racial background on the basis of genetic information (Edwards, 2003; Witherspoon et al., 2007).

Nevertheless, race has remained an important variable in demography. Brawley and Freeman (1999)

point out that "race medicine" dominated the last few centuries. Race medicine was based on the belief that diseases behave differently in different races and was promoted by prominent 18th-century scientists whose opinions were used as the justification for slavery. However, medical research consistently shows that diseases function equivalently in people of different racial backgrounds (Freeman & Payne, 2000). Furthermore, equivalent treatment typically produces equivalent benefit for those of different racial backgrounds (Ellis, 2008). Nevertheless, there are substantial disparities in the amount and quality of care that is available to those of different racial groups. This discrimination in access to health care may be the best explanation for the disparity in health outcomes among people of different races (Flores & Tomany-Korman, 2008).

status puts them at a disadvantage. Other studies suggest that reporting multiple race identity can be a source of tension or anxiety (Kaplan et al., 2011; Spencer, Logel, & Davies, 2016).

The Traditional Defense of Testing

This chapter focuses on a central issue: Are standardized tests as valid for African Americans and other minority groups as they are for whites? All of the types of evidence for validity we discussed in Chapter 5 come into play when the issue of test bias is considered (Kline, 2015; Lane, Raymond, & Haladyna, 2015; Worrell & Roberson, 2016). Some psychologists argue that the tests are differentially valid for African Americans and whites. Because **differential validity** is so controversial, it has forced psychologists to think carefully about many issues in test validation. Differences among ethnic groups on test performance do not necessarily indicate test bias. The question is whether the test has different meanings for different groups. In psychometrics, validity defines the meaning of a test. Some researchers still argue that there are important differences in performance across racial groups. For example, Roth and colleagues summarized studies on differences in job performance. They compared differences between African American and white employees on subjective measures such as supervisor ratings versus objective measures based on more formal evaluations. Their analysis suggested that the objective measures showed even larger differences between African American and white employees than the subjective evaluations for measures of work quality, quantity, and absenteeism. Differences between Hispanic and white employees were not as large as those between African American and white employees (Roth, Huffcutt, & Bobko, 2003).

Content-Related Evidence for Validity

Articles have been published in the popular media on cultural fairness in testing. A *Newsweek* article listed several items from the general information portion of the Stanford-Binet scale that people with disadvantaged backgrounds might find problematic. Test constructors and users were accused of being biased because some children never have the opportunity to learn about some of the items; furthermore, members of ethnic groups might answer some items differently but still correctly.

Many researchers also argued that scores on intelligence tests are affected by language skills inculcated as part of a white, middle-class upbringing but foreign to inner-city children (Silva & Cain, 2015). Children who are unfamiliar with the language have no chance of doing well on standardized IQ tests. For example, an American child does not usually know what a *shilling* is, but a British child probably does. Similarly, the American child would not know where one puts the *petrol*; a British child would. Some psychologists argue that privileged children are more likely to have been exposed to some of the words and concepts used on IQ tests. As a result, tests may provide an advantage to children from wealthier homes. Evidence suggests that scores on the SAT and other aptitude tests are systematically related to family income and parental education (Cottrell et al., 2015) (see Figure 19.6).

In response to this focus on the language and content of individual test items, Flaugher (1978) concluded that many perceived test bias problems are based on misunderstandings about the way tests are usually interpreted. Many people feel that a fair test asks questions they can answer. By contrast, a biased test does not ask about things a test taker knows. Flaugher argued that the purpose of aptitude and achievement tests is to measure performance on items sampled from a wide range of information. Not

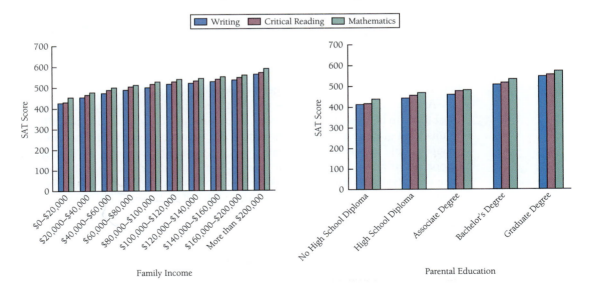

FIGURE 19.6

Relationship between family income and parental education and average performance on the SAT writing, critical reading, and mathematics tests. Data from College Board, 2015 college-bound seniors total group profile report.

Data from College Board, 2015 collegebound seniors total group profile report particularly concerned about individual items, test developers focus on test performance, making judgments about it based on correlations between the tests and external criteria. Many test critics, though, focus attention on specific items. For example, D. Owen (1985) reported that several intelligent and well-educated people had difficulty with specific items on the SAT and Law School Admission Test (LSAT) examinations. He also asserted that some items on standardized tests are familiar only to those with a middle-class background. Test developers are indifferent to the opportunities people have to learn the information on the tests. Again, the meaning they eventually assign to the tests comes from correlations of test scores with other variables.

Furthermore, some evidence suggests that the linguistic bias in standardized tests does not cause the observed differences (Scheuneman, 1987). Many years ago, Quay (1971) administered the Stanford-Binet test to 100 children in an inner-city Head Start program. Half of the children took a version of the test that used African American dialect, while the others took the standard version. The results demonstrated that the advantage produced by having the test in African American dialect translates into less than a 1-point increase in test scores. This finding is consistent with other research findings demonstrating that African American children can comprehend standard English about as well as they can comprehend African American dialect (Clarizio, 1979a; Copple & Succi, 1974). This finding does not hold for white children, who seem to comprehend only the standard dialect.

Some studies have failed to demonstrate that biased items in well-known standardized tests account for the differences in scores among ethnic groups (Drasgow, Whetzel, & Oppler, 2016). In one approach, developers ask experts to judge the unfairness of particular items. When tests are scored without the items that had been judged to be unfair, then there should be fewer differences between racial and ethnic groups. Unexpectedly, the many attempts to "purify" tests using this approach have not eliminated differences between groups. In one study, 16% of the items in an elementary reading test were eliminated after experts reviewed them and labeled them as potentially biased toward the majority group. However, when the "purged" version of the test was used, the differences between the majority and the minority school populations were no smaller than they had been originally (Bianchini, 1976).

Another approach to the same problem is to find those classes of items that are most likely to be missed by members of a particular minority group. If a test is biased against that group, then significant differences between minority and nonminority groups should appear in certain categories of items. These studies are particularly important; if they identify certain *types* of items that discriminate among groups, then these types of items can be avoided on future tests. Again, the results have not been encouraging; studies have not clearly identified such categories of items (Wild, McPeek, Koffler, Braun, & Cowell, 1989). The studies show that groups differ for certain items but not whether these are real or chance differences (Letukas, 2015).

Differential Item Functioning (DIF) Analysis

Another approach to the analysis of test bias has been developed by the Educational Testing Service (ETS) (Rawls, Zhang, & Hendrickson, 2016). The ETS creates and administers a variety of aptitude tests, including the Graduate Record Examination (GRE), the SAT, and the LSAT. In each of these programs, the performance of white test takers differs significantly from the performances of other racial and ethnic groups on verbal and analysis measures. On quantitative measures, Asian Americans tend to have the highest scores. On the GRE, men and women score equivalently on critical reading and women have a slight advantage on writing. Men, however, obtain higher scores on the mathematics test and this difference between men and women has been approximately unchanged between 1972 and 2015 (College Board data reported in 2016).

DIF analysis attempts to identify items that are specifically biased against any ethnic, racial, or gender group (Atar, 2016). The analysis first equates groups on the basis of overall score. For example, it would find subgroups of test takers who obtain equivalent scores. These might be groups of men and women who obtain scores of approximately 500 on the verbal portion of the GRE. Using these groups, it evaluates differences in performance between men and women on particular items. Items that differ significantly between the groups are thrown out and the entire test is rescored.

Similarly, items that show differences among racial and ethnic groups can be eliminated and the test rescored. In one study, 27 items from the original SAT were eliminated because ethnic groups consistently answered them differently. Then the test was rescored for everyone. Although it seems this procedure should have eliminated the differences between the two groups, it actually had only slight effects because the items that differentiated the groups tended to be the easiest items in the set. When these items were eliminated, the test was harder for everyone (Flaugher & Schrader, 1978; Park, 2016).

There is at least some evidence that test items that depict people do not accurately portray the distribution of genders and races in the population. Zores and Williams (1980) reviewed the Wechsler Adult Intelligence Scale (WAIS), Wechsler Intelligence Scale for Children–Revised (WISC-R), Stanford-Binet, and Slosson Intelligence test items for race and gender characterization and found that white male characterization occurred with disproportionate frequency. Nevertheless, no one has yet established that the frequency of different groups appearing in items affects the outcome of tests. Studies have failed to demonstrate serious bias in item content. Most critics argue that the verbal content of test items is most objectionable because it is unfamiliar to minority groups. However, Scheuneman (1981) reviewed the problem and concluded that the verbal material reflected the life experiences of African Americans more closely than did the nonverbal material. In a related example, studies that manipulate gender bias by creating neutral, male, and female items demonstrate little effect on the performance differences between male and female test takers (McCarty, Noble, & Huntley, 1989). Other studies have used DIF to help understand the experiences of discrimination in the community (Cunningham et al., 2011) and to show that DIF has only small effects on race and sex differences for children with ADHD (Wiesner, Windle, Kanouse, Elliott, & Schuster, 2015).

In spite of the many studies, the role of item bias remains poorly understood (Warne, 2016). For example, those students who have taken the most tests may be best able to answer questions that are irrelevant to the knowledge base being assessed. Because such test-wise students tend to get these items correct, item analysis may incorrectly identify the irrelevant items as useful. These problems magnify the differences between high-achieving and low-achieving students (Masters, 1988). Or, tests that are most similar to the core components of traditional IQ tests may show more group differences, regardless of their validity (Warne, 2016).

In summary, studies have not supported the popular belief that items have different meanings for different groups (Letukas, 2015); however, we must continue to scrutinize the content of tests. On some occasions, careful reviews of tests have turned up questionable items. Many tests are carelessly constructed, and every effort should be taken to purge items that have the potential for being biased. New technologists, including crowdsourcing, may allow draft test items to be scrutinized for objectionable content (Sadler, Sonnert, Coyle, & Miller, 2016).

Criterion-Related Sources of Bias

Weather forecasts are readily available on your smartphone. Usually you can get an estimate of what weather to expect for the next week or 10 days. If such forecasts are consistently accurate, we come to depend on them. In evaluating the weather report, we make a subjective assessment of validity. Similarly, we evaluate tests by asking whether they forecast future performance accurately. Standardized tests such as the SAT have been found to satisfactorily predict performance during the first year of college. These tests clearly do not give us all of the information needed for perfect prediction, but they give enough information to make us pay attention to them.

College administrators who use the test scores face difficult problems. On the average, minority applicants have lower test scores than do nonminority applicants. At the same time, most universities and colleges are attempting to increase their minority enrollments. Because minority applicants are considered as a separate category, we should ask whether the tests have differential predictive power for the two groups of applicants.

As we mentioned in Chapter 5, we assess the criterion-related evidence for validity of a test by the coefficient of correlation between the test and some criterion. The higher the correlation, the more confident we can feel about making predictions. If college grades are the criterion (the variable we are trying to forecast), then the validity of a test such as the SAT is represented by the correlation between the SAT score and first-year college grades. If students who score well on the SAT do well in college and students who score poorly on it get lower grades, then the test might be considered valid for helping administrators decide which college students to admit.

In Chapter 3, we reviewed the interpretation of regression plots as they relate to the validity of psychological tests. Showing plots like the one in Figure 19.7, we explained how to obtain a predicted criterion score from a test score. First, you find the test score on the horizontal axis of the graph and draw a line directly upward until it hits the regression line. Then you draw a line directly left until it comes to the vertical axis. This gives the predicted criterion score. The only difference between Figure 19.7 and Figure 3.8 is that we have added an ellipse, called an **isodensity curve**, around the regression line. This ellipse is used to encircle a specified portion of the cases that constitute a particular group.

FIGURE 19.7

A sample regression plot. The slope of the line shows the relationship between a test and a criterion. The steeper the slope of the line, the better the prediction of the criterion score.

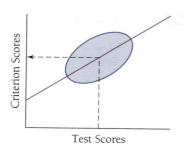

Test Scores

Criterion Scores

FIGURE 19.8

A single regression slope predicts performance equally well for two groups. However, the means of the groups differ.

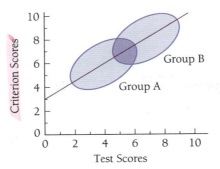

Figure 19.8 shows a regression line that represents two groups equally well. Group A appears to be performing less well than Group B on both the test (predictor) and the criterion scores. You can demonstrate this for yourself by selecting some points from the test scores for Group A and finding the expected scores on the criterion. By repeating this exercise for a few points in Group B, you will find that Group A is expected to do poorly on the criterion because it did more poorly on the test. However, for both Group A and Group B, the relationship between the test score and performance on the criterion is the same. Thus, Figure 19.8 shows there is little evidence for test bias.

Figure 19.9 represents a different situation—a separate regression line for each group. Because their slopes are the same, the lines are parallel. However, the intercepts, or the points where the regression lines cross the vertical axis, differ. If you pick a particular test score, you get one expected criterion score if you use regression line A and another if you use B. For a test score of 8, the expected criterion score from regression line A is 6, whereas the expected criterion score from regression line B is 10. The broken line in Figure 19.9 is based on a combination of regression lines A and B. Now try finding the predicted score for a test score of 8 from this combined (broken) regression line. You should get 8. The combined regression line actually overpredicts performance on the criterion for Group A and underpredicts it for Group B. According to this example, the use of a single regression line produces discrimination in favor of Group A and against Group B.

FIGURE 19.9

Regression lines with equal slopes but different intercepts.

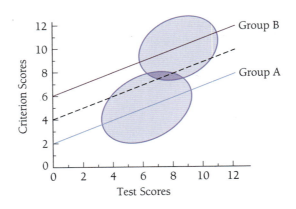

This situation seems to fit the use of the SAT (Cucina, Peyton, Su, & Byle, 2016). Each of these studies showed that the relationship between college performance and SAT scores was best described by two separate regression equations. The commonly used combined regression equation overpredicts how well minority students will do in college and underpredicts the performance of majority group students (Kobrin, Patterson, Shaw, Mattern, & Barbuti, 2008). In other words, it appears that the SAT used with a single regression line yields biased predictions in favor of minority groups and against majority groups.

The equal slopes of the lines in Figure 19.9 suggest equal predictive evidence for validity. Most standardized intelligence, aptitude, and achievement tests in fact do confirm the relationships shown in the figure (Kobrin et al., 2008). Thus, there is little evidence that tests such as the SAT predict college performance differently for different groups or that IQ tests have different correlations with achievement tests for African American, white, or Latino and Latina children. This finding has been reported for the SAT (Beard & Marini, 2015), preschool tests (Reynolds, 1980), and IQ tests such as the WISC-R (Sattler, 2014). Whether separate or combined regression lines are used depends on different definitions of bias. (We shall return to this issue later in the chapter. As you will see, the interpretation of tests for assessing different groups can be strongly influenced by personal and moral convictions.) The situation shown in Figure 19.9 is independent of differences in mean scores, which are equal to the differences between the two regression lines (Kobrin et al., 2008).

Some studies have shown that these problems are not specific to U.S. culture. Psychometric aptitude tests are currently used by all Israeli universities. A wide variety of cultural and ethnic groups makes up Israeli society. As in the United States, there is interest in determining whether or not aptitude tests include biases against specific ethnic or cultural groups. In a study of 1538 Israeli college candidates of varying ethnic backgrounds, the predictive test-criterion relationship was the same across groups in spite of mean differences among the groups (Zeidner, 1987).

A third situation outlined by Cleary et al. (1975) is shown in Figure 19.10. The two regression lines are not parallel; the coefficient of one group differs from that of the other. In the situation presented in Figure 19.10, each group was best represented by its own regression line. Using a common regression line causes error in predicting the scores for each group. However, the situation depicted in Figure 19.10 is not hopeless, and indeed some psychologists feel that this situation is useful because it may help increase the accuracy of predictions (Cleary, 1968). In Figure 19.10, however, the test is differentially valid for the two groups, meaning that the test has an entirely different meaning for each group. Although empirical studies have rarely

FIGURE 19.10

Regression lines with different slopes suggest that a test has different meanings for different groups. This is the most clear-cut example of test bias.

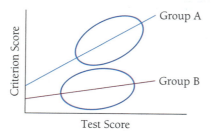

turned up such a case, there are some known examples of differential slopes (Mercer, 1979). For example, a test that is designed to predict performance in a mechanical training program would show differential validity if it predicted performance much better for men than for women. Women who have traditionally had less previous experience with mechanical concepts than men may score more poorly. However, when taking the course, many women would easily acquire this information and perform well. Thus, the test would provide relatively little information about how these women would perform in the program, but it would tend to predict how men would perform. Focused Example 19.4 illustrates the application of both content- and criterion-related evidence of validity.

19.4 FOCUSED EXAMPLE

The Bell Curve: 25 Years Later

In 1994, Richard Herrnstein, a noted Harvard psychologist, and Charles Murray, a professional writer, published a controversial book titled *The Bell Curve: Intelligence and Class Structure in American Life*. The controversial book provoked an immediate reaction from the mass media and serious scholars alike. Some praised the book as important scholarship, but many regarded it as "scientific racism." In contrast to the many testing professionals who question the value of intelligence tests, Herrnstein and Murray argued that, indeed, intelligence tests are the primary correlates of success in American life. Consistent with Spearman, they argued that the *g* factor is essential to a variety of different skills and abilities.

The Bell Curve used data from the National Longitudinal Study of Youth, which had begun in 1979. The study has involved a representative sample of 12,686 youths who were between 14 and 21 years old in 1979 and who have been restudied each year. The book used data collected through 1990. For the analysis, testers used the Armed Services Vocational Aptitude Battery (ASVAB). Various analyses showed that IQ scores are related to a wide variety of indexes of success in life ranging from completion of a college degree through the attainment of substantial income. Some researchers argued that IQ tests predict who will fill the important leadership roles in society. According to the book, those with low IQs are likely to become involved in crime and delinquency, to end up on welfare, and to have illegitimate children.

Herrnstein and Murray were unusually optimistic about the relationship between job performance and IQ. From their data, they suggested that the correlation is .53 between IQ and job-performance rating, .22 between education and job performance, and .11 between college grades and performance. They even argued that the Supreme Court case of *Griggs v. Duke Power Company* (see Chapter 20), which restricted the use of IQ testing for job selection, has cost U.S. companies billions of dollars because it prevented the most-qualified individuals from being selected for various jobs. They attributed most social problems—such as school dropout rates, unemployment, and work-related injury and crime—to low intelligence. Furthermore, they suggested that the differences in economic attainment for various ethnic groups probably reflect differences in IQ. They concluded by arguing that the United States must face up to differences in intelligence. Finally, they suggested that we must recognize that not all people are created equal and that traditional approaches to these problems will simply not work.

Upon publication, *The Bell Curve* was robustly attacked for a variety of reasons. First, many complained about its arrogant writing style. For example, Herrnstein and Murray described themselves as classicists who favor the traditional view of *g* intelligence. They discussed alternative views of intelligence proposed by "revisionists" and "radicals." They then wrote off these theories as approaches that scholars do not take seriously, even though scholars do seriously

(continues)

consider them. Critics of the book's statistical methods focused on the simplified analyses. For example, many of the correlations between IQ and outcome depend highly on those in the lowest decimal of intelligence. Indeed, it may be that those with low IQs under 80 may have difficulty in various aspects of their lives. However, removing the bottom decile from the analyses would significantly reduce the relationship between IQ and several of the outcome variables.

Others have attacked *The Bell Curve* for not using measures of intelligence but measures of developed ability as captured by the ASVAB. Leman (1995) claimed that people from higher social classes would be expected to do better on the ASVAB because the test better reflects their culture. Finally, there is concern that comparisons on the basis of race have little meaning because race is not clearly defined. Gould (1996) argued persuasively that it is inappropriate to compare racial groups in countries such as the United States. In the biological sciences, races are considered to be biological subspecies defined by well-identified genetic markers. Today, there are few individuals who represent biologically distinct subgroups. To some extent, all human races are intermingled; we are all genetically linked. We tend to use racial terms in a social rather than a biological sense (Suzuki & Valencia, 1997).

Now, nearly 20 years after the publication of the *Bell Curve*, new evidence is forcing us to rethink many of the basic foundations of the genetic determinism argument. We now know that genes are affected by environment and that the structure of the brain itself is a function of early experiences.

The science of early childhood development has progressed rapidly in the last few decades (Shonkoff, 2011; Shonkoff et al., 2012). In particular, there has been an explosion of research on the development of the brain and the nervous system. Evidence now suggests that from the time of conception through the earliest stages of life, the brain is highly "plastic," suggesting that it is very adaptable to environmental stimulation (Shonkoff & Levitt, 2010). Children are born with many more synapses or connections between neurons than they will ever use. We are all born with the neurological capacity to learn virtually any language in the world. However, exposure to particular languages shapes the

neurological pathways that will be developed. Many of these experiences occur early in life. Pathways that are not used eventually are pruned, suggesting that the unused neural pathways may go away. Early life experiences shape the development of the functioning brain. Abusive or neglectful care might provide a dangerous environment for the developing brain (Garner et al., 2012). However, brains develop to the environments they are exposed to. Children exposed to language and music early in life may develop brains that have highly developed processing pathways for these fields. Children who grow up in environments that require physical adaptation to survive might develop neural pathways that are best able to cope with these threatening experiences. Each brain becomes highly adapted to the situations it faces, but not all brains develop in the same way.

These insights on human brain development, which were first described in a National Academy of Sciences report titled "From Neurons to Neighborhoods: A Science of Early Child Development" [Shonkoff & Phillips, National Research Council (U.S.), Board on Children Youth and Families, and Institute of Medicine (U.S.), 2000]. The report became one of the most important challenges to the idea that nature and nurture are independent forces in human development. Biology, to a large extent, can be determined by environmental influences. The most recent analysis shows limited evidence from modern gene sequencing studies that educational outcomes are well predicted from specific genes and even less evidence that we are becoming genetically segmented (Conley & Domingue, 2016).

In the era when *The Bell Curve* was written, there was a clear distinction between biological and environmental determinants of behavior. Now, there is strong evidence that environment influences biology. Following the completion of the human genome project, there was a seismic shift in thinking about the nature versus nurture. Basic biological scientists believed that inherited traits were coded within the DNA. Thus, whatever information is transmitted by the genetic code determines characteristics such as growth, behaviors, and intelligence. However, as basic scientists learned more about the process of inheritance, they came to realize that environmental circumstances can cause errors that alter the DNA sequence. Environmental experiences can cause large sequences of the genome to be removed or to be duplicated. This might be analogous to having pages of a book ripped out or having the same pages appear multiple times. In some cases, only a single protein sequence is modified and in other cases larger components might be affected. In addition, epigenetic modifications can affect the way the genetic code is read. This might be analogous to changes in punctuation that affect our interpretation of written language. Epigenetic modifications determine whether genes are turned off or turned on. For example, a person might have the genetic disposition for a certain biological or behavioral trait, but whether or not that trait is observed depends on whether the gene is expressed. Epigenetic phenomena determine whether the gene is expressed or not. Factors that affect epigenetic modification include stress, environmental toxins, and learning (Sweatt, 2015). The development of the new science of epigenetics has dramatically changed our thinking about nature versus nurture. In particular, we now know that nature and nurture are not independent of one another. In fact, the environment (nurture) can affect genetic expression (nature).

Other Approaches to Testing Minority Group Members

To many U.S. psychologists, the defense of psychological tests has not been totally satisfactory. Although some consider the defense of the tests strong enough, others emphasize that developers must try to find selection procedures that will end all discriminatory practices and protect the interests of minority group members. Those who do not think that the tests are fair suggest one of two alternatives: outlaw the use of psychological tests for minority students (Williams, 1974) or develop psychological assessment strategies that suit minority children. Advocates of the first alternative have launched a legal battle to restrict the use of tests. (This battle is discussed in detail in Chapter 20.) In this section, we review various approaches to the second alternative. In particular, we look at three different assessment approaches: the Chitling Test, the Black Intelligence Test of Cultural Homogeneity (BITCH), and the System of Multicultural Pluralistic Assessment (SOMPA). Though each approach differs, they are all based on one common assumption: Minority children have not had the opportunity to learn how to answer items on tests that reflect traditional, white, middle-class values.

Ignorance Versus Stupidity

In a California trial about the use of testing in public schools, *Larry P. v. Wilson Riles*, the judge made an abrasive but insightful comment. Both sides in the case agreed that minority children perform more poorly than white children on standardized tests. The main issue debated was the meaning of the scores. One side argued that the scores reflect the underlying trait of intelligence. In other words, the tests allegedly measure how smart a child is. Witnesses for the other side suggested that the tests measure only whether the child has learned the appropriate responses needed to perform well on the test. This position claims that the tests do not measure how smart the child is but only whether the child has been exposed to the information on the test. Studies do show that it is possible to teach people to perform better on IQ tests (Cottrell et al., 2015). After hearing the testimony for the different points of view, the judge commented that the issue was really one of ignorance versus stupidity. Although this comment appears insensitive and racist, it deserves reflection. There are two potential explanations for why some children do more poorly on standardized tests than do other children. One explanation is that they are less intelligent—the "stupidity" explanation. The other is that some children do more poorly because they are ignorant of the right responses for a particular test. If ignorance is the explanation, then differences in IQ scores are of less concern because they can be changed. The stupidity explanation is more damning because it implies that the lower test scores obtained by some students are a product of some deficit that cannot be changed.

Ignorance implies that differences can be abolished. It also implies that IQ test performance is relative to content for whites as well as for minorities. Just as some minority children have not learned how to answer items that might predict success in white, middle-class culture, so many white, middle-class children have not learned how to succeed in the inner city. This proposition is illustrated by several tests that show minority children outperform majority children.

Originally named the Dove Counterbalance General Intelligence Test, the Chitling Test was developed to demonstrate that there is a body of information about which the white middle class is ignorant (Dove, 1968). A major aim in developing this was to show that African Americans and whites are just not talking the same language. And the results confirmed this belief. African American children obtained significantly higher scores. However, there was no clear evidence that scores on the Chitling Test predicted academic success or even success in the children's home environment.

Other tests were built on the assumption that the use of intelligence tests is a subtle and dangerous form of racism because the tests are purportedly supported by scientific validity studies (Garcia, 1981). R. L. Williams (1974) has labeled this phenomenon *scientific racism*. He views IQ and standardized achievement tests as "nothing but updated versions of the old signs down South that read 'For Whites Only'" (1974, p. 34). Of particular interest to Williams and his colleagues is the assessment of the ability to survive in the African American community. They believe that the assessment of survival potential with a survival quotient (SQ) is more important than assessment of IQ, which indicates only the likelihood of succeeding in the white community. As a beginning, Williams developed The Black Intelligence Test of Cultural Homogeneity (BITCH), which asks respondents to define 100 vocabulary words relevant to African American culture. The words came from the *Afro-American Slang Dictionary* and from Williams's personal experience interacting with African Americans. African American people obtain higher scores than do their white counterparts on the BITCH. When Williams administered the BITCH to 100 16- to 18-year-olds from each group, the average score for African American subjects was 87.07 (out of 100). The mean score for the whites was significantly lower (51.07). Williams argues that traditional IQ and achievement tests are nothing more than culture-specific tests that assess how much white children know about white culture. The BITCH is also a culture-specific test, but one on which African American subjects outperform whites.

However, little convincing validity data on the BITCH are available. Although the test manual does report some studies, the samples are small and do not represent any clearly defined population (Cronbach, 1978).

Another challenge to traditional beliefs about testing was The System of Multicultural Pluralistic Assessment (SOMPA) (Mercer, 1979) that was adopted by several states in the 1980s.

Mercer, who developed the SOMPA, asserted that beliefs about what is fair and what knowledge exists are related to the social structure. One important philosophical assumption underlies the development of the SOMPA—that all cultural groups have the same average potential. Any differences among cultural groups are assumed to be caused by differences in access to cultural experiences. Those who do not perform well on the tests are not well informed about the criteria for success usually set forth by the dominant group. Within groups that have had the same cultural experiences, however, not all individuals are expected to be the same, and assessment of these differences is a better measure of ability than is assessment of differences among cultural groups.

The basic point of divergence between the SOMPA and earlier approaches to assessment was that the SOMPA attempts to integrate three different approaches to assessment: medical, social, and pluralistic.

The SOMPA attempts to assess children relative to each of these models. The medical portion of the SOMPA includes physical measures such as tests of vision, hearing, and motor functioning. The social-system portion resembles most assessment procedures in that the entire WISC-R is given and evaluated according to the regular criteria. Finally, the pluralistic portion evaluates WISC-R scores against those for groups that have similar social and cultural backgrounds. In other words, the WISC-R scores are adjusted for socioeconomic background. These adjusted scores are known as **estimated learning potentials (ELPs)**. The main dispute between Mercer and her many critics centered on the validity of the SOMPA. The correlation between ELPs and school achievement is approximately .40, whereas the correlation between the WISC-R and school achievement is nearly .60 (Oakland, 1979). Thus, ELPs are a poorer predictor of school success than are WISC-R scores.

Over the years since its introduction, the use of the SOMPA has decreased significantly. Although it is still discussed in articles about multicultural assessment (Hudson & Casey, 2016), use of the SOMPA has become uncommon.

Suggestions for Solutions

Focusing on problems associated with ethnic differences in test scores, we have presented many different arguments from various perspectives. In the following pages, we offer some solutions; however, we must warn you that these solutions depend on different social and political beliefs about the definition of bias.

Ethical Concerns and the Definition of Test Bias

It is difficult to define *test bias*; different authors present various views (Babad, 2016; Cabieses et al., 2016; Chu et al., 2016; Cottrell et al., 2015; Hudson & Casey, 2016;

Kamenetz, 2015; Letukas, 2015; Walton, Spencer, & Erman, 2013). These definitions represent commitments to ethical viewpoints about the way one should treat certain groups. Many years ago, Hunter and Schmidt (1976) identified three ethical positions that set the tone for much of the debate: unqualified individualism, the use of quotas, and qualified individualism. These positions focus on the use of tests to select people either for jobs or for training programs (including college).

Supporters of *unqualified individualism* would use tests to select the most qualified individuals they could find (Kuncel & Hezlett, 2007). In this case, users of tests would remain indifferent to the race or gender of applicants. The goal would be to predict those who would perform best on the job or in school. According to this viewpoint, a test is fair if it finds the best candidates for the job or for admission to school. If race or gender was a valid predictor of performance over and above the information in the test, then the unqualified individualist would see nothing wrong with considering this information in the selection process.

In a quite different ethical approach to selection, one uses *quotas*, which explicitly recognize race and gender differences. If the population of a state is 20% African American, then supporters of a quota system might argue that 20% of the new medical students in the state-supported medical school should also be African American. Selection procedures are regarded as biased if the actual percentage of applicants admitted differs from the percentage in the population; each group should demonstrate a fair share of the representation (Gordon & Terrell, 1981). This fair-share process places less emphasis than does testing on how well people in the different groups will do once selected (Markham, 2011).

The final moral position considered by Hunter and Schmidt might be viewed as a compromise between unqualified individualism and a quota system. Like unqualified individualism, *qualified individualism* embraces the notion that one should select the best-qualified people. But unqualified individualists also take information about race, gender, and religion into consideration if it helps to predict performance on the criterion—that is, if not to do so results in underprediction of performance for one group and overprediction for another. Qualified individualists, however, recognize that although failing to include group characteristics (race, gender, and religion) may lead to differential accuracy in prediction, this differential prediction may counteract known effects of discrimination. It may, for example, lead to underprediction of performance for the majority group and overprediction for the minority group. The qualified individualist may choose not to include information about personal characteristics in selection because ignoring this information may serve the interests of minority group members. Many people have argued that increased minority hiring will result in lower average job performance because some applicants with lower test scores will be hired. However, systematic study of this issue has not always supported these arguments. In fact, universities and business typically benefit from increasing the diversity of their workforce. Further, the broader goals of organizations are likely to benefit from greater diversity (Hamdani & Buckley, 2011).

One can relate each of these ethical positions to a particular statistical definition of test bias. Table 19.1 shows several different models of test bias, based on different definitions of fairness. All these models are based on regression lines. These models also apply to tests used for selection purposes, such as job placement and college, or for advanced degree programs.

TABLE 19.1 Different Models of Test Fairness

Model	Use of regression	Rationale	Effect on minority selection	Effect on average criterion performance
Regression	Separate regression lines are used for different groups. Those with predicted criterion scores are selected.	This is fair because those with the highest estimated level of success are selected.	Few minority group members selected	Good performance on criteria
Constant ratio	Points equal to approximately half of the average difference between the groups are added to the test scores of the group with the lower score. Then a single regression line is used, and those with the highest predicted scores are selected.	This is fair because it best reflects the potential of the lower-scoring group.	Some increase in the number of minority group members selected	Somewhat lower
Cole/ Darlington	Separate regression equations are used for each group, and points are added to the scores of those from the lower group to ensure that those with the same criterion score have the same predictor score.	This is fair because it selects more potentially successful people from the lower group.	Larger increase in the number of minority group members selected	Lower
Quota	The proportion of people to be selected from each group is predetermined. Separate regression equations are used to select those from each group who are expected to perform highest on the criterion.	This is fair because members of different subgroups are selected based on their proportions in the community.	Best representation of minority groups	About the same as for the Cole/Darlington model

Based on Dunnette and Borman (1979).

The regression model described in this table represents unqualified individualism. The result of this approach is that a large number of majority group members may be selected. This approach maintains that an employer or a school should be absolutely color- and gender-blind. The reason for considering ethnicity or gender is to improve the prediction of future performance. This approach has been favored by business because it ensures the highest employee productivity.

At the other extreme is the quota system. To achieve fair-share representation, separate selection procedures are developed. One procedure, for example, is used to select the best available African American applicants, and another to select the best available non-African American applicants. If a community has 42% African American residents, then the first procedure would be used to select 42% of the employees, the other procedure to select the other 58%.

The quota system may lead to greater rates of failure among some groups. Suppose that a test devised to select telephone operators did indeed predict who would succeed on the job, but it selected 70% women and 30% men. The quota system would encourage the use of separate cutoff scores so that the proportion of men selected would approach 50%. But because the women scored higher on the average, they would perform better on the job, resulting in a higher rate of failure among the men. Thus, although quota systems often increase the selection of underrepresented groups, they also make it likely that the underrepresented groups will experience failure.

Table 19.1 shows two other models, which represent compromises between the quota and the unqualified individualism points of view. Each of these cases reflects an attempt to select the most qualified people, yet there is some adjustment for minority-group members. When people from two different groups have the same test score, these procedures give a slight edge to those from the lower group and put those from the higher group at a slight disadvantage.

Although these approaches have been attacked for faulty logic (Hunter & Schmidt, 1976, 1978), plausible defenses have been offered. These procedures increase the number of people selected from underrepresented groups. However, these procedures also reduce the average performance score on the criterion. More recently, some methods have been proposed to address the quandary between maximizing performance on the criterion and increasing opportunity of underrepresented groups. As noted above, emphasizing performance on the criterion may result in adverse selection for some groups (unqualified individualism). However, there may be reasonable tradeoffs between the philosophical positions. One method attempts to find the best decision when there are competing goals, such as criterion performance and diversity in the workforce. A decision is considered *Pareto optimal* when it balances competing goals, in this case between criterion performance and ethnic or racial balance. The term *Pareto* derives from the work of the 19th-century Italian economist and philosopher Vilfredo Pareto. In the ideal "Pareto improvement, at least one person is made better off, without making anybody worse off." Using mathematical decision-modeling methods originally developed for engineering science, Pareto optimization methods attempt to balance these competing goals. The methods systematically balance selection and expected performance (De Corte, Lievens, & Sackett, 2007).

We cannot tell you which of these approaches is right and which is wrong. That decision depends on your own values and judgment about what is fair.

Despite the many problems and controversies surrounding psychological testing, surveys show that psychologists and educational specialists generally have positive attitudes about intelligence and aptitude tests. In one survey, 1020 experts agreed that there were some sociocultural biases in the tests (Snyderman & Rothman, 1987). However, these experts also generally agreed that the tests were valid for predictive purposes. Their main concerns involved the interpretation and application of test results by elementary and secondary schools. A more recent study surveyed opinions about psychological tests among experts from diverse communities, including different countries, regions, such as Finland, East Asia, sub-Saharan Africa, Southern Europe, the Arabian-Muslim world, Latin America, Israel, Jews in the West, Roma (gypsies), and Muslim immigrant. They found that education was the most commonly listed reason for international differences in cognitive ability. Genetics and cultural factors were identified as the second and third most commonly listed reasons, respectively. (Rindermann, Becker, & Coyle, 2016).

In general, industrial and organizational psychologists tend to feel that ability testing does not discriminate by race. In one study of 703 members of the Society of Industrial and Organizational Psychology, there appeared to be consensus that cognitive ability tests are valid and fair. However, the I/O psychologists also felt that tests provide an incomplete picture of human abilities and that job selection should consider tests as only one component.

Perhaps the most controversial defense of testing was presented in a 1994 book entitled *The Bell Curve*. This book is reviewed in Focused Example 19.4.

Thinking Differently: Finding New Interpretations of Data

Clearly, the observed differences between minority and nonminority groups on standardized tests pose a problem. Sometimes a problem stimulates us to think differently; in the words of the famous entrepreneur Henry Kaiser, "A problem is an opportunity in work clothes." The opportunity for test developers and users is to see test results in new ways.

For example, instead of indicating genetic variations or social handicaps, differences in test scores may reflect patterns of problem solving that characterize different subcultures. Knowing how groups differ in their approaches to problem solving can be helpful for two reasons. First, it can teach us important things about the relationship between socialization and problem-solving approaches. This information can guide the development of pluralistic educational programs (Pitts, 2012). Second, knowing more about the ways different groups approach problems can lead to the development of improved predictors of success for minority groups (Jeltova et al., 2011; Sternberg & Sternberg, 2016).

Developing Different Criteria

Criterion-related evidence for validity is the correlation between the test and the criterion. But what are the criteria used to validate the tests for assessing the potential of children? Most of these tests are simply valid predictors of how well children will do on other standardized tests. In other words, most standardized tests are evaluated against other standardized tests. However, the criterion simply may be the test dressed in different clothes. For example, one may evaluate an intelligence test to determine how well it predicts performance on a standardized achievement test. This means that the intelligence test really measures achievement, not native ability. Differences in scores on this test between minority and nonminority groups are therefore the result of the opportunity to learn rather than the ability to learn. This is recognized by the ETS, which requests special care in interpreting SAT and GRE scores for students who have had "an educational and cultural experience somewhat different from that of the traditional majority" (GRE Guide, 2016). These concerns forced the ETS to change their tests. Beginning in 2005, the test was modified to include more on writing skills and less on analogies and traditional word problems.

When Tests Harm

A basic principle in health care is, "first do no harm." Testing instruments are usually justified on the basis of potential to gain greater insight into individuals and to help them live better and more productive lives. In the best of all worlds, a psychological or educational test would identify strengths and weaknesses and inform a plan of action that might result in a happier, healthier person. Unfortunately, it doesn't always work this way. There is increasing evidence that test results are used to label people, to discriminate against them, and to interfere with personal growth.

Some of the best evidence that tests can harm comes from a program of research that was first initiated by Stanford psychologist Carol Dweck. Dweck and her colleagues identified mindset as a crucial ingredient of intellectual growth of children and young adults (Dweck, 2016). Mindsets are implicit theories about the determinants of success and failure. There is an important distinction between a fixed mindset and a growth mindset. A fixed mindset embraces the idea that skills are difficult, if not impossible, to change. For example, a young woman might be told that, "girls can't do math." Mathematics is challenging for almost everyone and a few failure experiences might reinforce the idea that, "I just can't do math." This fixed mindset or the belief that you can't succeed in a subject area might lead to avoidance of mathematics courses, a failure to persist in trying to learn math, and in many cases the selection of a different career course.

In contrast to the fixed mindset that emphasizes the belief that important intellectual and physical skills cannot be changed, a growth mindset underscores the malleability of human capabilities. In contrast to fixed mindsets that are promoted by parents or teachers who communicate that someone does not have the inherent skill, growth mindsets are engendered by parents and teachers who emphasize the importance of skill development. Growth mindsets underscore the belief that abilities can grow. For example, they might communicate that mathematics is difficult for everyone and those who succeed work hard at it. Mindsets are particularly important with regard to intelligence. Those with fixed intelligence mindset believe that intelligence cannot be changed, perhaps because it has a genetic root. A growth intelligence mindset is associated with the implicit theory that intelligence can be changed through experience.

Tests might feed into the development of fixed mindsets. Poor scores on large standardized tests might communicate that someone does not have the ability to succeed in a particular subject. We now have plenty of evidence that most human abilities are not fixed. With good instruction and determination, most people can succeed in mathematics and in many other academic subjects. A test result could provide an inappropriate signal to give up.

A convincing series of studies show that mindsets can be changed. With proper feedback about the malleability of human abilities, students persist longer and have higher achievement. One large-scale study showed that a relatively simple growth mindset intervention increased university enrollment among students from economically disadvantaged backgrounds. Further, the intervention that was evaluated in a systematic experiment raised first-year college grade point average and resulted in between a 31% and 40% reduction in the achievement gap between advantaged and disadvantaged students (Yeager, Walton, et al., 2016). In addition, these studies have gone to scale. The University of Texas, for example, has engaged in large-scale interventions to promote growth mindset for college freshmen. Early results are quite encouraging. Relatively simple manipulations resulted in greater student satisfaction and achievement (Yeager, Romero, et al., 2016).

Does It Matter? More Testing and Less Testing

We live in an interesting time. There has been an increase in testing and there has been a decrease in testing. The increase is reflected in the overuse of tests in schools. Recent evaluations suggested that the average child takes 112 mandated tests between pre-kindergarten and graduation from high school (Hart et al., 2015). In many countries that are achieving better educational outcomes, students complete standardized tests only three times prior to graduation from high school.

By 2015, the tide against excessive testing in the schools began to change. In the last year of his presidency, Barack Obama surprised many in the policy community when he argued that there was too much testing in the schools (see https://www.youtube.com/watch?v=zYZ4qtN6KVM). The president proclaimed, "learning is about so much more than just filling in the right bubble." He went on to say, "So we're going to work with states, school districts, teachers, and parents to make sure that we're not obsessing about testing." The announcement was a surprise because the Obama administration had promoted the use of standardized tests. Former Secretary of Education Arnold Duncan, following the No Child Left Behind momentum from the George W. Bush presidency, had initiated several programs that accelerated the use of these tests. Some of these programs were highly controversial. For example, accountability programs were created in which teachers were evaluated, and sometimes even fired, on the basis of improvements in standardized test scores. Most research methodologists agree that deciding whether or not to retain a teacher based on student test scores is a pretty bad idea. The difficulty is that the sample size of students in the classroom is typically much too small to gain a reliable estimate of teachers' performance. Nevertheless, school districts in several states have fired teachers when students do not perform well on standardized tests. Yet these policies had become politically sensitive. One Gallup poll showed that 63% of parents with children in school were against using test scores of students as part of the evaluation of their teachers.

The president's shift in policy was stimulated by an evaluation study conducted by the Council of the Great City Schools (Hart et al., 2015). The evaluation was conducted in 66 large school districts. Among the many problems identified in the report was a lack of standardization. Within the 66 districts that participated in the study, 401 different tests were administered during the 2014–2015 school year. The average student took about eight standardized tests per year, and the amount of time spent on testing was completely uncorrelated with performance in math or reading. There was no correlation between how much time was spent in testing and how well students performed in reading and math. Perhaps the biggest concern was the time that it took to take the tests. In 2015, students in the 66 largest school districts were spending 20 to 25 hours each school year taking standardized tests (Hart et al., 2015). The act of completing standardized tests was using more than 2% of classroom time (Hart et al., 2015).

In addition to the time actually spent in taking the test, it was estimated that a considerably larger number of hours were spent preparing the students to take the exams. This left less time for other forms of classroom instruction. The standardized tests that were the focus of the study were independent of the tests used by teachers to evaluate their students. In 71% of the districts participating in the study, students were required to take final exam or end-of-course tests in addition to the state-required tests. In 40% of the school districts in one national study, test results were not available until the next academic year. As a result, the test findings could not be used by the current teachers to adjust educational approach. In nearly half the districts, students also took career and technical education tests.

The word *test* itself raises some concerns. For example, as part of the evaluation, parents were asked if they agreed or strongly agreed with the statement "accountability for how well my child is educated is important, and it begins with accurate measurement of what he/she is learning in school." This high level of support drops very significantly if the word *accurate measurement* is substituted with *test*. Parents also reacted negatively to the words *harder* or *more rigorous* tests.

At the other end of the spectrum, there is growing evidence that testing is becoming irrelevant for some purposes. This seems particularly true in college admissions. A growing number of universities have made the SAT optional. By 2016, the rebellion against standardized tests had gained significant momentum. Colleges and universities began challenging the value of testing for making admissions decisions. According to the website "FairTest," more than 850 institutions are now test optional. This means that taking the SAT or ACT is no longer required of all applicants. In 2015 alone, 47 major institutions announced new test-optional policies. Institutions deciding they catch requiring tests included some of the most elite and selective universities in the country.

The decision to go test optional was supported by systematic research. William Hiss, a former dean of admissions at Bates College, published an evaluation involving 33 private and public universities that had adopted a test-optional policy. It had been assumed that those who got into college without test score evidence would be less likely to perform well or to graduate. But this is not what Hiss found. There were no difference in graduation rates between those who submitted test scores and those who did not. Further, cumulative GPA for those who submitted test scores (2.88) were not statistically distinguishable from GPAs of students who did not submit test scores (2.83). On the other hand, those who did not submit test scores were more likely to be first-generation college attenders from underrepresented ethnic and minority groups (Hiss & Franks, 2014). Going test optional may result in a more diversified student body without reducing academic preparedness.

Finally, suspicion about the testing industry remains. The Educational Testing service has vigorously defended it's practices. It even supports publications designed to debunk criticisms of the SAT (Letukas, 2015). Yet its public documents on understanding SAT scores never even mention the reliability and validity of the test (Board, 2016). You can find the validity report online, but it requires some poking around. And, the meaning of the report has been challenged. For example, the SAT developers assume that the relationship between a test score and performance on a criterion is constant. It has been reported that the correlation between the SAT Critical Reasoning test and first-year college GPA is 0.40. But, we must also ask if that relationship holds for subgroups. Is it 0.40 for men, and is the correlation different for men than it is for women? The correlation between test and criterion defines the criterion validity of the test. Is this validity equal for African American and for white students?

In the most recent version of *Standards for Educational and Psychological Testing* (Worrell & Roberson, 2016), the term *predictive bias* was coined to describe different patterns of association between test scores and criterion variables for different ethnic, racial, or study differences between male and female performance, and between performance of African American and white students and white and Hispanic students using hundreds of thousands of test-taker groups. Technically, predictive bias occurs when there are different slopes or intercepts for different groups.

One challenge in using tests to predict academic performance is in deciding how generalizable the relationship between tests and performance might be. The Educational Testing Service and a variety of different research investigators have assumed that the relationship between test scores and academic performance is the same for different groups and for different institutions. The older studies validated tests such as the SAT in a limited number of institutions. The early studies by Cleary (Cleary, 1968), which form the basis for contemporary policy (Worrell & Roberson, 2016), were based on only three colleges. Later investigations by Temp and others used only 13 institutions. More recently, larger-scale investigations have been conducted (Mattern, Patterson, & Wyatt, 2013). Most of these studies averaged results across institutions and concluded that the relationship between SAT scores and first-year college performance did not differ appreciably across institutions. However, recent and more detailed analyses challenge this assumption. These studies used over 300,000 test takers to compare the validity of the SAT for male versus female students, African American versus white students, and Hispanic versus white students. They observed that the relationship between test scores and first-year college performance varied substantially across institutions. Not all colleges and universities are the same. Further, the differences between groups in slopes of the relationship between SAT score and college performance also vary considerably. Using 348 samples from 176 different colleges and universities, many different relationships were observed. So, the question needs to be much more specifically focused. Institutions need to know how well the test performs for their particular admissions decisions (Aguinis, Culpepper, & Pierce, 2016; Beard & Marini, 2015).

If we do not accept standardized tests as a validity criterion for other tests, then how can we determine the meaning of the tests? A considerable debate concerns whether classroom grades should serve as this criterion. Supporters of the use of classroom grades claim that these grades are the only independent measure of how well the child is doing. It is no surprise, they maintain, that a correlation exists between IQ tests and scores on standardized achievement tests because both measure similar content. However, they argue that because they do not predict classroom grades for minority children, IQ tests are not valid for such youngsters. The support for this position comes from studies like one by R. D. Goldman and Hartig (1976). This study found scores on the WISC to be unrelated to teacher ratings of classroom performance for minority children. For the nonminority children, it found a significant relationship between IQ and teacher ratings. If the criterion becomes classroom grades rather than another standardized test, the IQ test appears valid for nonminority but not for minority children.

Supporters of the use of the tests give three reasons not to use grades as the criterion. First, teacher-assigned grades are unstandardized and open to subjective bias (Sattler, 2014). For example, teachers sometimes reward effort more than ability (Graham & Taylor, 2016; Weiner, 2011). Second, few available studies have used grades as the criterion. Third, the most frequently cited study (Goldman & Hartig, 1976) is open to other explanations. In this study, the teachers rated the classroom performance of nearly all of the minority children as poor. These low ratings resulted in little variance on the criterion measure. As we saw in Chapter 3, any variable for which there is no variability cannot correlate well with other variables.

The problem with criterion measures becomes even more apparent in relation to measures used with adults. For example, the Medical College Admissions Test (MCAT) predicts success in medical school. Yet, it does not predict who will be a successful doctor. Similarly, the LSAT predicts performance in law school, yet there is little evidence that it predicts who will be a good attorney. The professional school admission tests may thus be eliminating people who are potentially better doctors and lawyers than those who are admitted. Imagine, for example, that an Anglo and a Latina doctor, trained equally well in the science of medical care, both practice in a public hospital in a Latino neighborhood. The Latina doctor will more likely be effective because she understands the culture and the language of the patients and thus can better understand specific complaints and symptoms. The Anglo doctor may do a poorer job at diagnosing the problems. The MCAT would have done its job poorly by focusing on the short-term criterion of medical school grades. More work is needed to develop measures that are good predictors of the long-range goal of clinical success (Altmaier, Smith, O'Halloran, & Franken, 1992). See Focused Example 19.5, which discusses controversies relevant to law school admission.

A related problem is that many tests are not normed for different cultural groups. For example, cross-cultural norms are not available for most neuropsychological tests (Nell, 2000).

Changing the Social Environment

It is not hard to determine that majority and minority children grow up in different social environments. You can learn this by reading any sociology textbook or by getting in your car and driving around awhile (Soares, 2015). Given this disparity in environment, it is not surprising that tests favor the majority (Chu et al., 2016). Many critics of tests, though, seem to hold the tests responsible for inequality of opportunity (Mukherjee, 2016).

Another view claims that test scores accurately reflect the effects of social and economic inequality (Cottrell et al., 2015). We know, for instance, that family income is one of the best predictors of performance on standardized tests. Figure 19.6 (see page 521), shows the relationship between family income and performance on the SAT-V and SAT-M components. The graph summarizes the performance of all students who completed the test in 2015.

19.5 FOCUSED EXAMPLE

Does Affirmative Action Cause African American Students to Fail the Bar Exam?

In addition to the psychology and education fields, the issue of test bias can also be found in the legal literature. One controversy was spearheaded by Richard Sander, a professor at the UCLA School of Law, who developed a "mismatch" hypothesis. Sander contends that affirmative action at U.S. law schools has been responsible for the high rate of failure of the California Bar Exam. Passing the bar exam is required for the practice of law. Sander published "A Systematic Analysis of Affirmative Action in American Law Schools" (2004). In this analysis, he reported that African American students are more than two and a half times more likely than white students not to graduate from law school and four times more likely to fail the bar exam on their first attempt. Further, they are six times more likely to fail the bar exam after multiple attempts. He argued that this gap in performance is explained by overall lower average scores on the LSAT and lower undergraduate grade point averages for African American students who are admitted to law school. This same argument has been applied to other areas of college performance in challenging majors (Luppino & Sander, 2015).

Sander's position was not well received by other legal scholars. They contend that his analysis did not offer a fair comparison. In particular, they produced evidence showing that African Americans and white law students do not enter law school with equal backgrounds. For the data in Sander's analysis, African American students did not have the same exposure to the highest quality undergraduate education.

When African American and white students are matched by quality of their undergraduate training experience, differences in passing the bar exam go away (Ho, 2005). Other research has also challenged the idea that minority students who are given a boost through affirmative action programs fail to compete academically. One large study found that students who entered the university through special admissions programs did not earn lower grades or leave school earlier than other students admitted to the same campuses (Massey & Mooney, 2007). Nevertheless, Sandler provided a brief on his analysis and it became an important focus of attention in the 2016 U.S. Supreme Court case of *Fisher v. the University of Texas*. That case will be discussed in more detail in Chapter 20.

To understand these arguments, one must consider the purpose of testing. In educational settings, tests such as the SAT and the GRE or even IQ tests are usually considered to be tests of aptitude: They measure some inborn trait that is unlikely to change with environment. But most experts now agree that tests measure not just inborn potential but also the effects of cumulative experience. The University of California decided in 2001 to drop the aptitude-focused SAT in favor of the SATI, which is more clearly an achievement test. The impact of this decision is discussed in Focused Example 19.6. Verbal and numerical abilities are acquired through experience, so with proper nurturing, a student can change his or her score. Thus, low test scores should not be viewed as insurmountable problems; they can improve.

This chapter summarizes some studies identifying differences between minority and nonminority students in test performance. Although tests may have contributed to this problem, we think the problem is much deeper. Many minority students do well on the tests, which accurately predict that these students will do well on the criterion. An African American student and a white student who both achieve a score of 1100 on the SAT are predicted to do equally well in college, and studies

19.6 FOCUSED EXAMPLE

Consequences of the University of California Decision to Drop the SAT

In Chapter 5 (Focused Example 5.4, page 144), we discussed the University of California's decision to reject the SAT. The University of California decision underscores many of the issues that challenge testing today. For example, the decision raised the important distinction between aptitude and achievement tests. When Carl Brigham from Princeton University stimulated the earliest work on the SAT, his intention was to develop an IQ-like test. Brigham and other early leaders eventually turned against the idea that aptitude tests were precise enough to select college students. Later in his life, Alfred Binet rejected the idea that IQ tests could be used to provide reliable distinctions between individuals at the higher end of the IQ continuum. The SAT has always been considered an aptitude test, whereas the SATI was designed as an achievement test. As we reported in Chapter 5, a large study of 78,000 University of California freshmen demonstrated that the SATI was a better predictor of college grades than the SAT. In addition, statistically controlling for socioeconomic background did not affect the predicted value of the SATI but had a significant effect on the predictive value of the SAT. Once the SATI and high-school grades are in a statistical equation, adding the SAT contributes essentially no new information. Thus, the achievement-oriented SATI was less influenced by social background than the aptitude-focused SAT.

The decision by the University of California to drop the SAT was interpreted by many people as a rejection of college admissions testing. In fact, the University of California has retained its policy of requiring the SATI. Furthermore, the decision stimulated the College Board to rethink the content of the SAT. In particular, the University of California decision emphasized the need for tests to include both a writing sample and higher levels of mathematics. The current SAT has been modified to reflect these concerns.

It took little time for the decision to have a significant impact. The University of California decision was announced in 2001. One year later, the College Board acknowledged that it would create a new SAT that included writing samples and higher-level mathematics. Use of the new test began in 2006. In response to the new SAT, high schools began revising their curricula to include more math and more essay writing experiences for college-bound students. Framers of the test can help improve curricula and the quality of public education (Atkinson, 2004).

show that indeed they do perform at about the same level. However, the test is a relatively weak predictor for both white and African American studies because the tests have limitations in predicting who will be successful.

There is little question that wealthy students have greater access to programs that might enhance their test scores. Although the value of special test preparation courses has been debated, it appears that coaching does provide some benefit and that less access to test preparation may explain some of the difference between groups in test performance (Aaronson et al., 2011; Letukas, 2015). However, blaming the tests for observed differences between groups may be a convenient way to avoid a much larger problem. No one has suggested that the tuberculin test is unfair because it demonstrates that poor people have the disease more often than wealthy people. Public health officials have correctly concluded that some people live in environments that predispose them to the disease. Along the same lines, getting rid of scales that identify overweight children will not cure obesity (Flaugher, 1978). Although measuring intelligence may not be the same as testing for tuberculosis or measuring weight, the analogy may be worth considering.

If unequal access to adequate education and to stimulating experiences results in differences in test scores, it would be more useful to change the social environment than to bicker continuously about the tests. The tests may merely be the bearers of bad news. By documenting the problem's severity, the tests may be telling us that overcoming this problem will be expensive, difficult, and time-consuming. Blaming the tests for a problem that they did not cause seems to be shortsighted and nonproductive (Shenk, 2011a). Focused Example 19.7 describes how early environmental intervention can make an important difference.

19.7 FOCUSED EXAMPLE

The Value of Prekindergarten Intervention

One of the most compelling arguments for investment in early childhood education has been advanced by James Heckman, a Nobel Prize-winning economist from the University of Chicago. Heckman argues that poor literacy skills are responsible for many major social problems, including crime, teenage pregnancy, and poor health (Heckman, 2012). He also posits that the measurement of cognitive abilities through IQ tests misses some of the most important contributors to success, including socioemotional skills, physical and mental health, motivation, and self-confidence (Conti & Heckman, 2010).

Heckman believes that early intervention to improve socioemotional abilities is valuable and that it is cost effective. His work suggests that early stimulation, which may be crucial for emotional and cognitive development, is more difficult for nontraditional families, where parents have less time to spend with their children. However, very early intervention may be an appropriate remedy for some of these problems. One well-known study is the Perry Preschool Program, which was designed to enrich the lives of low-income African American children whose IQs were estimated to be below 85 at age 3. The program provided 2.5 hours a day of interaction 5 days a week for a period of approximately 2 years during the academic school year (October to May). It also involved home visits. When the children were followed, those in the treatment group improved IQ scores by nearly 15 points in comparison to only about 4 points in a control group. However, by age 10 the scores had come back together. When the children were followed into early adulthood, an economic analysis showed that those who had participated in the preschool program were more likely to be gainfully employed and to have avoided other legal difficulties. The economists estimated that the rate of return for investment in the preschool program was about 7% to 10% per year, which was better rate of return on investment than investing in the stock market (Heckman, Moon, Pinto, Savelyev, & Yavitz, 2010). Other programs, such as the Abecedarian program, have shown improvements in IQ that last over an extended period of time (Heckman & Lafontaine, 2010).

Overall, the Heckman study suggests that early significant investments in skill development pay dividends in terms of long-term changes in IQ, job skill, and participation in society. Further, Heckman and his associates argue that the return on investment for these early interventions avoids later costs associated with public assistance programs and criminal corrections. The investment in early education produces dividends at a rate that exceeds other conservative investments. Linking to the work on brain development, the argument suggests that intervention should occur early in life, prior to entrance into preschool.

Summary

In this chapter, we examined two sides of the issue of test bias. Table 19.2 offers a summary of some of the arguments for and against the use of tests. As the table shows, there are strong differences of opinion about the value of intelligence and aptitude tests for minority group members. As a result of the challenge to traditional tests, approaches such as the Chitling Test, the BITCH, and the SOMPA have been developed. All of these approaches are based on the assumption that social groups do not differ in their average potential. These approaches have been challenged because they do not have the same sort of validity evidence that traditional tests have.

Part of the debate about test bias results from different moral views about what is fair. Some have argued that a testing and selection program is fair if it selects the best-suited people, regardless of their social group. This approach is called *unqualified individualism*. It may lead to overrepresentation of one group. Another moral position supports *quotas*, or the selection of members from different racial and ethnic groups according to their proportions in the general population. A third

TABLE 19.2   For and Against the Use of Tests

Against	For
The Stanford-Binet was standardized on only 1000 children and 400 adults. None of these people were African American (Guthrie, 1976).	Although not originally standardized on minority group members, modern tests are validated using representative samples from most major ethnic and minority groups. The tests appear to have the same validity for minority students as they do for majority students. Therefore, neglecting to include minorities in the original validation studies was not relevant (Fiscella et al., 2011; Sattler, 2014).
The use of intelligence tests can have a damaging social impact. For example, the IQ scores of ethnic groups were used to limit immigration of certain groups into the United States during the early years of the 20th century (Mukherjee, 2016).	Examination of the *Congressional Record* covering the debates about the 1924 Immigration Act failed to uncover discussion of intelligence test data or claims that the mean IQ of Americans would decline if the immigration of certain groups was allowed (DuBois, 1972).
If a teacher just thinks some children have higher IQs, the actual test scores of those children will improve (Rosenthal & Rubie-Davies, 2015).	Studies that document the effects of self-fulfilling prophecies and teacher expectations overinterpreted their original data, contained some results that are statistically impossible, and cannot be depended on (Elashoff & Snow, 1971; Snow, 1969; Thorndike, 1968).
Minority children can only be damaged by the continued use of psychological tests (Spencer et al., 2016).	Psychological tests can be used to identify the most capable members of each group. Without the tests, people will be selected on the basis of personal judgment, which might be more racist than the tests (Ones, Chockalingam, & Schmidt, 1995).
The validity of IQ tests was documented using other standardized tests as the criterion rather than measures of classroom performance (Mercer, 1988).	The objective tests are better validity criteria than classroom performance, which is more subjective. Teachers may grade on the basis of effort rather than ability (Weiner, 2011).

moral position, *qualified individualism*, is a compromise between the other two. New methods have been introduced to balance the objectives of these competing belief systems. For example, the methods attempt to address the goals of criterion performance and racial and ethnic diversity.

Although test bias will surely remain an area of considerable controversy, some positive potential solutions have come to light. For example, differences in test scores may reflect patterns of problem solving that characterize different subcultures. Also, one might evaluate tests against outcome criteria relevant to minority groups.

A current controversy rages on about the nature of differences in test performance (Letukas, 2015; Soares, 2015). One group believes the differences are biological in origin (Herrnstein, 1982; Rushton, 1991; Vandenburg & Vogler, 1985), while another believes the differences result from the influence of social environment (Chu et al., 2016; Cottrell et al., 2015). Some people believe is the best evidence for supports and interaction between genetic and environmental explanations (Ansari, 2011; Simos, Breznitz, & Berninger, 2011). Further, we now have evidence that gene expression is affected by environments. The social environment explanation (Gould, 1981) seems to be the most popular. If people accept this view, then differences in test performance might suggest that people need to escalate their efforts to wipe out inequality. If one endorses the genetic position, then one acknowledges that little can be done to equalize performance among different groups.

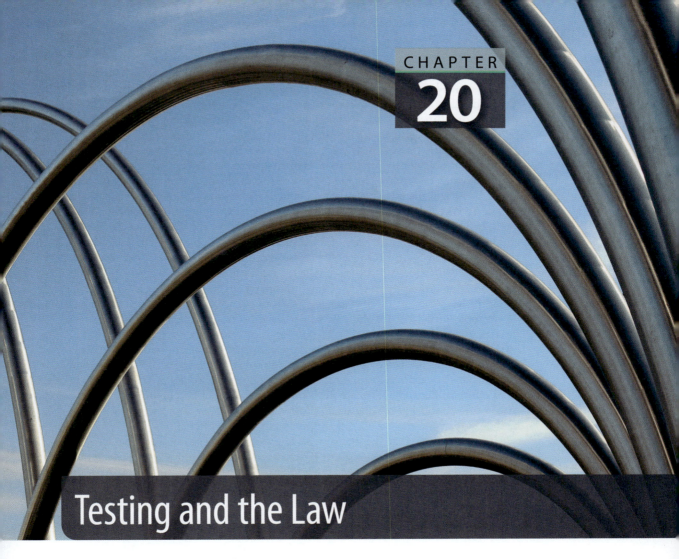

Testing and the Law

LEARNING OBJECTIVES

When you have completed this chapter, you should be able to:

► Describe the basis on which the federal government can regulate the use of psychological tests

► Describe the EEOC guidelines and their importance

► Describe how the New York Truth in Testing Law affects the use of psychological tests

► Discuss the impact of PL 94-142

► Discuss the importance of *Hobson v. Hansen*

► Describe the issue in *Diana v. State Board of Education* and how it differs from the major issue in *Larry P. v. Wilson Riles*

► Compare and contrast the decisions in *Larry P. v. Wilson Riles* and *Parents in Action on Special Education v. Hannon*

► Discuss the importance of *Parents v. Seattle*

► Describe how the courts are involved in the use of personnel tests

► Discuss the events that led to the Civil Rights Act of 1991

► Review the issues relevant to the No Child Left Behind Act

► Explain why *Ricci v. DeStefano* may be regarded as a setback for the civil rights movement

547

n 1969, the California Department of Education began requiring the use of standardized IQ tests to diagnose developmental disabilities. Students who scored below 85 on the Wechsler Intelligence Scale for Children (WISC) or the Stanford-Binet were sent to special classes for the educable mentally retarded (EMR).[1] Larry P. was one of approximately 6000 African American children assigned to EMR classes on the basis of the tests. However, a few years later, Larry P. and five of his African American schoolmates were retested by African American psychologists, who reported higher IQ scores. On the basis of these new, higher test scores, Larry and the others were placed back in the regular school track.

Larry P.'s battle was not as simple as being retested to gain an appropriate placement. Instead, a class-action lawsuit was filed on behalf of the six African American children (representing the class of all similar students). This case challenged the right of the state to use IQ tests for classroom placement, arguing that the tests discriminated by race and therefore violated both the California Constitution and the 14th Amendment to the U.S. Constitution, which guarantees equal protection under the law.

It took until 1977 for the case to be heard in the U.S. District Court. After hearing and reviewing more than 11,000 pages of testimony by psychologists and interested parties, Judge Robert Peckham released a 131-page opinion in October 1979 forbidding the placement of African American children in EMR classes on the basis of standardized test scores. The same judge reversed his own decision in a 1992 opinion. Thus, the ultimate decision about the use of psychological tests was made not by trained psychologists, professional educators, or interested citizens, but by the courts.

The same year that the decision in Larry P.'s case was released, the state of New York passed its Truth in Testing Law, and a similar bill was introduced in the U.S. House of Representatives. In addition, a Florida judge ruled that African American students who did not receive all their education in integrated schools could not be denied a high-school credential on the basis of a minimum competence test. By the end of the 1970s, the use of psychological tests had become a major legal issue. In the 1980s, 1990s, and the first two decades of the 21st century, the focus broadened to employment testing. These courtroom and legislative battles over the appropriate use of psychological tests set the stage for the many current conflicts over testing.

In this chapter, we present major legal issues concerning the use of psychological tests. We begin by covering some of the basic laws that regulate the use of tests, and then we examine how the courts have interpreted some of these laws. Focused Example 20.1 discusses the meaning of the word *law*.

---

[1]This chapter places evaluation of testing and the law in historical context. Many of the cases concerned individuals labeled as "mentally retarded." That term has fallen into disfavor and is often regarded as an insult. The difficulty is that, over time, various terms have been used and later dropped. The term *mental retardation* became popular in the mid-20th century as a replacement for "feeble minded." The terms now most commonly favored are *intellectual disability* or *intellectually challenged*. In this chapter, we continue to use the older term, *mentally retarded*, if that was the term used in the legal proceeding.

FOCUSED EXAMPLE

What Is a Law?

As common as it is to refer to laws, many people are confused about what exactly constitutes the law. Most people think of law only as statutes or the rules written by legislative bodies at any level of government. Before proposed statutes become law, they are called *bills* or *propositions*.

In addition to statutes, constitutions have the force of law. In the United States, there is a federal Constitution, and each state has its own constitution. In lawsuits (or litigation), lawyers frequently argue that a policy violates a constitutional rule or principle. The U.S. Constitution is considered the supreme law of the land; any federal, state, or local law is invalid if judged to conflict with it. State or local laws inconsistent with a state constitution can also be declared invalid.

Statutes and constitutions are typically worded in general terms. Often, they give authority to a specific agency to write regulations. These regulations are also laws. For example, the Civil Rights Act of 1964 (a statute) created the Equal Employment Opportunity Commission (EEOC), which wrote guidelines for fair employment practices; these guidelines are regulations. Although not created by any elected officials, they are laws that one must follow.

The final form of law is judicial opinion. Statutes, constitutions, and regulations must be applied to specific facts. Thus, courts of law are frequently called on to interpret the law in view of a given situation. In doing so, the courts offer opinions that consider specific cases against the background of statutes, constitutions, and regulations. Once a court offers an opinion on a specific case, the opinion becomes law (Wing, 1976). For example, in the case of *Larry P. v. Wilson Riles*, a judge rendered the opinion that IQ tests could not be used to place African American children in EMR classes. That policy remains in effect today in California, but not in other states (Frisby & Henry, 2016).

Laws Governing the Use of Tests

Federal Authorities

Many people believe that the federal government has unlimited authority to regulate almost any activity. Actually, the circumstances under which the federal government can regulate are limited. Until fairly recently, the most commonly used authority for regulation was interstate commerce.

Interstate Commerce

The U.S. Constitution gives most of the ruling power to the states. Each state has its own constitution, which defines the general relationship between the state and its citizens. The states must make policies for the other administrative units, such as cities and counties, that exist within them. The U.S. Constitution does not directly recognize cities, counties, or school districts. The only restriction on the states' authority to pass laws is that no state can pass or enforce a law that is inconsistent with the U.S. Constitution.

Because each state has only that authority necessary to attend to its own affairs, the federal government regulates interstate commerce or any business activity involving two or more states. For example, a test developed by a New Jersey company and shipped to Kansas to be administered for profit clearly involves interstate commerce. Some legal authorities now believe that interstate commerce involves almost all activities. The federal government can regulate many activities under this umbrella.

The regulation of interstate commerce is clear and direct. Federal agencies such as the Federal Trade Commission create policies to regulate specific products and activities. Congress also devotes much of its energy to creating laws that regulate specific business activities. These extensive and well-documented policies represent direct regulation. The other form of government regulation—the power to control spending—is indirect.

Control of Spending

The U.S. government is a big spender—so big, in fact, that virtually all major U.S. business institutions depend to some extent on federal revenues. This spending gives the federal government considerable leverage. It can withhold money whenever federal authorities consider it just to do so. In effect, the government has the right to say, "Do it our way or we will not pay."

This policy is straightforward when the government is a customer. For example, when the federal government is paying for the development of a test, it has the right to withhold payment unless the work is done according to government standards. However, this power is frequently exercised indirectly. For example, the government can withhold grant money, saying in effect, "Conform to our employment guidelines or we will not pay you to develop a test."

Most school districts are happy to receive federal funds to implement certain programs; however, they may not be enthusiastic about implementing government policies. For example, a district may have a lunch program for underprivileged children. What happens if the government asks the district to build ramps for handicapped children? If the district does not follow through, there is no criminal penalty for deciding not to build the ramps; however, the government has the authority to withhold the funds for the lunch program until the district agrees to the ramps.

Virtually all public and most major private institutions can be regulated this way because of their dependence on federal contracts and grants. Institutions in the private sector that do not depend as heavily on federal funds can be regulated through interstate commerce. Government regulation is thus difficult to escape.

Guidelines of the Equal Employment Opportunity Commission (EEOC)

The government exercises its power to regulate testing in large part through interpretations of the 14th Amendment to the Constitution. This amendment guarantees all citizens due process and equal protection under the law. Over time, the way in which these principles are implemented has been carefully refined. The clearest statement to date from the federal government concerns employee testing and personnel procedures.

During the presidency of Lyndon Johnson, Congress enacted the Civil Rights Act of 1964, one of the most important pieces of legislation in the 20th century. Title VII of the act and its subsequent amendments created an EEOC. In 1970, the EEOC released a set of guidelines that defined fair employee-selection procedures.

In 1978, the guidelines were revised and simplified, published as the *Uniform Guidelines on Employee Selection Procedures,* and jointly adopted by the EEOC, the Civil Service Commission, and the Departments of Justice, Labor, and the Treasury. These guidelines thus affect most public employment and institutions that receive government funds, and they remain very much the same as when they were introduced nearly 40 years ago.

The guidelines clearly state that an employer cannot discriminate on the basis of race, color, gender, national origin, or religion. Selection procedures that might have adverse impact receive particular attention. *Adverse impact* is interpreted according to one of the most controversial components of the guidelines, the **four-fifths rule**:

> A selection rate of any race, sex, or ethnic group which is less than four-fifths (4/5) (or 80%) of the rate for the group with the highest rate will generally be regarded by the federal enforcement agencies as evidence of adverse impact, while a greater than four-fifths rate will generally not be regarded by federal enforcement agencies as evidence of adverse impact.

In applying the four-fifths rule, employers place applicants in different categories, such as white women, African American women, and Latinas. If an employer hires 90% of the white female applicants and only 20% of African American female applicants, then the selection procedure violates the four-fifths rule. The employer then has to demonstrate that extenuating circumstances make the standard unreasonable. Suppose that an employer hires 60% of the applicants from the white female pool. Using the four-fifths rule, the employer must hire $4/5 \times 60\% = 48\%$ of the applicants from any other group. If there were 1000 white female applicants and 60% were hired, then there would be 600 new white female workers. Suppose that only 50 Latinas applied (and became members of the applicant pool). According to the four-fifths rule, the employer would need to hire 24 Latinas. This is calculated as:

$$\frac{4}{5} \times 60\% = 48\%$$

$$48\% \times 50 \text{ Latina applicants} = 24 \text{ Latinas selected}$$

Interestingly, by actively recruiting members of many minority groups, an employer can hire a smaller percentage of each group and still maintain the four-fifths rule. Thus, this rule, which was designed to protect minorities, may actually discourage the aggressive recruiting of these groups. The EEOC acknowledges these problems and has developed exceptions for particular circumstances. The authorization of these exceptions for specific individual cases is left up to the EEOC and in many cases has been left to the courts (Campbell & Marcum, 2016).

The guidelines include many careful definitions of terms such as *validity*. Whenever using a psychological test or other selection device results in adverse impact (or overselection in one group), the employer must present extensive evidence for the validity of the selection procedure. Much of the text of the EEOC guidelines is devoted to a discussion of the minimum requirements for the validity of a selection procedure. These guidelines parallel the discussion presented in Chapter 5. If prospective employees feel they have been treated unfairly, they can file complaints with the commission. The EEOC's regional and district offices handle approximately 70,000 complaints each year. The EEOC also gathers information.

20.2 FOCUSED EXAMPLE

Content Validity and Sexual Harassment During a Paramedic Exam

The EEOC guidelines make it clear that questions asked on employment tests and during employment interviews must relate to performance on the job. However, not all agencies are in full compliance with this regulation, particularly in regard to job interviews. This noncompliance irritated Sandra Buchanan when she appeared before the Los Angeles City Fire Department to interview for a paramedic job. During the interview, she was asked as much about her sex life as she was about her 4 years of paramedic training and experience. For example, she was asked: "Have you ever had semipublic sex?" "Have you had sex on the beach?" "Have you had sex in a parked car?" "Have you ever exposed yourself indecently?" "Have you molested any children?" "Do you have any homosexual contacts?"

Buchanan was so disturbed by these questions that she filed a complaint with the Civil Service Commission. In the ensuing investigation, the fire department was asked to show how the questions about sex related to the paramedic job.

Its response was that the questions create stress and therefore give the department a chance to observe how a person handles him- or herself in stressful situations. The department also argued that it needed to delve deeply into the backgrounds of applicants because paramedics are entrusted with important responsibilities. One member of the fire department argued that the question on indecent exposure was necessary because "they have a dormitory situation that is quite different from other jobs; the nature of this job makes some of the questions job related that would not be related in other jobs." The commission decided that the department had to review the questions and eliminate those that were not job related, and then reinterview Buchanan. It appeared that the commission agreed with Buchanan's attorney who argued, "It is time that the city of Los Angeles stop asking 'How's your sex life' and get back to the business of finding the most qualified person for the job of Los Angeles paramedic" (*Los Angeles Times,* June 29, 1979). Even though several decades have passed, we are still faced with problems associated with employment decisions based on personal and physical characteristics. In the 2005 case *Gonzalez v. Abercrombie & Fitch,* the retail clothing outlet reached a settlement in a case in which it was accused of discriminating against Latino, African American, Asian American, and female applicants. The retailer agreed to cease the practice of targeting fraternities, sororities, and specific colleges in their recruitment efforts. The settlement required Abercrombie and Fitch to pay $40 million to those who had been discriminated against and another $10 million in attorney fees. Other major companies who have been required to compensate underrepresented minority group members or women for discrimination include Home Depot, Federal Express, and UPS.

Any organization with more than 100 employees must complete a form each year that describes the number of women and members of four different minority groups employed in nine different job categories within the organization. The specific minority groups are African American, Hispanic (Cuban, Spanish, Puerto Rican, or Mexican), Asian, and American Indian. After collecting these forms from 260,000 organizations, the EEOC can estimate broad patterns of discrimination. Each year, the EEOC is involved in hundreds of lawsuits concerning discrimination.

Although the validity requirements apply specifically to psychological tests, they also apply to other selection devices such as employment forms and interviews, as well as job requirements, including education and work experience (see Focused Example 20.2). In summary, the EEOC guidelines provide clear, unambiguous regulations for the use of any assessment device in the selection of employees.

Sexism in Other Countries

The fairness in employment policies that characterizes some Western countries is not observed throughout the world. Consider this advertisement that appeared in a 1985 Hong Kong newspaper:

Obedient Young Secretary. Very obedient young woman required by American Director of position as Secretary/Personal Assistant. Must be attractive and eager to submit to authority, have good typing and filing skills, and be free to travel. Knowledge of Mandarin an advantage. Most important, she should enjoy following orders without question and cheerfully accept directions. Send handwritten resume on unlined paper and recent photo to G.P.O. Box 6132, Hong Kong.

From Cascio (1987, p. 29).

As you might expect, many employers were furious when the EEOC guidelines first came out. They saw them as government interference in their business and as a barrier to hiring the best person for a job. Although one can easily sympathize with their concern about bureaucratic red tape, historical evidence supports the implementation of the guidelines. The basic rationale for the EEOC guidelines was provided by the equal protection clause in the 14th Amendment. Though ratified in the post–Civil War era, this clause did not strongly affect public policy for nearly 100 years—until the court battles over school desegregation and the activities of the civil rights movement led to the passage of the 1964 Civil Rights Act. Even then, many employers did not follow fair employment practices. The specific EEOC guidelines were therefore necessary to enforce the law. Before these specific guidelines, more than 100 years had passed without employers recognizing the legal requirements of equal protection.

In 1980, the EEOC added specific guidelines on sexual harassment in the workplace. *Sexual harassment* was defined as unsolicited sexual advances, requests for sexual favors, or any other implicit or explicit conduct that might be interpreted as a condition of an individual's employment. The EEOC ruled that a company is always liable for sexual harassment by supervisors even when company officials are unaware of the problem, but the Supreme Court overturned this policy in a 1986 decision. Nevertheless, the Supreme Court affirmed that sexual harassment is sexual discrimination and underscored the need for employers to eliminate any form of sexual harassment (Wermiel & Trost, 1986). Most workplaces and universities now have specific guidelines, procedures for investigation, and training relevant to sexual harassment (Rothlin & McCann, 2016). When traveling abroad, some Americans are surprised by evidence of sexual discrimination and the sexist standards apparent in job-selection procedures. Consider the advertisement in Focused Example 20.3.

Specific Laws

Other regulatory schemes attempt to control the use of tests. An example is the New York Truth in Testing Law of 1979.

Truth in Testing Laws

One of the most controversial measures in the testing field, the New York Truth in Testing Law sprang from an extensive investigation of the Educational Testing Service (ETS) by the New York Public Interest Research Group (NYPIRG). Though it affects other testing companies, the New York law was written specifically for the ETS.

In 1948, the ETS was created by the College Entrance Examination Board, the American Council on Education, and the Carnegie Foundation. Its original and best-known mission was to create and administer aptitude tests such as the SAT Reasoning Test. ETS is responsible for more than 300 testing programs, including the Graduate Management Admission Test (GMAT), the Graduate Record Examination (GRE), the Multistate Bar Exam, and the Law School Admission Test (LSAT). The assets and income of the company are substantial.

Though apparently upset by the wealth and success of ETS, NYPIRG objected even more to the power ETS wielded. Even now, each year several million people take tests designed and administered by ETS, and the results of these tests profoundly affect their lives (Soares, 2015). Many educational programs take the scores seriously. Students who score poorly on the LSAT, for example, may be denied entrance to law school. Higher scores might have brought them higher income, occupational status, and self-esteem (Gilmore, 2016). In its investigation, NYPIRG became dissatisfied with the available information on test validity, the calculation of test scores, and the financial accounting of the ETS. The Truth in Testing Law addresses these objections by requiring testing companies to (1) disclose all studies on the validity of a test; (2) provide a complete disclosure to students about what scores mean and how they were calculated; and (3) on request by a student, provide a copy of the test questions, the correct answers, and the student's answers.

The first two portions are relatively noncontroversial. The test developers argue that they already disclose all pertinent information on validity and release many public documents that highlight the strengths and weaknesses of their tests. Furthermore, the ETS strongly encourages institutions that use its tests to perform local validity studies. Any of these studies can be published in scholarly journals (found in most college libraries) with no interference from the ETS. However, the NYPIRG provided some evidence that the ETS and other testing companies have files of secret data that they do not make public because these data may reflect poorly on the product. The second aspect of the law was included because the ETS sometimes reports index scores to schools without telling students how the index was calculated and the exact index value being reported.

The controversial third portion of the law may seriously decrease the value of testing programs. Requiring that the test questions be returned to students means that the same questions cannot be used in future versions of the test. Several problems have resulted from this policy. First, it decreases the validity of the test. With the items constantly changing, the test essentially becomes a new test each time the items change. As a result, it is impossible to accumulate a record of construct validity. Second, new items make it difficult to equate scores across years. For example, a graduate school must often consider students who took the GRE in different years. Because the test itself differs each year, comparing the scores of students who took the test at different times is difficult. Although the bill eventually adopted in New York did allow testing companies to keep some of the items secret for equating purposes, this practice falls short of a satisfactory solution. Equating can be accomplished, but only at the risk of increasing the chances of error. Third, and most serious, the disclosure of test items increases costs, which the ETS passes on to the consumer.

The College Board that oversees the SAT does make booklets available to the public that present information on the scoring system, validity, reliability, and standard error of measurement for each of their tests. After completing this testing course, you will have little difficulty interpreting the manuals, but it has taken you a long term of hard study to get to this point. People with no background in testing will probably not comprehend all of this information. The authors of the bills fail to recognize that the proper use of tests and test results requires technical training in advanced courses such as psychological testing. After all, we do not expect people to be able to practice medicine without medical school training. Testing experts tend to agree that primary and secondary schools misuse test scores. Those who do not understand the limitations of tests may rely too much on test scores (Yudof, Levin, Moran, Ryan, & Bowman, 2011).

Consider the ultimate impact of the truth-in-testing legislation. One side argues that the laws have made for a fairer and more honest testing industry. The other argues that students now have to pay a higher price for a poorer product. As a result of these laws, other tests are given on only a limited number of occasions, and test items are not reused. With the distribution of test items, tests are not as thoroughly validated before their use as they were 30 years ago. This may cause greater error in selecting students. In addition, continuing the development of the tests has increased expense. Ultimately, students may need to pay more to take a lower-quality test. In response to these concerns, the ETS argues that the concurrent validity of the tests is still significant (www.collegeboard.com).

Federal Initiatives in Education

One of the major criticisms of public education is that schools are not held accountable for the product they produce—a college-ready or workforce-ready young adult. Starting in the 1990s, several organizations called for higher standards and greater accountability in K-12 education. This effort resulted in the No Child Left Behind legislation. The NCLB Act (Public Law 107-110) was an attempt to coordinate different federal programs designed to improve performance of students in both primary and secondary schools. The NCLB legislation was based on the assumption that accountability could improve school performance. The law included a wide variety of provisions. For example, it offered parents more flexibility in the schools they selected for their children. By reauthorizing the Elementary and Secondary Education Act of 1965, the legislation promoted a focus on reading and basic skills. The law was passed by the U.S. House of Representatives in May 2001 and signed into law in June 2001. It was enacted in January 2002 and later reauthorized in 2004. It was replaced by the Every Student Succeeds Act (Klein, 2015) in 2015.

NCLB was controversial for a variety of reasons. One of the most important components of NCLB was the use of tests to assess student progress. These tests were used to hold schools accountable. Poorly performing schools would lose funding or even be forced to close. The testing component of NCLB came to be labeled as "test and punish." From a civil rights perspective, it appeared that teachers were being punished for working with students with the greatest needs and that the children who needed the most attention were likely to have their school facilities closed (Trujillo, 2016).

Another controversial provision the of NCLB required school districts to distribute the names, phone numbers, and addresses of students to military recruiters unless the students' parents specifically asked that this information be kept confidential. Further, the bill was challenged because it used tests to determine which schools should be rewarded and which schools should be punished. Many believed that the focus on tests motivated teachers to simply "teach to the test." In other words, schools gave up much of their basic curriculum and instead started focusing on the narrow bit of information they expected to be included on the tests. NCLB did not create a national test. Rather, each state created its own test and its own standards. Many states chose the least expensive alternative. States could also choose whether they wanted norm-based or criterion-based tests and these decisions varied from state to state.

Critics of NCLB found little evidence that performance had improved and offered other evidence that performance gaps had widened. The use of test scores as a way of achieving accountability for schools formed the core of the criticism. Legal challenges to NCLB also became common. One comparison of test performance in states that enacted or did not enact NCLB suggested that 4th graders improved math scores but not reading scores (Dee & Jacob, 2011; Yudof et al., 2011). Critics reported that NCLB was a failure because it did not address serious long-term reforms that could have reduced large gaps in opportunity for minority students. A variety of critics challenged the effect of the NCLB law and argued for new types of accountability systems. By 2012, it was apparent that the NCLB policy faced significant challenges. For example, it was projected that 82% of U.S. public schools would not meet the 2011 adequacy standard. Most importantly, critics argued that test-based accounting systems did not offer the type of feedback that was required to produce equal opportunity for all children (Sunderman, 2008).

The Common Core

In 2004, a report entitled, "Ready or Not: Creating A High School Diploma That Counts" outlined the need for a more demanding school curriculum in English language arts and mathematics (Conley, 2007). The report suggested that many students entered college or the workforce without the skills necessary for them to succeed. They needed a curriculum geared toward the challenges they would face after K-12 education. In order to address these concerns, students needed comprehensive assessment tools that identify learning deficits and progress toward achievement goals.

In 2009, The Common Core State Standards Initiative was introduced in an attempt to define what students should know in language arts and mathematics at the end of each grade (Jacob, 2015). The initiative got a major boost through endorsement by the National Governors Association and the Council of Chief State School Officers (Association, 2010).

Initially, the program went very well. Forty-two of the 50 U.S. states and the District of Columbia became collaborators on the Common Core State Standards Initiative. The only states not adopting the initiative were Oklahoma, Texas, Virginia, Alaska, Nebraska, Indiana, and South Carolina. Minnesota adopted the language arts component but declined to participate in the mathematics standards. Some of the states that were not participating originally adopted the common core but later decided to bow out. These states included Indiana, Oklahoma, and South Carolina (https://en.wikipedia.org/wiki /Common_Core_State_Standards_Initiative#cite_note-3).

Part of the launch for the common core was a program known as Race to the Top that provided grants to states that were willing to adopt internationally recognized standards and assessments that would prepare students for further education or for the workplace. Additional money was provided by the Bill and Melinda Gates Foundation, the Pearson publishing company, and the Charles Stewart Mott Foundation. In 2015, the Congress formally gave up on the No Child Left Behind Act and replaced it with a new program called the Every Student Succeeds Act (Klein, 2015). The new legislation drove a nail in the coffin of NCLB by expressly prohibiting the U.S. Department of Education from providing any incentives to adopt the Common Core State Standards.

Much of the political trouble encountered by the Common Core State Standards concerned formal assessment and testing (Ravitch, 2016). The original goal was to use a common standardized test to assess progress toward standardized educational goals. However, that approach did not work well because different states and jurisdictions set different performance standards. In some states, such as California, the bar was set very high. In other states, the criterion for success was lower.

To make matters worse, states in different jurisdictions adopted different testing programs. Nineteen jurisdictions formed a "Partnership For Assessment of Readiness For College and Careers." The partnership was based on the Race to the Top program. A separate effort was adopted by 31 states and territories. This was known as the Smarter Balance Assessment Consortium (Consortium, 2016). However, after participating in the consortium for just more than a year, 11 of 31 states and territories dropped out and a variety of states decided to go their own ways.

Reaction to the common core has been all over the map. Some observers feel that it is one of the most important attempts to level playing field in public education. Supporters come from both educational establishments and from industry. On the other side, the program has been attacked because it gives the federal government too much influence over the educational process in states and in school districts.

The testing component has also drawn significant criticism. Some parents felt that the tests were too hard and that they cause too much stress for their children. Others railed against the use of traditional test construction principles. They asked why the tests had been developed by testing experts and groups that included few teachers and parents. Perhaps the most serious criticisms implicated the test developers. In particular, critics pointed out that creating the tests was expensive and sometimes required the use of computer equipment. They felt that the process had been captured by for-profit corporations (Ravitch, 2016).

Major Lawsuits That Have Affected Psychological Testing

Legislation is not the only way to change policy. One option used with increasing frequency is litigation, usually considered a last resort for resolving conflicts. For example, if you feel you have been wronged but cannot persuade those who have offended you through other legal means, then you may file a lawsuit. In doing so, you trust the court to make a fair judgment about your case.

There have already been many lawsuits concerning the use of psychological tests, and we expect the number to increase. We shall now discuss some of the most important of these. Keep in mind that each of these complex cases involved considerably more evidence than we can cite here.

Early Desegregation Cases

The 14th Amendment requires that all citizens be granted equal protection under the law. At the end of the 19th century, some people argued that segregated schools did not offer such protection. In the famous 1896 case of *Plessy v. Ferguson*, the Supreme Court ruled that schools could remain segregated but that the quality of the schools must be equal. This was the famous separate-but-equal ruling.

Perhaps the most influential ruling in the history of American public school education came in the case of *Brown v. Board of Education* in 1954. In this case, the Supreme Court overturned the *Plessy v. Ferguson* decision by ruling that the schools must provide nonsegregated facilities for African American and white students. In this opinion, the Court raised several issues that would eventually affect the use of psychological tests.

The most important pronouncement of *Brown* was that segregation denied equal protection. In coming to its decision, the Court made extensive use of testimony by psychologists that suggested that African American children could be made to feel inferior if the school system kept the two races separate.

The story of the *Brown* case is well known, but what is less often discussed is the ugly history that followed. Many school districts did not want to desegregate, and the battle over busing and other mechanisms for desegregation continues even today. Many of the current arguments against desegregation are based on fears of children leaving their own neighborhoods or the stress on children who must endure long bus rides. The early resistance to the *Brown* decision was more clearly linked to the racist belief in African American inferiority.

Brown v. Board of Education is regarded as one of the most important civil rights decisions in American history. Although the decision had a revolutionary impact in some dimensions, severe problems in equal access to quality education remain. May 2004 marked the 50th anniversary of the *Brown* decision. At that time, many looked back critically at the progress made during that half century. The *Plessy v. Ferguson* decision of 1896 argued that schools could be racially separate but emphasized that the quality of the separate schools must be equal. The decision stood for more than half a century until the Supreme Court ruled on the *Brown* case in 1954. Fifty years following the *Brown* decision and more than 100 years following *Plessy v.*

Ferguson, many people believe that today's public schools are often still separate and that they remain unequal. Have we made significant progress toward resolving the issue during the last century? In 2004, it was reported that 38% of African American students and 42% of Hispanic students were in extremely segregated schools with more than 90% minority enrollment.

An important 2004 study by the California-based Center for the Future of Teaching and Learning raised some disturbing issues. The state of California, responding to a teacher shortage, significantly increased the number of classroom teachers. In the 2002–2003 academic year, nearly 310,000 people were employed as public school teachers in California. In response to the demand for teachers, school districts had hired about 37,000 (12% of the workforce) that had not completed formal teacher training or were teaching a subject in which they had no formal training. These teachers were described as "underprepared." Many of these teachers did not even have a preliminary teaching credential. The problem is that the under-prepared teachers tend to end up in schools with high percentages of minority students. For example, some schools still have 90% or more minority students while other schools have 30% or less minority students. In the schools with high concentrations of minority students, 20% of the teachers were underprepared, while in schools with low minority populations, only 4% of the teachers were underprepared. In other words, schools with large minority student populations were more than five times as likely to have underprepared teachers as those with low percentages of minority students. Further, students in poverty area schools were about three times as likely to have teachers who were underprepared as students in low-poverty areas.

It might be argued that schools that have poor academic performance are the ones that need the best-prepared teachers. Poorly performing students need more help. Yet in 2002–2003, schools scoring low on California's Academic Performance Index (API) had students who were 4.5 times more likely to be taught by someone who was underprepared than schools in the top quartile of academic performance.

Now, nearly 60 years following the landmark *Brown* decision and more than 115 years after the *Plessy* decision, our schools remain only partially desegregated, and the quality of the educational experience for many disadvantaged youths remains substandard.

Stell v. Savannah-Chatham County Board of Education

The most significant reactionary court case occurred when legal action was taken to desegregate the school system of Savannah, Georgia, on behalf of a group of African American children. The conflict began when the attorneys for two white children intervened. They argued that they were not opposed to desegregating on the basis of race but that African American children did not have the ability to be in the same classrooms as whites. Testimony from psychologists indicated that the median IQ score for African American children was 81, whereas that for white children was 101. Because there was such a large difference in this trait (assumed to be genetic), the attorneys argued that it could be to the mutual disadvantage of both groups to teach them in the same schools. Doing so might create even greater feelings of inferiority among African American children and might create frustration that would eventually result in antisocial behavior.

The court essentially agreed with this testimony and ruled that the district should not desegregate. The judge's opinion reflected his view of the best interest of all the children. Later, this decision was reversed. In doing so, the Supreme Court used the precedent set forth by *Brown* as the reason for requiring the Savannah district to desegregate. It is important to note that the validity of the test scores—the primary evidence—was never discussed (Bersoff, 1979, 1981).

Hobson v. Hansen

Stell was just one of many cases that attempted to resist the order set forth in the *Brown* desegregation case. Like *Stell*, many of these cases introduced test scores as evidence that African American children were genetically incapable of learning or being educated in the same classrooms as white children. The courts routinely accepted this evidence. Given the current controversy over the use of psychological tests, it is remarkable that several years passed before the validity of the test scores became an issue.

The first major case to examine the validity of psychological tests was *Hobson v. Hansen*. This case is relevant to many current lawsuits. Unlike the early desegregation cases, it did not deal with sending African American and white children to different schools. Instead, it concerned the placement of children once they arrived at a school. Although the courts had consistently required schools to desegregate, they tended to take a hands-off approach toward placement within schools.

The *Hobson* case contested the use of group standardized ability tests to place students in different learning tracks. Julius W. Hobson was the father of two African American children placed in a basic track by the District of Columbia School District. Carl F. Hansen was its superintendent. Within the district, children were placed in honors, regular, general, and basic tracks on the basis of group ability tests. The honors track was designed to prepare children for college, while the basic track focused on preparation for blue-collar jobs. Placement in the basic track made it essentially impossible to prepare for a high-income, high-prestige profession.

In *Hobson*, lawyers argued that the tracking system segregated groups by placing African American children in the basic track and white children in the other tracks. Psychological tests were the primary mechanism used to justify this separation.

The *Hobson* case was decided in 1967. Just 2 years before the decision, the Supreme Court had ruled that a group is not denied equal protection by "mere classification" (Bersoff, 1979). Nevertheless, Judge Skelly Wright ruled against classification based on group ability tests. After extensive expert testimony on the validity of the tests for minority children, the judge concluded that the tests discriminated against them. An interesting aspect of the opinion was that it claimed that grouping would be permissible if based on innate ability. The judge asserted that ability test scores were influenced by cultural experiences, and that the dominant cultural group had an unfair advantage on the tests and thereby gained admission to the tracks that provided the best preparation for high-income, high-prestige jobs. The Hobson case was unique because the court suggested that the tracking of students constituted intentional racial segregation. There has been only one similar decision (*People Who Care v. Rockford Board of Education*, 1997), but it was reversed by an appellate court.

Diana v. State Board of Education

The decision in *Hobson v. Hansen* opened the door for a thorough examination of the use of standardized tests for the placement of students in EMR tracks. The case of *Diana* has particular implications for the use of standardized tests for bilingual children. Diana was one of nine Mexican American elementary school children placed in EMR classes on the basis of scores on the WISC or Stanford-Binet test. Representing bilingual children, these nine students brought a class-action suit against the California State Board of Education, contending that the use of standardized IQ tests for placement in EMR classes denied equal protection, because the tests were standardized only for whites and had been administered by a non-Spanish-speaking psychometrist. Although only 18% of the children in Diana's school district had Spanish surnames, this group made up nearly one-third of the enrollment in EMR classes.

When tested in English, Diana had achieved an IQ score of only 30. However, when retested in Spanish and English, her IQ bounced to 79, high enough to keep her out of EMR classes. Seven of the other eight plaintiffs also achieved high enough scores on the retest to be taken out of the EMR classes.

Faced with this evidence, the California State Board of Education decided not to take the case to court. Instead, it adopted special provisions for testing Mexican American and Chinese American children, including the following:

1. The children would be tested in their primary language.
2. Questions based on vocabulary and information that the children could not be expected to know would be eliminated.
3. The Mexican American and Chinese American children already assigned to EMR classes would be reevaluated with tests that used their primary language and nonverbal items.
4. New tests would be developed by the state that reflected Mexican American culture and that were normed for Mexican American children (Bersoff, 1979).

Later studies confirmed that bilingual children do score higher when tested in their primary language (Bialystok, 2016).

The combination of the judgment in *Hobson* and the change in policy brought about by *Diana* forced many people to question seriously the use of IQ tests for the assignment of children to EMR classes. However, these decisions were quite specific to the circumstances in each case. *Hobson* dealt with group tests but not individual ones, even though individual tests are used more often than group tests to make final decisions for EMR placement. The ruling in *Diana* was limited strictly to bilingual children. These two cases thus did not apply to African American children placed in EMR classes on the basis of individual IQ tests. This specific area was left for the most important court battle of them all—*Larry P. v. Wilson Riles*.

Larry P. v. Wilson Riles

In October 1979, Judge Robert Peckham of the Federal District Court for the Northern District of California handed down an opinion that declared that "the use of IQ tests which had a disproportionate effect on Black children violated the Rehabilitation Act, the Education for All Handicapped Children Act, Title VII, and the 14th Amendment when used to place children in EMR classes." Attorneys for Larry P., one of six African American elementary-school students assigned to EMR classes on the basis of IQ test results, had argued that the use of standardized IQ tests to place African American children in EMR classes violated both the California constitution and the equal protection clause of the 14th Amendment, as well as the laws mentioned (Frisby & Henry, 2016).

During the trial, both sides geared up for a particularly intense battle. Wilson Riles, an African American, was the superintendent of public instruction in California; he had instituted many significant reforms that benefited minority children. Thus, it was particularly awkward to have a nationally recognized spokesperson for progressive programs named as the defendant for an allegedly racist scheme.

In defense of the use of tests, Riles and the state called many nationally recognized experts on IQ tests, including Lloyd Humphreys, Jerome Sattler, Robert Thorridike, Nadine Lambert, and Robert Gordon. These witnesses presented extensive evidence that IQ tests, particularly the Stanford-Binet and the WISC (used to test Larry and the others), were not biased against African Americans. Although the tests had not originally been normed for African American populations, studies had demonstrated that they were equally valid for African American and white children. (Many of the arguments that support the use of tests for all races are summarized in Chapter 19.) If the tests were not biased, then why did Larry and the others receive higher scores when they were retested by African American psychologists? The defense argued that the African American psychologists did not follow standard testing procedures and that IQ test scores are not changed when standardized procedures are followed.

Statements from special education teachers were also presented. The teachers argued that the children involved in the case could not cope with the standard curriculum and that they required the special tutoring available in the special education classes, which at the time were called Educationally Mentally Retarded (EMR) classes. Although EMR classes were officially designated as remedial education, it was widely believed that assignment to the EMR track was a dead end that assured the child would not gain access to life opportunities. African American children were disproportionately assigned to these classes on the basis of IQ tests. In other words, IQ tests were seen as the key tool used to deny African American children access to a good education (Frisby & Henry, 2016).

The Larry P. side of the case also had its share of distinguished experts, including George Albee, Leon Kamin, and Jane Mercer. The arguments for Larry varied widely. His lawyers argued that all humans are born with equal capacity and that any test that assigns disproportionate numbers of children from one race to an EMR category is racist and discriminatory. The witnesses testified that, throughout history, dominant social groups had used devices such as IQ tests to discriminate against less powerful social groups and that the school district had intentionally discriminated against African American children by using unvalidated IQ tests. Specifically, the tests were used to keep African Americans in dead-end classes for the mentally retarded in which they would not get the training they needed to move up in the social strata. Furthermore, the plaintiffs suggested that labeling someone as EMR has devastating social consequences. Children labeled as EMR lose confidence and self-esteem; eventually, the label becomes a self-fulfilling prophecy (Rosenthal & Rubie-Davies, 2015).

In other words, labeling a child as mentally retarded may cause the child to behave as though he or she really is mentally retarded.

Clearly persuaded by the plaintiffs, the judge declared that the tests "are racially and culturally biased, have a discriminatory impact on African American children, and have not been validated for the purpose of (consigning) African-American children into educationally dead-end, isolated, and stigmatizing classes." Furthermore, the judge stated that the Department of Education had "desired to perpetuate the segregation of minorities in inferior, dead-end, and stigmatizing classes for the retarded."

The effect of the ruling was a permanent discontinuance of IQ testing to place African American children in EMR classes. The decision immediately affected all African American California schoolchildren who had been labeled as EMR. More than 6000 of these children had to be reassessed in some other manner.

There are strong differences of opinion about the meaning of the *Larry P.* decision. Harold Dent, one of the African American psychologists who had retested Larry P. and the other children, hailed the decision as a victory for African American children:

> For more than 60 years, psychologists had used tests primarily to justify the majority's desire to "track" minorities into inferior education and dead-end jobs. The message of *Larry P.* was that psychologists must involve themselves in the task mandated in the last sentence of the court's opinion: "This will clear the way for more constructive educational reform." (Quoted in Opton, 1979)

Others did not share the belief that the *Larry P.* decision was a social victory. Nadine Lambert, an expert witness for the state, felt it was a terrible decision: "I think the people who will be most hurt by it are the African-American children" (quoted in Opton, 1979). Banning the use of IQ tests opens the door to completely subjective judgments, perhaps even more racist than the test results. Opponents of the *Larry P.* decision cite many instances in which gifted African American children were assumed to be average by their teachers but were recognized as highly intelligent because of IQ test scores.

The *Larry P.* decision has been frequently cited in subsequent cases, some of which are actually remote from the issues in that case. For example, in *Ana Maria R. v. California Department of Education,* parental rights were terminated on the grounds that the mother was mentally retarded. However, the mother was Spanish-speaking, and *Larry P.* was cited as precedent that tests used for classification of mental retardation discriminate against African Americans and Hispanics. In contrast to the case of *Ana Maria R.,* the factual situation in an Illinois case strongly resembled that of *Larry P.,* as you will see in the following section.

Following the Larry P. ruling and a series of affirmations in the courts, the California Department of Education has enforced a complete ban of IQ test administration to African American students in the State of California. Although IQ tests cannot be used for assessing African American Students in California, that state remains unique. The ban has not been adopted by other states (Frisby & Henry, 2016).

Parents in Action on Special Education v. Hannon

Just as *Larry P.* was making headlines in California, a similar case came to trial in Illinois: a class-action lawsuit filed on behalf of two African American children who had been placed in special classes for the educable mentally handicapped (EMH) on the basis of IQ test scores. Attorneys for the two student plaintiffs argued that the children were inappropriately placed in EMH classes because of racial bias in the IQ tests. They suggested that the use of IQ tests for African American children violates the equal protection clause of the constitution and many federal statutes.

In their presentation to the court, the plaintiffs relied heavily on the *Larry P.* decision, which held that the Wechsler Intelligence Scale for Children (WISC), the revised Wechsler Intelligence Scale for Children (WISC-R), and the Stanford-Binet IQ tests are biased and inappropriate for testing minority children. However, Judge John Grady came to exactly the opposite conclusion that Judge Robert Peckham had in *Larry P.* Judge Grady found evidence for racial bias in the three major IQ tests to be unconvincing. In his opinion, he noted that the objectionable items comprised only a fraction of the entire test. For example, witnesses for the plaintiffs never mentioned whole subtests on the WISC and WISC-R such as arithmetic, digit span, block design, mazes, coding, and object assembly. The judge noted that these subtests were not biased in favor of either African American or white children because most youngsters of both groups would never have confronted problems of this type before. The items for which there were legitimate objections were too few to affect test scores.

Thus, less than 1 year after the historic *Larry P.* case, another court concluded, "Evidence of racial bias in standardized IQ tests is not sufficient to render their use as part of classification procedures to place African-American children in 'educable mentally handicapped' classes violative of statutes prohibiting discrimination in federal funded programs." Focused Example 20.4 presents further conflicting statements from the two judges in these cases.

Crawford et al. v. Honig et al.

In 1986, the court modified the *Larry P.* court order to expand the intelligence testing ban to all African American children. The California Department of Education and the public interest lawyers who represented Larry P. gained an order from Judge Peckham to ban the use of standardized intelligence tests for African American children for assignment to special education programs. However, African American children could take intelligence tests to be considered for the state-supported gifted and talented education program (GATE).

After the 1986 strengthening of the *Larry P.* decision, several new problems arose. One of them is represented by the case of *Crawford v. Honig.* Some children do have special needs and may benefit from special education programs. Indeed, such programs were developed to identify learning problems and to provide special assistance. Under the 1986 modification of the *Larry P.* decision, one can evaluate white, Latino, Latina, Asian American, and Native American students with intelligence tests for placement in special education. However, these tests cannot be used for African American children. In fact, these tests cannot be given to African American children even if the families request them. Crawford's mother was African American, but her father was not. Recognizing that the child was struggling in school, the mother requested testing.

Citing *Larry P.*, the school denied the request because the child had been identified as African American. However, the mother was told that if she changed the

20.4 FOCUSED EXAMPLE

Different Opinions From Different Judges

People often think that two judges looking at the same evidence will come to the same conclusion. However, judges often differ sharply in this regard. When confronted with different opinions from Judges Peckham (*Larry P. v. Wilson Riles*) and Grady (*Parents in Action on Special Education v. Hannon*), Sattler (1980) juxtaposed quotes from the two judges on selected issues in the cases. Below are some of the statements demonstrating how differently the judges viewed the issues.

What are the functions of special classes for the educable mentally retarded or educable mentally handicapped?

Judge Robert Peckham

"EMR classes are designed to separate out children who are incapable of learning in the regular classes.... Further, the curriculum was not and is not designed to help students learn the skills necessary to return to the regular instructional program.... Finally, consistent with the first two aspects of EMR classes, the classes are conceived of as 'dead-end classes.' Children are placed there, generally at about eight to ten years of age, because they are thought to be incapable of learning the skills inculcated by the regular curriculum. They are provided with instruction that deemphasizes academic skills in favor of adjustment, and naturally they will tend to fall farther and farther behind the children in the regular classes."

Judge John Grady

The EMH curriculum is designed for the child who cannot benefit from the regular curriculum. It is designed for children who learn slowly, who have short attention spans, slow reaction time, and difficulty retaining material in both the short term and the long term. The curriculum also recognizes the difficulty an EMH child has in seeing similarities and differences, in learning by implication, in generalizing and in thinking abstractly. The curriculum thus involves much repetition and concrete teaching. Subjects are taught for short periods of time, in recognition of the children's short attention spans."

How much emphasis is given to the IQ in placing children in mentally retarded or educable mentally handicapped classes?

"The available data suggest very strongly that, even if in some districts the IQ scores were not always determinative, they were pervasive in the placement process.... Retardation is defined in terms of the IQ tests, and a low score in effect establishes a prima facie case of retardation."

"The IQ score is not the sole determinant of whether a child is placed in an EMH class. First, the score itself is evaluated by the psychologist who administers the test. The child's responses are recorded verbatim, and the significance of his numerical score is a matter involving judgment and interpretation.... The examiner who knows the milieu of the child can correct for cultural bias by asking the questions in a sensitive and intelligent way.... Finally, the IQ test and the psychologist's evaluation of the child in the light of that test are only one component of several which form the basis for an EMH referral."

(continues)

To what extent do socioeconomic factors account for the findings that black children score lower than white children on intelligence tests?

"It is clear that socioeconomic status by itself cannot explain fully the undisputed disparities in IQ test scores and in EMR placements.... The insufficiency of the above explanation leads us to question the cultural bias of IQ tests. The first important inferential evidence is that the tests were never designed to eliminate cultural biases against Black children, it was assumed in effect that Black children were less 'intelligent' than Whites."

"It is uncontradicted that most of the children in the EMH classes do in fact come from the poverty pockets of the city. This tends to suggest that what is involved is not simply race but something associated with poverty. It is also significant that many Black children who take the tests score at levels high enough to preclude EMH placement. Plaintiffs have not explained why the alleged cultural bias of the tests did not result in EMH-level scores for these children. Plaintiffs' theory of cultural bias simply ignores the fact that some Black children perform better than most Whites. Nationally, 15 to 20% of the Blacks who take the tests score above the White mean of 100."

To what extent does black children's use of nonstandard English affect their performance on intelligence tests?

"At the outset, it is undeniable that to the extent Black children speak other than standard English, they will be handicapped in at least the verbal component of the tests.... Dr. [Asa] Hilliard and other witnesses pointed out that Black children are more likely to be exposed to nonstandard English, and that exposure will be reflected in IQ scores."

"The evidence does not establish how the use of nonstandard English would interfere with performance on the Wechsler and Stanford-Binet tests.... Dr. [Robert J.] Williams testified that a Black child might say, 'John go to town' instead of 'John is going to town,' or 'John book' instead of 'John's book'.... What is unclear is how the use of such nonstandard English would handicap a child either in understanding the test items or in responding to them.... Moreover, responding to a test item in nonstandard English should not affect a child's score on the item, since the examiners are specifically instructed by the test manuals to disregard the form of the answer so long as the substance is correct.... But there are no vocabulary items on the IQ tests, so far as I can tell, which are peculiar to White culture."

Was the issue of test validity important in the trial?

"If defendants could somehow have demonstrated that the intelligence tests had been 'validated' for the purpose of EMR placement of Black children, those tests could have been utilized despite their disproportionate impact.... However, defendants did not make these showings."

"We do not address the broader questions of whether these IQ tests are generally valid as measures of intelligence, whether individual items are appropriate for that purpose, or whether the tests could be improved. Those questions are not involved in this case."

To what extent do differences between black culture and white culture affect black children's performance on intelligence tests?

"To the extent that a 'Black culture'—admittedly a vague term—exists and translates the phenomenon of intelligence into skills and knowledge untested by the standardized intelligence tests, those tests cannot measure the capabilities of Black children…. On the basis of their different cultural background, which results particularly in lower scores on IQ tests, Black children are subjected to discrimination analogous to that borne by many San Francisco Chinese, who, because of their cultural background, could not communicate effectively in English. Certainly many Chinese Americans would succeed in those schools even without remedial English. Nevertheless, the failure to provide English-language teaching foreclosed substantial numbers of students from any meaningful educational opportunity. This same result occurs from the use of IQ tests and a biased placement process."

"Dr. Williams did not explain how he relates the other characteristics of Black culture to performance on the tests. It is not clear, for instance, how the extended family as opposed to the nuclear family would pertain to performance on the tests. Like Dr. [Leon] Kamin's description of the racist attitudes of Goddard, Yerkes and Terman, Dr. Williams's description of African-American culture has not been connected to the specific issue in this case…. Dr. Kamin's argument that the Black child does not obtain the same 'information,' and Dr. [George] Albee's argument that the Black child does not share in the dominant White culture, seem inapplicable to most items on all three of the tests in question. As already noted, many of the categories of test items have no precise counterpart in the experience of any children, of whatever race. Others have almost precise counterparts in the everyday experience of American children of all races. Any number of test items could be cited to illustrate this point."

Generally, to what extent are intelligence tests racially biased?

"The answer, as should be clear from the earlier discussion of the history and biases of IQ tests, is that validation has been assumed, not established, for Blacks. The tests were developed and standardized in the United States on White, essentially middle-class groups."

"All but a few of the items on their face appear racially neutral…. I conclude that the possibility of the few biased items on these tests causing an EMH placement that would not otherwise occur is practically nonexistent."

Does the use of intelligence tests violate some provisions of Public Law 94-142 (Education for All Handicapped)?

"Defendants have failed to take the steps necessary to assure the tests' validity. They have committed a serious error that Title VII regulations warn against in the employment situation: 'Under no circumstances will the general reputation of a test, its author, or its publisher, or casual reports of test utility be accepted in lieu of evidence of validity.' Whether or not the tests in fact do what they are supposed to do, the law is that defendants must come forward and show that they have been validated for each minority group with which they are used. This minimal burden has not been met for diagnosing the kind of mental retardation justifying EMR placement."

"The requirement that 'materials and procedures' used for assessment be nondiscriminatory, and that no single procedure be the sole criterion for assessment, seems to me to contemplate that the process as a whole be nondiscriminatory. It does not require that any single procedure, standing alone, be affirmatively shown to be free of bias. The very requirement of multiple procedures implies recognition that one procedure, standing alone, could well result in bias and that a system of cross-checking is necessary."

From Sattler (1980).

child's racial identification to match the father's, testing would be permitted. The lawsuit that followed claimed that California Superintendent of Public Education Bill Honig and the California Board of Education violated Crawford's civil rights by denying a public service on the basis of race. The arguments in court suggested that a race-conscious testing policy promoted inequities and indignities. Eventually, the case was heard by Judge Peckham, the same judge who had issued the *Larry P.* ruling and the 1986 modification strengthening the original judgment. Crawford's case was vigorously opposed by the California Department of Education. However, since this 1991 case was not a class-action suit, it was uncertain whether or not the ruling would apply to all children. The plaintiffs petitioned the court to extend the judgment to all similar African American children (Bredemeier, 1991). In September 1992, Judge Peckham issued an order reversing the earlier ban on IQ tests for African American students.

Marchall v. Georgia

One of the first major decisions that had opposed the 1979 *Larry P.* judgment was *Marchall et al. v. Georgia.* This class-action suit was filed in 1981 on behalf of a group of African American students. Allegedly, students had received unfair treatment by being disproportionately placed in EMR classes and underrepresented in classes for learning disabilities (LD). The defendants in the case were 13 school districts, most in the state of Georgia. The key witness for the plaintiff was Robert Calfee, an educational psychologist from Stanford University. Calfee noted that racial differences accounted for differential performance in school more than did socioeconomic status. Through a series of complex analyses, Calfee concluded that the school experience itself was actually creating differences between groups. Thus, the practice of assigning students to groups was damaging. As a remedy, Calfee suggested that students be assigned to classrooms on a random basis.

The defense argued that placement into certain classrooms did provide benefits for students, and the court ultimately agreed. Furthermore, the court allowed the use of tests to separate students because these procedures ultimately resulted in better outcomes. The critical result of the decision was that the focus shifted from possible test bias to the ultimate benefit to students. An important issue in the case was the focus on curriculum-based assessment rather than IQ testing. Perhaps the most important difference between the *Marchall* decision and previous court cases was the judge's belief that test information could be used to structure interventions that would help the children (*Marchall et al. v. Georgia*, 1984, 1985; Reschly, Kicklighter, & McKee, 1988; Reschly & Ward, 1991).

Debra P. v. Turlington

Some people feel that a test is biased if it contains questions that particular test takers cannot answer. One 1979 lawsuit in Florida involved 10 African American students, including Debra P., who had failed in their first attempt to pass Florida's minimum competence test, the State Student Assessment Test. In Hillsborough County, where the suit was filed, approximately 19% of the students in the public school system were African American; however, African American students constituted 64% of those who failed the test.

More than 30 states had adopted minimum competence tests similar to the one used in Florida, and 19 states required the exam for graduation. If they meet other requirements, students who do not pass the exam receive a certificate of completion, which acknowledges that they attended high school but does not carry the same status as a high-school diploma. Examples of items from a minimum competence test are shown in Table 20.1.

TABLE 20.1   Examples of Items From a Minimum Competence Test

Use the following table to answer question 1:

12 inches = 1 foot	1760 yards = 1 mile
3 feet = 1 yard	5280 feet = 1 mile

1. Sara needs to wrap string around 8 boxes. Each box needs a piece of string 72 inches long. How many yards of string does she need?

   A. 8 yards   B. 16 yards   C. 48 yards   D. 576 yards

2. The Florida sales tax on cars is 4%. The sticker price on a car including extras, title, transportation, and dealer preparation is $3200. What is the total cost of the car, including sales tax?

   A. $3204   B. $3212   C. $3314   D. $3328

3. The graph below shows the changes in the cost of coffee during a 1-year period. According to this graph, how much did the cost of a pound of coffee change from April 1 to July 1?

   A. $.50   B. $1.00   C. $1.50   D. $2.50

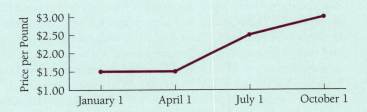

Chocolate Chip Cookies

1 cup brown sugar	2 eggs	1 tsp. salt
1 cup white sugar	1 tsp. baking soda	1 tsp. vanilla
1 cup shortening	$2\frac{1}{4}$ cups flour	1 pkg. chocolate chips

Preheat oven to 350 degrees. In a medium-sized mixing bowl, combine sugar and shortening. Add vanilla and eggs. In another bowl sift together flour, salt, and baking soda. Add sifted ingredients to sugar and shortening mixture. Add chocolate chips. Mix all ingredients together and drop by teaspoon on a cookie sheet. Bake for 10 minutes.

4. From the above recipe, what should be sifted with baking soda?

   A. vanilla and eggs   B. sugar and shortening   C. flour and salt   D. chocolate chips and salt

Answers to sample questions: 1) B,   2) D,   3) B,   4) C

From *State Student Assessment Test. Part II: Answers to Your Questions.* Reprinted with permission of the State of Florida, Department of Education.

The Florida suit charged that the test should not be used for those minority students taught primarily in segregated schools. The dispute was therefore over whether the same test should be used for students with unequal opportunities to learn in school. Attorneys for the students argued that their clients had attended inferior schools and had suffered continued discrimination; thus, they should not be held to the standards for majority students, who had received better opportunities.

Ralph D. Turlington was the commissioner of education and one of the defendants in the case. He argued that basic minimum standards must be applied to certify that students have enough information to perform in situations that require a high-school education. These standards, he argued, must be absolute. Either students know the basic information or they do not. According to the commissioner, "To demand that a 12th-grade student with a 3rd-grade reading level be given a diploma is silly." The Florida case pitted two sides with reasonable arguments against each other. One side argued that minority children have worked hard in school under great disadvantage and cannot be expected to have learned the things majority children know. In recognition of their work, they deserve a diploma. The other side argued that there should be an absolute standard for basic information (Seligmann, Coppola, Howard, & Lee, 1979). These arguments are very similar to contemporary debates about the use of standards-based testing in public schools.

The court essentially sided with the commissioner. The judge did not challenge the validity of the test. However, he did suspend the use of the test for 4 years, after which all the students who had any part of their education in segregated schools would have graduated. Then, according to the opinion, the test could be used.

In a 1981 article, Lerner argued that minimum competence exams, such as the SSAT II used in the state of Florida, benefit both students and society. As an attorney, she found little legal justification for court involvement. However, the court reopened the *Debra P.* case that same year. This new consideration came after those students who had begun their education under a segregated system had graduated, and thus differences in performance could not be attributed to segregation. In the new evaluation, the U.S. District Court of Appeals considered the validity of the test. It stated that the test would violate the equal protection clause if "the test by dividing students into two categories, passers and failers, did so without a rational relation to the purpose for which it was designed." However, in this case, the court concluded that the test did have adequate construct validity and that it could be used to evaluate functional literacy. In the same opinion, the court stressed that the test must reflect what is taught in school and that continual surveillance of test fairness is warranted.

Claims such as those in *Debra P.* are less common today than they were in the 1980s because few school districts engage in explicit racial discrimination. However, many of the arguments in *Debra P.* were used in cases involving the use of tests to withhold high-school diplomas from Mexican American students. An important case in Texas considered the use of English-based tests to deny high-school diplomas to students who used Spanish as their primary language (GI Forum v. Texas Education Agency, 1997).

Various arguments have been used in defense of grouping students in special education classes. In *Simmons on Behalf of Simmons v. Hooks* (1994), school officials argued that African American students benefited from being grouped in a slower educational track. The court rejected their arguments.

Regents of the University of California v. Bakke

Alan Bakke was an engineer in his 30s who decided to apply to medical school at the University of California, Davis, in the early 1970s. Although Bakke had a high grade point average and good Medical College Admission Test (MCAT) scores, he was denied admission. Bakke decided to investigate the matter. He discovered that his test scores were higher than those of minority students who had gained admission to the medical school under a special affirmative action program.

The United States Commission on Civil Rights defines Affirmative Action as "any measure, beyond simple termination of a discriminatory practice, that permits the consideration of race, national origin, sex, or disability, along with other criteria, and which is adopted to provide opportunities to a class of qualified individuals who have either historically or actually been denied those opportunities and/or to prevent the recurrence of discrimination in the future." Bakke eventually sued the university on the grounds that he had been discriminated against because he was not a minority group member. The suit ended in the Supreme Court. The case gained particular attention because it raised the issue of "reverse discrimination," or race-based discrimination against a majority group member.

A major argument in *Bakke* concerned the use of test scores. Under the affirmative action program, the cutoff value for MCAT scores was higher for nonminority than for minority students. The defense argued that the tests were not meaningful (valid) for minority students. However, evidence was also presented that the tests were equally meaningful for both groups.

The Supreme Court ruling did not specifically address the use of tests, but it ruled that the university had to admit Bakke and that it had denied him due process in the original consideration of the case. It also implied that the use of different cutoff scores was not appropriate. However, the court did acknowledge that race could be taken into consideration in selection decisions. The EEOC interpreted this acknowledgment as a green light for affirmative action programs based on numerical quotas (Norton, 1978). However, the *Bakke* case signified a change in attitude about affirmative action programs.

Former president Ronald Reagan openly opposed selection goals and affirmative action and made a political issue out of "racial quotas." He appointed several people to key positions who agreed with his beliefs. For example, his assistant attorney general for civil rights, Bradford Reynolds, became an advocate for unqualified individualism (see Chapter 19). He argued for "color blind" equal opportunity in which skin color is not considered in selection decisions. According to Reynolds, selecting African Americans with lower test scores to remediate past discrimination would be "borrowing the tools of the racist." He emphasized that government must "never support the use of quotas or any other numerical formulas" (Bareak & Lauter, 1991, p. A18). In 1996, California voters passed Proposition 209, which made affirmative action illegal. However, in 2008, the courts heard continuing legal challenges. California institutions also continued a variety of programs designed to increase racial balance.

Golden Rule Insurance Company et al. v. Washburn et al.

In 1976, the Golden Rule Insurance Company of Lawrenceville, Illinois, sued ETS and the Illinois Department of Insurance over "cultural bias" in the Illinois Insurance Licensing Examination, created by the ETS for the state of Illinois. A 1978 study showed that 77% of white applicants passed the exam, while only 52% of African Americans passed. The case was settled out of court. ETS made no admission of guilt but did agree to change the test, mainly in the way items are selected for it. An expert committee of insurance officials and testing experts now oversee the selection of the items on the criterion that the proportions of correct answers for white and African American test takers differ by no more than .15.

When the *Golden Rule* case was settled in 1984, civil rights experts predicted that there would be a major revision in the way insurance tests were administered in 22 other states. Approximately 200,000 applicants for insurance licenses take these tests every year ("Insurance License Exams Will Be Revised," 1984, p. 5). In 1985, a related case, *Allen v. Alabama State Board of Education*, followed similar lines of reasoning. However, in *Allen*, a much more stringent rule was used. The Alabama State Board of Education agreed to use items for which the African American to white proportion of correct answers differed by no more than .05. The *Golden Rule* case is important because it sets a new precedent within the testing industry. Although ETS admitted no guilt, it clearly agreed to revise its method of operation.

Adarand Constructors, Inc. v. Peña, Secretary of Transportation, et al.

In 1995, the U.S. Supreme Court weakened the legal basis for affirmative action. The case involved Adarand Constructors, which was competing for a subcontract from the federal government. Before 1995, most federal contracts had included a compensation clause that gave the primary contractor a financial incentive to hire as subcontractors small businesses controlled by socially and economically disadvantaged individuals. This particular case involved a contract from the U.S. Department of Transportation. After submitting the low bid to complete construction work, Adarand Constructors was denied the job in favor of a small business controlled by minority group members. The Supreme Court, by a vote of 5-4, suggested that giving business to firms owned by minority group members violated the equal protection component of the 14th Amendment. This policy, the court argued, denied Adarand and other contractors their due process. The decision had an immediate impact. Hundreds of millions of dollars in federal grants had been awarded under special preference programs, and these practices were ended. The ultimate impact of the decision on affirmative action programs will be determined by future policies and decisions.

Affirmative Action in Higher Education

In addition to *Adarand*, other cases concerning higher education have weakened affirmative action. For example, the early 1990s saw the beginning of a new type of lawsuit that held that affirmative action programs did not necessarily benefit all minority groups. For example, Asian students have historically done especially well on college admissions tests such as the SAT. Some people have argued that affirmative action programs systematically discriminate against both minority and majority students. In 1991, a California congressman requested an investigation of the University of California, San Diego (UCSD). The university admits approximately 60% of its first-year class according to grade point average and SAT scores. Admission to the university is extremely competitive. Those who are admitted often have a nearly perfect grade point average and high SAT scores. However, in the early 1990s, 40% of the spots were reserved for students admitted under special considerations, including special achievements in fields such as music, athletics, or student government. In addition, the supplemental criteria can include race and ethnicity. Students admitted under these criteria were often from traditionally underrepresented groups such as Latinos, Latinas, and African Americans. The UCSD case was initiated by a Filipino student denied admission under both standard and supplemental criteria. However, if all students had been admitted under the standard criteria, this student would probably have been admitted, because both his grade point average and SAT scores were high. The congressman argued that Asian Americans had been systematically denied admission because of their race. They did not receive extra consideration under the supplemental criteria, because they were not underrepresented in the first 60% of students selected. On the other hand, their test scores and grade point averages were higher than other minority-group members who were selected under the special admissions policies.

Similar complaints were filed at other University of California campuses. The university's defense was that it does not discriminate on the basis of race. Selection criteria are not ironclad. In other words, the university reserves the right to have some flexibility in its decision to select students. Ethnic diversity, they argued, is an appropriate goal for a public university. In 1995, the Regents of the University of California voted to give up all affirmative action programs (see Focused Example 20.5). The decision had a dramatic effect on admissions to professional schools within the University of California system.

Grutter v. Bollinger and *Gratz v. Bollinger*

The question of affirmative action reached the U.S. Supreme Court once again in June 2003. Two lawsuits challenged the University of Michigan admissions policy. The first case involved Barbara Grutter (*Grutter v. Bollinger*), who was denied admission to the law school in 1996. Grutter discovered that the university had given extra points to underrepresented students, and this created a bias against white students. The Court ruled by a margin of 5-4 in favor of the law school admission policy, ruling that it benefited the university by enriching the campus with racial diversity and helping to improve cross-racial understanding. The law school policy allowed membership in an underrepresented racial or ethnic group as a positive factor among the many factors that are considered in the admissions process. The second decision (*Gratz v. Bollinger*) by a vote of 6-3 reversed the university's undergraduate policy that allowed race to be considered but still allowed consideration of race among other factors in admission decisions. The Court argued that the policy did not provide for flexibility when considering applicants with various backgrounds. However, the Court agreed that race could be considered but not specifically quantified. These cases raised several important issues. For example, the decisions noted the need for incorporating time limits into admissions policies and for considering race-neutral alternatives. The Court also took into consideration extra burdens on nonminority students imposed by consideration of racial and economic background (Holden, 2003; "A Victory for Affirmative Action," 2003).

20.5 FOCUSED EXAMPLE

The Twists and Turns of University Affirmative Action Policies

Federal regulation of college admissions policies has taken many interesting twists and turns. Initially, affirmative action policies were designed to guarantee that institutions of higher learning would be ethnically diverse. Indeed, most disciplinary actions have been taken because universities had not successfully attracted an ethnically diverse student body. However, some institutions have been thoroughly successful. For example, Boalt Hall, the School of Law at the University of California, Berkeley, has made aggressive efforts to attract an ethnically diverse student body. In the class of 1996 (made up of students admitted in 1992), 39% of the students were from minority groups.

In September 1992, Boalt Hall's admissions policies came under scrutiny. The U.S. Department of Education's Office of Civil Rights argued that the university had engaged in policies inconsistent with Title VII of the 1964 Civil Rights Act in that the law school had allowed discrimination on the basis of race, color, or national origin. Because Boalt Hall set aside a portion of its entering class positions for minority students and used separate decision processes for minority and nonminority students, it was argued that discrimination was taking place against Asians and to some extent Caucasians.

When faced with the complaint, the university agreed to alter its admissions policies. It was required to report by 1994 the number of applicants in each racial and ethnic category and to list how many of these applicants were admitted. By the time the 1994 report was completed, the university faced several similar lawsuits. In 1995, the regents of the university decided to end their affirmative action programs. In 1996, California voters passed an initiative restricting affirmative action programs. The result has been a dramatic decline in the number of African American and Hispanic students. However, a 2003 California initiative that would have forbidden the collection of any information about race was rejected by the voters.

Most recently, the U.S. Supreme Court case of *Fisher v. University of Texas* allowed an affirmative action program to continue. The program allows universities to consider a variety of factors, including racial diversity, in their admissions decisions. The court asked for continued scrutiny and evaluation of the admissions process but signaled that some of the affirmative action is constitutional.

Some believe that the Michigan decisions ushered in a new era of appreciation for civil rights. However, the decision also had opponents. For example, Ward Connerly, a noted African American conservative activist, cited the U.S. Constitution proclamation that "all men are created equal" and the equal protection clause of the 4th Amendment, which states, "nor shall any state deprive any person of life, liberty, or property, without due process of law; nor deny any person within its jurisdiction to equal protection of the law." Connerly believes that the Michigan decision violated the law by allowing race to be considered in law school acceptance decisions. In contrast, Mary Sue Coleman, the University of Michigan president, stated, "I believe these rulings in support of affirmative action will go down in history as among the great landmark decisions of the Supreme Court." Dr. Coleman also argued, "The court has provided two important signals. The first is a green light to pursue diversity in the college classroom. The second is a road map to get us there. We will modify our undergraduate system to comply with today's ruling, but make no mistake; we will find the root that continues our commitment to a richly diverse student body." See Focused Example 20.6.

20.6 FOCUSED EXAMPLE

Contrasting Views on Affirmative Action

Crosby and colleagues provided a detailed review of affirmative action and social policy. Several initiatives have made the issue more controversial (Crosby et al., 2003). In 1996, California voters passed Proposition 209; Washington voters passed Initiative 200 in 1998. Both of these ballot measures made the preferential treatment based on demographic characteristics illegal. Despite an enormous debate on the issue, we still do not have definitive evidence that supports some of the arguments. For example, Crosby and colleagues suggested that affirmative action has driven a wedge into the African American community by separating those who are lucky enough to gain entrance into universities and those who are not. It may enhance the perception of relative deprivation (Carrillo, Corning, Dennehy, & Crosby, 2011). However, there is a strong sense of community for many ethnic groups. The United States has great disparities between the rich and poor. This is known as the problem of income inequality and it has been getting worse over the last 40 years. Despite lower median incomes among Hispanic and African American citizens, there is growing evidence that successful members of ethnic minority groups are generous in giving money back to their communities.

There is strongly compelling evidence that affirmative action policies do undermine self-confidence. Many years of research have documented that white men question the skills of women and of minority group members who have been chosen under affirmative action policies (Crosby et al., 2003). Some research shows that stigmatization toward African Americans can be reduced if people think employees or school applicants are being evaluated on merit. In one study, 178 students and 168 corporate employees evaluated descriptions of African American and white employees who were working under different conditions. In one case, the employees were described as being selected by an illegal policy that favored minority candidates. In a second case, the subjects were told that the employees were selected by a legal policy that had the same effect as the illegal policy. In the third case, subjects were told that the employees were selected under an equal opportunity policy. When the subjects believed that the employees were selected by an illegal policy, they rated achievement-related traits for African American employees lower than those for white employees. However, the same effect did not occur when the judges were told that the employees were selected by a fair and legal process (Evans, 2003).

Parents v. Seattle

In 2007, affirmative action suffered a significant setback. An important case involved Jill Kurfirst and her son Andy, who lived in Seattle, Washington. Jill wanted Andy to go to the best school and thus reviewed test performance, college acceptance rates, and other statistics for 10 schools in the Seattle area. She chose Ballard, Roosevelt, and Hale High Schools as appropriate for Andy and designated Ballard as the first choice.

However, when school assignments were distributed, Andy did not get into any of his first three choices. Instead, he was sent to Ingraham High School, a campus that did not offer advanced academic programs or college preparatory classes. The reason that Andy did not get into Ballard was that the Seattle Public School District gave preference to minority students, and Andy was white. The school acknowledged that it considered racial balance as a criterion for student assignment. The race of a student was considered if he or she could make each school appear closer to the district-wide average of 40% white and 60% minority students.

A group of parents got together and filed a lawsuit, claiming that the district's policy violated the Constitution, the Civil Rights Act of 1964, and a state of Washington initiative that prohibited preferential treatment on the basis of race, ethnicity, or gender. The district court of appeals argued that the school district had a "compelling interest in securing the educational and social benefits of racial (and ethnic) diversity." This opinion allowed the school districts to continue to consider race in their assignment of students to schools. The case was appealed to the U.S. Supreme Court. The Supreme Court was sharply divided and ruled by a narrow 5-4 margin to overturn the lower court ruling. The majority argued that the school district had not demonstrated the appropriateness of considering racial composition in its policy of assigning students to schools. Justices in both the majority and minority cited the *Brown v. School Board of Education* decision in their opinions.

Meredith v. Jefferson County Board of Education

This case was very similar to the *Seattle* case, and the Supreme Court heard the two cases together. The *Meredith* case asked if the desire to achieve racial balance in a student body is a valid goal for an elementary or a high school district. Jefferson County, Kentucky, enacted a plan to ensure that there was racial balance in its schools. The school district required that each school maintain an African American population that was no greater than 50% of the student body, but no less than 15%.

Enactment of this plan required that some students be bused across the county and that these students spend more time commuting to school than was deemed reasonable. A group of Jefferson County parents brought a civil suit against the county arguing that their children's constitutional rights had been violated. They suggested that the school district policy violated the Equal Protection Clause of the 14th Amendment. The district policy had been upheld by the 6th Circuit Court of Appeals. However, in June 2007, the U.S. Supreme Court released its opinions on this case and the *Seattle* case.

In effect, the Court found that Jefferson County policy was unconstitutional. Chief Justice John Roberts, writing for the majority, argued that the goal of achieving racial balance in the schools did not justify what he considered to be "extreme" burdens on individual students. The vocal minority, led by Justice Anthony Kennedy, argued that school districts in the U.S. have a strong moral and ethical obligation to achieve integration. Overall, the *Seattle* and *Jefferson County* cases reversed the tide by emphasizing individual burdens over the societal objective of racial balance. They were taken as evidence that a new and more conservative Supreme Court would undermine decades of progress toward racial integration.

Fisher v. University of Texas

As the book was in the final stages of production, one more case was working its way to the U.S. Supreme Court. This case involves Abigall Fisher who applied to the University of Texas in 2008. The University of Texas guarantees automatic admission to the top 10% of high school graduates. Ms. Fisher had a SAT score of 1180 that did not quite make the cut for the 1218 slots the university set aside for high-performing Texas high school students. However, Ms. Fisher's lawyers argued that the University of Texas had engaged in a policy that used different criteria for students with different ethnic or racial backgrounds. The lawyers argued that students from other ethnic or racial groups were admitted with SAT scores lower than those achieved by Ms. Fisher.

At first, the University tried to downplay the case. They argued that the court case was moot because Ms. Fisher was accepted to Louisiana State University in 2008 and graduated in 2012. It is also noteworthy that Ms. Fisher's claims were fairly modest. She asked only for the return of her $50 application fee and for the $50 housing deposit, both of which were not refundable.

The oral arguments in the Fisher case were heard on June 29, 2015 and they drew particular public reaction. Justice Antonin Scalia asked whether African American students might be better off in less selective institutions. He cited the "mismatch hypothesis" (see Chapter 19, Focused Example 19.7), which argues that students with lower LSAT scores who are admitted to top-tier schools in affirmative action programs are less likely to succeed if they had attended less competitive law schools. Specifically, Scalia said "There are those who contend that it does not benefit African Americans to get them into the University of Texas, where they do not do well, as opposed to having them go to a less-advanced school, a slower-track school where they do well. One of the briefs pointed out that most of the black scientists in this country don't come from schools like the University of Texas. They come from lesser schools where they do not feel that they're being pushed ahead in classes that are too fast for them." (Mencimer, 2015). The comment met with significant outrage and hinted to some that Justice Antonin Scalia would vote against the affirmative action program at the University of Texas. But, Scalia never got the opportunity to vote. He died unexpectedly in February of 2016. Because 2016 was an election year, the congress refused to approve any nominee to replace Scalia. In addition, Justice Elena Kagan recused herself because she had worked on the Fisher case when she was employed as the solicitor general. As a result, the case was decided by seven rather than nine justices.

Ultimately, the court voted 4-3 to uphold the University of Texas policy. The majority opinion noted the contribution of diversity to the mission of the university. However, the majority also noted that in future admission decisions "…race plays no greater role than is necessary to meet its compelling interest." The conclusion was that affirmative action programs, such as the one at the University of Texas, were lawful and can continue with the provision that universities continually examine data on the demographics of the student populations.

Personnel Cases

Several important lawsuits have dealt with testing in employment settings. Through a series of Supreme Court decisions, specific restrictions have been placed on the use of tests for the selection of employees. The most important of these cases are *Griggs v. Duke Power Company*, *Albemarle Paper Company v. Moody*, and *Washington v. Davis*. In effect, these decisions have forced employers to define the measure of job performance as well as how it relates to test scores. However, none of the decisions denies that tests are valuable tools in the personnel field and that the use of tests can continue.

In Chapter 5, we mentioned *Griggs v. Duke Power Company*. The case involved 14 African American employees of the Duke Steam Plant in North Carolina who were concerned about their lack of opportunity. In the steam plant, few employees, either African American or white, had graduated from high school. In 1966, the most an African American employee could earn was $1.65 per hour, while whites started at $1.81. Furthermore, white men generally rose through the ranks of the company and became managers or supervisors, with comfortable offices and bathrooms down the hall. Though assigned to clean the toilets in those bathrooms, African American men were not allowed to use them. Instead, the company built a "colored" bathroom and placed it across the railroad tracks behind the coal pile. The leader of the African American employees, Willie Boyd, had learned about the EEOC and become acquainted with a civil rights leader who persuaded Boyd and his coworkers to file a complaint. When they presented their complaint to the company, they were told that education and training were necessary for advancement. However, only 15 white employees had finished high school. The company reacted by creating a test and telling the African American employees that they needed to pass it in order to gain advancement. The test included 50 items such as this:

> In printing an article of 24,000 words, a printer decides to use two sizes of type. With the larger type, a printed page contains 900 words. With the smaller type, a page contains 1200 words. The article is allotted 21 full pages in the magazine. How many pages must be in small type?

None of the African American employees passed this difficult test. Neither did any of the white employees. The validity of the test became the central issue in the lawsuit that followed. Specifically, evidence was required on the relationship between the test and the job duties. Although Boyd led the group, the lawsuit was filed under the name of Willie Griggs, the youngest of the group with the least seniority and the least to lose. After 5 years, the case worked its way to the U.S. Supreme Court, which ruled that employment tests must be valid and reliable. The *Griggs* case set the tone for the next two decades of civil rights action in the United States (Bareak & Lauter, 1991; Crosby, Iyer, Clayton, & Downing, 2003).

In the 1988 Supreme Court case, *Watson v. Fort Worth Bank and Trust,* it was argued that any procedure that appears to discriminate because of the ratio of minorities selected violates the law. The case involved Clara Watson, an African American employee of the Fort Worth Bank and Trust. After being passed over for promotion to a supervisory position, Watson filed suit. She argued that African Americans made up 13% of the bank's workforce and 10% of Fort Worth's population. However, the bank had only one African American supervisor. Thus, there was a misrepresentation in selection for higher jobs. The lower courts had rejected Watson's petition, arguing that statistical evidence for bias applied only to objective selection devices, such as psychological tests, and that subjective judgments could be defended when there was evidence of "business necessity." The Supreme Court disagreed, suggesting that employers could protect themselves from discrimination suits by adding just one subjective item to objective tests. The court affirmed that statistical selection ratios are sufficient evidence of adverse impact.

Wards Cove and the 1991 Civil Rights Act

Sometimes trends in one direction spur reactions in another. Legislation like California's Proposition 209 reacted to earlier affirmative action developments by emphasizing the "color blind" selection of employees. *Watson* was one of the first important civil rights cases decided by a conservative group of Supreme Court justices. The next major case that came to the court was *Wards Cove Packing Company v. Antonio*. The case concerned salmon canneries in Alaska. Most of the workers were unskilled Filipinos and Eskimos who sliced up the fish during fishing season. Because these jobs were unsteady and dirty, they were the worst in the company. The employees claimed that the company was biased against them and kept them out of the better-paying skilled jobs, such as machinery repair. The nine Supreme Court justices decided not to hear the case, returning it to the lower courts. This decision reversed a central theme of the *Griggs* decision. In refusing to hear the case, the Court noted that the burden of proof should be shifted from the employer to the employee. In other words, instead of requiring the employer to show that a psychological test is valid and reliable, the burden fell to the employee to demonstrate that it did not have these properties. This may seem like a minor point, but in practice it could have had an enormous impact. Employers know how to interpret their own tests, financial records, and selection procedures. Requiring the plaintiff to discredit these procedures gives him or her an almost impossible task. Even the most skilled lawyers felt that the long fight for equal employment opportunity had been lost (Bareak & Lauter, 1991).

The *Wards Cove Packing Company v. Antonio* decision upset the Democratic-controlled 1991 Congress. In response to court actions, it proposed new and stronger legislation that culminated in the 1991 Civil Rights Act. Here are the purposes of the act:

1. Provide appropriate redress for intentional discrimination and unlawful harassment in the workplace.
2. Overrule proof burdens and the meaning of business necessity in *Wards Cove Packing Company v. Antonio* and codify the proof burdens and the meaning of business necessity used in *Griggs v. Duke Power Company*.
3. Confirm the basic aspects of the 1964 Civil Rights Act.
4. Provide a clear response to the Supreme Court decision.

In short, the act placed the burden of proof back on the employer. One provision of the 1991 Civil Rights Act deals specifically with test scores. Section 9, "Prohibition Against Discriminatory Use of Test Scores," states,

> It shall be an unlawful employment practice for a respondent in connection with the selection or referral of applicants or candidates for employment or promotion to adjust the scores of, use different cutoff scores, or otherwise alter the results of employment related tests on the basis of race, color, religion, sex, or natural origin.

This part of the bill appears to outlaw the use of differential cutoff scores by race, gender, or ethnic backgrounds. Thus, it may cause a shift away from the use of quotas. See Focused Example 20.7 to see how African Americans and whites see these issues differently.

Ricci v. DeStafano (129 S. Ct. 2658, 2671, 174 L Ed. 2d. 490 [2009]).

In 2009, the Supreme Court ruled on a lawsuit against the city of New Haven, Connecticut. The suit was brought by 20 firefighters who did not get promoted and believed that they were discriminated against on the basis of race. Among the 20

20.7 FOCUSED EXAMPLE

Different Views of Affirmative Action

African Americans and whites differ in their views of affirmative action. The Pew Research Center conducts continuing polls to monitor the values of representative samples of the U.S. population. For example, when asked if African Americans or other minorities should be given preferential treatment to make up for past discrimination, only 22% of white non-Hispanic respondents agreed in comparison to 58% of African American and 53% of Hispanic respondents (see Figure 20.1).

When asked if they favored or opposed affirmative action programs "to help the African Americans and other minorities get better jobs and education," 37% of white non-Hispanics said they opposed the programs in comparison to 17% of Hispanic respondents and only 6% of African American respondents (see Figure 20.2).

The Pew group has been following attitudes toward affirmative action since the mid-1990s. In 1995, 36% of the American public were opposed to affirmative action programs. Since then, the opposition rate has steadily declined to about 25% in 2007 (see Figure 20.3).

FIGURE 20.1

Differences between racial/ethnic groups favoring preferential treatment to improve the position of African Americans and other minorities.

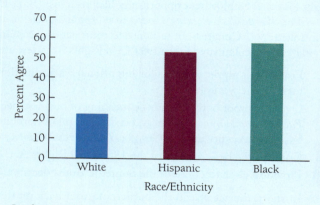

Data from 2009 report of Pew Research Center Values Survey (art original).

plaintiffs, 20 were white and 1 was Hispanic. All of the plaintiffs had passed a standardized test that was needed to obtain the promotion. However, the city of New Haven Fire Department had decided not to use the test results because none of the African American fire fighters had obtained scores high enough to be considered for advanced positions. The city argued that using the test might have placed them in the position of using an instrument that would result in race-based discrimination. The Supreme Court heard the case in April 2009 and in late June 2009 revealed a 5-4 decision in favor of the plaintiffs. In particular, the court argued that New Haven's decision to ignore high test performance by the white and Hispanic fire fighters violated Title VII of the Civil Rights Act of 1964.

FIGURE 20.2

Differences between racial/ethnic groups favoring preferential treatment to help African Americans and other minorities get better jobs or educational placements.

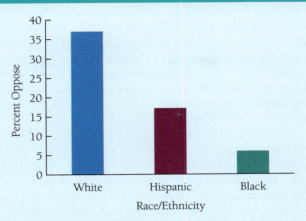

Data from the 2009 report of the Pew Research Center Values Survey (art original) (pewresearch.org/pubs/1240/sotomayor-supreme-court-affirmative-action-minority-preferences; accessed January 1, 2012).

FIGURE 20.3

Percent of the U.S. population opposed to affirmative action in Pew surveys completed in 1995, 2003, 2005, and 2007.

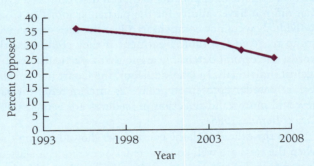

Data from the 2009 report of Pew Research Center Values Survey (art original) (pewresearch.org/pubs/ 1240/sotomayor-supreme-court-affirmative-action-minority-preferences; accessed January 1, 2012).

The impact of the *Ricci* decision remains to be evaluated. Some argue that it promotes the notion of judicial color blindness because it rewards good test performance regardless of the race of the test taker. On the other hand, it has also been argued that job-related assessment tools can be used to correct racial imbalance that might also be illegal. Further, New Haven failed to use high standards in the design and application of the test that was applied to the fire fighters. Its test did not necessarily select the applicants who were most likely to succeed, but New Haven may have unnecessarily perpetuated the status quo racial discrimination among its fire fighters (Harris & West-Faulcon, 2010).

Test Administration and Validity

The courts have sometimes been asked to decide on issues of test administration. For example, because of a low test score, an employee of the Detroit Edison Company was not promoted. In his defense, his union suggested that the low score might have been an error and requested a copy of the test to check the scoring. Detroit Edison did not want to release the test because it feared that the union would distribute the items to other employees. By a 5–4 vote, the Supreme Court ruled on the side of Detroit Edison in *Detroit Edison Co. v. N.L.R.B.* It is interesting that in a major decision such as this, a single vote can make a difference in policy (Cronbach, 1980).

A 1982 Supreme Court decision, *Connecticut v. Teal*, considered the issue of discrimination against an individual when there has been no adverse impact. In this case, a written test unrelated to any specific job was used as an initial screening device. This screening device significantly reduced the number of African Americans in the application pool. However, at the next step in the screening process, African Americans who had passed the test had a better chance of being hired than did whites. In short, the total number of African Americans hired did not reflect an adverse impact.

On review of the situation, the U.S. Supreme Court ruled that Title VII protects individuals, not just the groups to which they belong. Thus, it ruled that African American applicants had been discriminated against by the use of a test that did not have validity for the particular job. The Court suggested that these individuals were not compensated just because other members of their minority group received favorable treatment if they could pass the initial test. In other words, one cannot defensibly argue that a particular result justifies discrimination against individuals. In later decisions, the Court has upheld hiring goals that favor formerly underrepresented groups as interim relief for past discrimination while new and more valid selection procedures are being established (*United States v. City of Buffalo*, 1985).

On the other hand, the courts have allowed testing that excludes some groups when the tests are well constructed. For example, a class-action suit in California demonstrated that a teacher certification test had a higher failure rate for Mexican American teachers than for non-Hispanic Caucasian teachers. However, the court ruled that the test could still be used. The decision was based on three arguments. First, teacher educators and content experts had agreed to the items on the test before the measure was administered. Second, content-analysis and job-analysis studies had been conducted and questionable items had been eliminated. Third, the cutoff scores for failure had been established using acceptable methods (*Association of Mexican-American Educators v. California*, 1996).

In one summary article, Hogan and Quigley (1986) reviewed all of the cases that involved physical standards used in employment decisions. Physical tests, including height, weight, and physical strength, must be subjected to the same validity criteria as psychological tests. We expect many future lawsuits to arise concerning these issues.

A major issue that has plagued job discrimination cases is the evidence that one can use to prove bias. Proof of discrimination has often been difficult. In blue-collar jobs, employers have defended their hiring practices on the basis of the validity of aptitude tests. Challenges were typically based on the test criterion validity and the ratio of minority applicants that the test selected. In contrast, decisions about the selection and advancement of people in white-collar jobs have been based on subjective impressions of job performance and interviews. This promotes a double standard. White-collar employees have promoted the use of tests even though tests are not used for white-collar evaluations.

Cases Relevant to the Americans With Disabilities Act (ADA)

One of the major challenges in test administration was created by the passage of the ADA in 1991. The major focus of the ADA is the removal of physical barriers that make it difficult for people with disabilities to gain employment and education. However, according to some interpretations of the act, people with learning or other disabilities may request accommodations including substantially more time, rest breaks, or testing over multiple days.

The ADA, in effect, made private entities responsible for the same requirements that public agencies had addressed under Section 504 of the 1973 Rehabilitation Act. Section 504 creates a specific conflict with regard to testing:

> A recipient (of federal funds) shall make reasonable accommodations to the known physical or mental limitations of an otherwise qualified handicapped applicant or employee unless the recipient can demonstrate that the accommodation would impose an undue hardship on the operation of its program.

This passage has been interpreted to mean that those with disabilities should be afforded extra time or other accommodations in the completion of psychological or achievement tests. This policy contrasts with the *APA Standards for Educational and Psychological Tests.*

In typical applications, test administrators should follow carefully the standardized procedures for administration and scoring specified by the test publisher. Specifications regarding instructions to test takers, time limits, a form of item presentation or response, and test materials or equipment should be strictly observed. Exceptions should be made only on the basis of carefully considered professional judgment, primarily in clinical applications (Geisinger, 1994).

The ADA defines reasonable accommodation as modifications in the job-application process, work environment, or benefits and privileges of employment that enable the disabled person to be considered for, perform the essential job functions, or enjoy the benefits of employment of similarly situated employees without disabilities (U.S. Equal Employment Opportunity Commission, 2003; see www. eeoc.gov). There are a variety of ways in which employees can be accommodated. For example, shifting responsibility to other employees for some job task that the employee cannot perform is a form of accommodation. Employers can also restructure a job to allow a person with a disability to perform it. For example, a department store salesperson who has arthritis of the hands and cannot wrap packages might be relieved of this responsibility while still being able to perform sales activities. Some accommodations are not considered reasonable. For example, the ADA does not require an employer to change the supervisor of a disabled person. However, they may ask that the supervisor's behavior, such as their method of communicating assignments, be changed.

The ADA has provoked a variety of lawsuits. One of the earliest cases, *Brookhart v. Illinois State Board of Education* (1983), concerned minimum competency tests. Because they failed a minimum competency test, several disabled students were denied high-school diplomas. They filed a lawsuit arguing that they had completed individualized educational programs and therefore qualified for a diploma. The test, they argued, denied them due process. In particular, the disabled students, including those with learning disabilities, may have had difficulty completing the test within the required time. In their decision, the federal court suggested that schools must provide accommodations for disabled students. However, the court argued that the test administrator did not have to modify the test substantially. Further, the court noted that the test need not be modified to ensure a passing grade for a person unable to learn because of a disability. On the other hand, the court left unanswered many decisions about the degree of accommodation required of test administrators.

In another case, the Hawaii Department of Education refused to allow a reader to assist a learning-disabled boy in a statewide graduation test. Because the student did not have impaired vision, the court decided that the use of a reader for the reading portions of the test would be inappropriate; that is, the decision by the Hawaii Department of Education was not discriminatory. However, the court also concluded that readers could be provided for aspects of the test that did not measure reading competency. Furthermore, the ruling suggested that denying a reader for these portions of the test did constitute unlawful discrimination against those with disabilities (Phillips, 1994).

A Critical Look at Lawsuits

We can expect more court battles over the use of psychological tests. The problems that psychologists cannot resolve themselves will eventually be turned over to someone else for a binding opinion. This move, though, may not be in the best interest of the field of psychology or of the people whom the profession serves.

Inconsistencies in court decisions are commonplace. Even worse, judges who make important decisions about the use of tests often have little background in psychology or testing. On completing this course, you should be better able to evaluate most of the evidence than can some judges. Often, judges obtain their entire education about testing during the course of a trial.

In the near future, society must grapple with many difficult issues. For example, many current social problems seem related to the differential distribution of resources among the races in the United States. Changing the income distribution seems to be one of the only ways to effect social change. To accomplish this redistribution, society must get minority children in appropriate educational tracks, into professional schools, and into high-income positions. In some cases, the courts have ruled that psychological tests are blocking this progress.

Psychologists themselves are not of one mind regarding the use of psychological tests. Though some researchers do not agree with the predominant court opinion, the courts have the power, and their judgment is law.

Summary

With increasing frequency, tests are coming under legal regulation. Created by the Civil Rights Act of 1964, the EEOC has issued strict guidelines for the use of tests. The guidelines clearly spell out the minimum criteria for validity and reliability of psychological measures. The role of the EEOC became the focus of considerable debate in the 1980s, and the power of the commission was questioned by two court decisions at the end of that decade. However, the 1991 Civil Rights Bill breathed new life into affirmative action programs.

Tests have also come to be regulated by statute. The states of California and New York were among the first to pass truth-in-testing laws that place many requirements on commercial testing companies. These laws have required testing companies to disclose actual test items to test takers. In the past, test items were protected by copyright. Items on tests affected by these laws must now be rewritten frequently, and this procedure may damage the reliability and the validity of the tests. In 1975, Congress passed PL 94-142, which outlined standards for the assessment of potential among children with developmental disabilities. This law continues to affect the use of tests in the educational system.

Many lawsuits have also affected the use of tests. In *Stell v. Savannah–Chatham County Board of Education*, the court ruled that differences between African Americans and whites in IQ scores could not justify segregation. In *Hobson v. Hansen*, group tests were found to be inappropriate for the assignment of African American children to EMR classes. The concern over IQ tests was extended in *Diana v. State Board of Education*. Settled out of court, this case established that IQ tests could not be used with bilingual children, and it stimulated the development of new methods of assessment for these children. The impact of each of these decisions was magnified in *Larry P. v. Wilson Riles*, in which tests were banned as a means of assigning African American children to EMR classes. In 1980, a court apparently reversed this decision in the case of *Parents in Action on Special Education v. Hannon*. In *Debra P. v. Turlington*, a court ruled that a minimum competence test could be used only when the students had received their entire education in integrated schools. The courts have created new challenges in the *Adarand* case, which eliminated affirmative action. The U.S. Supreme Court has made several important rulings relevant to affirmative action. The most recent of these is *Fisher v. University of Texas*. That decision allows the university of consider a wide range of factors in admission decisions, including racial background. Test scores and grade point average are recognized as important data, but universities are allowed to consider other factors and to value diversity.

The regulation of testing through statute (laws passed by legislators), regulation (rules created by agencies), and litigation (lawsuits) has only recently become common. The passage of the Americans with Disabilities Act is one example of a set of laws likely to affect the testing industry. More legal challenges to the use of psychological tests can be expected in the years to come.

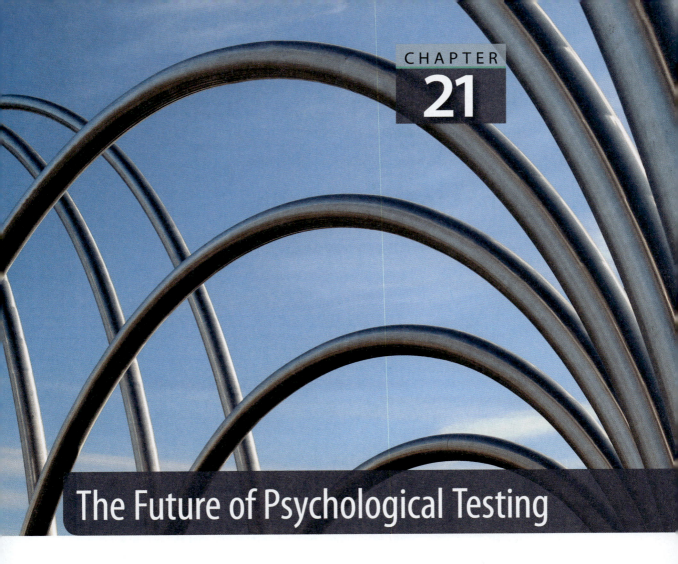

The Future of Psychological Testing

LEARNING OBJECTIVES

When you have completed this chapter, you should be able to:

▶ Explain why the question of whether people possess stable traits is an issue in the testing field

▶ Explain the issue of actuarial versus clinical prediction

▶ Identify human rights as they pertain to testing

▶ Explain the problem of labeling

▶ Explain the issue of divided loyalties

▶ Identify some important responsibilities of test users and constructors

▶ Identify four important current trends in the testing field

▶ Describe the future prospects of testing

The future of psychological testing is unfolding before our eyes. The most recent tests, such as the WISC-V, and the new SAT are based on technology and an awareness of the populations under study that was unheard of over 40 years ago when we wrote the first edition of psychological testing. Yet, the same forces, such as professional and moral issues, continue to shape the field. To understand where the field has come from, and where it is going, we conclude our discussion of testing with a look at the broad forces underlying the field.

Issues Shaping the Field of Testing

The concerns that currently shape testing include professional, moral, and social issues. Ethical issues underlie each of these concerns.

Professional Issues

Three major professional issues continually play an especially important role in the current status and the future of psychological testing: theoretical concerns, the adequacy of tests, and actuarial versus clinical prediction (see Figure 21.1).

Theoretical Concerns

One of the most important considerations underlying tests is the dependability (reliability) of test results (Thomas & Selthon, 2003; Tryon & Bernstein, 2003). Reliability places an upper limit on validity. A test that is totally unreliable (unstable) has no meaning. There may be exceptions to this rule, but current practice generally demands that tests possess some form of stability.

Each test must possess the type of reliability that is appropriate to the test's uses (AERA, APA, & NCME, 1999; APA, 2002; Slaney, Storey, & Barnes, 2011; Wyse & Reckase, 2011).

Most existing tests measure a presumably stable entity—either the individual as he or she currently functions or some temporally stable characteristic of the individual. In describing current functioning, psychologists imply that the person functions this way in a fairly stable, though perhaps short-term, manner that is independent of the situation or environment. In other words, they assume that they can describe the person in absolute terms, as if in a vacuum. They may say something like, "The person is emotionally unstable" or "The person is out of contact with reality" or else provide a diagnostic label such as "schizophrenic" or "neurotic." Similarly, and even more strikingly, psychologists purport to measure enduring qualities that will manifest themselves over time regardless of immediate or long-term external (situational, environmental, etc.) factors. Again, they assume that what they are measuring exists in absolute terms.

FIGURE 21.1
Schematic summary
of professional issues.

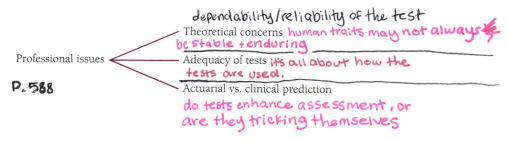

[handwritten annotations:] dependability/reliability of the test

Professional issues — Theoretical concerns *human traits may not always be stable + enduring*

Adequacy of tests *it's all about how the tests are used.*

Actuarial vs. clinical prediction

do tests enhance assessment, or are they tricking themselves

P. 588

Whether measuring current functioning or a temporally stable characteristic, testers always assume that the systematic source of variance measured by the test results entirely from the person rather than some other factor. When we try to measure a stable characteristic of an individual and find less than perfect temporal reliability, we assume that the imperfections proceed from test-related inadequacies, such as measurement error, or from minor fluctuating subject variables, such as fatigue. Presumably, then, the characteristic or variable being measured is stable, it exists, and only the test instrument limits one's ability to measure it. Therefore, the more accurate a test, the more stable the results should be.

However, many empirical investigations (Samuel et al., 2011) show that even the best tests have yet to achieve such temporal stability. In other words, testers cannot readily attribute differences over time solely to measurement error or fluctuating subject variables. Hence, this primary assumption underlying tests is not entirely correct. As is obvious, the social environment affects behavior (Hawkley, Lavelle, Berntson, & Cacioppo, 2011; Kendler et al., 2011). The trait question applies to psychology as a whole and to personality psychology in particular (Spear, 2007). Early formulations of human personality tended to view personality as comprising stable and lasting traits (behavioral dispositions). Freud and many of his followers, for example, believed that early experiences, memories, traumas, and anxieties often resulted in behavioral dispositions that persisted throughout life. Views such as Freud's, however, were challenged by those who saw human personality as changing rather than fixed and stationary, as well as by those who saw that situations and external factors influence behavior.

Most of the tests discussed in this text are based on the assumption that one can measure human characteristics independently of the context in which these characteristics occur, a theory not only disputable but also without significant support (Bandura, 1986; Mischel, 1968; Ziskin, 1995). Psychological tests can be no better than the science of psychology that underlies them. As the science clarifies basic theoretical issues, testing conforms to the available knowledge. In the meantime, perhaps the single most important theoretical assumption of tests—that human characteristics are stable and can be measured independently of the environment—is debatable. Thus, the new technologies of testing would be well served by measuring behavior in the social context, which might be accomplished by advances in virtual reality, for example.

After reviewing the psychometric qualities and the limits of mental ability and personality tests, we have concluded that, although people exhibit a core of stability, they continually change. Certainly, one explanation for the relatively poor long-term reliability of personality tests is that as the individual adjusts to the environment, he or she changes. Indeed, most definitions of intelligence include the ability to adapt or change according to circumstances. The fact is, people change all the time.

The Adequacy of Tests

A second professional issue in testing with strong overtones concerns the adequacy of existing tests. This entire book has been aimed at providing you with the knowledge you need to evaluate tests. To this end, the book is filled with statements about standardization, norms, scoring, interpretation, test design, reliability, and validity. Thus far, however, we have evaluated tests relative to traditionally accepted psychometric standards rather than absolute external criteria. David Shakow, who is to many the father of modern clinical psychology, posited that we have not quite reached our goal of providing objective and psychometrically sound assessment of personality and psychological function (Barlow, 2011, pp. 10–11). This was his conclusion after practicing clinical psychology in a career that spanned nearly 50 years. And now, nearly three quarters of a century after Shakow, his insights are almost as fresh as though they were made yesterday.

As we have noted repeatedly, the real issue in testing is how tests are used. No test at all is better than a test that often leads to an incorrect conclusion. In the end, how tests are used may be determined by law or by the threat of litigation. Tests that lead to selection biases are suspect. If an aptitude test consistently underselects African Americans, Latinos, and Latinas for college, then we have to ask how accurate these tests are, how much they add to prediction, and whether loss of diversity is justified by increased prediction (Geiser & Studley, 2001; Moore & Bell, 2011; Rosner, 2003; Shultz & Zedeck, 2011). In the end, it may be the U.S. Supreme Court or Congress that tells us whether the use of a test is justified.

Actuarial Versus Clinical Prediction

A third issue concerns the accuracy of predictions made by test users. Throughout this book, we have argued that tests provide a standard setting in which practitioners can observe behavior. Further, they can use this situation in conjunction with experience and local norms to gain accuracy in their observations and decisions. However, test users rarely, if ever, receive feedback on the accuracy of their predictions and decisions based on tests. Do tests, then, truly enhance assessment, or are practitioners fooling themselves, repeating their errors, and teaching them to students?

One can examine this question from all sides (see Campbell, 2003; Monahan, 2003; Ogloff & Douglas, 2003). The early work of Meehl (Meehl, 1954; Meehl & Rosen, 1955) and Little and Shneidman (1959) drew attention to the limits of test data even in the hands of trained practitioners more than half a century ago. Sawyer (1966) and Sines (1970) reviewed studies that compared an actuarial approach, in which test results were interpreted by using a set of rules, with a clinical approach, in which trained professionals interpreted test results (Quinsey, Harris, Rice, & Cormier, 2006). These reviews indicated that the set of rules was more accurate than the trained professional practitioners, even when the practitioners knew the rules. This research confirmed Meehl's (1954) earlier finding that trained practitioners could not surpass predictions based on statistical formulas. Ziskin (1995) and Dawes (1999) have argued that simple tables of actuarial data, such as number of prior arrests and severity of crime, predict recidivism better than do tests or clinical judgments. Do we really need trained clinicians and sophisticated tests to make decisions? The issue of actuarial versus clinical prediction has more recently reemerged with the proliferation of computerized test interpretations (Brooks & Barlow, 2011). As discussed in Chapter 15, computers are taking a prominent role in the scoring of tests, reporting of results, and diagnosis of clients (Frase et al., 2003). Can a computer accurately interpret a psychological test? The many problems inherent in such interpretations have fostered much debate about the computer's potential as a diagnostician (Drigas, Koukianakis, & Papagerasimou, 2011; Ponniah et al., 2011; Saccuzzo, 1994). As Hartman (1986) noted, several potential abuses accompany the use of computer software to interpret psychological tests, including trivialization of assessment, use of software inappropriate to the client, and inadequate contribution of the clinician to the assessment process. Further, the question remains as to whether the computer's interpretations can ever be as good as, let alone better than, those of the clinician. Regardless of whether clinicians rely on a computer-generated diagnosis, a testing service, or on their own interpretation of results, the APA guidelines entitled *Ethical Principles of Psychologists and Code of Conduct* specify that it is the clinician who retains responsibility for the appropriateness of the analysis (APA, 2002). Interestingly, with all the available technology, a 2011 survey of the practices of independent practitioners, very few relied on technology in their practices, and most were unsure about what uses of computer technology in practice was and was not ethical (McMinn, Bearse, Heyne, Smithberger, & Erb, 2011). Perhaps the Ph.D. programs that teach testing to doctoral students might consider some training in computers. If not, maybe the technology will pass them by.

Moral Issues

Professional issues alone will not determine the future of testing. The field is also being shaped by moral issues—human rights, labeling, and invasion of privacy (see Figure 21.2). Two other important ethical issues are divided loyalties and the responsibilities of test users and test constructors.

Human Rights

Several different kinds of human rights are relevant to psychological testing, including the right not to be tested. Individuals who do not want to subject themselves to testing should not, and ethically cannot, be forced to do so. Nevertheless, exceptions to this directive are noted in the 2010 APA guidelines. Specifically, informed consent to testing is not required when "testing is mandated by law or government," when "informed consent is implied because testing is conducted as a routine educational, institutional, or organizational activity," or when "the purpose of the testing is to evaluate decisional capacity" (p. 13). Clearly, these exceptions negate the right not to be tested in an inestimable number of situations. Swindell et al. (2010) provide a review of the literature regarding the right to refuse testing, covering such issues as autonomy, decision-making capacity, capacity for voluntariness, beneficence, and right to confidentiality (Swindell, Coverdale, Crisp-Han, & McCullough, 2010); what they found parallels the guidelines propagated by the APA.

Another right due test takers is their right to know their test scores and interpretations as well as the bases of any decisions that affect their lives. In the past, guarding the security of tests was of paramount importance. Today, one must still take all precautions to protect test security but not at the expense of an individual's right to know the basis of detrimental or adverse decisions. Test publishers who hide behind the veil of U.S. copyright laws and special rules protecting secure tests have

FIGURE 21.2
Schematic summary of moral issues.

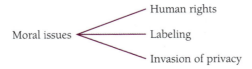

Moral issues
— Human rights
— Labeling
— Invasion of privacy

a responsibility to provide public sufficient information to allow users to make a truly informed decision of their adequacy. If the test has a selection bias, then this bias should be openly identified and not hidden by deceptive or misleading advertising. This is especially true of professional licensing exams such as those for physicians and attorneys, as these exams are the last barrier into a profession and would be suspect of bias if they underselected a disproportionate number of women and minorities.

Other human rights, some of which are only now being widely accepted, are the right to know who will have access to test data and the right to confidentiality of test results. The current frequent use of Internet and computer-based services has induced the APA to add a requirement for clinicians to warn clients of the risk to privacy and limits of confidentiality resulting from electronic transmission of information (APA, 2010).

Test interpreters have an ethical obligation to protect human rights. Potential test takers are responsible for knowing and demanding their rights. The increasing awareness among test users and the public of human rights is an important influence on the testing field.

Labeling

In standard medical practice, a person's disease or disorder is first identified (diagnosed). Once diagnosed, the disease can be labeled and standard medical intervention procedures implemented. It is no embarrassment to be diagnosed as having gall bladder or kidney disease. However, labeling people with certain medical diseases, such as acquired immunodeficiency syndrome (AIDS), and psychiatric disorders can be extremely damaging. The public has little understanding of the label schizophrenia, for example. Therefore, those who receive this label are often stigmatized, perhaps for life (Thoits, 2011). Labels may also affect one's access to help. Chronic schizophrenia, for example, has no cure. Labeling someone a chronic schizophrenic may be a self-fulfilling prophecy (McReynolds, Ward, & Singer, 2002). Because the disorder is incurable, nothing can be done. Because nothing can be done, why should one bother to help? Because no help is given, the person is a chronic case (Corrigan, 2007).

Still another problem with labels, which people unfortunately often justify with psychological tests, is theoretical. As Szasz (1961) originally noted, a medical label such as schizophrenia implies that a person is ill or diseased. Because no one can be blamed for becoming ill, a medical or psychiatric label implies that the person is not responsible for the condition. However, it may well be that those who are labeled as psychiatrically disturbed must take responsibility for their lives if they are to get better.

When we take responsibility for our lives, we believe that we can exercise some degree of control over our fates (after all, what is intelligence?) rather than simply being the victims of uncontrollable external forces. Individuals who feel a sense of control or responsibility for themselves should be able to tolerate more stress, frustration, and pain than do those who feel like passive victims (Sherrer, 2011). Certainly, a person who feels responsible or in control has more incentive to alter negative conditions than one who does not.

Labels that imply a person is not responsible may increase the risk that the person so labeled will feel passive. Thus, the labeling process may not only stigmatize the person but also lower tolerance for stress and make treatment more difficult. In view of the potentially negative effects of labels, a person should have the right not to be labeled. When testing is necessary, a test such as the Rorschach, which has been shown to overpathologize test takers (Carstairs, 2011; Drogin, Dattilio, Sadoff, & Gutheil, 2011; Finn, 2011), should not be relied on to determine pathology (Erard, 2005).

Invasion of Privacy

When people respond to psychological tests, they have little idea what is being revealed, but they often feel that their privacy has been invaded in a way not justified by the test's benefits. Public concern over this issue once became so strong that tests were investigated by the Senate Subcommittee on Constitutional Rights and the House Subcommittee on invasion of privacy. Neither found evidence of deliberate and widespread misuse of tests (see Brayfield, 1965).

The ethical code of the APA (1992, 2002) includes confidentiality. Guaranteed by law in most states that have laws governing the practice of psychology, this principle means that, as a general rule, personal information obtained by the psychologist from any source is communicated only with the person's consent. Exceptions include circumstances in which withholding information causes danger to the person or society, as well as cases that require subpoenaed records. Therefore, people have the right to know the limits of confidentiality and to know that test data can be subpoenaed and used as evidence in court (Benjamin & Gollan, 2003; Kocsis, 2011) or in employment decisions (Ones et al., 1995).

Divided Loyalties

Jackson and Messick (1967, Chapter 69) argued long ago that no one has formulated a coherent set of ethical principles that govern all legitimate uses of testing. Today, just like many of the other issues we have discussed, this is still true. The core of the problem lies in divided loyalties—the often conflicting commitments of the psychologist who uses tests. Despite the more than 50 years that have elapsed since Jackson and Messick first articulated the problem, the issue of divided loyalties remains a central dilemma to all psychologists who use tests in clinics, schools, business, industry, government, the military, and so forth. The question is, who is the client—the individual or the institution that ordered the test?

A conflict arises when the individual's welfare is at odds with that of the institution that employs the psychologist. For example, a psychologist working for an industrial firm to identify individuals who might break down under stress has a responsibility to the institution to identify such individuals as well as a responsibility to protect the rights and welfare of clients who are seeking employment with the firm. Thus, the psychologist's loyalty is divided. Similarly, the psychologist must not only maintain test security but also not violate the client's right to know the basis for an adverse decision. However, if the basis for an adverse decision is explained to one client, this information may leak out, and others with the same problem might then outsmart the test. Again, the test user is trapped between two opposing forces and principles.

The conflict is currently being resolved as follows. Ethically, psychologists must inform all concerned where their loyalty lies. They must tell clients or subjects in advance how tests are to be used and describe the limits of confidentiality. To the institution, they provide only the minimum information needed, such as "This subject has a low probability of breaking down under stress, and the probability that this conclusion is accurate is 68/100." Unnecessary or irrelevant personal information remains confidential.

In addition, the person's right to know the basis of an adverse decision may override issues of test security. Either the results are explained to the client or they are given to a representative of the client who is qualified to explain them (AERA, APA, & NCME, 1999; APA, 2010).

Responsibilities of Test Users and Test Constructors

A second overarching ethical issue in testing concerns the responsibilities of test users. Because even the best test can be misused, the testing profession has become increasingly stringent and precise in outlining the ethics of responsible test use. Almost any test can be useful in the right circumstances, but even the best test, when used inappropriately, can hurt the subject. Of particular concern is the use of tests with different populations. A test that is valid and reliable for one group may not be valid and reliable for another. In light of this issue, the 2002 version of the APA Code of Ethics added two subsections that direct psychologists who administer tests to "use assessment instruments whose validity and reliability have been established for use with members of the population being tested" and to "use assessment methods that are appropriate to an individual's language preference and competence." In addition, when interpreting test results, psychologists are instructed to take into account "characteristics of the person being assessed, such as situational, personal, linguistic, and cultural differences that might affect psychologists' judgments or reduce the accuracy of their interpretations" (p. 13). To reduce potential damage, the APA (1974, 2002) makes users of tests responsible for knowing the reason for using the test, the consequences of using the test, and the procedures necessary to maximize the test's effectiveness and to minimize unfairness. Test users must thus possess sufficient knowledge to understand the principles underlying the construction and supporting research of any test they administer. They must also know the psychometric qualities of the test being used as well as the literature relevant to the test. In addition, they are to ensure that interpretations based on the test are justified and that the test is properly used. A test user cannot claim ignorance: "I didn't realize normative data were not representative." The test user is responsible for finding out all pertinent information before using any test (APA, 1992, 2002, 2010).

The test developer is responsible for providing the necessary information (Franklin, 2003). Current standards for test use state that test constructors must provide a test manual with sufficient data to permit appropriate use of the test, including adequate validity and reliability data, clearly specified scoring and administration standards, and a clear description of the normative sample (AERA, APA, & NCME, 1999; APA, 2010).

Social Issues

In addition to professional and moral issues, social issues play an important role in the testing field. We discuss three of these issues: dehumanization, the usefulness of tests, and access to psychological testing sources (see Figure 21.3).

FIGURE 21.3

Schematic summary
of social issues.

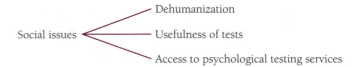

Dehumanization

One social issue in the testing field concerns the dehumanizing tendencies that lurk
in the testing process. For example, some corporations provide computerized analyses of the Minnesota Multiphasic Personality Inventory-2 (MMPI-2) and other
test results. Such technology tends to minimize individual freedom and uniqueness.
With high-speed computers and centralized data banks, the risk that machines will
someday make important decisions about our lives is always increasing. Thus, society
must weigh the risks against the benefits of the growing application of modern technology to the testing field. People must make this evaluation now before an undesirable but unalterable situation develops. As psychologists and the public allow test
results to be stored and analyzed by computers, it may become extremely difficult
to reverse this trend. U.S. society is founded on principles of individual rights and
freedom. Anything that might threaten these principles—such as computerized test
interpretations—must be evaluated. Only when the benefits far outweigh the risks
and the risks are minimized can the decision be socially acceptable.

Usefulness of Tests

Tests need not be perfect in all ways. Society often finds uses for initially crude
tools that become precise with research and development. For example, when Western society believed the sun revolved around the earth, the available formulas and
principles were useful in that they led to some accurate predictions, even though
the underlying theories were incorrect. Similarly, the assumptions underlying today's
tests may be fundamentally incorrect and the resulting test instruments far from perfect. However, the tests may still be useful as long as they provide information that
leads to better predictions and understanding than can otherwise be obtained. A
test may be useful to society even if all of the principles that underlie it are totally
incorrect.

   Thus, the crucial social issue in testing is not whether tests are perfect but
whether they are useful to society. Obviously, the answer to this question to date
has been a strong but disputed and controversial "Yes." However, as new knowledge
is gained, society must continually weigh the risks of tests against the benefits. The
risks, of course, include the possible misuse of tests, which in turn may adversely
affect the life of an individual or may discriminate systematically against a specific
cultural group (see Fish, 2002). The benefits include the potential for increased precision and fairness in the decision-making process. Obviously, the resolution of this
recurring issue will profoundly affect the field of testing.

   Society has used modern tests on a wide scale. First the military, then the schools
and psychiatric facilities, and finally business and industry have found important
uses for psychological tests. Indeed, there appears to be no end to the proliferation
of tests, despite criticism and heated debate. If the pervasiveness of tests in

society's opinion of their usefulness, then certainly society has found them useful. As long as tests continue to serve a function, they will most likely be used.

Access to Psychological Testing Services

Who will have access to psychological testing services? Being tested can be expensive. A practitioner in a large metropolitan area often commands a fee of several thousand dollars or more to administer a full battery of individual tests, score and interpret the findings, and produce a written report. In fact, the cost of a custody evaluation in Southern California can run as high as more than $25,000. Fees for extensive neurological testing, particularly in a legal battle, can be even higher. Moreover, like the cost of drugs, the cost of test materials continues to skyrocket.

As it stands now, the expensive test batteries for neurological and psychiatric assessment are available to those who can afford them and to those who have enough insurance. For example, anyone with a developmental disability in California may be eligible to receive Medi-Cal, which provides free medical care, including the services of a psychologist. The individual may also be eligible for federal assistance such as Medicare and SSI, which provide cash benefits. Further, in California, developmentally disabled people (e.g., persons with mental retardation) or those with suspected developmental disabilities have access to psychological testing services at regional centers throughout the state. Unless California laws are changed, anyone suspected of having a handicap that originated during the developmental years can request (or have someone request on his or her behalf) an evaluation that may include a medical examination and psychological testing. The service is free, and if a team of specialists finds the person developmentally disabled, then additional services are available. Thus, current California and federal laws and policies help ensure that certain disabled people will have access to psychological testing services. However, such guarantees are not available in all states, and only certain people are covered.

Current Trends

Professional, moral, social, and even legal issues have interacted to produce today's trends in testing. These trends can be placed into four main categories: the proliferation of new tests; higher standards, improved technology, and increased objectivity; greater public awareness and influence; and computer and Internet applications.

The Proliferation of New Tests

New tests keep coming out all the time, with no end in sight. If we count revised and updated tests, we find hundreds of new tests being published each year. The impetus for developing these new tests comes from professional disagreement over the best strategies for measuring human characteristics, over the nature of these characteristics, and over theories about the causes of human behavior. The impetus also stems from public and professional pressure to use only fair, accurate, and unbiased instruments. Finally, if tests are used, then the authors and publishers of tests stand to profit financially. As long as someone can make a profit publishing tests, then new tests will be developed and marketed.

An examination of major reference books on tests indicates that the majority of new tests are based on the same principles and underlying theories as the more established tests. Indeed, most newly developed tests are justified on the grounds that they are either psychometrically superior to the existing tests or more specific and thus more appropriate for particular problems. However, as you saw in Chapter 15, some of the newer tests are based on models, theories, and concepts that fundamentally differ from those that underlie traditional tests. These nontraditional tests stem from modern concepts and theories from learning, social, physiological, and experimental psychology. Most of these newer tests are rooted in empirically derived data.

The proliferation of nontraditional tests is related to two other trends in testing. First, it reflects the increasing role of the science of psychology in testing. Even critics of testing must admit that a responsiveness to criticism and an honest and persistent effort to improve the quality of tests have characterized testing. The application of insights and empirical findings from psychological laboratories currently reflects this responsiveness.

Second, efforts are being made to integrate tests with other aspects of applied psychology (Aidman & Shmelyov, 2002; Wiederhold, Jang, Kim, & Wiederhold, 2002). Many psychologists, especially the cognitive–behaviorally oriented, have long regretted the poor relationship among clinical assessment, traditional tests, and subsequent treatment interventions. They prefer test results that not only have a direct relationship to treatment but also can be used to assess the effectiveness of treatment. Because psychologists continually try to devise such procedures, their products add to the list of the many new tests published each year.

Higher Standards, Improved Technology, and Increasing Objectivity

Various pressures and issues have led to another current trend. The minimum acceptable standards for tests are becoming higher. Before the APA (1974) clearly and specifically defined their responsibilities, test constructors had neither a uniform nor a widely accepted set of guidelines. As a result, the quality of newly published tests varied greatly. With published standards, test constructors no longer have to work in the dark. An increasing percentage of new tests provides the information necessary for test users to make a fully informed choice in test selection, thus maximizing the chance of proper test use.

Higher standards of test construction have encouraged better use of tests (Clauser, 2002). The 1999 and 2010 standards have helped considerably by reemphasizing the critical importance of proper test use and by articulating the responsibilities of test users (AERA, APA, & NCME, 1999; APA, 2002, 2010). Related to higher standards, improved technology has greatly benefited the testing. Primarily because of advances in computer technology, statistical procedures such as factor analysis and item analysis can be performed with great ease. This technology thus contributes to the current trend toward better tests.

Also related to high standards is the trend toward increasing objectivity in test interpretation. Attacks on the Rorschach have become continuous and merciless (see Bornstein & Masling, 2005; Carstairs, 2011; Drogin, Dattilio, Sadoff, & Gutheil, 2011; Finn, 2011; Masling, 2006; Masling & Bornstein, 2005; Wood et al., 2003).

As a result, practitioners tend to rely heavily on objective data such as that provided by the MMPI-2. One can readily see this trend in how the relative proportion of references devoted to the Rorschach and the MMPI in the *Mental Measurements Yearbook* and other sources has changed.

The continuing research interest in testing also reflects the trend toward objectivity in the field. In view of the tens of thousands, if not hundreds of thousands, of published studies directly or indirectly related to psychological tests, a casual observer might conclude that little remains to be done. This conclusion is far from correct. Despite the thousands of articles already devoted to the MMPI and MMPI-2, for example, hundreds more creative and scientifically rigorous articles are published each year on these tests, not to mention the hundreds of other tests listed in the *Mental Measurements Yearbook* and other resource books. As long as tests are anything but perfect, and in this regard they have a long way to go, psychological researchers will no doubt keep conducting investigations to facilitate the objective use of tests.

Greater Public Awareness and Influence

Greater public awareness of the nature and use of psychological tests has led to increasing external influence on testing. At one time, the public knew little about psychological tests; psychologists played an almost exclusive role in governing how tests were used. With the public's greater assertiveness during the 1990s, the days when psychologists alone called the shots are gone forever (Saccuzzo, 1994). Today, one can simply perform a Google or other Internet search and find considerable information on just about any test. We believe this trend has affected the field positively.

Public awareness has led to an increased demand for psychological services, including testing services. This demand is balanced by the tendency toward restrictive legislative and judicial regulations and policies such as the judicial decision that restricts the use of standard intelligence tests in diagnosing mental retardation. These restrictions originate in real and imagined public fears. In short, the public seems to be ambivalent about psychological testing, simultaneously desiring the benefits yet fearing the power they attribute to tests.

Perhaps the greatest benefit of increased public awareness of tests has been the extra focus on safeguarding human rights. As more individuals share the responsibility of encouraging the proper use of tests by becoming informed of their rights and insisting on receiving them, the probability of misuse and abuse of tests will be reduced. The commitment of the field of psychology to high ethical standards can be easily seen in the published guidelines, position papers, and debates that have evolved during the relatively short period beginning in 1947 with the development of formal standards for training in clinical psychology (Shakow, Hilgard, Kelly, Sanford, & Shaffer, 1947). Practitioners of psychology, their instructors, and their supervisors show a deep concern for social values and the dignity of the individual human being. However, the pressure of public interest in psychological tests has led practitioners to an even greater awareness about safeguarding the rights and dignity of the individual.

Interrelated with all of these issues is the trend toward greater protection for the public. Nearly every state has laws that govern the use of psychological tests. Several factors give the public significant protection against the inherent risks of testing: limiting testing to reduce the chance that unqualified people will use psychological tests, sensitivity among practitioners to the rights of the individual, relevant court decisions, and a clearly articulated set of ethical guidelines and published standards for proper test use.

The Computerization of Tests

Throughout this book, we have discussed how computers are being applied to testing on a rapid and widespread basis. The computerization of tests is a major trend, and computers, as you saw in Chapter 15, are being used in many different ways.

In adaptive computerized testing, different sets of test questions are administered via computer to different individuals, depending on each individual's status on the trait being measured (Mills, Potenza, Fremer, & Ward, 2002; Weiss, 1983, 1985). In ability testing, for example, the computer adjusts the level of item difficulty according to the subject's response. If the subject's answer is incorrect, then an easier item is given; if correct, then a more difficult item appears next. Such an approach individualizes a test and reduces total testing time. By the year 2025, most students will probably be taking tests such as the SAT, Graduate Record Examination (GRE), and Law School Admission Test (LSAT) through adaptive computer programs. There are currently adaptive versions of several important knowledge and aptitude tests, such as the Armed Services Vocational Aptitude Test, GRE, SAT, and TOEFL (Díaz, Abad, Ponsoda Gil, Aguado, & Díaz, 2011).

Computers are also being used to administer, score, and even interpret psychological tests, as we've seen with the dual, coordinated iPads in the WISC-V. In addition, computers are being used to generate tasks that cannot be presented by traditional methods (see Chapter 15). Through computer technology, one might be able to tap a whole new range of abilities heretofore beyond the scope of traditional tests (Saccuzzo, Johnson, & Guertin, 1994). Objective personality tests such as the MMPI-2 can be processed by a computer that generates a typed report. Each year, developers create more programs that score tests and produce written reports. The use of the computer extends to all types of tests, including behavioral assessment.

Testing on the Internet

According to Crespin and Austin (2002), one of the most important future applications of psychological testing is through its use on the Internet. Imagine the possibility of taking a test from a website and having the results immediately sent to your doctor.

Future Trends

Having analyzed the major relevant issues and forces in testing and identified current trends, we are now ready to venture a few guesses about what the future holds for the field. Certainly, we are reasonably safe in stating that the current trends will continue and become established in the field. However, our predictions for the future are educated guesses based on limited knowledge.

Future Prospects for Testing Are as Promising as Ever Before

We continue to believe that testing has a promising future. Indeed, there were times when it almost looked like the end of psychological testing in America, but here it stands taller than ever before with more and better tests than many could have imagined. On a less lofty note, testing is a multibillion-dollar industry, and even relatively small testing companies can gross millions of dollars per year. With so much at stake, testing is certain to stay. The field gained its first real status from its role in the development of screening tests for the military in World War I. Later, psychologists' creativity and skill in the testing field during World War II no doubt numbered among the factors that ultimately led to government funding through the Veterans Administration to encourage the development of professional psychology. Indeed, this federal funding, first earmarked for psychology in 1945, played an important role in the birth of clinical psychology and formal training standards.

As indicated, the central role played by testing in the development and recognition of psychology does not alone ensure an important future role for testing. Despite division within psychology about the role and value of testing, it remains one of the few unique functions of the professional psychologist. When one sees psychological testing as encompassing not only traditional but also new and innovative uses—as in cognitive-behavioral assessment, psychophysiology, evaluation research, organizational assessment, community assessment, and investigations into the nature of human functioning—one can understand just how important tests are to psychologists.

Thus, with this fundamental tie to testing, psychologists remain the undisputed leaders in the field. It is unlikely that attacks on and dissatisfaction with traditional psychological tests will suddenly compel psychologists to abandon tests. Instead, psychologists will likely continue to take the lead in this field to produce better and better tests, and such a direction will benefit psychologists, the field, and society. Even if this doesn't happen, testing corporations that publish and sell widely used high-stakes standardized tests will no doubt continue to market their products aggressively.

Moreover, tests are used in most institutions—schools, colleges, hospitals, industry, business, the government, and so forth—and new applications and creative uses continue to emerge in response to their demands. Tests will not suddenly disappear with nothing to replace them. If anything, current tests will continue to be used until they are replaced by still better tests, which of course may be based on totally new ideas. Though current tests may gradually fade from the scene, we believe psychological testing will not simply survive but will flourish through the 21st century.

Controversy, Disagreement, and Change Will Continue

It doesn't matter whether the topic is testing or animal learning—disagreement and controversy are second nature to psychologists. Disagreement brings with it new data that may ultimately produce some clarification along with brand new contradictions and battle lines. Psychologists will probably never agree that any one test is perfect, and change will be a constant characteristic of the field. We continue to be optimistic because we see the change as ultimately resulting in more empirical data, better theories, continuing innovations and advances, and higher standards.

The Integration of Cognitive Science and Computer Science Will Lead to Several Innovations in Testing

As you saw in Chapter 15, concepts from basic psychological sciences have worked their way into the field: learning theory in the 1970s and 1980s, and psychophysiological and psychophysical concepts in the 1980s and 1990s. Today, the integration of concepts from experimental cognitive psychology, computer science, neuroscience, and psychometrics are rapidly shaping the field (Miller & Kinsbourne, 2011; Spear, 2007; Wetherell, 2011).

Multimedia computerized tests form the most recent cutting edge in the new generation of assessment instruments. The test taker sits in front of a computer that presents realistically animated situations with full color and sound. The program is both interactive and adaptive. The computer screen freezes and asks the test taker to provide a response. If the response is good, then a more difficult item is presented. For example, in research programs recently developed at companies such as IBM, the computer may show a scene involving sexual harassment. The screen freezes just after an employee has made an inappropriate joke. The test taker, who is applying for a manager's job, is given four choices to deal with the situation. If an effective choice is made, the computer moves on to an even more difficult situation, such as a threat from the offensive employee.

The computer offers test developers unlimited scope in developing new technologies: from interactive virtual reality games that measure and record minute responses to social conflict within a digital world to virtual environments that are suitable for measuring physiological responses while offering safe and effective systematic desensitization experiences to individuals with phobias. As we noted at the outset, the computer holds one of the major keys to the future of psychological testing.

Summary

The future of psychological testing depends on many issues and developments. Professional issues include theoretical concerns, such as the usefulness of the trait concept as opposed to index of adjustment; the adequacy of tests; and actuarial versus clinical prediction. Moral issues include human rights such as the right to refuse testing, the right not to be labeled, and the right to privacy. Another ethical issue that concerns test users and developers is the divided loyalty that can result from administering a test to an individual for an institution: Whose rights come first? Also, professionals have an ethical duty to provide and understand the information needed to use a test properly. Finally, social issues such as dehumanization, the usefulness of tests, and access to testing services also inform the field of testing today.

Current trends include the proliferation of new tests, higher standards, improved technology, increasing objectivity, greater public awareness and influence, the computerization of tests, and testing on the Internet.

As for the future, anything is possible, especially in a field as controversial as testing. Psychology is now better equipped in technique, methodology, empirical data, and experience than ever before, and the members of this new and expanding field, as a group, are relatively young. Therefore, it does not seem unrealistic or overly optimistic to expect that the next 50 years will see advances equal to those of the last 50. On the other hand, psychology has come so far in the last 50 years that a comparable advance in the next 50 could easily produce results unimaginable today. What happens to testing in the future will depend on the goals and objectives chosen by those in the field and by their persistence and creativity in accomplishing their goals.

Appendix 1

Areas of a Standard Normal Distribution

PART I Percentiles Associated With Various *Z* Scores

Z	% Rank	Z	% Rank
−3.0	.13	0	50.00
−2.9	.19	.1	53.98
−2.8	.26	.2	57.93
−2.7	.35	.3	61.79
−2.6	.47	.4	66.54
−2.5	.62	.5	69.15
−2.4	.82	.6	72.57
−2.3	1.07	.7	75.80
−2.2	1.39	.8	78.81
−2.1	1.79	.9	81.59
−2.0	2.28	1.0	84.13
−1.9	2.87	1.1	86.43
−1.8	3.59	1.2	88.49
−1.7	4.46	1.3	90.32
−1.6	5.48	1.4	91.92
−1.5	6.68	1.5	93.32
−1.4	8.08	1.6	94.52
−1.3	9.68	1.7	95.54
−1.2	11.51	1.8	96.41
−1.1	13.57	1.9	97.13
−1.0	15.87	2.0	97.72
−.9	18.41	2.1	98.21
−.8	21.19	2.2	98.61
−.7	24.20	2.3	98.93
−.6	27.43	2.4	99.18
−.5	30.58	2.5	99.38
−.4	34.46	2.6	99.53
−.3	38.21	2.7	99.65
−.2	42.07	2.8	99.74
−.1	46.02	2.9	99.81
0	50.00	3.0	99.87

PART II Areas Between Mean and Various Z Scores

Z	.00	.01	.02	.03	.04	.05	.06	.07	.08	.09
.0	.0000	.0040	.0080	.0120	.0160	.0199	.0239	.0279	.0319	.0359
.1	.0398	.0438	.0478	.0517	.0557	.0596	.0636	.0675	.0714	.0753
.2	.0793	.0832	.0871	.0910	.0948	.0987	.1026	.1064	.1103	.1141
.3	.1179	.1217	.1255	.1293	.1331	.1368	.1406	.1443	.1480	.1517
.4	.1554	.1591	.1628	.1664	.1700	.1736	.1772	.1808	.1844	.1879
.5	.1915	.1950	.1985	.2019	.2054	.2088	.2123	.2157	.2190	.2224
.6	.2257	.2291	.2324	.2357	.2389	.2422	.2454	.2486	.2517	.2549
.7	.2580	.2611	.2642	.2673	.2704	.2734	.2764	.2794	.2823	.2852
.8	.2881	.2910	.2939	.2967	.2995	.3023	.3051	.3078	.3106	.3133
.9	.3195	.3186	.3212	.3238	.3264	.3289	.3315	.3340	.3365	.3389
1.0	.3413	.3438	.3461	.3485	.3508	.3531	.3554	.3577	.3599	.3621
1.1	.3643	.3665	.3686	.3708	.3729	.3749	.3770	.3790	.3810	.3830
1.2	.3849	.3869	.3888	.3907	.3925	.3944	.3962	.3980	.3997	.4015
1.3	.4032	.4049	.4066	.4082	.4099	.4115	.4131	.4147	.4162	.4177
1.4	.4192	.4207	.4222	.4236	.4251	.4265	.4279	.4292	.4306	.4319
1.5	.4332	.4345	.4357	.4370	.4382	.4394	.4406	.4418	.4429	.4441
1.6	.4452	.4463	.4474	.4484	.4495	.4505	.4515	.4525	.4535	.4545
1.7	.4554	.4564	.4573	.4582	.4591	.4599	.4608	.4616	.4625	.4633
1.8	.4641	.4649	.4656	.4664	.4671	.4678	.4686	.4693	.4699	.4706
1.9	.4713	.4719	.4726	.4732	.4738	.4744	.4750	.4756	.4761	.4767
2.0	.4772	.4778	.4783	.4788	.4793	.4798	.4803	.4808	.4812	.4817
2.1	.4821	.4826	.4830	.4834	.4838	.4842	.4846	.4850	.4854	.4857
2.2	.4861	.4864	.4868	.4871	.4875	.4878	.4881	.4884	.4887	.4890
2.3	.4893	.4896	.4898	.4901	.4904	.4906	.4909	.4911	.4913	.4916
2.4	.4918	.4920	.4922	.4925	.4927	.4929	.4931	.4932	.4934	.4936
2.5	.4938	.4940	.4941	.4943	.4945	.4946	.4948	.4949	.4951	.4952
2.6	.4953	.4955	.4956	.4957	.4959	.4960	.4961	.4962	.4963	.4964
2.7	.4965	.4966	.4967	.4968	.4969	.4970	.4971	.4972	.4973	.4974
2.8	.4974	.4975	.4976	.4977	.4977	.4978	.4979	.4979	.4980	.4981
2.9	.4981	.4982	.4982	.4983	.4984	.4984	.4985	.4985	.4986	.4986
3.0	.4987	.4987	.4987	.4988	.4988	.4989	.4989	.4989	.4900	.4990

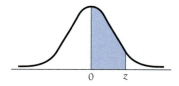

Standard score values are listed in the column headed "Z." To find the proportion of the total area occurring between the mean and any given Z score, locate the entry indicated by the Z score. For example, a Z score of $+1.85$ is located by reading across to the column for .05 from the value of 1.8 in the "Z" column. The value in the table is .4678. Since the total area above the mean is equal to .5000, this means that only .0322 of the area is beyond the Z score of $+1.85$.

Appendix 2

Critical Values of *r* for α = .05 and α = .01 (Two-Tailed Test)

df*	α = .05	α = .01	df*	α = .05	α = .01
1	.99692	.999877	17	.456	.575
2	.9500	.99000	18	.444	.561
3	.878	.9587	19	.433	.549
4	.811	.9172	20	.423	.537
5	.754	.875	25	.381	.487
6	.707	.834	30	.349	.449
7	.666	.798	35	.325	.418
8	.632	.765	40	.304	.393
9	.602	.735	45	.288	.372
10	.576	.708	50	.273	.354
11	.553	.684	60	.250	.325
12	.532	.661	70	.232	.302
13	.514	.641	80	.217	.283
14	.497	.623	90	.205	.267
15	.482	.606	100	.195	.254
16	.468	.590			

*df are equal to N–2, where N is the number of paired observations.

Reprinted with permission from Table IX-1. Percentage Points. Distribution of the Correlation Coefficient. When $p = 0$, *CRC Handbook of Tables for Probability and Statistics* (2nd ed.). Copyright 1968, CRC Press, Inc., Boca Raton, Florida.

Appendix 3

Critical Values of *t**

For any given *df*, the table shows the values of *t* corresponding to various levels of probability. Obtained *t* is significant at a given level if it is equal to or greater than the value shown in the table.

* Appendix 3 is taken from Table III of R. A. Fisher and R. Yates, 1967, *Statistical Tables for Biological, Agricultural and Medical Research* (6th ed.), New York: Hafner. With permission of the authors and publishers.

df	Level of significance for one-tailed test					
	.10	.05	.025	.01	.005	.0005
	Level of significance for two-tailed test					
	.20	.10	.05	.02	.01	.001
1	3.078	6.314	12.706	31.821	63.657	636.619
2	1.886	2.920	4.303	6.965	9.925	31.598
3	1.638	2.353	3.182	4.541	5.841	12.941
4	1.533	2.132	2.776	3.747	4.604	8.610
5	1.476	2.015	2.571	3.365	4.032	6.859
6	1.440	1.943	2.447	3.143	3.707	5.959
7	1.415	1.895	2.365	2.998	3.499	5.405
8	1.397	1.860	2.306	2.896	3.355	5.041
9	1.383	1.833	2.262	2.821	3.250	4.781
10	1.372	1.812	2.228	2.764	3.169	4.587
11	1.363	1.796	2.201	2.718	3.106	4.437
12	1.356	1.782	2.179	2.681	3.055	4.318
13	1.350	1.771	2.160	2.650	3.012	4.221
14	1.345	1.761	2.145	2.624	2.977	4.140
15	1.341	1.753	2.131	2.602	2.947	4.073
16	1.337	1.746	2.120	2.583	2.921	4.015
17	1.333	1.740	2.110	2.567	2.898	3.965
18	1.330	1.734	2.101	2.552	2.878	3.922
19	1.328	1.729	2.093	2.539	2.861	3.883
20	1.325	1.725	2.086	2.528	2.845	3.850
21	1.323	1.721	2.080	2.518	2.831	3.819
22	1.321	1.717	2.074	2.508	2.819	3.792
23	1.319	1.714	2.069	2.500	2.807	3.767
24	1.318	1.711	2.064	2.492	2.797	3.745
25	1.316	1.708	2.060	2.485	2.787	3.725
26	1.315	1.706	2.056	2.479	2.779	3.707
27	1.314	1.703	2.052	2.473	2.771	3.690
28	1.313	1.701	2.048	2.467	2.763	3.674
29	1.311	1.699	2.045	2.462	2.756	3.659
30	1.310	1.697	2.042	2.457	2.750	3.646
40	1.303	1.684	2.021	2.423	2.704	3.551
60	1.296	1.671	2.000	2.390	2.660	3.460
120	1.289	1.658	1.980	2.358	2.617	3.373
∞	1.282	1.645	1.960	2.326	2.576	3.291

Appendix 4

Code of Fair Testing Practices in Education

Prepared by the Joint Committee on Testing Practices[1]

The Code of Fair Testing Practices in Education, reaffirmed again and again, states the major obligations to test takers or professionals who develop or use educational tests. The Code is meant to apply broadly to the use of tests in education (admissions, educational assessment, educational diagnosis, and student placement). The Code is not designed to cover employment testing, licensure or certification testing, or other types of testing. Although the Code has relevance to many types of educational tests, it is directed primarily at professionally developed tests such as those sold by commercial test publishers or used in formally administered testing programs. The Code is not intended to cover tests made by individual teachers for use in their own classrooms.

The Code addresses the roles of test developers and test users separately. Test users are people who select tests, commission test development services, or make decisions on the basis of test scores. Test developers are people who actually construct tests as well as those who set policies for particular testing programs. The roles may, of course, overlap as when a state education agency commissions test development services, sets policies that control the test development process, and makes decisions on the basis of the test scores.

The Code presents standards for educational test developers and users in four areas:

A. Developing/Selecting Tests

B. Interpreting Scores

C. Striving for Fairness

D. Informing Test Takers

---

[1]The Code has been developed by the Joint Committee on Testing Practices, a cooperative effort of several professional organizations, that has as its aim the advancement, in the public interest, of the quality of testing practices. The Joint Committee was initiated by the American Educational Research Association, the American Psychological Association, and the National Council on Measurement in Education. In addition to these three groups, the American Association for Counseling and Development/Association for Measurement and Evaluation in Counseling and Development and the American Speech-Language-Hearing Association are now also sponsors of the Joint Committee.

This is not copyrighted material. Reproduction and dissemination are encouraged. Please cite this document as follows:

Code of Fair Testing Practices in Education. (1988) Washington, D.C. Joint Committee on Testing Practices. (Mailing Address: Joint Committee on Testing Practices, American Psychological Association, 1200 17th Street, NW, Washington, D.C. 20036.)

609

Organizations, institutions, and individual professionals who endorse the Code commit themselves to safeguarding the rights of test takers by following the principles listed. The Code is intended to be consistent with the relevant parts of the *Standards for Educational and Psychological Testing* (AERA, APA, NCME, 1985). However, the Code differs from the Standards in both audience and purpose. The Code is meant to be understood by the general public; it is limited to educational tests, and the primary focus is on those issues that affect the proper use of tests. The Code is not meant to add new principles over and above those in the Standards or to change the meaning of the Standards. The goal is rather to represent the spirit of a selected portion of the Standards in a way that is meaningful to test takers and/or their parents or guardians. It is the hope of the Joint Committee that the Code will also be judged to be consistent with existing codes of conduct and standards of other professional groups who use educational tests.

Developing/Selecting Appropriate Tests[2]

Test developers should provide the information that test users need to select appropriate tests.

Test users should select tests that meet the purpose for which they are to be used and that are appropriate for the intended test-taking populations.

Test Developers Should:

1. Define what each test measures and what the test should be used for. Describe the population (s) for which the test is appropriate.
2. Accurately represent the characteristics, usefulness, and limitations of tests for their intended purposes.
3. Explain relevant measurement concepts as necessary for clarity at the level of detail that is appropriate for the intended audience(s).
4. Describe the process of test development. Explain how the content and skills to be tested were selected.
5. Provide evidence that the test meets its intended purpose(s).
6. Provide either representative samples or complete copies of test questions, directions, answer sheets, manuals, and score reports to qualified users.

Test Users Should:

1. First define the purpose for testing and the population to be tested. Then, select a test for that purpose and that population based on a thorough review of the available information.
2. Investigate potentially useful sources of information, in addition to test scores, to corroborate the information provided by tests.
3. Read the materials provided by test developers and avoid using tests for which unclear or incomplete information is provided.
4. Become familiar with how and when the test was developed and tried out.
5. Read independent evaluations of a test and of possible alternative measures. Look for evidence required to support the claims of test developers.
6. Examine specimen sets, disclosed tests or samples of questions, directions, answer sheets,

---

[2] Many of the statements in the Code refer to the selection of existing tests. However, in customized testing programs, test developers are engaged to construct new tests. In those situations, the test development process should be designed to help ensure that the completed tests will be in compliance with the Code.

7. Indicate the nature of the evidence obtained concerning the appropriateness of each test for groups of different racial, ethnic, or linguistic backgrounds who are likely to be tested.
8. Identify and publish any specialized skills needed to administer each test and to interpret scores correctly.

manuals, and score reports before selecting a test.
7. Ascertain whether the test content and norms group(s) or comparison group(s) are appropriate for the intended test takers.
8. Select and use only those tests for which the skills needed to administer the test and interpret scores correctly are available.

Interpreting Scores

Test developers should help users interpret scores correctly.

Test Developers Should:

9. Provide timely and easily understood score reports that describe test performance clearly and accurately. Also explain the meaning and limitations of reported scores.
10. Describe the population(s) represented by any norms or comparison group(s), the dates the data were gathered, and the process used to select the samples of test takers.
11. Warn users to avoid specific, reasonably anticipated misuses of test scores.
12. Provide information that will help users follow reasonable procedures for setting passing scores when it is appropriate to use such scores with the test.
13. Provide information that will help users gather evidence to show that the test is meeting its intended purpose(s).

Test users should interpret scores correctly.

Test Users Should:

9. Obtain information about the scale used for reporting scores, the characteristics of any norms or comparison group(s), and the limitations of the scores.
10. Interpret scores taking into account any major differences between the norms or comparison groups and the actual test takers. Also take into account any differences in test administration practices or familiarity with the specific questions in the test.
11. Avoid using tests for purposes not specifically recommended by the test developer unless evidence is obtained to support the intended use.
12. Explain how any passing scores were set and gather evidence to support the appropriateness of the scores.
13. Obtain evidence to help show that the test is meeting its intended purpose(s).

Striving for Fairness

Test developers should strive to make tests that are as fair as possible for test takers of different races, gender, ethnic backgrounds, or handicapping conditions.

Test users should select tests that have been developed in ways that attempt to make them as fair as possible for test takers of different races, gender, ethnic backgrounds, or handicapping conditions.

Test Developers Should:

14. Review and revise test questions and related materials to avoid potentially insensitive content or language.
15. Investigate the performance of test takers of different races, gender, and ethnic backgrounds when samples of sufficient size are available. Enact procedures that help to ensure that differences in performance are related primarily to the skills under assessment rather than to irrelevant factors.
16. When feasible, make appropriately modified forms of tests or administration procedures available for test takers with handicapping conditions. Warn test users of potential problems in using standard norms with modified tests or administration procedures that result in noncomparable scores.

Test Users Should:

14. Evaluate the procedures used by test developers to avoid potentially insensitive content or language.
15. Review the performance of test takers of different races, gender, and ethnic backgrounds when samples of sufficient size are available. Evaluate the extent to which performance differences may have been caused by inappropriate characteristics of the test.
16. When necessary and feasible, use appropriately modified forms of tests or administration procedures for test takers with handicapping conditions. Interpret standard norms with care in the light of the modifications that were made.

Informing Test Takers

Under some circumstances, test developers have direct communication with test takers. Under other circumstances, test users communicate directly with test takers. Whichever group communicates directly with test takers should provide the information described as follows.

Test Developers or Test Users Should:

17. When a test is optional, provide test takers or their parents/guardians with information to help them judge whether the test should be taken, or if an available alternative to the test should be used.
18. Provide test takers the information they need to be familiar with the coverage of the test, the types of question formats, the directions, and appropriate test-taking strategies. Strive to make such information equally available to all test takers.

Under some circumstances, test developers have direct control of tests and test scores. Under other circumstances, test users have such control. Whichever group has direct control of tests and test scores should take the steps described as follows.

Test Developers or Test Users Should:

17. Provide test takers or their parents/guardians with information about rights test takers may have to obtain copies of tests and completed answer sheets, retake tests, have tests rescored, or cancel scores.
18. Tell test takers or their parents/guardians how long scores will be kept on file and indicate to whom and under what circumstances test scores will or will not be released.
19. Describe the procedures that test takers or their parents/guardians may use to register complaints and have problems resolved.

Note: The membership of the Working Group that developed the Code of Fair Testing Practices in Education and of the Joint Committee on Testing Practices that guided the Working Group was as follows:

Theodore P. Bartell
John R. Bergan
Esther E. Diamond
Richard P. Duran
Lorraine D. Eyde
Raymond D. Fowler
John J. Fremer
(Co-chair, JCTP and Chair,
    Code Working Group)

Edmund W. Gordon
Jo-Ida C. Hansen
James B. Lingwall
George F. Madaus
(Co-chair, JCTP)
Kevin L. Moreland
Jo-Ellen V. Perez
Robert J. Solomon
John T. Stewart

Carol Kehr Tittle
(Co-chair, JCTP)
Nicholas A. Vacc
Michael J. Zieky
Debra Boltas and Wayne
Camara of the American
    Psychological Association
    served as staff liaisons.

Glossary

A

achievement Previous learning.

acquiescence The tendency to agree or to endorse a test item as true.

age differentiation Discrimination based on the fact that older children have greater capabilities than do younger children.

age scale A test in which items are grouped according to age level. (The Binet scale, for example, grouped into one age level items that two-thirds to three-quarters of a representative group of children at a specific age could successfully pass.)

anxiety An unpleasant emotional state marked by worry, apprehension, and tension.

aptitude Potential for learning or acquiring a specific skill (for example, musical aptitude).

B

basal The level at which a minimum criterion number of correct responses is obtained.

base rate In decision analysis, the proportion of people expected to succeed on a criterion if they are chosen at random.

biserial correlation An index used to express the relationship between a continuous variable and an artificially dichotomous variable.

C

category format A rating-scale format that often uses the categories 1 to 10.

ceiling A certain number of incorrect responses in a test that indicate the items are too difficult.

class interval The unit for the horizontal axis in a frequency distribution.

coefficient alpha A generalized method for estimating reliability. Alpha is similar to the KR_{20} formula, except that it allows items to take on values other than 0 and 1.

coefficient of alienation In correlation and regression analysis, the index of nonassociation between two variables.

coefficient of determination The correlation coefficient squared; gives an estimate of the percentage of variation in Y that is known as a function of knowing X (and vice versa).

COGAT Form 7 Cognitive Abilities Test (COGAT) Form 7 is a standardized test that measures fluid intelligence. It provides three separate scores: verbal, quantitative, and nonverbal.

concurrent validity evidence Evidence for criterion validity in which the test and the criterion are administered at the same point in time.

construct validity evidence A process used to establish the meaning of a test through a series of studies. To evaluate evidence for construct validity, a researcher simultaneously defines some construct and develops the instrumentation to measure it. In the studies, observed correlations between the test and other measures provide evidence for the meaning of the test. See also *convergent evidence* and *discriminant evidence*.

content validity evidence The evidence that the content of a test represents the conceptual domain it is designed to cover.

convergent evidence Evidence obtained to demonstrate that a test measures the same attribute as do other measures that purport to measure the same thing. A form of construct validity evidence.

correction for attenuation Correction of the reduction, caused by low reliability, in the estimated correlation between a test and another measure. The correction for attenuation formula is used to estimate what the correlation would have been if the variables had been perfectly reliable.

correlation coefficient A mathematical index used to describe the direction and the magnitude of a relationship between two variables. The correlation coefficient ranges between —1.0 and 1.0.

criterion-referenced test A test that describes the specific types of skills, tasks, or knowledge of an individual relative to a well-defined mastery criterion. The content of criterion-referenced tests is limited to certain well-defined objectives.

criterion validity evidence The evidence that a test score corresponds to an accurate measure of interest. The measure of interest is called the *criterion*.

cross validation The process of evaluating a test or a regression equation for a sample other than the one used for the original studies.

D

deciles Points that divide the frequency distribution into equal tenths.

descriptive statistics Methods used to provide a concise description of a collection of quantitative information.

developmental quotient (DQ) In the Gesell Developmental Schedules, a test score that is obtained by assessing the presence or absence of behaviors associated with maturation.

dichotomous format A test item format in which there are two alternatives for each item.

differential validity The extent to which a test has different meanings for different groups of people. For example, a test may be a valid predictor of college success for white but not for African American students.

discriminability analysis In item analysis, how well an item performs in relation to some criterion. For example, items may be compared according to how well they separate groups who score high and low on the test. The index of discrimination would then be the association between performance on an item and performance on the whole test.

discriminant analysis A multivariate data analysis method for finding the linear combination of variables that best describes the classification of groups into discrete categories.

discriminant evidence Evidence obtained to demonstrate that a test measures something different from what other available tests measure. A form of construct validity evidence.

distractors Alternatives on a multiple-choice exam that are not correct or for which no credit is given.

dyslexia A specific reading disorder characterized by reading backwardness.

E

estimated learning potentials (ELPs) In the SOMPA system, WISC-R scores adjusted for the socioeconomic background of the children. ELPs take the place of IQ scores.

expectancy effects The tendency for results to be influenced by what experimenters or test administrators expect to find (also known as the *Rosenthal effect*, after the psychologist who has studied this problem intensively).

F

face validity The extent to which items on a test appear to be meaningful and relevant. Actually not evidence for validity because face validity is not a basis for inference.

factor analysis A method of finding the minimum number of dimensions (characteristics, attributes), called *factors*, to account for a large number of variables.

false negatives In test-decision theory, a case in which the test suggests a negative classification, yet the correct classification is positive.

false positive In test-decision analysis, a case in which the test suggests a positive classification, yet the correct classification is negative.

frequency distribution The systematic arrangement of scores on a variable or a measure to reflect how frequently each value occurred.

G

general cognitive index (GCI) In the McCarthy Scales of Children's Abilities, a standard score with a mean of 100 and standard deviation of 16.

group test A test that a single test administrator can give to more than one person at a time.

H

hit rate In test-decision analysis, the proportion of cases in which a test accurately predicts success or failure.

human ability Behaviors that reflect either what a person has learned or the person's capacity to emit a specific behavior; includes *achievement*, *aptitude*, and *intelligence*.

I

individual tests Tests that can be given to only one person at a time.

inferences Logical deductions (from evidence) about something that one cannot observe directly.

inferential statistics Methods used to make inferences from observations of a small group of people, called a *sample*. These inferences are then used to estimate the characteristics of a larger group of individuals, known as a *population*.

intelligence General potential independent of previous learning. It refers to a person's ability to solve problems, adapt to changing circumstances, think abstractly, and profit from experience.

intelligence quotient (IQ) A unit for expressing the results of intelligence tests. The intelligence quotient is based on the ratio of the individual's mental age (MA) (as determined by the test) to actual or chronological age (CA): $IQ = MA/CA \times 100$.

intercept On a two-dimensional graph, the point on the Y axis where X equals 0. In regression, this is the point at which the regression line intersects the Y axis.

interquartile range The interval of scores bounded by the 25th and the 75th percentiles.

interval scale A scale that one can use to rank order objects or individuals. It has the properties of magnitude and equal intervals but not absolute zero.

interview A method of gathering information by talk, discussion, or direct questions.

ipsative score A test result presented in relative rather than absolute terms. Ipsative scores compare the individual against him- or herself. Each person thus provides his or her own frame of reference.

item A specific stimulus to which a person responds overtly and that can be scored or evaluated.

item analysis A set of methods used to evaluate test items. The most common techniques involve assessment of item difficulty and item discriminability.

item characteristic curve A graph prepared as part of the process of item analysis. One graph is prepared for each test item and shows the total test score on the X axis and the proportion of test takers passing the item on the Y axis.

item difficulty A form of item analysis used to assess how difficult items are. The most common index of difficulty is the percentage of test takers who respond with the correct choice.

item discriminability In item analysis, how well an item performs in relation to some criterion. For example, items may be compared according to how well they separate groups who score high and low on the test. The index of discrimination would then be the association between performance on an item and performance on the whole test.

K

Kuder-Richardson 20 A formula for estimating the internal consistency of a test. The KR_{20} (or KR_{20}) method is equivalent to the average split-half correlation obtained from all possible splits of the items. For the KR_{20} formula to be applied, all items must be scored either 0 or 1.

L

Likert format A format for attitude scale items in which subjects indicate their degree of agreement to statements using these categories: strongly disagree, disagree, neither disagree nor agree, agree, strongly agree.

M

McCall's *T* A standardized score system with a mean of 50 and a standard deviation of 10. McCall's *T* can be obtained from a simple linear transformation of *Z* scores ($T = 10Z + 50$).

mean The arithmetic average score in a distribution.

median The point on a frequency distribution marking the 50th percentile.

mental Relates to intellectual activities and matters of the mind

multiple regression A multivariate data analysis method that considers the relationship between a continuous outcome variable and the linear combination of two or more predictor variables.

multivariate analysis A set of methods for data analysis that considers the relationships between combinations of three or more variables.

N

nominal scales Systems that arbitrarily assign numbers to objects. Mathematical manipulation of numbers from a nominal scale is not justified. For example, numbers on the backs of football players' uniforms are a nominal scale.

norm-referenced test A test that evaluates each individual relative to a normative group.

O

ordinal scale A scale that one can use to rank order objects or individuals without disclosing the meaning of the differences between the ranks.

P

parallel forms reliability The method of reliability assessment used to evaluate the error associated with the use of a particular set of items. Equivalent forms of a test are developed by generating two forms using the same rules. The correlation between the two forms is the estimate of parallel forms reliability.

Pearson product moment correlation An index of correlation between two continuous variables.

percentile band The range of percentiles that are likely to represent a subject's true score. It is created by forming an interval one standard error of measurement above and below the obtained score and converting the resulting values to percentiles.

percentile rank The proportion of scores that fall below a particular score.

personality tests Tests that measure overt and covert dispositions of individuals (the tendency that individuals will show a particular behavior or response in any given situation). Personality tests measure typical human behavior.

polytomous format A format for objective tests in which three or more alternative responses are given for each item. This format is popular for multiple-choice exams. Also called *polychotomous format*.

Q

quartiles Points that divide the frequency distribution into equal fourths.

R

ratio scale A scale that one can use to rank order objects or individuals. It has the properties of magnitude, equal intervals, and an absolute zero.

regression line The best-fitting straight line through a set of points in a scatter diagram.

reliability It refers to the accuracy, dependability, consistency, or repeatability of test results.

representative sample A sample drawn in an unbiased or random fashion so that it is composed of individuals with characteristics similar to those for whom the test is to be used.

predictive validity evidence The evidence that a test forecasts scores on the criterion at some future time.

projective hypothesis The proposal that when a person attempts to understand an ambiguous or vague stimulus, his or her interpretation reflects needs, feelings, experiences, prior conditioning, thought processes, and so forth.

projective personality test Tests in which the stimulus or the required response or both are ambiguous. The general idea behind projective tests is that a person's interpretation of an ambiguous stimulus reflects his or her unique characteristics.

psychological test A set of items designed for measuring characteristics of human beings that pertain to overt (observable) and covert (intraindividual) behavior. A psychological test measures past, present, or future human behavior. It is also known as *educational test*.

psychological testing It refers to all of the possible uses, applications, and underlying concepts of psychological and educational tests. The tests evaluate individual differences or variations among individuals.

residual The difference between predicted and observed values from a regression equation.

response style The tendency to mark a test item in a certain way irrespective of content.

restricted range problem In correlation and regression, variability on one measure is used to forecast variability on a second measure. If the variability is restricted on either measure, the observed correlation is likely to be low. For example, the correlation between the GRE and performance among students in an elite graduate program is likely to be low because GRE scores among students admitted to the program might have very little variability. The true correlation considering all students at all universities may be higher.

Rosenthal effect See *expectancy effect*.

S

scales Tools that relate raw scores on test items to some defined theoretical or empirical distribution.

scatter diagram A picture of the relationship between two variables. For each individual, a pair of observations is obtained, and the values are plotted in a two-dimensional space created by variables *X* and *Y*.

selection ratio In test decision analysis, the proportion of applicants who are selected.

self-report questionnaires A questionnaire that provides a list of statements about an individual and requires him or her to respond in some way to each, such as "True" or "False."

shrinkage Many times a regression equation is created for one group and used to predict the performance of another group of subjects. This procedure tends to overestimate the magnitude of the relationship for the second group.

The amount of decrease in the strength of the relationship from the original sample to the sample with which the equation is used is known as *shrinkage*.

Spearman's rho A method for finding the correlation between two sets of ranks.

standard deviation The square root of the average squared deviation around the mean (or the variance). It is used as a measure of variability in a distribution of scores.

standard error of estimate An index of the accuracy of a regression equation. It is equivalent to the standard deviation of the residuals from a regression analysis. Prediction is most accurate when the standard error of estimate is small.

standard error of measurement An index of the amount of error in a test or measure. The standard error of measurement is a standard deviation of a set of observations for the same test.

stanine system A system for assigning the numbers 1 through 9 to a test score. The system was developed by the U.S. Air Force. The standardized stanine distribution has a mean of 5 and a standard deviation of approximately 2.

structured personality tests Tests that provide a statement, usually of the self-report variety ("I like rock and roll music"), and require the subject to choose between two or more alternative responses ("True" or "False," for example). Sometimes called *objective personality tests*.

T

Taylor-Russell tables A series of tables one can use to evaluate the validity of a test in relation to the amount of information it contributes beyond what would be known by chance.

test A measurement device or technique that quantifies behavior or aids in its understanding and prediction.

test administration The act of giving a test.

test administrator Person giving a test.

test anxiety Anxiety that occurs in test-taking situations.

test batteries Two or more tests used in conjunction to appraise an individual.

third variable A variable that may account for the observed relationship between two other variables.

tracking The tendency to stay at about the same level of growth or performance relative to peers who are the same age.

traits Enduring or persistent characteristics of an individual that are independent of situations. Traits distinguish one individual from another.

***T* score** On the MMPI, a standard score with a mean of 50 and a standard deviation of 10. (See also *McCall's* T.)

two-tailed test A nondirectional test of the null hypothesis. In contrast to a one-tailed test which states a specific direction, the two-tailed test is used to evaluate whether observations are significantly different from chance in either the upper or lower end of the sampling distribution.

V

validity It refers to the meaning and usefulness of test results, or the degree to which a certain inference or interpretation based on a test is appropriate.

variance The average squared deviation around the mean; the standard deviation squared.

A victory for affirmative action. (2003). *Lancet, 352*(9377), 1.

Aamodt, M. G. (2004). *Applied industrial/organizational psychology* (4th ed.). Belmont, CA: Wadsworth.

Aamodt, M. G. (2016). Conducting background checks for employee selection. Society for human resource management. Arlinington, VA.

Aaronson, N., Choucair, A., Elliott, T., Greenhalgh, J., Michele Halyard, Hess, R., et al. (2011). *User's guide to implementing patient-reported outcomes assessment in clinical practice.* Amsterdam: International Society for Quality of Life Research.

Abbott, R. D., Amtmann, D., & Munson, J. (2003). Exploratory and confirmatory methods in learning disabilities research. In H. L. Swanson & K. R. Harris (Eds.), *Handbook of learning disabilities* (pp. 471–482). New York: Guilford Press.

Abed, M. A., Hall, L. A., & Moser, D. K. (2011). Spielberger's State Anxiety Inventory: Development of a shortened version for critically ill patients. *Issues in Mental Health Nursing, 32*(4), 220–227.

Abel, J. S., & Russell, P. S. S. (2005). Communication and symbolic behaviour deficits in children with autism: Are they related to other autistic domains? *Autism, 9*(3), 333–334.

Abell, S. C., Horkheimer, R., & Nguyen, S. E. (1998). Intellectual evaluations of adolescents via human figure drawings: An empirical comparison of two methods. *Journal of Clinical Psychology, 54,* 811–815.

Abramovitch, A., Abramowitz, J. S., Mittelman, A., Stark, A., Ramsey, K., & Geller, D. A. (2015). Research Review: Neuropsychological test performance in pediatric obsessive–compulsive disorder–a meta-analysis. *Journal of Child Psychology and Psychiatry, 56*(8), 837–847.

Abramson, L. Y., Alloy, L. B., & Metalsky, G. I. (1995). Hopelessness depression: Explanatory style. In G. M. Buchanan & E. P. Seligman (Eds.), *Explanatory style* (pp. 113–134). Hillsdale, NJ: Erlbaum.

Abramson, T. (1969). The influence of examiner race on first-grade and kindergarten subjects' Peabody Picture Vocabulary Test scores. *Journal of Educational Measurement, 6,* 241–246.

Accardo, P. (2013). 50 years ago in the journal of pediatrics: The pedictability of Gesell Developmental Scales in mongolism. *The Journal of Pediatrics, 162*(1), 55.

Ackerman, M. J., & Pritzl, T. B. (2011). Child custody evaluation practices: A 20-year follow-up. *Family Court Review, 49,* 618–628. doi: 10.1111/j.1744-1617.2011.01397.x.

Acklin, M. W. (1995). Rorschach assessment of the borderline child. *Journal of Clinical Psychology, 51*(2), 294–302.

Adnot, M., Dee, T., Katz, V., & Wyckoff, J. (2016). *Teacher turnover, teacher quality, and student achievement in DCPS.* **NBER Working Paper No. 21922,** Charlotsville, CA National Bureau of Economic Researh

Ægisdóttir, S., Spengler, P. M., & White, M. J. (2006). Should I pack my umbrella?: Clinical versus statistical prediction of mental health decisions. *Counseling Psychologist, 34*(3), 410–419.

Ægisdóttir, S., White, M. J., Spengler, P. M., Maugherman, A. S., Anderson, L. A., Cook, R. S., et al. (2006). The meta-analysis of clinical judgment project: Fifty-six years of accumulated research on clinical versus statistical prediction. *Counseling Psychologist, 34*(3), 341–382.

Affleck, G., Termen, H., Urrows, S., & Higgins, P. (1994). Person and contextual features of daily stress reactivity: Individual differences in relations of undesirable daily events with mood disturbance and chronic pain intensity. *Journal of Personality and Social Psychology, 66*(2), 329–340.

Aguinis, H., Culpepper, S. A., & Pierce, C. A. (2016). Differential prediction generalization in college admissions testing. *Journal of Educational Psychology,* Published online ahead of print. http://dx.doi.org/10.1037/edu0000104

Ahern, S., & Beatty, J. (1979). Pupillary responses vary during information processing with scholastic aptitude test score. *Science, 205,* 1289–1292.

Aidman, E. V., & Shmelyov, A. G. (2002). Mimics: A symbolic conflict/cooperation simulation program, with embedded protocol recording and automatic psychometric assessment. *Behavior Research Methods, Instruments, and Computers, 34*(1), 83–89.

Aiken, L. R. (1987). *Assessment of intellectual functioning.* Newton, MA: Allyn & Bacon.

Aiken, L. S. (2008). Doctoral training in statistics, measurement, and methodology in psychology: Replication and extension of Aiken, West, Sechrest, and Reno's (1990) survey of PhD programs in North America. *American Psychologist, 63*(1), 32.

Ajayi, L. (2016). A review of: The Test: Why our schools are obsessed with standardized testing—But you don't have to be. *Wisdom in Education, 6*(1), 5.

Akehurst, L., & Vrij, A. (1999). Creating suspects in police interviews. *Journal of Applied Social Psychology, 29,* 192–210.

Akutagawa, D. A. (1956). *A study in construct validity of the psychoanalytic concept of latent anxiety and a test of projection distance hypothesis.* Unpublished doctoral dissertation, University of Pittsburgh, PA.

Albert, D. (2012). *Neurodevelopmental substrates of peer influences on adolescents' choice evaluation and decision making.* Philadelphia: Temple University.

Albrecht, M. A., Masters, C., Ames, D., & Foster, J. (2016). Impact of mild head injury on neuropsychological performance and cognitive decline in cognitively healthy older adults: Longitudinal assessment in the AIBL cohort. *Frontiers in Aging Neuroscience*, *8*, 105.

Alessandri, G., Vecchione, M., Caprara1, G., & Letzring, T. D. (2011). The Ego Resiliency Scale revised: A cross-cultural study in Italy, Spain, and the United States. *European Journal of Psychological Assessment*, 1–8. doi: 10.1027/1015-5759/a000102.

Alexopoulos, D., Haritos-Fatouros, M., Sakkas, D., Skaltsas, A., & Vlachos, O. (2000). Reliability and validity of the WISC-R for the age range 6 to 11 years in Greece. *Psychology: Journal of the Hellenic Psychological Society*, *7*(1), 35–45.

Alger, S. (2016). Is this reliable enough? Examining classification consistency and accuracy in a criterion-referenced test. *International Journal of Assessment Tools in Education (IJATE)*, *3*(2).

Al-Heeti, K., Hamid, A., & Alghorani, M. (2012). The irrational beliefs inventory: Psychometric properties and cross-cultural validation of its arabic version. *Psychological Reports*, *111*(1), 47.

Ali, U., & Aslam, S. (2011). Ordinal position of birth and individual's psychological needs on edwards personal preference schedule. *Pakistan Journal of Clinical Psychology*, *10*(1), 53–63.

Allard, G., & Faust, D. (2000). Errors in scoring objective personality tests. *Assessment*, *7*(2), 119–129.

Allen, K. D., DeVellis, R. F., Renner, J. B., Kraus, V. B., & Jordan, J. M. (2007). Validity and factor structure of the AUSCAN Osteoarthritis Hand Index in a community-based sample. *Osteoarthritis Cartilage*, *15*(7), 830–836.

Allen, M. J., & Yen, W. M. (1979). *Introduction to measurement theory*. Pacific Grove, CA: Brooks/Cole.

Allison, J., Blatt, S. J., & Zimet, C. N. (1968). *The interpretation of psychological tests*. New York: Harper & Row.

Allport, G. W., & Odbert, H. S. (1936). Trait-names, a psycholexical study. *Psychological Monographs*, *47*(1).

Almkvist, O., Adveen, M., Henning, L., & Tallberg, I. M. (2007). Estimation of premorbid cognitive function based on word knowledge: The Swedish Lexical Decision Test (SLDT). *Scandinavian Journal of Psychology*, *48*(3), 271–279.

Alonso, P., Moscoso, S., & Salgado, J. F. (2016). Structured behavioral interview as a legal guarantee for ensuring equal employment opportunities for women: A meta-analysis. *The European Journal of Psychology Applied to Legal Context*.

Online ahead of print. http://dx.doi.org/10.1016/j.ejpal.2016.03.002

Altmaier, E. M., Smith, W. L., O'Halloran, C. M., & Franken, E. A., Jr. (1992). The predictive utility of behavior-based interviewing compared with traditional interviewing in the selection of radiology residents. *Investigative Radiology*, *27*(5), 385–389.

Alvarado, N. (1994). Empirical validity of the Thematic Appercention Test. *Journal of Personality Assessment*, *63*(1), 59–79.

American Educational Research Association (AERA), American Psychological Association (APA), & National Council on Measurement in Education (NCME). (1999). *Standards for educational and psychological testing*. Washington, DC: American Educational Research Association.

American Educational Research Association, American Psychological Association, American Council on Measurement in Education. (2012). *Standards for educational and psychological testing* (Preliminary Release for Comment).

American Psychiatric Association. (1995). *Diagnostic and statistical manual of mental disorders* (4th ed.). Washington, DC: American Psychiatric Association.

American Psychological Association (APA), American Educational Research Association (AERA), & National Council on Measurement in Education (NCME). (1999). *Standards for educational and psychological testing*. Washington, DC: AERA.

American Psychological Association (APA). (1954). *Psychology and its relations with other professions*. Washington, DC: American Psychological Association.

American Psychological Association (APA). (1974). *Standards for educational and psychological tests*. Washington, DC: American Psychological Association.

American Psychological Association (APA). (1992). *APA code of conduct*. Washington, DC: American Psychological Association.

American Psychological Association (APA). (2010). 2010 amendments to the 2002 "Ethical principles of psychologists and code of conduct". *American Psychologist*, *65*(5), 493.

American Psychological Association. (2002). *The ethical principles of psychologists and code of conduct*. Retrieved from www.apa.org/ethics/code2002.html

Ames, L. B., Metraux, R. W., & Walker, R. N. (1971). *Adolescent Rorschach responses*. New York: Brunner/Mazel.

Amutio, A., & Smith, J. (2007). The factor structure of situational and dispositional versions of the smith irrational beliefs inventory in a spanish student population. *International Journal of Stress Management*, *14*(3), 321–328.

Anastasi, A. (1984). The K-ABC in historical and contemporary perspective. *Journal of Special Education*, *78*(3), 357–366.

Anastasi, A. (1995). Psychology evolving: Linkages, hierarchies, and dimensions. In F. Kessel (Ed.), *Psychology, science, and human affairs: Essays in honor of William Bevan* (pp. 245–260). Boulder, CO: Westview.

Anastasi, A., & Urbina, S. (1997). *Psychological testing* (7th ed.). Upper Saddle River, NJ: Prentice-Hall.

Anderson, M. (2001). Conceptions of intelligence. *Journal of Child Psychology and Psychiatry and Allied Disciplines*, *42*(2), 287–298.

Anderson, M. (2013). What is intelligence? *Psychologist*, *26*(3), 162–163.

Anderson, M. J. (2016). Learning assessment methods that enhance learning outcomes in adult distance learning courses. Presented at the 13th Annual Symposium on Teaching and Learning effectiveness, Daytona Beach, FL.

Anderson, N. B., & McNeilly, M. (1991). Age, gender, and ethnicity as variables in psychophysiological assessment: Socio-demographics in context. *Psychological Assessment: A Journal of Consulting and Clinical Psychology*, *3*, 376–384.

Annalakshmi, N. (2006). TAT responses in relation to induced motivational set and reasoning ability. *Journal of the Indian Academy of Applied Psychology*, *32*(3), 331–336.

Antony, M. M. (2001). Measures for specific phobia. In M. M. Antony & S. M. Orsillo (Eds.), *Practitioner's guide to empirically based measures of anxiety. AABT clinical assessment series* (pp. 133–158). New York: Klumer Academic/ Plenum.

Anusic, I., & Schimmack, U. (2016). Personality processes and individual differences: Stability and change of personality traits, self-esteem, and well-being: Introducing the meta-analytic stability and change model of retest correlations. *Journal of Personality and Social Psychology*, *110*(5), 766–781.

Arbisi, P. A., Ben-Porath, Y. S., & Mc-Nulty, J. (2002). A comparison of MMPI-2 validity in African American and Caucasian psychiatric inpatients. *Psychological Assessment, 14*(1), 3–15.

Archer, E. M., Hagan, L. D., Mason, J., Handel, R., & Archer, R. P. (2011, February 2). MMPI-2-RF characteristics of custody evaluation litigants. *Assessment.* Retrieved from http://asm.sage-pub.com/content/early/2011/01/28/1073191110397469.abstract. doi: 10.1177/1073191110397469.

Archer, R. P., Maruish, M., Imhof, E. A., & Piotrowski, C. (1991). Psychological test usage with adolescent clients: 1990 survey. *Professional Psychology: Research and Practice, 22,* 247–252.

Archer, R., Buffington-Vollum, J., Stredny, R., & Handel, R. (2006). A survey of psychological test use patterns among forensic psychologists. *Journal of Personality Assessment, 87*(1), 84–94.

Arentoft, A., Van Dyk, K., Thames, A., Sayegh, P., Thaler, N., et al. (2016). Comparing the unmatched count technique and direct self-report for sensitive health-risk behaviors in hiv+ adults. *AIDS Care, 28*(3), 370–375.

Arita, A. A., & Baer, R. A. (1998). Validity of selected MMPI-A content scales. *Psychological Assessment, 10,* 59–63.

Arkes, H. R. (1991). Costs and benefits from judgment errors: Implications for debiasing. *Psychological Bulletin, 110,* 486–489.

Aron, A., & Aron, E. (2003). *Statistics for psychology* (3rd ed.). Upper Saddle River, NJ: Prentice-Hall.

Aronow, E., Reznikoff, M., & Moreland, K. L. (1995). The Rorschach: Projective technique or psychometric test? *Journal of Personality Assessment, 64*(3), 213–228.

Aronson, J., Fried, C. B., & Good, C. (2002). Reducing the effects of stereotype threat on African American college students by shaping theories of intelligence. *Journal of Experimental Social Psychology, 38*(2), 113–125.

Aronson, J., Lustina, M. J., Good, C., Keough, K., Steele, C. M., & Brown, J. (1999). When white men can't do math: Necessary and sufficient factors in stereotype threat. *Journal of Experimental Social Psychology, 35*(1), 29–46.

Arrindell, W. A., van Nieuwenhuizen, C., & Lutejin, F. (2001). Chronic psychiatric status and satisfaction with life. *Personality and Individual Differences, 31*(2), 145–155.

Arthur, G. (1930). *Arthur point scale of performance tests.* Chicago: Stoelting.

Arvey, R. D., & Campion, J. E. (1982). The employment interview: A summary and review of recent research. *Personnel Psychology, 35,* 281–322.

Asher, J. J., & Sciarrino, J. A. (1974). Realistic work sample tests: A review. *Personnel Psychology, 27,* 519–533.

Ashton, M. C. (1998). Personality and job performance: The importance of narrow traits. *Journal of Organizational Behavior, 19,* 289–303.

Ashwin, P. W. H. (2016). Teaching to the test. *University World News,* (395). ISSN 1756-297X Unpublished.

Association of Mexican-American Educators v. California. (1996). 836 F. Supp. 1534.

Association, N. G. (2010). *Common core state standards.* Washington, DC: National Governors Association.

Asún, R. A., Rdz-Navarro, K., & Alvarado, J. s. M. (2016). Developing multidimensional Likert Scales using item factor analysis. *Sociological Methods & Research, 45*(1), 109–133.

Atabakhsh, M., & Mazaheri, M. (2016). Responsiveness of the SF-36 questionnaire to the treatment outcome: A comparison of the mental and the physical patients. *Modern Applied Science, 10*(6), 183.

Atar, B. (2016). Differential item functioning analyses for mixed response data using IRT likelihood-ratio test, logistic regression, and GLLAMM procedures. Doctoral Dissertation, Florida State University.

Atkinson, A. P., & Adolphs, R. (2011). The neuropsychology of face perception: Beyond simple dissociations and functional selectivity [Review]. *Philosophical Transactions of the Royal Society of London. Series B, Biological Sciences, 366*(1571), 1726–1738. doi: 10.1098/rstb.2010.0349.

Atkinson, J. W. (1981). Studying personality in the context of an advanced motivational psychology. *American Psychologist, 36,* 117–128.

Atkinson, L. (1990). Reliability and validity of ratio developmental quotients from the Cattell Infant Intelligence Scale. *American Journal of Mental Retardation, 95,* 215–219.

Atkinson, R. C, & Geiser, S. (2009). Reflections on a century of college admission tests. *Educational Researcher, 38*(9), 665–676.

Audulv, Å., Packer, T., Hutchinson, S., Roger, K. S., & Kephart, G. (2016). Coping, adapting or self-managing—what is the difference? A concept review based on the neurological literature. *Journal of Advanced Nursing.* Published online. doi: 10.1111/jan.13037.

Augustine, A. A., Mehl, M. R., & Larsen, R J. (2011). A positivity bias in written and spoken English and its moderation by personality and gender. *Social Psychological and Personality Science, 2,* 508–513. Retrieved from http://spp.sagepub.com/content/2/5/508.

Avolio, B. J., & Waidman, D. A. (1990). An examination of age and cognitive test performance across job complexity and occupational types. *Journal of Applied Psychology, 75,* 43–50.

Ax, A. F. (1953). The physiological differentiation between fear and anger in humans. *Psychosomatic Medicine, 15,* 433–442.

Aylward, G. P. (2011). Neuropsychological assessment of newborns, infants, and toddlers. In A. S. Davis (Ed.), *Handbook of pediatric neuropsychology* (pp. 201–212). New York: Springer Publishing.

Azad, T. D., Li, A., Pendharkar, A. V., Veeravagu, A., & Grant, G. A. (2016). Junior Seau: An illustrative case of chronic traumatic encephalopathy and update on chronic sports-related head injury. *World Neurosurgery, 86,* 515. e511-515. e516.

Babad, E. (2016). Pygmalion and the classroom after 50 years. In S. Trusz & P. Babel (Eds.), *Interpersonal and intrapersonal expectancies* (pp. 125–132). New York: Routledge.

Baddeley, A. D., Wilson, B. A., & Watts, F. N. (1995). *Handbook of memory disorders.* Chichester, England: Wiley.

Baehr, M. (1987). A review of employee evaluation procedures and a description of "high potential" executives and professionals. *Journal of Business and Psychology, 1,* 172–202.

Baer, R. A., & Sekirnjak, G. (1997). Detection of underreporting on the MMPI-2 in a clinical population: Effects of information about validity scales. *Journal of Personality Assessment, 69,* 555–567.

Bai, X., Wu, C., Zheng, R., & Ren, X. (2011). The psychometric evaluation of the Satisfaction with Life Scale using a nationally representative sample of China. *Journal of Happiness Studies, 12*(2), 183–197. doi: 10.1007/s10902-010-9186-x.

Bain, S., & Gray, R. (2008). Kaufman Assessment Battery for Children, Second edition. *Journal of Psychoeducational Assessment, 26*(1), 92–101.

Bajrić, E., Kobašlija1, S., & Hrvoje J. (2011). Children's Fear Survey Schedule (CFSS-DS) in children in Bosnia and Herzegovina. *Bosnian Journal of Basic Medical Science, 11*(4), 214–218.

Baker, B. D., Farrie, D., & Sciarra, D. G. (2016). Mind the gap: 20 years of progress and retrenchment in school funding and achievement gaps. Princeton, NJ: ETS Research Report Series.

Bakker, A. B., Demerouti, E., & Ten Brummelhuis, L. L. (2011). Work engagement, performance, and active learning: The role of conscientiousness. *Journal of Vocational Behavior.* Retrieved from http://www.sciencedirect.com/science/article/pii/S0001879111001151.

Bandura, A. (1986). The explanatory and predictive scope of self-efficacy theory. *Journal of Social & Clinical Psychology, 4,* 359–373.

Bandura, A. (1994). Regulative function of perceived self-efficacy. In M. G. Rumsey, C. B. Walker, & J. H. Harris (Eds.), *Personnel selection and classification* (pp. 261–271). Hillsdale, NJ: Erlbaum.

Bangerter, A., Roulin, N., & König, C. J. (2012). Personnel selection as a signaling game. *Journal of Applied Psychology, 97,* 719–738.

Barak, A., & Cohen, L. (2002). *Empirical examination of an online version of the Self-Directed Search.* Thousand Oaks, CA: Sage.

Barber, T. X., & Silver, M. J. (1968). Fact, fiction, and the experimenter bias effect. *Psychological Bulletin Monograph Supplement, 70,* 1–29.

Bareak, B., & Lauter, D. (1991, November 5). 1991 rights bill a return to earlier path of bias redress. *Los Angeles Times,* pp. A1, A18.

Barker, R. G. (1979). Settings of a professional lifetime. *Journal of Personality and Social Psychology, 37,* 2137–2157.

Barker, R. G., & Schoggen, P. (1973). *Qualities of community life.* San Francisco: Jossey-Bass.

Barlow, D. H. (2011). A prolegomenon to clinical psychology: Two 40-year odysseys. In D. H. Barlow (Ed.), *The Oxford handbook of clinical psychology* (pp. 3–22). New York: Oxford Press.

Baron, I. S., & Fennell, E. B. (2000). Neuropsychological and intellectual assessment of children. In B. J. Sadock & V. A. Sadock (Eds.), *Comprehensive textbook of psychiatry* (7th ed., Vol. 1, pp. 722–732). Philadelphia: Lippincott, Williams & Wilkins.

Baron, R. A. (1986). Self-presentation in job interviews: When there can be "too much" of a good thing. *Journal of Applied Social Psychology, 16,* 16–28.

Barrett, G. V., & Dupinet, R. L. (1991). A reconsideration of testing for confidence rather than for intelligence. *American Psychologist, 46,* 1012–1024.

Barrick, M. R., Dustin, S. L., Giluk, T. L., Stewart, G. L., Shaffer, J. A., & Swider, B. W. (2011). Candidate characteristics driving initial impressions during rapport building: implications for employment interview validity. *Journal of Occupational and Organizational Psychology.* doi: 10.1111/j.2044-8325.2011.02036.x.

Barrick, M. R., Mount, M. K., & Judge, T. A. (2001). Personality and performance at the beginning of the new millennium: What do we know and where do we go next? *Personality and Performance, 9*(1–2), 9–30.

Bartell, S. S., & Solanto, M. V. (1995). Usefulness of the Rorschach Inkblot Test in assessment of attention deficit hyperactivity disorder. *Perceptual and Motor Skills, 80*(2), 531–541.

Bartholomew, D. J., & Knott, M. (1999). *Latent variable models and factor analysis.* New York: Oxford University Press.

Bartlett, C. J., & O'Leary, B. S. (1989). A differential prediction model to moderate the effects of heterogeneous groups in personnel selection and classification. *Personnel Psychology, 22,* 117.

Bartley, C. E., & Roesch, S. C. (2011). Coping with daily stress: The role of conscientiousness. *Personality and Individual Differences, 50*(1), 79–83. Retrieved from http://www.sciencedirect.com/science/article/pii/S0191886910004290.

Bartone, P. T. (1995). *A short hardiness scale.* Paper presented at the Annual Convention of the American Psychological Society, New York.

Bartone, P. T. (2007). Test–retest reliability of the Dispositional Resilience Scale-15, a Brief Hardiness Scale. *Psychological Reports, 101*(3), 943–944.

Bartone, P. T., Wright, K. M., Ingraham, L. H., & Ursano, R. J. (1989). The impact of a military air disaster on the health of assistance workers. *Journal of Nervous and Mental Disease, 177,* 317–328.

Basgul, S. S., Uneri, O. S., Akkaya, G. B., Etiler, N., & Coskun, A. (2011). Assessment of drawing age of children in early childhood and its correlates. *Psychology, 2*(4), 376–381. doi: 10.4236/psych.2011.24059.

Bates, T. C., & Shieles, A. (2003). Crystallized intelligence as product of speed and drive for experience: The relationship of inspection time and

openness to g and Gc. *Intelligence, 31*(3), 275–287.

Baudin, N., Aluja, A., Rolland, J. P., & Blanch, A. (2011). The roll of personality in satisfaction with life and sport. *Behavioral Psychology/Psicología Conductual, 19*(2), 333–345.

Baxter, D. J., Barbaree, H. E., & Marshall, W. L. (1986). Sexual responses to consenting and forced sex in a large sample of rapists and nonrapists. *Behaviour Research and Therapy, 24,* 513–520.

Bay, M. (1998). An exploratory factor analysis of the Leiter-R. *Dissertation Abstracts International: Section B. The Physical Sciences and Engineering, 58,* 4513.

Bayles, K. A. (1990). Language and Parkinson disease. *Alzheimer's Disease and Associated Disorders, 4,* 171–180.

Bayley, N. (1969). *Manual: Bayley Scales of Infant Development.* New York: Psychological Corporation.

Beal, J. A. (1991). Methodological issues in conducting research on parent-infant attachment. *Journal of Pediatric Nursing, 6,* 11–15.

Beal-Alvarez, J. S., Lederberg, A. R., & Easterbrooks, S. R. (2011). Grapheme–phoneme acquisition of deaf preschoolers. *Journal of Deaf Studies and Deaf Education, 16*(4), 66–78.

Beard, J., & Marini, J. P. (2015). Validity of the SAT® for predicting first-year grades: 2012 SAT validity sample. Statistical Report 2015 2. *College Board.*

Beato, L., Cano, T. R., & Belmonte, A. (2003). Relationship of dissociative experiences to body shape concerns in eating disorders. *European Eating Disorders Review, 11*(1), 38–45.

Bech, P., Carrozzino, D., Austin, S., Møller, S., & Vassend, O. (2016). Measuring euthymia within the Neuroticism Scale from the Neo Personality Inventory. *Journal of Affective Disorders, 193,* 99–102.

Beck, A. T. (1967). *Depression: Clinical, experimental, and theoretical aspects.* New York: Harper & Row.

Beck, A. T. (1976). *Cognitive therapy and the emotional disorders.* New York: International Universities Press.

Beck, A. T., & Rector, N. A. (2002). Delusions: A cognitive perspective. *Journal of Cognitive Psychotherapy, 16*(4), 455–468.

Beck, A. T., Brown, G., Steer, R. A., & Weissman, A. N. (1991). Factor analysis of the Dysfunctional Attitude Scale in a clinical population. *Psychological Assessment: Journal of Consulting and Clinical Psychology, 3,* 478–583.

Beck, S. J. (1933). Configurational tendencies in Rorschach responses. *American Journal of Psychology, 45*, 433–443.

Beck, S. J. (1944). *Rorschach's Test: Vol. 1. Basic processes.* New York: Grune & Stratton.

Beck, S. J. (1945). *Rorschach's Test: Vol. 2. A variety of personality pictures.* New York: Grune & Stratton.

Beck, S. J. (1952). *Rorschach's Test: Vol. 3. Advances in interpretation.* New York: Grune & Stratton.

Becker, B. J. (2003). Introduction to the special section on metric in meta-analysis. *Psychological Methods, 8*(4), 403–405.

Behrwind, S. D., Dafotakis, M., Halfter, S., Berthold-Losleben, M., Cieslik, E. C., & Eickhoff, S. B. (2011). Executive control in chronic schizophrenia: A perspective from manual stimulus-response compatibility task performance. *Behavioral Brain Research, 223*(1), 24–29.

Beilock, S. L., Rydell, R. J., & McConnell, A. R. (2007). Stereotype threat and working memory: Mechanisms, alleviation, and spillover. *Journal of Experimental Psychology: General, 136*(2), 256.

Bell, N. L., Lassiter, K. S., Matthews, T. D., & Hutchinson, M. B. (2001). Comparison of the Peabody Picture Vocabulary Test–Third Edition and Wechsler Adult Intelligence Scale–Third Edition with university students. *Journal of Clinical Psychology, 57*(3), 417–422.

Bell, N. L., Matthews, T. D., Lassiter, K. S., & Leverett, J. (2002). Validity of the Wonderlic Personnel Test as a measure of fluid or crystallized intelligence: Implications for career assessment. *North American Journal of Psychology, 4*(1), 113–120.

Bell, T. K. (1990). Rapid sequential processing in dyslexic and ordinary readers. *Perceptual and Motor Skills, 71*, 1155–1159.

Bellack, A. S. (Ed.). (1998). *Behavioral assessment: A practical handbook* (4th ed.). Needham Heights, MA: Allyn & Bacon.

Bellak, L. (1975). *The TAT, CAT, and SAT in clinical use* (3rd ed.). New York: Grune & Stratton.

Bellak, L. (1986). *The TAT, CAT, and SAT in clinical use* (4th ed.). New York: Grune & Stratton.

Bellak, L. (1996). *The TAT, CAT, and SAT in clinical use* (6th ed.). New York: Grune & Stratton.

Bellak, L., & Bellak, S. S. (1973). *Manual: Senior apperception technique.* Larchmont, NY: CPS.

Bem, D. J., & Allen, A. (1974). On predicting some of the people some of the time: The search for cross-situational consistencies in behavior. *Psychological Review, 81*, 506–520.

Bem, D. J., & Funder, D. C. (1978). Predicting more of the people more of the time: Assessing the personality of situations. *Psychological Review, 85*, 485–501.

Benjamin, G. A., & Gollan, J. K. (2003). Evidentiary standards and rules of evidence. In G. A. Benjamin & J. K. Gollan (Eds.), *Family evaluation in custody litigation: Reducing risks of ethical infractions and malpractice. Forensic practice guidebook* (pp. 17–28). Washington, DC: American Psychological Association.

Bennouna-Greene, M., Berna, F., Conway, M. A., Rathbone, C, J., Vidailhet, P., & Danion, J. M. (2011). Self-images and related autobiographical memories in schizophrenia. *Consciousness and Cognition.* Retrieved October 29, 2011, from http://www.sciencedirect.com/science/article/pii/S1053810011002662.

Bentler, P. M. (1990). Comparative fit indexes in structural models. *Psychological Bulletin, 107*(2), 238–246.

Bentler, P. M. (1991). Modeling of intervention effects. *Nida Research Monograph, 107*, 159–182.

Bentler, P. M. (1994). On the quality of test statistics in covariance structure analysis: Caveat emptor. In C. R. Reynolds (Ed.), *Cognitive assessment: A multidisciplinary perspective. Perspectives on individual differences* (pp. 237–260). New York: Plenum.

Bentler, P. M. (2015). New methods for test reliabilty based on structural equation modeling. Invited Address, 27th APS Convention, New York, May.

Bentler, P., & de Leeuw, J. (2011). Factor analysis via components analysis. *Psychometrika, 76*(3), 461–470. doi: 10.1007/s11336-011-9217-5.

Bentley, T. G., Palta, M., Paulsen, A. J., Cherepanov, D., Dunham, N. C., Feeny, D., ... Fryback, D. G. (2011). Race and gender associations between obesity and nine health-related quality-of-life measures. *Quality of Life Research, 20*(5), 665–674.

Benton, A. L., & Sivan, A. B. (2007). Clinical neuropsychology: A brief history. *Dis Mon, 53*(3), 142–147.

Bereby-Meyer, Y., Meyer, J., & Flascher, O. M. (2002). Prospect theory analysis of guessing in multiple choice tests. New York: Wiley.

Berg, K. C., Peterson, C. B., Frazier, P., & Crow, S. J. (2011). Convergence of scores on the interview and questionnaire versions of the eating disorder examination: A meta-analytic review. *Psychological Assessment, 23*(3), 714–724. doi: 10.1037/a0023246.

Bergan, A., McManis, D. L., & Melchert, P. A. (1971). Effects of social and token reinforcement on WISC block design performance. *Perceptual and Motor Skills, 32*, 871–880.

Bergan, J. R., & Parra, E. B. (1979). Variations in IQ testing and instruction and the letter learning and achievement of Anglo and bilingual Mexican-American children. *Journal of Educational Psychology, 71*, 819–826.

Berger, S. P., Hopkins, J., Bae, H., Hella, B., & Strickland, J. (2010). Infant assessment. In J. G. Bremner & T. D. Wachs (Eds.), *Wiley-Blackwell handbook of infant development, volume 2* (2nd ed.). Oxford, UK: Wiley-Blackwell. doi: 10.1002/9781444327588.ch9.

Berger, S. (2012). The rise and demise of the sat: The university of California generates change for college admissions. *American Educational History Journal, 39*(1), 165–180.

Bergner, M., Babbitt, R. A., Carter, W. B., & Gilson, B. S. (1981). The sickness impact profile: Development and final revision of a health status measure. *Medical Care, 19*, 787–788.

Bergstrom, B. A., & Lunz, M. E. (1999). CAT for certification and licensure. In F. Drasgow & J. B. Olson-Buchanan (Eds.), *Innovations in computerized assessment* (pp. 67–91). Mahwah, NJ: Erlbaum.

Bermant, G., Talwar, C., & Rozin, P. (2011). To celebrate positive psychology and extend its horizons. In K. M. Sheldon, T. B. Kashdan, & M. F. Steger (Eds.), *Designing positive psychology: Taking stock and moving forward* (pp. 430–439). New York: Oxford University Press.

Berninger, V., Abbott, R., Cook, C. R., & Nagy, W. (2016). Relationships of attention and executive functions to oral language, reading, and writing skills and systems in middle childhood and early adolescence. *Journal of Learning Disabilities*, Published online before print January 8, 2016, doi: 10.1177/0022219415617167.

Berry, L. M. (2003). *Employee selection.* Belmont, CA: Wadsworth.

Bersoff, D. N. (1979). Regarding psychologists testily: Legal regulation of psychological assessment in the public schools. In B. Sales & M. Novick (Eds.), *Perspectives in law and psychology: Testing and evaluation* (Vol. 3). New York: Plenum.

Bersoff, D. N. (1981). Testing and the law. *American Psychologist, 36*, 1047–1057.

Bewley, S. (2011). The NHS breast screening programme needs independent review. *British Medical Journal, 343*, d6894.

Bhave, A., Bhargava, R., & Kumar, R. (2011). Validation of a new Lucknow Intelligence Screening Test for Indian children aged 9 to 15 yr. *Journal of Pediatric Neurology, 9*(2), 215.

Bialystok, E. (2016). Bilingual education for young children: Review of the effects and consequences. *International Journal of Bilingual Education and Bilingualism*, 1–14. doi: 10.1080/13670050.2016.1203859.

Bianchini, J. C. (1976, May). *Achievement tests and differentiated norms*. Paper presented at the U. S. Office of Education invitational conference on achievement testing of disadvantaged and minority students for educational program evaluation, Reston, VA.

Bickel, W. K., Christensen, D. R., & Marsch, L. A. (2011). A review of computer-based interventions used in the assessment, treatment, and research of drug addiction. *Substance Use & Misuse, 46*(1), 4–9.

Bigler, E. D. (2003). Neurobiology and neuropathology underlie the neuro-psychological deficits associated with traumatic brain injury. *Archives of Clinical Neuropsychology, 18*(6), 595–621, 623–627.

Bilder, R. M. (2011). Neuropsychology 3.0: Evidence-based science and practice [Historical Article]. *Journal of the International Neuropsychological Society, 17*, 7–13.

Bills, D. B., & Kaufman, E. (2016). Affirmative action. The Wiley Blackwell Encyclopedia of Race, Ethnicity, and Nationalism. 30 December 2015. doi: 10.1002/9781118663202.wberen636.

Bina, R., & Harrington, D. (2016). The Edinburgh Postnatal Depression Scale: Screening tool for postpartum anxiety as well? Findings from a confirmatory factor analysis of the Hebrew version. *Maternal and Child Health Journal, 20*(4), 904–914.

Binet, A. (1890a). Perceptions d'enfants. *La Revue Philosophique, 30*, 582–611.

Binet, A. (1890b). Recherches sur les mouvements de quelques jeunes enfants. *La Revue Philosophique, 29*, 297–309.

Binet, A., & Henri, V. (1895). La psychologie individuelle. *L'Année Psychologique, 2*, 411–463.

Binet, A., & Henri, V. (1896). La psychologie individuelle. *L'Année Psychologique, 3*, 296–332.

Binet, A., & Simon, T. (1905). Methodes nouvelles pour le diagnostic du niveau intellectuel des anormaux. *L'Année Psychologique, 11*, 191–244.

Birk, J. M. (1974). Interest inventories: A mixed blessing. *Vocational Guidance Quarterly, 22*, 280–286.

Bishop, P. A., & Herron, R. L. (2015). Use and misuse of the Likert item responses and other ordinal measures. *International Journal of Exercise Science, 8*(3), 10.

Biswas, P., Malhotra, S., Malhotra, A., & Gupta, N. (2006). Comparative study of neuropsychological correlates in schizophrenia with onset in childhood, adolescence, and adulthood. *European Child & Adolescent Psychiatry, 15*(6), 360–366.

Black issues in higher education. (2001). *Black Issues in Higher Education, 17*(24), 14.

Black, P., & Wiliam, D. (2007). Large-scale assessment systems: Design principles drawn from international comparisons. *Measurement: Interdisciplinary Research and Perspectives, 5*(1), 1–53.

Black, S. (2003). Distance learning. *Nursing Standards, 17*(19), 18–19.

Blais, M. A., Norman, D. K., Quintar, B., & Herzog, D. B. (1995). The effect of the administration method: A comparison of the Rapaport and Exner Rorschach systems. *Journal of Clinical Psychology, 51*(1), 119–121.

Blasczyk-Schiepa, S., Kazénb, M., Kuhlb, J., & Grygielskic, M. (2011). Appraisal of suicidal risk among adolescents and young adults through the Rorschach Test. *Journal of Personality Assessment, 93*(5), 518–526. doi: 10.1080/00223891.2011.594130.

Blatt, S. J. (1990). The Rorschach: A test of perception or an evaluation of representation? *Journal of Personality Assessment, 55*, 394–416.

Blazar, D., Litke, E., & Barmore, J. (2016). What does it mean to be ranked a "high" or "low" value-added teacher? Observing differences in instructional quality across districts. *American Educational Research Journal, 53*(2), 324–359.

Blazek, N. L., & Forbey, J. D. (2011). A comparison of validity rates between paper-and-pencil and computerized testing with the MMPI-2. *Assessment, 18*(1), 63–66.

Bleske-Rechek, A., & Browne, K. (2014). Trends in gre scores and graduate enrollments by gender and ethnicity. *Intelligence, 46*, 25–34.

Block, J. (1961). *The Q-sort method in personality assessment and psychiatric research*. Springfield, IL: Thomas.

Board of Professional Affairs, American Psychological Association. (1998). Awards for distinguished professional contributions: John Exner. *American Psychologist, 53*, 391–392.

Board, C. (2016). *SAT: Understanding scores 2016*. Princeton, NJ: Educational Testing Service.

Bobic, J., Pavicevic, L., & Gomzi, M. (2000). Cognitive functional inefficiency in alcoholics. *Studia Psychologa, 42*(1–2), 105–110.

Bödecs, T., Horváth, B., Szilágyi, E., Gonda, X., Rihmer, Z., & Sándor, J. (2011). Effects of depression, anxiety, self-esteem, and health behaviour on neonatal outcomes in a population-based Hungarian sample. *European Journal of Obstetrics, Gynecology and Reproductive Biology, 154*(1), 45–50.

Boegels, S. M., van der Vleuten, C. P. M., Blok, G., & Kreutzkamp, R. (1996). Assessment and validation of diagnostic interviewing skills for mental health professionals. *Journal of Psychopathology and Behavioral Assessment, 17*, 217–230.

Boelema, S. R., Harakeh, Z., Van Zandvoort, M. J., Reijneveld, S. A., Verhulst, F. C., Ormel, J., & Vollebergh, W. A. (2016). Executive functioning before and after onset of alcohol use disorder in adolescence. A TRAILS study. *Journal of Psychiatric Research, 78*, 78–85.

Bohil, C. J., Alicea, B., & Biocca, F. A. (2011). Virtual reality in neuroscience research and therapy. *Nature Reviews Neuroscience, 12*, 752–762. doi: 10.1038/nrn3122.

Bolen, L. M., Hewett, J. B., Hall, C. W., & Mitchell, C. C. (1992). Expanded Koppitz Scoring System of the Bender Gestalt Visual-Motor Test for adolescents: A pilot study. *Psychology in the Schools, 29*(2), 113–115.

Bolino, M., Long, D., & Turnley, W. (2016). Impression management in organizations: Critical questions, answers, and areas for future research. *Annual Review of Organizational Psychology and Organizational Behavior, 3*, 377–406.

Bolt, D. (2003). Essays on item response theory. *Psychometrika, 68*(1), 155–158.

Bombardier, C., Ware, J., Russell, I. J., Larson, M., Chalmers, A., & Read, J. L. (1986). Auranofin therapy in quality of life for patients with rheumatoid arthritis: Results of a multicenter trial. *American Journal of Medicine, 81,* 565–578.

Bondi, M. W., Houston, W. S., Salmon, D. P., Corey-Bloom, J., Katzman, R., Thal, L. J., et al. (2003). Neuropsychological deficits associated with Alzheimer's disease in the very old: Discrepancies in raw vs. standardized scores. *Journal of the International Neuropsychology Society, 9*(5), 783–795.

Bootzin, R. R., & McKnight, P. E. (2006). *Strengthening research methodology: Psychological measurement and evaluation.* Washington, DC: American Psychological Association.

Borman, W. C, & Hallman, G. L. (1991). Observational accuracy for assessors of work-sample performance: Consistency across task and individual differences correlate. *Journal of Applied Psychology, 76,* 11–18.

Borman, W. C., Brantley, L. B., & Hanson, M. A. (2014). Progress toward understanding the structure and determinants of job performance: A focus on task and citizenship performance. *International Journal of Selection and Assessment, 22*(4), 422–431.

Bornstein, M. H., Hahn, C, Suwalsky, J. T. D., and Haynes, O. M. (2003). Socioeconomic status, parenting, and child development: The hollingshead four-factor index of social status and the socioeconomic index of occupations. In M. H. Bornstein & R. H. Bradley (Eds.), *Socioeconomic status, parenting, and child development: Monographs in parenting series* (pp. 29–82). Mahwah, NJ: Erlbaum.

Bornstein, R. F., & Masling, J. M. (2005). *Scoring the Rorschach: Seven validated systems.* Mahwah, NJ: Lawrence Erlbaum Associates Publishers.

Borsboom, D. (2015). Zen and the art of validity theory. *Assessment in Education: Principles, Policy & Practice,* 1–7. doi: 10.1080/0969594X.2015.1073479.

Borsboom, D., Mellenbergh, G. J., & van Heerden, J. (2002). Different kinds of DIF: A distinction between absolute and relative forms of measurement invariance and bias. Thousand Oaks, CA: Sage.

Bos, J. S. (1996). Factor structure of the field edition of the Leiter International Performance Scale—Revised. *Dissertation Abstracts International: Section B.*

The Physical Sciences and Engineering, 57, 1494.

Bosshardt, M. J., Carter, G. W., Gialluca, K. A., Dunnette, M. D., & Ashworth, S. D. (1992). Predictive validation of an insurance agent support person selection battery [Special Issue: Test validity yearbook I]. *Journal of Business and Psychology, 7,* 213–224.

Botet, F., de Caceres, M. L., Rosales, S., & Costas, C. (1996). Behavior assessment of newborns from diabetic mothers. *Behavioral Neurology, 9*(1), 1–4.

Boudreau, J. W., & Ramstad, P. M. (2003). *Strategic industrial and organizational psychology and the role of utility analysis models.* New York: Wiley.

Bowling, A. (2005). Mode of questionnaire administration can have serious effects on data quality. *Journal of Public Health (Oxford), 27*(3), 281–291.

Bracken, B. A. (1985). A critical review of the Kaufman Assessment Battery for Children (K-ABC). *School Psychology Review, 14,* 21–35.

Bradley-Johnson, S. (2001). Cognitive assessment for the youngest children: A critical review of tests. *Journal of Psychoeducational Assessment, 19*(2), 19–44.

Bragger, J., Kutcher, E. J., Schettino, G., Muzyczyn, B., Farago, P., & Fritzky, E. (2016). The job interview and cognitive performance: Does structure reduce performance on selection batteries, and can explanation of purpose improve it? *Performance Improvement Quarterly, 29*(2), 97–124.

Brandt, J. (2007). 2005 INS presidential address: Neuropsychological crimes and misdemeanors. *The Clinical Neuropsychologist, 21*(4), 553–568.

Bratko, D., & Marusic, I. (1997). Family study of the big five personality dimensions. *Personality and Individual Differences, 23,* 365–369.

Brawley, O. W., & Freeman, H. P. (1999). Race and outcomes: Is this the end of the beginning for minority health research? [editorial]. *Journal of the National Cancer Institute, 91*(22), 1908–1909.

Bray, J. H. (2009). Vision for the future of psychology practice. *American Psychological Association Monitor, 40*(2), 5. Retrieved from http://www.apa.org/monitor/2009/02/pc.aspx.

Brayfield, A. H. (Ed.). (1965). Testing and public policy. *American Psychologist, 20,* 857–1005.

Brazelton, T. B. (1973). *Neonatal Behavioral Assessment Scale.* Philadelphia: Lippincott.

Brazelton, T. B. (1984, November–December). *Neonatal Behavioral Assessment Scale* (2nd ed.). Philadelphia: Lippincott.

Brazelton, T. B. (1993). Why children and parents must play while they eat: An interview with T. Berry Brazelton, MD [interview by Nancy I. Hahn]. *Journal of the American Dietetic Association, 93*(12), 1385–1387.

Bredemeier, M. (1991, November–December). IQ test ban for blacks called unconstitutional. *California Associations of School Psychologists Today,* pp. 22–23.

Breen, N., Cronin, K., Meissner, H. I., Taplin, S. H., Tangka, F. K., Tiro, J. A., et al. (2007). Reported drop in mammography: Is this cause for concern? *Cancer, 109*(12), 2405–2409.

Breggin, P. R. (2002). Empathetic self-transformation in therapy. In P. R. Breggin, G. Breggin, & F. Bemak (Eds.), *Dimensions of empathic therapy* (pp. 177–189). New York: Springer.

Breithaupt, K. J., Mills, C. N., & Melican, G. J. (2006). Facing the opportunities of the future. In D. Bartram & R. K. Hambleton (Eds.), *Computer-based testing and the Internet: Issues and advances* (pp. 219–251). New York: John Wiley & Sons, Inc.

Brennan, R. L. (1994). Variance components in generalizability theory. In C. R. Reynolds (Ed.), *Cognitive assessment: A multidisciplinary perspective* (pp. 175–207). New York: Plenum.

Brenner, L. A. (2011). Neuropsychological and neuroimaging findings in traumatic brain injury and post-traumatic stress disorder [Review]. *Dialogues in Clinical Neuroscience, 13*(3), 311–323.

Bridgeman, B., & Schmitt, A. (1997). Fairness issues in test development and administration. In W. W. Willingham & N. S. Cole (Eds.), *Gender and fair assessment* (pp. 185–226). Mahwah, NJ: Erlbaum.

Bridges, K. R. (2001). Using attributional style to predict academic performance: How does it compare to traditional methods? *Personality and Individual Differences, 31*(5), 723–730.

Bridges, K. R., & Harnish, R. J. (2010). Role of irrational beliefs in depression and anxiety: A review. *Health, 2*(8), 862–877. doi: 10.4236/health.2010.28130.

Bridges, K. R., & Sanderman, R. (2002). The irrational beliefs inventory: Cross-cultural comparisons between American and Dutch samples. *Journal* of *Rational-Emotive and Cognitive Therapy, 20*(1), 65–71.

Briggs, D. C., & Weeks, J. P. (2011). The persistence of school-level value-added. *Journal of Educational and Behavioral Statistics, 36*(5), 616–637.

Britton, J., & Propper, C. (2016). Teacher pay and school productivity: Exploiting wage regulation. *Journal of Public Economics, 133*, 75–89.

Broaden, H. E. (1946). On the interpretation of the correlation coefficient as a measure of predictive efficiency. *Journal of Educational Psychology, 37*, 65–76.

Broaden, H. E. (1949). When tests pay off. *Personnel Psychology, 2*, 171–183.

Broks, P. (2003). *Into the silent land: Travels in neuropsychology.* New York: Atlantic Monthly Press.

Brookhart v. Illinois State Board of Education. (1983). 697 F. 2d. 179. 7th Cir.

Brooks, B. L., & Barlow, K. M. (2011). A methodology for assessing treatment response in Hashimoto's Encephalopathy: A case study demonstrating repeated computerized neuropsychological testing. *Journal of Child Neurology, 26*(6), 786–791. doi: 10.1177/08830738 10391532.

Brown, D. C. (1994). Subgroup norming: Legitimate testing practice or reverse discrimination? *American Psychologist, 49*(11), 927–928.

Brown, D. S., Jia, H., Zack, M. M., Thompson, W. W., Haddix, A. C., & Kaplan, R. M. (2013). Using health-related quality of life and quality-adjusted life expectancy for effective public health surveillance and prevention. *Expert Review of Pharmacoeconomics & Outcomes Research, 13*(4), 425–427.

Brown, E. A., Kenardy, J., Chandler, B., Anderson, V., McKinlay, L., & Le Brocque, R. (2016). Parent-reported health-related quality of life in children with traumatic brain injury: A prospective study. *Journal of Pediatric Psychology, 41*(2), 244–255.

Brown, F. G. (1979a). The algebra works—But what does it mean? *School Psychology Digest, 80*, 213–218.

Brown, F. G. (1979b). The SOMPA: A system of measuring potential abilities? *School Psychology Digest, 8*, 37–46.

Brown, J. S., & Burton, R. B. (1978). Diagnostic models for procedural bugs in basic mathematical skills. *Cognitive Science, 2*, 155–192.

Brown, S. D., & Lent, R. W. (2016). Vocational psychology: Agency, equity, and well-being. *Annual Review of Psychology, 67*, 541–565.

Brown, T. A. (2015). *Confirmatory factor analysis for applied research.* New York: Guilford Press.

Buck, J. N. (1948). The H-T-P technique as a qualitative and quantitative scoring manual. *Journal of Clinical Psychology, 4*, 317–396.

Buckwalter, J. G., Carter, S. R., Forgatch, G. T., Parsons, T. D., & Warren, N. C. (2013). Method and system for identifying people who are likely to have a successful relationship. *Google Patents.*

Bureau-Chalot, F., Novella, J. L., Jolly, D., Ankri, J., Guillemin, F., & Blanchard, F. (2002). Feasibility, acceptability and internal consistency reliability of the nottingham health profile in dementia patients. *Gerontology, 48*(4), 220–225.

Burke, M. J., & Doran, L. I. (1989). A note on the economic utility of generalized validity coefficients. *Journal of Applied Psychology, 73*, 171–175.

Burke, R. J. (2016). *The fulfilling workplace: The organization's role in achieving individual and organizational health*: New York: Routledge.

Burnham, J. J. (2005). Fears of children in the United States: An examination of the American fear survey schedule with 20 new contemporary fear items. *Measurement and Evaluation in Counseling and Development, 38*(2), 78–91.

Burnham, S. C., Bourgeat, P., Doré, V., Savage, G., Brown, B., Laws, S., … Martins, R. N. (2016). Clinical and cognitive trajectories in cognitively healthy elderly individuals with suspected non-Alzheimer's disease pathophysiology (SNAP) or Alzheimer's disease pathology: A longitudinal study. *The Lancet Neurology.*

Burns, R. C., & Kaufman, S. H. (1970). *Kinetic Family Drawings (KF-D): An introduction to understanding through kinetic drawings.* New York: Brunner/Mazel.

Burns, R. C., & Kaufman, S. H. (1972). *Actions, styles, and symbols in Kinetic Family Drawings (K-F-D).* New York: Brunner/Mazel.

Burnsa, G. N., & Christiansen, N. D. (2011). Methods of measuring faking behavior. *Human Performance, 24*(4), 358–372. doi: 10.1080/08959285. 2011.597473.

Buros, O. K. (Ed.). (1970). *Personality tests and reviews.* Highland Park, NJ: Gryphon Press.

Burtona, D. L., Dutyb, K. J., & Leibowitzc, G. S. (2011). Differences between sexually victimized and nonsexually victimized male adolescent sexual

abusers: Developmental antecedents and behavioral comparisons. *Journal of Child Sexual Abuse, 20*(1), 77–93. doi: 10.1080/10538712.2011.541010.

Burtt, H. E. (1926). *Principles of employment psychology.* Boston: Houghton Mifflin.

Bush, J. W. (1984). Relative preferences versus relative frequencies in health-related quality of life evaluations. In N. K. Wenger, M. E. Mattson, C. D. Furberg, & J. Elinson (Eds.), *Assessment of quality of life in clinical trials of cardiovascular therapies.* New York: LaJacq.

Butcher, H. L. (1972). Review of cooperative school and college ability tests: Series 2. In O. K. Buros (Ed.), *The seventh mental measurements yearbook* (Vol. 1). Highland Park, NJ: Gryphon Press.

Butcher, J. N. (1989). *MMPI-2 users' guide.* Minneapolis, MN: Natural Computer Systems.

Butcher, J. N. (1990). *MMPI-2 in psychological treatment.* New York: Oxford University Press.

Butcher, J. N., Aidwin, C. M., Levenson, M. R., & Ben-Porath, Y. S. (1991). Personality and aging: A study of the MMPI-2 among older men. *Psychology and Aging, 6*, 361–370.

Butcher, J. N., Graham, J. R., Dahlstrom, W. G., Tellegen, A. M., & Kaernmer, B. (1989). *MMPI-2 manual for administrators and scoring.* Minneapolis: University of Minnesota Press.

Butcher, J. N., Graham, J. R., Williams, C. L., & Ben-Porath, Y. S. (1990). *Development and use of the MMPI-2 Content Scales.* Minneapolis: University of Minnesota Press.

Butters, N., Delis, D. C., & Lucas, J. A. (1995). Clinical assessment of memory disorders in amnesia and dementia. *Annual Review of Psychology, 46*, 493–523.

Byers, C. (2001). Interactive assessment: An approach to enhance teaching and learning. *Journal of Interactive Learning Research, 12*(4), 359–374.

Byrd, D. A., Fellows, R. P., Morgello, S., Franklin, D., Heaton, R. K., Deutsch, R., et al. (2011). Neurocognitive impact of substance use in HIV infection [Research Support, N.I.H., Extramural]. *Journal of Acquired Immune Deficiency Syndromes, 58*(2), 154–162.

Cabieses, B., Pickett, K. E., & Wilkinson, R. G. (2016). The impact of socioeconomic inequality on children's health and well-being. In J. Komlos, & I. Kelly (Eds.), *The Oxford handbook of economics and human biology* (pp. 244–265). Oxford University Press.

Cacioppo, J. T., Berntson, G. G., & Anderson, B. L. (1991). Physiological approaches to the evaluation of psychotherapeutic process and outcome, 1991: Contributions from social psychophysiology. *Psychological Assessment Journal of Consulting and Clinical Psychology, 3*, 321–336.

Caffrey, E. D. (2009). Assessment in elementary and secondary education: A primer. In *Congressional research service report for congress.* Darby, PA: Diane Publishing.

Cahan, S., & Noyman, A. (2001). The Kaufman Ability Battery for Children Mental Processing Scale: A valid measure of "pure" intelligence? *Educational and Psychological Measurement, 61*(5), 827–840.

Caldwell, M. B., & Knight, D. (1970). The effects of Negro and white examiners on Negro intelligence test performance. *Journal of Negro Education, 39*, 177–179.

Callahan, S., Roge, B., Cardenal, M., Cayrou, S., & Sztulman, H. (2001). Ego control and ego resiliency: French translation of a scale measuring these concepts and initial reliability and validity status. *Journal de Therapie Comportementale et Cognitive, 11*(4), 144–150.

Callinan, M., & Robertson, I. T. (2000). *Work sample testing.* London, United Kingdom: Blackwell.

Camaioni, L., Ercolani, A. P., Penge, R., Riccio, M., & Bernabei, P. (2001). Typical and atypical profiles of referential communication ability: A comparison of normal Ss and Ss with a specific learning disorder. *Psicologia Clinica Dello Sviluppo, 5*(1), 77–94.

Camara, W. J., & Schneider, D. L. (1994). Integrity tests: Facts and unresolved issues. *American Psychologist, 49*(2), 112–119.

Campbell, D. (2002). *The history and development of the campbell interest and skill survey.* Thousand Oaks, CA: Sage.

Campbell, D. P. (1974). *Manual for the SVIB-SCII strong-campbell interest inventory* (2nd ed.). Stanford, CA: Stanford University Press.

Campbell, D. P. (1995, August). *The campbell interest and skills survey (SCII).* Paper presented at the annual meeting of the American Psychological Association, New York.

Campbell, D. P., Hyne, S. A., & Nilsen, D. (1992). *Manual for the campbell interest*

and skill survey. Minneapolis, MN: National Computer Systems.

Campbell, D. T., & Fiske, D. W. (1959). Convergent and discriminant validation by the multitrait-multimethod matrix. *Psychological Bulletin, 56*, 81–105.

Campbell, E. A., & Marcum, T. M. (2016). Search for equality through the rule of law, *The University of Detroit Mercy Law Review, 93*, 1.

Campbell, J. M., Bell, S. K., & Keith, L. K. (2001). Concurrent validity of the Peabody Picture Vocabulary Test–Third Edition as an intelligence and achievement screener for low SES African American children. *Assessment, 8*(1), 85–94.

Campbell, K. A., Rohlman, D. S., Storzbach, D., & Binder, L. M. (1999). Test–retest reliability of psychological and neurobehavioral tests self-administered by computer. *Assessment, 6*(1), 21–32.

Campbell, M. L. (2015). Multiple-choice exams and guessing: Results from a one-year study of general chemistry tests designed to discourage guessing. *Journal of Chemical Education, 92*(7), 1194–1200.

Campbell, S. L. (2011). Chaos theory and social work treatment. In F. J. Turner (Ed.), Social work treatment: Interlocking theoretical approaches (5th ed., pp. 48–57). New York: Oxford University Press.

Campbell, V. L. (2000). A framework for using tests in counseling. In C. E. Watkins Jr. & Vicki L. Campbell (Eds.), *Testing and assessment in counseling practice* (2nd ed., pp. 3–11). Mahwah, NJ: Erlbaum.

Campion, J. E. (1972). Work sampling for personnel selection. *Journal of Applied Psychology, 56*, 40–44.

Campion, M. A., Palmer, D. K., & Campion, J. E. (1997). A review of structure in the selection interview. *Personnel Psychology, 50*(3), 655–702. doi: 10.1111/j.1744-6570.1997.tb00709.x.

Canals, J., Hernández-Martínez, C., Esparó, G., & Fernández-Ballart, J. (2011). Neonatal Behavioral Assessment Scale as a predictor of cognitive development and IQ in full-term infants: A 6-year longitudinal study. *Acta Paediatrica, 100*, 1331–1337. doi: 10.1111/j.1651-2227.2011.02306.x.

Canivez, G. L. (2008). Stanford-Benet Intelligence Scales. In E. Anderman & L. H. Anderman (Eds.), *Psychology of classroom learning: An encyclopedia* (pp. 884–886). New York: MacMillon.

Canivez, G. L. (2015). Factor structure of the Wechsler Intelligence Scale for Children–Fifth Edition: Exploratory factor analyses with the 16 primary and secondary subtests). *Psychological Assessment.* Note—this has no volume or page numbers

Cannell, C. F., & Henson, R. (1974). Incentives, motives, and response bias. *Annals of Economic and Social Measurement, 3*, 307–317.

Caravale, B., Mirante, N., Vagnoni, C, & Vicari, S. (2011). Change in cognitive abilities over time during preschool age in low risk preterm children. *Early Human Development, 88*(6), 363–367.

Carkhuff, R. R. (1969). *Helping and human relations: I Selection and training; II. Practice and research.* New York: Holt, Rinehart & Winston.

Carkhuff, R. R., & Berenson, B. C. (1967). *Beyond counseling and therapy.* New York: Holt, Rinehart & Winston.

Carle, A. C., Riley, W., Hays, R. D., & Cella, D. (2015). Confirmatory factor analysis of the patient reported outcomes measurement information system (PROMIS) adult domain framework using item response theory scores. *Medical care, 53*(10), 894–900.

Carless, S. A. (1999). Career assessment: Holland's vocational interests, personality characteristics, and abilities. *Journal of Career Assessment, 7*(2), 125–144.

Carlin, J. B., & Rubin, D. B. (1991). Summarizing multiple-choice tests using three information statistics. *Psychological Bulletin, 110*, 338–349.

Carlozzia, N. E., Stoutbc, J. C, Millsde, J. A., Dufff, K., Beglingerd, L. J., & Aylwardg, E. H. (2011). Estimating premorbid IQ in the prodromal phase of a neurodegenerative disease. *The Clinical Neuropsychologist, 25*(5), 757–777. doi: 10.1080/13854046.2011.577811.

Carlson, R. E., Thayer, P. W., Mayfield, E. C, & Peterson, D. A. (1971). Improvements in the selection interview. *Personnel Journal, 50*, 268–275.

Carper, M., McHugh, R., & Barlow, D. (2011). The dissemination of computer-based psychological treatment: A preliminary analysis of patient and clinician perceptions. *Administration and Policy in Mental Health and Mental Health Services Research*, 1–9. Retrieved from http://dx.doi.org/10.1007/s10488-011-0377-5.

Carr, M. A., Sweet, J. J., & Rossini, E. (1986). Diagnostic validity of the Luria-Nebraska Neuropsychological Battery— Children's revision. *Journal* of *Consulting and Clinical Psychology, 54*, 354–358.

Carstairs, K. S. (2011). Rorschach assessment of parenting capacity: A case study. *Rorschachiana, 32*(1), 91–116. doi: 10.1027/1192-5604/a000017.

Carver, C, & Schier, M. (2012). *Perspectives on personality* (7th ed.). Boston: Pearson.

Casaletto, K., Cattie, J., Franklin, D., Moore, D., Woods, S., et al. (2014). The wide range achievement test-4 reading subtest "holds" in hiv-infected individuals. *Journal of Clinical and Experimental Neuropsychology, 36*(9), 992–1001.

Cascio, W. F. (1998). *Applied psychology in human resource management.* Englewood Cliffs, NJ: Prentice-Hall.

Cascio, W. F., & Ramos, R. A. (1986). Development and application of a new method for assessing job performance in behavioral economic terms. *Journal of Applied Psychology, 71*, 20–28.

Casey, B., Somerville, L. H., et al. (2011). Behavioral and neural correlates of delay of gratification 40 years later. *Proceedings of the National Academy of Sciences, 108*(36), 14998–15003.

Cash, T. F. (1985). The impact of grooming style on the evaluation of women in management. In M. Solomon (Ed.), *The psychology of fashion* (pp. 343–355). New York: Lexington Press.

Caspi, A., Roberts, B. W., & Shiner, R. L. (2005). Personality development: Stability and change. *Annual Review of Psychology, 56*, 453–484.

Castellino, S., Tooze, J., Flowers, L., & Parsons, S. (2011). The Peabody Picture Vocabulary Test as a pre-screening tool for global cognitive functioning in childhood brain tumor survivors. *Journal of Neuro-Oncology, 104*(2), 559–563. doi: 10.1007/s11060-010-0521-1.

Castenell, L. A., & Castenell, N. E. (1988). Norm-referenced testing in low-income blacks. *Journal of Counseling and Development, 67*, 205–206.

Cattell, J. M. (1890). Mental tests and measurements. *Mind, 15*, 373–380.

Cattell, R. B., & Scheier, I. H. (1961). *The meaning and measurement of neuroticism and anxiety.* New York: Ronald Press.

Cattell, R., & Cattell, H. (1995). Personality structure and the new 5th-edition of the 16pf. *Educational and Psychological Measurement, 55*(6), 926–937.

Cautela, J. R., & Upper, D. (1976). The Behavioral Inventory Battery: The use of self-report measures in behavioral analyses and therapy. In M. Hersen &

A. S. Bellack (Eds.), *Behavioral assessment.* New York: Pergamon Press.

Cesare, S. J. (1996). Subjective judgment and the selection interview: A methodological review. *Public Personnel Management, 25*, 291–306.

Chabanne, V., Peruch, P., & Thinus-Blanc, C. (2003). Virtual to real transfer of spatial learning in a complex environment: The role of path network and additional features. *Spatial Cognition and Computation, 31*(1), 43–59.

Chambers, L. W. (1996). The McMaster Health Index Questionnaire. In B. F. Spilker (Ed.), *Quality of life and pharmcoeconomics in clinical trials* (2nd ed., pp. 267–279). New York: Raven.

Champney, H., & Marshall, H. (1939). Optimal refinement of the rating scale. *Journal of Applied Psychology, 23*, 323–331.

Chan, G., Gelernter, J., Oslin, D., Farrer, L., & Kranzler, H. R. (2011). Empirically derived subtypes of opioid use and related behaviors. *Addiction, 106*(6), 1146–1154. doi: 10.1111/j.1360-0443. 2011.03390.x.

Chang, C. H., Ferris, D. L., Johnson, R. E., Rosen, C. C., & Tan, J. A. (2011, September 12). Core self-evaluations: A review and evaluation of the literature. *Journal of Management.* doi: 10.1177/0149206311419661. Retrieved from http://jom.sagepub.com/content/ early/2011/09/09/01492 06311419661.

Chang, H. Y., Yang, Y. L., Jensen, M. P., Lee, C.N., & Lai, Y. H. (2011). The experience of and coping with lumbopelvic pain among pregnant women in Taiwan. *Pain Medicine, 12*(6), 846–853. doi: 10.1111/j.1526-4637.2011. 01151.x.

Chang, T. (2005). The validity and reliability of student ratings: Comparison between paper-pencil and online survey. *Chinese Journal of Psychology, 47*(2), 113–125.

Checa, P., & Rueda, M. R. (2011). Behavioral and brain measures of executive attention and school competence in late childhood [Research Support, Non-U.S. Gov't]. *Developmental neuropsychology, 36*(8), 1018–1032. doi: 10.1080/87565641. 2011.591857.

Chen, E., Touyz, S. W., Beumont, P. J. V., Fairburn, C. G., Griffiths, R., Butow, P., et al. (2003). Comparison of group and individual cognitive-behavioral therapy for patients with bulimia nervosa. *International Journal of Eating Disorders, 33*(3), 241–254.

Chen, H., Donaldson, S., et al. (2011). Validity frameworks for outcome evaluation. *New Directions for Evaluation, 130*, 5–16.

Cheng, P.-Y., & Liao, W.-R. (2016). The relationship between test anxiety and achievement in accounting students with different cognitive styles: The mediating roles of self-regulation. *International Research in Education, 4*(2), 14–33.

Chico-Libran, E. (2002). Dispositional optimism as a predictor of strategies coping. *Psicothema, 14*(3), 544–550.

Child, D. (2006). *The essentials of factor analysis* (3rd ed.). New York: Continuum International Publishing Group.

Chingos, M. M., & Peterson, P. E. (2011). It's easier to pick a good teacher than to train one: Familiar and new results on the correlates of teacher effectiveness. *Economics of Education Review, 30*(3), 449–465.

Chinta, S., Walker, K., Halliday, R., Loughran-Fowlds, A., & Badawi, N. (2014). A comparison of the performance of healthy australian 3-year-olds with the standardised norms of the Bayley Scales of Infant and Toddler Development (Version-iii). *Archives of Disease in Childhood, 99*(7), 621–624.

Chong, B. H. (2000). Early childhood gifted education: Relationship of screening tests with measured intelligence. *Dissertation Abstracts International: Section A. The Humanities and Social Sciences, 61*, 5A.

Chu, J. P., Maruyama, B. A., Elefant, A., & Bongar, B. (2016). Diversity and assessment. In R. B. Weiner & R. L. Greene (Eds.), *The Wiley handbook of personality assessment* (pp. 134–145).

Chuang, A., Shen, C. T., & Judge, T. A. (2016). Development of a multidimensional instrument of person–environment fit: The Perceived Person–Environment Fit Scale (PPEFS). *Applied Psychology, 65*(1), 66–98.

Chung, C. Y., Liu, W. Y., Chang, C. J., Chen, C. L., Tang, S. F., & Wong, A. M. (2010). The relationship between parental concerns and final diagnosis in children with developmental delay. *Journal of Child Neurology, 26*, 413–419. doi: 10.1177/0883073810381922.

Clapham, M. M. (1998). Structure of Figural Forms A and B of the Torrance Tests of Creative Thinking. *Educational and Psychological Measurement, 58*, 275–283.

Clarizio, H. F. (1979a). In defense of the IQ test. *School Psychology Digest, 8*(1), 79–88.

Clarizio, H. F. (1979b). SOMPA: A symposium continued: Commentaries. *School Psychology Digest, 8*(2), 207–209.

Clark, L. A., & Watson, D. (1998). Assessment. In A. E. Kazdin (Eds.), *Methodological issues and strategies in clinical research* (2nd ed., pp. 193–281). Washington, DC: American Psychological Association.

Clarke, R., Emberson, J. R., Parish, S., Palmer, A., Shipley, M., Linksted, P., et al. (2007). Cholesterol fractions and apolipoproteins as risk factors for heart disease mortality in older men. *Archives of Internal Medicine, 167*(13), 1373–1378.

Clay, E. J., Lankford, J. S., & Wilson, S. E. (1992). The effects of computerized versus paper-and-pencil administration on measures of negative affect. *Computers in Human Behavior, 8*(2–3), 203–209.

Cleary, M. J., & Scott, A. J. (2011). Developments in clinical neuropsychology: Implications for school psychological services [Review]. *The Journal of School Health, 81*(1), 1–7. doi: 10.1111/j.1746-1561.2010.00550.x.

Cleary, T. A. (1968). Test bias: Prediction of grades of Negro and white students in integrated colleges. *Journal of Educational Measurement, 5*, 115–124.

Cleary, T. A., Humphreys, L. G., Kendrick, S. A., & Wesman, A. (1975). Educational uses of tests with disadvantaged populations. *American Psychologist, 30*, 15–41.

Coalson, D., Wahlstrom, D., Raiford, S., & Holdnack, J. (2011). Psychometric and clinical properties of new working memory and inhibition control subtests on the wechsler primary and Preschool Scale of Intelligence-Fourth Edition (wppsi-iv). *Archives of Clinical Neuropsychology, 26*(6), 498.

Coffey, C., Cummings, J., & George, M. (Eds.). (2011). *Textbook of geriatric neuropsychiatry* (3rd ed.). New York: American Psychiatric Publishing.

Cohen, J. (1960). A coefficient of agreement for nominal scales. *Educational and Psychological Measurement, 20*, 37–46.

Cohen, S., & Lichtenstein, E. (1990). Partner behaviors that support quitting smoking. *Journal of Consulting and Clinical Psychology, 58*, 304–309.

Cohen, T. R., Wolf, S. T., Panter, A. T., & Insko, C. A. (2011). Introducing the GASP scale: A new measure of guilt and shame proneness. *Journal of Personality and Social Psychology, 100*(5), 947–966. doi: 10.1037/a0022641.

Coid, J., Yang, M., Roberts, A., Ullrich, S., Moran, P., Bebbing-ton, P., et al. (2006). Violence and psychiatric morbidity in the national household population of Britain: Public health implications. *British Journal of Psychiatry, 189*(1), 12–19.

Cole, N. S. (1973). Bias in selection. *Journal of Educational Measurement, 10*, 237–255.

Cole, N. S. (1981). Bias in testing. *American Psychologist, 36*, 1067–1077.

Coleman, M. R., Buysse, V., & Neitzel, J. (2006). *Recognition and response: An early intervening system for young children at-risk for learning disabilities*. Retrieved from http://www.ldonline.org.

Colom, R., & Garcia-Lopez, O. (2002). Sex differences in fluid intelligence among high school graduates. *Personality and Individual Differences, 32*(3), 445–451.

Colom, R., Flores-Mendoza, C., & Rebello, I. (2003). Working memory and intelligence. *Personality and Individual Differences, 34*(1), 33–39.

Colom, R., Flores-Mendoza, C., Quiroga, M. Á., & Privado, J. (2005). Working memory and general intelligence: The role of short-term storage. *Personality and Individual Differences, 39*(5), 1005–1014.

Concurrent validity of the Bayley Scales of infant & toddler development-3rd edition and neuro sensory motor developmental assessment in preterm infants. (2015). *Developmental Medicine & Child Neurology, 57*, 55.

Conklin, M. H., & Desselle, S. P. (2007). Development of a multidimensional scale to measure work satisfaction among pharmacy faculty members. *American Journal of Pharmaceutical Education, 71*(4), 61.

Conley, D. T. (2007). The challenge of college readiness. *Educational Leadership, 64*(7), 23.

Conley, D., & Domingue, B. (2016). The Bell curve revisited: Testing controversial hypotheses with molecular genetic data. *Sociological Science, 3*, 520–539.

Connolly, J. J., Kavanagh, E. J., & Viswesvaran, C. (2007). The convergent validity between self and observer ratings of personality: A meta-analytic review. *International Journal of Selection and Assessment, 15*(1), 110–117.

Constantine, M. G., & Watt, S. K. (2002). Cultural congruity, womanist identity attitudes, and life satisfaction among African American college women attending historically Black and predominately White institutions. *Journal of College Student Development, 43*(2), 184–194.

Constantino, G., & Malgady, R. G. (1999). The Tell-Me-A-Story Test: A multicultural offspring of the Thematic Apperception Test. In L. G. Gieser & M. I. Stein (Eds.), *Evocative images: The Thematic Apperception Test and the art of projection*. Washington, DC: American Psychological Association.

Constantino, G., Malgady, R. G., Colon-Malgady, G., & Bailey, J. (1992). Clinical utility of the TEMAS with nonminority children. *Journal of Personality Assessment, 59*(3), 433–438.

Cook, D. A., & Beckman, T. J. (2006). Current concepts in validity and reliability for psychometric instruments: Theory and application. *American Journal of Medicine, 119*(2), 166–167.

Cook, D., Lee, E.-K., & Majumder, M. (2016). Data visualization and statistical graphics in big data analysis. *Annual Review of Statistics and Its Application, 3*, 133–159.

Cook, M. (2016). *Personnel selection: Adding value through people–A changing picture*. New York: John Wiley & Sons.

Cook, M. L., & Peterson, C. (1986). Depressive irrationality. *Cognitive Therapy and Research, 10*, 293–298.

Cooley, P. C., Rogers, S. M., Turner, C. F., Al-Tayyib, A. A., Willis, G., & Ganapathii, L. (2001). Using touch screen audio-CASI to obtain data on sensitive topics. *Computers in Human Behavior, 17*(3), 285–293.

Copple, C. E., & Succi, G. J. (1974). The comparative ease of processing standard English and black nonstandard English by lower-class black children. *Child Development, 45*, 1048–1053.

Corballis, M. C. (2011). A frontal approach to intelligence. *Brain: A Journal of Neurology, 134*(9), 2787–2790. doi: 10.1093/brain/awr186.

Cordes, A. K. (1994). The reliability of observational data: I. Theories and methods for speech-language pathology. *Journal of Speech and Hearing Research, 37*(2), 264–278.

Cormier, D. C., McGrew, K. S., Evans, J. J. (2011). Quantifying the degree of linguistic demand in spoken intelligence test directions. *Journal of Psychoeducational Assessment*.

Corrigan, J. D., Bogner, J. A., Mysiw, W. J., Clinchot, D., & Fugate, L. (2001). Life satisfaction after traumatic brain injury. *Journal of Head Trauma Rehabilitation*, *16*(6), 543–555.

Corrigan, P. W. (2007). How clinical diagnosis might exacerbate the stigma of mental illness. *Social Work*, *52*(1), 31–39.

Costa Jr., P. T., & McCrae, R. R. (1985). *The NEO personality inventory: Manual*. New York: Psychological Assessment Resources.

Costa Jr., P. T., & McCrae, R. R. (1995). Domains and facets: Hierarchical personality assessment using the revised NEO Personality Inventory. *Journal of Personality Assessment*, *64*(1), 21–50.

Costa Jr., P. T., McCrae, R. R., & Kay, G. G. (1995). Persons, places, and personality: Career assessment using the revised NEO Personality Inventory. *Journal of Career Assessment*, *76*(2), 123–139.

Costa Jr., P. T., McRae, R. R., & Jonsson, F. H. (2002). Validity and utility of the revised NEO personality inventory: Examples from Europe. In B. de Raad (Ed.), *Big five assessment* (2nd ed., pp. 61–72). Ashland, OH: Hogrefe & Huber.

Costa, R. M. E., De Carvalho, L. A. V., Drummond, R., Wauke, A. P. T., & De Sa Guimaraes, M. (2002). The UFRJ-UERJ group: Interdisciplinary virtual reality experiments in neuropsychiatry. *Cyberpsychology and Behavior*, *5*(5), 423–431.

Costa, R., Figueiredo B., Tendais I., Conde A., Pacheco A., & Teixeira C. (2010). Brazelton Neonatal Behavioral Assessment Scale: A psychometric study in a Portuguese sample. *Infant Behavior and Development*, *33*(4), 510–517.

Costantino, G., Dana, R. H., & Malgady, R. G. (2007). *TEMAS (tell-me- A-story) assessment in multicultural societies*. Mahwah, NJ: Lawrence Erlbaum Associates Publishers.

Costello, J., & Dickie, J. (1970). Leiter and Stanford-Binet IQ's of preschool disadvantaged children. *Developmental Psychology*, *2*, 314.

Cottraux, J. (2005). Recent developments in research and treatment for social phobia (social anxiety disorder). *Current Opinion in Psychiatry*, *18*(1), 51–54.

Cottrell, J. M., Newman, D. A., & Roisman, G. I. (2015). Explaining the black–white gap in cognitive test scores: Toward a theory of adverse impact. *Journal of Applied Psychology*, *100*(6), 1713.

Cox, D. R. (2006). *Principles of statistical inference*. Cambridge, New York: Cambridge University Press.

Coyle, H., Traynor, V., & Solowij, N. (2015). Computerized and virtual reality cognitive training for individuals at high risk of cognitive decline: Systematic review of the literature. *The American Journal of Geriatric Psychiatry*, *23*(4), 335–359.

Cramer, P. (1999). Future directions for the Thematic Apperception Test. *Journal of Personality Assessment*, *72*, 74–92.

Creamer, M., O'Donnell, M. L., Carboon,. I, Lewis, V., Densley, K., McFarlane, A., Silove, D., Bryant, R. A. (2009). Evaluation of the Dispositional Hope Scale in injury survivors. *Journal of Research in Personality*, *43*(4), 613–617.

Crespin, T. R., & Austin, J. T. (2002). Computer technology applications in industrial and organizational psychology. *Cyber Psychology and Behavior*, *5*(4), 279–303.

Crespo-Facorro, B., Barbadillo, L., Pelayo-Teran, J. M., & Rodriguez-Sanchez, J. M. (2007). Neuropsychological functioning and brain structure in schizophrenia. *International Review of Psychiatry*, *19*(4), 325–336.

Crocker, L. M., & Algina, J. (1986). *Introduction to classical and modern test theory*. New York: Holt, Rinehart & Winston.

Crome, E., Baillie, A., Slade, T., & Ruscio, A. M. (2010). Social phobia: further evidence of dimensional structure. *Australian and New Zealand Journal of Psychiatry*, *44*(11), 1012–1020.

Cronbach, L. J. (1951). Coefficient alpha and the internal structure of tests. *Psychometrika*, *16*, 297–334.

Cronbach, L. J. (1975). Five decades of public controversy over mental testing. *American Psychologist*, *30*, 1–14.

Cronbach, L. J. (1978). Black Intelligence Test of Cultural Homogeneity: A review. In O. K. Buros (Ed.), *The eighth mental measurements yearbook* (Vol. 1). Highland Park, NJ: Gryphon Press.

Cronbach, L. J. (1980). Validity on parole: How can we go straight? *New Directions for Testing and Measurement*, *5*, 99–108.

Cronbach, L. J. (1989). Construct validation after thirty years. In R. Linn (Ed.), *Intelligence: Measurement, theory, and public policy*. Urbana: University of Illinois Press.

Cronbach, L. J. (1995). Giving method variance its due. In P. E. Shrout & S. T. Fiske (Eds.), *Personality research, methods, and theory: A festschrift honoring Donald W. Fiske* (pp. 145–157). Hillsdale, NJ: Erlbaum.

Cronbach, L. J., & Furby, L. (1970). How we should measure "change"—Or should we? *Psychological Bulletin*, *74*, 68–80.

Cronbach, L. J., & Gleser, G. C. (1965). *Psychological tests and personnel decisions*. Urbana: University of Illinois Press.

Cronbach, L. J., & Meehl, P. E. (1955). Construct validity in psychological tests. *Psychological Bulletin*, *52*, 281–302.

Cronk, B. C, & West, J. L. (2002). Personality research on the Internet: A comparison of Web-based and traditional instruments in take-home and in-class settings. *Behavior Research Methods, Instruments, and Computers*, *34*(2), 177–180.

Crosby, F. J., Iyer, A., Clayton, S., & Downing, R. A. (2003). Affirmative action. Psychological data and the policy debates. *American Psychologist*, *58*(2), 93–115.

Crowe, T. V (2003). Self-esteem scores among deaf college students: An examination of gender and parents' hearing status and signing ability. *Journal of Deaf Studies and Deaf Education*, *8*(2), 199–206.

Cubelli, R., & Sala, S. D. (2007). What are neuropsychologists up to? *Cortex*, *43*(8), 1122–1124.

Cubelli, R., Pedrizzi, S., & Della Sala, S. (2016). The role of cognitive neuropsychology in clinical settings: The example of a single case of Deep Dyslexia. In A. B. J. Macniven (Ed.), *Neuropsychological formulation: A clinical casebook* (pp. 15–27). Cham: Springer International Publishing.

Cucina, J. M., Peyton, S. T., Su, C., & Byle, K. A. (2016). Role of mental abilities and mental tests in explaining high-school grades. *Intelligence*, *54*, 90–104.

Cumella, E. J., & O'Connor, J. L. (2009). Assessing adolescents with the MMPI-A. In J. N. Butcher (Ed.), *Oxford handbook of clinical and personality assessment* (pp. 485–500). New York: Oxford University Press.

Cundick, B. P. (1985). Review of incomplete sentences task. In J. V. Mitchell (Ed.), *Ninth mental measurements yearbook* (Vol. 1, pp. 681–682). Highland Park, NJ: Gryphon Press.

Cunningham, T. J., Berkman, L. F., Gortmaker, S. L., Kiefe, C. I., Jacobs Jr., D. R., Seeman, T. E., & Kawachi, I. (2011). Assessment of differential item functioning in the experiences of discrimination index. *American Journal of Epidemiology*, *174*(11), 1266–1274.

Cureton, E. E., Cronbach, L. J., Meehl, P. E., Ebel, R. L., & Ward, A. W. (1996). Validity. In A. W. Ward, H. W. Stoker, & M. Murray-Ward (Eds.), *Educational measurement: Origins, theories and explications, Vol. 1: Basic concepts and theories* (pp. 125–243). Lanham, MD: University Press of America.

Cyranowski, J. M., Shear, M. K., Rucci, P., Fagiolini, A., Frank, E., Grochocinski, V. J., et al. (2002). Adult separation anxiety: Psychometric properties of a new structure clinical interview. *Journal of Psychiatric Research, 36*(2), 77–86.

Dahlstrom, W. G. (1969a). Invasion of privacy: How legitimate is the current concern over this issue? In J. N. Butcher (Ed.), *MMPI: Research developments and clinical applications.* New York: McGraw-Hill.

Dahlstrom, W. G. (1969b). Recurrent issues in the development of the MMPI. In J. N. Butcher (Ed.), *MMPI: Research developments and clinical applications.* New York: McGraw-Hill.

Dahlstrom, W. G., & Welsh, G. S. (1960). *An MMPI handbook. A guide to use in clinical practice and research.* Minneapolis: University of Minnesota Press.

Daini, S., & Bernardini, L. (2007). Emotional feelings in eating disorders: A Rorschach test quantitative analysis. *Journal of Projective Psychology & Mental Health, 14*(1), 76–84.

Dale, B.A., McIntosh, D.E., Rothlisberg, B.A., Ward, K. E., & Bradley, M. (2011). Profile analysis of the Kaufman Assessment Battery for Children, Second Edition, with African American and Caucasian preschool children. *Psychology in the Schools, 48*(5), 476–487.

Dalton, E. D., Hammen, C. L., Brennan, P. A., & Najman, J. M. (2016). Pathways maintaining physical health problems from childhood to young adulthood: The role of stress and mood. *Psychology & Health*, 1–17. doi: 10.1080/08870446.2016.1204448.

Dana, R. H. (2000). *Handbook of cross-cultural and multicultural personality assessment.* Mahwah, NJ: Erlbaum.

Danaher, K., & Crandall, C. S. (2008). Stereotype threat in applied settings re-examined. *Journal of Applied Social Psychology, 38*(6), 1639–1655.

Dangel, H. L. (1970). *The biasing effect of pretest information on the MSC scores of mentally retarded children.* (Doctoral dissertation, Pennsylvania State University). (UMI No. 7116,588).

Dantzker, M. L. (2011). Psychological preemployment screening for police candidates: Seeking consistency if not standardization. *Professional Psychology: Research and Practice, 42*(3), 276–283. doi: 10.1037/a0023736.

Darlington, R. B. (1971). Another look at "cultural fairness". *Journal of Educational Measurement, 8*, 71–82.

Darlington, R. B. (1978). Cultural test bias: Comment on Hunter and Schmidt. *Psychological Bulletin, 85*, 673–674.

Darolia, C. R., & Joshi, H. L. (2004). Psychometric evaluation of a short form of Holtzman Inkblot technique. *Journal of Projective Psychology & Mental Health, 11*(2), 124–132.

Das, H. P., & Sahoo, M. (2015). Talent search: A challenge for employers. *Parikalpana: KIIT Journal of Management, 11*(1), 120.

Das, J. P. (1973). Cultural deprivation and cognitive competence. In N. R. Ellis (Ed.), *International review of research in mental retardation* (Vol. 6). New York: Academic Press.

Datta, L. (1975). Foreword. In E. E. Diamond (Ed.), *Issues of sex bias and sex fairness in career interest measurement.* Washington, DC: National Institutes of Education.

Davidson, J. E., & Kemp, I. A. (2011). Contemporary models of intelligence. In R. Sternberg & S. Kaufman (Eds.), *The Cambridge handbook of intelligence* (pp. 58–85). New York: Cambridge University Press.

Davis, R. N. (1999). Web-based administration of a personality questionnaire: Comparison with traditional methods. *Behavior Research Methods, Instruments and Computers, 31*(4), 572–577.

Dawes, R. M. (1999). Two methods for studying the incremental validity of a Rorschach variable. *Psychological Assessment, 11*, 297–302.

Dawson, J. K., & Grant, I. (2000). Alcoholics' initial organization and problem-solving skills predict learning and memory performance on the Rey-Osterrieth complex figure. *Journal of the International Neuropsychological Society, 6*(1), 12–19.

Day, D. V. (2016). The Leadership Quarterly Yearly Review (LQYR) for 2018. *The Leadership Quarterly.* Retrived from http://www.journals.elsevier.com/the-leadership-quarterly/call-for-papers/the-leadership-quarterly-yearly-review-lqyr-for-2018

Day, D. V., & Sulsky, L. M. (1995). Effects of frame-of-reference training and information configuration on memory organization and rating accuracy.

Journal of Applied Psychology, 80, 158–167.

De Ayala, R., & Santiago, S. (2016). An introduction to mixture item response theory models. *Journal of School Psychology.* Published online in advance of print April 2016, http://dx.doi.org/10.1016/j.jsp.2016.01.002.

De Corte, W., Lievens, F., & Sackett, P. R. (2007). Combining predictors to achieve optimal trade-offs between selection quality and adverse impact. *Journal of Applied Psychology, 92*(5), 1380–1393.

de Haan, E., Grant, A. M., Burger, Y., & Eriksson, P.-O. (2016). A large-scale study of executive and workplace coaching: The relative contributions of relationship, personality match, and self-efficacy. *Consulting Psychology Journal: Practice and Research, 68*(3), 189–207.

De Marco, A. P., & Broshek, D. K. (2016). Computerized cognitive testing in the management of youth sports-related concussion. *Journal of Child Neurology, 31*(1), 68–75.

Dearborn, G. (1897). Blots of ink in experimental psychology. *Psychological Review, 4*, 390–391.

Deary, I. J., Penke, L., & Johnson, W. (2010). The neuroscience of human intelligence differences. *Neuroscience, 11*, 201–211. doi: 10.1038/nrn2793.

Deaton, A., & Stone, A. A. (2016). Understanding context effects for a measure of life evaluation: How responses matter. *Oxford Economic Papers*, gpw022.

Dee, T. S., & Jacob, B. (2011). The impact of No Child Left Behind on student achievement. *Journal of Policy Analysis and Management, 30*(3), 418–446.

Deffenbacher, J. L., Swerner, W. A., Whisman, M. A., Hill, R. A., & Sloan, R. D. (1986). Irrational beliefs and anxiety. *Cognitive Therapy and Research, 10*, 281–292.

Delhees, K. H., & Cattell, R. B. (1971). *Manual for the Clinical Analysis Questionnaire (CAQ).* Champaign, IL: Institute for Personality and Ability Testing.

Delis, D. C., & Wetter, S. R. (2007). Cogniform disorder and cogniform condition: Proposed diagnoses for excessive cognitive symptoms. *Archives of Clinical Neuropsychology, 22*(5), 589–604.

Delis, D. C., Filoteo, J. V., Massman, P. J., Kaplan, E., & Kramer, J. H. (1994). The clinical assessment of memory disorders. In L. S. Cermak (Eds.),

Neuropsychological explorations of memory and cognition: Essays in honor of Nelson Butters (pp. 223–239). New York: Plenum.

Delis, D. C., Jacobson, M., Bondi, M. W., Hamilton, J. M., & Salmon, D. P. (2003). The myth of testing construct validity using factor analysis or correlations with normal or mixed clinical populations: Lessons from memory assessment. *Journal of the International Neuropsychological Society*, 9(6), 936–946.

Delis, D. C., Kramer, J. H., Kaplan, E., & Holdnack, J. (2004). Reliability and validity of the Delis-Kaplan executive function system: An update. *Journal of the International Neuropsychological Society*, 10(2), 301–303.

Delis, D. C., Kramer, J. H., Kaplan, E., & Ober, B. A. (1987). *The California Verbal Learning Test* (Research ed.). San Diego: Harcourt Brace Jovanovich.

Delis, D. C., Magsman, P. J., Butters, N., Salmon, D. P., Cermak, L. S., & Kramer, J. H. (1991). Profiles of demented and amnesic patients on the California Verbal Learning Test: Implications for the assessment of memory disorders. *Psychological Assessment: A Journal of Consulting and Clinical Psychology*, 3, 19–26.

DeMars, C. (2010). *Item response theory.* New York: Oxford University Press.

Deogun, J., & Spaulding, W. (2010). Conceptual development of mental health ontologies. In Z. Ras & L. Tsay (Eds.), *Advances in intelligent information systems* (pp. 265, 299–333). Berlin: Springer. doi: 10.1007/978-3-642-05183-8_13.

DeRosa, A., & Patalano, F. (1991). Effects of familiar proctor on fifth and sixth grade students' test anxiety. *Psychological Reports*, 68, 103–113.

DeRue, D. S., & Morgeson, F. P. (2007). Stability and change in person-team and person-role fit over time: The effects of growth satisfaction, performance, and general self-efficacy. *Journal of Applied Psychology*, 92(5), 1242.

Deskovitz, M., Weed, N., Chakranarayan, C., Williams, J., & Walla, P. (2016). Interpretive reliability of two common mmpi-2 profiles. *Cogent Psychology*, 1161287.

Detwiler, F. R., & Ramanaiah, N. V. (1996). Structure of the Jackson personality inventory from the perspective of the five-factor model. *Psychological Reports*, 79, 411–416.

DeVellis, R. F. (2006). Classical test theory. *Medical Care*, 44(11, Suppl. 3), S50–S59.

Devoe, E. R., & Faller, K. C. (2002). Question strategies in interviews with children who may have been sexually abused. *Child Welfare*, 81(1), 5–31.

Dewey, D., Creighton, D. E., Heath, J. A., Wilson, B. N., Anseeuw-Deeks, D., Crawford, S. G., & Sauve, R. (2011). Assessment of developmental coordination disorder in children born with extremely low birth weights [Research Support, Non-U.S. Gov't]. *Developmental Neuropsychology*, 36(1), 42–56. doi: 10.1080/87565641.2011.540535.

DeWitt, M. B., Schreck, K. A., & Mulick, J. A. (1998). Use of Bayley Scales in individuals with profound mental retardation: Comparison of the first and second editions. *Journal of Developmental and Physical Disabilities*, 10, 307–313.

Dhar, J., & Mishra, J. (2014). Human personality behavior based on family structure using a Thematic Apperception Test. *Journal of Human Behavior in the Social Environment*, 24(7), 751–758.

di Blasi, F. D., Elia, F., Buono, S., Ramakers, G. J. A., & di Nuovo, S. F. (2007). Relationships between visual-motor and cognitive abilities in intellectual disabilities. *Perceptual and Motor Skills*, 104(3), 763–772.

Di Fabio, A., & Busoni, L. (2007). Fluid intelligence, personality traits and scholastic success: Empirical evidence in a sample of Italian high school students. *Personality and Individual Differences*, 43(8), 2095–2104.

Diamond, E. E. (1979). Sex equality and measurement practices. *New Directions for Test and Measurement*, 3, 61–78.

Diamond, E. E., & Zytowski, D. G. (2000). The kuder occupational interest survey. In C. E. Watkins Jr. & V. L. Campbell (Eds.), *Testing and assessment in counseling practice* (2nd ed., pp. 263–294). Mahwah, NJ: Erlbaum.

Díaz, J. O., Abad, F. J., Ponsoda Gil, V., Aguado, D., & Díaz, J. (2011). Development, psychometric properties and new validity evidences of the web-based computerized adaptive test of English eCat. *Revista Electrónica de Metodología Aplicada*, 16(1), 50–65.

DiBello, L. V., Stout, W. F., & Roussos, L. A. (1995). Unified cognitive/ psychometric diagnostic assessment likelihood-based classification techniques. In P. D. Nichols, S. F. Chipman, & R. L. Brennan (Eds.), *Cognitively*

diagnostic assessment (pp. 361–389). Hillsdale, NJ: Erlbaum.

DiCaccavo, A. (2010). All in the mind: cognitive behavioural therapy. *Psychology Review*, 16(2). ISSN 1750–3469.

Diener, E., Emmons, R. A., Larsen, R. J., & Griffin, S. (1985). The Satisfaction with Life Scale. *Journal of Personality Assessment*, 49, 71–75.

Diercke, K., Ollinger, I., Bermejo, J. L., Stucke, K., Lux, C. J., & Brunner, M. (2012). Dental fear in children and adolescents: A comparison of forms of anxiety management practised by general and paediatric dentists. *International Journal of Paediatric Dentistry*, 22, 60–67. doi: 10.1111/j.1365-263X. 2011.01158.x.

Dierdorff, E. C., & Wilson, M. A. (2003). A meta-analysis of job analysis reliability. *Journal of Applied Psychology*, 88(4), 635–646.

Dige, N., & Wik, G. (2005). Adult attention deficit hyperactivity disorder identified by neuropsychological testing. *International Journal of Neuroscience*, 115(2), 169–183.

Dillard, J. P., & Marshall, L. J. (2003). Persuasion as a social skill. In J. O. Greene & B. R. Burleson (Eds.), *Handbook of communication and social interaction skills* (pp. 479–513). Mahwah, NJ: Erlbaum.

DiSantis, D. J., Ayoob, A. R., & Williams, L. E. (2015). Journal club: Prevalence of flawed multiplecChoice questions in continuing medical education activities of major radiology journals. *American Journal of Roentgenology*, 204(4), 698–702.

Dishion, T. J., Andrews, D. W., & Crosby, L. (1995). Antisocial boys and their friends in early adolescence: Relationship characteristics, quality, and interactional process. *Child Development*, 66, 139–151.

DiStefano, C., & Dombrowski, S. C. (2006). Investigating the theoretical structure of the Stanford-Binet, fifth edition. *Journal of Psychoeducational Assessment*, 24(2), 123–136.

Dobkin, B. H., & Dorsch, A. (2011). The promise of mHealth. *Neurorehabilitation and Neural Repair*, 25(9), 788–798.

Dobko, P., & Kehoe, J. F. (1983). On the fair use of bias: A comment on Drasgow. *Psychological Bulletin*, 93, 604–608.

Dockray, S., Grant, N., Stone, A. A., Kahneman, D., Wardle, J., & Steptoe, A. (2010). A comparison of affect ratings obtained with ecological momentary assessment and the day reconstruction method. *Social Indicators Research, 99*(2), 269–283. doi: 10.1007/s11205-010-9578-7.

Doctor, R. (1972). Review of the Porteus Maze Test. In O. K. Buros (Ed.), *The seventh mental measurements yearbook* (Vol. 1). Highland Park, NJ: Gryphon Press.

Dodrill, C. B., & Warner, M. H. (1988). Further studies of the Wonderlic Personnel Test as a brief measure of intelligence. *Journal of Consulting and Clinical Psychology, 59,* 145–147.

Doerries, L. E., & Ridley, D. R. (1998). Time sensitivity and purpose in life: Contrasting theoretical per-spectives of Myers-Briggs and Victor Frankl. *Psychological Reports, 83,* 67–71.

Doherty, E. M., & Nugent, E. (2011). Personality factors and medical training: A review of the literature. *Medical Education, 45*(2), 132–140. doi: 10.1111/j.1365-2923.2010.03760.x.

Dolezal, C., Marhefka, S., Santamaria, E., Leu, C. S., Brackis-Cott, E., & Mellins, C. (2011). A comparison of audio computer-assisted self-inter-views to face-to-face interviews of sexual behavior among perinatally HIV-exposed youth. *Archives of Sexual Behavior,* 1–10. doi: 10.1007/s10508-011-9769-6.

Donahue, D., & Sattler, J. M. (1971). Personality variables affecting WAIS scores. *Journal of Consulting and Clinical Psychology, 36,* 441.

Dougherty, T. W., Turban, D. B., & Call-ender, J. C. (1994). Confirming first impressions in the employment interview: A field study of interviewer behavior. *Journal of Applied Psychology, 79*(5), 659–665.

Douglas, J. (2002). Psychological treatment of food refusal in young children. *Child and Adolescent Mental Health, 7*(4), 173–180.

Dove, A. (1968). Taking the Chitling Test. *Newsweek, 72,* 51–52.

Drasgow, F. (1982). Biased test items and differential validity. *Psychological Bulletin, 92,* 526–531.

Drasgow, F., Whetzel, D. L., & Oppler, S. H. (2016). Strategies for test validation and refinement. *Applied Measurement: Industrial Psychology in Human Resources Management,* New York: Routledge.

Dretsch, M., Parish, R., Kelly, M., Coldren, R., & Russell, M. (2015). Eight-day temporal stability of the automated neuropsychological assessment metric (ANAM) in a deployment

environment. *Applied Neuropsychology: Adult, 22*(4), 304–310.

Drieling, R. L., LaCroix, A. Z., Beresford, S. A., Boudreau, D. M., Kooperberg, C., & Heckbert, S. R. (2016). Valid-ity of self-reported medication use compared with pharmacy records in a cohort of older women: Findings from the Women's Health Initiative. *American Journal of Epidemiology, 184*(3), 233–238.

Drigas, A., Koukianakis, L., & Papagerasi-mou, Y. (2011). Towards an ICT-based psychology: E-psychology. *Computers in Human Behavior, 27*(4), 1416–1423. doi: 10.1016/j.chb.2010.07.045.

Drogin, E. Y., Dattilio, F. M., Sadoff, R. L., & Gutheil, T. G. (2011). Child custody and parental fitness. In *Handbook of forensic assessment: Psychological and psychiatric perspectives* (pp. 443–458). Hoboken, NJ: John Wiley & Sons, Inc. doi: 10.1002/9781118093399.

Dror, R., Malinger, G., Ben-Sira, L., Lev, D., Pick, C. G., & Lerman-Sagie, T. (2009). Developmental outcome of children with enlargement of the cis-terna magna identified in utero. *Journal of Child Neurology, 24,* 1486–1492. doi: 10.1177/0883073808331358.

Drummond, M. F., Sculpher, M. J., Claxton, K., Stoddart, G. L., & Torrance, G. W. (2015). *Methods for the economic eval-uation of health care programmes.* New York: Oxford university press.

Du, Y. B., Lee, C. T., Christinam, D., Belfer, M. L., Betancourt, T. S., O'Rourke, E. J., et al. (2011). The living environ-ment and children's fears following the Indonesian tsunami. *Disasters.* doi: 10.1111/j. 1467-7717.2011.01271.x.

DuBois, P. H. (1970). *A history of psychological testing.* Boston: Allyn & Bacon.

DuBois, P. H. (1972). Increase in edu-cational opportunity through mea-surement. In *Proceedings of the 1971 Invitational Conference on Testing Problems.* Princeton, NJ: Educational Testing Service.

Dubow, E. F., Huesmann, L. R., Boxer, P., & Smith, C. (2016). Childhood and adolescent risk and protective factors for violence in adulthood. *Journal of Criminal Justice, 45,* 26–31.

Dubowitz, H., Villodas, M. T., Litrownik, A. J., Pitts, S. C., Hussey, J. M., Thompson, R., et al. (2011). Psycho-metric properties of a youth self-report measure of neglectful behavior by parents. *Child Abuse & Neglect, 35*(6), 414–424.

Dunn, D. M., & Dunn, L. M. (2007). *Pea-body Picture Vocabulary Test* (4th ed. PPVT-4™). Minneapolis, MN: NCS Pearson, Inc. Retrieved from http://psychcorp.pearsonassessments.com.

Dunn, J. A. (1972). Review of the Goode-nough-Harris Drawing Test. In O. K. Buros (Ed.), *The seventh mental mea-surements yearbook* (Vol. 1). Highland Park, NJ: Gryphon Press.

Dunn, L. M., & Dunn, D. M. (2007). *Pea-body Picture Vocabulary Test* (4th ed. PPVT™-4). Retrieved from http://www.pearsonassessments.com.

Dunn, L. M., & Dunn, I. M. (1981). *Pea-body Picture Vocabulary Test–Revised.* Circle Pines, MN: American Guidance Service.

Dunnette, M. D. (1967). The assessment of managerial talent. In F. R. Wickert & D. E. McFarland (Eds.), *Measur-ing executive effectiveness.* New York: Appleton-Century-Crofts.

Dunnette, M. D. (1972). *Validity study results for jobs relevant to the petroleum refining industry.* Washington, DC: American Petroleum Institute.

Dunnette, M. D., & Borman, W. C. (1979). Personnel selection and classification systems. *Annual Review of Psychology, 30,* 477–525.

Durand, M. (2016). Employing critical incident technique as one way to dis-play the hidden aspects of post-merger integration. *International Business Review, 25*(1), 87–102.

Dush, D. M. (1985). Review of incomplete sentences task. In J. V. Mitchell (Ed.), *The ninth mental measurements yearbook* (Vol. 1, pp. 682–683). Highland Park, NJ: Gryphon Press.

Duty, S. M., Christian, L., Loftus, J., & Zappi, V. (2016). Is cognitive test-tak-ing anxiety associated with academic performance among nursing students? *Nurse Educator, 41*(2), 70–74.

Dvir, T., Eden, D., & Banjo, M. (1995). Self-fulfilling prophecy and gen-der: Can women be Pygmalion and Galatea? *Journal of Applied Psychology, 80,* 253–270.

Dweck, C. S. (2016). The remarkable reach of growth mind-sets. *Scientific Ameri-can Mind, 27*(1), 36–41.

Dwight, S. A., & Feigelson, M. E. (2000). A quantitative review of the effect of computerized testing on the measure-ment of social desirability. *Educational and Psychological Measurement, 60*(3), 340–360.

Dytham, C. (2011). *Choosing and using statistics: A biologist's guide* (3rd ed.).

Chichester, West Sussex, UK; Hoboken, NJ: Wiley-Blackwell.

Eaton, N. K., Wing, H., & Mitchell, K. J. (1985). Alternative methods of estimating the dollar value of performance. *Personnel Psychology, 38*, 27–40.

Ebmeier, H., Dillon, A., & Ng, J. (2007). *Employment selection instruments—What we have learned from ten years of research*. Lawrence: University of Kansas. Retrieved from http://people.ku.edu/~howard/.

Eby, M. D., Chin, J. L., Rollock, D., Schwartz, J. P., & Worrell, F. C. (2011). Professional psychology training in the era of a thousand flowers: Dilemmas and challenges for the future. *Training and Education in Professional Psychology, 5*(2), 57–68. doi: 10.1037/a0023462.

Economides, A. A., & Roupas, C. (2007). Evaluation of computer adaptive testing systems. *International Journal of Web-Based Learning and Teaching Technologies, 2*(1), 70–87.

Edelstein, B., & Kalish, K. (1999). Clinical assessment of older adults. In C. C. John & S. K. Whitbourne (Eds.), *Gerontology: An interdisciplinary perspective* (pp. 269–304). New York: Wiley.

Edelstein, K., DAgostino, N., Bernstein, L. J., Nathan, P. C, Greenberg, M. L., Hodgson, D. C, et al. (2011). Longterm neuro cognitive outcomes in young adult survivors of childhood acute lymphoblastic leukemia. *Journal of Pediatric Hematology/Oncology, 33*(6), 450–458. doi: 10.1097/MPH.0b013e31820d86f2.

Educational Testing Service. (1991). *Sex, race, ethnicity, and performance on the GRE general test*. Princeton, NJ: Educational Testing Service.

Educational Testing Service. (2011). About the GRE® revised general test. Retrieved from http://www.ets.org/gre/revised_general/about.

Edwards, A. L. (1954). *Manual for the edwards personal preference schedule*. New York: Psychological Corporation.

Edwards, A. L. (1959). *Edwards personal preference schedule*. New York: Psychological Corporation.

Edwards, A. W. F. (2003). Human genetic diversity: Lewontin's fallacy. *BioEssays, 25*(8), 798–801.

Edwards, O. W., & Oakland, T. D. (2006). Factorial invariance of Woodcock-Johnson III scores for African Americans and Caucasian Americans. *Journal of Psychoeducational Assessment, 24*(4), 358–366.

Edwards, T. C., Fredericksen, R. J., Crane, H. M., Crane, P. K., Kitahata, M. M., Mathews, W. C., ... Solorio, R. (2016). Content validity of Patient-Reported Outcomes Measurement Information System (PROMIS) items in the context of HIV clinical care. *Quality of Life Research, 25*(2), 293–302.

Eggen, T. J., & Stobart, G. (2015). *High-stakes testing in education: Value, fairness and consequences*. New York: Routledge.

Egger, J. I. M., Gringhuis, M., Breteler, M. A., De Mey, H. R. A., Wingbermühle, E., Derksen, J. J. L., et al. (2007). MMPI-2 clusters of alcohol-dependent patients and the relation to Cloninger's temperament-character inventory. *Acta Neuropsychiatrica, 19*(4), 238–243.

Egger, J. I., De May, H. R., Hubert, R. A., Dersen, J. J. L., & van der Staak, C. P. F. (2003). Cross-cultural replication of the five-factor model and comparison of the NEO-PI-R and MMPI-2 PSY-5 Scales in a Dutch psychiatric sample. *Psychological Assessment, 15*(1), 81–88.

Eggly, S. (2002). Physician-patient coconstruction of illness narratives in the medical interview. *Health Communication, 14*(3), 339–360.

Ehrhart, K., & Makransky, G. (2007). Testing vocational interests and personality as predictors of person-vocation and person-job fit. *Journal of Career Assessment, 15*(2), 206–226.

Einarsdottir, S. (2002). Structural equivalence of vocational interests across culture and gender: Differential item functioning in the strong interest inventory (Iceland). *Dissertation Abstracts International: Section B. The Physical Sciences and Engineering, 62*, 8B.

Eisenberg, N., Duckworth, A., Spinrad, T., & Valiente, C. (2014). Conscientiousness: Origins in childhood? *Developmental Psychology, 50*(5), 1331–1349.

Eisenberger, R., & Cameron, J. (1998). Reward, intrinsic interest, and creativity: New findings. *American Psychologist, 53*(6), 676–679.

Ekman, P. (2003). *Emotions revealed: Recognizing faces and feelings to improve communication and emotional life*. New York: Times Books/Holt.

Ekman, P., Levenson, R. W., & Friesen, W. V. (1983). Autonomic nervous system activity distinguishes among emotions. *Science, 221*, 1208–1210.

Ekren, U. W. (1962). *The effect of experimenter knowledge of subjects' scholastic standing on the performance of a task*. Unpublished master's thesis, Marquette University, WI.

El-Ansarey, B. M. (1997). The psychometric properties of NEO Five-Factor Inventory (NEO-FFI-S) based on the Kuwaiti society [Arabic]. *Derasat Nafseyah, 7*, 277–310.

Elashoff, J., & Snow, R. E. (Eds.). (1971). *Pygmalion revisited*. Worthington, OH: C. A. Jones.

Elder, C., McNamara, T., & Congdon, P. (2003). Rasch techniques for detecting bias in performance assessments: An example comparing the performance of native and nonnative speakers on a test of academic English. *Journal of Applied Measurement, 4*(2), 181–197.

El-Dib, M., Massaro, A. N., Glass, P., & Aly, H. (2011). Neurodevelopmental assessment of the newborn: An opportunity for prediction of outcome. *Brain and Development, 33*(2), 95–105. ISSN 0387-7604; doi: 10.1016/j.braindev.2010.04.004.

Ellis, A. (1946). The validity of personality questionnaires. *Psychological Bulletin, 43*, 385–440.

Ellis, M. (2008). Race and medicine in nineteenth- and early twentieth-century America. *Social History of Medicine, 21*(1), 207.

Elmir, R., Schmied, V., Jackson, D., & Wilkes, L. (2011). Interviewing people about potentially sensitive topics. *Nurse Researcher, 19*(1), 12.

Embretson, S. E., & Hershberger, S. L. (1999). *The new rules of measurement: What every psychologist and educator should know*. Mahwah, NJ: Erlbaum.

Emory, E. K., Tynan, W. D., & Dave, R. (1989). Neurobehavioral anomalies in neonates with seizures. *Journal of Clinical and Experimental Neuropsychology, 11*, 231–240.

Endler, N. S., & Parker, J. D. A. (1990). *Coping intervention for stressful situations*. Towanda, NY: Mulit-Health Systems Inc.

Endler, N. S., Kantor, L., & Parker, J. D. A. (1994). State-trait coping, state-trait anxiety and academic performance. *Personality and Individual Differences, 16*(5), 663–670.

Endler, N. S., Parker, J. D. A., Bagby, R. M., & Cox, B. J. (1991). Multidimensionality of state and trait anxiety: Factor structure of the Endler Multidimensional Anxiety Scales. *Journal of Personality and Social Psychology, 60*, 919–926.

Epstein, J., & Klinkenberg, W. D. (2001). From Eliza to internet: A brief history of computerized assessment. *Computers in Human Behavior, 17*(3), 295–314.

Epstein, J., & Klinkenberg, W. D. (2002). Collecting data via the internet: The development and deployment of a web-based survey. *Journal of Technology in Human Services, 19*(2–3), 33–47.

Epstein, J., & Rotunda, R. J. (2000). The utility of computer versus clinician-authored assessments in aiding the prediction of patient symptomatolgy. *Computers in Human Behavior, 16*(5), 519–536.

Erard, R. E. (2005). What the Rorschach can contribute to child custody and parenting time evaluations. *Journal of Child Custody, 2*(1), 119–142.

Erdberg, S. P. (1969). *AIMPI differences associated with sex, race, and residence in a Southern sample.* Unpublished doctoral dissertation, University of Alabama, Birmingham.

Erdman, H. P., Klein, M. H., & Greist, J. H. (1985). Direct patient computer interviewing. *Journal of Consulting and Clinical Psychology, 53*(6), 760–773.

Erez, A., & Judge, T. A. (2001). Relationship of core self-evaluations to goal setting, motivation, and performance. *Journal of Applied Psychology, 86*(6), 1270–1279.

Ergene, T. (2003). Effective interventions on test anxiety reduction: A meta-analysis. *School Psychology International, 24*(3), 313–328.

Erickson, S. K., Lilienfeld, S. O., & Vitacco, M. J. (2007). Failing the burden of proof: The science and ethics of projective tests in custody evaluations. *Family Court Review, 45*(2), 185–192.

Erlanger, D., Feldman, D., Kutner, K., Kaushik, T., Kroger, H., et al. (2003). Development and validation of a web-based neuropsychological test protocol for sports-related return to play decision making. *Archives of Clinical Neuropsychology, 18*(3), 293–316.

Espenshade, T. J., & Chung, C. Y. (2010). *Standardized admission tests, college performance, and campus diversity.* Princeton, New Jersey: Office of Population Research, Princeton University. Retrieved from https://www.princeton.edu/~tje/files/Standardized%20AdmissionTests. pdf.

Evert, T. F., & Lang, B. A. (2016). Variables that affect the complexity of board/superintendent interactions. *Working toward success: Board and superintendent interactions, relationships, and hiring*

issues, In Van Deuren, A. E., Evert, T. F., & Lang, B. A.(Eds.), *Working toward success: Board and superintendent interactions, relationships, and hiring issues* (pp. 57–74). Lanhan, MD: Rowman & Littlefield.

Ewart, C. K. (1991). Social action theory for a public health psychology. *American Psychologist, 46*, 931–946.

Ewing-Cobbs, L., Barnes, M., Fletcher, J. M., Levin, H. S., Swank, P. R., & Song, J. (2004). Modeling of longitudinal academic achievement scores after pediatric traumatic brain injury. *Developments in Neuropsychology, 25*(1–2), 107–133.

Exner, J. E. (1976). Projective techniques. In I. B. Weiner (Ed.), *Clinical methods in psychology.* New York: Wiley.

Exner, J. E. (1993). *The Rorschach: A comprehensive system: Vol. 1. Basic foundation* (3rd ed.). New York: Wiley.

Exner, J. E. (1995). Narcissism in the comprehensive system for the Rorschach—Comment. *Clinical Psychology—Science and Practice, 2*(2), 200–206.

Exner, J. E. (1999). The Rorschach: Measurement concepts and issues of validity. In S. E. Embretson & S. L. Hershberger (Eds.), *The new rules of measurement.* Mahwah, NJ: Erlbaum.

Exner, J. E. (2003). *The Rorschach: A comprehensive system* (4th ed.). New York: Wiley.

Exner, J. E., & Farber, J. G. (1983). Peer nominations among female college students living in a dormitory setting. In *Workshops study 290* [unpublished]. Bayville, NY: Rorschach Workshops.

Exner, J., & Erdberg, P. (2005). *The Rorschach: A comprehensive system* (Vol. II, 3rd ed.). Hoboken, NJ: Wiley & Sons.

Exterkate, C. C., Bakker-Brehm, D. T., & de Jong, C. A. J. (2007). MMPI-2 profiles of women with eating disorders in a Dutch day treatment sample. *Journal of Personality Assessment, 88*(2), 178–186.

Eysenck, H. J. (1991). Raising IQ through vitamin and mineral supplementation: An introduction. *Personality and Individual Differences, 12*, 329–333.

Fagundes, D. D., Haynes, W. O., Haak, N. J., & Moran, M. J. (1998). Task variability effects on the language test performance of Southern lower socioeconomic class African American and Caucasian five-year-olds. *Language, Speech, and Hearing Services in Schools, 29*(3), 148–157.

Fairtest. (2007). *Examining the GRE: Myths, misuses, and alternatives. The National*

Center for Fair and Open Testing. Retrieved from http://www.fairtest.org/facts/gre.htm.

FairTest. (2011). *The national center for fair and open testing.* Retrieved from http://fairtest.org.

Falk, C. F., & Savalei, V. (2011). The relationship between unstandardized and standardized alpha, true reliability, and the underlying measurement model. *Journal of Personality Assessment, 93*(5), 445–453.

Fancher, R. E. (2011). The intelligence men: Makers of the IQ controversy. New York: W. W. Norton & Company.

Faria, C. D., Teixeira-Salmela, L. F., Nascimento, V. B., Costa, A. P., Brito, N. D., & Rodrigues-De-Paula, F. (2011). Comparisons between the Nottingham health profile and the short form-36 for assessing the quality of life of community-dwelling elderly [Research Support, Non-U.S. Gov't]. *Revista brasileira de fisioterapia, 15*(5), 399–405.

Farr, J. L., & Tippins, N. T. (2013). *Handbook of employee selection.* New York: Routledge.

Fazel, S., & Bjørkly, S. (2016). Methodological considerations in risk assessment research. In J. P. Singh, S. Bjørkly, & S. Fazel (Eds.), *International perspectives on violence risk assessment* (pp. 16–25). New York: Oxford University Press.

Feldman, S. E., & Sullivan, D. S. (1960). Factors mediating the effects of enhanced rapport on children's performances. *Journal of Consulting and Clinical Psychology, 36*, 302.

Feng, L., & Sass, T. R. (2016). Teacher quality and teacher mobility. *Education Finance and Policy.* Published online ahead of print. doi: 10.1162/EDFP_a_00214.

Fenster A., Markus, K. A., Wiedemann, C. F., Brackett, M. A. & Fernandez, J. (2001). Selecting tomorrow's forensic psychologists: A fresh look at familiar predictors. *Educational and Psychological Measurement, 61*(2), 336–348.

Fenton, K. A., Mercer, C. H., McManus, S., Erens, B., Wellings, K., Macdowall, W., et al. (2005). Ethnic variations in sexual behaviour in Great Britain and risk of sexually-transmitted infections: A probability survey. *Lancet, 365*(9466), 1246–1255.

Ferguson, J. E., & Redish, A. D. (2011). Wireless communication with implanted medical devices using the conductive properties of the body. *Expert Review of Medical Devices, 8*(4), 427–433. doi: 10.1586/erd.11.16.

Ferrando, P. J. (1999). Likert scaling using continuous, censored, and graded response models: Effects on criterionrated validity. *Applied Psychological Measurement, 23*(2), 161–175.

Ferrario, S. R., Zotti, A. M., Massara, G., & Nuvolone, G. (2003). A comparative assessment of psychological and psycho-social characteristics of cancer patients and their caregivers. *Psycho-Oncology, 12*(1), 1–7.

Feuer, M. J., National Research Council (U.S.) Committee on Equivalency and Linkage of Educational Tests, National Research Council (U.S.) Commission on Behavioral and Social Sciences and Education, & Board on Testing and Assessment. (1999). *Uncommon measures: Equivalence and linkage among educational tests*. Washington, DC: National Academy Press.

Fidler, L. J., Plante, E., & Vance, R. (2001). Identification of adults with developmental language impairments. *American Journal of Speech-Language Pathology, 20*(2). doi: 10.1044/1058-0360(2010/09-0096.

Field, T., Diego, M., & Hernandez-Reif, M. (2010). Prenatal depression effects and interventions: A review. *Infant Behavior and Development, 33*(4), 409–418. ISSN 0163-6383; doi: 10.1016/j.infbeh.2010.04.005.

Field, T., Diego, M., Hernandez-Reif, M., Schanberg, S., & Kuhn, C. (2002). Relative right versus left frontal EEG in neonates. *Developmental Psychobiology, 41*(2), 147–155.

Fielding-Barnsley, R., & Purdie, N. (2003). Early intervention in the home for children at risk of reading failure. *Support for Learning, 18*(2), 77–82.

Finkel, E. J., Eastwick, P. W., Karney, B. R., Reis, H. T., & Sprecher, S. (2012). Online dating: A critical analysis from the perspective of psychological science. *Psychological Science in the Public Interest, 13*(1), 3–66.

Finn, S. E. (2011). Journeys through the valley of death: Multimethod psychological assessment and personality transformation in long-term psychotherapy. *Journal of Personality Assessment, 93*(2), 123–141.

Finnigan, K. M., & Corker, K. S. (2016). Do performance avoidance goals moderate the effect of different types of stereotype threat on women's math performance? *Journal of Research in Personality, 63*, 36–43.

Fiscella, K., Ransom, S., Jean-Pierre, P., Cella, D., Stein, K., Bauer, J. E., et al. (2011). Patient-reported outcome measures suitable to assessment of patient navigation [Review]. *Cancer, 117*(15 Suppl.), 3603–3617. doi: 10.1002/ cncr.26260.

Fischer, Smith, Spillane & Cyders. (2005). Urgency: Individual differences in reaction to mood and implications for addictive behaviors. In A. V. Clark (Ed.), *Psychology of Moods* (pp. 86–103). New York: Nova Science Publishers Inc.

Fish, D. D. (2001). The mechanisms of homogeneity: Individual and social structure influences on selection outcomes. *Dissertation Abstracts International Section B. The Physical Sciences and Engineering, 61*, 9B.

Fish, J. M. (2002). *Race and intelligence: Separating science from myth*. Mahwah, NJ: Erlbaum.

Fiske, D. W., & Baughman, E. E. (1953). Relationships between Rorschach scoring categories and the total number of responses. *Journal of Abnormal and Social Psychology, 48*, 25–32.

Fitts, W. H., & Warren, W. L. (1996). *Tennessee Self-Concept Scale* (2nd ed.). Los Angeles: Western Psychological Services.

Fitzgerald, C. (1997). The MBTI and leadership development: Personality and leadership reconsidered in changing times. In C. Fitzgerald & L. K. Kirby (Eds.), *Developing leaders: Research and applications in psychological type and leadership development: Integrating reality and vision, mind and heart* (pp. 33–59). Palo Alto, CA: Davies-Black.

Fitzgerald, P., & Leudar, I. (2010). On active listening in person-centered, solution-focused psychotherapy. *Journal of Pragmatics, 42*(12), 3188–3198.

Fitzgerald, S., Gray, N. S., & Snowden, R. J. (2007). A comparison of WAIS-R and WAIS-III in lower IQ range: Implications for learning disability diagnosis. *Journal of Applied Research in Intellectual Disabilities, 20*(4), 323–330.

Flanagan, D. P., McGrew, K. S., & Ortiz, S. 0. (2000). *The Wechsler Intelligence Scale and Gf-Gc theory: A contemporary approach to interpretation* (p. 424). Needham Heights, MA: Allyn & Bacon..

Flanagan, J. C. (1954). The critical incident technique. *Psychological Bulletin, 51*, 327–358.

Flanagan, R. (1995). The utility of the Kaufman Assessment Battery for Children (K-ABC) and the Wechsler Intelligence Scales for Linguistically Different Children: Clinical considerations. *Psychology in the Schools, 32*(1), 5–11.

Flaugher, R. L. (1978). The many definitions of test bias. *American Psychologist, 33*, 671–679.

Fleishman, E. A., & Quaintance, M. K. (1984). *Taxonomies of human performance: The description of human tasks*. Orlando, FL: Academic Press.

Fleiss, J. L. (1971). Measuring nominal scale agreement among many raters. *Psychological Bulletin, 76*, 378–382.

Fleiss, J. L. (1981). *Statistical methods for rates and proportions*. New York: Wiley.

Fletcher, J. M., Taylor, H. G., Levin, H., & Satz, P. (1995). Neuropsychological and intellectual assessment of children. In H. I. Kaplan & B. J. Saddock (Eds.), *Comprehensive textbook of psychiatry* (6th ed., pp. 581–601). Baltimore: Williams & Wilkens.

Fletcher, R. B., & Hattie, J. (2011). *Intelligence and intelligence testing*. New York: Routledge.

Fletcher, S. W. (1997). Whither scientific deliberation in health policy recommendations? Alice in the Wonderland of breast-cancer screening. *New England Journal of Medicine, 336*(16), 1180–1183.

Flett, G. L., & Blankstein, K. R. (1994). Worry as a component of test anxiety: A multidimensional analysis. In G. C. L. Davey & Frank Tallis (Eds.), *Worrying: Perspectives on theory, assessment and treatment* (pp. 219–239). Chichester, England: Wiley.

Florell, D. (2011). Using advancing technologies in the practice of school psychology, In T. M. Lionetti, E. P. Snyder, & R. W. Christner (Eds.), *A practical guide to building professional competencies in school psychology* (pp. 227–244). New York: Springer US. doi: 10.1007/978-1-4419-6257-7_14.

Flores, G., & Tomany-Korman, S. C. (2008). Racial and ethnic disparities in medical and dental health, access to care, and use of services in US children. *Pediatrics, 121*(2), e286.

Floyd, R. G., McCormack, A. C., Ingram, E. L., Davis, A. E., Bergeron, R., & Hamilton, G. (2006). Relations between the Woodcock-Johnson III clinical clusters and measures of executive functions from the Delis-Kaplan executive function system. *Journal of Psychoeducational Assessment, 24*(4), 303–317.

Flynn, D., Schaik, P., & van Wersch, A. (2004). A comparison of multi-item

Likert and Visual Analogue Scales for the assessment of transactionally defined coping function. *European Journal of Psychological Assessment, 20*(1), 49–58.

Flynn, J. R. (1999). Searching for justice: The discovery of IQ gains over time. *American Psychologist, 54*(1), 5–20.

Flynn, J. R. (2016). *Does your family make you smarter?: Nature, nurture, and human autonomy.* New York: Cambridge University Press.

Foley, K. L., Reed, P. S., Mutran, E. J., & DeVellis, R. F. (2002). *Measurement adequacy of the CES-D among a sample of older African-Americans.* London, United Kingdom: Elsevier Science.

Folkman, S. (2010). Stress, coping, and hope. *Psycho-Oncology, 19*(9), 901–908. doi: 10.1002/pon.1836.

Forer, B. R. (1949). The fallacy of personal validation: A classroom demonstration of gullibility. *Journal of Abnormal and Social Psychology, 44,* 118–123.

Forsterling, F. (1988). *Attribution theory in clinical psychology.* New York: Wiley.

Forsyth, R. A. (1991). Do NAEP scales yield valid criterion-referenced interpretations? *Educational Measurement: Issues and Practice, 10,* 16.

Foster, C. E., Webster, M. C., Weissman, M. M., Pilowsky, D. J., Wickramaratne, P. J., Rush, A. J., et al. (2008). Course and severity of maternal depression: Associations with family functioning and child adjustment. *Journal of Youth and Adolescence, 37*(8), 906–916. doi: 10.1007/ s10964-007-9216-0.

Frampton, I., & Warner-Rogers, J. (2011). Developmental neuropsychology in clinical practice [Editorial, Introductory Journal Article]. *Clinical Child Psychology and Psychiatry, 16*(2), 163–164.

Franceschina, E., Dorz, S., & Bari, M. (2001). Computer and traditional administration of the cognitive behavioral assessment 2.0. *Bollettino di Psicologia Applicata, 235*(48), 57–62.

Frank, G. (1995). On the assessment of self representations and object representations from the Rorschach: A review of the research and commentary. *Psychological Reports, 76*(2), 659–671.

Frank, L. K. (1939). Projective methods for the study of personality. *Journal of Psychology, 8,* 343–389.

Franklin, R. D. (2003). *Prediction in forensic and neuropsychology: Sound statistical practices.* Mahwah, NJ: Erlbaum.

Frase, L. T., Almond, R. G., Burstein, J., Kukich, K., Sheehan, K. M., Steinberg, L. S., et al. (2003). Technology and assessment. In H. F. O'Neil & R. S.Perez (Eds.), *Technology applications in education: A learning view* (pp. 213–244). Mahwah, NJ: Erlbaum.

Fredrickson, B. L. (2001). The role of positive emotions in positive psychology: The broaden-and-build theory of positive emotions. *American Psychologist, 56,* 218–226.

Freeman, F. S. (1955). *Theory and practice of psychological testing.* New York: Holt.

Freeman, H. P., & Payne, R. (2000). Racial injustice in health care. *New England Journal of Medicine, 342*(14), 1045–1047.

Freeman, L., & Miller, A. (2001). *Normreferenced, criterion-referenced, and dynamic assessment: What exactly is the point?* United Kingdom: Pitman Publishing.

Freire, C., Ramos, R., Puertas, R., Lopez-Espinosa, M. J., Julvez, J., Aguilera, I., et al. (2010). Association of traffic-related air pollution with cognitive development in children. *Journal of Epidemiology and Community Health, 64,* 223–228. doi: 10.1136/ jech.2008.084574.

Frey, B., Petersen, S., Edwards, L., Pedrotti, J., & Peyton, V. (2005). Item-writing rules: Collective wisdom. *Teaching and Teacher Education, 21*(4), 357–364.

Frick, P. J., Barry, C. T., & Kamphaus, R. W. (2010). Structured diagnostic interviews. *Clinical Assessment of Child and Adolescent Personality and Behavior, 2,* 253–270, 253. doi: 10.1007/978-1-4419-0641-0_11.

Fried, Y., & Tiegs, R. B. (1995). Supervisors' role conflict and role ambiguity differential relations with performance ratings of subordinates and the moderating effect of screening ability. *Journal of Applied Psychology, 80,* 282–296.

Frisby, C. L. (1998). Culture and cultural differences. In J. H. Sandoval, C. L. Frisby, & K. F. Geisinger (Eds.), *Test interpretation and diversity: Achieving equity in assessment* (pp. 51–73). Washington, DC: American Psychological Association.

Frisby, C. L., & Henry, B. (2016). Science, politics, and best practice: 35 years after Larry P. *Contemporary School Psychology, 20*(1), 46–62.

Froehlich, L., Martiny, S. E., Deaux, K., Goetz, T., & Mok, S. Y. (2016). Being smart or getting smarter: Implicit theory of intelligence moderates stereotype threat and stereotype lift effects. *British Journal of Social Psychology.* Published online ahead of print. doi: 10.1111/bjso.12144.

Frumkin, R. M. (1997). Significant neglected sociocultural and physical factors affecting intelligence. *American Psychologist, 52*(1), 76–77.

Fryback, D. G., Dunham, N. C., Palta, M., Hanmer, J., Buechner, J., Cherepanov, D., et al. (2007). US norms for six generic health-related quality-of-life indexes from the national health measurement study. *Medical Care, 45*(12), 1162–1170.

Fuchs, D., & Fuchs, L. S. (1986). Test procedure bias: A meta-analysis of examiner familiarity effects. *Review of Educational Research, 56,* 243–262.

Fuertes, J. N., & Sedlacek, W. E. (1994). Predicting the academic success of Hispanic college students using SAT scores. *College Student Journal, 28,* 350–352.

Fuller, G. B., & Vance, B. (1995). Interscorer reliability of the Modified Version of the Bender-Gestalt Test for Preschool and Primary School Children. *Psychology in the Schools, 32,* 264–266.

Funder, D. C. (2010). *The personality puzzel* (5th ed.). New York: W. W. Norton & Company.

Funder, D. C. (2015). *The personality puzzle: Seventh International Student Edition*: New York: WW Norton & Company.

Funder, D. C. (2015). Taking situations seriously: The situation construal model and the riverside situational Q-sort. *Current Directions in Psychological Science, 25*(3), 203–208.

Funder, D. C., & West, S. G. (1993). Consensus, self-other agreement, and accuracy in personality judgment: An introduction. *Journal of Personality, 61,* 457–476.

Funder, D. C., Parke, R. D., Tomhnson-Keasey, C., & Widaman, K. (Eds.). (1993). *Studying lives through time: Personality and development.* Washington, DC: American Psychological Association.

Furnham, A., & Petrides, K. V. (2003). Trait emotional intelligence and happiness. *Social Behavior and Personality, 31*(8), 815–824.

Furnham, A., Guenole, N., Levine, S., & Chamorro-Premuzic, T. (2013). The neo personality inventory–revised: Factor structure and gender invariance from exploratory structural equation modeling analyses in a high-stakes setting. *Assessment, 20*(1), 14–23.

Gacano, C. B., & Meloy, J. R. (1994). *The Rorschach assessment of aggressive and psychopathic personalities*. Hillsdale, NJ: Erlbaum.

Gacono, C. B., & Evans, F. B. (2007). *The handbook of forensic rorschach assessment* (p. 83). New York: Taylor & Francis.

Gadermann, A., Guhn, M., & Zumbo, B. (2011). Investigating the substantive aspect of construct validity for the Satisfaction with Life Scale Adapted for Children: A focus on cognitive processes. *Social Indicators Research, 100*(1), 37–60. doi: 10.1007/s11205-010-9603-x.

Gafni, N. (2016). Comments on implementing validity theory. *Assessment in Education: Principles, Policy & Practice, 32*(2), 284–286.

Gallego, M. J., Emmelkamp, P. M. G., van der Kooij, M., & Mees, H. (2011). The effects of a Dutch version of an Internet-based treatment program for fear of public speaking: A controlled study. *International Journal of Clinical and Health Psychology, 11*(3), 459–472.

Galli, F., Pozzi, G., Frustaci, A., Allena, M., Anastasi, S., Chirumbolo, A., et al. (2011). Differences in the personality profile of medication-overuse headache sufferers and drug addict patients: A comparative study using MMPI-2. *Headache: The Journal of Head and Face Pain, 51*(8), 1212–1227. Retrieved from http://dx.doi.org/10.1111/j.1526-4610.2011.01978.x. doi: 10.1111/j.1526-4610.2011.01978.x.

Gallo, M., & Rinaldo, V. (2010). Intrinsic versus extrinsic motivation: A study of undergraduate student motivation in science. *Teaching and Learning, 6*(1), 95–106.

Galton, F. (1869). *Hereditary genius: An inquiry into its laws and consequences.* London: Collins.

Galton, F. (1879). Psychometric experiments. *Brain, 2,* 149–162.

Galton, F. (1883). *Inquiries into human faculty and its development.* London: Macmillan.

Gamble, K. R. (1972). The Holtzman Inkblot Technique: A review. *Psychological Bulletin, 77,* 172–194.

Gao, F., Tilse, C., Wilson, J., Tuckett, A., & Newcombe, P. (2015). Perceptions and employment intentions among aged care nurses and nursing assistants from diverse cultural backgrounds: A qualitative interview study. *Journal of Aging Studies, 35,* 111–122.

Garayzábal Heinze, E., Lens Villaverde, M., Moruno López, E., Conde Magro, T., Moura, L. F., Fernández, M., et al. (2011). General cognitive functioning and psycholinguistic abilities in children with Smith-Magenis syndrome. *Psicothema, 23*(4), 725–731.

Garb, H. N. (1998). *Studying the clinician: Judgment research and psychological assessment.* Washington, DC: American Psychological Association.

Garb, H. N. (1999). Call for a moratorium on the use of the Rorschach Inkblot in clinical and forensic settings. *Assessment, 6,* 313–315.

Garb, H. N. (2007). Computer-administered interviews and rating scales. *Psychological Assessment, 19*(1), 4–13.

Garb, H. N., Wood, J. M., Lilienfeld, S. O., & Nezworski, M. T. (2005). Roots of the Rorschach controversy. *Clinical Psychology Review, 25*(1), 97–118.

Garb, H. N., Wood, J. M., Nezworski, M. T., Grove, W. M., & Stejskal, W. J. (2001). Toward a resolution of the Rorschach Controversy. *Psychological Assessment, 13*(4), 433–448.

Garcia, H. A., Kelley, L. P., Rentz, T. O., & Lee, S. (2011). Pretreatment predictors of dropout from cognitive behavioral therapy for PTSD in Iraq and Afghanistan war veterans. *Psychological Services, 8*(1), 1–11.

Garcia, J. (1981). The logic and limits of mental aptitude testing. *American Psychologist, 36,* 1172–1180.

Garcia, S. F., Cella, D., Clauser, S. B., Flynn, K. E., Lai, J. S., Reeve, B. B., et al. (2007). Standardizing patient-reported outcomes assessment in cancer clinical trials: A patient-reported outcomes measurement information system initiative. *Journal of Clinical Oncology, 25*(32), 5106–5112.

Garcia-Palacios, A., Hoffman, H. G., Carlin, A., Furness, T. A., & Botella, C. (2002). Virtual reality in the treatment of spider phobia: A controlled study. *Behavior & Research Therapy, 40*(9), 983–993.

Garcia-Palacios, A., Hoffman, H. G., See, S. K., Tsai, A., & Botella, C. (2001). Redefining therapeutic success with virtual reality exposure therapy. *Cyberpsychology and Behavior, 4*(3), 341–348.

Gardner, E. F., Rudman, H. C., Karlsen, B., & Merwin, J. C. (1982). *The Stanford Achievement Test* (7th ed.). New York: Harcourt Brace Jovanovich.

Gardner, H. (1983). *Frames of mind: The theory of multiple intelligences.* New York: Basic Books.

Gardner, H. (1993). The relationship between early giftedness and later achievement. In B. R. Block & K. Acrill (Eds.), *The origins and development of high ability* (pp. 175–186). Ciba Foundation Symposium: Vol. 178. Chichester, England: Wiley.

Gardner, H., Krechevsky, M., Sternberg, R. J., & Okagaki, L. (1994). Intelligence in context: Enhancing students' practical intelligence for school. In K. McGilly (Ed.), *Classroom lessons: Integrating cognitive theory and classroom practice* (pp. 105–127). Cambridge, MA: MIT Press.

Garfield, S. L., & Sineps, J. (1959). An appraisal of Taulbee and Sisson's "Configurational analysis of MMPI profiles of psychiatric groups". *Journal of Consulting Psychology, 23,* 333–335.

Garner, A. S., Shonkoff, J. P., Committee on Psychosocial Aspects of, Child, Family, Health, Committee on Early Childhood, Adoption, Dependent, Care, Behavioral, Pediatrics. (2012). Early childhood adversity, toxic stress, and the role of the pediatrician: translating developmental science into lifelong health. *Pediatrics, 129*(1), e224–e231. doi: 10.1542/peds.2011-2662.

Gass, C. S., & Curiel, R. E. (2011). Test anxiety in relation to measures of cognitive and intellectual functioning. *Archives of Clinical Neuropsychology, 26*(5), 396–404.

Gasser, C, Larson, L., & Borgen, F. (2007). Concurrent validity of the 2005 strong interest inventory: An examination of gender and major field of study. *Journal of Career Assessment, 15*(1), 23–43.

Gasser, C. E., Larson, L. M., & Borgen, F. H. (2004). Contributions of personality and interests to explaining the educational aspirations of college students. *Journal of Career Assessment, 12*(4), 347–365. doi: 10.1177/106907270 4266644.

Gaston, M. F., Nelson, W. M., Hart, K. J., Quatman, G., et al. (1994). The equivalence of the MMPI and MMPI-2. *Assessment, 1,* 415–418.

Gati, I., & Tikotzki, Y. (1989). Strategies for collection and processing of occupational information in making career decisions. *Journal of Counseling Psychology, 36,* 430–439.

Geer, J. H. (1965). The development of a scale to measure fear. *Behaviour Research and Therapy, 3,* 45–53.

Geiselman, R. E., Woodward, J. A., & Beatty, J. (1982). Individual differences in verbal memory performance: A test of alternative information-processing models. *Journal of Experimental Psychology: General, 111*, 109–134.

Geiser, S., & Studley, R. (2001). *UC and the SAT: Predictive validity and differential impact of the SAT I and SAT II at the University of California.* Retrieved from www.ucop.edu/sas/research/researchand-planning/pdf/sat_study.pdf.

Geisinger, K. F. (1994). Crosscultural normative assessment: Translation and adaption issues influencing the normative interpretation of assessment instruments. *Psychological Assessment, 6*(4), 304–312.

Geisinger, K. F., Spies, R. A., Carlson, J. F., & Plake, B. S. (Eds.). (2007). *The seventeenth mental measurements yearbook.* Lincoln, NE: Buros Institute of Mental Measurements.

Gentner, D. (2010). Psychology in cognitive science: 1978–2038. *Topics in Cognitive Science, 2*, 328–344.

Gershon, R. C., Wagster, M. V., Hendrie, H. C., Fox, N. A., Cook, K. F., & Nowinski, C. J. (2013). NIH toolbox for assessment of neurological and behavioral function. *Neurology, 80*(11 Supplement 3), S2–S6.

Gesell, A. (1925). Monthly increments of development in infancy. *Journal of Genetic Psychology, 32*, 203–208.

Gesell, A., Halverson, H. M., Thompson, H., Ilg, F. L., Castner, B. M., Ames, L. B., et al. (1940). *The first five years of life: A guide to the study of the preschool child.* New York: Harper & Row.

Gibby, R. G., Miller, D. R., & Walker, E. L. (1953). The examiner's influence on the Rorschach protocol. *Journal of Consulting Psychology, 17*, 425–428.

Gibby, R., & Zickar, M. (2008). A history of the early days of personality testing in American industry: An obsession with adjustment. *History of Psychology, 11*(3), 164–184.

Gilberstadt, H., & Duker, J. (1965). *A handbook for clinical and actuarial MMPI interpretation.* Philadelphia: Saunders.

Gillingham, W. H. (1970). An investigation of examiner influence on Wechsler Intelligence Scale for Children scores. *Dissertation Abstracts International, 31*, 2178. (UMI No. 70-20, 458).

Gilmore, H. (2016). SAT, LSAT, and discrimination: Professor Gilmore again responds to Professor Subotnik, *Law & Inequality, 34*, 153.

Gilpin, E. A., & Pierce, J. P. (2003). Concurrent use of tobacco products by California adolescents. *Preventive Medicine, 36*(5), 575–584.

Ginther, D. K., Schaffer, W. T., Schnell, J., Masimore, B., Liu, F., Haak, L. L., & Kington, R. (2011). Race, ethnicity, and NIH research awards. *Science, 333*(6045), 1015–1019. doi: 333/6045/1015 [pii] 10.1126/science.1196783.

Glaesmer, H., Grande, G., Braehler, E., & Roth, M. (2011). The German version of the Satisfaction with Life Scale (SWLS): Psychometric properties, validity, and population-based norms. *European Journal of Psychological Assessment, 27*(2), 127–132. doi: 10.1027/1015-5759/a000058.

Glaser, B. A., Calhoun, G. B., & Petrocelli, J. V. (2002). Personality characteristics of male juvenile offenders by adjudicated offenses as indicated by the MMPI-A. *Criminal Justice & Behavior, 29*(2), 183–201.

Godlee, F. (2011). Mammography wars. *British Medical Journal, 343*, d7623.

Golden, C. J. (1981). A standardized version of Luria's neuropsychological tests: Quantitative and qualitative approach in neuropsychological evaluation. In F. E. Filskov & T. J. Boll (Eds.), *Handbook of clinical neuropsychology.* New York: Wiley.

Golden, C. J. (2015). The influence of Ralph Reitan on the development of the Luria-Nebraska neuropsychological battery. *Archives of Clinical Neuropsychology, 30*(8), 768–769.

Goldhaber, D. (2016). In schools, teacher quality matters most. *Education Next, 16*(2), 1–2.

Goldman, R. D. (1973). Hidden opportunities in the prediction of college grades for different subgroups. *Journal of Educational Measurement, 10*(3), 205–210.

Goldman, R. D., & Hartig, L. (1976). The WISC may not be a valid predictor of school performance for primary-grade minority children. *American Journal of Mental Deficiency, 80*, 583–587.

Goldstein, D. J., Fogle, E. E., Wieber, J. L., & O'Shea, T. M. (1995). Comparison of the Bayley Scales of Infant Development-Second Edition and the Bayley Scales of Infant Development with premature infants. *Journal of Psychoeducational Assessment, 13*, 391–396.

Goldstein, G., & Beers, S. R. (2004). *Comprehensive handbook of psychological assessment, intellectual and neuropsychological assessment.* New York: John Wiley & Sons.

Goldstein, G., Minshew, N. J., Allen, D. N., & Seaton, B. E. (2002). High-functioning autism and schizophrenia: A comparison of an early and late onset neurodevelopmental disorder. *Archives of Clinical Neuropsychology, 17*(5), 461–475.

Goldstein, L. H., Canavan, A. G., & Polkey, C. E. (1988). Verbal and abstract designs paired associate learning after unilateral temporal lobectomy. *Cortex, 24*, 41–52.

Golomb, B. A., Stattin, H., & Mednick, S. (2000). *Low cholesterol and violent crime.* United Kingdom: Elsevier Science.

Good, C., Aronson, J., & Harder, J. A. (2008). Problems in the pipeline: Stereotype threat and women's achievement in high-level math courses. *Journal of Applied Developmental Psychology, 29*(1), 17–28.

Goodman, J. (1977). The diagnostic fallacy: A critique of Jane Mercer's concept of mental retardation. *Journal of School Psychology, 15*, 197–206.

Goodman, J. (1979). "Ignorance" versus "stupidity"—The basic disagreement. *School Psychology Digest, 8*(2), 218–223.

Goodyear-Brown, P. (2011). Comprehensive and therapeutic assessment of child sexual abuse: A bridge to treatment. In P. Van Eys & A. Truss (Eds.), *Handbook of child sexual abuse* (pp. 143–170). John Wiley & Sons, Inc. doi: 10.1002/9781118094822.ch7.

Gordon, B. (2004). Review of the Wechsler Preschool and Primary Scale of Intelligence, third edition (WPPSI-III). *Canadian Journal of School Psychology, 19*(1), 205–220.

Gordon, E. W., & Terrell, M. D. (1981). The changed social context of testing. *American Psychologist, 36*, 1167–1171.

Gordon, M. F., Lenderking, W. R., Duhig, A., Chandler, J., Lundy, J. J., Miller, D. S., … Gauthier, S. (2016). Development of a patient-reported outcome instrument to assess complex activities of daily living and interpersonal functioning in persons with mild cognitive impairment: The qualitative research phase. *Alzheimer's & Dementia, 12*(1), 75–84.

Gorham, D. R., Moseley, E. C, & Holtzman, W. H. (1968). Norms for the computer-scored Holtzman Inkblot Technique. *Perceptual and Motor Skills, 26*(3), 1279–1305.

Gorman, J. (2011). Team coordination dynamics and the interactive approach: Emerging evidence and future work. In D. Schmorrow & C. Fidopiastis (Eds.), *Foundations of augmented cognition. Directing the future of adaptive systems* (pp. 298–307). Berlin: Springer. doi: 10.1007/978-3-642-21852-1_36.

Gotkin, T. D., & Reynolds, C. R. (1981). Factorial similarity of the WISC-R white and black children from the standardization sample. *Journal of Educational Psychology, 73*, 227–231.

Gottfredson, L. S. (1980). Construct validity of Holland's occupational typology in terms of prestige, census, Department of Labor, and other classification systems. *Journal of Applied Psychology, 65*, 697–714.

Gottfredson, L. S. (1994). The science and politics of race-norming. *American Psychologist, 49*, 955–963.

Gottlib, I. H., & Cine, D. B. (1989). Self-report assessment of depression and anxiety. In P. C. Kendill & D. Watson (Eds.), *Anxiety and depression: Distinctive and overlapping features* (pp. 131–169). San Diego: Academic Press.

Gough, H. G. (1960). The adjective checklist as a personality assessment research technique. *Psychological Reports, 6*, 107–122.

Gough, H. G. (1987). *California psychological inventory, revised manual.* Palo Alto, CA: Consulting Psychologists Press.

Gough, H. G. (1995). Career assessment and the California psychological inventory. *Journal of Career Assessments, 30*, 101–122.

Gough, H. G. (1996). *California psychological inventory.* Retrieved February 2, 2003, from www.stevejudah.com/DescCalifornia.htm.

Gough, H. G., & Heilbrun Jr., A. B. (1980). *The adjective checklist manual (revised).* Palo Alto, CA: Consulting Psychologists Press.

Gould, S. J. (1981). The *mismeasure of man.* New York: Norton.

Gould, S. J. (1996). *The mismeasure of man* (Rev. ed.). New York: Norton.

Graham, F. K., & Kendall, B. S. (1960). Memory-for-Designs Test: Revised general manual. *Perceptual Motor Skills, 11*, 147–190.

Graham, S., & Taylor, A. Z. (2016). Attribution theory and motivation in school. In K. R. Wentzel & D. B. Miele (Eds.), *Handbook of motivation at school* (2nd ed., pp. 11–32). New York: Routledge.

Grant, I., & Adams, K. M. (Eds.). (1996). *Neuropsychological assessment of neuro-psychiatric disorders* (2nd ed.). New York: Oxford University Press.

Graves, L. V., Holden, H. M., Delano-Wood, L., Bondi, M. W., Woods, S. P., Corey-Bloom, J., ... Gilbert,

P. E. (2016). Total recognition discriminability in Huntington's and Alzheimer's disease. *Journal of Clinical and Experimental Neuropsychology*, 1–11.

Gravetter, F., & Wallnau, L. (2016). *Statistics for the behavioral sciences.* Belmont, CA: Cengage Learning.

Gray, J. R. (2003). Neural mechanisms of general fluid intelligence. *Nature Neuro-science, 6*, 316–322.

Gray, P. (2010). *Psychology* (6th ed.). New York: Worth.

GRE guide to the use of scores. (2012). Princeton, NJ: Educational Testing Service.

GRE News Release. (2010). *GRE® general test now accepted by more than 500 MBA programs worldwide.* Princeton, NJ (April 28, 2011). Retrieved from http://www.ets.org/gre/news/now_accepted_mba.

Green Jr., D. F., & Wing, H. (1988). *Analysis of job performance measurement data: Report of a workshop.* Washington, DC: National Academy Press.

Green, B. F. (1978). In defense of measurement. *American Psychologist, 33*, 664–670.

Green, D. R., & Draper, J. F. (1972, September). *Exploratory studies of bias and achievement.* Paper presented at the meeting of the American Psychological Association, Honolulu, HI.

Green, K. E. (1983). Subjective judgment of multiple choice item characteristics. *Educational & Psychological Measurement, 43*, 563–570.

Green, P. (2003). Welcoming a paradigm shift in neuropsychology. *Archives of Clinical Neuropsychology, 18*(6), 625–627.

Green, S. B., & Yang, Y. (2009). Reliability of summed item scores using structural equation modeling: An alternative to coefficient alpha. *Psychometrika, 74*(1), 155–167.

Greene, R. L. (2000). *The MMPI-2: An interpretive manual.* Boston: Allyn & Bacon.

Greenea, R. L. (2011). Some considerations for enhancing psychological assessment. *Journal of Personality Assessment, 93*(3), 198–203. doi: 10.1080/00223891.2011.558879.

Grégoire, J., Coalson, D., & Zhu, J. (2011). Analysis WAIS-IV index score scatter using significant deviation from the mean index score. *Assessment, 18*(2), 168–177.

Greisinger, K. F. (2003). Testing and assessment in cross-cultural psychology. In J. R. Graham & J. A. Naglieri (Eds.), *Handbook of psychology: Assessment*

psychology (Vol. 10, pp. 95–117). New York: Wiley.

Gresham, F. M., McIntyre, L. L., Olson-Tinker, H., Dolstra, L., McLaughlin, V., & Van, M. (2004). Relevance of functional behavioral assessment research for schoolbased interventions and positive behavioral support. *Research in Developmental Disabilities, 25*(1), 19–37.

Greve, K. W., Bianchini, K. J., Mathias, C. W., & Houston, R. J. (2003). Detecting malingering performance on the Wechsler Adult Intelligence Scale. *Archives of Clinical Neuropsychology, 18*, 245–260.

Griggs v. Duke Power Company. (1971). 401 U.S. 424(a).

Grodberg, D., Weinger, P., Halpern, D., Parides, M., Kolevzon, A., et al. (2014). The autism mental status exam: Sensitivity and specificity using dsm-5 criteria for autism spectrum disorder in verbally fluent adults. *Journal of Autism and Developmental Disorders, 44*(3), 609–614.

Groessl, E. J., Kaplan, R. M., & Cronan, T. A. (2003). Quality of wellbeing in older people with osteoarthritis. *Arthritis and Rheumatology, 49*(1), 23–28.

Groessl, E. J., Kaplan, R. M., Rejeski, W. J., Katula, J. A., King, A. C., Frierson, G., et al. (2007). Health-related quality of life in older adults at risk for disability. *American Journal of Preventive Medicine, 33*(3), 214–218.

Groessl, E. J., Kaplan, R. M., Sweet, C. M. C., Church, T., Espeland, M. A., Gill, T. M., ... Manini, J. (2016). Cost-effectiveness of the LIFE physical activity intervention for older adults at increased risk for mobility disability. *The Journals of Gerontology Series A: Biological Sciences and Medical Sciences*, glw001.

Groth-Marnat, G. (2003). *Handbook of psychological assessment* (4th ed.). New York, NY: Wiley.

Groth-Marnat, G. (2009a). *Handbook of psychological assessment.* New York: Wiley.

Groth-Marnat, G. (2009b). *Handbook of psychological assessment* (p. 80). Hoboken, NJ: John Wiley & Sons, Inc.

Groth-Marnat, G., & Shumaker, J. (1989). Computer-based psychological testing: Issues and guidelines. *American Journal of Orthopsychiatry, 59*, 257–263.

Gruber, N., & Kreuzpointner, L. (2013). Measuring the reliability of picture story exercises like the tat: E79450. *PLoS One, 8*(11).

Guarnaccia, V., Dill, C. A., Sabatino, S., & Southwick, S. (2001). Scoring accuracy using the comprehensive system for the Rorschach. *Journal of Personality Assessment, 77*, 464–474.

Gudjonsson, G. H., & Sigurdsson, J. F. (2003). The relationship of compliance with coping strategies and self-esteem. *European Journal of Psychological Assessment, 19*(2), 117–123.

Guedalia, J., Finkelstein, Y., Drukker, A., & Frishberg, Y. (2000). The use of Luria's method for the neurobehavioral assessment of encephalopathy in an adolescent: Application in a rehabilitation setting. *Archives of Clinical Neuropsychology, 15*(2), 177–184.

Guilford, J. P., & Zimmerman, W. S. (1956). Fourteen dimensions of temperament. *Psychological Monographs, 70*(10), 1–26.

Guion, R. M., & Ironson, G. H. (1983). Latent trait theory for organizational research. *Organizational Behavior and Human Performance, 31*, 54–87.

Gupta, S., Vaida, F., Riggs, K., Jin, H., Grant, I., Cysique, L., et al. (2011). Neuropsychological performance in mainland china: the effect of urban/rural residence and self-reported daily academic skill use [Research Support, N. I. H., Extramural]. *Journal of the International Neuropsychological Society, 17*(1), 163–173. doi: 10.1017/S135561771 0001384.

Guttman, L. (1950). Relation of scalogram analysis to other techniques. In S. A. Stouffer (Eds.), *Measurement and prediction* (pp. 172–212). Princeton, NJ: Princeton University Press.

Guzzetta, F. (2009). Psychomotor development; the beginning of cognition, In F. Guzzetta & J. Libby (Eds.), *Neurology of the infant* (pp. 37–54). Montrouge, France: Eurotext.

Hagell, P., Whalley, D., McKenna, S. P., & Lindvall, O. (2003). Health status measurement in Parkinson's disease: Validity of the PDQ-39 and Nottingham Health Profile. *Movement Disorders, 18*(7), 773–783.

Hale, J. B., Hoeppner, J. B., & Fiorello, C. A. (2002). Analyzing digit span components for assessment of attention processes. *Journal of Psychoeducational Assessment, 20*(2), 128–143.

Hambleton, R. K. (1994). The rise and fall of criterion-referenced measurement? *Educational Measurement: Issues and Practice, 13*, 21–26.

Hambrick, D. Z., Rench, T. A., Poposki, E. M., Darowski, E. S., Roland, D., Bearden, R. M., et al. (2011). The relationship between the ASVAB and multitasking in navy sailors: A process-specific approach. *Military Psychology, 23*(4), 365–380.

Hamdani, M. R., & Buckley, M. R. (2011). Diversity goals: Reframing the debate and enabling a fair evaluation. *Business Horizons, 54*(1), 33–40.

Hamel, M., Shaffer, T. W., & Erdberg, P. (2000). A study of nonpatient preadolescent Rorschach protocols. *Journal of Personality Assessments, 75*, 280–294.

Hammer, A. L., & Marting, M. S. (1985). *Manual for the coping resources inventory*. Palo Alto, CA: Consulting Psychologists Press.

Hammond, S. (2006a). Multivariate data analysis. In G. Breakwell, S. Hammond, C. Fife-Schaw, & J. Smith (Eds.), *Research methods in psychology* (pp. 414–443). Thousand Oaks, CA: Sage.

Hammond, S. (2006b). Using psychometric tests. In G. Breakwell, S. Hammond, C. Fife-Schaw, & J. Smith (Eds.), *Research methods in psychology* (3rd ed., pp. 182–209). Thousand Oaks, CA: Sage.

Hampson, E., & Kimura, D. (1988). Reciprocal effects of hormonal fluctuations on human motor and perceptual-spatial skills. *Behavioral Neuroscience, 102*, 456–459.

Hand, D. J. (2011). Introduction to psychometric theory by Tenko Raykov, George A. Marcoulides. *International Statistical Review, 79*(2), 298–299.

Handel, R. W., Arnau, R. C., Archer, R. P., & Dandy, K. L. (2006). An evaluation of the MMPI-2 and MMPI-A true response inconsistency (TRIN) scales. *Assessment, 13*(1), 98–106.

Haney, W. (1981). Validity, vaudeville, and values: A short history of social concerns over standardized testing. *American Psychologist, 36*, 1021–1034.

Hanford, G. H. (1986). The SAT and statewide assessment: The distinction between measurement and evaluation. *Vital Speeches of the Day, 52*(24), 765–768.

Hanmer, J., Cherepanov, D., Palta, M., Kaplan, R. M., Feeny, D., & Fryback, D. G. (2016). Health condition impacts in a Nationally representative cross-sectional survey vary substantially by preference-based health index. *Medical Decision Making, 36*(2), 264–274.

Hanmer, J., Hays, R. D., & Fryback, D. G. (2007). Mode of administration is important in US national estimates of health-related quality of life. *Medical Care, 45*(12), 1171–1179.

Hansen, B. M., Dinesen, J., Hoff, B., & Greisen, G. (2002). Intelligence in preterm children at four years of age as a predictor of school function: A longitudinal controlled study. *Developmental Medicine and Child Neurology, 44*(8), 517–521.

Hansen, I., & Leuty, M. (2007). Evidence of validity for the Skill Scale scores of the Campbell Interest and Skill Survey. *Journal of Vocational Behavior, 71*(1), 23–44.

Hansen, J. C., & Campbell, D. P. (1985). *Manual for the SVIB-SCII* (4th ed.). Stanford, CA: Stanford University Press.

Hansen, J. –I. C. (2000). Interpretation of the strong interest inventory. In C. E. Watkins Jr. & V. L. Campbell (Eds.), *Testing and assessment in counseling practice* (2nd ed., pp. 227–262). Mahwah, NJ: Erlbaum.

Hanson, M. A., Borman, W. C., Kubisiak, U. C., & Sager, C. E. (1999). Cross-domain analyses. In N. G. Peterson, M. D. Mumford, & W. C. Borman (Eds.), *An occupational information system for the 21st century: The development of O*NET* (pp. 247–258). Washington, DC: American Psychological Association.

Hanten, G., Dennis, M., Zhang, L., Barnes, M., Roberson, G., Archibald, J., et al. (2004). Childhood head injury and metacognitive processes in language and memory. *Developments in Neuropsychology, 25*(1–2), 85–106.

Hanton, S., Evans, L., & Neil, R. (2003). Hardiness and the competitive trait anxiety response. *Anxiety, Stress, & Coping, 16*(2), 167–184.

Harasym, P. H., Woloschuk, W., Mandin, H., & Brundin-Mather, R. (1996). Reliability and validity of interviewer's judgments of medical school candidates. *Academic Medicine, 71*, 540–542.

Hardle, W., & Simar, L. (2007). *Applied multivariate statistical analysis*. New York: Springer.

Hardy, J. B., Welcher, D. W., Mellits, E. D., & Kagan, J. (1976). Pitfalls in the measurement of intelligence: Are standardized intelligence tests valid for measuring the intellectual potential of urban children? *Journal of Psychology, 94*, 43–51.

Haren, E. G., & Mitchell, C. W. (2003). Relationship between the five-factor personality model and coping styles.

Psychology and Education: An Interdisciplinary Journal, 40(1), 38–49.

Harkness, A. R., McNulty, J. L., & Ben-Porath, Y. S. (1995). The personality psychopathology—5 (Psy5): Construct and MMPI-2 scales. *Psychological Assessment, 7*(1), 104–114.

Harlow, G., Boulmetis, J., Clark, P. G., Willis, G. H. (2003). Computer-assisted life stories. *Computers in Human Behavior, 19*(4), 391–406.

Harmon, L. W., Cole, N., Wysong, E., & Zytowski, D. G. (1973). AMEG commission report on sex bias in interest measurement. *Measurement and Evaluation in Guidance, 6,* 171–177.

Harrati, S., Mazoyer, V., & Vavassori, D. (2014). Thematic apperception test and insecure models of attachment of criminal women. *L'Evolution Psychiatrique, 79*(3), 513.

Harris, C. I., & West-Faulcon, K. (2010). Reading ricci: Whitening discrimination, racing test fairness. *UCLA Law Review, 58,* 73.

Harris, D. B. (1963). *Children's drawings as measures of intellectual maturity: A revision and extension of the Goodenough Draw-a-Man Test.* New York: Harcourt, Brace, & World.

Harris, F. C, & Lahey, B. B. (1982). Subject reactivity in direct observational assessment: A review and critical analysis. *Clinical Psychology Review, 2,* 523–538.

Harris, W. G., Neider, D., Feldman, C, Fink, A., & Johnson, J. H. (1981). An online interpretive Rorschach approach: Using Exner's comprehensive system. *Behavior Research Methods and Instrumentation, 13*(4), 588–591.

Harrison, R. (1940a). Studies in the use and validity of the Thematic Apperception Test with mentally disordered patients: II. A quantitative validity study. *Character and Personality, 9,* 192–133.

Harrison, R. (1940b). Studies in the use and validity of the Thematic Apperception Test with mentally disordered patients: III. Validation by blind analysis. *Character and Personality, 9,* 134–138.

Hart, R., Casserly, M., Uzzell, R., Moses, P., Corcoran, A., & Spurgeon, L. (2015). *Student testing in America's great city schools: An inventory and preliminary analysis.* Washington, DC: Council of the Great City Schools.

Hart, B., & Spearman, C. (1912). General ability, its existence and nature. *British Journal of Psychology, 5,* 51–84.

Hart, S. A., Petrill, S. A., Deckard, K. D., & Thompson, L. A. (2007). SES and CHAOS as environmental mediators

of cognitive ability: A longitudinal genetic analysis. *Intelligence, 35*(3), 233–242.

Hartigan, J., & Wigdor, A. (1989). Fairness in employment testing. *Science, 245,* 14.

Hartman, D. E. (1986). On the use of clinical psychology software: Practical, legal, and ethical concerns. *Professional Psychology: Research and Practice, 17,* 473–475.

Hartman, E. (2001). Rorschach administration: A comparison of the effect of two instructions. *Journal of Personality Assessment, 76*(3), 461–471.

Hartman, J. G., & Looney Jr., M., (2003). *Norm-referenced and criterion-referenced reliability and validity of the back-saver sit-and-reach.* Mahwah, NJ: Erlbaum.

Hartung, P. J., & Santilli, S. (2017). The theory and practice of career construction. In M. McMahon (Ed.), *Career counselling: Constructivist approaches 2nd Edition,* in press. New York: Routledge.

Harwood, T. M., Beutler, L. E., & Groth-Marnat, G. (2011). *Integrative assessment of adult personality* (3rd ed.). New York: Guilford Press.

Hase, H. D., & Goldberg, L. R. (1967). Comparative validity of different strategies of constructing personality inventory scales. *Psychological Bulletin, 67,* 231–248.

Haskard, K. B., Williams, S. L., DiMatteo, M. R., Heritage, J., & Rosenthal, R. (2008). The provider's voice: Patient satisfaction and the content-filtered speech of nurses and physicians in primary medical care. *Journal of Nonverbal Behavior, 32*(1), 1–20.

Hathaway, S. R., & McKinley, J. C. (1943). *Manual for the Minnesota multiphasic personality inventory.* New York: Psychological Corporation.

Hawkins-Gilligan, J., Dygdon, J. A., & Conger, A. J. (2011). Examining the nature of fear of flying. *Aviation, Space, and Environmental Medicine, 82*(10), 964–971.

Hawkley, L. C., Lavelle, L. A., Berntson, G. G., & Cacioppo, J. T. (2011). Mediators of the relationship between socioeconomic status and allostatic load in the Chicago Health, Aging, and Social Relations Study (CHASRS). *Psychophysiology, 48*(8), 1134–1145. doi: 10.1111/j.1469-8986.2011. 01185.x.

Hayes, F. B., & Martin, R. P. (1986). Effectiveness of the PPVT-R in the screening of young gifted children. *Journal of Psychoeducational Assessment, 4,* 27–33.

Hayes, N., & Joseph, S. (2003). Big 5 correlates of three measures of subjective

well-being. *Personality and Individual Differences, 34*(4), 723–727.

Hayes, R. D., Morales, L. S., & Reise, S. P. (2000). Item response theory and health outcomes measurement in the 21st century. *Med Care, 38* (9 Suppl.), II28–42.

Haynes, S. N. (1992). Behavioral assessment. In M. Hersen, A. Kazdin, & A. Bellack (Eds.), *The clinical psychology handbook* (2nd ed., pp. 430–446). New York: Pergamon Press.

Haynes, S. N. (1995). Introduction to the special section on chaos theory and psychological assessment. *Psychological Assessment, 7*(1), 3–4.

Hays, M. (2004). Illustration clinique de l'observation selon la méthode de brazelton, dans une circonstance particulière d'accouchement: Processus de transformation des angoisses vitales en potentiel de lien vivant. *Neuropsychiatrie de l'enfance et de l'adolescence, 52*(3), 166–174.

Hays, P. A. (2001). Putting culture to the test: Considerations with standardized testing. In P. A. Hays (Ed.), *Addressing cultural complexities in practice: A framework for clinicians and counselors* (pp. 111–127). Washington, DC: American Psychological Association.

Hays, R. D., Brown, J., Brown, L. U., Spritzer, K. L., & Crall, J. J. (2006). Classical test theory and item response theory analyses of multi-item scales assessing parents' perceptions of their children's dental care. *Medical Care, 44*(11 Suppl. 3), S60–S68.

Hays, R. D., Liu, H., Spritzer, K., & Cella, D. (2007). Item response theory analyses of physical functioning items in the medical outcomes study. *Medical Care, 45*(5 Suppl. 1), S32–S38.

Healy, W., & Fernald, G. M. (1911). Tests for practical mental classification. *Psychological Monographs, 13*(54), 34–40.

Hearst, E. (1979). One hundred years: Themes and perspectives. In E. Hearst (Ed.), *The first century of experimental psychology.* Hillsdale, NJ: Erlbaum.

Heatherton, T. F., & Wyland, C. L. (2003). Assessing self-esteem. In S. J. Lopez & C. R. Snyder (Eds.), *Positive psychological assessment: A handbook of models and measures* (pp. 219–233). Washington DC: American Psychological Association.

Heaton, R. K., Franklin, D. R., Ellis, R. J., McCutchan, J. A., Letendre, S. L., Leblanc, S., et al. (2011). HIV-associated neurocognitive disorders before and during the era of combination antiretroviral therapy: Differences in rates, nature, and predictors. *Journal of NeuroVirology, 17,* 3–16.

Heider, F. (1944). Social perception and phenomenal causation. *Psychological Review, 51,* 358–374.

Heider, F. (1958). *The psychology of interpersonal relations.* New York: Wiley.

Heilbrun Jr., A. B. (1972). Edwards personal preference schedule. In O. K. Buros (Ed.), *The seventh mental measurements yearbook* (Vol. 1). Highland Park, NJ: Gryphon Press.

Heimberg, R. C., Keller, K. E., & Peca-Baker, T. (1986). Cognitive assessment of social-evaluative anxiety in the job interview: Job interview self-statement schedule. *Journal of Counseling Psychology, 33,* 190–195.

Heimberg, R. G. (2001). Current status of psychotherapeutic interventions for social phobia. *Journal of Clinical Psychiatry, 62*(1), 36–42.

Heller, D., Judge, T. A., & Watson, D. (2002). The confounding role of personality and trait affectivity in the relationship between job and life satisfaction. *Journal of Organizational Behavior, 23*(7), 815–835.

Heller, K. (1971). Laboratory interview research as an analogue to treatment. In A. E. Bergin & S. L. Garfield (Eds.), *Handbook of psychotherapy and behavior change* (pp. 126–153). New York: Wiley.

Helmbold, N., & Rammsayer, T. (2006). Timing performance as a predictor of psychometric intelligence as measured by speed and power tests. *Journal of Individual Differences, 27*(1), 20–37.

Henry, P., & Bardo, H. R. (1990). Relationship between scores on developing cognitive abilities test and scores on medical college admissions test for nontraditional premedical students. *Psychological Reports, 67,* 55–63.

Henry, P., Bryson, S., & Henry, C. A. (1990). Black student attitudes toward standardized tests. *College Student Journal, 23,* 346–354.

hepard, L. (1992). Psychometric properties of the gesell developmental assessment: A critique. *Early Childhood Research Quarterly, 7*(1), 47–52.

Herbert, W. (1982). Intelligence tests: Sizing up a newcomer. *Science News, 122,* 280–281.

Hermans, H., van der Pas, F. H., & Evenhuis, H. M. (2011). Instruments assessing anxiety in adults with intellectual disabilities: A systematic review.

Research in Developmental Disabilities, 32(3), 861–870. doi: 10.1016/j.ridd.2011.01.034.

Hernandez, M., Avery, D. R., Tonidandel, S., Hebl, M. R., Smith, A. N., & McKay, P. F. (2016). The role of proximal social contexts: Assessing stigma-by-association effects on leader appraisals. *Journal of Applied Psychology, 101*(1), 68.

Hernández-Martínez, C, Canals, J., Aranda, N., Ribot, B., Escribano, J., & Arija, V. (2011). Effects of iron deficiency on neonatal behavior at different stages of pregnancy. *Early Human Development, 87*(3), 165–169. ISSN 0378-3782; doi: 10.1016/j. earlhumdev.2010.12.006. Retrieved from http://www.sciencedirect.com/science/article/pii/S0378378210007176.

Hernstein, R. J. (1982, August). IQ testing and the media. *Atlantic Monthly,* pp. 68–74.

Hersen, M., Kazdin, A. E., & Bellack, A. S. (1991). *The clinical psychology handbook* (2nd ed.). New York: Pergamon Press.

Hersh, J. B. (1971). Effects of referral information on tester. *Journal of Consulting and Clinical Psychology, 37,* 116–122.

Hertz, M. R. (1937). Discussion on "Some recent Rorschach problems". *Rorschach Research Exchange, 2,* 53–65.

Hertz, M. R. (1938). Scoring the Rorschach Inkblot Test. *Journal of Genetic Psychology, 52,* 16–64.

Heubert, J. P., & Hauser, R. M. (1999). *High stakes: Testing for tracking, promotion and graduation.* Washington, DC: National Academy Press.

Heuchert, J. W. P., Parker, W. D., Stumpf, H., & Myburgh, C. P. H. (2000). The five-factor model of personality in South African college students. *American Behavioral Scientist, 44*(1), 112–125.

Hewitt, M. (2002). Attitudes toward interview mode and comparability of reporting sexual behavior by personal interview and audio computer-assisted self-interviewing: Analysis of the 1995 National survey of family growth. *Sociological Methods and Research, 31*(1), 3–26.

Hewitta, C. E., Perryb, A. E., Adams, B., & Gilbodyd, S. M. (2011). Screening and case finding for depression in offender populations: A systematic review of diagnostic properties. *Affective Disorders, 128*(1–2), 72–82.

Hicks, K. L., Harrison, T. L., & Engle, R. W. (2015). Wonderlic, working memory capacity, and fluid intelligence. *Intelligence, 50,* 186–195.

Higgins, C. A. (2001). The effect of applicant influence tactics on recruiter perceptions of fit. *Dissertation Abstracts International, 61,* 9A.

Highhouse, S., Doverspike, D., & Guion, R. M. (2015). *Essentials of personnel assessment and selection.* New York: Routledge.

Hill, H. C., Kapitula, L., & Umland, K. (2011). A validity argument approach to evaluating teacher value-added scores. *American Educational Research Journal, 48*(3), 794–831.

Hilsenroth, M. J., Fowler, J. C., & Padawer, J. R. (1998). The Rorschach Schizoprenia Index (SCZI): An examination of reliability, validity, and diagnostic efficiency. *Journal of Personality Assessment, 70,* 514–534.

Hinton, D., & Stevens-Gill, D. (2016). Online psychometric assessment. In A. Attrill & C. Fullwood (Eds.), *Applied cyberpsychology* (pp. 236–255). New York: Springer.

Hinz, A., Klaiberg, A., Schumacher, J., & Brahler, E. (2003). The psychometric quality of the Nottingham Health Profile (NHP) in the general population. *Psychotherapy and Psychosomatic Medical Psychology, 53*(8), 353–358.

Hiscock, M., Inch, R., & Gleason, A. (2002). Raven's progressive matrices performance in adults with traumatic brain injury. *Applied Neuropsychology, 9*(3), 129–138.

Hiss, W. C., & Franks, V. W. (2014). Defining promise: Optional standardized testing policies in American college and university admissions. *Report of the National Association for College Admission Counseling (NACAC).* Retrieved from http://www. nacacnet. org/research/research-data/nacac-research/Documents/DefiningPromise.pdf.

Hoekstra, R. A., Bartels, M., Hudziak, J. J., Van Beijsterveldt, T. C., & Boomsma, D. I. (2007). Genetic and environmental covariation between autistic traits and behavioral problems. *Twin Research and Human Genetics, 10*(6), 853–860.

Hoekstra, R. A., Happé, F., Baron-Cohen, S. & Ronald, A. (2010). Limited genetic covariance between autistic traits and intelligence: Findings from a longitudinal twin study. *American Journal of Medical Genetics Part B: Neuropsychiatric Genetics, 153B,* 994–1007. doi: 10.1002/ajmg.b.31066.

Hoertel, N., López, S., Peyre, H., Wall, M. M., González-Pinto, A., Limosin, F., & Blanco, C. (2015). Are symptom features of depression during pregnancy, the postpartum period and outside the peripartum period distinct? Results from a nationally representative sample using item response theory (IRT). *Depression and Anxiety, 32*(2), 129–140.

Hofer, J., & Chasiotis, A. (2011). Implicit motives across cultures. *Online readings in psychology and culture, unit 4.* Retrieved from http://scholarworks.gvsu.edu/orpc/vol4/iss1/5.

Hoff, K. (2010). Test review of the Wide Range Achievement Test 4. In R. A. Spies, J. F. Carlson, & K. F. Geisinger (Eds.), *The eighteenth mental measurements yearbook*. Retrieved from http://www.unl.edu/buros.

Hoffman, M., Kahn, L. B., & Li, D. (2015). *Discretion in hiring.* National Bureau for Economic Research. doi: 10.3386/w21709.

Hogan, J., & Quigley, A. M. (1986). Physical standards for employment and the courts. *American Psychologist, 41*, 1193–1217.

Hogarth, L., Dickinson, A., & Duka, T. (2005). Explicit knowledge of stimulus-outcome contingencies and stimulus control of selective attention and instrumental action in human smoking behaviour. *Psychopharmacology, 177*(4), 428–437.

Hogarth, L., Dickinson, A., Wright, A., Kouvaraki, M., & Duka, T. (2007). The role of drug expectancy in the control of human drug seeking. *Journal of Experimental Psychology: Animal Behavior Processes, 33*(4), 484–496.

Holaday, M., Smith, D. A., & Sherry, A. (2000). Sentence completion test: A review of the literature and results of a survey of members of the society for personality assessment. *Journal of Personality Assessment, 74*, 71–385.

Holahan, C. J. (1986). Environmental psychology. *Annual Review of Psychology, 37*, 381–407.

Holahan, C. J., & Moos, R. H. (1986). Personality, coping, and family support in stress resistance: A longitudinal analysis. *Journal of Personality and Social Psychology, 51*, 389–395.

Holden, C. (2003). Affirmative action. Careful use of race is OK, high court tells colleges. *Science, 300*(5628), 2012.

Holden, K., Kellett, S., Davies, J., & Scott, S. (2016). The experience of working with people that hoard: A Q-sort exploration. *Journal of Mental Health*, 1–7. Published online ahead of print, April 2016.

Holifield, J. E., Nelson, W. M., III, & Hart, K. J. (2002). MMPI profiles of sexually abused and nonabused outpatient adolescents. *Journal of Adolescent Research, 17*(2), 188–195.

Holland, J. L. (1975). *Manual for the vocational preference inventory.* Palo Alto, CA: Consulting Psychologists Press.

Holland, J. L. (1985). *The self-directed search: professional manual.* Odessa, FL: Psychological Assessment Resources.

Holland, J. L. (1997). *Making vocational choices: A theory of vocational personalities and work environments* (3rd ed.). Odessa, FL: Psychological Assessment Resources.

Holland, J. L. (2013). Self-directed search. In W. B. Walsh & S. H. Osipow (Eds.), *Advances in vocational psychology: Volume 1: The assessment of interests* (pp. 55-81).

Holland, J. L., & Gottfredson, G. D. (1976). Using a typology of persons and environments to explain careers: Some extensions and clarifications. *Counseling Psychologist, 6*, 20–29.

Hollingworth, H. L. (1922). *Judging human character.* New York: Appleton-Century-Crofts.

Holmes, C. B., & Beishline, M. J. (1996). Correct classification, false positives, and false negatives in predicting completion of the Ph. D. from GRE scores. *Psychological Reports, 79*, 939–945.

Holt, R. R. (1967). Diagnostic testing: Present status and future prospects. *Journal of Nervous and Mental Disease, 141*, 444–464.

Holtzman, W. H., & Sells, S. B. (1954). Prediction of flying success by clinical analysis of test protocols. *Journal of Abnormal and Social Psychology, 49*, 485–490.

Holtzman, W. H., Thorpe, J. S., Swartz, J. D., & Herron, E. W. (1961). *Inkblot perception and personality.* Austin: University of Texas Press.

Hölzl, R., Kleinböhl, D., & Huse, E. (2005). Implicit operant learning of pain sensitization. *Pain, 115*(1), 12–20.

Hooper, S. R., & March, J. S. (1995). Neuropsychology. In J. S. March (Ed.), *Anxiety disorders in children and adolescents* (pp. 35–60), New York: Guilford Press.

Hooper, S. R., Conner, R. E., & Umansky, W. (1986). The Cattell Infant Intelligence Scale: A review of the literature. *Developmental Review, 6*, 146–164.

Hooper, V. S., & Mee Bell, S. (2006). Concurrent validity of the universal nonverbal intelligence test and the

Leiter International Performance Scale-Revised. *Psychology in the Schools, 43*(2), 143–148.

Hopko, D. R., Hunt, M. K., & Armento, M. E. A. (2005). Attentional task aptitude and performance anxiety. *International Journal of Stress Management, 12*(4), 389–408.

Hoppmann, C. A., & Ho, A. (2016). Ecological momentary assessment. *The Encyclopedia of Adulthood and Aging.* Published Online: 20 DEC 2015.doi:10.1002/9781118521373.wbeaa10.

Horn, J. L. (1994). Theory of fluid and crystallized intelligence. In R. J. Sternberg (Ed.), *Encyclopedia of human intelligence* (pp. 443–451). New York: Macmillan.

Horn, J. L., & Blankson, N. (2005). In D. P. Flanagan, & P. L. Harrison (Eds.), *Foundations for better understanding of cognitive abilities*. New York: Guilford Press.

Horn, J. L., & Cattell, R. B. (1966). Refinement and test of the theory of fluid and crystallized intelligence. *Journal of Educational Psychology, 57*, 253–276.

Horn, J. L., & Noll, J. (1997). Human cognitive capabilities: *Gf-Gc* theory. In D. P. Flanagan, J. L. Genshaft, & P. L. Harrison (Eds.), *Contemporary intellectual assessment: Theories, tests, and issues* (pp. 53–91). New York: Guilford Press.

Horn, J., & Masunaga, H. (2006). In K. A. Ericsson, N. Charness, P. J. Feltovich, & R. R. Hoffman (Eds.), *A merging theory of expertise and intelligence*. New York: Cambridge University Press.

Horney, D. J., Smith, H. E., McGurk, M., Weinman, J., Herold, J., Altman, K., et al. (2011). Associations between quality of life, coping styles, optimism, and anxiety and depression in pretreatment patients with head and neck cancer. *Head & Neck, 33*(1), 65–71. doi: 10.1002/hed.21407.

Horowitz, J. A., Murphy, C. A., Gregory, K. E., & Wojcik, J. (2009). Best practices: Community based post-partum depression screening: Results from the care study. *Psychiatric Services, 60*, 1432–1434. doi: 10.1176/appi.ps.60.11.1432.

Horowitz, M. J., & Wilner, N. (1980). Life events, stress, and coping. In L. Poon (Ed.), *Aging in the eighties* (pp. 363–374). Washington, DC: American Psychological Association.

Horváth, A., Montana, X., Lanquart, J.-P., Hubain, P., Szűcs, A., Linkowski, P., & Loas, G. (2016). Effects of state and trait anxiety on sleep structure: A polysomnographic study in 1083 subjects. *Psychiatry Research, 244*, 279–283.

House, J. D. (1997). Predictive validity of graduate record examination scores for outcomes of American Indian/Alaska native students. *Psychological Reports, 81*, 337–338.

House, J. D. (1998). Age differences in prediction of student achievement from graduate record examination scores. *Journal of Genetic Psychology, 159*, 379–382.

House, J. D., & Johnson, J. J. (1998). Predictive validity of the graduate record examination for grade performance in graduate psychology courses. *Psychological Reports, 82*, 1235–1238.

House, J. D., & Keeley, E. J. (1995). Gender bias in prediction of graduate grade performance from Miller Analogies Test scores. *Journal of Psychology, 129*, 353–355.

House, J. D., & Keeley, E. J. (1996). Differential prediction of adult student performance from Miller Analogies Test scores. *Journal of Genetic Psychology, 157*, 501–503.

Howard, J. L., & Ferris, G. R. (1996). The employment interview context: Social and situational influences on interviewer decisions. *Journal of Applied Social Psychology, 26*, 112–136.

Howell, D. (2008). *Fundamental statistics for the behavioral sciences* (6th ed.). Belmont, CA: Wadsworth.

Hsieh, F., Ferrer, E., Chen, S., Mauss, I. B., John, O., & Gross, J. J. (2011). A network approach for evaluating coherence in multivariate systems: An application to psychophysiological emotion data. *Psychometrika, 76*(1), 124–152, doi: 10.1007/s11336-010-9194-0.

Hu, C., Cui, Z., Dai, X., Chen, X., Gao, B., Hou, Y., et al. (2002). Coping style, mental health status, and personality of policemen. *Chinese Mental Health Journal, 16*(9), 642–643.

Hu, C., Szapary, P. O., Yeilding, N., & Zhou, H. (2011). Informative dropout modeling of longitudinal ordered categorical data and model validation: Application to exposure-response modeling of physician's global assessment score for ustekinumab in patients with psoriasis. *Journal of Pharmacokinetics Pharmacodynamics, 38*(2), 237–260.

Huang, C. D., Church, A. T., & Katigbak, M. S. (1997). Identifying cultural differences in items and traits: Differential item functioning in the NEO personality inventory. *Journal of Cross-Cultural Psychology, 28*, 192–218.

Huang, C., & Dong, N., (2011). Factor structures of the Rosenberg Self-Esteem Scale: A meta-analysis of pattern matrices. *European Journal of Psychological Assessment*, 1–7. Retrieved from http://www.psycontent.com/content/y7r153tg271h216n/?references Mode=Show.

Huang, H., & Wang, W. (2014). Multilevel higher-order item response theory models. *Educational and Psychological Measurement, 74*(3), 495–515.

Hubbs-Tait, L., Culp, A. M., Culp, R. E., & Miller, C. E. (2002). Relation of maternal cognitive stimulation, emotional support, and intrusive behavior during Head Start to children's kindergarten cognitive abilities. *Child Development, 73*(1), 110–131.

Huber, A., Oldridge, N., & Höfer, S. (2016). International SF-36 reference values in patients with ischemic heart disease. *Quality of Life Research*, 1–12. Published online ahead of print. doi: 10.1007/s11136-016-1316-4.

Hudson, M. K., & Casey, E. M. (2016). Focus on middle school: Assessing and planning for second language literacy success with middle level refugee children. *Childhood Education, 92*(2), 158–160.

Huffcutt, A. I. (2011). An empirical review of the employment interview construct literature. *International Journal of Selection and Assessment, 19*(1), 62–81.

Huffcutt, A. I., & Roth, P. L. (1998). Racial group differences in employment interview evaluations. *Journal of Applied Psychology, 83*, 179–189.

Huffcutt, A. I., & Youngcourt, S. (2007). Employment interviews. In D. Whetzel, & G. Wheaton (Eds.), *Applied measurement: Industrial psychology in human resources management* (pp. 181–200). Mahwah, NJ: Routledge.

Huffcutt, A. I., Roth, P.L., & McDaniel, M. A. (1996). A meta-analytic investigation of cognitive ability in employment interview evaluations: Moderating characteristics and implications for incremental validity. *Journal of Applied Psychology, 81*, 459–473.

Huibregtse, I., Admiraal, W., & Meara, P. (2002). *Scores on a yes–no vocabulary test: Correction for guessing and response style*. London, United Kingdom: Hodder Arnold.

Humphreys, K. L., Foley, K. M., Feinstein, B. A., Marx, B. P., Kaloupek, D. G., & Keane, T. M. (2011). The influence of externalizing comorbidity on psychophysiological reactivity among veterans with posttraumatic stress disorder. *Psychological Trauma: Theory, Research, Practice, and Policy*. Retrieved from http://psycnet.apa.org/psycinfo/2011-06225-001/. doi: 10.1037/a0022644.

Hunsley, J., & Bailey, J. M. (2001). Whither the Rorschach? An analysis of the evidence. *Psychological Assessment, 13*, 472–485.

Hunsley, J., & DiGiulio, G. (2001). Norms, norming, and clinical assessment. *Clinical Psychology: Science and Practice, 8*, 378–382.

Hunt, T. V. (1978). Review of McCarthy Scales of Children's Abilities. In O. K. Buros (Ed.), *The eighth mental measurements yearbook* (Vol. 1). Highland Park, NJ: Gryphon Press.

Hunter, J. E., & Schmidt, F. L. (1976). Critical analysis of statistical and ethical implications of various definitions of test bias. *Psychological Bulletin, 83*, 1053–1071.

Hunter, J. E., & Schmidt, F. L. (1978). Bias in defining test bias: Reply to Darlington. *Psychological Bulletin, 85*, 675–676.

Hurlburt, R. T. (2003). *Comprehending behavioral statistics* (3rd ed.). Belmont, CA: Wadsworth.

Iacoboni, M., & Mazziotta, J. C. (2007). Mirror neuron system: Basic findings and clinical applications. *Annals of Neurology, 62*(3), 213–218.

Iliescu, D., Ispas, D., Sulea, C., & Ilie, A. (2015). Vocational fit and counterproductive work behaviors: A self-regulation perspective. *Journal of Applied Psychology, 100*(1), 21.

Imada, A. S., & Hakel, M. D. (1977). Influences of nonverbal communication and rater proximity on impressions and decisions in simulated employment interviews. *Journal of Applied Psychology, 62*, 295–300.

Ironson, G. H., & Sebkovial, N. J. (1979). A comparison of several methods for assessing item bias. *Journal of Educational Measurement, 16*, 209–225.

Isaksen, S. G., & Puccio, G. J. (1988). Adaption-innovation and the Torrance Tests of Creative Thinking: The levelstyle issue revisited. *Psychological Reports, 63*, 659–670.

Ispas, D., Iliescu, D., Ilie, A., & Johnson, R. (2014). Exploring the cross-cultural generalizability of the five-factor model of personality: The romanian neo pi-r. *Journal of Cross-Cultural Psychology, 45*(7), 1074–1088.

Istepanian, R., Philip, N., Wang, X., & Laxminarayan, S. (2011). Non-telephone healthcare: The role of 4G and emerging mobile systems for future m-Health systems. *Future Visions on Biomedicine and Bioinformatics 2*, 9–16.

Iverson, G. L., Franzen, M. D., & Hammond, J. A. (1995). Examination of inmates' ability to malinger on the MMPI-2. *Psychological Assessment, 7*(1), 118–121.

Iwata, N., Mishima, N., Shimizu, T., Mizoue, T., Fukuhara, M., Hidano, T., et al. (1998). Positive and negative affect in the factor structure of the state-trait anxiety inventory for Japanese workers. *Psychological Reports, 82*(2), 651–656.

Jablonski, N. G., & Chaplin, G. (2010). Colloquium paper: human skin pigmentation as an adaptation to UV radiation. *Proceedings of National Academy of Sciences USA, 107* (Suppl. 2), 8962–8968. doi: 10.1073/pnas.0914628107.

Jackle, A., Lynn, P., Sinibaldi, J., & Tipping, S. (2013). The effect of interviewer experience, attitudes, personality and skills on respondent co-operation with face-to-face surveys. *Survey Research Methods, 7*(1), 1–15.

Jackson, D. N. (1967). *Personality research form manual.* Goshen, NY: Research Psychologists Press.

Jackson, D. N. (1976a). *Jackson personality inventory.* Goshen, NY: Research Psychologists Press.

Jackson, D. N. (1976b). *Manual for the Jackson personality inventory.* Goshen, NY: Research Psychologists Press.

Jackson, D. N. (1997). *Jackson personality inventory–Revised.* London Ontario: Sigma Assessment Systems.

Jackson, D. N. (2002). *The constructs in people's heads.* Mahwah, NJ: Erlbaum.

Jackson, D. N., & Livesley, W. J. (1995). Possible contributions from personality assessment to the classification of personality disorders. In W. J. Livesley (Ed.), *The DSM-IV personality disorders: Diagnosis and treatment of mental disorders* (pp. 459–481). New York: Guilford Press.

Jackson, D. N., & Messick, S. (Eds.). (1967). *Problems in human assessment.* New York: McGraw-Hill.

Jackson, D. N., Paunonen, S. V., Fraboni, M., & Goffin, R. D. (1996). A five-factor versus six-factor model of personality structure. *Personality and Individual Differences, 20*, 33–45.

Jackson, J. C., Sinnott, P. L., Marx, B. P., Murdoch, M., Sayer, N. A., Alvarez, J. M., Greevy, R. A., & Schnurr, P. P. (2011). Variation in practices and attitudes of clinicians assessing ptsd-related disability among veterans. *Journal of Traumatic Stress, 24*, 609–613. doi: 10.1002/jts.20688.

Jacob, B. A. (2011). Do principals fire the worst teachers? *Educational Evaluation and Policy Analysis, 33*(4), 403–434.

Jacob, W. J. (2015). A review of the common core state standards initiative in the United States: Historical background and international relevance. *Jiaoyu Yanjiu Yuekan* (255, 5–19.

Jacobs, R. R., Conte, J. M., Day, D. V., Silva, J. M., & Harris, R. (1996). Selecting bus drivers: Multiple predictors, multiple perspectives on validity, and multiple estimates of utility. *Human Performance 9*(3), 199–217.

Jacobson, M. W., Bondi, M. W., & Salmon, D. P. (2002). Do neuropsychological tests detect preclinical Alzheimer's disease: Individual test versus cognitive discrepancy score analysis. *Neuropsychology, 16*(2).

Jacobson, M. W., Delis, D. C., & Bondi, M. W. (2002). Do neuropsychological tests detect preclinical Alzheimer's disease: Individual-test versus cognitive score analyses. *Neuropsychology, 16*(2), 132–139.

James, A., & Rix, K. (2013). Working on working memory. *Psychologist, 26*(11), 791.

Jamieson, S. (2004). Likert Scales: How to (ab)use them. *Medical Education, 38*(2), 1117–1118.

Janssen, A. J., Akkermans, R. P., Steiner, K., de Haes, O., Oostendorp, R., Kollée, L., et al. (2011). Unstable longitudinal motor performance in preterm infants from 6 to 24 months on the Bayley Scales of Infant Development—Second Edition. *Research in Developmental Disabilities, 32*(5), 1902–1909. ISSN 0891-4222; doi: 10.1016/j.ridd.2011.03.026.

Janssen, E. (2002). Psychophysiological measurement of sexual arousal. In M. W. Wiederman & B. E. Whitley Jr. (Eds.), *Handbook for conducting research on human sexuality* (pp. 139–171). Mahwah, NJ: Erlbaum.

Jantz, P., Bigler, E., Froehlich, A., Prigge, M., Cariello, A., et al. (2015). Wide range achievement test in autism spectrum disorder: Test-retest stability. *Psychological Reports, 116*(3), 674–684.

Jayawickreme, E., & Blackie, L. (2014). Post-traumatic growth as positive personality change: Evidence, controversies and future directions. *European Journal of Personality, 28*(4), 312–331.

Jeanneret, P. R., Borman, W. C, Kubisiak, U. C, & Hanson, M. A. (1999). Generalized work activities. In N. G. Peterson & M. D. Mumford (Eds.), *An occupational information system for the 21st century: The development of O*NET* (pp. 105–125). Washington, DC: American Psychological Association.

Jeltova, I., Birney, D., Fredine, N., Jarvin, L., Sternberg, R. J., & Grigorenko, E. L. (2011). Making instruction and assessment responsive to diverse students' progress: Group-ad ministered dynamic assessment in teaching mathematics. *Journal of Learning Disabilities, 44*(4), 381–395.

Jensen, A. R. (1969). How much can we boost IQ and scholastic achievement? *Harvard Educational Review, 39*, 1–23.

Jensen, A. R. (1972). *Genetics and education.* New York: Harper & Row.

Jensen, A. R. (1984). The black-white difference on the K-ABC: Implication for future tests. *Journal of Special Education, 18*, 377–408.

Jensen, A. R. (1985). The nature of black-white differences on various psychometric tests: Spearman's hypothesis. *Behavioral and Brain Sciences, 8*, 193–263.

Jensen, C. L., Voigt, R. G., Llorente, A. M., Peters, S. U., Prager, T. C., Zou, Y. L., et al. (2010). Effects of early maternal docosahexaenoic acid intake on neuropsychological status and visual acuity at five years of age of breast-fed term infants. *Journal of Pediatrics, 157*(6), 900–905. ISSN 0022-3476; doi: 10.1016/j.jpeds.2010.06.006.

Ji, C. C. (1998). Predictive validity of the graduate record examination in education. *Psychological Reports, 82*, 899–904.

Jing, G., Deqing, T., & Longhui, L. (2001). Visual-motor deficits in children with learning disabilities. *Chinese Mental Health Journal, 15*(6), 388–390.

Johansson, C. B. (1976). *Manual for the career assessment inventory.* Minneapolis, MN: National Computer Systems.

Johansson, C. B., & Johansson, J. C. (1978). *Manual supplement for the career assessment inventory.* Minneapolis, MN: National Computer Systems.

Johansson, G., Johnson, J. V., & Hall, E. M. (1991). Smoking and sedentary behavior as related to work organization.

Social Science and Medicine, 32(7), 837–846.

Johnson, A. (2013). Knots in the pipeline for prospective lawyers of color: The lsat is not the problem and affirmative action is not the answer. *Stanford Law & Policy Review, 24*(2), 379.

Johnson, J. H., Null, C, Butcher, J. N., & Johnson, K. N. (1984). Replicated items level factor analysis of the full MMPI. *Journal of Personality and Social Psychology, 47,* 105–114.

Johnson, J. L. (1994). The Thematic Apperception Test and Alzheimer's disease. *Journal of Personality Assessment, 62*(2), 314–319.

Johnson, M. R. (2003). Neonatal assessment. In T. H. Ollendick & C. S. Schroeder (Eds.), *Encyclopedia of clinical child and pediatric psychology* (pp. 400–402). New York: Plenum Publishers.

Johnson, N. E., Saccuzzo, D. P., Larson, G. E., Guertin, T. L., Christianson, L., & Longley, S. (1993). *The San Diego Test of Reasoning Ability (S. A. N. T. R. A.).* [Available from N. E. Johnson, Ph. D., & D. P. Saccuzzo, Ph. D., 6363 Alvarado Court, Suite 103; San Diego, CA 92120–4913]

Johnstone, B., Holland, D., & Larimore, C. (2000). Language and academic abilities. In G. Groth-Marnat (Ed.), *Neuropsychological assessment in clinical practice: A guide to test interpretation and integration* (pp. 335–354). New York: Wiley.

Jones, E. E., & Nisbett, R. E. (1971). *The actor and observer: Divergent perceptions of the causes of behavior.* Morristown, NJ: General Learning Press.

Jones, P. W., & Kaplan, R. M. (2003). Methodological issues in evaluating measures of health as outcomes for COPD. *European Respiration Journal Supplement, 41,* 13s–18s.

Jones, R. A. (1968). *A factored measure of Ellis' irrational belief system with personality and maladjustment correlates.* Unpublished doctoral dissertation, Texas Technological College, Lubbock.

Jong, Y., & Jung, C. (2015). The development of interview techniques in language studies: Facilitating the researchers' views on interactive encounters. *English Language Teaching, 8*(7), 30.

Joseph, D. L., Jin, J., Newman, D. A., & O'Boyle, E. H. (2015). Why does self-reported emotional intelligence predict job performance? A meta-analytic investigation of mixed EI. *Journal of Applied Psychology, 100*(2), 298.

Joshi, A., Neely, B., Emrich, C., Griffiths, D., & George, G. (2015). Gender research in AMJ: An overview of five decades of empirical research and calls to action thematic issue on gender in management research. *Academy of Management Journal, 58*(5), 1459–1475.

Joy, S., Kaplan, E., & Fein, D. (2004). Speed and memory in the WAIS-III digit symbol–coding subtest across the adult lifespan. *Archives of Clinical Neuropsychology, 19*(6), 759–767.

Judge, T. A., & Bono, J. E. (2000). Five factor model of personality and transformational leadership. *Journal of Applied Psychology, 85*(5), 751–765.

Judge, T. A., & Larsen, R. J. (2001). Dispositional affect and job satisfaction: A review and theoretical extension. *Organizational Behavior and Human Decision Processes, 86*(1), 67–98.

Judge, T. A., Erez, A., Bono, J. E., & Thoresen, C. J. (2002). Are measures of self-esteem, neuroticism, locus of control, and generalized self-efficacy indicators of a common core construct? *Journal of Personality and Social Psychology, 83*(3), 693–710.

Judge, T. A., Locke, E. A., Durham, C. C., & Kluger, A. N. (1998). Dispositional effects on job and life satisfaction: The role of core evaluations. *Journal of Applied Psychology, 83*(1), 17–34.

Judiesch, M. K., Schmidt, F. L., & Hunter, J. E. (1993). Has the problem of judgment in utility analysis been solved? *Journal of Applied Psychology, 78,* 903–911.

Jung, C. G. (1910). The association method. *American Journal of Psychology, 21,* 219–269.

Kabuba, N., Menon, J. A., Franklin Jr, D. R., Heaton, R. K., & Hestad, K. A. (2016). Use of Western Neuropsychological Test Battery in detecting HIV-associated neurocognitive disorders (HAND) in Zambia. *AIDS and Behavior,* 1–11. Published online ahead of print doi:10.1007/s10461-016-1443-5.

Kagan, J., Moss, H. A., & Siegel, I. E. (1963). Psychological significance of styles of conceptualization. *Monographs of the Society for Research in Child Development, 28*(2, Serial No. 86), 73–124.

Kager, M. B. (2000). Factors that affect hiring: A study of age discrimination and hiring. *Dissertation Abstracts International: Section A. The humanities and social sciences, 60,* 11A.

Kamenetz, A. (2015). *The test: Why our schools are obsessed with standardized testing but you don't have to be.* PublicAffairs.

Kamin, L. J. (1974). *The science and politics of IQ.* Hillsdale, NJ: Eribaum.

Kammeier, M. L., Hoffman, H., & Loper, R. G. (1973). Personality characteristics of alcoholics as college freshmen and at time of treatment. *Quarterly Journal of Studies on Alcohol, 34,* 390–399.

Kanazawa, S. (2011). Intelligence and physical attractiveness. *Intelligence, 39*(1), 7–14.

Kane, M. J., & Engle, R. W. (2002). *The role of prefrontal cortex in working-memory capacity, executive attention, and general fluid intelligence: An individual-differences perspective.* US: Psychonomic Society,Retrieved from http://www.psychonomic.org.

Kane, R. L., Roebuck-Spencer, T., Short, P., Kabat, M., & Wilken, J. (2007). Identifying and monitoring cognitive deficits in clinical populations using Automated Neuropsychological Assessment Metrics (ANAM) tests. *Archives of Clinical Neuropsychology, 22*(Suppl. 1), S115–126.

Kantrowitz, T., Dawson, C., & Fetzer, M. (2011). Computer adaptive testing (CAT): A faster, smarter, and more secure approach to pre-employment testing. *Journal of Business and Psychology, 26*(2), 227–232. doi: 10.1007/s10869-011-9228-3.

Kaplan, R. M. (1973). Components of trust: Note on use of Rotter's Scale. *Psychological Reports, 33,* 13–14.

Kaplan, R. M. (1982). Nader's raid on the Educational Testing Service: Is it in the best interest of the consumer? *American Psychologist, 37,* 15–23.

Kaplan, R. M. (1985). The controversy related to the use of psychological tests. In B. B. Wolman (Ed.), *Handbook of intelligence: Theories, measurements, and applications.* New York: Wiley.

Kaplan, R. M. (1990). Behavior as the central outcome in health care. *American Psychologist, 45,* 1211–1220.

Kaplan, R. M. (1993). *The hippocratic predicament.* San Diego, CA: Academic Press.

Kaplan, R. M. (1994). Value judgment in the Oregon Medicaid experiment. *Medical Care, 32*(10), 975–988.

Kaplan, R. M. (1999). Health-related quality of life in mental health services evaluation. In N. E. Miller & K. M. Magruder (Eds.), *Cost-effectiveness of psychotherapy: A guide for practitioners, researchers, and policymakers* (pp. 160–173). New York: Springer.

Kaplan, R. M. (2000). Two pathways to prevention. *American Psychologist, 55*(4), 382–396.

Kaplan, R. M. (2002). *Quality of life and chronic illness*. Malden, MA: Blackwell.

Kaplan, R. M. (2003). The significance of quality of life in health care. *Quality of Life Research, 12*(Suppl. 1), 3–16.

Kaplan, R. M. (2004). Achievements of the veterans health study. *Journal of Ambulatory Care Management, 27*(1), 66–67.

Kaplan, R. M. (2009). *Diseases, diagnoses, and dollars*. New York: Springer.

Kaplan, R. M., & Ernst, J. (1983). Do category rating scales produce biased preference weights for a health index? *Medical Care, 21*, 193–207.

Kaplan, R. M., & Golomb, B. A. (2001). *Cost-effectiveness of statin medications*. Washington, DC: American Psychological Association.

Kaplan, R. M., & Groessl, E. J. (2002). Applications of costeffectiveness methodologies in behavioral medicine. *Journal of Consulting Clinical Psychology, 70*(3), 482–493.

Kaplan, R. M., & Ries, A. L. (2007). Quality of life: Concept and definition. *COPD: Journal of Chronic Obstructive Pulmonary Disease, 4*(3), 263–271.

Kaplan, R. M., & Stone, A. A. (2013). Bringing the laboratory and clinic to the community: Mobile technologies for health promotion and disease prevention a. *Annual Review of Psychology, 64*, 471–498.

Kaplan, R. M., & Toshima, M. T. (1992). Does a reduced fat diet cause retardation in child growth? *Preventive Medicine, 21*, 33–52.

Kaplan, R. M., Anderson, J. P., Patterson, T. L., McCutchan, J. A., Weinrich, J. D., Heaton, R. K., et al. (1995). Validity of the Quality of Well-Being Scale for persons with human immunodeficiency virus infection. HNRC Group. HIV Neurobehavioral Research Center. *Psychosomatic Medicine, 57*, 138–147.

Kaplan, R. M., Criqui, M. H., Denenberg, J. O., Bergan, J., & Fronek, A. (2003). Quality of life in patients with chronic venous disease: San Diego population study. *Journal of Vascular Surgery, 37*(5), 1047–1053.

Kaplan, R. M., Ganiats, T. G., Sieber, W. J., & Anderson, J. P. (1998). The Quality of Well-Being Scale: Critical similarities and differences with SF-36. *International Journal for Quality in Health Care, 10*(6), 509–520.

Kaplan, R. M., Navarro, A. M., Castro, F. G., Elder, J. P., Mishra, S. I., Hubbell, A., et al. (1996). Increased use of mammography among Hispanic women: Baseline results from the NCI cooperative group on cancer prevention in hispanic communities. *American Journal of Preventive Medicine, 12*(6), 467–471.

Kaplan, R. M., Ries, A. L., Prewitt, L. M., & Eakin, E. (1994). Self-efficacy expectations predict survival for patients with chronic obstructive pulmonary disease. *Health Psychology, 13*, 366–368.

Kaplan, R. M., Tally, S., Hays, R. D., Feeny, D., Ganiats, T. G., Palta, M., & Fryback, D. G. (2011). Five preference-based indexes in cataract and heart failure patients were not equally responsive to change [Comparative Study]. *Journal of Clinical Epidemiology, 64*(5), 497–506.

Kaplan, R., Howard, V., Manely, J., & Howard, G. (2017). Comparison of simple efficient clinical and self-reported predictors of mortality in the REGARDS cohort. *Unpublished manuscript, Stanford University.*

Kar, B. R., Rao, S. L., Chandramouli, B. A., & Thennarasu, K. (2011). Growth patterns of neuropsychological functions in Indian children. *Frontiers in Psychology, 2*, 240. doi: 10.3389/fpsyg.2011.00240.

Karageorgiou, E., Schulz, S., Gollub, R., Andreasen, N., Ho, B. C., Lauriello, J., et al. (2011). Neuropsychological testing and structural magnetic resonance imaging as diagnostic biomarkers early in the course of schizophrenia and related psychoses. *Neuroinformatics, 9*(4), 321–333. doi: 10.1007/s12021-010-9094-6.

Karim, J., Weisz, R., & Ur Rehman, S. (2011). International positive and negative affect schedule short-form (I-PANAS-SF): Testing for factorial invariance across cultures. *Procedia—Social and Behavioral Sciences, 15*, 2016–2022.

Karp, S. A. (Ed.). (1999). *Studies of objective/projective personality tests*. Brook/Andville, MD: Tests, Inc.

Kaszniak, A. W., & Christenson, G. (1994). Differential diagnosis of dementia and depression. In M. Storandt & G. R. VandenBos (Eds.), *Neuropsychological assessment of dementia and depression in older adults: A clinician's guide* (pp. 81–117). Washington, DC: American Psychological Association.

Kataoka, H. C., Latham, G. P., & Whyte, G. (1997). The relative resistance of the situational, patterned behavior, and conventional structured interviews to anchoring effects. *Human Performance, 10*(1), 47–63.

Katigbak, M. S., Church, A. T., Guanzon-Lapena, M. A., Carlota, A. J., & del Pilar, G. H. (2002). Are indigenous personality dimensions culture specific? Philipinne inventories and the five-factor model. *Journal of Personality & Social Psychology, 82*(1), 89–101.

Kaufman, A. S. (1978). Review of Columbia Mental Maturity Scale. In O. K. Buros (Ed.), *The eighth mental measurements yearbook* (Vol. 1). Highland Park, NJ: Gryphon Press.

Kaufman, A. S. (1984). K-ABC and controversy. *Journal of Special Education, 18*(3), 409–444.

Kaufman, A. S. (1990). *Assessment of adolescent and adult intelligence*. Boston: Allyn & Bacon.

Kaufman, A. S., & Kaufman, N. (2004). *KABC-II manual*. Circle Pines, MN: American Guidance Service.

Kaufman, A. S., & Kaufman, N. L. (1983a). *K-ABC administration and scoring manual*. Circle Pines, MN: American Guidance Service.

Kaufman, A. S., & Kaufman, N. L. (1983b). *K-ABC interpretive manual*. Circle Pines, MN: American Guidance Service.

Kaufman, A. S., Kaufman, R. W., & Kaufman, N. L. (1985). The Kaufman Assessment Battery for Children (K-ABC). In C. S. Newmark (Ed.), *Major psychological assessment instruments* (pp. 205–245). Newton, MA: Allyn & Bacon.

Kaufman, A. S., Lichtenberger, E. O., Fletcher-Janzen, E., & Kaufman, N. L. (2005). *Essentials of KABC-II assessment*. Hoboken, NJ: John Wiley & Sons, Inc.

Kaufman, J. C. (2009). Creativity, intelligence, and culture: Connections and possibilities. In P. Meusburger, J. Funke, E. Wunder, & P. Meusburger, (Eds.), *Milieus of creativity* (pp. 155–168). Netherlands:New York: Springer.

Kaufman, S. B., DeYoung, C. G., Reis, D. L., & Gray, J. R. (2011). General intelligence predicts reasoning ability even for evolutionarily familiar content. *Intelligence, 39*(5), 311–322.

Kazdin, A. E. (2004). *Research design in clinical psychology* (4th ed.). Needham Heights, MA: Allyn & Bacon.

Kefyalew, F. (1996). The reality of child participation in research: Experience from a capacity-building program. *Childhood, 3*, 203–213.

Keiser, R. E., & Prather, E. N. (1990). What is the TAT? A review of ten years of research. *Journal of Personality Assessment, 55*, 800–803.

Kelemen, W. L., Winningham, R. G., & Weaver, C. A., III. (2007). Repeated testing sessions and scholastic aptitude in college students' metacognitive accuracy. *European Journal of Cognitive Psychology, 19*(4), 689–717.

Keller, S. D., Ware Jr., J.E., Hatoum, H.T., & Kong, S. X. (1999). The SF-36 Arthritis-Specific Health Index (ASHI): II. Tests of validity in four clinical trials. *Medical Care, 37*(5 Suppl.), MS51–60.

Kelly, H. H. (1967). Attribution theory in social psychology. In D. Levine (Ed.), *Nebraska symposium on motivation* (pp. 192–238). Lincoln: University of Nebraska Press.

Kendler, K. S., Eaves, L. J., Loken, E. K., Pedersen, N. L., Middeldorp, C. M., Reynolds, C., et al. (2011). The impact of environmental experiences on symptoms of anxiety and depression across the life span. *Psychological Science, 22*, 1343–1352. doi: 10.1177/0956797611417255.

Kennedy, R. B. (1994). The employment interview. *Journal of Employment Counseling, 31*, 110–114.

Kent, G. H., & Rosanoff, A. J. (1910). A study of association in insanity. *American Journal of Insanity, 67*, 37–96, 317–390.

Kent, R. N., Kanowitz, J., O'Leary, K. D., & Cheiken, M. (1977). Observer reliability as a function of circumstances of assessment. *Journal of Applied Behavior Analysis, 10*, 317–324.

Kerner, D. N., Patterson, T. L., Grant, I., & Kaplan, R. M. (1998). Validity of the quality of well-being scale for patients with Alzheimer's disease. *Journal of Aging and Health, 10*(1), 44–61.

Kerner, J. (1857). Klexographien (Pt. VI). In R. Pissin (Ed.), *Kerners Werke*. Berlin, Germany: Bong.

Kersten-Alvarez, L. E., Hosman, C. M., Riksen-Walraven, J. M., van Doesum, K. T., Smeekens, S., & Hoefnagels, C. (2012). Early school outcomes for

children of postpartum depressed mothers: Comparison with a community sample. *Child Psychiatry & Human Development, 43*(2), 201–218.

Kessler, R. C. (2003). Epidemiology of women and depression. *Journal of Affective Disorders, 74*(1), 5–13.

Khanna, D., Ahmed, M., Furst, D. E., Ginsburg, S. S., Park, G. S., Hornung, R., et al. (2007). Health values of patients with systemic sclerosis. *Arthritis and Rheumatism, 57*(1), 86–93.

Khanna, D., Maranian, P., Palta, M., Kaplan, R. M., Hays, R. D., Cherepanov, D., & Fryback, D. G. (2011). Health-related quality of life in adults reporting arthritis: analysis from the National health measurement study. [Research Support, N.I. H., Extramural]. *Quality of Life Research, 20*(7), 1131–1140. doi: 10.1007/s11136-011-9849-z.

Khanna, M., Aschenbrand, S. G., & Kendall, P. C. (2007). New frontiers: Computer technology in the treatment of anxious youth. *The Behavior Therapist, 30*(1), 22–25.

Kim, B. H. (2011). Deception and applicant faking: Putting the pieces together. *International Review of Industrial and Organizational Psychology, 26*, 181–217. doi: 10.1002/9781119992592.ch7.

Kim, J.-y., & Lee, J.-h. (2016). A study on the psychological characteristics of Korean medicine students: Focus on the Minnesota multiphasic personality inventory-2, the state-trait anxiety inventory. *Journal of Oriental Neuropsychiatry, 27*(1), 33–40.

Kim, K. (2011). The creativity crisis: The decrease in creative thinking scores on the Torrance Tests of creative thinking. *Creativity Research Journal, 23*(4), 285–295.

Kim, K. H. (2006a). Can we trust creativity tests? A review of the Torrance Tests of Creative Thinking (TTCT). *Creativity Research Journal, 18*(1), 3–14.

Kim, K. H. (2006b). Is creativity unidimensional or multidimensional? Analyses of the Torrance Tests of Creative Thinking. *Creativity Research Journal, 18*(3), 251–259.

Kim, K. H., Cramond, B., & Bandalos, D. L. (2006). The latent structure and measurement invariance of scores on the Torrance Tests of Creative Thinking-figural. *Educational and Psychological Measurement, 66*(3), 459–477.

Kimble, G. A., & Wertheimer, M. (Eds.). (2003). *Portraits of pioneers in psychology* (Vol. 5). Mahwah, NJ: Erlbaum.

Kimura, D. (1999). *Sex and cognition*. Cambridge, MA: MIT Press.

Kirkland, A., & Hansen, B. (2011). "How do i bring diversity?" Race and class in the college admissions essay. *Law & Society Review, 45*(1), 103–138.

Kirkpatrick, E. A. (1900). Individual tests of school children. *Psychological Review, 7*, 274–280.

Kirsch, I. (Ed.). (1999). *How expectancies shape experience*. Washington, DC: American Psychological Association.

Kirton, M. (1976). Adaptors and innovators: A description and measure. *Journal of Applied Psychology, 61*(5), 622–629.

Kirton, M. J. (1978). Wilson and Patterson's Conservatism Scale: A shortened alternative form. *British Journal of Social and Clinical Psychology, 17*, 319–323.

Kirton, M. J. (1987). *Kirton adaption-innovation inventory manual*. Hatfield, UK: Occupational Research Centre.

Kirton, M. J. (1989). *Adaptors and innovators*. London: Routledge.

Kitaeff, J. (2011). *Handbook of police psychology*. New York: Routledge.

Klauer, K. C., Voss, A., & Stahl, C. (2011). *Cognitive methods in social psychology*. New York: Guilford Publications, Inc.

Klausen, O., Moller, P., Holmeford, A., Reiseaeeter, S., & Asbjornsen, A. (2000). Lasting effects of orbitis media with effusion on language skills and listening performance. *Acta Oto-Laryngoloca, 120*(Suppl. 543), 73–76.

Klein, A. (2015). ESEA reauthorization: The Every Student Succeeds Act explained. *Education Week*.

Klein, S. P. (2002). Law school admissions, LSATs, and the bar. *Academic Questions, 15*(1), 33–39.

Klimstra, T. A., Crocetti, E., Hale, W. W. III, Fermani, A., & Meeus, W. H. J. (2011). Big five personality dimensions in Italian and Dutch adolescents: A cross-cultural comparison of mean-levels, sex differences, and associations with internalizing symptoms. *Journal of Research in Personality, 45*(3), 285–296. ISSN 0092-6566; doi: 10.1016/j.jrp.2011.03.002. Retrieved from http://www.sciencedirect.com/science/article/pii/S0092656611000365.

Kline, P. (2015a). *A handbook of test construction (Psychology revivals): Introduction to psychometric design*. New York: Routledge.

Kline, P. (2015b). *Personality (Psychology revivals): Measurement and theory*. New York: Routledge.

Klopfer, B., & Davidson, H. H. (1944). Form level rating: A preliminary proposal for appraising mode and level of thinking as expressed in Rorschach records. *Rorschach Research Exchange, 8*, 164–177.

Klopfer, B., & Davidson, H. H. (1962). *The Rorschach technique: An introductory manual.* Orlando: Harcourt Brace.

Klopfer, B., & Kelley, D. (1942). *The Rorschach technique.* Yonkers, NY: World Book.

Klopfer, B., & Kelly, D. M. (1946). *The Rorschach technique* (2nd ed.). Yonkerson-Hudson, NY: World Book.

Knafl, K., Deatrick, J., Gallo, A., Holcombe, G., Bakitas, M., Dixon, J., et al. (2007). The analysis and interpretation of cognitive interviews for instrument development. *Research in Nursing & Health, 30*(2), 224–234.

Knox, H. A. (1914). A scale based on the work at Ellis Island for estimating mental defect. *Journal of the American Medical Association, 62*, 741–747.

Kobasa, S. C. (1979). Stressful life events, personality and health: An inquiry into hardiness. *Journal of Personality and Social Psychology, 37*, 1–11.

Kobrin, J. L., Patterson, B. F., Shaw, E. J., Mattern, K. D., & Barbuti, S. M. (2008). Validity of the SAT® for predicting first-year college grade point average. Research Report No. 2008-5. *College Board.*

Kocsis, R. N. (2011). The structured interview of reported symptoms 2nd Edition (SIRS-2): The new benchmark towards the assessment of malingering. *Journal of Forensic Psychology Practice, 11*(1), 73–81.

Koedel, C., & Betts, J. R. (2011). Does student sorting invalidate value-added models of teacher effectiveness? An extended analysis of the Rothstein Critique. *Education Finance and Policy, 6*(1), 18–42.

Kohli, M. A., Salyakina, D., Pfennig, A., Lucae, S., Horstmann, S., Menke, A., et al. (2010). Association of genetic variants in the neurotrophic receptor–encoding gene NTRK2 and a lifetime history of suicide attempts in depressed patients. *Archives of General Psychiatry, 67*(4), 348–359.

Kohnen, S., & Nickels, L. (2010). Teaching children with developmental spelling difficulties in a one-on-one context. *Australian Academic Press, 34*(1), 36–60. doi: 10.1375/ajse. 34.1.36.

Kohs, S. C. (1923). *Intelligence measurement: A psychological and statistical study based upon the blockdesign tests.* New York: Macmillan.

Konradt, U., Syperek, S., & Hertel, G. (2011). Testing on the internet: Faking in a web-based self-administered personality measure. *Journal of Business and Media Psychology, 2*(1), 1–10. Retrieved from www.journal-bmp.de.

Koppitz, E. M. (1964). *The Bender Gestalt Test for young children.* New York: Grune & Stratton.

Korbin, J., Sinharay, S., et al. (2011). An investigation of the fit of linear regression models to data from the SAT validity study. *Technical Report Series,* Educational Testing Service. 2011 (1)

Kosinski, M., Keller, S. D., Ware Jr., J. E., Hatoum, H. T., & Kong, S. X. (1999). The SF-36 Health survey as a generic outcome measure in clinical trials of patients with osteoarthritis and rheumatoid arthritis: Relative validity of scales in relation to clinical measures of arthritis severity. *Medical Care, 37*(5 Suppl.), MS23–MS39.

Kossowska, M. (2002). Relationship between cognitive strategies, intelligence, and personality. *Polish Psychological Bulletin, 33*(2), 47–54.

Kossowsky, J., Wilhelm, F. H., Roth, W. T., & Schneider, S. (2011). Separation anxiety disorder in children: Disorder-specific responses to experimental separation from the mother. *Journal of Child Psychology and Psychiatry.* doi: 10.1111/j.1469-7610.2011.02465.x.

Kounti, F., Tsolaki, M., & Kiosseoglou, G. (2006). Functional Cognitive Assessment Scale (FUCAS): A new scale to assess executive cognitive function in daily life activities in patients with dementia and mild cognitive impairment. *Human Psychopharmacology: Clinical and Experimental, 21*(5), 305–311.

Kraepelin, E. (1912). *Lehrbuch der psychiatric.* Leipzig: Barth.

Kraiger, K., Hakel, M. D., & Cornelius, E. T., III. (1984). Exploring fantasies of TAT reliability. *Journal of Personality Assessments, 48*, 365–370.

Krasa, N. (2007). Is the Woodcock-Johnson III a test for all seasons?: Ceiling and item gradient considerations in its use with older students. *Journal of Psychoeducational Assessment, 25*(1), 3–16.

Krause, S., Back, M., Egloff, B., & Schmukle, S. (2014). Implicit interpersonal attraction in small groups: Automatically activated evaluations predict actual behavior toward social partners. *Social Psychological and Personality Science, 5*(6), 671–679.

Kreiner, D. S., & Ryan, J. J. (2001). Memory and motor skill components of the WAIS-III Digit Symbol-Coding Subtest. *Clinical Neuro-psychologist, 15*(1), 109–113.

Kreutzer, J. S., DeLuca, J., Caplan, B., & SpringerLink (Online service). (2011). *Encyclopedia of clinical neuropsychology.* Retrieved from http://dx.doi.org/10.1007/978-0-387-79948-3.

Krikorian, R., & Bartok, J. A. (1998). Developmental data for the Porteus Maze Test. *Clinical Neuropsychologist, 12*, 305–310.

Krishnamurthy, R., Archer, R. P., & Groth-Marnat, G. (2011). The Rorschach and performance-based assessment. In T. M. Harwood, L. E. Beutler, G. Groth-Marnat, & A. L. Austin (Eds.), *Integrative assessment of adult personality* (3rd ed., pp. 276–328, 280). New York: Guilford Press.

Kroese, J. M. (2003). Cognitive abilities and assessment of children with language impairment. In C. R. Reynold & R. W. Kamphaus (Eds.), *Handbook of psychological and educational assessment of children* (2nd ed., pp. 615–627). New York: Guilford Press.

Kröhne, U., & Martens, T. (2011). 11 computer-based competence tests in the National Educational Panel Study: The challenge of mode effects. *Zeitschrift für Erziehungswissenschaft, 14*, 169–186. doi: 10.1007/s11618-011-0185-4.

Kuder, G. F. (1979). *Manual, Kuder occupational interest survey, 1979 revision.* Chicago: Science Research Associates.

Kuder, G. F., & Richardson, M. W. (1937). The theory of the estimation of reliability. *Psychometrika, 2*, 151–160.

Kugler, L. M. (2007). *Methadone maintenance therapy and its effects on executive functioning.* US: ProQuest Information & Learning.

Kugu, N., Akyuez, G. Dogan, O., Ersan, E., & Izgic, F. (2002). Prevalence of eating disorders in a university population and the investigation of its relation with self-esteem, family functions, childhood abuse and neglect. *Psikiyatri Psikoloji Psikofarmakoloji Dergisi, 10*(3), 255–266.

Kuh, G. D., & Hu, S. (1999). Unraveling the complexity of the increase in college grades from the mid-1980s to the mid-1990s. *Educational Evaluation and Policy Analysis, 21*(3), 297–320.

Kuncel, N. R., & Hezlett, S. A. (2007). Assessment: Standardized tests predict graduate students' success. *Science, 315*(5815), 1080–1081.

Kuncel, N. R., Hezlett, S. A., & Ones, D. S. (2001). A comprehensive meta-analysis of the predictive validity of the graduate record examination: Implications for graduate student selection and performance. *Psychological Bulletin, 127*(1), 162–181.

Kuncel, N. R., Wee, S., Serafin, L., & Hezlett, S. A. (2010). The validity of the graduate record examination for master's and doctoral programs: A meta-analytic investigation. *Educational and Psychological Measurement, 70*(2), 340–352. doi: 10.1177/0013164409344508.

Kushnir, J., Gothelf, D., & Sadeh, A. (2015). Assessing fears of preschool children with nighttime fears by a parent version of the fear survey schedule for preschool children. *The Israel Journal of Psychiatry and Related Sciences, 52*(1), 61.

Kwon, P. (2002). Comment on "Effects of acculturation on the MMPI-2 scores of Asian American students". *Journal of Personality Assessment, 78*(1), 187–189.

Laborde, S., Guillen, F., Dosseville, F., & Allen, M. (2015). Chronotype, sport participation, and positive personality-trait-like individual differences. *Chronobiology International, 32*(7), 942–951.

Lachman, R., Lachman, J. L., & Butterfield, E. C. (2015). *Cognitive psychology and information processing: An introduction.* New York: Psychology Press.

Ladd, B. O., Tomlinson, K., Myers, M. G., & Anderson, K. G. (2016). Feasibility and reliability of a coding system to capture in-session group behavior in adolescents. *Prevention Science, 17*(1), 93–101.

Lahikainen, A. R., Kraav, I., Kirmanen, T., & Taimalu, M. (2006). Child-parent agreement in the assessment of young children's fears: A comparative perspective. *Journal of Cross-Cultural Psychology, 37*(1), 100–119.

Lai, T. J., Guo, Y. I., Guo, N. W., & Hsu, C. C. (2001). Effects of prenatal exposure to polychlorinated biphenyls on cognitive development in children: A longitudinal study in Taiwan. *British Journal of Psychiatry, 178*(40), s49–s52.

Lakin, J. M., & Lai, E. R. (2011). Multigroup generalizability analysis of verbal, quantitative, and nonverbal ability tests for culturally and linguistically diverse students. *Educational and Psychological Measurement.*

Retrieved from http://epm.sagepub.com/content/early/2011/07/19/0013164411408074. abstract?rss=1. doi: 10.1177/0013164411408074.

Lamb, S. (2011). Pathways to school completion: An international comparison. In *School Dropout and Completion* (Part 1, pp. 21–73). Retrieved from http://www.springerlink.com/content/1693211238729870/.

Lamont, R. A., Swift, H. J., & Abrams, D. (2015). A review and meta-analysis of age-based stereotype threat: Negative stereotypes, not facts, do the damage. *Psychology and Aging, 30*(1), 180.

Lamp, R. E., & Krohn, E. J. (2001). A longitudinal predictive validity investigation of the SB: FE and KABC with at-risk children. *Journal of Psychoeducational Assessment, 19*(4), 334–349.

Landis, C. (1936). Questionnaires and the study of personality. *Journal of Nervous and Mental Disease, 83*, 125–134.

Landis, C., Zubin, J., & Katz, S. E. (1935). Empirical evaluation of three personality adjustment inventories. *Journal of Educational Psychology, 26*, 321–330.

Landy, F. J. (2003). *Validity generalization: Then and now.* Mahwah, NJ: Erlbaum.

Landy, F. J., & Shankster, L. J. (1994). Personnel selection and placement. *Annual Review of Psychology, 45*, 261–296.

Landy, F. J., Farr, J. L., & Jacobs, R. (1982). Utility concepts in performance measurement. *Organizational Behavior and Human Performance, 30*, 15–40.

Landy, F. J., Vance, R. J., Barnes-Farrell, J. L., & Steele, J. W. (1980). Statistical control of halo error in performance ratings. *Journal of Applied Psychology, 65*, 501–506.

Landy, F., & Conte, J. (2006). *Work in the 21st century: An introduction to industrial and organizational psychology.* New York: Blackwell.

Lane, S., Raymond, M. R., & Haladyna, T. M. (2015). *Handbook of test development.* New York: Routledge.

Langdon, D. W., Rosenblatt, N., & Mellanby, J. H. (1998). Discrepantly poor verbal skills in poor readers: A failure of learning or ability? *British Journal of Psychology, 89*, 177–190.

Langenbucher, J. W., Labouvie, E., Martin, C. S., Sanjuan, P. M., Bavly, L., Kirisci, L., et al. (2004). An application of item response theory analysis to alcohol, cannabis, and cocaine criteria in DSM-IV. *Journal of Abnormal Psychology, 113*(1), 72–80.

Langer, N., Pedroni, A., Gianotti, L. R., Hänggi, J., Knoch, D., & Jäncke, L.

(2011). Functional brain network efficiency predicts intelligence. *Human Brain Mapping.* doi: 10.1002/hbm.21297. Retrieved from http://onlinelibrary.wiley.com/doi/10.1002/hbm.21297/full.

Lanyon, B. P., & Lanyon, R. I. (1980). *Incomplete sSentences task: Manual.* Chicago: Stoelting.

Larrabee, L. L., & Kleinsaser, L. D. (1967). *The effect of experimenter bias on WISC performance.* Unpublished manuscript.

Larson, L. (2011). Testing requirements in particular. In M. Bender (Ed.), *Employment discrimination.* Albany: LexusNexus.

Latham, G. P., & Whyte, G. (1994). The futility of utility analysis. *Personnel Psychology, 47*(1), 31–46.

Laub, D. (2002). Testimonials in the treatment of genocidal trauma. *Journal of Applied Psychoanalytic Studies, 4*(1), 63–87.

Law School Admissions Council. (2011). *Diversity in law school: Racial/ethnic minority applicants.* Retrieved from http://www.lsac.org/.

Lawlor, S., Richman, S., & Richman, C. L. (1997). The validity of using the SAT as a criterion for black and white students' admission to college. *College Student Journal, 31*, 507–515.

Lawrence, I., et al. (2002). A Historical Perspective on the SAT® 1926-2001. Research Report No. 2002-7. *College Entrance Examination Board.*

Lazarus, R. S., & Folkman, S. (1984). *Stress, appraisal, and coping.* New York: Springer-Verlag.

Lazarus, R. S., Lazarus, B. N., & ebrary Inc. (2006). *Coping with aging.* Retrieved from http://site.ebrary.com/lib/yale/Doc?id=10160516. Online book.

Leavitt, W. M., Lombard, J. R., & Morris, J. C. (2011). Examining admission factors in an MPA program. *Journal of Public Affairs Education, 17*(3), 447–460.

Lee, J. (2014). Conducting cognitive interviews in cross-national settings. *Assessment, 21*(2), 227–240.

Lee, J. M., Ku, J. H., Jang, D. P., Kim, D. H., Choi, Y. H., Kim, I. Y., et al. (2002). Virtual reality system for treatment of the fear of public speaking using image-based rendering and moving pictures. *Cyberpsychology and Behavior, 5*(3), 191–195.

Leekham, S. R., Libby, S. J., Wing, L., Gould, J., & Taylor, C. (2002). The diagnostic interview for social and communication disorders: Algorithms for ICD-10 childhood autism and Wing and Gould autistic spectrum disorder. *Journal of Child Psychology and Psychiatry, 43*(3), 327–342.

Leibovitch, A. (2015). Relative judgments. *Available at SSRN 2622585.*

Leichsenring, F. (1990). Discriminating borderline from neurotic patients: A study with the Holtzman Inkblot Technique. *Psychopathology, 23,* 21–26.

Leichsenring, F. (1991). Primary process thinking, primitive defensive operations and object relations in borderline and neurotic patients. *Psychopathology, 24,* 39–44.

Leman, N. (1995, September). The great sorting. *Atlantic Monthly,* pp. 84–100.

Lemke, S., & Moos, R. H. (1986). Quality of residential settings of elderly adults. *Journal of Gerontology, 41,* 268–276.

Leshem, R., & Glicksohn, J. (2007). The construct of impulsivity revisited. *Personality and Individual Differences, 43*(4), 681–691.

Leslie, L. K., Gordon, J. N., Ganger, W., & Gist, K. (2002). Developmental delay in young children in child welfare by initial placement type. *Infant Mental Health Journal, 23*(5), 496–516.

Lesser, G. S., Fifer, G., & Clark, D. H. (1965). Mental abilities of children from different social-class and cultural groups. *Monographs of the Society for Research in Child Development, 30*(4, Serial No. 102), 1–115.

Lessler, J. T., Caspar, R. A., Penne, M. A., & Barker, P. R. (2000). Developing computer assisted interviewing (CAI) for the National household survey on drug abuse. *Journal of Drug Issues, 30*(1), 9–34.

Letendre, S., Marquie-Beck, J., Capparelli, E., Best, B., Clifford, D., Collier, A. C., et al. (2008). Validation of the CNS penetration-effectiveness rank for quantifying antiretroviral penetration into the central nervous system. *Archives of Neurology, 65*(1), 65–70.

Letukas, L. (2015). Nine facts about the SAT that might surprise you. Statistical Report. *College Board.*

Leung, S. F., French, P., Chui, C., & Arthur, D. (2007). Computerized mental health assessment in integrative health clinics: A cross-sectional study using structured interview. *International Journal of Mental Health Nursing, 16*(6), 441–446.

Levashina, J., Hartwell, C., Morgeson, F., & Campion, M. (2014). The structured employment interview: Narrative and quantitative review of the research

literature. *Personnel Psychology, 67*(1), 241–293.

Levenson, H., Olkin, R., Herzoff, N., & DeLancy, M. (1986). MMPI evaluation of erectile dysfunction: Failure of organic vs. psychogenic decision rules. *Journal of Clinical Psychology, 42,* 752–754.

Leventhal, A. M., Gelernter, J., Oslin, D., Anton, R. F., Farrer, L. A., & Kranzler, H. R. (2011). Agitated depression in substance dependence. *Drug and Alcohol Dependence, 116*(1–3), 163–169. doi: 10.1016/j.drugalcdep.2010.12.012.

Levine, D. W., Lewis, M. A., Bowen, D. J., Kripke, D. F., Kaplan, R. M., Naughton, M. J., et al. (2003). *Reliability and validity of Women's Health Initiative Insomnia Rating Scale.* Washington, DC: American Psychological Association.

Levinson, W., Lesser, C. S., & Epstein, R. M. (2010). Developing physician communication skills for patient-centered care. *Health Affairs, 29*(7), 1310–1318. doi: 10.1377/hlthaff.2009.0450.

Levitas, A. S., Hurley, A. D., & Pary, R. (2002). The mental status examination in patients with mental retardation and developmental disabilities. *Mental Health Aspects of Developmental Disabilities, 4*(1), 2–16.

Lewandowski, D. G., & Saccuzzo, D. P. (1976). The decline of psychological testing: Have traditional procedures been fairly evaluated? *Professional Psychology, 7,* 177–184.

Lewin, T. (2009). A new look for graduate entrance test. *New York Times.* Retrieved from http://www.nytimes.com/2009/12/06/education/06gre.html.

Lewinsohn, P. N., & Teri, L. (1982). Selection of depressed and nondepressed subjects on the basis of self-report data. *Journal of Consulting and Clinical Psychology, 50,* 590–591.

Lezak, M. D. (1983). *Neuropsychological assessment* (2nd ed.). New York: Oxford University Press.

Lezak, M. D. (1995). *Neuropsychological assessment* (3rd ed.). New York: Oxford University Press.

Li, F., Wang, E., & Zhang, F. (2002). The multitrait-multirater approach to analyzing rating biases. *Acta Psychologica Sinica, 34*(1), 98–96.

Lighthouse, A. G. (2006). *The relationship between SAT scores and grade point averages among post-secondary students with disabilities.* US: ProQuest Information & Learning.

Likert, R. (1932). A technique for the measurement of attitudes. *Archives of Psychology, 22*(140), 55.

Lilienfeld, S. O., Alliger, G., & Mitchell, K. (1995). Why integrity testing remains controversial. *American Psychologist, 50*(6), 457–458.

Lilienfeld, S. O., Garb, H. N., & Wood, J. M. (2011). Unresolved questions concerning the effectiveness of psychological assessment as a therapeutic intervention: Comment on Poston and Hanson (2010). *Psychological Assessment, 23*(4), 1047–1055. doi: 10.1037/a0025177.

Lilienfeld, S. O., Wood, J. M., & Garb, H. N. (2000). The scientific status of projective techniques. *Psychological Science in the Public Interest, 1,* 27–66.

Lin, K., Taylor, M. J., Heaton, R., Franklin, D., Jernigan, T., Fennema-Notestine, C., et al. (2011). Effects of traumatic brain injury on cognitive functioning and cerebral metabolites in HIV-infected individuals. [Research Support, N.I.H., Extramural]. *Journal of Clinical and Experimental Neuropsychology, 33*(3), 326–334. doi: 10.1080/13803395.2010.518140.

Lin, W.-Y., Zhang, X., Song, H., & Omori, K. (2016). Health information seeking in the Web 2.0 age: Trust in social media, uncertainty reduction, and self-disclosure. *Computers in Human Behavior, 56,* 289–294.

Lindgren, T., Carlsson, A. M., & Lundbäck, E. (2007). No agreement between the Rorschach and self-assessed personality traits derived from the comprehensive system. *Scandinavian Journal of Psychology, 48*(5), 399–408.

Lindsey, M. L. (1998). Culturally competent assessment of African American clients. *Journal of Personality Assessment, 70*(1), 43–53.

Lindstrom, J. H., & Gregg, N. (2007). The role of extended time on the SAT® for students with learning disabilities and/or attention-deficit/hyperactivity disorder. *Learning Disabilities Research & Practice, 22*(2), 85–95.

Lindzey, G. (1952). The Thematic Apperception Test: Interpretive assumptions and related empirical evidence. *Psychological Bulletin, 49,* 1–25.

Linehan, M. M. (2016). Behavior therapy: Where we were, where we are and where we need to be going. *Cognitive and Behavioral Practice.* In press, published online ahead of print, http://dx.doi.org/10.1016/j.cbpra.2015.12.002.

Ling, J., & Cavers, M. (2015). Student-weighted multiple choice tests. Unpublished, available at http://prism.ucalgary.ca/handle/1880/50553

Linn, R. L. (1994a). *Criterion-referenced measurement: A valuable perspective clouded by surplus meaning*. Annual Meeting of the American Educational Research Association: Criterion-referenced measurement: A 30-year retrospective (1993, Atlanta, Georgia). *Educational Measurement: Issues and Practice, 13*, 12–14.

Linn, R. L. (1994b). Fair test use: Research and policy. In M. G. Rumsey, C. B. Walker, & J. H. Harris (Eds.), *Personnel selection and classification* (pp. 363–375). Hillsdale, NJ: Erlbaum.

Linn, R. L., & Burton, E. (1994). Performance-based assessment: Implications of task specificity. *Educational Measurement: Issues and Practice, 13*, 15.

Lis, A., Parolin, L., Calvo, V., Zennaro, A., & Meyer, G. (2007). The impact of administration and inquiry on Rorschach comprehensive system protocols in a national reference sample. *Journal of Personality Assessment, 89*(1), 193–200.

Litcher-Kelly, L., Martino, S. A., Broderick, J. E., & Stone, A. A. (2007). A systematic review of measures used to assess chronic musculoskeletal pain in clinical and randomized controlled clinical trials. *Journal of Pain, 8*(12), 906–913.

Little, K. B., & Schneidman, E. S. (1959). Congruencies among interpretations of psychological test and anamnestic data. *Psychological Monographs, 73*(6).

Liu, O., Bridgeman, B., Gu, L., Xu, J., & Kong, N. (2015). Investigation of response changes in the gre revised general test. *Educational and Psychological Measurement, 75*(6), 1002–1020.

Llorente, A., Brouwers, P., Charurat, M., Magder, L., Malee, K., Mellins, C., et al. (2003). Early neurodevelopmental markers predictive of mortality in infants infected with HIV-1. *Developmental Medicine and Child Neurology, 45*(2), 76–84.

Lobbestael, J., Leurgans, M., & Arntz, A. (2010). Inter-rater reliability of the Structured Clinical Interview for DSM-IV Axis I Disorders (SCID I) and Axis II Disorders (SCID II). *Clinical Psychological Psychotherapy, 18*, 75–79.

Lochman, J. E. (1995). Conduct problems prevention research group: Screening of child behavior problems for prevention programs at school entry [Special Section: Prediction and prevention of child and adolescent antisocial behavior]. *Journal of Consulting and Clinical Psychology, 63*, 549–559.

Locke, S. D., & Gilbert, B. O. (1995). Method of psychological assessment, self-disclosure, and experiential differences: A study of computer, questionnaire, and interview assessment formats. *Journal of Social Behavior and Personality, 10*, 255–263.

Locke, S., McGrew, K. S., & Ford, L. (2011). A multiple group confirmatory factor analysis of the structural invariance of the Cattell-Horn-Carroll theory of cognitive abilities across matched Canadian and U.S. samples. *WMF Press Bulletin, No. 1*. Retrieved from http://woodcockmunoz-foundation.org/press/pressbulletins.html.

Lockwood, C. A., Mansoor, Y., Homer-Smith, E., & Moses Jr., J. A. (2011). Factor structure of the Benton Visual Retention Tests: Dimensionalization of the Benton Visual Retention Test, Benton Visual Retention Test—Multiple choice, and the Visual Form Discrimination Test. *The Clinical Neuropsychologist, 25*(1), 90–107.

Loevinger, J. (1998). *Technical foundations for measuring ego development: The Washington University Sentence Completion Test*. Mahwah, NJ: Erlbaum.

Loffredo, D. A., & Opt, S. K. (1998). Relating the MBTI to communication apprehension, receiver apprehension, and argumentativeness. *Journal of Psychological Type, 47*, 21–27.

Lohman, D. F. (2012). *Cognitive abilities test, form 7: Research and development guide*. Rolling Meadows, IL: Riverside Publishing.

Long, P. A., & Anthony, J. J. (1974). The measurement of retardation by a culture-specific test. *Psychology in the Schools, 11*, 310–312.

Longe, O., Maratos, F. A., Gilbert, P., Evans, G., Volker, F., Rockliff, H., et al. (2010). Having a word with yourself: Neural correlates of self-criticism and self-reassurance. *NeuroImage, 49*(2), 1849–1856. doi: 10.1016/j.neuroimage.2009.09.019.

Lopatovska, I., & Arapakis, I. (2011). Theories, methods and current research on emotions in library and information science, information retrieval and human–computer interaction. *Information Processing & Management, 47*(4), 575–592. doi: 10.1016/j.ipm.2010.09.001.

Lord, E. (1950). Experimentally induced variations in Rorschach performance. *Psychological Monographs, 64*(10, Whole No. 316), 1–34.

Lorenzo-Seva, U. (2003). A factor simplicity index. *Psychometrica, 68*(1), 49–60.

Lorian, C. N., Titov, N., & Grisham, J. R. (2011). Changes in risk-taking over the course of an Internet-delivered cognitive behavioral therapy treatment for generalized anxiety disorder. *Journal of Anxiety Disorders*. Retrieved from http://www.sciencedirect.com/science/article/pii/S0887618511001678.

Lounsbury, J. W., Sundstrom, E. D., Gibson, L. W., Loveland, J. M., & Drost, A. W. (2016). Core personality traits of managers. *Journal of Managerial Psychology, 31*(2), 434–450.

Löve, J., Moore, C., & Hensing, G. (2011). Validation of the Swedish translation of the general self-efficacy scale. *Quality of Life Research*, 1–5. doi: 10.1007/s11136-011-0030-5. Retrieved from http://www.springerlink.com/content/e076624407873776/.

Lowman, R. L. (1991). *The clinical practice of career assessment*. Washington, DC: American Psychological Association.

Lowndes, C., Jayachandran, A., Banandur, P., Ramesh, B., Washington, R., Sangameshwar, B., et al. (2011). Polling booth surveys: A novel approach for reducing social desirability bias in HIV-related behavioural surveys in resource-poor settings. *AIDS and Behavior*, 1–9. doi: 10.1007/s10461-011-0004-1.

Loy, D. L. (1959). The validity of the Taulbee-Sisson MMPI Scale pairs in female psychiatric groups. *Journal of Clinical Psychology, 15*, 306–307.

Lozano, L. M., García-Cueto, E., et al. (2008). Effect of the number of response categories on the reliability and validity of rating scales. *Methodology: European Journal of Research Methods for the Behavioral and Social Sciences, 4*(2), 73–79.

Lubin, B., & Sands, E. W. (1992). Bibliography of the psychometric properties of the Bender Visual-Motor Gestalt Test: 1970–1991. *Perceptual and Motor Skills, 75*(2), 385–386.

Lubin, B., Larsen, R., & Matarazzo, J. (1984). Patterns of psychological test usage in the United States: 1935–1982. *American Psychologist, 39*, 451–454.

Lubin, B., Wallis, H. R., & Paine, C. (1971). Patterns of psychological test usage in the United States: 1935–1969. *Professional Psychology, 2*, 70–74.

Lucas, J. L., Wanberg, C. R., & Zytowski, D. G. (1997). Development of a career Task Self-Efficacy Scale: The Kuder Task Self-Efficacy Scale. *Journal of Vocational Behavior, 50*(3), 432–459.

Lucas, R. E., Diener, E., & Larsen, R. J. (2003). Measuring positive emotions. In S. J. Lopez & C. R. Snyder (Eds.), *Positive psychological assessment: A handbook of models and measures* (pp. 201–218). Washington, DC: American Psychological Association.

Lui, Z., Chen, X., Qin, S., Xue, J., Hao, W., Lu, X., et al. (2002). Risk factors for female criminals. *Chinese Mental Health Journal, 16*(2), 106–108.

Lundqvist, C., & Sabel, K. G. (2000). Brief report: The Brazelton Neonatal Assessment Scale detects differences among newborn infants of optimal health. *Journal of Pediatric Psychology, 25*(8), 577–582.

Lundqvist-Persson, C., Lau, G., Nordin, P., Bona, E., & Sabel, K. G. (2011, November 29). Preterm infants' early developmental status is associated with later developmental outcome. doi: 10.1111/j.1651-2227.2011.02526.x.

Luo, D., Thompson, L. A., & Detterman, D. K. (2003). The causal factor underlying the correlation between psychometric *g* and scholastic performance. *Intelligence, 31*(1), 67–83.

Luppino, M., & Sander, R. (2015). College major peer effects and attrition from the sciences. *IZA Journal of Labor Economics, 4*(1), 1.

Luria, A. R. (1966). *Higher cortical functions in man.* New York: Basic Books.

Luria, A. R. (1973). *The working brain.* New York: Basic Books.

Lysaker, P. H., Clements, C. A., Wright, D. E., Evans, J., & Marks, K. A. (2001). Neurocognitive correlates of helplessness, hopelessness, and well-being in schizophrenia. *Journal of Nervous and Mental Disease, 189*(7), 457–462.

Mabon, H. (1998). Utility aspects of personality and performance. *Human Performance, 11,* 289–304.

Mabry, L. (1995). Review of the Wide Range Achievement Test–3. In O. Buros (Ed.), *The 12th mental measurements yearbook* (pp. 1108–1110). Lincoln, NE: Buros Institute of Mental Measurements.

Macan, T. (2009). The employment interview: A review of current studies and directions for future research. *Human Resource Management Review, 19*(3), 201–218.

Machado, P., Beutler, L. E., Harwood, T. M., Mohr, D., & Lenore, S. (2011). The integrative clinical interview. In T. Harwood, L. Beutler, G. Groth-Marnat, A. Austin & P. Machado (Eds.), *Integrative assessment of adult personality* (pp. 80–114). New York: Guilford Press.

Machover, K. (1949). *Personality projection in the drawings of the human figure: A method of personality investigation.* Springfield, IL: Thomas.

Mack, L. J., & Rybarczyk, B. D. (2011). Behavioral treatment of insomnia: A proposal for a stepped-care approach to promote public health. *Nature and Science of Sleep, 3,* 87–99. Retrieved from http://dx.doi.org/10.2147/NSS.S12975.

Madden, M., & Lenhart, A. (2013). *Online dating.* Pew Internet and American Life Project. March 5.

Madrid, R., Kalpakjian, C., Hanks, R., & Rapport, L. (2015). Using cognitive interviews for women's health research in TBI. *Archives of Physical Medicine and Rehabilitation, 96*(10), e24.

Madsen, B., & SpringerLink (online service). (2011). *Statistics for nonstatisticians.* Retrieved from http://dx.doi.org/10.1007/978-3-642-17656-2.

Magalette, P. R., & Oliver, J. M. (1999). The hope construct, will, and ways: Their relations with self-efficacy, optimism, and general well-being. *Journal of Clinical Psychology, 55*(5), 539–551.

Maj, M., Gaebel, W., Lopez-Ibor, J. J., & Sartorius, N. (Eds.). (2002). *Psychiatric diagnosis and classification.* New York: Wiley.

Majnemer, A., & Mazer, B. (1998). Neurologic evaluation of the newborn infant: Definition and psychometric properties. *Developmental Medicine and Child Neurology, 40,* 708–715.

Makkonen, I., Riikonen, R., Kuikka. J. T., Kokki, H., Bressler, J. P., Marshall, C., et al. (2011). Brain derived neurotrophic factor and serotonin transporter binding as markers of clinical response to fluoxetine therapy in children with autism. *Journal of Pediatric Neurology, 9*(1), 1–8. doi: 10.3233/JPN-2010-0446.

Malda, M., van de Vijver, F., Srinivasan, K., Transler, C., & Sukumaar, P. (2010). Traveling with cognitive tests: Testing the validity of a KABC-II adaptation in India. *Assessment, 17,* 107–115.

Malgady, R. G., Constantino, G., & Rogler, L. H. (1984). Development of a Thematic Apperception Test (TEMAS) for urban hispanic children. *Journal of Consulting and Clinical Psychology, 52*(6), 986–996.

Malinchoc, M., Oxford, K. P., Colligan, R. C., & Morse, R. M. (1994). The Common Alcohol Logistic–Revised Scale (CAL-R): A revised Alcoholism Scale for the MMPI and MMPI-2. *Journal of Clinical Psychology, 50*(3), 436–445.

Maltby, J., Wood, A. M., Day, L., & Pinto, D. (2011). The position of authenticity within extant models of personality. *Personality and Individual Differences.* ISSN 0191-8869; doi: 10.1016/j.paid.2011.10.014. Retrieved from http://www.sciencedirect.com/science/article/pii/S0191886911004697.

Maltby, N., Kirsch, I., Mayers, M., & Allen, G. J. (2002). Virtual reality exposure therapy for the treatment of fear of flying: A controlled investigation. *Journal of Consulting & Clinical Psychology, 70*(5), 1112–1118.

Mammen, P., Russell, P., Nair, M., Russell, S., Kishore, C., & Shankar, S. (2013). Development and psychometric validation of the Brief Intellectual Disability Scale for use in low-health resource, high-burden countries. *Journal of Clinical Epidemiology, 66*(1), 30–35.

Mandes, E., & Gessner, T. (1988). Differential effects on verbal performance achievement levels on the WAIS-R as a function of progressive error rate on the Memory for Designs Test (MFD). *Journal of Clinical Psychology, 44,* 795–798.

Mangiante, E. M. S. (2011). Teachers matter: Measures of teacher effectiveness in low-income minority schools. *Educational Assessment Evaluation and Accountability, 23*(1), 41–63.

Manners, J., & Derkin, K. (2001). A critical review of the validity of ego development theory and its measurement. *Journal of Personality Assessment, 77,* 541–567.

Mannheim, K. (1936). *Ideology and utopia.* London: Kegan, Paul, Trench, Trubner.

Mao, T. (2011). Study on word association knowledge and reading ability. *Applied Mechanics and Materials, 109,* 699–702. doi: 10.4028/www.scientific.net/AMM.109.699.

Marceau, E. M., Lunn, J., Berry, J., Kelly, P. J., & Solowij, N. (2016). The Montreal Cognitive Assessment (MoCA) is sensitive to head injury and cognitive impairment in a residential alcohol and other drug therapeutic community. *Journal of Substance Abuse Treatment, 66,* 30–36.

Marchall et al. v. Georgia. (1985). U.S. district court for the southern district of Georgia, CV482-233 (June 28, 1984), *aff'd*, 11th cir no 848771 (Oct. 29, 1985).

Marchand, Y., Lefebvre, C. D., & Connolly, J. F. (2006). Correlating digit span performance and event-related potentials to assess working memory. *International Journal of Psychophysiology*, 62(2), 280–289.

Marchman, V. A., Saccuman, C., & Wulfeck, B. (2004). Productive use of the English past tense in children with focal brain injury and specific language impairment. *Brain and Language*, 88, 202–214.

Marcus, S., Lopez, J. F., McDonough, S., MacKenzie, M. J., Flynn, H., Neal Jr., C. R., et al. (2011). Depressive symptoms during pregnancy: Impact on neuroendocrine and neonatal outcomes. *Infant Behavior and Development*, 34(1), 26–34. ISSN 0163-6383; 10.1016/j. infbeh.2010.07.002.

Mark, J. C. (1993). Review of the book The Thematic Apperception Test, the Children's Apperception Test, and the Senior Apperception Technique in clinical use, 5th edition. *Contemporary Psychology*, 38(9), 971–972.

Markham, I. S. (2011). Assessing the prediction of employee productivity: A comparison of OLS vs. CART. *International Journal of Productivity and Quality Management*, 8(3), 313–332.

Marques, R. C., Dórea, J. G., Bernardi, J. V. E., Bastos, W. R., & Malm, O. (2009). Prenatal and postnatal mercury exposure, breastfeeding and neurodevelopment during the first 5 years. *Cognitive & Behavioral Neurology*, 22(2), 134–141. doi: 10.1097/WNN.0b013e3181 a72248.

Marsh, H. W., & Bazeley, P. (1999). Multiple evaluations of grant proposals by independent assessors: Confirmatory factor analysis evaluations of reliability, validity, and structure. *Multivariate Behavioral Research* 34(1), 1–30.

Marshalek, B., Lohman, D. F., & Snow, R. E. (1983). The complexity continuum in the radex and hierarchical models of intelligence. *Journal of Intelligence*, 7, 107–127.

Martin, A., & Swinson, R. P. (2000). Cognitive strategies. In A. Martin & R. P. Swinson (Eds.), *Phobic disorders and panic in adults: A guide to assessment and treatment* (pp. 239–254). Washington, DC: American Psychological Association.

Martin, P., Johnson, M., Poon, L. W., Clayton, G. M., & Olsen, S. F. (1994). Group or individual testing: Does it make a difference? *Educational Gerontology*, 20, 171–176.

Martin, R. A., Berry, G. E., Dobranski, T., Horne, M., & Dodgson, P. G. (1996). Emotion perception threshold: Individual differences in emotional sensitivity. *Journal of Research in Personality*, 30, 290–305.

Martin, R. C., Grier, T., Canham-Chervak, M., Anderson, M. K., Bushman, T. T., DeGroot, D. W., & Jones, B. H. (2016). Validity of self-reported physical fitness and body mass index in a military population. *The Journal of Strength & Conditioning Research*, 30(1), 26–32.

Martino, V., Grattagliano, I., Bosco, A., Massaro, Y., Lisi, A., et al. (2016). A new index for the mmpi-2 test for detecting dissimulation in forensic evaluations: A pilot study. *Journal of Forensic Sciences*, 61(1), 249–253.

Masling, J. (2006). When Homer nods: An examination of some systematic errors in Rorschach scholarship. *Journal of Personality Assessment*, 87(1), 62–73.

Masling, J. M., & Bornstein, R. F. (2005). Scoring the Rorschach: Retrospect and prospect. In R. F. Bornstein & J. M. Masling (Eds.), *Scoring the Rorschach: Seven validated systems* (pp. 1–24). Mahwah, NJ: Lawrence Erlbaum Associates Publishers.

Massey, D., & Mooney, M. (2007). The effects of America's three affirmative action programs on academic performance. *Social Problems*, 54(1), 99–117.

Masters, B. N. (1988). Item discrimination: One more is worse. *Journal of Educational Measurement*, 25, 15–29.

Masters, W., & Johnson, V. (1966). *Human sexual response*. Boston: Little, Brown.

Masuda, A., Twohig, M. P., Stormo, A. R., Feinstein, A. B., Chou, Y. Y., & Wendell, J. W. (2010). The effects of cognitive defusion and thought distraction on emotional discomfort and believability of negative self-referential thoughts. *Journal of Behavior Therapy and Experimental Psychiatry*, 41(1), 11–17. doi: 10.1016/j. jbtep.2009.08.006.

Matarazzo, J. D. (1986). Computerized clinical psychological test interpretations: Unvalidated plus all mean and no sigma. *American Psychologist*, 41, 14–24.

Matarazzo, J. D. (1990). Psychological assessment versus psychological

testing: Validation from Binet to the school, clinic, and court room. *American Psychologist*, 45, 999–1017.

Matheny, K. B., Curlette, W. L., Aysan, F., Herrington, A., Gfroerer, C. A., Thompson, D., et al. (2002). Coping resources, perceived stress and life satisfaction among Turkish and American university students. *International Journal of Stress Management*, 9(2), 81–97.

Mather, N., & Schrank, F. A. (2001). *Use of the WJ III discrepancy procedures for learning disabilities identification and diagnosis* (Assessment bulletin no. 3). Itasca, IL: Riverside.

Mattern, K. D., Patterson, B. F., & Wyatt, J. N. (2013). How useful are traditional admission measures in predicting graduation within four years? Research Report 2013-1. *College Board*.

Mattlar, C. (2004). The Rorschach comprehensive system is reliable, valid, and cost-effective. In A. Andronikof (Ed.), *Rorschachiana XXVI: Yearbook of the international Rorschach society* (pp. 158–186). Ashland, OH: Hogrefe & Huber Publishers.

Mattson, D. C. (2011). Standardizing the Formal Elements Art Therapy Scale (FEATS) rotation scale with computerized technology: A pilot study. *The Arts in Psychotherapy*, 38(2), 120–124. ISSN 0197-4556; doi: 10.1016/j. aip.2011.02.003. Retrieved from http://www.sciencedirect.com/science/article/pii/S0197455611000207.

Mau, W., & Lynn, R. (2001). Gender differences on Scholastic Aptitude Test, the American College Test, and college grades. *Educational Psychology*, 21(2), 133–136.

Maul, A., Irribarra, D. T., & Wilson, M. (2016). On the philosophical foundations of psychological measurement. *Measurement*, 79, 311–320.

Maurer, T. J., & Alexander, R. A. (1991). Contrast effects in behavioral measurement: An investigation of alternative process explanations. *Journal of Applied Psychology*, 76, 3–10.

Maurer, T. J., Solamon, J. M., Andrews, K. D., &Troxtel, D. D. (2001). Interviewee coaching, preparation strategies, and response strategies in relation to performance in situational employment interviews: An extension of Maurer, Solamon, and Troxtel (1998). *Journal of Applied Psychology*, 86, 709–717.

May, M., Tuvblad, C., Baker, L., & Raine, A. (2015). Heritability and longitudinal stability of planning and behavioral disinhibition based on the porteus maze test. *Behavior Genetics, 45*(6), 672–673.

Mayer, D. M., & Hanges, P. J. (2003). Understanding the stereotype threat effect with "culture-free" tests: An examination of its mediators and measurement. *Human Performance, 16*(3), 207–230.

Mazaheri, M., Nikneshan, S., Daghaghzadeh, H., & Afshar, H. (2015). The role of positive personality traits in emotion regulation of patients with irritable bowel syndrome (ibs). *Iranian Journal of Public Health, 44*(4), 561–569.

Mazar, N., Amir, O., & Ariely, D. (2008). The dishonesty of honest people: A theory of self-concept maintenance. *Journal of Marketing Research, 45*(6), 633–644.

Mazerolle, M., Régner, I., Rigalleau, F., & Huguet, P. (2015). Stereotype threat alters the subjective experience of memory. *Experimental Psychology, 62,* 395–402.

McCabe, S. E., Boyd, C. J., Couper, M. P., Crawford, S., & D'Arcy, H. (2002). Mode effects for collecting alcohol and other drug use data: Web and U.S. mail. *Journal of Studies on Alcohol, 63*(6), 755–761.

McCall, R. B. (2001). *Fundamental statistics for behavioral sciences* (8th ed.). Belmont, CA: Wadsworth.

McCallum, R. S., Karnes, F. A., & Oehler-Stinnett, J. (1985). Construct validity of the K-ABC for gifted children. *Psychology in the Schools, 22,* 254–259.

McCarthy, A., Lee, K., Itakura, S., &Muir, D. W. (2008). Gaze display when thinking depends on culture and context. *Journal of Cross-Cultural Psychology, 39*(6), 716–729. doi: 10.1177/0022022108323807.

McCarthy, J. M., Van Iddekinge, C. H., & Campion, M. A. (2010). Are highly structured job interviews resistant to demographic similarity effects? *Personnel Psychology, 63*(2), 325–359.

McCarty, J. R., Noble, A. C, & Huntley, R. M. (1989). Effects of item wording on sex bias. *Journal of Educational Measurement, 26,* 285–293.

McCaulley, M. H., & Martin, C. R. (1995). Career assessment and the Myers-Briggs type indicator. *Journal of Career Assessment, 3,* 219–239.

McClelland, D. C. (1994). The knowledge-testing-educational complex strikes back. *American Psychologist, 490,* 66–69.

McClelland, D. C. (1999). How the test lives on: Extensions of the Thematic Apperception Test approach. In L. G. Gieser & M. I. Stein (Eds.), *Evocative images: The Thematic Apperception Test and the art of projection.* Washington, DC: American Psychological Association.

McCormick, E. J., & Ilgen, D. (1980). *Industrial psychology* (7th ed.). Englewood Cliffs, NJ: Prentice-Hall.

McCrae, R. R., & Costa, P. T. (2003). *Personality in adulthood: A five factor theory perspective* (2nd ed.). New York: Guilford Press.

McCrae, R. R., Costa, P. T., Del Pilar, G. H., Rolland, J. P., & Parker, W. D. (1998). Cross-cultural assessment of the five-factor model: The revised NEO personality inventory. *Journal of Cross-Cultural Psychology, 29,* 171–188.

McDaniel, M. A. (1989). Biographical constructs for predicting employee suitability. *Journal of Applied Psychology, 74,* 964–970.

McDaniel, M. A., Whetzel, D. L., Schmidt, F. L., & Maurer, S. D. (1994). The validity of employment interviews: A comprehensive review and meta-analysis. *Journal of Applied Psychology, 79,* 599–616.

McDermott, P., Watkins, M., & Rhoad, A. (2014). Whose IQ is it?–Assessor bias variance in high-stakes psychological assessment. *Psychological Assessment, 26*(1), 207–214.

McDonald, C. R., Taylor, J., Hamberger, M., Helmstaedter, C., Hermann, B. P., & Schefft, B. (2011). Future directions in the neuropsychology of epilepsy [Research Support, N.I.H., Extramural]. *Epilepsy and Behavior, 22*(1), 69–76.

McDowell, I. (2006). *Measuring health: A guide to rating scales and questionnaires* (3rd ed.). Oxford; New York: Oxford University Press.

McEwen, J. (1992). The Nottingham health profile. In S. R. Walker & R. M. Rosser (Eds.), *Quality of life assessment: Key issues for the 1990s* (pp. 111–137). Dordreht, Netherlands: Kluwer Academic Publishers.

McFall, R. M., & McDonell, A. (1986). The continuous search for units of analysis in psychology: Beyond persons, situations, and their interactions. In R. O. Nelson & S. C. Hays (Eds.), *Conceptual foundations of behavioral assessment* (pp. 201–241). New York: Guilford Press.

McGill-Evans, J., & Harrison, M. J. (2001). Parent-child interactions, parenting stress, and developmental outcomes at 4 years. *Children's Health Care, 30*(2), 135–140.

McGlone, M., & Pfiester, R. (2007). The generality and consequences of stereotype threat. *Sociology Compass, 1*(1), 174–190.

McGraw, K. O., Tew, M. D., & Williams, J. E. (2000). The integrity of web-delivered experiments: Can you trust the data? *Psychological Science, 11*(6), 502–506.

McGregor, C. M. (2001). Test review of the Neonatal Behavioral Assessment Scale (NBAS). In R. A. Spies, J. F. Carlson, & K. F. Geisinger (Eds.), *The fourteenth mental measurements yearbook.* Retrieved from http://www.unl.edu/buros.

McHorney, C. A. (1999). Health status assessment methods for adults: Past accomplishments and future challenges. *Annual Review of Public Health, 20*(3), 309–335.

McKenna, P., Clare, L., & Baddeley, A. D. (1995). Schizophrenia. In A. D. Baddeley, B. A. Wilson, & F. N. Watts (Eds.), *Handbook of memory disorders* (pp. 271–292). Chichester, England: Wiley.

McKown, C. (2007). Concurrent validity and clinical usefulness of several individually administered tests of children's social-emotional cognition. *Journal of Clinical Child and Adolescent Psychology, 36*(1), 29–41.

McLennan, N. A., & Arthur, N. (1999). Applying the cognitive information processing approach to career problem solving and decision making to women's career development. *Journal of Employment Counseling, 36*(2), 82–96.

McMinn, M. R., Bearse, J., Heyne, L. K. Smithberger, A., & Erb, A. L. (2011). Technology and independent practice: Survey findings and implications. *Professional Psychology: Research and Practice, 42*(2), 176–184. doi: 10.1037/a0022719.

McNemar, O. W., & Landis, C. (1935). Childhood disease and emotional maturity in the psychopathic woman. *Journal of Abnormal and Social Psychology, 30,* 314–319.

McReynolds, C. J., Ward, D. M., & Singer, O. (2002). Stigma, discrimination, and invisibility: Factors affecting successful integration of individuals diagnosed with schizophrenia. *Journal of Applied Rehabilitation Counseling, 33*(4), 32–39.

Medoff-Cooper, B., McGrath, J. M., & Bilker, W. (2000). Nutritive sucking and neurobehavioral development in preterm infants from 34 weeks PCA to term. *American Journal of Maternal Child Nursing, 25*(2), 64–70.

Meehl, P. E. (1951). *Research results for counselors.* St. Paul, MN: State Department of Education.

Meehl, P. E. (1954). *Clinical versus statistical prediction: A theoretical analysis and a review of the evidence.* Minneapolis: University of Minnesota Press.

Meehl, P. E. (1956). Wanted—A good cookbook. *American Psychologist, 11,* 263–272.

Meehl, P. E. (1957). When shall we use our heads instead of the formula? *Journal of Counseling Psychology, 4,* 268–273.

Meehl, P. E. (1995). Utiles, hedons, and the mind-body problem, or, who's afraid of Vilfredo? In P. E. Shrout & S. T. Fiske (Eds.), *Personality research, methods, and theory: A festschrift honoring Donald W. Fiske* (pp. 45–66). Hillsdale, NJ: Erlbaum.

Meehl, P. E. (1997). Credentialed persons, credentialed knowledge. *Clinical Psychology: Science and Practice, 4,* 91–98.

Meehl, P. E., & Dahlstrom, W. G. (1960). Objective configural rules for discriminating psychotic from neurotic MMPI profiles. *Journal of Consulting Psychology, 24,* 375–387.

Meehl, P. E., & Rosen, A. (1955). Antecedent probability and the efficiency of psychometric signs, patterns or cutting scores. *Psychological Bulletin, 52,* 194–216.

Meersand, P. (2011). Psychological testing and the analytically trained child psychologist. *Psychoanalytical Psycholologist, 28,* 117–131.

Megargee, E. I. (1972). *The California Psychological inventory handbook.* San Francisco: Jossey-Bass.

Mehl, M. R., Pennebaker, J. W., Crow, D. M., Dabbs, J., & Price, J. H. (2001). The Electronically Activated Recorder (EAR): A device for sampling naturalistic daily activities and conversations. *Behavior Research Methods, Instruments, and Computers, 33*(4), 517–523.

Meichenbaum, D. (1976). A cognitive-behavior modification approach to assessment. In M. Hersen & A. S. Bellack (Eds.), *Behavioral assessment.* New York: Pergamon Press.

Meichenbaum, D. (2003). Cognitive behavior therapy: Folktales and the unexpurgated history. *Cognitive Therapy & Research, 27*(1), 125–129.

Meijer, R. R. (2003). *Diagnosing item score patterns on a test using item response theory-based person-fit statistics.* Washington, DC: American Psychological Association.

Meikle, S., & Gerritse, R. (1970). NIMPI cookbook pattern frequencies in a psychiatric unit. *Journal of Clinical Psychology, 26,* 82–84.

Melchert, T. P. (1998). Support for the validity of the graduate record examination. *American Psychologist, 53,* 573–574.

Melei, J. P., & Hilgard, E. R. (1964). Attitudes toward hypnosis, self predictions, and hypnotic susceptibility. *International Journal of Clinical and Experimental Hypnosis, 12,* 99–108.

Mellenbergh, G. J. (1999). A note on simple gain precision. *Applied Psychological Measurement, 23*(1), 87–89

Meloy, J. R., & Singer, J. (1991). A psychoanalytic view of the Rorschach comprehensive system "Special scores". *Journal of Personality Assessment, 56,* 202–217.

Mencimer, S. (2015, December 9). Justice Scalia suggests blacks belong at "slower" colleges. *Mother Jones.*

Ment, L. R., Vohr, B., Allan, W., Katz, K. H., & Schneider, K. C, Westerveld, M., et al. (2003). Change in cognitive function over time in very low-birth-weight infants. *Journal of the American Medical Association, 289*(6), 705–711.

Mercer, J. R. (1971). Sociocultural factors in labeling mental retardates. *Peabody Journal of Education, 48,* 188–203.

Mercer, J. R. (1972, September). *Anticipated achievement: Computerizing the self-fulfilling prophecy.* Paper presented at the meeting of the American Psychological Association, Honolulu, HI.

Mercer, J. R. (1979). In defense of racially and culturally nondiscriminatory assessment. *School Psychology Digest, 8*(1), 89–115.

Merrell, K. W. (1999). *Behavioral, social, and emotional assessment of children and adolescents.* Mahwah NJ: Erlbaum.

Merrell, K. W. (2003). *Behavioral, social, and emotional assessment of children and adolescents* (2nd ed.). Mahwah, NJ: Erlbaum.

Messick, S. J. (1998a). Alternative modes of assessment, uniform standards of validity. In M. D. Hakel (Ed.), *Beyond multiple choice: Evaluating alternatives to traditional testing for selection* (pp. 59–74). Mahwah, NJ: Erlbaum.

Messick, S. J. (1998b). Test validity: A matter of consequence. *Social Indicators Research, 45*(1–3), 35–44.

Metzger, M. B. (2005). Bridging the gaps: Cognitive constraints on corporate controls & ethics education. University of Florida. *Journal of Law and Public Policy, 16,* 435, FN: 220.

Meyer, G. J. (1999). Introduction to the special series on the utility of the Rorschach for clinical assessment. *Psychological Assessment, 11,* 235–239.

Meyer, G. J., Finn, S. E., Eyde, L. D., Kay, G. G., Moreland, K. L., Dies, R. R., et al. (2003). Psychological testing and psychological assessment: A review of evidence and issues. In A. E. Kazdin (Ed.), *Methodological issues and strategies in clinical research* (3rd ed., pp. 265–345). Washington, DC: American Psychological Association.

Meyer, G. J., Mihura, J. L., & Smith, B. L. (2005). The inter-clinician reliability of Rorschach Interpretation in four data sets. *Journal of Personality Assessment, 84,* 296–314.

Meyer, R. G. (1993). *The clinician's handbook: Integrated diagnostics, assessment, and intervention in adult and adolescent psychopathology* (3rd ed.). Boston: Allyn & Bacon.

Michel, J. S., & LeBreton, J. M. (2011). Leadership coherence: An application of personality coherence theory to the study of leadership. *Personality and Individual Differences, 50*(5), 688–694.

Michel, N., Goldberg, J., Heinrichs, R., Miles, A., Ammari, N., et al. (2013). Wais-iv profile of cognition in schizophrenia. *Assessment, 20*(4), 462–473.

Miele, F. (2002). *Intelligence, race, and genetics: Conversations with Arthur R. Jensen.* Boulder, CO: Westview Press.

Miettunen, J., Veijola, J., Isohanni, M., Paunio, T., Freimer, N., Jääskeläinen, E., et al. (2011). Identifying schizophrenia and other psychoses with psychological scales in the general population. *Journal of Nervous & Mental Disease, 199*(4), 230–238. doi: 10.1097/NMD.0b013e3182125d2c.

Miller, E. T., Neal, D. J., Roberts, L. J., Baer, J. S., Cressler, S. O., Metrik, J., et al. (2002). Test-retest reliability of alcohol measures: Is there a difference between internet-based assessment and traditional methods? *Psychology of Addictive Behaviors, 16*(1), 56–63.

Miller, J. (2015). Dredging and projecting the depths of personality: The thematic apperception test and the narratives of the unconscious. *Science in Context, 28*(1), 9–30.

Miller, J. A. L., Scurfield, B. K., Drga, V., Galvin, S. J., & Whitmore, J. (2002).

Nonparametric relationships between single-interval and two-interval forced-choice tasks in the theory of signal detectability. *Journal of Mathematical Psychology, 46*(4), 383–417.

Miller, J. G., & Kinsbourne, M. (2011). Culture and neuroscience in developmental psychology: Contributions and challenges. *Child development perspectives*. Retrieved from http://onlinelibrary.wiley.com/doi/10.1111/j.1750-8606.2011.00188.x/full. doi: 10.1111/j.1750-8606.2011.00188.x.

Miller, J. O., & Phillips, J. (1966). *A preliminary evaluation of the head start and other metropolitan Nashville kindergartens*. Unpublished manuscript, George Peabody College for Teachers, TN.

Miller, L. A., & Lovler, R. L. (2015). *Foundations of psychological testing: A practical approach*. Beverly Hills: Sage Publications.

Miller, M. D., Linn, R. L., & Gronlund, N. E. (2012). *Measurement and assessment in teaching*. Pearson Higher Ed. Unpublished, available from Person website.

Miller-Loncar, C., Lester, B. M., Seifer, R., Lagasse, L. L., Bauer, C. R., Shankaran, S., et al. (2005). Predictors of motor development in children prenatally exposed to cocaine. *Neurotoxicology and Teratology, 27*(2), 213–220.

Millett, G. A., Ding, H., Marks, G., Jeffries, W., Bingham, T., Lauby, J., et al. (2011). Mistaken assumptions and missed opportunities: Correlates of undiagnosed HIV infection among black and Latino men who have sex with men. *Journal of Acquired Immune Deficiency Syndromes, 58*(1), 64–71.

Mills, C. N., Potenza, M. T., Fremer, J. J., & Ward, W. C. (2002). *Computer based testing: Building the foundation for future assessments*. Mahwah, NJ: Erlbaum.

Milne, S., McDonald, J., & Comino, E. (2012). The use of the Bayley Scales of infant and toddler development III with clinical populations: A preliminary exploration. *Physical & Occupational Therapy in Pediatrics, 32*(1), 24–33.

Min, K. H., Kim, J. H., Hwang, S. H. S., & Jahng, S. M. (1998). Variations in emotion response patterning across genders, generations, and personality types. *Korean Journal of Social & Personality Psychology, 12*(2), 119–140.

Minguez-Milio, J. A., Alcázar, J. L., Aubá, M., Ruiz-Zambrana, A., & Minguez, J. (2011). Perinatal outcome and long-term follow-up of extremely low birth weight infants depending on the mode of delivery. *Journal of Maternal-Fetal and Neonatal Medicine, 24*(10), 1235–1238.

Minton, H. L., & Schneider, F. W. (1980). *Differential psychology*. Pacific Grove, CA: Brooks/Cole.

Mirsky, A. F. (1989). The neuropsychology of attention: Elements of a complex behavior. In E. Perecman (Eds.), *Integrating theory and practice in clinical neuropsychology* (pp. 75–91). Hillsdale, NJ: Erlbaum.

Mirsky, A. F. (1996). Disorders of attention: A neuropsychological perspective. In G. Reid Lyon & N. A. Krasnegor (Eds.), *Attention, memory, and executive function* (pp. 71–95). Baltimore: Williams & Wilkins.

Mirsky, A. F., Kugelmass, S., Ingraham, L. J., & Frenkel, E. (1995). Overview and summary: Twenty-five-year followup of high-risk children. *Schizophrenia Bulletin, 21*(2), 227–239.

Mischel, W. (1968). *Personality and assessment*. New York: Wiley.

Mischel, W. (1984). Convergences and challenges in the search for consistency. *American Psychologist, 39*, 351–364.

Mislevy, R. J. (2002). *Psychometric principles in student assessment*. Los Angeles, CA: Center for the Study of Evaluation National Center for Research on Evaluation Standards and Student Testing Graduate School of Education & Information Studies University of California Los Angeles.

Misri, S., Corral, M., Wardrop, A. A., & Kendrick, K. (2006). Quetiapine augmentation in lactation: A series of case reports. *Journal of Clinical Psychopharmacology, 26*(5), 508–511.

Moe, V. (2002). Foster placed and adopted children exposed to in utero opiates and other substances: Prediction and outcome at four and a half years. *Journal of Developmental and Behavioral Pediatrics, 23*(5), 330–339.

Moneta, G., & Wong, F. (2001). Construct validity of the chinese adaptation of Four Thematic Scales of the personality research form. *Social Behavior and Personality: An International Journal, 29*(5), 459–475.

Moore, W. L., & Bell, J. M. (2011). Maneuvers of whiteness: 'Diversity' as a mechanism of retrenchment in the affirmative action discourse. *Critical Sociology, 37*(5), 597–613. doi: 10.1177/0896920510380066.

Moos, R. H. (1973). Conceptualizations of human environment. *American Psychologist, 28*, 652–665.

Moos, R. H. (1986). *Work Environment Scale* (2nd ed.). Palo Alto, CA: Consulting Psychologist Press.

Moos, R. H. (1987). Person-environment congruence in work, school, and health care settings. *Journal of Vocational Behavior, 31*, 231–247.

Moos, R. H. (2003). *Social contexts: Transcending their power and their fragility*. Netherlands: Kluwer Academic Publishers.

Moreland, K. L. (1985). Validation of computer-based test interpretations: Problems and prospects. *Journal of Consulting and Clinical Psychology, 53*, 816–825.

Moreno, G., & Mickie, W. L. (2011). Practical considerations for working with Latino and Asian-American students and families. *Multicultural Learning and Teaching, 6*(4). Retrieved from http://www.bepress.com/mlt/vol16/iss/4.

Moreno, K. E., Segall, D. O., & Hetter, R. D. (1997). The use of computerized adaptive testing in the military. In R. F. Dillon (Eds.), *Handbook on testing* (pp. 204–219). Westport, CT: Greenwood.

Morera, O. F., & Stokes, S. M. (2016). Coefficient α as a measure of test score reliability: Review of 3 popular misconceptions. *American Journal of Public Health, 106*(3), 458–461.

Morgan, J. E., & Ricker, J. H. (2016). *Textbook of clinical neuropsychology*. New York: Taylor & Francis.

Morin, S. F., Steward, W. T., Charlebois, E. D., Remien, R. H., Pinkerton, S. D., Johnson, M. O., et al. (2005). Predicting HIV transmission risk among HIV-infected men who have sex with men: Findings from the healthy living project. *JAIDS Journal of Acquired Immune Deficiency Syndromes, 40*(2), 226–235.

Morris, S. B., Daisley, R. L., Wheeler, M., & Boyer, P. (2015). A meta-analysis of the relationship between individual assessments and job performance. *Journal of Applied Psychology, 100*(1), 5.

Morrison, T., & Morrison, M. (1995). A meta-analytic assessment of the predictive validity of the quantitative and verbal components of the Graduate Record Examination with graduate grade point average representing the criterion of graduate success. *Educational and Psychological Measurement, 55*(2), 309–316.

Morrow, C. E., Bandstra, E. S., Emmalee, S., Anthony, J. C, Ofir, A. Y., Xue, L., et al. (2001). Influence of prenatal cocaine exposure on full-term infant neurobehavioral functioning. *Neurotoxicology and Teratology, 23*(6), 533–544.

Moscoso, S. (2000). Selection interviews: A review of validity evidence, adverse impact and applicant reactions. *International Journal of Selection and Assessment, 8*, 237–247.

Moses, J. A., Pritchard, D. A., & Faustman, W. O. (1994). Modal profiles for the Luria-Nebraska Neuropsychological Battery. *Archives of Clinical Neuropsychology, 9*, 15–30.

Motowidlo, S. J., Carter, G. W., Dunnette, M. D., Tippins, N., Werner, S., Burnett, J. R., et al. (1992). Studies of the structured behavioral interview. *Journal of Applied Psychology, 77*, 571–587.

Mottram, L., & Donders, J. (2005). Construct validity of the California Verbal Learning Test–Children's Version (CVLT-C) after pediatric traumatic brain injury. *Psychological Assessment, 17*(2), 212.

Moun, T. (1998). Mode of administration and interviewer effects in self-reported symptoms of anxiety and depression. *Social Indicators Research, 45*(1–3), 279–318.

Mühlberger, A., Bülthoff, H. H., Wiedemann, G., & Pauli, P. (2007). Virtual reality for the psychophysiological assessment of phobic fear: Responses during virtual tunnel driving. *Psychological Assessment, 19*(3), 340–346.

Mühlberger, A., Weik, A., Pauli, P., & Wiedemann, G. (2006). One-session virtual reality exposure treatment for fear of flying: 1-year follow-up and graduation flight accompaniment effects. *Psychotherapy Research, 16*(1), 26–40.

Mukherjee, S. (2016). *The gene: An intimate history*. New York: Simon and Schuster.

Mulhollen, C. (2007). *The relationship between multiple intelligences and attitude toward independent learning in a high transactional distance environment*. US: ProQuest Information & Learning.

Mulsant, B. H., Kastango, K. B., Rosen, J., Stone, R. A., Mazumdar, S., & Pollock, B. G. (2002). *Interrater reliability in clinical trials of depressive disorders*. Washington, DC: American Psychiatric Association.

Munsinger, H. (1975). The adopted child's I.Q.: A critical review. *Psychological Bulletin, 82*, 623–659.

Münte, T. F., & Klump, G. (2008). Active listening. *Brain Research, 12*(20).

Muris, P., & Field, A. P. (2011). The "normal" development of fear. In W. K. Silverman & A. P. Field (Eds.), *Anxiety disorders in children and adolescents* (2nd ed., pp. 76–89). New York: Cambridge University Press.

Murisa, P., Huijdinga, J., Mayera, B., & de Vriesa, H. (2011). Does "yuck" mean "eek"? Fear responses in children after a disgust manipulation. *Journal of Behavior Therapy and Experimental Psychiatry, 43*(2), 765–769.

Murphy, K. R. (2003a). *The logic of validity generalization*. Mahwah, NJ: Erlbaum.

Murphy, K. R. (Ed.). (2003b). *Validity generalization: A critical review*. Mahwah, NJ: Erlbaum.

Murphy, K. R., & Dzieweczynski, J. L. (2005). Why don't measures of broad dimensions of personality perform better as predictors of job performance. *Human Performance, 18*(4), 343–357.

Murphy, R. (2010). *Front matter, in dynamic assessment, intelligence and measurement*. Chichester, UK: John Wiley & Sons, Ltd. doi: 10.1002/9780470977484.fmatter.

Murray, D. M., Kaplan, R. M., Ngo-Metzger, Q., Portnoy, B., Olkkola, S., Stredrick, D., ... O'Connell, M. E. (2015). Enhancing coordination among the US Preventive Services Task Force, Agency for Healthcare Research and Quality, and National Institutes of Health. *American Journal of Preventive Medicine, 49*(3), S166–S173.

Murray, H. A. (1938). *Explorations in personality*. New York: Oxford University Press.

Murstein, B. I. (1963). *Theory and research in projective techniques*. New York: Wiley

Museum of Modern Art. (1955). *The family of man*. New York: Maco Magazine Corporation.

Musewicz, J., Marczyk, G., Knauss, L., & York D. (2009). Current assessment practice, personality measurement, and Rorschach usage by psychologists. *Journal of Personality Assessment, 91*(5), 453–461.

Naar-King, S., Ellis, D. A., & Frey, M. A. (2003). *Assessing children's well being: A handbook of measures*. Mahwah, NJ: Erlbaum.

Naglieri, J. A. (1985). Review of the Gesell Preschool Test. In J. V. Mitchell (Ed.), *The ninth mental measurements yearbook* (Vol. 1). Highland Park, NJ: Gryphon Press.

Naglieri, J. A., & Ford, D. Y. (2003). Addressing underrepresentation of gifted minority children using the Naglieri Nonverbal Ability Test (NNAT). *Gifted Child Quarterly, 47*(2), 155–160.

Naglieri, J. A., & Goldstein, S. (2009). Understanding the strengths and weaknesses of intelligence and achievement tests. In J. Naglieri & S. Goldstein (Eds.), *Practitioner's guide to assessing intelligence and achievement* (pp. 3–10). Hoboken, NJ: John Wiley & Sons.

Nathanson, J. T., Connolly, J. G., Yuk, F., Gometz, A., Rasouli, J., Lovell, M., & Choudhri, T. (2016). Concussion incidence in professional football position-specific analysis with se of a novel metric. *Orthopaedic Journal of Sports Medicine, 4*(1), 2325967115622621.

National Center for Education Statistics. (1995). *The condition of education 1995/ Indicator 21: Graduate Record Examination (GRE) scores*. Washington, DC: U.S. Department of Education.

National Center for Education Statistics. (2011). Average scores on General Record Examination (GRE) general subjects tests: 1965 through 2009. *Digest of Education Statistics*. Retrieved from http://nces.ed.gov/programs/digest/d10/tables/dt10_344.asp.

Naughton, M. J., & Shumaker, S. A. (2003). The case for domains of function in quality of life assessment. *Quality of Life Research, 12*(Suppl. 1), 73–80.

Neisser, U., Boodoo, G., Bouchard Jr., T. J., Boykin, A. W., Brody, N. Ceci, S. J., et al. (1996). Intelligence: Knowns and unknowns. *American Psychologist, 51*, 77–101.

Nelson, D. V., Novy, D. M., Averill, P. M., & Berry, L. A. (1996). Ethnic comparability of the MMPI in pain patients. *Journal of Clinical Psychology, 52*, 485–497.

Neto, F. (2002). Social adaptation difficulties of adolescents with immigrant backgrounds. *Social Behavior and Personality, 30*(4), 335–346.

Nevo, B., & Jager, R. S. (Eds.). (1993). *Educational and psychological testing: The test taker's outlook*. Gottingen, Germany: Huber.

Newman, C., Leahy, R. L., Beck, A. T., Reilly-Harrington, N. A., & Gyulia, L., (2003). Bipolar disorder: A cognitive therapy approach. *Behavioral & Cognitive Psychotherapy, 31*(1), 113–114.

Newman, J., Grobman, W. A., & Greenland, P. (2008). Combination polypharmacy for cardiovascular disease prevention in men: A decision analysis and cost-effectiveness model. *Preventive Cardiology, 11*(1), 36–41.

Newman, M. G., Szkodny, L. E., Llera, S. J., & Przeworski, A. (2011). A review of technology-assisted self-help and minimal contact therapies for drug and alcohol abuse and smoking addiction: Is human contact necessary for therapeutic efficacy? *Clinical Psychology Review, 31*(1), 178–186. doi: 10.1016/j.cpr.2010. 10.002.

Newton, R. L. (1954). The clinician as judge: Total Rorschachs and clinical case material. *Journal of Consulting Psychology, 18*, 248–250.

Nezworski, M. T., & Wood, J. M. (1995). Narcissism in the comprehensive system for the Rorschach. *Clinical Psychology—Science and Practice, 2*, 179–199.

Nguyen, J., Williams, T., Silverman, E., & Levy, D. (2015). *Validating the Pediatric Automated Neuropsychological Assessment Metrics Cognitive Performance Scores in the screening of neurocognitive impairment in childhood-onset systemic lupus erythematosus.* Paper presented at the Clinical and Experimental Rheumatology Association. Santa Maria.

Nichols, D. S., & Greene, R. L. (1997). Dimensions of deception in personality assessment: The example of the MMPI-2. *Journal of Personality Assessment, 68*, 251–266.

Nijenhuis, J., & van der Flier, H. (2007). The secular rise in IQs in the Netherlands: Is the Flynn effect on g? *Personality and Individual Differences, 43*(5), 1259–1265.

Nisbett, R. E. (2005). Heredity, environment, and race differences in IQ: A commentary on Rushton and Jensen (2005). *Psychology, Public Policy, and Law, 11*(2), 302–310.

Nisbett, R. E., & Miyamoto, Y. (2005). The influence of culture: Holistic versus analytic perception. *Trends in Cognitive Science, 9*, 467–473.

Nittono, H. (1997). Personality needs and short-term memory. *Psychological Reports, 81*, 19–24.

Norcross, J. C., VandenBos, G. R., Freedheim, D. K., & Domenech Rodríguez, M. M. (2016). *APA handbook of clinical psychology: Roots and branches* (Vol. 1). Washington: APA.

Nordhov, S. M., Rønning, J. A., Dahl, L. B., Ulvund, S. E., Tunby, J., & Kaaresen, P.

I. (2010). Early intervention improves cognitive outcomes for preterm infants: Randomized controlled trial. *Pediatrics, 126*(5), 1088–1094. doi: 10.1542/peds.2010-0778.

Nores, M., & Barnett, W. S. (2010). Benefits of early childhood interventions across the world: (Under) investing in the very young. *Economics of Education Review, 29*(2), 271–282.

Norlin, J. W. (2003). *The special educator 2003 desk book.* Palm Beach Gardens, FL: LRP Publications.

Norman, G. (2003). Hi! How are you? Response shift, implicit theories and differing epistemologies. *Quality of Life Research, 12*(3), 239–249.

Norman, R., King, M. T., et al. (2010). Does mode of administration matter? Comparison of online and face-to-face administration of a time trade-off task. *Quality of Life Research, 19*(4), 499–508.

Norris, J. T., Pauli, R., & Bray, D. E. (2007). Mood change and computer anxiety: A comparison between computerised and paper measures of negative affect. *Computers in Human Behavior, 23*(6), 2875–2887.

North, M. M., North, S. M., & Coble, J. R. (2002). Virtual reality therapy: An effective treatment for psychological disorders. In K. M. Stanney (Ed.), *Handbook of virtual environments: Design, implementation, and applications. Human factors and ergonomics* (pp. 1065–1078). Mahwah, NJ: Erlbaum.

Norton, E. H. (1978, July). *The Bakke decision and the future of affirmative action.* Statement of the Chair, U.S. Equal Employment Opportunity Commission, at the convention of the National Association for the Advancement of Colored People.

Notelaers, G., Vermunt, J. K., Baillien, E., Einarsen, S., & De Witte, H. (2011). Exploring risk groups workplace bullying with categorical data. *Ind Health, 49*(1), 73–88.

Novick, M. R. (1981). Federal guidelines and professional standards. *American Psychologist, 36*, 1035–1046.

Nugent, J. (2013). The competent newborn and the Neonatal Behavioral Assessment Scale: T. Berry Brazelton's legacy. *Journal of Child and Adolescent Psychiatric Nursing, 26*(3), 173–179.

Nugent, W. R. (2003). *A psychometric study of the Multi-Problem Screening Inventory depression subscale using item response and generalizability theories.* Thousand Oaks, CA: Sage.

Nunnally, J. C., & Bernstein, I. H. (1994). *Psychometric theory* (3rd ed.). New York: McGraw-Hill.

Nyborg, H., & Jensen, A. R. (2000). Blackwhite differences on various psychometric tests: Spearman's hypothesis tested on American armed services veterans. *Personality and Individual Differences, 28*(3), 593–599.

Nykodym, N., & Ruud, W. N. (1985). Intraview: Career development through business communication. *Journal of Employment Counseling, 22*, 161–165.

Nykodym, N., & Simonetti, J. L. (1981). *Communication: The key to business and organizational effectiveness.* Toledo, OH: Management Skills Books.

Nystul, M. S. (1999). *Introduction to counseling: An art and science perspective.* Boston, MA: Allyn & Bacon.

O'Connell, M. S., Hartman, N. S., McDaniel, M. A., Grubb, W. L., & Lawrence, A. (2007). Incremental validity of situational judgment tests for task and contextual job performance. *International Journal of Selection and Assessment, 15*(1), 19–29.

O'Connor, E., Rossom, R. C., Henninger, M., Groom, H. C., & Burda, B. U. (2016). Primary care screening for and treatment of depression in pregnant and postpartum women: Evidence report and systematic review for the US Preventive Services Task Force. *JAMA, 315*(4), 388–406.

O'Donnell, J., Hawkins, J. D., & Abbott, R. D. (1995). Predicting serious delinquency and substance use among agres-sive boys [Special Section: Prediction and prevention of child and adolescent antisocial behavior]. *Journal of Consulting and Clinical Psychology, 63*, 529–537.

O'Hare, A., & Dien, J. (2008). The fear survey schedule as a measure of anxious arousal: Evidence from ERPS. *Neuroscience Letters, 441*(3), 243–247.

O'Leary, K. D., & Kent, R. N. (1973). Behavior modification for social action: Research tactics and problems. In L. A. Hamerlynck, P. O. Davidson, & L. E. Acker (Eds.), *Critical issues in research and practice.* Champaign, IL: Research Press.

Oakland, T. (1979). Research on the ABIC and ELP: A revisit to an old topic. *School Psychology Digest, 8*, 209–213.

Oakland, T., & Feigenbaum, D. (1979). Multiple sources of test bias on the WISC-R and the Bender-Gestalt Test.

Journal of Consulting and Clinical Psychology, 47, 968–974.

Oakland, T., & Parmelee, R. (1985). Mental measurement of minoritygroup children. In B. B. Wolman (Ed.), *Handbook of intelligence: Theories, measurements, and applications*. New York: Wiley-Interscience.

Oakland, T., & Wechsler, S. M. (2016). Guidelines for preparing psychological specialists: An entry-level course on intellectual assessment. *International Journal of School & Educational Psychology, 4*(3), 179–186.

Oberlander, T. F., Jacobson, S. W., Weinberg, J., Grunau, R. E., Molteno, C. D., & Jacobson, J. L. (2010). Prenatal alcohol exposure alters biobehavioral reactivity to pain in newborns. *Alcoholism: Clinical and Experimental Research, 34*(4), 575–749. doi: 10.1111/j.1530-0277.2009.01137.x.

Oei, T. P. S., Evans, I., & Crook, G. M. (1990). Utility and validity of the STAI with anxiety disorder patients. *British Journal of Clinical Psychology, 29*, 429–432.

Ofiesh, N., Mather, N., & Russell, A. (2005). Using speeded cognitive, reading, and academic measures to determine the need for extended test time among university students with learning disabilities. *Journal of Psychoeducational Assessment, 23*(1), 35–52.

Okazaki, S., & Sue, S. (2003). *Methodological issues in assessment research with ethnic minorities*. Washington, DC: American Psychological Association.

Olson, K., & Bilgen, I. (2011). The role of interviewer experience on acquiescence. *Public Opinion Quarterly, 75*(1), 99.

Ones, D. S., Chockalingam, V., & Schmidt, F. L. (1995). Integrity tests: Overlooked facts, resolved issues, and remaining questions. *American Psychologist, 50*(6), 456–457.

Oostdam, R., & Meijer, J. (2003). *Influence of test anxiety on measurement of intelligence*. Washington, DC: Psychological Reports.

Opton, E. (1979, December). A psychologist takes a closer look at the recent landmark *Larry P.* opinion. *APA Monitor*, pp. 1–4.

Oral, E., Güleç, M., Aydin, N., Ozan, E., & Kırpınar, I. (2011). Severe generalize cortical atrophy inconsistent with her age, and neurocognitive impairment in an untreated schizophrenia patient: A case report. *European Psychiatry, 26*(1),

1463. doi: 10.1016/S0924-9338(11)73168-6.

Orfield, G., & Kornhaber, M. L. (2001). *Raising standards or raising barriers? Inequality and high-stakes testing in public education*. New York: Century Foundation Press.

Osberg, T. M., & Poland, D. L. (2002). Comparative accuracy of the MMPI-2 and the MMPI-A in the diagnosis of psychopathology in 18-year-olds. *Psychological Assessment, 14*(2), 164–169.

Osipow, S. H. (1983). *Theories of career development* (3rd ed.). Englewood Cliffs, NJ: Prentice-Hall.

Osipow, S. H. (1999). Assessing career indecision. *Journal of Vocational Behavior, 55*(1), 147–154.

Othmer, E., & Othmer, S. C. (2002). *The clinical interview using DSM-IVTR: Vol. 2. The difficult patient*. Washington, DC: American Psychiatric Publishing.

Ottem, E. (2002a). Confirmatory factor analysis of ITPA models with language-impaired children. *Scandinavian Journal of Psychology, 43*(4), 299–305.

Ottem, E. (2002b). The complementary nature of ITPA and WISC-R results for language-impaired children. *Scandinavian Journal of Educational Research, 46*(2), 145–160.

Owen, D. (1985). *None of the above: Behind the myth of scholastic aptitude*. Boston: Houghton Mifflin.

Palaniappan, A. K., & Torrance, E. P. (2001). Comparison between regular and streamlined versions of scoring of Torrance Tests of Creative Thinking. *Korean Journal of Thinking and Problem Solving, 11*(2), 5–7.

Palm, J. A. (2005). *Comprehensive system indices, constellations, and supplemental aggression ratings for the Rorschach inkblot method: Reliability and validity in a child and adolescent outpatient sample*. US: ProQuest Information & Learning. *ETD Collection for Fordham University*. Paper AAI3159396.

Palta, M., Chen, H. Y., Kaplan, R. M., Feeny, D., Cherepanov, D., & Fryback, D. G. (2011). Standard error of measurement of 5 health utility indexes across the range of health for use in estimating reliability and responsiveness. [Research Support, N.I.H., Extramural]. *Medical Decision Making, 31*(2), 260–269. doi: 10.1177/0272989X10380925.

Paolini, L., Yanez, A. P., & Kelly, W. E. (2006). An examination of worry and life satisfaction among college students.

Individual Differences Research, 4(5), 331–339.

Parducci, A. (1968). The relativism of absolute judgments. *Scientific American, 219*(6), 84–90.

Parducci, A. (1995). *Happiness, pleasure, and judgment: The contextual theory and its applications*. Mahwah, NJ: Erlbaum.

Parissea, C., & Maillartb, C. (2009). Specific language impairment as systemic developmental disorders. *Journal of Neurolinguistics, 22*(2), 109–122.

Park, C. L., Malone, M. R., Suresh, D. P., Bliss, D., & Rosen, R. I. (2008). Coping, meaning in life, and quality of life in congestive heart failure patients. *Quality of Life Research, 17*(1), 21–26.

Park, S. (2011). Unexpected direction of differential item functioning. Doctoral Dissertation Florida State University.

Parker, J. D., Endler, N. S., & Bagby, R. M. (1993). If it changes, it might be unstable: Examining the factor structure of the ways of coping questionnaire. *Psychological Assessment, 5*(3), 361–368.

Parker, K. (1983). A meta-analysis of the reliability and validity of the Rorschach. *Journal of Personality Assessment, 42*, 227–231.

Parnell, B., Dunivan, G., Connolly, A., Jannelli, M., Wells, E., & Geller, E. (2011). Validation of web-based administration of the Pelvic Organ Prolapse/Urinary Incontinence Sexual Function Questionnaire (PISQ-12). *International Urogynecology Journal, 22*(3), 357–361. doi: 10.1007/s00192-010-1297-8.

Parsons, O. A. (1970). Clinical neuropsychology. In C. D. Spielberger (Ed.), *Current topics in clinical and community psychology* (Vol. 2). New York: Academic Press.

Parsons, T. D. (2016). Neuropsychological assessment 2.0: Computer-automated assessments. In T. D. Parsons (Ed.), *Clinical neuropsychology and technology* (pp. 47–63). New York: Springer.

Pascanu, R., & Jaeger, H. (2011). A neurodynamical model for working memory. *Neural Networks, 24*(2), 199–207. ISSN 0893-6080; doi: 10.1016/j.neunet.2010.10.003.

Pashley, P., Thornton, A., & Duffy, J. (2005). Access and diversity in law school admissions. In W. J. Camara & E. W. Kimmel (Eds.), *Choosing students: Higher education admissions tools for the 21st century* (pp. 231–249). Mahwah, NJ: Lawrence Erlbaum Associates Publishers.

Patrianakos-Hoobler, A. I., Msall, M. E., Huo, D., Marks, J. D., Plesha-Troyke, S. & Schreiber, M. D. (2010). Predicting school readiness from neurodevelopmental assessments at age 2 years after respiratory distress syndrome in infants born preterm. *Developmental Medicine & Child Neurology, 52*(4), 379–385. doi: 10.1111/j.1469-8749.2009.03343.x.

Patrick, D. L., Bushnell, D. M., & Rothman, M. (2004). Performance of two self-report measures for evaluating obesity and weight loss. *Obesity Research, 12*(1), 48–57.

Patterson, M., Slate, J. R., Jones, C. H., & Steger, H. S. (1995). The effects of practice administrations in learning to administer and score the WAIS-R: A partial replication. *Educational and Psychological Measurement, 55*(1), 32–37.

Patterson, T. L., Kaplan, R. M., Grant, I., Semple, S. J., Moscona, S., Koch, W. L., et al. (1996). Quality of well-being in late-life psychosis. *Psychiatry Research, 63*(2–3), 169–181.

Pattishall, E. (1992). Smoking and body weight. *Health Psychology, 11*(Suppl.), 32–33.

Paul, R., Cohen, R., Moser, D., Ott, B., Zawacki, T., & Gordon, N. (2001). Performance on the Hooper Visual Organizational Test in patients diagnosed with subcortical vascular dementia: Relation to naming performance. *Neuropsychiatry, Neuropsychology, and Behavioral Neurology, 14*(2), 93–97.

Paunonen, S. V., & Ashton, M. C. (1998). The structured assessment of personality across cultures. *Journal of Cross-Cultural Psychology, 29*, 150–170.

Pawling, R., Kirkham, A. J., Tipper, S. P., & Over, H. (2016). Memory for incidentally perceived social cues: Effects on person judgment. *British Journal of Psychology.* doi: 10.1111/bjop.12182.

Pearson, K. (1901). *Mathematical contributions to the theory of evolution.* London: Dulau & Co.

Pelletier, J. E., Lytle, L. A., & Laska, M. N. (2016). Stress, health risk behaviors, and weight status among community college students. *Health Education & Behavior, 43*(2), 139–144.

Peluso, P. R., Liebovitch, L. S., Gottman, J. M., Norman, M. D., & Su, J. (2011). A mathematical model of psychotherapy: An investigation using dynamic nonlinear equations to model the therapeutic relationship. *Psychotherapy Research.* Retrieved from

http://www.tandfonline.com/doi/abs/10.1080/10503307.2011.622314.

Penfield, R. D. (2003). A score method of constructing asymmetric confidence intervals for the mean of a rating scale item. *Psychological Methods, 8*(2), 149–163.

People Who Care v. Rockford Board of Education School District No. 205. (1997). 111 F. 3d 528 (7th Cir. 1997).

Peoples, V. Y. (1975). Measuring the vocational interest of women. In S. H. Osipow (Ed.), *Emerging women: Career analysis and outlooks.* Columbus, OH: Merrill.

Perkins, D. N., & Grotzer, T. A. (1997). Teaching intelligence. *American Psychologist, 52*(10), 1125–1133.

Perkos, S., Theodorakis, Y., & Chronni, S. (2002). Enhancing performance and skill acquisition in novice basketball players with instructional self-talk. *Sport Psychologist, 16*(4), 368–383.

Pernas, A., Iraurgi C. I., Bermejo, P., Basebe, N., Carou, M., Paez, D., et al. (2001). Coping and affectivity in persona with HIV/AIDS. *Psiquis: Revista de Psiquiatria, Psicologia Medica y Psicosomatica, 22*(5), 30–35.

Perez, M., Wilhelm, P., Schoebi, D., & Horner, M. (2001). Simultaneous computer-assisted assessment of causal attribution and social coping in families. In J. Fahrenberg & U. Freilberg (Eds.), *Progress in ambulatory assessment: Computer assisted psychological and psycho-physiological methods in monitoring and field studies* (pp. 25–43). Kirkland, WA: Hogrefe & Huber.

Perry, W., Sprock, J., Schaible, D., & McDougall, A. (1995). Amphetamine on Rorschach measures in normal subjects. *Journal of Personality Assessment, 64*(3), 456–465.

Petchkovsky, L., Petchkovsky, M., Morris, P., Dickson, P., Montgomery, D., et al. (2013). FMRI responses to Jung's word association test: Implications for theory, treatment and research. *Journal of Analytical Psychology, 58*(3), 409–431.

Peterson, N. G., Mumford, M. D., Levin, K. Y., Green, J., & Waksberg, J. (1999). Research method: Development and field testing of the content model. In N. G. Peterson, M. D. Mumford, & W. C. Borman (Eds.), *An occupational information system for the 21st century: The development of O*NET* (pp. 31–47). Washington, DC: American Psychological Association.

Pettigrew, T. F. (1964). *A profile of the American Negro.* New York: Van Nostrand Reinhold.

Pettit, F. A. (2002). A comparison of worldwide web and paper-and-pencil personality questionnaires. *Behavior Research Methods, Instruments, & Computers, 34*(1), 6–18.

Pfaffenberger, A. H., & Marko, P. W. (2011). Exceptional maturity of personality: An emerging field. In A. H. Pfaffenberger, P. W. Marko, & A. Combs (Eds.), *The postconventional personality: Assessing, researching, and theorizing higher development* (pp. 1–8). Albany: New York Press.

Pfeifer, C., & Sedlacek, W. (1971). The validity of academic predictors for black and white students at a predominantly white university. *Journal of Educational Measurement, 8*, 253–261.

Phares, E. J., & Trull, T. J. (2000). *Clinical psychology* (6th ed.). Pacific Grove, CA: Brooks/Cole.

Phillips, S. E. (1994). High-stakes testing accommodations: Validity versus disabled rights. *Applied Measurement in Education, 7*(2), 93–120.

Picard, R. W., & Klein, J. (2002). Computers that recognize and respond to user emotion: Theoretical and practical implications. *Interacting with Computer, 14*(2), 141–169.

Pickett, K. E., & Wilkinson, R. G. (2015). Income inequality and health: A causal review. *Social Science & Medicine, 128*, 316–326.

Picone, L., Regine, A., & Ribaudo, F. (2001). Factorial validity of the McCarthy Scales of Children's Abilities by measuring cognitive ability in young children. *Bollettino di Psicologia Applicata, 234*(48), 21–31.

Piers, V. P., Harris, D. B., & Herzberg, D. S. (1999). *Piers Harris Children's Self-Concept Scale–Second Edition.* Los Angeles: Western Psychological Services.

Piotrowski, C, Sherry, D., & Keller, J. W. (1985). Psychodiagnostic test usage: Survey of the Society for Personality Assessment. *Journal of Personality Assessment, 49*, 115–119.

Piotrowski, C. (1984). The status of projective techniques: Or, "wishing won't make it go away". *Journal of Clinical Psychology, 40*, 1495–1499.

Piotrowski, C. (1995). A review of the clinical and research use of the Bender-Gestalt Test. *Perceptual and Motor Skills, 81*, 1272–1274.

Piotrowski, Z. (1947). Rorschach compendium. *Psychiatric Quarterly, 21*, 79–101.

Piotrowski, Z. (1964). Digital computer interpretation of inkblot test data. *Psychiatric Quarterly, 38,* 1–26.

Piotrowski, Z. A. (1980). CPR: The psychological X-ray in mental disorders. In J. B. Sidowski, J. H. Johnson, & T. A. Williams (Eds.), *Technology in mental health care delivery systems* (pp. 85–108). Norwood, NJ: Ablex.

Pirelli, G., Gottdiener, W. H., & Zapf, P. A. (2011). A meta-analytic review of competency to stand trial research. *Psychology, Public Policy, and Law, 17*(1), 1–53. doi: 10.1037/a0021713.

Pitts, T. W. (2012). *Common schools: Classical schools citizenship education in a pluralistic state.* Charlottesville: University of Virginia.

Plaisted, J. R., Gustavson, J. L., Wilkening, G. N., & Golden, C. J. (1983). The Luria-Nebraska Neuropsychological Battery Children's revision: Theory and current research findings. *Journal of Clinical Child Psychology, 12,* 13–21.

Ployhart, R. E., & Holtz, B. C. (2008). The diversity-validity dilemma: Strategies for reducing racioethnic and sex subgroup differences and adverse impact in selection. *Personnel Psychology, 61,* 153–172. doi: 10.1111/j.1744-6570.2008.00109.x.

Polansky, N., Freeman, W., Horowitz, M., Irwin, L., Papanis, N., Rapaport, D., et al. (1949). Problems of interpersonal relations in research on groups. *Human Relations, 2,* 281–291.

Policy Analysis for California Education and Rennie Center for Education Research & Policy (Pace). (2011). *The road ahead for state assessments.* Cambridge, MA: Rennie Center for Education Research & Policy.

Pomplun, M., & Custer, M. (2005). The construct validity of the Stanford-Binet 5 measures of working memory. *Assessment, 12*(3), 338–346.

Ponniah, K., Weissman, M. W., Bledsoe, S. E., Verdeli, H., Gameroff, M. J., Mufson, L., et al. (2011). Training in structured diagnostic assessment using DSM-IV criteria. *Research on Social Work Practice, 21*(4), 452–457. doi: 10.1177/1049731511398151.

Pons, D., Atienza, F. L., Balaguer, I., & Garcia-Merita, M. (2002). Psychometric properties of Satisfaction with Life Scale in elderly. *Revista Iberoamericana de Diagnostico y Evaluacion Psicologica, 13*(1), 71–82.

Pope, K. S., Butcher, J. N., & Seelen, J. (2000). *The MMPI, MMPI-2, & MMPI-A in court: A practical guide for expert witnesses and attorneys* (2nd ed.). Washington, DC: American Psychological Association.

Popham, W. J. (1994). The instructional consequences of criterion-referenced clarity. *Educational Measurement: Issues and Practice, 13*(4), 15–18, 30.

Popham, W. J. (2001). *The truth about testing: An educator's call to action.* New York: Association for Supervision & Curriculum Development.

Poropat, A. (2009). A meta-analysis of the five-factor model of personality and academic performance. *Psychological Bulletin, 135*(2), 322–338.

Porter, S. C., Forbes, P., Manzi, S., & Kalish, L. A. (2010). Patients providing the answers: Narrowing the gap in data quality for emergency care. *Quality and Safety in Health Care, 19*(5), 1–5. doi: 10.1136/qshc.2009.032540.

Portoghese, C., Buttiglione, M., De Giacomo, A., Lafortezza, M., Lecce, P. A., Martinelli, D., et al. (2010). Leiter-R versus developmental quotient for estimating cognitive function in preschoolers with pervasive developmental disorders. *Neuropsychiatric Disease and Treatment, 6,* 337–342.

Posthuma, R. A., Morgeson, F. P., & Campion, M. A. (2002). Beyond employment interview validity: A comprehensive narrative review of recent research and trends over time. *Personnel Psychology, 55*(1), 1–81.

Potvin, D., Keith, T., Caemmerer, J., & Trundt, K. (2015). Confirmatory factor structure of the Kaufman Assessment Battery for Children-second edition with preschool children: Too young for differentiation? *Journal of Psychoeducational Assessment, 33*(6), 522–533.

Potvin, O., Bergua, V., Meillon, C., Le Goff, M., Bouisson, J., Dartigues, J. F., & Amieva, H. (2011). Norms and associated factors of the STAI-Y State anxiety inventory in older adults: Results from the PAQUID study. *International Psychogeriatrics, 1*(1), 1–11.

Power, M. J., Katz, R., McGuffin, P., & Duggan, C. F. (1994). The Dysfunctional Attitude Scale (DAS): A comparison of Form A and Form B and proposals for a new subscaled version. *Journal of Research in Personality, 28*(3), 263–276.

Powers, D. E. (2001). *Validity of GRE general test scores for admission to colleges of veterinary medicine* (No. GRE Board 98-09R). Princeton, NJ: Educational Testing Service.

Price, K. H., & Garland, H. (1983). Compliance with a leader's suggestions as a function of perceived leader/member competence and potential reciprocity. *Journal of Applied Psychology, 66,* 329–336.

Priede, C., Jokinen, A., Ruuskanen, E., & Farrall, S. (2014). Which probes are most useful when undertaking cognitive interviews? *International Journal of Social Research Methodology, 17*(5), 559–568.

Primi, C., Morsanyi, K., Chiesi, F., Donati, M. A., & Hamilton, J. (2015). The development and testing of a new version of the cognitive reflection test applying item response theory (IRT). *Journal of Behavioral Decision Making.* Published online June 2015. doi: 10.1002/bdm.1883.

Primi, R. (2002). Complexity of geometric inductive reasoning tasks: Contribution to the understanding of fluid intelligence. *Intelligence, 30*(1), 41–70.

Prince, R. J., & Guastello, S. J. (1990). The Barnum effect in a computerized Rorschach interpresentation system. *Journal of Psychology, 124,* 217–222.

Prinstein, M. J. (2004). The interview. In C. Williams-Nickelson (Ed.), *Internships in psychology: The APAGS workbook for writing successful applications and finding the right match* (pp. 79–92). Washington, DC: American Psychological Association.

ProEd. *ITPA-3: Illinois Test of Psycholinguistic Abilities–Third Edition.* Retrieved November 29, 2011, from http://www.proedinc.com/customer/productView.aspx?ID=788.

Prout, H. T., & Sheldon, K. L. (1984). Classifying mental retardation in vocational rehabilitation: A study of diagnostic practices and their adherence to accepted guidelines. *Rehabilitation Counseling Bulletin, 28,* 125–128.

Puccio, G. J., Joniak, A. J., & Talbot, R. J. (1995). Person-environment fit: Examining the use of Commensurate Scales. *Psychological Reports, 76,* 931–938. doi: 10.2466/pr0.1995.76.3.931.

Pugh, R. C. (1968). Evidence for the validity of the behavioral dimensions of Teaching-Characteristics Schedule Scales. *Educational and Psychological Measurement, 28*(4), 1173–1179.

Pugliese, M. D., Lifshitz, F., Grad, G., Fort, P., & Marks-Katz, M. (1983). Fear of obesity: A cause of short stature and delayed puberty. *New England Journal of Medicine, 309,* 513–518.

Pull, C. B. (2005). Current status of virtual reality exposure therapy in anxiety disorders. *Current Opinion in Psychiatry, 18*(1), 7–14.

Pupo, M. C., Jorge, M. R., Schoedl, A. F., Bressan, R. A., Andreoli, S. B., Mello, M. F., et al. (2011). The accuracy of the Clinician-Administered PTSD Scale (CAPS) to identify PTSD cases in victims of urban violence. *Psychiatry Research, 185*(1–2), 157–160.

Pyburn Jr., K. M., Ployhart, R. E., & Kravitz, D. A. (2008). The diversity-validity dilemma: Overview and legal context. *Personnel Psychology, 61,* 143–151.

Pyne, J. M., Sieber, W. J., David, K., Kaplan, R. M., Hyman Rapaport, M., & Keith Williams, D. (2003). Use of the quality of well-being self-administered version (QWB-SA) in assessing health-related quality of life in depressed patients. *Journal of Affect Disord, 76*(1–3), 237–247.

Qi, C. H., Kaiser, A. P., Milan, S., & Hancock, T. (2006). Language performance of low-income, African American and European American preschool children on the Peabody Picture Vocabulary Test-III. *Language, Speech, Hearing Services in Schools, 37,* 1–12.

Quay, L. C. (1971). Language dialect, reinforcement, and the intelligence-test performance of Negro children. *Child Development, 42,* 5–15.

Quenk, N. L. (2000). *Essentials of Myers-Briggs type indicator assessment.* New York: Wiley.

Quinsey, V. L., Harris, G. T., Rice, M. E., & Cormier, C. A. (2006). Criticisms of actuarial risk assessment. In V. L. Quinsey, G. T. Harris, M. E. Rice, & C. A. Cormier (Eds.), *Violent offenders: Appraising and managing risk* (2nd ed., pp. 197–223). Washington, DC: American Psychological Association.

Rabin, B. A., Lewis, C. C., Norton, W. E., Neta, G., Chambers, D., Tobin, J. N., … Glasgow, R. E. (2016). Measurement resources for dissemination and implementation research in health. *Implementation Science, 11*(1), 1.

Raju, N. S., Burke, M. J., Normand, J., & Lezotte, D. V. (1993). What would be if what is wasn't? Rejoinder to Judiesch, Schmidt, and Hunter (1993). *Journal of Applied Psychology, 78,* 912–916.

Ralston, S. M. (1988). The effect of applicant race upon personnel selection decisions: A review with recommendations. *Employee Responsibilities and Rights Journal, 1,* 215–226.

Ramírez, J. M., & Andreu, J. M. (2006). Aggression, and some related psychological constructs (anger, hostility, and impulsivity): Some comments from a research project. *Neuroscience & Biobehavioral Reviews, 30*(3), 276–291.

Rammsayer, T. H., & Brandler, S. (2002). On the relationship between general fluid intelligence and psychophysical indicators of temporal resolution in the brain. *Journal of Research in Personality, 36*(5), 507–530.

Randolph, D. L., Smart, T. K., & Nelson, W. (1997). The personality research form as a discriminator of attachment styles. *Journal of Social Behavior and Personality, 12,* 113–127.

Rapaport, D., Gill, M. M., & Schafer, R. (1945–1946). *Diagnostic psychological testing* (2 vols.). Chicago: Yearbook Publishers.

Rapaport, D., Gill, M. M., & Schafer, R. (1968). *Diagnostic psychological testing* (Rev. ed., R. R. Holt, Ed.). New York: International Universities Press.

Rapp, D., Hinze, S., Kohlhepp, K., & Ryskin, R. (2014). Reducing reliance on inaccurate information. *Memory & Cognition, 42*(1), 11–26.

Rappaport, N. B., & McAnulty, D. P. (1985). The effect of accented speech on the scoring of ambiguous WISC-R responses by prejudiced and nonprejudiced raters. *Journal of Psychoeducational Assessment, 3,* 275–283.

Rasulis Jr., R., Schuldberg, D., & Murtagh, M. (1996). Computer administered testing with the Rotter incomplete sentences blank. *Computers in Human Behavior, 12*(4), 497–513.

Raven, J. (1986). *Manual for Raven's Progressive Matrices and Vocabulary Scales: Research supplement No. 3.* London: H. K. Lewis.

Raven, J. (1990). *Raven manual research supplement 3: American and international norms.* London: Oxford Psychologist Press.

Raven, J. (2000). The Raven's Progressive Matrices: Change and stability over culture and time. *Cognitive Psychology, 41*(1), 1–48.

Raven, J., Raven, J. C., & Court, J. H. (1998). *Standard progressive matrices, 1998 edition.* Oxford, England: Oxford University Press.

Ravitch, D. (2016). *The death and life of the great American school system: How testing and choice are undermining education.* New York: Basic Books.

Ravitch, D. (2016). *The death and life of the great American school system: How testing and choice are undermining education.* New York: Basic Books.

Rawls, A., Zhang, X., & Hendrickson, A. (2016). Identifying with more than one ethnic and/or racial group: Another examination of the impact on differential item functioning statistics. Statistical Report 2016-1. *College Board.*

Raykov, T., & Marcoulides, G. A. (2010). *Introduction to psychometric theory.* New York: Taylor & Francis.

Raykov, T., & Zinbarg, R. E. (2011). Proportion of general factor variance in a hierarchical multiple-component measuring instrument: A note on a confidence interval estimation procedure. *British Journal of Mathematical and Statistical Psychology, 64*(Pt 2), 193–207. doi: 10.1348/000711009X479714.

Reardon, R. C., & Lenz, J. G. (1999). Holland's theory and career assessment. *Journal of Vocational Behavior, 55*(1), 102–113.

Reardon, R., & Lenz, J. (2015). *Handbook for using the self-directed search: Integrating RIASEC and CIP theories in practice.* Odessa, FL: Psychological Assessment Resources.

Reardon, S. F., Nicole, A., Allison, A., & Michal, K. (2010). Effects of failing a high school exit exam on course taking, achievement, persistence, and graduation. *Educational Evaluation and Policy Analysis, 32,* 498–520.

Reece, T. (2009). Seal the deal: First impressions are important, but so are last impressions. Here are some dos and don'ts for the end of a job interview. *Career World, a Weekly Reader Publication, 38*(3), 23.

Reed, J. C., & Reed, H. B. (2015). Contributions to neuropsychology of Reitan and associates: Neuropsychology Laboratory, Indiana University Medical Center, 1960s. *Archives of Clinical Neuropsychology, 30*(8), 751–753.

Reed, S. B. (2000). An investigation of the physical attractiveness stereotype. *Dissertation Abstracts International Section B. The Physical Sciences and Engineering, 60,* 12B.

Reeves, T. D., & Marbach-Ad, G. (2016). Contemporary test validity in theory and practice: A primer for discipline-based education researchers. *CBE-Life Sciences Education, 15*(1), rm1.

Regenwetter, M. (2006). *Behavioral social choice: Probabilistic models, statistical inference, and applications.* Cambridge; New York: Cambridge University Press.

Reh, V., Schmidt, M., Lam, L., Schimmelmann, B., Hebebrand, J., et al. (2015).

Behavioral assessment of core ADHD symptoms using the Qbtest. *Journal of Attention Disorders, 19*(12), 1034–1045.

Reid, J. B. (1970). Reliability assessment of observation data: A possible methodological problem. *Child Development, 41*, 1143–1150.

Reid, J. B., & DeMaster, B. (1972). The efficacy of the spotcheck procedure in maintaining the reliability of data collected by observers in quasinatural settings: Two pilot studies. *Oregon Research Institute Research Bulletin, 12*.

Reidy, T. J., Sorensen, J. R., & Davidson, M. (2016). Testing the predictive validity of the Personality Assessment Inventory (PAI) in relation to inmate misconduct and violence. *Psychological Assessment, 28*(8), 871–884.

Reilly, J. L., Hill, S. K., Gold, J. M., Keefe, R. S., Clementz, B. A., Gershon, E., … Sweeney, J. A. (2016). Impaired context processing is attributable to global neuropsychological impairment in schizophrenia and psychotic bipolar disorder. *Schizophrenia Bulletin*, Published online ahead of print. doi: 10.1093/schbul/sbw081.

Reise, S. P., & Waller, N. G. (2003). How many IRT parameters does it take to model psychopathology items? *Psychological Methods, 8*(2), 164–184.

Reitan, R. M. (1968). Theoretical and methodological bases of the Halstead-Reitan Neuropsychological Test Battery. In I. Grant & K. N. Adams (Eds.), *Neuro-psychological assessment of neuropsychiatric disorders.* New York: Oxford University Press.

Reitan, R. M. (1976). Neuropsychology: The vulgarization that Luria always wanted. *Contemporary Psychology, 21*, 737–738.

Reitan, R. M., & Wolfson, D. (1997). Consistency of neuropsychological test scores of head-injured subjects involved in litigation compared with head-injured subjects not involved in litigation: Development of the retest consistency index. *Clinical Neuropsychologist, 11*(1), 69–76.

Reitan, R. M., & Wolfson, D. (1999). The two faces of mild head injury. *Archives of Clinical Neuropsychology, 14*(2), 191–202.

Rentz, D. M., Dekhtyar, M., Sherman, J., Burnham, S., Blacker, D., Aghjayan, S. L., … Chenhall, T. (2016). The feasibility of at-home iPad cognitive testing for use in clinical trials. *The Journal of Prevention of Alzheimer's Disease, 3*(1), 8.

Reschly, D. J. (1981). Psychological testing in educational classification and placement. *American Psychologist, 36*, 1094–1102.

Reschly, D. J., & Sabers, D. L. (1979). Analysis of test bias in four groups with the regression definition. *Journal of Educational Measurement, 16*, 1–9.

Reschly, D. J., & Ward, S. M. (1991). Use of adaptive behavior measures and over-representation of black students in programs for students with mild mental retardation. *American Journal on Mental Retardation, 96*, 257–268.

Reschly, D. J., Kicklighter, R., & McKee, P. (1988). Recent placement of litigation part III: Analysis of differences in Larry P., Marshal and S-1, and implications for future practices. *School Psychology Review, 17*, 39–50.

Resnick, S. M., Trotman, K. M., Kawas, C., & Zonderman, A. B. (1995). Age-associated changes in specific errors on the Benton Visual Retention Test. *Journals of Gerontology Series B—Psychological Sciences and Social Sciences, 50B*, 171–178.

Reynolds, C. R. (1980). An examination of Bias in a Pre-School Battery across race and sex. *Journal of Educational Measurement, 17*, 137–146.

Reynolds, C. R. (1982). Determining statistically reliable strengths and weaknesses in the performance of single individuals on the Luria Nebraska Neuropsychological Battery. *Journal of Consulting and Clinical Psychology, 50*, 525–529.

Reynolds, C. R. (1986). Wide Range Achievement Test (WRAT-R), 1984 edition. *Journal of Counseling and Development, 64*, 540–541.

Reynolds, C. R., & Kamphaus, R. W. (1997). The Kaufman Assessment Battery for Children: Development, structure, and applications in neuropsychology. In A. M. Horton, D. Wedding, & J. Webster (Eds.), *The neuropsychology handbook: Vol. 1. Foundations and assessment* (2nd ed., pp. 290–330). New York: Springer.

Reynolds, C. R., & Livingston, R. B. (2012). *Mastering modern psychological testing: Theory & methods.* New York: Pearson Education.

Reynolds, C. R., & Nigl, A. J. (1981). A regression analysis of differential validity: An intellectual assessment for black and white inner-city children. *Journal of Clinical and Child Psychology, 10*, 176–179.

Reynolds, C. R., & Ramsay, M. C. (2003). Bias in psychological assessment: An

empirical review and recommendations. In J. R. Graham & J. A. Naglieri (Eds.), *Handbook of psychology: Assessment psychology* (Vol. 10, pp. 67–93). New York: Wiley.

Richards, J. E., Sanchez, C., Phillips-Meek, M., & Xie, W. (2016). A database of age-appropriate average MRI templates. *Neuroimage, 124*, 1254–1259.

Richeson, N., & Thorson, J. A. (2002). The effect of autobiographical writing on the subjective well-being of older adults. *North American Journal of Psychology, 4*(3), 395–404.

Ridenour, T. A., Treloar, J. H., & Dean, R. S. (2003). Utility analysis for clinical decision-making in small treatment settings. *International Journal of Neurosciences, 113*(3), 417–430.

Ridge, S., Campbell, W., & Martin, D. (2002). Striving towards an understanding of Conscious Identification: Its definition and its effects. *Counseling Psychology Quarterly, 15*(1), 91–105.

Ridgers, N. D., Stratton, G., & McKenzie, T. L. (2011). Reliability and validity of the System for Observing Children's Activity and Relationships during Play (SOCARP). *Journal of Physical Activity & Health, 7*(1), 17–25.

Rieke, M. L., & Guastello, S. J. (1995). Unresolved issues in honesty and integrity testing. *American Psychologist, 50*, 458–459.

Riggio, R. E., Murphy, S. E., & Pirozzolo, F. J. (Eds.) (2002). *Multiple intelligences and leadership.* Mahwah, NJ: Erlbaum.

Righetti-Veltema, M., Bousquet, A., & Manzano, J. (2003). Impact of postpartum depressive symptoms on mother and her 18-month-old infant. *European Child and Adolescent Psychiatry, 12*(2), 75–83.

Rindermann, H., Becker, D., & Coyle, T. R. (2016). Survey of expert opinion on intelligence: Causes of international differences in cognitive ability tests. *Frontiers in Psychology, 7*, 399–406.

Rips, L. J. (2011). *Lines of thought: Central concepts in cognitive psychology.* New York: Oxford University Press, Inc.

Ritzler, B. A., & Alter, B. (1986). Rorschach teaching in APA-approved clinical graduate programs: Ten years later. *Journal of Personality Assessment, 50*, 44–49.

Ritzler, B. A., Sharkey, K. J., & Chudy, J. F. (1980). A comprehensive projective alternative to the TAT. *Journal of Personality Assessment, 44*, 358–362.

Roberts, B. W., Harms, P. D., Caspi, A., & Moffitt, T. E. (2007). Predicting the counterproductive employee in a child-to-adult prospective study. *Journal of Applied Psychology, 92*(5), 1427–1436.

Roberts, J.S., Laughlin, J.E., & Wendel, D.H. (1999). Validity issues in the Likert and Thurstone approaches to attitude measurement. *Educational and Psychological Measurement, 59*(2), 211–233.

Roberts, K. E., Hart, T. A., & Eastwood, J. D. (2016). Factor structure and validity of the state-trait inventory for cognitive and somatic anxiety. *Psychological Assessment, 28*(2), 134.

Robins, J., & Antrim, P. (2013). Planning for rti. *Knowledge Quest, 42*(1), 44–47.

Rock, R. (2007). Active listening: Can it reduce pain? *Clinical Nurse Specialist, 21*(2), 116–117.

Rodger, S. C. (2002). Teacher clarity and student anxiety: An aptitude-treatment interaction experiment. *Dissertation Abstracts International: Section B. The Physical Sciences and Engineering, 63*, 4B.

Rodriguez, M. (2005). Three options are optimal for multiple-choice items: A meta-analysis of 80 years of research. *Educational Measurement: Issues and Practice, 24*(2), 3–13.

Rodriguez, M. (2016). *College instructor's guide to writing test items: Measuring student learning outcomes in the … College classroom.* New York: Routledge.

Roeckelein, J. E. (2002). A demonstration of undergraduate students' first impression and their ratings of pathology. *Psychological Reports, 90*(2), 613–618.

Rogers, C. R. (1959a). A Tentative Scale for the measurement of process in psychotherapy. In E. A. Rubinstein & M. B. Parloff (Eds.), *Research in psychotherapy.* Washington, DC: American Psychological Association.

Rogers, C. R. (1959b). A theory of therapy, personality, and interpersonal relationships, as developed in the client-centered framework. In S. Koch (Ed.), *Psychology: A study of science* (Vol. 3, pp. 185–252). New York: McGraw-Hill.

Rogers, C. R. (1961). *On becoming a person.* Boston: Houghton Mifflin.

Rogers, C. R. (1980). *A way of being.* Boston: Houghton Mifflin.

Rogers, R., Sewell, K. W., Harrison, K. S., & Jordan, M. J. (2006). The MMPI-2 Restructured Clinical Scales: A paradigmatic shift in scale development. *Journal of Personality Assessment, 87*(2), 139–147.

Rogers, W. H., Lerner, D., & Adler, D. A. (2010). Technological approaches to screening and case finding for depression. In A. Mitchell & J. C. Coyne (Eds.), *Screening for depression in clinical practice: An evidence-based guide* (pp. 19–25). New York: Oxford University Press.

Roid, G. H. (2003a). *Stanford Binet Intelligence Scales* (5th ed.). Itasca, IL: Riverside.

Roid, G. H. (2003b). *Stanford Binet Intelligence Scales* (5th ed.), Examiners Manual. Itasca, IL: Riverside.

Roid, G. H. (2003c). *Stanford Binet Intelligence Scales* (5th ed.), Technical Manual. Itasca, IL: Riverside.

Roid, G. H. (2014). *A message from Leiter-3 author, Dr. Gale Roid.* Wood Dale, IL: Stoelting Co.

Roid, G. H., Miller, L. J., Pomplun, M., & Koch, C. (2013). *Leiter International Performance Scale* (3rd ed.). Wood Dale, IL: Stoelting Co.

Roland, M., & Dudley, R. A. (2015). How financial and reputational incentives can be used to improve medical care. *Health services research, 50*(S2), 2090–2115.

Rolland, J. P., Parker, W. D., & Stumpf, H. (1998). A psychometric examination of the French translations of the NEO-PI-R and NEO-FFI. *Journal of Personality Assessment, 71*, 269–291.

Rollnick, J. D., Borsutsky, M., Huber, T. J., Mogk, H., Seifert, J., Emrich, H. M., & Schneider, U. (2002). Short-term cognitive improvement in schizophrenics treated with typical and atypical neuroleptics. *Neuropsychobiology, 45*(2), 74–80.

Rosenberg, M. (1965). *Society and the adolescent self-image.* Princeton, New Jersey: Princeton University Press.

Rosenfeld, P., Doherty, L. M., Vicino, S. M., Kantor, J., & Greaves, J. (1989). Attitude assessment in organizations: Testing three microcomputer-based survey systems. *Journal of General Psychology, 116*, 145–154.

Rosenstein, R., & Glickman, A. S. (1994). Type size and performance of the elderly on the Wonderlic Personnel Test. *Journal of Applied Gerontology, 13*(2), 185–192.

Rosenthal, R. (1966). *Experimenter effects in behavioral research.* New York: Appleton-Century-Crofts.

Rosenthal, R. (2002a). *Experimenter and clinician effects in scientific inquiry and clinical practice.* Washington, DC: American Psychological Assocation.

Rosenthal, R. (2002b). *The Pygmalion effect and its mediating mechanisms.* San Diego, CA: Academic Press.

Rosenthal, R. (2015). Reflections on the origins of meta-analysis. *Research Synthesis Methods, 6*(3), 240–245.

Rosenthal, R., & Fode, K. L. (1963). The effects of experimenter bias on the performance of the albino rat. *Behavioral Science, 8*, 183–189.

Rosenthal, R., & Jacobson, L. (1968). *Pygmalion in the classroom.* New York: Holt, Rinehart & Winston.

Rosenthal, R., & Rosnow, R. L. (1991). *Essentials of behavioral research: Method and data analysis* (2nd ed.). New York: McGraw-Hill.

Rosenthal, R., & Rubie-Davies, C. M. (2015). Bob Rosenthal's lifetime of research into interpersonal expectancy effects. In C. M. Rubie-Davies, J. M. Stephens, & P Watson (Eds.), *The Routledge International Handbook of Social Psychology of the Classroom* (pp. 285–295). New York: Routledge.

Rosner, J. (2003, April 14). On white preferences. *The Nation.*

Rossier, J. (2015). Personality assessment and career interventions. In P. J. Hartung, M. L. Savickas, & W. B. Walsh (Ed.), *APA handbook of career intervention, Volume 1: Foundations* (pp. 327–350). Washington, DC, US: American Psychological Association,

Rostami, A., Abdollahi, H., & Maeder, M. (2016). Enhanced target factor analysis. *Analytica Chimica Acta, 119*, 35–41.

Roth, P. L., Huffcutt, A. I., & Bobko, P. (2003). Ethnic group differences in measures of job performance: A new meta-analysis. *Journal of Applied Psychology, 88*(4), 694–706.

Rothbaum, B. O., Anderson, P., Zimand, E., Hodges, L., Lang, D., & Wilson, J. (2006). Virtual reality exposure therapy and standard (in vivo) exposure therapy in the treatment of fear of flying. *Behavior Therapy, 37*(1), 80–90.

Rothlin, S., & McCann, D. (2016). Employees: Discrimination and sexual harassment. In S. Rothlin & D. McCann (Eds.), *International business ethics* (pp. 179–201). New York: Springer.

Rothstein, H. R. (2003). *Progress is our most important product: Contributions of validity generalization and meta-analysis to the development and communication of knowledge in I/O psychology.* Mahwah, NJ: Erlbaum.

Rotter, J. B. (1967). A new scale for the measurement of interpersonal trust. *Journal of Personality, 35*, 651–665.

Rotter, J. B., & Rafferty, J. E. (1950). *Manual: The Rotter incomplete sentences blank*. San Antonio, TX: Psychological Corporation.

Rottinghaus, P., Coon, K., Gaffey, A., & Zytowski, D. (2007). Thirty-year stability and predictive validity of vocational interests. *Journal of Career Assessment, 15*(1), 5–22.

Roy, D. D., & Deb, N. C. (1999). Item-to-tal-score correlations of state anxiety inventory across different months in Antarctic expedition. *Psychological Studies, 44*(1–2), 43–45.

Royal, K. D., & Guskey, T. R. (2015). On the appropriateness of norm-and-criterion-referenced assessments in medical education. *Ear, Nose and Throat Journal, 94*(7), 252–254.

Rubie-Davies, C. M., Peterson, E. R., Sibley, C. G., & Rosenthal, R. (2015). A teacher expectation intervention: Modelling the practices of high expectation teachers. *Contemporary Educational Psychology, 40,* 72–85.

Rubin, Z. (1979, February 21). Los Angeles says it with love on a scale. *Los Angeles Times.*

Rubio, D. M., Berg-Weger, M., Tebb, S. S., Lee, E. S., & Rauch, S. (2003). Objectifying content validity: Conducting a content validity study in social work research. *Social Work Research, 27*(2), 94–104.

Ruiz, F., Suárez-Falcón, J., Barón-Rincón, D., Barrera-Acevedo, A., Martínez-Sánchez, A., et al. (2016). Factor structure and psychometric properties of the Dysfunctional Attitude Scale Revised in colombian undergraduates. *Revista Latinoamericana De Psicología, 48*(2), 81–87.

Ruiz, F., Suarez-Falcon, J., Odriozo-la-Gonzalez, P., Barbero-Rubio, A., Lopez-Lopez, J., et al. (2015). Factor structure and psychometric properties of the spanish version of the "Dysfunctional Attitude Scale-Revised". *Behavioral Psychology-psicologia Conductual, 23*(2), 287–303.

Rumsey, M. G. (2013). The future: A research agenda. *Personnel Selection and Classification,* In M. G. Rumsey, C. B. Walker, & J. H. Harris (Eds.), *Personnel selection and classification* (pp. 457–474). Hillsdale NJ: Psychology Press.

Ruscio, J., & Walters, G. D. (2011). Differentiating categorical and dimensional data with taxometric analysis: are two variables better than none? *Psychol Assess, 23*(2), 287–299. doi: 10.1037/a0022054.

Rushton, J. P. (1991). Do r-K strategies underlie human race differences? *Canadian Psychology, 32,* 29–42.

Rushton, J. P., & Irwing, P. (2011). The general factor of personality: Normal and abnormal. In T. Chamorro-Premuzic, S. von Stumm, & A. Furnham (Eds.), *The Wiley Blackwell handbook of individual differences* (pp. 132–162). West Sussex, UK: Blackwell Publishing.

Rushton, J., & Irwing, P. (2009). A general factor of personality in 16 sets of the big five, the guilford–zimmerman temperament survey, the california psychological inventory, and the temperament and character inventory. *Personality and Individual Differences, 47*(6), 558–564.

Rushton, P., & Jensen, A. R. (2005). Thirty years of research on race differences in cognitive ability psychology. *Public Policy, and Law, 11*(2), 235–294.

Russell, E. W. (2000). The application of computerized scoring programs to neuropsychological assessment. In R. D. Vanderploeg (Ed.), *Clinician's guide to neuropsychological assessment* (pp. 483–515). Mahwah, NJ: Erlbaum.

Russell, L. B. (1986). *Is prevention better than cure?* Washington, DC: Brookings Institution.

Russo, M. (2011). Aptitude testing over the years. *Interpreting, 13*(1), 5–30.

Rust, J., & Golombok, S. (2009). *Modern psychometrics: The science of psychological assessment* (3rd ed.). London; New York: Routledge.

Rutherford, C., Costa, D., Mercieca-Bebber, R., Rice, H., Gabb, L., & King, M. (2015). Mode of administration does not cause bias in patient-reported outcome results: A meta-analysis. *Quality of Life Research, 25*(3), 559–574.

Saccuzzo and Lewandowski (1976a)

Saccuzzo, D. P. (1975). Canonical correlation as a method of assessing the correlates of good and bad therapy hours. *Psychotherapy: Theory, Research and Practice, 12,* 253–256.

Saccuzzo, D. P. (1994, August). *Coping with complexities of contemporary psychological testing: Negotiating shifting sands.* Invited presentation for the G. Stanley Hall Lecture Series, American Psychological Association 102nd Annual Meeting, Los Angeles.

Saccuzzo, D. P. (1999). Still crazy after all these years: California's persistent use of the MMPI as character evidence in criminal cases. *University of San Francisco Law Review, 33,* 379–400.

Saccuzzo, D. P., & Johnson, N. E. (1995). Traditional psychometric test and proportionate representation: An intervention and program evaluation study. *Psychological Assessment, 7*(2), 183–194.

Saccuzzo, D. P., & Johnson, N. E. (2000). *The 5-minute IQ test: Item characteristics and reliability.* San Diego, CA: Applications of Psychology to Law.

Saccuzzo, D. P., & Kaplan, R. M. (1984). *Clinical psychology.* Boston: Allyn & Bacon.

Saccuzzo, D. P., & Lewandowski, D. G. (1976b). The WISC as a diagnostic tool. *Journal of Clinical Psychology, 32,* 115–124.

Saccuzzo, D. P., Braff, D. L., Shine, A., & Lewandowski, D. G. (1981, April). *A differential WSC pattern in the retarded as a function of sex and race.* Paper presented at the meeting of the Western Psychological Association, Los Angeles.

Saccuzzo, D. P., Johnson, N. E., & Russell, G. (1992). Verbal versus performance IQs for gifted African-American, Caucasian, Filipino, and Hispanic children. *Psychological Assessment, 4,* 239–244.

Saccuzzo, D., Kewley, S., & Johnson, N., et al. (2003). *An examination of positive affect measures* (Naval Health Research Center Rep. No. TCN 02109/D. I. 0118).

Sackett, P. R. (1998). Performance assessment in education and professional certification: Lessons for personnel selection? In M. D. Hakel (Eds.), *Beyond multiple choice: Evaluating alternatives to traditional testing for selection* (pp. 113–129). Mahwah, NJ: Erlbaum.

Sackett, P. R. (2003). *The status of validity generalization research: Key issues in drawing inferences from cumulative research findings.* Mahwah, NJ: Erlbaum.

Sackett, P. R., & Lievens, F. (2008). Personnel selection. *Annual Review of Psychology, 59,* 1–32.

Sackett, P. R., & Wilk, S. L. (1994). Within-group norming and other forms of score adjustment in pre-employment testing. *American Psychologist, 49,* 929–954.

Sackett, P. R., Borneman, M. J., & Connelly, B. S. (2008). High-stakes testing in higher-education and employment: Appraising the evidence for validity and fairness. *American Psychologist, 63,* 215–227.

Sadler, P. M., Sonnert, G., Coyle, H. P., & Miller, K. A. (2016). Identifying promising items: The use of crowdsourcing in the development of assessment instruments. *Educational Assessment, 21*(3), 196–214.

Safir, M., & Wallach, H. (2011). Current trends and future directions for virtual reality enhanced psychotherapy. In S. Brahman & L. Jain (Eds.), *Advanced computational intelligence paradigms in healthcare: Virtual reality in psychotherapy, rehabilitation, and assessment, Studies in computational intelligence 337* (Vol. 3, pp. 32–45). Berlin: Springer. doi: 10.1007/978-3-642-17824-5_3.

Saine, N. L., Lerkkanen, M. -K., Ahonen, T., Tolvanen, A., & Lyytinen, H. (2011). Computer-assisted remedial reading intervention for school beginners at risk for reading disability. *Child Development, 82*(3), 1013–1028. doi: 10.1111/j.1467-8624.2011.01580.x.

Sakuragi, A. (2006). *The applicability of Exner's comprehensive system of the Rorschach to a Japanese population*. US: ProQuest Information & Learning.

Salgado, J. F., Moscoso, S., & Anderson, N. (2016). Corrections for criterion reliability in validity generalization: The consistency of Hermes, the utility of Midas. *Revista de Psicología del Trabajo y de las Organizaciones, 32*(1), 17–23.

Sallis, J. F., Cerin, E., Conway, T. L., Adams, M. A., Frank, L. D., Pratt, M., … Cain, K. L. (2016). Physical activity in relation to urban environments in 14 cities worldwide: A cross-sectional study. *The Lancet, 387*(10034), 2207-2217.

Saltzman, J., Strauss, E., Hunter, M., & Spellacy, F. (1998). Validity of the Wonderlic Personnel Test as a brief measure of intelligence in individuals referred for evaluation of head injury. *Archives of Clinical Neuropsychology, 13*, 611–616.

Salzinger, K. (2005). Clinical, statistical, and broken-leg predictions. *Behavior and Philosophy, 33*, 91–99.

Samuel, D. B., Hopwood, C. J., Ansell, E. B., Morey, L. C., Sanislow, C. A., Markowitz, J. C., et al. (2011). Comparing the temporal stability of self-report and interview assessed personality disorder. *Journal of Abnormal Psychology, 120*(3), 670–680. doi: 10.1037/a0022647.

Sander, N., Johann, R., Wilhelm, O., & Wittmann, W. (2000). Promise and impact of structuring interviews: Personnel selection of textile. *International Journal of Psychology, 35*(3–4), 381.

Sanderson, T., Hewlett, S., Richards, P., Morris, M., & Calnan, M. (2011). Utilizing qualitative data from nominal groups: Exploring the influences on treatment outcome prioritization with rheumatoid arthritis patients. *Journal of Health Psychology*.

Sands, W. A., Waters, B. K., & McBride, J. R. (1997). *Computerized adaptive testing: From inquiry to operation*. Washington, DC: American Psychological Association.

Sangwan, S. (2001). Ecological factors as related to I.Q. of children. *PsychoLingua, 31*(2), 89–92.

Santangelo, G., Sacco, R., Siciliano, M., Bisecco, A., Muzzo, G., Docimo, R., … Tedeschi, G. (2016). Anxiety in multiple sclerosis: Psychometric properties of the state-trait anxiety inventory. *Acta Neurologica Scandinavica*. Published online ahead of print. *doi:* 10.1111/ane.12560.

Santosa, C. M., Strong, C. M., Nowakowska, C., Wang, P. W., Rennicke, C. M., & Ketter, T. A. (2007). Enhanced creativity in bipolar disorder patients: A controlled study. *Journal of Affective Disorders, 100*(1), 31–39.

Sapp, M. (1999). *Test anxiety: Applied research, assessment, and treatment interventions* (2nd ed.). Lanham, MD: University Press of America.

Sarason, I. G., Sarason, B. R., & Pierce, G. R. (1990). *Social support: An interactional view*. New York: Wiley.

Sarason, I., & Sarason, B. (2004). *Abnormal psychology: The problem of maladaptive behavior* (11th ed.). Boston: Pearson.

Satre, D. D., Chi, F. W., Eisendrath, S., & Weisner, C. (2011). Subdiagnostic alcohol use by depressed men and women seeking outpatient psychiatric services: Consumption patterns and motivation to reduce drinking. *Alcoholism: Clinical and Experimental Research, 35*, 695–702. doi: 10.1111/j.1530-0277.2010.01387.x.

Sattler, J. M. (1970). Racial "experimenter effects" in experimentation, testing, interviewing, and psychotherapy. *Psychological Bulletin, 73*, 137–160.

Sattler, J. M. (1973a). Intelligence testing of ethnic minority-group and culturally disadvantaged children. In L. Mann & D. Sabatino (Eds.), *The first review of special education* (Vol. 2). Philadelphia: JSE Press.

Sattler, J. M. (1973b). Racial experimenter effects. In K. S. Miller & R. M. Dreger (Eds.), *Comparative studies of blacks and whites in the United States*. New York: Seminar Press.

Sattler, J. M. (1979a, April). *Intelligence tests on trial: Larry P. et al. v. Wilson Riles et al.* Paper presented at the meeting of the Western Psychological Association, San Diego, CA.

Sattler, J. M. (1979b). Standard intelligence tests are valid for measuring the intellectual potential of urban children: Comments on pitfalls in the measurement of intelligence. *Journal of Psychology, 102*, 107–112.

Sattler, J. M. (1982). *Assessment of children's intelligence and special abilities*. Boston: Allyn & Bacon.

Sattler, J. M. (1988). *Assessment of children* (3rd ed.). San Diego, CA: J. M. Sattler.

Sattler, J. M. (1998). *Clinical and forensic interviewing of children and families: Guidelines for the mental health, education, pediatric, and child maltreatment fields*. San Diego, CA: J. M. Sattler.

Sattler, J. M. (2002). *Assessment of children: Behavioral and clinical applications* (4th ed.). La Mesa, CA: J. M. Sattler.

Sattler, J. M. (2004). *Assessment of children: WISC-IV and WPPSI-III SUPPLEMENT*. La Mesa, CA: J. M. Sattler.

Sattler, J. M. (2014). *Foundaitons of behavioral, social, and clinical assessment of children* (6th ed.). La Mesa, CA: Jerome M. Sattler, Publishers.

Sattler, J. M., & Gwynne, J. (1982). Ethnicity and Bender Visual Motor Test performance. *Journal of School Psychology, 20*, 69–71.

Sattler, J. M., & Theye, F. (1967). Procedural, situational, and interpersonal variables in individual intelligence testing. *Psychological Bulletin, 68*, 347–360.

Sattler, J. M., & Winget, B. M. (1970). Intelligence testing procedures as affected by expectancy and IQ. *Journal of Clinical Psychology, 26*, 446–448.

Sattler, J. M., Hillix, W. A., & Neher, L. A. (1970). Halo effect in examiner scoring of intelligence test responses. *Journal of Consulting and Clinical Psychology, 34*, 172–176.

Sauerberger, K. S., & Funder, D. C. (2016). Behavioral change and consistency across contexts. *Journal of Research in Personality*. Published online ahead of print http://dx.doi.org/10.1016/j.jrp.2016.04.007.

Saunders, B. T., & Vitro, F. T. (1971). Examiner expectancy and bias as a function of the referral process in cognitive assessment. *Psychology in the Schools, 8*, 168–171.

Savage, G. (2016). Cognitive Neuropsychological Formulation. In A. B. J. Macniven (Ed.), *Neuropsychological Formulation: A Clinical Casebook* (pp. 221–239). Cham: Springer International Publishing.

Savickas, M. L. (2000). Assessing career decision making. In C. E. Watkins

Jr. & V. L. Campbell (Eds.), *Testing and assessment in counseling practice* (2nd ed., pp. 429–477). Mahwah, NJ: Erlbaum.

Savickas, M. L. (2015). Career counseling paradigms: Guiding, developing, and designing. In P. J. Hartung, M. L. Savickas, & W. B. Walsh (Ed.), *APA handbook of career intervention, Volume 1: Foundations* (pp. 129–143). Washington, DC, US: American Psychological Association.

Sawyer, J. (1966). Measurement and prediction, clinical and statistical. *Psychological Bulletin, 66*, 178–200.

Sawyer, R. (2007). Indicators of usefulness of test scores. *Applied Measurement in Education, 20*(3), 255–271.

Schaefer, B. A., Koeter, M. W. J., Wouters, L., Emmelkamp, P. M. G., & Schene, A. H. (2003). What patient characteristics make clinicians recommend brief treatment? *Acta Psychiatrica Scandinavica, 107*(3), 188–196.

Schaefer, J. A., & Moos, R. H. (1996). Effects of work stressors and work climate on long-term care staff's job morale and functioning. *Research in Nursing and Health, 19*(1), 63–73.

Schalet, B. D., Hays, R. D., Jensen, S. E., Beaumont, J. L., Fries, J. F., & Cella, D. (2016). Validity of PROMIS physical function measures in diverse clinical samples. *Journal of Clinical Epidemiology, 73*, 112–118.

Scheier, M. F., & Carver, C. S. (1985). Optimism, coping, and health: Assessment and implications of generalized outcome expectancies. *Health Psychology, 4*, 219–247.

Scheier, M. F., Weintraub, J. K., & Carver, C. S. (1986). Coping with stress: Divergent strategies of optimists and pessimists. *Journal of Personality and Social Psychology, 51*(6), 1257–1264.

Scheuneman, J. D. (1987). An experimental, exploratory study of causes of bias in test items. *Journal of Educational Measurement, 24*, 97–118.

Schleicher, A., & Tamassia, C. (2000). *Measuring student knowledge and skills: The PISA Assessment of Reading, Mathematical, and Scientific Literacy.* Retrieved April 16, 2003, from www.pisa.oecd.org/knowledge/home/intro.htm.

Schmidt, A. E. (2000). An approximation of a hierarchical logistic regression model used to establish the predictive validity of scores on a nursing licensure exam. *Educational & Psychological Measurement, 60*(3), 463–478.

Schmidt, F. L., & Hunter, J. E. (1983). Individual differences in productivity: An empirical test of estimates derived from studies of selection procedure utility. *Journal of Applied Psychology, 68*, 407–414.

Schmidt, F. L., & Rothstein, H. R. (1994). Application of validity generalization to biodata scales in employment selection. In G. S. Stokes, M. D. Mumford, & W. A. Owens (Eds.), *Biodata handbook: Theory, research, and use of biographical information in selection and performance prediction* (pp. 237–260). Palo Alto, CA: CPP Books.

Schmidt, F. L., Law, K., Hunter, J. E., Rothstein, H. R., Pearlman, K., & McDaniel, M. (1993). Refinements in validity generalization methods: Implications for the situational specificity hypothesis. *Journal of Applied Psychology, 78*, 3–12.

Schmidt, F., & Hunter, J. (2003). *History, development, evolution, and impact of validity generalization and meta-analysis methods, 1975–2001.* Mahwah, NJ: Erlbaum.

Schmitt, N. (2012). *The Oxford handbook of personnel assessment and selection.* New York: Oxford University Press.

Schmukle, S. C., Egloff, B., & Burns, L. R. (2002). The relationship between positive and negative affect in the positive and negative affect schedule. *Journal of Research in Personality, 36*(5), 463–475.

Schneider, A., Kotronoulas, G., Papadopoulou, C., McCann, L., Miller, M., McBride, J., … Kearney, N. (2016). Trajectories and predictors of state and trait anxiety in patients receiving chemotherapy for breast and colorectal cancer: Results from a longitudinal study. *European Journal of Oncology Nursing, 24*, 1–7.

Schneider, L. M., & Briel, J. B. (1990). *Validity of the GRE: 1988–1989 summary report.* Princeton, NJ: Educational Testing Service.

Schneider, L., Powell, D., & Roulin, N. (2015). Cues to deception in the employment interview. *International Journal of Selection and Assessment, 23*(2), 182–190.

Schneider, R. J., Goff, M., Anderson, S., & Borman, W. C. (2003). Computerized adaptive rating scales for measuring managerial performance. *International Journal of Selection & Assessment, 11*(2–3), 237–246.

Schneider, S., & Stone, A. A. (2016). Ambulatory and diary methods can facilitate the measurement of patient-reported outcomes. *Quality of Life Research, 25*(3), 497–506.

Schneider, S., Stone, A. A., Schwartz, J. E., & Broderick, J. E. (2011). Peak and end effects in patients' daily recall of pain and fatigue: A within-subjects analysis [Research Support, N.I.H., Extramural]. *The Journal of Pain, 12*(2), 228–235. doi: 10.1016/j.jpain.2010.07.001.

Schnipke, D. L., Stilwell, L. A., & Reese L. M. (2011). LSAT performance with regional, gender, and racial/ethnic breakdowns. Retrieved from www.lsac.org

Schoenberg, M. R., Scott, J. G., & SpringerLink (Online service). (2011). *The little black book of neuropsychology a syndrome-based approach.* Retrieved from http://dx.doi.org/10.1007/978-0-387-76978-3.

Schoggen, P. (1979). Roger G. Barker and behavioral settings: A commentary. *Journal of Personality and Social Psychology, 37*, 2158–2160.

Scholz, U., Dona, B. G., Sud, S., & Schwarzer, R. (2002). Is general self-efficacy a universal construct? Psychometric findings from 25 countries. *European Journal of Psychological Assessment, 18*(3), 242–251.

Schouten, B. C., & Meeuwesen, L. (2006). Cultural differences in medical communication: A review of the literature. *Patient Education and Counseling, 64*(1–3), 21–34.

Schrank, F. A., Flanagan, D. P., Woodcock, R. W., & Mascolo, J. T. (2002). *Essentials of WJ III cognitive abilities assessment.* New York: Wiley.

Schrank, F. A., Mather, N., & McGrew, K. S. (2014). *Woodcock-Johnson IV Tests of Achievement.* Rolling Meadows, IL: Riverside.

Schrank, F. A., McGrew, K. S., & Woodcock, R. W. (2001). *Technical abstract* (Assessment service bulletin no. 2). Itasca, IL: Riverside.

Schroeder, H. E., & Kleinsaser, L. D. (1972). Examiner bias: A determinant of children's verbal behavior on the WISC. *Journal of Consulting and Clinical Psychology, 39*, 451–454.

Schuerger, J. M. (1995). Career assessment and the sixteen personality factor questionnaire. *Journal of Career Assessment, 3*, 157–175.

Schuerger, J. M., Tait, E., & Tavernelli, M. (1982). Temporal stability of personality by questionnaire. *Journal of Personality and Social Psychology, 43*, 176–182.

Schulenberg, S. E., & Yutrzenka, B. A. (1999). The equivalence of computerized and paper-and-pencil psychological instruments: Implications for measures of negative affect. *Behavior Research Methods, Instruments and Computers, 31*(2), 315–321.

Schuler, H. (1993). Is there a dilemma between validity and acceptance in the employment interview? In B. Nevo & R. S. Jager (Eds.), *Educational and psychological testing: The test taker's outlook* (pp. 239–250). Gottingen, Germany: Huber.

Schultz, C. B., & Sherman, R. H. (1976). Social class, development, and differences in reinforcer effectiveness. *Review of Educational Research, 46,* 25–59.

Schultz, D. S., & Loving, J. L. (2012). Challenges since Wikipedia: The availability of Rorschach information online and Internet users' reactions to online media coverage of the Rorschach–Wikipedia debate. *Journal of Personality Assessment, 94*(1), 73–81.

Schwager, I., Hülsheger, U., Lang, J., & Bridgeman, B. (2015). Graduate student selection: Graduate record examination, socioeconomic status, and undergraduate grade point average as predictors of study success in a western european university. *International Journal of Selection and Assessment, 23*(1), 71–79.

Schwartz, A. (2014). A review of the Rorschach Inkblot Test: An interpretive guide for clinicians. *Journal of Personality Assessment, 96*(4), 482–483.

Schwarz, L. R., Gfeller, J. D., & Oliveri, M. V. (2006). Detecting feigned impairment with the digit span and vocabulary subtests of the Wechsler Adult Intelligence Scale-Third edition. *Clinical Neuropsychologist, 20*(4), 741–753.

Schweder, T., & Hjort, N. L. (2016). *Confidence, likelihood, probability* (Vol. 41). Cambridge, UK: Cambridge University Press.

Scott, L. H. (1981). Measuring intelligence with the Goodenough-Harris Drawing Test. *Psychological Bulletin, 89,* 483–505.

Scurich, N., & John, R. (2011). A Bayesian approach to the group versus individual prediction controversy in actuarial risk assessment. *Law and Human Behavior,* 1–11. Retrieved from http://www.springerlink.com/content/l957226475617406/. doi: 10.1007/s10979-011-9286-0.

Sechrest, L., Stickle, T. R., & Stewart, M. (1998). The role of assessment in clinical psychology. In A. Bellack, M.

Hersen (Series Ed.), & C. R. Reynolds (Vol. Ed.), *Comprehensive clinical psychology* (Vol. 4, Chap. 1). New York: Pergamon Press.

Seewaldt, V. A. (2006). *Using the CCRT to interpret the TAT: Understanding the phenomenon of 'card pull'.* US: ProQuest Information & Learning.

Segre, L. S., O'Hara, M. W., Arndt, S., & Stuart, S. (2007). The prevalence of postpartum depression: The relative significance of three social status indices. *Social Psychiatry and Psychiatric Epidemiology, 42*(4), 316–321.

Seguin, E. (1907). *Idiocy: Its treatment by the physiological method.* New York: Bureau of Publications, Teachers College, Columbia University. (Original work published 1866).

Seidman, L. J., Buka, S. L., Goldstein, J. M., & Tsuang, M. T. (2006). Intellectual decline in schizophrenia: Evidence from a prospective birth cohort 28-year follow-up study. *Journal of Clinical and Experimental Neuropsychology, 28*(2), 225–242.

Seligmann, J., Coppola, V., Howard, L., & Lee, E. D. (1979, May 28). A really final exam. *Newsweek,* pp. 97–98.

Senior, C., Phillips, M. L., Barns, J., & David, A. S. (1999). An investigation into the perception of dominance from schematic faces: A study using the World-Wide Web. *Behavior Research Methods, Instruments and Computers, 31*(2), 341–346.

Serfass, D., & Sherman, R. (2013). Personality and perceptions of situations from the Thematic Apperception Test. *Journal of Research in Personality, 47*(6), 708–718.

Sethuraman, R., Kerin, R. A., & Cron, W. L. (2005). A field study comparing online and offline data collection methods for identifying product attribute preferences using conjoint analysis. *Journal of Business Research, 58*(5), 602–610.

Shackleton, V. (2015). Recruitment and selection. In *Spurgeon.* And. A. J. Chapman (Eds.), *Elements of applied psychology* (pp. 153–192). Mountain View, CA: Google Books.

Shaffer, D., Fisher, P., Lucas, C. P., Dulcan, M. K., Schwab-Stone, M. E. (2000). NIMH Diagnostic Interview Schedule for Children Version IV (NIMH DISC-IV): Description, differences from previous versions, and reliability of some common diagnoses. *Journal of the American Academy of Child and Adolescent Psychiatry, 39*(1), 28–38.

Shaffer, L. (1953). Of whose reality I cannot doubt. *American Psychologist, 8,* 608–623.

Shaffer, T. W., & Erdberg, P. (1996, July). *Cooperative movement in the Rorschach response: A qualitative approach.* Paper presented at the 15th International Congress of Rorschach and Projective Methods, Boston, MA.

Shaffer, T. W., Erdberg, P., & Horaian, J. (1999). Current nonpatient data for the Rorschach, WAIS-R, and MMPI-2. *Journal of Personality Assessment, 73,* 305–316.

Shakow, D., Hilgard, E. R., Kelly, E. L., Sanford, R. N., & Shaffer, L. F. (1947). Recommended graduate training in clinical psychology. *American Psychologist, 2,* 539–558.

Sharkey, K. J., & Ritzler, B. A. (1985). Comparing diagnostic validity of the TAT and a new Picture Projective Test. *Journal of Personality Assessment, 49,* 406–412.

Shattuck, D. W., Mirza, M., Adisetiyo, V., Hojatkashani, C., Salamon, G., Narr, K. L., et al. (2008). Construction of a 3d probabilistic atlas of human cortical structures. *Neuroimage, 39*(3), 1064–1080.

Shavelson, R. J., & Ruiz-Primo, M. A. (2000). On the psychometrics of assessing science understanding. In J. J. Mintzes, J. H. Wandersee, & J. D. Novak (Eds.), *Assessing science understanding: A human constructivist view* (pp. 303–341). San Diego, CA: Academic Press.

Shavitt, S., Cho, Y. I., Johnson, T. P., Jiang, D., Holbrook, A., & Stavrakantonaki, M. (2016). Culture moderates the relation between perceived stress, social support, and mental and physical health. *Journal of Cross-Cultural Psychology, 47*(7), 956–980.

Sheldon, B. (2011). *Cognitive-behavioural therapy.* New York: Routledge.

Shenk, D. (2011a). *The genius in all of us: New insights into genetics, talent, and IQ.* New York: Anchor.

Shenk, D. (2011b). *The genius in all of us: Why everything you've been told about genetics, talent, and IQ is wrong.* New York: Anchor.

Shermer, M. (2015). Willpower and won't power: A review of the marshmallow test: Mastering self-control by Walter Mischel. *Skeptic, 20*(2), 58–60.

Shermis, M. D., Mzumara, H. R., & Bublitz, S. T. (2001). On test and computer anxiety: Test performance under CAT and SAT conditions. *Journal of*

Educational Computing Research, 24(1), 57–75.

Sherrer, M. V. (2011). The role of cognitive appraisal in adaptation to traumatic stress in adults with serious mental illness: A critical review. *Trauma Violence & Abuse, 12*(3), 151–167. doi: 10.1177/1524838011404254.

Shibata, S. (2002). A Macintosh and Windows program for assessing body-image disturbance using adjustable image distortion. *Behavior Research Methods, Instruments, and Computers, 34*(1), 90–92.

Shiffman, S., Fischer, L. A., Paty, J. A., Gnys, M., Hickox, M., & Kassel, J. D. (1995). Drinking and smoking: A field study of their association. *Annals of Behavioral Medicine, 16*(3), 203–209.

Shirzad, G. (2016). The role of the Myers-Briggs Personality Type and emotional intelligence in marital satisfaction among married female students at Tehran University. *Global Journal of Health Science, 8*(10), 50.

Shonkoff, J. P. (2011). Protecting brains, not simply stimulating minds. *Science, 333* (6045), 982–983. doi: 10.1126/science.1206014.

Shonkoff, J. P., & Levitt, P. (2010). Neuroscience and the future of early childhood policy: moving from why to what and how. *Neuron, 67*(5), 689–691. doi: 10.1016/j.neuron. 2010.08.032.

Shonkoff, J. P., Garner, A. S., Committee on Psychosocial Aspects of, Child, Family, Health, Committee on Early Childhood, Adoption, Dependent, Care, Behavioral, Pediatrics. (2012). The lifelong effects of early childhood adversity and toxic stress. *Pediatrics, 129*(1), e232–e246. doi: 10.1542/peds.2011-2663.

Short, P., Cernich, A., Wilken, J. A., & Kane, R. L. (2007). Initial construct validation of frequently employed ANAM measures through structural equation modeling. *Archives of Clinical Neuropsychology, 22* (Suppl. 1), S63–S77.

Shrout, P. E., Spitzer, R. L., & Fleiss, J. L. (1987). Quantification of agreement in psychiatric diagnosis revisited. *Archives of General Psychiatry, 44*(2), 172–177.

Shull-Senn, S., Weatherly, M., Morgan, S. K., & Bradley-Johnson, S. (1995). Stability reliability for elementary-age students on the Woodcock-Johnson Psychoeducational Battery—Revised (Achievement section) and the Kaufman Test of Educational

Achievement. *Psychology in the Schools, 32,* 86–92.

Shultz, M. M., & Zedeck, S. (2011). Predicting lawyer effectiveness: Broadening the basis for law school admission decisions. *Law & Social Inquiry, 36*(3), 620–661. doi: 10.1111/j.1747-4469.2011.01245.x.

Sidick, J. T., Barrett, G. V., & Doverspike, D. (1994). Three alternative multiple choice tests: An attractive option. *Personnel Psychology, 47,* 829–835.

Sijtsma, K., & Verweij, A. C. (1999). Knowledge of solution strategies and IRT modeling of items for transitive reasoning. *Applied Psychological Measurement, 23*(1), 55–68.

Silk-Eglit, G. M., Stenclik, J. H., Miele, A. S., Lynch, J. K., & McCaffrey, R. J. (2015). Performance validity classification accuracy of single-, pairwise-, and triple-failure models using the Halstead-Reitan Neuropsychological Battery for adults. *Applied Neuropsychology: Adult, 22*(4), 271–281.

Silva, J. M., & Jacobs, R R. (1993). Performance as a function of increased minority hiring. *Journal of Applied Psychology, 78,* 591–601.

Silva, M., & Cain, K. (2015). The relations between lower and higher level comprehension skills and their role in prediction of early reading comprehension. *Journal of Educational Psychology, 107*(2), 321.

Silver, N. C, & Dunlap, W. P. (1987). Averaging correlation coefficients: Should Fisher's Z transformation be used? *Journal of Applied Psychology, 72,* 146–148.

Silverman, W., Miezejeski, C., Ryan, R., Zigman, W., Krinsky-McHale, S., et al. (2010). Stanford-binet and wais IQ differences and their implications for adults with intellectual disability (aka mental retardation). *Intelligence, 38*(2), 242–248.

Sim, J., & Wright, C. C. (2005). The kappa statistic in reliability studies: Use, interpretation, and sample size requirements. *Physical Therapy, 85*(3), 257–268.

Sim, S., Saperia, J., Brown, J., Bernieri, F., & Hackett, J. (2015). Judging attractiveness: Biases due to raters' own attractiveness and intelligence. *Cogent Psychology, 2*(1), 996316.

Simms, L. J., Goldberg, L. R, Roberts, J. E., Watson, D., Welte, J., & Rotterman, J. H. (2011). Computerized adaptive assessment of personality disorder: Introducing the CAT-PD

project. *Journal of Personality Assessment, 93*(4), 380–389. doi: 10.1080/00223891.2011.577475.

Simos, P. G., Breznitz, Z., & Berninger, V. (2011). Introduction to the special issue on advancing neuroscience through a systems approach [Editorial]. *Developmental Neuropsychology, 36*(7), 807–809.

Sines, J. O. (1970). Actuarial versus clinical prediction in psychopathology. *British Journal of Psychiatry, 116,* 129–144.

Sines, L. K. (1959). The relative contribution of four kinds of data to accuracy in personality assessment. *Journal of Counseling Psychology, 23,* 483–492.

Singh, L. (1986). Standardization of n-power measuring instrument (T. A. T.). *Journal of Psychological Researches, 28,* 14–20.

Sivas, F., Ercin, O., Tanyolac, O., Barca, N., Aydog, S., & Ozoran, K. (2003). The Nottingham health profile in rheumatoid arthritis: Correlation with other health status measurements and clinical variables. *Rheumatology International, 24*(4), 203–206.

Skipper, Y., & Douglas, K. (2011). Is no praise good praise? Effects of positive feedback on children's and university students' responses to subsequent failures. *British Journal of Educational Psychology.* doi: 10.1111/j.2044-8279.2011.02028.x.

Slaney, K. L., Storey, J. E., & Barnes, J. (2011). Is my test valid? Guidelines for the practicing psychologist for evaluating the psychometric properties of measures. *International Journal of Forensic Mental Health, 10*(4), 261–283.

Slatkoff, J. (2007). *Validity of the MMPI-A structural summary in a forensic sample: Effects of ethnicity, gender, and age.* US: ProQuest Information & Learning.

Sletten, I. W., Ulett, G., Altman, H., & Sundland, D. (1970). The Missouri Standard System of Psychiatry (SSOP): Computer generated diagnosis. *Archives of General Psychiatry, 23*(1), 73–79.

Smarter Balance Assessment Consortium. (2016). What is smarter balance. Retrieved from http://www.smarterbalanced.org

Smith Jr., E. V., Wakely, M. B., De Kruif, R. E. L., & Swartz, C. W. (2003). *Optimizing rating scales for self-efficacy (and other) research.* Thousand Oaks, CA: Sage.

Smith, B., & Sechrest, L. (1991). Treatment of aptitude X treatment interactions.

Journal of Consulting and Clinical Psychology, 59, 233–244.

Smith, M., & George, D. (1994). Selection methods. In C. L. Cooper & I. T. Robertson (Eds.), *Key reviews in managerial psychology: Concepts and research for practice* (pp. 54–96). New York: Wiley.

Smith, R. (2005). *Mental functioning of children with HIV infection: The preschool and early school-age years.* US: ProQuest Information & Learning.

Smith, T. W., Pope, M. K., Rhodewalt, F., & Poulton, J. L. (1989). Optimism, neuroticism, coping, and symptom reports: An alternative interpretation of the Life Orientation Test. *Journal of Personality and Social Psychology, 56*, 640–648.

Snelbaker, A. J., Wilkinson, G. S., Robertson, G. J., & Glutting, J. J. (2001). Wide Range Achievement Test 3 (WRAT-3). In W. I. Dorfman & M. Hersen (Eds.), *Understanding psychological assessment. Perspective on individual differences* (pp. 259–274). New York: Kluwer Academic/ Plenum.

Snow, J. H. (1998). Clinical use of the Benton Visual Retention Test for children and adolescents with learning disabilities. *Archives of Clinical Neuropsychology, 13*, 629–636.

Snow, R. E. (1991). Aptitude treatment interaction as a framework for research on individual differences in psychotherapy. *Journal of Consulting and Clinical Psychology, 59*, 205–216.

Snyder, C. R., Harris, C., Anderson, J. R., Holleran, S. A., Irving, L. M., Sigman, S. T., et al. (1991). The will and the ways: Development and validation of an individual differences measure of hope. *Journal of Personality and Social Psychology, 60*(4), 570–585.

Snyder, C. R., Shorey, H. S., Cheavens, J., Pulvers, K. M., Adams, V. G., & Wiklund, C. (2002). Hope and academic success in college. *Journal of Educational Psychology, 94*(4), 820–826.

Snyder, C. R., Sympson, S. C., Michael, S. T., & Cheavens, J. (2001). Optimism and hope constructs: Variants on a positive expectancy theme. In E. C. Chang (Ed.), *Optimism & pessimism: Implications for theory, research, and practice* (pp. 101–125). Washington, DC: American Psychological Association.

Snyderman, M., & Rothman, S. (1987). Survey of expert opinion in intelligence and aptitude testing. *American Psychologist, 42*, 137–144.

Soares, J. A. (2015). *SAT wars: The case for test-optional college admissions.* New York: Teachers College Press.

Soares, J. A. (2015). *SAT wars: The case for test-optional college admissions.* New York: Teachers College Press.

Sostek, A. M. (1978). Review of the Brazelton Neonatal Assessment Scale. In O. K. Buros (Ed.), *The eighth mental measurements yearbook* (Vol. 1). Highland Park, NJ: Gryphon Press.

South, M., Larson, M. J., White, S. E., Dana, J., & Crowley, M. J. (2011). Better fear conditioning is associated with reduced symptom severity in autism spectrum disorders. *Autism Research, 4*(6), 412–421. doi: 10.1002/aur.221.

Spear, J. H. (2007). Prominent schools or other active specialties? A fresh look at some trends in psychology. *Review of General Psychology, 11*, 363–380.

Spear, S. E., Shedlin, M., Gilberti, B., Fiellin, M., & McNeely, J. (2016). Feasibility and acceptability of an audio computer-assisted self-interview version of the Alcohol, Smoking and Substance Involvement Screening Test (ASSIST) in primary care patients. *Substance Abuse, 37*(2), 299–305.

Spearman, C. E. (1923). *The nature of intelligence and the principles of cognition.* London: Macmillan.

Spencer, R. J., & Adams, K. M. (2016). Clinical neuropsychology. In J. C. Norcross, G. R. VandenBos, D. K. Freedheim, & M. M. Domenech Rodríguez (Ed.), *APA handbook of clinical psychology: Roots and branches* (Vol. 1, pp. 259–278, xxviii, 572). Washington, DC, US: American Psychological Association.

Spencer, S. J., Logel, C., & Davies, P. G. (2016). Stereotype threat. *Annual Review of Psychology, 67*, 415–437.

Spencer, S. J., Steele, C. M., & Quinn, D. M. (1999). Stereotype threat and women's math performance. *Journal of Experimental Social Psychology, 35*(1), 4–28.

Spielberger, C. D., & Sydeman, S. J. (1994). State-Trait anxiety inventory and State-Trait anger expression inventory. In M. E. Maruish (Ed.), *The use of psychological testing for treatment planning and outcome assessment* (pp. 292–321). Hillsdale, NJ: Erlbaum.

Spielberger, C. D., Anton, W. D., & Bedell, J. (2015). The nature and treatment of test anxiety. In M. Zuckerman & C. D. Spielderger (Eds.), *Emotions and anxiety: New concepts, methods, and applications* (pp. 317–344). New York: Psychology Press.

Spielberger, C. D., Auerbach, S. M., Wadsworth, A. P., Dun, T. M., & Taulbee, E. S. (1975). Emotional reactions to surgery. *Journal of Consulting and Clinical Psychology, 40*, 33–38.

Spielberger, C. D., Foreyt, J. P., Reheiser, E. C., & Poston, W. S. C. (1998). Motivational, emotional, and personality characteristics of smokeless tobacco users compared with cigarette smokers. *Personality and Individual Differences, 25*(5), 821–832.

Spielberger, C. D., Gorsuch, R. L., & Lushene, R. E. (1970). *Manual for the state-trait anxiety inventory.* Palo Alto, CA: Consulting Psychologists Press.

Spiers, P. A. (1982). The Luria Nebraska Neuropsychological Battery revisited: A theory in practice or just practicing? *Journal of Consulting and Clinical Psychology, 50*, 301–306.

Spilker, B. (Ed.). (1996). *Quality of life and pharmacoeconomics in clinical trials* (2nd ed.). New York: Raven Press.

Spirrison, C. L., & Choi, S. (1998). Psychometric properties of a Korean version of the revised NeoPersonality inventory. *Psychological Reports, 83*, 263–274.

Spitzer, R. L., & Wakefield, J. C. (1999). DSM-IV diagnostic criterion for clinical significance: Does it help solve the false positives problem? *American Journal of Psychiatry, 156*(12), 1856–1864.

Spitzer, R. L., Williams, J. B. W., Gibbon, M., & First, M. B. (1990). *Structured clinical interview for DSM-III-R—patient edition* (SCIDP, 9/l/89 version). Washington DC: American Psychiatric Press.

Spokane, A. R., & Catalano, M. (2000). The Self-Directed Search: A theory-driven array of self-guiding career interventions. In C. E. Watkins Jr. & V. L. Campbell (Eds.), *Testing and assessment in counseling practice* (2nd ed., pp. 339–370). Mahwah, NJ: Erlbaum.

Squire, L. R., & Butters, N. (1984). *The neurosychology of memory.* New York: Guilford Press.

Srsic, C. S., Stimac, A. P., & Walsh, W. B. (2001). *Self-directed search.* Dordrecht, Netherlands: Kluwer Academic Publishers.

Stallones, R. A., (1983). Ischemic heart disease and lipids in blood and diet. *Annual Review of Nutrition, 3*, 155–185.

Stankov, L. (2003). Complexity in human intelligence. In R. J. Sternberg & J. Lautrey (Eds.), *Models of intelligence: International perspectives* (pp. 27–42). Washington, DC: American Psychological Association.

Stanley, J. C. (1971). Reliability. In R. L. Thorndike (Ed.), *Educational measurement.* Washington, DC: American Council on Education.

Steadman, H. J., Mulvey, E. P., Monahan, J., Robbins, P. C., Appelbaum, P. S., Grisso, T., et al. (1998). Violence by people discharged from acute psychiatric inpatient facilities and by others in the same neighborhoods. *Archives of General Psychiatry, 55*(5), 393–401.

Steele, C. M. (1997). A threat in the air: How stereotypes shape intellectual identity and performance. *American Psychologist, 52*(6), 613–629.

Steele, C. M., & Aronson, J. (1998). Stereotype threat and the test performance of academically successful African Americans. In C. Jencks & M. Phillips (Eds.), *The black–white test score gap* (pp. 401–427). Washington, DC: American Psychological Association.

Steele, C. M., & Aronson, J. A. (2004). Stereotype threat does not live by Steele and Aronson (1995) alone. *American Psychologist, 59*(1), 47–48.

Steele, C. M., & Davies, P. G. (2003). Stereotype threat and employment testing: A commentary. *Human Performance, 16*(3), 311–326.

Stein, A. T., Hearon, B. A., Beard, C., Hsu, K. J., & Björgvinsson, T. (2016). Properties of the dialectical behavior therapy ways of coping checklist in a diagnostically diverse partial hospital sample. *Journal of Clinical Psychology, 72*(1), 49–57.

Stein, A., Woolley, H., Cooper, S., & Winterbottom, J., Fairburn, C. G., & Cortina-Borja, M. (2006). Eating habits and attitudes among 10-year-old children of mothers with eating disorders: Longitudinal study. *The British Journal of Psychiatry, 189*, 324–329. doi: 10.1192/bjp. bp.105.014316.

Stephenson, W. (1953). *The study of behavior.* Chicago: University of Chicago Press.

Stern, D. N. (2010). A new look at parent–infant interaction. In B. M. Lester & J. D. Sparrow (Eds.), *Nurturing children and families: Building on the legacy of T. Berry Brazelton* (pp. 73–82). Oxford, UK: Wiley-Blackwell. doi: 10.1002/9781444324617.ch7.

Stern, W. (1912). *Die psychologische Methoden der Intelligenzprufung.* Leipzig, Germany: Barth.

Sternberg, R. J. (1984). The Kaufman Assessment Battery for Children: An information processing analysis and critique. *Journal of Special Education, 180*, 269–279.

Sternberg, R. J. (1986). *Intelligence applied: Understanding and increasing your*

intellectual skills. San Diego, CA: Harcourt Brace Jovanovich.

Sternberg, R. J. (1988). *The triarchic mind: A theory of human intelligence.* New York: Viking.

Sternberg, R. J. (2000). *Handbook of intelligence.* Cambridge: Cambridge University Press.

Sternberg, R. J., & Kaufman, S. B. (2011). *The Cambridge handbook of intelligence.* Cambridge: Cambridge University Press.

Sternberg, R. J., & Williams, W. M. (1997). Does the graduate record examination predict meaningful success in the graduate training of psychologists? *American Psychologist, 52*, 630–641.

Sternberg, R. J., Mio, J., & Mio, J. S. (2009). *Cognitive psychology* (5th ed., pp. 1–660). Belmont, CA: Wadsworth.

Sternberg, R., & Sternberg, K. (2016). *Cognitive psychology.* Nelson Education.

Stevens, S. S. (1966). A metric for the social consensus. *Science, 151*, 530–541.

Steverink, N., Veenstra, R., Oldehinkel, A., Gans, R., & Rosmalen, J. (2011). Is social stress in the first half of life detrimental to later physical and mental health in both men and women? *European Journal of Ageing, 8*(1), 21–30. Retrieved from http://dx.doi.org/10.1007/s10433-011-0178-4. doi: 10.1007/s10433-011-0178-4.

Stewart, A. L., & Ware, J. E. (Eds.). (1992). *Measuring functioning and well-being: The medical outcomes study approach.* Durham, NC: Duke University Press.

Stewart, J. L. (2007). *External correlates of the MMPI-2 Restructured Clinical Scales in an American Indian outpatient sample.* US: ProQuest Information & Learning.

Stewart, O. T., Moudon, A. V., Saelens, B. E., Lee, C., Kang, B., & Doescher, M. P. (2016). Comparing associations between the built environment and walking in rural small towns and a large metropolitan area. *Environment and Behavior, 48*(1), 13–36.

Stochl, J., Böhnke, J., Pickett, K., & Croudace, T. (2015). Computerized adaptive testing of population psychological distress: Simulation-based evaluation of GHQ-30. *Social Psychiatry and Psychiatric Epidemiology.*

Stokols, D. (2000). *Theory development in environmental psychology: A prospective view.* Dordrecht, Netherlands: Kluwer Academic Publishers.

Stokols, D., Clitheroe, C., & Zmuidzinas, M. (2002). *Qualities of work*

environments that promote perceived support for creativity. Mahwah, NJ: Erlbaum.

Stone, A. A., & Broderick, J. E. (2007). Realtime data collection for pain: Appraisal and current status. *Pain Medicine, 8*(Suppl. 3), S85–S93.

Stone, A. A., Broderick, J. E., & Schwartz, J. E. (2010). Validity of average, minimum, and maximum end-of-day recall assessments of pain and fatigue. [Research Support, N.I.H., Extramural]. *Contemporary Clinical Trials, 31*(5), 483–490.

Stone, E., & Davey, T. (2011). *Computer-adaptive testing for students with disabilities: A review of the literature* (Educational Testing Service: (Research Report ETS RR–11-32)). Retrieved from http://www.ets.org/Media/Research/pdf/RR-11-32.pdf.

Strassberg, D. S. (1997). A crossnational validity study of four MMPI-2 Content Scales. *Journal of Personality Assessment, 69*, 596–606.

Strauss, M. E., & Brandt, J. (1990). Are there neuropsychologic manifestations of the gene for Huntington's disease in asymptomatic, at-risk individuals? *Archives of Neurology, 47*, 905–908.

Streiner, D. L., Norman, G. R., & Cairney, J. (2014). *Health Measurement Scales: A practical guide to their development and use.* USA: Oxford University Press.

Stricker, L. J., Rock, D. A., & Bridgeman, B. (2015). Stereotype threat, inquiring about test takers' race and gender, and performance on low-stakes tests in a Large-Scale Assessment. *ETS Research Report Series, 2015*(1), 1–12.

Stricker, L., & Rock, D. (2015). An "Obama effect" on the gre general test? *Social Influence, 10*(1), 11–18.

Strong Jr., E. K., & Campbell, D. P. (1966). *Manual for strong vocational interest blank.* Stanford, CA: Stanford University Press.

Strong, M., Gargani, J., & Hacifazlioglu, O. (2011). Do we know a successful teacher when we see one? Experiments in the identification of effective teachers. *Journal of Teacher Education, 62*(4), 367–382.

Stronge, J. H., Ward, T. J., & Grant, L. W. (2011). What makes good teachers good? A cross-case analysis of the connection between teacher effectiveness and student achievement. *Journal of Teacher Education, 62*(4), 339–355.

Studer, L. H., Aylwin, A. S., Sribney, C., & Reddon, J. R. (2011). Uses, misuses, and abuses of risk assessment with sexual offenders. *International Perspectives on the Assessment and Treatment of Sexual Offenders*, 193–212.

Stumpf, H., & Stanley, J. C. (2002). Group data on high school grade point average and scores on academic aptitude tests as predictors of institutional graduation rates. *Educational and Psychological Measurement*, 62(6), 1042–1052.

Sue, S. (1999). Science, ethnicity, and bias. *American Psychologist*, 54(12), 1070–1077.

Sue, S. (2003). *Science, ethnicity, and bias: Where have we gone wrong?* Washington, DC: American Psychological Association.

Sullivan, J., Beech, A. R., Leam A. C., & Gannon T. A. (2011). Comparing intra-familial and extra-familial child sexual abusers with professionals who have sexually abused children with whom they work. *International Journal of Offender Therapy and Comparative Criminology*, 55, 56–74, doi: 10.1177/0306624X0935 9194.

Summerfeldt, L. J., & Antony, M. M. (2002). Structured and semistructured diagnostic interviews. In M. M. Antony & D. H. Barlow (Eds.), *Handbook of assessment and treatment planning for psychological disorders* (pp. 3–37). New York: Guilford Press.

Sun, J., & Buys, N. (2013). Using the Illinois test of psycholinguistic ability to assess visual and auditory abilities in Chinese children with learning difficulties. *International Public Health Journal*, 5(4), 435.

Sun, Q., Chen, Y.-L., Yu, Z.-B., Han, S.-P., Dong, X.-Y., Qiu, Y.-F., et al. (2011, February 4). Long-term consequences of the early treatment of children with congenital hypothyroidism detected by neonatal screening in Nanjing, China: A 12-year follow-up study. *Journal of Tropical Pediatrics*. Retrieved from http://tropej.oxfordjournals.org/content/early/2011/02/03/tropej.fmr010 .abstract. doi: 10.1093/tropej/fmr010.

Sun, Q., Pan, J., & Tong, R. (2004). Sexual behavior of neurotic patients. *Chinese Mental Health Journal*, 18(11), 791–793.

Sunderman, G. (2008). *Holding NCLB accountable: Achieving accountability, equity, and school reform*. New York: Corwin Press.

Super, D. E., & Hall, D. T. (1978). Career development: Exploitation and planning. *Annual Review of Psychology*, 29, 333–372.

Supple, A., Su, J., Plunkett, S., Peterson, G., & Bush, K. (2013). Factor structure of the Rosenberg Self-Esteem Scale. *Journal of Cross-Cultural Psychology*, 44(5), 748–764.

Sutherland, S. (1992). *Irrationality: Why we don't think straight!* New Brunswick, NJ: Rutgers University Press.

Sutin, A. R., & Costa, P. T. (2011). The five factor model of personality traits. In S. J. Lopez (Ed.), *The encyclopedia of positive psychology* (Vol. 1). Hoboken, NJ: Wiley-Blackwell.

Suzuki, L. A., & Valencia, R. R. (1997). Race-ethnicity and measured intelligence: Educational implications. *American Psychologist*, 52, 1103–1114.

Svensson, T., Inoue, M., Sawada, N., Yamagishi, K., Charvat, H., Saito, I., … Shibuya, K. (2016). Coping strategies and risk of cardiovascular disease incidence and mortality: The Japan Public Health Center-based prospective study. *European Heart Journal*, 37(11), 890–899.

Swanda, R. M., Haaland, K. Y., & LaRue, A. (2000). Clinical neuropsychology and intellectual assessment of adults. In B. J. Sadock & V. A. Sadock (Eds.), *Comprehensive textbook of psychiatry* (Vol. 1, pp. 689–702). Philadelphia: Lippincott Williams & Wilkins.

Swann, W., Chang-Schneider, C., & McClarty, K. (2007). Do people's self-views matter?: Self-concept and self-esteem in everyday life. *American Psychologist*, 62(2), 84–94.

Sweatt, J. D. (2015). Epigenetic mechanisms in memory formation. Retrieved from *National Institutes of Health: Office of Behavioral and Social Sciences Research*.

Sweet, J. J., Wolfe, P., Sattlberger, E., Numan, B., Rosenfeld, J. P., Clingerman, S., & Nies, K. J. (2000). Further investigation of traumatic brain injury versus insufficient effort with the California Verbal Learning Test. *Archives of Clinical Neuropsychology*, 15(2), 105–113.

Sweet, R. C. (1970). Variations in the intelligence test performance of lower-class children as a function of feedback or monetary reinforcement. *Dissertation Abstracts International*, 31(2A), 648–649. (UMI No. 70-37, 21).

Swider, B. W., Barrick, M. R., & Harris, T. B. (2016). Initial impressions: What they are, what they are not, and how they influence structured interview outcomes. *Journal of Applied Psychology*, 101(5), 625–638

Swindell, J. S., Coverdale, J. H., Crisp-Han, H., & McCullough, L. B. (2010). Focus on patient management: Responsibly managing psychiatric inpatient refusal of medical or surgical diagnostic work-up. *Psychiatric Services*, 61(9), 868–870.

Syeda, M., & Climie, E. (2014). Test review: Wechsler Preschool and Primary Scale of Intelligence. *Journal of Psychoeducational Assessment*, 32(3), 265–272.

Symonds, P. M. (1924). On the loss of reliability in ratings due to coarseness of the scale. *Journal of Experimental Psychology*, 7, 456–461.

Szasz, T. S. (1961). *The myth of mental illness*. New York: Harper & Row.

Tabak, L. A., & Collins, F. S. (2011). Sociology. Weaving a richer tapestry in biomedical science. *Science*, 333(6045), 940–941. doi: 333/6045/940[pii]10.1126/science.1211704.

Taghavi, M. R., Goodarzi, M. A., Kazemi, H., & Ghorbani, M. A. (2006). Irrational beliefs in major depression and generalized anxiety disorders in an Iranian sample: A preliminary study. *Perceptual and Motor Skills*, 102(1), 187–196.

Takahiko, M., Ellsworth, P. C., Mesquita, B., Leu, J., Tanida, S., & Van de Veerdonk, E. (2008). Placing the face in context: Cultural differences in the perception of facial emotion. *Journal of Personality and Social Psychology*, 94(2), 365–381. doi: 10.1037/0022-3514.94.3.365.

Tallent, N. (1987). Computer-generated psychological reports: A look at the modern psychometrics machine. *Journal of Personality Assessment*, 51(1), 95–108.

Tan, U., & Tan, M. (1998). Curvelinear correlations between total testosterone levels and fluid intelligence in men and women. *International Journal of Neuroscience*, 95, 77–83.

Taplin, P. S., & Reid, J. B. (1973). Effects of instructional set and experimenter influence on observer reliability. *Child Development*, 44, 547–554.

Tarafder, S., Mukhopadhyay, P., & Basu, S. (2004). Personality profile of siblings of children with autism: A comparative study. *Journal of Projective Psychology & Mental Health*, 11(1), 52–58.

Tate, K. M. (2016). The Impact of Myers-Briggs Type Indicator (MBTI) on team success in the workplace.

Taylor, H. C., & Russell, J. T. (1939). The relationship of validity coefficients to the practical effectiveness of tests in selection: Discussion and tables. *Journal of Applied Psychology, 23*, 565–578.

Taylor, L. A., Livingston, L. A., Kreutzer, J. S., & West, D. D. (2016). neuropsychologists as family service providers after the onset of neurological disorders in older adults. *Geriatric Neuropsychology: Practice Essentials*, 453.

Taylor, M., Pietrobon, R., Taverniers, J., Leon, M., & Fern, B. (2011). Relationships of hardiness to physical and mental health status in military men: A test of mediated effects. *Journal of Behavioral Medicine*, 1–9. Retrieved from http://www.springerlink.com/content/d5767251073t3447/.doi: 10.1007/s10865-011-9387-8.

Taylor, R. L., Sternberg, L., & Partenio, I. (1986). Performance of urban and rural children on the SOMPA: Preliminary investigation. *Perceptual and Motor Skills, 63*, 1219–1223.

Taylor, T. R. (1994). A review of three approaches to cognitive assessment, and a proposed integrated approach based on a unifying theoretical framework. *South African Journal of Psychology, 24*, 183–193.

Tazaki, M., & Landlaw, K. (2006). Behavioural mechanisms and cognitive-behavioural interventions of somatoform disorders. *International Review of Psychiatry, 18*(1), 67–73.

te Nijenhuis, J., Jongeneel-Grimen, B., & Armstrong, E. L. (2015). Are adoption gains on the g factor? A meta-analysis. *Personality and Individual Differences, 73*, 56–60.

te Nijenhuis, J., Willigers, D., Dragt, J., & van der Flier, H. (2016). The effects of language bias and cultural bias estimated using the method of correlated vectors on a large database of iq comparisons between native dutch and ethnic minority immigrants from non-western countries. *Intelligence, 54*, 117–135.

Tellegen, A. (2003). *Introducing the new MMPI-2 Restructured Clinical (RC) Scales—The first variant version of the Clinical Scales*. Minneapolis: University of Minnesota Press Test Division.

Temp, G. (1971). Test bias: Validity of the SAT for blacks and whites in thirteen integrated institutions. *Journal of Educational Measurement, 8*, 245–251.

Tempel, T., & Neumann, R. (2016). Taming test anxiety: The activation of failure-related concepts enhances cognitive test performance of test-anxious students. *The Journal of Experimental Education, 84*(4), 702–722.

Templin, J. (2016). Item response theory. *The Encyclopedia of Adulthood and Aging*. Published Online: 20 December 2015. doi: 10.1002/9781118521373.wbeaa320

Ten Berge, M., & Veerkamp, J. S. J. (2005). The impact of behavioural and emotional problems in children's dental fear development. In P. L. Gower (Ed.), *New research on the psychology of fear* (pp. 141–151). Hauppauge, NY: Nova Science Publishers.

Teng, E. L., Wimer, C., Roberts, E., Damasio, A. R., Eslinger, P. J., Folstein, M. F., et al. (1989). Alzheimer's dementia: Performance on parallel forms of the Dementia Assessment Battery. *Journal of Clinical and Experimental Neuropsychology, 11*, 899–912.

Tennen, H., Affleck, G., & Tennen, R. (2002). Clipped feathers: The theory and measurement of hope. *Psychological Inquiry, 13*(4), 311–317.

Tenopyr, M. L. (1998). Measure me not: The test taker's new bill of rights. In M. D. Hakel (Ed.), *Beyond multiple choice: Evaluating alternatives to traditional testing for selection* (pp. 17–22). Mahwah, NJ: Erlbaum.

Terman, L. M. (1916). *The measurement of intelligence*. Boston: Houghton Mifflin.

Terraciano, A., McCrae, R. R., & Costa, P. T. (2003). Factorial and construct validity of the Italian Positive and Negative Affect Schedule (PANAS). *European Journal of Psychological Assessment, 19*(2), 131–141.

Terrell, F., Taylor, J., & Terrell, S. L. (1978). Effects of type of social reinforcement on the intelligence test performance of lower-class black children. *Journal of Consulting and Clinical Psychology, 46*, 1538–1539.

Terrill, D. R., Friedman, D. G., Gottschalk, L. A., & Haaga, D. A. F. (2002). Construct validity of the Life Orientation Test. *Journal of Personality Assessment, 79*(3), 550–563.

Thalmayer, A. G., Saucier, G., & Eigenhuis, A. (2011). Comparative validity of brief to medium-length big five and big six personality questionnaires. *Psychological Assessment, 23*(4), 995–1009. doi: 10.1037/a0024165.

Thayer, P. W. (1992). Construct validation: Do we understand our criteria? *Human Performance, 5*, 97–108.

Thayer, P. W., & Kalat, J. W. (1998). Questionable criteria. *American Psychologist, 53*, 566.

The College Board. (2010a). *The college board total group report: College-bound seniors 2010*. For Professionals/Educator. Retrieved from http://professionals.collegeboard.com.

The College Board. (2010b). *PSAT/NMSQT 2010 state summary reports*. Retrieved from http://professionals.collegeboard.com/data-reports-research/psat/cb-jr-soph.

The Gesell Institute. (2010). *Gesell Institute 2009–2010 annual report*, 7. Retrieved from http://www.gesellinstitute.org/pdf/Gesell0910AR.pdf.

The Gesell Institute. (2011). *Gesell developmental observation*. Retrieved from http://www.gesellinstitute.org/pdf/GDOR_Overview_2011_11-08-11.pdf.

The Psychological Corporation. (2001). *Administering and calculating conversion scores for reading comprehension*. San Antonio, TX: The Psychological Corporation.

Theorell, T., Hammarström, A., Aronsson, G., Bendz, L. T., Grape, T., Hogstedt, C., … Hall, C. (2015). A systematic review including meta-analysis of work environment and depressive symptoms. *BMC Public Health, 15*(1), 1.

Thissen, D., Liu, Y., Magnus, B., Quinn, H., Gipson, D. S., Dampier, C., … Reeve, B. B. (2016). Estimating minimally important difference (MID) in PROMIS pediatric measures using the scale-judgment method. *Quality of Life Research, 25*(1), 13–23.

Thoits, P. A. (2011). Resisting the stigma of mental illness. *Social Psychology Quarterly, 74*(1), 6–28. doi: 10.1177/0190272511398019.

Thomas, J. C., & Selthon, L. (2003). Planning data collection and performing analysis. In J. C. Thomas & M. Hersen (Eds.), *Understanding research in clinical and counseling psychology.* (pp. 319–339). Mahwah, NJ: Erlbaum.

Thomas, M. L. (2012). Modern psychometric theory in clinical assessment. Phoenix: Arizona State University.

Thompson, D. E., & Thompson, T. A. (1982). Court standards for job analysis in test validation. *Personnel Psychology, 35*, 865–874.

Thompson, F. E., Dixit-Joshi, S., Potischman, N., Dodd, K. W., Kirkpatrick, S. I., Kushi, L. H., … Sundaram, M. E. (2015). Comparison of interviewer-administered and automated self-administered 24-hour dietary recalls in 3 diverse integrated health systems. *American Journal of Epidemiology, 181*(12), 970–978.

Thompson, S. B. N., Ennis, E., Coffin, T., & Farman, S. (2007). Design and evaluation of a computerised version of the Benton Visual Retention Test. *Computers in Human Behavior, 23*(5), 2383–2393.

Thompson, S. B., & Chinnery, H. (2011). Normative values for 18–30 age group of Benton Visual Retention Test scores and pre-morbid intelligence quotients: New data comparisons for diagnosing memory and visual spatial deficits in Alzheimer's disease and stroke. *Brain, 2*(5), WMC001918.

Thorndike, E. L. (1904). *An introduction to the theory of mental and social measurements.* New York: Science Press.

Thorndike, E. L. (1920). A constant error in psychological rating. *Journal of Applied Psychology, 4*, 25–29.

Thorndike, E. L. (1921). Intelligence and its measurement: A symposium. *Journal of Educational Psychology, 12*, 123–147, 195–216.

Thorndike, R. L. (1968). *Review of pygmalion in the classroom* by R. Rosenthal and L. Jacobson. *American Educational Research Journal, 5*, 708–711.

Thorndike, R. L. (1971). Concepts of culture-fairness. *Journal of Educational Measurement, 8*, 63–70.

Thorndike, R. L. (1973). *Stanford-Binet Intelligence Scale, Form L-M, 1972 norms tables.* Boston: Houghton Mifflin.

Thorndike, R. L., Hagen, E. P., & Sattler, J. M. (1986). *Technical manual: Stanford-Binet Intelligence Scale: Fourth Edition.* Chicago: Riverside.

Thorsen, C., Gustafsson, J., & Cliffordson, C. (2014). The influence of fluid and crystallized intelligence on the development of knowledge and skills. *British Journal of Educational Psychology, 84*(4), 556–570.

Thorson, J. A., & Powell, F. C. (1996). Women, aging, and sense of humor. *Humor: International Journal of Humor Research, 9*, 169–186.

Thurstone, L. L. (1938). Primary mental abilities. *Psychometric Monographs*, Chicago, University of Chicago Press.

Timbrook, R. E., & Graham, J. R. (1994). Ethnic differences on the MMPI-2? *Psychological Assessment, 6*(3), 212–217.

Timmerman, M. E., & Kiers, H. A. L. (2003). Four simultaneous component models for the analysis of multivariate time series from more than one subject to model intraindividual and interindividual differences. *Psychometrica, 68*(1), 105–121.

Tittle, C. K. (1983). Studies of the effects of career interest inventories: Expanding outcome criteria to include women's experience. *Journal of Vocational Behavior, 22*, 148–158.

Todd, M., H. Tennen, Carney, M. A., Armeli, S., & Affleck, G. (2004). Do we know how we cope? Relating daily coping reports to global and time-limited retrospective assessments. *Journal of Personal and Social Psychology, 86*(2), 310–319.

Toga, A. W., & Mazziotta, J. C. (2015). *Brain mapping.* New York: Elsevier, Incorporated.

Tolin, D. F., Gilliam, C., Wootton, B. M., Bowe, W., Bragdon, L. B., Davis, E., … Hallion, L. S. (2016). Psychometric properties of a structured diagnostic interview for DSM-5 anxiety, mood, and obsessive-compulsive and related disorders. *Assessment,* Published online ahead of print. doi: 1073191116638410.

Tolomeo, S., Christmas, D., Jentzsch, I., Johnston, B., Sprengelmeyer, R., Matthews, K., & Steele, J. D. (2016). A causal role for the anterior mid-cingulate cortex in negative affect and cognitive control. *Brain,* aww069.

Tomes, Y. I. (2011). Building competency in cross-cultural school psychology. In T. M. Lionetti, E. P. Snyder, & R. W. Christner (Eds.), *A practical guide to building professional competencies in school psychology* (pp. 35–49). US: Springer.

Tong, F., & Zhu, L. (2006). An investigation of the relationship between psycholinguistic abilities and intelligence structure in children with learning disabilities. *Chinese Journal of Clinical Psychology, 14*(6), 578–579.

Tong, S., Baghurst, P., Vimpani, G., & McMichael, A. (2007). Socioeconomic position, maternal IQ, home environment, and cognitive development. *Journal of Pediatrics, 151*(3), 284–288, 288 e281.

Torrance, E. P., & Yun Horng, R. (1980). Creativity and style of learning and thinking characteristics of adaptors and innovators. *The Creative Child and Adult Quarterly, 5*, 80–85.

Torras-Mana, M., Guillamon-Valenzuela, M., Ramirez-Mallafre, A., Brun-Gasca, C., & Fornieles-Deu, A. (2014). Usefulness of the Bayley Scales of infant and toddler development, third edition, in the early diagnosis of language disorder. *PSICOTHEMA, 26*(3), 349–356.

Torstrick, A., McDermut, W., Gokberk, A., Bivona, T., & Walton, K. (2015). Associations between the rotter incomplete sentences blank and measures of personality and psychopathology. *Journal of Personality Assessment, 97*(5), 494–505.

Tourangeau, R., Couper, M. P., & Steiger, D. M. (2003). Humanizing self-administration surveys: Experiments on social presence in web and IVR surveys. *Computers in Human Behavior, 19*(1), 1–24.

Towne, R. L. (2003). Test review of the Illinois Test of Psycholinguistic Abilities, Third Edition. In B. S. Plake, J. C. Impara, & R. A. Spies (Eds.), *The fifteenth edition mental measurements yearbook.* Retrieved from http://www.unl.edu/buros.

Treisman, G. J., & Clark, M. R. (2011). Chronic pain and addiction: A behaviorist perspective. *Advances in Psychosomatic Medicine, 30*, 8–21. doi: 10.1159/000324063.

Tronick, E., & Brazelton, T. B. (1975). Clinical uses of the brazelton neonatal behavioral assessment. In B. Friedlander, G. Sterritt, & G. Kirk (Eds.), *Exceptional infant* (Vol. 3). New York: Brunner/Mazel.

Trotter, M. A., & Endler, N. S. (1999). An empirical test of the interaction model of anxiety in a competitive equestrian setting. *Personality and Individual Differences, 27*(5), 861–875.

Truax, C. B., & Carkhuff, R. R. (1967). *Toward effective counseling and psychotherapy: Training and practice.* Chicago: Aldine Atherton.

Truax, C. B., & Mitchell, K. M. (1971). Research on certain therapist interpersonal skills in relation to process and outcome. In A. E. Bergin & S. L. Garfield (Eds.), *Handbook of psychotherapy and behavior change.* New York: Wiley.

Trujillo, T. (2016). Why the federal school improvement grant program triggers civil rights complaints. In E. Frankenbert, L. M. Garces, & M. Hopkins (Eds.), *School integration matters: Research-based strategies to advance equity* (pp. 89-104). New York: Teachers College Press.

Truxillo, D. M., Seitz, R., & Bauer, T. N. (2008). The role of cognitive ability in self-efficacy and self-assessed test performance 1. *Journal of Applied Social Psychology, 38*(4), 903–918.

Tryon, W. W. (1991). *Activity measurement in psychology and medicine.* New York: Plenum.

Tryon, W. W., & Bernstein, D. (2003). Understanding measurement. In J. C.

Thomas & M. Hersen (Eds.), *Understanding research in clinical and counseling psychology* (pp. 27–68). Mahwah, NJ: Erlbaum.

Tsatsanis, K. D., Dartnall, N., Cicchetti, D., Sparrow, S. S., Klin, A., & Volkmar, F. R. (2003). Concurrent validity and classification accuracy of the Leiter and Leiter-R in low-functioning children with autism. *Journal of Autism and Developmental Disorders, 33*(1), 23–30.

Tuel, B. D., & Betz, N. E. (1998). Relationships of career self-efficacy expectations to the Myers-Briggs Type Indicator and the Personal Styles Scales. *Measurement and Evaluation in Counseling and Development, 31,* 150–163.

Tukey, J. W. (1977). *Exploratory data analysis.* Reading, MA: Addison- Wesley.

Tulsky, D. S., & Rosenthal, M. (2003). Measurement of quality of life in rehabilitation medicine: Emerging issues. *Archives of Physical and Medical Rehabilitation, 84*(4 Suppl. 2), S1–2.

Tulsky, D. S., Carlozzi, N. E., & Cella, D. (2011). Advances in outcomes measurement in rehabilitation medicine: Current initiatives from the National institutes of health and the National institute on disability and rehabilitation research. *Archives of Physical Medicine and Rehabilitation, 92*(10), S1–S6.

Tulsky, D., Zhu, J., & Ledbetter, M. (1997). *WAIS-III WMS-III technical manual.* San Antonio, TX: Psychological Corporation.

Turgeon, L., & Chartrand, E. (2003). *Psychometric properties of the French Canadian version of the State-Trait anxiety inventory for children.* Thousand Oaks, CA: Sage.

Turkheimer, E. (1991). Individual and group differences in adoption studies of IQ. *Psychological Bulletin, 110,* 392–405.

Turner, D. R. (1966). Predictive efficiency as a function of amount of information and level of professional experience. *Journal of Projective Techniques and Personality Assessment, 30,* 4–11.

Turpin, G. (1991). The psychophysiological assessment of anxiety disorders: Three-systems measurement and beyond. *Psychological Assessment: A Journal of Consulting and Clinical Psychology, 3,* 366–375.

Tyler, L. E., & Walsh, W. B. (1979). *Tests and measurements* (3rd ed.). Englewood Cliffs, NJ: Prentice-Hall.

Uber, J. W. (2005). *An example of ethical errors in assessment: Differentiating*

psychiatric diagnoses with a modified Bender Visual Motor Gestalt Test. New York, US: ProQuest Information & Learning.

United States Office of Personnel Management, Structured Interviews: A practical guide. 2008. Retrieved from http:// apps. opm.gov/ADT/ContentFiles/ SIGuide09.08.08.pdf.

United States v. City of Buffalo. (1985). 37 U.S. 628 (W.D. N.Y. 1985).

Uutela, T., Hakala, M., & Kautiainen, H. (2003). Validity of the Nottingham health profile in a finnish out-patient population with rheumatoid arthritis. *Rheumatology* (Oxford), *42*(7), 841–845.

Vale, C. D., Keller, L. S., & Bentz, V. J. (1986). Development and validation of a computerized interpretation system for personnel tests. *Personnel Psychology, 39*(3), 525–542.

Valencia, R. R., Rankin, R. J., & Livingston, R. (1995). K-ABC content bias: Comparisons between Mexican American and white children. *Psychology in the Schools, 32,* 153–169.

Valsan, N., Veetil, S. A., & Beevi, S. (2016). *Executive dysfunction in alcohol dependent individuals: A case control study. Journal of Evidence Based Medicine. Healthcare, 3*(47), 2351–2356. doi: 10.18410/jebmh/2016/519.

van de Vijver, F., Schweizer, K., & DiStefano, C. (2016). The use of standards in test development. In K. Schweizer & C. DiStefano (Eds.), *Principles and methods of test construction: Standards and recent advancements* (pp. 7–25). Goettingen, Germany: Hogrefe.

van der Linden, D., te Nijenhuis, J., & Bakker, A. B. (2010). The general factor of personality: A meta-analysis of big five intercorrelations and a criterion-related validity study. *Journal of Research in Personality, 44,* 315–327.

van der Linden, W. J. (2016). *Handbook of item response theory, volume two: Statistical tools* (Vol. 21). Boca Raton, FL: CRC Press.

van der Linden, W. J., Scrams, D. J., & Schnipke, D. L. (1999). Using response-time constraints to control for differential speededness in computerized adaptive testing. *Applied Psychological Measurement, 23*(3), 195–210.

van Leeuwen, M., van den Berg, S., & Boomsma, D. (2008). A twin-family study of general IQ. *Learning and Individual Differences, 18,* 76–88.

Vandenburg, S. G., & Vogler, G. P. (1985). Genetic determinants of intelligence.

In B. B. Wolman (Ed.), *Handbook of intelligence.* New York: Wiley.

Vandevijer, F. J. R., & Harsveld, M. (1994). The incomplete equivalence of the paper-and-pencil and computerized versions of the General Aptitude Test Battery. *Journal of Applied Psychology, 79*(6), 852–859.

Vasishth, S., Broe, M., & SpringerLink (online service). (2011). The foundations of statistics: A simulation-based approach. Retrieved from http://dx. doi.org/10.1007/978-3-642-16313-5.

Vassend, O., & Skrondal, A. (2011). The neo personality inventory revised (neo-pi-r): Exploring the measurement structure and variants of the five-factor model. *Personality and Individual Differences, 50*(8), 1300–1304.

Vassend, O., Quale, A. J., Røise, O., & Schanke, A. K. (2011). Predicting the long-term impact of acquired severe injuries on functional health status: The role of optimism, emotional distress and pain. *Spinal Cord, 49,* 1193–1197. doi: 10.1038/sc.2011.70.

Vatrapu, R., & Pérez-Quiñones, M. A. (2006). Culture and usability evaluation: The effects of culture in structured interviews. *Journal of Usability Studies, 1,* 156–170.

Vecchione, M., Alessandri, G., & Barbaranelli, C. (2011). Paper-and-pencil and web-based testing: The measurement invariance of the big five personality tests in applied settings. *Assessment, 18*(4). doi: 10.1177/1073191111419091.

Velox, A. J. (2005). *Use of the Rorschach as personality assessment tool with African American students.* Doctoral dissertation, Texas A&M University. Texas A&M University. Available electronically from http: //hdl.handle.net/1969 .1/2265.

Venkatesan, S. (2015). Test session behaviors of children with academic problems. *Guru Journal of Behavioral and Social Sciences, 3*(3), 421–430.

Verdon, B. (2011). The case of thematic tests adapted to older adults: On the importance of differentiating latent and manifest contents in projective tests. *Rorschachiana, 32*(1), 46–71. doi: 10.1027/1192-5604/a000015.

Vernon, S. W., Tiro, J. A., Vojvodic, R. W., Coan, S., Diamond, P. M., Greisinger, A., et al. (2008). Reliability and validity of a questionnaire to measure colorectal cancer screening behaviors: Does mode of survey administration matter? *Cancer Epidemiology*

Biomarkers and Prevention, 17(4), 758–767.

Vicario, C. M., Martino, D., Spata, F., Defazio, G., Giacchè, R., Martino, V., et al. (2010). Time processing in children with Tourette's syndrome. *Brain and Cognition, 73*(1), 28–34. ISSN 0278-2626; doi: 10.1016/j.bandc.2010.01.008.

Viera, A. J., & Garrett, J. M. (2005). Understanding interobserver agreement: The kappa statistic. *Family Medicine, 37*(5), 360–363.

Viglione, D. (1999). A review of recent research addressing the utility of the Rorschach. *Psychological Assessment, 11,* 251–265.

Viglione, D. J., & Hilsenroth, M. K. (2001). The Rorschach: Facts, fictions, and future. *Psychological Assessment, 13*(4), 452–471.

Villarreal, V. (2015). Test review: Schrank, f. a., mather, n., & mcgrew, k. s. (2014). Woodcock-Johnson iv tests of achievement. *Journal of Psychoeducational Assessment, 33*(4), 391–398.

Vincelli, F., & Riva, G. (2000). Immersive virtual reality in clinical psychology and psychotherapy. *Rivista di Psichiatria, 35*(4), 153–162.

Vlaeyen, J. W. S., de Jong, J. R, Onghena, P., Kerckhoffs-Hanssen, M., & Kole-Snijders, A. M. J. (2002). Can pain-related fear be reduced? The application of cognitive-behavioural exposure in vivo. *Pain Research and Management, 7,* 144–153.

Vogt, E., Dolan, B., & Hoelzle, J. (2015). 5, 4, 3, 2, 1? wisc-v factor structure. *Clinical Neuropsychologist, 29*(3), 374.

Vogt, W. P., & Johnson, R. B. (2015). *The SAGE dictionary of statistics & methodology: A nontechnical guide for the social sciences.* Beverly Hills: SAGE Publications.

von Stumm, S., Chamorro-Premuzic, T., & Ackerman, P. L. (2011) Re-visiting intelligence-personality associations. In T. Chamorro-Premuzic, S. von Stumm, & A. Furnham (Eds.), *The Wiley-Blackwell handbook of individual differences.* Oxford, UK: Wiley-Blackwell. doi: 10.1002/9781405184359.ch8.

Vorstenboscha, V., Antonya, M. M., Koernera, N., & Boivinb, B. K. (2012). Assessing dog fear: Evaluating the psychometric properties of the Dog Phobia Questionnaire. *Journal of Behavior Therapy and Experimental Psychiatry, 43*(2), 780–786.

Vraniak, D. (1997). Mapping contexts for supporting American Indian families

of youth with disabilities. *Families, Systems and Health, 15*(3), 283–302.

Wagner, E. E., & Flamos, O. (1988). Optimized split-half reliability for the Bender Visual Motor Gestalt Test: Further evidence for the use of the maximization procedure. *Journal of Personality Assessment, 52,* 454–458.

Wagner, E. E., Alexander, R. A., Roos, G., & Adair, H. (1986). Optimum split-half reliabilities for the Rorschach: Projective techniques are more reliable than we think. *Journal of Personality Assessment, 50,* 107–112.

Wagner, R. (1949). The employment interview: A critical review. *Personnel Psychology, 2,* 17–46.

Wagner, R. K. (1997). Intelligence, training, and employment. *American Psychologist, 52*(10), 1059–1069.

Wainer, H. (2014). Musing about changes in the sat: Is the college board getting rid of the bulldog? *Chance, 27*(3), 59.

Wainwright, D., & Calnan, M. (2002). *Work stress: The making of a modern epidemic.* Phildelphia: Open University Press.

Wald, J., & Taylor, S. (2000). Efficacy of virtual reality exposure therapy to treat driving phobia: A case report. *Journal of Behavior Therapy and Experimental Psychology, 31*(3–4), 249–257.

Waldman, I. D., Weinberg, R. A., & Scarr, S. (1994). Racial-group differences in IQ in the Minnesota transracial adoption study: A reply to Levin and Lynn. *Intelligence, 19,* 29–44.

Walker, A. M., Rablen, R. A., & Rogers, C. R. (1960). Development of a scale to measure process changes in psychotherapy. *Journal of Clinical Psychology, 16,* 79–85.

Walker, M. T. (2001). Practical applications of the Rogerian perspective in post-modern psychotherapy. *Journal of Systematic Therapies, 20*(2), 41–57.

Walker, R. (1992). The gesell development assessment: Psychometric properties. *Early Childhood Research Quarterly, 7*(1), 21–43.

Walker, S., Spohn, C., & DeLone, M. (2011). *The color of justice: Race, ethnicity, and crime in America.* Belmont, CA: Wadsworth Pub Co.

Walrath, R. (2014). Test review: Insight test of cognitive abilities. *Journal of Psychoeducational Assessment, 32*(6), 567–572.

Walsh, W. B., & Osipow, S. H. (2013). *Advances in vocational psychology: Volume 1: The assessment of interests.* New York: Routledge.

Walton, G. M., Murphy, M. C., & Ryan, A. M. (2015). Stereotype threat in

organizations: Implications for equity and performance. *Annual Review of Organizational Psychology and Organizational Behavior, 2*(1), 523–550.

Walton, G. M., Spencer, S. J., & Erman, S. (2013). Affirmative meritocracy. *Social Issues and Policy Review, 7*(1), 1–35.

Walton, G. M., Spencer, S. J., & Erman, S. (2013). Affirmative meritocracy. *Social Issues and Policy Review, 7*(1), 1–35.

Wang, C., Chang, H.-H., & Huebner, A. (2011). Restrictive Stochastic item selection methods in cognitive diagnostic computerized adaptive testing. *Journal of Educational Measurement, 48*(3), 255–273. doi: 10.1111/j.1745-3984.2011.00145.x.

Wang, S., Jiao, H., Young, M., Brooks, T., & Olson, J. (2008). Comparability of computer-based and paper-and-pencil testing in K–12 reading assessments: A meta-analysis of testing mode effects. *Educational and Psychological Measurement, 68*(1), 5–24.

Wang, S., Lin, H., Chang, H., & Douglas, J. (2016). Hybrid computerized adaptive testing: From group sequential design to fully sequential design. *Journal of Educational Measurement, 53*(1), 45–62.

Wang, Z., & Thompson, B. (2007). Is the Pearson r^2 Biased, and if so, what is the best correction formula? *Journal of Experimental Education, 72*(2), 109–125.

Wao, J. O., Ries, R., Flood, I., Lavy, S., & Ozbek, M. E. (2016). Relationship between admission GRE scores and graduation GPA scores of construction management graduate students. *International Journal of Construction Education and Research, 12*(1), 37–53.

Ward, T. J., Hooper, S. R., & Hannafin, K. M. (1989). The effect of computerized tests on the performance and attitudes of college students. *Journal of Educational Computing Research, 5,* 327–333.

Wards Cove Packing Company v. Antonio. (1989). 490 U.S. 642.

Ware Jr., J. E. (2003). Conceptualization and measurement of health-related quality of life: Comments on an evolving field. *Archives of Physical and Medical Rehabilitation, 84*(4 Suppl. 2), S43–S51.

Ware Jr., J. E. (2000). SF-36 health survey update. *Spine, 25*(24), 3130–3139.

Ware Jr., J. E., & Gandek, B. (1998). Overview of the SF-36 health survey and the International Quality of Life Assessment (IQOLA) project. *Journal of Clinical Epidemiology, 51*(11), 903–912.

Ware, J. E., & Kosinski, M. (2001). Interpreting SF-36 summary health measures: A response. *Quality of Life Research, 10*(5), 405–413, 415–420.

Ware Jr., J. E., Kosinski, M., Bayliss, M. S., McHorney, C. A., Rogers, W. H., & Raczek, A. (1995). Comparison of methods for the scoring and statistical analysis of SF-36 health profile and summary measures: Summary of results from the Medical Outcomes Study. *Medical Care, 33,* AS264–AS279.

Warne, R. (2015). Test review: Cognitive Abilities Test, Form 7 (CogAT7). *Journal of Psychoeducational Assessment, 33*(2), 188–192.

Warne, R. T. (2016). Testing Spearman's hypothesis with advanced placement examination data. *Intelligence, 57,* 87–95.

Warner-Benson, D. M. (2001). The effect of a modified test administration procedure on the performance of male and female African American inner-city school children on a group administered intelligence test. *Dissertation Abstracts International: Section A. The Humanities and Social Sciences, 61,* 10A.

Warren, J. (2011). School counselor consultation: Teachers' experiences with rational emotive behavior therapy. *Journal of Rational-Emotive & Cognitive-Behavior Therapy,* 1–15. doi: 10.1007/s10942-011-0139-z.

Warren, N. C. (1994). *Finding the love of your life: Ten principles for choosing the right marriage partner.* Simon and Schuster.

Warrens, M. J. (2015). Five ways to look at Cohen's Kappa. *Journal of Psychology & Psychotherapy, 5,* 197. doi: 10.4172/2161-0487.1000197.

Watkins Jr., C. E., Campbell, V. L., Nieberding, R., & Hallmark, R. (1995). Contemporary practice of psychological assessment by clinical psychologists. *Professional Psychology: Research and Practice, 26,* 54–60.

Watkins, M., & Beaujean, A. (2014). Bifactor structure of the Wechsler Preschool and Primary Scale of Intelligence—Fourth edition. *School Psychology Quarterly, 29*(1), 52.

Watson, C. W., & Klett, W. G. (1975). The Henmon-Nelson, Cardall-Miles, Slosson, and Quick Tests as predictors of NAIS IQ. *Journal of Clinical Psychology, 31,* 310–313.

Watson, D. (1988). The vicissitudes of mood measurement: Effects of varying descriptors, time frames, and response formats on measures of positive and negative affect. *Journal of Personality and Social Psychology, 55,* 128–141.

Watson, D., Clark, L. A., & Tellegen, A. (1988). Development and validation of brief measures of positive and negative affect: The PANAS Scales. *Journal of Personality and Social Psychology, 54,* 1063–1070.

Watson, W. (2015). *Putting up a fight: Exploring a youth of color social justice praxis.* n.p. New York: ProQuest Dissertations Publishing.

Webster, E. C. (1964). *Decision making in the employment interview.* Montreal: Industrial Relations Center, McGill University.

Webster, J. S., & Dostrow, V. (1982). Efficacy of a decision-tree approach to the Luria-Nebraska Neuropsychological Battery. *Journal of Consulting and Clinical Psychology, 50,* 313–315.

Wechsler, D. (1939). *The measurement of adult intelligence.* Baltimore: Williams & Wilkins.

Wechsler, D. (1955). *Manual: Wechsler Adult Intelligence Scale.* New York: Psychological Corporation.

Wechsler, D. (1958). *The measurement and appraisal of adult intelligence* (4th ed.). Baltimore: Williams & Wilkins.

Wechsler, D. (2002). *The Wechsler Preschool and Primary Scale of Intelligence* (3rd ed. WPPSI-III). San Antonio, TX: The Psychological Corporation.

Wechsler, D. (2003). *WISC-IV administration and scoring manual.* San Antonio: The Psychological Corporation.

Wechsler, D. (2012). *The Wechsler Preschool and Primary Scale of Intelligence* (4th ed. WPPSI-IV). San Antonio, TX: The Psychological Corporation.

Wechsler, D., Coalson, D. L., & Engi Raiford, S. (2008). *WAIS-IV: Technical and interpretive manual.* San Antonio, TX: The Psychological Corporation.

Wechsler, D., Raiford, S., & Holdnack, J. A. (2014). *WISC-V: Technical and interpretive manual.* San Antonio, TX: The Psychological Corporation.

Weiner, B. (1991). Metaphors in motivation and attribution. *American Psychologist, 46,* 921–930.

Weiner, B. (2011a). An attribution theory of motivation. *Handbook of Theories of Social Psychology, 1,* 135.

Weiner, B. (2011b). Ultimate and proximal determinants of motivation given an attribution perspective and the metaphors guiding attribution theory. *Group & Organization Management, 36*(4), 526.

Weiner, B., Graham, S., Peter, O., & Zmuidinas, M. (1991). Public confession and forgiveness. *Journal of Personality, 59,* 281–312.

Weiner, I. B. (2003). *Principles of Rorschach interpretation* (2nd ed.) Mahwah, NJ: Erlbaum.

Weiner, I. B., & Craighead, W. E. (2010). *The Corsini encyclopedia of psychology, volume 4* (pp. 1776–1777). Hoboken, NJ: John Wiley & Sons.

Weiss, D. J. (1985). Adaptive testing by computer. *Journal of Consulting and Clinical Psychology, 53,* 774–789.

Weiss, D. J. (Ed.). (1983). *New horizons in testing.* New York: Academic Press.

Weiss, L. G., Oakland, T., & Aylward, G. (2010). *Bayley-III clinical use and interpretation.* Burlington, MA: Elsevier.

Weissman, A. N. (1979). The Dysfunctional Attitude Scale: A validation study. *Dissertation Abstracts International, 40,* 1389A–1390B. (UMI No. 7919,533)

Weissman, A. N., & Beck, A. T. (1978, November). *Development and validation of the Dysfunctional Attitude Scale: A preliminary investigation.* Paper presented at the meeting of the Association for the Advancement of Behavior Therapy, Chicago.

Weissman, M. M., Sholomskas, D., Pottenger, M., Prusoff, B. A., & Locke, B. Z. (1977). Assessing depressive symptoms in five psychiatric populations: A validation study. *American Journal of Epidemiology, 106,* 203–214.

Welch, H. G. (2004). *Should I be tested for cancer?* Berkeley: University of California Press.

Welsh, G. S. (1948). An extension of Hathaway's MMPI profile coding system. *Journal of Consulting Psychology, 12,* 343–344.

Welsh, K., Butters, N., Hughes, J., Mobs, R., & Hayman, A. (1991). Detection of abnormal memory decline in mad cases of Alzheimer's disease using CERAD neuropsychological measures. *Archives of Neurology, 48,* 278–281.

Wermiel, S., & Trost, C. (1986, June 20). Justices say hostile job environment due to sex harrassment violates rights. *Wall Street Journal,* 2.

Werner, H. (1937). Process and achievement: The basic problem of education and developmental psychology. *Hayward Educational Review, 7,* 353–368.

Wertz, F. J., Charmaz, K., McMullen, L. M., Josselson, R., Anderson, R., & McSpadden, E. (2011). Contemporary movement, methodological pluralism, and challenges. In F. J. Wertz,

K. Charmaz, L. M. McMullen, et al. (Eds.), *Five ways of doing qualitative analysis: Phenomenological psychology* (pp. 75–110). New York: Guilford Press.

Westenberg, P. M., Gullone, E., Bokhorst, C. L., Heyne, D.A., & King, N.J. (2007). Social evaluation fear in childhood and adolescence: Normative developmental course and continuity of individual differences. *British Journal of Developmental Psychology, 25*(3), 471–483.

Westrick, P. A., Le, H., Robbins, S. B., Radunzel, J. M., & Schmidt, F. L. (2015). College performance and retention: A meta-analysis of the predictive validities of ACT® scores, high school grades, and SES. *Educational Assessment, 20*(1), 23–45.

Wetherell, M. (2011). The winds of change: Some challenges in reconfiguring social psychology for the future. *British Journal of Social Psychology, 50*(3), 399–404. doi: 10.1111/j.2044-8309.2011.02038.x.

Wheeler, L., & Reitan, R. M. (1962). A presence and alaterality of brain damage predicted from response to a short aphasia screening test. *Perceptual and Motor Skills, 15*, 783–799.

Whetzel, D., & Wheaton, G. (2007). *Applied measurement: Industrial psychology in human resources management.* Mahwah, NJ: Routledge.

Whipple, C. M. (1910). *Manual of mental and physical tests.* Baltimore: Warwick & York.

Whisman, M.A., Johnson, D.P., & Smolen, A. (2011). Dysfunctional attitudes and the serotonin transporter promoter polymorphism (5-HTTLPR). *Behavior Therapy, 42*(2), 300–305. doi: 10.1016/j.beth.2010.08.007.

Whiteside-Mansell, L., & Corwyn, R. F. (2003). Mean and covariance structures analysis: An examination of the Rosenberg Self-Esteem Scale among adolescents and adults. *Educational and Psychological Measurement, 63*(1), 163–173.

Whittington, D. (2004, April 5). The achievement gap: Should we rely on SAT scores to tell us anything about it? *Education Policy Analysis Archives, 12*(12).

Whyte, G., & Latham, G. (1997). The futility of utility analysis revisited: When even an expert fails. *Personnel Psychology, 50*(3), 601–610.

Wiberg, M. (2003). An optimal design approach to criterion-referenced computerized testing. *Journal of Educational and Behavioral Statistics, 28*(2), 97–110.

Wichers, M., Lothmann, C., Simons, C. J. P., Nicolson, N. A., & Peeters, F. (2011). The dynamic interplay between negative and positive emotions in daily life predicts response to treatment in depression: A momentary assessment study. *British Journal of Clinical Psychology.* doi: 10.1111/j.2044-8260.2011.02021.x.

Wicker, A. W. (1979). Ecological psychology: Some recent and prospective developments. *American Psychologist, 34*, 755–765.

Wicker, A. W., & Kirmeyer, S. L. (1976). From church to laboratory to national park. In S. Wapner, S. B. Conen, & B. Kaplan (Eds.), *Experiencing the environment.* New York: Plenum.

Wiederhold, B. K., Gervirtz, R. N., & Spira, J. L. (2001). Virtual reality exposure therapy vs. imagery desensitization therapy in the treatment of flying phobia. In G. Riva & C. Galimberti (Eds.), *Towards cyberpsychology: Mind, cognition and society in the internet age* (pp. 253–273). Washington, DC: IOS.

Wiederhold, B. K., Jang, D. P., Kim, S. I., & Wiederhold, M. D. (2002). Physiological monitoring as an objective tool in virtual reality therapy. *Cyberpsychology and Behavior, 5*(1), 77–82.

Wiesner, M., Windle, M., Kanouse, D. E., Elliott, M. N., & Schuster, M. A. (2015). DISC Predictive Scales (DPS): Factor structure and uniform differential item functioning across gender and three racial/ethnic groups for ADHD, conduct disorder, and oppositional defiant disorder symptoms. *Psychological assessment, 27*(4), 1324.

Wiesner, W. H., & Cronshaw, S. F. (1988). A meta-analytic investigation of the impact of interview format and degree of structure on the validity of the employment interview. *Journal of Occupational Psychology, 61*, 275–290.

Wiggan, G. (2007). Race, school achievement, and educational inequality: Toward a student-based inquiry perspective. *Review of Educational Research, 77*(3), 310.

Wiggins, J. G. (1994). Would you want your child to be a psychologist? *American Psychologist, 49*(6), 485–492.

Wiggins, J. S. (1973). *Personality and prediction: Principles of personality assessment.* Reading, MA: Addison-Wesley.

Wilcox, K. C., & Youngsmith, D. M. (2015). Overview of equal employment opportunity laws. *California Employment Law, 2.*

Wild, C. L., McPeek, W. M., Koffler, S. L., Braun, H. I., & Cowell, W. (1989). *Concurrent validity of verbal item types for ethnic and gender subgroups. GRE Publication Report 84–10p.* Princeton, NJ: Educational Testing Service.

Wilder, J. (1950). The law of initial values. *Psychosomatic Medicine, 12*, 392–401.

Wilkins, C., Rolfhus, E., Weiss, L., & Zhu, J. J. (2005). *A new method for calibrating translated tests with small sample sizes.* Paper presented at the 2005 annual meeting of the American Educational Research Association, Montreal, Canada.

Wilkinson, G. S., & Robertson, G. J. (2006). Wide Range Achievement Test 4 (WRAT4) professional manual. *Psychological Assessment Resources, Inc.* Retrieved from http://portal.wpspublish.com/portal/page?_pageid=53,118660&_dad=portal&_schema=PORTAL.

Wilkinson, L. (1999). Statistical methods in psychology journals: Guidelines and explanations. *American Psychologist, 54*(8), 594–604.

Williams, J. E. (1994). Anxiety measurement: Construct validity and test performance. *Measurement and Evaluation in Counseling and Development, 27*, 302–307.

Williams, J. M., Voelker, S., & Ricciardi, P. W. (1995). Predictive validity of the K-ABC for exceptional preschoolers. *Psychology in the Schools, 32*, 178–185.

Williams, M. (2016). Techniques for job interview success in today's competitive job market. Abstract available at http://commons.lib.jmu.edu/celebrationofscholarshipgrad/2016/PosterPresentations/13/

Williams, R. L. (1974). Scientific racism and I.Q.: The silent mugging of the black community. *Psychology Today, 7*, 32–41.

Williamson, L. G., Campion, J. E., Malos, S. B., Roehling, M. V., & Campion, M. (1997). Employment interview on trial: Linking interview structure with litigation outcomes. *Journal of Applied Psychology, 82*, 900–912.

Williamson, W. D., Wilson, G. S., Lifschitz, M. H., & Thurbers, S. A. (1990). Nonhandicapped very-low-birth-weight infants at one year of age developmental profile. *Pediatrics, 85*, 405–410.

Willis, J. O., Dumont, R., & Kaufman, A. S. (2011). Factor-analytic models of intelligence. In R. Sternberg &

S. Kaufman (Eds.), *The Cambridge handbook of intelligence* (pp. 39–58). New York: Cambridge University Press.

Wilson, M., De Boeck, P., Moss, P., & Draney, K. (2003). Welcome. *Measurement: Interdisciplinary Research and Perspectives, 1*(1), 1–12.

Winkler, M. H., Weyers, P., Mucha, R. F., Stippekohl, B., Stark, R., & Pauli, P., (2011). Conditioned cues for smoking elicit preparatory responses in healthy smokers. *Psychopharmacology, 213*(4), 781–789. doi: 10.1007/s00213-010-2033-2.

Winter, D. G., & Stewart, A. J. (1977). Power motive reliability, as a function of retest instructions. *Journal of Consulting and Clinical Psychology, 42,* 436–440.

Wise, S. L., Finney, S. J., Enders, C. K., Freeman, S. A., & Severance, D. D. (1999). Examinee judgments of changes in item difficulty: Implications for item review in computerized adaptive testing. *Applied Measurement in Education, 12*(2), 185–199.

Wissler, C. (1901). The correlation of mental and physical tests. *Psychological Review, 3* (Monograph Supp. 16).

Witherspoon, D. J., Wooding, S., Rogers, A. R., Marchani, E. E., Watkins, W. S., Batzer, M. A., et al. (2007). Genetic similarities within and between human populations. *Genetics, 176*(1), 351.

Witmer, J. M., Bernstein, A. V., & Dunham, R. M. (1971). The effects of verbal approval and disapproval upon the performance of third and fourth grade children of four subtests of the Wechsler Intelligence Scale for Children. *Journal of School Psychology, 9,* 347–356.

Wittenborn, J. R., & Sarason, S. B. (1949). Exceptions to certain Rorschach criteria of pathology. *Journal of Consulting Psychology, 13,* 21–27.

Wolach, A. H., & McHale, M. A. (2002). Computer program to generate operant schedules. *Behavior Research Methods, Instruments, and Computers, 34*(2), 245–249.

Wolpe, J., & Lang, P. J. (1964). A fear survey schedule for use in behavior therapy. *Behaviour Research and Therapy, 2,* 27–30.

Wong, K. F. E., & Kwong, J. Y. Y. (2007). Effects of rater goals on rating patterns: Evidence from an experimental field study. *Journal of Applied Psychology, 92*(2), 577.

Wong, P. S., & Jamadi, M. (2010). Projective tests. In C. S. Clauss-Ehlers

(Eds.), *Encyclopedia of cross-cultural school psychology* (pp. 763–766). New York: Springer. doi: 10.1007/978-0-387-71799-9_335.

Wood, D. P., Murphy, J., Center, K., McLay, R., Reeves, D., Pyne, J., et al. (2007). Combat-related post-traumatic stress disorder: A case report using virtual reality exposure therapy with physiological monitoring. *CyberPsychology & Behavior, 10*(2), 309–315.

Wood, J. M., Lilienfeld, S. O., Garb, H. N., & Nezworski, M. T. (2000). Limitations of the Rorschach as a diagnostic tool: A reply to Garfield (2000), Lerner (2000), and Weiner (2000). *Journal of Clinical Psychology, 56*(3), 441–448.

Wood, J. M., Lilienfeld, S. O., Nezworski, M. T., & Garb, H. N. (2001). Coming to grips with negative evidence for the comprehensive system for the Rorschach: A comment on Gacono, Loving, and Bodholdt; Ganellen; and Bornstein. *Journal of Personality Assessment. 77*(1), 48–70.

Wood, J. M., Lilienfeld, S. O., Nezworski, M. T., Garb, H. N., Allen, K. H., & Wildermuth, J. L. (2010). Validity of Rorschach Inkblot scores for discriminating psychopaths from nonpsychopaths in forensic populations: A meta-analysis. *Psychological Assessment, 22*(2), 336–349. doi: 10.1037/a0018998.

Wood, J. M., Nezworski, M. T., Garb, H. N., & Lilienfeld, S. O. (2001). The misperception of psychopathology: Problems with the norms of the Comprehensive System for the Rorschach. *Clinical Psychology: Science and Practice, 8,* 350–373.

Wood, J. M., Nezworski, M. T., Lilienfeld, S. O., & Garb, H. N. (2003). *What's wrong with the Rorschach? Science confronts the controversial inkblot test.* San Francisco: Jossey-Bass.

Wood, J. M., Nezworski, T., & Stejskal, W. J. (1996). The comprehensive system for the Rorschach: A critical examination. *Psychological Science, 7,* 3–10.

Wood, J. M., Nezworski, T., Lilienfeld, S. O., & Garb, H. N. (2011). *What's wrong with the Rorschach: Science confronts the controversial inkblot test.* Hoboken, NJ: John Wiley & Sons.

Wood, K., & McMurran, M. (2013). A treatment goal checklist for people with personality disorder. *Personality and Mental Health, 7*(4), 298–306.

Woodcock, R. W., McGrew, K. S., & Mather, N. (2001). *Woodcock-Johnson III Battery.* Itasca, IL: Riverside.

Woods, S. P., Iudicello, J. E., Moran, L. M., Carey, C. L., Dawson, M. S., & Grant, I. (2008). HIV-associated prospective memory impairment increases risk of dependence in everyday functioning. *Neuropsychology, 22*(1), 110–117.

Woods, S. P., Iudicello, J. E., Morgan, E. E., Cameron, M. V., Doyle, K. L., Smith, T. V., … Ellis, R. J. (2016). Health-related everyday functioning in the Internet Age: HIV-associated neurocognitive disorders disrupt online pharmacy and health chart navigation skills. *Archives of Clinical Neuropsychology,* acv090.

Woodworth, R. S. (1920). *Personal data sheet.* Chicago: Stoelting.

Woolfson, L. M., Taylor, R. J., & Mooney, L. (2011). Parental attributions of controllability as a moderator of the relationship between developmental disability and behaviour problems. *Child: Care, Health and Development, 37,* 184–194. doi: 10.1111/j.1365-2214.2010.01103.x.

Worling, J. A. (2001). Personality-based typology of adolescent male sexual offenders: Differences in recidivism rates, victim-selection characteristics, and personal victimization histories. *Sexual Abuse: Journal of Research and Treatment, 13*(3), 149–166.

Worrell, F. C., & Roberson, C. C. (2016). 2014 standards for educational and psychological testing: Implications for ethnic minority youth. In S. L. Graves & J. J. Blake (Eds.), *Psychoeducational assessment and intervention for ethnic minority children: Evidence-based approaches* (pp. 41–57, xiv, 289). Washington, DC, USA: American Psychological Association. http://dx.doi.org/10.1037/14855-004.

Worrell, Frank, C., Roberson, C. C. B. (2016). Psychoeducational assessment and intervention for ethnic minority children: Evidence-based approaches. In S. L. Graves, J. J. Blake (Eds.), (pp. 41–57). Washington, DC, US: American Psychological Association.

Wright, M. J., Woo, E., Birath, J. B., Siders, C. A., Kelly, D. F., Wang, C., … Cantu, R. C. (2016). An index predictive of cognitive outcome in retired professional American football players with a history of sports concussion. *Journal of Clinical and Experimental Neuropsychology, 38*(5), 561–571.

Wright, T. L., & Tedeschi, R. G. (1975). Factor analysis of the Interpersonal Trust Scale. *Journal of Consulting and Clinical Psychology, 43,* 470–477.

Wrightsman, L. F. (1998). *Psychology and the legal system* (4th ed.). Belmont, CA: Wadsworth.

Wu, H., Sears, L. E., Coberley, C. R., & Pope, J. E. (2016). Overall well-being and supervisor ratings of employee. *Journal of Occupational and Environmental Medicine. 58*, 35–40.

Wuyek, L. A., Antony, M. M., & McCabe, R. E. (2011). Psychometric properties of the Panic Disorder Severity Scale: Clinician-administered and self-report versions. *Clinical Psychology & Psychotherapy, 18*(3), 234–243. doi: 10.1002/cpp.703.

Wyman, P. (1998). Integrating the MBTI and the Enneagram in psychotherapy: The core self and the defense system. *Journal of Psychological Type, 46*, 28–40.

Wyse, A. E., & Reckase, M. D. (2011). Examining rounding rules in Angofftype standard-setting methods. *Educational and Psychological Measurement*. Retrieved from http://epm.sage-pub.com/citmgr?gca=s-pepm;0013164411413572v1. doi: 10.1177/00131644114 13572.

Xu, F., Fu, G., & Zhang, T. (1996). A use of the Bender-Gestalt Test (BGT) in mentally retarded children [Chinese]. *Chinese Mental Health Journal, 10*, 208–209.

Xu, H., & Tracey, T. J. (2016). Stability and change in interests: A longitudinal examination of grades 7 through college. *Journal of Vocational Behavior, 93*, 129–138.

Yan, L., Yang, X., & Wang, H. (2001). Effects of gingo bilboa on cognition of patients at the early stage of Alzheimer's disease. *Chinese Mental Health Journal, 15*(1), 31–32.

Yanai, H. (2003). *New developments in psychometrics: Proceedings of the International Meeting of the Psychometric Society (Tokyo)*. New York: Springer.

Yang, C., Richard, G., & Durkin, M. (2016). The association between Myers-Briggs Type Indicator and Psychiatry as the specialty choice. *International Journal of Medical Education, 7*, 48.

Yarcheski, T. J., Mahon, N. E., & Yarcheski, A. (2003). Social support, self-esteem, and positive health practices of early adolescents. *Psychological Reports, 92*(1), 99–103.

Yeager, D. S., Romero, C., Paunesku, D., Hulleman, C. S., Schneider, B., Hinojosa, C., … Roberts, A. (2016). Using design thinking to improve psychological interventions: The case of the growth mindset during the transition to high school. *Journal of Educational Psychology, 108*(3), 374–391.

Yeager, D. S., Walton, G. M., Brady, S. T., Akcinar, E. N., Paunesku, D., Keane, L., …Urstein, R. (2016). Teaching a lay theory before college narrows achievement gaps at scale. *Proceedings of the National Academy of Sciences, 113*(34), 3341–3348.

Yeh, Y.-c. (2012). Aptitude-treatment interaction. In N. M. Seel (Ed.), *Encyclopedia of the sciences of learning* (pp. 295–298). New York: Springer.

Yoon, K., Schmidt, F., & Ilies, R. (2002). Cross-cultural construct validity of the five-factor model of personality among Korean employees. *Journal of Cross-Cultural Psychology, 33*(3), 217–235.

Yu, C. K. (2011). The mechanisms of defense and dreaming. *Dreaming, 21*(1), 51–69. doi: 10.1037/a0022867.

Yu, Y., Hsieh, W., Hsu, C., Chen, L., Lee, W., et al. (2013). A psychometric study of the Bayley Scales of Infant and Toddler Development—3rd edition for term and preterm taiwanese infants. *Research in Developmental Disabilities, 34*(11), 3875–3883.

Yudof, M., Levin, B., Moran, R., Ryan, J., & Bowman, K. (2011). Educational policy and the law. *MSU Legal Studies Research Paper No. 09–15.*

Yurong, H., Dun, X., & Xiurong, X. (2001). Clinical analysis of 95 children with autistic disorder. *Chinese Mental Health Journal, 15*(6), 396–397.

Zanarini, M., Frankenburg, F., & Vujanovic, A. (2002). The interrate & test-retest reliability of the revised diagnostic interview for borderlines (dib-r)). *Journal of Personality Disorders, 16*, 270–276.

Zane, K., Emmert, N., Gfeller, J., Roskos, P., Merz, Z., & Bucholz, R. (2016). *An exploration of the Automated Neuropsychological Assessment Metrics (ANAM) mood scales in predicting neurocognitive performance in traumatic brain injury.* Paper presented at the Clinical Neuropsychologist, Taylor & Francis Inc, 530 Walnut Street, STE 850, Philadelphia, PA 19106 USA.

Zavis, A., & Barboza, T. (2010). Teacher's suicide shocks school : Rigoberto Ruelas, a fifth-grade teacher at Miramonte Elementary in South L.A., was hailed as a caring teacher. *Los Angeles Times*, September 28.

Zedeck, S., & Blood, M. R. (1974). *Foundations of behavioral science research in organizations.* Pacific Grove, CA: Brooks/Cole.

Zedeck, S., & Cascio, W. F. (1984). Psychological issues in personnel decisions. *Annual Review of Psychology, 35*, 461–518.

Zedeck, S., Tziner, A., & Middlestadt, S. E. (1983). Interviewer validity and reliability: An individual analysis approach. *Personnel Psychology, 36*, 355–370.

Zeidner, M. (1987). Test of the cultural bias hypothesis: Some Israeli findings. *Journal of Applied Psychology, 72*, 38–48.

Zeidner, M. (1990). Does test anxiety bias scholastic aptitude performance by gender and sociocultural group? *Journal of Personality Assessment, 55*, 145–160.

Zhou, X., Booth, J. R., Lu, J., Zhao, H., Butterworth, B., Chen, C., & Dong, Q. (2011). Age-independent and age-dependent neural substrate for single-digit multiplication and addition arithmetic problems [Research Support, N.I.H., Extramural]. *Developmental Neuropsychology, 36*(3), 338–352.

Zimbardo, P. G., & Boyd, J. N. (2015). Putting time in perspective: A valid, reliable individual-differences metric. In S. Stolarski (Ed.), *Time perspective theory: Review, research and application: Essays in Honor of Philip G. Zimbardo* (pp. 17–55). Zurich: Springer.

Zimmerman, M., & Coryell, W. (1987). The Inventory to Diagnose Depression (IDD): A self-report scale to diagnose major depressive disorders. *Journal of Consulting and Clinical Psychology, 55*, 55–59.

Ziskin, J. (1995). *Coping with psychiatric and psychological testimony* (5th ed.). Los Angeles: Law and Psychology Press.

Zores, L. S., & Williams, P. B. (1980). A look at the content bias in IQ tests. *Journal of Educational Measurement, 17*, 313–322.

Zubin, J. (1954). Failures of the Rorschach technique. *Journal of Projective Techniques, 18*, 303–315.

Zubin, J. (1972). Discussion of symposium on newer approaches to personality assessment. *Journal of Personality Assessment, 36*, 427–434.

Zuckerman, M. (1960). The development of an affect adjective check list measure of anxiety. *Journal of Consulting Psychology, 24*, 457–462.

Zuckerman, M. (1971). Physiological measures of sexual arousal in the human. *Psychological Bulletin, 75*, 297–329.

Zuckerman, M. (1990). Some dubious premises in research and theory on racial differences. *American Psychologist, 45*, 1297–1303.

Zuckerman, M., & Spielberger, C. D. (2015). *Emotions and anxiety (PLE: Emotion): New concepts, methods, and applications* (Vol. 12). New York: Psychology Press.

Zunker, V. G. (2011). *Career counseling: A holistic approach.* Salt Lake City, UT: Brooks/Cole Pub Co.

Zwick, R., & Green, J. G. (2007). New perspectives on the correlation of SAT scores, high school grades, and socioeconomic factors. *Journal of Educational Measurement, 44*(1), 23–45.

Zytowski, D. G. (1976). Predictive validity of the Kuder occupational interest survey: A 12–19 year follow-up. *Journal of Counseling Psychology, 23*, 921–233.

Zytowski, D. G. (1977). The effects of being interest inventoried. *Journal of Vocational Behavior, 11*, 153–158.

Zytowski, D. G. (1985). *Kuder occupational interest survey form DD manual supplement.* Chicago: Science Research Associates.

Zytowski, D. G. (1992). Three generations: The continuing evolution of Frederic Kuder's interest inventories. *Journal of Counseling and Development, 71*, 245–248.

Zytowski, D. G. (1996). Three decades of interest inventory results: A case study. *Career Development Quarterly, 45*(2), 141–148.

Name Index

A

Aamodt, M. G., 493
Abad, F. J., 599
Abbott, R. D., 230, 460
Abel, J. S., 274
Abell, S. C., 325
Abrams, D., 191
Abramson, T., 190
Accardo, P., 275
Ackerman, M. J., 384, 395
Ackerman, P. L., 331
Acklin, M. W., 377, 380
Adams, K. M., 445
Adams, M. A., 504
Adams, V. G., 364
Adisetiyo, V., 445
Admiraal, W., 165
Adnot, M., 495
Adveen, M., 253
Affleck, G., 364, 467
Aghjayan, S.L., 199
Aguado, D., 599
Aguilera, I., 280
Ahern, S., 415
Ahonen, T., 422
Aidman, E. V., 420, 421, 597
Aidwin, C. M., 346
Aiken, L. R., 283
Aiken, L. S., 181
Ajayi, L., 514
Akehurst, L., 208
Akkaya, G. B., 398
Akkermans, R. P., 277
Akutagawa, D. A., 409
Akyuez, G., 362
Alcázar, J. L., 281–282
Alessandri, G., 363, 417
Alexander, R. A., 384
Alexopoulos, D., 325
Alfonso, V. C., 276, 277
Algina, J., 112
Alicea, B., 420, 421
Allard, G., 418
Allen, D. N., 256
Allen, G. J., 256, 421
Allen, K. D., 161
Allen, K. H., 19, 383
Allen, M. J., 104, 174, 175, 358
Allena, M., 346
Allison, A., 3
Allison, J., 375
Allport, G. W., 350
Almkvist, O., 253

Almond, R. G., 590
Al-Tayyib, A. A., 417
Alter, B., 373
Altmaier, E. M., 540
Altman, H., 418
Altman, K., 364
Aluja, A., 361
Alvarado, N., 390, 392
Alvarado, J. S. M., 166
Aly, H., 273
Ames, D., 447
Ames, L. B., 274, 377
Amtmann, D., 230
Anastasi, A., 50, 154, 162, 283
Anastasi, S., 346
Anderson, B. L., 167
Anderson, J. P., 69, 152, 475
Anderson, J. R., 364
Anderson, K. G., 115
Anderson, M., 226
Anderson, M.J., 185
Anderson, M.K., 500
Anderson, N. B., 415, 506
Anderson, N. H., 167
Anderson, P., 421
Anderson, S., 182
Anderson, V., 472
Andreasen, N., 293
Andreoli, S. B., 347
Andreu, J. M., 409
Andrews, D. W., 242
Andrews, K.D., 218
Ankri, J., 474
Annalakshmi, N., 391
Ansell, E. B., 589
Anthony, J. C., 273
Anton, R. F., 416
Anton, W. D., 416
Antony, M. M., 409, 410
Aranda, N., 273
Arapakis, I., 418
Arbisi, P. A., 346
Archer, E. M., 342
Archer, R., 334
Archer, R. P., 342, 345, 372
Archibald, J., 446
Arentoft, A., 403
Arija, V., 273
Arita, A. A., 345
Armento, M. E. A., 255
Armstrong, E. L., 517
Arnau, R. C., 345
Arndt, S., 141
Aronow, E., 372, 380

Aronson, J. A., 191, 192, 517
Aronsson,G., 509
Arrindell, W. A., 365
Arthur, G., 257
Arthur, N., 438
Arvey, R. D., 221
Asbjornsen, A., 289
Aschenbrand, S. G., 420
Asher, J. J., 139
Ashton, M. C., 355, 356
Ashwin, P. W. H., 186
Association, N. G., 556
Atienza, F. L., 365
Atkinson, J. W., 394
Atkinson, L., 278
Atkinson, R. C., 3
Atlis, M. M., 419
Aubá, M., 281–282
Auerbach, S. M., 465
Austin, J. T., 419, 599
Austin, S., 359
Averill, P. M., 346
Avolio, B. J., 326
Ax, A. F., 414
Aydin, N., 396
Aydog, S., 474
Aylward, G. P., 272, 276, 277
Ayoob, A. R., 163

B

Babbitt, R. A., 472
Back, M., 209
Badawi, N., 276
Bae, H., 273
Baer, J. S., 419
Baer, R. A., 345
Bagby, R. M., 508
Baghurst, P., 515
Bai, X., 365
Bailey, J., 395
Baillie, A., 416
Baker, B.D., 517
Baker, L., 287
Baker, T., 485
Bakker, A. B., 361
Bakker-Brehm, D. T., 347
Balaguer, I., 365
Banandur, P., 417
Bandalos, D. L., 295
Bandura, A., 358, 589
Barbaranelli, C., 417
Barbaree, H. E., 415
Barber, T. X., 194

Barbuti, S. M., 526
Barca, N., 474
Bardo, H. R., 311
Bareak, B., 571, 578, 579
Bari, M., 420
Barker, P. R., 417
Barlow, D. H., 420, 590
Barlow, K. M., 590
Barmore, J., 496
Barnes, J., 588
Barnes, M., 446
Barnett, W. S., 281
Barns, J., 199
Baron, I. S., 449, 451, 459
Baron, R. A., 485
Baron-Cohen, S., 280
Barrett, G. V., 163
Barrick, M. R., 361, 484
Bartell, S. S., 377
Bartels, M., 515
Bartley, C. E., 361
Bartok, J. A., 287
Bartone, P. T., 363
Basebe, N., 366
Basgul, S. S., 398
Bastos, W. R., 274
Basu, S., 377
Bates, T. C., 231, 361
Batzer, M. A., 520
Baudin, N., 361
Bauer, C. R., 277
Bauer, J. E., 544
Bauer, T. N., 510
Baughman, E. E., 385
Baxter, D. J., 415
Bay, M., 286
Bayles, K. A., 285
Bayley, N., 275
Bayliss, M. S., 472
Beal, J. A., 273
Beal-Alvarez, J. S., 285
Beard, C., 466
Beard, J., 526, 539
Bearden, R. M., 327
Bearse, J., 591
Beato, L., 363
Beatty, J., 415
Beaumont, J. L., 183
Bech, P., 359
Beck, A. T., 411
Beck, S. J., 375
Becker, D., 535
Bedell, J., 201
Beech, A. R., 347
Beevi, S., 447
Behrwind, S. D., 253
Beishline, M. J., 316
Bell, J. M., 590
Bell, N. L., 285
Bell, S. K., 285
Bell, T. K., 290
Bellak, L., 391, 392–393, 395
Bellak, S. S., 395
Belmonte, A., 363
Bem, D. J., 509
Bender, L., 293
Bendz, L. T., 509
Benjamin, G. A., 593
Bennouna-Greene, M., 413
Ben-Porath, Y. S., 346, 347

Ben-Sira, L., 274
Bentler, P. M., 101, 349
Benton, A. L., 446
Bentz, V. J., 418
Bereby-Meyer, Y., 164–165
Berenson, B. C., 217
Berg, K, C., 347
Bergan, A., 197
Bergan, J., 152
Berger, S., 3
Berger, S. P., 273
Bergner, M., 472
Berkman, L. F., 523
Bermant, G., 358
Bermejo, J. L., 409
Bermejo, P., 366
Berna, F., 413
Bernabei, P., 285
Bernardi, J. V. E., 274
Bernardini, L., 378
Bernieri, F., 219
Bernstein, A. V., 189
Bernstein, D., 588
Bernstein, I. H., 104, 123
Bernstein, L. J., 285
Berntson, G. G., 589
Berry, J., 446
Berry, L. A., 346
Bersoff, D. N., 560–561
Berzon, R., 473
Beutler, L. E., 207, 347
Bhargava, R., 272
Bhave, A., 272
Bialystok, E., 561
Bianchini, J. C., 522
Bianchini, K. J., 451
Bickel, W. K., 420
Bigler, E., 296
Bilker, W., 273
Binet, A., 227, 228, 331, 374
Bingham, T., 416
Biocca, F. A., 420, 421
Birk, J. M., 437
Bishop, P. A., 166
Biswas, P., 294
Black, P., 21
Blacker, D., 199
Blais, M. A., 376, 378, 387
Blanch, A., 361
Blanchard, F., 474
Blankson, N., 230
Blasczyk-Schiepa, S., 372
Blatt, S. J., 372, 375
Blazar, D., 496
Blazek, N. L., 199, 200, 417
Bledsoe, S. E., 590
Block, J., 169
Blok, G., 218
Blood, M. R., 506
Board, C., 538
Bobic, J., 294
Bobko, P., 506, 520
Bödecs, T., 362
Boegels, S. M., 218
Boelema, S. R., 448
Bogner, J. A., 365
Bohil, C. J., 420, 421
Boivinb, B. K., 410
Bokhorst, C. L., 409
Bolen, L. M., 294

Bolino, M., 485
Bolt, D., 180
Bombardier, C., 152
Bona, E., 273
Bondi, M. W., 292, 415, 461
Bono, J. E., 361, 366
Boodoo, G., 300
Boomsma, D. I., 515
Borgen, F., 430
Borgen, F. H., 330
Borman, W. C., 182, 199, 494, 507, 533
Bornstein, M. H., 227
Bornstein, R. F., 597
Borsboom, D., 154
Borsutsky, M., 293
Bos, J. S., 286
Bosco, A., 345
Bosshardt, M. J., 501
Botella, C., 421
Bouchard, T. J., Jr., 300
Boudreau, D. M., 500
Boudreau, J. W., 494
Bourgeat, P., 446
Bousquet, A., 277
Bowen, D. J., 153
Bowers, K. S., 508
Bowling, A., 200
Boyd, C. J., 419
Boyd, J. N., 161
Boyer, P., 484
Boykin, A. W., 300
Bracken, B. A., 283
Brackett, M. A., 316
Bradley, M., 283
Bradley-Johnson, S., 286
Braehler, E., 365
Brahler, E., 474
Brandler, S., 326
Brandt, J., 294
Brantley, L. B., 494
Bratko, D., 362
Braun, H. I., 522
Brawley, O. W., 520
Bray, D. E., 418
Brayfield, A. H., 593
Brazelton, T. B., 272, 273
Bredemeier, M., 568
Breggin, G., 208
Breggin, P. R., 208
Bressan, P. A., 464
Bressler, J. P., 286
Bridgeman, B., 3, 192, 316
Bridges, K. R., 412
Briel, J. B., 300
Brody, N., 300
Brooks, B. L., 590
Brooks, T., 200
Broshek, D. K., 463
Brouwers, P., 277
Brown, B., 446
Brown, D. C., 53, 326
Brown, D. S., 472
Brown, E. A., 472
Brown, G., 411
Brown, J. S., 185
Brown, S. D., 429, 472
Brown, T. A., 87, 91, 113, 127, 137
Brun-Gasca, C., 277
Bublitz, S. T., 417

Bucholz, R., 445, 463
Buck, J. N., 398
Buckwalter, J. G., 441
Buechner, J., 152
Buffington-Vollum, J., 334
Buka, S. L., 253
Bülthoff, H. H., 421
Buono, S., 294
Bureau-Chalot, F., 474
Burger, Y., 502
Burke, M. J., 494
Burke, R. J., 484
Burnett, J. R., 501
Burnham, J. J., 409
Burnham, S., 199
Burnham, S. C., 446
Burns, L. R., 365
Burns, R. C., 398
Burnsa, G. N., 355
Buros, O. K., 388
Burstein, J., 590
Burton, R. B., 185
Burtona, D.L., 348
Burtt, H. E., 219
Bush, K., 362
Bushman, T. T., 500
Busoni, L., 361
Butcher, J. N., 19, 342, 343, 345–346,
     418, 419
Butters, N., 447
Buttiglione, M., 286
Buysse, V., 288
Byers, C., 421
Byle, K.A., 526

C

Cacioppo, J. T., 589
Cahan, S., 283
Cain, K., 521
Calhoun, G. B., 347
Callahan, S., 363
Callinan, M., 139
Calvo, V., 379
Camaioni, L., 285
Cameron, J., 196
Cameron, M. V., 445
Campbell, D. P., 90, 427, 428, 429, 430, 437,
     438
Campbell, D. T., 149
Campbell, E. A., 551
Campbell, J. M., 285
Campbell, M. L., 165
Campbell, V. L., 334. 373, 508
Campbell, W., 208
Campion, J. E., 221, 484
Campion, M., 206, 207, 484
Campion, M. A., 218, 220, 221
Canals, J., 273
Canavan, A. G., 294
Canham-Chervak, M., 500
Cannell, C. F., 197
Cano, T. R., 363
Cantu, R. C., 452
Caprara1, G., 363
Cardenal, M., 363
Carkhuff, R. R., 215, 217
Carlin, A., 421
Carlin, J. B., 165
Carlota, A. J., 421

Carlson, J. F., 276
Carlson, R. E., 221
Carou, M., 366
Carper, M., 420
Carr, M. A., 458
Carrozzino, D., 359
Carstairs, K. S., 593, 597
Carter, G. W., 501
Carter, S. R., 441
Carter, W. B., 472
Carver, C. S., 364, 440
Cascio, W. F., 139
Casey, B., 440
Casey, E. M., 531
Cash, T. F., 485
Caspar, R. A., 417
Casserly, M., 537, 538
Castellino, S., 285, 286
Castner, B. M., 274
Cattell, H., 350
Cattell, J. M., 13
Cattell, R., 350
Cattell, R. B., 240, 352, 465
Cautela, J. R., 410
Cayrou, S., 363
Ceci, S. J., 300
Cella, D., 182, 183
Center, K., 421
Cermak, L. S., 461
Chakranarayan, C., 342
Chambers, D., 193
Chambers, L. W., 472
Chamorro-Premuzic, T., 331, 359
Champney, H., 167
Chan, G., 416
Chandler, B., 472
Chandler, J., 201
Chandramouli, B. A., 287
Chang, C. H., 366
Chang, C. J., 277
Chang, D., 303
Chang, H. Y., 413, 476
Chang, H.-H., 366, 422
Chang-Schneider, C., 357
Chartrand, E., 465
Charurat, M., 277
Chasiotis, A., 390
Cheavens, J., 364
Chen, C. L., 277
Chen, E., 363
Chen, S., 414
Chen, X., 347361
Chen, Y. -L., 274
Cherepanov, D., 108, 152, 472, 473, 474
Chi, F. W., 417
Chico-Libran, E., 364
Chiesi, F., 182
Chinnery, H., 293
Chinta, S., 276, 277
Chirumbolo, A., 346
Cho, Y. I., 464
Chockalingam, V., 544
Choi, S., 362
Choi, Y. H., 421
Chong, B. H., 311
Christensen, D. R., 420
Christiansen, N. D., 355
Christianson, L., 323, 324
Christinam, D., 409
Chronni, S., 413

Chudy, J. F., 395
Chun, K., 90
Chung, C. Y., 3, 277
Church, A. T., 362
Church, T., 472
Cicchetti, D., 286
Cine, D. B., 140
Clapham, M. M., 295
Clarizio, H. F., 522
Clark, L. A., 167–168
Clark, M. R., 407
Clarke, R., 145
Clauser, B. E., 597
Clay, E. J., 417
Clayton, G. M., 201
Clayton, S., 578
Cleary, T. A., 526, 539
Clements, C. A., 257
Cliffordson,C., 231
Clinchot, D., 365
Clingerman, S., 462
Coalson, D., 262, 266
Coalson, D. L., 256
Coan, S., 200
Coble, J. R., 421
Coffin, T., 293
Cohen, J., 116
Cohen, R., 257
Coid, J., 416
Coleman, M. R., 288
Colligan, R. C., 346
Collins, F. S., 195
Colom, R., 240, 322, 324, 326
Colon-Malgady, G., 395
Comino, E., 276
Conde, A., 272
Conde Magro, T., 289
Conger, A. J., 409
Conner, R. E., 279
Connolly, A., 417
Connolly, J. F., 255
Connolly, J. G., 452
Connolly, J. J., 500
Constantine, M. G., 365
Constantino, G., 395
Conte, J. M., 495
Conway, M. A., 413
Conway, T. L., 504
Cook, K. F., 471
Cook, M., 484, 494, 501
Cook, M. L., 412
Cooley, P. C., 417
Coon, K., 435
Copple, C. E., 522
Coppola, V., 570
Corballis, M. C., 251
Corcoran, A., 537
Corey-Bloom, J., 461, 462
Corker, K. S., 190
Cormier, C. A., 590
Cormier, D. C., 11, 193
Cornelius, E. T., III., 394
Corral, M., 277
Corrigan, J. D., 365
Corrigan, P. W., 592
Corwyn, R. F., 363
Coryell, W. 140, 141
Coskun, A., 398
Costa, A.P., 474
Costa, D., 198

Costa, P. T., 359, 362, 365
Costa, P. T., Jr., 359
Costa, R. M. E., 421
Costa R., 272
Costantino, G., 395
Cottraux, J., 421
Cottrell, J. M., 514, 515, 521, 530, 531, 540, 545
Couper, M. P., 417, 419
Court, J. H., 322
Coverdale, J. H., 591
Cowell, W., 522
Cox, B. J., 508
Coyle, H., 517
Coyle, H. P., 524
Coyle, T.R., 535
Craig, H. K., 285
Craighead, W. E., 390
Cramer, P., 394
Cramond, B., 295
Crandall, C. S., 192
Crane, H. M., 137
Crane, P. K., 137
Crawford, S., 419
Creamer, M., 364
Creed, P. A., 364
Crespin, T. R., 419, 599
Criqui, M. H., 152
Crisp-Han, H., 591
Crocetti, E., 362
Crocker, L. M., 112
Crome, E., 416
Cron, W. L., 419
Cronan, T. A., 152
Cronbach, L. J., 101, 112, 115, 137, 149, 495,
    496, 514, 531, 582
Cronk, B. C., 419
Cronshaw, S. F., 484
Crosby, F. J., 575, 578
Crow, D. M., 420
Crow, S. J., 347
Crowe, T. V., 363
Crowley, M. J., 414
Cubelli, R., 445, 451
Cucina, J. M., 526
Cui, Z., 361
Culp, A. M., 281
Culp, R. E., 281
Cumella. E. J., 347
Cundick, B. P., 397
Cunningham, T. J., 523
Cureton, E. E., 137
Curiel, R. E., 255
Custer, M., 240

D

Dabbs, J., 420
DAgostino, N., 285
Dahl, L. B., 280
Dahlstrom, W. G., 18, 341, 342, 345
Dai, X., 361
Daini, S., 378
Daisley, R. L., 484
Dale, B. A., 283
Dana, J., 414
Dana, R. H., 395
Danaher, K., 192
Dandy, K. L., 345
Dantzker, M. L., 348
Darnasio, A. R., 294

Darowski, E. S., 327
Dartnall, N., 286
Das, H. P., 510
Das, J. P., 226
Datta, L., 427
Dave, R., 273
Davey, T., 417
David, A. S., 199
David, K., 152
Davidson, H. H., 375, 380–381
Davidson, J. E., 254
Davidson, M., 489
Davies, J., 170
Davies, P. G., 191, 518, 520
Davis, R. N., 419
Dawes, R. M., 590
Dawson, C., 422
Dawson, J. K., 448
Day, D. V., 495
Day, L., 361
De Ayala, R., 180
De Carvalho, L. A. V., 421
De Corte, W., 534
De Giacomo, A., 286
De Haan, E., 502
De Haes, O., 277
De Jong, C. A. J., 347
De Jong, J. R., 407
De Kruif, R. E. L., 182
De Leeuw, J., 349
De Marco, A. P., 463
De Sa Guimaraes, M., 421
De Vriesa, H., 409
Dearborn, G., 375
Deckard, K. D., 227
Dee, T., 495
Dee, T. S., 556
Defazio, G., 286
Deffenbacher, J. L., 412
DeGroot, D. W., 500
Dekhtyar, M., 199
Del Pilar, G. H., 362
DeLancy, M., 347
Delano-Wood, L., 461, 462
Delhees, K. H., 352
Delis, D. C., 292, 447, 460, 461, 462
Della Sala, S.(2016)., 451
DeMay, H. R., 362
Demerouti, E., 361
Denenberg, J. O., 152
Dennis, M., 446
Deqing, T., 294
Derkin, K., 397
Derksen, J. J. L., 362
DeRosa, A., 189
DeRue, D. S., 510
Deskovitz, M., 342
Detterman, D. K., 311
Detwiler, F. R., 361
DeVellis, R. F., 104, 161
Devoe, E. R., 210
DeWitt, M. B., 277
DeYoung, C. G., 257
Dhar, J., 390
Di Blasi, F. D., 294
Di Fabio, A., 361
Di Nuovo, S. F., 294
Diamond, E. E., 432, 437
Diamond, P. M., 200
Díaz, J. O., 599

DiCaccavo, A., 404
Dickinson, A., 407
Dickson, P., 396
Diego, M., 273
Diener, E., 365
Diercke, K., 409
Dierdorff, E. C., 506
Dige, N., 292
DiGiulio, G., 373
Dill, C. A., 383
Dillard, J. P., 209
Dillon, A., 222
DiMatteo, M. R., 196
Dinesen, J., 280
Ding, H., 416
DiSantis, D. J., 163
DiStefano, C., 199, 226, 244
Dobkin, B. H., 476, 477
Doctor, R., 287
Dodrill, C. B., 502
Doerries, L. E., 502
Dogan, O., 362
Doherty, E. M., 348
Doherty, L. M., 198
Dolezal, C., 416–417
Dombrowski, S. C., 226, 244
Dona, B. G., 363
Donahue, D., 196
Donati, M. A., 182
Donders, J., 460
Dong, N., 362
Dong, X. Y., 274
Doré, V., 446
Dórea, J. G., 274
Dorsch, A., 476, 477
Dorz, S., 420
Dostrow, V., 458
Douglas, J., 303, 407
Douglas, K., 197
Dove, A., 530
Doverspike, D., 139, 163
Downing, R. A., 578
Drasgow, F., 522
Drigas, A., 590
Dror, R., 274
Drukker, A., 457
Drummond, M.F., 494
Drummond, R., 421
Du, Y. B., 409
Duan, C., 209
DuBois, P. H., 11, 544
Dubowitz, H., 410
Duckworth, A., 361
Dudley, R. A., 495
Duffy, J., 3
Duggan, C. F., 411
Duka, T., 407
Duker, J., 341
Dun, T. M., 465
Dun, X., 274
Dunham, N. C., 152, 474
Dunham, R. M., 189
Dunivan, G., 417
Dunlap, W. P., 104
Dunn, D. M., 286
Dunn, I. M., 285
Dunn, J. A., 325
Dunn, L. M., 285, 286
Dunnette, M. D., 139, 143, 501, 533
Durham, C. C., 366

Dush, D. M., 397
Dutyb, K.J., 348
Dwight, S. A., 417
Dygdon, J. A., 409

E

Easterbrooks, S. R., 285
Eastwick, P. W., 441
Eaves, L. J., 589
Ebel, R. L., 137
Ebmeier, H., 222
Economides, A. A., 422
Edelstein, B., 197
Edelstein, K., 285
Edwards, A. L., 353
Edwards, A. W. F., 520
Edwards, L., 173
Eggen, T. J., 494
Egger, J. I., 362
Egger, J. I. M., 346
Eggly, S., 207
Egloff, B., 209, 365
Ehrhart, K., 140, 341
Eigenhuis, A., 361
Einarsdottir, S., 438
Eisenberg, N., 361
Eisenberger, R., 196
Eisendrath, S., 417
Ekman, P., 414
El-Ansarey, B. M., 362
Elashoff, J., 194, 544
El-Dib, M., 273
Elia, F., 294
Elliott, M. N., 523
Ellis, A., 336
Ellis, M., 520
Ellis, R.J, 445
Elmir, R., 208
Embretson, S. E., 180, 181
Emmelkamp, P. M. G., 362, 413
Emmert, N., 445, 463
Emmons, R. A., 365
Emory, E. K., 273
Emrich, C., 437
Emrich, H. M., 293
Enders, C. K., 422
Endler, N. S., 366, 465, 508, 589
Engi Raiford, S., 256
Engle, R. W., 231, 502
Ennis, E., 293
Epstein, J., 416, 418, 419
Epstein, R. M., 218
Erard, R. E., 384, 593
Erb, A. L., 519
Ercin, O., 474
Ercolani, A. P., 285
Erdberg, P., 377, 378, 384
Erdberg, S. P., 346
Erens, B., 416
Erez, A., 366
Ergene, T., 464
Erickson, S. K., 374
Eriksson, P.-O., 502
Erlanger, D., 452, 453
Erman, S., 190, 532
Ernst, J., 167
Ersan, E., 362
Escribano, J., 273
Eslinger, P. J., 294

Esparó, G., 273
Espeland, M. A., 472
Espenshade, T. J., 3
Etiler, N., 398
Evans, F. B., 372, 377, 378, 383
Evans, G., 413
Evans, J., 257, 281
Evans, J. J., 11, 193
Evans, L., 363
Evenhuis, H. M., 409
Ewing-Cobbs, L., 446
Exner, J. E., 373, 374, 376, 378, 380, 384, 387, 388
Exterkate, C. C., 347
Eysenck, H. J., 515

F

Fagundes, D. D., 190
Faller, K. C., 210
Farber, J. G., 378
Farman, S., 293
Farr, J. L., 143, 493
Farrer, L., 416
Faust, D., 418
Faustman, W. O., 458
Feeny, D., 108, 474
Feigelson, M. E., 417
Feigenbaum, D., 531
Fein, D., 257
Feinstein, A. B., 413
Feinstein, B. A., 414
Feldman, D., 452, 453
Feldman, S. E., 188
Fennell, E. B., 449, 451, 459
Fenster A., 316
Fenton, K. A., 416
Fermani, A., 362
Fern, B., 363
Fernandez, J., 316
Fernández, M., 289
Fernández-Ballart, J., 273
Ferrario, S. R., 365
Ferrer, E., 414
Ferrer, D. L., 366
Fetzer, M., 422
Feuer, M. J., 184
Fidler, L. J., 285
Field, A. P., 407, 409
Field, T., 273
Fielding-Barnsley, R., 285
Fiellin, M., 199
Figueiredo, B., 272
Filoteo, J. V., 365
Finkel, E. J., 441
Finkelstein, Y., 457
Finn, S. E., 347, 593, 597
Finney, S. J., 422
Finnigan, K. M., 190
Fiorello, C. A., 255
Fiscella, K., 544
Fischer, L. A., 467
Fish, D. D., 220
Fish, J. M., 595
Fiske, D. W., 385
Fitts, W. H., 357
Fitzgerald, P., 217
Flamos, O., 294
Flanagan, D. P., 257, 290
Flanagan, J. C., 507
Flascher, O. M., 164–165

Flaugher, R. L., 521, 523, 542
Fleiss, J. L., 116, 119
Fletcher, J. M., 453
Fletcher, R. B., 226
Fletcher-Janzen, E., 283
Florell, D., 416
Flores, G., 520
Flores-Mendoza, C., 240, 322
Florio, C. M., 384
Flowers, L., 285
Flynn, D., 166
Flynn, H., 273
Flynn, J. R., 516
Fode, K. L., 194
Fogle, E. E., 277
Foley, K. L., 161
Foley, K. M., 414
Folkman, S., 466
Folstein, M. F., 294
Forbes, P., 416
Forbey, J. D., 199, 200, 417
Ford, D. Y., 269
Forer, B. R., 382
Foreyt, J. P., 465
Fornieles-Deu, A., 277
Fort, P., 57
Fowler, J. C., 380
Fox, H. R., 471
Fraboni, M., 361
Franceschina, E., 420
Frank, G., 377, 388
Frank, L. D., 504
Frank, L. K., 373
Franken, E. A., Jr., 540
Franklin, D., 296
Franklin, D. R., Jr., 447
Franklin, R. D., 594
Franklin, R. D., Jr., 447
Franks, V. W., 143, 538
Franzen, M. D., 347
Frase, L. T., 590
Frazier, P., 347
Fredrickson, B. L., 363
Freeman, F. S., 226
Freeman, H. P., 520
Freeman, S. A., 422
Freeman, W., 407
Freire, C., 280
Fremer, J. J., 599
Frenkel, E., 451
Frey, B., 173
Fried, C. B., 191
Fried, Y., 500
Friedman, D. G., 364
Frierson, G., 152
Fries, J.F., 183
Friesen, W. V., 414
Frisby, C. L., 549, 562, 563
Frishberg, Y., 457
Fronek, A., 152
Frustaci, A., 346
Fryback, D. G., 200, 474, 475, 520
Fu, G., 294
Fuchs, D., 189
Fuchs, L. S., 189
Fugate, L., 365
Fuller, G. B., 294
Funder, D. C., 508, 509, 510
Furby, L., 115, 496
Furness, T. A., 421

Furnham, A., 230, 359

G

Gacano, C. B., 378
Gadermann, A., 365
Gaebel, W., 214
Gaffey, A., 435
Gallego, M. J., 413
Galli, F., 346
Gallo, M., 407
Galton, F., 12, 229, 237, 396
Gamble, K. R., 389
Gameroff, M. J., 590
Ganapathii, L., 417
Gandek, B., 473
Ganger, W., 277
Ganiats, T. G., 152, 475, 520
Gannon T. A., 347
Gans, R., 335
Gao, B., 361
Gao, F., 207
Garayzábal Heinze, E., 289
Garb, H. N., 19, 372, 374, 384, 385, 388
Garcia, H. A., 347
Garcia, J., 530
Garcia, S. F., 182
Garcia-Lopez, O., 326
Garcia-Merita, M., 365
Garcia-Palacios, A., 421
Gardner, E. F., 305
Gardner, H., 226
Garfield, S. L., 341
Garland, H., 485
Garner, A. S., 528
Gass, C. S., 255
Gasser, C. E., 330, 430
Gaston, M. F., 345
Geer, J. H., 409
Geiselman, R. E., 415
Geiser, S., 3, 590
Geisinger, K. F., 276, 277, 583
Gelernter, J., 416
Geller, D. A., 447
Geller, E., 417
Gerritse, R., 341
Gervirtz, R. N., 421
Gesell, A., 274
Gessner, T., 294
Gfeller, J., 445, 463
Gfeller, J. D., 253
Ghorbani, M. A., 412
Giacchè, R., 286
Gialluca, K. A., 501
Gianotti, L. R., 415
Gibby, R., 335
Gibby, R. G., 378
Giesen, J., 409
Gilberstadt, H., 341
Gilbert, B., 199
Gilbert, P., 413
Gilbert, P. E., 461, 462
Gilberti, B., 199
Gill, D., 502
Gill, M. M., 375, 396
Gill, T. M., 472
Gilmore, H., 554
Gilpin, E. A., 504
Gilson, B. S., 472
Gist, K., 277

Glaesmer, H., 365
Glaser, B. A., 347
Glasgow, R. E., 193
Glass, P., 273
Gleason, A., 324
Gleser, G. C., 495
Glickman, A. S., 502
Glicksohn, J., 287
Glutting, J. J., 296
Gnys, M., 467
Goff, M., 182
Goffin, R. D., 361
Goldberg, J., 253
Golden, C. J., 445, 457, 459
Goldhaber, D., 496
Goldman, R. D., 539, 540
Goldstein, D. J., 277
Goldstein, G., 256
Goldstein, J. M., 253
Goldstein, L. H., 294
Goldstein, S., 227
Gollan, J. K., 593
Gollub, R., 293
Golomb, B. A., 145
Gomzi, M., 294
Good, C., 191, 192
Goodarzi, M. A., 412
Goodyear-Brown, P., 395
Gordon, B., 266
Gordon, E. W., 532
Gordon, J. N., 277
Gordon, N., 257
Gorham, D. R., 418
Gortmaker, S. L., 523
Gothelf, D., 406
Gottdiener, W. H., 395
Gottfredson, G. D., 509
Gottfredson, L. S., 54, 429
Gottlib, I. H., 140
Gottschalk, L. A., 364
Gough, H. G., 192, 330, 347, 348, 357
Gould, S. J., 227, 528, 545
Grad, G., 57
Graham, F. K., 294
Graham, J. R., 346
Grande, G., 365
Grant, A. M., 502
Grant, G. A., 452
Grant, I., 66, 152, 448, 624
Grant, L. W., 499
Grape, T., 509
Grattagliano, I., 345
Graves, L. V., 461, 462
Gravetter, F., 24, 25, 29, 84, 87
Gray, J. R., 257, 322
Gray, R., 282
Green, J., 507
Green, J. G., 481
Green, K. E., 422
Green, P., 446
Green, S. B., 167
Greenberg, M.L., 285
Greevy, R. A., 208
Greve, K. W., 451
Grier, T., 500
Grodberg, D., 218
Groessl, E. J., 148, 152
Gronlund,N.E., 185
Gross, J. J., 414
Groth-Marnat, G., 347, 372

Gruber, N., 394
Gu, L., 316
Guillamon-Valenzuela, M., 277
Gustafsson, J., 231

H

Haaga, D. A. F., 364
Haak, L. L., 194, 195
Haak, N. J., 190
Haaland, K. Y., 448, 449
Hackett, J., 219
Hagan, L. D., 342
Hagell, P., 474
Hagen, E. P., 238
Hahn, C., 227
Hakala, M., 474
Haladyna, T.M. 25, 170, 198, 520
Hale, J. B., 254–255
Hale, W. W. III., 362
Hall, C., 509
Hall, C. W., 294
Hall, D. T., 426
Halliday, R., 276
Hallmark, R., 334, 373
Halpern, D. F., 218
Halverson, H. M., 274
Hambrick, D. Z., 327
Hamel, M., 384
Hamilton, J., 182
Hamilton, J. M., 461
Hammarström, A., 509
Hammer, A. L., 466
Hammond, J. A., 347
Han, S. P., 274
Hancock, T., 286
Handel, R., 334, 342, 345, 372
Handel, R. W., 334
Haney, W., 514
Hanford, G. H., 312
Hanges, P. J., 518
Hänggi, J., 415
Hanmer, J., 108, 200, 472, 473
Hansen, B., 3
Hansen, B. M., 280
Hansen, I., 430
Hansen, J. C., 428
Hanson, M. A., 199, 494, 507
Hanten, G., 446
Hanton, S., 363
Hao, W., 347
Happé, F., 280
Harakeh, Z., 448
Haren, E. G., 361
Haritos-Fatouros, M., 325
Harkness, A. R., 347
Harnish, R. J., 412
Harrati, S., 390
Harris, C., 364
Harris, C.I., 581
Harris, D. B., 325, 357
Harris, G. T., 590
Harris, K. S., 342
Harris, L. M., 419
Harris, R., 495
Harris, T. B., 484, 485, 500
Harris, T. L., 502
Harrison, K. S., 342
Harrison, M. J., 281
Harrison, R., 394

Harrison, T. L., 502
Harsveld, M., 326
Hart, B., 331
Hart, K. J., 345
Hart, S. A., 227
Hart, T. A., 465
Hartig, L., 539, 540
Hartigan, J., 54
Hartman, D. E., 590
Hartman, E., 379, 387
Hartman, J. G., 58
Hartwell, C., 206
Harwood, T. M., 207, 347
Haskard, K. B., 196
Hathaway, S. R., 341
Hauser, R. M., 143, 154
Hawkins, J. D., 409
Hawkins-Gilligan, J., 409
Hawkley, L. C., 589
Hayes, F. B., 285
Hayes, N., 361
Haynes, O. M., 227
Haynes, W. O., 190
Hays, M., 272
Hays, P. A., 227
Hays, R. D., 182, 200
Hearst, E., 13
Heatherton, T. F., 362
Heaton, R. K., 69, 447
Hedge, J. W., 199
Heilbrun, A. B., Jr., 355, 357
Heimberg, R. C., 485
Heimberg, R. G., 120
Heinrichs, R., 253
Hella, B., 273
Heller, D., 366
Heller, K., 208
Helmbold, N., 226
Henning, L., 253
Henninger, M., 467
Henri, V., 331, 374
Henry, B., 549, 562, 563
Henry, C. A., 311
Henry, P., 311
Hensing, G., 363
Henson, R., 197
Herbert, W., 283
Heritage, J., 196
Hermans, H., 409
Hernandez, M., 507
Hernández-Martínez, C., 273
Hernandez-Reif, M., 273
Herold, J., 364
Herrnstein, R. J., 545
Herron, E. W., 389
Herron, R. L., 166
Hertel, G., 418
Hertz, M. R., 375
Herzberg, D. S., 357
Herzoff, N., 347
Herzog, D. B., 376
Hetter, R. D., 327
Heubert, J. P., 143, 154
Heuchert, J. W. P., 361
Hewett, J. B., 294
Hewitt, M., 417
Heyne, D. A., 419
Heyne, L. K., 591
Hezlett, S. A., 409
Hicks, K. L., 502

Higgins, P., 467
Hilgard, E. R., 20, 598
Hill, H.C., 496
Hill, R.A., 412
Hill, S.K., 447
Hillix, W. A., 196
Hilsenroth, M. J., 380
Hilsenroth, M. K., 388
Hinojosa, C., 537
Hinton, D., 502
Hinz, A., 474
Hinze, S., 219
Hiscock, M., 324
Hiss, W. C., 143, 538
Hjort, N. L., 24–25
Ho, A., 466, 467
Ho, B. C., 293
Hodges, L., 421
Hodgson, D. C., 285
Hoefnagels, C., 467
Hoekstra, R. A., 280, 515
Hoeppner, J. B., 254–255
Hofer, J., 390, 391
Höfer, S., 473
Hoff, B., 280
Hoff, K., 296
Hoffman, H., 346
Hoffman, H.G., 421
Hoffman, M., 154
Hogan, J., 582
Hogarth, L., 407
Hogstedt,C., 509
Hojatkashani, C., 445
Holaday, M., 397
Holahan, C. J., 504
Holbrook, A., 464
Holden, C., 573
Holden, H.M., 461, 462
Holden, K., 170
Holger B., 391
Holifield, J. E., 347
Holland, D., 296
Holland, J. L., 428, 436, 437, 509
Holleran, S. A., 364
Hollingworth, H. L., 219
Holmeford, A., 289
Holmes, C. B., 316
Holt, R. R., 20
Holtzman, W. H., 382, 385, 389, 418
Hölzl, R., 407
Homer-Smith, E., 293
Hooper, S. R., 279, 286
Hooper, V. S., 286
Hopkins, J., 273
Hopko, D. R., 255
Hoppmann, C. A., 466, 467
Hopwood, C. J., 589
Horaian, J., 384
Horkheimer, R., 325
Horn, J. L., 229, 230, 231, 240
Horner, M., 414
Horney, D. J., 364
Horowitz, M., 407
Horowitz, M. J., 466
Horstmann, S., 416
Horváth, A., 465
Horváth, B., 362
Hosman, C. M., 467
Hou, Y., 361
House, J. D., 316, 319

Houston, R. J., 451
Houston, W. S., 461
Howard, G., 500
Howard, L., 570
Howard, V., 500
Howell, D., 25
Hrvoje J., 409
Hsieh, F., 414
Hsieh, W., 277
Hsu, C., 277
Hsu, C. C., 277
Hsu, K. J., 466
Hu, C., 361
Hu, S., 317
Huang, C. D., 362
Huang, H., 229
Hubbs-Tait, L., 281
Huber, A., 473
Huber, T. J., 293
Hudson, M. K., 531
Hudziak, J. J., 515
Huebner, A., 422
Huffcutt, A. I., 207, 222, 484, 485, 520, 560
Huibregtse, I., 165
Huijdinga, J., 409
Hulleman, C. S., 537
Hülsheger, U., 3
Humphreys, K. L., 414
Humphreys, L.G., 526
Hunsley, J., 373, 388
Hunt, M. K., 255
Hunter, J., 155
Hunter, J. E., 494, 532, 534
Hunter, M., 502
Huntley, R. M., 523
Huo, D., 277
Hurley, A. D., 218
Huse, E., 407
Hutchinson, M. B., 285
Hutchinson, S., 466
Hwang, S. H. S., 363
Hyman Rapaport, M., 152
Hyne, S. A., 429

I

Ilg, F. L., 274
Ilie, A., 362, 427
Ilies, R., 362
Iliescu, D., 362, 427
Inch, R., 324
Ingraham, L. H., 363
Ingraham, L. J., 451
Iraurgi C. I., 366
Irribarra, D. T., 24
Irving, L. M., 364
Irwin, L., 407
Irwing, P., 348, 350, 361
Isohanni, M., 347
Ispas, D., 362, 427
Itakura, S., 220
Iudicello, J. E., 445
Iverson, G. L., 347
Iyer, A., 578
Izgic, F., 362

J

Jackson, D. N., 208, 355, 361, 436, 460
Jacob, B. A., 495, 556

Jacob, W. J., 556
Jacobs, R., 143
Jacobs, R. R., 495
Jacobs Jr., D.R., 523
Jacobson, J. L., 273
Jacobson, L., 515
Jacobson, M., 461
Jacobson, M. W., 292, 415
Jacobson, S. W., 273
Jaeger, H., 258
Jager, R. S., 220
Jahng, S. M., 363
Jamadi, M., 389
James, A., 258
Jäncke, L., 415
Jang, D. P., 420
Jannelli, M., 417
Janssen, A. J., 277
Janssen, E., 415
Jayachandran, A., 417
Jeanneret, P. R., 507
Jean-Pierre, P., 544
Jeffries, W., 416
Jensen, A. R., 280, 283, 515
Jensen, M. P., 366, 413, 422, 476
Jensen, S. E., 183
Jerusalem, M., 363
Ji, C. C., 316
Jiang, D., 464
Jiao, H., 200
Jing, G., 294
Johansson, C. B., 436
JohanssonJohansson, J. C., 436
John, O., 414
Johnson, A., 272, 321
Johnson, D. P., 411
Johnson, J. H., 345
Johnson, J. J., 316
Johnson, J. L., 230, 257
Johnson, K. N., 345
Johnson, M., 201
Johnson, M. O., 416
Johnson, M. R., 272
Johnson, N., 367
Johnson, N. E., 260, 300, 324
Johnson, R., 362
Johnson, R. B., 87, 257, 265
Johnson, R. E., 366, 413, 422, 476
Johnson, T. P., 464
Johnson, V., 415
Johnson, W., 226
Johnston, B., 453
Johnstone, B., 296
Jolly, D., 474
Jones, B. H., 500
Jones, C. H., 193
Jones, P. W., 227
Jones, R. A., 412
Jongeneel-Grimen, B., 517
Joniak, A. J., 295
Jonsson, F. H., 359
Jordan, J. M., 161
Jordan, M. J., 342
Jorge, M. R., 347
Joseph, D.L., 500
Joseph, S., 361
Joy, S., 257
Judge, T. A., 361, 366, 385, 510
Judiesch, M. K., 494

Julvez, J., 280
Jung, C., 206
Jung, C. G., 396

K

Kaaresen, P. I., 280
Kabat, M., 463
Kaernmer, B., 342
Kaiser, A. P., 286
Kalat, J. W., 300
Kalish, K., 197
Kalish, L. A., 416
Kaloupek, D. G., 414
Kamin, L. J., 515
Kammeier, M. L., 346
Kamphaus, R. W., 282
Kane, M. J., 231
Kane, R. L., 463
Kanfer, F. H., 403
Kanouse, D.E., 523
Kantor, J., 198
Kantrowitz, T., 422
Kaplan, E., 257, 460, 461, 462
Kaplan, R. M., 20, 57, 66, 90, 108, 117, 142,
    145, 148, 152, 153, 167, 201, 227, 257,
    456, 458, 466, 468, 472, 473, 474, 500
Kar, B. R., 287
Karageorgiou, E., 293
Karim, J., 365
Karlsen, B., 305
Karnes, F. A., 283
Karney, B. R., 441
Karp, S. A., 394
Kataoka, H. C., 494
Katigbak, M. S., 362
Katula, J. A., 152
Katz, K. H., 285
Katz, M., 57
Katz, R., 411
Katz, S. E., 336
Katz, V., 495
Katzman, R., 461
Kaufman, A. S., 230, 253, 256, 282, 283, 285
Kaufman, E., 134
Kaufman, J. C., 283
Kaufman, N. L., 282, 283
Kaufman, R. W., 282, 283
Kaufman, S. B., 257
Kaufman, S. H., 398
Kaushik, T., 452, 453
Kautiainen, H., 474
Kavanagh, E. J., 500
Kawachi, I., 523
Kawas, C., 293
Kay, G. G., 359
Kazemi, H., 412
Kazénb, M., 372
Keane, T. M., 414
Kearney, N., 465
Keeley, E. J., 319
Keiser, R. E., 390
Keith, L. K., 285
Keith, T., 283
Keith Williams, D., 152
Keller, J. W., 373
Keller, K. E., 485
Keller, L. S., 418
Kellett, S., 170

Kelley, D., 375
Kelley, L. P., 347
Kemp, I. A., 254
Kenardy, J., 472
Kendall, B. S., 294
Kendall, P. C., 294
Kendler, K. S., 589
Kendrick, K., 277
Kendrick, S.A., 526
Kennedy, R. B., 485
Kent, G. H., 396
Kerckhoffs-Hanssen, M., 407
Kerin, R. A., 419
Kerner, D. N., 151
Kerner, J., 374
Kerr, M., 152
Kersten-Alvarez, L. E., 467
Kessler, R. C., 467
Khanna, M., 420
Kicklighter, R., 568
Kiefe, C. I., 523
Kiers, H. A. L., 230
Kim, B. H., 355
Kim, D. H., 421
Kim, I. Y., 421
Kim, J. H., 363
Kim, J. -y., 65, 465
Kim, K., 295
Kim, K. H., 295
Kim, S. I., 420, 421
Kimble, G. A., 275
King, A. C., 152
King, M., 198
King, N. J., 409
Kinsbourne, M., 601
Kiosseoglou, G., 404
Kirkham, A. J., 196
Kirkland, A., 3
Kirkpatrick, E. A., 375
Kirkpatrick, S. I., 139
Kirmanen, T., 409
Kirsch, I., 421
Kishore, C., 274
Kitahata, M. M., 137
Kivlighan, D. M., Jr., 209
Klaiberg, A., 474
Klausen, O., 289
Klein, A., 555, 557
Klein, J., 418
Klein, S. P., 321
Kleinböhl, D., 407
Klett, W. G., 311
Klimstra, T. A., 362
Klin, A., 286
Kline, P., 100, 101, 104, 112
Klinkenberg, W. D., 416, 419
Klopfer, B., 375, 380–381, 382
Kluger, A. N., 366
Knauss, L., 372
Knoch, D., 415
Knox, H. A., 272
Kobasa, S. C., 358
Kobašlija1, S., 409
Kobrin, J. L., 526
Koch, C., 286
Koch, W. L., 152
Kocsis, R. N., 593
Koernera, N., 410
Koeter, M. W. J., 362

Koffler, S. L., 522
Kohlhepp, K., 219
Kohli, M. A., 416
Kohnen, S., 289
Kohs, S. C., 257
Kokki, H., 286
Kole-Snijders, A. M. J., 407
Kolevzon, A., 218
Kollée, L., 277
Kong, N., 316
Konradt, U., 418
Koopmans, P. C., 412
Koppitz, E. M., 294
Kossowska, M., 331
Kossowsky, J., 415
Kotronoulas, G., 465
Koukianakis, L., 590
Kounti, F., 404
Kouvaraki, M., 407
Kraav, I., 409
Kraepelin, E., 13
Kraiger, K., 394
Kramer, J. H., 460, 461, 462
Kranzler, H. R., 416
Kraus, V. B., 161
Krause, S., 209
Kreiner, D. S., 256
Kremen, A., 363
Kreutzkamp, R., 218
Kreuzpointner, L., 394
Krikorian, R., 287
Krinsky-McHale, S., 244
Kripke, D. F., 153
Krishnamurthy, R., 372
Kroese, J. M., 284
Kroger, H., 452, 453
Krohn, E. J., 283
Kröhne, U., 199, 417–418
K?rp?nar, I., 396
Ku, J. H., 421
Kubisiak, U. C., 507
Kuder, G. F., 111
Kugelmass, S., 451
Kugler, L. M., 287
Kugu, N., 362
Kuh, G. D., 317
Kuhlb, J., 372
Kuhn, C., 273
Kuikka, J. T., 286
Kukich, K., 590
Kumar, R., 272
Kuncel, N. R., 147, 316, 532
Kushnir, J., 409
Kutner, K., 452–453
Kwon, P., 347
Kwong, J. Y. Y., 506

L

Lafortezza, M., 286
Lagasse, L. L., 277
Lahikainen, A. R., 409
Lai, E.R., 311
Lai, T. J., 277
Lai, Y. H., 413
Lakin, J. M., 311
Lam, D., 411
Lam, L., 402
Lamp, R. E., 283

Landis, C., 336
Landlaw, K., 407
Landy, F. J., 143, 144, 154, 484
Lane, S., 25, 170, 198, 520
Lang, B. A., 502
Lang, D., 421
Lang, J., 3
Lang, P. J., 409
Langdon, D. W., 311
Langer, N., 415
Lankford, J. S., 417
Lanyon, B. P., 397
Lanyon, R. I., 397
Larimore, C., 296
Larsen, R., 334
Larsen, R. J., 208, 365, 366
Larson, G. E., 323, 324
Larson, L., 139
Larson, L. M., 139, 330, 430
Larson, M., 152
Larson, M. J., 414
LaRue, A., 448, 449
Laska, M. N., 464
Lassiter, K. S., 285
Latham, G. P., 494
Lau, G., 273
Lauby, J., 416
Lauriello, J., 293
Lauter, D., 571, 578–579
Lavelle, L. A., 589
Law, K., 494
Lazarus, R. S., 466
Le, H., 139
Le Brocque, R., 429, 472
Leach, J., 347
Leahy, R. L., 411
Leam, A. C., 347
Leavitt, W. M., 300, 316
Leblanc, S., 610
Lecce, P. A., 286
Ledbetter, M., 258
Lederberg, A. R., 285
Lee, C., 504
Lee, C. N., 366, 413, 476
Lee, C. T., 409
Lee, E. D., 570
Lee, E.-K., 65
Lee, J. M., 421
Lee, J.-h., 465
Lee, K., 220
Lee, K. J., 220
Lee, S., 347
Lefebvre, C. D., 255
Leibovitch, A., 167
Leibowitzc, G. S., 348
Leichsenring, F., 390
Leman, N., 528
Lens Villaverde, M., 289
Lenz, J., 437
Leon, M., 363
Lerkkanen, M.-K., 422
Lerman-Sagie, T., 274
Leshem, R., 287
Leslie, L. K., 277
Lesser, C. S., 218
Lessler, J. T., 417
Lester, B. M., 277
Letukas, L., 522, 523, 532, 538, 542, 545
Letzring, T. D., 363

Leuty, M., 4301
Lev, D., 274
Levashina, J., 206, 207
Levenson, H., 347
Levenson, M. R., 346
Levenson, R. W., 414
Leventhal, A. M., 416
Levin, B., 555–556
Levin, H., 453
Levin, K. Y., 507
Levine, D. W., 153
Levine, S., 359
Levitas, A. S., 218
Lewandowski, D. G., 20, 379
Lewin, T., 314
Lewinsohn, P. N., 140
Lewis, C. C., 193
Lewis, M. A., 153
Lewis, V., 364
Lezak, M. D., 459–460
Li, A., 452
Li, D., 154
Li, F., 219
Lichtenberger, E. O., 283
Lievens, F., 485, 492, 534
Lifschitz, M. H., 275
Lifshitz, F., 57
Likert, R., 165
Lilienfeld, S. O., 19, 372, 374, 376, 383, 385, 388, 390, 392, 394
Lindvall, O., 474
Lindzey, G., 393, 399
Linn, R. L., 182, 185
Lis, A., 379, 383
Lisi, A., 345
Litke, E., 496
Litrownik, A. J., 410
Little, K. B., 382, 385, 394
Liu, F., 194
Liu, H., 182
Liu, O., 316
Liu, W. Y., 277
Liu, Y., 183
Livesley, W. J., 436
Livingston, L.A., 447
Livingston, R., 514
Livingston, R.B., 514
Llera, S. J., 420
Llorente, A. M., 277, 280
Lochman, J. E., 489
Locke, B. Z., 140
Locke, E. A., 366
Lockwood, C. A., 293
Loevinger, J., 397
Lohman, D. F., 311, 322
Loken, E. K., 589
Lomax, C. L., 411
Lombard, J. R., 300, 316
Long, D., 485
Longe, O., 413
Longhui, L., 294
Longley, S., 323–324
Looney, M., Jr., 58
Lopatovska, I., 418
Loper, R. G., 346
Lopez, J. F., 273
Lopez, S., 467
Lopez-Espinosa, M. J., 280
Lopez-Ibor, J. J., 214

Lopez-Lopez, J., 411
Lord, E., 376
Lorenzo-Seva, U., 230
Lorian, C. N., 420
Lothmann, C., 414
Loughran-Fowlds, A., 276, 277
Löve, J., 363
Lovler, R. L., 137
Lowndes, C., 417
Loy, D. L., 341
Lu, X., 347
Lubin, B., 294, 334, 353
Lucae, S., 416
Lucas, J. A., 447
Lucas, J. L., 435
Lucas, R. E., 365
Lui, Z., 347
Lundqvist, C., 273
Lundqvist-Persson, C., 273
Luo, D., 311
Luppino, M., 541
Luria, A. R., 457
Lutejin, F., 365
Lynch, J. K., 455
Lynn, P., 209
Lysaker, P. H., 257
Lytle, L. A., 464
Lyytinen, H., 422

M

Mabon, H., 502
Mabry, L., 296
Macdowall, W., 416
Machover, K., 398
Mack, L. J., 404
MacKenzie, M. J., 273
Magalette, P. R., 364
Magder, L., 277
Mahon, N. E., 263
Maillartb, C., 269
Maj, M., 214
Majnemer, A., 273
Makkonen, I., 286
Makransky, G., 140, 431
Malda, M., 283
Malee, K., 277
Malgady, R. G., 395
Malhotra, A., 294
Malhotra, S., 294
Malinchoc, M., 346
Malm, O., 274
Malos, S. B., 484
Maltby, J., 361
Maltby, N., 421
Mammen, P., 274
Mandes, E., 294
Manely, J., 500
Manini, T., 472
Manners, J., 397
Manning, C., 199
Mansoor, Y., 293
Manzano, J., 277
Manzi, S., 416
Mao, T., 396
Maratos, F. A., 413
Marbach-Ad, G., 135, 136
Marchand, Y., 255
Marchani, E. E., 520
Marchman, V. A., 285

Marcum, T. M., 551
Marcus, S., 273
Marczyk, G., 372
Marhefka, S., 416–417
Marini, J., 526, 539
Mark, J. C., 395
Marko, P. W., 397
Markowitz, J. C., 589
Marks, G., 416
Marks, J. D., 277
Marks, K. A., 257
Marks-Katz, M., 57
Markus, K. A., 316
Marques, R. C., 274
Marsch, L. A., 420
Marshalek, B., 322
Marshall, C., 286
Marshall, H., 167
Marshall, L. J., 209
Marshall, W. L., 415
Martens, T., 199, 417–418
Martin, A., 413
Martin, D., 208
Martin, P., 201
Martin, R. P., 285
Martin, R.C., 500
Martinelli, D., 286
Marting, M. S., 466
Martino, D., 286
Martino, V., 345
Martins, R. N., 446
Marusic, I., 362
Marx, B. P., 414
Mascolo, J. T., 290
Masling, J. M., 597
Mason, J., 342
Massara, G., 365
Massaro, A. N., 273
Massaro, Y., 345
Massey, D., 541
Massman, P. J., 462
Masters, B. N., 523
Masters, C., 447
Masters, W., 415
Masuda, A., 413
Masunaga, H., 231
Matarazzo, J. D., 199, 334
Matheny, K. B., 365
Mather, N., 290
Mathews, W. C., 137
Mathias, C. W., 451
Mattern, K. D., 526, 539
Matthews, K., 453
Matthews, T. D., 285
Mattlar, C., 372, 374, 383
Mattson, D. C., 303
Maul, A., 24
Maurer, S. D., 500
Maurer, T. J., 218
Mauss, I. B., 414
May, M., 287
Mayer, D. M., 518
Mayera, B., 409
Mayers, M., 421
Mayfield, E. C., 221
Mazer, B., 273
Mazoyer, V., 626
Mazziotta, J. C., 456
McAnulty, D. P., 196
McBride, J., 465

McBride, J. R., 327, 465
McCabe, R. E., 410
McCabe, S. E., 419
McCaffrey, R. J., 455
McCall, R. B., 25, 27
McCallum, R. S., 283
McCann, L., 465
McCardle, P., 292
McCarthy, J. M., 220
McCarty, J. R., 523
McClelland, D. C., 390
McCrae, R. R., 359, 362, 365
McCullough, L. B., 591
McCutchan, J. A., 69, 475
McDaniel, M., 494
McDaniel, M. A., 222, 493, 500
McDermott, P., 277
McDonald, J., 276
McDonough, S., 273
McDougall, A., 378
McEwen, J., 472
McGill-Evans, J., 281
McGrath, J. M., 273
McGraw, K. O., 419s
McGregor, C. M., 273
McGrew, K. S., 11, 193, 257, 290
McGuffin, P., 411
McGurk, M., 364
McHale, M. A., 420
McHorney, C. A., 472
McHugh, R., 420
McIntosh, D. E., 283
McKay, P. F., 507
McKee, P., 568
McKenna, S. P., 474
McKinlay, L., 429, 472
McKinley, J. C., 341
McLay, R., 421
McLennan, N. A., 438
McManis, D. L., 197
McManus, S., 416
McMichael, A., 515
McMinn, M. R., 591
McNeely, J., 199
McNeilly, M., 415
McNemar, O. W., 336
McNulty, J., 346
McPeek, W. M., 522
McRae, R. R., 359
McReynolds, C. J., 592
Meara, P., 165
Mednick, S., 145
Medoff-Cooper, B., 273
Mee Bell, S., 286
Meehl, P. E., 137, 149, 341, 382, 500, 590
Meersand, P., 395
Mees, H., 413
Meeus, W. H. J., 362
Megargee, E. I., 348
Mehl, M. R., 208, 420
Meichenbaum, D., 413
Meijer, R. R., 201, 464
Meikle, S., 341
Melchert, P. A., 197
Melchert, T. P., 316
Mellanby, J. H., 311
Mellenbergh, G. J., 115
Mellins, C., 277, 416–417
Mello, M. F., 347
Meloy, J. R., 373, 378, 388

Menke, A., 416
Ment, L. R., 285
Menzies, R. G., 418
Mercer, C. H., 416
Mercer, J. R., 527, 531
Merrell, K. W., 196
Merwin, J. C., 305
Merz, Z., 445, 463
Messick, S. J., 137, 155, 593
Metraux, R. W., 377
Meyer, G., 379
Meyer, G. J., 372
Meyer, J., 164
Meyer, R. G., 352
Michael, S. T., 364
Michel, J. S., 508
Michel, N., 253
Middeldorp, C. M., 589
Miele, A.S., 455
Miettunen, J., 347
Miezejeski, C., 244
Milan, S., 286
Miles, A., 253
Miller, B., 292
Miller, C. E., 281
Miller, D. R., 379
Miller, D. S., 201
Miller, E. T., 419
Miller, J., 390
Miller, J. G., 601
Miller, K. A., 524
Miller, L. A, 137
Miller, L. J, 286
Miller, M., 465
Miller, M. D, 185
Miller-Loncar, C., 277
Millett, G. A., 416
Mills, C. N., 599
Milne, S., 276
Min, K. H., 363
Minguez, J., 282
Minguez-Milio, J. A., 281
Minshew, N. J., 256
Minton, H. L., 438
Mirsky, A. F., 451
Mirza, M., 445
Mischel, W., 440, 589
Mishra, J., 390
Misri, S., 277
Mitchell, C. C., 294
Mitchell, C. W., 361
Mitchell, K. M., 217
Moe, V., 277
Mogilka, H. J., 199
Mogk, H., 293
Moller, P., 289
Møller, S., 359
Molteno, C. D., 273
Moneta, G., 356
Montgomery, D., 396
Mooney, L., 335
Mooney, M., 541
Moore, C., 363
Moore, D., 296
Moore, W. L., 590
Moos, R. H., 503–505
Moran, M. J., 190
Moran, P., 416
Moran, R., 555
Moreland, K. L., 372, 380

Moreno, G., 11
Moreno, K. E., 327
Morera, O. F., 108
Morey, L. C., 589
Morgan, E. E., 445
Morgan, J. E, 445–447
Morgeson, F., 206, 207
Morgeson, F. P., 206, 218, 510
Morin, S. F., 416
Morris, J. C., 300, 316
Morris, P., 396
Morris, S. B., 484
Morrison, A. M., 316
Morrison, T., 316
Morrow, C. E., 273
Morsanyi, K., 182
Morse, R. M., 346
Moruno López, E., 289
Moscona, S., 152
Moseley, E. C., 418
Moser, D., 257
Moses, J. A., Jr., 293, 458
Moses, P., 537–538
Motowidlo, S. J., 501
Mottram, L., 460
Moun, T., 200
Mount, M. K., 361
Moura, L. F., 289
Msall, M. E., 277
Mucha, R. F., 407
Mufson, L., 590
Mühlberger, A., 421
Muir, D., 220
Mukherjee, S., 514, 515, 540, 544
Mukhopadhyay, P., 377
Mulhollen, C., 230
Mulick, J. A., 277
Mumford, M. D., 507
Munsinger, H., 515
Munson, J., 230
Murdoch, M., 208
Muris, P., 407, 409
Murisa, P., 409
Murphy, J., 421
Murphy, K. R., 146, 155
Murphy, M. C., 192
Murphy, R., 422
Murphy, S. E., 230
Murray, D. M., 468
Murray, H. A., 353, 390
Murstein, B. I., 392
Murtagh, M., 418
Musewicz, J., 372–373
Mutran, E. J., 161
Myburgh, C. P. H., 361
Mysiw, W. J., 365
Mzumara, H. R., 417

N

Naglieri, J. A., 227, 269
Nair, M., 274
Narr, K. L., 445
Nathan, P. C., 285
Naughton, M. J., 153, 473
Neal, C. R., Jr., 273
Neal, D. J., 419
Neher, L. A., 196
Neil, R., 363
Neisser, ., 300

Neitzel, J., 288
Nell, V., 540
Nelson, D. V., 346
Nelson, W., 355
Nelson, W. M., 345, 347
Neta, G., 193
Neto, F., 365
Neumann, R., 464
Nevo, B., 220
Newcombe, P., 207
Newman, C., 411
Newman, D. A., 500, 514
Newman, M. G., 420
Newton, R. L., 385
Nezworski, M. T., 19, 372, 374, 376, 383, 385, 388
Ng, J., 222
Ngo-Metzger, Q., 468
Nguyen, J., 463
Nguyen, S. E., 325
Nichols, D. S., 346
Nickels, L., 289
Nicolson, N. A., 414
Nieberding, R., 334, 373
Nies, K. J., 462
Nijenhuis, J., 227, 361, 517
Nilsen, D., 429
Nisbett, R. E., 515
Nittono, H., 353
Noble, A. C., 523
Noll, J., 230, 240
Nordhov, S. M., 280
Nordin, P., 273
Nores, M., 281
Norlin, J. W., 268–269
Norman, D. K., 376
Norman, G., 167
Norman, G. R., 28
Norman, J., 494
Norris, J. T., 418
North, M. M., 421
North, S. M., 421
Norton, E. H., 571
Norton, W. E., 193
Novella, J. L., 474
Novick, B. Z., 288
Novy, D. M., 346
Noyman, A., 283
Nugent, E., 348
Nugent, J., 272
Nugent, W. R., 182
Null, C., 345
Numan, B., 462
Nunnally, J. C., 104, 123
Nuvolone, G., 365
Nyborg, H., 515

O

Oakland, T., 193, 277, 531
Ober, B. A., 460
Oberlander, T. F., 273
O'Connell, M.E., 468
O'Connor, E., 467–468
O'Connor, J. L., 347
Odbert, H. S., 350
O'Donnell, J., 364
Oehler-Stinnett, J., 283
Ofiesh, N., 290
Ogloff, J. R. P., 590
O'Halloran, C. M., 540

O'Hara, M. W., 141
Oldehinkel, A., 335
Oldridge, N., 473
Oliver, J. M., 364
Oliveri, M. V., 253
Olkin, R., 347
Olkkola, S., 468
Ollinger, I., 409
Olson, J., 200
Ones, D. S., 316, 593
Onghena, P., 407
Oostdam, R., 201, 464
Oostendorp, R., 277
Opton, E., 563
Oral, E., 396
Ortiz, S. O., 257
Osberg, T. M., 346
O'Shea, T. M., 277
Osipow, S. H., 436
Oslin, D., 416
Ott, B., 257
Ottem, E., 289
Over, H., 196
Owen, D., 522
Oxford, K. P., 346
Ozan, E., 396
Ozoran, K., 474

P

Pacheco A., 272
Padawer, J. R., 380
Paez, D., 366
Paine, C., 353
Palaniappan, A. K., 295
Palm, J. A., 383
Palta, M., 108, 152, 474–475, 520
Pan, J., 390
Paolini, L., 365
Papadopoulou, C., 465
Papagerasimou, Y., 590
Papanis, N., 407
Parducci, A., 167–168
Parides, M., 218
Parissea, C., 269
Parker, J. D. A., 366, 508
Parker, K., 384
Parker, W. D., 361
Parnell, B., 417
Parolin, L., 379
Parsons, O. A., 446
Parsons, S., 285
Parsons, T. D., 441, 463
Partenio, I., 550
Pary, R., 218
Pascanu, R., 258
Pashley, P., 3
Patalano, F., 189
Patrianakos-Hoobler, A. I., 277
Patterson, B. F., 526, 539
Patterson, M., 193
Patterson, T. L., 69, 152
Paty, J. A., 467
Paul, R., 257
Pauli, P., 407, 421
Paunesku, D., 192, 537
Paunonen, S. V., 355, 361
Pavicevic, L., 294
Pawling, R., 196
Payne, R., 519–520

Pearson, K., 101
Peca-Baker, T., 485
Pedersen, N. L., 589
Pedrizzi, S., 451
Pedroni, A., 415
Pedrotti, J., 173
Peeters, F., 414
Pelletier, J. E., 464
Penfield, R. D., 168
Penge, R., 285
Penne, M. A., 417
Pennebaker, J. W., 420
Peoples, V. Y., 437
Perkos, S., 413
Pernas, A., 366
Perrez, M., 414
Perry, J. N., 419
Perry, W., 378
Petchkovsky, L., 396
Petchkovsky, M., 396
Peters, S. U., 280
Petersen, S., 173
Peterson, C., 412
Peterson, C. B., 347
Peterson, D. A., 221
Peterson, E. R., 194
Peterson, G., 362
Peterson, N. G., 507
Peterson, P. E., 496
Petrides, K. V., 230
Petrill, S. A., 227
Petrocelli, J. V., 347
Pettit, F. A., 419–420
Peyton, S. T., 526
Peyton, V., 173
Pfaffenberger, A. H., 397
Pfennig, A., 416
Phares, E. J., 256–257
Phelps, P., 280
Phillips, M. L., 199
Phillips, S. E., 584
Phillips-Meek, M., 445
Picard, R. W., 418
Pick, C. G., 274
Pickett, K., 416
Pickett, K. E., 514, 531
Picone, L., 80
Piedmont, R. L., 361
Pierce, C. A., 539
Pierce, J. P., 504
Piers, V. P., 357
Pietrobon, R., 363
Pinto, D., 361
Piotrowski, C., 373–374
Piotrowski, Z. A., 374–375
Pirelli, G., 395
Pirozzolo, F. J., 230
Plaisted, J. R., 457
Plake, B. S., 276
Plante, E., 285
Plesha-Troyke, S., 277
Poland, D. L., 346
Polansky, N., 407
Polkey, C. E., 294
Pomplun, M., 240, 286
Ponniah, K., 590
Pons, D., 365
Ponsoda Gil, V., 599
Poon, L. W., 201
Pope, J. E., 506

Pope, K. S., 418
Pope, M. K., 364
Poposki, E. M., 327
Porter, S. C., 416
Portnoy, B., 468
Portoghese, C., 286
Posthuma, R. A., 218, 220
Poston, W. S. C., 465
Potenza, M. T., 599
Pottenger, M., 140
Potvin, D., 283
Poulton, J. L., 364
Powell, D. H., 207
Powell, F. C., 353
Power, M. J., 411
Powers, D. E., 148
Pozzi, G., 346
Prager, T. C., 280
Prather, E. N., 390
Price, J. H., 420
Price, K. H., 485
Primi, C., 182
Primi, R., 231
Prinstein, M. J., 218
Pritchard, D. A., 458
Pritzl, T. B., 384, 395
Privado, J., 240
Prout, H. T., 285
Prusoff, B. A., 140
Przeworski, A., 420
Puccio, G. J., 295
Puertas, R., 280
Pugh, R. C., 14
Pugliese, M. D., 57
Pull, C. B., 421
Pulvers, K. M., 364
Pupo, M. C., 347
Purdie, N., 285
Pyne, J. M., 152, 421

Q

Qin, S., 347
Qiu, Y. -F., 274
Quale, A. J., 364
Quatman, G., 345
Quay, L. C., 522
Quenk, N. L., 501–502
Quigley, A. M., 582
Quinsey, V. L., 590
Quintar, B., 376
Quiroga, M. Á., 240

R

Rabin, B. A., 193
Rablen, R. A., 215
Raczek, A., 472
Radunzel, J. M., 139
Rafferty, J. E., 397
Raju, N. S., 494
Ralston, S. M., 220
Ramakers, G. J. A., 294
Ramanaiah, N. V., 361
Ramesh, B., 417
Ramírez, J. M., 409
Ramirez-Mallafre, A., 277
Rammsayer, T. H., 226, 326
Ramos, R., 280
Ramsay, M. C., 227
Ramstad, P. M., 494

Randolph, D. L., 355
Rankin, R. J., 283
Ransom, S., 544
Rao, S. L., 287
Rapaport, D., 375, 396, 407
Rapp, D., 219
Rappaport, N. B., 196
Rasulis, R., Jr., 418
Rathbone, C, J., 413
Raven, J., 322, 324
Raymond, M. R., 25, 170, 198, 520
Reardon, R. C., 437
Reardon, S. F., 3
Rebello, I., 322
Reckase, M. D., 588
Reed, H. B., 454
Reed, J. C., 454
Reed, P. S., 161
Reed, S. B., 220
Reeve, B. B., 183
Reeves, D., 421
Reeves, T. D., 135–136
Regine, A., 280
Reheiser, E. C., 465
Reidy, T. J., 489
Reijneveld, S. A., 448
Reilly-Harrington, N. A., 411
Reis, D. L., 257
Reis, H. T., 441
Reise, S. P., 182
Reiseaeeter, S., 289
Reitan, R. M., 455, 457
Rejeski, W. J., 152
Ren, X., 265
Rench, T. A., 327
Renner, J. B., 161
Rentz, D. M., 199
Rentz, T. O., 347
Reschly, D. J., 568
Resnick, S. M., 293
Reynolds, C., 589
Reynolds, C. R., 227, 282–283, 458, 514, 526
Reznikoff, M., 372, 380
Rhoad, A., 227
Rhodewalt, F., 364
Ribaudo, F., 280
Ribot, B., 273
Ricciardi, P. W., 283
Riccio, M., 285
Rice, H., 198
Rice, M. E., 590
Richards, J. E., 445
Richardson, M. W., 111
Richeson, N. 365
Ricker, J. H., 44, 445, 446
Ridge, S., 208
Ridley, D. R., 502
Ries, A. L., 108, 152, 474
Ries, R., 491
Riggio, R. E., 230
Righetti-Veltema, M., 277
Riikonen, R., 286
Riksen-Walraven, J. M., 467
Rinaldo, V., 407
Rindermann, H., 535
Ritzler, B. A., 373, 395
Riva, G., 421
Rix, K., 258
Robbins, S. B., 139
Roberson, C. C., 135, 137, 170, 520, 539

Roberson, G., 446
Roberts, A., 192, 416, 537
Roberts, E., 294
Roberts, K. E., 465
Roberts, L. J., 419
Robertson, G. J., 296
Robertson, I. T., 139
Rockliff, H., 413
Rodriguez, M., 160, 163, 444
Roebuck-Spencer, T., 463
Roeckelein, J. E., 204
Roehling, M. V., 484
Roesch, S. C., 361
Roge, B., 363
Rogers, A. R., 520
Rogers, C. R., 214, 215, 217, 330, 358
Rogers, R., 342
Rogers, S. M., 417
Rogers, W. H., 472
Rogler, L. H., 472
Roid, G. H., 226, 229, 230, 241, 244, 286
Røise, O., 364
Roisman,G.I., 514
Roland, D., 327
Roland, M., 495
Rolland, J. P., 361, 362
Rollnick, J. D., 293
Romero, C., 537
Ronald, A., 280
Rønning, J. A., 280
Rosanoff, A. J., 396
Rosen, A., 341, 590
Rosen, C. C., 366
Rosenberg, M., 362
Rosenblatt, N., 311
Rosenfeld, J. P., 462
Rosenfeld, P, 198
Rosenstein, R., 502
Rosenthal, R., 194, 196, 515, 544, 562
Roskos,P., 445, 463
Rosmalen, J., 335
Rosner, J., 321, 590
Rossier, J., 429
Rossini, E., 458
Roth, M., 365, 415
Roth, P. L., 506, 520
Roth, W. T., 415
Rothbaum, B. O., 421
Rothlin, S., 553
Rothlisberg, B.A., 283
Rothman, S., 534
Rothstein, H. R., 155, 494
Rotter, J. B., 90, 397
Rottinghaus, P., 435
Rotunda, R. J., 418
Roulin, N., 207, 484
Roupas, C., 422
Rozin, P., 358
Rubin, D. B., 165
Rubin, Z., 150
Rudman, H. C., 305
Ruiz, F., 411
Ruiz-Zambrana, A., 281–282
Ruscio, A. M., 428
Rushton, J. P., 372, 533, 565
Rushton, J.,348, 350, 361
Rushton, P., 283
Russell, A., 304
Russell, E. W., 430, 431
Russell, G., 267

Russell, I. J., 151
Russell, J. T., 505
Russell, L. B., 488
Russell, P., 274
Russell, P. S. S., 286
Russell, S., 274
Ruud, W. N., 501
Ryan, A. M., 192
Ryan, J., 555, 556
Ryan, J. J., 256
Ryan, R., 244
Rybarczyk, B. D., 404
Ryskin, R., 219

S

Sabatino, S., 383
Sabel, K. G., 273
Saccuman, C., 285
Saccuzzo, D., 367
Saccuzzo, D. P., 11, 20, 209, 230, 257, 260, 300, 324, 347, 367, 379, 388, 590, 598, 599
Sackett, P. R., 54, 146, 149, 155, 485, 492, 494, 534
Sadeh, A., 409
Sadler, P. M., 524
Safir, M., 421
Sager, C. E., 509
Sahoo, M., 510
Saine, N. L., 422
Sakkas, D., 325
Saklofske, D. H., 251
Sakuragi, A., 383
Sala, S., 451
Sala, S. D., 445
Salamon, G., 445
Salmon, D. P., 415, 461, 462
Saltzman,J., 502
Salyakina, D., 416
Samuel, D. B., 589
Sanchez, C., 445
Sander, N., 220
Sander, R., 541
Sanderman, R., 412
Sands, E. W., 294
Sands, W. A., 327
Sanford, R. N., 20, 598
Sangameshwar, B., 417
Sangwan, S., 227
Sanislow, C. A., 589
Santamaria, E., 416–417
Santiago, S., 180
Santosa, C. M., 295
Saperia, J., 219
Sarason, S. B., 382
Sartorius, N., 214
Saslow, G., 405
Satishchandra, P., 287
Satre, D. D., 417
Sattlberger, E., 462
Sattler, J. M., 189, 190, 196, 197, 238, 526, 540, 544, 565, 567
Satz, P., 453
Saucier, G., 361
Savage, G., 447
Savickas, M. L., 426
Sawyer, J., 590
Sayegh, P., 403
Sayer, N. A., 208
Schaefer, B. A., 362
Schaefer, J. A., 504

Schafer, R., 375, 396
Schaible, D., 378
Schaik, P., 166
Schalet, B. D., 183
Schanberg, S., 273
Schanke, A. K., 364
Scheier, I. H., 465
Scheier, M. F., 364
Schene, A. H., 362
Scheuneman, J. D., 522
Schleicher, A., 3
Schmidt, A. E., 422
Schmidt, F., 180, 181, 362
Schmidt, F. L., 139, 155, 402, 494, 500, 532, 534
Schmidt, M., 402
Schmied, V., 208
Schmitt, N., 484, 485
Schmukle, S., 209
Schmukle, S. C., 365
Schneider, A., 465
Schneider, B., 192
Schneider, F. W., 438
Schneider, K. C., 285
Schneider, L., 207
Schneider, L. M., 300
Schneider, R. J., 182
Schneider, S., 465, 467
Schneider, U., 293
Schneidman, E. S., 382, 385, 394
Schnipke, D. L., 182
Schnurr, P. P., 208
Schoebi, D., 414
Schoedl, A. F., 347
Scholz, U., 363
Schrader, W. B., 523
Schrank, F. A., 290
Schreck, K. A., 277
Schreiber, M. D., 277
Schuerger, J. M., 350, 352
Schuldberg, D., 418
Schulz, S., 293
Schuster, M. A., 523
Schwager, I., 3, 21
Schwartz, A., 373
Schwarz, L. R., 253
Schwarzer, R., 363
Schweder, T., 24–25
Sciarrino, J. A., 139
Scott, L. H., 325
Scott, S., 17
Scrams, D. J., 182
Sears, L. E., 506
Seaton, B. E., 256
Sechrest, L., 374, 510
See, S. K., 421
Seelen, J., 418
Seeman, T. E., 523
Seewaldt, V. A., 392
Segall, D. O., 327
Segre, L. S., 141
Seguin, E., 13, 272
Seidman, L. J., 253
Seifer, R., 277
Seifert, J., 293
Seitz, R., 510
Sekirnjak, G., 345
Seligmann, J., 570
Sells, S. B., 382, 385
Selthon, L., 588
Semple, S. J., 152

Senior, C., 199
Serafin, L., 147
Serfass, D., 390
Sethuraman, R., 419
Severance, D. D., 422
Sewell, K. W., 342
Shackleton, V., 500
Shaffer, J. A., 220
Shaffer, L., 20
Shaffer, L. F., 20, 598
Shaffer, T. W., 378, 384
Shakow, D., 20, 598
Shankar, S., 274
Shankaran, S., 277
Shankster, L. J., 144
Sharkey, K. J., 395
Shattuck, D. W., 445
Shavitt, S., 464
Shaw, E. J., 526
Shedlin, M., 199
Sheehan, K. M., 590
Sheldon, B., 404
Sheldon, K. L., 285
Sherman, J., 199
Sherman, R., 390
Shermis, M. D., 417
Sherrer, M. V., 592
Sherry, A., 397
Sherry, D., 373
Shibata, S., 420
Shieles, A., 231
Shiffman, S., 467
Shirzad, G., 502
Shmelyov, A. G., 420, 421, 597
Sholomskas, D., 140
Shonkoff, J. P., 528
Shorey, H. S., 364
Short, P., 463
Shultz, M. M., 321, 590
Shumaker, J., 199
Shumaker, S. A., 473
Sidick, J. T., 163
Sieber, W. J., 152
Sigman, S. T., 364
Sigurdsson, J. F., 362
Sijtsma, K., 182
Silk-Eglit, G. M., 455
Silva, J. M., 495
Silva, M., 521
Silver, M. J., 194
Silver, N. C., 104
Silverman, W., 244
Sim, S., 219
Simon, T., 228
Simons, C. J. P., 414
Sineps, J., 341
Sines, J. O., 590
Singer, J., 373, 388
Singer, O., 592
Singh, L., 395
Sinnott, P. L., 208
Sivan, A. B., 446
Sivas, F., 474
Skaltsas, A., 325
Slade, T., 416
Slaney, K. L., 588
Slate, J. R., 193
Slatkoff, J., 346
Sletten, I. W., 418
Smart, T. K., 355

Smeekens, S., 467
Smith, A. N., 507
Smith, B., 510
Smith, B. L., 372
Smith, C., 488
Smith, D. A., 397
Smith, E., 293
Smith, E. V., Jr., 182
Smith, H. E., 293
Smith, J., 412
Smith, R., 280, 372
Smith, T. V., 445
Smith, T. W., 364
Smithberger, A., 591
Smolen, A., 411
Snelbaker, A. J., 296
Snow, J. H., 293
Snow, R. E., 194, 322, 544
Snyder, C. R., 364
Snyderman, M., 534
Soares, J. A., 540, 545, 554
Sohn, W. J., 352
Solamon, J. M., 218
Solanto, M. V., 377
Solorio, R., 137
Somerville, L. H., 440
Song, H., 199`
Sonnert, G., 524
Sorensen, J. R., 489
Sostek, A. M., 272
South, M., 414
Southwick, S., 383
Spangler, W. D., 395
Sparrow, S. S., 286
Spata, F., 286
Spear, J. H., 589, 601
Spear, S. E., 199
Spearman, C., 331
Spearman, C. E., 226
Spellacy, F., 502
Spencer, R. J., 445, 544
Spencer, S. J., 191, 192, 193, 518, 520, 532
Sperry, R. W., 282
Spielberger, C. D., 201, 465
Spiers, P. A., 458
Spies, R. A., 276
Spinrad, T., 361
Spira, J. L., 421
Spirrison, C. L., 362
Sprecher, S., 441
Spritzer, K., 182
Sprock, J., 378
Spurgeon, L., 537, 538
Srinivasan, K., 283
Srsic, C. S., 436
Stallones, R. A., 145
Stankov, L., 231
Stanley, J. C., 101, 314
Stannard, L., 280
Stark, A., 447
Stark, R., 407
Stattin, H., 145
Stavrakantonaki, M., 464
Steele, C. M., 190, 517, 518
Steele, J. D., 453
Steer, R. A., 411
Steger, H. S., 193
Steiger, D. M., 417
Stein, A. T., 466
Stein, K., 544

Steinberg, L. S., 590
Steiner, K., 277
Stejskal, W. J., 372, 388
Stenclik, J. H., 455
Stephenson, W., 169
Stern, D. N., 273
Stern, W., 234
Sternberg, K., 535
Sternberg, L., 226
Sternberg, R., 535
Sternberg, R. J., 147, 226, 251, 283, 300, 497
Stevens, S. S., 167
Stevens-Gill, D., 502
Steverink, N., 335
Stewart, A. J., 394
Stewart, A. L., 473
Stewart, G. L., 220
Stewart, J. L., 346
Stewart, M., 374
Stewart, O. T., 504
Stickle, T. R., 374
Stimac, A. P., 436
Stippekohl, B., 407
Stobart, G., 494
Stokes, S. M., 108
Stone, A. A., 117, 466, 467
Stone, E., 417
Storey, J. E., 588
Stormo, A. R., 413
Strassberg, D. S., 345
Strauss, E., 502
Strauss, M. E., 294
Stredny, R., 334
Stredrick, D., 468
Strickland, J., 273
Strong, E. K., Jr., 427
Strong, M., 495
Stuart, S., 141
Studley, R., 590
Stumpf, H., 314, 361
Su, C., 526
Su, J., 362
Succi, G. J., 522
Sud, S., 363
Sukumaar, P., 283
Sulea, C., 427
Sullivan, D. S., 188
Sullivan, J., 347
Sulsky, L. M., 500
Sun, J., 290
Sun, Q., 274, 390
Sunderman, G., 556
Sundland, D., 418
Super, D. E., 426
Sutherland, S., 383
Sutin, A. R., 359
Suwalsky, J. T. D., 227
Suzuki, L. A., 528
Swallen, K. C., 519
Swanda, R. M., 448, 449
Swartz, C. W., 182
Swartz, J. D., 389
Sweeney, J. A., 447
Sweet, C. M. C., 472
Sweet, J. J., 458, 462
Sweet, R. C., 196
Swindell, J. S., 591
Swinson, R. P., 413
Sydeman, S. J., 465
Symonds, P. M., 167

Sympson, S. C., 364
Syperek, S., 418
Szasz, T. S., 592
Szilágyi, E., 362
Szkodny, L. E., 420
Sztulman, H., 363

T

Taghavi, M. R., 412
Taimalu, M., 409
Tait, E., 352
Talbot, R. J., 295
Tallberg, I. M., 253
Tallent, N., 418
Talwar, C., 358
Tamassia, C., 3
Tan, J. A., 366
Tan, M., 325
Tan, U., 325
Tang, S. F., 277
Tanyolac, O., 474
Tarafder, S., 377
Taulbee, E. S., 465
Tavernelli, M., 352
Taverniers, J., 363
Taylor, A. Z., 540
Taylor, H. C., 489
Taylor, H. G., 453, 454
Taylor, L. A., 447
Taylor, M., 363
Taylor, R. J., 335
Taylor, S., 421
Taylor, T. R., 226
Tazaki, M., 407
Te Nijenhuis, J., 227, 361, 517
Tedeschi, G., 465
Tedeschi, R. G., 90
Teixeira, C., 272
Tellegen, A., 347, 365
Tellegen, A. M., 342, 345, 346
Tempel, T., 464
Ten Berge, M., 409
Ten Brummelhuis, L. L., 361
Tendais I., 272
Teng, E. L., 294
Tennen, H., 364
Tennen, R., 364
Tenopyr, M. L., 143
Teri, L., 140
Terman, L. M., 14, 226, 331
Termen, H., 467
Terraciano, A., 365
Terrell, M. D., 532
Terrill, D. R., 364
Tew, M. D., 419
Thal, L. J., 461
Thaler, N., 403
Thalmayer, A. G., 361
Thames, A., 403
Thayer, P. W., 221, 300
Thennarasu, K., 287
Theodorakis, Y., 413
Theorell, T., 509
Thoits, P. A., 592
Thomas, J. C., 588
Thomas, M. L., 100, 104
Thompson, B., 84
Thompson, D., 365
Thompson, D. E., 139

Thompson, F. E., 200
Thompson, H., 274
Thompson, L. A., 227, 311
Thompson, R., 410
Thompson, S. B., 293
Thompson, S. B. N., 293
Thompson, T. A., 139
Thompson, W. W., 472
Thoresen, C. J., 366
Thorndike, E. L., 219, 331
Thorndike, R. L., 194, 238, 544
Thornton, A., 3
Thorpe, J. S., 389
Thorsen, C., 231
Thorson, J. A., 353, 365
Thurbers, S. A., 275
Thurstone, L. L., 240
Tiegs, R. B., 500
Tilse, C., 207
Timbrook, R. E., 346
Timmerman, M. E., 230
Tipper, S. P., 196
Tippins, N., 501
Tippins, N. T., 493
Tiro, J. A., 200
Titov, N., 420
Tittle, C. K., 437
Tobin, J. N., 193
Toga, A. W., 456
Tolvanen, A. 422
Tomany-Korman, S. C., 520
Tomes, Y. I., 283
Tong, F., 290
Tong, R., 390
Tong, S., 515
Tooze, J., 285
Torrance, E. P., 295
Torrance, G. W., 494
Torras-Mana, M., 277
Toshima, M. T., 57
Tourangeau, R., 417
Towne, R. L., 290
Tracey, T., 428, 440
Transler, C., 283
Traynor, V., 517
Treisman, G. J., 407
Tronick, E. Z., 273
Trost, C., 553
Trotman, K. M., 293
Trotter, M. A., 465
Troxtel, D. D., 218
Truax, C. B., 215, 217
Truckett, E., 505
Trujillo, T., 556
Trull, T. J., 256, 257
Trumbo, D., 221
Truxillo, D. M., 510
Tryon, W. W., 588
Tsai, A., 421
Tsatsanis, K. D., 286
Tsolaki, M., 404
Tsuang, M. T., 253
Tuckett, A., 207
Tukey, J. W., 24
Tulsky, D., 258, 260, 262
Tunby, J., 280
Turgeon, L., 465
Turkheimer, E., 515
Turner, C. F., 417
Turner, D. R., 382

Turpin, G., 414
Tuvblad, C., 287
Twohig, M. P., 413
Tyler, L. E., 428
Tynan, W. D., 273

U

Uber, J. W., 294
Ulett, G., 418
Ulrich, L., 221, 222
Ulvund, S. E., 280
Umansky, W., 279
Uneri, O. S., 398
Upper, D., 410
Ur Rehman, S., 365
Urbina, S., 50, 154, 162
Urrows, S., 467
Ursano, R. J., 363
Uutela, T., 473
Uzzell, R., 537, 538

V

Vale, C. D., 418
Valencia, R. R., 283, 528
Valiente, C., 361
Valsan, N., 447
Van Beijsterveldt, T. C., 515
Van de Vijver, F., 199, 283
Van den Berg, S., 515
Van der Flier, H., 227, 517
Van der Kooij, M., 413
Van der Linden, D., 361
Van der Linden, W. J., 180, 182
Van der Pas, F. H., 409
Van der Staak, C. P. F., 362
Van der Vleuten, C. P. M., 218
Van Doesum, K. T., 467
Van Dyk, K., 403
Van Iddekinge, C. H., 220, 221
Van Leeuwen, M., 515
Van Nieuwenhuizen, C., 365
Van Wersch, A., 166
Van Zandvoort, M. J., 448
Vance, B., 294
Vance, R., 285
VandenBos, G. R., 444
Vandenburg, S. G., 545
Vandevijer, F. J. R., 326
Vassend, O., 359, 364
Vavassori, D., 390
Vecchione, M., 363, 417
Veenstra, R., 335
Veerkamp, J. S. J., 409
Veetil, S. A., 447
Veijola, J., 347
Velox, A. J., 388
Verdeli, H., 590
Verdon, B., 395
Verhulst, F. C., 448
Vernon, S. W., 200
Verweij, A. C., 182
Vicario, C. M., 286
Vicino, S. M., 198
Viglione, D. J., 388
Villodas, M. T., 410
Vimpani, G., 515
Vincelli, F., 421

Viswesvaran, C., 500
Vitacco, M. J., 374
Vlachos, O., 325
Vlaeyen, J. W. S., 407
Voelker, S., 283
Vogler, G. P., 545
Voigt, R. G., 280
Vojvodic, R. W., 200
Volker, F., 413
Volkmar, F. R., 286
Von Stumm, S., 331
Vorstenboscha, V., 410
Vrij, A., 208

W

Wadsworth, A. P., 465
Wagner, E. E., 294, 384
Wagner, R., 221
Waidman, D. A., 326
Wainer, H., 3
Wakely, M. B., 182
Waksberg, J., 507
Wald, J., 421
Walker, A. M., 215
Walker, E. L., 379
Walker, K., 276, 277
Walker, M. T., 214
Walker, R., 275
Walker, R. N., 377
Walla, P., 342
Wallach, H., 421
Waller, N. G., 182
Wallis, H. R., 353
Wallnau, L., 24, 25, 29, 84, 87
Walsh, W. B., 428, 436
Wanberg, C. R., 435
Wang, C., 422
Wang, E., 219
Wang, H., 293
Wang, P. W., 295
Wang, S., 200, 303
Wang, W., 229
Wang, X., 476
Wang, Z., 84
Ward, A. W., 137
Ward, D. M., 592
Ward, K. E., 283
Ward, S. M., 568
Ward, T. J., 198, 499
Ward, W. C., 599
Wardrop, A. A., 277
Ware, J., 152
Ware, J. E., 473
Ware, J. E., Jr., 472, 473
Warner, M. H., 502
Warren, J., 412
Warren, N. C., 441
Warren, W. L., 357
Washington, J. A., 285
Washington, R., 417
Waters, B. K., 327
Watkins, C. E., Jr., 334, 373
Watkins, M., 227
Watkins, W. S., 520
Watson, C. W., 311
Watson, D., 165, 167, 168, 365, 366
Watson, W., 16
Watt, S. K., 365

Wauke, A. P. T., 359, 421
Webster, E. C., 485
Webster, J. S., 458
Wechsler, D., 16, 249, 251, 256, 257, 260, 264, 265
Wechsler, S. M., 193
Wee, S., 147
Weed, N., 342
Weik, A., 421
Weinberg, J., 273
Weiner, B., 540, 544
Weiner, I. B., 373, 390
Weinger, P., 218
Weinman, J., 364
Weinrich, J. D., 69, 475
Weintraub, J. K., 364
Weisner, C., 417
Weiss, D. J., 181, 599
Weiss, L., 257
Weiss, L. G., 251, 253, 277
Weissman, A. N., 411
Weissman, M. M., 140
Weissman, M. W., 590
Weisz, R., 365
Welch, H. G., 120
Welch, E. L., 379
Wellings, K., 416
Wells, E., 417
Welsh, G. S., 345
Wermiel, S., 553
Werner, H., 459
Werner, S., 501
Wertheimer, M., 275
West, D. D., 447
West, J. L., 419
West, S. G., 510
Westenberg, P. M., 409
Westrick, P. A., 139
Wetherell, M., 601
Wetter, S. R., 460
Weyers, P., 407
Whalley, D., 474
Wheeler, L., 455
Wheeler, M., 484
Whetzel, D. L., 500, 522
Whipple, C. M., 375
Whisman, M. A., 411, 412
White, S. E., 414
Whiteside-Mansell, L., 363
Whittington, D., 517
Whyte, G., 494
Wiberg, M., 58
Wichers, M., 414
Wieber, J. L., 277
Wiedemann, C. F., 316
Wiedemann, G., 421
Wiederhold, B. K., 420, 421, 597
Wiederhold, M. D., 420, 421, 597
Wiesner, M., 523
Wiesner, W. H., 484
Wigdor, A., 54
Wiggan, G., 515
Wiggins, J. G., 360
Wiggins, J. S., 12, 333
Wik, G., 292
Wiklund, C., 364
Wild, C. L., 522
Wilder, J., 415
Wildermuth, J. L., 19, 383
Wilhelm, F. H., 415

Wilhelm, O., 220
Wilhelm, P., 414
Wiliam, D., 21
Wilk, S. L., 54
Wilken, J. A., 463
Wilkening, G. N., 457
Wilkes, L. 208
Wilkins, C., 257
Wilkinson, G. S., 296
Wilkinson, L., 65
Wilkinson, R. G., 514
Williams, C. L., 346
Williams, J., 342
Williams, J. M., 283
Williams, P. B., 523
Williams, R. L., 529
Williams, S. L., 2008
Williams, W. M., 147, 300
Williams, L.E., 163
Williamson, L. G., 484
Williamson, W. D., 275
Willis, G., 417
Willis, J. O., 230
Wilner, N., 466
Wilson, M., 24, 506
Wilson, M. A., 506
Wilson, S. E., 417
Wimer, C., 294
Windle, M., 523
Winget, B. M., 196
Winkler, M. H., 407
Winter, D. G., 394
Wise, S. L., 422
Wissler, C., 228
Witherspoon, D. J., 520
Witmer, J. M., 189
Wittenborn, J. R., 382
Wolach, A. H., 420
Wolfe, P., 462
Wolfgang, C. H., 280
Wolfson, D., 455
Wolk, R. B., 395
Wolk, R. L., 395
Wolpe, J., 409
Wong, A. M., 277
Wong, F., 356
Wong, K. F. E., 506
Wong, P. S., 389
Wood, A. M., 361

Wood, D. P., 421
Wood, J. M., 19, 372, 373, 374, 377,
    382, 383, 385, 388, 389, 390, 397,
    398, 597
Wood, K., 336
Woodcock, R. W., 290
Wooding, S., 520
Woods, S., 296
Woods, S. P., 445, 461, 462
Woodward, J. A., 415
Woodworth, R. S. 334
Woolfson, L. M., 335
Worling, J. A., 348
Worrell, F. C., 135, 137, 170, 520, 539
Wouters, L., 362
Wright, A., 407
Wright, D. E., 257
Wright, K. M., 363
Wright, M. J., 452
Wright, T. L., 90
Wrightsman, L. F., 321
Wu, C., 365
Wu, H., 506
Wulfeck, B., 285
Wuyek, L. A., 410
Wyatt, J.N., 539
Wyckoff, J., 495
Wyland, C. L., 362
Wyse, A. E., 588

X

Xie, W., 445
Xiurong, X., 274
Xu, F., 294
Xu, H., 428, 440
Xu, J., 316
Xue, J., 347
Xue, L., 273

Y

Yan, L., 293
Yanez, A. P., 365
Yang, C., 502
Yang, M., 416
Yang, X., 293
Yang, Y., 167

Yang, Y. L., 413
Yarcheski, A., 363
Yarcheski, T. J., 363
Yeager, D. S., 192, 537
Yen, W. M., 104, 174, 175
Yerkes, R. M., 15
Yoon, K., 362
York, D., 371, 372–373
Young, M., 200
Youngcourt, S., 484
Yu, C. K., 397
Yu, Y., 277
Yu, Z.-B., 274
Yurong, H., 274

Z

Zack, M. M., 472
Zane, K., 445, 463
Zapf, P. A., 395
Zawacki, T., 257
Zedeck, S., 139, 321, 506, 590
Zeidner, M., 466, 526
Zennaro, A., 379
Zhang, F., 219
Zhang, L., 446
Zhang, T., 294
Zhang, X., 199, 522
Zheng, R., 365
Zhu, J., 258, 260, 262
Zhu, J. J., 257
Zhu, L., 290
Zickar, M., 335
Zigman, W., 244
Zimand, E., 421
Zimbardo, P. G., 161
Zimet, C. N., 375
Zimmerman, M., 140
Zimmerman, W. S., 349
Ziskin, J., 589, 590
Zonderman, A. B., 293
Zores, L. S., 523
Zotti, A. M., 365
Zou, Y. L., 280
Zubin, J., 336, 381, 382, 389
Zuckerman, M., 201, 415, 515
Zumbo, B., 365
Zurawski, R. M., 412
Zytowski, D. G., 432, 434, 435

Subject Index

A

Ability tests, 8, 321–327
  See also Individual ability tests
Absolute 0, 26–27
Achievement, need for, 390
Achievement tests
  aptitude tests *vs.*, 305–306
  defined, 8
  evolution of, 14–16
  group tests, 305–308
  individual, 296
  intelligence tests *vs.*, 296
  SATI, 541–542
Acquiescence, 345
ACT (American College Test), 313–314
Active listening, 217
Actuarial prediction, 590–591
*Adarand Constructors, Inc. v. Pena, Secretary of
  Transportation et al.* (1995), 572
Adjective Checklist, 357
Admissions, norms for university, 59
  See also College entrance tests
Advanced Placement (AP) calculus test, 192
Adolescents, Junior Senior High School
  Personality Questionnaire, 352
Adult neuropsychology, 453–459
Adverse impact, 551, 578
Affirmative action, 541, 571–575, 580–581, 585
  See also Quotas
Affordable Care Act (2010), 477
African Americans. *See* Race and ethnicity
Afro-American Slang Dictionary, 530
Age, apperception tests and, 395
Age bias, 318–319
Age differentiation, 228–229, 244
Age-related norms, 54–58
Age scale, 232–233
Agreeableness, 360–361
Alabama State Board of Education, 572
Alcoholism, 358, 447
Allen v. Alabama State Board of Education, 572
Alpha coefficient, 129
Alzheimer's disease, 461–463
American Bar Association, 320
American Civil Service Commission, 12
American College Test (ACT), 142, 327
American Council on Education, 554
American Educational Research Association
  (AERA), 121, 135, 193
American Journal of Psychology, 101
American Psychological Association (APA),
  20, 121, 135, 144, 591, 593–594, 597
  Task Force on Statistical Inference, 65

Americans with Disabilities Act (ADA),
  583–585
Analysis of variance, 508
*Ana Maria R. v. California Department of
  Education,* 563
Ansell-Casey Life Skills Assessment, 417
Antimode, 184
Anxiety
  assessments, 463–464
  computer-based treatments, 420
  defined, 464
  state, 464–465
  stress and, 464
  test, 463–464, 482
  trait, 464
*APA Standards for Educational and Psychological
  Tests,* 583
Apperception tests, 390–395
Aptitude tests
  achievement tests *vs.*, 305, 306
  bias in, 526
  defined, 8
  industry for, 142–143
  intelligence tests *vs.*, 305
  prevalence of, 22
Aptitude-treatment interaction, 509
Armed Services Vocational Aptitude Battery
  (ASVAB), 161, 326–328, 527
Army Alpha test, 15
Army Beta test, 15
Artificially dichotomous variables, 80
Assertive Behavior Survey Schedule (ABSS), 410
Assertiveness, 409–410
Assessment interview, 224
Assessments, defined, 372
Association for Evaluation in Guidance, 437
*Association of Mexican-American Educators v.
  California,* 582
Attention, 450–451
Attenuation, reliability and, 127–128
Automated Neuropsychological Metrics
  (ANAM), 462–463

B

Barnum effect, 382
Basal, 243
Base rates and hit rates, 486–501
  basic principles, 486–489
  decision analysis, 493–494
  incremental validity, 499–501
  Taylor-Russell Tables, 489–493
  utility theory, 493–494
Bayley Scales of Infant Development, 297

Bayley Scales of Infant Development Third
  Edition (BSID-III), 275–278
Beck Depression Inventory, 140, 417–418
Behavioral deficits, 405
Behavioral excesses, 405
Behavioral observation studies, reliability in,
  115–116
Behavior assessment, 402
  See also Cognitive-behavioral assessment *vs.*
  medical model
Behavior, overt *vs.* covert, 6
Bell Adjustment Inventory, 335
Bell Curve, The (Herrnstein and Murray),
  527–529, 535
Bender Visual Motor Gestalt Test (BVMGT),
  293–294, 297
Benton Visual Retention Test–Fifth Edition
  (BVRT-V), 292–293
Bernreuter Personality Inventory, 335
Best-fitting line, 68–74
Betas, 88
Bias
  age, 318–319
  confirmation, 382–383
  in interviews, 219–222
  item, 523
  See also Test bias
Big Data, 61
  behavioral observation in, 117–118
  measurement error in, 127
Bills, 549
Binet-Simon Scale
  background, 14–15, 231
  1905 scale, 231–232
  1908 scale, 232–233
  Wechsler Intelligence Scales compared to,
  249–251
  See also Stanford-Binet Intelligence Scale
Biserial correlation, 80–81
Bivariate distributions, 64–65
Black Intelligence Test of Cultural
  Homogeneity (BITCH), 529–531
Boalt Hall, School of Law, University of
  California-Berkeley, 574
Boston Diagnostic Aphasia Examination, 450
Brain
  functioning of, 448, 455
  plasticity of, 450
  See also Neuropsychology
Brain imaging, 322–323
Brazelton Neonatal Assessment Scale (BNAS),
  272–274
Britain, 12
British Journal of Psychology, 101

Brookhart v. Illinois State Board of Education (1983), 584
Brown v. Board of Education (1954), 558
Business. *See* Industrial psychology; Jobs and careers

C

California, 571, 596
California Department of Education, 548, 563, 568
California Psychological Inventory (CPI), 165, 330, 347–349
California Verbal Learning Test (CVLT), 459–462
Campbell Interest and Skill Survey (CISS), 429–430
Career Assessment Inventory (CAI), 436
Carnegie Foundation, 554
Carnegie Interest Inventory, 427
Carroll Depression Scale, 141
Carryover effect, 107
Category format for test items, 166–168
Cattell-Horn-Carroll (CHC) theory of intelligence, 290
Cattell Infant Intelligence Scale (CIIS), 278–279
Causation, and correlation, 84
Ceiling, 243
Center for Epidemiologic Studies Depression Scale (CES-D), 41, 140–141
Center for the Future of Teaching and Learning, 559
Central Intelligence Agency (CIA), 33
Checklists
    items written as, 168–170
    job analysis using, 506
Child Behavior Checklist, 450
Child Development Inventory, 450
Child psychology, 21
Children
    California Verbal Learning Test-Children (CVLT-C), 462
    Children's Apperception Test (CAT), 395
    Children's Personality Questionnaire, 352
    individual ability tests, 279–284
    neuropsychology, 449–453
Children's Apperception Test (CAT), 395, 402
Children's State-Trait Anxiety Scale, 450
China, 11–12
Chitling Test, 529
Cholesterol tests, 145
Chronological age, and IQ, 234–235
Civil Rights Act (1964)549–550, 553, 574, 576, 579, 585
    See also Title VII, Civil Rights Act (1964)
Civil Rights Act (1991), 54, 326, 578–579
Civil service testing, 11–12
Clarification statements, 213
Classical test theory, 101–105, 108, 180
Class intervals, 31
Classroom placement, 548
Clinical Analysis Questionnaire (CAQ), 352
Clinical neuropsychology, 444–449
Clinical prediction, 590–591
Clinical psychology, 20
Closed-ended questions, 211, 223
Coefficient alpha (α)
    reliability estimation and, 112–113
    in split-half reliability, 111, 130

Coefficient of alienation, 83, 92
Coefficient of determination, 83, 92
Cognitive Abilities Test (COGAT) Form 7, 311
Cognitive approach to intelligence, 226
Cognitive-behavioral assessment *vs.* medical model
    cognitive-functional analysis, 412–414
    computerization of, 420
    Dysfunctional Attitude Scale (DAS), 411
    Irrational Beliefs Inventory (IBI), 412
    Irrational Beliefs Test (IBT), 411–412
    operant conditioning and, 405–407
    self-reports, 407–411
    steps in, 405
    traditional assessment *vs.*, 403–404
Cognitive-functional analysis, 412–414
College Board, 515, 542
College Entrance Examination Board, 554
College entrance tests, 312–314
    See also Admissions, norms for university; Graduate school entrance tests
"Color blind" policies, 571, 578
Columbia Mental Maturity Scale-Third Edition (CMMS), 284–285, 297
Common Core State Standards, 557
Common variance, 352
Comprehensive System, for scoring Rorschach tests, 379–380, 383
Computers, 416–422
    adaptive testing using, 181–182, 421–422, 599
    ASVAB and, 327
    California Verbal Learning Test (CVLT), 459–462
    cognitive-behavioral assessment and, 420
    dehumanization and, 595
    diagnosis using, 418–419, 591
    factor analysis and, 349
    human-computer interaction, 416
    interviews using, 416–417
    multimedia tests, 601
    neuropsychological assessment, 462–463
    scoring of tests by, 418–419
    test administration using, 327, 417–418, 420–421, 599, 601
    trends in use of, 597, 599
    virtual reality programs, 420–421
    See also Internet
Concurrent validity, 139, 157
Concussion resolution index (CRI), 452
Confabulatory response (DW), 377
Confidence intervals, 122–123
Confidentiality, 591–593
Confirmation bias, 382
Confirmatory data analysis, 24
Conflict, 464
Confrontation, 223
Connecticut v. Teal (1982), 582
Conscientiousness, 360–361
Construct, defined, 149
Construct-irrelevant variance, 138
Construct-related validity, 154
Construct underrepresentation, 137
Construct validity, 149–155, 157
    convergent evidence, 149–152
    criterion-referenced tests, 155
    discriminant evidence, 152–155
    establishing evidence of, 149
Content validity, 137, 157, 521–524
Context, value ratings and, 168–169

Continuous variables, 80
Contrast, 33
Convergent evidence, 149–152, 157
Co-operation and Development (OECD), 3–5
Cooperative movement, in Rorschach test, 378
Coping, 466
Coping Intervention for Stressful Situations (CISS), 366
Coping Inventory, 466
Coping Resources Inventory, 466
Core Self-Evaluations, 366
Correction for attenuation, 127–128
Correlation, 66
    causation and, 85
    regression and, 70–72
    restricted range problem, 86
    terms and issues, 82–86
Correlation-causation problem, 86
Correlation coefficients, 92
    biserial correlation, 80–81
    calculation of, 96–97
    coefficient of determination, 83
    defined, 66
    Pearson product moment correlation coefficient, 70, 80
    reciprocal nature of, 72
    selection of, 80
    Spearman's rho, 80–81
    statistical significance of, 74–76
Counseling, 20
    occupational interest inventories, 426–439
    personal characteristics inventories, 439–441
Covariance
    defined, 68
    *KR*20 formula and, 112
    shrinkage and, 84
    variance and, 74
Covert behavior, 6
Crawford et al. v. Honig et al., 564, 568
Creativity, 294–296
Criterion group, 333
Criterion-group approach, 333, 336–349
Criterion-referenced tests, 58–59, 186
    items for, 184–185
    validity of, 155
Criterion-related validity, 154
Criterion validity, 138–148
    GRE, 300
    LSAT, 300
    predictive and concurrent evidence, 138–140
    regression plots and, 76
    test bias and, 525–529, 535–536
    validity coefficients, 140, 142–148
Criterion validity evidence, 76, 138
Critical incidents, 507
Critical Reading, 143
Cronbach's coefficient alpha (*a*), 110–111
Cross validation, 84, 146, 341
Crystallized abilities, 240
Crystallized intelligence, 231, 245, 258
Cultural considerations
    Armed Services Vocational Aptitude Battery (ASVAB), 326–327
    Children's Apperception Test (CAT), 395
    Cognitive Abilities Test (COGAT), 311
    Culture Fair Intelligence Test, 325–326
    Henmon-Nelson Test (H-NT), 310–311
    interviews and, 220–221
    item writing and, 161

Cultural considerations *(Continued)*
   Kaufman Assessment Battery for Children, Second Edition (KABC-II), 282–284
   language, 189–190, 521
   Minnesota Multiphasic Personality Inventory (MMPI), 345
   norming, 53–54, 326
   personality models, 362
   Raven Progressive Matrices (RPM), 324
   reinforcing responses and, 196–197
   SAT Reasoning Test, 312
   Sixteen Personality Factor Questionnaire (16PF), 350–352
   stereotyping, 518
   See also Discrimination; Race and ethnicity; Test bias
Culture Fair Intelligence Test, 325–326
Current trends, 596–599
   computerization of tests, 599
   proliferation of tests, 596–597
   public awareness/influence, 598
   standards, 597–598
   testing on internet, 599
Cutting score, 184–185, 486–487

D

Debra P. v. Turlington, 568–570, 585
Deciles, 50
Decision analysis, 493–494
Deductive strategies, in personality tests, 331–332
Degrees of freedom (df), 74–76
Dehumanization, 595
Depression Scale (CES-D), 41
Depression, self-report validity on, 140–141
Descriptive statistics, 25
Desegregation court cases, 558–559
Detection rate, 488
Deterioration, 252–253
Determinants, in Rorschach test, 378
Detroit Edison Co. v. N.L.R.B., 582
Developing adolescent brain, 455
Developmental neuropsychology, 449–453
Developmental quotient (DQ), 274–275
Deviation IQ, 237–238, 245
Diagnostic interviews, 206
Diagnostic Interview Schedule, 141
Diana v. State Board of Education, 561, 585
Dichotomous format for test items, 161–162, 186
Dichotomous variables, 80–82
Dictionary of Occupational Titles (U.S. Department of Labor), 507
Difference scores, 113–115
Differential item functioning (DIF) analysis, 522–524
Differential prediction, 148
Differential validity, 520, 527
Difficulty, 112
Disabilities
   Americans with Disabilities Act (ADA), 583–585
   educable mentally retarded/handicapped548, 565–567
   Education for All Handicapped Children Act (PL 94-142), 561–562, 585
   individual ability tests, 284–287
   Individuals with Disabilities Education Act (IDEA), 288
   learning disabilities, 287–296, 451

minimum competence exams, 568, 570, 584–585
   test administration, 583
Discrepancies, in testing, 304
Discriminability
   item analysis and, 175–177
   Likert scales and, 165–166
   reliability and, 126–127
Discriminability analysis, 127
Discriminant analysis, 88–89, 92
Discriminant evidence, 152–155, 157
Discrimination
   court cases concerning, 558–572
   employment, 134, 506, 551, 553, 577–579
   sexual, 552
   See also Affirmative action; Gender bias; Test bias
Discrimination index, 175, 186
Dispositional Resilience Scale (DRS), 363
Distractors, 162–163
Distributions. *See* Frequency distributions
Divergent validation, 153
Divided loyalties, 591, 593–594
Domain sampling model, 103–104, 124–125
Double-barreled items, 160
Dove Counterbalance General Intelligence Test, 530
Draw-a-Clock task, 450
Draw-a-Person Test, 398
Drawing tests, 398
DSM-IV, 141
Ductal carcinoma in situ (DCIS), 120
Dysfunctional Attitude Scale (DAS), 411
Dyslexia, 451

E

Ecological Momentary Assessment (EMA), 466–467
Edinburgh Postnatal Depression Scale (EPDS), 468–470
Educable mentally handicapped (EMH), 563–567
Educable mentally retarded (EMR), 548–549, 561, 563, 565–567, 585
Educational psychology, 20
Educational Testing Service (ETS), 142, 165, 314, 436, 522, 554, 571–572
Educational tests. *See* Psychological tests
Education for All Handicapped Children Act (PL 94-142), 561–562, 585
Edwards Personal Preference Schedule (EPPS), 353–355
EEOC guidelines, 550–553
Ego Resiliency Scale (ER89), 363
Ego Resiliency Scale Revised, 363
eHarmony, 441
Elementary and Secondary Education Act (1965), 555
Eligibility in Local Context (ELC) program, 59
Emotional intelligence, 363
Empathy
   in interviews, 213–214
   measuring, 215–217
Empirical strategies, in personality tests, 331–334
Employment. *See* Jobs and careers
Encode, in mental processing, 451
English East India Company, 12
Environments, classification of, 503–505

EPDS. *See* Edinburgh Postnatal Depression Scale (EPDS)
Equal Employment Opportunity Commission (EEOC), 549–553
   See also EEOC guidelines
Equal intervals, 26
Equal protection clause, 553, 562, 564, 570, 574, 576
   See also Fourteenth Amendment, U.S. Constitution
Equivalent forms reliability, 109–110
Error, 129
   conceptualization of, 100–101
   defined, 100
   interviews and, 219–223
   random *vs.* systematic, 102–103
   sources of, 106–107, 119–120
   standard error of measurement, 103
   test-retest method, 106
Error variance, 352, 509
Essay exams, 165
Estimated learning potentials (ELPs), 531
Ethical considerations
   APA code of ethics, 594
   divided loyalties, 591, 593–594, 601
   human rights, 591–592, 598, 601
   labeling, 591–593
   privacy, 591, 593
   public awareness/influence, 598–599
   test bias, 531–535
   test construction, 594
   test use, 594
Ethical Principles of Psychologists and Code of Conduct (American Psychological Association), 591
Every Student Succeeds Act, 557
Examiners, 7
   expectations of, 193–194
   race of, 189–190
   reinforcing responses from, 196–197
   role of, 302
   Rorschach inkblot test, 374–383
   test taker's relationship to, 188–189
   training of, 193
Executive function, 451
Expectancy effects, 193–194
Experimental psychology, 13
Exploratory data analysis, 24
External validity, 193
Extraversion, 359, 361
Extreme group method, 176
Extroversion, 359

F

Face validity, 136, 157, 322, 335–336
Factor analysis, 89–92
   computers, 349
   defined, 19
   intelligence and, 230
   reliability and, 113, 126–127
Factor analytic strategy, in personality tests, 334, 349–353
Factor and item analysis, 127
Factor loadings, 89
Factors, 19, 89, 230
Fairness. *See* Cultural considerations; Test bias
Faking, on personality tests, 336, 338, 340, 354–355, 364
False negatives, 487–488

False positives, 335, 487–488
Family income, and test performance, 521, 540
Fear and phobias
  computer-based treatments, 421
  psychophysiological assessment, 415
Fear Survey Schedule (FSS), 409, 421
Federal Express, 552
Federal government. See U.S. government
Figure drawing tests, 398
First impressions, 219–220, 485
Five-factor model of personality, 359–362
Fluid-analytic abilities, 240
Fluid intelligence, 231, 244–245, 257–258, 261
Focus execute, in mental processing, 451
Food and Drug Administration, 472
Football head injuries, 452
Ford and Ford v. Long Beach Unified School
  District, 268
Forensic psychology, 21
Form quality, in Rorschach test, 380
Four-fifths rule, 551
Fourteenth Amendment, U.S. Constitution,
  548, 550, 553, 575, 562, 572, 576
  See also Equal protection clause
France, 12, 227
Free association, 376
Frequency distributions, 29–32
  mean, 37–38
  standard deviation, 38–40
  standard normal deviation, 41–48
Frequency polygon, 31
Frustration, 464–466
Full-scale IQ (FSIQ), 252, 258–259
Future trends, 599–601

G

Gain-score information, 115
Gender bias
  content validity, 522–523
  interest measurement, 437–439
  LSAT and, 320–321
  Revised Wechsler Intelligence Scale for
    Children (WISC-R), 523
  Slosson Intelligence Test, 523
  Stanford-Binet Intelligence Scale, 523
  Strong Vocational Interest Blank
    (SVIB), 428
  Wechsler Adult Intelligence Scale
    (WAIS), 523
General Aptitude Test Battery (GATB), 53,
  326, 328
General cognitive index (GCI), 280–281
General (g) factor of intelligence, 230,
  238–239, 322, 515
Generalizability, 148
General Management Aptitude Test
  (GMAT), 422
General mental ability, 229–231
General Self-Efficacy Scale (GSE), 363
General standoutishness, 219, 226
Genes, IQ and, 516–517
Germany, 12
Gerontological Apperception Test, 395
Gesell Developmental Schedules (GDS),
  274–275
gf-gc theory of intelligence, 230–231, 238–240
GI Forum v. Texas Education Agency, 570
GMAT (Graduate Management Aptitude
  Test), 422

Golden Rule Insurance Company et al. v.
  Washburn et al., 571–572
Gonzalez v. Abercrombie & Fitch, 552
Goodenough Draw-a-Man Test, 398
Goodenough-Harris Drawing Test (G-HDT),
  324–325, 328, 398
Government. See U.S. government
GPA (grade point average), 138
  ACT and, 313
  as criterion, 535, 540
  GRE and, 314–318
  LSAT and, 300, 320–321
  Miller Analogies Test and, 318–319
  SAT Reasoning Test and, 49
Grades
  case study, 260–262
  grade inflation, 317–318
  See also GPA (grade point average)
Graduate Management Admission Test
  (GMAT), 554
Graduate school entrance tests, 314–321
Gratz v. Bollinger (2003), 573–574
GRE (Graduate Record Exam),
  314–318, 554
  computer-adaptive testing, 422
  computer-administered, 599
  criticisms of, 142–143
  impact of, 3, 300
  predictive validity, 147, 300, 314–318
  quantitative ability sample items, 317
  score trends, 316
  test bias, 522, 527
  verbal ability sample items, 315
  verbal and quantitative, 316
Griggs v. Duke Power Company (1972), 527,
  577–578
Group tests, 8, 229–328
  achievement tests, 305–311
  advantages, 302–303
  characteristics, 303
  civil service tests, 326
  college entrance tests, 312–314
  graduate/professional school entrance tests,
    314–321
  individual tests compared to, 301–303
  intelligence tests, 308–311
  military testing, 326–327
  nonverbal ability tests, 321–327
  overview, 303–305
  predictive validity, 300
  schools, 305–311
  selection of, 303–304
  using information on, 304–305
Grutter v. Bollinger (2003), 573–574
Guessing, on multiple-choice tests, 163–165
Guessing threshold, 165
Guilford-Zimmerman Temperament
  Survey, 349

H

Halo effect, 219, 224
Halstead-Reitan Neuropsychological Battery,
  418, 453–456
Hamilton Rating Scale for Depression, 141
Handicapped. See Disabilities
Hardiness, 358, 363
Hawaii Department of Education, 584
Health, definitions of, 472
Health index, 148, 150–152

Health psychology, 21, 444–482
  anxiety and stress assessment, 463–467
  neuropsychological assessment, 444–471
  quality-of-life assessment, 472–482
Healy-Fernald Test, 272
Henmon-Nelson Test (H-NT), 310–311
Hereditary Genius (Galton), 12, 229
Hero, in Thematic Apperception Test (TAT), 392
High stakes testing, 2–3
High Stakes: Testing for Tracking, Promotion,
  and Graduation, 143
Histograms, 30–31
History
  antecedents of psychological testing, 11–12
  current environment, 21
  evolution of tests, 14–16
  individual differences, concept of, 12–13
  intelligence tests, 14–16
  mid-twentieth century developments, 20
  personality tests, 16–18
  psychophysical measurement, 13
Hit rates. See Base rates and hit rates
Hobson v. Hansen, 560
Holtzman Inkblot Test, 389–390, 418
Home Depot, 552
Hope Scale, 364
House-Tree-Person Test, 398
Human ability, 8
Human-figure drawing tests, 324–325
Human needs, 353, 390
Human rights, 591, 594–595, 598, 601

I

Idiosyncratic concepts, 254
Idiot, defined, 231
Ignorance, stupidity vs., 529–531
Illinois Department of Insurance, 571–572
Illinois Insurance Licensing Examination,
  571–572
Illinois Test of Psycholinguistic Abilities
  (ITPA), 289–292
Illness, test performance and, 201
Imbecile, defined, 231
Incomplete Sentences Task, 397
Incremental validity, 499–501
Index, 252
Individual ability tests, 267–297
  advantages, 301–303
  Binet and Wechsler Scales compared to,
    268–270
  comparisons among, 270–272
  early examples of, 272
  group tests compared to, 301–303
  infants, 272–287
  learning disabilities, 287–296
  persons with disabilities, 284–287
  strengths/weaknesses of, 269
  young children, 279–284
Individual achievement tests, 296
Individual differences, Charles Darwin and, 12–13
Individualism
  qualified, 532, 544–545
  unqualified, 532–533, 544, 571
Individuals with Disabilities Education Act
  (IDEA), 288
Individual tests, 7
Industrial psychology, 20, 484–511
  decision analysis, 493–494
  employee selection, 484–485, 494, 501

Industrial psychology *(Continued)*
  job analysis, 505–507
  person-job fit, 501–502
  person-situation interaction, 508–510
  test bias, 534–535
  test use, 502
  test validity and, 139
  utility theory, 493–494
  work setting assessment, 503–505
Infant mortality, 33
Infants, individual ability tests for, 272–279
Inferences, 24
Inferential statistics, 25
Information-processing approach to
    intelligence, 226
Information-processing model, 289–290
Information processing, neuropsychological
    assessment of, 449, 541–542
Information-processing speed computer-
    assisted assessment, 452
Informed consent, 591
Initiative 200 (Washington), 575
Inquiry, 377
Inquiry phase of Rorschach test, 377
Institute for Personality and Ability Testing
    (IPAT) Anxiety Scale, 465
Intelligence
  Binet's model, 231–233
  Cattell-Horn-Carroll model, 290
  defining, 226–228
  measurement of, 26
  Modern Binet, 238–244
  multidimensional model, 240
  research approaches, 226–227
  Spearman's model, 229–233
  Terman's Stanford-Binet, 234–238
Intelligence quotient (IQ), 234–235, 245
  calculation of, 234–235
  deviation IQ, 237–238
  full-scale IQ, 252, 258–259
  genes and, 516–517
  Gesell Developmental Schedules, 274–275
  intervals and, 26
  performance IQ, 16
  Stanford-Binet Intelligence Scale, 14–15,
    234–238
Intelligence tests
  achievement tests *vs.*, 296
  aptitude tests *vs.*, 305
  Binet's principles of construction, 228–229
  classroom placement and, 548, 563
  computer-adaptive testing, 421–423
  criticisms of, 227
  defined, 8
  evolution of, 14–16
  fairness of, 226–227
  group tests, 308–311
  history of, 226–227
  norms in, 51
  race/ethnicity and, 189–190
Interactive process, 223
Intercept, 68, 92
Interest inventories. *See* Occupational
    interests
Interjudge reliability, 115
Internal consistency, 106–107, 119
  coefficient alpha (a), 112–113
  *KR*20 formula, 111–112
  split-half reliability, 109–111
Internal criteria, 182

Internet
  dating, 440–441
  distance learning, 185
  psychological testing, 419–420, 599
Interobserver reliability, 115–116
Interpersonal attraction, 209
Interpersonal influence, 209
Interquartile range, 50
Interrater reliability, 115, 120
Interscorer reliability, 115
Interstate commerce, 549–550
Interval scales, 28, 61
Interviews, 203–224
  attitudes for, 209
  bias in, 219–222
  case history interviews, 224
  closed-ended questions in, 211
  computer-assisted, 416–417
  defined, 10
  diagnostic, 206
  effective interviewing, 208–218
  empathy in, 213–214
  employment, 484–485
  first impressions, 204
  flow of, maintaining, 212–215
  hostile statements in, 210
  importance of, 208
  judgmental statements in, 209
  mental status examinations, 271–218, 224
  open-ended questions in, 211
  probing statements in, 209–210
  reassuring statements in, 210
  reciprocal nature of, 208
  reliability of, 222–223
  responses, effective and ineffective, 209–210
  selection, 206
  skills development for, 218
  sources of error, 219–223
  stress, 209
  structured, 206, 221–222, 484, 518
  as tests, 207–208
  types, 224
  unstructured, 204, 215, 223
  validity of, 219–222
*Introduction to the Theory of Mental and Social
    Measurements, An* (Thorndike), 101
Inventory to Diagnose Depression (IDD), 141
Iowa Test of Educational Development
    (ITED), 313
IPAT Culture Fair Intelligence Test, 325–326, 328
Ipsative scores, 353–355
IQ. *See* Intelligence quotient (IQ)
Irrational Beliefs Inventory (IBI), 412
Irrational Beliefs Test (IBT), 411–412
Isodensity curve, 524
Item analysis, 173–186
  criterion-referenced tests, 184–185
  difficulty, 173–174
  discriminability, 175–177
  external criteria and, 182
  item characteristic curve, 177–182
  item response theory, 180–182
  limitations of, 185–186
  linking uncommon measures, 182–184
Item characteristic curve, 177–182, 186
Item difficulty, 173–174
Item discriminability, 175
  extreme group method, 176
Item formats, 161–173
  category format, 166–168

checklists, 168–170
dichotomous format, 161–162
guessing, 163–170
Likert format, 165–166
polytomous format, 162–163
Q-sort, 196
Item loadings, 90
Item pools, 160
Item response theory (IRT), 104–105,
    180–182, 186
  medicine and, 183
Items, 160–186
  analysis of, 173–186
  defined, 6
  writing, 160–173
Item sampling, 108–109, 119

J

Jackson Personality Inventory Revised (JPI-R),
    355–357
Jackson Vocational Interest Survey (JVIS), 435
Job analysis, 505–507
Job performance, 501, 505, 532
Jobs and careers
  court cases concerning, 577–583
  employee selection, 484–485, 495, 501
  interests assessment, 426–439
  personal characteristics, 439–441, 501–503
  person-job fit, 501–503
  personnel psychology, 484–485, 501–503
  person-situation interaction, 508–510
  work setting assessment, 503–505
  See also Interviews
Job satisfaction, 366, 501
Judicial opinion, 549
Junior Senior High School Personality
    Questionnaire, 352

K

Kappa statistic, 116
Kaufman Assessment Battery for Children
    (KABC), 279
Kaufman Assessment Battery for Children,
    Second Edition (KABC-II), 282–284, 297
Kaufman Test of Educational Achievement,
    Second Edition (KTEA-II), 282
Kinetic Family Drawing Test, 398
Korsakoff's syndrome, 461
*KR*20 formula, 111–113, 130–132
*KR*21 formula, 112
Kuder Occupational Interest Survey (KOIS),
    432–436, 438–439, 442
Kuder Preference Survey, 427, 432
Kuder-Richardson 20 formula, 111–113
Kuhlmann-Anderson Test (KAT)–Eighth
    Edition, 308–310

L

Labeling, 591–593
Language, and test performance, 193, 521
Larry P. v. Wilson Riles, 529, 549, 561–563,
    565, 585
Law, 548–585
  affirmative action cases, 572–577
  cases, 558–577
  defined, 549
  disabilities cases, 583–584

influential lawsuits, 558–584
judicial opinion and, 549
personnel cases, 577–583
use of tests, 549–557
Law School Admissions Council, 321
Learning disabilities
developmental neuropsychology and, 451
testing, 287–296
Leiter International Performance Scale-Third
Edition (LIPS-3), 250, 286–287
Life Orientation Test-Revised (LOT-R), 364
Life satisfaction, 365–366
Likert scales, 165–166
Linear combination of variables, 87
Location chart, for Rorschach test, 377
Locus of control, 366
Logical-content strategy, in personality tests,
332, 334–336
Long-delay savings, 462
Los Angeles City Fire Department, 552
Love, meaning of, 150–151
Low scores, interpreting, 304
Loyalties, divided, 591, 593–594, 601
LSAT (Law School Admission Test), 319–321,
327, 554
bias in, 321
computer-administered, 599
impact of, 3
predictive validity, 300, 540
questions on, 2
test bias, 522
Luria-Nebraska Neuropsychological Battery,
444, 457–459

M

Magnitude, 25
Major depressive disorders (MDDs), 467
Marchall v. Georgia, 568
MCAT (Medical College AdmissionTest), 540
McCall's *T*, 48–49, 341
McCarthy Scales of Children's Abilities
(MSCA), 279–282, 297
McMaster Health Index Questionnaire, 472
Mean, 37–38, 61
symbols for, 38, 40
Measurement, 25
See also Scales
Measurement error. *See* Error
Median, quartiles and, 50–51
Medical college admission test (MCAT), 477–481
Medical Decision Making (journal), 494
Medical model, 403
Medical Outcome Study Short Form-36
(SF-36), 472–473
Memory
assessments, 447
California Verbal Learning Test(CVLT),
459–462
short-term, 240
working, 252
Memory Assessment Scales (MAS), 447
Memory-for-Designs (MFD) Test, 294
Mental age, 14, 229, 232–236, 245
Mental Measurements Yearbook, 322, 427, 598
Mental processing factors, 451
Mental status examinations, 217–218, 224
Mental tests, 13
Meredith v. Jefferson County Board of Education
(2007), 576

Meta-analysis, 384
Methods of rotation, 91
Metropolitan Achievement Test (MAT),
306–308, 327
mHealth, 476–477
defined, 476
Military testing
Armed Services Vocational Aptitude
Battery (ASVAB), 161, 326–327
computer-adaptive testing, 422
personality tests, 331, 335
Raven Progressive Matrices (RPM), 324
Woodworth Personal Data Sheet, 334–335
Miller Analogies Test (MAT), 318–319, 327
Minimum competence exams, 568, 570, 584–585
Minnesota Multiphasic Personality Inventory
(MMPI), 198, 336–347, 368–369, 372
administration of, 338
California Psychological Inventory (CPI)
compared to, 347–349
clinical scales, 336–337
computer-administered, 417, 599
computer scoring of, 418
content scales, 337
criterion groups, 339
current status, 347
development of, 338–341
format of, 165
Halstead-Reitan Battery and, 455
interpretation of, 341
Meehl's extension of empirical approach,
341–342
MMPI-2, 336–337, 340–345, 346, 372, 595,
598–599
original scales, 345, 347
principles of, 19
problems covered by, 345–346
profile sheet, 337
psychometric properties, 345–347
purpose of, 338
reliability, 345
restandardization of, 342–345
standardization samples, 340, 344
validity, 346
validity scales, 336–337, 340–341, 345
Mooney Problem Checklist, 335–336
Moral considerations. *See* Ethical
considerations
Moron, defined, 231
Multimedia computerized tests, 601
Multiple-choice tests, 162–163
Multiple regression, 87, 92
Multi-State Bar Exam, 554
Multivariate analysis, 87, 92
Myers-Briggs Type Indication (MBTI),
501–502

N

National Academy of Sciences, 54, 123
National Research Council, 143
National Assessment of Educational Progress
(NAEP), 183
National Cancer Institute, 200
National Center for Health Services Research,
472
National Council on Measurement in
Education (NCME), 121, 135, 588, 597
National Enquirer, 92
National Institutes of Health (NIH), 183

National Longitudinal Study of Youth, 527
National Research Council, 184
Needs
human, 353, 390
in Thematic Apperception Test (TAT), 392
Negative correlation, 66–67
Negative stereotype, 190–191
NEO Personality Inventory–Revised
(NEOPI-R), 369–372
Neuroimaging, 445
Neuropsychological assessment
Automated Neuropsychological Metrics
(ANAM), 462–463
California Verbal Learning Test (CVLT),
459–462
clinical neuropsychology, 444–449
depression, 467–470
developmental neuropsychology, 449–453
Halstead-Reitan Neuropsychological
Battery, 453–456
Luria-Nebraska Neuropsychological Battery,
457–459
NIH Toolbox, 470–471
quantitative *vs.* qualitative, 459
uses of, 447
Neuropsychology, 21
adult, 453–459
alcoholism and, 450
clinical, 444–449
developmental, 449–453
football head injuries, 452
rehabilitation process, 453, 459
Neuroticism, 359–361, 366
Newsweek (magazine), 521
New York, 548, 553–554
New York Public Interest Research Group
(NYPIRG), 554
NIH grants, race and ethnicity in, 195
NIH toolbox, 470–471
No Child Left Behind (NCLB) Act, 59–60,
555–556
Nominal scales, 27, 61
Nonpictorial projective procedures, 395–398
Nonverbal group ability tests, 321–327
Normalization, *vs.* standardization, 49
Norm-referenced tests, 58
Norms, 51–61
age-related, 54–58
criterion-referenced tests, 58–61
defined, 51
norm-referenced tests, 58–61
Rorschach inkblot test, 383
tracking and, 54–58
university admissions and, 59
within-group controversy, 53–54
Nottingham Health Profile (NHP), 472, 474
Null hypothesis, 74

O

Objectivity, in testing field, 597–598
Observation, job analysis using, 507
Observers. *See* Examiners
Obtained scores. *See* Raw scores
Occupational Information Network
(O*NET), 507
Occupational interests, 432–436
aptitudes and, 439
Campbell Interest and Skill Survey (CISS),
429–430

Occupational interests *(Continued)*
  Career Assessment Inventory (CAI), 436
  gender bias, 437–439
  Jackson Vocational Interest Survey
    (JVIS), 435
  Kuder Occupational Interest Survey
    (KOIS), 432–436, 438–439, 442
  personality and, 509
  personality traits and, 440
  Self-Directed Search (SDS), 436–437
  Strong-Campbell Interest Inventory (SCII),
    428–429
  Strong Interest Inventory (SII), 430
  Strong Vocational Interest Blank (SVIB),
    427–428
Odd-even system, 109
Open-ended questions, 211
Openness, 359
Openness to experience, 360
Operant conditioning, 405–407
Ordinal scales, 27, 61
Organizational psychology. *See* Industrial
  psychology
Origin of Species, The (Darwin), 12
Otis Self-Administering Tests of Mental
  Ability, 502
Outcomes, in Thematic Apperception Test
  (TAT), 392
Overpathologizing, 384
Overselection, 53
Overt behavior, 6

P

Parallel forms reliability, 106, 108
Paraphrasing, 213
*Parents in Action on Special Education v.
  Hannon*, 563–565, 585
Parents v. Seattle (2007), 575–576
Pareto-optimal decisions, 534
Patient Health Questionnaire (PHQ), 468
Patient Reported Outcomes Measurement
  Information System (PROMIS), 183
Pattern analysis, 260
Peabody Picture Vocabulary Test-Third
  Edition (PPVT-III), 285–286
Pearson product moment correlation, 70,
  80, 109
Percentile bands, 308
Percentile ranks, 32–36, 45–47
  Z scores and, 45–47
Percentiles, 36–37
Performance evaluation, 506
Performance IQ, 16, 259–260
Performance scale, 250–251, 266
Personality
  characteristics, 330
  core of, 366
  defined, 330
  five-factor model of, 359–362
  occupational interests and, 509
  states, 330
  types, 330
  See also Personality traits
Personality Research Form (PRF), 355–357
Personality tests
  combination strategies, 358–362
  criterion-group strategy, 333, 336–349
  deductive strategies, 332
  defined, 8

empirical strategies, 331–332
evolution of, 16–18
factor analytic strategy, 334, 349–353
logical-content strategy, 332, 334–336
new approaches, 18–19
positive personality measurement, 358–367
projective, 8, 18, 331, 371–399
structured, 8, 17–19, 331–334
summary of, 19
theoretical strategy, 332, 353–358
types, 8
Personality traits
  Cattell's research on, 350–352
  defined, 7, 16, 330
  occupational interests and, 440
  positive measurement of, 362–367
  source traits, 350–351
  stability of, 440
  surface traits, 350
Personnel psychology, 484–485, 501–503
  decision analysis, 493–494
  employee selection, 484–485
  person-job fit, 501–503
  utility theory, 493–494
Person-situation interaction, 508–510
Phi coefficient, 81–82
Phobias. *See* Fear and phobias
Piers-Harris Children's Self-Concept Scale-
  Second Edition, 357
PL 94-142 (Education for All Handicapped
  Children Act), 561, 585
Plessy v. Ferguson (1896), 558–559
Pluripotentiality, 457
Point biserial correlation, 81, 175–177
Point scale, 249–250, 266
Polytomous format for test items,
  162–163, 186
Population
  defined, 25
  domain sampling model and, 103–104
  symbols for, 39–40
Porteus Maze Test (PMT), 287
Positive and Negative Affect Schedule
  (PANAS), 365
Positive correlation, 66–67
Positive manifold, 230
Positive personality research
  analysis of, 367
  frequently used measures, 362–366
  Personality Inventory–Three (NEO-PI-3),
    358–359
Positive skew, 30
Practice effects, 107–108
Prediction, actuarial *vs.* clinical, 590–591
Predictive bias, 539
Predictive validity
  family income, 540
  GRE (Graduate Record Exam), 147,
    314–318
  LSAT (Law School Admission Test),
    300, 540
  MCAT (Medical College Admission
    Test), 540
  medical tests, 145
  SAT Reasoning Test, 138, 524
Predictive validity evidence, 138, 157
Predictor variables, 138
Prekindergarten intervention, 543
Preschool Language Assessment
  Instrument, 190

Press, in Thematic Apperception Test
  (TAT), 392
Pressure, 464
Principal components, 89, 349
Principle of least squares, 67, 69
Principles of psychological testing, 10
Privacy, 591, 593
Processing intensity, 415
Professional issues, 588–591
  actuarial *vs.* clinical prediction, 590–591
  adequacy of tests, 589–590
  theoretical concerns, 588–589
Professional school entrance tests, 319–321
Programme for International Student
  Assessment (PISA), 3–4
Projective hypothesis, 373–374
Projective personality tests, 8, 17, 371–399
  administration of, 376
  controversial nature of, 372
  defined, 331
  drawing tests, 398
  Holtzman Inkblot Test, 389
  interpretation of, 374
  nonpictorial, 395–398
  other apperception procedures, 395
  prevalence of, 372–373
  projective hypothesis, 373–374, 398
  Rorschach inkblot test, 374–389, 398–399
  Thematic Apperception Test (TAT), 18,
    390–395
  See also Rorschach inkblot test
PROMIS initiative, 183
Proposition 209 (California), 571, 575, 578
Propositions, 549
Psychodiagnostik (Rorschach), 375
Psychological deficit, 292
Psychological testing
  access to, 596
  applications, 10–11
  controversial issues, 11
  criticisms of, 16, 20
  current trends, 596–599
  future trends, 599–601
  historical perspective, 11–21
  moral issues, 591–594
  principles, 10
  professional issues, 588–591
  purpose, 9
  social issues, 594–596
  traditional defense of, 520–529
Psychological tests
  adequacy of, 589–590
  defined, 6
  proliferation of, 596–597
  usefulness of, 595–596
Psychometric approach to intelligence, 226
Psychometric *g*, 230
Psychophysical measurement, 13
Psychophysiological procedures, 414–415
Psychotherapy, 20
Public awareness/influence, 598–599
Public Law 107-110, 555
Pure form response, in Rorschach test, 378

Q

Q-global scoring and reporting, 264
Q-sort, 169, 358
Qualified individualism, 532, 545
Quality-of-life assessment, 472–481

Quality of Well-Being Scale, 472
Quartiles, 50–51
Questionnaires, for job analysis, 507
Quotas, 532, 534, 544, 571, 579
See also Affirmative action

R

Race and ethnicity
    concept of race, 519–520
    examiners', 189–190
    intelligence tests and, 189
    item writing and, 161
    NIH grants, 195
    reinforcing responses and, 196–197
    See also Affirmative action; Cultural
        considerations; Discrimination; Test bias
Race to the Top program, 557
Racism, scientific, 530, 527
RAND Corporation, 473
RANDT Memory Test (RMT), 447
Ratio scales, 28, 61
Raven Progressive Matrices (RPM),
    322–324, 328
Raw regression coefficients, 88
Raw scores
    symbol for, 38
    Wechsler Intelligence Scales, 257
Reaction time
    Rorschach inkblot test, 376
    Thematic Apperception Test (TAT), 392
Reasonable accommodation, 583
Referral, 304–305
*Regents of the University of California v.
    Bakke*, 571
Regression, 67–80
    best-fitting line, 68–74
    correlation and, 70–72
    interpretation of, 76–80, 88
    multiple, 87
    origin of term, 72
    regression lines, 67–68
    statistical definition of, 72–74
    test bias and, 524–526, 532–533
Regression coefficients, 67, 88, 92
Regression equations, 67–68
    calculation of, 93–96
    cross validation, 84
    residuals, 82–83
    shrinkage, 84
Regression lines, 67–68, 77, 79, 92
Regression plots, 76–80, 524–526, 532–533
Rehabilitation Act, 561, 583
Reinforcement
    computer-generated schedules, 420
    test taking affected by, 196–197
    See also Operant conditioning
Reliability, 100–132
    behavioral observation studies, 115–118
    Brazelton Neonatal Assessment Scale
        (BNAS), 273
    campbell interest and skill survey, 430
    Career Assessment Inventory (CAI), 436
    coefficient, 106
    coefficient alpha (*a*), 112–113
    decline in, 161
    defined, 10, 100
    difference scores, 113–115
    domain sampling model, 103–104, 124
    estimate, 123–124

estimation of, 105
    guidelines, 121
    history of, 100–103
    internal consistency, 106–107, 119
    interrater, 124, 273, 506
    of interviews, 222–223
    item response theory, 104–105
    item sampling, 108–109, 119
    Jackson Vocational Interest Survey
        (JVIS), 436
    job analysis, 506
    *KR*20 formula, 111–112, 130–132
    low, 124–129
    Minnesota Multiphasic Personality
        Inventory (MMPI), 345
    models, 106–115, 119–121
    parallel forms, 106, 108
    Rorschach inkblot test, 384, 388
    sources of error, 106–107, 119–121
    split-half method, 109–111
    Stanford-Binet Intelligence Scale,
        236–237, 244
    State-Trait Anxiety Inventory (STAI), 465
    strength of, 123
    Strong Vocational Interest Blank (SVIB), 427
    test-retest method, 107–108
    Thematic Apperception Test (TAT), 394
    theoretical concerns, 588–589
    time sampling, 107–108, 119
    using information on, 122–129
    validity and, 154–155
    Wechsler Intelligence Scales, 263, 265
    Wonderlic Personnel Test (WPT), 502
Representative samples, 14, 146
Residuals, 69, 82–83, 92
Resilience, 363
Response acquiescence, 160
Response style, 346
Restatement, 213
Restricted range problem, 86, 147–148
Revised Wechsler Intelligence Scale for
    Children (WISC-R), 462, 523, 526,
    531, 564
Reynolds Depression Scale, 450
"Right to know," 591–594
Rorschach inkblot test, 8, 374–389, 398–399
    administration of, 375–380, 385–389
    Card 1, 18, 375–376
    clinical validation, 380–383
    confabulatory responses (DW), 377, 380
    controversial nature of, 379–381
    determinants, 377–378
    diagnosis in relation to, 385
    early use, 18
    form quality, 380
    history of, 374–375
    interpretation of, 377–380, 386–387
    location choices, 377
    movement response, 378
    norms, 383
    overpathologizing, 384
    popular responses, 379
    prevalence of, 372–373
    psychometric properties, 380–389
    pure form response, 378
    reliability, 388
    responses ("R"), 385
    scoring, 379–385, 388
    space responses, 385
    stimuli in, 391

Thematic Apperception Test (TAT)
    compared to, 390–391
    validity, 380–383, 388
Rosenberg Self-Esteem Scale, 362–363
Rosenthal effects, 194, 196
Rotter Incomplete Sentence Blank,
    397, 418
Rubber yardsticks, 100, 103, 122–123

S

Samples
    defined, 25
    domain sampling model, 103–104
    representativeness, 14
    symbols for, 39–40
    See also Standardization sample
Sampling error, 101
SATI, 142, 144
Satisfaction with Life Scale (SWLS), 365
SAT Reasoning Test (SAT-I; formerly Scholastic
    Aptitude Test), 49, 312–313, 554
    computer-administered, 599
    criticisms of, 142–143
    current version of, 52
    family income and, 540
    norms of, 51–52
    predictive validity, 138, 524
    standardized scores in, 49
    test bias, 522–523, 536
    University of California and, 144, 542
SAT scores, 138
SAT Suite of Assessments, 312
Scaled scores, 257–258, 266
Scales, 25–29, 465
    defined, 7
    permissible operations, 28–29
    properties, 25–27
    types, 27–28
Scatter diagrams, 64–66, 92
Scatter plots, 89
Schemas, 411
Schizophrenia, 260, 592
Scholastic Aptitude Test. *See* SAT Reasoning
    Test (SAT-I; formerly Scholastic
    Aptitude Test)
School psychology, 20
Schools, group tests in, 305–311
    See also College entrance tests; Graduate
        school entrance tests
Scientific racism, 530, 527
Seguin Form Board Test, 13, 272
Selection interviews, 206
Selection ratio, 490–493
Self-concept, 330, 357–358
Self-Directed Search (SDS), 436–437
Self-efficacy, 363, 366, 435
Self-esteem, 362–363, 366
Self-handicapping, 191
Self-reports, 407–411
    assertiveness, 409–410
    behavior and, 500
    evaluation of, 410–411
    example, 407
    Fear Survey Schedule (FSS), 409
    procedures, 410–411
    questionnaires, 441
    test administration and, 200
    test items, 9
    validity of, 140–141, 500

Self, Rogers's model of, 358
Self-statements, 413
Senior Apperception Technique, 395
Sentence completion tasks, 396–397
Separate-but-equal principle, 558
Sequential processing, 282
Sequential-simultaneous distinction, 282
Sexism, 553
Sexual harassment, 552
SF-36 (Medical Outcome Study Short Form-36), 472–473
Shift, in mental processing, 451
Short Hardiness Scale, 363
Short-term memory, 240
Shrinkage, 84
Sickness Impact Profile (SIP), 473
Simultaneous processing, 282
Sixteen Personality Factor Questionnaire (16PF), 19, 350–352
Skew, 30–31
Slope, 68, 92
Slosson Intelligence Test, 523
Slow learner case study, 261–262
Smarter Balance Assessment Consortium, 557
Social desirability, 353–354
Social facilitation, 208, 223
Social issues, 594–596
   access to services, 596
   dehumanization, 595
   usefulness of tests, 595–596
Society for Medical Decision Making, 494
Society of Industrial and Organizational Psychology, 535
Socioeconomic considerations, 227
Source traits, 350
Space responses, in Rorschach test, 385
Spearman-Brown formula, 109–111, 125–126
Spearman's rho, 80–81
Special Educator 2003 Desk Book (Norlin), 268
Spelling achievement test, 8
Split-half method, 129
Split-half reliability, 109–113
   coefficient alpha (*a*) for estimating, 130
Standard conditions, 14
Standard deviation, 38–40, 61
   formula for, 39
   standard error of measurement and, 103, 122, 124
   symbols for, 39–40
Standard error of estimate, 83, 92
Standard error of measurement, 103, 122–123, 263
Standardization
   normalization *vs.*, 49
   in test administration, 197
Standardization sample, 14
   Columbia Mental Maturity Scale-Third Edition, 285
   Gesell Developmental Schedules, 275
   Stanford-Binet Intelligence Scale, 234, 236
   Wechsler Intelligence Scales, 250, 262
Standardized interview, 206, 223
Standardized regression coefficients (*B*'s or betas), 88
Standardized testing and reporting (STAR) system, 60
Standardized tests, 14–15
   See also Group tests
Standard normal distribution, 41–48
Standards, 135

Standards-based testing, 60
Standards for Educational and Psychological Testing, 539
Standards for Educational and Psychological Testing (AERA, APA, and NCME), 135, 144, 155, 197
Stanford Achievement Test (SAT), 15, 305, 308, 312, 327
Stanford-Binet Intelligence Scale, 234, 236
   alternatives compared to, 268–270
   Cattell Infant Intelligence Scale and, 278
   classroom placement and, 548, 564
   cover page, 239
   development of, 14–15
   gender bias, 523
   modern scale, 238–244
   1916 scale, 234–235
   1937 scale, 16, 235–237
   1960 scale (SB-LM), 237–238
   1986 scale, 16, 240, 242
   psychometric properties, 243–244
   race of examiner and, 190
   reliability, 237, 244
   standardization samples, 234, 236, 238, 243
   2003 scale, 242–244
   validity, 244
Stanine system, 50–51
Start point, 243
State anxiety, 464
State-Trait Anxiety Inventory (STAI), 418, 464–465, 482
Statistics, uses of, 24–25
Stell v. Savannah-Chatham County Board of Education, 559–560, 585
Stereotype threat, 190–201
   computer-assisted test administration, 197–199
   damaging effects of, 192
   expectancy effects, 193–196
   mode of administration, 199–200
   reinforcing responses effect, 196–197
   remedy of, 192–193
   subject variables, 201
   test administrators training, 193
   test taker language, 193
Stereotyping, 518
Stress
   anxiety and, 463–464
   components of, 464
   coping with, 466
   Ecological Momentary Assessment (EMA), 466–467
   effects of, 463
   See also Anxiety
Stress interviews, 209
Strong-Campbell Interest Inventory (SCII), 428–430
Strong Interest Inventory (SII), 139–140, 430
Strong Vocational Interest Blank (SVIB), 427–428
Structured clinical interviews, 193, 224
Structured Clinical Interview for DSM-V (SCID), 193
Structured interviews, 206, 211, 220–223, 484, 500
Structured personality tests, 8, 16–18, 331–334
Stupidity, ignorance *vs.*, 529–531
Summarizing statements, 213
Summation sign, 38

Sum of squares, 67, 72
Surface traits, 350
Sustain, in mental processing, 451
Symbols, 38–40
Symmetrical binomial probability distribution, 44
System for Observing Children's Activity and Relationships during Play (SOCARP), 116
System of Multicultural Pluralistic Assessment (SOMPA), 529, 531

T

Tabloid news report, 64
TAT. *See* Thematic Apperception Test (TAT)
Taylor Manifest Anxiety Scale, 465
Taylor-Russell Tables, 489–493, 511
t distribution, 74
Technological improvements, 597–598
Tell Me a Story Test (TEMAS), 395
Template-matching technique, 509
Tennessee Self-Concept Scale-Second Edition, 357
Test administration, 188–201
   computer-assisted, 181–182, 197–199, 327, 417–418, 420–421, 599, 601
   defined, 10
   examiner's race and, 189–190
   examiner-test taker relationship, 188–189
   expectancy effects, 193–196
   language and, 193
   mode of, 199–200
   reinforcing responses and, 196–197
   subject variables and, 201
   training and, 193
Test administrators, 7–8
Test anxiety, 201, 463–464, 482
Test batteries, 11
Test bias, 514–545
   alternate approaches for minority group testing, 529–531
   Chitling Test, 529–530
   content validity, 521–524
   controversial nature of, 514–520
   criterion validity, 524–529, 535–536
   defense of testing, 520–529, 535
   defining, 531–532
   ethical considerations, 531–535
   ignorance *vs.* stupidity, 529–531
   interpretation of data, 535
   legal issues, 520
   regression and, 524–529, 532–533
   social changes, 540–543
   suggested solutions, 531–543
   See also Gender bias
Test construction, ethics of, 594
Test fairness. *See* Test bias
Testing industry, 142–143
Test of English as a Foreign Language (TOEFL), 422, 599
Test-preparation courses, 542
Test-retest method, 129
Test-retest reliability, 107–108
   carryover effects, 107–108
   Minnesota Multiphasic Personality Inventory (MMPI), 345
   practice effects, 107–108
   State-Trait Anxiety Inventory (STAI), 464–465
   Thematic Apperception Test (TAT), 394
   time interval, 108

Tests, 24
 defined, 6–7
 types, 7–9
Test score theory, 101–103
 See also Classical test theory
Test takers
 examiner's relationship to, 188–189
 expectancy effects, 193–196
 language of, 193
 reinforcing responses and, 196–197
 variables in, 201
Test use, ethics of, 594
Tetrachoric correlation, 81
Thematic Apperception Test (TAT), 18,
  390–395, 399
 administration of, 391–392
 Card 12F, 391
 interpretation of, 392–394
 interviews and, 207
 psychometric properties, 394–395
 reliability, 395
 Rorschach inkblot test compared to, 390
 scoring, 392
 stimuli in, 375–376
 themes, in, 392
 theory of needs and, 390
 validity, 394
Theoretical strategy, in personality tests, 332,
  353–358
Third variable, 85, 92
Time sampling, 107–108, 119
Title VII, Civil Rights Act (1964), 550, 574, 580
Torrance Tests of Creative Thinking (TTCT),
  294–296
Tracking, 54–58
Trail Making Tests, 451, 456
Trait anxiety, 464
Traits. *See* Personality traits
True dichotomous variables, 80
True-false tests, 161–162, 173
True score, 104
Trust, factor analysis of, 90–91
Truth in Testing Law, 548, 554–555
T score, 49
Two-point codes, 341
Two-tailed tests, 76
2016 SAT, 312–313

U

Understanding. *See* Empathy
Unidimensional tests, 127
*Uniform Guidelines on Employee Selection
 Procedures* (Equal Employment
 Opportunity Commission), 551
Unique variance, 352
United States
 civil service testing, 12, 326
 intelligence testing, 234
United States National Institutes of Health
  (NIH), 195
United States v. City of Buffalo (1985), 582
University admissions, within high-school
  norms for, 59, 142–143
University of California, 59, 144, 542,
  571–573
University of Michigan, 573
Unqualified individualism, 532–534, 544, 571
Unstructured interviews, 206, 215, 223
UPS (United Parcel Service), 522

U.S. Centers for Disease Control and
  Prevention (CDC), 56
U.S. Civil Service Commission, 12, 551
U.S. Constitution, 548–549, 574
U.S. Department of Defense, 462
U.S. Department of Justice, 551
U.S. Department of Labor, 53, 507, 551
U.S. Department of the Treasury, 551
U.S. Department of Transportation, 572
U.S. government
 interstate commerce, 549–550
 role of, in test regulation, 549–553
 spending control, 550
U.S. House Subcommittee on Invasion of
  Privacy, 593
US News & World Report (magazine), 430
U.S. Preventive Services Task Force
  (USPSTF), 467
U.S. Senate Subcommittee on Constitutional
  Rights, 593
U.S. Veterans Administration, 600
Utility theory, 493–495

V

Validity
 aspects, 136–148
 automated neuropsychological metrics
  (ANAM), 463
 Brazelton Neonatal Assessment Scale
  (BNAS), 277
 California Verbal Learning Test
  (CVLT), 460
 concurrent-related evidence, 139
 construct-related evidence, 149–155
 content-related evidence, 136–138,
  521–524
 criterion-related evidence, 138–148,
  524–529, 535–536
 defined, 10, 135, 155
 differential, 520, 527
 external, 193
 face validity, 136
 Holtzman Inkblot Test, 389
 incremental, 499–501
 of interviews, 219–222
 Jackson Vocational Interest Survey
  (JVIS), 436
 Kuder Occupational Interest Survey
  (KOIS), 435
 Minnesota Multiphasic Personality
  Inventory (MMPI), 336–337, 340–342,
  345–346
 nottingham health profile (NHP), 474
 predictive validity, 138, 145
 reliability and, 155–156
 Rorschach inkblot test, 380–383, 388
 Self-Directed Search (SDS), 437
 SF-36, 473
 Stanford-Binet Intelligence Scale, 244
 State-Trait Anxiety Inventory (STAI), 465
 Strong Vocational Interest Blank
  (SVIB), 427
 Taylor-Russell Tables, 489–493
 Thematic Apperception Test (TAT), 394
 Wonderlic Personnel Test (WPT), 502
Validity coefficients, 140–144
 changing relationships and, 145–146
 criterion-predictor problems and, 146
 criterion reliability and validity, 146

defined, 140
 differential prediction and, 148
 evaluating, 144
 generalization and, 148
 sample representativeness and, 146
 size of, 141, 143
Value-added employee assessments, 495–499
Value ratings, context and, 168–169
Variability, standard deviation and, 39
Variables
 continuous, 80
 defined, 37
 dichotomous, 80
 symbol for, 38
Variance
 analysis of, 508
 common, 352
 covariance and, 73–74
 defined, 39, 61, 72
 error, 352, 509
 formula for, 39
 *KR*20 formula and, 112
 reliability and, 106
 shrinkage and, 84
 symbol for, 39
 unique, 352
Verbal IQ (VIQ), 258–263
Verbatim playback, 212–213
Virtual reality, 420–421
Visiographic tests, 292–294
Visual analogue scale, 167
Vocabulary, 252

W

Wards Cove Packing Company v. Antonio, 579
Washington University Sentence Completion
 Test (WUSCT), 397
Watson v. Fort Worth Bank and Trust
  (1988), 578
Ways of Coping Scale, 466
Wechsler Adult Intelligence Scale (WAIS),
  251, 523
Wechsler Adult Intelligence Scale, Fourth
  Edition (WAIS-IV), 248, 252, 256
 downward extensions, 264–266
 hierarchical model, 258–259
 index scores, 253
 reliability coefficients, 263
 subtest scaled score, 257
 validity, 263
 Wechsler–Bellevue scale, 251
Wechsler Adult Intelligence Scale-Revised
  (WAIS-R), 193, 251
Wechsler Adult Intelligence Scale, Third
  Edition (WAIS-III), 251
 arithmetic subtest, 254
 block design subtest, 257
 comprehension subtest, 255–256
 digit span subtest, 254–255
 digit symbol-coding subtest, 256
 evaluation of, 263–264
 full-scale IQ (FSIQ), 258–259
 hypothetical case studies, 260–262
 index comparisons, 259–260
 index scores, 253, 258
 information subtest, 255
 interpretative features, 259–262
 letter–number sequencing subtest, 256
 matrix reasoning subtest, 257

Wechsler Adult Intelligence Scale *(Continued)*
  pattern analysis, 260
  performance IQ (PIQ), 259
  psychometric properties, 262–263
  raw scores, 257
  reliability263
  similarities subtest, 253–254
  standardization samples, 262
  subtests, 251–257
  symbol search subtest, 257
  validity, 263
  verbal IQ (VIQ), 258–263
  vocabulary subtest, 252–253
Wechsler-Bellevue Intelligence Scale (W-B),
    16, 249, 251
Wechsler Intelligence Scale for Children
    (WISC)
  classroom placement and, 548, 564
  Revised Wechsler Intelligence Scale for
    Children (WISC-R), 462, 523, 526,
    531, 564

Wechsler Intelligence Scale for Children, Fifth
    Edition (WISC-V), 248, 250, 264–265, 402
Wechsler Intelligence Scales
  alternatives compared to, 268–271
  Binet-Simon Scale compared to, 249–250
  performance scale concept, 250–251
  point scale concept, 249–251
Wechsler Memory Scale-Revised
    (WMS-R), 447
Wechsler Preschool and Primary Scale
    of Intelligence, Fourth Edition
    (WPPSI-IV), 248, 264–266
Wernicke's aphasia, 448
What's Wrong with the Rorschach? (Wood
    et al.), 383
Why is My Child Having Trouble at School
    (Novick and Arnold), 288
Wide Range Achievement Test-4 (WRAT-4),
    296–297
Within-group norming controversy,
    53–54, 326

Women's Health Initiative Insomnia Rating
    Scale (WHIIRS), 153
Wonderlic Personnel Test (WPT), 502–503
Woodcock-Johnson IV, 290
Woodworth Personal Data Sheet, 17, 334–335,
    368, 410
Word association tests, 396
Working memory, 252
Work satisfaction. *See* Job satisfaction
Work setting, assessment of, 503–505
World Health Organization (WHO), 472
World War I, 15, 600
World War II, 20, 600

Z

Z scores, 40–41
  formula for, 40
  grades and, 48
  normal distributions and, 45
  percentile ranks and, 45–47